IMPORTANT BIRD AREAS IN EUROPE

compiled by

R. F. A. GRIMMETT and T. A. JONES

INTERNATIONAL COUNCIL FOR BIRD PRESERVATION
EUROPEAN CONTINENTAL SECTION

INTERNATIONAL WATERFOWL AND WETLANDS
RESEARCH BUREAU

sponsored by

ROYAL SOCIETY FOR THE PROTECTION OF BIRDS

ICBP Technical Publication No. 9

Cover illustration: Dalmatian Pelican *Pelecanus crispus*, by Trevor Boyer.

Second Reprint 1991

British Library Cataloguing in Publication Data

Grimmett, R. F. A. *1960-*
Important bird areas in Europe
1. Europe. Birds
I. Title II. Jones, T. A. *1965-*
III. Series
598.294

ISBN 0-946888-17-5

Published by International Council for Bird Preservation, Cambridge, U.K.

Printed and bound by Page Bros. (Norwich) Ltd, Norfolk, U.K.

IMPORTANT BIRD AREAS IN EUROPE

compiled by

R. F. A. Grimmett and T. A. Jones

Project Steering Committee:

P. Devillers, A. B. Gammell (Chairman), P. D. Goriup,
E. de Juana, M. R. W. Rands, M. Smart, J. Temple Lang

Main contributors:

M. Bouvier (Albania); M.-J. Dubourg (Andorra); K. Bauer, A. Grüll, H. Schifter (Austria); R.-M. Lafontaine, M. des N. van der Elst, P. Devillers (Belgium); T. Michev (Bulgaria); C. J. L. Bennett (Cyprus); J. Hora, A. Randík (Czechoslovakia); B. Søgaard, P. U. Jepsen, F. Danielsen, S. Brøgger-Jensen (Denmark); B. Olsen (Faroe Islands); D. Boertmann, K. Kampp, H. Meltofte, B. Søgaard, P. U. Jepsen, P. G. H. Evans (Greenland); O. Järvinen (Finland); M. Thauront, F. de Beaufort (France); E. Rutschke, J. Naacke (German Democratic Republic); W. Winkel, M. Frantzen, the late R. Berndt (Federal Republic of Germany); B. Hallmann, Hellenic Ornithological Society (Greece); F. Márkus (Hungary); A. Gardarsson, O. K. Nielsen (Iceland); O. J. Merne, D. Norriss, H. J. Wilson, R. Sheppard, R. Nairn (Republic of Ireland); N. Baccetti, F. Spina, P. Gelati, M. Lambertini (Italy); G. Willi (Liechtenstein); D. Crowther, J.-P. Schmitz (Luxembourg); J. Sultana (Malta); E. R. Osieck, J. Rooth, J. Vink (Netherlands); J. Sandvik, R. Barrett (Norway); P. E. Fjeld (Svalbard and Jan Mayen); Z. Krzeminski, A. Dyrcz (Poland); A. M. Teixeira, A. Araújo, R. Neves, M. V. Pinto, R. Rufino (Portugal); G. Le Grand (Azores); M. J. Biscoito, F. Zino (Madeira); D. Munteanu (Romania); E. de Juana, L. M. Carrascal, C. Saéz-Royuela (Spain); K. W. Emmerson, A. Martín, G. Delgado, M. Nogales, V. Quilis (Canary Islands); T. Larsson, H. Lindahl (Sweden); O. Biber, N. Zbinden, C. Marti, L. Schifferli (Switzerland); M. Kasparek, A. Kiliç-Kasparek, A. Ertan (Turkey); D. E. Pritchard, C. A. Galbraith, C. J. Murphy (United Kingdom); J. P. Cullen (Isle of Man); J. C. Finlayson (Gibraltar); V. Zubakin, J. Vīksne, M. G. Wilson (USSR); J. Mužinić, the late J. Soti, B. Garovnikov, G. Sušić, B. Grubač, J. Gregori, J. Fištrović (Yugoslavia); T. Salathé and N. Varty (ICBP); S. Bräger (IWRB).

Illustrations by

Norman Arlott

Maps by

Craig Robson

INTERNATIONAL COUNCIL FOR BIRD PRESERVATION

ICBP is the longest-established worldwide conservation organisation. Its primary aim is the protection of wild birds and their habitats as a contribution to the preservation of biological diversity. Founded in 1922, it is a federation of 330 member organisations in 100 countries. These organisations represent a total of over ten million members all over the world.

Central to the successful execution of ICBP's mission is its global network of scientists and conservationists specialising in bird protection. This network enables it to gather and disseminate information, identify and enact priority projects, and promote and implement conservation measures. Today, ICBP's Conservation Programme includes some 120 projects throughout the world.

ICBP provides expert advice to governments on bird conservation matters, management of nature reserves, and such issues as the control of trade in endangered species. Through interventions to governments on behalf of conservation issues ICBP can mobilise and bring to bear the force of international scientific and popular opinion at the highest levels. Conferences and symposia by its specialist groups help to attract worldwide attention to the plight of endangered birds.

ICBP maintains a comprehensive databank concerning the status of all the world's threatened birds and their habitats, from which the Bird Red Data Books are prepared. A series of Technical Publications gives up-to-date and in-depth treatment of major bird conservation issues, while monographs provide comprehensive, modern information on specific or regional issues relating to bird conservation.

ICBP now has a membership scheme, the World Bird Club, and issues a topical quarterly newsletter, *World Birdwatch.*

ICBP, 32 Cambridge Road, Girton, Cambridge CB3 0PJ, U.K. U.K. Charity No. 286211

INTERNATIONAL WATERFOWL AND WETLANDS RESEARCH BUREAU

IWRB was founded in 1954 as an independent non-governmental organisation which aims to stimulate and coordinate research into the conservation of waterfowl and their wetland habitats, worldwide. It has an Executive Board, which comprises delegates from almost forty member countries and coordinators of seventeen Research Groups. The Bureau has its headquarters at Slimbridge, England. IWRB has a small staff which, by acting in a catalytic fashion, helps IWRB to achieve goals well beyond the means of its modest financial resources. IWRB played an instrumental role in the creation of the Ramsar Convention, and now hosts a section of the Ramsar secretariat, to which it provides technical support.

IWRB's Waterfowl Division coordinates the monitoring of waterfowl populations in over sixty countries through the International Waterfowl Census. The results of this and of studies coordinated through a number of Research Groups are used to formulate management plans for waterfowl populations and recovery plans for threatened species. IWRB's Wetland Division coordinates activities through a Wetland Management Group. Activities include the compilation of regional wetland inventories, analyses of the functions and values of wetlands, the preparation and implementation of management plans, publication of wetland management handbooks, organisation of wetland workshops and training courses.

IWRB organises numerous scientific symposia and publishes many reports and special publications. The *IWRB Bulletin*, published in January and July each year, carries information about these and other activities.

IWRB, Slimbridge, Gloucester GL2 7BX, U.K.

CONTENTS

FOREWORD

by Christoph Imboden, Director, ICBP, and
Mike Moser, Director, IWRB

While international conservation organisations, quite rightly, concentrate the majority of their efforts on the immense ecological problems of the tropical developing countries which harbour the largest share of global biodiversity, we should not forget that the situation is not so encouraging in Europe either; and this despite the fact that there is a relatively high conservation awareness among the governments and peoples of most European countries. Many of the changes here are more subtle, and not as quick and dramatic as, for example, in areas where vast tracts of tropical forest are destroyed each year, but cumulatively they have given rise to profound ecological changes with serious consequences for Europe's wildlife.

Monitoring programmes in many European countries consistently indicate a steady reduction in the abundance and distribution of many European birds. The list of species contained in individual national Red Data Books is constantly growing. Many factors are responsible for this, and different species are affected by different factors, but ultimately most are linked to the one problem: our increasingly intensive use of our environment, through higher agricultural production, pollution, and more recreational activities.

If we are to achieve our objective of maintaining Europe's birds in their present diversity, abundance and distribution, many adjustments are needed in the use and management of our land. Sustainable instead of intensive use will have to be one of the key concepts – a use that is based on sound ecological principles which will not change the characteristics of the ecosystems themselves. For a 'bird-rich' Europe we need a diversity of healthy ecosystems and landscapes with a diversity of natural features.

Indeed, in order to work towards a general biodiversity strategy for Europe there can be no better way of starting than with the birds, since we know more about them than about any other group of animals or plants. In this study, the birds are the indicators for the selection of sites that are important for conserving our European wildlife, because, besides the birds they harbour, most of them are of general ecological significance as habitats for a broad diversity of other animal and plant species.

If we are to put our vision of maintaining a diverse European natural heritage into practice we need, among other measures, an integrated supra-national approach to the planning of conservation sites across the whole continent. We believe that this study is a milestone in reaching such a goal. For the first time, individual sites in each European country have been evaluated in a standard way, based on as objective criteria as possible. For the first time, there is a concrete proposal for a continent-wide network of areas that *must* be protected from man-induced ecological changes or even restored through careful management. The sites identified in this study constitute a key element of the European bird conservation agenda and will determine much of ICBP's and IWRB's future conservation activities in Europe. We greatly hope that they will also be accepted as a planning basis by many European governments and inter-governmental organisations.

Much as we see the great value and importance of this study, we are aware, too, that to advocate the conservation of individual sites has the inherent danger of implying to politicians and decision-makers that other sites are expendable. Therefore we must stress that the conservation of individual sites is not our only objective: good and comprehensive land-use planning in the whole of Europe, and the introduction of proper land-use practices in vulnerable ecosystems and habitats, will likewise have a decisive influence on the future of the avifauna of Europe.

This book is based on many years of data-collecting and would not have been possible without the help of the large number of amateur and professional ornithologists and scientists making up the ICBP and IWRB network of experts. We are deeply grateful to them and hope they find reward and take pride in the achievement presented here.

Some collaborators have asked us to keep certain sites confidential. The authors have followed this where evidence clearly indicated that disclosure could result in detrimental disturbances. However, some might feel that we should have kept many more sites confidential (e.g. in the Mediterranean area). The reply must surely be, how can we expect these sites to be protected if we do not tell the public and government officials about them?

Finally we wish to thank very warmly our two staff members, Richard Grimmett and Tim Jones (and, in the early stages, Stefan Bräger), for their hard and extremely dedicated work in compiling the information, editing submitted texts and writing a lot of it themselves. Their work was guided with great enthusiasm by a steering committee of experts: P. Devillers, A. B. Gammell (Chairman), P. D. Goriup, E. de Juana, M. R. W. Rands, M. Smart, and J. Temple Lang, and many other staff and outside persons have assisted in various aspects. To all of them, to The Royal Society for the Protection of Birds (U.K.), which sponsored the work very generously, and the European Community (DGXI), which helped in the compilation of data on wetlands through a grant to IWRB (ACE 6611/84/07-5), we, and ultimately the birds of Europe, are greatly indebted.

ACKNOWLEDGEMENTS

A great many people have assisted us with our work. First and foremost we would like to acknowledge the debt we owe the many hundreds of amateur and professional birdwatchers and scientists who, through their fieldwork and/or coordinating efforts, have provided the data which form the basis of this book. It is impossible to acknowledge everyone who has contributed, since many remain anonymous. We hope that in a small way our efforts will repay their dedication and will contribute to the conservation of the sites which they care so much about.

Those persons who have provided a considerable amount of data, many acting as coordinators in their country or regions, are acknowledged on the inside title-page. Without their assistance, enthusiasm and great kindness this book would not have been possible. We would particularly like to mention M. Thauront and E. de Juana, who have made a major contribution. Within each country account, we give as full an acknowledgement as is possible to those who have provided material, usually in the form of data-sheets, personal notes or unpublished reports, and to the people who have written introductions to the site inventories. We thank these people for their considerable generosity, commitment to the conservation of important bird areas, and enthusiastic support.

The stimulus for this book came from A. B. Gammell (International Department of the Royal Society for the Protection of Birds), who arranged for the major financing of the work and gathered together and chaired the project's Steering Committee (P. Devillers, P. D. Goriup, E. de Juana, M. R. W. Rands, M. Smart, and J. Temple Lang). All the Steering Committee members gave freely of their time and expertise; A. B. Gammell was always available for advice and guidance and J. Temple Lang was tireless in his commitment to the project and kept us going with advice and criticism. Members of the Executive Committee of the European Continental Section of ICBP, and especially its chairman J. Sultana, have provided advice on a number of occasions.

A major source of data has been the very important work carried out by the ICBP European Community Working Group, with major data-gathering exercises completed in 1981 by E. R. Osieck and M. F. Mörzer Bruyns, in 1982 by B. Hallmann, and in 1984 by W. G. Braakhekke, and A. B. Gammell and Z. Karpowicz. Major contributions to the 1981 study were made by D. A. Scott (IWRB), L. Marion and F. de Beaufort (for France), and by S. Allavena (for Italy). For the 10 European Community countries covered by the above studies our work essentially involved the updating and expanding of their work. The project undertaken by J. A. van der Ven in 1984 for the Council of Europe was also useful when preparing the site inventories for a number of non-EEC countries.

We also acknowledge the extensive use of data collected by the Protected Areas Data Unit (of the World Conservation Monitoring Centre [WCMC], Cambridge). Friends at PADU – Z. Karpowicz, J. Harrison, and G. Drucker – have always been generous with their assistance. We also acknowledge the access and extensive reference to data collected for the Biotopes Project of the European Community CORINE Programme. In particular we wish to thank B. K. Wyatt and D. Moss for their help and the Institute of Terrestrial Ecology, Natural Environment Research Council, for making the data available to us while they were contractors for the CORINE Biotopes Project.

R.F.A.G. has received considerable encouragement and guidance from staff at the ICBP Secretariat: P. D. Goriup and T. A. Urquhart provided much help at the early stages, and Ch. Imboden, M. R. W. Rands and N. J. Collar have guided the project from the earliest days. The book would not have emerged without N. J. Collar's skilful handling of the final stages.

T.A.J. would like to thank colleagues at IWRB: D. A. Scott, M. Smart, J. A. van der Ven, J.-Y. Pirot, J.-Y. Mondain-Monval, and M. Moser. G. V. T. Matthews, former Director of IWRB, encouraged close collaboration with ICBP, and S. Bräger, who coordinated the project for IWRB in the early stages, helped establish the site selection criteria and set the project on a steady course.

At the ICBP Secretariat G. Pfaff and I. Hughes typed the entire text, prepared the camera-ready copy with great skill (battling with a whole variety of accents!), and worked for long hours – involving many evenings and weekends – with enthusiasm, perseverance and total professional dedication: their cheerfulness and loyalty in the face of impossible workloads has been one of the wonders of the world, and our indebtedness to them is total. I. Hughes was of great help during R.F.A.G.'s absence from the office by organising the circulation of draft texts and keeping everything in order. At IWRB, K. Russell and S. McKean were of great help to T.A.J.

Friends and colleagues at ICBP helped in many ways: T. Salathé translated a great deal of data from French and German (including all the data-sheets from the Federal Republic of Germany); N. Varty undertook much of the updating of information for the Italian inventory, whilst N. J. Collar, M. J. Crosby, A. C. Dunn, J. H. Fanshawe, J. Fenton, A. Gretton, I. R. Hepburn, T. H. Johnson, M. R. W. Rands, T. Salathé, A. J. Stattersfield, and N. Varty helped with proof-reading and made useful comments. J. Sharpe, S. Shutes and S. Usui helped in many important ways. C. FitzGibbon and A. Craig also very kindly helped with proof-reading, and N. Bousson translated some information into English.

R.F.A.G. received considerable support from Helen Taylor and parents, Frank and Molly Grimmett, during the course of the project.

P. D. Moore commented on the section covering the vegetation of Europe, S. Lyster commented on the section covering the international conventions, B. Soto-Largo of the Commission of the European Communities (DGXI) provided useful information on Special Protection Areas, and in addition to the major funders mentioned in the directors' foreword, the Nature Conservancy Council (U.K.), World Wide Fund for Nature (International), and the Ornithological Society of the Middle East provided some financial support.

Finally, we would like to thank N. Arlott for his excellent black-and-white drawings, C. R. Robson for painstakingly preparing the maps and checking many of the coordinates, A. C. Dunn for help with marking-up the book, P. M. Cocker for copy-editing most of the text, J. Eames for assisting at the very end of the project, M. Bramwell for assisting with publication of the book, T. Boyer for the cover illustration, and S. C. Commons of Page Bros. for being so patient in the face of passing deadlines.

INTRODUCTION

Following the last ice-age, Europe became covered mainly in a climax vegetation of mixed broadleaved forest with areas of evergreen forest in the Mediterranean basin, coniferous forest and wetlands in the north, steppe grasslands in the extreme east, and tundra on mountain tops and at high latitudes. The spread of mankind, and in particular the development of pastoral and arable agriculture, resulted in large-scale deforestation, cultivation of natural grasslands, and drainage and cultivation of wetlands. Today, where natural habitats remain, they are by and large highly fragmented and degraded; only in remote parts of northernmost Europe can substantial tracts of climax vegetation still be found.

The consequences of primary habitat destruction for the original (post-glacial) European avifauna were profound. Those species dependent on undisturbed climax vegetation suffered a marked decline. However, in place of climax vegetation new habitats emerged, ranging from semi-natural secondary forest to highly modified areas of cultivation and settlement. Open landscapes, and edge habitats formerly of very restricted distribution, became widespread, and with them a range of 'new' European environments emerged. Initially such developments must have increased the diversity of Europe's avifauna, and a number of formerly scarce species became more widespread and abundant.

Recent agricultural development, particularly in the twentieth century, has been largely detrimental to European bird populations. Intensification of agriculture (including extensive use of fertilisers, pesticides, drainage and irrigation), greater specialisation (segregation of traditional mixed farming into arable or pastoral), and intensification of forestry, have reduced habitat diversity and degraded habitat quality. Many species that thrived in, or were at least tolerant of, low-intensity forestry or mixed agriculture are severely threatened by twentieth-century practices; rapid urbanisation and industrialisation (which has brought with it serious problems of air and water pollution) have further contributed to environmental degradation.

Today, then, conservation in Europe faces challenges on many fronts. This book is one response to these challenges, by identifying some of the most important areas that remain to us in the European natural heritage.

Aims of the study

The conservation of birds and any other form of wildlife can, broadly speaking, be approached in three ways:

1. protection of the species from direct persecution (including egg-collecting);
2. conservation of sites by establishing protected areas such as national parks or nature reserves and preserving or managing them according to the needs of their fauna and flora;
3. conservation of the environment in general by regulating economic activities that will modify habitats and landscape, and by controlling pollution of air, soil and water.

All are of importance and are complementary; we will be unsuccessful in our objective of maintaining the distribution and abundance of Europe's bird fauna if one of these is ignored. Nevertheless, this study is aimed at the promotion of the second approach by providing, in handbook form, key information on sites of major importance for the conservation of Europe's avifauna. It is intended for international agencies, governmental and non-governmental nature conservationists, land-use planners and professional and amateur ornithologists. The book, the result of a two-year study, describes 2444 sites and provides an indication of the degree to which they are unprotected or under threat. It represents the first comprehensive basis for the promotion of a network of protected sites for birds throughout Europe from the Urals to the Atlantic and from Greenland to the Euphrates.

Specifically, the inventory of sites is considered to serve five functions:

1. to guide the implementation of national conservation strategies and in particular to promote the development of national protected-area programmes;
2. to inform decision-makers at all levels of the existence of these vital habitats and thereby to enable them to oppose land-use proposals which would be incompatible with their conservation;
3. to provide an indication of the sites which are currently threatened and/or inadequately protected to assist the lobbying activities of national and international conservation bodies;
4. to serve the conservation activities of international governmental organisations, particularly the Council of Europe, the Council for Mutual Economic Assistance (COMECON), the European Community (EEC), the Nordic Council, the United Nations Economic Commission for Europe, and the United Nations Educational, Scientific and Cultural Organisation (UNESCO);
5. to promote the implementation of global agreements such as the Ramsar Convention on Wetlands of International Importance Especially as Waterfowl Habitat, the Bonn Convention on the Conservation of Migratory Species of Wild Animals, the Convention Concerning the Protection of World Cultural and Natural Heritage, and regional measures such as the Bern Convention on the Conservation of European Wildlife and Natural Habitats, the Barcelona Convention for the Protection of the Mediterranean Sea Against Pollution, and the EEC Directive and Resolution on the Conservation of Wild Birds.

The aim has been to identify sites of importance for four groups of birds:

1. regularly occurring migratory species which concentrate at and are dependent on particular sites either when breeding, on migration, or during the winter;
2. globally threatened species (i.e. species at risk of total extinction);
3. species and subspecies threatened throughout all or large parts of their range in Europe but not globally;
4. species that have relatively small total world ranges with important populations in Europe.

This publication is intended to be an exhaustive inventory based on current knowledge. However, for reasons of confidentiality some sites, although known to us, have not been listed and there are inevitably other areas probably of equal importance to some of those listed, which are missing because of a lack of sufficient information. We urge all readers who know of sites which should have been included to inform ICBP/IWRB using the forms at the back of this book. The omission of a site from the inventory does not mean, therefore, that it is not important and does not require conservation measures.

The need and options for Important Bird Area protection

This inventory is, then, a list of sites which, in ICBP and IWRB's view, require effective protection in Europe. A large proportion of the sites listed here are not just important because of their bird species, but have their own intrinsic value as ecosystems with a great variety of other animal and plant species.

The preparation of this inventory comes at a time when 29 species of the European avifauna are believed to be threatened with global extinction (Collar and Stuart 1985, Collar and Andrew 1988). A further 185 species and subspecies, many with clearly decreasing populations, are considered to be threatened throughout all, or a major part, of their range in Europe (this study). If action is not taken across Europe, then the continent's birdlife will be drastically impoverished by the beginning of the twenty-first century.

At least on paper, every country in Europe has its own framework for the designation of protected areas. The existence of such areas is crucial for effective conservation, although the degree and efficacy of protection varies considerably, both within and between countries. In every country, however, there are not enough conservation areas (or they are too small or too isolated). Furthermore, many existing protected areas are inadequately or inappropriately managed, or are threatened by some form of human activity.

The type of habitat protection needed will vary from site to site (according to size, habitat, species, immediacy of threats etc.) but the options immediately available will largely be dictated by the protected-area legislation now in force in each country. Appropriate protection will vary from strictly protected nature reserves, where man-made disturbances are minimised and public access prohibited, to protected landscapes where the management objective is to maintain the landscape character whilst permitting or promoting traditional land-uses and maintaining ecological diversity. The inventory is not, therefore, a list of sites which should all be strictly protected. At many of the sites, some economic activities are compatible with conservation and in some cases may be vital in the maintenance of particular habitats. In such cases, existing land-uses may need to be supported rather than restricted, and legislation controlling the use of specified habitats may be as important as designating protected areas.

Most states in Europe are parties to one or more of the international legal measures (described below) set up to conserve wildlife and their habitats. This inventory of important bird areas should be regarded as a list of sites which need to be designated or protected under the terms of one or more of the six measures. There are several international programmes which are also significant for the conservation of important bird areas; these include UNESCO's Man and the Biosphere Programme, and the Biogenetic Reserves Programme of the Council of Europe. The conservation activities of the UN Economic Commission for Europe, the Nordic Council, and the Council for Mutual Economic Assistance could also contribute to the welfare of these sites.

This inventory is not an end in itself but a prerequisite for more effective continental planning of protected areas. It is intended to be the basis for something more important and more ambitious than has so far been attempted – the setting up of a scientifically planned network of protected areas for birds throughout Europe, disregarding national frontiers, conceived as a whole, and designed so as to safeguard a significant proportion of Europe's bird populations throughout the next century. Such a network can only be set up if there is wider cooperation between European countries and if the promotion of such a network is given greater priority. The existing international and European Community measures summarised below already provide a good framework for taking the first steps towards an integrated European network of protected areas for birds.

Limits to the Important Bird Area concept

A proportion of Europe's bird species, because of their dispersed distribution, cannot be protected fully at any time in their life-cycle by the protection of the sites in this inventory. Whilst some important bird areas have been listed which hold significant numbers of such species, only a small proportion of their total population can ever be covered by a network of protected areas. Most Accipitridae, Falconidae, Tetraonidae, Phasianidae, Strigidae and Picidae, for example, as well as many passerines, fall into this category. Furthermore, most species that do congregate, and which benefit most from the identification and protection of sites, do not do so throughout the year. Most Anatidae, Charadriidae and Scolopacidae are widely distributed during the breeding season and only a small proportion of their breeding habitat can ever be protected by an important bird area network. Conversely, most Laridae, Sternidae and Alcidae, which usually nest in dense concentrations, are mostly widely dispersed on migration and during the winter.

It is therefore clear that the protection of the sites listed in this inventory goes only some way towards our objective of maintaining the diversity, abundance and distribution of Europe's bird fauna. The use and management of the areas in between and outside these sites, even if the sites themselves were all protected, is required, based on sound ecological principles and as part of an overall land-use strategy to preserve a 'bird-rich' Europe. Regulations governing forestry and agriculture, and in particular the use of certain fragile habitats, are urgently needed throughout Europe. In the European

Community, the proposed EEC Habitats Directive may help rectify the inadequacy of the existing legislation within the community countries (Everett 1988).

Furthermore, sites can be seriously affected by the pollution of air and water (e.g. acid rain), often of international origin. A bird-rich Europe not only requires a comprehensive network of sites and an overall land-use strategy, but also effective international controls on pollution.

The need to regulate farming and forestry practices is of particular importance, and generally is more relevant than the protection of individual sites in countries with vast expanses of relatively uniform habitats, such as in Norway, Sweden and Finland. The protection of individual sites in such regions, in the sense of setting them aside as protected areas, is less important than introducing effective regulations ensuring that whatever use is made of such ecosystems by man does not affect their long-term ecological integrity and change their natural characteristics.

Despite these provisos, the important bird areas concept must become a corner-stone of conservation planning and implementation for most European countries, and should represent a major component of any strategy to conserve the European natural heritage.

The European Region

The region covered by this study (Figure 1) includes Iceland, Fennoscandia, the USSR west of the Ural Mountains and Caspian Sea, Turkey, and the Atlantic islands which form part of the territory of Spain and Portugal. Important sites for Palearctic species in Greenland have also been included. The region lies entirely within the Palearctic biogeographic realm, except Greenland which is in the Nearctic realm (Udvardy 1975). Important bird areas have been identified in all the European states except Monaco, San Marino, and Vatican City, which therefore have no national chapter in this volume.

Some countries have been divided with overseas territories treated separately. This is either because they are quite different biogeographically and/or because they have a considerable degree of political independence. Thus the Faroe Islands and Greenland have been treated separately from Denmark, Svalbard and Jan Mayen have been treated separately from Norway, the Azores and Madeira have been treated separately from Portugal, the Canary Islands have been treated separately from Spain, and the Isle of Man, Channel Islands and Gibraltar have been treated separately from the United Kingdom.

Variation in the number of sites per country

Even making allowances for differences in the size of the countries covered, there is considerable variation between countries in the number of sites included in this inventory, for the following main reasons:

- Albania, Bulgaria, Romania, Turkey and Yugoslavia are not fully covered because of incomplete information on the status and distribution of birds;
- some countries have a comparatively large number of seabird colonies and wetland sites which are easier to distinguish and record than other types of sites (e.g. United Kingdom, Ireland);
- some countries are largely covered by homogeneous habitats where the most important bird areas are difficult to identify because their boundaries cannot be defined (Finland, Norway, Sweden, northern USSR).

Background to the study

ICBP and IWRB have, for a number of years, compiled data on important bird areas. One of the earlier published accounts was IWRB's *Preliminary inventory of wetlands of international importance for waterfowl in West Europe and Northwest Africa* (Scott 1980) which covered 15 European countries. Working in collaboration with IWRB, the ICBP EEC Working Group at the same time compiled information on behalf of the Commission of the European Community. That work listed sites in Belgium, Denmark, France, Federal Republic of Germany, Ireland, Italy, Luxembourg, the Netherlands and the United Kingdom (Osieck and Mörzer Bruyns 1981). Follow-up studies expanded the list of sites for these nine countries (and covered Greece, Spain and Portugal for the first time) and also identified sites under threat, highlighting those seriously and immediately threatened (Hallmann 1982, Gammell and Karpowicz 1984, Grimmett and Gammell 1987).

On behalf of the Council of Europe, ICBP also compiled information on sites for 81 species in need of special protection in Europe (after Parslow and Everett 1981). The study (van der Ven 1984) was of a preliminary nature and covered 22 countries (21 Member States of the Council of Europe, plus Finland).

These studies have been helpful to planners and conservationists and have enabled ICBP, IWRB and others to lobby for greater protection of sites in Europe and to present effective arguments for the conservation of threatened sites. Scott's inventory of 1980 has been widely considered as a list of internationally important wetlands that deserve to be protected under the Ramsar Convention, whilst the other reports have been used by the Commission of the European Community and by the Council of Europe in developing their conservation activities. However, these studies (except Scott 1980) remain unpublished and are therefore not readily available.

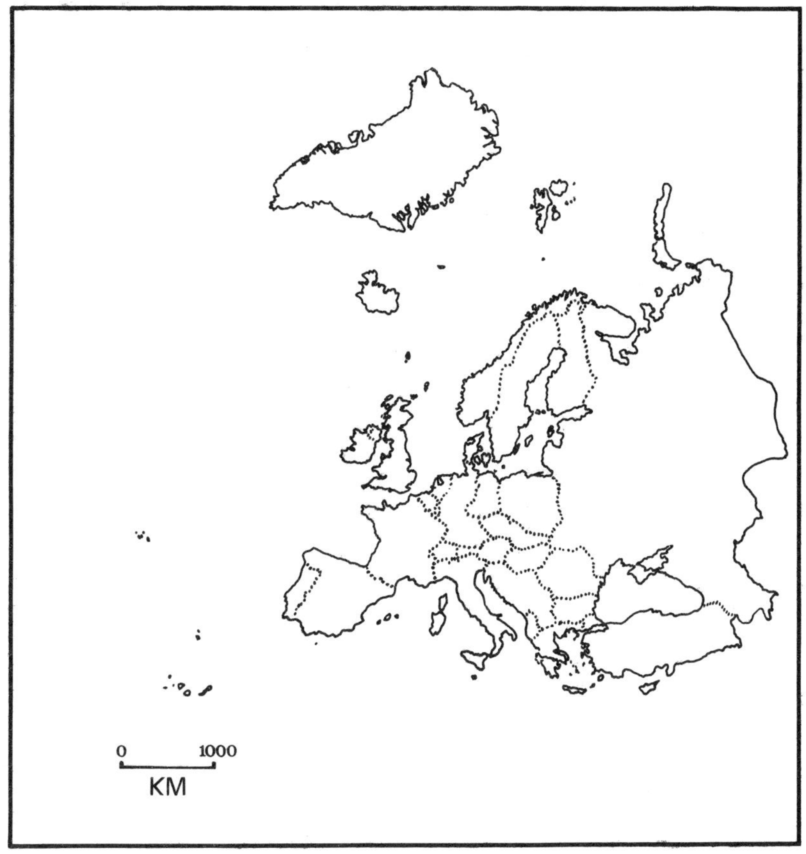

Figure 1: Map of region covered by study

Not mentioned above, but of value to the Important Bird Areas project, was the *Directory of wetlands of international importance in the Western Palearctic* (Carp 1980). This directory covered all of Europe and provided detailed information on a selected number of wetlands in each country. The site accounts were of a general nature and covered faunal, floral, and limnological aspects of the wetlands.

The study on which this book is based has extensively updated and expanded the inventory of important bird areas held by ICBP and IWRB. It covers a total of 32 countries, eight of which were not covered at all by the studies mentioned above. Readers familiar with the earlier studies will notice a change in the number of sites in all countries. This is either because of changed circumstances (some sites have lost their importance) or improved knowledge.

Methods

The compilation of this inventory has involved the collection of data by two principal methods:

- The circulation of a questionnaire to ICBP's sections and representatives, and IWRB's delegates, as well as to a limited number of additional experts, throughout Europe. This usually resulted in the establishment of an unofficial 'coordinator', who in turn consulted appropriate sources in his or her area of responsibility.
- The analysis of published and unpublished material held by ICBP and IWRB, including data from previous questionnaire surveys. Draft inventories for some countries (or overseas territories) were compiled using data on file at ICBP and IWRB, and were circulated for comments and updating of information. All material previously compiled by ICBP for the EEC and Council of Europe has been taken into account. For many countries IWRB has drawn on its database of winter waterfowl counts.

Because of time constraints on the project, a complete review of the literature was not possible for most countries (nor overseas territories), although this was sometimes undertaken by the 'coordinators', for their particular countries or regions.

Further information on methods is given in the sections below on 'Site selection' and 'Data presentation'.

Updating and adding to the inventory

ICBP and IWRB would be pleased to receive corrections or up-to-date information regarding the sites included in this inventory. Persons wishing to submit data for new sites are asked to complete one of the questionnaires (preferably both for wetland sites) which can be found at the back of this book.

INTERNATIONAL MEASURES FOR CONSERVATION

The various international and regional conventions and programmes, and the EEC Wild Birds Directive, represent a strong basis for international cooperation in the protection of natural resources in Europe. In this section we briefly describe those which are relevant to the protection of important bird areas in Europe. The inventory of sites in this book is viewed as a technical companion to such conventions and programmes, since a proper understanding of the location and importance of valuable sites is essential for their effective implementation.

Six international conventions or directives (three global, two European, one Mediterranean) adopted since 1975, and two international programmes, are particularly relevant to the conservation of birds and their habitats.

Convention on Wetlands of International Importance Especially as Waterfowl Habitat

This Convention, known as the Ramsar Convention, came into force in December 1975 and was the first treaty to concern itself exclusively with habitat conservation. The main undertakings accepted by the Contracting Parties are to:

> designate suitable wetlands within (their) territory for inclusion in a List of Wetlands of International Importance (Article 2,1)

and

> formulate and implement their planning so as to promote the conservation of the wetlands included in the List, and as far as possible, the wise use of wetlands in their territory (Article 3,1)

and

> promote the conservation of wetlands and waterfowl by establishing nature reserves on wetlands whether they are included in the list or not, and provide adequately for their wardening (Article 4,1).

Each Contracting Party must designate at least one site for inclusion in the List at the time it joins the Convention (Article 2,4).

As of November 1988, there were 278 European (including Greenland) sites on the list. However, not all of these are ornithologically important. Of the six conventions or directives covered here, Ramsar is the most widely applicable in terms of geographical coverage, with 24 Contracting Parties in Europe, and it has had a very positive impact on wetland conservation in many European states. The 'wise use' concept, which applies to all wetlands whether or not they are included in the List, is receiving increasing attention.

Convention on the Conservation of Migratory Species of Wild Animals

Also called the Bonn Convention, it is relatively new and came into force in November 1983. Its fundamental objective is to protect migratory species (not only birds but mammals, fish and invertebrates) in recognition of the fact that protection is needed throughout every part of their migratory range, and that this requires international cooperation and action. If a party to the Convention is a Range State of a migratory species listed in Appendix I or Appendix II it accepts an obligation to provide strict protection for species in Appendix I and to conclude Agreements with other Range States for the conservation and management of species in Appendix II. Appendix I species are in danger of extinction throughout all or a major part of their range, and Appendix II species are those which would benefit from international cooperation in their conservation and management.

For Appendix I species, Parties that are Range States are obliged to endeavour, amongst other things, to:

> conserve and, where feasible and appropriate, restore those habitats of the species which are of importance in removing the species from danger of extinction (Article III 4a);

and with regard to the Agreements which Parties are obliged to sign for Appendix II species, each Agreement should, where appropriate and feasible, provide for the:

> maintenance of a network of suitable habitats appropriately disposed in relation to the migration routes.

By September 1988, 12 countries in Europe and the European Community were full Parties to the Convention, and an additional two countries had signed but not ratified the Convention. A number of globally threatened species occurring in Europe are on Appendix I and some of their Range States have ratified the Convention (e.g. *Haliaeetus albicilla* – Hungary, Federal Republic of Germany, Norway and Sweden; *Larus audouinii* – Italy and Spain). However, a number of globally threatened species occurring in Europe are currently not on Appendix I, although some of their Range States are Contracting Parties (*Pterodroma feae* – Portugal; *Marmaronetta angustirostris* – Spain; *Crex crex* – all European Contracting Parties). To date, no Agreements between Range States for species on Appendix II have been concluded, although a draft Agreement has been prepared for *Ciconia ciconia* and another for ducks and geese in the Western Palearctic has been agreed as a high priority.

Convention concerning the Protection of the World Cultural and Natural Heritage

Known as the World Heritage Convention, it came into force in December 1975, its objective being the protection of cultural and natural heritage of outstanding universal value. For the purposes of the Convention the following is considered as 'natural heritage' (Article 2):

> natural features consisting of physical and biological formations or groups of such formations, which are of outstanding universal value from the aesthetic or scientific point of view

and

> geological and physiographical formations and precisely delineated areas which constitute the habitat of threatened species of animals and plants of outstanding universal value from the point of view of science or conservation

and

> natural sites or precisely delineated areas of outstanding universal value from the point of view of science, conservation or natural beauty.

Article 4 of the Convention states that each Party recognises its duty to ensure the identification, protection, conservation, presentation and transmission to future generations of the natural heritage situated on its territory, and requires that it does all it can do to further this end. Each Party identifies sites of natural heritage as described in Article 2 and is required, in so far as is possible, to:

> submit to the World Heritage Committee an inventory of property forming part of the cultural and natural heritage, situated in its territory and suitable for inclusion in the list (Article 11).

The list is the World Heritage List which is managed by the World Heritage Committee, and an appropriate proposal from a Party is required before a site can be considered for selection. Parties to the Convention accept a legal duty to do all they can to protect sites which are on the list. By April 1988, 20 European states were Parties to the Convention, but only 12 natural sites had been listed (with no natural World Heritage Sites designated by 13 European Contracting Parties). However, several important bird areas are included (notably Srébarna Nature Reserve, Bulgaria; Bialowieza National Park, Poland), and there are clearly many more sites, identified by this inventory, which qualify for listing.

Convention on the Conservation of European Wildlife and Natural Habitats

This Convention, known as the Bern Convention, was opened for signature in September 1979 and came into force in June 1982. By December 1988, 18 European states and the European Community were Parties to the Convention and a further two countries had signed but not ratified the Convention.

Contracting Parties are required to maintain populations of wild flora and fauna and give particular emphasis to endangered and vulnerable species, including endangered and vulnerable migratory species. Specifically, each Contracting Party undertakes to:

> take appropriate and necessary legislative and administrative measures to ensure the conservation of the habitats of the wild flora and fauna species especially those specified in the Appendices I and II and the conservation of endangered natural habitats (Article 4,1)

and to

> give special attention to the protection of areas that are of importance for the migratory species specified in Appendix II and III and which are appropriately situated in relation to migration routes, as wintering, staging, feeding, breeding or moulting areas (Article 4,3)

and to prohibit the

> deliberate damage to or destruction of breeding or resting sites [of Appendix II] species (Article 6,b).

Article 6,b is very specific and strict; however the explanatory report of the Convention states that it should apply only to important breeding and resting sites.

As Lyster (1985) has pointed out, implementation of Article 6,b necessitates the identification of important breeding and resting sites for species on Appendix II. Parties may make exceptions to their obligations under Articles 4 and 6, but only in very limited circumstances (such as interests of public health and safety) and use of the exception must never be detrimental to the survival of the population concerned (Article 9).

Appendix I is a list of plants. Appendix II is a long list of strictly protected faunal species which includes a high proportion of the European avifauna, with Appendix III covering almost all the bird species not included in Appendix II, with the exception of 11 species.

Directive and Resolution of the Council of the European Community on the Conservation of Wild Birds

This Directive, adopted in April 1979, came into force in April 1981 and requires the 12 Member States to maintain populations of naturally occurring wild birds and to preserve a sufficient diversity and area of habitats for their conservation. The Directive (and Resolution; see below) imposes strict legal requirements on Member States, and the European Commission is responsible for closely supervising enforcement, and is able to take a case to the European Court of Justice if a Member State is considered to have violated the terms of the Directive. Article 4(1,2 and 4) requires that:

> The species mentioned in Annex I shall be the subject of special conservation measures concerning their habitat in order to ensure their survival and reproduction in their area of distribution

and that Member States

> shall classify in particular the most suitable territories in number and size as special protection areas for the conservation of these species, taking into account their protection requirements in the geographical sea and land area where this Directive applies

and that

> Member States shall take similar measures for regularly occurring migratory species not listed in Annex I, bearing in mind their need for protection in the geographical sea and land area where this Directive applies, as regards their breeding, moulting and wintering areas and staging posts along their migration routes. To this end, Member States shall pay particular attention to the protection of wetlands and particularly to wetlands of international importance

and that

> Member States shall take appropriate steps to avoid pollution or deterioration of habitats or any disturbances affecting the birds, in so far as these would be significant having regard to the objectives of this Article.

The sentence regarding wetlands of international importance is widely interpreted as a clear reference to the Ramsar Convention. Annex I is a list of species and subspecies which, in the European Community, are either in danger of extinction, or vulnerable to specific changes in their habitats, or rare because of small populations or restricted local distribution, or are species requiring particular attention for reasons of the specific nature of their habitat. It was amended by a Directive in 1985 and now comprises a list of 144 species and subspecies. With the accession of Spain and Portugal to the Community in 1986, a list of additional species and subspecies has been drawn up and it is expected that Annex I will again be amended to include these.

In a Resolution of 2 April 1979, the Council of the European Community called upon Member States to notify the Commission within 24 months following the adoption of the Directive of "the special protection areas designated for Annex I species" and "to take similar measures for regularly occurring migratory species not listed in Annex I". By February 1989, 757 Special Protection Areas had been designated according to Article 4 of the Directive, of which 387 were in the Federal Republic of Germany.

Conventions and other multinational legal measures relevant to the conservation of important bird areas.

	Ramsar[1]	Bonn[2]	World Heritage[3]	Bern[4]	EEC Wild Birds Directive[5]	Barcelona Convention MSPA Protocol[6]
Albania	-	-	-	-	¤	-
Andorra	-	-	-	-	¤	¤
Austria	*	-	-	*	¤	¤
Belgium	*	-	-	+	*	¤
Bulgaria	*	-	*	-	¤	¤
Cyprus	-	-	*	*	¤	x
Czechoslovakia	-	-	-	-	¤	¤
Denmark	*	*	*	*	*	¤
Faroe Islands	c	c	-	-	¤	¤
Greenland	c	-	-	-	¤	¤
Finland	*	-	*	*	¤	¤
France	*	+	*	+	*	*
German DR	*	-	-	-	¤	¤
FR Germany	*	*	*	*	*	¤
Greece	*	+	*	*	*	*
Hungary	*	*	*	-	¤	¤
Iceland	*	-	-	-	¤	¤
Ireland	*	*	-	*	*	¤
Italy	*	*	*	*	*	*
Liechtenstein	-	-	-	*	¤	¤
Luxembourg	-	*	*	*	*	¤
Malta	*	-	*	-	¤	+
Netherlands	*	*	-	*	*	¤
Norway	*	*	*	*	¤	¤
Svalbard	c	c	c	-	¤	¤
Poland	*	-	*	-	¤	¤
Portugal	*	*	*	*	*	¤
Azores	c	c	c	c	c	¤
Madeira	c	c	c	c	c	¤
Romania	-	-	-	-	¤	¤
Spain	*	*	*	*	*	+
Canary Islands	c	c	c	c	c	¤
Sweden	*	*	*	*	¤	¤
Switzerland	*	-	*	*	¤	¤
Turkey	-	-	*	*	¤	*
United Kingdom	*	*	*	*	*	-
Isle of Man	-	-	c	-	¤	¤
Channel Islands	c[7]	-	c	-	¤	¤
Gibraltar	c	-	c	-	c	-
USSR	*	-	-	-	¤	¤
Yugoslavia	*	-	*	-	¤	*
European Community	¤	*	-	*		*

Notes:

1. * = Party to the Convention; c = covered by the Convention (as overseas territory); - = not covered by the Convention; ¤ = Convention is not applicable. Situation as of November 1988.

2. * = Party to the Convention; + = signed but not ratified the Convention; c = covered by the Convention (as overseas territory); - = not covered by the Convention. Situation as of September 1988.

3. * = Party to the Convention; c = covered by the Convention (as overseas territory); - = not covered by the Convention. Situation as of April 1988.

4. * = Party to the Convention; + = signed but not ratified the Convention; c = covered by the Convention (as overseas territory); - = not covered by the Convention. Situation as of December 1988.

5. * = Member State of European Community; ¤ = Directive is not applicable; c = covered by the Directive (as overseas territory within the Community).

6. MSPA = Barcelona Convention's Protocol concerning Mediterranean Specially Protected Areas; * = Party to the Convention and has ratified Protocol; - = not covered by the Convention but with coastline bordering Mediterranean Sea; + = Party to the Convention and signed but not ratified Protocol; x = Party to the Barcelona Convention but not signed/ratified Protocol; ¤ = no coastline bordering Mediterranean Sea. - for U.K. refers to its overseas territory of Gibraltar. Situation as of February 1988.

7. Jersey but not Guernsey is covered by the United Kingdom being a Party to the Ramsar Convention.

Convention for the Protection of the Mediterranean Sea against Pollution

In 1976, the governments of countries surrounding the Mediterranean signed this Convention, generally referred to as the Barcelona Convention. One important Protocol associated with the Convention was adopted in 1982 and is entitled the Protocol concerning Mediterranean Specially Protected Areas. It was adopted to provide special protection to endangered Mediterranean species as well as to habitats considered vital for their conservation. Contracting Parties have agreed to:

> take all appropriate measures with a view to protecting those marine areas which are important for the safeguarding of the natural resources and natural sites of the Mediterranean Sea Area (Article 1)

and

> establish protected areas and...endeavour to undertake the action necessary in order to protect those areas and, as appropriate, restore them, as rapidly as possible.

Such areas are to be be established in order to safeguard in particular: (a) sites of biological and ecological value (the genetic diversity, as well as satisfactory population levels, of species, and their breeding grounds and habitats; representative types of ecosystems, as well as ecological processes); (b) sites of particular importance because of their scientific, aesthetic, historical, archaeological, cultural or educational interest (Article 3).

By February 1988, the Protocol had been ratified by the European Community and by five European countries, and signed by a further three European countries. The five countries that had ratified the protocol by November 1988 had between them designated 41 Mediterranean Specially Protected Areas.

UNESCO's Man and the Biosphere Programme

The Man and the Biosphere Programme of UNESCO (United Nations Educational, Scientific and Cultural Organisation) was launched in 1970 and aimed, amongst other things, to:

> develop within the natural and social services a basis for the rational use and conservation of the resources of the biosphere.

The MAB project 8 (one of 14 international themes or projects in the Programme) is "the conservation of natural areas and the genetic material they contain". The objective was to create a worldwide network of reserves (Biosphere Reserves), with each reserve qualifying under one or more of the following categories:

1. representative examples of natural biomes;
2. unique communities or areas with unusual natural features of exceptional interest such as a population of a globally rare species;
3. examples of harmonious landscapes resulting from traditional patterns of land-use;
4. examples of modified or degraded ecosystems capable of being restored to more natural conditions.

Each Biosphere Reserve needs to be large enough to comprise an effective conservation unit and must have adequate long-term protection.

A number of countries in Europe are very active in the MAB programme (e.g. Bulgaria, France, Poland, Spain, USSR) and a total of 90 Biosphere Reserves have been designated in 22 countries in Europe. As the network in Europe grows, it will make an increasingly important contribution to the conservation of ecosystems and improve the conservation standing of existing protected areas.

European Network of Biogenetic Reserves

In 1976, the Committee of Ministers of the Council of Europe adopted a resolution on the European Network of Biogenetic Reserves with the aim of conserving representative examples of Europe's fauna, flora and natural areas. A Biogenetic Reserve means a protected area enjoying legal status and characterised by one or more typical, unique, endangered or rare habitats, biocoenoses or ecosystems. Each Member State was asked to compile an inventory of the different types of habitats (defined as biological and physico-chemical sites constituting the environment of the individuals of one of more species in a given place and permitting their proper development), biocoenoses (defined as balanced communities of plants and animals inhabiting a given environment and their interaction) and ecosystems (defined as characteristic wholes comprising a number of biocoenoses) in its country.

The Committee of Ministers asked that a list of these priority environments be established as soon as possible, so that the rarest and most endangered could be preserved and designated as a contribution to the Biogenetic Reserves Network. The present inventory is regarded as a contribution to the compilation of such a list, and many of the sites are clearly suitable for inclusion in the Biogenetic Reserves Network (although a significant proportion will require national protection before qualifying). By the end of 1987, 140 sites, covering an area of 1,784,500 ha, had been proposed by the ten countries then participating in the Network (though by no means all of these are relevant to birds).

SITE SELECTION

Definition of an area or site

Some types of area or site are clearly easier to identify and delimit than others. For example, wetland sites are usually much easier to distinguish from their surroundings than are agricultural or forest sites. For the purposes of this study a site has been defined so that, as far as possible, it should:

1. be different in character or habitat or ornithological importance from the surrounding land; and
2. exist as an actual or potential protected area, with or without buffer zones, or be an area which can be managed in some way for nature conservation; and
3. alone or with other sites, be a self-sufficient area which provides all the requirements of the birds (that it is important for) which use it during the time they are present.

In parts of Europe where there are extensive tracts of continuous habitat which are important for birds, only characteristics (2) and (3) apply.

This definition is not applicable to the identification of bottleneck sites, where large numbers of migratory birds occur because of a site's geographical location or physical structure.

Important areas in which the habitat is protected for bird conservation should be large enough to provide all the requirements of the birds using them, while they are present. However, for various reasons, not all the areas listed in this book meet this requirement. Those which do not (mostly relatively small areas; usually seabird breeding sites) will therefore not be satisfactorily safeguarded unless some appropriate steps are taken to conserve the habitats (e.g. surrounding seas) in the neighbouring areas which the birds need to use while they are present.

A subsite is generally a much smaller area (such as a heronry or seabird colony) which is clearly distinct from, and more vulnerable than, the main site of which it forms a part, and which requires or receives stricter conservation measures.

Criteria used to select sites

The following categories of sites have been selected, using criteria which are outlined below:

CATEGORY 1: Sites for migratory species which congregate (either when breeding, or on passage, or in winter) in important numbers.

Criteria:
1. The site regularly holds one per cent of a species's world population; or
2. the site regularly holds one per cent of a species's European population (or EEC population for EEC Member States only); or
3. the site regularly holds one per cent of a species's biogeographical population; or

4. it is a 'bottleneck site' where over 5000 storks (Ciconiidae) or over 3000 raptors (Accipitridae) regularly pass on spring or autumn migration.

See notes 1, 2 and 3, and Appendices 1a and 1b, all given below.

CATEGORY 2: Sites for globally threatened species.

Criterion:

1. The site regularly holds a significant number of the species.

See note 4 and Appendix 2, given below.

CATEGORY 3: Sites for species and subspecies which are threatened throughout all or large parts of their range in Europe (but are not globally threatened).

Criteria:

1. The site is one of the five most important in the European region in question for the species or subspecies, or one of the ten most important in the European region in question for the species or subspecies (if the region is particularly large and is subdivided into comparatively small political units; the regions used when applying the criteria are given in Appendix 5); or
2. the site is one of the 100 most important in Europe for the species or subspecies; or
3. the site is one of the 100 most important for the species or subspecies in the European Community.

See notes 5, 6, 7, 8, 9, and 10, and Appendices 3 and 5, all given below.

CATEGORY 4: Sites for species which have relatively small total world ranges with important populations in Europe.

Criteria:

1. The site is one of the five most important in the European region in question for the species, or one of the ten most important in the European region in question for the species (if the region is particularly large and is subdivided into comparatively small political units; the regions used when applying the criteria are given in Appendix 5); or
2. the site is one of the 100 most important in Europe for the species.

See notes 5, 6, 11 and 12 and Appendices 4 and 5, all given below.

It is important to note that some sites have been included in this inventory which do not meet the criteria discussed above. These have been included for other reasons which are described in the section 'comments on the inventory' in the introduction for each country (or overseas territory).

Comparison with previous studies covering the European Community

Readers familiar with Osieck and Mörzer Bruyns (1981), Hallmann (1982) and Grimmett and Gammell (1987) will notice that slightly different criteria have been used to select the sites that are listed in these reports (which only cover countries in the European Community). The essential difference is that, in the above studies, numerical criteria were used to select sites for non-waterfowl/non-seabird species which were based on a sound understanding of each species's status, characteristics of dispersion, and habitat preference within the European Community. These criteria could not be applied outside the Community (this study has selected sites in 20 countries outside the Community) because such information about these species is not known for many of the countries. The important point to make is that all the EEC sites included in this book would qualify according to the criteria applied by the above-mentioned studies.

Notes on the criteria

1. The criteria 'one per cent of a species's world population' and 'one per cent of a species's European or EEC population' have only been applied to sites for seabirds (Appendix 1a). The criterion 'one per cent of a species's biogeographic population' has only been applied to sites for waterfowl (Appendix 1b). Waterfowl sites have

also been selected where they regularly hold 20,000 or more waterfowl. Some of these species are also covered by the criteria in categories 2-4.

2. The numerical criteria for waterfowl have been developed in connection with the Ramsar Convention and were adopted by the Conference of Parties to the Convention in May 1987.
3. The numerical criteria for bottleneck sites cause the inclusion of most of the important sites in this category. Birds using these sites are particularly vulnerable because they concentrate in large numbers, and at some of these sites they are subject to human disturbance, exploitation or persecution.
4. Twenty-nine species have been considered when applying the criterion in category 2 (Appendix 2). They are either included in Collar and Stuart (1985) or Collar and Andrew (1988).
5. In applying the criteria in categories 3 and 4 the importance of a site has been determined, where possible, after consideration of: (a) the numbers of the species at the site; (b) the density of the species at the site; and (c) the completeness of the site as defined above.
6. Regions used when applying the criteria in categories 3 and 4 are listed in Appendix 5.
7. One hundred and eighty-five species and subspecies, regarded as threatened throughout all or large parts of their range in Europe, have been selected for this study and have been considered when applying the criteria in category 3 (Appendix 3). These are additional to those relevant to the application of the category 2 criterion. This list includes:
   (a) species and subspecies in danger of extinction or declining in numbers or reducing their range in Europe;
   (b) species and subspecies which are threatened in an important or representative part of their range in Europe;
   (c) species and subspecies with a restricted range within Europe which are vulnerable to particular changes in habitat;
   (d) species and subspecies which are confined, when breeding, wintering, on passage, or when roosting, to particular habitats which are threatened throughout all or large parts of Europe.
8. All species and subspecies on Annex I of the EEC Wild Birds Directive have been considered when applying the criteria in categories 2 and 3, as have all the species and subspecies in need of conservation measures in Spain and Portugal and which seem likely to be added to Annex I when it is amended. The list of species and subspecies which are threatened throughout all or large parts of their range in Europe is, therefore, believed to be complete regarding taxa occurring in the European Community. Due to the time constraints on this project, it was not possible, however, to undertake a thorough review of the status of all European species and subspecies, and some parts of Europe may be under-represented by the list of taxa used when applying the category 3 criteria.
9. Some species and subspecies considered when applying the criteria in category 3 (e.g. *Philomachus pugnax*, *Tringa glareola*, *Phalaropus lobatus*, *Melanocorypha calandra*, *Calandrella brachydactyla*, *C. rufescens*, *Galerida theklae*, *Lullula arborea*, *Anthus campestris*, *Luscinia svecica*, *Sylvia undata*, *Lanius collurio*, and *Emberiza hortulana*) are, in parts of their range, numerous and are unlikely to be threatened, and in these regions to attempt the selection of important sites would be unrealistic and also of limited value. This has been taken into account in the site selection process. Species which have a small breeding population but are widely distributed outside Europe and which are not threatened by habitat changes or human persecution have not been considered when applying the criteria in category 3.
10. Subspecies have been considered when applying the criteria in category 3, but not by the criterion in category 2. The decision to exclude subspecies from the third edition of the ICBP/IUCN Red Data Book is explained at length by Collar and Stuart (1985),

on the grounds that with so many threatened species still requiring conservation attention, subspecies had to take second place at a global level. ICBP remains concerned about the status of subspecies in Europe and elsewhere and, because of this, and because they are given an equal place on Annex I of the EEC Wild Birds Directive, they have been considered when applying the category 3 criteria.

11. Thirty-five species have been considered when applying the criteria in category 4 (Appendix 4). None of these species is globally threatened or is threatened in Europe as defined above. Europe does, however, have a major responsibility for their conservation. Some of these species (e.g. *Alectoris rufa*, *Hippolais polyglotta*, *Sylvia cantillans*, *S. melanocephala*, *Regulus ignicapillus*, *Certhia brachydactyla* and *Serinus serinus*) are widespread and not uncommon, and in some countries, the identification of sites for them would be unrealistic or of negligible value.
12. The criteria in category 4 has only been applied to select a site, when the site does not qualify according to the criteria in categories 1, 2 or 3.

Confidentiality

Especially sensitive information has been dealt with in one of three ways:
- the site has been totally excluded from the inventory; or
- the site has been included but the sensitive species has not been mentioned; or
- a description of the site has been included but the site name, coordinates and area have not been mentioned.

In such cases, the maintenance of site confidentiality was considered to be necessary. However, some sites and species vulnerable to egg-collectors and illegal hunting are nevertheless included in the inventory. Information of such a sensitive nature has not been disclosed before consideration and evaluation of the factors affecting each site or species. As a result, confidentiality has only been sacrificed where threats such as habitat loss are considered to exceed the risks involved in publishing site details.

DATA PRESENTATION

A short introduction to each inventory is provided. The introduction has either been prepared by someone closely involved in the data-gathering for the country (or overseas territory), is based on a contribution received from such a person with material added by the compilers, or has been entirely written by the compilers. Each introduction has the following subsections:

General information

This provides a very brief overview of the country or overseas territory, covering human population, location, topography, main vegetation, and land-use.

Ornithological importance

This provides a very brief overview of bird habitats and populations in a European context, and covers breeding species, and importance during migration periods and in winter.

Conservation infrastructure and protected-area system

This covers the protected areas referred to in the inventory (with, where known, a brief explanation of the protection provided, as well as an indication of the main authority responsible for nature conservation).

International measures relevant to the conservation of sites

Information is given regarding the main international conventions (Ramsar, World Heritage, Bern, Bonn, and Barcelona), and whether or not sites have been designated according to UNESCO's Man and the Biosphere Programme, the Council of Europe's Biogenetic Reserves Network, and the EEC's Wild Birds Directive (Special Protection Areas).

Overview of the inventory

This provides an overview of the sites included in the inventory, and the extent to which they are protected, unprotected or experiencing changes or problems. If certain types of species or important bird habitats have not been adequately covered, this is also discussed.

Acknowledgements

Mention is made of all persons and organisations known to have contributed data.

References

In a work of this scale and scope, it has proved impossible to provide references for all the information presented, and we have simply provided a list of main references at the end of most country accounts. However, the following references have been widely used when preparing the introductions to the inventories:

Baldock, D., Holzner, J. and Bennett, G. (1988) *The organisation of nature conservation in selected EC countries.* London: Institute for European Environmental Policy.

Carp, E. (1980) *A directory of Western Palearctic wetlands.* Gland, Switzerland: IUCN.

Cerovský, J. (1988) *Nature conservation in the socialist countries of East Europe.* Praha: Ministry of Culture of the Czech Socialist Republic.

Council of Europe (1987) *Management of Europe's natural heritage: twenty-five years of activity.* Strasbourg: Environment Protection and Management Division, Council of Europe.

Cramp, S. (ed.) (1985) *Handbook of the birds of Europe, the Middle East and North Africa.* Vol. 4. Oxford: Oxford University Press.

Cramp, S. and Simmons, K. E. L. (eds.) (1977-1983) *Handbook of the birds of Europe, the Middle East and North Africa.* Vols. 1-3. Oxford: Oxford University Press.

Croxall, J. P., Evans, P. G. H. and Schreiber, R. W. eds. (1984) *Status and conservation of the world's seabirds.* Cambridge, U.K.: International Council for Bird Preservation, Techn. Publ. No.2.

EEC (1980) *Protected areas in the European Community: an approach to a common classification.* Commission of the European Communities.

Gensbøl, B. (1986) *Collins guide to the birds of prey of Britain and Europe, North Africa and the Middle East.* London: Collins.

Imboden, E. ed. (1987) *Riverine forests in Europe: status and conservation.* Cambridge: ICBP.

IUCN (1966) *Plants in danger: what do we know?* Gland, Switzerland and Cambridge: IUCN.

IUCN (1987a) *Protected landscapes: experience around the word.* Gland, Switzerland and Cambridge: IUCN.

IUCN (1987b) *Directory of wetlands of international importance.* Gland, Switzerland and Cambridge: IUCN.

IUCN (1988) *Internationally recognised protected areas.* Cambridge: IUCN World Conservation Monitoring Centre.

Jacob J.-P., Lafontaine, R.-M., Chiwy, B., Devillers, P., De Visscher, M.-N. and Ledant, J.-P. (1985) Fiches d'information sur les espèces enumérées dans l'annexe I de la Directive 79/409/CEE. Institut Royal des Sciences Naturelles de Belgique.

Koester, V. (1980) *Nordic countries' legislation on the environment with special emphasis on conservation: a survey.* Gland, Switzerland: IUCN

Piersma, T. (1986) Breeding waders in Europe: a review of population size estimates and a bibliography of information sources. Wader Study Group Bulletin. 48 Supplement.

Polunin, O. and Walters, M. *A guide to the vegetation of Britain and Europe.* Oxford: Oxford University Press.

Poore, D. and Gryn-Ambroes, P. (1980) *Nature conservation in northern and western Europe.* Gland, Switzerland: IUCN.

The Times atlas of the world (1982) Comprehensive (sixth) edition. London: Times Books.

Table of sites (with a summary of the criteria used to select sites)

Following the introduction, a table of sites is given which gives the site number (No.), the site name, and the name of the region where the site can be found. The * in columns 1(i) – 4 refers to the criteria used to select the site for inclusion in the inventory. The * in column 0 (for some countries or overseas territories only) indicates that the site has been selected for other reasons, with the reasons for inclusion noted in the section 'Comments on the inventory'. The criteria have not been applied to subsites. A summary of the criteria which were used to select the sites is given below (see the section 'Site selection' above for details).

0 = Selected for other reasons. See 'Comments on the inventory' for each country (or overseas territory).
1(i) = One per cent of the world population of a seabird species.
1(ii) = One per cent of the European (or EEC population) of a seabird species.
1(iii) = One per cent of the biogeographic population of a waterfowl species; or 20,000 waterfowl.
1(iv) = Bottleneck site for migrating raptors and/or storks.
2 = Regularly holds a significant number of a globally threatened species.
3 = For a species or subspecies which is threatened throughout all or large parts of its range in Europe, *either* one of the five most important sites in the region in question *or* one of the ten most important sites in the region in question if the region is particularly large and is subdivided into comparatively small political units *or* one of the 100 most important sites in Europe (or EEC for Member States of the Community). See Appendix 5 for the regions of Europe which have been used when applying the criteria.
4 = For a species which has a relatively small total world range with important populations in Europe, *either* one of the five most important sites in the region in question *or* one of the ten most important sites in the region in question if the region is particularly large and is subdivided into comparatively small political units *or* one of the 100 most important sites in Europe. See Appendix 5 for the regions of Europe which have been used when applying the criteria.

It must be stressed that many of the sites in this inventory are important for reasons additional to the justification given in these tables of sites, and if other data were available, some sites would certainly qualify by meeting the other criteria.

Furthermore, the justification for inclusion of a site may not always be the same as the reason the site was submitted for inclusion in the inventory.

Site inventory

Following the table of sites, an account (effectively a summary of the data held on file at ICBP and/or IWRB) is given for each site. For a large proportion of the sites, ICBP and/or IWRB have more data than that published, which usually includes a map of the site showing at least its approximate boundaries. Each site account is presented in a standard format depicted graphically below.

Site name (alternative name or English name) (region)

Coordinates Area International Protection Status

National Protection Status

Site description

Ornithological information

1. Site names
Where possible these are given in the national (or regional) language. For some countries (e.g. Portugal, Sweden) the contributors have chosen to give the name of the site in English only. For some countries (and overseas territories), an alternative site name or the English name is given in parentheses. A glossary giving English translations of commonly used words is provided for some countries (and overseas territories). For some sites, the site name is followed by the name of an administrative or geographical unit. Finally, the region in which the site can be found is given in parentheses. For most countries the regions used when applying the site selection criteria are the same as the regions given in parentheses at the end of the site name. For each country (and overseas territory), the site name is described in the section 'Comments on the inventory', as are the regions used when applying the site selection criteria.

2. Coordinates
These are the geographical coordinates.

3. Area
This is the area of the site in hectares (100 ha = 1 sq km) and is usually taken from returned questionnaires. Many of the areas given are estimates, sometimes rounded off to the nearest 100 ha or even 1000 ha. For some sites no area is given, usually because the boundaries of the site have not been defined.

4. International protection status
This refers to the site's designation (entirely or partly) either as a Ramsar Site (Ramsar Convention; as of September 1988), World Heritage Site (World Heritage Convention; as of April 1988), Biosphere Reserve (UNESCO's Man and the Biosphere Programme; as of April 1988), Mediterranean Specially Protected Area (Barcelona Convention's Protocol concerning Mediterranean Specially Protected Areas; as of November 1988), EEC Special Protection Area (EEC Wild Birds Directive; as of September 1988, for some countries January 1989), or Biogenetic Reserve (Council of Europe's Biogenetic Reserves Programme; as of May 1988).
For some countries it has not been possible to determine (generally because of a lack of time) whether some sites are (entirely or partly) Mediterranean Specially Protected Areas, EEC Special Protection Areas (Federal Republic of Germany only), or Biogenetic Reserves. Where no area (ha) is given alongside the designation, the protection status, as far as is known, applies to the whole site (but see 'Comments on the inventory' for some countries).

5. National protection status
This refers to the site's protection status at a national level. For most countries, only the English translation of the protected-area category is given, and, where possible, an explanation of the protection afforded is given in the introduction to the inventory. Many sites are covered by two or more types of protected area and often it has not been possible to determine whether they overlap or are complementary. Where no area (ha) is given alongside the designation, the protection status, as far as is known, applies to the whole site (but see the 'Comments on the inventory' for some countries).

6. Site description
This covers three principal aspects: description of location and main habitats, information on main land-use and management, and a summary of the main problems, changes or threats. The site descriptions are generally those provided in returned questionnaires, and the contributors have used their own interpretation of 'heathland', 'moorland', 'bog', 'marsh', 'woodland', and 'forest' etc. For some countries, other important fauna and flora occurring at the site are also mentioned.

7. Ornithological importance

This provides a summary of the ornithological importance of each site, and deals first with breeding species, and then with species occurring on passage and/or in winter. The data were, for most countries, compiled in 1987 and/or 1988. Emphasis is usually given to the presence of globally threatened species, species or subspecies which are threatened throughout all or major parts of their European range, and migratory species occurring in internationally important numbers as defined by the criteria. Other species of particular interest may also be mentioned. The reader should assume that a variety of other species (some of interest in a European context) also occur at most sites (at some in large numbers). The scientific nomenclature (full species only) follows Voous (1977) except where it differs from Collar and Stuart (1985) or Collar and Andrew (1988), in which case the nomenclature they have adopted has been used.

Data for breeding species (often the figures are only rough estimates) are usually given as the number of 'pairs'. A great majority of species form pairs when breeding; some European species are, however, polygamous (e.g. *Circus* spp.) or form no bond (*Tetrao* spp., *Otis tarda*, *Philomachus pugnax*) and the use of the word 'pair' should be interpreted with caution (some, but not all, contributors have chosen to use 'breeding females', 'males' or 'birds' for such species). Where known, data for breeding Alcidae (i.e. *Uria aalge*, *U. lomvia*, *Alca torda*) have been given as a count of birds, but this has not always been possible (because the contributors have chosen to give the data as pairs).

Data for species occurring at sites on passage (spring and/or autumn passage) have been impossible to standardise. For some countries, the information is given as the total number of a species occurring during the season, for other countries as the maximum count on a single day or average maximum count over a number of years. Where necessary, an explanation regarding passage counts is given in the section 'Comments on the inventory' preceding the site inventories.

Data for species occurring at sites in winter are either expressed as an average maximum, or maximum count or as a range. Except for certain species of birds of prey, as far as is known the data refer to the number of the species occurring at any one time.

The data are provided in order to give a general impression about the importance of a site, and to provide a basis for comparison between sites (both within and between countries).

We hope readers will understand that it was impossible to be more consistent given that the project did not have the time nor financial resources to promote field surveys and that it has been necessary to rely on data from many different sources (with quite different approaches to data-gathering, analysis and storage amongst individuals, organisations, and countries).

REFERENCES

Collar, N. J. and Stuart, S. N. (1985) *Threatened birds of Africa and related islands: the ICBP/IUCN Red Data Book*, Part I. 3rd Edition. Cambridge, U.K. and Gland, Switzerland: International Council for Bird Preservation and International Union for the Conservation of Nature and Natural Resources.

Collar, N. J. and Andrew, P. (1988) *Birds to watch: the ICBP world checklist of threatened birds*. Cambridge, U.K.: International Council for Bird Preservation, Techn. Publ. No. 7.

Carp, E. ed. (1980) *Directory of wetlands of international importance in the Western Palearctic*. Gland, Switzerland: IUCN-UNEP.

Cramp, S. (1977) *Bird conservation in Europe*. London: HMSO.

Everett, S. (1988). European habitat protection: the draft directive. *Ecos* 9(3): 37-40.

Evans, P. G. H. (1986) Monitoring seabirds in the North Atlantic. Pp. 179-206 in Medmaravis and Monbailliu, X. eds. *Mediterranean marine avifauna*. Berlin, Heidelberg: Springer-Verlag.

Gammell, A. and Karpowicz, Z. (1984) Important bird areas in the European Community under serious threat. Unpublished report to the Commission of the European Communities.

Grimmett, R. F. A. and Gammell, A. (1987) Preliminary inventory of important bird areas in Spain and Portugal. Unpublished report to the Commission of the European Communities.

Hallmann, B. (1982) Important bird areas in the European Community: preliminary list of important bird areas in Greece. Unpublished report to the Commission of the European Communities.

King, W. B. (1981) *Endangered birds of the world: the ICBP bird red data book.* Washington, D.C.: Smithsonian Institution Press in cooperation with the International Council for Bird Preservation.

Lyster, S. (1985) *International wildlife law.* Cambridge, U.K.: Grotius.

Osieck, E. R. and Mörzer Bruyns, M. F. (1981) Important bird areas in Europe. Unpublished report to the Commission of the European Communities.

Parslow, J. and Everett, M. (1981) Birds in need of special protection in Europe. Council of Europe.

Pirot, J.-Y., Laursen, K., Madsen, J. and Mondain-Monval, J.-Y. (in press) Population estimates of swans, geese, ducks and coot in the Western Palearctic and Sahelian Africa. IWRB Special Publication no. 9.

Scott, D. (1980) *A preliminary inventory of wetlands of international importance for waterfowl in West Europe and North-west Africa.* IWRB Special Publ. No. 2. Slimbridge: IWRB.

Temple Lang, J. (1982) The European Community Directive on Bird Conservation. *Biol. Conserv.* 22: 11-26.

Udvardy, M. D. F. (1975) *A classification of the biogeographic provinces of the world.* Morges, Switzerland: International Union for the Conservation of Nature and Natural Resources, Occasional Paper No. 18.

van der Ven, J. A. (1984) Eighty-one bird species in need of special protection in Council of Europe countries. Unpublished report to the Council of Europe.

APPENDICES

APPENDIX 1 **Numerical criteria used to select sites for migratory species:** see criteria category 1

The one per cent criteria have been used for the species and subspecies listed in Appendices 1a and 1b only

APPENDIX 1a **Selected colonial nesting seabirds**

Species	*c.*1% world (pairs)	*c.*1% Europe (pairs)	*c.*1% EEC (pairs)
Fulmarus glacialis		16,000	3000
Pterodroma feae	1	1	1
P. madeira	1	1	1
Bulweria bulwerii		100	100
Calonectris diomedea	6000	5800	5800
Puffinus puffinus	2400	2400	2400
P. assimilis		100	100
Pelagodroma marina		1000	1000
Hydrobates pelagicus	1300	1300	700
Oceanodroma leucorhoa		100	100
O. castro		100	100
Sula bassana	2600	2200	2100
Phalacrocorax carbo carbo		280	100
P. aristotelis	670	670	390
Stercorarius skua	135	135	70
Larus audouinii	50	50	50
L. argentatus		10,700	5900
L. argentatus cachinnans		1100	1100
L. fuscus	1700	1700	860
L. marinus	1600	1400	250
L. melanocephalus	1500	1500	40
L. genei		1000	10
L. hyperboreus		290	
Rissa tridactyla		20,000	5700
Gelochelidon nilotica		40	15
Sterna caspia		30	
S. sandvicensis		480	400
S. hirundo			440
S. paradisaea		3000	850
S. dougallii		15	15
S. albifrons			140
Uria aalge		24,000	7800
U. lomvia	53,000	39,000	
Alca torda	3000	2800	1400
Alle alle	80,000	80,000	
Fratercula arctica	35,000	35,000	7200

Notes:

1. The above figures are largely based on Evans (1986) and P. G. H. Evans (*in litt.* 1987). Populations in Greenland have been taken into account when determining the one per cent criteria. Minimum population estimates have been used when determining the criteria.

APPENDIX 1b **Selected waterfowl species**

The following numerical criteria have been developed to identify wetlands of international importance in the context of the Ramsar Convention.

Species	*c.*1% breeding (pairs)	*c.*1% passage/winter (birds)	Region applicable
Phalacrocorax carbo sinensis	200	600	Europe except Black Sea and USSR
Pelecanus onocrotalus	50	-	Mediterranean and Black Sea
Botaurus stellaris	25	-	Europe except Black Sea and USSR
Nycticorax nycticorax	440	1320	Europe except Black Sea and USSR
Ardeola ralloides	40	120	Europe except Black Sea and USSR
Bubulcus ibis	500	1800	SW Europe
Egretta garzetta	190	285	Europe except Black Sea and USSR
E. alba	7	20	E Mediterranean and Black Sea
Ardea cinerea	500	-	Europe
A. purpurea	65	200	Europe except Black Sea and USSR
Plegadis falcinellus	10	75	E Mediterranean and Black Sea
Platalea leucorodia	6	20	W Europe
	20	60	E Mediterranean and Black Sea
Phoenicopterus ruber	200	650	Europe
Cygnus olor	-	1800	NW and Central Europe
	-	200	E Mediterranean and Black Sea
C. columbianus	-	170	Europe
C. cygnus	-	170	Iceland, UK and Ireland
	-	250	NW Continental Europe
	-	170	E Mediterranean and Black Sea
Anser fabalis fabalis	-	800	Breeding range: N Scandinavia, W Russia; Winter range: NW Europe
A. f. rossicus	-	3000	Breeding range: N Russia, Siberia; Winter range: Europe
A. brachyrhynchus	-	1100	Breeding range: Iceland, E Greenland; Winter range: UK and Ireland
	-	250	Breeding range: Svalbard; Winter range: NW Europe

continued

Appendix 1b (contd)

Species	*c.*1% breeding (pairs)	*c.*1% passage/winter (birds)	Region applicable
Anser albifrons albifrons	-	3000	Breeding range: Siberia; Winter range: NW Europe
	-	1000	Breeding range: Siberia; Winter range: Central Europe
	-	2500	Breeding range: Siberia; Winter range: E Mediterranean and Black Sea
A. a. flavirostris	-	220	Breeding range: W Greenland; Winter range: UK and Ireland
A. anser	-	1000	Breeding range: Iceland; Winter range: UK and Ireland
	-	20	Breeding range: N Scotland; Winter range: N Scotland
	-	1300	Breeding range: NW Europe; Winter range: Spain and Netherlands
	-	200	Breeding range: Central Europe; Winter range: NE Africa
	-	200	Breeding range: SE Europe; Winter range: E Mediterranean and Black Sea
Branta leucopsis	-	700	Breeding range: N Russia and Sweden; Winter range: Netherlands
	-	300	Breeding range: E Greenland; Winter range: Scotland and Ireland
	-	100	Breeding range: Svalbard; Winter range: SW Scotland
B. bernicla bernicla	-	1700	Breeding range: N Siberia; Winter range: W Europe
B. b. hrota	-	200	Breeding range: NE Canada and NE Greenland; Winter range: Ireland
	-	40	Breeding range: Svalbard; Winter range: Denmark and E England
Tadorna ferruginea	-	15	W Mediterranean
	-	200	Black Sea and E Mediterranean
T. tadorna	-	2500	NW Europe
	-	150	W Mediterranean
	-	600	Black Sea and E Mediterranean
Anas penelope	-	7500	NW Europe
	-	6000	Black Sea and Mediterranean
A. strepera	-	120	NW Europe
	-	750	Black Sea and Mediterranean
A. crecca	-	4000	NW Europe
	-	10,000	Black Sea and Mediterranean
A. platyrhynchos	-	50,000	NW Europe
	-	40,000	Black Sea and Mediterranean

continued

Appendix 1b (contd)

Species	*c.*1% breeding (pairs)	*c.*1% passage/winter (birds)	Region applicable
Anas acuta	-	700	NW Europe
	-	3000	Black Sea and Mediterranean
A. clypeata	-	1400	NW Europe
	-	3750	Black Sea and Mediterranean
Netta rufina	-	200	Central and SW Europe
	-	500	Black Sea and E Mediterranean
Aythya ferina	-	3500	NW Europe
	-	12,500	Black Sea and Mediterranean
A. nyroca	-	500	Black Sea and Mediterranean
A. fuligula	-	7500	NW Europe
	-	6000	Black Sea and Mediterranean
A. marila	-	1500	NW Europe
	-	500	Black Sea and Mediterranean
Somateria m. mollissima	-	30,000	Western Palearctic
S. spectabilis	-	1000	N Scandinavia
Polysticta stelleri	-	150	N Scandinavia
Histrionicus histrionicus	-	65	Iceland
Clangula hyemalis	-	20,000	NW Europe
Melanitta nigra	-	8000	Western Palearctic
M. fusca	-	2500	Western Palearctic
Bucephala islandica	-	25	Iceland
B. clangula	-	3000	NW Europe
	-	200	Black Sea and Mediterranean
Mergus albellus	-	150	NW Europe
	-	650	Black Sea and E Mediterranean
M. serrator	-	1000	NW Europe
	-	500	Black Sea and Mediterranean
M. merganser	-	1250	NW Europe
	-	100	Black Sea and E Mediterranean
Porphyrio porphyrio	5	15	S Europe
Fulica atra	-	15,000	NW Europe
	-	25,000	Black Sea and Mediterranean
F. cristata	All	All	SW Europe
Grus grus	-	500	NW and W Europe
	-	200	Central Europe
Haematopus ostralegus	-	7500	Europe
Himantopus himantopus	50	150	Europe
Recurvirostra avosetta	115	260	Atlantic Europe
	100	250	Mediterranean
Glareola pratincola	30	100	Europe
Charadrius hiaticula	-	1000	Europe
C. alexandrinus	100	250	Europe
Pluvialis apricaria	-	10,000	Europe

continued

Appendix 1b (contd)

Species	*c.*1% breeding (pairs)	*c.*1% passage/winter (birds)	Region applicable
Pluvialis squatarola	-	800	Europe
Vanellus vanellus	-	20,000	Europe
Calidris canutus	-	3500	NW Europe
	-	6500	Wadden Sea (migration)
C. alba	-	500	Europe
	-	150	NW Europe (winter)
C. minuta	-	400	W Europe
C. ferruginea	-	1500	W Europe
C. alpina	-	20,000	Europe
Philomachus pugnax	-	10,000	W Europe
Gallinago gallinago	-	10,000	W Europe
Limosa limosa limosa	-	3500	Europe
L. l. islandica	-	400	NW and W Europe
L. lapponica	-	5500	Europe
Numenius phaeopus	-	500	Europe
N. arquata	-	3000	Europe
Tringa erythropus	-	500	W Europe
T. totanus totanus	-	2000	W Europe
T. t. robusta/britannica	-	2000	NW and W Europe
T. nebularia	-	500	W Europe
Arenaria interpres	-	500	W Europe

Notes:

1. The numerical criteria for the waders have been taken from (and have not been revised since) Scott (1980) and are therefore provisional criteria only.

2. The following waterfowl species are globally threatened and all breeding, passage and wintering sites qualify as internationally important: *Phalacrocorax pygmeus, Pelecanus crispus, Anser erythropus, Branta ruficollis, Marmaronetta angustirostris, Oxyura leucocephala* and *Numenius tenuirostris.*

3. The numerical criteria for swans, geese, ducks, and coot have been derived from Pirot *et al.* (in press).

APPENDIX 2 **Globally threatened species**: see criteria category 2

Key

EEC = EEC Directive on the Conservation of Wild Birds with * = included in Annex I and + = additional species (or subspecies) which are expected to be added to Annex I when it is next amended; Bern = Bern Convention with * = included in Appendix II; Bonn = Bonn Convention with * = included in Appendix I and + = included in Appendix II, with some species in Appendices I and II

	EEC	Bern	Bonn
Pterodroma feae	+	*	
P. madeira	+	*	
Phalacrocorax pygmeus	*	*	
Pelecanus crispus	*	*	*+
Geronticus eremita		*	*
Anser erythropus	*	*	+
Branta ruficollis	*	*	+
Marmaronetta angustirostris	+	*	+
Oxyura leucocephala	*	*	+
Milvus milvus	*	*	+
Haliaeetus albicilla	*	*	*+
Aegypius monachus	*	*	+
Aquila adalberti	*	*	+
A. heliaca	*	*	+
Falco naumanni	*	*	+
Crex crex	*	*	
Tetrax tetrax	*	*	
Chlamydotis undulata	+	*	*+
Otis tarda	*	*	+
Haematopus meadewaldoi			
Chettusia gregaria			+
Numenius tenuirostris	*	*	*+
Larus audouinii	*	*	*
Columba trocaz	+		
C. bollii	+	*	
C. junoniae	+	*	
Saxicola dacotiae	+	*	+
Acrocephalus paludicola	*	*	+
Fringilla teydea	+	*	

Notes:

1. The importance of conservation measures in Europe, for some species in particular, should be emphasised: seven are endemic or near-endemic residents (*Milvus milvus, Aquila adalberti, Columba trocaz, C. bollii, C. junoniae, Saxicola dacotiae*, and *Fringilla teydea*); three breed entirely or almost entirely in Europe, dispersing/migrating to regions outside Europe (*Pterodroma madeira, Larus audouinii*, and *Acrocephalus paludicola*); and one winters almost entirely in Europe (*Branta ruficollis*).

2. *Falco peregrinus* (included in King 1981) will not be included in future editions of the Red Data Book because effective conservation measures have been taken and the threat from pesticides has been significantly reduced.

3. *Haematopus meadewaldoi* is almost certainly extinct (Collar and Stuart 1985).

APPENDIX 3 **Species and subspecies which are threatened throughout all or large parts of their range in Europe (but not globally)**: see criteria category 3

Key as for Appendix 2

	EEC	Bern	Bonn
Gavia stellata	*	*	
G. arctica	*	*	
G. immer	*	*	
G. adamsii		*	
P. auritus	*	*	
Puffinus puffinus mauretanicus	+	*	
Bulweria bulwerii	+	*	
Calonectris diomedea	*	*	
Puffinus assimilis	+	*	
Pelagodroma marina	+	*	
Hydrobates pelagicus	*	*	
Oceanodroma leucorhoa	*	*	
O. castro	+	*	
Phalacrocorax carbo sinensis	*		
P. aristotelis desmarestii	*		
Pelecanus onocrotalus	*	*	*
Botaurus stellaris	*	*	
Ixobrychus minutus	*	*	
Nycticorax nycticorax	*	*	
Ardeola ralloides	*	*	
Egretta garzetta	*	*	
E. alba	*	*	
Ardea purpurea	*	*	
Ciconia nigra	*	*	+
C. ciconia	*	*	+
Plegadis falcinellus	*	*	+
Platalea leucorodia	*	*	+
Phoenicopterus ruber	*	*	+
Cygnus columbianus	*	*	+
C. cygnus	*	*	+
Anser albifrons flavirostris	*		+
Branta leucopsis	*	*	+
Tadorna ferruginea	*	*	+
Aythya nyroca	*		+
Polysticta stelleri		*	+
Histrionicus histrionicus		*	+
Bucephala islandica		*	+
Pernis apivorus	*	*	+
Elanus caeruleus	+	*	+
Milvus migrans	*	*	+
Gypaetus barbatus	*	*	+
Neophron percnopterus	*	*	+
Gyps fulvus	*	*	+
Circaetus gallicus	*	*	+
Circus aeruginosus	*	*	+
C. cyaneus	*	*	+
C. macrourus	*	*	+
C. pygargus	*	*	+
Accipiter gentilis arrigonii	*	*	+
A. nisus granti	+	*	+
A. brevipes	*	*	+
Buteo rufinus	*	*	+
Aquila pomarina	*	*	+
A. clanga	*	*	+

continued

Appendix 3 (contd)

	EEC	Bern	Bonn
Aquila rapax		*	+
A. chrysaetos	*	*	+
Hieraaetus pennatus	*	*	+
H. fasciatus	*	*	+
Pandion haliaetus	*	*	+
Falco vespertinus		*	+
F. columbarius	*	*	+
F. eleonorae	*	*	+
F. biarmicus	*	*	+
F. cherrug		*	+
F. rusticolus		*	+
F. peregrinus	*	*	+
F. pelegrinoides	+	*	+
Bonasa bonasia	*		
Lagopus mutus pyrenaicus/	*		
L. m. helveticus	*		
Tetrao tetrix	*		
T. mlokosiewiczi			
T. urogallus	*		
Tetraogallus caspius			
Alectoris graeca saxatilis/	*		
A. g. whitakeri	*		
A. barbara	*		
Francolinus francolinus			
Perdix perdix italica/	*		
P. p. hispaniensis	+		
Turnix sylvatica	+	*	
Porzana porzana	*	*	
P. parva	*	*	
P. pusilla	*	*	
Porphyrio porphyrio	*	*	
Fulica cristata	+	*	
Anthropoides virgo		*	+
Grus grus	*	*	+
Himantopus himantopus	*	*	+
Recurvirostra avosetta	*	*	+
Burhinus oedicnemus	*	*	+
Cursorius cursor	+	*	
Glareola pratincola	*	*	+
G. nordmanni		*	+
Charadrius leschenaultii		*	+
C. morinellus	*	*	+
Pluvialis apricaria	*		+
Hoplopterus spinosus	*	*	+
Limicola falcinellus		*	+
Philomachus pugnax	*		+
Gallinago media	*	*	+
Limosa limosa			+
Tringa stagnatilis		*	+
T. glareola	*	*	+
Xenus cinereus		*	+
Phalaropus lobatus	*	*	+
P. fulicarius		*	+
Larus ichthyaetus			
Larus melanocephalus	*	*	
L. genei	*	*	
Rhodostethia rosea			
Pagophila eburnea		*	
Gelochelidon nilotica	*	*	

continued

Appendix 3 (contd)

	EEC	Bern	Bonn
Sterna caspia	*	*	
S. sandvicensis	*	*	
S. dougallii	*	*	
S. hirundo	*	*	
S. paradisaea	*	*	
S. albifrons	*	*	
Chlidonias hybridus	*	*	
C. niger	*	*	
C. leucopterus		*	
Uria aalge ibericus	+		
U. lomvia			
Pterocles orientalis	+	*	
P. alchata	*	*	
Columba palumbus azorica	+		
Bubo bubo	*	*	
Nyctea scandiaca	*	*	
Surnia ulula		*	
Glaucidium passerinum	*	*	
Strix uralensis		*	
S. nebulosa		*	
Asio flammeus	*	*	
Aegolius funereus	*	*	
Caprimulgus europaeus	*	*	
C. ruficollis	+	*	
Halcyon smyrnensis		*	
Alcedo atthis	*	*	
Ceryle rudis		*	
Merops superciliosus			
Coracias garrulus	*	*	+
Picus canus	*	*	
Dryocopus martius	*	*	
Dendrocopos major canariensis/	+	*	
D. m. thanneri	+	*	
D. syriacus	*	*	
D. medius	*	*	
D. leucotos	*	*	
Picoides tridactylus	*	*	
Apus caffer	+	*	
Chersophilus duponti	+	*	
Melanocorypha calandra	*	*	
M. leucoptera		*	
M. yeltoniensis		*	
Calandrella brachydactyla	*	*	
C. rufescens	+	*	
Galerida theklae	*	*	
Lullula arborea	*		
Anthus campestris	*	*	
Troglodytes t. fridariensis	*	*	
Cercotrichas galactotes	+	*	+
Luscinia svecica	*	*	+
Oenanthe leucura	*	*	+
Acrocephalus melanopogon	*	*	+
Hippolais olivetorum	*	*	+
Sylvia sarda	*	*	+
S. undata	*	*	+
S. rueppelli	*	*	+
S. nisoria	*	*	+
Ficedula parva	*	*	+
F. semitorquata	*	*	+

continued

Appendix 3 (contd)

	EEC	Bern	Bonn
Ficedula albicollis	*	*	+
Sitta krueperi	*	*	
S. whiteheadi	*	*	
Lanius collurio	*	*	
L. minor	*	*	
Pyrrhocorax pyrrhocorax	*	*	
Fringilla coelebs ombriosa	+		
Pyrrhula pyrrhula murina	+		
Loxia scotica	*	*	
Bucanetes githagineus	+	*	
Emberiza cineracea	*	*	
E. hortulana	*		
E. caesia	*	*	

Notes:

1. The importance of conservation measures in Europe, for some of these species in particular, should be emphasised. Some species in this category are confined (as a resident, breeding visitor or winter visitor) entirely or almost entirely to Europe, and have a limited range or restricted breeding habitat requirement (e.g. *Calonectris diomedea, Hydrobates pelagicus, Branta leucopsis, Accipiter brevipes, Falco eleonorae, Porzana parva, Larus melanocephalus, Sterna sandvicensis, Hippolais olivetorum, Sylvia sarda, Ficedula semitorquata, Sitta krueperi, S. whiteheadi, Loxia scotica, Emberiza cineracea* and *E. caesia*).

2. All Annex I species and subspecies (of the EEC Wild Birds Directive) and additional species (and subspecies) which are expected to be added to Annex I when it is next amended are included (unless they are listed in Appendix 2; globally threatened species).

3. *Tetrao urogallus cantabrius* is in Appendix II of the Bern Convention.

APPENDIX 4 **Additional species which have relatively small total world ranges with important populations in Europe**: see criteria category 4

Key as for Appendix 2

	EEC	Bern	Bonn
Puffinus puffinus		*	
Sula bassana			
Phalacrocorax aristotelis			
Anser brachyrhynchus			+
Tetraogallus caucasicus			
Alectoris graeca			
A. rufa			
Stercorarius skua			
Alca torda			
Apus unicolor		*	
Anthus berthelotii		*	
Prunella ocularis		*	
Irania gutturalis		*	+
Oenanthe cypriaca		*	+
Turdus torquatus			+
Hippolais polyglotta		*	+
Sylvia conspicillata		*	+
S. cantillans		*	+
S. melanocephala		*	+
S. melanothorax		*	+
Phylloscopus nitidus		*	+
P. bonelli		*	+
Regulus ignicapillus		*	+
Parus lugubris		*	
Sitta neumayer		*	
Certhia brachydactyla		*	
Lanius nubicus		*	
Cyanopica cyana		*	
Sturnus unicolor		*	
Serinus serinus		*	
S. canaria			
S. citrinella		*	
Loxia pytyopsittacus		*	
Rhodopechys sanguinea			
Emberiza cirlus		*	

Notes:

1. The importance of conservation measures in Europe, for some species in particular, should be emphasised. Some are confined to a comparatively small number of coastal breeding sites (*Puffinus puffinus*, *Sula bassana*, *Stercorarius skua* and *Alca torda*), or are restricted to small mountain ranges (*Tetraogallus caucasicus* and *Prunella ocularis*), or small islands and island groups (*Anthus berthelotii* and *Sylvia melanothorax*).

2. Subspecies of some species in Appendix 4 are included in Appendix 3.

APPENDIX 5 **Regions of Europe used when applying the site-selection criteria:** see criteria categories 3 and 4

Country	Region	One of the 5/10 most important sites for a species (see criteria categories 3 and 4) 5	10
Albania	Albania	*	
Andorra	Andorra	*	
Austria	Austria		*
Belgium	NUTS level 1: Wallonne; Vlaams Gewest	*	
Bulgaria	Bulgaria		*
Cyprus	Cyprus	*	
Czechoslovakia	Czech Republic	*	
	Slovak Republic	*	
Denmark	NUTS level 0: Denmark	*	
Faroe Islands	Faroes	*	
Greenland	Greenland		*
Finland	Finland		*
France	NUTS level 2	*	
German DR	German DR		*
FR Germany	NUTS level 1: Länder	*	
Greece	NUTS level 2	*	
Hungary	Hungary		*
Iceland	Iceland		*
Ireland	NUTS level 3	*	
Italy	NUTS level 2	*	
Liechtenstein	Liechtenstein	*	
Luxembourg	NUTS level 0: Luxembourg	*	
Malta	Malta	*	
Netherlands	NUTS level 0: Netherlands	*	
Norway	Norway		*
Svalbard	Svalbard	*	
Poland	Poland		*
Portugal	NUTS level 2	*	
Azores	Azores	*	
Madeira	Madeira	*	
Romania	Romania		*
Spain	NUTS level 1	*	
Canary Islands	Canary Islands	*	
Sweden	Sweden		*
Switzerland	Switzerland	*	
Turkey	Turkey		*

continued

Appendix 5 (contd)

Country	Region	One of the 5/10 most important sites for a species (see criteria categories 3 and 4) 5	10
United Kingdom	NUTS level 1	*	
Channel Islands	Channel Islands	*	
Isle of Man	Isle of Man	*	
Gibraltar	Gibraltar	*	
Yugoslavia	Republics and autonomous provinces of Yugoslavia	*	
USSR			
Republics except RSFSR	Belorussia		*
	Ukraine		*
	Azerbaijan	*	
	Georgia	*	
	Moldavia	*	
	Lithuania	*	
	Armenia	*	
	Latvia	*	
	Estonia	*	
	Kazakhstan (part of)	*	
RSFSR	Autonomous Soviet Socialist Republics and Oblasts	*	

Notes:

1. The regions in the European Community are the administrative regions which have been designated by the Statistical Office of the European Commission (Nomenclature des Unités Territoriales Statistiques: NUTS). Each country is divided into administrative units at levels on which statistics are systematically collected in Member States. This project has followed the CORINE Biotopes Project (an inventory of sites of importance for nature conservation in the European Community) in its subdivision of the European Community into NUTS regions (at various levels) when applying the site-selection criteria. Further explanation of these NUTS regions is given in the 'Comments on the inventory' for European Community countries.

2. Several of the above-mentioned regions are comparatively small, such that one or two sites per species is the maximum that can realistically be selected when applying the criteria in categories 3 and 4.

ALBANIA

Pygmy Cormorant *Phalacrocorax pygmeus*

INTRODUCTION

General information

Albania is bordered by south-west Yugoslavia, north-west Greece, and the southern Adriatic Sea. It is one of the smaller European states, having a surface area of just 28,750 sq km. About two-thirds of the country's 2.9 million inhabitants (an average population density of 100 persons per sq km) live in rural settlements, whilst the largest urban area is the capital city Tiranë, which holds approximately 220,000 people.

Topographically, Albania can be divided into four zones: an alpine zone, north of the River Drin, with peaks over 2000 m; a mountainous zone between the Drin and Osum valleys with alternating forested mountains and cultivated depressions; a region of limestone mountains and valleys south of the Osum valley; and a coastal plain which is up to 60 km wide and bisected by the Rivers Vijosë, Seman, Shkumbin, Drin, and Erzen. There are four very large lakes shared with Yugoslavia and/or Greece, namely: Liqen i Shkodrës (Lake Shkodra, or Skadarsko Jezero in Yugoslavia), Liqen i Ohrit (Lake Ohrid, or Ohridsko Jezero in Yugoslavia); Liqen i Prespa (Lake Megali Prespa, or Limni Megali Prespa in Greece, or Prespansko Jezero in Yugoslavia) and Liqen i Prespes (Lake Mikri Prespa, or Limni Mikri Prespa in Greece).

The flora is rich and diverse, reflecting a varied topography. Despite intensification of agriculture and a rapidly growing human population, there are still some extensive tracts of relatively undisturbed forested/mountainous terrain.

The littoral zone formerly held large areas of marshes and lagoons, but these have been largely drained in a post-war drive towards increased agricultural productivity and the extermination of malaria. Between 1946 and 1974, 60,000 ha were drained and a further 170,000 ha were 'improved' for agriculture. Breeding sites for *Phalacrocorax pygmeus* and *Pelecanus crispus* are known to have been drained. However, socio-economic reforms have also resulted in the creation of artificial wetlands such as reservoirs and canals, although these are thought to be not as important for birds.

Ornithological importance

Published details of ornithological observations and other environmental studies are few and fragmented; furthermore, communication with Albanian ornithologists has been extremely difficult.

In the 1950s and 1960s Albania was known to be of world importance for breeding *Phalacrocorax pygmeus* and *Pelecanus crispus*. The latter species was thought to have become extinct (as an Albanian breeder) by the early 1980s, but a population of at least 11 pairs was located in 1985. The present status of *Phalacrocorax pygmeus* is far from clear, with a large colony suspected at Liqen i Shkodrës. However, significant declines are thought to have occurred as a result of wetland modification and destruction.

Other species which are known still to breed include a variety of heron species, *Haliaeetus albicilla*, *Himantopus himantopus*, and *Recurvirostra avosetta*.

Given our understanding of the species breeding across the border in Yugoslavia and Greece, it is reasonable to assume that Albania still supports populations of *Gypaetus barbatus*, *Neophron percnopterus*, *Gyps fulvus*, *Aegypius monachus*, *Falco naumanni*, *F. biarmicus*, *Tetrao urogallus*, *Alectoris graeca* (several protected areas hold this species), and *Dendrocopos leucotos*.

Conservation infrastructure and protected-area system

There is a state body with responsibility for nature conservation, presumably within the Ministry of Forest and Water Economy.

Two categories of protected areas have been distinguished (Bouvier *in litt.* 1988): National Parks and Natural Reserves. Five National Parks have been designated, covering 19,000 ha. These are strictly protected with grazing, forestry, and hunting all prohibited. Natural Reserves are created for the management of one or more species; 18 sites have been designated covering 35,000 ha.

International measures relevant to the conservation of sites

Albania is not a party to any of the main conservation treaties referred to in the introduction to this book, and is the only Mediterranean country that is not a party to the Barcelona Convention.

Overview of the inventory

Only 13 sites are included that represent no more than a sample of the important bird areas in the country, with much of the information extracted from recent literature (see references). Nine of the sites are wetlands or areas of rocky coast, four are mountainous sites. Six of the sites are unprotected, including Liqen i Shkodrës which is possibly the most important site in the country; three sites are covered by Natural Reserves, and four sites by National Parks. There are clear deficiencies, but these reflect the shortage of information described above.

Acknowledgements

Unpublished material was provided by M. Bouvier, and this includes data provided by F. Lamani. Z. Karpowicz and M. Fasola provided some useful references.

INVENTORY

No.	Site name	Region	Criteria used to select site [see p.18] 0	1(i)	1(ii)	1(iii)	1(iv)	2	3	4
001	Liqen i Shkodrës	SR	*							
002	Liqen i Ohrit	PC	*							
003	Liqen i Prespa	KË	*							
004	Liqen i Prespes	KË	*							
005	Karaburun, Sazan, and Gjol i Nartës	VË						*		
006	Kënet'e Karavastas	LË,FR				*		*	*	
007	Wetlands of Shëngjin, Lesh, and Kunes	SR,LZ	*							
008	Thethi	SR	*							
009	Lura	PI	*							
010	Llogara	VË	*							
011	Pishe Poro	VË						*		
012	Marshabit	CI	*							
013	Liqen i Butrintit	SË	*							

SR=Shkodër PC=Pogradec KË=Korçë VË=Vlorë LË=Lushnjë
FR=Fier LZ=Lezhë PI=Peshkopi CI=Curri SË=Sarandë

Comments on the inventory

1. The site descriptions given should not be regarded as anything more than tentative outlines. It is hoped that this clear lack of information may stimulate further efforts towards filling a large gap in European ornithological knowledge.
2. Many sites fail to meet the site-selection criteria (see column 0 of above table). It has been difficult to apply the criteria because of the lack of information on these sites; they are included because of their suspected importance or because they are part of sites included in the Greek and/or Yugoslavian site inventories.
3. The area (ha) of two of the sites is not known.
4. The site name is followed by the name of the district or rreth, given in parentheses, where the site can be found. Albania has been treated as a single 'region' when applying the site-selection criteria (category 3).

Glossary

The following Albanian words have been used in the inventory: gjol = pond; liqen = lake; kënet = marsh.

---

001 Liqen i Shkodrës (Lake Shkodra or Skadarsko Jezero) (Shkodër)

42°10'N, 19°20'E *c.*35,000 ha (*c.*40 per cent in Albania)

Unprotected

A large freshwater lake in north-east Albania, on the border with Yugoslavia. Oligotrophic and generally shallow except for a few very deep parts. Overlaps with IBA no. 043 (Skadarsko Jezero) in Yugoslavia.

Formerly important for breeding waterfowl such as *Phalacrocorax pygmeus, Pelecanus crispus, Ardeola ralloides*, and *Aythya nyroca*. However, the lake shores in the Albanian sector have been heavily reclaimed for agriculture and some authorities consider the area to be of only minor importance, with the species mentioned above no longer nesting;

although observers in Yugoslavia believe that the large numbers of *Phalacrocorax pygmeus* which occur at the lake (*c.*2000 pairs) actually breed on the Albanian side. Birds seen in May 1985 and May 1987 included: *Ardeola ralloides*, *Egretta garzetta*, *E. alba*, *Circus aeruginosus*, *Coturnix coturnix* (many calling from lakeside fields), *Charadrius dubius* (common on dried-up fish-ponds next to the lake), *Sterna hirundo*, *Chlidonias hybridus*, *C. niger*, *Alcedo atthis*, and *Acrocephalus arundinaceus*.

002 Liqen i Ohrit (Lake Ohrid or Ohridsko Jezero) (Pogradec)

41°00'N, 20°45'E 34,800 ha (9700 ha in Albania)

Unprotected

A large freshwater lake on the border with south-west Yugoslavia. Overlaps with IBA no. 059 (Ohridsko Jezero) in Yugoslavia.

Formerly important for breeding waterfowl, and of great limnological and ichthyological interest. Recent visitors to the Albania sector have reported that the area is now of minor ornithological importance owing to reclamation for agriculture. The only species of note reported in May 1985 was *Ixobrychus minutus*. *Otis tarda*, *Glareola pratincola*, and *Sturnus roseus* have also been recorded. There is no information on wintering wildfowl from the Albanian sector, (but see the Yugoslavian account).

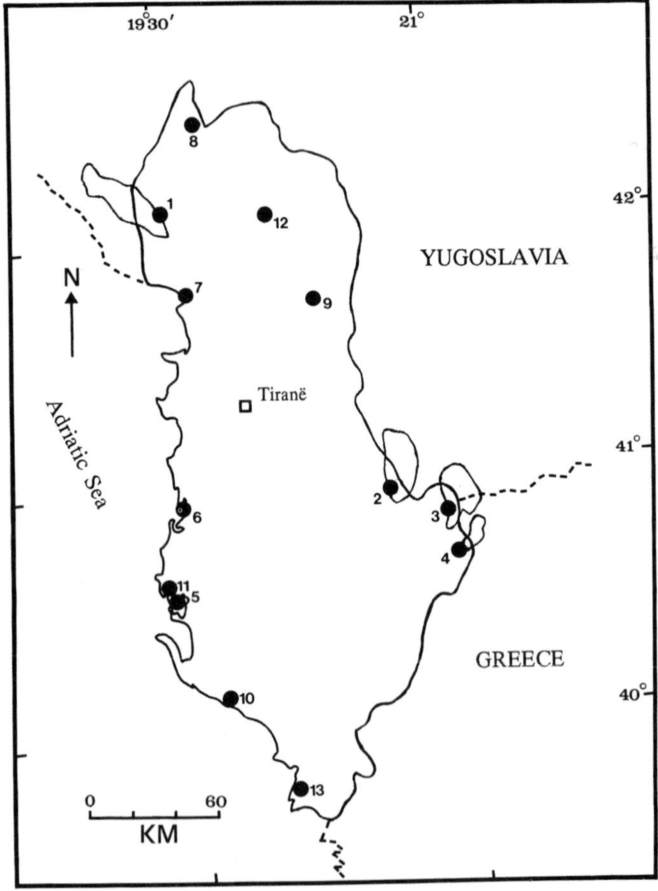

Figure 2: Map showing the location of the sites in Albania

003 Liqen i Prespa (Lake Megali Prespa or Limni Megali Prespa or Prespansko Jezero) (Korçë)

40°53'N, 20°57'E 30,000+ ha (approx. 10,000 ha in Albania)

Unprotected

Part of an extensive freshwater, mountain-basin lake which also extends into Greek and Yugoslavian territories. Formerly, the lake margins were marshy and supported important breeding waterfowl populations. These areas have now been largely drained and cultivated. Overlaps with IBA no. 032 (Limni Megali Prespa) in Greece and IBA no. 060 (Prespansko Jezero) in Yugoslavia.

Pelecanus crispus no longer nests and it is unlikely that anything remains of former colonies of *Phalacrocorax pygmeus* and *Pelecanus onocrotalus*. Important bird populations are still to be found in the Greek and Yugoslavian sectors of the lake.

004 Liqen i Prespes (Lake Mikri Prespa or Limni Mikri Prespa) (Korçë)

40°50'N, 21°05'E *c.*6000 ha (800 ha in Albania)

Unprotected

The western end of a large freshwater lake shared with Greece. As in the case of neighbouring Liqen i Prespa, its former importance (in the Albanian sector) has been greatly reduced by reclamation for agriculture. Overlaps with IBA no. 032 (Limni Mikri Prespa) in Greece.

Pelecanus spp. no longer nest on the Albanian side of the lake. No additional information available, though significant waterfowl populations still exist in the Greek sector of the lake.

005 Karaburun, Sazan, and Gjol i Nartës (Vlorë)

40°30'N, 19°18'E

Natural Reserve (Karaburun peninsula)

Sazan is a small rocky island off the Karaburun peninsula. Both these areas are a few kilometres west-south-west of Gjol i Nartës, which is a large coastal lagoon with a narrow opening to the sea. The whole area includes several saltpans and extensive rocky coastlines.

Gyps fulvus occurs and *Haliaeetus albicilla* breeds. This is the only area in Albania where Mediterranean Monk Seal *Monachus monachus* has been seen in recent years, and where *Canis aureus* is common.

006 Kënet'e Karavastas (Divjaka) (Lushnjë, Fier)

40°53'N, 19°25'E 4000 ha

National Park

A large coastal lagoon with a narrow opening to the sea. Public access is restricted, although commercial fishing is allowed. As one of the few Albanian coastal wetlands which remain more or less intact, this site is very important for waterfowl. Particularly significant was the discovery in 1985 of nesting *Pelecanus crispus*, previously thought to be extinct as a breeding species in the country.

The following species were noted in May 1985 (singles or small numbers unless otherwise stated) on the north side of the lagoon: *Pelecanus crispus* (11 nests; fisheries manager reported other colonies present in the area), *Haematopus ostralegus* (a few breeding), *Glareola pratincola*, *Charadrius alexandrinus*, *Numenius arquata*, *Sterna hirundo* (breeding in small numbers), *S. albifrons* (colony of *c.*200 breeding pairs), and *Lanius collurio*. Government documentation notes the presence of *Pelecanus onocrotalus* (50-100), which visit the site from Mikra Prespa in Greece, and *Haliaeetus albicilla* (4-5 pairs).

007 Wetlands of Shëngjin, Lesh, and Kunes (Shkodër, Lezhë)

41°47'N, 19°37'E

Includes four Natural Reserves (covering 5500 ha)

A complex of relatively intact coastal lakes and marshes near the mouth of the River Drin. The coastal lowlands are quite narrow in this part of the country, quickly rising to mountain foothills.

The area has long been known as important for breeding waterfowl, but the present status of species such as *Phalacrocorax carbo sinensis*, *P. pygmeus*, *Plegadis falcinellus*, and *Platalea leucorodia* is uncertain. *Phalacrocorax pygmeus* and *Plegadis falcinellus* have apparently bred at least during the last decade. It is probable that all the species mentioned above have (at least) seriously declined since former times. Species noted in May 1985 included (small numbers unless otherwise stated): *Phalacrocorax carbo sinensis*, *Nycticorax nycticorax*, *Egretta garzetta* (numerous), *Platalea leucorodia*, *Anas querquedula*, *Milvus migrans*, *Alectoris graeca*, *Rallus aquaticus*, *Haematopus ostralegus*, *Himantopus himantopus* (fairly common), *Charadrius dubius* (common), *C. alexandrinus*, *Calidris ferruginea* (many), *Tringa totanus*, *Arenaria interpres*, *Larus argentatus*, *Sterna hirundo* (small breeding colony), *S. albifrons* (fairly common), *Chlidonias niger*, *Alcedo atthis*, *Merops apiaster*, *Acrocephalus arundinaceus*, *Hippolais pallida*, and *Sturnus roseus*.

008 Thethi (Shkodër)

42°30'N, 19°45'E 4500 ha

National Park

A mountainous area (1200-2500 m) with forests of *Fagus* and *Abies alba*, thickets of *Pinus heldreichii*, and alpine pastures at high altitude.

The National Park has been designated partly because of its populations of large raptors and *Tetrao urogallus*. The mammals *Ursus arctos*, *Lynx lynx*, and *Rupicaria rupicaria* are also present.

009 Lura (Peshkopi)

41°45'N, 20°15'E 4000 ha

National Park

A mountainous area (900-2100 m) with forests of *Fagus* and *Abies alba*, lakes and bogs with *Pinus mugo*, and areas of *Taxus baccata*.

The National Park has been designated partly because of its populations of *Aquila chrysaetos*, *Tetrao urogallus*, and *Alectoris graeca*. *Ursus arctos* and *Lynx lynx* are also present. *Picoides tridactylus* was noted in May 1987, as well as other bird species typical of old mountain forests.

010 Llogara (Vlorë)

40°10'N, 19°40'E 3500 ha

National Park

A mountainous area (500-1600 m) with forests of *Pinus austriaca* and flora typical of calcareous soil.

The National Park has been designated partly because of its population of *Aquila chrysaetos* (min. 4 pairs). The diversity of habitats supports a wide variety of birds, with over 40 species of passerines seen in 1987, including *Ficedula parva*.

011 Pishe Poro (Vlorë)

40°45'N, 19°20'E 5500 ha

Natural Reserve

A section of coast adjacent to Levan, which possibly includes the sea bay 'Gjol i Nartës'; and possibly overlaps with site no. 005.

The Natural Reserve was selected because of its population of waterbirds and *Haliaeetus albicilla*. In May 1987 the following birds were observed: *Bubulcus ibis*, *Egretta alba*, *Ardea purpurea*, *Netta rufina*, *Circus aeruginosus*, *Circus cyaneus*, *Buteo rufinus*, *Haematopus ostralegus*, *Tringa totanus*, and *Larus melanocephalus*. Tracks of the mammal *Lutra lutra* were also noted.

012 Marshabit (Curri)

42°05'N, 20°07'E *c.*1000 ha

Unprotected

A mountainous area (1000-1500 m) with heterogeneous forests containing five major tree species: *Pinus austrica*, *Abies alba*, *Fagus* sp., *Tilia cordata*, and *Castanea sativa*. Although the area is unprotected there is no forestry, and the structure of the woods is typical of old mountainous forests.

In May 1986, at an altitude of 1100 m, six different species of raptors were observed *Buteo rufinus*, *Aquila chrysaetos*, *Hieraaetus fasciatus*, *Falco tinnunculus*, *F. subbuteo*, and *F. peregrinus*. Among the birds observed in May 1987, six different species of woodpeckers were noted including *Dryocopus martius*, and *Dendrocopos medius*. *Bonasa bonasia* is killed every year by local hunters and *Tetrao urogallus* is present. Tracks of the mammals *Ursus arctos*, *Canis lupus*, and *Martes martes* have been seen in the area.

013 Liqen i Butrintit (Sarandë)

39°50'N, 20°00'E *c.*1000 ha

Unprotected

A large, coastal, brackish-water lagoon without any opening to the sea. The major part of the shores are covered with typical forests (*Laurus nobilis*, *Fraxinus* spp., *Populus alba*, *Quercus* spp.) and marshes.

Bird species seen during very short visits to the area (in May 1986 and May 1987) included *Ardeola ralloides*, *Egretta alba*, *Ardea purpurea*, *Ciconia ciconia*, *Netta rufina*, *Neophron percnopterus*, *Circaetus gallicus*, *Circus aeruginosus*, *Alcedo atthis*, *Melanocorypha calandra*, *Hippolais olivetorum*, and *Lanius minor*. The area is also thought to be the richest in Albania for reptiles and amphibians.

MAIN REFERENCES

Barbieri, F., Bogliani, G. and Prigioni, C. (1986) Note sull'ornitofauna dell'Albania. *Riv. ital. Orn.* Milano 56 (1-2): 53-66.

Bogliani, G., Barbieri, F. and Prigioni, C. (1987) Ornithological research in Albania: an annotated bibliography. *Avocetta* 11: 63-66.

Bouvier, M. and Kempf, C. (1987) La Nature en Albanie. *Le Courier de la Nature* no. 109.

Lamani, F. and Zeko, I. (1983) L'Albanie, pays propre à l'hivernage des anseriformes. *Bilogia Gallo-Hellenica*. Vol. X, 1: 333-337.

ANDORRA

Chough *Pyrrhocorax pyrrhocorax*

INTRODUCTION

General information

The Principality of Andorra is located on the southern slopes of the eastern Pyrenees on the border between France and Spain. It has an area of 467.8 sq km and a population (in 1987) of 48,933 (an average population density of 105 persons per sq km), scattered in seven parishes. The country contains narrow valleys and gorges, surrounded by high mountains, and ranges in altitude from 860 m up to 2946 m. The cultivation of tobacco, potatoes, and hay, and grazing of free-range cattle are the main agricultural activities. Tourism is the main industry.

More than a third of the country is covered with forests of *Pinus*, *Abies*, *Quercus*, and *Betula*, and rich alpine meadows are also widespread.

Ornithological importance

The most important breeding species are *Circaetus gallicus* (2+ pairs), *Aquila chrysaetos* (3 pairs), *Falco peregrinus* (3+ pairs), *Tetrao urogallus* (10+ pairs), and *Lagopus mutus*. *Gypaetus barbatus* occurs on foraging flights but does not breed. Owing to the altitude of the high passes, the extent of visible migration depends mainly on the weather and during spring northerly winds trap birds in the valleys. Passage migrants include *Ciconia ciconia*, *Pernis apivorus*, and *Milvus migrans*.

Conservation infrastructure and protected-area system

There are no protected areas except one reserve where hunting is prohibited until 1992. All birds of prey have been protected by law since February 1988.

International measures relevant to the conservation of sites

Andorra is not a member of the European Community, nor has it signed any of the major conservation treaties referred to in the introduction to this book.

Overview of the inventory

A single important bird area is listed which includes much of the country and all of the montane and plateau areas. It is basically unprotected and subject to heavy human pressure which includes tourism and skiing (many of the mountain slopes have been developed for skiing, causing much damage), the use of four-wheel-drive vehicles, scrambling motorbikes, and skidoos. Hunting and the use of poisoned baits are also problems.

Acknowledgements

The following site account has been compiled from information provided by M.-J. Dubourg (Associació per a la Defensa de la Natura, Andorra), who also helped with the preparation of the introduction, and the Spanish Ornithological Society (Sociedad Española de Ornitología).

INVENTORY

No.	Site name	Region	Criteria used to select site [see p.18]							
			0	1(i)	1(ii)	1(iii)	1(iv)	2	3	4
001	Pirineo de Andorra	Andorra							*	

Comments on the inventory

1. Andorra has been treated as a single 'region' when applying the site-selection criteria (category 3).

---

001 Pirineo de Andorra (Andorra)

42°35'N, 01°35'E 40,000 ha

Unprotected

A mountainous area (1600-2900 m), which comprises much of Andorra except the Valira Valley, with coniferous woodland (*Pinus sylvestris*), and alpine grasslands. Human activities include tourism, skiing, tobacco-growing/manufacturing, and stock-farming.

Important for birds of forest and high mountains including *Circaetus gallicus*, *Aquila chrysaetos*, *Lagopus mutus*, *Tetrao urogallus*, *Perdix perdix hispaniensis*, *Dryocopus martius*, and *Pyrrhocorax pyrrhocorax*.

MAIN REFERENCE

IUCN (1986) Plants in Danger: What do we know? IUCN: Gland, Switzerland and Cambridge.

AUSTRIA

Middle Spotted Woodpecker *Dendrocopos medius*

INTRODUCTION

General information

The Federal Republic of Austria occupies a central geographical position in Europe and has borders with Switzerland, Liechtenstein, the Federal Republic of Germany, Czechoslovakia, Hungary, Yugoslavia, and Italy. The country's total territory extends to some 84,000 sq km and the population exceeds 7.5 million people (an average population density of 90 persons per sq km in 1981).

Much of Austria is above 500 m, and the south-western part of the country is dominated by the Alps, which reach 3660 m. The Danube plain east of Vienna, which is largely below 200 m, is the most extensive lowland area in the country. The major rivers are the River Inn along the border with the Federal Republic of Germany, the Danube (Donau), which divides the north-east part of the country, and the March that runs along the border with Czechoslovakia and joins the Danube east of Vienna. The main lakes are Lake Constance (Bodensee) in the west, the Attersee east of Salzburg, and Lake Neusiedl (Neusiedler See) in the east.

At present, 38 per cent of Austria is covered by forest, a large proportion of which comprises montane and subalpine forests of *Quercus*, *Abies*, and particularly *Picea*. The lowland *Quercus*/*Carpinus* forests have been lost to agriculture and viticulture, and larger forests of this type are left only on the hills and lower mountains. Even in the sub-montane zone, most of the forests in the valleys have been replaced by arable land.

Forests still dominate in mountainous areas, and large parts (by comparison with most central European countries) have retained their original vegetational character. However, even in this region, forests have been replaced by alpine pastures and grasslands.

The plains of eastern Austria (northern Burgenland, eastern Niederösterreich) form part of the western fringe of the Pannonian forest steppe with islands of oak-shrub and primary grassland covering rock, sand, gravel, or loess in xerothermic situations. The same area is noteworthy for its wetlands – alkali flats and wet meadows with a distinct eastern flora – and its surviving patches of secondary 'steppe' of puszta-type.

Only remnants of the formerly very extensive moorlands have survived (mostly in the west), but the Rivers Danube and March still have extensive and impressive tracts of annually flooded riverine forests. In the south and south-east (eastern Tirol, Kärnten, Steiermark) sub-Mediterranean influences are evident. The Alps support a full range of vegetation zones from *Pinus nigra* (with *Pinus sylvestris* forests along the eastern fringes and in the arid inner valleys) through *Picea abies* and *Pinus cembra* to *P. mugo*, with alpine heath and grassland above the tree line, and rock and permanent snow at the highest altitudes.

Ornithological importance

Internationally, the most important bird habitats are the quite unique wetlands of Neusiedler See and Seewinkel with adjoining meadows, remnant moorland, alkaline pans, and shallow lakes, as well as the equally outstanding complex of rivers, oxbow lakes, riverine forest, and flood-plain meadows along the Danube, March, and Thaya. Further areas of major conservation value are the granitic plateau of the Waldviertel with its deeply incised meandering valleys (some still clean enough for *Lutra lutra* and Freshwater Pearl Mussel *Margaritifera margaritifera*), the vegetationally rich forests of the Wienerwald with its eastern fringe of forest-steppe rich in xerothermophilic plants and animals, and the multifaceted alpine complex of the Hohe Tauern National Park, which includes the highest ranges of the eastern Alps.

The important breeding species (approximate number of pairs, unless otherwise stated) are as follows: *Botaurus stellaris* (200-300), *Egretta alba* (250), *Ardea purpurea* (100), *Ciconia nigra* (60-65), *C. ciconia* (290), *Platalea leucorodia* (50), *Aythya nyroca* (100), *Milvus migrans* (30-35), *Circus aeruginosus* (150), *C. pygargus* (5-10), *Aquila chrysaetos* (70-100), *Falco peregrinus* (30), *F. cherrug* (5), *Otis tarda* (60-80 birds), *Bonasa bonasia* (10,000 birds), *Tetrao tetrix* (10,000 birds), *T. urogallus* (10,000 birds), *Porzana parva* (3000), *Recurvirostra avosetta* (50-100), *Charadrius morinellus* (10), *Limosa limosa* (70-130), *Sterna hirundo* (120), *Bubo bubo* (200-250), *Glaucidium passerinum* (1000), *Asio flammeus* (10), *Aegolius funereus* (1000), *Caprimulgus europaeus* (500), *Alcedo atthis* (500), *Coracias garrulus* (10), *Dryocopus martius* (5000), *Dendrocopos leucotos* (100), *D. medius* (1000), *Picoides tridactylus* (5000), *Lullula arborea* (100-200), *Anthus campestris* (10), *Luscinia svecica cyaneculus* (300), *L. s. svecica* (50), *Acrocephalus melanopogon* (several thousand), *Lanius minor* (10), *Emberiza hortulana* (10), and *Serinus citrinella* (1000). Passage migrants and winter visitors include: geese, with (autumn maxima) *Anser fabalis* (20,000), *A. albifrons* (6000-9000), and *A. anser* (5000-10,000); ducks and waders (autumn maxima), with *Anas clypeata* (2500), *A. strepera* (5000), *Netta rufina* (1000), and *Limosa limosa* (800). Midwinter numbers of some waterfowl species include *Podiceps cristatus* (1000), *Anas platyrhynchos* (5000-20,000), *Aythya ferina* (6000), *A. fuligula* (11,000), *Bucephala clangula* (2000-5000), *Mergus merganser* (400), and *Fulica atra* (20,000-30,000).

Conservation infrastructure and protected-area system

Categories for habitat protection in individual provinces are not always comparable. In general, however, the categories of protection in the inventory may be defined as follows:

1. Landscape Protection Areas (Landschaftsschutzgebiet)
   Operations which would change the appearance of the landscape are forbidden; this helps to control building programmes, but alterations in the type of land-use are, however, generally permitted.

2. Partial Nature Reserves (Teilnaturschutzgebiet)
   Permits traditional agricultural use within certain restrictions in favour of protected plants or animals (mostly regulations like postponing mowing until after the flowering/fruiting period).

3. Nature Reserves (Vollnaturschutzgebiet)
   Any operation (including entry) is, as a rule, forbidden, and only certain forms of usage (e.g. hunting, fishing) can be permitted.

Nature conservation in Austria is not the responsibility of the national government but is taken care of by the Federal States (Bundesländer). This is the reason for a lot of (mostly minor) regional differences, but does not interfere with these major categories. A rather unusual speciality of Austrian nature-conservation legislation is, that even in (full) nature reserves, hunting and fishing might be allowed.

International measures relevant to the conservation of sites

Austria has ratified the Ramsar Convention and Bern Convention. It has designated five Ramsar Sites (covering 102,370 ha; four out of five included in this inventory), four Biosphere Reserves (two included in this inventory), but no Biogenetic Reserves.

Overview of the inventory

The inventory includes Austria's internationally most important wetlands: Donau-March-Thaya-Auen, Neusiedler See and Seewinkel (covered by two site accounts in this inventory), the Rhine delta (Vorarlberger Rheindelta), and the reservoirs of the lower Inn along the German border (Innstauseen). From an ornithological viewpoint, the Neusiedler See area is the richest. It is the only area in Austria for some 14 breeding species of special concern and provides habitat for most of the country's breeding and passage waders and nearly all of the passage and wintering geese.

Land-bird areas were chosen not only on the basis of quantitative criteria, but also in order to include a representative cross-section of Austria's main bird habitats, from the plains to the high montane landscapes. As far as possible, sizeable, contiguous landscape units, which are capable of functioning ecologically, were given priority. There is one major gap: the complex of alpine river landscapes, severely threatened by hydroelectric engineering projects and other 'development', is not yet adequately represented. Not only from an Austrian but from a European point of view, such landscapes are scarce and still being damaged. The very sketchy available information indicates that the valley, gorges, and (particularly) extensive gravel-beds of the upper Lech (from Vorarlberg to the Tirol-Federal Republic of Germany border, infringed but not yet irreparably damaged by hydrotechnology), would qualify as a representative and highly valuable important bird area. Research beginning there now should guarantee that in a future edition of this inventory the area, which supports breeding *Mergus merganser*, *Actitis hypoleucos*, and one of the very last breeding populations of *Charadrius dubius* in its natural habitat (instead of gravel-pits), will be adequately covered.

Unfortunately, the most important areas (not only for birds, but also because of their uniqueness, their ecological fragility, and the floral and faunal richness of their habitats) are still in grave danger (in spite of some degree of legal protection). In 1984 a nationwide uproar prevented the damming of the Danube east of Vienna and with it the destruction of the most valuable remaining tract of riverine forest along the whole stretch of Europe's second largest river. Despite this, new plans are proposed. At Neusiedler Seewinkel, agriculture and development are responsible for continuing habitat loss and dangerous eutrophication of the lakes and inflowing waters.

Acknowledgements

The site descriptions were compiled from information provided by K. Bauer, J. Gressel, A. Grüll, E. Hable, K. Kirchberger, H.-J. Lauermann, F. Samwald, O. Samwald, and H. Schifter. M. Leitner helped with the final text. The introduction to this inventory was written by K. Bauer, A. Grüll and H. Schifter. In addition, G. Dick and G. Aubrecht submitted data-sheets to IWRB.

INVENTORY

No.	Site name	Region	Criteria used to select site [see p.18]							
			0	1(i)	1(ii)	1(iii)	1(iv)	2	3	4
001	Neusiedler See	BD				*			*	
002	Seewinkel	BD				*			*	
003	Hanság	BD						*	*	
004	Parndorfer Platte	BD						*	*	
005	Donau-March-Thaya-Auen	NH						*	*	
006	Braunsberg-Hundsheimer Berg	NH							*	
007	Zentrales Marchfeld	NH						*		
008	Wienerwald	NH,WN							*	
009	Ötscher – Dürrenstein	NH							*	
010	Waldviertel	NH							*	
011	Innstauseen	OH				*			*	
012	Nockberge	SK,KN							*	
013	Südoststeirisches Hügelland	SK							*	
014	Seetaler Alpen	SK							*	
015	Puxberg	SK							*	
016	Niedere Tauern	SG,SK							*	
017	Radtstätter Tauernpass including Hundesfeld	SG							*	
018	Hohe Tauern and Rauristal	KN,SG,TL							*	
019	Karwendel	TL							*	
020	Vorarlberger Rheindelta	VG				*			*	

BD=Burgenland NH=Niederösterreich WN=Wien OH=Oberösterreich
SK=Steiermark KN=Kärnten SG=Salzburg TL=Tirol VG=Vorarlberg

Comments on the inventory

1. The regions following the site names in parentheses are the Federal States. Austria has been treated as a single 'region' when applying the site-selection criteria (category 3).
2. The application of the criteria in category 3 as depicted in the above table is provisional only; as stated in the 'overview of the inventory', some land-bird areas were chosen primarily in order to include a representative cross-section of Austria's bird habitats.

Glossary

The following German words have been used in the inventory: Alpen = alps; Auen = river plains; Berg = mountain; Hügelland = hillside area; See = lake.

---

001 Neusiedler See (Burgenland)

47°42'-47°57'N, 16°40'-16°51'E 25,000-30,000 ha

Included in Ramsar Site (Neusiedler See region: 57,000-62,500 ha) and Biosphere Reserve (25,000 ha)

Landscape Protection Area; Partial Nature Reserves and several Nature Reserves

An alkaline and eutrophic salt-lake, the largest in Europe, with an average depth of 1 m. There are extensive reedbeds of *Phragmites australis* up to 6 km wide in places. The salt content results mainly from carbonates and sulphates in the underground water, which reaches the surface through fissures in the rock. Water-levels fluctuate because of evaporation in summer.

Breeding species include *Botaurus stellaris*, *Ixobrychus minutus*, *Egretta alba* (*c.*250 pairs), *Ardea purpurea* (*c.*100 pairs), *Platalea leucorodia* (*c.*50 pairs), *Anser anser* (*c.*300 pairs), *Aythya nyroca*, *Circus aeruginosus* (min. 130 pairs), *Porzana porzana*, *P. parva*, and *Luscinia svecica*; also impressive numbers of commoner reed birds, for example *Rallus aquaticus* (*c.*10,000 pairs). In autumn, moderate numbers of Anatidae occur and have included *Anas strepera* (2200), *A. crecca* (7000), and *A. clypeata* (2300).

002 Seewinkel (Burgenland)

47°42'-47°51'N, 16°45'-16°57'E 30,000 ha

Included in Ramsar Site (Neusiedler See region: 57,000-62,500 ha)

Landscape Protection Area; Partial Nature Reserves and several Nature Reserves

Seewinkel is adjacent to Neusiedler See and is an extension of the Hungarian steppe (puszta). Mainly dry alkaline grasslands with several salt-lakes (some frequently drying out in summer) and marshes. There is some agricultural land and vineyards. The extension of the vineyards is detrimental to the area.

Breeding species include *Podiceps nigricollis* (40 pairs), *Ciconia ciconia* (20 pairs), *Anas querquedula* (*c.*40 pairs), *A. clypeata* (50 pairs), *Circus pygargus* (*c.*5 pairs), *Porzana porzana* (max. 10 pairs), *P. pusilla* (max. 1 pair), *Recurvirostra avosetta* (50-100 pairs), *Limosa limosa* (50-130 pairs), *Tringa totanus* (150-200 pairs), *Larus melanocephalus* (max. 2 pairs), *Sterna hirundo* (60 pairs), *Asio flammeus* (max. 10 pairs), *Tyto alba* (max. 5 pairs), and *Lanius minor* (*c.*10 pairs). Large numbers of ducks and waders occur on spring and autumn passage with *Philomachus pugnax* (max. 4000) in spring, and *Anser fabalis* (max. 22,000), *A. albifrons* (max. 7000), *A. anser* (max. 5000), *Anas strepera* (max. 1000), *A. crecca* (max. 4000), *A. clypeata* (max. 1000), and *Limosa limosa* (max. 800) in autumn.

003 Hanság (Burgenland)

47°45'N, 17°02'E *c.*2500 ha Included in Ramsar Site (Neusiedler See region)

Mainly unprotected; partly a Nature Reserve (*c.*130 ha)

Agricultural land and bogs with some deciduous woodland.

Breeding species include *Circus pygargus* (1 pair), *Limosa limosa* (5 pairs), *Numenius arquata* (2 pairs), *Otis tarda* (*c.*30 resident birds with 5 breeding females; decreasing), and *Asio flammeus* (5 pairs). *Aquila pomarina* regularly frequents the site and in winter up to 200 *Otis tarda* occur.

004 Parndorfer Platte (Burgenland)

47°53'-48°02'N, 16°51'-17°05'E *c.*18,000 ha

Partly a Nature Reserve (Zurndorfer Eichenwald) and some smaller protected areas

A low, flat, plateau, which is largely treeless in the western part, to the north-east of Neusiedler See; bisected only by a little-used railway line in the western part and a district road in the less important eastern part. An area of intensive agriculture with patches of dry grassland and grassland with scrub and a *Quercus* wood. There is a plan to build an international motorway (Autobahn) that would bisect the area and destroy some of the valuable non-agricultural sites.

An important area for *Otis tarda* (max. 26 birds). Other breeding species include *Burhinus oedicnemus*, *Anthus campestris*, *Sylvia nisoria*, and *Lanius collurio*. It is of major importance as a hunting area for raptors breeding in the Neusiedler See area, particularly *Circus aeruginosus* and *C. pygargus*, and is regularly used by oversummering and passage raptors that breed in Czechoslovakia and Hungary, such as *Milvus migrans*, *M. milvus*, *Aquila pomarina*, *Falco vespertinus*, and *F. cherrug*.

005 Donau-March-Thaya-Auen (Niederösterreich)

48°12'N, 16°28'E – 48°11'N, 16°58'E and 48°11'N, 16°58'E – 48°43'N, 16°53'E 38,500 ha

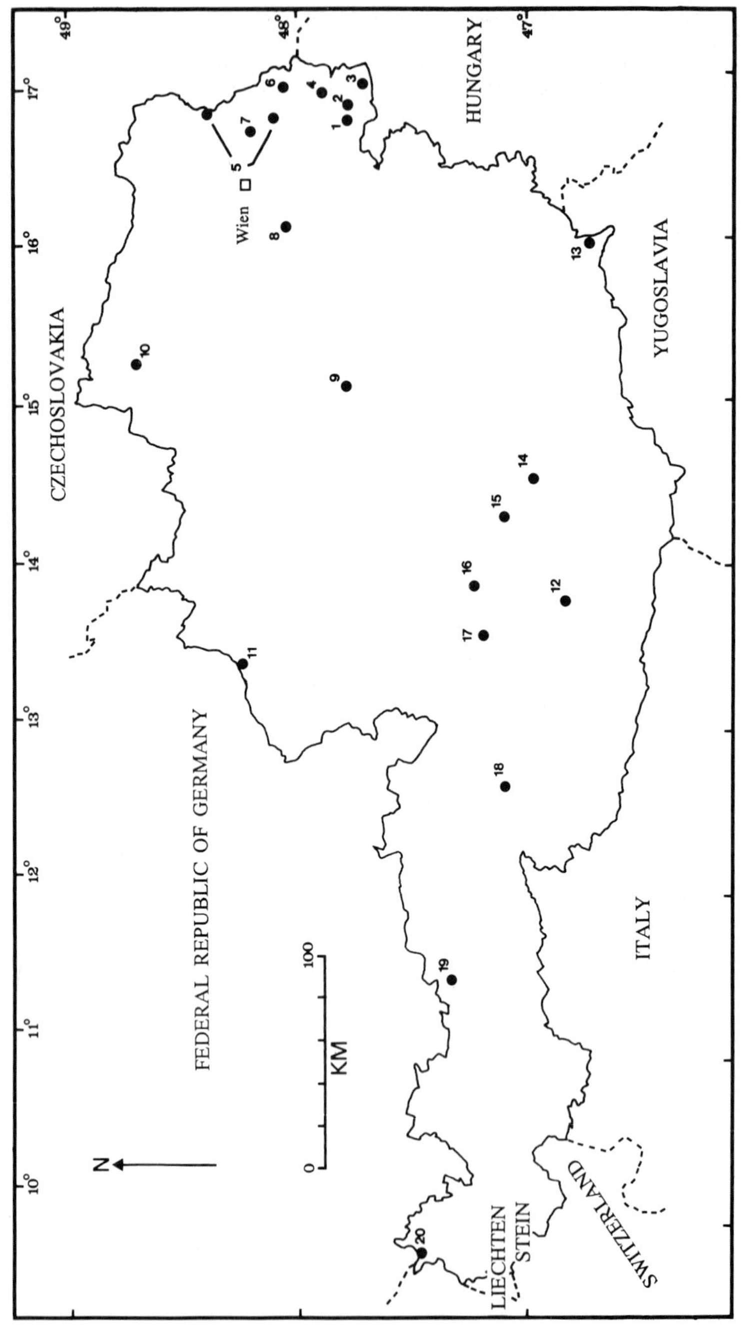

Figure 3: Map showing the location of the sites in Austria

Ramsar Site (Donau-March-Auen: 38,500 ha) and Biosphere Reserve (1000 ha)

Partly a Nature Reserve (Marchauen-Marchegg: 1120 ha) and Landscape Protection Area (2000 ha)

A complex of riverine and flood-plain forests including meadows, backwaters, and oxbows. Includes the Donau (Danube) between Wien (Vienna) and Hainburg, the March between Hainburg and Hohenau, and the Thaya between Hohenau and Bernhardsthal. These areas comprise the largest remaining tract of near-natural to natural riverine and flood-plain forest in central Europe. The stretch of the March is quite different floristically to the Donau (it is referred to as the 'westernmost forest-steppe river'), with stands of *Fraxinus angustifolia* and the westernmost locality for *Acer tataricum*, *Vitis sylvestris*, *Urtica kioviensis*, and *Leucojum aestivum*. The intensification of forestry management (use of *Populus* hybrids and heavy machinery) and reclamation of meadows continues slowly to reduce the value of the area, and a major threat is the continuing possibility of hydroelectric development between Wien and Hainburg.

Breeding species include *Ciconia nigra* (6+ pairs), *C. ciconia* (30 pairs), *Pernis apivorus*, *Milvus migrans* (10 pairs), *Circus aeruginosus*, *C. pygargus*, *Crex crex*, *Alcedo atthis*, *Picus canus*, *Dryocopus martius*, *Dendrocopos medius*, *Sylvia nisoria*, *Ficedula albicollis*, and *Lanius collurio*. The area is also the stronghold for *Locustella fluviatilis* in Austria. *Haliaeetus albicilla* irregularly oversummers and possibly breeds, with up to 10 in winter. *Falco cherrug* also occurs throughout the year.

006 Braunsberg-Hundsheimer Berg (Niederösterreich)

48°06'N, 16°56'E 210 ha

Nature Reserve

Chalk grassland and xerothermophytic shrubs on the steep, southward face of two isolated calcareous rocks (which although south of the Danube are geologically part of the Carpathian chain), with *Pinus* and *Quercus/Carpinus* forest on the western, northern, and eastern slopes. An area of exceptional botanical and entomological interest. There are no problems at present but existing quarrying rights might become a problem in future.

Breeding species include *Sylvia nisoria*, *Lullula arborea*, and *Lanius collurio*. *Pernis apivorus*, *Picus canus*, *Dendrocopos syriacus*, and *D. medius* breed in the adjacent wooded parts.

007 Zentrales Marchfeld (Niederösterreich)

48°10'-48°20'N, 16°35'-16°55'E *c.*30,000 ha

Partly covered by several Nature Reserves (Sandberge Oberweiden, Weikendorfer Remise, Schlosspark Obersiebenbrunn, and Wacholderheide Obersiebenbrunn)

Mainly an intensively cultivated area (partly under irrigation) with remnant natural or near-natural (floristically rich) dry grassland on consolidated sand-dunes and gravel; there is also dry forest. Parts of the area are managed for the conservation of *Otis tarda*.

An important area for *Otis tarda* with 6-7 breeding females and 22 wintering birds. Other breeding species include *Caprimulgus europaeus*, *Dendrocopos syriacus*, *Sylvia nisoria*, *Lanius collurio*, and possibly *Circus aeruginosus*, *Burhinus oedicnemus*, and *Anthus campestris*. *Haliaeetus albicilla* (1-5) and *Falco peregrinus* occur in winter.

008 Wienerwald (Wien, Niederösterreich)

47°57'-48°20'N, 15°47'-16°21'E 120,000 ha

Landscape Protection Area with one large and several small Nature Reserves (Lainzer Tiergarten: *c.*2000 ha; Eichkogel: 34 ha; Glaslauterriegl: 6 ha)

A forested area to the west of Wien (Vienna) with: deciduous forest (*Fagus*, *Carpinus*, *Quercus cerris*, *Q. petraea*) in the north-eastern part; deciduous and coniferous forest (*Abies*, *Picea*, *Pinus sylvestris*, *Larix*) in the north-western part; *Pinus nigra* forest in the south-eastern part, and mixed deciduous and coniferous forest on calcareous rock in the south-western part. The main human activities are forestry and tourism. Lainzer

Tiergarten is a former imperial hunting reserve and there is degradation of the natural vegetation from overgrazing; the encroachment of settlements is also a problem.

Breeding species include *Ciconia nigra* (1-2 pairs), *Pernis apivorus*, *Bubo bubo*, *Caprimulgus europaeus*, *Alcedo atthis*, *Picus canus*, *Dryocopus martius*, *Dendrocopos medius*, *D. leucotos* (1-2 pairs), *Lullula arborea*, *Sylvia nisoria*, *Ficedula parva*, *F. albicollis*, *Lanius collurio*, and *Emberiza hortulana*.

009 Ötscher – Dürrenstein (Niederösterreich)

47°48'-48°00'N, 14°00'-15°25'E 80,000 ha

Landscape Protection Area and Nature Reserves (Lechnergraben: 200 ha; Rothwald: 600 ha; Stockgrund-Kothbergtal: 40 ha)

A varied and dissected part of the calcareous and dolomitic northern Alps and pre-Alps, covered by submontane, montane, subalpine, and alpine vegetation belts. The main vegetation consists of a mosaic of climax stands dominated by *Abies*, *Picea*, and *Fagus*, and relict forests of *Pinus sylvestris* and *Larix*. Economic activities include forestry, tourism, agriculture (dairying), and apiculture. Encroachment of the area for the exploitation of hydroelectric power is an increasing problem.

Breeding species include *Pernis apivorus*, *Aquila chrysaetos*, *Falco peregrinus*, *Bonasa bonasia*, *Lagopus mutus*, *Tetrao tetrix*, *T. urogallus*, *Bubo bubo*, *Glaucidium passerinum*, *Aegolius funereus*, *Alcedo atthis*, *Picus canus*, *Dryocopus martius*, *Dendrocopos leucotos*, *Picoides tridactylus*, *Ficedula parva*, *F. albicollis*, and *Lanius collurio*.

010 Waldviertel (Niederösterreich)

48°10'-49°01'N, 14°42'-15°59'E 490,000 ha

The region includes seven Nature Reserves, four Landscape Protection Areas

A rich faunal area with dry areas, deep natural river gorges, and hillside woodlands of different compositions. The manifold habitats are threatened by the intensification of agriculture and forestry, flooding to create dams for electricity generation, road construction, the cutting of old trees, and the drainage and infilling of small rivers. There are also conflicts with anglers (who cause disturbance and call for the control of fish-eating birds).

Breeding species include *Ixobrychus minutus* (less than 5 pairs), *Ciconia nigra* (15-20 pairs), *C. ciconia* (*c.*10 pairs), *Aythya nyroca* (*c.*5 pairs), *Pernis apivorus* (*c.*50 pairs), *Circus aeruginosus* (1-2 pairs), *Bonasa bonasia* (less than 50 pairs), *Tetrao tetrix* (less than 50 pairs; about 700 pairs in 1960), *T. urogallus* (less than 30 pairs; about 200 pairs in 1960), *Bubo bubo* (*c.*30 pairs), *Aegolius funereus* (less than 5 pairs), *Caprimulgus europaeus* (less than 10 pairs), *Dryocopus martius* (more than 200 pairs), *Dendrocopos syriacus* (*c.*10 pairs), *D. medius* (*c.*30 pairs), *Picoides tridactylus* (less than 10 pairs), *Lullula arborea* (less than 50 pairs), *Sylvia nisoria* (50-70 pairs), and *Ficedula parva* (*c.*5 pairs). Wintering species include *Haliaeetus albicilla* (0-2) and *Circus cyaneus* (*c.*20).

011 Innstauseen (Oberösterreich)

48°14'N, 13°01'E - 48°27'N, 13°26'E 1955 ha Ramsar Site (870 ha)

Partly a Nature Reserve (Unterer Inn: 870 ha)

A 50 km length of the River Inn between the mouth of the River Salzach and Schärding on the border with the Federal Republic of Germany, comprising four reservoirs (dammed stretches) with riverine forest in places, and islands and sandflats. The water is mainly 0-1 m deep; deeper only in the vicinity of power-plants. There are electricity-generating plants; also fishing and hunting (which are problems at the site).

Breeding species include *Ixobrychus minutus*, *Nycticorax nycticorax* (12-13 pairs), *Pernis apivorus*, *Circus aeruginosus*, *Limosa limosa*, *Sterna hirundo*, *Alcedo atthis*, *Picus canus*, *Luscinia svecica*, and *Lanius collurio*. A considerable variety of species occurs on passage, some in large numbers, including *Cygnus olor* (500), *Anas strepera* (1900), *A. platyrhynchos* (12,000), *Aythya ferina* (13,000), *A. fuligula* (20,000), *Bucephala clangula*

(4000), *Philomachus pugnax* (13,400), and *Fulica atra* (13,000). Other passage species include *Tringa glareola* and *Chlidonias niger*.

012 Nockberge (Steiermark, Kärnten)

46°50'N, 13°40'E 32,840 ha

National Park and a complex of Nature Reserves and Landscape Protection Areas

High montane, subalpine, and extensive alpine zones. Human activities include tourism, forestry, and agriculture. Problems include road building and winter tourism.

Particularly important for *Charadrius morinellus* (5 pairs) as one of the few breeding sites in the Alps. Other breeding species include *Bonasa bonasia*, *Lagopus mutus*, *Tetrao tetrix*, *T. urogallus*, *Alectoris graeca*, *Bubo bubo*, *Glaucidium passerinum*, *Aegolius funereus*, *Dryocopus martius*, and *Picoides tridactylus*.

013 Südoststeirisches Hügelland (Steiermark)

46°45'-46°51'N, 15°51'-16°00'E 10,000 ha

Landscape Protection Area

A rich farmland area with riverine forest (*Quercus*), hillside forests, vineyards, and orchards. Human activities include traditional farming and modern agriculture. There are some villages and many scattered farms. The replacement of grassland areas with maize cultivation, and the clearance of forest and orchards are a threat to the bird populations at this site.

Breeding species include *Ciconia ciconia* (1 pair), *Coracias garrulus* (9 pairs plus 3 individuals; rapidly declining), *Picus canus* (*c.*5 pairs), *Ficedula albicollis* (10-20 pairs), and *Lanius collurio* (30-40 pairs).

014 Seetaler Alpen (Steiermark)

47°02'-47°06'N, 14°32'-14°35'E 2000 ha

Nature Reserve (Bird Reserve)

Alpine meadows, ledges exposed to wind, and forest zone with *Pinus cembra*. Human activities include cattle- and sheep-grazing, game hunting, and military training. During the breeding season the region is wardened and no military training takes place.

Breeding species include *Aquila chrysaetos* (1 pair), *Lagopus mutus* (10-12 pairs), *Tetrao tetrix* (5 pairs), *Charadrius morinellus* (3-4 pairs), *Aegolius funereus* (2 pairs), *Picoides tridactylus* (4 pairs), *Alectoris graeca* (1 pair; not seen since 1982), and *Turdus torquatus* (13-15 pairs).

015 Puxberg (Steiermark)

47°08'N, 14°20'E 875 ha

Landscape Protection Area and partly a Nature Reserve

A calcareous south-facing cliff with dry forest (*Abies*, *Larex*) and scattered forest below the sunny cliff. The south-facing cliff provides a microhabitat for flora and fauna. Human activities are few, with some hunting of *Tetrao* spp. but not *Bonasa bonasia*.

Breeding species include *Falco peregrinus* (1 pair until 1968 when the nest was robbed; no breeding since), *Aquila chrysaetos* (1 pair), *Tetrao tetrix* (2 pairs), *T. urogallus* (30 pairs), *Bubo bubo* (1 pair), *Glaucidium passerinum* (3 pairs), and *Aegolius funereus* (2 pairs).

016 Niedere Tauern (Salzburg, Steiermark)

47°15'N, 13°45'E *c.*10,000 ha

Landscape Protection Area and proposed National Park

Montane, subalpine, and alpine zones, with deciduous and coniferous forests and alpine grasslands and rocks. There are *c.*300 permanent lakes. The south-western border-zone contains some interesting moors. Human activities include agriculture, forestry, and some tourism. Encroachment of the area for the exploitation of hydroelectric power is an increasing problem.

Breeding species include *Aquila chrysaetos*, *Bonasa bonasia*, *Lagopus mutus*, *Tetrao tetrix*, *T. urogallus*, *Bubo bubo*, *Picus canus*, *Dryocopus martius*, *Picoides tridactylus*, and *Luscinia svecica svecica*.

017 Radtstätter Tauernpass including Hundsfeld (Salzburg)

47°12'-47°16'N, 13°30'-13°36'E 3714 ha

Landscape Protection Area

A mountainous area (1300-2000 m) with forests of *Picea*, *Pinus*, *Acer*, and *Larix* and bog vegetation, with rocks and lichens above the treeline. The area is being adversely affected by ski-resort development. The site includes the Hundsfeld, an area of blanket and raised bog (80 ha), that supports an important alpine population of *Luscinia svecica svecica*. Development of this area has proceeded unabated with no legal protection in existence (although included in the Landscape Protection Area this provides inadequate protection), thus drainage of one of the main bogs to build an indoor tennis court and tourist accommodation was allowed, and houses and roads have been built at the edge of the bog.

Breeding species include *Tetrao tetrix* (12-14 birds), *T. urogallus* (4-5 birds), *Bubo bubo* (1 pair), *Ptyonoprogne rupestris* (4 pairs), *Monticola saxatilis* (2 pairs), and *Luscinia svecica svecica* (14 pairs).

018 Hohe Tauern and Rauristal (Kärnten, Salzburg, Tirol)

46°53'-47°17'N, 12°05'-13°30'E 10,000 ha

National Park (Hohe Tauern, although not declared in Tirol) and Landscape Protection Area (Rauristal)

The central part of the Alps with montane and alpine zones. The vegetation is largely coniferous (*Picea*, *Larix*, *Pinus sylvestris*, *P. cembra*) with extensive areas of shrubs (*Alnus*, *Rhododendron*, *Vaccinium*) and alpine grasslands, with rocks and glaciers above the treeline. Economic activities include agriculture (with dairy farming), haymaking, forestry, and tourism. Hydroelectric projects have prevented the declaration of the final part of the National Park in Tirol.

Rauristal is the release site for the *Gypaetus barbatus* reintroduction project (14 free-flying birds). There is also an oversummering population of *Gyps fulvus* (from a breeding population on the Dalmatian coast, Yugoslavia). Other breeding species include *Pernis apivorus*, *Aquila chrysaetos*, *Bonasa bonasia*, *Lagopus mutus*, *Tetrao tetrix*, *T. urogallus*, *Alectoris graeca*, *Bubo bubo*, *Glaucidium passerinum*, *Aegolius funereus*, *Picus canus*, *Dryocopus martius*, *Dendrocopos leucotos*, *Picoides tridactylus*, *Luscinia svecica*, and *Lanius collurio*.

019 Karwendel (Tirol)

47°16'-47°35'N, 11°11'-11°44'E 69,000 ha

Nature Reserve

A representative part of the calcareous northern Alps (with valley bottoms to alpine peaks). The forest vegetation merges from deciduous and coniferous (*Fagus*, *Abies*, *Picea abies*) to coniferous (*Pinus resinosa*, *P. sylvestris*, *Picea abies*), with large areas of more or less barren rock above the treeline. Human activities include forestry and tourism; in immediate danger of further human encroachment including development of the winter-sports industry.

Breeding species include *Pernis apivorus*, *Aquila chrysaetos*, *Falco peregrinus*, *Bonasa bonasia*, *Lagopus mutus*, *Tetrao tetrix*, *T. urogallus*, *Glaucidium passerinum*, *Aegolius funereus*, *Picus canus*, *Dryocopus martius*, *Dendrocopos leucotos*, *Picoides tridactylus*, and *Lanius collurio*. *Alectoris graeca* possibly breeds.

020 Vorarlberger Rheindelta (Vorarlberg)

47°28'-47°31'N, 09°33'-09°41'E 1960 ha Ramsar Site

Nature Reserve (1400 ha)

The site includes the freshwater delta of the Rhine where it enters the Bodensee and an adjacent area of the Bodensee (Lake Constance). There are reedbeds, watermeadows, and alluvial sand islands at the mouth of the river.

Breeding species include *Podiceps cristatus* (200 pairs), *Ixobrychus minutus* (7-12 pairs), *Ardea purpurea* (1-5 pairs), *Anas strepera* (5 pairs), *A. clypeata* (5 pairs), *Netta rufina* (10-20 pairs), *Crex crex* (1-2 pairs), *Gallinago gallinago* (30-50 pairs), *Limosa limosa* (12-15 pairs), *Numenius arquata* (10-15 pairs), and *Sterna hirundo* (50-150 pairs). During spring and autumn passage, moderate numbers of grebes, ducks, and waders occur, including *Podiceps nigricollis* (100 in autumn), *Anas strepera* (700 in autumn), *Netta rufina* (1000 in autumn), and *Numenius arquata* (1000 in autumn). Large numbers of *Podiceps cristatus* (1000) and ducks overwinter.

MAIN REFERENCES

Aubrecht, G. *et al.* (1987) *Wasservögel. Ökologie als Abenteuer.* Kataloge des Oberöst. Landesmuseums, Neue Folge 8, Linz.

Aubrecht, G. and Böck, F. (1985) *Österreichische Gewässer als Winterrastplätze für Wasservögel.* Grüne Reihe des Bundesministeriums für Gesundheit und Umweltschutz 3, Wien.

Blum, V. (1977) *Die Vögel des Vorarlberger Rheindeltas.* Konstanz.

Dick, G. (1987) The significance of the Lake Neusiedl area of Austria for migrating geese. *Wildfowl* 38: 19-27.

Dvorak, M., Grüll, A. and Kohler, B. (1986) Verbreitung und Bestand gefährdeter und ökologisch wichtiger Brutvögel im Neusiedlerseegebiet 1984. *BFB-Bericht* 59: 1-25.

Grüll, A. (1988) Zur Bedeutung des südlichen Neusiedlersee-Beckens für den Vogelschutz. *BFB-Bericht* 67: 3-19.

Kraus, E. (1984) Die Bedeutung der Teichlandschaft im nördlichen Waldviertel für die Wasservogelwelt Österreichs. *Wiss. Mitt. Niederösterr. Landesmus.* 3: 99-135.

Lauermann, H. (1976) Die Vögel des Forstes Trübenbach im nordöstlichen Waldviertel (Niederösterreich). *Egretta* 19: 23-60.

Orn. Arbeitsgemeinschaft Bodensee (1983) *Die Vögel des Bodenseegebietes.* Konstanz.

Spitzenberger, F. ed. (1988) *Artenschutz in Österreich.* Grüne Reihe des Bundesministeriums für Familie und Umwelt 8, Wien.

Wendland, V. (1963) Die Vögel des Rauristales (Hohe Tauern). *Egretta* 6: 60-75.

Willi, P. (1985) Langfristige Bestandstaxierungen im Rheindelta. *Egretta* 28: 1-62.

Winding, N. (1985) Gemeinschaftsstruktur, Territorialität und anthropogene Beeinflussungen der Kleinvögel im Glocknergebiet (Hohe Tauern, Österreichische Zentralalpen). *Veröff. Österr. MaB-Programm* 9: 133-173.

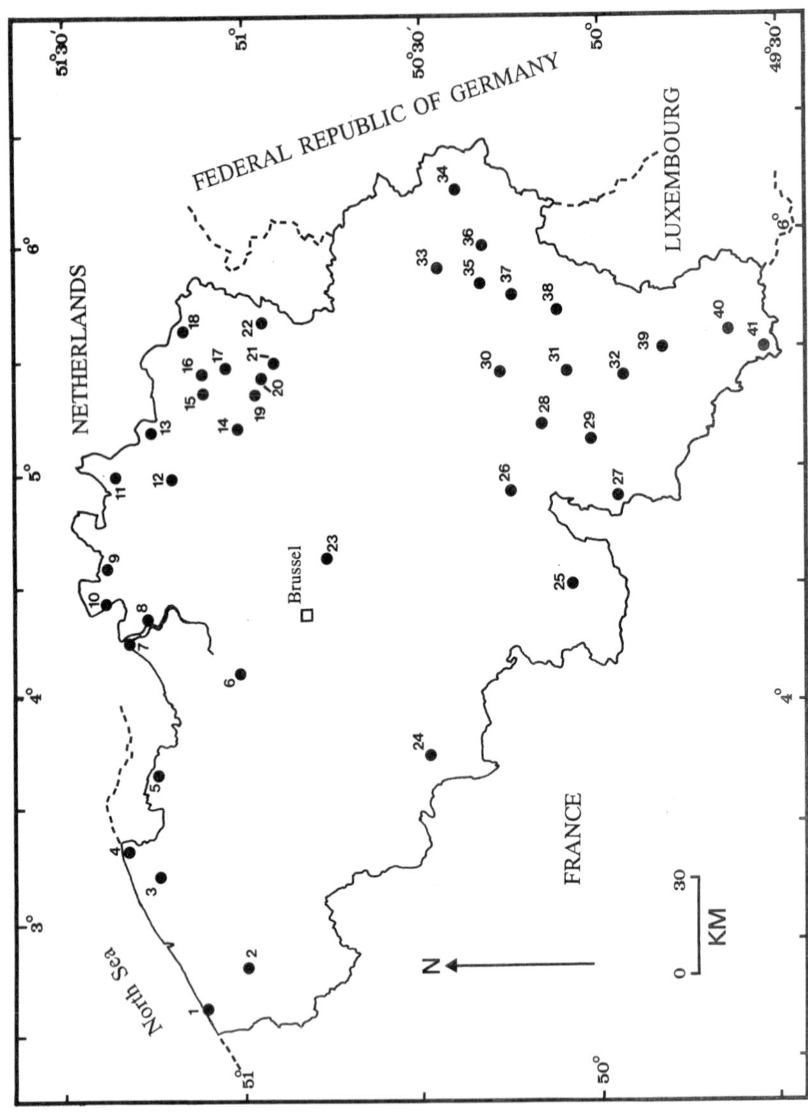

Figure 4: Map showing the location of the sites in Belgium

BELGIUM

Bluethroat *Luscinia svecica*

INTRODUCTION

General information

Belgium has a surface area of 30,521 sq km and an average population density of 324 persons per sq km (with the highest densities north of the riverine lowlands of Sambre and Meuse). Urban zones occupy a considerable part of the country.

The largest part of the country comprises the basins of the Rivers Escaut/Schelde and Meuse, and the basin of the River IJzer covers part of West Flanders. Two small regions are drained by tributaries of the Moselle into the Rhine and by the River Oise and its smaller tributaries to the River Seine. Belgium can be divided into three regions according to altitude, from west to east: lowland Belgium from the coast to the regions of Kempen, Brabant and Hainaut with altitudes below 50 m above sea-level; medium-altitude Belgium between 50 and 200 m up to the riverine lowlands of Sambre and Meuse and upland Belgium which reaches 694 m. These three main regions are further divided into a number of geological and hydrographical zones, from west to east:

- A low sandy coastal area including a shallow water zone (Vlaamse Banken). A line of dunes runs along the coast, although this zone is almost completely built up. The preservation of the small remaining natural areas is thus of great importance.
- A reclaimed plain, inland from the dunes, which is between 10 and 15 km wide. It is a very fertile area consisting of drained fields which normally lie below the high-tide

level. This wide belt, parallel to the coast, extends up to Antwerp on the Dutch border.

- Interior Flanders, which consists of a lightly undulating plain with sandy soils in the north, and a hilly region on sandy-silty soils in the south.
- The Kempen region with its heathland on sandy soils. In many parts, the heathland has been replaced by *Pinus* plantations, and boggy depressions have often been used to create artificial ponds. This region rises from west to east and consists of a low plain in the west followed by a higher plain (50 – 100 m) in the east.
- A transition zone (Petit Brabant, Kempen Brabançonne, Hageland) which lies between the Kempen and the alluvial regions of Brabant and Hesbaye.
- A region of low plains, south of Flanders and Kempen as far as the Rivers Sambre, Meuse, and Vesdre. Distinguishable from west to east are the following plains: Plateau Hennuyer, Plateau Brabançon, Plateau Hesbignon, and Plateau de Herve between the Rivers Meuse and Vesdre. The first is well separated and lightly undulating with many meadows. The Plateau Brabançon is distinguished by its principally sandy soil below an upper layer of clay and by the presence of many forest patches (remnants of an ancient large forest). To the east lies Plateau Hesbignon, a mainly cultivated high plain, and the Plateau de Herve ends this eastward succession of high plains.
- The river lowlands of Sambre and Meuse which are densely populated with important industrial areas. South of this area is the upland region of Belgium.
- The depression of Fagne-Famenne, between Condroz and the Ardennes, with soil of limited value for agriculture and thus covered by grassland and forests. The region contains many marshy depressions which have often been transformed into ponds. At its southern limit chalk predominates, resulting in the Calestienne geological formation at the foothill of the Ardennes.
- The Ardennes, between 300 and 694 m high, which form an extensive high plateau with a line of flat summits between the Signal de Botrange (694 m) in the east and the Croix-Scaille (505 m) in the west. Some very good peatbogs lie on the highest plateaus, and the slopes are covered with deciduous forests and conifer plantations.
- Finally the Lorraine, south of the Ardennes, which is characterised by the alternation of hard calcareous rocks and softer marl and clay. Three main sections can be distinguished, of which Sinémurienne and Bajocienne are the most important. The steep northern slopes are covered with forests, while the southern slopes are cultivated or serve as pastures.

Ornithological importance

The Belgian part of the North Sea is shallow and offers only limited foraging possibilities for seabirds. There is, however, a remarkable migration of Gaviidae, Podicipedidae, *Sula bassana*, Stercorariidae, *Rissa tridactyla*, Sternidae and seaducks along the coast. The shallow zone close to the coast is an important wintering area for *Melanitta* spp. (mainly *M. nigra*).

In summer the coast is heavily disturbed by tourists and this prevents *Charadrius alexandrinus* and *Sterna albifrons* from breeding, although these species have started to breed on newly created beaches such as those alongside the large harbour constructions at Zeebrugge. The remnant saltmarshes, notably the Zwin and the banks of the River Schelde north of Antwerp, are important breeding sites for *Tadorna tadorna* and *Recurvirostra avosetta*. The reclaimed areas are important for wintering geese, mainly *Anser brachyrhynchus* (max. 22,000 birds) and *A. albifrons* (max. 80,000 birds) and also *Cygnus columbianus*. They are equally important breeding sites for *Limosa limosa*.

Few natural marshes and ponds remain, but an important number of artificial ponds have been created for various human purposes. The freshwater wetlands of lowland and medium-altitude Belgium are wintering and breeding sites for many Anatidae; in particular the population of *Anas strepera* in the vicinity of Antwerp is of international importance.

The wetlands of the Haine basin support very important populations of *Luscinia svecica* as well as breeding *Botaurus stellaris* and *Cettia cetti* (the latter at the northernmost extent of its distribution). *Ixobrychus minutus* (declining) can be found in these marshes and *Porzana porzana* breeds in a few sedgebeds of the Kempen and Gaume regions.

The wet and dry heaths of Kempen and the foothills of the Ardennes have lost much of their native avifauna but still have a population of *Tetrao tetrix*. The Hautes-Fagnes population is probably one of the last viable populations of the north-west European plains. The heaths of the Kempen region, preserved partially due to the establishment of large military training areas, have a typical avifauna, with species such as *Caprimulgus europaeus, Lullula arborea*, and *Anthus campestris* which are declining in parts of Europe.

Forests are mainly located in the southern part. The four important forest belts in the Ardennes and Lorraine are essential for the survival of *Bonasa bonasia*; here a population survives in pure deciduous forests. These forests are equally important for *Accipiter gentilis, Picus canus, Dryocopus martius*, and *Dendrocopos medius*. In the Haute-Ardennes, *Aegolius funereus* occupies small stands of *Fagus sylvatica* within old *Picea abies* plantations which, in turn, if they still hold small peatbogs, are inhabited by *Nucifraga caryocatactes* (since an invasion of the species in 1968).

Agricultural land and built-up areas lie mainly in lowland and medium-altitude Belgium, but also cover considerable surfaces in parts of upland Belgium. Increasing agricultural exploitation has left little room for certain specialised species, which are dependent on traditional land-use techniques and are found mainly in the Famenne, the Belgian Lorraine and the Kempen Plateau. In these regions and on the high plateaus of the Ardennes a rich avifauna survives in areas effectively protected because of the presence of military training camps or the difficulties of exploitation due to the poor quality or humidity of the soils. *Crex crex, Saxicola rubetra*, and *Lanius collurio* are amongst the more interesting species in these regions. *Emberiza hortulana* now only breeds in the Kempen region, where rye is still cultivated in a landscape with copses and *Quercus* hedges.

Conservation infrastructure and protected-area system

Nature conservation and the establishment of protected areas is the responsibility of the Water and Forest Administration (of the Ministry of Agriculture). A number of independent nature conservation organisations have also established nature reserves.

Belgium possesses the following types of protected areas:

1. NATURE RESERVES

   These include reserves owned or leased by the state, and reserves owned by private individuals and/or organisations. The degree of protection at these private and independent reserves varies greatly. The State Reserves are supervised by the Water and Forest Administration. The large reserves may have zones where the public is excluded.

2. NATURAL PARK

   The aim of a Natural Park is to preserve the character, diversity and scientific value of the countryside and its fauna and flora, and also to provide for recreation and tourism. Natural Parks may include Nature Reserves and Forestry Reserves.

3. FORESTRY RESERVES

   These are areas of forest where human activities are restricted or totally prohibited.

Other types of protected area, which are incorporated into regional plans, include Protected Landscapes and Green Zones.

International measures relevant to the conservation of sites

Belgium is a member of the European Community and is bound by the terms of the EEC Wild Birds Directive. It is a party to the Ramsar Convention and has signed but not ratified the Bern Convention. The country has designated six Ramsar Sites (all included in this inventory), 33 EEC Special Protection Areas, and a number of Biogenetic Reserves.

Overview of the inventory

The inventory includes 41 sites covering a total area of over 544,000 ha. Twenty-three of the sites are in the Flemish part of the country (Vlaams Gewest) and 19 sites are in the Wallonne Region (one site is shared by both regions).

The inventory is very complete for Belgium and covers all important sites for bird conservation. A substantial number (33) have already been designated by the Belgian authorities as EEC Special Protection Areas. The remaining sites will certainly be designated in the near future, which will enable Belgium to preserve its avifaunal natural heritage in a comprehensive way.

Acknowledgements

The inventory was compiled from information provided by the Institut Royal des Sciences Naturelles de Belgique and has incorporated data from the CORINE Biotopes Project and van Vessem and Kuijken (1986). The introduction ('General information' and 'Ornithological importance') was written by R.-M. Lafontaine, M. des N. van der Elst, and P. Devillers of the Institut Royal des Sciences Naturelles de Belgique.

INVENTORY

No.	Site name	Region	Criteria used to select site [see p.18]							
			0	1(i)	1(ii)	1(iii)	1(iv)	2	3	4
001	Vlaamse Banken en Westkust	VG				*			*	
002	IJzervallei-De Blankaart	VG				*			*	
003	Polderkomplex: Hoeke, Damme, Meetkerke, Uitkerke, Nieuwmunster and Wenduine	VG				*		*	*	
004	Het Zwin	VG				*			*	
005	Krekengebied	VG				*			*	
006	Durme/Middenloop Schelde	VG							*	
007	Beneden Schelde: Doelse Polder and Schorren	VG				*			*	
008	Kuifeend and Blokkersdijk	VG				*			*	
009	De Maatjes-Wuustwezel Heide and Groot Schietveld	VG				*			*	
010	Kalmthoutse Heide	VG				*			*	
011	Gebieden ten noorden van Turnhout en Ravels	VG							*	
012	Zegge	VG				*			*	
013	Ronde Put and Wateringen, Mol-Postel	VG							*	
014	Schulensbroek, Gorenbroek and Stamprooierbroek	VG						*		
015	Leopoldsburg – Zwarte Beek	VG							*	
016	Peer	VG							*	
017	Helchteren-Meeuwen	VG							*	
018	Hamonterheide, Hageven, Buitenheide, Mariahof and Stamprooierbroek	VG							*	
019	Vijverkomplex van Midden Limburg	VG							*	
020	Bokrijk	VG							*	
021	De Maten	VG							*	
022	Mechelse Heide/Vallei Ziepbeek	VG							*	
023	Vallée de la Dyle/Dijle Vallei	VG,RW							*	
024	Bassin de la Haine	RW				*			*	
025	Entre-Sambre-et-Meuse	RW						*	*	
026	Haute Meuse	RW							*	
027	Croix-Scaille	RW						*	*	
028	Lesse et Lomme	RW						*	*	

No.	Site name	Region	Criteria used to select site [see p.18]							
			0	1(i)	1(ii)	1(iii)	1(iv)	2	3	4
029	Daverdisse	RW							*	
030	Marche en Famenne	RW						*	*	
031	Saint-Hubert	RW							*	
032	Ochamp-Freux	RW							*	
033	Malchamps	RW						*	*	
034	Hautes Fagnes/Eifel	RW				*		*	*	
035	Vallée de la Lienne	RW							*	
036	Wanne-Logbiermé	RW							*	
037	Tailles	RW							*	
038	Deux Ourthes	RW							*	
039	Haute Sûre/Ardennes méridionale	RW						*	*	
040	Sinémurienne	RW						*	*	
041	Côte Bajocienne	RW						*	*	

VG=Vlaams Gewest RW=Région Wallonne

Comments on the inventory

1. The figures for passage birds are the maximum daily counts.
2. It has not been possible to determine whether or not a number of sites are protected (partly) as Nature Reserves or Protected Landscapes etc. (although some of these are protected as EEC Special Protection Areas).
3. The site name is followed by the NUTS level 1 region which is given in parentheses.
4. The NUTS level 1 regions are the 'regions' used when applying the site-selection criteria.

Glossary

See glossaries for France and the Netherlands. EEC SPA = European Community Special Protection Area

---

001 Vlaamse Banken en Westkust, West-Vlaanderen (Vlaams Gewest)

51°08'N, 02°40'E 60,000 ha Ramsar Site (1900 ha); EEC SPA (1415 ha)

State Reserve (De Westhoek: 340 ha); Nature Reserve (IJzermonding: 20 ha); partly unprotected

Largely offshore waters (58,900 ha) with sandbanks. Includes the most important stretch of sand-dunes along the Belgian coast (from De Panne to Nieuwpoort) and the salt-marshes and mudflats of the IJzer Estuary. Human activities include fishing, yachting, and recreation. Problems include sand extraction at sea with a lowering of the water-table inland, extraction of drinking water affecting De Westhoek, pollution of the River IJzer, intensive recreation and residential building.

Passage species include *Charadrius alexandrinus* (100), *Numenius arquata* (815), *Larus melanocephalus* (3), *Sterna hirundo* (500+), and *Asio flammeus* (5). Wintering species include *Melanitta nigra* (8500), *Calidris alba* (350), and *C. maritima* (150).

002 IJzervallei-De Blankaart, West-Vlaanderen (Vlaams Gewest)

51°00'N, 02°50'E 5100 ha Ramsar Site (De Blankaart: 160 ha); EEC SPA

Two Nature Reserves

An area of flat and regularly flooded grasslands along the River IJzer. Includes Blankaart which is a shallow freshwater lake with extensive reedbeds, regularly inundated by the River IJzer. Human activities include arable and stock-farming, fish-farming, hunting, and recreation, and there is scattered human habitation. There are plans to lower the water-table for agricultural development and drainage to prevent flooding; also eutrophication, siltation, and water pollution are affecting Blankaart.

Breeding species include *Ardea cinerea* (200 pairs), *Anas querquedula* (5 pairs), *A. clypeata* (5 pairs), *Circus aeruginosus* (3+ pairs), and *Philomachus pugnax* (20+ 'pairs'). Species occurring on passage include *Botaurus stellaris*, *Pandion haliaetus*, *Porzana porzana*, *P. parva*, *Pluvialis apricaria* (15,000), *Philomachus pugnax* (600), *Limosa limosa* (3300), *Chlidonias niger* (100), and *Asio flammeus* (15). Winter visitors include *Phalacrocorax carbo* (200), *Cygnus columbianus* (70), *Branta leucopsis* (2000; only in cold winters), *Anas penelope* (35,000), *A. crecca* (3500), *A. platyrhynchos* (25,000), *A. clypeata* (800), and *Circus cyaneus* (25).

003 Polderkomplex: Hoeke, Damme, Meetkerke, Uitkerke, Nieuwmunster and Wenduine; West-Vlaanderen (Vlaams Gewest)

51°15'N, 03°13'E 9,600 ha EEC SPA

Two small Nature Reserves

The area includes the most interesting parts of the coastal polders to the north of Brugge which consist of grasslands with ditches, canals, and marshy places. It includes the claypits at Wenduine which have overgrown banks and large reedbeds, and also coastal sand-dunes and sand beaches. Human activities include arable and stock-farming, forestry, fishing, hunting, and there is scattered human habitation. Problems include the intensification of agriculture (more intensive use of fertilisers) and drainage; industrial, residential and recreational development and recreation and hunting pressure.

Breeding species include *Botaurus stellaris* (1 pair), *Ixobrychus minutus* (1 pair), *Tadorna tadorna* (75 pairs), *Anas querquedula* (10 pairs), *A. clypeata* (40 pairs), *Philomachus pugnax*, *Limosa limosa* (60 pairs), *Tringa totanus* (55 pairs), and *Asio flammeus*. Birds occurring on passage include *Botaurus stellaris* (15), *Circus cyaneus* (80), *Falco columbarius* (10), *Pluvialis apricaria* (35,000), *Philomachus pugnax* (3000), *Numenius arquata* (3000), and *Asio flammeus* (75). Winter visitors include *Cygnus columbianus* (100), *Anser fabalis* (3000), *A. brachyrhynchus* (5500), *A. albifrons* (28,000), *A. erythropus* (2), *Branta leucopsis* (500), *B. ruficollis* (2), *Anas penelope* (15,000+), *A. crecca* (10,000+), and *A. clypeata* (3000).

004 Het Zwin, West-Vlaanderen (Vlaams Gewest)

51°20'N, 03°21'E 1950 ha Ramsar Site (550 ha); EEC SPA

Nature Reserve (Het Zwin: 125 ha and 1500 ha buffer zone); Protected Landscape

An important area of saltmarshes and mudflats (a remnant of a former estuary) with a dune system and some lakes and neighbouring polders. Human activities include arable and stock-farming, fishing, hunting and there is scattered human habitation. The 300,000 visitors a year are well controlled.

Breeding species include *Circus aeruginosus*, *Tadorna tadorna* (80 pairs), *Himantopus himantopus*, *Recurvirostra avosetta* (70 pairs), *Larus melanocephalus* (10 pairs), *Sterna dougallii* (1 pair), *S. hirundo* (370 pairs), *S. paradisaea* (1 pair), and *Asio flammeus*. A considerable variety of species occur on passage including *Botaurus stellaris* (10), *Ardea purpurea* (10+), *Platalea leucorodia* (100), *Tadorna tadorna* (1250), *Pandion haliaetus* (3), *Recurvirostra avosetta* (540), *Charadrius morinellus* (5), *Philomachus pugnax* (1200), *Numenius phaeopus* (950), *N. arquata* (1600), *Tringa glareola* (60), and *Asio flammeus* (11). In winter, waterfowl occurring include *Cygnus columbianus* (60), *C. cygnus* (20), *Anser fabalis* (1300), *A. albifrons* (4000), *Branta leucopsis* (100), *Anas penelope* (3500), and *Mergus albellus* (190). Other wintering species include *Circus cyaneus* (22) and *Falco columbarius* (7).

005 Krekengebied, Oost-Vlaanderen (Vlaams Gewest)

51°15'N, 03°40'E 8500 ha EEC SPA

Two small Nature Reserves

A complex of old sea inlets ('kreken') with brackish and fresh water areas in a polder landscape. Diverse habitats from remnant saltmarshes to oligotrophic and acid marshes and wet woodlands. The polder landscape is mainly arable land characterised by closely connected dykes with rows of *Populus* interspersed by marshes. Human activities include arable and stock-farming, fish-farming, hunting, and recreation. Problems include recreation, ploughing of reedbeds, and illegal dumping.

Breeding species include *Botaurus stellaris* (1 pair), *Circus aeruginosus* (10+ pairs), *Recurvirostra avosetta* (10 pairs), and *Luscinia svecica* (25 pairs). *Circus cyaneus* (10), *Pandion haliaetus*, *Porzana porzana*, *Recurvirostra avosetta* (30), *Pluvialis apricaria* (700), *Philomachus pugnax* (25), *Chlidonias niger* (30), and *Asio flammeus* (3) occur on passage, and winter visitors include *Cygnus columbianus* (90) and *Anser fabalis* (1000).

006 Durme/Middenloop Schelde, Antwerpen and Oost-Vlaanderen (Vlaams Gewest)

51°03'N, 04°06'E 5200 ha EEC SPA

State Reserve (De Schorren van de Durme: 23.5 ha); six Nature Reserves

The area includes long portions of the Rivers Schelde and Durme with regularly flooded marshes, oxbows, and wet meadows. The mouth of the River Durme is one of the few intact tidals river marshes in Flanders with mudflats, marshes, and reedbeds. Human activities include arable and stock-farming, forestry, hunting, recreation, and river transport. Problems include excessive recreation in some places, intensive agriculture, excessive hunting, drainage, water pollution, inappropriate management of reed borders along rivers, broadening of dykes, and the damming and cultivation of saltmarsh.

Breeding species include *Ardea cinerea* (80 pairs), *Anas querquedula* (6 pairs), *Milvus migrans* (1 pair), *Circus aeruginosus* (1 pair), *Limosa limosa* (3 pairs), *Alcedo atthis* (5 pairs), and *Luscinia svecica* (60 pairs). Passage species include *Botaurus stellaris* (4), *Ardea purpurea* (5), *Circus aeruginosus* (3), *C. cyaneus* (10), *Porzana porzana*, *Philomachus pugnax* (40), and *Asio flammeus* (2+), and winter visitors include *Anas clypeata* (800).

007 Beneden Schelde: Doelse Polder and Schorren, Antwerpen and Oost-Vlaanderen (Vlaams Gewest)

51°19'N, 04°15'E 5600 ha Ramsar Site (417 ha); EEC SPA

Nature Reserve (Groot Buitenschoor: 216 ha); Protected Landscape

The Schelde Estuary (becoming the Westerschelde in the Netherlands) with mud and sandflats and saltmarshes, and neighbouring polders with grazing-meadows and agricultural land. There is stock-farming, agriculture, industry, scattered human habitation, and port facilities. Groot Buitenschoor is, with Paardeschoor, the only remaining brackish marsh in Belgium. Problems include industrialisation and pollution. Connected to site no. 050 Westerschelde in the Netherlands.

Breeding species include *Tadorna tadorna* (20-35 pairs), *Circus aeruginosus* (2+ pairs), *Recurvirostra avosetta* (350 pairs), *Tringa totanus* (16 pairs), and *Luscinia svecica* (26 pairs). Important for passage wildfowl and waders with *Anser fabalis* (4000), *A. albifrons* (3000), *A. anser* (620), *Tadorna tadorna* (4000), *Anas crecca* (3200), *A. clypeata* (1700), *Recurvirostra avosetta* (1800), *Pluvialis apricaria* (2000), and *Limosa limosa* (800); *Cygnus columbianus* (30) occurs in winter.

008 Kuifeend and Blokkersdijk, Antwerpen (Vlaams Gewest)

51°16'N, 04°21'E 200 ha EEC SPA

Nature Reserves (De Kuifeend: 69 ha and Blokkersdijk: 50 ha)

Kuifeend is an area of freshwater pools and marshes, whilst Blokkersdijk is a deep freshwater lake surrounded by marshes, wet meadows, and dry grasslands. Surrounded by residential areas, motorways, and railway lines. Industrialisation is affecting part of the site by lowering the water-table.

A site for *Botaurus stellaris* (2 pairs), *Tadorna tadorna* (40-50 pairs), *Anas strepera* (100 pairs), *A. acuta* (2 pairs), *A. querquedula* (2 pairs), *A. clypeata* (25-30 pairs), *Circus aeruginosus* (2 pairs), *Recurvirostra avosetta* (10 pairs), *Limosa limosa* (6 pairs), and *Luscinia svecica* (25-30 pairs). Passage species include *Anas strepera* (300-700) and *A. clypeata* (1400).

009 De Maatjes-Wuustwezel Heide and Groot Schietveld, Antwerpen (Vlaams Gewest)

51°23'N, 04°34'E 4100 ha EEC SPA

Partly a Protected Landscape (De Maatjes)

The area includes grasslands and marshes (De Maatjes), and heaths in military camps (De Heide and Groote Schietveld). Human activities include arable and stock-farming, forestry, and military training. Part of the site is threatened by the drainage of marshes for agricultural development. The building of weekend cottages and pollution are other problems.

Breeding species include *Circus aeruginosus* (1 pair), *Falco subbuteo* (13 pairs), *Tetrao tetrix* (6 males), *Porzana porzana* (1 pair), *Limosa limosa* (10 pairs), *Numenius arquata* (40 pairs), *Asio flammeus* (1 pair), *Caprimulgus europaeus* (10+ pairs), *Lullula arborea* (6 pairs), and *Luscinia svecica* (5 pairs). Passage species include *Botaurus stellaris*, *Circus aeruginosus* (2), *C. cyaneus* (2), *Philomachus pugnax* (40), and *Numenius phaeopus* (900-1000).

010 Kalmthoutse Heide, Antwerpen (Vlaams Gewest)

51°24'N, 04°26'E 2200 ha Ramsar Site (4045 ha); EEC SPA

State Reserve (910 ha); Protected Landscape

A very important and extremely diverse area of dry and wet heaths, fens, and inland sand-dunes of the Antwerpse Kempen. Human activities include arable and stock-farming, forestry, and recreation. Problems include excessive recreational pressure, eutrophication of heathland, and the surrounding zones are being adversely affected by the extraction of drinking water (lowering the water-table) and agricultural intensification.

Breeding species include *Anas clypeata*, *Aythya ferina*, *A. fuligula*, *Pernis apivorus* (1 pair), *Tetrao tetrix* (4 males), *Porzana porzana*, *Numenius arquata* (14-18 pairs), *Caprimulgus europaeus* (3 pairs), and *Lullula arborea* (10 pairs). Passage waders include *Limosa limosa* (900), *Numenius phaeopus* (3000-6000), and *N. arquata* (3000+). Wintering species include *Circus cyaneus* (8).

011 Gebieden ten noorden van Turnhout en Ravels, Antwerpen (Vlaams Gewest)

51°23'N, 05°00'E 7100 ha EEC SPA

Nature Reserve (De Liereman: 167 ha); Protected Landscape

An area of grasslands, agricultural land, deciduous and coniferous woodland, and heaths with oligotrophic fens. There is also an ancient park with neglected orchards and lakes. Human activities include arable and stock-farming, forestry, recreation, military training, and there is scattered human habitation. Problems include drainage, eutrophication, excessive recreation, and building of weekend cottages.

Breeding species include *Falco subbuteo* (7 pairs), *Tetrao tetrix* (6 males), *Limosa limosa* (68 pairs), *Numenius arquata* (50 pairs), *Tringa totanus* (64 pairs), *Caprimulgus europaeus* (5 pairs), *Alcedo atthis* (3 pairs), *Dryocopus martius* (9 pairs), *Lullula arborea* (10 pairs), and *Luscinia svecica* (2 pairs).

012 Zegge, Antwerpen (Vlaams Gewest)

51°11'N, 04°56'E 90 ha EEC SPA

Nature Reserve (95 ha)

A remnant of the once-extensive fen of Kleine Nete. It is a varied site, ranging from open pools and low moorland to overgrown grasslands and alder swamps. Human activities are negligible.

Breeding species include *Botaurus stellaris* (1 pair), *Ixobrychus minutus*, *Anas strepera* (31 pairs), *A. acuta* (2 pairs), *A. querquedula* (2 pairs), *A. clypeata* (30 pairs), *Aythya ferina* (27 pairs), *A. fuligula* (96 pairs), *Recurvirostra avosetta* (10 pairs), *Limosa limosa* (6 pairs), *Alcedo atthis*, and *Luscinia svecica* (30 pairs). *Ardea purpurea*, *Anas strepera* (300-700), *A. clypeata* (1170), and *Porzana porzana* occur on passage.

013 Ronde Put and Wateringen, Mol-Postel; Antwerpen (Vlaams Gewest)

51°17'N, 05°11'E 5450 ha EEC SPA

Nature Reserves (De Maat: 65 ha and De Ronde Put: 40 ha)

An area of the Turnhoutse Kempen covered with deciduous and coniferous woodlands, and with interesting marshes and ponds. Human activities include arable and stock-farming, forestry, hunting, and recreation. Problems include intensive recreation, and there are plans for a vast recreation park which would have disastrous consequences for nature conservation.

Breeding species include *Ixobrychus minutus* (1 pair), *Botaurus stellaris* (4 pairs), *Pernis apivorus* (5 pairs), *Circus aeruginosus* (4 pairs), *Chlidonias niger*, *Caprimulgus europaeus* (4 pairs), *Alcedo atthis* (4 pairs), *Dryocopus martius* (8 pairs), *Lullula arborea* (6 pairs), and *Luscinia svecica* (8 pairs). Passage species include *Pandion haliaetus* (4) and *Falco peregrinus* (2). *Circus cyaneus* and *Falco columbarius* occur in winter.

014 Schulensbroek, Gorenbroek; Hasselt (Vlaams Gewest)

51°01'N, 05°11'E 140 ha EEC SPA

A large alluvial depression at the confluence of the Rivers Demer, Merk, Gete, Velp, and Mangelbeek, with grasslands and small areas of alluvial forests and *Quercus* woods. Human activities include stock-farming, tourism, and leisure.

Breeding species include *Anas querquedula* (3 pairs), *Circus aeruginosus* (0-1 pair), *Crex crex*, *Limosa limosa* (4 pairs), and *Luscinia svecica* (5 pairs).

015 Leopoldsburg – Zwarte Beek, Limburg (Vlaams Gewest)

51°07'N, 05°20'E 10,150 ha EEC SPA

Nature Reserve (De Zwarte Beek: 86 ha)

Extensive heathland of the Kempen Plateau with oligotrophic fens, sand-dune system and the wet valley of the Zwarte Beek with a well-preserved, semi-natural landscape (bogs, moorland, marsh, woodland, meadows, and arable land). A large part of the valley is included in the military camp of Leopoldsburg. Human activities include military training, arable farming, forestry, recreation, and there is scattered human habitation. Problems include drainage of valuable parts for agriculture, recreation pressure, and vegetational succession.

Breeding species include *Botaurus stellaris* (2 pairs), *Pernis apivorus* (1 pair), *Circus aeruginosus* (1 pair), *C. pygargus* (1 pair), *Tetrao tetrix* (20 pairs), *Crex crex* (1 pair), *Pluvialis apricaria* (1 pair), *Limosa limosa* (10 pairs), *Numenius arquata* (25 pairs), *Asio flammeus* (1 pair), *Caprimulgus europaeus* (15 pairs), *Alcedo atthis* (3 pairs), *Lullula arborea* (25 pairs), *Anthus campestris* (3 pairs), *Luscinia svecica* (40+ pairs), and *Lanius collurio* (10 pairs). A variety of raptors occur on passage including *Circus cyaneus* (15), *Pandion haliaetus*, and *Falco columbarius*, as well as *Grus grus* (150).

016 Peer, Limburg (Vlaams Gewest)

51°07'N, 05°25'E 10,100 ha EEC SPA

An extensive area of grassland and cultivation crossed by valleys with old humid hay-meadows, fens, and wet woodlands. Of particular importance are the Abeek, Dommel, and Bollisterbeek valleys. The low-quality agricultural land is important for the local avifauna, especially *Emberiza hortulana*. Human activities include arable and stock-farming and hunting, and there is scattered human habitation and an aerodrome. Problems include agricultural intensification (loss of hedgerows and introduction of maize cultivation).

Breeding species include *Pernis apivorus* (1 pair), *Alcedo atthis* (5 pairs), *Caprimulgus europaeus* (10 pairs), *Luscinia svecica* (10 pairs), and *Emberiza hortulana* (40 pairs).

017 Helchteren-Meeuwen, Limburg (Vlaams Gewest)

51°03'N, 05°26'E 2850 ha EEC SPA

Protected by a military camp

An extensive area of dry and wet heaths on the Kempen Plateau. Vegetation comprises fens, ponds, and marshes, inland dunes, and tree plantations. Mainly a military camp. Other human activities include agriculture, fish-farming, and recreation. The main problems are intensive fish-farming, recreation (motorcycling), and excessive hunting.

Breeding species include *Botaurus stellaris* (1 pair), *Anas querquedula* (4 pairs), *A. clypeata* (6+ pairs), *Pernis apivorus* (1 pair), *Circus aeruginosus* (2 pairs), *C. pygargus* (1 pair), *Tetrao tetrix* (30 pairs), *Porzana porzana* (5 pairs), *Limosa limosa* (5 pairs), *Numenius arquata* (30 pairs), *Caprimulgus europaeus* (5+ pairs), *Lullula arborea* (15+ pairs), and *Luscinia svecica* (25 pairs). *Pandion haliaetus* and *Grus grus* (20+) occur on passage.

018 Hamonterheide, Hageven, Buitenheide, Mariahof and Stamprooierbroek; Limburg (Vlaams Gewest)

51°10'N, 05°35'E 13,350 ha EEC SPA

Nature Reserves (Het Hageven: 160 ha; Mariahof: 28 ha and Stamprooierbroek: 37 ha)

The main habitats are heathlands, woodlands, poor wet grasslands, crops, ponds, and marshes. Includes the remote areas of the Kempen Plateau along the border with the Netherlands. Human activities include arable and stock-farming, forestry, fish-farming, hunting, and recreation. Problems include drainage, canalisation, hunting, poaching, recreation, and a lack of management.

A breeding site for *Botaurus stellaris* (3+ pairs), *Ixobrychus minutus* (1+ pair), *Pernis apivorus* (7+ pairs), *Circus aeruginosus* (3+ pairs), *Asio flammeus* (1 pair), *Alcedo atthis* (15+ pairs), *Dryocopus martius* (7+ pairs), *Luscinia svecica* (35 pairs), *Lullula arborea* (10+ pairs), and *Lanius collurio* (4+ pairs). *Grus grus* (100) occurs on passage.

019 Vijverkomplex van Midden Limburg, Limburg (Vlaams Gewest)

50°58'N, 05°18'E 2500 ha EEC SPA

State Reserve (De Platwijers: 101 ha); four Nature Reserves (500 ha); Protected Landscape (Bolderberg)

An important wetland area (by far the largest unbroken lake area in Belgium) including many ponds and marshes, humid grasslands, and wet woodlands. Includes parts of the Echelbeek, Slangbeek, Roosterbeek, and Lambeek. Human activities include agriculture, forestry, fish-farming, recreation, and there is scattered human habitation. Problems include excessive recreation, intensive fish-farming, pollution, illegal dumping, illegal weekend cottages, and excessive hunting pressure.

Breeding species include *Botaurus stellaris* (15+ pairs), *Ixobrychus minutus* (5+ pairs), *Ardea cinerea* (80 pairs), *A. purpurea* (2 pairs), *Anas crecca* (75 pairs), *A. querquedula* (5 pairs), *A. clypeata* (15+ pairs), *Aythya ferina* (150 pairs), *A. fuligula* (100 pairs), *Pernis apivorus* (2 pairs), *Circus aeruginosus* (2 pairs), *Porzana porzana* (5+ pairs), *Alcedo atthis* (15+ pairs), *Dryocopus martius* (3+ pairs), and *Luscinia svecica* (60+ pairs). Passage raptors include *Circus cyaneus* (5+) and *Pandion haliaetus* (6).

020 Bokrijk, Limburg (Vlaams Gewest)

50°57'N, 05°24'E 800 ha EEC SPA

Nature Reserves (Het Wik: 150 ha and De Borggraaf: 28 ha); Protected Landscape (Het Wik)

An area of lakes and marsh with deciduous, mixed and coniferous woodland. Includes Het Wik which is a complex of eutrophic lakes used for fish-farming surrounded by reedbeds. Human activities include agriculture, forestry, fish-farming, recreation, and there is scattered human habitation. Problems include excessive recreation at Het Wik and drainage of the Klotbroek which feeds the lakes via numerous brooks and ditches.

Breeding species include *Botaurus stellaris* (8 pairs), *Ixobrychus minutus* (3+ pairs), *Anas crecca* (20+ pairs), *A. clypeata* (3+ pairs), *Rallus aquaticus* (50+ pairs), *Porzana parva* (1 pair), *Alcedo atthis* (10 pairs), *Dryocopus martius* (3 pairs), and *Luscinia svecica* (30 pairs). In addition, *Circus aeruginosus* and *C. cyaneus* occur on passage.

021 De Maten, Limburg (Vlaams Gewest)

50°57'N, 05°27'E 600 ha EEC SPA

Nature Reserve (180 ha) and buffer zone

An extremely diverse area of heathland, marshes, oligotrophic and mesotrophic ponds, wet woodlands, and sand-dunes of the Kempen Plateau. Human activities include agriculture, fish-farming, recreation, and there is scattered human habitation. Problems include recreation, illegal dumping, and changing water-levels because of fish-farming.

Breeding species include *Ixobrychus minutus* (1+ pair), *Botaurus stellaris* (2+ pairs), *Circus aeruginosus*, *Alcedo atthis* (4 pairs), and *Luscinia svecica* (25+ pairs). *Pandion haliaetus* occurs on passage.

022 Mechelse Heide/Vallei Ziepbeek, Limburg (Vlaams Gewest)

50°57'N, 05°38'E 2350 ha EEC SPA

State Reserves (including De Mechelse Heide: 545 ha and Ziepbeek: 161 ha and Ven onder de Berg: 6 ha)

Includes the Ziepbeek and Asbeek valleys which represent one of the most important areas of wet and dry heath and fen of the Limburgse Kempen; De Mechelse Heide, an important area of wet and dry heath; and Ven onder de Berg, a quaking bog. Human activities include agriculture and recreation. The heathland is being adversely affected by sand and gravel extraction, and excessive recreation is a problem for *Tetrao tetrix*.

Breeding species include *Botaurus stellaris* (1 pair), *Anas crecca* (20 pairs), *Pernis apivorus* (3+ pairs), *Tetrao tetrix* (5+ pairs), *Coturnix coturnix* (15 pairs), *Rallus aquaticus* (20 pairs), *Numenius arquata* (5 pairs), *Caprimulgus europaeus* (10+ pairs), *Alcedo atthis* (2 pairs), *Dryocopus martius* (3 pairs), *Lullula arborea* (20 pairs), and *Luscinia svecica* (15 pairs). *Grus grus* (30+) occurs on passage.

023 Vallée de la Dyle/Dijle Vallei, Leuven and Nivelles (Vlaams Gewest and Région Wallonne)

50°47'N, 04°36'E 4000 ha EEC SPA (Flemish part of site only)

Humid valley and hillsides with ponds, marshes, grasslands, and woodlands. The site comprises a portion of the River Dyle between Leuven and Wavre and a portion of a tributary, the River Lasne. Human activities include arable and stock-farming, forestry, fishing, hunting, recreation, and there is a railway and scattered human habitation.

Breeding species include *Botaurus stellaris* (1 pair), *Anas clypeata* (10 pairs), *Aythya ferina* (70 pairs), *A. fuligula* (80 pairs), *Pernis apivorus* (1 pairs), *Milvus migrans* (1), *Circus aeruginosus* (2 pairs), *Porzana porzana* (2 pairs), *Alcedo atthis* (10 pairs), and *Dryocopus martius* (5 pairs). The site is particularly important for migratory birds and a considerable variety of species occur including small numbers of *Pernis apivorus*, *Milvu migrans*, *M. milvus*, and *Pandion haliaetus*, plus *Porzana porzana* (6), *Grus grus* (30) and *Chlidonias niger* (100). Wintering species include *Botaurus stellaris* (3), *Cygnu columbianus* (20), *C. cygnus* (10), *Circus cyaneus* (4), and *Asio flammeus* (2).

024 Bassin de la Haine, Hainaut (Région Wallonne)

50°30'N, 03°46'E 11,500 ha EEC SPA; Ramsar Site (Le Marais d'Harchies)

A complex of ponds, marshes, and grasslands in the Haine basin. Human activities include agriculture, forestry, recreation, and industry. Problems include the infilling of marshes.

Breeding species include *Botaurus stellaris* (5 pairs), *Ixobrychus minutus* (8 pairs), *Nycticorax nycticorax* (2 pairs), *Anas querquedula* (7 pairs), *Pernis apivorus* (7 pairs), *Circus aeruginosus* (5 pairs), *Porzana porzana* (1 pair), *Caprimulgus europaeus* (3+ pairs), *Alcedo atthis* (15 pairs), *Dryocopus martius* (5 pairs), *Luscinia svecica* (70 pairs), *Locustella luscinioides* (10 pairs), and *Acrocephalus arundinaceus* (4 pairs). Species occurring on passage include *Phalacrocorax carbo* (300), *Anas crecca* (5200), *Circus cyaneus* (12), *Porzana porzana* (10), *Recurvirostra avosetta* (30), *Pluvialis apricaria* (2000), *Philomachus pugnax* (50), and *Chlidonias niger* (70).

025 Entre-Sambre-et-Meuse, Hainaut and Namur (Région Wallonne)

50°05'N, 04°30'E 40,000 ha EEC SPA

An exceptionally varied zone including parts of the Fagne, Calestienne, and Ardennes, with semi-natural humid grasslands, dry calcareous grasslands, and deciduous woodland. Human activities include forestry, agriculture, and recreation. The site is threatened by forest destruction for the development of a firing range.

Breeding species include *Botaurus stellaris* (1 pair), *Pernis apivorus* (30 pairs), *Milvus migrans* (1 pair), *M. milvus* (2 pairs), *Circus aeruginosus* (1 pair), *Bonasa bonasia* (15+ pairs), *Crex crex* (1+ pair), *Asio flammeus* (1 pair), *Aegolius funereus* (1 pair), *Caprimulgus europaeus* (5+ pairs), *Alcedo atthis* (20 pairs), *Dryocopus martius* (10+ pairs), *Dendrocopos medius*, and *Lanius collurio* (4 pairs). *Circus cyaneus* (10) occurs on passage.

026 Haute Meuse, Namur (Région Wallonne)

50°15'N, 04°55'E 7700 ha

An interesting section of the River Meuse and its tributaries including hill slopes with woodlands, dry grasslands, and calcareous rocks. Human activities include agriculture, forestry, hunting, fishing, yachting, recreation, and there is scattered human habitation.

Breeding species include *Pernis apivorus* (6+ pairs), *Falco peregrinus*, *Caprimulgus europaeus* (3+ pairs), *Alcedo atthis* (20 pairs), and *Dryocopus martius* (2 pairs). Additional passage species include *Milvus migrans* and *M. milvus*.

027 Croix-Scaille, Luxembourg and Namur (Région Wallonne)

49°57'N, 04°55'E 39,000 ha

Comprises the Belgian part of the Croix-Scaille upland plateau and a stretch of the River Semois, with important deciduous woodlands and well-preserved rivers, and remnant bogs and heaths on the upland plateau. Human activities include arable and stock-farming, forestry, fish-farming, hunting, and recreation.

Breeding species include *Pernis apivorus* (18+ pairs), *Milvus milvus* (2 pairs), *Bonasa bonasia* (30 pairs), *Tetrao tetrix* (25 males, shared with habitat across the border in France), *Dryocopus martius* (12 pairs), *Dendrocopos medius* (less than 5 pairs), *Lullula arborea* (5 pairs), and *Lanius collurio* (10+ pairs). In addition *Circus cyaneus* (5+) occurs on passage.

028 Lesse et Lomme, Luxembourg and Namur (Région Wallonne)

50°10'N, 05°11'E 16,700 ha EEC SPA

Covers the most interesting parts of the Calestienne and Famenne along the River Meuse. Comprises a considerable variety of habitats including calcareous dry grasslands, and woodlands. Human activities include agriculture, forestry, and recreation.

Breeding species include *Pernis apivorus* (5 pairs), *Milvus milvus*, *Bonasa bonasia* (8 pairs), *Crex crex* (1 pair), *Caprimulgus europaeus* (5+ pairs), *Alcedo atthis* (15 pairs), *Dryocopus martius* (10 pairs), *Dendrocopos medius* (2 pairs), *Lullula arborea* (12 pairs), and *Lanius collurio* (5 pairs). *Pernis apivorus* (30) and *Circus cyaneus* (5+) occur on passage and wintering species include *Alcedo atthis* (100).

029 Daverdisse, Luxembourg and Namur (Région Wallonne)

50°02'N, 05°06'E 12,000 ha EEC SPA

A large area of old deciduous woodland in the northern Ardennes. Human activities include forestry.

Breeding species include *Pernis apivorus* (5 pairs), *Bonasa bonasia* (2+ pairs), *Alcedo atthis* (8 pairs), *Dryocopus martius* (8 pairs), *Dendrocopos medius* (30 pairs), and *Ficedula hypoleuca* (150 pairs).

030 Marche en Famenne, Luxembourg and Namur (Région Wallonne)

50°18'N, 05°25'E 5100 ha

A typical area of the Famennian depression covered by woodlands and pastures, and including the very important military camp of Marche en Famenne (which is free of agricultural disturbance) and a stretch of the River Ourthe. Additional human activities include arable and stock-farming, forestry, and recreation. Problems include residential development (holiday homes) on the dry grassland areas and the channelisation of watercourses.

Breeding species include *Pernis apivorus* (8+ pairs), *Bonasa bonasia* (1+ pair), *Crex crex* (2+ pair), *Caprimulgus europaeus* (2+ pairs), *Alcedo atthis* (5+ pairs), *Dryocopus martius* (3+ pairs), *Lullula arborea* (12+ pairs), and *Lanius collurio* (10+ pairs). *Milvus milvus*, *M. migrans*, *Circus cyaneus* (5), and *Grus grus* (200) occur on passage.

031 Saint-Hubert, Luxembourg (Région Wallonne)

50°05'N, 05°24'E 16,700 ha

A large area of old deciduous woodland in the central, high Ardennes with well-preserved rivers and streams, remnant peatbogs, and heaths. Human activities include arable and stock-farming, forestry, hunting, recreation, and there is scattered human habitation.

Breeding species include *Pernis apivorus* (8 pairs), *Bonasa bonasia* (3 pairs), *Alcedo atthis* (5 pairs), *Dryocopus martius* (10 pairs), *Dendrocopos medius* (15 pairs), *Ficedula hypoleuca* (150 pairs), and *Lanius collurio* (5 pairs). *Milvus milvus*, *M. migrans*, and *Circus cyaneus* occur on passage.

032 Ochamp-Freux, Luxembourg (Région Wallonne)

49°57'N, 05°23'E 10,900 ha

A woodland area of the high Ardennes including many ponds and humid grasslands. Human activities include arable and stock-farming, forestry, fish-farming, hunting, recreation, and there is scattered human habitation.

Breeding species include *Ciconia nigra*, *Pernis apivorus* (3 pairs), *Alcedo atthis* (5 pairs), *Dryocopus martius* (4 pairs), *Saxicola rubetra* (30 pairs), and *Lanius collurio* (2 pairs). *Circus cyaneus* (5) and *Grus grus* (less than 200) occur on passage.

033 Malchamps, Liège (Région Wallonne)

50°28'N, 05°50'E 14,500 ha EEC SPA

Includes important area of woodland, the western ridge of the Fagnes Plateau which is covered by bogs, heaths, and fens, and remnant dry heaths and peaty heaths in southern

Spa. Human activities include agriculture, forestry, and recreation. The site is threatened by road construction.

Breeding species include *Pernis apivorus* (5+ pairs), *Milvus migrans* (1 pair), *M. milvus* (1 pair), *Bonasia bonasia* (1+ pair), *Tetrao tetrix* (4 pairs), *Aegolius funereus* (1 pair), *Caprimulgus europaeus* (12+ pairs), *Alcedo atthis* (5 pairs), and *Dryocopus martius* (less than 7 pairs). *Circus cyaneus* (3+) and *Grus grus* (less than 300) occur on passage.

034 Hautes Fagnes/Eifel, Liège (Région Wallonne)

50°24'N, 06°12'E 70,000 ha EEC SPA

Natural Park

Comprises the Natural Park and includes the high plateau of the eastern Ardennes covered by peatbogs and fens, and woodland. Human activities include agriculture, forestry, and recreation.

Breeding species include *Pernis apivorus* (25+ pairs), *Milvus milvus* (3+ pairs), *Tetrao tetrix* (41+ 'pairs'), *Crex crex* (2+ pairs), *Asio flammeus*, *Aegolius funereus* (less than 10 pairs), *Caprimulgus europaeus* (less than 10 pairs), *Alcedo atthis* (10+ pairs), *Picus canus* (less than 8 pairs), *Dryocopus martius* (20 pairs), *Dendrocopos medius* (5 pairs), *Lullula arborea* (less than 10 pairs), and *Lanius collurio* (30 pairs). Passage birds include *Milvus milvus* (40), *Circus cyaneus* (10+), *Grus grus* (5000), and *Saxicola rubetra* (150).

035 Vallée de la Lienne, Liège and Luxembourg (Région Wallonne)

50°20'N, 05°47'E 8500 ha

An example of the traditional grassland landscape of a high Ardennes valley and surrounding woodland. Human activities include arable and stock-farming, forestry, recreation, and there is scattered human habitation.

Breeding species include *Pernis apivorus* (4+ pairs), *Bonasa bonasia* (2+ pairs), *Aegolius funereus* (less than 4 pairs), *Alcedo atthis* (5+ pairs), and *Dryocopus martius* (8+ pairs). *Milvus milvus*, *M. migrans*, *Circus cyaneus* (3+), and *Grus grus* (30+) occur on passage.

036 Wanne-Logbiermé, Liège (Région Wallonne)

50°19'N, 05°57'E 5700 ha

A high plateau covered mainly by spruce plantations with remnant acid fens and beech woodland. Human activities include arable and stock-farming, forestry, and recreation.

Breeding species include *Pernis apivorus* (3 pairs), *Bonasa bonasia* (1+ pair), *Aegolius funereus* (4+ pairs), and *Dryocopus martius* (5 pairs).

037 Tailles, Liège and Verviers (Région Wallonne)

50°15'N, 05°44'E 5600 ha EEC SPA

An area of peatbogs, mires and heaths in a woodland, and grassland landscape in the Ardennes. Human activities include agriculture, and forestry. The site is adversely affected by a motorway near a peatbog which supports *Tetrao tetrix*.

Breeding species include *Pernis apivorus* (5+ pairs), *Bonasa bonasia* (2+ pairs), *Tetrao tetrix* (10+ pairs), *Aegolius funereus* (2+ pairs), *Alcedo atthis* (5 pairs), *Dryocopus martius* (6+ pairs), and *Lanius collurio* (2 pairs). *Circus cyaneus* (5) and *Grus grus* (300+) occur on passage.

038 Deux Ourthes, Luxembourg (Région Wallonne)

50°07'N, 05°40'E 23,500 ha

An undisturbed part of the Ourthe Valley with slopes covered by woodlands. Human activities include forestry, fish-farming, hunting, recreation, and there is scattered human habitation. Channelisation of watercourses is a problem.

Breeding species include *Pernis apivorus* (4+ pairs), *Milvus milvus* (1-2 pairs), *Bonasa bonasia* (5+ pairs), *Alcedo atthis* (10-15 pairs), *Dryocopus martius* (5 pairs), and *Lanius collurio*.

039 Haute Sûre/Ardennes méridionale, Luxembourg (Région Wallonne)

49°51'N, 05°28'E 65,000 ha EEC SPA

An important area of woodland at the southern limit of the Ardennes and the upper basin of the River Sûre with many old humid grasslands. Human activities include agriculture and forestry.

Breeding species include *Ciconia nigra*, *Pernis apivorus* (25 pairs), *Milvus migrans* (1 pair), *M. milvus* (3 pairs), *Bonasa bonasia* (10+ pairs), *Crex crex*, *Alcedo atthis* (15 pairs), *Dryocopus martius* (25 pairs), *Dendrocopos medius* (100 pairs), *Saxicola rubetra* (75 pairs), and *Lanius collurio* (20 pairs). Passage raptors include *Milvus milvus* (20), *Circus cyaneus* (15), and *C. pygargus* (5).

040 Sinémurienne, Luxembourg (Région Wallonne)

49°38'N, 05°35'E 22,500 ha EEC SPA

Includes forests on sandstone in the Sinémurienne region and the marshes of the upper River Semois.

Breeding species include *Pernis apivorus* (25+ pairs), *Milvus migrans* (1 pair), *M. milvus* (2 pairs), *Circus pygargus* (10 pairs), *Bonasa bonasia* (15 pairs), *Tetrao tetrix* (2+ pairs), *Rallus aquaticus* (40 pairs), *Crex crex* (1 pair), *Caprimulgus europaeus* (20 pairs), *Alcedo atthis* (5 pairs), *Picus canus* (1+ pair), *Dryocopus martius* (8 pairs), *Dendrocopos medius* (75 pairs), *Lullula arborea* (35 pairs), and *Lanius collurio* (30 pairs). *Circus cyaneus* (15) and *Grus grus* (50) occur on passage.

041 Côte Bajocienne, Luxembourg (Région Wallonne)

49°32'N, 05°30'E 8000 ha EEC SPA

Comprises the limestone ridge of the Bajocienne and covered mainly by woodlands, dry grasslands, copses, and marshes. Human activities include agriculture and forestry.

Breeding species include *Pernis apivorus* (5 pairs), *Milvus migrans* (1 pair), *M. milvus* (2 pairs), *Circus aeruginosus* (1 pair), *C. pygargus* (less than 12 pairs), *Porzana porzana* (3 pairs), *Crex crex* (1 pair), *Alcedo atthis* (less than 4 pairs), *Dendrocopos medius* (15 pairs), *Lullula arborea* (5 pairs), and *Lanius collurio* (45 pairs). In addition, *Milvus migrans* (5), *M. milvus* (10), *Circus cyaneus* (5), and *Grus grus* (200) occur on passage.

MAIN REFERENCES

IRSNB (1987) Inventaire des zones de grand intérêt pour la conservation des oiseaux sauvages dans la Communauté européenne – Belgique. Unpublished report.

van Vessem, J. and Kuijken, E. (1986) *Contribution to the determination of special protection areas for bird conservation in Flanders*. Hasselt: Institute of Nature Conservation, Ministry of the Flemish Community.

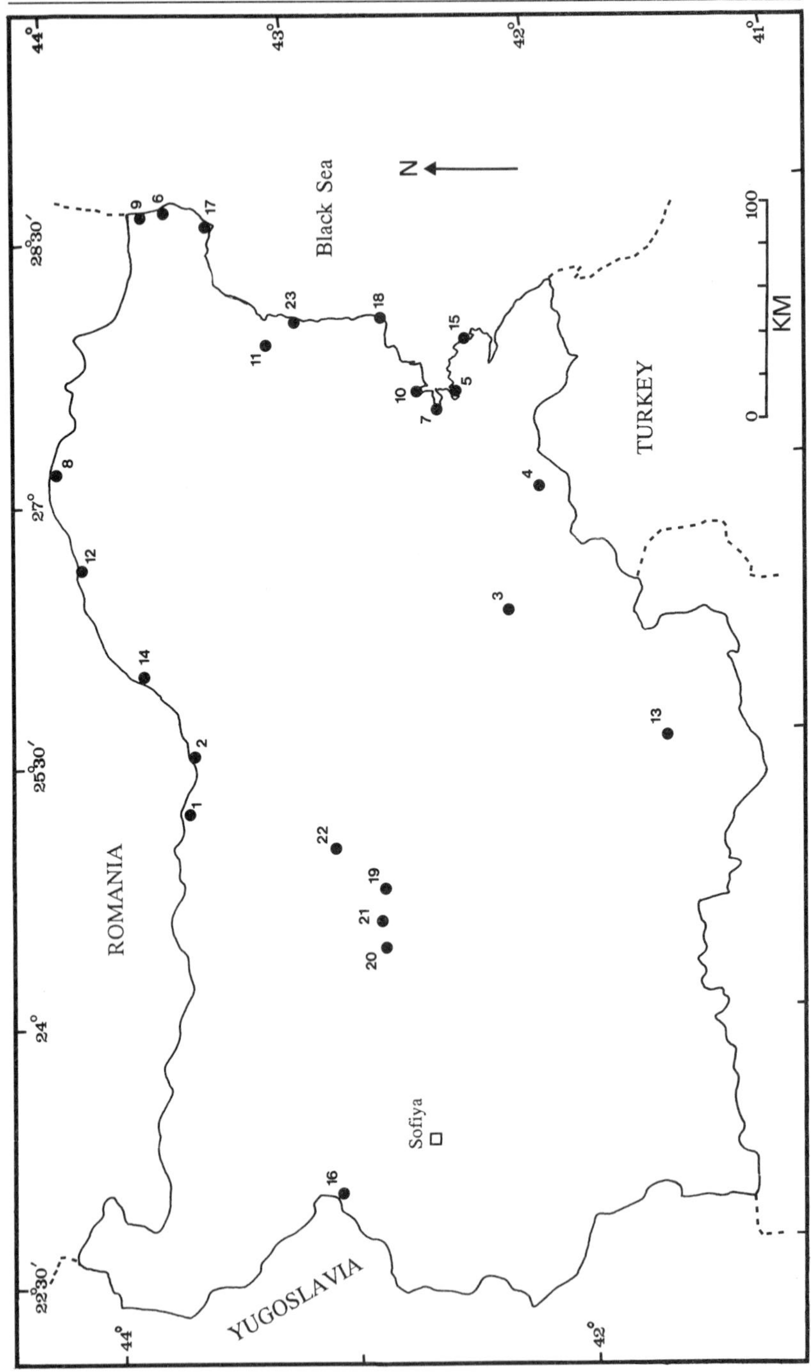

Figure 5: Map showing the location of the sites in Bulgaria

BULGARIA

Black-winged Stilt *Himantopus himantopus*

INTRODUCTION

General information

Bulgaria covers an area of 110,911 sq km and in 1983 had a population of 8,929,332 (an average population density of 80 persons per sq km). The country can be roughly divided into five main regions: the fertile Danube plain along the border with Romania; the Stara Planina mountains, a 600-km chain running east-west and dividing the country, with the highest point at 2376 m (Botev); the central plain and valleys of the River Maritsa immediately south of the Stara Planina; the high Rila Planina, Pirin Planina, and Rodopi Planina mountains in the south-west, with the highest point at 2925 m (Musala); and the Black Sea coast, which forms the eastern frontier of the country and is mostly flat (with some sea cliffs in the north).

The lowlands of Bulgaria have been largely converted to agricultural land. In 1982 agricultural land covered 61,815 sq km (56 per cent of the land surface), of which 46,547 sq km (41 per cent of the land surface) were cultivable. In 1982 forests covered 38,590 sq km (35 per cent of the land surface), of which 34 per cent were coniferous and 26 per cent *Quercus* spp. The climax vegetation is *Quercus* up to 1000 m, *Fagus* between 1000 and 1500 m, and coniferous woodland up to 2200 m. Forests of *Pinus peuce* are particularly well developed, forming stands above 1700 m in the Rila, Pirin, and Rodopi mountains. However, vast areas in the uplands have been devastated by grazing, mainly by sheep.

Furthermore, the development of tourism and recreation including skiing is a contemporary problem affecting undisturbed mountain areas.

The main wetlands lie along the Danube and Black Sea coast. Many of Bulgaria's marshlands and coastal lakes have been drained or modified since 1944; mainly for agriculture, but also because of development for tourism and industry. The north-eastern part of the Black Sea coast has some remnant steppe, and is similar to the adjacent Dobrogea of Romania.

Ornithological importance

The remaining marshes and lakes along the Danube and the Black Sea coastal wetlands are particularly important for breeding Ardeidae, especially *Nycticorax nycticorax, Ardeola ralloides, Egretta garzetta,* and *Ardea purpurea*; there are also important, although not large, populations of *Phalacrocorax pygmeus, Pelecanus crispus* (breeding now at a single site: Lake Srébarna), *Plegadis falcinellus, Platalea leucorodia, Milvus migrans* and *Haliaeetus albicilla*. Bulgaria also has a sizeable population of *Ciconia ciconia* (5000 pairs). *Tadorna ferruginea, Himantopus himantopus, Recurvirostra avosetta, Glareola pratincola*, and *Gelochelidon nilotica* breed along the coast, and there is a small colony of *Phalacrocorax aristotelis* on the cliffs at Cape Kaliakra. The wetlands are particularly important for summering and passage *Pelecanus onocrotalus* (the species formerly breeding at at least one site: Lake Mandra). Large numbers of geese, particularly *Anser anser*, occur in winter. The lakes in the north-east (Shabla-Ezeretz and Durankulak) also hold up to 15,000 *Branta ruficollis* and are of particular significance for this species when the weather in more northerly parts of the Black Sea is harsh.

Bulgaria supports good populations of some birds of prey, although the widespread use of strychnine baits up until the mid 1960s has been responsible for the extinction or drastic reduction of scavengers such as *Gypaetus barbatus* and *Aegypius monachus*. Raptor populations include *Neophron percnopterus* (80-100 pairs), *Gyps fulvus* (1-5 pairs), *Circaetus gallicus* (10-100 pairs), *Accipiter brevipes* (10-100 pairs), *Buteo rufinus* (50 pairs; increasing), *Aquila pomarina* (10-100 pairs), *A. heliaca* (4-20 pairs), *A. chrysaetos* (100-150 pairs), *Hieraaetus pennatus* (10-100 pairs), *Falco naumanni* (10-100 pairs), and *F. cherrug* (10-15 pairs).

The mountain forests, as well as supporting many of the raptor species mentioned above, also hold populations of *Bonasa bonasia, Tetrao urogallus*, a variety of owls including a small population of *Strix uralensis*, and a variety of woodpeckers including *Dendrocopos leucotos* and *Picoides tridactylus*.

Soaring migrants concentrate at particular sites along the Black Sea coast, with large numbers of *Pelecanus onocrotalus*, storks, and a variety of raptors occurring mainly on autumn migration.

Conservation infrastructure and protected-area system

The Committee for Conservation of the Natural Environment (KOPS) is the central authority concerned with nature conservation, and the Research and Coordination Centre for Conservation and Restoration of the Environment is the institute coordinating ecological research within the Bulgarian Academy of Sciences.

There are four types of protected areas relevant to nature conservation: National Parks, Protected Landscapes, Nature Reserves, and Natural Monuments.

1. National Parks
   These are territories distinguished by their outstanding natural beauty; they cover comparatively large areas and are suitable for recreation and tourism.

2. Protected Landscapes
   These are parts of the natural scenery (such as mountain ridges and gorges) and other characteristic landscapes which are suitable for rest and recreation.

3. Nature Reserves
   These are territories characterised by rare plant or animal communities of scientific value. Activities, including agricultural or industrial activities, which may adversely affect the site are strictly prohibited. Admittance to and movement within the reserves is strictly controlled.

4. Natural Monuments
These are natural phenomena where preservation is a matter of public interest.

International measures relevant to the conservation of sites

Bulgaria has ratified the Ramsar Convention and the World Heritage Convention and has designated four Ramsar Sites (all included in this inventory except Arkoutino) and two natural World Heritage Sites (of which one, Lake Srébarna, is included).

Bulgaria is an active participant in UNESCO's Man and the Biosphere Programme and has designated 17 Biosphere Reserves.

Overview of the inventory

A total of 22 sites are included. Wetlands along the coast and the important reservoirs are well covered, although several sites are without protection, including Lake Mandra, Shabla-Ezeretz, and Lake Burgas. A number of sites along the Danube have also been included, most notably Lake Srébarna, although some are rather small and can only cover the actual nesting sites (e.g. Vardim Island). Coverage of those waterbird species mentioned above is good to excellent (at least of their nesting sites). However, there are certain to be other wetlands along the Danube and other main rivers (including the Maritsa), especially areas of riverine forest and flood-meadows, which need to be identified and protected.

Only a selection of non-wetland sites are included, and further research is needed to identify other important bird areas (for raptors, grouse, woodpeckers etc.), including further areas in the Stara Planina as well as in the mountains in the south of the country. Michev (1985) has pointed out that there is a lack of adequate protected areas containing typical habitats for various species of raptors, and that action is needed to create large protected areas along the borders with Yugoslavia, Greece, and Turkey.

Acknowledgements

The following site accounts were compiled largely from information provided by T. Michev (Bulgarian Academy of Sciences). Additional information was received from J. Spiridonov and J. Lawton Roberts. Information from Michev *et al.* (1981) has also been incorporated.

INVENTORY

No.	Site name	Region	Criteria used to select site [see p.18]							
			0	1(i)	1(ii)	1(iii)	1(iv)	2	3	4
001	Belene Island	PN				*		*	*	
002	Vardim Island	TO				*		*	*	
003	Ovtcharitza Reservoir	SN				*				
004	Malko Sharkovo Reservoir	YL						*		
005	Lake Mandra	BS				*		*	*	
006	Shabla-Ezeretz complex	TN				*		*	*	
007	Lake Burgas or Vaya	BS				*		*	*	
008	Lake Srébarna	SA				*		*	*	
009	Lake Durankulak	TN				*		*	*	
010	Atanasovsko Ezero (Atanassovo Lake)	BS				*	*	*	*	
011	Yatata Reservoir	VA				*			*	
012	Island in the Danube near Nova Cherna	RD				*		*	*	
013	Studen Kladenetz	KO						*	*	
014	Rusenski Lom	RS						*	*	
015	Alepu Ezero	BS				*		*	*	
016	Gintzi	SF							*	
017	Cape Kaliakra	VA				*	*	*	*	
018	Cape Emine	BS					*			
019	Steneto	LH						*	*	

No.	Site name	Region	Criteria used to select site [see p.18] 0	1(i)	1(ii)	1(iii)	1(iv)	2	3	4
020	Boatin	LH							*	
021	Tzarichina (Tsaritchina)	LH							*	
022	Kamtchia Biosphere Reserve	VA							*	

PN=Pleven TO=Turnovo SN=Sliven YL=Yambol BS=Burgas TN=Tolbukhin
SA=Silistra VA=Varna RD=Razgrad KO=Khaskovo RS= Rus SF=Sofia LH=Lovech

Comments on the inventory

1. Much of the information was compiled and was up to date in 1987, although published material from 1981, which analysed all previous waterfowl counts, has been included. The passage figures, where given, refer to total counts during the season.
2. The site name is followed by the name of the province (okrug), which is given in parentheses. Bulgaria has been treated as a single 'region' when applying the site-selection criteria (category 3).

---

001 Belene Island (Pleven)

43°40'N, 25°10'E

Nature Reserve (385 ha) with buffer zone (551 ha) and Natural Monument (719 ha)

The largest Bulgarian island in the Danube, with two large marshes (Martvoto and Pischina) and several smaller marshes, surrounded by seasonally flooded *Salix* forest and wet meadows. In drier summers the marshes completely dry out. Land-uses include hunting, agriculture, and forestry.

Breeding species include *Phalacrocorax carbo* (60-138 pairs), *P. pygmeus* (1-40 pairs), *Nycticorax nycticorax* (82-1412 pairs), *Ardeola ralloides* (58-5197 pairs), *Egretta garzetta* (60-2084 pairs), *Ardea purpurea* (1-70 pairs), *Plegadis falcinellus* (60-695 pairs), *Platalea leucorodia* (22-61 pairs), *Anser anser* (20 pairs), *Haliaeetus albicilla* (1 pair), and *Chlidonias hybridus* (100 pairs). Wintering species include *Egretta alba* and *Anser albifrons*.

002 Vardim Island (Turnovo)

43°37'N, 25°28'E

Partly a Nature Reserve (72 ha), with plans to protect the whole island

An island in the Danube with temporary sandbars, covered in forests of *Quercus*, *Populus*, and *Salix*. In spring the island is almost completely flooded, but dry in autumn and winter. Outside the reserve land-uses include hunting and forestry.

Breeding species include *Phalacrocorax carbo* (350 pairs), *P. pygmeus* (20 pairs), *Nycticorax nycticorax* (300 pairs), *Ardeola ralloides* (200 pairs), *Plegadis falcinellus* (50 pairs), *Platalea leucorodia* (10 pairs), *Haliaeetus albicilla* (1 pair), and *Egretta garzetta* (200 pairs).

003 Ovtcharitza Reservoir (Sliven)

42°13'N, 26°10'E 630 ha

Unprotected, although proposed Natural Monument

A reservoir (which does not freeze in winter) on the River Ovtcharitza, surrounded by low hills with arable land (mainly winter wheat). There is a thermoelectric power-station on the northern shore and hunting in winter.

A wintering site for *Anser albifrons* (av. 15,000). Other wintering species include *Gavia arctica*, *Podiceps grisegena*, *Egretta alba*, and *Mergus albellus*.

004 Malko Sharkovo Reservoir (Yambol)

42°05'N, 26°50'E 380 ha

Unprotected, although proposed Natural Monument

A water-storage reservoir, surrounded by low hills with arable land (mainly winter wheat). Human activities include hunting and fishing.

Wintering species include *Phalacrocorax pygmeus*, *Egretta alba*, and *Anser albifrons* (av. 1600).

005 Lake Mandra (Burgas)

42°25'N, 27°28'E 1000 ha

Unprotected, although plans to protect southern and eastern parts

A brackish coastal lake which has been turned into a water reservoir (now fed only by inflowing rivers) with a remnant, brackish coastal lagoon (Uzun-geren) with an outlet to the sea; surrounded by wet meadows, marshes, and hills. The lake is used for fishing, hunting, and irrigation. A steel-manufacturing plant, currently under construction, is likely to be detrimental to the site.

Breeding species include *Phalacrocorax pygmeus*, *Nycticorax nycticorax*, *Ardeola ralloides*, *Egretta garzetta*, *E. alba* (occasionally), *Ardea purpurea*, *Plegadis falcinellus*, *Platalea leucorodia* (10-35 pairs), *Himantopus himantopus*, *Recurvirostra avosetta*, *Sterna albifrons*, and *S. hirundo*. *Pelecanus onocrotalus* and *P. crispus* formerly bred. Wintering species include *Phalacrocorax pygmeus* (av. 180), *Pelecanus onocrotalus*, *P. crispus* (occasionally), *Egretta alba* (av. 16), *Anser albifrons* (av. 1250), and *Oxyura leucocephala* (av. 5) (total figures for waterfowl: av. 20,300).

006 Shabla-Ezeretz complex (Tolbukhin)

43°30'N, 28°35'E 300 ha

Unprotected, although hunting prohibited (403 ha)

Two lakes connected by an artificial canal and separated from the Black Sea by a sandbar; both with indented shorelines covered with *Phragmites*. There is a hyper-saline lake (Shablenska tuzla: 19 ha) just south of this complex. Hunting and fishing remain a problem at the site.

Breeding species include *Tadorna ferruginea* (10 pairs) and *Aythya nyroca*. Very important for wintering waterfowl, with *Cygnus olor* (av. 110), *Anser albifrons* (av. 30,600), *Branta ruficollis* (av. 7600, max. 17,000+), and *Anas platyrhynchos* (av. 27,600, max. 66,515). Other wintering species include *Gavia arctica*, *Phalacrocorax pygmeus*, *Egretta alba*, and *Mergus albellus*.

007 Lake Burgas or Vaya (Burgas)

42°30'N, 27°20'E 2800 ha

Unprotected, except for Protected Landscape (70 ha)

A brackish to freshwater lake situated close to Burgas, connected to the Black Sea by a canal with a sluice. There is a belt of reeds along the northern, western, and southern shores. Land-uses include intensive fishing and controlled hunting, with agriculture and stock-grazing in the surrounding area. The lake is polluted by oil derivatives.

Breeding species include *Phalacrocorax pygmeus*, *Nycticorax nycticorax*, *Ardeola ralloides*, *Egretta garzetta*, *Ardea purpurea*, *Plegadis falcinellus* (100-200 pairs), *Aythya nyroca*, *Himantopus himantopus*, *Recurvirostra avosetta*, *Glareola pratincola*, and *Sterna hirundo*.

Wintering species include *Phalacrocorax pygmeus, Pelecanus crispus* (occasionally), and *Egretta alba* (av. 16, max. 95).

008 Lake Srébarna (Silistra)

44°05'N, 27°07'E 600 ha

Ramsar Site; Biosphere Reserve; World Heritage Site

Nature Reserve

A freshwater lake close to the Danube with emergent vegetation dominated by *Phragmites*. The connection with the Danube was closed in 1949 by a dam which prevented annual flooding, but the lake was reconnected in 1978. Surrounded by forests, vineyards, arable land, and areas of steppe. All economic and touristic activities are prohibited. The adjacent parts of the Danube, although ecologically connected, are not included in the site.

The lake supports the only breeding population of *Pelecanus crispus* in Bulgaria (29-127 pairs). Other breeding species include *Podiceps grisegena, Phalacrocorax pygmeus* (20 pairs), herons (*Ixobrychus minutus, Nycticorax nycticorax, Ardeola ralloides, Egretta garzetta, Ardea cinerea* and *A. purpurea*: *c.*1000 pairs), *Egretta alba* (3-10 pairs), *Plegadis falcinellus* (50-500 pairs), *Platalea leucorodia* (3-10 pairs), *Haliaeetus albicilla* (1 pair), *Circus aeruginosus, Chlidonias hybridus,* and *C. niger*. *Anser albifrons* (av. 5300) and *A. anser* (av. 437) occur in winter. Other species occurring include *Cygnus cygnus, Anser erythropus, Branta ruficollis,* and *Mergus albellus*.

009 Lake Durankulak (Tolbukhin)

43°38'N, 28°30'E 350 ha Ramsar Site

Protected Landscape

A brackish to freshwater coastal lake with some reedbeds. Human activities are few.

Breeding species include *Botaurus stellaris, Ixobrychus minutus, Anser anser, Circus aeruginosus,* and *Glareola pratincola*. Important for wintering *Branta ruficollis* (av. 400; max. 1710). Other wintering species include *Gavia arctica, Phalacrocorax pygmeus, Cygnus cygnus, Anser albifrons* (av. 17,000; max. 34,060), *A. anser* (av. 430; max. 890), and *Mergus albellus*, with an average of 27,000 wintering swans, geese, and ducks.

010 Atanasovsko Ezero (Atanassovo Lake) (Burgas)

42°30'N, 27°30'E 1690 ha Ramsar Site (1050 ha)

Nature Reserve plus buffer zone (several hundred ha)

A complex of saltpans with smaller settling pools for salt extraction, surrounded by a freshwater canal (which is wide in places) with reedbeds. There is salt extraction, but fishing and grazing are prohibited. The site is threatened by pollution of the canal (by industry to the north of the Reserve and by pig farms), erosion, and general deterioration of the dykes (on which many of the birds breed). The breeding colonies are also accessible to mammalian predators.

Breeding species (breeding data mainly from 1977) include *Ixobrychus minutus* (many pairs), *Ardea purpurea* (2+ pairs), *Anas acuta, Aythya nyroca* (2+ pairs), *Circus aeruginosus* (3 pairs), *Himantopus himantopus* (22 pairs), *Recurvirostra avosetta* (725 pairs), *Burhinus oedicnemus, Glareola pratincola* (5 pairs), *Gelochelidon nilotica* (35 pairs; the only Bulgarian breeding locality), *Sterna sandvicensis, S. hirundo* (90 pairs), *S. albifrons* (30+ pairs), and probably *Tadorna ferruginea, Porzana porzana, P. parva,* and *Chlidonias niger*. An extremely important bottleneck site for migratory birds (averages of seasonal counts over five autumns unless stated) with *Phalacrocorax pygmeus* (autumn max. 225), *Pelecanus onocrotalus* (14,800), *P. crispus* (195), *Ciconia nigra* (2860), *C. ciconia* (135,800), *Platalea leucorodia* (autumn max. 200), *Pernis apivorus* (3680), *Circaetus gallicus* (400), *Aquila pomarina* (5680), *Grus grus* (1790), *Recurvirostra avosetta* (autumn max. 7570), *Larus melanocephalus* (autumn max. 4100), *L. genei* (autumn max. 1385), and *Gelochelidon nilotica* (1390).

011 Yatata Reservoir (Varna)

43°11'N, 27°42'E 154 ha

Natural Monument

A former sedimentation reservoir near to Beloslav now covered with *Typha latifolia* and other emergent vegetation, and with areas of open water. Formerly connected with the Varna – Devnya Canal, and a reconnection with the Canal has been recommended.

Breeding species include *Himantopus himantopus* (10 pairs) and *Recurvirostra avosetta* (20 pairs). Considerable numbers of *Pelecanus onocrotalus* and *Ciconia* spp. occur on spring and autumn passage. Other passage species include *Tadorna ferruginea, Pernis apivorus, Milvus migrans, Circaetus gallicus, Circus aeruginosus, C. cyaneus, C. pygargus, Aquila pomarina*, and *Hieraaetus pennatus*.

012 Island in the Danube near Nova Cherna (Razgrad)

44°03'N, 26°28'E 560 ha

Unprotected, although protection proposed

A comparatively young unnamed island in the Danube covered with periodically flooded forests of *Salix alba*. There is no land-use or management.

A breeding site for *Phalacrocorax pygmeus* (5 pairs) and over 500 pairs of *Nycticorax nycticorax, Ardeola ralloides*, and *Egretta garzetta*.

013 Studen Kladenetz (Khaskovo)

41°36'N, 25°30'E *c.*20,000 ha

Nature Reserve (Valchi dol: 774 ha)

An artificial lake created some 30 years ago in a rocky gorge of the River Arda. There are numerous vertical cliffs and precipitous banks with scant vegetation. Land-uses include forestry, stock-farming, apiculture, and a small amount of agriculture.

Breeding species include *Ciconia nigra* (*c.*50 pairs), *C. ciconia* (*c.*10 pairs), *Pernis apivorus* (10-20 pairs), *Neophron percnopterus* (*c.*40 pairs), *Gyps fulvus* (1-9 pairs), *Circaetus gallicus* (1-2 pairs), *Accipiter brevipes* (2-3 pairs), *Buteo rufinus* (2+ pairs), *Aquila pomarina* (a few pairs), *A. heliaca* (a few pairs), *A. chrysaetos* (2+ pairs), *Hieraaetus pennatus* (a few pairs), *Falco naumanni* (a few pairs), *Bubo bubo*, and *Coracias garrulus*. *Gyps fulvus* (*c.*30) and *Aegypius monachus* (max. 29) occur in winter.

014 Rusenski Lom (Ruse)

43°50'N, 25°57'E 3260 ha

National Park

The river valleys of the Beli Lom, Cherni Lom, and Malki Lom which join to form the Rusenski Lom, with vertical limestone walls, broadleaved forests, meadows, and some arable land. Land-uses include haymaking, grazing, and some horticulture. Pollution of the Beli Lom is a problem.

Breeding species include *Ciconia nigra, C. ciconia* (*c.*10 pairs), *Tadorna ferruginea, Neophron percnopterus, Buteo rufinus, Aquila pomarina, A. chrysaetos, Falco naumanni, F. cherrug, Bubo bubo, Coracias garrulus*, and possibly *Aquila heliaca*.

015 Alepu Ezero (Burgas)

42°22'N, 27°43'E 14 ha

Natural Monument

A brackish coastal marsh with *Phragmites* and *Typha* beds and two areas of open water, alongside a sandy beach on the Black Sea coast. There is the need for a buffer zone to separate a nearby tourist complex from the lake.

Breeding species include *Ixobrychus minutus, Ardea purpurea,* and *Aythya nyroca.* During spring and autumn *Phalacrocorax pygmeus* (*c.*50), *Pelecanus onocrotalus* (thousands), and *P. crispus* (a few) occur.

016 Gintzi (Sofia)

43°04'N, 23°06'E 10 ha
Natural Monument

An area of vertical limestone cliffs, rocky outcrops, large caves, secondary *Fagus sylvatica* forest and open areas sparsely covered with *Juniperus.* Land-uses include livestock-grazing and hiking.

Breeding species include *Buteo rufinus, Falco cherrug,* and *Pyrrhocorax graculus* (*c.*50 pairs).

017 Cape Kaliakra (Varna)

43°20'N, 28°30'E 688 ha

Nature Reserve

A coastal headland with vertical limestone cliffs and many caves, with relict steppe vegetation inland.

Breeding species include *Phalacrocorax aristotelis desmarestii* and *Oenanthe pleschanka,* and possibly *Neophron percnopterus* and *Bubo bubo.* The cape acts as a bottleneck for birds on autumn passage with many *Phalacrocorax pygmeus, Pelecanus onocrotalus, Ciconia nigra, C. ciconia, Pernis apivorus, Milvus migrans, Circus aeruginosus, C. cyaneus, C. pygargus, Accipiter brevipes, Buteo rufinus, Aquila pomarina,* and *Hieraaetus pennatus* occurring. Wintering species include *Branta ruficollis* (hundreds) and *Otis tarda* (30+).

018 Cape Emine (Burgas)

42°42'N, 27°54'E 100 ha

Unprotected

A coastal headland and the easternmost point of the Stara Planina mountains. Rocky coast with vertical cliffs and xerophytic vegetation and sparse stands of secondary *Quercus* sp.

A very important bottleneck site with very large numbers of birds occurring during autumn passage, including *Pelecanus onocrotalus* (*c.*10,000), *Ciconia nigra* (*c.*1500), *C. ciconia* (100,000+), *Pernis apivorus* (*c.*2000), *Milvus migrans* (*c.*200), *Circaetus gallicus* (*c.*300), *C. aeruginosus* (100), *Aquila pomarina* (*c.*4000), and *Grus grus* (*c.*500).

019 Steneto (Lovech)

42°48'N, 24°40'E 5487 ha Biosphere Reserve (2889 ha)

Nature Reserve (2635 ha); National Park, and buffer zone (2598 ha)

An area with outstanding limestone karst topography, with ancient forests of *Fagus sylvatica* (2000 ha) and *Picea abies* (550 ha). In the buffer zone there are forests, pastures, subalpine scrub, and grasslands (*Juniperus sibirica, Vaccinium* sp. etc.). Economic activities are prohibited in the Nature Reserve, with summer grazing and hiking in the buffer zone.

Breeding species include *Pernis apivorus* (1-2 pairs), *Buteo rufinus* (1-2 pairs), *Aquila heliaca, A. chrysaetos, Bonasa bonasia, Tetrao urogallus* (a few pairs), *Alectoris graeca, Glaucidium passerinum* (2+ pairs), *Strix uralensis* (1-3 pairs), *Picus canus* (10 pairs), *Dryocopus martius* (8-10 pairs), *Dendrocopos medius* (several pairs), *D. leucotos lilfordi* (*c.*15 pairs), *Lullula arborea* (10-20 pairs), *Ficedula parva, Lanius collurio,* and two subspecies endemic to the Balkans: *Eremophila alpestris balcanica* and *Prunella collaris subalpina. Aquila pomarina, Hieraaetus pennatus,* and *Falco cherrug* possibly breed, whilst *Aegypius monachus* is now extinct.

020 Boatin (Lovech)

42°52'N, 24°20'E 2223 ha Biosphere Reserve (1281 ha)

Nature Reserve (1281 ha) and buffer zone (942 ha)

Ancient forests of *Fagus sylvatica* (1350 ha) and *Picea abies* (300 ha) on the northern slopes of the Stara Planina; with meadows, young *Fagus sylvatica* woodland, subalpine scrub (*Juniperus sibirica, Pinus mugo,* and *Vaccinium* sp.) and grassland. No economic activities are permitted in the Nature Reserve, whilst there is summer grazing and hiking in the buffer zone.

Breeding species include *Pernis apivorus* (1 pair), *Aquila chrysaetos* (1 pair), *Falco peregrinus, Bonasa bonasia, Alectoris graeca, Bubo bubo* (1 pair), *Strix uralensis* (1-3 pairs), *Aegolius funereus* (1-2 pairs), *Picus canus* (2-3 pairs), *Dryocopus martius* (5-6 pairs), *Dendrocopos leucotos lilfordi* (10-12 pairs), *Turdus torquatus* (*c.*500 pairs), *Ficedula parva* (10-20 pairs), *F. semitorquata* (*c.*20 pairs), and two subspecies endemic to the Balkans: *Eremophila alpestris balcanica* and *Prunella collaris subalpina*. *Gyps fulvus* possibly breeds, whilst *Tetrao urogallus* is now extinct.

021 Tzarichina (Tsaritchina) (Lovech)

42°50'N, 24°30'E 2482 ha Biosphere Reserve (1420 ha)

Nature Reserve (1420 ha) and buffer zone (1062 ha)

Ancient forests of *Fagus sylvatica, Abies alba, Picea abies,* and *Pinus peuce* (a Balkan endemic) on the northern slopes of the Stara Planina; with subalpine forests of *Picea abies* and *Pinus peuce,* subalpine scrub, grassland, and alpine meadows. No economic activities are permitted in the Nature Reserve, whilst there is summer grazing and hiking in the buffer zone.

Breeding species include *Pernis apivorus* (1 pair), *Circaetus gallicus* (1 pair), *Aquila chrysaetos* (1 pair), *Falco peregrinus* (1 pair), *Bonasa bonasia* (30-50 pairs), *Tetrao urogallus* (a few birds), *Alectoris graeca* (20-40 pairs), *Bubo bubo* (1-2 pairs), *Glaucidium passerinum, Strix uralensis* (1-3 pairs), *Aegolius funereus* (1-3 pairs), *Caprimulgus europaeus, Picus canus* (2-3 pairs), *Dryocopus martius* (5-6 pairs), *Dendrocopos leucotos lilfordi* (12-15 pairs), *Turdus torquatus* (500-1000 pairs), and two subspecies endemic to the Balkans: *Eremophila alpestris balcanica* and *Prunella collaris subalpina*. *Gyps fulvus* and *Aquila pomarina* possibly breed.

022 Kamtchia Biosphere Reserve (Varna)

43°02'N, 27°50'E 842 ha

Nature Reserve

An area of remnant riverine forest at the mouth of the River Kamtchia, dominated by mature *Fraxinus oxyphylla* and *Quercus pedunculiflora,* with marshes along the river bank. All economic activities are prohibited, but drainage and forestry plans have been proposed in the past.

Breeding species include *Egretta garzetta* (a small colony), *Ciconia nigra,* and *Ficedula semitorquata.*

MAIN REFERENCES

Michev, T. (1985) Status and conservation of raptors in Bulgaria. *Bull. WWG Birds of Prey* 2: 32-36.

Michev, T., Pomakov, V., Nankinov, D. and Ivanov, B. (1981) Wetlands of international importance in Bulgaria. *Proceed. Reg. Symp. under Project 8. MAB, UNESCO.*

IUCN (1986) Biosphere Reserves compilation 4, October 1986. Cambridge: IUCN.

Stoilov, D., Noshtev, V. Gerasimov, S. and Velev, V. (1981) *Protected natural sites in the People's Republic of Bulgaria.* Sofia: Scientific Research Centre for the Protection of the Natural Environment and Water Resources.

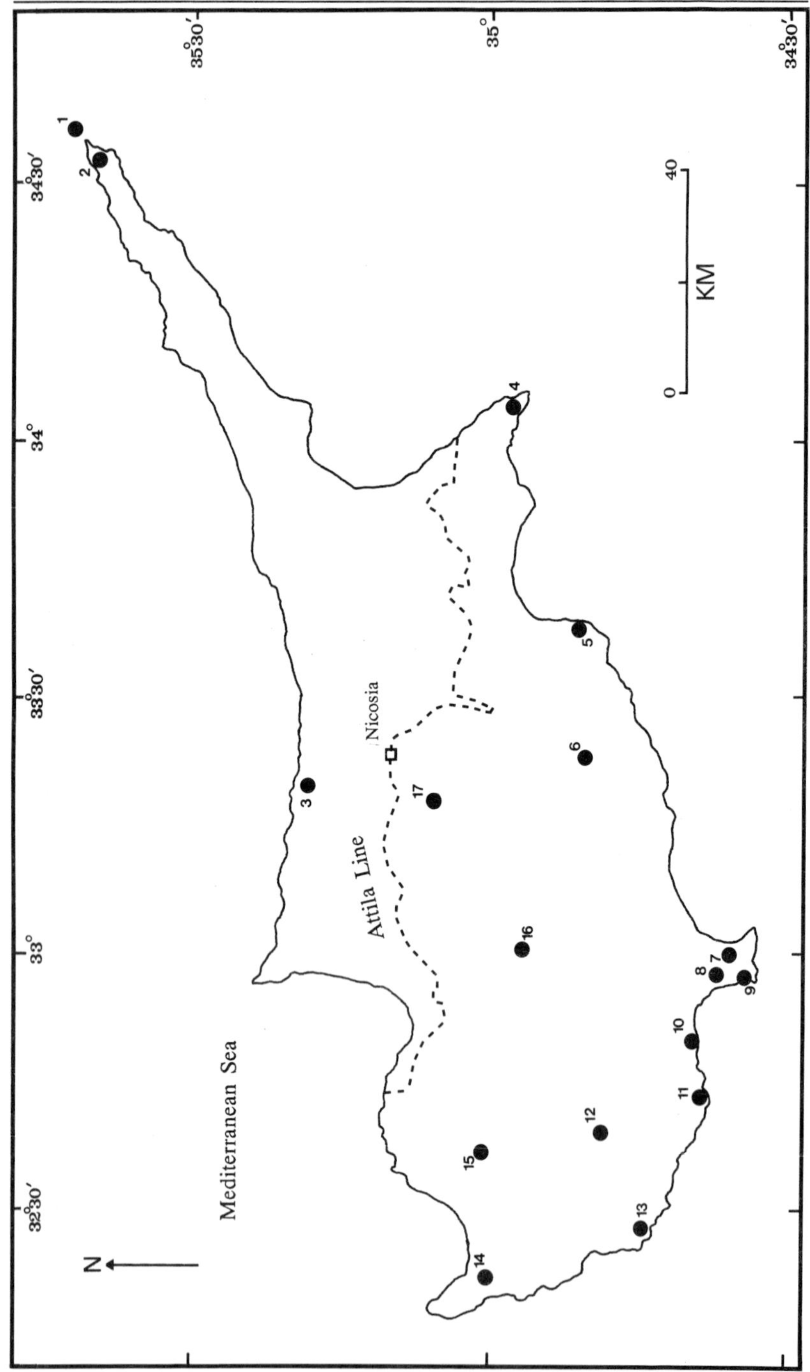

Figure 6: Map showing the location of the sites in Cyprus

CYPRUS

Cyprus Warbler *Sylvia melanothorax*

INTRODUCTION

General information

Cyprus lies south of Turkey in the easternmost Mediterranean between 34°33'-35°45'N and 32°17'-34°35'E. The island's total surface area is 9251 sq km, with a human population of 655,100 (in 1983); an average population density of 70.8 persons per sq km.

In the western half of the island the shoreline is generally rocky with offshore reefs; there are occasional sandy bays but these are few and far between. The cliffs in this part of the island vary up to 100 m in height, particularly in the area around Cape Aspro. The eastern part of Cyprus is more low lying with considerable stretches of sand, particularly on the east coast throughout the Famagusta district.

Cyprus is the most thoroughly cultivated land in the eastern Mediterranean (46 per cent of the land area; much of it of indifferent quality). The narrow coastal strip along the north coast especially in the Kyrenia area is fairly intensively cultivated; lemons and olives are the main crops, with vegetables and cereals being grown in places unsuitable for citrus groves. Flocks of sheep and goats are maintained in the more arid areas in the foothills. This plain is bounded on the south side by the narrow northern or Kyrenia range of hills, which stretch from Cape Kormakiti in the west, to Cape Andreas in the east; the highest point (about 900 m) is at the western end.

Between this range, the Troodos massif in the south-west and the coast in the south-east, lies the Mesaoria or central plain. This is the 'bread-basket' of Cyprus where the rain-irrigated crops of barley and wheat are grown, and flocks of sheep and goats range over the whole area. The fertile red-soil areas of the south-east corner are where potatoes and other vegetables are grown.

The northern slopes of the Troodos massif are fruit-growing areas; citrus fruits predominate in the foothills and on the plains surrounding Morphou, while the bulk of the island's soft fruit is grown in the main river valleys in the Solea District, which is in the same area but deeper into the massif. The southern slopes and the south-western corner of the island form the main vineyard area, but with the advent of irrigation, bananas, citrus fruits, and early vegetables are becoming increasingly popular crops.

Clearance over many centuries and the unrestricted grazing by goats, have destroyed much of the island's original forest, which is now confined mainly to the Troodos and Kyrenia Mountains. Paphos Forest in the western part of the Troodos range contains about two-thirds of the islands trees, mainly *Pinus halepensis* and *Quercus albifolia*. On Troodos Mountain, *Pinus nigra* forms pure forest above *c.*1600 m. Open forests of *Pinus halepensis* and *Cupressus sempervirens* are found in the Kyrenia range, but much of the range is covered by scrub, although efforts have been made to reafforest the southern slopes. High maquis, mostly *Juniperus phoenicea*, occurs mainly in the east of Cyprus, or on coastal promontories such as Karpas, Cape Greco and Akrotiri, and Akamas. The uncultivated low ground and hills are mainly covered by low maquis or, in drier areas, by open garigue.

The island has no perennial rivers (except for a few streams in the Troodos area) and usually none reaches the sea during the summer. There are shallow salt-lakes on the Akrotiri peninsula and south of Larnaca, and also a number of dams, with large expanses of fresh water, particularly on the southern slopes of the Troodos range.

The killing of migratory birds is a serious problem. Although the island's hunting (shooting) regulations are fairly comprehensive, the enforcement of the laws is inadequate and thousands of birds of many species are illegally shot each year. Other problems include liming and netting.

Liming (using sticks covered in glue to trap birds) is a traditional method of catching birds for food, but is now strictly illegal. However, it still takes place continuously from August to May on a massive scale, with little or no effort being made to stop it. The illegal use of nets to catch birds, almost unknown until the late 1960s, is now also a problem.

Ornithological importance

Nearly 200 species occur as regular passage migrants in Cyprus, and spring and autumn migration is the most prominent aspect of the ornithological year. Millions of migrants stop over on spring and autumn passage, particularly nocturnal migrants such as *Erithacus rubecula*, *Turdus philomelos*, *Sylvia atricapilla*, *Phylloscopus collybita*, and *P. trochilus*, and diurnal migrants such as *Merops apiaster*, hirundines, *Alauda arvensis*, and *Anthus pratensis*. Falls of nocturnal migrants occur throughout the islands and form dense concentrations in the scrub behind the departure coast.

In autumn there is a substantial passage west along the north coast of *Anas* spp. Ardeidae, and *Larus* spp. with many birds resting offshore. In spring waterfowl move east along the south coast. Large soaring birds, such as storks and *Aquila* eagles, tend to avoid Cyprus; however, many medium to small birds of prey migrate through Cyprus in autumn. Other passage birds include *Anthropoides virgo* (a concentrated passage from mid-August to early September with flocks of 100+ seen daily and some birds stopping to roost at Akrotiri) and *Grus grus* (passing in mid-October to early November).

Ninety species regularly winter, with large numbers of *Erithacus rubecula*, *Turdus philomelos*, *Phylloscopus collybita*, and several species of finches. The salt-lakes of Akrotiri and Larnaca hold up to 10,000 wintering *Phoenicopterus ruber*. Akrotiri also holds several thousand ducks in winter, and the freshwater dams are supporting increasing numbers of wintering (and passage) ducks and waders.

Seventy-three species regularly breed. Cyprus has two endemic species: *Oenanthe cypriaca* and *Sylvia melanothorax*. Both species are common and widespread throughout the islands; *Oenanthe cypriaca* is particularly numerous in the more rocky and open wooded areas of the Troodos. There are a further five endemic subspecies (some authorities recognise more) including *Loxia curvirostra guillemardi*. Other breeding species include *Phalacrocorax aristotelis*, *Gyps fulvus* (10+ pairs), *Aquila heliaca* (1-2 pairs), *Falco eleonorae*, *Francolinus francolinus* (fairly common resident), *Larus audouinii* (15 pairs), and *Pterocles orientalis* (scarce resident).

Conservation infrastructure and protected-area system

The two major categories of protected areas that protect birds from hunting are the Permanent Game Reserve and the Temporary Game Reserve. The former category is self-explanatory and those parts of the island designated include all urban areas, plus the whole of the Paphos Forest in the central and western parts of the Troodos massif, the southern part of the Paphos Plain, together with a few smaller areas. Temporary Game Reserves cover areas (such as dams) designated from time to time by the government, usually to protect possible breeding areas which are being too heavily hunted. The designated areas are marked on the ground by boards, on maps available to all hunters, and enjoy the same protection as Permanent Game Reserves; anyone caught infringing the regulations is subject to fairly strong penalties. Hunting is permitted outside these areas but it is regulated, in theory, in that the number of days on which shooting can take place is clearly defined, as are the periods for which licences are granted; thus one area may be available for daily hunting, whilst another area may be for Sundays and Wednesday afternoons only. In this way, the government aims to maintain some sort of control over hunting. Apart from these restrictions, the licences issued to cover each open season clearly stipulate which species may be shot. However, although experienced hunters may be able to differentiate between species, the vast majority are unable to do so and, as a consequence, birds are shot indiscriminately, posing a major conservation problem. Although the government is attempting to bring some order to the present chaos, there is a powerful anti-reform lobby. In addition, the enforcement of hunting laws on the ground is grossly inadequate. Thus there are frequent glaring infringements of the law with little chance of legal action being taken.

There are proposals to establish a National Park at the Akamas peninsula to control the use of the area by tourists. There are no Nature Reserves as such in the southern part of the island, the only reserves in this region being Game Reserves.

Akrotiri Salt-lake, Phasouri Reedbeds, Akrotiri Cliffs and Episkopi Cliffs are within the U.K. Sovereign Base Area. The conservation of the first two is the responsibility of the Republic, who invariably consult the SBA Authorities before making any change in the status of either area. The SBA Authorities normally agree with any changes proposed unless defence considerations dictate otherwise. The Akrotiri Cliffs site is inside the Akrotiri Garrison area and is the responsibility of the SBA Authorities, but, since access is strictly prohibited, their conservation is not a problem. The majority of the cliffs at Episkopi are within the Episkopi Garrison area and are thus offered the same protection; the small part of the site outside the Garrison area is extremely dangerous and difficult to reach, so again its conservation is not a problem.

Following the Turkish invasion of Cyprus, the island was divided, and the northern half was unilaterally declared as the Turkish Republic of Northern Cyprus which has international recognition only from Turkey. In the northern part, there are National Forest Parks, Natural Forest Reserves and Nature Conservation Areas. Natural Forest Parks are forested areas established for recreational and scenic value; Natural Forest Reserves and Nature Conservation Areas tend to be established to conserve forests and wildlife. There is also a single National Park (Zafer Burnu or Karpas Peninsula).

International measures relevant to the conservation of sites

Cyprus is a Party to the World Heritage Convention (but has not designated any natural World Heritage Sites) and the Bern Convention. Cyprus has ratified the Barcelona Convention but has not signed this Convention's Protocol concerning Mediterranean Specially Protected Areas.

Overview of the inventory

A total of 17 sites are included in this inventory, of which three are in the northern part of the island. Of the 17, four are islands or rocky sections of coast, included because of their breeding populations of *Phalacrocorax aristotelis*, *Gyps fulvus*, *Falco peregrinus*, *F. eleonorae*, and *Larus audouinii*; five are wetlands included because of their importance for passage and wintering waterbirds (two sites being particularly important for wintering *Phoenicopterus ruber*: Larnaca Salt-lakes and Akrotiri Salt-lake). The other sites, which include areas of agricultural land, scrub (maquis and garigue) and woodland, have been included because of their breeding birds of prey, *Francolinus francolinus*, and *Pterocles orientalis*, or their importance for passage migrants. Thirteen of the 17 sites receive some form of protection usually as Permanent or Temporary Game Reserves. Three of the island's most important sites, Larnaca Salt-lakes, Akrotiri Salt-lake and Phasouri Reedbeds are threatened by a variety of factors.

Acknowledgements

The site descriptions were compiled from information provided in 1987 by C. J. L. Bennett (Cyprus Ornithological Society 1957), who also prepared the introduction, and in 1984, by M. Charalambides. Additional material was provided by G. Magnin (ICBP), J. van der Ven (IWRB), A. R. Johnson (Tour du Valat), and A. Demetropoulos (Fisheries Department, Ministry of Agriculture and Natural Resources). G. Drucker (WCMC Protected Areas Data Unit) provided useful information on the protected areas in the northern part of the island. G. F. A. Munns was extremely helpful on a number of occasions.

INVENTORY

No.	Site name	Region	Criteria used to select site [see p.18]							
			0	1(i)	1(ii)	1(iii)	1(iv)	2	3	4
001	Klidhes Islands							*	*	
002	Karpas Peninsula								*	
003	Kyrenia Range between Kornos and Pentadactylos Mountains								*	
004	Cape Greco								*	
005	Larnaca Salt-lakes					*			*	
006	Dhypotamos Dam								*	
007	Akrotiri Salt-lake including Bishop's Pool					*			*	
008	Phasouri Reedbeds							*	*	
009	Akrotiri Cliffs								*	
010	Episkopi Cliffs								*	
011	Cape Aspro								*	
012	Asprokremmos Dam								*	
013	Paphos Plain							*	*	
014	Polis and the Akamas Peninsula					*			*	
015	Stavros-tis-Psokas							*	*	
016	Adelphi Forest							*		
017	Yeri near Nicosia								*	

Comments on the inventory

1. The names of the sites are anglicised in so far as words such as island, peninsula etc. have been used.
2. Cyprus has been treated as a single 'region' when applying the site-selection criteria (category 3).
3. No area (ha) is given for a number of sites because their boundaries have not been determined.

---

001 Klidhes Islands

35°42'N, 34°36'E

Nature Conservation Area; included in Zafer Burnu National Park

A chain of nine small, rocky islands off the north-east point of Cyprus. The main island is surrounded by low cliffs with vegetation dominated by grasses, *Salicornia* and *Atriplex* forming low, dense swards in places. Apart from a lighthouse, the islands are uninhabited, but are occasionally visited by fishermen. Human predation of gull eggs occurs but is not thought to be significant at present.

A breeding site for *Phalacrocorax aristotelis desmarestii* (25+ pairs in 1987), *Falco peregrinus* (2 pairs), and *Larus audouinii* (36 adults and 15 nests in 1987).

002 Karpas Peninsula (Zafer Burnu) Burnu

35°35'N, 34°25'E 8000+ ha

National Park (8000 ha)

A long, narrow peninsula north-east of Rizo Karpasso (with small offshore islands) with sandy and rocky shores and cliffs in places. The centre of the peninsula is dominated by a ridge of grass and scrub-covered hills with strips of farmland; there is maquis towards the coast. Human activities include goat- and sheep-grazing and agriculture dependent on rainfall. The marine turtles, *Caretta caretta* and *Chlidonias midas* breed along the coast.

An important area for *Francolinus francolinus*, which is increasing because shooting has been prohibited. Large numbers of passerine migrants occur, particularly in spring.

003 Kyrenia Range between Kornos and Pentadactylos Mountains

35°18'N, 33°08'E - 35°17'N, 33°28'E

State Forest (precise category of protection not known)

A long, narrow ridge of rocky mountains (600-800 m) covered (except for rocky outcrops) with a mixture of coniferous woodland, scrub, maquis, and grassland. There is some forestry, with goat- and sheep-grazing in all suitable areas. There is no recent accurate information on bird populations.

Breeding species include *Gyps fulvus* (possibly 6 pairs) and *Falco peregrinus* (probably 1-2 pairs). *Hieraaetus fasciatus* used to breed, but there is no recent information.

004 Cape Greco

34°57'N, 34°05'E

Temporary Game Reserve (headland only)

A rocky escarpment ending in steep cliffs on the southern, seaward side. Mainly covered in scrub (with rocky outcrops) and some cultivation, with the Cape closed to the public because of a radio station. There is intensive, illegal human predation by liming, netting, and trapping with considerable numbers of birds killed each year.

Breeding species include *Oenanthe cypriaca* (max. 10 pairs), *Sylvia melanothorax* (10+ pairs), and *Emberiza caesia* (2-3 pairs). An important site for migrants (particularly passerines, but also for raptors), providing the first arrival point for northbound birds in spring. Migrants include *Pandion haliaetus* (1-2 in spring and autumn), *Ficedula albicollis* (max. 10 in spring), *Lanius collurio* (4-5 in spring; max. 10 in autumn), *L. minor* (10+ in autumn), and *Emberiza hortulana* (max. 10 in spring). Small numbers of *Calandrella brachydactyla* winter.

005 Larnaca Salt-lakes

34°52'-34°54'N, 33°37'E 678 ha

Temporary Game Reserve (lakes only)

Four salt-lakes (three of which are interconnected) which dry out in summer, partially surrounded by agricultural land and *Salicornia fruticosa* scrub. The north-east corner is bordered by the suburbs of Larnaca and military camps, whilst Larnaca International Airport is on the eastern side (with one of the lakes intersected by the runway). The area is threatened by pollution from the airport, airport expansion plans, encroachment of the Larnaca suburbs, and possible tourist development of the lakes and surrounding area.

Breeding species include *Himantopus himantopus* (3-4 pairs; if water-level suitable), *Melanocorypha calandra* (tens of pairs), *Oenanthe cypriaca* (tens of pairs), and *Sylvia melanothorax* (max. 10 pairs). An important passage site, particularly in spring, with *Nycticorax nycticorax* (max. 10), *Ardeola ralloides* (*c.*50), *Egretta garzetta* (common), *Ardea purpurea* (10+), *Plegadis falcinellus* (10+), *Platalea leucorodia* (1-14), *Recurvirostra avosetta* (max. 20), *Hoplopterus spinosus* (1-10), *Philomachus pugnax* (100+), *Tringa glareola* (100+), *Larus genei* (10+), and *Calandrella brachydactyla* (100+). Wintering species include *Phoenicopterus ruber* (*c.*2000), *Anser albifrons* (max. 200), *Oxyura leucocephala* (scarce; max. 14), and *Burhinus oedicnemus* (*c.*50).

006 Dhypotamos Dam

34°50'N, 33°23'E 130 ha

Unprotected

A freshwater reservoir and scrub-covered valley with some citrus-fruit cultivation, surrounded by agricultural land. A comparatively new site and its full potential is not known.

Small numbers of *Pelecanus onocrotalus* (3), *Egretta alba* (2-3), and *Ciconia nigra* (max. 3) have been recorded.

007 Akrotiri Salt-lake including Bishop's Pool

34°36'N-34°38'N, 32°57'E-33°00'E 9400 ha

Permanent Game Reserve (lake only); shooting permitted in surrounding area; includes within U.K. Sovereign Base Area

A salt-lake which dries out in summer, surrounded by reedbeds and saltmarsh. There are vineyards and orange groves in the vicinity of Bishop's Pool, which is a man-made sump taking surplus treated effluent from the Akrotiri sewage-disposal works. Threatened by the construction of a dam on the River Kouris, which was one of the sources of water during the winter, by a shortage of water because of changing methods used to irrigate surrounding land, and the absorption of water by the surrounding *Eucalyptus* belt.

Breeding species include *Himantopus himantopus* (max. 10 pairs when water-level suitable), *Oenanthe cypriaca* (10-20 pairs), *Sylvia melanothorax* (3-4 pairs), and *Passer moabiticus* (50 pairs). Of major importance during spring and autumn passage. Species occurring in spring include *Ardeola ralloides* (tens), *Ardea purpurea* (5-10), *Ciconia ciconia* (occasionally hundreds), *Plegadis falcinellus* (tens), *Platalea leucorodia* (max. 10), *Circus aeruginosus* (max. 10), *C. cyaneus* (2-3), *C. macrourus* (1-2), *C. pygargus* (1-2), *Grus grus* (hundreds; thousands in autumn), *Anthropoides virgo* (max. 100; resting overnight), *Charadrius leschenaultii* (10-20), *Tringa stagnatilis* (tens), and *Gelochelidon nilotica* (5-10). Very important for wintering *Phoenicopterus ruber* (max. 10,000). Other wintering species include *Anas acuta* (3000), *Tadorna tadorna* (1000), and *T. ferruginea* (10-15). There are no recent records of *Oxyura leucocephala* (formerly 5-10 in winter).

008 Phasouri Reedbeds

34°37'N, 32°58'E

Permanent Game Reserve (reedbeds only); remaining area unprotected; included within U.K. Sovereign Base Area

An extensive area of reedbeds and water-meadows (unique in Cyprus), adjacent to Akrotiri Salt-lake. Threatened by the dam on the River Kouris, which formerly supplied water to the area. The reedbeds are being extensively damaged by unmanaged reed-cutting and burning, and there is encroachment for grazing and indiscriminate shooting.

Breeding species include *Nycticorax nycticorax* (max. 5 pairs), *Porzana pusilla* (3 pairs), *Oenanthe cypriaca* (2-3 pairs), and *Sylvia melanothorax* (3-4 pairs). Very important during spring and autumn passage. Species occurring include *Ixobrychus minutus* (max. 10), *Nycticorax nycticorax* (max. 20), *Ardeola ralloides* (max. 50), *Egretta garzetta* (tens), *Ardea purpurea* (max. 10), *Ciconia ciconia* (occasionally hundreds), *C. nigra* (max. 10 in autumn),

Plegadis falcinellus (tens), and a variety of raptors including *Circus aeruginosus* (max. 10), *Aquila heliaca* (1-2), and *Hieraaetus fasciatus* (2-3).

009 Akrotiri Cliffs

34°34'N, 32°57'E

Permanent Game Reserve; included within U.K. Sovereign Base Area

Sea cliffs and rocky coasts.

A breeding site for *Phalacrocorax aristotelis desmarestii* (5-10 pairs) and *Falco eleonorae* (8-11 pairs), although there have been no recent surveys. In addition, large numbers of birds pass on migration.

010 Episkopi Cliffs

34°41'N, 32°49'E

Permanent Game Reserve; included within U.K. Sovereign Base Area

Sea cliffs and rocky coasts with occasional beaches.

A breeding site for *Phalacrocorax aristotelis desmarestii* (5-10 pairs), *Gyps fulvus* (2-4 pairs; with up to 20 in winter), *Falco peregrinus* (1 pair), and *F. eleonorae* (8-10 pairs).

011 Cape Aspro

34°39'N, 32°43'E

Unprotected

Sea cliffs and rocky coasts.

A breeding site for *Falco peregrinus* (2 pairs) and *F. eleonorae* (25-30 pairs), although there have been no recent surveys.

012 Asprokremmos Dam

34°44'N-34°46'N, 32°34'E 260 ha

Temporary Game Reserve

Reservoir formed as a result of the damming of the River Xeros, mainly surrounded by rough grassland (used for grazing goats and sheep) with some arable land planted with cash crops.

Breeding species include *Oenanthe cypriaca* (max. 10 pairs), *Sylvia melanothorax* (3-4 pairs), and *Emberiza caesia* (1-2 pairs). Species occurring on spring and autumn passage include (spring figures unless stated) *Ixobrychus minutus* (1-6), *Nycticorax nycticorax* (max. 10), *Ardeola ralloides* (max. 10), *Egretta garzetta* (4-5), *Ardea purpurea* (3-4), *Falco eleonorae* (max. 4 in autumn), *Grus grus* (max. 10), *Hoplopterus spinosus* (3-4), and *Coracias garrulus* (max. 4). Wintering species include *Egretta alba* (1-2) and *Gyps fulvus* (3-4).

013 Paphos Plain

34°41'N-34°54'N, 32°29'E-32°32'E

Permanent Game Reserve (south of Paphos); mainly unprotected

A fairly narrow coastal plain (from Ay Georghios to the mouth of the River Khapotami) with cliffs, a rocky shore and a few sandy bays on the seaward side, and low rolling hills inland. Bisected by the Rivers Ezousas and Dhiarizos. An irrigated area used to grow cash crops. The main problem is tourist development along the shoreline either side of Paphos.

One of the main breeding areas for *Francolinus francolinus*. Other breeding species include *Oenanthe Cypriaca* (tens) and *Sylvia melanothorax* (tens). A favoured resting place for migrants during spring and autumn, with passage species include *Ixobrychus minutus* (5-6), *Nycticorax nycticorax* (tens), *Ardeola ralloides* (tens), *Egretta garzetta* (max. 20), *Ardea purpurea* (max. 10), *Plegadis falcinellus* (tens), *Circus aeruginosus* (5-10), *C. cyaneus* (5-10), *C. macrourus* (2-3), *C. pygargus* (2-3), *Falco naumanni* (tens), *Glareola pratincola* (tens), *G. nordmanni* (max. 10), *Hoplopterus spinosus* (max. 10), *Coracias garrulus* (tens), *Melanocorypha calandra* (tens), and *Calandra brachydactyla* (tens). Wintering species include *Falco columbarius* (2-3) and *Burhinus oedicnemus* (tens).

014 Polis and the Akamas Peninsula

35°02'N, 32°17'E-32°27'E

Proposed National Park; unprotected (although access restricted to northern part because of firing range)

Narrow ridge of hills (covered with scrub and occasional pockets of coniferous woodland) with considerable areas of rank grassland; also patches of farmland and maquis. The coastline is rocky with cliffs and occasional beaches. The area is mainly used for grazing goats and sheep, with a small amount of arable farming and fruit growing. There is considerable pressure to allow the development of coastal areas for tourism.

An important breeding area for *Gyps fulvus* (2 pairs), *Falco peregrinus* (1 pair), and *Francolinus francolinus* (increasing). Other breeding species include *Oenanthe cypriaca* (tens of pairs) and *Sylvia melanothorax* (10-20 pairs). Passage species include *Ardeola ralloides* (tens), *Egretta garzetta* (hundreds), *Ardea purpurea* (tens), Anatidae (including sizeable rafts of *Anas crecca* and *A. querquedula* in autumn), *Grus grus* (thousands in autumn), *Coracias garrulus* (max. 20 in spring), *Sylvia rueppelli* (10-20), and *Ficedula albicollis* (10-20). The waterbirds usually occur along the northern shore of the peninsula, particularly in the autumn.

015 Stavros-tis-Psokas

35°01'N, 32°38'E

Permanent Game Reserve

Coniferous woodland (well managed by the Forestry Department) with rocky outcrops. There is a large replanting scheme covering an area which was decimated by fire in 1974.

Breeding species include *Gyps fulvus* (several pairs), *Aquila heliaca* (2 pairs), *Hieraaetus fasciatus* (3 pairs), and *Lullula arborea* (tens of pairs).

016 Adelphi Forest

35°02'N, 32°58'E

Temporary Game Reserve

Coniferous woodland

Formerly a site for breeding *Aquila heliaca* (2 pairs), but there have been no recent surveys.

017 Yeri near Nicosia

35°04'N, 33°19'E

Unprotected

Agricultural land and dry fields. A sensitive area close to the cease-fire line, with no recent ornithological information.

A breeding site for *Burhinus oedicnemus* (6 pairs) and *Pterocles orientalis* (10 pairs).

MAIN REFERENCES

Bannerman, D. A. and Bannerman, W. M. (1971) *Handbook of the birds of Cyprus and migrants of the Middle East.* Edinburgh: Oliver and Boyd.

Cyprus Ornithological Society (1957) Annual Reports Nos. 12-32 (1965-1985).

Cyprus Ornithological Society (1970) Annual Reports Nos. 1-14 (1970-1983).

Flint, P. R. and Stewart, P. F. (1983) *The birds of Cyprus.* (Checklist No. 6). London: British Ornithologists' Union.

Stewart, P. F. and Christensen, S. (1971) *A checklist of the birds of Cyprus 1971.* Plymouth: P. F. Stewart.

CZECHOSLOVAKIA

Tengmalm's Owl *Aegolius funereus*

INTRODUCTION

General information

Czechoslovakia covers an area of 127,896 sq km, in 1983 had a population of 15,395,970 (an average population density of 120 persons per sq km), and is largely an agricultural and heavily industrialised country.

The northern and southern borders of the Czech Republic are mountainous (with the Krkonoše and Jeseníky Mountains in the north, and Sumava Mountains in the south), whilst the Slovak Republic is particularly mountainous, dominated by the Malá Fatra, Vel'ká Fatra, Vysoké, and Nízké Tatry mountains.

Agricultural land covers 69,000 sq km (54 per cent of the land surface), of which 48,000 sq km are arable, 8000 sq km are meadow, and 8000 sq km are pasture. The remaining area of the country is largely covered by forests, with broad-leaved deciduous woodland at lower altitudes (extensively reafforested by *Picea* and *Pinus*) giving way to mixed coniferous and deciduous woodland at higher altitudes, and *Pinus* in subalpine zones. The forests of Czechoslovakia, particularly in the north-west, are amongst the most seriously affected by air pollution in Europe. In warmer areas, close to the Hungarian border, there are remains of steppe-woodland and steppe-grassland vegetation.

The alluvial plains of southern Bohemia, southern Moravia, the River Danube and River Morava (March), and Rivers Bodrog-Latorica-Ondava, which were originally covered by extensive riverine forests and marshes, have since the thirteenth and fourteenth centuries been converted into agricultural fields and fish-pond complexes. Important riverine forests remain along the Danube, in a narrow strip 5-10 km wide between Bratislava and Zlatná na Ostrove, and along lower reaches of the Dyje and Morava. Remnant swamps, marshes, and oxbows are scattered throughout the plains; the largest complex of open water and marsh is the fish-pond complex in the Třeboň basin.

Ornithological importance

The most restricted habitats are the remaining 'natural' wetlands, although their loss has been partly compensated for by the creation over the centuries of numerous fish-ponds. Breeding wetland birds include *Botaurus stellaris* (55-80 pairs), *Ixobrychus minutus* (450-800 pairs), *Nycticorax nycticorax* (300-500 pairs), *Ardea purpurea* (25-75 pairs), *Anser anser* (300-500 pairs), and *Chlidonias niger* (300-600 pairs).

Areas of lowland grassland, steppe, and unintensively cultivated land are also much reduced, and Czechoslovakia's populations of species such as *Otis tarda* (*c.*280 birds) and *Burhinus oedicnemus* (15-30 pairs) have declined considerably, whilst *Crex crex* has virtually disappeared from the lowlands (although still breeding in upland meadows). Other declining species include *Caprimulgus europaeus* and *Lullula arborea*.

The uplands, particularly the mountain ranges of Slovakia and the warmer limestone hills of the south, are of particular importance for breeding birds of prey, grouse, and woodpeckers. Breeding species include *Aquila pomarina* (300 pairs), *A. heliaca* (25 pairs), *A. chrysaetos* (50 pairs), *Falco cherrug* (25 pairs), *Bonasa bonasia* (12,000+ birds), *Tetrao tetrix* (2200 birds in 1975; declining), *T. urogallus* (less than 4000 birds), *Bubo bubo* (700-900 pairs), *Glaucidium passerinum*, *Strix uralensis* (70 pairs), *Aegolius funereus*, *Dendrocopos leucotos*, and *Picoides tridactylus*.

Other species threatened in a European context with significant populations in Czechoslovakia include *Ciconia nigra* (250-400 pairs; increasing), *C. ciconia* (1669 pairs in 1984), *Milvus milvus* (20 pairs), *Circus aeruginosus* (600 pairs), *C. cyaneus* (10 pairs), and *C. pygargus* (*c.*20 pairs).

Conservation infrastructure and protected-area system

The Ministry of Culture (Department for Nature Conservation) and its agency, the Centre for State Protection of Monuments and Nature, are responsible for nature conservation in the Czech Republic, and the Ministry of Culture (Department for Museums, Cultural Monuments, and Nature Conservation) and its agency, the Centre for State Nature Conservation, are responsible for nature conservation in the Slovak Republic. There are eight categories of protected areas: National Park, Protected Landscape Area, State Nature Reserve, Protected Finding Place (or Protected Habitat), Protected Study Area, Protected Park or Garden, Protected Natural Feature, and Protected Natural Monument. Of these, the following are referred to in the inventory (definitions from IUCN 1987):

1. National Park
   This is an area of outstanding importance for nature where human activity is controlled. The Park is strictly protected and exploitation of any kind is regulated. They are fully open to visitors (tourism is a main objective) and parts are zoned for recreational development.

2. Protected Landscape Area
   These are examples of areas where there has been a harmonious interaction between nature and man. Economic activities are not prohibited, but are required to be carried out in accordance with the interests of nature conservation.

3. State Nature Reserve
   These are areas where the habitat is subject to strict conservation (with habitat management when required).

4. Protected Finding Place/Protected Locality (Protected Habitat)
   These are sites where the occurrence of one or more plant or animal species is preserved by all available means.

5. Protected Study Area
   These are protected sites designated for research and teaching purposes.

6. Protected Natural Feature
These are similar in character and type of protection to State Nature Reserves and Protected Finding Places, but are established only by District National Committees.

International measures relevant to the conservation of sites

Czechoslovakia is one of the few European countries that is not a party to the Ramsar Convention. Also, it is not a party to the World Heritage Convention. It has, however, designated four Biosphere Reserves (three of which are included in this inventory).

Overview of the inventory

Twenty-nine sites are included in this inventory (some of which are extremely large with a number of subsites), covering a total of 1,527,000 ha (to nearest 1000 ha). Although a number of wetland areas have not been covered, particularly in the northern Czech Republic, the inclusion of the Třeboňsko area, Soutok, Záhorské močiare marshes, Podunaji (the Danube flood plain), and east Slovakian marshes (as well as several other important fish-ponds and reservoirs) means that wetlands and areas of riverine forest are covered well by the inventory, thus accounting for the majority or a significant proportion of the total population of the wetland species mentioned above. Třeboň basin is an existing Protected Landscape Area. All the other main wetland areas are proposed Protected Landscape Areas, but are currently being adversely affected by drainage, canalisation, agricultural development, and forestry, with the stretch of the Danube between Bratislava and Chl'aba (017-1) under threat from the Danube Water Scheme.

Populations of birds of prey, grouse, and woodpeckers are covered well by this inventory, with some species' distributions concentrated in the areas included, although the inclusion of additional upland areas in southern and eastern Slovakia (particularly the Slovenské Rudohorie mountains) would have ensured better coverage of Czechoslovakia's significant populations of *Aquila pomarina*, *A. heliaca*, and *Falco cherrug*.

All the species mentioned above are covered at least partly by the sites included in this inventory, although those which are more widely distributed in the country (e.g. *Ixobrychus minutus*, *Ciconia nigra*, *C. ciconia*, *Pernis apivorus*, and *Bubo bubo*) have a major proportion of their population lying outside these sites.

Acknowledgements

Information for the Czech Republic was provided by J. Flousek, P. Miles, P. Bürger, B. Kloubec, K. Pecl, M. Honců, L. Urbánek, J. Janda, J. Chytil, S. Kučera and K. Hudec, with the project coordinated by J. Hora and Z. Veselovský. Information for the Slovak Republic was provided by A. Randík.

INVENTORY

No.	Site name	Region	Criteria used to select site [see p.18]							
			0	1(i)	1(ii)	1(iii)	1(iv)	2	3	4
001	Krkonoše Mountains	BA						*	*	
001-1	Pančavská and Labská louka peatbogs	BA								
001-2	Úpská rašelina peatbog	BA								
002	Šumava Mountains	BA						*	*	
002-1	Mount Boubín	BA								
002-2	Vltavský luh	BA								
003	Třeboňsko Protected Landscape Area	BA				*		*	*	
003-1	Ruda peatbog and Horusický rybník pond	BA								
003-2	Velký and Malý Tisý ponds	BA								

No.	Site name	Region	Criteria used to select site [see p.18]							
			0	1(i)	1(ii)	1(iii)	1(iv)	2	3	4
003-3	River Stará řeka and Novořecké močály marshes	BA								
004	Dehtář pond	BA				*		*	*	
005	Řežabinec pond	BA							*	
006	Novozámecký rybník pond	BA						*	*	
007	Žehuňský rybník pond	BA						*	*	
008	Pálava Protected Landscape Area	MA							*	
009	Soutok	MA						*	*	
010	Lednické rybníky ponds	MA				*		*	*	
011	Pohořelické rybníky pond	MA				*		*	*	
012	Střední nádrž	MA				*		*	*	
013	Znojmo area	MA						*	*	
014	Záhorské močiare marshes	SA							*	
014-1	Jakubovské rybníky ponds	SA								
015	Šúr peatbog	SA							*	
016	Trnavské rybníky ponds	SA							*	
017	Podunají	SA						*	*	
017-1	River Danube between Bratislava and Chl'aba	SA								
017-2	Čičovské mrtvé rameno 'dead arm'	SA								
017-3	Istragov marsh	SA								
017-4	Zlatná na Ostrove	SA								
017-5	Parížske močiare marshes	SA								
018	Orava reservoir	SA				*		*		
019	Malá Fatra Mountains	SA							*	
020	Vel'ká Fatra Mountains	SA							*	
021	Tatra National Park	SA							*	
022	Nízké Tatry Mountains	SA							*	
023	Pieniny Mountains	SA							*	
024	Slovenský Kras karst	SA						*	*	
025	Slanské vrchy hills – southern part	SA						*	*	
026	Vihorlat Mountains	SA						*	*	
027	East Slovakia marshes	SA				*			*	
027-1	Zatínske močiare marshes	SA								
027-2	Tajba marshes	SA								
028	Senné-rybníky ponds	SA							*	
029	Zemplínská Sírava reservoir	SA							*	

BA=Bohemia MA=Moravia SA=Slovakia

Comments on the inventory

1. The presentation of site names is based on the method used by Czechoslovakian geographers and is as proposed by the Czech contributors to this inventory. In general, Czech or Slovak names have been given first, followed by the English word for the type of site (e.g. mountains, hills, peatbog, etc.).
2. The passage figures are daily figures rather than total numbers during a season.
3. The regions, given in parentheses following each site name, are Bohemia, Moravia (both in the Czech Socialist Republic), and Slovakia (Slovak Socialist Republic). The Czech Republic and Slovak Republic are the 'regions' which have been used when applying the site-selection criteria (category 3).

001 Krkonoše Mountains (Bohemia)

50°37'-50°47'N, 15°23'-15°53'E 54,700 ha

National Park (38,500 ha) with buffer zone (16,200 ha) and including seven State Nature Reserves

A mountainous region (max. 1602 m) mainly covered in *Fagus* and Fagus/*Picea* forest (500-900 m) and *Picea* forests (900-1250 m), with peatbogs, subalpine meadows, and alpine zones. Forestry is the most important economic activity; other land-uses include recreation and grazing. These activities are much restricted in the nature reserves. Seriously affected by air pollution (one of the worst affected national parks in Europe); the rapid destruction of the *Picea* forests has resulted in the continuous decline of forest bird populations. The impact of 8-10 million visitors a year is also considerable.

Breeding species include *Ciconia nigra* (*c.*5-7 pairs), *Pernis apivorus* (*c.*3 pairs), *Circus cyaneus* (*c.*1 pair), *Aquila pomarina* (1 pair), *Falco columbarius* (probably 1 pair), *F. peregrinus* (probably 1 pair), *Tetrao tetrix* (*c.*100 birds), *T. urogallus* (*c.*10 birds), *Crex crex* (*c.*15-20 pairs in 1987), *Charadrius morinellus* (regularly breeding until 1946; in 1986 1 pair probably bred), *Bubo bubo* (*c.*3 pairs), *Aegolius funereus* (*c.*30 pairs), *Alcedo atthis* (*c.*5 pairs), *Picus canus* (*c.*10 pairs), *Dryocopus martius* (*c.*30 pairs), *Dendrocopos medius* (*c.*3-5 pairs), *D. leucotos* (probably 1 pair), *Lullula arborea* (*c.*5-10 pairs), *Prunella collaris* (*c.*10 pairs; an isolated population and the most northerly breeding locality in Europe), *Luscinia svecica svecica* (*c.*15-20 pairs; the whole Czechoslovak population), *Ficedula parva* (*c.*25-30 pairs) and *Lanius collurio* (*c.*30-40 pairs).

001-1 Pančavská and Labská louka peatbogs (Bohemia)

50°46'N, 15°32'E *c.*130 ha

Included in a State Nature Reserve (Prameny Labe [source of the Elbe]) and in Krkonoše National Park

A raised peatbog of a subarctic character with numerous pools. The peatbog is covered by scattered stands of *Pinus mugo*. The area is managed for nature conservation but there is considerable pressure from tourism.

Breeding species include *Tetrao tetrix* (*c.*10 birds) and *Luscinia svecica svecica* (*c.*10 pairs; *c.*60 per cent of the Czechoslovak population). *Falco columbarius* (1 pair) probably breeds.

001-2 Úpská rašelina peatbog (Bohemia)

50°46'N, 15°43'E 73 ha

Included in Prameny Úpy (source of the River Úpa) State Nature Reserve and Krkonoše National Park

A peatbog in the subalpine zone with extensive stands of *Pinus mugo*. Problems result from industrial pollution and tourism, and there is the danger of some drainage because of the possible construction of a chalet nearby.

The peatbog supports an important population of *Luscinia svecica svecica* (4-6 pairs).

002 Šumava Mountains (Šumava Protected Landscape Area) (Bohemia)

48°40'-49°20'N, 13°15'-14°10'E 163,000 ha

Major parts are a proposed Biosphere Reserve

Protected Landscape Area and ten State Nature Reserves

A mountainous area on the border with the Federal Republic of Germany and Austria. About 60 per cent of the area is covered by *Picea* forest, with *Fagus/Abies* at lower altitudes that has been modified by commercial plantations of *Picea*. There is also a complex of raised peatbogs and numerous wetlands. Parts of the area are exploited for forestry and agriculture, which are unrestricted outside the nature reserves. The area is also extensively used for summer and winter recreation. The drainage of wetlands, application of pesticides and other chemicals in agriculture, and forestry, and exploitation

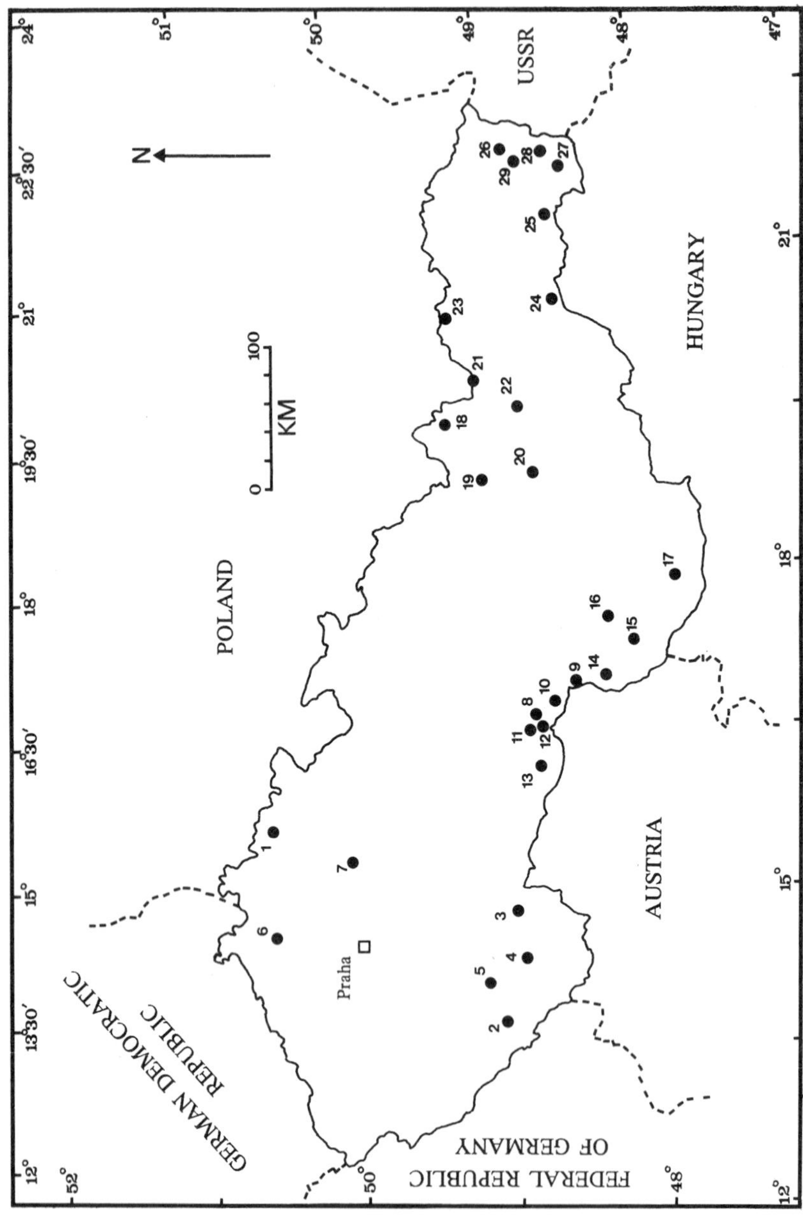

Figure 7: Map showing the location of the sites in Czechoslovakia

of the peatbogs are adversely affecting species such as *Tetrao tetrix*, *Crex crex*, *Lullula arborea*, and *Lanius collurio*.

Very important for breeding *Ciconia nigra* (3-5 pairs), *C. ciconia* (3 pairs), *Circus cyaneus* (2-4 pairs), *Aquila pomarina* (2-3 pairs), *Tetrao tetrix* (100-200 pairs), *T. urogallus* (50-60 pairs), *Crex crex* (10-20 pairs), *Bubo bubo* (*c.*10 pairs), *Glaucidium passerinum* (100-150 pairs), *Aegolius funereus* (100-150 pairs), *Dendrocopos leucotos* (2-5 pairs), and *Luscinia svecica cyaneculus* (2-3 pairs). In addition the area supports a comparatively high density for southern Bohemia of *Pernis apivorus* (tens of pairs), *Bonasa bonasia* (hundreds of pairs), *Picoides tridactylus* (hundreds of pairs), *Lullula arborea* (tens of pairs), *Ficedula parva* (tens of pairs), and *Lanius collurio* (tens of pairs).

002-1 Mount Boubín (Bohemia)

49°00'N, 13°15'E 6000 ha included in proposed Biosphere Reserve

State Nature Reserve (Boubínský prales primeval forest: 600+ ha); included in Protected Landscape Area

Comprises the Boubín and Bobík mountains which are covered with *Picea* and virgin *Fagus/Abies* forest. Economic activity is prohibited within the Nature Reserve, which protects the ancient *Fagus/Abies* forest.

An important ornithological area in the Šumava with breeding *Ciconia nigra* (1 pair), *Bonasa bonasia* (tens of pairs), *Tetrao urogallus* (possibly 1-2 pairs), *Bubo bubo* (1-2 pairs), *Glaucidium passerinum* (10-20 pairs), *Aegolius funereus* (10-20 pairs), *Dryocopus martius* (10-20 pairs), *Dendrocopos leucotos* (2 pairs), *Picoides tridactylus* (20-30 pairs), and *Ficedula parva* (3-5 pairs).

002-2 Vltavský luh (River Vltava flood plain) (Bohemia)

48°50'N, 13°50'E 2000 ha included in proposed Biosphere Reserve

Included in Protected Landscape Area; some peatbogs are State Nature Reserves

The valley of the River Vltava with a complex of peatbogs and marshes. Economic activities include agriculture. Agriculture, drainage of wetlands, and exploitation of the peatbogs are adversely affecting species such as *Tetrao tetrix* and *Crex crex*.

Breeding species include *Ciconia ciconia* (1 pair), *Pernis apivorus* (1-2 pairs), *Circus cyaneus* (1 pair), *Aquila pomarina* (1 pair), *Tetrao tetrix* (15-20 pairs), *Crex crex* (3-5 pairs), *Glaucidium passerinum* (less than 10 pairs), *Aegolius funereus* (less than 10 pairs), *Picoides tridactylus* (less than 5 pairs), *Luscinia svecica cyaneculus* (2 pairs), and *Lanius collurio* (*c.*10 pairs).

003 Třeboňsko Protected Landscape Area (Bohemia)

49°02'N, 14°49'E 70,000 ha Biosphere Reserve

Protected Landscape Area; the most valuable sites protected, or proposed, as State Nature Reserves

An extremely varied landscape with more than 500 fish-ponds. A large part of the area is covered in *Pinus*, *Abies* and *Picea* forest, with remnant broad-leaved forests in the river flood plains. There are also areas of wet *Alnus* woodland, peatbogs, wet meadows and numerous rivers, streams, and channels. Agriculture, forestry, and fish-farming are the main economic activities, which are not overly restricted outside the nature reserves. Problems include loss of meadows for cultivation, eutrophication and vegetational succession of important areas, aerial spraying of pesticides, exploitation of peat, and extraction of sand and minerals lowering the water-table.

Breeding species include *Phalacrocorax carbo* (*c.*120 pairs; increasing), *Botaurus stellaris* (several pairs), *Nycticorax nycticorax* (tens of pairs), *Ardea cinerea* (500 pairs), *A. purpurea* (1-2 pairs), *Ciconia nigra* (5-10 pairs), *C. ciconia* (max. 20 pairs), *Anser anser* (250 pairs), *Pernis apivorus* (max. 20 pairs), *Haliaeetus albicilla* (4 pairs), *Circus aeruginosus* (60-70 pairs), *C. cyaneus* (scarce), *C. pygargus* (scarce), *Bonasa bonasia* (scarce), *Tetrao tetrix* (scarce), *T. urogallus* (scarce), *Limosa limosa* (5 pairs), *Porzana porzana*, *P. parva*, *Crex crex* (3 pairs), *Sterna hirundo* (*c.*50 pairs), *Chlidonias niger* (14 pairs; irregularly max. 30 pairs), *Bubo bubo* (2 pairs), *Glaucidium passerinum* (max. 50 pairs), *Asio flammeus* (occasionally), *Aegolius funereus*, *Caprimulgus europaeus* (max. 50 pairs), *Alcedo atthis* (max. 10 pairs), *Picus canus* (*c.*50 pairs), *Dryocopus martius* (*c.*100 pairs) and *Dendrocopos medius* (max. 40 pairs).

003-1 Ruda peatbog and Horusický rybník pond (Bohemia)

49°09'N, 14°42'E 550 ha included in Biosphere Reserve

Included in Protected Landscape Area; partly a State Nature Reserve (*c.*150 ha)

A large fish-pond (Horusický rybník) and marshes, peatbog and *Pinus* forests. There is vegetational succession, and intensive fish-farming is sometimes detrimental to the avifauna (alternating the level of the water and removing emergent vegetation).

Breeding species include *Pernis apivorus* (1 pair), *Haliaeetus albicilla* (1 pair), *Circus aeruginosus* (1-2 pairs), *Limosa limosa* (1-2 pairs), *Sterna hirundo* (occasionally *c.*10 pairs), *Asio flammeus* (occasionally), *Alcedo atthis* (1-3 pairs), *Picus canus* (1-2 pairs), *Dryocopus martius* (1 pair), *Dendrocopos medius* (1 pair), *Luscinia svecica cyaneculus* (1-3 pairs), *Sylvia nisoria* (1-2 pairs), *Lanius collurio* (1-5 pairs), and *Ficedula albicollis* (5-10 pairs). *Anser anser* (max. 2000-3000) occurs on passage and *Haliaeetus albicilla* (1-5) occurs in winter.

003-2 Velký and Malý Tisý ponds (Bohemia)

49°03'N, 14°43'E 720 ha included in Biosphere Reserve

State Nature Reserve; included in Protected Landscape Area

An area of fish-ponds with extensive *Phragmites* beds, forests, meadows and arable land. Economic activities include fish-farming and agriculture. Vegetational succession and the maintenance of a high water-level are problems at the site.

Breeding species include *Botaurus stellaris* (1 pair), *Ardea purpurea* (1-5 pairs), *Pernis apivorus* (1 pair), *Haliaeetus albicilla* (1 pair), *Circus aeruginosus* (5-10 pairs), *Porzana porzana* (1-5 pairs), *P. parva*, *Limosa limosa* (1-3 pairs), *Sterna hirundo* (occasionally 15-20 pairs), *Picus canus* (1-2 pairs), *Dendrocopos medius* (3-5 pairs), *Luscinia svecica cyaneculus* (min. 10 pairs), and *Ficedula albicollis* (common). *Egretta alba* (5-10) and *Anser anser* (500-2000) occur on passage and *Haliaeetus albicilla* (5-10) occurs in winter.

003-3 River Stará řeka and Novořecké močály marshes (Bohemia)

49°02'N, 14°49'E *c.*1200 ha included in Biosphere Reserve

Partly a State Nature Reserve; included in Protected Landscape Area

A more-or-less natural river system with marshes, wet *Alnus* woodland, and forests (mainly *Pinus*, *Picea*). There is intensive forestry and the marshes are undergoing vegetational succession.

Breeding species include *Phalacrocorax carbo* (100 pairs), *Botaurus stellaris* (1 pair), *Ciconia nigra* (occasionally 1 pair), *Pernis apivorus* (1-2 pairs), *Haliaeetus albicilla* (1 pair), *Circus aeruginosus* (3-5 pairs), *Porzana porzana* (1-5 pairs), *Chlidonias niger* (irregularly max. 20 pairs), *Bubo bubo* (1 pair), *Glaucidium passerinum* (*c.*10 pairs), *Aegolius funereus* (1-5 pairs), *Caprimulgus europaeus* (max. 10-15 pairs), *Alcedo atthis* (1-2 pairs), *Picus canus* (3-5 pairs), *Dryocopus martius* (3-5 pairs), *Dendrocopos medius* (*c.*10 pairs), *Luscinia svecica cyaneculus* (1 pair), and *Ficedula albicollis* (common). *Haliaeetus albicilla* (1-2) occurs in winter.

004 Dehtář pond (Bohemia)

49°00'N, 14°17'E 250 ha

Unprotected but protection proposed

Fish-ponds (Dehtář and Posměch) in an agricultural landscape. A proposal for protection is in preparation which will divide Dehtář pond into zones for recreation and conservation. Existing problems result from recreation (weekend houses, bathing, and wind surfing), cultivation of the wet meadows, and pollution from agricultural chemicals.

Breeding species include *Nycticorax nycticorax* (tens of pairs), *Circus aeruginosus* (1-2 pairs), *C. pygargus* (1 pair), and *Limosa limosa* (max. 5 pairs). It is one of the most important sites for migrating waterbirds in southern Bohemia with *Gavia arctica*, *Podiceps grisegena*, *Platalea leucorodia*, *Anser anser* (max. 3000), *Circus cyaneus*, *Pandion haliaetus*, *Grus grus*, and numerous waders occurring. Wintering species include *Haliaeetus albicilla* (1-3) and *Circus cyaneus* (5-10).

005 Řežabinec pond (Bohemia)

49°15'N, 14°06'E 110 ha

State Nature Reserve; Protected Finding Place

Fish-pond with peatbog, wet and dry meadows, secondary woodland, and pools (Řežabinneckétuné tůne) which were formerly sand pits and are now flooded. Economic activities include fish-farming, with agriculture in the surrounding area. Important for educational and research activities.

Breeding species include *Botaurus stellaris* (1-3 pairs), *Ciconia ciconia* (1 pair; for the first time in 1987), *Circus aeruginosus* (1-5 pairs), *Porzana porzana* (1+ pairs), and *Sterna hirundo* (5 pairs). An important site for migrants with many species occurring. In winter *Haliaeetus albicilla* (occasionally) and *Circus cyaneus* (1-2) occur.

006 Novozámecký rybník pond (Bohemia)

50°40'N, 14°30'E 270 ha

State Nature Reserve

Fish-pond with reedbeds, wet meadows, peatbogs, and copses. Economic activities include fish-farming (in accordance with nature conservation requirements) and haymaking (only once a year after 1 July). There is eutrophication and vegetation succession with the water surface gradually disappearing. Ornithological research has been carried out here for over 100 years.

Breeding species include *Botaurus stellaris* (2-3 pairs), *Ixobrychus minutus* (1 pair), *Circus aeruginosus* (3-6 pairs), *Porzana porzana* (1-2 pairs), and *Locustella naevia* (20 pairs). A variety of species occurs on passage including *Haliaeetus albicilla*, *Pandion haliaetus*, *Crex crex*, and *Chlidonias niger*.

007 Žehuňský rybník pond (Bohemia)

50°10'N, 15°19'E 511 ha

State Nature Reserve

A large fish-pond on the River Cidlina between Žehuň and Choťovice with a rich emergent flora (*Phragmites*, *Typha*, *Carex*) and wet meadows along the river. Includes Obora forest (*Quercus*/*Carpinus*). Economic activities include fish-farming and agriculture. Recreation including water-sports (wind-surfing, sailing), pesticide use, and pollution of the River Cidlina are problems at the site.

Breeding species include *Podiceps nigricollis* (30-40 pairs), *Botaurus stellaris* (1-2 pairs), *Ciconia ciconia* (1 pair), *Pernis apivorus* (1 pair), *Milvus migrans* (1 pair), *Circus aeruginosus* (3-5 pairs), *Porzana parva* (1-2 pairs), *Limosa limosa* (1-6 pairs), *Alcedo atthis* (1 pair), *Sylvia nisoria* (5 pairs), and *Lanius collurio* (1-3 pairs). A variety of species occurs on passage including *Gavia arctica*, *G. stellata*, *Ciconia nigra*, *C. ciconia*, *Circus aeruginosus*, *Pandion haliaetus*, and *Chlidonias niger*; *Haliaeetus albicilla*, *Circus cyaneus*, and *Asio flammeus* occur in winter.

008 Pálava Protected Landscape Area (Moravia)

48°46'-48°53'N, 16°37'-16°45'E 7500 ha Biosphere Reserve

Protected Landscape Area including 12 State Nature Reserves and three Protected Natural Features

An area of limestone outcrops (Pavlovské vrchy hills) which dominate an otherwise rolling landscape of lowlands and hills. Vegetation includes forests of *Quercus* and *Carpinus*, forest-steppe and steppe. The steppe and forest-steppe habitats support vegetation communities at their northern and western limits. Includes the River Dyje (Thaya) flood-plain with remnant alluvial forest of *Quercus* and *Fraxinus*. Human activities include tourism, scientific research, and intensive agriculture. Existing problems include intensive tourism, overgrazing by moufflon, goats, and deer, lowering of the water-table, and canalisation of the River Dyje.

Breeding species include *Ciconia nigra* (1 pair), *C. ciconia* (4 pairs), *Pernis apivorus* (5-8 pairs), *Milvus migrans* (1 pair), *Bubo bubo* (3-4 pairs), *Dryocopus martius* (5-10 pairs), *Dendrocopos syriacus* (5-10 pairs), *D. medius* (several tens of pairs), *Sylvia nisoria* (many tens of pairs), *Ficedula albicollis* (several hundreds of pairs), and *Lanius collurio* (several hundreds of pairs).

009 Soutok (floodplain of the Rivers Morava and Dyje confluence) (Moravia)

48°37'-48°44'N, 16°53'-17°02'E *c.*7000 ha

Mainly unprotected but included in the proposed enlargement of the Pálava Protected Landscape Area and Biosphere Reserve. Currently three small State Nature Reserves (19 ha, 12 ha, 2 ha) protecting riverine forests.

The confluence of the Rivers Morava (March) and Dyje (Thaya) with riverine forests (*Quercus*, *Fraxinus*, *Salix*, *Carpinus*, *Populus*), marshes and wet meadows, and numerous backwaters and oxbows, channels, and pools. Regularly flooded in spring. Human activities include intensive forestry and game management. Problems include drainage, canalisation of the Morava and Dyje, overgrazing, and intensive forestry. *Falco cherrug* young have been illegally taken for the international falcon trade.

A very important area with breeding *Ciconia nigra* (3-5 pairs), *C. ciconia* (20-25 pairs), *Milvus migrans* (20 pairs), *M. milvus* (7 pairs), *Falco cherrug* (2-3 pairs), *Dryocopus martius* (10 pairs), *Dendrocopos medius* (20-30 pairs), and *Ficedula albicollis* (hundreds of pairs). *Haliaeetus albicilla* (2-4) occurs in winter.

010 Lednické rybníky ponds (Moravia)

48°43'-48°48'N, 16°42'-16°48'E 650 ha

State Nature Reserve; included in the proposed enlargement of the Pálava Protected Landscape Area and Biosphere Reserve

Five large fish-ponds with reedbeds. Economic activities include fish-farming and tourism. Botulism and disturbance by tourists are problems at the site.

Breeding species include *Botaurus stellaris* (1 pair; irregular), *Ixobrychus minutus* (10 pairs), *Nycticorax nycticorax* (80 pairs; max. 270 pairs in 1987), *Ardea purpurea* (1-3; irregular), *Ciconia ciconia* (1 pair), *Anser anser* (30-50 pairs), *Circus aeruginosus* (5 pairs), *Dendrocopos medius* (3-5 pairs). Important for species on passage including *Phalacrocorax carbo* (max. 800), *Egretta alba* (1-5), *Anser fabalis* (500-1000), *A. anser* (5000), *Anas clypeata* (1500-2000), *Netta rufina* (200-300), *Circus aeruginosus* (10-15), *Philomachus pugnax* (200-500), and *Chlidonias niger* (60-100). *Haliaeetus albicilla* (2-4) occurs in winter.

011 Pohořelické rybníky pond (Moravia)

48°50'-48°59'N, 16°30'-16°34'E *c.*500 ha

State Hunting Reserve, with hunting and protection regulations

Three large fish-ponds (Starý rybník, Novoveský rybník and Vrkoč) with islets and reedbeds in an agricultural landscape. The ponds are used for fish-farming and duck-farming, with intensive agriculture in the surrounding area. Problems include agricultural pollution with eutrophication, outbreaks of botulism, and conflicts between fish-farming and fish-eating birds.

Breeding species include *Botaurus stellaris* (1 pair), *Ixobrychus minutus* (3 pairs), *Ciconia ciconia* (3 pairs), *Aythya nyroca* (1 pair), *Circus aeruginosus* (5 pairs), and

Sterna hirundo (10 pairs). Passage species include *Nycticorax nycticorax* (10), *Anser fabalis* (5000 roosting), *A. anser* (2000 roosting), and *Chlidonias niger* (20). *Haliaeetus albicilla* (3) occurs in winter.

012 Střední nádrž (Nové Mlýny middle reservoir) (Moravia)

48°51'-48°54'N, 16°36'-16°39'E *c.*1080 ha

Unprotected, but proposed Protected Natural Feature

The middle reservoir of the Nové Mlýny reservoir complex (replacing an area of riverine forest) on the confluence of the Rivers Dyje (Thaya), Svratka, and Jihlava, with small islets, *Salix* vegetation, and some reedbeds. The reservoir was built to control flooding and provide water for irrigation. Existing problems include outbreaks of botulism, fluctuating water-levels, chemical pollution, and pressure from hunting.

Breeding species include *Phalacrocorax carbo* (50 pairs), *Ardea purpurea* (5-10 pairs), *Platalea leucorodia* (2-4 pairs), *Anser anser* (30 pairs), *Circus aeruginosus* (1 pair), *Larus melanocephalus* (1-5 pairs; irregular), and *Sterna hirundo* (70-100 pairs). An important passage site with *Gavia arctica* (10-30), *Phalacrocorax carbo* (500-1000; increasing), *Egretta alba* (20-50), *Platalea leucorodia* (10-30), *Anser fabalis* (15,000-20,000), *A. albifrons*, *A. anser* (5000-8000), *Circus aeruginosus* (10-30), *Pandion haliaeetus* (2-3), *Chlidonias niger* (50-100), and *Anas platyrhynchos* (15,000-25,000). In winter, *Egretta alba* (5-10), *Anser fabalis* (1000-10,000), *A. albifrons*, *Haliaeetus albicilla* (5-10), and *Circus aeruginosus* (5) occur.

013 Znojmo area (Moravia)

48°47'-48°51'N, 16°10'-16°16'E *c.*750 ha

Unprotected, but protection proposed

An agricultural landscape with sandy soils (alfalfa, winter wheat, barley, maize, and sugar-beet are grown), lines of trees as wind-breaks and small areas of dry grassland. Heavy machinery and agricultural chemicals are used and current problems include irrigation and tree-planting schemes.

The only site in the Czech Socialist Republic for *Otis tarda* (a resident population of 10 males and 20 females). Other breeding species include *Burhinus oedicnemus* (5 pairs), *Anthus campestris* (5 pairs), *Sylvia nisoria* (10 pairs), and *Lanius minor* (2 pairs). Wintering species include *Circus cyaneus* (10), *Falco cherrug* (1), and *Asio flammeus* (30).

014 Záhorské močiare marshes (Slovakia)

48°30'N, 17°00'E 27,522 ha

Currently protected by several small State Nature Reserves and Protected Study Areas; will be included in the proposed Záhorská Protected Landscape Area.

Comprises the flood-plain of the River Morava and its tributaries, the Myjava, Rudava, Malina, and Močiarka, with rolling country to the north. Includes Abrod peatbog, Zelenka peatbog, Červený rybník pond, Starý rybník pond, and Bezedné peatbog. Much of the area is covered by *Pinus sylvestris* plantations; also there are wet meadows, marshes, peatbogs, sand dunes, native forests of *Pinus sylvestris* and *Quercus* sp., with fragments of *Betula pendula* and *Salix*/*Populus* woodland in waterlogged areas and along riverbeds. The entire area is intensively used for forestry and agriculture. Water-management regulations, creation of artificial reservoirs and fish-ponds (replacing natural swampy biotopes), drainage, and agricultural intensification have had a detrimental effect on the area's birdlife. Following declaration as a Protected Landscape Area, economic activities will be managed in accordance with nature conservation.

Breeding species include *Botaurus stellaris* (2-5 pairs), *Ixobrychus minutus* (20-50 pairs), *Ardea purpurea* (1-5 pairs), *Ciconia nigra* (10-30 pairs), *C. ciconia* (50-80 pairs), *Pernis apivorus* (30-40 pairs), *Milvus migrans* (5-10 pairs), *Circus aeruginosus* (10-30 pairs), *Falco cherrug* (2-5 pairs), *Limosa limosa* (3-10 pairs), *Sterna hirundo* (5-10 pairs), *Chlidonias niger* (5-10 pairs), *Caprimulgus europaeus*, *Alcedo atthis*, *Picus canus*,

Dendrocopos medius, *Anthus campestris*, *Sylvia nisoria*, *Lanius collurio* (abundant), and *L. minor*. *Porzana parva* possibly breeds.

The most important localities are Abrod peatbog, Zelenka peatbog, Červený rybník pond, Starý rybník pond, Bezedné peatbog, and Jakubovské rybníky ponds (treated here as a subsite).

014-1 Jakubovské rybníky ponds (Slovakia)

16°57'N, 48°28'E *c.*50 ha

Protected Locality

Artificial fish-ponds with *Phragmites*, *Typha*, and *Carex* vegetation; the ponds are intensively utilised for fish and domestic-duck breeding. Hunting of waterfowl is limited.

A significant breeding and migration locality. Breeding species include *Podiceps nigricollis* (up to 50 pairs in small colonies), *Anas strepera* (5-10 pairs), *Aythya ferina* (50-100 pairs), *A. fuligula* (30-50 pairs), *Circus aeruginosus* (1-3 pairs), and *Larus ridibundus* (100-200 pairs). *Phalacrocorax carbo*, *Egretta alba*, *E. garzetta*, *Platalea leucorodia*, *Anser anser*, and *Larus minutus* are regular visitors; large numbers of waders occur on passage.

015 Šúr peatbog (Slovakia)

48°14'N, 17°13'E 1886 ha

State Nature Reserve (567 ha) and buffer zone (1319 ha)

Swampy *Alnus* forest in the western part of the Danube flood-plain, and flood-plain forest of *Salix*, *Alnus*, *Ulmus*, *Ulmus*/*Fraxinus*; also wet meadows, and *Quercus* forest. Economic activities are prohibited in the nature reserve, with controlled agriculture in the buffer zone. Drainage of the surrounding flood-plain 30-40 years ago has caused a gradual drying up of the site.

Over 70 species breed or probably breed including *Ixobrychus minutus* (1-3 pairs), *Circus aeruginosus* (1-2 pairs), *Falco cherrug*, *Crex crex*, *Alcedo atthis*, *Dendrocopos medius*, *Sylvia nisoria*, *Ficedula albicollis*, and *Lanius collurio* (abundant).

016 Trnavské rybníky ponds (Slovakia)

48°22'N, 17°33'E 61 ha

Protected Study Area (38 ha) and buffer zone (23 ha)

Four fish-ponds with overgrown banks and abundant aquatic vegetation in the catchment of the River Parná in rolling country. The ponds are used for fish-farming and there is disturbance by visitors from Trnava.

Breeding species include or probably include *Botaurus stellaris* (1-2 pairs), *Ixobrychus minutus* (2-5 pairs), *Aythya nyroca* (3-5 pairs), *Circus aeruginosus* (1-3 pairs), *Porzana porzana*, *Chlidonias hybridus*, *Alcedo atthis*, *Dendrocopos syriacus*, *Sylvia nisoria*, and *Lanius collurio* (abundant).

017 Podunají (Danube flood plain) (Slovakia)

47°45'-48°12'N, 17°00'-18°45'E 750,000 ha

Largely unprotected; after completion of the Danube Water Scheme, the Danube Protected Landscape Area will be established (in 1992-94).

The area comprises the flood-plain of the Danube with an extensive hydrographic network. There are fragments of lowland forest and marshes scattered throughout the area, as well as areas of steppe, meadow, and unintensively cultivated agricultural land. The territory is largely intensively utilised by agriculture, and agricultural development and water-management programmes are currently having a major impact on the area.

An important area for breeding and passage species. Species breeding include *Botaurus stellaris* (5-15 pairs), *Ixobrychus minutus* (20-50 pairs), *Nycticorax nycticorax*, *Ardea purpurea* (breeding in small colonies), *Ciconia nigra* (5-10 pairs), *C. ciconia* (abundant breeder), *Milvus milvus* (5-10 pairs), *Otis tarda* (30-50 birds), and *Crex crex.* It is also an important wintering locality for *Haliaeetus albicilla.*

Further information is provided for the following subsites:

017-1 River Danube between Bratislava and Chl'aba (Slovakia)

47°44'-48°07'N, 17°08'-18°51'E 170 km in length

Largely unprotected; proposed Protected Landscape Area

Comprises the Czechoslovakian stretch of the Danube, with numerous backwaters and islands particularly between Bratislava and Čičov. There is a strip of riverine forest inside the dammed flooding zone of the river between Bratislava and Zlatná na Ostrove, which is fragmented and dominated by *Salix/Populus*, *Fraxinus/Ulmus*, and *Crataegus.* In many areas the natural forest has been replaced by *Populus* monocultures. Outside the dams, there is little forest, but there are marshes around ditches, oxbow lakes, and canals. The Danube Water Scheme, which involves the construction of a large reservoir and canal between Bratislava and Gabcikovo, will have a major impact on the area and careful management will be needed to avoid serious ecological damage.

On the islands there are colonies of *Phalacrocorax carbo* (max. 50 pairs) and *Nycticorax nycticorax* (max. 30-50 pairs). The flood-plain forests support a typical avifauna with breeding *Milvus migrans, Locustella fluviatilis, Hippolais icterina, Muscicapa striata, Remiz pendulinus, Oriolus oriolus,* and *Fringilla coelebs,* and recently *Dryocopus martius.* It is an important migration and wintering site for waterfowl particularly *Anser fabalis, A. albifrons* (10,000-20,000 combined on passage), and *Anas platyrhynchos* (20,000-30,000); *Haliaeetus albicilla* (4-10) occurs in winter.

017-2 Čičovské mrtvé rameno 'dead arm' (Slovakia)

47°46'N, 17°43'E 80 ha

State Nature Reserve

A protected territory in the inundation zone of the Danube. An oxbow lake with well-developed aquatic and swampy vegetation, and surrounded by *Salix/Populus* flood-plain forest, some parts with thick jungle-like vegetation. The area is utilised for fishing with management controlled by the statutes of the reserve.

A significant breeding area for *Botaurus stellaris* (1-2 pairs), *Ardea purpurea* (1-2 pairs), *Circus aeruginosus* (1-3 pairs), *Aythya nyroca* (5-10 pairs), *Locustella fluviatilis,* and *L. luscinioides. Remiz pendulinus* also occurs.

017-3 Istragov marsh (Slovakia)

47°50'N, 17°35'E 14 ha

Protected Study Area

A swamp, overgrown with *Phragmites,* bordered by an oxbow lake and the main river bed of the Danube with flood-plain forests (*Salix/Populus*) and tangled jungle-like vegetation.

Breeding species include *Phalacrocorax carbo* (formerly max. 50 pairs) and *Ixobrychus minutus. Egretta alba* and *Ardea purpurea* use the site for feeding, and large numbers of *Anser* spp. use the site for roosting.

017-4 Zlatná na Ostrove (Slovakia)

47°45'N, 17°55'E 8218 ha

State Nature Reserve

An area of grassland and agricultural land.

An important area for *Otis tarda.*

017-5 Parížske močiare marshes (Slovakia)

47°52'N, 18°30'E 141 ha

State Nature Reserve

A wetland situated on alluvium of the Hron area, to the north of Gbelce. There is extensive dense growth of *Phragmites*, *Typha*, and *Carex*, with peatbog lakes. Peat exploitation has recently commenced in the northern part of the site and will certainly affect the water regime of the whole protected area. Wetland habitats have been degraded by water-management measures. Reed-cutting is carried out in winter.

Breeding species include *Botaurus stellaris* (3-10 pairs), *Ixobrychus minutus* (10-30 pairs), *Ardea purpurea* (5-30 pairs), *Ciconia ciconia* (in nearby villages), *Aythya nyroca* (5-20 pairs), *Circus aeruginosus* (10-15 pairs), *Porzana porzana*, *P. parva* (5-15 pairs), *Crex crex* (2-5 pairs), *Limosa limosa* (5-10 pairs), *Chlidonias hybridus*, *C. niger* (5-20 pairs), *Alcedo atthis*, *Luscinia svecica* (3-5 pairs), *Locustella naevia*, *L. luscinioides*, *Acrocephalus melanopogon* (1-3 pairs; occasionally), *Sylvia nisoria*, and *Lanius collurio*. *Tringa glareola* occurs on passage.

018 Orava reservoir (Slovakia)

49°24'N, 19°33'E *c.*50-100 ha

Partly a Protected Study Area; included in the Upper Orava Landscape Protection Area

An artificial reservoir that is a significant migration locality for waterfowl, especially the north-eastern part in which the Protected Study Area (an Ornithological Reserve) is situated. The rest of the territory is utilised for recreation and water sports. The use of the territory is controlled by the statutes of the Protected Landscape Area.

The more important species include *Ciconia ciconia* (breeding in the villages of the neighbourhood) and *Haliaeetus albicilla* (has attempted to breed). During migration *Anser anser* (200-500) occurs.

019 Malá Fatra Mountains (Malá Fatra National Park) (Slovakia)

49°07'-49°15'N, 18°53'-19°13'E 19,792 ha

National Park (19,792 ha) and buffer zone (26,532 ha)

A geomorphologically varied territory with the highest peak, Vel'ký Fatranský Kriváň, at 1711 m and extensive forests and diverse plant and animal communities. *Fagus* forests predominate, merging into *Picea*/*Abies* and *Picea* forests at higher altitudes. On the summit *Pinus mugo* is abundant. The territory is of importance for tourism and recreation.

The detached rocky masses provide breeding localities for birds of prey with *Aquila chrysaetos* (2 pairs) and *Falco peregrinus* (probably breeding). Other breeding species are *Bonasa bonasia*, *Tetrao tetrix*, *T. urogallus*, *Bubo bubo*, *Caprimulgus europaeus*, *Dendrocopos medius*, *D. leucotos*, *Anthus spinoletta*, *Monticola saxatilis*, *Ficedula parva*, *F. albicollis*, *Tichodroma muraria*, and *Lanius collurio*.

020 Vel'ká Fatra Mountains (Vel'ká Fatra Protected Landscape Area) (Slovakia)

48°48'-49°10'N, 18°53'-19°18'E 60,610 ha

Protected Landscape Area (60,610 ha) and buffer zone (20,500 ha)

A mountainous area (max. 1592 m) in the central Carpathians. The territory is geomorphologically varied with karst formations, calcareous detached masses, and deep valleys. Forest stands are formed by *Fagus sylvatica* and *Picea excelsa*, mixed with *Abies alba*, *Pinus sylvestris*, and *Acer* sp.; with *Pinus mugo* and scattered *Taxus baccata* on the ridges. Includes the Harmanec valley which is the richest locality for *Taxus baccata* in Europe. Rich in plants endemic to the Carpathians.

Breeding species include *Ciconia nigra*, *Pernis apivorus*, *Aquila pomarina*, *A. chrysaetos* (2 pairs), *Bonasa bonasia* (abundant), *Tetrao tetrix*, *T. urogallus*, *Bubo bubo*, *Aegolius funereus*, *Caprimulgus europaeus*, *Alcedo atthis*, *Picus canus*, *Dryocopus martius*,

Dendrocopos leucotos, *Picoides tridactylus* (possibly breeding), *Lullula arborea*, *Monticola saxatilis*, *Tichodroma muraria*, and *Lanius collurio*.

021 Tatra National Park (Vysoké Tatry Mountains) (Slovakia)

49°05'-49°18'N, 19°35'-20°20'E 50,965 ha

National Park (50,965 ha) and buffer zone (72,000 ha)

The territory encompasses the High Tatra and Belanské Tatry mountains (max. 2655 m) and has a varied geomorphology with rocky massifs, deep valleys, and cliffs. Vegetation zones alternate from the submontane to alpine with *Picea excelsa*, *Pinus sylvestris*, *Larix decidua*, *Abies alba*, *Fagus sylvatica*, *Pinus cembra*, and *P. mugo* predominating. The territory ranks amongst the most valuable areas in Czechoslovakia particularly for recreation and as a refuge area for rare relict fauna and flora.

Breeding species include *Ciconia nigra* (breeding rarely), *Aquila pomarina*, *A. chrysaetos* (4-5 pairs), *Falco peregrinus* (probably breeding sporadically), *Bonasa bonasia* (abundant), *Tetrao tetrix*, *T. urogallus*, *Crex crex*, *Bubo bubo*, *Glaucidium passerinum*, *Strix uralensis* (probably breeding), *Aegolius funereus*, *Caprimulgus europaeus*, *Alcedo atthis*, *Picus canus*, *Dryocopus martius*, *Dendrocopos medius*, *D. leucotos*, *Picoides tridactylus*, *Ficedula parva*, *F. albicollis*, and *Tichodroma muraria*.

022 Nízké Tatry Mountains (Nízké Tatry National Park) (Slovakia)

48°48'-49°04'N, 19°06'-20°18'E 81,095 ha

National Park (81,095 ha) and buffer zone (123,990 ha)

The territory encompasses the extensive mountain range of the Low Tatras. In the montane zone there are forests of *Fagus* and *Picea* with stands composed of *Abies alba*, *Pinus sylvestris*, and *Acer*. A valuable area for recreation and tourism.

Breeding species include *Ciconia nigra*, *Pernis apivorus*, *Aquila pomarina*, *A. clanga* (possibly breeding), *A. chrysaetos* (4-5 pairs), *Falco peregrinus* (possibly breeding), *Bonasa bonasia*, *Tetrao tetrix*, *T. urogallus*, *Crex crex*, *Bubo bubo* (abundant), *Glaucidium passerinum*, *Aegolius funereus*, *Caprimulgus europaeus*, *Alcedo atthis*, *Picus canus*, *Dryocopus martius*, *Dendrocopos medius*, *D. leucotos*, *Picoides tridactylus*, *Lullula arborea*, *Sylvia nisoria*, *Ficedula parva*, *F. albicollis*, and *Lanius collurio*.

023 Pieniny Mountains (Pieniny National Park) (Slovakia)

49°22'-49°26'N, 20°25'-20°30'E 2125 ha

National Park (2125 ha) and buffer zone (28,523 ha)

A very impressive landscape with rocky outcrops and a canyon-like valley. Includes forest of *Fagus*/*Abies*, *Picea*, and *Pinus sylvestris*, and supports several rare and endemic plants. The territory is important for tourism, recreation, and scientific research.

Breeding species include *Ciconia nigra* (possibly breeding), *Pernis apivorus* (possibly breeding), *Aquila pomarina*, *A. chrysaetos* (1 pair), *Bonasa bonasia*, *Crex crex*, *Bubo bubo* (several pairs), *Aegolius funereus*, *Caprimulgus europaeus*, *Alcedo atthis*, *Dryocopus martius*, *Turdus iliacus*, *Lanius collurio*, and *Carpodacus erythrinus*.

024 Slovenský Kras karst (Slovenský Kras Protected Landscape Area) (Slovakia)

48°30'-48°41'N, 20°25'-20°55'E 36,165 ha Biosphere Reserve

Protected Landscape Area (36,165 ha) and buffer zone (38,334 ha)

The largest and most outstanding limestone karst area in Czechoslovakia, with plateaus, gorges and deep canyons. The forests are largely *Carpinus betulus*, *Quercus petraea*, and *Fagus sylvatica*, with *Fraxinus ornus* and *Acer tataricum* particularly in areas of remnant forest-steppe. Botanically, it is one of the richest areas in central Europe, supporting over 900 species of vascular plants. There are also cultivated land, marshes, and meadows. Economic activities include controlled forestry and agriculture; limestone extraction for a cement factory partly devalues the eastern part.

Breeding species include *Ciconia ciconia, Pernis apivorus, Circaetus gallicus* (1-2 pairs), *Aquila pomarina, A. heliaca* (2-4 pairs), *Falco cherrug* (3-5 pairs), *F. peregrinus* (possibly breeding), *Bonasa bonasia, Tetrao tetrix, Bubo bubo, Strix uralensis, Aegolius funereus, Caprimulgus europaeus, Alcedo atthis, Coracias garrulus* (probably breeding), *Dryocopus martius, Dendrocopos syriacus, Lullula arborea, Sylvia nisoria, Ficedula parva, Lanius collurio* (abundant), and *L. minor*.

025 Slanské vrchy hills – southern part (Slovakia)

48°34'-48°38'N, 21°24'-21°32'E 35,600 ha

Unprotected; proposed Protected Landscape Area (Milíc)

The southern portion of the Slanské vrchy range. A forested landscape, mainly *Fagus*. Forestry is managed in accordance with the conservation needs of birds of prey. Nests are guarded to prevent disturbance and nest robbing.

An important area for breeding birds of prey with *Milvus milvus, Aquila pomarina, Falco cherrug*, and *F. peregrinus* (possibly breeding). Other breeding species include *Bonasa bonasia, Bubo bubo, Strix uralensis, Caprimulgus europaeus, Alcedo atthis, Picus canus, Dryocopus martius, Dendrocopos syriacus, D. medius, D. leucotos, Lullula arborea, Sylvia nisoria, Ficedula parva, F. albicollis*, and *Lanius collurio*.

026 Vihorlat Mountains (Vihorlat Protected Landscape Area) (Slovakia)

48°48'-48°57'N, 22°00'-22°20'E 4387 ha

Protected Landscape Area (4387 ha) and buffer zone (9912 ha)

The area covers the central part of the Vihorlat mountain range covered almost entirely by forest (mainly *Fagus, Acer, Carpinus*, and *Quercus*). The dominant economic activity is forestry.

Breeding species include *Milvus milvus, Pernis apivorus, Aquila pomarina, Bonasa bonasia, Bubo bubo, Glaucidium passerinum* (probably breeding), *Strix uralensis, Caprimulgus europaeus, Picus canus, Dryocopus martius, Dendrocopos leucotos, Sylvia nisoria, Ficedula parva, F. albicollis*, and *Lanius collurio*.

027 East Slovakia marshes (Slovakia)

48°21'-48°48'N, 21°40'-22°15'E 150,000 ha

Currently a number of State Nature Reserves, Protected Localities, and Protected Study Areas; proposed Protected Landscape Area (Latorica)

The flood-plain of the Rivers Bodrog and Latorica, between the rivers and the Hungarian border. The area has an extensive network of rivers and channels with numerous oxbow lakes, marshes, and remnant riverine forests along the Rivers Latorica, Laborec, Bodrog and Uh. An intensively utilised agricultural landscape; drainage and agricultural intensification in recent years has had a detrimental impact on the area.

Breeding species include *Botaurus stellaris* (15-30 pairs), *Ixobrychus minutus, Nycticorax nycticorax, Ardeola ralloides, Egretta garzetta, Ardea purpurea, Platalea leucorodia, Ciconia nigra, C. ciconia, Aythya nyroca, Milvus migrans, Circus aeruginosus, Aquila pomarina, Falco vespertinus, Porzana porzana, P. parva, Crex crex, Himantopus himantopus, Limosa limosa, Chlidonias hybridus, C. niger, C. leucopterus, Asio flammeus, Alcedo atthis* and *Lanius collurio*.

Additional information is provided for the following subsites:

027-1 Zatínske močiare marshes (Slovakia)

48°28'N, 21°55'-22°00'E 213 ha

State Nature Reserve

An oxbow lake of the River Latorica in the East Slovakian Plain, which is now swamps and water-logged meadows, with *Alnus/Betula* forests and rare flora and fauna.

Breeding species include *Botaurus stellaris*, *Ixobrychus minutus*, *Ardea purpurea* (sporadically), *Ciconia ciconia* (abundantly breeding in the nearby villages), *Aythya nyroca*, *Milvus migrans* (breeding in the nearby flood-plain forests), *Circus aeruginosus*, *C. pygargus*, *Porzana porzana*, *P. parva*, *Crex crex*, *Limosa limosa*, *Chlidonias niger*, *Coracias garrulus*, *Dendrocopos syriacus*, *Lanius collurio*, and *L. minor*. Also important for passage waterfowl.

027-2 Tajba marsh (Slovakia)

48°23'N, 21°54'E 27 ha

State Nature Reserve

A depression (formerly an oxbow lake of the River Bodrog) now an extensive swamp. The territory is economically untouched.

Breeding species include or probably include *Ixobrychus minutus*, *Ardea purpurea*, *Circus aeruginosus*, *Porzana parva*, *Chlidonias niger*, *Luscinia svecica cyaneculus*, and *Lanius collurio*.

028 Senné-rybníky ponds (Slovakia)

48°42'N, 22°05'E 424 ha

State Nature Reserve (213 ha) and buffer zone (211 ha)

A very important ornithological locality in the East Slovakian Plain, formerly part of the Cierna Voda, Laborec and Uh flood-plain. Fish-ponds were created, which are partly protected as a nature reserve.

Breeding species include *Botaurus stellaris* (1-3 pairs), *Ixobrychus minutus* (5-10 pairs), *Ardea purpurea* (3-5 pairs), *Ciconia ciconia* (breeding in neighbouring villages), *Platalea leucorodia*, *Circus aeruginosus* (3-5 pairs), *C. pygargus* (1-3 pairs), *Porzana porzana*, *Crex crex*, *Himantopus himantopus*, *Limosa limosa*, *Chlidonias hybridus*, *C. niger*, *Asio flammeus*, and *Acrocephalus paludicola* (rarely breeding). Passage species include *Gavia arctica*, *G. stellata*, *Ciconia nigra*, and *Grus grus*.

029 Zemplínská Šírava reservoir (Slovakia)

48°46'-48°50'N, 21°55'-22°05'E 622 ha

Protected Study Area (622 ha) and buffer zone (2037 ha)

The eastern part of an artificial reservoir. The area is marked off by buoys, and water-sports and hunting are prohibited.

Porzana porzana breeds. A very important passage site and species occurring include *Gavia immer*, *G. stellata*, *Podiceps auritus*, *Nycticorax nycticorax*, *Egretta garzetta*, *E. alba*, *Ardeola ralloides*, *Ciconia nigra*, *Anser anser*, *A. erythropus*, *Grus grus*, and *Gallinago media*.

MAIN REFERENCES

Hudec, K. The Morava-Dyje riverine forest system, Czechoslovakia. Pp.38-42 in Imboden, E. eds. (1987) *Riverine forests in Europe: status and conservation.* Cambridge: International Council for Bird Preservation.

IUCN (1987) *Protected landscapes: experience around the world.* Cambridge and Gland, Switzerland: International Union for the Conservation of Nature.

Marsaková-Nemejcová, M. and Mihálik, S. *et al.* (1987) *National parks, reserves and other protected territories in Czechoslovakia.* (in Czech) Praha: Academia.

Randík, A. The bird fauna of the riverine forests along the Danube in Czechoslovakia. Pp.43-45 in Imboden, E. eds. (1987) *Riverine forests in Europe: status and conservation.* Cambridge: International Council for Bird Preservation.

Štastný, K., Randík, A. and Hudec, K. (1987) *Atlas hnízdního rozšíření ptáku v ČSSR 1973/77* (The atlas of breeding birds in Czechoslovakia 1973/77). Praha: Academia.

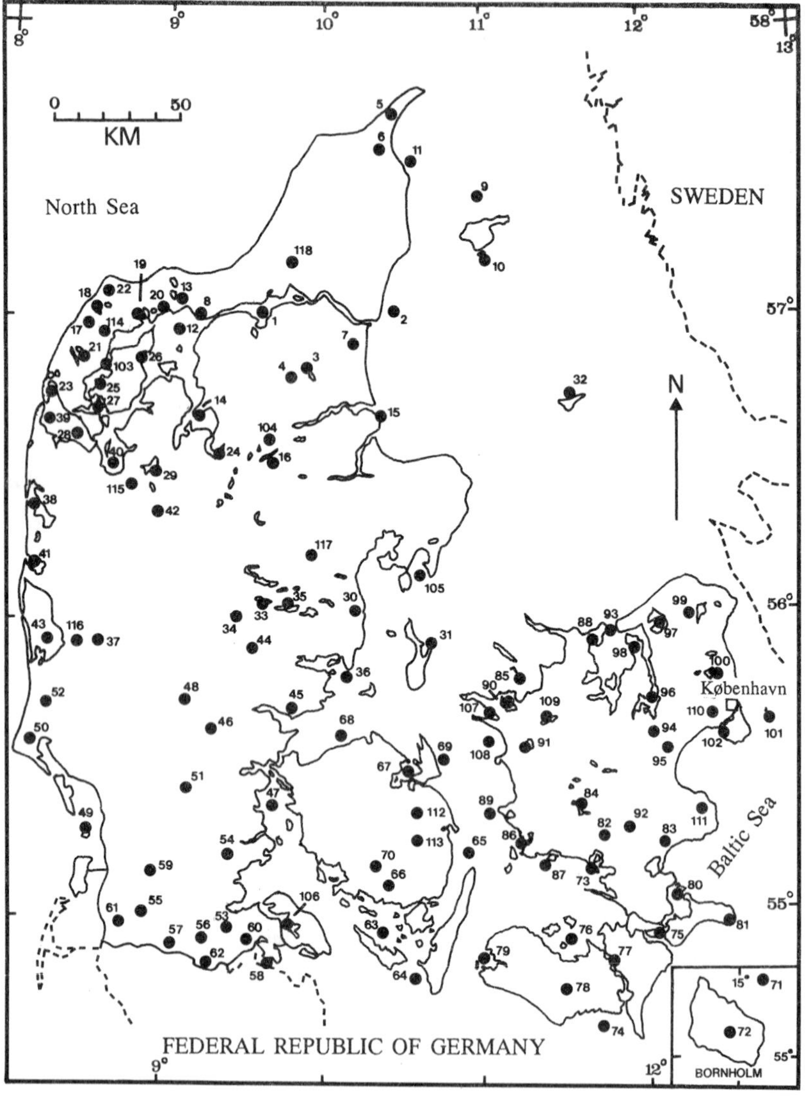

Figure 8: Map showing the location of the sites in Denmark

DENMARK

Long-tailed Duck *Clangula hyemalis* and Eider *Somateria mollissima*

INTRODUCTION

General information

In addition to Denmark itself, Danish Sovereign territory is composed of Greenland and the Faroe Islands. There are separate inventories of important bird areas for these two regions and this introduction is therefore confined to Denmark *per se* ('mainland').

Denmark is a physically complex country at the mouth of the Baltic Sea; it consists of a peninsula (Jylland), connected only narrowly with northern continental Europe, and extensive archipelagic waters. A few of the islands (notably Sjælland, Fyn and Lolland) are very large, but there are numerous smaller islands, islets, shoals, and banks. The coasts are characterised by a very high degree of indentation (the coastline is well over 7000 km in length) with an abundance of fjords, bays, straits, and peninsulas. Bornholm is an outlying Baltic island, about 150 km east of Sjælland, which marks the eastern limit of Danish territory.

The total area of Denmark extends to some 43,000 sq km and while the human population is small, at less than 5.5 million people, the corresponding population density of over 125 individuals per sq km is high in comparison with the other Scandinavian countries. Approximately 65 per cent of the country's area is agricultural land with a further 12 per cent afforested, although over 80 per cent of people live in large towns or cities such as København (Copenhagen), Odense and Ålborg.

Topographically, Denmark is dominated by lowlands, with the highest point barely reaching 175 m. Despite this fact, however, landscapes are typified by gentle undulation; flat plains are not extensive. Ninety per cent of the land surface has been extensively modified mainly by agriculture. Remaining areas of semi-natural vegetation include woods of *Quercus* and *Fagus* (which tend to be small and dispersed), sand-dunes mainly along the west coast, scattered inland heaths, and peatbogs.

Ornithological importance

The shallow waters around Denmark are of major international importance for moulting, staging, and wintering Gaviidae, Podicipedidae, Anatidae (notably seaducks), and Alcidae. Detailed knowledge of population sizes and principal concentrations of the non-breeding species is limited by the difficulties of surveying the huge sea areas involved. Recent (and on-going) surveys have, however, improved the information available for these groups, and it is clear that Denmark holds some of the most important populations in Europe of non-breeding *Gavia stellata, G. arctica, Aythya marila, Somateria mollissima, Clangula hyemalis, Melanitta nigra, M. fusca, Bucephala clangula, Mergus serrator*, and Alcidae.

The extensive intertidal areas (and adjoining land) of the archipelago, eastern Jylland, and the Vadehavet (Danish Wadden Sea) hold internationally important concentrations of non-breeding swans, geese, *Anas* spp., and waders. The more significant populations include those of *Cygnus olor, C. columbianus, C. cygnus, Anser brachyrhynchus, Branta bernicla hrota, Tadorna tadorna, Anas penelope, A. crecca, A. acuta, Haematopus ostralegus, Calidris canutus, C. alpina*, and *Limosa lapponica*.

The country's wetlands are also important for a number of breeding species including *Phalacrocorax carbo sinensis* (14,000 pairs), *Botaurus stellaris* (30-75 pairs), *Circus aeruginosus* (450-500 pairs), *Recurvirostra avosetta* (3500-4700 pairs), *Limosa limosa* (600-800 pairs), *Gelochelidon nilotica* (5-15 pairs), *Sterna sandvicensis* (3000-4000 pairs), *S. hirundo* (975-1100 pairs), *S. paradisaea* (6000-8000 pairs), *S. albifrons* (300-350 pairs), and *Chlidonias niger* (100-150 pairs).

The forests, heaths, bogs, and sand-dunes are principally of importance for breeding birds including *Pernis apivorus* (800 pairs), *Tetrao tetrix* (40-50 pairs), *Tringa glareola* (47-64 pairs), *Caprimulgus europaeus* (100-300 pairs), *Lullula arborea* (300-500 pairs), and *Lanius collurio* (1500-3000 pairs).

Conservation infrastructure and protected-area system

The national protected-areas network operates according to the provisions of the Conservation of Nature Act (1969; amended 1975, 1979, 1984), which contain measures for both general biotope conservation and protection of individual sites or 'Nature Conservation Areas'. The principal categories of protected areas in Denmark are outlined below.

1. Nature Conservation Area

   The conservation provisions vary from site to site; they may include restrictions on construction, agriculture, transport, recreation, and hunting. Management techniques may be specified in order to preserve particular habitat characteristics. Although (under section 73 of the Danish Constitution) landowners are liable to compensation where property must be surrendered, there is no clear mechanism for relating this to restrictions on land-use.

2. Scientific Reserves

   There are nine such sites covering *c.*25,000 ha; they are mostly sea areas. Hunting and egg-collection prohibited. Very limited public admittance. There are provisions for protection and conservation of habitats. Monitoring and scientific investigations are carried out by the Ministry of the Environment.

3. Wildlife (Game) Reserves

   There are 82 such sites covering *c.*120,000 ha; hunting is regulated. Also regulations and restrictions relating to other human activities.

In addition, the Conservation of Nature Act gives general protection to a number of habitats such as lakes and streams, heathlands and saltmarshes above a certain size.

It should be noted that sites which have been designated as EEC Special Protection Areas (sites designated according to the EEC Wild Birds Directive) are not necessarily covered by any other designated protected area.

International measures relevant to the conservation of sites

Denmark is a member of the European Community, and is a party to the Ramsar Convention, World Heritage Convention, Bern Convention, and Bonn Convention, and is bound by the EEC's Wild Birds Directive.

By May 1988, 27 Ramsar Sites (plus 11 in Greenland) had been designated, covering over 700,000 ha. The (National) Forest and Nature Agency (Skov-og Naturstyrelsen) had also designated 111 EEC Special Protection Areas (covering some 950,000 ha). Although Denmark participates in the identification of European Biogenetic Reserves, there are no Biogenetic Reserves and no natural sites have been nominated for the World Heritage List; there are also no Biosphere Reserves in mainland Denmark (although a large area of north-east Greenland has been designated).

Overview of the inventory

The inventory covers 118 sites, with a combined area exceeding 1 million ha; it includes all of the EEC Special Protection Areas, all Ramsar Sites, a large number of Nature Conservation Areas, and several Scientific/Wildlife Reserves. All but ten sites are at least partly protected and only 16 sites are not EEC SPAs. All of the principal sites for geese and waders are covered, but several important areas for Gaviidae, seaducks, and Alcidae have not yet been properly defined. However, it is thought that a representative sample of seaduck sites is included.

The forest, heath, and other non-wetland sites in the inventory are not exhaustive in their coverage of non-waterfowl species.

Acknowledgements

The following accounts for wetland sites have been compiled largely from data-sheets provided in 1987 by B. Søgaard and P. U. Jepsen on behalf of the Wildlife Administration of the Ministry of Agriculture, the Danish Ornithological Society (Dansk Ornitologisk Forening) and the (National) Forest and Nature Agency (Ministry of the Environment), whilst the accounts for other sites were compiled largely from information provided by F. Danielsen on behalf of the Danish Ornithological Society. S. Brøgger-Jensen has also been of considerable help in his coordination of the contribution from the Danish Ornithological Society.

INVENTORY

No.	Site name	Region	Criteria used to select site [see p.18]							
			0	1(i)	1(ii)	1(iii)	1(iv)	2	3	4
001	Ulvedybet and Nibe Bredning	ND			*	*			*	
002	Ålborg Bugt (northern part)	ND				*			*	
003	Madum Sø	ND				*				
004	Rold Skov	ND	*							
005	Råbjerg Mile and surrounding moorland and dunes	ND							*	
006	Jerup Hede, Råbjerg Mose, and Tolshave Mose	ND							*	
007	Lille Vildmose	ND							*	
008	Aggersborg Enge	ND				*			*	
009	Nordre Rønner	ND							*	
010	South Læsø and adjacent sea	ND				*			*	

No.	Site name	Region	Criteria used to select site [see p.18] 0	1(i)	1(ii)	1(iii)	1(iv)	2	3	4
011	Hirsholmene and Deget	ND			*				*	
012	Løgstør Bredning	ND				*			*	
013	Vejlerne	VG				*			*	
014	Lovns Bredning	VG,ND				*			*	
015	Parts of Randers and Mariager Fjords and adjoining sea areas	AS,ND				*			*	
016	Tjele Langsø	VG				*				
017	Alvand Klithede and Førby Sø	VG							*	
018	Vangså Hede	VG							*	
019	Lønnerup Fjord	VG				*			*	
020	Arup Holm and Hovsør Røn	VG							*	
021	Ove Sø	VG				*			*	
022	Hanstholm Reservatet	VG				*			*	
023	Agger Tange and Krik Vig	VG				*			*	
024	Hjarbæk Fjord	VG				*			*	
025	Mågerodde and Karbyodde	VG				*			*	
026	Dråby Vig	VG				*			*	
027	Glomstrup Vig, Agerø, Munkholm and Katholm Odde, Lindholm, and Rotholme	VG,RG				*			*	
028	Nissum Bredning	VG,RG				*				
029	Flyndersø	VG,RG				*				
030	Norsminde (Kysing) Fjord	AS				*				
031	Stavns Fjord and adjacent waters	AS				*			*	
032	Sea area north of Anholt Island	AS				*				
033	Salten Langsø	AS,VE							*	
034	Forest areas south of Silkeborg	AS	*							
035	Mossø	AS				*				
036	Horsens Fjord, Svanegrunden, and Endelave	AS,VE				*			*	
037	Borris Hede	RG							*	
038	Nissum Fjord	RG			*	*			*	
039	Harboøre Tange, Plet Enge, and Gjeller Sø	RG				*			*	
040	Venø, Venø Bugt, and Kås Bredning	VG,RG				*				
041	Stadil Fjord and Veststadil Fjord	RG				*			*	
042	Heath areas in Sønder Feldborg Plantage	VG							*	
043	Ringkøbing Fjord	RG			*	*			*	
044	Uldum Kær	VE						*	*	
045	Forest areas along the northern part of Vejle Fjord	VE							*	
046	Randbøl Hede	RE,VE							*	
047	Lillebælt	SD,VE,FN				*			*	
048	Heath areas near Store Råbjerg	RE							*	
049	Vadehavet (Wadden Sea)	RE,SD				*			*	
050	Kallesmæsks Hede, Grærup Langsø, and surrounding areas	RE							*	
051	Vejen Mose	RE							*	
052	Fiilsø	RE				*			*	
053	Hostrup Sø, Assenholm Mose, and Felsted Vestermark	SD							*	
054	Pamhule Skov	SD							*	
055	Kongens Mose	SD							*	
056	Tinglev Mose and Sø	SD							*	
057	Sønder Adal	SD							*	
058	Flensborg Fjord and Nybøl Nor	SD				*				

No.	Site name	Region	Criteria used to select site [see p.18]							
			0	1(i)	1(ii)	1(iii)	1(iv)	2	3	4
059	Lindet Skov, Hønning Plantage, Lovrup Skov, and Skråp	SD	*							
060	Forests near Gråsten	SD							*	
061	Kogsbøl and Skast Mose	SD							*	
062	Frøslev Mose	SD							*	
063	Sydfynske Ø-hav	FN				*			*	
064	Marstal Bugt and the coast of south-west Langeland	FN							*	
065	Vresen and adjacent sea	FN				*				
066	Forests near Brahetrolleborg	FN	*							
067	Odense Fjord	FN				*			*	
068	Nærå Coast and Aebelø area	FN				*			*	
069	Romsø and adjacent sea	FN				*				
070	Brændegård Sø, Nørresø, and Arreskov Sø	FN				*		*	*	
071	Ertholmene east of Bornholm	BM								*
072	Almindingen	BM							*	
073	Karrebæk, Dybsø, and Avnø Fjords	SM				*			*	
074	Sea area between Lolland and Falster, Rødsand, Bredningen, and Bøtø Nor	SM				*		*	*	
075	Ulfsund, Grønsund, Farø Fjord, and Fanefjord	SM				*			*	
076	Smålandshavet north of Lolland	SM				*			*	
077	Guldborgsund	SM				*			*	
078	Maribo lakes	SM				*			*	
079	Nakskov Fjord and Indre Fjord	SM				*			*	
080	Præstø Fjord, Ulfshale, Nyord, and Jungshoved Nor	SM				*			*	
081	Klinteskoven	SM	*							
082	Holmegårds Mose and Porsemose	SM,VD				*			*	
083	Forests near Vemmetofte	SM	*							
084	Tystrup – Bavelse Søerne	VD,SM				*			*	
085	Sejerø Bugt	VD				*				
086	Skælskør Nor, Skælskør Fjord, and Borreby Mose	VD				*			*	
087	Sea area between Skælskør Fjord and Glænø	VD				*			*	
088	Hovvig	VD				*			*	
089	Sprogø and Halsskov Rev	VD				*				
090	Saltbæk Vig	VD				*			*	
091	Tissø, Lille Åmose, and Hallenslev Mose	VD				*		*	*	
092	Bregentved and Gisselfeldt Lakes	VD,SM				*				
093	Sea area between Korshage and Hundested	VD,FG				*				
094	Wetland north of Gammel Havdrup	RD							*	
095	Ramsø Mose	RD							*	
096	Roskilde Fjord, Selsø, and Kattinge Søerne	FG,RD				*		*	*	
097	Arresø	FG				*			*	
098	Jægerspris Nordskov	FG							*	
099	Grib Skov	FG							*	
100	Furesø and Farum Sø	FG,KN				*				
101	Saltholm	KN				*			*	
102	Vestamager and adjacent sea area	KN				*		*	*	
103	Vilsund and Stokkær Odde	VG				*			*	
104	Klejtrup Sø	VG				*				

No.	Site name	Region	Criteria used to select site [see p.18]							
			0	1(i)	1(ii)	1(iii)	1(iv)	2	3	4
105	Kalø and Ebeltoft Vig including Hjelm and Begtrup Røn	AS				*				
106	Alssund and Augustenborg Fjord	SD				*				
107	Kalundborg Inderfjord	VD				*				
108	Sea area between Reersø and Røsnæs	VD				*				
109	Skarresø	VD	*							
110	Damhussøen	KN				*				
111	Møllesø and Gjorslev	SM				*				
112	Rønninge Søgård	FN	*							
113	Lykkesholm	FN	*							
114	Rosvang and Sjørring Sø	VG							*	
115	Karup Å	VG							*	
116	Skjern Å	RG,VE				*		*	*	
117	Gudenå, Nørreå, and Skals Å	VG,AS						*	*	
118	Ryå near Store Vildmose	ND						*		

ND=Nordjylland VG=Viborg AS=Århus RG=Ringkøbing VE=Vejle RE=Ribe SD=Sønderjylland FN=Fyn BM=Bornholm SM=Storstrøm VD=Vestsjælland FG=Frederiksborg RD=Roskilde KN=København

Comments on the inventory

1. The figures given for waterfowl are taken from the data-sheets mentioned above, which were in turn largely based on the references given at the end of the inventory. Because of the varying data sources, it has not been possible to qualify each figure in the text. In general, they are maximum counts.

2. The site names are as given on the data-sheets: 'proper names' are in Danish (see glossary below); descriptive text as part of a site name is given in English.

3. The regions, given in parentheses following the site names, are the counties (amtskommuner). The 'region' used when applying site-selection criteria (category 3) is NUTS level 0: Denmark (mainland).

4. The presence of certain species at sites in the inventory has been kept confidential.

5. The sequence of sites follows the Danish list of EEC SPAs, except that the Vadehavet (Wadden Sea) EEC SPAs have been grouped together to form a single site (049). The non-EEC SPAs have been grouped together at the end of the inventory (103-118).

6. A number of sites do not meet the site-selection criteria but have been included for other reasons (column 0 of table above). The following sites have been included because they are important for woodland species that are scarce in Denmark, and hold one or more EEC Wild Birds Directive Annex I species (*Pernis apivorus*, *Caprimulgus europaeus*, *Dryocopus martius*, although as far as is known the sites do not meet criteria category 3 for these species): 004, 034, 059, 066, 081, 083. The following sites have been included because of their large populations of *Anser anser* (although the populations do not quite meet the numerical criteria, category 1(iii)): 109, 112, 113.

Glossary

EEC SPA = European Community Special Protection Area designated according to the EEC's Wild Birds Directive. The following Danish words have been used in the inventory: å = river or brook; bredning = bay; bugt = bay; hede = heath; holm = islet or island; mose = bog or moor; odde = point or headland; skov = wood; sø = lake; sund = sound; vig = bay.

001 Ulvedybet and Nibe Bredning (Nordjylland)

57°02'N, 09°35'E 20,304 ha Ramsar Site; EEC SPA

Nature Conservation Area (23 ha); three Wildlife Reserves (*c*.1200 ha)

A coastal site with a diversity of habitats including shallow fjord areas, (with associated intertidal flats, islands, and islets), saltmarsh, reed-swamp, small freshwater lakes, and agricultural land. The Ulvedybet area is a brackish lake which has been dammed-off from the Limfjord. A moulting area for *Cygnus olor*, *Aythya ferina*, and *Bucephala clangula*.

Breeding species include *Recurvirostra avosetta* (100-170 pairs), *Gelochelidon nilotica* (0-5 pairs), *Sterna sandvicensis* (100-400 pairs), and *S. paradisaea* (150-180 pairs). Important for waterfowl outside the breeding season with *Podiceps cristatus* (500), *Cygnus olor* (2700), *C. columbianus* (350), *C. cygnus* (1800), *Anas penelope* (11,150), *A. crecca* (7000), *A. clypeata* (510), *Aythya ferina* (5000), *A. fuligula* (9000), *Mergus serrator* (2250), *M. merganser* (1500), *Recurvirostra avosetta* (300), *Pluvialis apricaria* (10,000), *Calidris minuta* (1000), and *C. alpina* (13,500).

002 Ålborg Bugt (northern part) (Nordjylland)

57°00'N, 10°25'E 22,200 ha EEC SPA

A shallow offshore site with shoals, banks, and islets.

Breeding species include *Sterna sandvicensis* (100-200 pairs), and *S. paradisaea* (200 pairs). Important for waterfowl outside the breeding season with *Aythya marila* (17,000), *Somateria mollissima* (55,000), *Melanitta nigra* (38,000), *M. fusca* (20,000), *Bucephala clangula* (4000), and *Mergus serrator* (1000).

003 Madum Sø (Nordjylland)

56°50'N, 09°55'E 250 ha EEC SPA

Nature Conservation Area

An oligotrophic freshwater lake with a sandy bottom, surrounded by forest.

Important for moulting *Bucephala clangula* (3000) and wintering *Aythya fuligula* (3000-5000).

004 Rold Skov (Nordjylland)

56°48'N, 09°50'E 7000 ha EEC SPA

Nature Conservation Areas (Rebild Bakker, Lindenborg Å, Troldeskoven)

A forested, hilly area with scattered glades and wetlands supporting a high diversity of forest birds.

Breeding species include *Pernis apivorus*, *Caprimulgus europaeus* (2 pairs), and other forest species which are scarce in Denmark.

005 Råbjerg Mile and surrounding moorland and dunes (Nordjylland)

57°33'N, 10°21'E 4200 ha EEC SPA

Nature Conservation Areas (Råbjerg Mile and Stene: 1620 ha)

A dune and moorland area with wetlands bordering agricultural land. Breeding species include *Tringa glareola* (0-2 pairs). During spring migration it is an important staging area for raptors.

006 Jerup Hede, Råbjerg Mose and Tolshave Mose (Nordjylland)

57°32'N, 10°22'E 2100 ha EEC SPA

Nature Conservation Area (98 ha)

A large heterogeneous moorland and peatbog area.

Important as a breeding site for several scarce moorland birds including *Numenius arquata* (6-8 pairs), *Tringa glareola* (2-5 pairs), and *Asio flammeus* (0-1 pair).

007 Lille Vildmose (Nordjylland)

56°52'N, 10°13'E 6800 ha EEC SPA

The largest raised bog in Denmark (and one of the best-preserved lowland raised bogs in north-west Europe) with small lakes, peaty ponds, and wooded areas. Now partly agricultural.

Breeding species include *Phalacrocorax carbo sinensis*, *Numenius arquata*, and *Tringa glareola* (3-4 pairs).

008 Aggersborg Enge (Nordjylland)

57°02'N, 09°10'E 1300 ha

Part of Vejlerne and Løgstør Bredning Ramsar Site; EEC SPA

Wildlife Reserve (233 ha)

A large area of coastal meadows and adjacent waters, with several small islands between Bygholm Vejle and Aggersund.

Breeding species include *Recurvirostra avosetta* (50 pairs). Waterfowl outside the breeding season include *Cygnus cygnus* (700), *Tadorna tadorna* (1500), *Anas penelope* (2000), and *Pluvialis apricaria* (1750).

009 Nordre Rønner (Nordjylland)

57°22'N, 10°56'E 2923 ha Ramsar Site; EEC SPA

Voluntary agreements governing recreational activities

A sea area with stony banks and uninhabited islands.

Breeding species include *Rissa tridactyla* (100 pairs), *Sterna sandvicensis* (100 pairs), *S. hirundo* (20 pairs), and *Cepphus grylle* (110 pairs).

010 South Læsø and adjacent sea (Nordjylland)

57°12'N, 11°10'E 67,840 ha Ramsar Site; EEC SPA

Nature Conservation Area (2000 ha)

A coastal site with intertidal flats, shoals, banks, islands, and islets. Also saltmarsh, coastal heathland, and a few cultivated areas with associated habitation. An important moulting area for seaducks.

Breeding species include *Recurvirostra avosetta* (170 pairs), *Philomachus pugnax*, *Numenius arquata*, *Tringa glareola* (1-2 pairs) and *Sterna paradisaea* (200 pairs). Important for waterfowl outside the breeding season with *Branta bernicla bernicla* (1950), *Somateria mollissima* (80,000), *Melanitta nigra* (38,000), *M. fusca* (11,000), *Mergus serrator* (2000), *Recurvirostra avosetta* (600), and *Calidris alpina* (45,000).

011 Hirsholmene and Deget (Nordjylland)

57°29'N, 10°38'E 600 ha Ramsar Site (480 ha); part of EEC SPA (4000 ha)

Nature Conservation Area (Hirsholmene and surrounding water)

A sea area with stony shoals, banks, and islands. Only the main island is inhabited. Important long-standing research area for marine biology.

An important site for breeding gulls and terns with *Larus ridibundus* (25,000 pairs), *L. fuscus* (330 pairs), *L. marinus* (280 pairs), *Sterna sandvicensis* (1000-1400 pairs), *S. hirundo* (40-90 pairs), and *S. paradisaea* (50-100 pairs). Other breeding species include *Cepphus grylle* (100-175 pairs) and *Anthus spinoletta* (57 pairs; the most important Danish site).

012 Løgstør Bredning (Nordjylland)

56°55'N, 09°10'E 38,300 ha

Part of Vejlerne and Løgstør Bredning Ramsar Site; two EEC SPAs (1300 ha and 37,000 ha)

Nature Conservation Area (*c*.300 ha); three Wildlife Reserves (*c*.1500 ha)

A shallow saline fjord area with shoals and islands, coastal saltmarsh, and agricultural land. A moulting area for *Melanitta fusca* and *Mergus serrator*.

Breeding species include *Recurvirostra avosetta* (50 pairs). Important for waterfowl outside the breeding season with *Cygnus cygnus* (700), *Anas penelope* (8000), *Aythya marila* (18,000), *Bucephala clangula* (12,000), *Melanitta fusca* (16,000), *Mergus serrator* (10,000), and *M. merganser* (2000).

013 Vejlerne (Viborg)

57°03'N, 09°00'E 6000 ha

Part of Vejlerne and Løgstør Bredning Ramsar Site; includes the whole and part of two EEC SPAs (3300 ha and 2350 ha)

Scientific Reserve/Nature Conservation Area

An area of partly drained fjords with lakes, reed-swamp, meadows, and saltmarsh.

Breeding species include *Botaurus stellaris* (28-36 pairs), *Anser anser* (370-464 pairs), *Circus aeruginosus*, *Porzana porzana*, *Recurvirostra avosetta* (200 pairs), and *Chlidonias niger* (70 pairs). Important for waterfowl outside the breeding season with *Cygnus columbianus* (884), *C. cygnus* (595), *Anser fabalis* (828), *A. brachyrhynchus* (496), *A. anser* (1500), *Anas penelope* (8086), *A. crecca* (13,000), *A. clypeata* (427), *Bucephala clangula* (3900), *Mergus serrator* (3847), *Recurvirostra avosetta* (505), and *Pluvialis apricaria* (8771).

014 Lovns Bredning (Viborg, Nordjylland)

56°40'N, 09°10'E 7300 ha EEC SPA

A shallow fjord area with coastal marshes and agricultural land. Important moulting area for *Aythya marila* and *Mergus serrator*.

Important for waterfowl outside the breeding season with *Cygnus cygnus* (130), *Anas crecca* (9000), *Aythya marila* (2000), *Bucephala clangula* (9000), *Mergus serrator* (10,000), and *M. merganser* (3000).

015 Parts of Randers and Mariager Fjords and adjoining sea areas (Århus, Nordjylland)

56°39'N, 10°10'E 41,400 ha Ramsar Site; EEC SPA

Nature Conservation Area (40 ha); Wildlife Reserve (76 ha)

A shallow sea and fjord area with small islands, coastal marshes, and cultivated land including large reclaimed areas near Overgaard. A moulting area for seaducks.

Breeding species include *Recurvirostra avosetta* (45 pairs), *Sterna hirundo* (20 pairs) and *S. paradisaea* (20 pairs). Important for waterfowl outside the breeding season with *Cygnus olor* (5000), *C. cygnus* (2000), *Branta bernicla hrota* (2500), *Tadorna tadorna* (4000), *Aythya marila* (3000), *Somateria mollissima* (47,000), *Melanitta nigra* (10,000), *M. fusca* (20,000), and *Mergus merganser* (1000).

016 Tjele Langsø (Viborg)

56°32'N, 09°40'E 1250 ha EEC SPA

A freshwater lake with adjacent agricultural land.

Important for wintering *Anser fabalis* (1200).

017 Ålvand Klithede and Førby Sø (Viborg)

56°57'N, 08°25'E 800 ha EEC SPA

Nature Conservation Area

A moor with peatbog, small wetlands, and moor lakes.
Important as a breeding site for several scarce moorland birds including *Numenius arquata* (2-3 pairs) and *Tringa glareola*. Waterfowl present outside the breeding season include *Anser brachyrhynchus* (150).

018 Vangså Hede (Viborg)

57°01'N, 08°28'E 1400 ha EEC SPA

Nature Conservation Area

A moor and dune area with small wetlands.
Important as a breeding site for several scarce moorland birds including *Numenius arquata* (2 pairs) and *Tringa glareola* (3+ pairs).

019 Lønnerup Fjord (Viborg)

57°00'N, 08°47'E 450 ha

Part of Vejlerne and Løgstør Bredning Ramsar Site; EEC SPA

Wildlife Reserve (141 ha)

A partly drained fjord area with lakes, lagoons, coastal meadows, saltwater and freshwater marshes, and an associated dyke and dam network.
Important for waterfowl outside the breeding season with *Cygnus columbianus* (372) and *C. cygnus* (550), and also *Pluvialis apricaria* (2000).

020 Arup Holm and Hovsør Røn (Viborg)

56°58'N, 08°52'E part of Vejlerne and Løgstør Bredning Ramsar Site; EEC SPA

A minor part is a Nature Conservation Area

A shallow sea area and meadows grazed by cattle.
Important as breeding site for waders including *Haematopus ostralegus* (14-34 pairs), *Recurvirostra avosetta* (18-45 pairs), *Charadrius hiaticula* (8-19 pairs), *Vanellus vanellus* (18-31 pairs), *Calidris alpina* (1-7 pairs), and *Tringa totanus* (8-21 pairs). Other breeding species include *Sterna paradisaea* (40-50 pairs) and *S. albifrons*. Species occurring outside the breeding season include *Cygnus columbianus*, *C. cygnus*, *Pluvialis apricaria* (6000), *Vanellus vanellus* (3000), and *Philomachus pugnax* (150).

021 Ove Sø (Viborg)

56°52'N, 08°30'E 650 ha EEC SPA

A freshwater lake with islets surrounded by grazing-meadows and arable land.
Important for wintering *Cygnus columbianus* (100), *C. cygnus* (400), and *Philomachus pugnax* (200).

022 Hanstholm Reservatet (Viborg)

57°07'N, 08°37'E 4800 ha EEC SPA

Nature Conservation Area; Wildlife Reserve (3846 ha)

An extensive coastal heath with sand hills, moorland, and a number of large and small oligotrophic lakes. There are also plantations and scattered habitation.
Breeding species include *Grus grus*, *Pluvialis apricaria* (0-4 pairs), and *Tringa glareola* (25-30 pairs). Important for waterfowl outside the breeding season with *Cygnus columbianus* (108), *C. cygnus* (430), and *Anser brachyrhynchus* (1450).

023 Agger Tange and Krik Vig (Viborg)

56°45'N, 08°15'E 6100 ha

Part of Nissum Bredning, Harboøre and Agger Ramsar Site; EEC SPA

Proposed Nature Conservation Area (Agger peninsula: 1400 ha); Wildlife Reserve (11 ha)

A coastal peninsula with a dyked brackish lagoon, saltmarsh, grazing-meadows, and a shallow fjord area with shoals, banks, intertidal flats, and saltmarsh seaward of the peninsula.

Breeding species include *Circus aeruginosus*, *Recurvirostra avosetta* (200 pairs), *Philomachus pugnax* (45 pairs), *Limosa limosa* (60 pairs), *Sterna sandvicensis* (150-300 pairs), *S. hirundo* (40 pairs), *S. paradisaea* (200 pairs), *S. albifrons* (40 pairs), and *Asio flammeus*. Important for waterfowl outside the breeding season with *Cygnus columbianus* (800), *C. cygnus* (700), *Anser brachyrhynchus* (3000), *Branta bernicla hrota* (420), *Anas penelope* (11,500), *A. crecca* (3000), *A. acuta* (1800), *Recurvirostra avosetta* (1000), *Pluvialis apricaria* (7000), *Calidris minuta* (920), and *C. alpina* (20,000).

024 Hjarbæk Fjord (Viborg)

56°33'N, 09°20'E 2700 ha Part of EEC SPA (3850 ha)

Wildlife Reserve (2681 ha)

A shallow brackish/freshwater arm of the Limfjord, separated from the main fjord by a road embankment and bordered by coastal marshes and agricultural land. An important waterfowl moulting area especially for *Podiceps cristatus*, *Bucephala clangula*, and *Fulica atra*.

Important for waterfowl outside the breeding season with *Podiceps cristatus* (3760), *Cygnus cygnus* (400), *Anas clypeata* (1140), *Aythya ferina* (5241), *A. fuligula* (7000), *Bucephala clangula* (7211), and *Mergus merganser* (1109). Other non-breeding species include *Cygnus columbianus* (50) and *Recurvirostra avosetta*.

025 Mågerodde and Karbyodde (Viborg)

56°45'N, 08°35'E 600 ha EEC SPA

A coastal area with saltmarsh and saline lagoons.

Breeding species include *Recurvirostra avosetta* (50 pairs) and *Sterna paradisaea* (35-40 pairs). Important for non-breeding *Pluvialis apricaria* (10,000-25,000). Other non-breeders include *Calidris minuta* (370).

026 Dråby Vig (Viborg)

56°50'N, 08°50'E 1650 ha EEC SPA

Bays and straits with coastal brackish/saline lagoons, tidal flats, and marshes.

Breeding species include *Recurvirostra avosetta* (20-25 pairs) and *Sterna paradisaea* (40-75 pairs). Important for non-breeding *Pluvialis apricaria* (21,000).

027 Glomstrup Vig, Agerø, Munkholm and Katholm Odde, Lindholm, and Rotholme (Viborg, Ringkøbing)

56°40'N, 08°35'E 5900 ha EEC SPA

DOF Bird Sanctuary at Agerø (130 ha)

A shallow fjord area with shoals, banks, and islands, and coastal areas with saltmarsh and agricultural land.

Breeding species include *Recurvirostra avosetta* (30-50 pairs) and *Sterna paradisaea* (25-60 pairs). Important for waterfowl outside the breeding season with *Branta bernicla hrota* (1417), *Bucephala clangula* (4000), *Mergus serrator* (2000), and *Pluvialis apricaria* (15,000).

028 Nissum Bredning (Viborg, Ringkøbing)

56°40'N, 08°20'E 12,800 ha

Part of Nissum Bredning, Harboøre and Agger Ramsar Site; EEC SPA

A shallow fjord area, with coastal lagoons and marshes in the western part of Nissum Bredning.

Important for waterfowl outside the breeding season with *Bucephala clangula* (3000), *Mergus serrator* (2000) and *M. merganser* (4000).

029 Flyndersø (Viborg, Ringkøbing)

56°30'N, 08°55'E 600 ha EEC SPA

Nature Conservation Area (500 ha)

A freshwater lake surrounded by plantations of conifers and oaks, moorland, and agricultural land.

Important for waterfowl outside the breeding season with *Mergus merganser* (2000). *Pandion haliaetus* also occurs.

030 Norsminde (Kysing) Fjord (Århus)

56°00'N, 10°20'E 334 ha EEC SPA (300 ha)

Nature Conservation Area (*c.*50 ha); Wildlife Reserve

A shallow, almost enclosed fjord area (connected to the open sea by sluices), surrounded by coastal marshes, meadows, and agricultural land with scattered habitation.

Waterfowl occurring outside the breeding season include *Anas penelope* (1800), *A. crecca* (900), *A. platyrhynchos* (3000), *A. acuta* (150), *A. clypeata* (160), *Aythya fuligula* (2200), *Mergus merganser* (47), *Fulica atra* (10,000), and *Vanellus vanellus* (3000).

031 Stavns Fjord and adjacent waters (Århus)

55°54'N, 10°40'E 16,320 ha Ramsar Site; EEC SPA

Nature Conservation Area; two Wildlife Reserves (1939 ha)

Sea and fjord areas with shallows, uninhabited islands, saltmarsh, and higher grassland, with some cultivation on a few islands. A moulting area for sea ducks, especially *Somateria mollissima*.

Breeding species include *Somateria mollissima* (2000 pairs; second largest colony in Denmark), *Recurvirostra avosetta* (25 pairs), *Larus fuscus* (375 pairs), *L. marinus* (200 pairs; the largest colony in Denmark), *Sterna paradisaea* (70 pairs), and *Cepphus grylle* (70 pairs). Important for waterfowl outside the breeding season with *Phalacrocorax carbo sinensis* (1902), *Cygnus olor* (2000), *C. cygnus* (200), *Somateria mollissima* (62,000), *Melanitta nigra* (9000), and *Mergus merganser* (1000).

032 Sea area north of Anholt Island (Århus)

56°42'N, 11°34'E 12,720 ha Ramsar Site; EEC SPA

Nature Conservation Area (Beaches and Totten: 100 ha)

A sea area with shoals and banks. Includes the eastern point of Anholt and the shores of its northern coast. A moulting area for *Somateria mollissima*.

Important for waterfowl outside the breeding season with *Somateria mollissima* (80,000) and *Melanitta nigra* (20,000).

033 Salten Langsø (Århus, Vejle)

56°06'N, 09°35'E 500 ha EEC SPA

Bordered to east by a Nature Conservation Area

A eutrophic freshwater lake with reed-swamp surrounded by forest, heathland, and agricultural land.

Breeding species include *Podiceps cristatus* (70-90 pairs). Non-breeding species include *Mergus merganser* (800) and *Pandion haliaetus*.

034 Forest areas south of Silkeborg (Århus)

56°01'N, 09°28'E 3850 ha EEC SPA

Large forests with several streams and lakes.

Breeding species include *Pernis apivorus*, *Caprimulgus europaeus*, *Alcedo atthis*, *Dryocopus martius*, and other forest species which are scarce in Denmark.

035 Mossø (Århus)

56°02'N, 09°48'E 1800 ha EEC SPA

Nature Conservation Area

A freshwater lake (third largest in Denmark) with reed-swamp, surrounded by forest and agricultural land.

Important for breeding *Podiceps cristatus* (300 pairs), *P. nigricollis* (130-150 pairs; the largest colony in north-west Europe), *Circus aeruginosus*, and non-breeding *Mergus merganser* (1200).

036 Horsens Fjord, Svanegrunden, and Endelave (Århus, Vejle)

55°51'N, 10°10'E 43,200 ha Ramsar Site; EEC SPA

Nature Conservation Area (1000 ha, including Vorsø scientific area); four small Wildlife Reserves (11-210 ha)

A shallow fjord and sea area with shoals and banks; three fairly large islands with coastal saltmarsh, lagoons, cultivated land, and scattered habitation. A moulting area for seaducks including *Somateria mollissima*, *Melanitta nigra*, and *M. fusca*.

Breeding species include *Phalacrocorax carbo sinensis* (3000 pairs), *Recurvirostra avosetta* (80 pairs), *Sterna sandvicensis* (300 pairs), *S. paradisaea* (450 pairs), *S. albifrons*, and *Cepphus grylle*. Important for waterfowl outside the breeding season with *Aythya marila* (5000), *Somateria mollissima* (80,000), *Melanitta nigra* (8000), *M. fusca* (3000), *Mergus serrator* (1000), *M. merganser* (1000), and waders (20,000).

037 Borris Hede (Ringkøbing)

55°55'N, 08°41'E 4600 ha EEC SPA

Nature Conservation Area (1830 ha)

A very large moorland area with streams and bogs.

Important for a number of moorland species including *Numenius arquata* (10-30 pairs), *Tringa glareola* (5-10 pairs), and *Asio flammeus* (1-2 pairs).

038 Nissum Fjord (Ringkøbing)

56°21'N, 08°14'E 11,600 ha Ramsar Site; EEC SPA

Nature Conservation Area (400 ha); Wildlife Reserve (7500 ha)

A shallow brackish fjord connected by sluices to the North Sea, with coastal saltmarsh and reed-swamp, and heathland vegetation on Fjandø island. Some marsh areas are becoming overgrown.

Breeding species include *Phalacrocorax carbo sinensis* (170 pairs), *Anas acuta* (16-20 pairs), *Recurvirostra avosetta* (294 pairs), *Calidris alpina* (43 pairs), *Philomachus pugnax* (20 pairs), *Limosa limosa* (30 pairs), *Sterna sandvicensis* (1230 pairs), *S. hirundo* (51 pairs), *S. paradisaea* (238 pairs), and *S. albifrons* (35 pairs). Important for waterfowl outside the breeding season with *Cygnus olor* (1276), *C. columbianus* (203), *C. cygnus* (313), *Anser brachyrhynchus* (5955), *Branta bernicla hrota* (2503), *Tadorna tadorna*

(4445), *Anas penelope* (4998), *A. crecca* (4640), *A. acuta* (1630), *Bucephala clangula* (3120), *Mergus merganser* (1358), *Recurvirostra avosetta* (891), *Pluvialis apricaria* (8690), *Vanellus vanellus* (10,345), *Calidris alpina* (14,163), *Limosa lapponica* (9715), and *Numenius arquata* (3028).

039 Harboøre Tange, Plet Enge, and Gjeller Sø (Ringkøbing)

56°40'N, 08°15'E 7200 ha

Part of Nissum Bredning, Harboøre and Agger Ramsar Site; EEC SPA

Nature Conservation Area (1500 ha); Wildlife Reserve (17 ha)

A narrow peninsula with shallow fjord area containing shoals and banks, with an intertidal zone and saltmarsh seaward of the peninsula, and brackish lagoons and grazing-meadows on the landward side. There are some cultivated areas with scattered habitation.

Breeding species include *Recurvirostra avosetta* (130 pairs), *Calidris alpina* (35-65 pairs), *Philomachus pugnax*, *Limosa limosa*, *Sterna albifrons* (2 pairs), and *Asio flammeus*. Important for waterfowl outside the breeding season with *Cygnus cygnus* (100-200), *Anser brachyrhynchus* (3100), *Branta bernicla hrota* (1340), and *Recurvirostra avosetta* (650).

040 Venø, Venø Bugt, and Kås Bredning (Viborg, Ringkøbing)

56°35'N, 08°40'E 6000 ha EEC SPA (2450 ha)

Wildlife Reserve (Nørskov Vig: 132 ha)

A shallow brackish fjord with a small area of saline lagoons and saltmarsh.

Breeding species include *Recurvirostra avosetta* (11 pairs), *Sterna paradisaea* (21 pairs), and *S. albifrons* (5 pairs). Important for waterfowl outside the breeding season with *Bucephala clangula* (15,000), *Mergus serrator* (3000), and *M. merganser* (1000).

041 Stadil Fjord and Veststadil Fjord (Ringkøbing)

56°11'N, 08°09'E 7184 ha Ramsar Site; EEC SPA

Nature Conservation Area (Veststadil Fjord and Husby Klit: 1500 ha)

A shallow fjord area with reed-swamps and meadows.

Breeding species include *Circus aeruginosus* and *Chlidonias niger*. Important for waterfowl outside the breeding season with *Cygnus columbianus* (500), *C. cygnus* (300), *Anser brachyrhynchus* (20,000), *Anas crecca* (5000), and *Anas acuta* (1000).

042 Heath areas in Sønder Feldborg Plantage (Viborg)

56°19'N, 08°58'E 300 ha EEC SPA

A moorland surrounded by small areas of forest.

An important breeding site for moorland birds including *Tringa glareola* (4 pairs).

043 Ringkøbing Fjord (Ringkøbing)

56°00'N, 08°15'E 27,240 ha Ramsar Site; EEC SPA

Nature Conservation Area (24,600 ha); Wildlife Reserve (49 ha)

A shallow brackish fjord with several small islands; connected by sluices to the North Sea, with low-lying meadows and reed-swamp to the south. The most important locality in Denmark for *Cygnus columbianus* and *Anas clypeata*. Moulting area for *Cygnus olor* and *Anas platyrhynchos*.

Breeding species include *Circus aeruginosus* (11 pairs), *Recurvirostra avosetta* (400-450 pairs), *Limosa limosa* (130-180 pairs), *Sterna sandvicensis* (800 pairs), and *Asio flammeus* (6 pairs). Important for waterfowl outside the breeding season with *Cygnus olor* (4300), *C. columbianus* (1100), *C. cygnus* (900), *Anser brachyrhynchus* (6670), *Branta bernicla bernicla* (3062), *Anas penelope* (30,000), *A. crecca* (11,000), *A. platyrhynchos* (22,000),

A. acuta (18,000), *A. clypeata* (900), *Bucephala clangula* (3200), *Mergus merganser* (6800), *Fulica atra* (40,000), *Pluvialis apricaria* (10,000), and *Calidris minuta* (1040).

044 Uldum Kær (Vejle)

55°52'N, 09°33'E 950 ha EEC SPA

Wet meadows, ponds, peatbogs, and moorland wetlands.

Breeding species include *Circus aeruginosus* (1 pair), *Crex crex*, *Tringa glareola* (2 pairs), and *Alcedo atthis*.

045 Forest areas along the northern part of Vejle Fjord (Vejle)

55°42'N, 09°45'E 2700 ha EEC SPA

Nature Conservation Area (1024 ha)

Deciduous forest along the northern part of the fjord.

Breeding species include *Pernis apivorus* (5-6 pairs), *Alcedo atthis*, and other forest species which are scarce in Denmark.

046 Randbøl Hede (Ribe, Vejle)

55°40'N, 09°09'E 900 ha EEC SPA

Nature Conservation Area (760 ha)

A moorland with bogs.

Important for several scarce moorland breeding species including *Numenius arquata*, *Tringa glareola* (1-2 pairs), and *Asio flammeus* (4-5 pairs).

047 Lillebælt (Sønderjylland, Vejle, Fyn)

55°21'N, 09°43'E 37,344 ha Ramsar Site; EEC SPA

Four small Wildlife Reserves (Gamborg: 130 ha; Hejlsminde Nor: 288 ha; Bastholm: 13 ha; Linderum: 16 ha)

A narrow sea area containing islands and peninsulas with coves, lagoons, saltmarsh, reedswamp, cultivated land, and some scattered habitation. A moulting area for seaducks, especially *Somateria mollissima*.

Breeding species include *Phalacrocorax carbo sinensis* (618 pairs), *Recurvirostra avosetta* (50 pairs), *Sterna hirundo* (15 pairs), *S. paradisaea* (400 pairs), and *S. albifrons* (10 pairs). Important for waterfowl outside the breeding season with *Cygnus cygnus* (1000), *Anser anser* (1400), *Anas acuta* (1000), *Aythya fuligula* (10,000), *A. marila* (40,000), *Somateria mollissima* (40,000), *Melanitta fusca* (5000), *Bucephala clangula* (5000), and *Mergus serrator* (4500).

048 Heath areas near Store Råbjerg (Ribe)

55°44'N, 09°00'E 600 ha EEC SPA

A moorland with bogs between Utoft and Gyttegårds Plantage.

Breeding species include *Tringa glareola* (2-3 pairs).

049 Vadehavet (Wadden Sea) (Ribe, Sønderjylland)

55°16'N, 08°32'E 140,830 ha

Ramsar Site; includes whole or part of nine EEC SPAs (totalling 142,450 ha)

Nature Conservation Area (120,000 ha); two Wildlife Reserves (including Vadehavet: 86,729 ha)

The Wadden Sea (divided between the Netherlands, Federal Republic of Germany, and Denmark) is characterised by intertidal mud- and sandflats between the mainland and barrier islands. The flats are flanked by deeper water channels. There are coastal marshes and reclaimed marshland behind the dykes. Coastal marshland is partly grazed by sheep and cattle, whilst reclaimed marshland has permanent grass and some arable land. The islands have heathland, sand-dunes, and arable land; some are inhabited. Potential ecological changes include those resulting from increasing pollution, drainage, cultivation, overcropping of shellfish, dredging, reclamation, and oil/gas exploration. Most important resting area in Denmark for surface-feeding ducks and most important Danish site for moulting *Melanitta nigra*.

Breeding species include *Botaurus stellaris*, *Circus aeruginosus*, *C. pygargus*, *Tadorna tadorna*, *Anas acuta*, *A. clypeata*, *Somateria mollissima*, *Haematopus ostralegus*, *Recurvirostra avosetta*, *Vanellus vanellus*, *Calidris alpina*, *Philomachus pugnax*, *Limosa limosa*, *Sterna paradisaea*, *S. albifrons*, and *Chlidonias niger*. Of major importance for waterfowl outside the breeding season with *Cygnus columbianus* (225), *C. cygnus* (488), *Anser brachyrhynchus* (16,000), *Branta leucopsis* (2109), *B. bernicla* (12,510), *Tadorna tadorna* (29,200), *Anas penelope* (58,600), *A. crecca* (16,700), *A. platyrhynchos* (26,350), *A. acuta* (3800), *A. clypeata* (2010), *Somateria mollissima* (64,800), *Melanitta nigra* (46,300), *Haematopus ostralegus* (46,200), *Recurvirostra avosetta* (11,365), *Pluvialis apricaria* (31,500), *P. squatarola* (3960), *Vanellus vanellus* (39,700), *Calidris canutus* (41,000), *C. alba* (790), *C. alpina* (374,000), *Limosa lapponica* (41,600), *Numenius arquata* (3800), *Tringa totanus* (3360), and *T. nebularia* (1420).

050 Kallesmæsks Hede, Grærup Langsø, and surrounding areas (Ribe)

55°36'N, 08°09'E 6800 ha EEC SPA

A minor part is a Nature Conservation Area

Large moor areas with small forests, lakes, bogs, and dunes.

Breeding species include *Tringa glareola* (3-5 pairs).

051 Vejen Mose (Ribe)

55°31'N, 09°05'E 350 ha EEC SPA

A peat bog.

Breeding species include *Tringa glareola* (0-2 pairs).

052 Fiilsø (Ribe)

55°42'N, 08°15'E 4320 ha Ramsar Site; includes EEC SPA (4000 ha)

Nature Conservation Area (400 ha)

Mainly open agricultural land (on former lake-bottom) and small plantations, but also two shallow lakes surrounded by marshy areas. The land turned over to forestry is increasing in area.

Breeding species include *Circus aeruginosus*, *C. pygargus*, and *Tringa glareola*. Important for waterfowl outside the breeding season with *Cygnus columbianus* (500), *C. cygnus* (300), *Anser brachyrhynchus* (25,000), and *Anas acuta* (5000).

053 Hostrup Sø, Assenholm Mose, and Felsted Vestermark (Sønderjylland)

54°57'N, 09°27'E 10 ha part of EEC SPA (1350 ha)

A relatively large lake surrounded by meadows and marshes.

Breeding species include *Botaurus stellaris* (0-1 pair), *Circus aeruginosus* (2-3 pairs), *Tringa glareola* (1 pair), and *Asio flammeus* (0-1 pair).

054 Pamhule Skov (Sønderjylland)

55°13'N, 09°23'E 1100 ha EEC SPA

An area of deciduous forest, meadows, and marshes.

Breeding species include *Pernis apivorus* (4 pairs), *Alcedo atthis* (3 pairs), and other forest species which are scarce in Denmark.

055 Kongens Mose (Sønderjylland)

55°02'N, 08°56'E 450 ha EEC SPA

Proposed Nature Conservation Area

A raised bog.
Breeding species include *Circus aeruginosus* (1-2 pairs), *C. pygargus* (1-2 pairs), *Tringa glareola* (5 pairs), *Chlidonias niger* (10-15 pairs), and *Asio flammeus* (1 pair).

056 Tinglev Mose and Sø (Sønderjylland)

54°56'N, 09°16'E 450 ha EEC SPA

Nature Conservation Area (94 ha)

A partly drained lake with large areas of swamps.
Breeding species include *Circus aeruginosus* (1-2 pairs) and *C. pygargus*.

057 Sønder Ådal (Sønderjylland)

54°54'N, 09°03'E 1700 ha EEC SPA

A river valley with meadows and marshes.
Breeding species include *Botaurus stellaris* (1 pair), *Circus aeruginosus* (1-2 pairs), *C. pygargus* (3-5 pairs), *Chlidonias niger* (5-10 pairs), and *Asio flammeus* (1-2 pairs).

058 Flensborg Fjord and Nybøl Nor (Sønderjylland)

54°50'N, 09°35'E 3300 ha EEC SPA

Wildlife Reserve (96 ha)

Nybøl Nor is a shallow fjord with only a narrow connection to the open water of Flensborg Fjord.
Important for waterfowl outside the breeding season with *Aythya fuligula* (26,000), *A. marila* (27,000), *Bucephala clangula* (4000), *Mergus serrator* (1000), and *Fulica atra* (15,000).

059 Lindet Skov, Hønning Plantage, Lovrup Skov, and Skråp (Sønderjylland)

55°09'N, 08°54'E 2150 ha EEC SPA

A minor part is a Nature Conservation Area

A deciduous and coniferous forest.
Breeding species include *Pernis apivorus* (2-3 pairs), *Certhia brachydactyla* (30-40 pairs), and several other forest species which are scarce in Denmark.

060 Forests near Gråsten (Sønderjylland)

54°56'N, 09°32'E 750 ha EEC SPA

Nature Conservation Area (16 ha)

A deciduous forest in a heterogeneous landscape.
Breeding species include *Pernis apivorus* (5 pairs), *Circus aeruginosus* (1-4 pairs), *Alcedo atthis* (1 pair), *Certhia brachydactyla* (38-40 pairs), and other forest species which are scarce in Denmark.

061 Kogsbøl and Skast Mose (Sønderjylland)

55°03'N, 08°42'E 600 ha EEC SPA

Nature Conservation Area (390 ha)

A moor with marshes and meadows.
Breeding species include *Circus aeruginosus* (1 pair), *C. pygargus* (3-4 pairs), *Tringa glareola* (0-3 pairs), *Chlidonias niger*, and *Asio flammeus*.

062 Frøslev Mose (Sønderjylland)

54°49'N, 09°14'E 350 ha EEC SPA

Nature Conservation Area

A moorland bog with oak scrub.

Breeding species include *Circus aeruginosus* (1-3 pairs), *C. pygargus* (2-3 pairs), *Numenius arquata* (3 pairs), *Tringa glareola* (2-4 pairs), and *Asio flammeus* (1-4 pairs).

063 Sydfynske Ø-hav (Fyn)

55°00'N, 10°20'E 39,200 ha Ramsar Site; EEC SPA

Nature Conservation Area (190 ha); four small Wildlife Reserves (150 ha)

A shallow archipelagic sea area with shoals and many, generally uninhabited, islands, with saltmarsh, reed-swamp, and small lakes. There is scattered habitation and cultivation on a few islands. An important moulting area for *Cygnus olor*.

Breeding species include *Botaurus stellaris*, *Anas acuta* (24 pairs), *A. clypeata* (35 pairs), *Circus aeruginosus*, *Recurvirostra avosetta* (125 pairs), *Sterna sandvicensis* (100 pairs), *S. paradisaea* (700 pairs) and *S. albifrons* (60 pairs). Important for waterfowl outside the breeding season with *Cygnus olor* (6000), *C. cygnus* (600), *Branta bernicla bernicla* (2345), *Aythya fuligula* (23,000), *A. marila* (19,000), *Somateria mollissima* (45,000), *Clangula hyemalis* (6000), *Melanitta fusca* (4000), *Bucephala clangula* (4000), *Mergus serrator* (1000), and *Fulica atra* (38,000).

064 Marstal Bugt and the coast of south-west Langeland (Fyn)

54°47'N, 10°40'E 4200 ha EEC SPA

Nature Conservation Area (128 ha)

A shallow coastal area surrounded by cultivated fields.

Important during the breeding and migration season and during warm winters for many species, including large numbers of waterfowl. Breeding species include *Botaurus stellaris*, *Circus aeruginosus*, and *Anas clypeata*. Non-breeding species include *Cygnus cygnus*.

065 Vresen and adjacent sea (Fyn)

55°10'N, 10°50'E 3100 ha EEC SPA

Wildlife Reserve (20 ha)

A shallow sea area between Fyn and Langeland with shoals and banks. Vresen is a small (5 ha) islet with a little vegetation. A moulting area for seaducks.

Important for *Somateria mollissima* (378 pairs; 24,000 non-breeding); non-breeding species include *Melanitta nigra* (5000) and *M. fusca* (600).

066 Forests near Brahetrolleborg (Fyn)

55°07'N, 10°23'E 2100 ha EEC SPA

Nature Conservation Area (532 ha)

Forests (mainly deciduous) around a large eutrophic lake.

Important throughout the year for a large number of forest species, including raptors. Breeding birds include *Pernis apivorus*.

067 Odense Fjord (Fyn)

55°30'N, 10°34'E 4800 ha EEC SPA

Nature Conservation Area (300 ha); Wildlife Reserve (3 ha)

A shallow fjord area with shoals and banks. Islands and coastal areas with saltmarsh, forest, and agricultural land.

Breeding species include *Circus aeruginosus*, *Recurvirostra avosetta* (60 pairs), *Sterna sandvicensis* (100-200 pairs), and *S. paradisaea* (400 pairs). Important for waterfowl outside the breeding season with *Cygnus olor* (10,000), *C. cygnus* (300), *Branta bernicla bernicla* (800), *Mergus serrator* (1000), *M. merganser* (1000), and *Fulica atra* (15,000).

068 Næra coast and Aebelø area (Fyn)

55°36'N, 10°13'E 13,800 ha Ramsar Site; EEC SPA

Nature Conservation Area (100 ha); Wildlife Reserve (20 ha)

A shallow sea area with islands and islets which have saltmarsh and drained and cultivated areas with scattered habitation.

Breeding species include *Phalacrocorax carbo sinensis* (452 pairs), *Circus aeruginosus*, *Recurvirostra avosetta* (50 pairs), *Sterna paradisaea* (170 pairs), and *S. albifrons* (2-4 pairs). Important for waterfowl outside the breeding season with *Phalacrocorax carbo sinensis* (931), *Cygnus olor* (2000), *Anser anser* (1200), *Somateria mollissima* (20,000), *Melanitta nigra* (4200), and *M. fusca* (2000).

069 Romsø and adjacent sea (Fyn)

55°30'N, 10°50'E 3600 ha EEC SPA

Nature Conservation Area (100 ha)

A shallow sea area between Hindsholm peninsula and Romsø island. Romsø is uninhabited and has saltmarsh and forest.

Important for moulting *Somateria mollissima* (20,000). Other non-breeding species include *Melanitta nigra* (6000).

070 Brændegård Sø, Nørresø, and Arreskov Sø (Fyn)

55°05'N, 10°20'E 800 ha EEC SPA

Nature Conservation Area (285 ha); Wildlife Reserve (775 ha)

Freshwater lakes surrounded by forest and agricultural land.

Supports a breeding colony of *Phalacrocorax carbo sinensis* (750 pairs). Important for waterfowl outside the breeding season with *Phalacrocorax carbo sinensis* (1000), *Anser anser* (2000), *Aythya ferina* (4000), and *A. fuligula* (7500). *Haliaeetus albicilla* and *Falco peregrinus* also occur.

071 Ertholmene east of Bornholm (Bornholm)

55°19'N, 15°11'E 1257 ha Ramsar Site; EEC SPA

Nature Conservation Area; Scientific Sanctuary (11 ha)

A sea area off Bornholm containing rocky islands with cliffs. Two islands are inhabited. The only Danish site for nesting *Uria aalge* and *Alca torda*.

Breeding species include *Somateria mollissima* (2000 pairs), *Larus fuscus* (20-30 pairs), *Uria aalge* (1600 pairs), and *Alca torda* (200 pairs).

072 Almindingen (Bornholm)

55°08'N, 14°58'E 5800 ha EEC SPA

Partly a Nature Conservation Area; partly a Game Reserve

A large forest with glades and wetlands.

Breeding species include *Pernis apivorus*, *Caprimulgus europaeus*, *Dryocopus martius* (15-20 pairs), and other forest species which are scarce in Denmark.

073 Karrebæk, Dybsø, and Avnø Fjords (Storstrøm)

55°10'N, 11°40'E 19,200 ha Ramsar Site; EEC SPA

Nature Conservation Area (300 ha); two Wildlife Reserves (14 ha and 925 ha)

A sea area with shoals and banks. Islands and peninsulas with cultivated land and scattered habitation as well as common land, saltmarsh, and reed-swamp.

Breeding species include *Recurvirostra avosetta* (50-100 pairs), *Sterna hirundo* (10-25 pairs), *S. paradisaea* (130 pairs), *S. albifrons* (45 pairs), *Sylvia nisoria*, and *Lanius collurio*. Important for waterfowl outside the breeding season with *Cygnus olor* (3300), *C. cygnus* (900), *Anser fabalis* (626), *Anas acuta* (1000-2500), *Aythya fuligula* (25,000), *Mergus merganser* (3000), and *Fulica atra* (14,000).

074 Sea area between Lolland and Falster, Rødsand, Bredningen, and Bøtø Nor (Storstrøm)

54°14'N, 11°45'E 36,800 ha

Ramsar Site; includes two EEC SPAs (800 ha and 34,500 ha)

Nature Conservation Area (270 ha); four Wildlife Reserves (*c*.800 ha)

A sea area with shoals and banks, coastal slopes, and uninhabited islands with saltmarsh and reed-swamp; some areas enclosed by dams. There is a small freshwater lake at Bøtø Nor.

Breeding species include *Recurvirostra avosetta* (25-30 pairs), *Limosa limosa*, *Sterna sandvicensis* (305 pairs), *S. hirundo* (75 pairs), *S. paradisaea* (250 pairs), and *S. albifrons* (10 pairs). Important for waterfowl outside the breeding season with *Phalacrocorax carbo sinensis* (2500), *Cygnus olor* (5700), *C. cygnus* (370), *Anser fabalis* (3000), *A. anser* (2000), *Branta bernicla* (2000), *Aythya fuligula* (6000), and *Fulica atra* (15,000). *Haliaeetus albicilla* and *Circus aeruginosus* also occur.

075 Ulfsund, Grønsund, Farø Fjord, and Fanefjord (Storstrøm)

54°55'N, 12°00'E 7100 ha EEC SPA

A shallow sea area with shoals, banks, and islands surrounded by saltmarsh and agricultural land.

Breeding species include *Anas acuta*, *Sterna hirundo*, and *S. paradisaea* (30 pairs). Important for waterfowl outside the breeding season with *Cygnus olor* (8000), *C. cygnus* (2000), *Aythya fuligula* (8000), *Clangula hyemalis* (1000-2000), *Bucephala clangula* (4000), *Mergus serrator* (2000), *M. merganser* (1500), and *Fulica atra* (15,000).

076 Smålandshavet north of Lolland (Storstrøm)

54°54'N, 11°30'E 42,000 ha

Includes Fejø and Femø Islands Ramsar Site; EEC SPA

Two Wildlife Reserves (*c*.130 ha)

A sea area with shoals, banks, and mainly uninhabited islands which have reed-swamp and saltmarsh. Two islands have cultivated land and scattered habitation. A moulting area for *Cygnus olor*.

Breeding species include *Somateria mollissima* (700 pairs), *Circus aeruginosus*, *Recurvirostra avosetta* (75 pairs), *Philomachus pugnax*, *Sterna hirundo*, *S. paradisaea* (100 pairs), and *S. albifrons* (15-20 pairs). Important for waterfowl outside the breeding season with *Cygnus olor* (6000), *C. cygnus* (700), *Anser anser* (1392), *Aythya fuligula* (6000), *Bucephala clangula* (5000), *Mergus serrator* (4000), *M. merganser* (1500), and *Fulica atra* (25,000).

077 Guldborgsund (Storstrøm)

54°50'N, 11°50'E 2700 ha EEC SPA

Wildlife Reserve (321 ha)

A long, narrow and shallow fjord area between Lolland and Falster islands.

Breeding species include *Circus aeruginosus*. Important for waterfowl outside the breeding season with *Cygnus olor* (3000), *C. cygnus* (350), *Aythya fuligula* (13,000), and *Mergus merganser* (2000).

078 Maribo lakes (Storstrøm)

54°46'N, 11°31'E 4400 ha Ramsar Site; EEC SPA

Nature Conservation Area (1200 ha) around lake

Freshwater lakes with wooded islands and peninsulas. Lake shores have parkland, reed-swamp, deciduous forest, meadows, fields, and scattered habitation.

Breeding species include *Anser anser* (280 pairs), *Anas clypeata* (26 pairs), and *Circus aeruginosus* (30 pairs). Important for waterfowl outside the breeding season with *Anser anser* (3735), *Aythya ferina* (7000-10,000), *A. fuligula* (15,000-20,000), and *Mergus merganser* (1200).

079 Nakskov Fjord and Indre Fjord (Storstrøm)

54°50'N, 11°02'E 8960 ha Ramsar Site; EEC SPA

Three Wildlife Reserves (*c.*200 ha)

A fjord area with shoals, banks, and islands (a few of which are inhabited) with saltmarsh, reed-swamp, and freshwater ponds. A moulting area for *Cygnus olor*.

Breeding species include *Recurvirostra avosetta* (30 pairs), *Philomachus pugnax*, *Sterna hirundo* (20 pairs), *S. paradisaea* (225 pairs), and *S. albifrons* (40 pairs). Important for waterfowl outside the breeding season with *Cygnus olor* (3000), *C. cygnus* (700), *Aythya fuligula* (12,000), and *Fulica atra* (19,000).

080 Præstø Fjord, Ulfshale, Nyord, and Jungshoved Nor (Storstrøm)

55°05'N, 12°15'E 25,960 ha Ramsar Site; EEC SPA

Nature Conservation Area (*c.*1800 ha); two Ornithological Sanctuaries (7 ha and 100 ha)

A sea area with shoals, banks, and islands. The islets and islands have saltmarsh, reed-swamp, cultivated land, and scattered settlements. A moulting area for *Cygnus olor*.

Breeding species include *Recurvirostra avosetta* (110 pairs), *Philomachus pugnax*, *Limosa limosa*, *Sterna sandvicensis* (200 pairs), *S. paradisaea* (100 pairs), and *S. albifrons* (20 pairs). Important for waterfowl outside the breeding season with *Phalacrocorax carbo sinensis* (750), *Cygnus olor* (6000), *C. cygnus* (1800), *Anser anser* (650), *Aythya fuligula* (19,000), *A. marila* (1500), *Clangula hyemalis* (5500), *Bucephala clangula* (5000), *Mergus serrator* (3000), *M. merganser* (2000), and *Fulica atra* (25,000).

081 Klinteskoven (Storstrøm)

54°58'N, 12°32'E 850 ha EEC SPA

Nature Conservation Area (330 ha); proposed Nature Conservation Area (remaining 520 ha)

A forest dominated by deciduous trees on steep cliffs. Also includes some agricultural areas with hedges.

Breeding species include *Pernis apivorus* and *Sylvia nisoria*.

082 Holmegårds Mose and Porsemose (Storstrøm, Vestsjælland)

55°20'N, 11°50'E 2200 ha EEC SPA

Nature Conservation Area (326 ha)

Bog areas with freshwater ponds, marshes, grazed meadows, cultivated land, and woodland.

Breeding species include *Podiceps grisegena* (20 pairs), *Pernis apivorus*, *Circus aeruginosus*, and *Limosa limosa*. Important for waterfowl outside the breeding season with *Cygnus columbianus* (41), *C. cygnus* (330), *Anser fabalis* (2200), and *A. anser* (600). *Aquila chrysaetos* also occurs.

083 Forests near Vemmetofte (Storstrøm)

55°15'N, 12°12'E 1950 ha EEC SPA

A mature deciduous forest.
Breeding species include *Pernis apivorus*.

084 Tystrup – Bavelse Søerne (Vestsjælland, Storstrøm)

55°22'N, 11°35'E 1900 ha EEC SPA

Nature Conservation Area

Two connected freshwater lakes surrounded by forest and agricultural land.
Important for waterfowl outside the breeding season with *Cygnus cygnus* (305), *Anser fabalis* (1200), *Aythya ferina* (4600), and *A. fuligula* (17,000). *Haliaeetus albicilla* and *Aquila chrysaetos* also occur.

085 Sejerø Bugt (Vestsjælland)

55°50'N, 11°18'E 36,100 ha

Part of Sejerø Bugt, Nekselø Bugt, and Saltbæk Vig Ramsar Site; EEC SPA

Nature Conservation Area (660 ha)

A sea area with shallow bays, peninsulas, coastal saltmarsh/reed-swamp, heath, sandy beaches, and clay cliffs. Also a cultivated island with scattered habitation. A moulting area for *Aythya marila*, *Somateria mollissima*, *Melanitta nigra*, and *M. fusca*.
Breeding species include *Sterna paradisaea* and *Cepphus grylle* (20-30 pairs). Important for waterfowl outside the breeding season with *Aythya marila* (4000), *Somateria mollissima* (37,000), *Melanitta nigra* (15,000), and *M. fusca* (12,000).

086 Skælskør Nor, Skælskør Fjord, and Borreby Mose (Vestsjælland)

55°15'N, 11°20'E 2600 ha

Part of Skælskør Nor and Glænø Ramsar Site; EEC SPA

Nature Conservation Area (*c*.800 ha); Wildlife Reserve (133 ha)

A coastal area with shallow seas, brackish lagoons, reed-swamp, freshwater meadows, marshes, agricultural land, and woodland.
Breeding species include *Podiceps nigricollis*, *Anas acuta*, and *Circus aeruginosus* (6 pairs). Important for waterfowl outside the breeding season with *Cygnus olor* (3000), *C. cygnus* (700), *Anser anser* (715), and *Aythya fuligula* (24,000).

087 Sea area between Skælskør Fjord and Glænø (Agersø, Omø, Sevedø, Basnæs Nor, and Holsteinborg Nor) (Vestsjælland)

55°10'N, 11°30'E 16,400 ha

Part of Skælskør Nor and Glænø Ramsar Site; EEC SPA

Nature Conservation Area (1000 ha); Wildlife Reserve (1105 ha)

A sea area with shallows and a cove protected by barrier islands. Islands with overgrown coastal slopes, dams, marshes (fresh and salt), grassland, and reed-swamp. Also cultivated land and scattered settlements.
Breeding species include *Phalacrocorax carbo sinensis* (2500 pairs), *Anas acuta* (12 pairs), *Recurvirostra avosetta* (250 pairs), *Sterna sandvicensis*, *S. paradisaea* (142 pairs), and *S. albifrons* (11 pairs). Important for waterfowl outside the breeding season with *Cygnus olor* (2700), *C. cygnus* (750), *Anser fabalis* (1500), *A. anser* (4700), *Anas acuta* (1500), *A. clypeata* (500), *Somateria mollissima* (10,000), *Melanitta nigra* (5000), and *M. fusca* (3000).

088 Hovvig (Vestsjælland)

55°55'N, 11°40'E 200 ha EEC SPA

Nature Conservation Area (130 ha)

A dyked lagoon with reed-swamp, surrounded by agricultural land.

Important for waterfowl outside the breeding season with *Cygnus columbianus* (139), *C. cygnus* (196), *Bucephala clangula* (3000), and *Mergus merganser* (2400).

089 Sprogø and Halsskov Rev (Vestsjælland)

55°20'N, 11°00'E 4700 ha EEC SPA

A shallow sea area with shoals and banks between Sprogø and Sjælland.
Breeding species include *Sterna sandvicensis*. Important for non-breeding *Somateria mollissima* (36,000).

090 Saltbæk Vig (Vestsjælland)

55°45'N, 11°10'E 2700 ha

Part of Sejerø Bugt, Nekselø Bugt, and Saltbæk Vig Ramsar Site; EEC SPA

Proposed Nature Conservation Area

A dyked fjord/lagoon area (a failed land-reclamation project) with saltmarsh, meadows (partly cultivated), reed-swamp, and wooded areas.
Breeding species include *Anser anser* (30 pairs), *Anas acuta*, *Circus aeruginosus*, *Recurvirostra avosetta* (15-25 pairs), *Philomachus pugnax*, and *Sterna albifrons* (10-15 pairs). Important for waterfowl outside the breeding season with *Cygnus cygnus* (150), *Anser fabalis* (605), *A. anser* (3000), and *Anas crecca* (5500).

091 Tissø, Lille Åmose, and Hallenslev Mose (Vestsjælland)

55°35'N, 11°20'E 2900 ha EEC SPA

Nature Conservation Area (100 ha)

A large, shallow freshwater lake with associated grazed meadows and reed-swamp. Inundated by seasonal river flooding.
Breeding species include *Anser anser* (75-100 pairs), *Circus aeruginosus* and *Sterna albifrons*. Important for waterfowl outside the breeding season with *Podiceps cristatus* (500), *Cygnus columbianus* (400), *C. cygnus* (190), and *Anser anser* (1700). Other species occurring include *Haliaeetus albicilla*, *Aquila chrysaetos*, *Pandion haliaetus*, *Philomachus pugnax* (500), and *Sterna caspia*.

092 Bregentved and Gisselfeldt Lakes (Vestsjælland, Storstrøm)

55°20'N, 12°00'E 700 ha EEC SPA

Freshwater lakes surrounded by reed-swamp, forest and agricultural land.
Important for non-breeding *Anser anser* (2880).

093 Sea area between Korshage and Hundested (Vestsjælland, Frederiksborg)

55°58'N, 11°50'E 4100 ha EEC SPA

A sea area connecting Isefjorden with Kattegat, and mouth of shallow fjord with beaches, saltmarsh, heath, and sand dunes.
Breeding species include *Dryocopus martius*, *Anthus campestris*, and *Lanius collurio*. Important for waterfowl outside the breeding season with *Somateria mollissima* (34,000), *Bucephala clangula* (3000), *Mergus serrator* (1000), and *M. merganser* (1700).

094 Wetland north of Gammel Havdrup (Roskilde)

55°34'N, 12°09'E 100 ha EEC SPA

A small wetland area surrounded by agricultural land.
Breeding species include *Circus aeruginosus* and *Chlidonias niger* (10 pairs).

095 Ramsø Mose (Roskilde)

55°35'N, 12°03'E 100 ha EEC SPA

A small wetland area surrounded by agricultural land.

Breeding species include *Chlidonias niger* (4-5 pairs) and *Asio flammeus*.

096 Roskilde Fjord, Selsø, and Kattinge Søerne (Frederiksborg, Roskilde)

55°45'N, 12°05'E 13,350 ha EEC SPA

Nature Conservation Area (3000 ha); three Wildlife Reserves (*c*.900 ha)

A long shallow fjord with islands and islets. Coastal areas with saltmarsh, agricultural land, and forested peninsulas.

Breeding species include *Circus aeruginosus*, *Recurvirostra avosetta* (75 pairs), *Sterna hirundo* (250 pairs), *S. paradisaea* (150 pairs), and *S. albifrons* (25 pairs). Important for waterfowl outside the breeding season with *Cygnus olor* (7000), *C. cygnus* (600), *Anser anser* (5000), *Aythya fuligula* (24,000), *Mergus merganser* (2500), and *Fulica atra* (25,000). *Haliaeetus albicilla* and *Aquila chrysaetos* also occur.

097 Arresø (Frederiksborg)

56°00'N, 12°10'E 600 ha part of EEC SPA (4600 ha)

Nature Conservation Area (150 ha)

A very shallow freshwater lake (largest in Denmark), surrounded by reed-swamp, marsh, cultivated areas, and woodland.

Breeding species include *Botaurus stellaris*, *Circus aeruginosus*, *Porzana porzana*, and *Acrocephalus arundinaceus*. Important for non-breeding *Mergus merganser* (2600). *Pandion haliaetus* also occurs.

098 Jægerspris Nordskov (Frederiksborg)

55°54'N, 11°59'E 1550 ha EEC SPA

Unprotected; proposed Nature Conservation Area

A heterogeneous forest area with glades, wetlands, and coastal meadows.

Breeding species include *Pernis apivorus* (4-6 pairs), *Tringa ochropus* (2-3 pairs), and *Dryocopus martius* (2-3 pairs).

099 Grib Skov (Frederiksborg)

55°58'N, 12°20'E 6000 ha EEC SPA

A minor part is a Nature Conservation Area (Strødam and Nørresø)

A very large forest area with glades and wetlands.

Breeding species include *Pernis apivorus* (8-10 pairs), *Tringa ochropus* (5-10 pairs), *Caprimulgus europaeus* (5 pairs), *Dryocopus martius* (16 pairs), and other forest species which are scarce in Denmark.

100 Furesø and Farum Sø (Frederiksborg, København)

55°48'N, 12°25'E 1000 ha EEC SPA

Nature Conservation Area (250 ha)

A relatively deep, eutrophic freshwater lake surrounded by reed-swamp and swampy thickets; close to urban areas.

Non-breeding species include important numbers of *Aythya fuligula* (17,600).

101 Saltholm (København)

55°40'N, 12°50'E 6800 ha EEC SPA

Proposed Nature Conservation Area (1600 ha); Wildlife Reserve (400 ha)

A large, flat, uncultivated island with saltmarshes, surrounded by a shallow sea with stony shoals, banks, and mudflats; includes the largest area of saltmarsh in Denmark outside Jylland.

Breeding birds include *Somateria mollissima* (5500 pairs), *Haematopus ostralegus* (650 pairs), *Recurvirostra avosetta* (60-120 pairs), *Philomachus pugnax*, *Larus marinus* (60 pairs), *Sterna paradisaea* (100-150 pairs), and *S. albifrons* (26 pairs). Important for waterfowl outside the breeding season with *Cygnus olor* (2300), *C. cygnus* (240), *Anser fabalis* (757), *Anser anser* (557), *Branta leucopsis* (2000), *Anas penelope* (8200), and *Pluvialis apricaria* (8000).

102 Vestamager and adjacent sea area (København)

55°35'N, 12°32'E 5300 ha EEC SPA

Nature Conservation Area (2000 ha); three Wildlife Reserves (*c*.3000 ha)

A shallow sea area and adjacent coast with saltmarshes; also includes a reclaimed area with freshwater lakes and reed-swamps.

Breeding species include *Circus aeruginosus*, *Haematopus ostralegus* (100 pairs), *Recurvirostra avosetta*, *Philomachus pugnax*, and *Sterna paradisaea* (200 pairs). Important for waterfowl outside the breeding season with *Phalacrocorax carbo sinensis* (260), *Cygnus olor* (1600), *Aythya fuligula* (20,000), *Mergus albellus* (400), *M. serrator* (2000), and *M. merganser* (1000). Also important for non-breeding raptors with *Haliaeetus albicilla*, *Circus cyaneus*, *Buteo lagopus* (80), *Aquila chrysaetos*, and *Falco columbarius*.

103 Vilsund and Stokkær Odde (Viborg)

56°50'N, 08°35'N 750 ha

Unprotected

A shallow fjord area with coastal saltmarsh and reed-swamp.

Breeding species include *Sterna paradisaea*. Important for waterfowl outside the breeding season with *Cygnus columbianus* (130), *Aythya ferina* (10,000), *A. fuligula* (9000), *Bucephala clangula* (3000), *Mergus serrator* (2100), *Recurvirostra avosetta* (400), and *Pluvialis apricaria* (10,000).

104 Klejtrup Sø (Viborg)

56°35'N, 09°40'E 150 ha

Unprotected

A freshwater lake surrounded by agricultural land and urban development.

Important for non-breeding *Mergus serrator* (1100) and *M. merganser* (1100).

105 Kalø and Ebeltoft Vig, including Hjelm and Begtrup Røn (Århus)

56°10'N, 10°20'E 25,000 ha

Wildlife Reserve (188 ha)

A shallow sea area with shoals, banks, and coastal saltmarsh. Some human habitation on islands. A moulting area for seaducks.

Breeding species include *Recurvirostra avosetta* (3-10 pairs), *Sterna sandvicensis* (11-13 pairs), *S. paradisaea* (10-15 pairs), and *Cepphus grylle* (2 pairs). Important for waterfowl outside the breeding season with *Phalacrocorax carbo sinensis* (383), *Aythya marila* (22,000), *Somateria mollissima* (25,000), and *Melanitta nigra* (7000).

106 Alssund and Augustenborg Fjord (Sønderjylland)

55°00'N, 09°35'E 7500 ha

Wildlife Reserve (62 ha)

A narrow strait and fjord area surrounded by agricultural land.

Breeding species include *Larus ridibundus* (7000 pairs), *L. canus* (2000 pairs), and *Sterna hirundo* (20 pairs). Important for non-breeding *Aythya marila* (2000).

107 Kalundborg Inderfjord (Vestsjælland)

55°40'N, 11°04'E 622 ha

Wildlife Reserve

A sea area in the inner part of Kalundborg Fjord, including Kalundborg harbour.
The area is important for waterfowl outside the breeding season with *Cygnus cygnus* (50) and *Aythya fuligula* (9000).

108 Sea area between Reersø and Røsnæs (Vestsjælland)

55°35'N, 11°10'E 20,000 ha

Unprotected

A shallow sea area with shoals and banks. A moulting area for *Somateria mollissima*, *Melanitta nigra*, and *M. fusca*.
Sterna paradisaea and *S. albifrons* breed on Reersø. The area holds important numbers of waterfowl outside the breeding season with *Somateria mollissima* (28,000) and *Melanitta nigra* (10,000).

109 Skarresø (Vestsjælland)

55°40'N, 11°20'E 200 ha

Unprotected

A freshwater lake surrounded by forest, with meadows on the western shore.
The area is important for non-breeding *Anser anser* (1200).

110 Damhussøen (København)

55°35'N, 12°30'E 35 ha

Unprotected

A freshwater lake in an urban area.
Important for wintering *Aythya fuligula* (6500-7500).

111 Møllesø and Gjorslev (Storstrøm)

55°25'N, 12°20'E 50 ha

Unprotected

A freshwater lake surrounded by agricultural land and forest.
Important for non-breeding *Anser anser* (1720).

112 Rønninge Søgård (Fyn)

55°20'N, 10°37'E 200 ha

Nature Conservation Area (Hindemæ: 110 ha)

A freshwater lake surrounded by meadows and agricultural land.
Non-breeding species include *Anser anser* (1000).

113 Lykkesholm (Fyn)

55°15'N, 10°36'E 200 ha

Unprotected

A freshwater lake with adjacent meadows and agricultural land.
Non-breeding species include *Anser anser* (1235).

114 Rosvang and Sjørring Sø (Viborg)

56°57'N, 08°34'E 400 ha

Unprotected

Mainly arable land with a few small meadows; a former lake, now drained.

Important for waterfowl outside the breeding season with *Cygnus cygnus* (200), *Anser fabalis* (680), *A. anser* (300), *Pluvialis apricaria* (7000), and *Vanellus vanellus* (10,000).

115 Karup Å (Viborg)

56°28'N, 08°58'E 500 ha

Nature Conservation Area (500 ha)

A river valley with grazed meadows, scrub, and moorland.

Breeding species include *Ciconia ciconia* (1 pair), *Anas crecca*, *A. querquedula*, *Circus aeruginosus*, *Gallinago gallinago*, *Numenius arquata*, *Tringa totanus*, *T. glareola* (3-5 pairs), and *Alcedo atthis* (1-2 pairs).

116 Skjern Å (Ringkøbing, Vejle)

56°56'N, 08°30'E 3850 ha

Unprotected

A river valley with meadows, marshes, and moorland. Although the river has been extensively canalised, the meadows are still important for breeding ducks and waders.

Breeding species include *Anas crecca*, *A. querquedula*, *Circus aeruginosus*, *Crex crex*, *Gallinago gallinago*, *Numenius arquata*, *Tringa totanus*, *T. glareola* (3-5 pairs), *Asio flammeus*, and *Alcedo atthis* (5-10 pairs). Non-breeding species include *Ciconia ciconia*, *Cygnus columbianus* (700), and *C. cygnus* (100).

117 Gudenå, Nørreå and Skals Å (Viborg, Århus)

56°24'N, 09°50'E

Nature Conservation Area (1000 ha)

River valleys with marshes, lakes, and large meadows grazed by cattle. The largest river system in Denmark.

Very important for breeding ducks and waders. Breeding species include *Podiceps cristatus* (250 pairs), *Ciconia ciconia* (2 pairs), *Anas querquedula* (5-10 pairs), *Circus aeruginosus* (3-5 pairs), and *Crex crex*.

118 Ryå near Store Vildmose (Nordjylland)

57°14'N, 09°43'E

Unprotected

An area of extensive meadows (flooded in winter) with cattle-grazing and hay production in summer.

Breeding species include *Crex crex* (0-10 pairs; irregular), *Vanellus vanellus*, *Gallinago gallinago*, *Numenius arquata*, and *Tringa totanus*.

MAIN REFERENCES

Bøgebjerg, B. (1986) Spættet sæl (Phoca vitulina) i Danmark 1976-1984. Danske Vildtundersøgelser, hæfte 42.

Brøgger-Jensen, S. and Falk, K. (1988) Overvågning af EF-fuglebeskyttelsesområder 1987. Skov-og Naturstyrelsen & Vildtforvaltningen.

Danielsen, F., Durinck, J. and Skov, H. (1986) Biological and environmental conditions in the Danish sector of the Wadden Sea with reference to oil spill impact. Annex A: Atlas of Birds. Preliminary determination of areas important to water birds with assessment of sensitivity to oil Production. København: Mærsk Oil and Gas A/S, Environment & Safety Department.

Dybbro, T. *et al.* (1983) Dansk Ornitologisk Forenings lokaliteseregistreringer. Amtsrapporter udgivet af Dansk Ornitologisk Forening.

Dybbro, T. (1985) *Status for Danske Fuglelokaliteter*. København: Dansk Ornitologisk Forening.

Eskildsen, J. (1986) Vandfugle På Samsø Øster Flak. Flytællinger juli 1984 – juli 1985. Rapport nr. 5, Vildtbiologisk Station.

Fredningsstyrelsen (1981-1984) Vejlerne. Årsrapport over observationer 1981-1984. Miljøministeriet.

Fredningsstyrelsen (1983) EF-fuglebeskyttelsesområder. Kortlægning og foreløbig udpegning i henhold til EF-fuglebeskyttelsesdirektivet. Miljøministeriet.

Joensen, A. H. (1974) Waterfowl populations in Denmark 1965-1973. *Danish Review of Game Biology* 9(1).

Laursen, K. (1987) Fældende dykænder i danske farvande 1985 og 1986 samt oplysninger om skarv og knopsvane. Rapport nr. 9, Vildtbiologisk Station.

Laursen, K. and Frikke, J. (in press) Surveys of waterfowl and gulls in the Danish Wadden Sea 1980-1983. Numbers, phenology and distribution in relation to tidal cycles and season. Vildtbiologisk Station.

Laursen, K., Rasmussen, L. M. and Frikke, J. (1986) International bird countings in the Danish Wadden Sea 1981-1986. Game Biology Station – Dansk Ornitologisk Forening.

Madsen, J. (1986a) Forsøgsreservater: Projektbeskrivelse og foreløbige resultater. Rapport nr. 8, Vildtbiologisk Station.

Madsen, J. (1986b) Danske rastepladser for gæs. Gåsetællinger 1980-1983. Fredningsstyrelsen, Miljøministeriet.

Madsen, J. and Laursen, K. (1985) Optælling af havfugle i det sydlige Kattegat, juni og juli 1985 i forbindelse med olieefterforskning. Rapport nr. 9, Vildtbiologisk Station.

Meltofte, H. (1980) Fugle i Vadehavet. Vadefugletællinger i Vadehavet 1974-1978. Fredningsstyrelsen, Miljøministeriet.

Meltofte, H. (1981) Danske rastepladser for vadefugle. Vadefugletællinger i Danmark 1974-1978. Fredningsstyrelsen, Miljøministeriet.

Scott, D. A. (1980) *Wetlands of international importance for waterfowl in Denmark*. Slimbridge: International Waterfowl Research Bureau.

Søgaard, B. (1985) Vildtreservaterne og vandfuglene. Vandfugletællinger i vildtreservaterne 1976-1984 (The wildlife reserves and the waterfowl. Waterfowl counts in the wildlife reserves 1976--1984). Vildtreservatkontoret, Landbrugsministeriets Vildtforvaltning.

Sørensen, U. G. and Dybbro, T. (1985) Counts of birds on 50 Danish EEC-localities and annual statements on a number of annex 1 species from the EEC-directive on the protection of wild birds. København: Dansk Ornithologisk Forening.

FAROE ISLANDS

INTRODUCTION

General information

The Faroe Islands (Føroyar) are a group of 18 islands in the north-east Atlantic at about 62°00'N and 07°00'W. The total area is 1399 sq km and the topography is dominated by mountains up to 882 m in height. The human population is 47,650 (in 1989) with an average population density of 34 persons per sq km.

The base rock is basalt, which is only partly covered by a thin and stony soil. The main vegetation is grass, with scattered areas of moor, but around the villages there are cultivated hayfields, gardens with trees, and a few small woods. There are many ponds and a few lakes, some of which are surrounded by peatbogs. The coasts are rugged with steep grass-covered slopes, and (especially on the north and west sides), the cliffs are very steep with boulder screes. Throughout the islands, sheep are grazed all year round; some areas are also grazed by cattle during the summer.

Ornithological importance

In all, more than 250 bird species have been recorded in the islands, but most of these are rare or irregular visitors, with only about 50 species breeding regularly.

Inland, species diversity is low (Bloch and Sørensen 1984), and the only species of international interest are the *c.*210 pairs of *Stercorarius skua* (which has a limited global range), and 10-15 pairs of *Gavia stellata*, breeding on some lakes.

The productive waters around the islands provide important foraging areas for seabirds all year round, and the steep cliffs, grass-covered slopes, and boulder screes facing the sea form ideal nesting sites. The only seabirds that have been censused are *Sula bassana* (Wanless 1987), *Uria aalge* (Dyck and Meltofte 1975, Olsen unpublished), and *Rissa tridactyla* (Olsen unpublished), although E. Mortensen and B. Olsen have estimated the sizes of the other populations. The most numerous species are *Fulmarus glacialis* (600,000 pairs), *Fratercula arctica* (550,000 pairs), *Hydrobates pelagicus* (250,000 pairs), *Rissa tridactyla* (230,000 pairs), and *Uria aalge* (175,000 pairs).

There has been a dramatic decline in the population of *Uria aalge* since the late 1950s (Dyck and Meltofte 1975, Olsen 1982, 1986), and the population of *Rissa tridactyla* has also been declining, but is now increasing again. The *Fulmarus glacialis* population has been increasing since colonisation 150 years ago, and the species is now the most numerous bird in the islands.

During the next few years hydrocarbon exploration will be carried out in Faroese waters. This may have consequences for the island's seabird populations.

Conservation infrastructure and protected-area system

According to the island's game legislation all birds are protected from hunting within the 200-nautical-mile fishing limit, except the following: *Fulmarus glacialis*, *Puffinus puffinus*, *Sula bassana*, *Phalacrocorax aristotelis*, *Stercorarius parasiticus*, *S. skua*, Laridae, *Uria aalge*, *Alca torda*, *Fratercula arctica*, *Corvus corone*, and *C. corax*.

The main quarry species is *Fulmarus glacialis* which can be hunted all year round. *Phalacrocorax aristotelis*, *Uria aalge*, *Alca torda*, *Fratercula arctica*, and young of *Puffinus puffinus* and *Sula bassana* are also hunted, but in restricted periods.

A recommendation for new game legislation is being discussed, which gives hope for improved conservation of the very important bird areas listed in this inventory.

International measures relevant to the conservation of sites

The Faroes are a self-governing region of the Kingdom of Denmark. Unlike mainland Denmark, the islands are not covered by the Bern Convention, or World Heritage Convention, nor the EEC Wild Birds Directive, but the Faroes, as part of Denmark, are covered by the Bonn Convention and the Ramsar Convention although no Ramsar Sites have been designated.

Overview of the inventory

Nineteen sites have been included. Of these, 18 have been included largely because of their breeding seabird populations (two of the 18 sites also have important breeding wader populations). One site (015) is included because it is outstanding for breeding waders. The huge seabird colonies are of major international importance. These areas are not protected as nature reserves/bird sanctuaries, although they are not currently threatened. Any exploitation must be approved by the island's Nature Conservancy Tribunal, and the shooting of birds closer than three nautical miles from *Uria aalge* colonies and half a nautical mile from *Fratercula arctica* colonies is forbidden.

No important sea areas are included. Ship-based surveys of the marine distribution of seabirds around the Faroes are currently being undertaken. A preliminary analysis has shown that the area between Suduroy and the Faroe Bank is of considerable importance for moulting *Uria aalge*; other important areas will be identified soon.

Acknowledgements

The site descriptions were compiled from information provided by B. Olsen (all seabird sites) and D. Bloch (Føroya Náttúrugripasavn [Museum of Natural History]). B. Olsen prepared the introduction.

INVENTORY

No.	Site name	Criteria used to select site [see p.18]							
		0	1(i)	1(ii)	1(iii)	1(iv)	2	3	4
001	Mykines and Mykineshólmur		*	*				*	
002	Vágar *		*	*				*	
003	Streymoy *		*	*				*	
004	Eysturoy *		*	*				*	
005	Kalsoy *		*	*				*	
006	Kunoy *							*	
007	Bordoy *							*	
008	Vidoy *			*				*	
009	Fugloy		*	*				*	
010	Svínoy *		*	*				*	
011	Nólsoy		*	*				*	
012	Koltur *		*	*				*	
013	Hestur *		*	*				*	
014	Sandoy *		*	*				*	
015	Vøtnini á Sandoy							*	
016	Skúvoy		*	*				*	
017	Stóra Dímun		*	*				*	
018	Lítla Dímun		*	*				*	
019	Suduroy *		*	*				*	

* alongside the site name = Seabird colonies only

Comments on the inventory

1. The breeding populations (at each site) of *Fulmarus glacialis*, *Puffinus puffinus*, *Oceanodroma leucorhoa*, *Phalacrocorax aristotelis*, *Alca torda*, *Cepphus grylle*, and

Fratercula arctica are believed to be accurate to ± 75 per cent of the figure given. Population figures for *Sula bassana, Stercorarius parasiticus, S. skua* and *Rissa tridactyla* are believed to be accurate to ± 25 per cent of the figure given. *Hydrobates pelagicus* populations are believed to be accurate to ± 75 per cent of the figure given, except at site numbers 003, 004, 006 and 007 (± 100 per cent).

2. Throughout the text, an * alongside the site name indicates that the site only comprises the seabird colonies (see map).
3. The Faroe Islands have been treated as a single 'region' when applying the site-selection criteria (category 3).
4. The coordinates given for the site refer to the centre of the island rather than the location of the seabird colony.

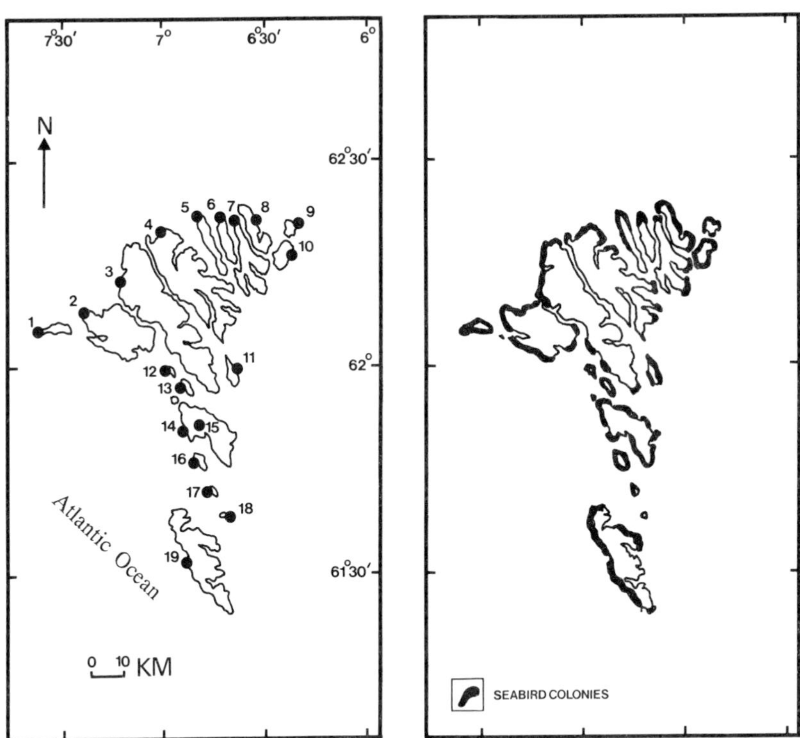

Figure 9: Map showing the location of the sites in the Faroe Islands

---

001 Mykines and Mykineshólmur

62°06'N, 07°37'W 1028 ha

Protected by game legislation

An island and islet with rugged coasts, steep cliffs, and grass-covered slopes. Land-uses include sheep-grazing.

Important for breeding seabirds with *Fulmarus glacialis* (50,000 pairs), *Puffinus puffinus* (2500 pairs), *Hydrobates pelagicus* (50,000 pairs), *Oceanodroma leucorhoa* (500 pairs), *Sula bassana* (2000 pairs), *Phalacrocorax aristotelis* (250 pairs), *Stercorarius parasiticus* (50 pairs), *S. skua* (2 pairs), *Rissa tridactyla* (23,100 pairs), *Sterna paradisaea* (50-500 pairs), *Uria aalge* (9500 birds), *Alca torda* (950 birds), *Cepphus grylle* (200 pairs), and *Fratercula arctica* (125,000 pairs).

002 Vágar *

62°05'N, 07°15'W 175 ha

Protected by game legislation

An island and two islets with rugged coasts and steep grass-covered slopes. Land-uses include sheep-grazing. The site comprises the seabird colonies that are mainly on the north-west, west and south-west coasts.

Important for breeding seabirds with *Fulmarus glacialis* (100,000 pairs), *Puffinus puffinus* (500 pairs), *Hydrobates pelagicus* (5000 pairs), *Phalacrocorax aristotelis* (500 pairs), *Stercorarius skua* (20 pairs), *Rissa tridactyla* (8400 pairs), *Sterna paradisaea* (50-500 pairs), *Uria aalge* (2700 birds), *Alca torda* (700 birds), *Cepphus grylle* (400 pairs), and *Fratercula arctica* (40,000 pairs).

003 Streymoy *

62°08'N, 07°00'W 125 ha

Protected by game legislation

An island with rugged coasts, steep cliffs, boulder screes, and grass slopes. Land-uses include sheep-grazing. The site comprises the seabird colonies that are mainly on the north-west coast.

Important for breeding seabirds with *Fulmarus glacialis* (75,000 pairs), *Puffinus puffinus* (500 pairs), *Hydrobates pelagicus* (2500 pairs), *Phalacrocorax aristotelis* (150 pairs), *Stercorarius skua* (120 pairs), *Rissa tridactyla* (9000 pairs), *Sterna paradisaea* (100-1000 pairs), *Uria aalge* (16,300 birds), *Alca torda* (1000 birds), *Cepphus grylle* (300 pairs), and *Fratercula arctica* (20,000 pairs).

004 Eysturoy *

62°13'N, 06°55'W 60 ha

Protected by game legislation

An island with rugged coasts, steep cliffs, boulder screes and grass slopes. Land-uses include sheep-grazing. The site comprises the seabird colonies that are on the north, north-east, and south-east coasts.

Important for breeding seabirds with *Fulmarus glacialis* (25,000 pairs), *Puffinus puffinus* (2500 pairs), *Hydrobates pelagicus* (500 pairs), *Phalacrocorax aristotelis* (50 pairs), *Rissa tridactyla* (4600 pairs), *Sterna paradisaea* (100-1000 pairs), *Uria aalge* (11,100 birds), *Alca torda* (350 birds), *Cepphus grylle* (300 pairs), and *Fratercula arctica* (5000 pairs).

005 Kalsoy *

62°18'N, 06°45'W 50 ha

Protected by game legislation

An island with rugged coasts, steep cliffs, boulder screes, and grass slopes. Land-uses include sheep-grazing. The site comprises the coastline of the northern half of the island.

Important for breeding seabirds with *Fulmarus glacialis* (25,000 pairs), *Puffinus puffinus* (500 pairs), *Hydrobates pelagicus* (5000 pairs), *Phalacrocorax aristotelis* (50 pairs), *Rissa tridactyla* (15,600 pairs), *Sterna paradisaea* (50-500 pairs), *Uria aalge* (10,700 birds), *Alca torda* (150 birds), *Cepphus grylle* (200 pairs), and *Fratercula arctica* (40,000 pairs).

006 Kunoy *

62°18'N, 06°40'W 20 ha

Protected by game legislation

An island with rugged coasts, steep cliffs, boulder screes, and grass slopes. Land-uses include sheep-grazing. The site comprises the coastline of the northern tip of the island.

Important for breeding seabirds with *Fulmarus glacialis* (15,000 pairs), *Puffinus puffinus* (250 pairs), *Hydrobates pelagicus* (250 pairs), *Phalacrocorax aristotelis* (50 pairs), *Sterna paradisaea* (50-500 pairs), *Cepphus grylle* (200 pairs), and *Fratercula arctica* (5000 pairs).

007 Bordoy *

62°15'N, 06°32'W 35 ha

Protected by game legislation

An island with rugged coasts, steep cliffs, boulder screes, and grass slopes. Land-uses include sheep-grazing. The site comprises the seabird colonies of the northern and south-eastern headlands.

Important for breeding seabirds with *Fulmarus glacialis* (5000 pairs), *Puffinus puffinus* (50 pairs), *Hydrobates pelagicus* (250 pairs), *Stercorarius skua* (5 pairs), *Sterna paradisaea* (50-500 pairs), *Cepphus grylle* (200 pairs), and *Fratercula arctica* (500 pairs).

008 Vidoy *

62°19'N, 06°30'W 75 ha

Protected by game legislation

An island with rugged coast, steep cliffs, boulder screes, and grass slopes. Land-uses include sheep-grazing. The site comprises the seabird colonies along the northern and eastern sides of the island.

Important for breeding seabirds with *Fulmarus glacialis* (25,000 pairs), *Puffinus puffinus* (500 pairs), *Hydrobates pelagicus* (500 pairs), *Phalacrocorax aristotelis* (50 pairs), *Stercorarius skua* (2 pairs), *Rissa tridactyla* (5300 pairs), *Sterna paradisaea* (50-500 pairs), *Uria aalge* (6700 birds), *Alca torda* (50 birds), *Cepphus grylle* (200 pairs), and *Fratercula arctica* (25,000 pairs).

009 Fugloy

62°20'N, 06°18'W 1118 ha

Protected by game legislation

An island with rugged coasts, steep cliffs, boulder screes, and grass slopes. Also moorland areas to 600 m. Land-uses include sheep-grazing.

Important for breeding seabirds with *Fulmarus glacialis* (15,000 pairs), *Puffinus puffinus* (50 pairs), *Hydrobates pelagicus* (25,000 pairs), *Phalacrocorax aristotelis* (100 pairs), *Stercorarius parasiticus* (65 pairs), *S. skua* (2 pairs), *Rissa tridactyla* (2500 pairs), *Sterna paradisaea* (50-500 pairs), *Uria aalge* (23,700 birds), *Alca torda* (1000 birds), *Cepphus grylle* (100 pairs), and *Fratercula arctica* (15,000 pairs). Also important for breeding waders with *Haematopus ostralegus* (100 pairs), *Pluvialis apricaria* (30 pairs), and *Numenius phaeopus* (50 pairs), The island also supports an extraordinarily high density of *Oenanthe oenanthe* and *Troglodytes troglodytes*, and is one of the few known breeding sites for *Plectrophenax nivalis* (1-3 pairs) in the Faroes.

010 Svínoy *

62°15'N, 06°25'W 100 ha

Protected by game legislation

An island with rugged coasts, steep cliffs, boulder screes, and grass slopes. Land-uses include sheep-grazing. The site comprises the seabird colonies that surround the island.

Important for breeding seabirds with *Fulmarus glacialis* (25,000 pairs), *Puffinus puffinus* (500 pairs), *Hydrobates pelagicus* (25,000 pairs), *Phalacrocorax aristotelis* (50 pairs), *Stercorarius skua* (8 pairs), *Rissa tridactyla* (50 pairs), *Sterna paradisaea* (50-500 pairs), *Cepphus grylle* (100 pairs), and *Fratercula arctica* (10,000 pairs).

011 Nólsoy

61°59'N, 06°38'W 1028 ha

Protected by game legislation

An island with rugged coasts, steep cliffs, boulder screes, and grass slopes with important seabird colonies. Inland there are heath and moorland areas. Land-uses include sheep-grazing.

Important for breeding seabirds with *Fulmarus glacialis* (10,000 pairs), *Puffinus puffinus* (500 pairs), *Hydrobates pelagicus* (50,000 pairs), *Stercorarius skua* (2 pairs), *Rissa tridactyla* (850 pairs), *Sterna paradisaea* (100-1000 pairs), *Cepphus grylle* (100 pairs), and *Fratercula arctica* (30,000 pairs). Other breeding species include *Gavia stellata* (1 pair), *Haematopus ostralegus* (200 pairs), *Gallinago gallinago* (60 pairs), and *Phalaropus lobatus* (1-3 pairs).

012 Koltur *

62°00'N, 06°59'W 30 ha

Protected by game legislation

An island with rugged coasts, steep cliffs, boulder screes, and grass slopes. Land-uses include sheep-grazing. The site comprises the seabird colonies that almost surround the island.

Important for breeding seabirds with *Fulmarus glacialis* (10,000 pairs), *Puffinus puffinus* (500 pairs), *Hydrobates pelagicus* (5000 pairs), *Stercorarius skua* (1 pair), *Sterna paradisaea* (10-100 pairs), *Cepphus grylle* (50 pairs), and *Fratercula arctica* (20,000 pairs).

013 Hestur *

61°58'N, 06°50'W 50 ha

Protected by game legislation

An island with rugged coasts, steep cliffs, boulder screes, and grass slopes. Land-uses include sheep-grazing. The site comprises the seabird colonies that almost surround the island.

Important for breeding seabirds with *Fulmarus glacialis* (15,000 pairs), *Puffinus puffinus* (250 pairs), *Hydrobates pelagicus* (5000 pairs), *Phalacrocorax aristotelis* (50 pairs), *Rissa tridactyla* (26,100 pairs), *Sterna paradisaea* (20-200 pairs), *Uria aalge* (2300 birds), *Cepphus grylle* (50 pairs), and *Fratercula arctica* (25,000 pairs).

014 Sandoy *

61°51'N, 06°48'W 250 ha

Protected by game legislation

An island with rugged coasts, steep cliffs, boulder screes, and grass slopes. Land-uses include sheep-grazing. The site comprises the seabird colonies that almost surround the island.

Important for breeding seabirds with *Fulmarus glacialis* (50,000 pairs), *Puffinus puffinus* (5000 pairs), *Hydrobates pelagicus* (50,000 pairs), *Phalacrocorax aristotelis* (150 pairs), *Stercorarius skua* (15 pairs), *Rissa tridactyla* (20,500 pairs), *Sterna paradisaea* (50-500 pairs), *Uria aalge* (29,500 birds), *Alca torda* (500 birds), *Cepphus grylle* (400 pairs), and *Fratercula arctica* (70,000 pairs).

015 Vøtnini á Sandoy (Lakes of Sandoy)

61°50'N, 06°49'W c.1000 ha

Protected by game legislation

Includes the lowland areas around Sandur with moorland and peat bogs, and the lakes Gróthúsvatn, Sandsvatn, Stóravatn, and Lítlavatn. There is hay cultivation and sheep-grazing.

An outstanding area for breeding waders (with very high densities of the commoner species) with *Haematopus ostralegus* (200-400 pairs), *Pluvialis apricaria* (20-30 pairs), *Numenius phaeopus* (100-150 pairs), *Tringa totanus* (4-6 pairs; one of the few places in the Faroes), and *Phalaropus lobatus* (15-20 pairs; a high proportion of the Faroes' population). Other breeding species include *Gavia stellata* (1-2 pairs).

016 Skúvoy

61°46'N, 06°50'W 999 ha

Protected by game legislation

An island with rugged coasts, steep cliffs, boulder screes, and coastal grass slopes. Land-uses include sheep-grazing.

Important for breeding seabirds with *Fulmarus glacialis* (50,000 pairs), *Puffinus puffinus* (10,000 pairs), *Hydrobates pelagicus* (20,000 pairs), *Phalacrocorax aristotelis* (50 pairs), *Stercorarius parasiticus* (100 pairs), *S. skua* (25 pairs), *Rissa tridactyla* (22,900 pairs), *Sterna paradisaea* (10-100 pairs), *Uria aalge* (135,300 birds), *Alca torda* (2300 birds), *Cepphus grylle* (150 pairs), and *Fratercula arctica* (40,000 pairs). Other breeding species include *Haematopus ostralegus* (120 pairs), *Pluvialis apricaria* (40 pairs), *Calidris maritima* (3-5 pairs; rare in the Faroes), *Gallinago gallinago* (50 pairs), and *Numenius phaeopus* (40 pairs).

017 Stóra Dímun

61°42'N, 06°45'W 265 ha

Protected by game legislation

A small island with rugged coasts, steep cliffs, boulder screes, and grass slopes. Land-uses include sheep-grazing.

Important for breeding seabirds with *Fulmarus glacialis* (15,000 pairs), *Puffinus puffinus* (250 pairs), *Hydrobates pelagicus* (15,000 pairs), *Phalacrocorax aristotelis* (100 pairs), *Stercorarius skua* (1 pair), *Rissa tridactyla* (36,900 pairs), *Uria aalge* (29,600 birds), *Alca torda* (450 birds), *Cepphus grylle* (50 pairs), and *Fratercula arctica* (40,000 pairs).

018 Lítla Dímun

61°38'N, 06°43'W 82 ha

Protected by game legislation

A small island with rugged coasts, steep cliffs, boulder screes, and grass slopes. Land-uses include sheep-grazing.

Important for breeding seabirds with *Fulmarus glacialis* (2000 pairs), *Puffinus puffinus* (50 pairs), *Hydrobates pelagicus* (5000 pairs), *Phalacrocorax aristotelis* (25 pairs), *Rissa tridactyla* (13,100 pairs), *Uria aalge* (6200 birds), *Alca torda* (50 birds), *Cepphus grylle* (25 pairs), and *Fratercula arctica* (10,000 pairs).

019 Suduroy *

61°31'N, 06°50'W 200 ha

Protected by game legislation

An island with rugged coasts, steep cliffs, boulder screes, and grass slopes. The site comprises the seabird colonies that are mainly along the western side of the island.

Important for breeding seabirds with breeding *Fulmarus glacialis* (100,000 pairs), *Puffinus puffinus* (250 pairs), *Hydrobates pelagicus* (2500 pairs), *Phalacrocorax aristotelis* (200 pairs), *Stercorarius skua* (7 pairs), *Rissa tridactyla* (39,200 pairs), *Sterna paradisaea* (100-1000 pairs), *Uria aalge* (31,900 birds), *Alca torda* (350 birds), *Cepphus grylle* (400 pairs), and *Fratercula arctica* (20,000 pairs).

MAIN REFERENCES

Bloch, D. and Sørensen, S. (1984) *Checklist of Faroese birds.* Tórshavn, Føroya Skúlabókagrunnur.

Dyck, J. and Meltofte, H. (1975) The Guillemot *Uria aalge* population of the Faroes 1972. *Dansk Orn. Foren. Tidsskr.* 69: 55-64.

Joensen, A. H. (1966) *Fuglene på Færøerne* (The birds on the Faroe Islands). Rhodos, København.

Nørrevang, A. (1977) *Fuglefangsten på Færøerne* (Bird-catching in the Faroe Islands). Rhodos, København.

Olsen, B. and Permin, M. (1974) Bestanden av Sule *Sula bassana* på Mykineshólmur 1972 (The population of Gannet *Sula bassana* on Mykineshólmur 1972). *Dansk Orn. Foren. Tidsskr.* 68: 39-42 (English summary).

Olsen, B. (1982) Nogle årsager til nedgangen i den færøske lomviebestand vurderet ud fra mønsteret i tilbagegangen og ringmærkningsresultater (Some of the reasons for the decline of the Faroese Guillemot population as revealed by the pattern of the decline and ringing results). *Viltrapport* 21: 24-30.

Olsen, B. (1986) Stødan hjá tí føroyska lomviga- og álkustovninum (Status of the Faroese Guillemot and Razorbill population). Tórshavn, Report distributed by the Fisheries Laboratory.

Wanless, S. (1987) A survey of the numbers and breeding distribution of the North Atlantic Gannet *Sula bassana* and an assessment of the changes which have occurred since Operation Seafarer 1969/70. Nature Conservation Series no. 4.

GREENLAND

Brunnich's Guillemot *Uria lomvia*

INTRODUCTION

General information

Greenland covers some 2.2 million sq km. It is part of the Danish kingdom, although the country obtained autonomy over most of its domestic affairs in 1979 with the Greenland Home Rule Act. Many Danes have settled in Greenland, as administrators, skilled workers, teachers, etc., although the native people and their language are of Inuit origin. Officially, and in practice, the country is bilingual. The population has increased rapidly this century and now amounts to about 53,000 people.

West Greenland is divided into 15 'kommuner' (municipalities), each of which contains a town and a number of smaller settlements; 90 per cent of the population lives in this area. In East Greenland there are two 'kommuner' with around 3300 people, and in North Greenland one 'kommune' (Avanersuaq or Thule) with less than 800 people. Most of the rest of North and East Greenland is uninhabited (apart from a couple of weather stations and the *Sirius*-patrol) and exists outside the municipality system.

Some 80 per cent of Greenland's land surface is covered by ice. However, an ice-free zone of some 384,000 sq km borders the coast. It is generally quite narrow, but broadens to 200-300 km in central West Greenland, at Scoresby Sound in East Greenland, and in Peary Land (North Greenland).

Throughout Greenland, the country is much influenced by sea ice. Polar basin ice blocks the north and north-east coast permanently and pack ice regularly drifts south along the east coast, forming an extensive belt. During spring and summer, this 'storis' ('big ice') drifts around Kap Farvel and northwards along West Greenland, usually to 61-62°N, but in some years as far as 65°N.

The country is underlain by bedrock of Precambrian origin, which is exposed in almost all of West and East Greenland, but covered by younger volcanic or sedimentary rock in some places, including most of North Greenland. The landscape is mountainous with lowlands effectively confined to the coastal zone and to valley floors.

The climate is Arctic, but given the island's north-south extension of 2670 km (from 59°46' – 83°40'N), there is some variation. South of Melville Bay in the west, and the Blosseville coast in the east, the climate is low-Arctic, while it is high-Arctic to the north of this line. The transition between low- and high-Arctic is gradual, but generally the low-Arctic areas are rather humid, and experience extended summers, while precipitation is low or very low and the growth season is short in the high-Arctic. In the extreme south, shielded inland valleys may be characterised as subarctic.

In most high-Arctic and/or alpine areas, the vegetation is very sparse. Much of low-Arctic Greenland is covered by dwarf-shrub heaths; extensive *Salix* shrubs reach heights of about 1 m in more sheltered places; and in the subarctic, so-called *Betula* 'woods' occur, reaching a height of 2-4 m. All over Greenland, it is only along lakes, streams, and in marshy areas, that the vegetation is relatively luxuriant: such areas often form biological 'oases'.

Apart from sheep-farming in South Greenland and haymaking in a few places, no agriculture takes place.

Originally, the Inuit people were hunters, and for people in the 'outer districts' (North, East and parts of West Greenland), subsistence hunting is still their main occupation. They are green-card permit holders, a status which entitles them to hunt traditionally. Almost all male Greenlanders do some hunting; either as a secondary occupation (red-card permit holders) or for sport. Harpoons and kayaks are giving way to firearms and powered boats.

Ornithological importance

The avifaunas of high- and low-Arctic Greenland differ, with the former occurring almost throughout East and North Greenland, and the latter in West Greenland. Throughout, species diversity is low, with both zones harbouring an impoverished mixture of Pale-arctic and Nearctic high-latitude faunas (and some endemic subspecies). In the Thule area, Nearctic forms are more strongly represented, particularly waterfowl and waders (e.g. *Anser caerulescens*, *Calidris bairdii*). Seabirds, both offshore feeders like auks and inshore/coastal feeders like gulls and seaducks, are much more numerous in the low-Arctic than in the truly high-Arctic zone.

Twenty species of seabird breed in Greenland, mainly on the west coast. The region supports over 80 per cent of the world population of *Alle alle*, and large populations of *Fulmarus glacialis*, *Rissa tridactyla*, *Uria lomvia*, and *Cepphus grylle*. In addition, three species of Laridae (*Larus sabini*, *Rhodostethia rosea*, *Pagophila eburnea*) breed here and, apart from Svalbard, nowhere else in the region covered by this book.

Compared with the rest of Europe, Greenland has large breeding populations of *Gavia immer*, *Anser albifrons flavirostris* (breeding only here), *Anser brachyrhynchus*, *Branta leucopsis* (all goose species stop-over on passage in Iceland and winter almost entirely in the United Kingdom and Ireland), *Falco rusticolus*, *Phalaropus fulicarius*, and *Nyctea scandiaca*. Greenland's population of *Haliaeetus albicilla* is also significant. The country supports large populations of breeding waders, including *Charadrius hiaticula*, *Calidris canutus*, *C. alpina*, and *Arenaria interpres*, that winter in Europe, or migrate along the Atlantic seaboard to winter along the western coast of Africa.

The combination of increased human population, increased mobility, and modern firearms has led to local depletion of seabird populations. In particular, *Uria lomvia* has proved vulnerable owing to its concentration at a few, large breeding colonies; although even *Somateria mollissima* has experienced a widespread decline this century.

Conservation infrastructure and protected-area system

Bird hunting was largely uncontrolled until 1978, when general regulations were introduced in West Greenland. Since people's knowledge of these rules has been poor, their effect has been slight. However, they were revised and extended to all of Greenland in 1988 and a public information campaign was initiated. It is still too early to tell how effectively these steps will increase protection for the most vulnerable bird populations.

The rules now prohibit all shooting and other disturbance within 200 m of breeding colonies of gulls and terns, and within 5 km of bird cliffs with *Rissa tridactyla*, *Uria lomvia*, and other seabird species. The present rules prohibit hunting of all birds in West Greenland between 1 June and 15 August with extended closed seasons for some species. All shooting and other necessary disturbance is prohibited. Moreover, some areas, including bird cliffs, have been declared Breeding Reserves for Birds, where no trespassing or traffic within 500 m is allowed between 1 June and 31 August.

Most of the uninhabited parts of Greenland are gazetted as a National Park, with strict regulations on human activities and prohibition of hunting (except traditional hunting by inhabitants of Thule and Scoresbysund). The North-east Greenland National Park (the largest in the world) was established in 1974, comprising all of East and North Greenland north of approximately 72°N and west of approximately 62°W.

In 1980, the coast and islands of Melville Bay acquired similar status, as a National Wildlife Reserve.

International measures relevant to the conservation of sites

Recently, the Greenland Home Rule designated 11 Ramsar Sites. In addition, the North-east Greenland National Park has been declared a Biosphere Reserve, under UNESCO's Man and the Biosphere Programme. Unlike mainland Denmark, Greenland is not covered by the World Heritage Convention, Bonn Convention, Bern Convention, or by the EEC Wild Birds Directive.

Overview of the inventory

There are 65 sites in the Greenland inventory, of which 25 or more have been included (at least partly) for breeding or moulting/passage geese, and at least 30 have been included because of breeding seabirds.

The inventory includes all 11 of the country's Ramsar Sites (covering a total area of 1,044,000 million ha); ten sites are part of the North-east Greenland National Park and Biosphere Reserve (including two of the Ramsar Sites), and eight are Breeding Reserves for Birds. However, 38 sites are not covered by any protected area status (although some protection is provided by the hunting regulations).

Few areas of major importance to birds are threatened by urbanisation, mining activities, planned hydroelectric development, etc. Due to the small human population and the widespread distribution of most bird species, this is likely to hold true in the foreseeable future. Only in the case of the current oil-exploration activities in Jameson Land has some concern been expressed, and this is because of the extreme sensitivity of moulting geese to disturbance. If, however, oil is discovered, and shipped out in the future, the polynia (open water amongst sea ice) at the entrance to Scoresby Sound entrance and the nearby colonies of *Uria lomvia* and *Alle alle* would be at risk from accidents.

The principal threats to Greenland bird populations are disturbance and hunting, and these chiefly concern species with slow population turn-overs, such as seabirds and geese.

Acknowledgements

The following inventory was compiled from data-sheets completed by D. Boertmann, K. Kampp and H. Meltofte of the Danish Ornithological Society (DOF), and by B. Søgaard and P. U. Jepsen of the Ministry of Agriculture's Wildlife Administration, together with information provided by P. G. H. Evans. The individuals mentioned also contributed valuable follow-up advice and background material. A. Fox (Wildfowl Trust) also helped by providing information about sites for *Anser albifrons flavirostris*. K. Kampp prepared the introduction.

INVENTORY

No.	Site name	Region	Criteria used to select site [see pp.18] 0	1(i)	1(ii)	1(iii)	1(iv)	2	3	4
001	Myggbukta					*			*	
002	Østersletten and Knudshoved					*			*	
003	Tobias Dal								*	
004	Stordal – Moskusoksefjord – Badlanddal – Loch Fyne					*			*	
005	Hochstetter Forland					*			*	
006	Shannon								*	
007	Hvalrosodden – Slamodden								*	
008	Flade Bugt								*	*
009	Danmarks Havn and surrounding area, including Skibsso								*	
010	Kilen					*			*	
011	Ørsted Dal and Coloradodal					*			*	
012	River valleys entering Fleming Fjord					*			*	
013	Kjoveland					*			*	
014	Hurry Fjord including Fame Øer and Kap Stewart					*			*	
015	Nuna masarsuttalik Jameson Land – imiittoq kitaanittoq	II				*			*	
016	Liverpool Land coast and Scoresbysund			*	*				*	
017	Kap Brewster and Volquart Boon's Coast			*	*				*	
018	Kitsissut Avalliit	QQ							*	
019	Foxfaldet, Ilorput	PT							*	
020	Ikkattoq tamatumalu kitaaniittut Qeqertat	NK						*		
021	Taateraat	MQ							*	
022	Sermilinnguaq	MQ							*	
023	Søndre Isortoq	MQ							*	
024	Tasersuaq	ST				*			*	
025	Itinnera	ST							*	
026	Eqalummiut Nunaat – Nassuttuup Nunaa	ST,KQ				*			*	
027	Rifkol	KQ	*							
028	Nunatsiaq	AT	*							
029	Naternaq	QT,KQ				*			*	
030	Kitsissunnguit	QT,AT			*				*	
031	Sarqaqdalen	IT							*	
032	Appat, Ritenbenk	IT			*				*	
033	Aqajarua – Sullorsuaq	QE				*			*	
034	Assissut near Kronprinsens England	QE							*	
035	Nipissat, Diskofjord	QE	*							
036	Kuannersuit Kuussuat	QE							*	
037	Qinnguata Marraa – Kuussuaq	QE							*	
038	Qegertat	UK							*	
039	Sanderson's Hope	UP							*	
040	Appatsiaat	UP							*	
041	Kingittoq Apparsuit	UP							*	
042	Issortussoq	UP							*	
043	Saatoq	UP							*	
044	Uigorluk	UP							*	
045	Kitsissorsuit	UP	*							
046	Kingittuarsuk II	UP							*	
047	Kingittuarsuk III	UP	*							

No.	Site name	Region	Criteria used to select site [see pp.18]							
			0	1(i)	1(ii)	1(iii)	1(iv)	2	3	4
048	Avannarleq	UP	*							
049	Aarrussaq	UP	*							
050	Torqussaarsuk	UP	*							
051	Torqussaq	UP							*	
052	Appalersalik	UP	*							
053	Kippaku	UP							*	
054	Apparsuit	UP		*	*				*	
055	Timmiakulussuit	UP			*				*	
056	Appat Appai	AQ			*				*	
057	Parker Snow Bugt	AQ			*				*	
058	Appat	AQ		*	*				*	
059	Kitsissut	AQ							*	
060	Appaarsuit	AQ							*	
061	Lyon Øer	AQ	*							
062	Saatut	AQ	*							
063	Booth Sund area	AQ	*							
064	Igannaq	AQ	*							
065	Qeqertaarsuit	AQ	*							

II=Ittoqqortoormiit QQ=Qaqortoq PT=Paamiut NK=Nuuk MQ=Maniitsoq ST=Sisimiut KQ=Kangaatsiaq AT=Aasiaat QT=Qasigiannguit IT=Ilulissat QE=Qeqertarsuaq UK=Uummannaq UP=Upernavik AQ=Avanersuaq

Comments on the inventory

1. Information on bird populations in Greenland is comparatively scant, and even the distribution of several species is poorly known. This is especially true of North and East Greenland, although in West Greenland information about different districts also varies considerably. One result of this is a bias, to some extent, in favour of the better-explored areas, and the inventoryshould be regarded as preliminary.
2. *Falco rusticolus* visits many of the seabird sites in late summer to feed on young seabirds.
3. For sites 001-010 'part of Biosphere Reserve' indicates that the site is part of the North-east Greenland National Park Biosphere Reserve (70 million ha).
4. The area (ha) has not been determined for a number of sites, often because field-work is required before boundaries can be determined.
5. Inuit, Danish and English names are all used as place names in Greenland. In general, where the site is within a kommune (municipality), the Inuit name is used (sometimes followed by an alternative Inuit or Danish name in parentheses); this is then followed by the kommune name in parentheses. Many sites lie outside the municipality system, and in general their names are in Danish and English, and there is no kommune name in parentheses.
6. All of the sites are believed to qualify for inclusion in the inventory according to the site-selection criteria, except eight that have been included because of their nationally important populations of *Fratercula arctica* and/or *Cepphus grylle*. One (035) has been included because it is considered to be an important wetland for which numerical data are lacking, and five sites (061-065) are listed because of their populations of two Nearctic species: *Anser caerulescens* and *Larus sabini*.
7. Greenland has been treated as a single 'region' when applying the site criteria (category 3).

Glossary
The following list gives English translations of some commonly used Danish words which occur in the site names: bugt = bay; dal = valley; odde = narrow peninsula; sø = lake; ø = island (øer = islands).

---

001 Myggbukta, Hold With Hope

73°29'N, 21°34'W

Part of Biosphere Reserve (North-east Greenland National Park: 70 million ha)

Part of North-east Greenland National Park

A coastal plain at the junction of south Hold With Hope and Hudson Land. At the head of a fjord, the area consists of low-altitude tundra with many bogs, ponds, and lakes, dammed by a well developed and preserved quaternary beach-ridge system. Includes Ternholme which is a low, level island, 2.5 km offshore. Results of a particularly thorough survey in 1979 (covering only 610+ ha), provide the basis of the information for this site.

Breeding species include *Gavia stellata* (5 pairs), *Anser brachyrhynchus* (scarce in 1979, with only 3 pairs nesting in the area censused and a few others outside), *Somateria mollissima* (100 pairs on Ternholme), *S. spectabilis* (18 pairs), *Clangula hyemalis* (7 pairs), *Lagopus mutus* (sporadic breeder), *Charadrius hiaticula* (12 pairs), *Calidris alba* (11 pairs), *Calidris alpina* (14 pairs), *Arenaria interpres* (numerous on slopes outside the censused area), *Stercorarius parasiticus* (1-2 pairs), *S. longicaudus* (6 pairs; also common outside the censused area), *Sterna paradisaea* (sizeable colony thought to be present on Ternholme), and *Nyctea scandiaca* (scarce). *Phalaropus lobatus* and *P. fulicarius* occur and possibly breed. Passage species include *Anser brachyrhynchus* and *Branta leucopsis* (both in internationally important numbers), *Somateria mollissima* and *S. spectabilis* (pre-breeding and moulting rafts), and *Falco rusticolus* (formerly more numerous; perhaps breeds sporadically).

002 Østersletten and Knudshoved, Hold With Hope

73°35'N, 20°30'W *c.*15,000 ha part of Biosphere Reserve

Part of North-east Greenland National Park

Two coastal, lowland tundra embayments (about 10 km apart) connected by a narrow coastal strip, in east Hold With Hope. Knudshoved is at the mouth of the valley Tobias Dal.

Breeding species include *Anser brachyrhynchus*, possibly *Branta leucopsis* (2 pairs with goslings in July 1973), *Lagopus mutus*, *Charadrius hiaticula*, and *Calidris alpina*. *Anser brachyrhynchus* (560+, Aug. 1973), *Branta leucopsis* (315+, Aug. 1973), and *Falco rusticolus* occur on passage.

003 Tobias Dal, Hold With Hope

73°45'N, 21°10'W *c.*10,000 ha part of Biosphere Reserve

Part of North-east Greenland National Park

A recently glaciated valley with a coastal tundra plain at its mouth (see entry for Østersletten and Knudshoved). The valley floor carries seasonal stream channels and contains some small water bodies.

Breeding species include *Anser brachyrhynchus* (8 pairs with goslings in July 1973; presumed local), *Lagopus mutus*, *Charadrius hiaticula*, *Calidris canutus*, and *C. alpina*. *Branta leucopsis* (60, July 1973) and *Nyctea scandiaca* occur on passage.

004 Stordal – Moskusoksefjord – Badlanddal – Loch Fyne

73°30'N, 22°00'W *c.*300,000 ha part of Biosphere Reserve

Part of North-east Greenland National Park

A series of converging, wide, glacial valleys in otherwise mountainous terrain, containing fjords, seasonal stream channels and water bodies, and tundra vegetation on thick superficial deposits. Moskusoksefjord and Loch Fyne are long, narrow, sea inlets that continue inland as valleys.

Breeding species include *Gavia stellata*, *Anser brachyrhynchus* and *Branta leucopsis* (several pairs of both species with goslings in 1973; local breeding not proved), *Charadrius hiaticula*, *Calidris canutus*, *C. alba*, *C. alpina*, *Arenaria interpres*, *Stercorarius parasiticus*, *S. longicaudus*, and *Sterna paradisaea*. *Anser brachyrhynchus* (200+, Aug. 1973), *Branta leucopsis* (440+, Aug. 1973), *Falco rusticolus*, and *Nyctea scandiaca* occur on passage. In addition, the wide valley of Badlanddal, leading down to the coast at Myggbukta, appears to be an important migration corridor for waders.

005 Hochstetter Forland

75°10'-75°45'N, 19°30'-20°30'W 140,000 ha Ramsar Site; part of Biosphere Reserve

Part of North-east Greenland National Park

An extensive area of coastal tundra with river valleys and a mountainous hinterland.

Anser brachyrhynchus (50 pairs) and *Branta leucopsis* (*c.*50 pairs) breed, as do *Gavia stellata*, *G. immer*, *Somateria mollissima*, *S. spectabilis*, *Clangula hyemalis*, *Charadrius hiaticula*, *Calidris canutus*, *C. alba*, *C. alpina*, *Phalaropus fulicarius*, and *Stercorarius longicaudus*. Non-breeding species include *Anser brachyrhynchus* (min. 3000; second most important moulting site in Greenland) and *Branta leucopsis* (400+).

006 Shannon

75°15'N, 18°30'W part of Biosphere Reserve

Part of North-east Greenland National Park

Important for *Branta leucopsis*: breeding (30 pairs) and non-breeding (214).

007 Hvalrosodden – Slamodden, Germania Land

76°50'N, 20°00'W 10,000+ ha part of Biosphere Reserve

Part of North-east Greenland National Park

A wide (5-10 km) gravel 'desert' of moraines and raised sea floor, separating the large fjord-like Lake Saelsöen from Dove Bugt. The area is crossed by several rivers, notably Lakseelven, and there are numerous small lakes and ponds with narrow fringes of vegetation. Arctic heath grows on the slopes rising up towards the hinterland.

Breeding species include *Branta leucopsis* (10-40 pairs), *Clangula hyemalis* (several pairs), *Falco rusticolus* (scarce), *Lagopus mutus* (common), *Charadrius hiaticula* (widespread), *Calidris canutus*, *C. alba*, *C. alpina* (common and widespread), *Arenaria interpres* (widespread), *Stercorarius longicaudus*, and *Larus hyperboreus*. Non-breeding birds include *Gavia stellata* (common along south coast), *Anser brachyrhynchus* (max. 400 moulting birds), *Branta leucopsis* (small flocks of up to 40 on spring passage; also presumed moulting site), and *Clangula hyemalis* (several hundred).

008 Flade Bugt, Germania Land

77°15'N, 19°45'W 10,000 ha part of Biosphere Reserve

Part of North-east Greenland National Park

A large bay off northern Germania Land. The coast is mainly barren gravel slopes with Arctic heath vegetation in a few sheltered places.

Anser brachyrhynchus (more than 400 moulting birds) occur.

009 Danmarks Havn and surrounding area, including Skibsso

76°50'N, 18°50'W *c.*4,000 ha part of Biosphere Reserve

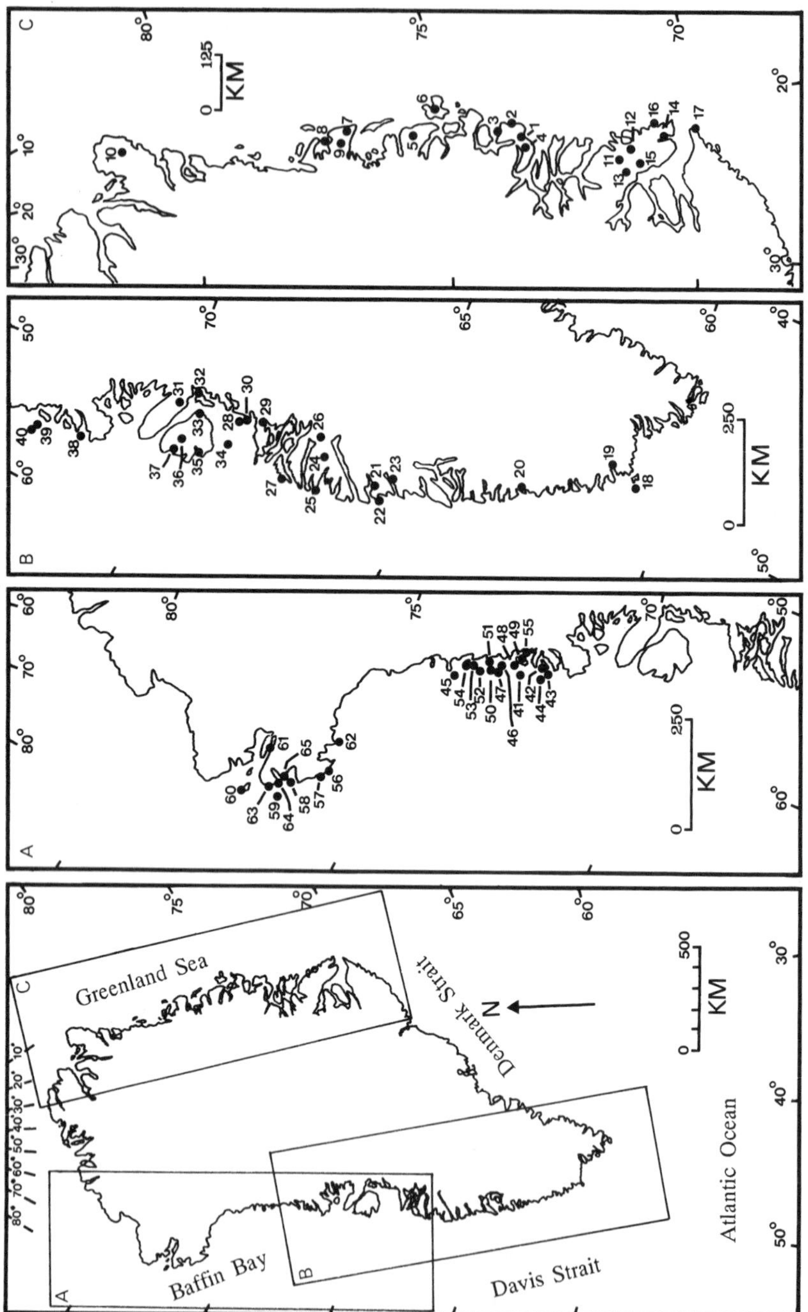

Figure 10: Map showing the location of the sites in Greenland

Part of North-east Greenland National Park.

A coastal area composed of swampy meadows or marshes with dense vegetation, stony slopes of clay and gravel (some sparsely vegetated, others more thickly), cliffs, and barren stone and boulder fields with sporadic vegetation. Surrounded by mountains to the north, east and west.

Breeding species include *Gavia stellata*, *Somateria spectabilis*, *Clangula hyemalis*, *Lagopus mutus*, *Charadrius hiaticula* (*c.*8 pairs per 100 ha), *Calidris alba* (max. 4 pairs per 100 ha), *C. alpina* (max. 7-10 pairs per 100 ha), and *Arenaria interpres* (1.8 pairs per 100 ha). *Phalaropus fulicarius* (probably bred in 1970); and *Stercorarius longicaudus*, and *Anser brachyrhynchus* possibly breeds. Non-breeding species include *Anser brachyrhynchus* (max. 40 in spring and max. 80 in autumn), *Branta leucopsis* (max. 80 in spring and autumn; also moulting flocks), *Falco rusticolus*, passage Charadriidae, and *Nyctea scandiaca*.

010 Kilen

81°15'N, 12°00'W 3000 ha Ramsar Site; part of Biosphere Reserve

Part of North-east Greenland National Park

Northernmost ice-free land area in East Greenland; wide valley containing rivers and other water bodies.

Breeding species include *Anser caerulescens* (2-3 pairs; most easterly known site), *Branta bernicla hrota* (70 pairs; largest known colony in Greenland), *Larus sabini* (30 pairs; largest known colony in Greenland), and *Pagophila eburnea* (35 pairs). Also non--breeding *Branta bernicla hrota* (625).

011 Ørsted Dal and Coloradodal, Scoresby Land and Jameson Land

71°30'-71°51'N, 22°45'-24°00'W 40,000+ ha

Unprotected

A valley *c.*60 km long containing bogs, lakes, and ponds, bisecting a plateau (700-1000 m) in north-east Jameson Land.

Breeding species include *Anser brachyrhynchus* (*c.*60 pairs in small colonies of 2-5 nests) and *Branta leucopsis* (*c.*100 pairs). Non-breeding species include *Anser brachyrhynchus* (900) and *Branta leucopsis* (1600).

012 River valleys entering Fleming Fjord, Jameson Land

71°35'-71°40'N, 23°00'-23°15'W 20,000+ ha

Unprotected

River valley containing extensive bogs in north-east Jameson Land.

Breeding species include *Anser brachyrhynchus* (small colonies) and *Branta leucopsis* (small colonies). Non-breeding species include *Anser brachyrhynchus* (200) and *Branta leucopsis* (400).

013 Kjoveland

71°18'-71°27'N, 24°35'-25°00'W 20,000+ ha

Unprotected

A heath with lakes and rivers, several bogs, and one large lake in western Jameson Land.

Breeding species include *Gavia immer* (1 pair) and *Pluvialis apricaria* (1 pair found in 1983/84). Non-breeding species include *Anser brachyrhynchus* (400) and *Branta leucopsis* (400).

014 Hurry Fjord including Fame Øer and Kap Stewart, Jameson Land

70°49'-70°57'N, 22°20'-22°40'W 25,000+ ha

Unprotected

Arctic tundra heath and bogs containing many stream/river channels and ponds in south-east Jameson Land.

Breeding species include *Branta leucopsis* (a few pairs at Fame Øer and Kap Stewart) and *Sterna paradisaea* (on Fame Øer), and non-breeding *Branta leucopsis* (400) occurs.

015 Nuna masarsuttalik Jameson Land – imiittoq kitaanittoq (Heden) (Ittoqqortoormiit)

70°40'-71°20'N, 23°40'-24°35'W 125,000 ha Ramsar Site

Unprotected

The western part of Jameson Land, comprising flat tundra with many rivers, lakes, and ponds. The tundra vegetation is mainly dwarf-scrub heath. The primary habitats for geese are graminoid marshes and wet grasslands adjacent to lakes and streams.

Breeding species include *Gavia stellata* (a few pairs), *Anser brachyrhynchus* (50 pairs), *Branta leucopsis* (a few pairs), *Calidris alba*, *Numenius phaeopus* (11 pairs), *Arenaria interpres*, *Phalaropus lobatus*, *P. fulicarius*, *Stercorarius longicaudus*, and *Larus sabini* (1-4 pairs). Non-breeding species include *Anser brachyrhynchus* (4000; most important moulting area in Greenland: *c.*5 per cent of Greenland population), *Branta leucopsis* (2000-3000; most important moulting area in Greenland: *c.*10 per cent of Greenland population), and *Larus sabini* (10-35).

016 Liverpool Land coast and Scoresbysund

70°30'-71°30'N, 21°40'W 60,000+ ha

Unprotected

A rocky sea coast with cliffs and small offshore islands. Scoresbysund is the mouth of a wide fjord between Liverpool Land coast and Kap Brewster (see separate entry for Kap Brewster and associated coastline), which remains ice-free for much of the year because of strong tidal currents. The nutrient-rich waters of Scoresbysund provide excellent feeding for seabirds. Raffles Ø and Rathbone Ø are islands off Liverpool Land coast.

Breeding auks include *Uria lomvia* (at least 1000 pairs at Raffles Ø), *Cepphus grylle*, *Alle alle* (extremely numerous on all islands and headlands with 1-5 million pairs; making this one of the most important locations in the world), and possibly *Fratercula arctica*. In addition, there are a few pairs of breeding *Anser brachyrhynchus* and *Branta leucopsis*.

017 Kap Brewster and Volquart Boon's Coast, Scoresbysund

70°10'N, 22°05'-24°40'W several thousand ha

Unprotected

Rocky coast with cliffs south of Scoresbysund.

Breeding species include *Fulmarus glacialis*, *Somateria mollissima*, *Larus hyperboreus*, *Rissa tridactyla* (300 pairs), *Uria lomvia* (30,000 pairs), *Alle alle* (1-5 million pairs), and possibly *Fratercula arctica*.

018 Kitsissut Avalliit (Ydre Kitsissut or Ydre Kitsigsut) (Qaqortoq)

60°45'N, 48°30'W 8000 ha Ramsar Site

Breeding Reserve for Birds

Group of small, low, rocky, offshore islands with sparse vegetation.

May support the most diverse seabird colony in Greenland. Breeding species include *Gavia stellata*, *Fulmarus glacialis* (*c.*150 pairs in 1985), *Larus hyperboreus* (25 pairs), *Rissa tridactyla* (25 pairs), *Uria aalge* (*c.*900 pairs in 1985), *U. lomvia* (5500 pairs in 1985), *Alca torda* (200 pairs in 1985), *Cepphus grylle* (500 pairs), and *Fratercula arctica* (at least 30 pairs). *Phalacrocorax carbo*, *Histrionicus histrionicus*, and *Calidris maritima* also occur.

019 Foxfaldet, Ilorput (Arsuk Fjord) (Paamiut)

61°20'N, 48°00'W

Unprotected

A cliff-dominated coastline.
Breeding species include (1986 figures) *Larus glaucoides* (200 pairs), *Rissa tridactyla* (5000 pairs), *Uria lomvia* (1600 pairs), and *Alca torda* (a few pairs).

020 Ikkattoq tamatumalu kitaaniittut Qeqertat (Ikkattoq Fjord and islands to the west) (Nuuk)

62°35'-62°52'N, 49°50'-50°30'W 35,000 ha Ramsar Site

Unprotected

A fjord containing several islands, rocky and sandy coastal stretches, and large intertidal flats.
Breeding species include *Clangula hyemalis*, *Haliaeetus albicilla* (3-4 pairs), *Stercorarius parasiticus* (10-20 pairs), and *Sterna paradisaea* (100 pairs). Non-breeding species include *Somateria mollissima* (100-500), *Clangula hyemalis* (500 moulting), and *Mergus serrator* (500-1000; an important moulting area and the largest concentration known in Greenland).

021 Taateraat (Maniitsoq)

66°00'N, 52°33'W

Unprotected

Sea cliffs.
A site with breeding *Uria lomvia* (9000 birds in 1988).

022 Sermilinnguaq (Maniitsoq)

65°40'N, 52°37'W

Unprotected

Sea cliffs.
A site with breeding *Uria lomvia* (11,500 birds in 1987).

023 Søndre Isortoq (Maniitsoq)

65°26'N, 52°10'W

Unprotected

Sea cliffs.
A site with breeding *Uria lomvia* (2200 birds in 1988).

024 Tasersuaq (Sisimiut)

67°00'N, 51°45'W 3,000 ha

Unprotected

A lake situated in a typical U-shaped glacial valley. Gentle lake-shelf gradients characterised by marine and glacial deposits with an abundance of species such as *Triglochin palustris*, which form a valuable source of nutrition for migrating geese in spring.
A non-breeding site for *Anser albifrons flavirostris* (200+; possibly a regular staging site for birds from a large part of Greenland, and may be of particular importance in years with a late spring).

025 Itinnera (Sisimiut)

67°00'N, 52°20'W

Unprotected

The northern branch of Ikertooq-fjordens, Maligiaq.
Large flocks of *Anser albifrons flavirostris* occur on spring passage.

026 Eqalummiut Nunaat – Nassuttuup Nunaa (Sisimiut, Kangaatsiaq)

67°00'-67°50'N, 50°00'-52°00'W *c.*500,000 ha Ramsar Site

Unprotected

A plateau adjacent to the ice-cap, with deeply incised glacial valleys and associated wetlands that are important feeding and staging areas for geese in the spring. Mid--altitude areas, characterised by grasslands and Arctic scrub, are important for nesting geese; whilst high-altitude lakes are used as moulting grounds. Most important site in Greenland for *Anser albifrons flavirostris*.
Breeding species include *Gavia stellata*, *G. immer*, *Anser albifrons flavirostris* (100 pairs; a significant percentage of the number which nests in Greenland each year), *Somateria mollissima*, *Clangula hyemalis*, *Mergus serrator*, *Haliaeetus albicilla*, *Falco rusticolus*, *F. peregrinus*, *Lagopus mutus*, *Charadrius hiaticula* (small numbers), and *Phalaropus lobatus* (most common breeding wader). Very important for non-breeding *Anser albifrons flavirostris* (2500; more than 10 per cent of the world population).

027 Rifkol (Kangaatsiaq)

67°58'N, 53°50'W

Unprotected

A rocky island.
Breeding *Fratercula arctica*.

028 Nunatsiaq (Rotten) (Aasiaat)

68°52'N, 53°22'W

Breeding Reserve for Birds

A small island.
Breeding *Fratercula arctica*.

029 Naternaq (Lersletten) (Qasigiannguit, Kangaatsiaq)

68°15'-68°35'N, 51°00'-52°30'W 150,000 ha Ramsar Site

Unprotected

An uplifted plain of marine sediments with vast expanses of grassland and numerous shallow lakes and rivers.
Anser albifrons flavirostris breeds (no detailed figures available, but more than one per cent of the total breeding population and large numbers on passage). Probably an important staging area for a range of migratory species.

030 Kitsissunnguit (Gronne Ejland) (Qasigiannguit, Aasiaat)

68°50'N, 51°50'W 16,000 ha Ramsar Site

Hunting prohibited; skerries to the north-west are a Breeding Reserve for Birds

Several small islands, mainly covered with heath vegetation, but also some small lakes and bogs.
Breeding species include *Phalaropus lobatus* (100 pairs), *P. fulicarius* (15 pairs), *Rhodostethia rosea* (a single breeding record in 1979), *Sterna paradisaea* (25,000 pairs; one of the largest colonies in Greenland), *Stercorarius longicaudus* (a few pairs), *Alle alle* (200 pairs), and *Fratercula arctica* (200 pairs). The archipelago is important as a staging area for passage waders.

031 Sarqaqdalen (Ilulissat)

70°07'N, 52°10'W 10,000 ha

Unprotected

A river valley, the lower part of which is marshy and well vegetated. Two channels run through the area, separated by a 300 m ridge near to the valley-head. The flat bottom is vegetated by dwarf-scrub heath and moorland, with willow scrub and grassland in other places. The surrounding area is Precambrian with sandstone massifs rising sharply to over 1000 m.

Important for *Anser albifrons flavirostris* (very significant gathering area in spring, with variable numbers breeding annually in the hinterland). Other breeding species include *Gavia stellata*, *Lagopus mutus*, *Falco rusticolus*, *Calidris maritima*, and *Phalaropus lobatus*.

032 Appat, Ritenbenk (Ilulissat)

69°48'N, 51°13'W

Breeding Reserve for Birds

Sea cliffs.

Breeding species include (1984 figures) *Phalacrocorax carbo* (10 pairs), *Rissa tridactyla* (30,000 pairs; probably the largest colony in Greenland), *Uria lomvia* (4500 pairs), and *Alca torda* (a few pairs).

033 Aqajarua – Sullorsuaq (Mudderbugten and Kvandalen) (Qeqertarsuaq)

69°42'N, 51°50'-52°40'W 30,000 ha Ramsar Site

Unprotected

Sullorsuaq is a broad, U-shaped valley with its flat lower reaches containing glacial melt-water channels. There are also raised flats of heath and dwarf scrub, with large areas of freshwater marsh at low altitude. Aqajarua is a shallow offshore area. There is an important eutrophic lake just north of the main valley floor.

Breeding species include *Anser albifrons flavirostris* (more than 10 pairs), *Branta canadensis*, *Phalaropus lobatus*, and *Stercorarius parasiticus* (large numbers). In addition, moulting *Somateria spectabilis* (30,000; probably the most important concentration in Greenland) occur in Aqajarua.

034 Assissut (Braendvinsskaerene) near Kronprinsens England (Qeqertarsuaq)

69°04'N, 53°31'W

Breeding Reserve for Birds

Three small islands almost devoid of vegetation.

Breeding species include *Phalaropus lobatus*, *P. fulicarius*, *Sterna paradisaea* (200 pairs), *Alle alle* (20 pairs), *Fratercula arctica* (100 pairs), and possibly *Alca torda*. *Histrionicus histrionicus* also occurs.

035 Nipissat, Diskofjord (Qeqertarsuaq)

69°27'N, 54°14'W

Unprotected

Coastal area with several lakes and ponds and shallow offshore waters.

A staging area for geese, ducks and shorebirds, and *Clangula hyemalis* (100-150) occurs in spring.

036 Kuannersuit Kuussuat (Kuannesuit at Sorte Hak, Disko) (Qeqertarsuaq)

69°40'N, 53°17'W 4500 ha Ramsar Site

Unprotected

A barren tundra valley with melt-water channels, and several small lakes and ponds.

Breeding species include *Gavia stellata* (a few pairs), *Somateria mollissima*, *Clangula hyemalis* (dense population), and *Phalaropus lobatus* (very common). Large numbers of *Anser albifrons flavirostris* (moulting) also occur.

037 Qinnguata Marraa – Kuussuaq (Nordfjord and adjacent valley) (Qeqertarsuaq)

69°56'N, 54°17'W 6000 ha Ramsar Site

Unprotected

A fjord and valley with lakes and ponds.

Breeding species include *Gavia stellata* (very dense population), *Anser albifrons flavirostris*, and *Branta canadensis*. Non-breeding species include *Anser albifrons flavirostris* (100+), *Somateria mollissima* (200), *S. spectabilis* (200), and *Mergus serrator* (large summering and moulting flocks at eastern end of fjord).

038 Qegertat (Schades Øer) (Uummannaq)

71°23'N, 53°50'W

Unprotected

Small rocky islands.

An important site for breeding *Sterna paradisaea*.

039 Sanderson's Hope (Upernavik Apparsuit), island of Qaersorssuaq (Upernavik)

72°42'N, 56°10'W

Breeding Reserve for Birds

Rocky coast and sea cliffs.

Breeding seabirds include *Rissa tridactyla* (500 pairs in 1987) and *Uria lomvia* (max. 2000 pairs).

040 Appatsiaat (Agpatsiait), island of Qaersorssuaq (Upernavik)

72°42'N, 55°49'W

Unprotected

Rocky coast and sea cliffs.

Breeding seabirds include *Rissa tridactyla* (1200 pairs in 1987) and *Uria lomvia* (900 birds in 1987).

041 Kingittoq Apparsuit (Kingigtoq Agparssuit), island of Qaersorssuaq (Upernavik)

72°39'N, 55°53'W

Unprotected

Sea cliffs.

Breeding seabirds include *Rissa tridactyla* (1250 pairs in 1987), *Uria lomvia* (8500 birds in 1987), and *Alca torda* (8 birds in 1987).

042 Issortussoq (Ivsortussoq) (Upernavik)

72°15'N, 55°43'W

Unprotected

Rocky island with sea cliffs.

A site with breeding *Sterna paradisaea* (500-1000 pairs in 1987).

043 Saatoq (Store Fladø) (Upernavik)

72°15'N, 55°55'W 1600 ha

Unprotected

A low grassy island with pools.

A site with breeding (data from 1974) *Gavia stellata* (1 pair), *Somateria mollissima* (10-20 pairs), *Clangula hyemalis* (max. 10 pairs), *Phalaropus lobatus* (1 pair), *P. fulicarius* (1 pair), *Stercorarius longicaudus* (6-10 pairs), and *Sterna paradisaea* (several hundred pairs).

044 Uigorluk (Lille Fladø) (Upernavik)

72°18'N, 55°58'W 96 ha

Unprotected

A low grassy island.

A site with breeding (data from 1974) *Somateria mollissima* (1-10 pairs), *Clangula hyemalis* (1-5 pairs), *Phalaropus fulicarius* (1 pair), and *Sterna paradisaea* (1000+ pairs).

045 Kitsissorsuit (Ederfugleøer) (Upernavik)

74°02'N, 57°50'W 100-200 ha

Unprotected

Three rocky islands with sea cliffs.

Breeding species include *Somateria mollissima* (1500 pairs) and *Cepphus grylle* (620 birds).

046 Kingittuarsuk (Kingigtuarsuk) II (Upernavik)

72°56'N, 56°38'W

Breeding Reserve for Birds

A small rocky island.

Supports a breeding colony of *Uria lomvia* (40 birds in 1987; previously much larger), *Alca torda* (25 pairs in 1974), *Cepphus grylle* (50-100 pairs in 1974), and *Fratercula arctica* (50 pairs in 1974).

047 Kingittuarsuk (Kingigtuarsuk) III (Upernavik)

73°15'N, 56°50'W 5 ha

Unprotected

A small rocky island, max. 58 m in height. A former colony of *Uria lomvia* is now extinct.

Breeding species include *Somateria mollissima* (200 pairs), *Alca torda* (25 birds), and *Fratercula arctica* (100 birds).

048 Avannarleq (Nordø) (Upernavik)

72°45'N, 56°25'W 50 ha

Unprotected

A small, low, rocky island.

Breeding auks in 1974 included *Cepphus grylle* (*c.*100 pairs) and *Fratercula arctica* (25-50 pairs).

049 Aarrussaq (Hvalø) (Upernavik)

72°41'N, 56°18'W

Unprotected

A small, low, rocky island.
Breeding *Fratercula arctica* (several hundred burrows and 175 birds in 1965).

050 Torqussaarsuk (Torqussarssuk) (Upernavik)

73°22'N, 56°40'W 25 ha

Unprotected

A rocky island with sea cliffs.
Breeding seabirds include *Alca torda* (*c.*50 pairs in 1974), *Cepphus grylle* (30 pairs in 1974), and *Fratercula arctica* (*c.*300 pairs in 1974; possibly largest colony in Greenland).

051 Torqussaq (Upernavik)

73°22'N, 56°38'W 532 ha

Breeding Reserve for Birds

A rocky island with sea cliffs.
Breeding seabirds (data from 1987) include *Rissa tridactyla* (10 pairs), *Uria lomvia* (550-600 birds), *Alca torda* (60 birds), *Cepphus grylle* (300-350 birds), and *Fratercula arctica* (*c.*10 pairs).

052 Appalersalik (Horse Head) (Upernavik)

73°38'N, 57°02'W 300 ha

Unprotected

A rocky island with sea cliffs.
Breeding seabirds include *Alca torda* (1-10 pairs in 1974), *Cepphus grylle* (*c.*200-300 pairs in 1987), *Alle alle* (*c.*6000 pairs in 1974), and *Fratercula arctica* (100-200 pairs in 1987).

053 Kippaku (Kipako) (Upernavik)

73°43'N, 56°45'W 15 ha

Unprotected

A small rocky island with sea cliffs on north-west and north side, sloping gradually to the south/south-west.
Breeding seabirds include *Rissa tridactyla* (2000 pairs in 1987), *Uria lomvia* (13,000 birds in 1987), *Alca torda* (25 pairs in 1988), and *Cepphus grylle* (*c.*60 pairs in 1988).

054 Apparsuit (Agparssuit or Kap Shackleton) (Upernavik)

73°47'N, 56°45'W 247.5 ha

Breeding Reserve for Birds

A high rocky island with sea cliffs particularly on the south coast, with one (sometimes two) pools.
Breeding seabirds include *Rissa tridactyla* (3900 pairs in 1987), *Uria lomvia* (*c.*187,000 birds in 1987; largest colony in west Greenland), *Alca torda* (13 birds in 1987), *Cepphus grylle* (76 pairs in 1987), and *Fratercula arctica* (1-5 pairs in 1987).

055 Timmiakulussuit (Tingmiakulugssuit), island of Nutaarmiut (Upernavik)

72°39'N, 55°45'W

Unprotected

High sea cliffs (*c.*800 m high).
Breeding seabirds include (data from 1987) *Fulmarus glacialis* (19,000-20,000 pairs), *Rissa tridactyla* (470 pairs), *Uria lomvia* (400 birds), and *Alca torda* (9 birds).

056 Appat Appai (Avanersuaq)

76°05'N, 68°25'W

Unprotected

Sea cliffs.
Important for breeding *Uria lomvia* (48,000 birds in 1987).

057 Parker Snow Bugt (Avanersuaq)

76°10'N, 68°30'W

Unprotected

Sea cliffs.
Important for breeding *Uria lomvia* (50,000 birds in 1987).

058 Appat (Saunders Ø) (Avanersuaq)

76°34'N, 70°03'W

Unprotected

Island with sea cliffs.
Important for breeding *Fulmarus glacialis* and *Uria lomvia* (143,000 birds in 1987).

059 Kitsissut (Carey Øer) (Avanersuaq)

76°44'N, 73°04'W

Unprotected

Islands with sea cliffs.
Breeding seabirds in 1987 included *Uria lomvia* (7000 birds; mainly on Isbjørneø), *Alca torda* (at least 12 birds), and *Fratercula arctica* (*c.*60 birds).

060 Appaarsuit (Hakluyt Ø) (Avanersuaq)

77°26'N, 72°38'W

Unprotected

Island with sea cliffs.
Breeding seabirds in 1987 included *Uria lomvia* (37,000 birds), *Alca torda* (2 birds), and *Fratercula arctica* (30-40 birds).

061 Lyon Øer (Avanersuaq)

77°29'N, 66°42'W 15 ha

Breeding Reserve for Birds

Small islands.
Breeding species include *Larus sabini* (a few pairs) and *Sterna paradisaea*.

062 Saatut (Sabine Øer) (Avanersuaq)

75°30'N, 60°13'W 40 ha

Included in the Melville Bay National Wildlife Reserve

Small islands.
Breeding species include *Larus sabini* (30 pairs in 1978) and *Sterna paradisaea* (100 pairs in 1978).

063 Booth Sund area (Avanersuaq)

76°53'N, 70°50'W *c.*1200 ha

Unprotected

A well-vegetated plain south of the inlet, with heath and marshes, and several shallow lakes.

Breeding species include *Gavia stellata* (several pairs), *Anser caerulescens* (*c.*100 pairs in 1987; also moulting site for non-breeders), and waders (e.g. *Calidris canutus* and *C. maritima*).

064 Igannaq (Dalrymple Rock) (Avanersuaq)

76°28'N, 70°13'W 15 ha

Unprotected

Small rocky island with sea cliffs.

Breeding species include *Anser caerulescens, Somateria mollissima* (400 nests in 1988), and *Fratercula arctica* (100 pairs in 1988).

065 Qeqertaarsuit (Ederfugleøer) (Avanersuaq)

76°30'N, 70°05'W 5 ha

Unprotected

Small islands.

Breeding species include *Anser caerulescens* and *Somateria mollissima* (1000 nests in 1988).

MAIN REFERENCES

Boertmann, D., Madsen, J. and Mortensen, C. E. (1985) Sjældnerefugle i Jameson Land, Østgrønland, Somrene 1982-84. *Dansk Orn. Foren. Tidsskr.* 81: 151-152.

Evans, P. G. H. (1984) The seabirds of Greenland: their status and conservation. Pp. 49-84 in Croxall, J. P., Evans, P. G. H. and Schreiber, R. W. *Status and conservation of the world's seabirds.* Cambridge, U.K.: International Council for Bird Preservation, Tech. Publ. No. 2: 49-84.

Hjort, C., Håkansson, E. and Mølgaard, P. (1987) Brent Geese, Snow Geese and Barnacle Geese on Kilen, Kronprins Christian Land, Northeast Greenland, 1985. *Dansk Orn. Foren. Tidsskr.* 81: 121-128.

Kampp, K., Meltofte, H. and Mortensen, C. E. (1987) Population size of the Little Auk *Alle alle* in East Greenland. *Dansk Orn. Foren. Tidsskr.* 81: 129-136.

Meltofte, H. (1985) Populations and breeding schedules of waders, Charadrii, in high Arctic Greenland. *Meddr. Grønland, Biosci.* 16: 1-43.

Meltofte, H., Elander, M. and Hjort, C. (1981) Ornithological observations in Northeast Greenland between 74°30'N and 76°00'N, 1976. *Meddr. Grønland, Biosci.* 3: 1-53.

FINLAND

Broad-billed Sandpiper *Limicola falcinellus*

INTRODUCTION

General information

Finland lies at the head of the Baltic Sea, with the Gulf of Bothnia and the Gulf of Finland adjoining the country's south-western and southern shorelines respectively. Norway and Sweden border to the north and north-west, whilst the Soviet Union lies to the east.

In common with its two Scandinavian neighbours, Finland has a rather long north-south extension, from approximately 59°50'N to more than 70°N. This latitudinal elongation is reflected in zonation of climate and vegetation.

The total area of Finland is around 337,000 sq km (one of the larger national territories in Europe) but the human population is relatively small at about 5 million: population density is, therefore, extremely low (an average density of 13.2 persons per sq km in 1978). For example, the average population of a square kilometre in Finland is at least twenty-five times lower than the corresponding density in the Netherlands. There are few very large centres of population, and extensive tracts of land with no permanent human occupation.

Topographically, much of central and southern Finland is rather low-lying, with very few areas exceeding 200 m above sea-level. The country's extensive fringe of coastal lowlands reflects the continuing rise of land (relative to sea-level) around the Gulfs of Bothnia and Finland. The north of the country, however, is more rugged with high-level plateaus and deep river valleys which cut into the ancient rocks of the Fenno-Scandian shield.

The coastline of Finland is extremely complex, with numerous peninsulas and inlets, and archipelagic waters containing tens of thousands of islands and islets. However, probably the most striking physical features of the country are Finland's lakes, which exceed 60,000 in number, and vast peatland areas. Together with extensive taiga forests, the lakes and peatlands provide a combination of habitats which support a variety of internationally important bird populations.

Ornithological importance

The enormous area of Finnish wetlands is reflected in correspondingly important populations of breeding and passage waterfowl. However, the country's north-easterly position means that all but a relatively small minority of wetland habitats are frozen during the winter months.

In common with other countries dealt with in this volume, much of Finland's great importance for birds results from the sheer extent of habitats holding relatively few species at rather low densities. It is, therefore, important to bear in mind that preservation of the country's ornithological importance can only be achieved through conservation of huge tracts of often homogeneous habitats. A site-orientated approach such as that undertaken during the Important Bird Areas project must be considered against this background.

Three breeding species are globally threatened: *Anser erythropus* (less than 10 pairs), *Haliaeetus albicilla* (50 pairs), and *Crex crex* (100-500 males; in some years more than 1000; population has increased since 1950s). Amongst Finland's more important breeding populations are those of *Gavia stellata*, *G. arctica*, *Podiceps grisegena*, *P. auritus*, *Anser fabalis*, *A. anser*, *Anas* spp., *Aythya* spp. *Melanitta* spp., *Bucephala clangula*, *Mergus* spp., *Pernis apivorus* (800-900 pairs), *Circus cyaneus* (600 pairs), *Pandion haliaetus* (900-1000 pairs), *Falco columbarius* (1600 pairs), *F. rusticolus* (minimum 20-25 pairs), *Tetrao tetrix* (225,000 females), *T. urogallus* (135,000 females), *Grus grus*, *Charadrius morinellus* (800 pairs), *Pluvialis apricaria* (100,000 pairs), *Calidris temminckii* (2000 pairs), *Limicola falcinellus* (8000 pairs), *Lymnocryptes minimus* (10,000 pairs), *Sterna caspia* (1000 pairs), *Nyctea scandiaca*, *Surnia ulula*, *Strix uralensis*, and *Asio flammeus*.

Many of these and other species (particularly waterfowl) occur in important numbers during passage to and from more northerly/easterly breeding sites.

Conservation infrastructure and protected-area system

The Nature Protection Act (1923) provides for the establishment under law of general and special nature reserves on state-owned land for sites more than 50 ha in extent (reserves can also be designated on private land, subject to a decision of the relevant provincial authority). Reserves of less than 50 ha are designated by statute.

1. General Reserve (Iuonnonpuisto)
   These are strict nature reserves used mainly for research work, where public access is strictly limited. The Bird Sanctuaries, included in this category and referred to in the inventory, are mainly designated by the state.

2. Special Reserve/National Park (Kansalispuisto)
   These should have educational value and be valuable and typical examples of a landscape-type, etc.

Other protected areas include those on National Forestry Board and Royal Forest Research Institute land. Both these bodies are controlled by the Ministry of Agriculture and Forestry. Categories of protection include 'primeval forest', 'special conservation forest', and 'peatland protected from drainage'.

A National Wetland Conservation Programme (Valtakunnallinen Lintuvesiensuojeluohjelma) was initiated in 1981 by the Ministry of Agriculture and Forestry.

International relations relevant to the conservation of sites

Finland is a party to the Ramsar Convention and Bern Convention, and has designated 11 Ramsar Sites, all of which are included in the following inventory. Although Finland is also a party to the World Heritage Convention, no natural sites have been designated; nor has the country designated any Biosphere Reserves.

Overview of the inventory

Thirty-five areas are included. The inventory should be considered in the light of factors outlined in the section 'Ornithological importance'. It is largely impossible strictly to define important bird areas for breeding species in Finland according to the principles which have been used for many central and southern European states.

Similarly, with passage and wintering species, birds simply do not congregate in numbers when vast tracts of homogeneous suitable habitat are available. These points highlight the importance of conserving sufficiently extensive examples of the various biotopes involved (the most important biotope in Finland being taiga forest).

In view of these difficulties, the following inventory also includes:

(a) Major wetland areas, some designated as Ramsar sites, supporting a variety of breeding waterfowl species;
(b) Examples of biotopes rare in Finland (e.g. large sandy beaches);
(c) Sites of exceptional educational and/or scientific interest (e.g. sites supporting a very high number of species in a small area).

The inventory, therefore, includes a limited selection of areas which cover *some* of the habitats and species requiring conservation measures on a national scale. It is not suggested that the protection of the listed sites would conserve the character of Finland's undoubtedly rich avifauna.

Acknowledgements

The following site accounts are based on data-sheets completed on behalf of the Finnish ICBP Section, and O. Järvinen and P. Koskimies provided assistance and advice. Data received from J. Valste by J. van der Ven has been incorporated in the introduction.

INVENTORY

No.	Site name	Region	Criteria used to select site [see p.18]							
			0	1(i)	1(ii)	1(iii)	1(iv)	2	3	4
001	Sammuttijänkä	LI	*							
002	Lätäseno	LI	*							
003	Patvinsuo National Park	PK	*							
004	Islands of Kainuunkylä, River Tornionjoki	LI	*							
005	Martimoaapa – Lumiaapa	LI	*							
006	Krunnit Nature Reserve	OU			*				*	
007	Hailuodon ranta-alueet; Isomatala Maasyvänlahti, Viinikanlahti, Põllä-Itänenä, Pökönnokka-Vesanniityt, Lahdenperä, and Kirkkosalmi	OU				*			*	
008	Merikylänlahti – Ulkonokka, Siikajokisuu, Säikänlahti, and Hientaniitynlahti	OU				*		*		
009	Liminganlahti – Lumijoenselkä	OU				*		*	*	
010	Letto and Vihaspauha	OU	*							

No.	Site name	Region	Criteria used to select site [see p.18]							
			0	1(i)	1(ii)	1(iii)	1(iv)	2	3	4
011	Ainali, Apaja, Haapalampi, Korkatti, Kypärä, Köyrylampi, Litukka, and Suojärvi	OU	*							
012	Valsörarna – Björkögrunden	VA							*	
013	Vassorfjärden – Österfjärden – Söderfjärden	VA				*			*	
014	Sundominlahti: southern part	VA				*			*	
015	Härkmerifjärden	VA	*							
016	Niemijärvi – Itäjärvi	TP	*							
017	Preiviikinlahden perä, Yyteri – Riitsaranlahti and Enäjärvi	TP	*							
018	Kokemäenjoen suisto	TP							*	
019	Halkkoaukko – Oukkulanlahti, Rukanaukko, and Louhisaarenlahti	TP	*							
020	Signilskär Bird Sanctuary	TP								*
021	Southern part of archipelagic seas: Föglö – Dragsfjärd	TP				*			*	
022	Svanvik – Henriksberg, Täcktbukten – Österfjärden and Västerfjärden	UA	*							
023	Viiki Nature Reserve	UA	*							
024	Östersundominlahti	UA	*							
025	Kaupunginselkä – Stensbölefjärden	UA	*							
026	Pernajanlahti	UA							*	
027	Teutjärvi and Suvijärvi	UA							*	
028	Santaniemenselkä – Tyyslahti	KI	*							
029	Kirkon – Vilkkiläntura	KI				*			*	
030	Gulf of Finland	KI,UA				*			*	
031	Siikalahti	KI	*							
032	Kesonsuo – Juurikkasuo – Piitsonsuo	PK	*							
033	Koitilaiskaira	LI	*							
034	Kiesjärvi, Hautalampi – Jokilampi and Jouhtenuslampi	PK	*							
035	Heinä – Suvanto – Suvantojärvi	KS				*				

LI=Lappi PK=Pohjois-Karjala OU=Oulu VA=Vaasa
TP=Turku-Pori UA=Uusimaa KI=Kymi KS=Keski-Suomi

Comments on the inventory

1. The site name is followed by the name of the province (given in (parentheses), where the site can be found.
2. The whole of Finland has been treated as a single region when applying the site-selection criteria. The application of the criteria as depicted in the above table is provisional only. Many of the sites do not meet the criteria and have been included for other reasons (column 0; see 'overview of the inventory').

---

001 Sammuttijänkä (Lappi)

69°30'N, 27°30'E 100,000 ha

Unprotected

A large marsh complex with several hundred small ponds and lakes.

An important area for waders, with 14 breeding species.

002 Lätäseno (Lappi)

68°35'N, 22°20'E 26,000 ha

Unprotected

A large marsh region along the rivers Lätäseno and Hieta, with hundreds of small ponds. Together with site no. 001, this is the most important area in Finland for breeding subarctic wetland birds.

Thirteen wader species nest in the area.

003 Patvinsuo National Park (Pohjois-Karjala)

63°05'N, 30°35'E 9400 ha Ramsar Site

National Park

A large peatland area with fenlands, raised bogs, and small brackish pools, centred around the oligotrophic Lake Suomujärvi. A river runs through the area, draining into the larger Lake Koitere.

An important breeding area for waterfowl and waders, including *Cygnus cygnus*, *Anser fabalis*, *Anas acuta*, *Mergus albellus*, *Grus grus*, *Limicola falcinellus*, and *Lymnocryptes minimus*. Other breeding species include *Aquila chrysaetos*, *Pandion haliaetus*, and *Bubo bubo*. Passage migrants include *Anser albifrons*, *Branta leucopsis*, and *B. bernicla*.

004 Islands of Kainuunkylä, River Tornionjoki (Lappi)

66°13'N, 23°42'E 1440 ha

Unprotected

An inland delta of the River Tornionjoki, where the river divides into numerous channels separating several islands. The flora of the area is exceptional, holding many rarities. *Equisetum* dominates the bank vegetation; floating vegetation is rather sparse. The islands themselves make up the largest area of regularly flooded meadowland in Finland. The meadows were formerly well grazed, but this practice has steadily declined so that some areas are becoming overgrown.

The area is important for both breeding and migrating wildfowl, and waders.

005 Martimoaapa – Lumiaapa (Lappi)

65°49'N, 25°15'E 8000 ha includes Ramsar Site (7400 ha)

A bog with several small ponds and lakes.

An important breeding area for waterfowl and waders, with *Gavia stellata*, *G. arctica*, *Podiceps auritus*, *Anser fabalis* (10 pairs), *Grus grus* (5 pairs), *Limicola falcinellus*, *Lymnocryptes minimus*, *Tringa erythropus*, and *Phalaropus lobatus*. Also important as a resting area for migrating wetland birds.

006 Krunnit Nature Reserve (Oulu)

65°21'-65°26'N, 24°45'-25°09'E 4600 ha (360 ha land) Ramsar Site

Nature Reserve

A complex of four island groups including seven larger and 15 smaller morainic islands. The islands display important botanical successions.

There is a rich avifauna of breeding waterfowl and seabirds, including *Sterna caspia* (*c.*100 pairs).

007 Hailuodon ranta-alueet; Isomatala Maasyvänlahti, Viinikanlahti, Pöllä-Itänenä, Pökönnokka-Vesanniityt, Lahdenperä, and Kirkkosalmi (Oulu)

65°00'N, 24°45'E 2550 ha

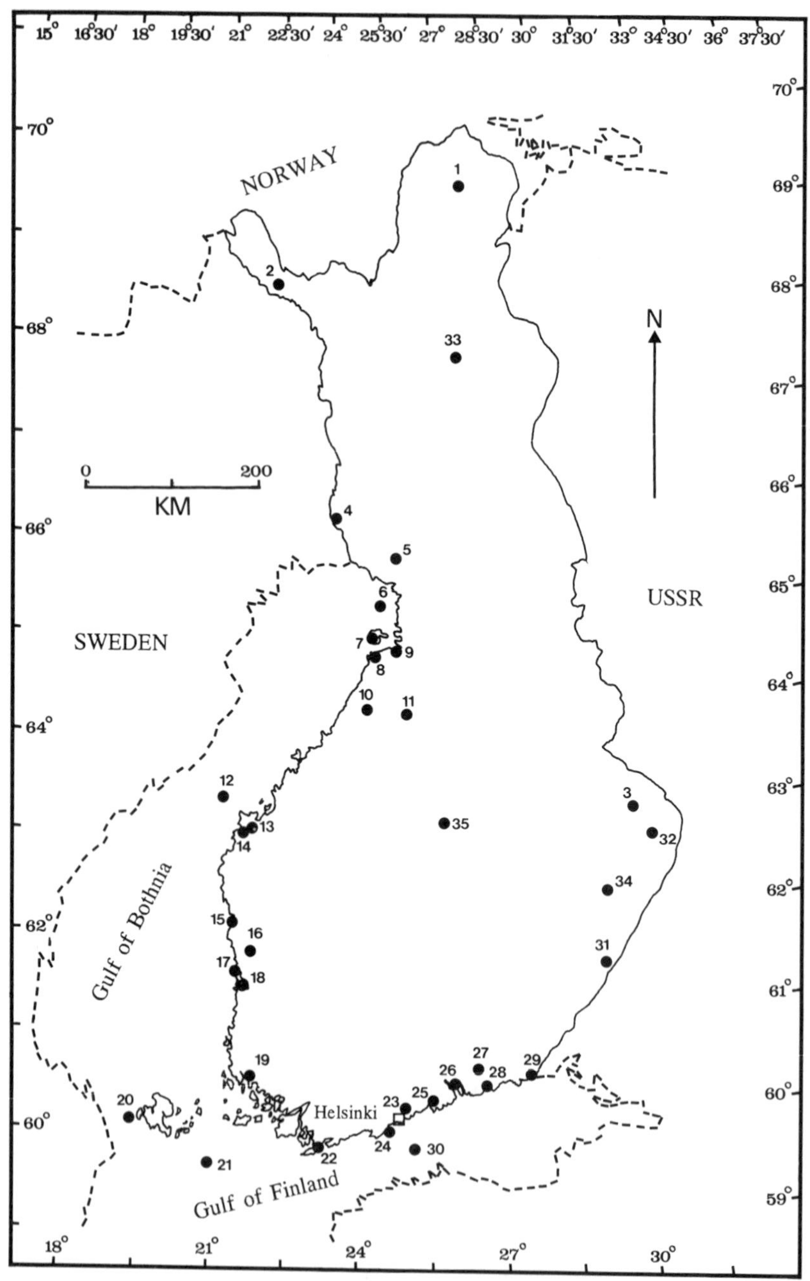

Figure 11: Map showing the location of the sites in Finland

Unprotected

A series of areas on the offshore island of Hailuoto. Typical features include extensive reedbeds bordered by meadows of tall, wild grasses. The island is permanently inhabited and human activities include fishing and hunting. Cottage development and hunting cause disturbance of the area.

Species occurring on passage include *Cygnus cygnus* (autumn av. 3000; spring av. 200) and *Anser anser* (autumn av. 200).

008 Merikylänlahti – Ulkonokka, Siikajokisuu, Säikänlahti, and Hientaniitynlahti (Oulu)

64°49'N, 24°42'E 1370 ha

Unprotected

Merikylänlahti is an open sea bay, the western end of which is called Ulkonokka. Säikänlahti and Hietaniitynlahti lie just to the south and are former bays, now separated from the sea by a narrow strip of land. Siikajokisuu is the mouth of the River Siika where it flows into Merikylänlahti; there are many large sandbars in this particular area. The shores of the main bay include long stretches of shingle in the west. Adjacent land is characterised by fields of grasses merging into reeds. The bay is extensively fished, and the whole area is a popular resort for tourists and day-trippers. Plans to dredge the river-mouth could threaten the important sandbar habitats.

Breeding species include *Sterna albifrons* (10 pairs), whilst *Anser erythropus* (spring av. 20) occurs on passage.

009 Liminganlahti – Lumijoenselkä (Oulu)

64°50'N, 25°20'E 10,825 ha

Proposed for protected status

The inner and outer zones of Liminka Bay. The adjacent coastal areas are rising very rapidly (8-10 mm per year) relative to sea-level and the land is very flat. Habitats include open water, deciduous forest (mainly *Betula*), grass meadows, and reedbeds. A number of medium sized rivers flow into Liminka Bay carrying large amounts of dissolved nutrients arising from agricultural fertilisers. The area is a popular fishing and hunting resort and is in danger from development pressures.

Breeding species include *Circus aeruginosus* (6 pairs). An important area for passage waterfowl with *Cygnus cygnus* (spring av. 2000), *Anser fabalis fabalis* (spring av. 10,000), *A. erythropus* (spring av. 50), and *Tringa erythropus* (spring max. 500).

010 Letto and Vihaspauha (Oulu)

64°17'N, 24°40'E 200 ha

Unprotected

An area including wide sandy shores, coastal meadows and many small ponds, and lagoons. Human activities include recreational use of the area (e.g. horse-riding, summer cottage development).

There is a rich avifauna of shorebirds, e.g. *Calidris alpina schinzii*, *Phalaropus lobatus*, and *Sterna albifrons*. Other species include *Emberiza aureola*.

011 Ainali, Apaja, Haapalampi, Korkatti, Kypärä, Köyrylampi, Litukka, and Suojärvi (Oulu)

64°13'N, 25°25'E 1600 ha

Unprotected

A series of small lakes lying along the upper reaches of the River Piipsa. The surroundings are marshy with abundant *Equisetum* but there are few reedbeds. There is intensive hunting of wildfowl in autumn, and digging of further ditches in the marshy areas could seriously damage the ecosystem.

An important nesting area for Anatidae with a total of *c.*850 breeding pairs, including *Anas penelope*, *A. crecca*, *A. platyrhynchos*, *A. acuta*, *A. querquedula*, *Aythya ferina*, *A. fuligula*, *Melanitta fusca*, and *Bucephala clangula*.

012 Valsörarna – Björkögrunden (Vaasa)

63°21'-63°28'N, 21°01'-21°09'E 17,700 ha (600 ha land)

Ramsar Sites (Valassaaret: 11,800 ha; Björkögrunden: 5900 ha)

Bird Sanctuaries

Two very shallow areas of archipelagic waters in the Gulf of Bothnia, with more than 100 islands and islets, most of which are treeless though a few have deciduous trees. The largest island is Storskar, which is part of the Valassaaret group. About 2 ha of new land-surface are created in the Valassaaret region each year owing to rapid rise of land relative to sea-level. Björkögrunden is a group of stony islets to the south of Valassaaret. There is a Bird Observatory and the area is also of important botanical interest. The are two small settlements on Storskar.

Breeding birds include *Aythya fuligula*, *A. marila*, *Melanitta fusca*, *Mergus serrator*, *Arenaria interpres*, *Tringa totanus*, *Larus canus*, *L. fuscus*, and *Sterna caspia* (one colony). The islands lie on an important migration route in the Gulf of Bothnia.

013 Vassorfjärden – Österfjärden – Söderfjärden (Vaasa)

63°11'N, 21°57'E 1257 ha

Unprotected

The shallow delta region of the River Kyrö. The distribution of vegetation zones is very complex, reflecting the variety of sediment deposits. Reedbeds alone cover tens of hectares. The eastern part of Vassorfjärden is extensively built upon, and across the site as a whole several hundred hectares have been lost to embankment construction and land reclamation. Fishermen have cut some of the reed areas, and there are plans for sewage pipes to be placed on the south side of Vassorfjärden.

The delta is an important area for passage *Grus grus* (autumn av. 1300).

014 Sundominlahti: southern part (Vaasa)

63°03'N, 21°40'E 624 ha

Unprotected

A large shallow sea bay. Several rivers flow into the bay, the largest of which are the Rivers Sulva and Laihian. In places, there is a zone of coastal *Typha* vegetation. Over 1000 ha of land were reclaimed in the 1960s, but the part of the remaining bay included as an important bird area has been fairly well preserved because of its local importance as a fishery. The main refuse-tip serving the city of Vaasa (population 70,000) is located on the opposite (northern) side of the bay. The site would be degraded by further reclamation or spreading of the refuse-tip.

Passage birds include *Cygnus cygnus* (spring/autumn av. 350).

015 Härkmerifjärden (Vaasa)

62°10'N, 21°27'E 530 ha

Unprotected

A former sea bay, now connected to the sea only by a channel *c.*500 m in length. There are numerous small islands and many typical sea bay features are still retained, such as extensive reedbeds and saltwater plants. The only human activity in the area is tourism in the form of day-trippers; the islands have not yet been developed for summer houses. Water-level is immediately threatened with drastic reduction owing to alterations to a nearby stream.

The entire area is important for breeding and migrating wildfowl.

016 Niemijärvi – Itäjärvi (Turku-Pori)

61°51'N, 21°50'E 686 ha

Unprotected

Formerly a 'lake'-bulge in the River Siikais, the area was subjected to water-level reduction in the 1960s (owing to hydrological regulation) and is now a complex of reedbeds, water plants and floating vegetation. The flora of the area is exceptionally diverse and holds several national rarities. There is a constant threat to the site from possible raising of the River Siikais to its former level.

The site supports very high densities of breeding Anatidae.

017 Preiviikinlahden perä, Yyteri – Riitsaranlahti and Enäjärvi (Turku-Pori)

61°33'N, 21°33'E 1087 ha

Unprotected

An extensive sea bay with a relatively simple shoreline broken by Riitasaari cove and Yyteri beach. Enäjärvi is a small, partly overgrown lake which is connected with Riitasaari by a stream *c.*2 km in length. There are wild meadows between the lake and the bay. Principal bird habitats include Yyteri beach, Enäjärvi reedbeds, and surrounding meadows. The site is exceptional in Finland for a high diversity of habitats in a relatively small area. High levels of tourism cause disturbance, as do visiting ornithologists deviating from marked paths.

An important area for passage waders in autumn, especially *Calidris* spp.

018 Kokemäenjoen suisto (Turku-Pori)

61°30'N, 21°30'E 982 ha

Unprotected

The largest delta in Finland, also holding the country's largest area of uninterrupted reedbeds. In the 1940s the delta was growing shallower by 3 cm per year and extending seaward by 40 m at the same time. Surrounding thickets and meadows are also of importance for birds. The River Kokemäki is threatened by high pollution levels from nearby industry. The industrial infrastructure (railways, power-lines etc.) are threatening the delta itself, which is also endangered by drainage.

The area holds approximately 1000 breeding pairs of Anatidae, including *Anas penelope*, *A. crecca*, *A. platyrhynchos*, *A. acuta*, *A. querquedula*, *A. clypeata*, *Aythya ferina*, *A. fuligula*, and *Bucephala clangula*. Other breeding birds include *Circus aeruginosus* (8-10 pairs).

019 Halkkoaukko – Oukkulanlahti, Rukanaukko, and Louhisaarenlahti (Turku-Pori)

60°34'N, 21°52'E 659 ha

Unprotected

A series of rather small, contiguous sea bays within the northern part of a much larger bay: Naantali-Askainen. All of the bays are shallow and eutrophic, with borders of extensive reedbeds passing into drier fields of wild grasses. The bays are locally important fisheries. Summer cottages have spread to virtually all parts of the coastline which are suitable for building on, and some fields have been earmarked for drainage and cultivation.

An important area for passage waterfowl, mostly *Cygnus* spp. and dabbling ducks.

020 Signilskär Bird Sanctuary (Turku-Pori)

60°09'N, 19°20'-19°25'E 11,600 ha Ramsar Site

Bird Sanctuary

An offshore archipelago and surrounding sea, centred on Signilskär Island (1.5 km long). Most of the 50 islands and islets are treeless.

The islands support large numbers of *Somateria mollissima*, *Alca torda*, *Cepphus grylle*, and Laridae.

021 Southern part of archipelagic seas: Föglö – Dragsfjärd (Turku-Pori)

59°45'N, 20°00'-23°00'E many thousand hectares

Includes Ramsar Site (Björkör and Lågskär: 5760 ha)

National Park; Nature Reserve (Björkör); Bird Sanctuary (Lågskär); private reserve (Klåvskär)

A very extensive archipelagic area. The Ramsar Site consists of two separate areas containing two wooded islands with freshwater pools, over 150 islets (mostly treeless), and open sea areas. Human activities include commercial shipping and intensive recreational boating in summer. Summer cottages are increasing in number.

Breeding seabirds include *Sterna caspia*. There is an important pre-moult gathering of male *Somateria mollissima* (150,000); a considerable proportion of these remain to moult.

022 Svanvik – Henriksberg, Täcktbukten – Österfjärden and Västerfjärden (Uusimaa)

59°51'N, 23°25'E 322 ha

Unprotected

A series of four shallow bays, two of which (Österfjärden and Västerfjärden) are becoming separated from the sea. All of the bays have flats which are at least partly exposed during low tide. The site remains unfrozen in autumn for a longer period than surrounding areas. Svanvik and Täktbukten are bordered by hayfields, otherwise only summer cottages disturb the shores. Large numbers of visiting birdwatchers sometimes cause problems with disturbance.

Passage waterfowl includes *Cygnus cygnus* (autumn av. 200) and *Anser anser* (autumn av. 600).

023 Viiki Nature Reserve (Uusimaa)

60°13'N, 25°00'E 247 ha Ramsar Site

Nature Reserve

An area of the Vantaa river mouth just north-east of Helsinki, including a small island (Lammassaari Farholmen), marshlands, and the shallow estuarine waters of the coastal inlet. The marshes are dominated by reedbeds. The reserve is surrounded by densely populated suburbs of Helsinki, and there is a major motorway which forms the site's north-west border. Water pollution is a potential threat.

The area supports a large population of breeding birds including *Podiceps cristatus*, *Anas platyrhynchos*, *Larus ridibundus*, and *Acrocephalus schoenobaenus*.

024 Östersundominlahti (Uusimaa)

60°00'N, 25°13'E 110 ha

Unprotected

A sea bay bordered by thick bushes, *Betula* woods, and several large reedbeds. Sheltered areas of the bay have abundant floating vegetation. Construction of a pier is proposed for one of the major islands in Östersundom; this will greatly increase boat traffic if the plans are implemented.

Breeding birds include *Porzana porzana*, *Crex crex*, and *Acrocephalus arundinaceus* (0-3; fluctuates annually).

025 Kaupunginselkä – Stensbölefjärden (Uusimaa)

60°15'N, 25°36'E 541 ha Includes Ramsar Site (Ruskis Nature Reserve 235 ha)

Nature Reserve (Ruskis 235 ha)
The delta of the River Porvoo with many large reedbeds and a rich flora including a number of national rarities. The Ramsar Site includes the inshore island of Svino and surrounding marshlands near the river mouth. Svino is linked to the mainland by a causeway and there are several settlements in the area. Sewage pollution arising from Porvoo city is a problem.
Breeding species include *Podiceps cristatus*, *Botaurus stellaris*, *Anas platyrhynchos*, *Aythya ferina*, *A. fuligula*, *Circus aeruginosus*, *Fulica atra*, and *Larus ridibundus*. *Mergus albellus* (autumn max. 120) occurs on passage.

026 Pernajanlahti (Uusimaa)

60°27'N, 26°02'E 642 ha

Partly protected (460 ha) under National Conservation Law

A long (*c.*10 km) and narrow sea bay with several small inshore islands. Part of the shoreline consists of fields, but the main features are extensive reedbeds, over 200 m wide in places. Some of the islands are covered with deciduous forest. Eutrophication, arising from nearby settlements, has affected the bay.
Breeding birds include *Circus aeruginosus* (3-5 pairs). The site is also an important staging area for swans, geese, and *Grus grus*.

027 Teutjärvi and Suvijärvi (Uusimaa)

60°36'N, 26°30'E 552 ha

Unprotected

Teutjärvi is a lake formed at the junction of two rivers (Teutjoki and Kymijoki), whilst Suvijärvi is a lake-like widening of the River Kymi itself. The most important habitat is formed by extensive reedbeds. Teutjärvi is regularly fished and its water-level has been artificially reduced in the past to prevent flooding.
Breeding species (pairs) include *Botaurus stellaris* (3) and *Circus aeruginosus* (3).

028 Santaniemenselkä – Tyyslahti (Kymi)

60°27'N, 26°36'E 448 ha

Unprotected

The estuarine mouth of a tributary of the River Kymi. The water is shallow, and sediment deposited by the incoming channel continuously shifts the shoreline seaward. Vegetation zones are therefore also in constant flux. The area is notable for several large reedbeds. The bay is traversed by an actively used shipping lane.
Large numbers of Anatidae breed in the reedbed areas.

029 Kirkon – Vilkkiläntura (Kymi)

60°32'N, 27°45'E 192 ha

Unprotected

A small sea bay on the western edge of the Bay of Virolahti. The shores are bordered by a number of large meadows of sedges and grasses. The area has been partly drained, and is used for wildfowling in autumn. The site's future may be threatened by further drainage, disturbance from fishermen and birdwatchers, and construction of summer cottages. However, planning permission for holiday homes has so far been consistently refused.
Passage waterfowl include *Cygnus columbianus* (spring av. 200) and *C. cygnus* (spring av. 400), which feed on coastal meadows.

030 Gulf of Finland (Kymi, Uusimaa)

*c.*60°00'N, 23°00'-27°00'E several hundred thousand ha

Includes Ramsar Sites (Aspskär: 369 ha; Söderskär and Långören: 9632 ha)

National Parks (Itäisen Suomenlahden; Tammisaari); Bird Sanctuaries (Aspskär; Nothamn), Nature Reserves (Långören; Tvärminne)

A vast area of archipelagic waters and open sea. Oil spillages and leakages from tankers and other vessels cause pollution problems, whilst summer houses and recreational boating cause disturbance to breeding birds.

The archipelagic islands are important breeding sites for seabirds including *Larus canus*, *L. fuscus*, *L. argentatus*, *L. marinus*, *Sterna paradisaea*, *Uria aalge*, *Alca torda*, and *Cepphus grylle*. Other breeding species include *Aythya fuligula*, *Somateria mollissima*, and *Tringa totanus*. The sea areas are important for resting boreal and arctic migrants in May and June, with Gaviidae (25,000), *Clangula hyemalis* (1,000,000+), *Melanitta nigra* (200,000+), Stercorariidae, and waders (resting on islets). Tens of thousands of male *Somateria mollissima* congregate in the outer archipelago prior to moulting.

031 Siikalahti (Kymi)

61°34'N, 29°35'E 400 ha

Fully protected

A sheltered, shallow bay of Lake Simpele, with floating vegetation and extensive reedbeds. Parts of the lake shores are cultivated. Since the area was purchased by the state in the mid-1980s, problems of sewage/waste disposal, wildfowling, and holiday home construction have been alleviated.

Breeding species include *Botaurus stellaris*, *Circus aeruginosus*, *Pandion haliaetus*, *Porzana porzana*, *Locustella fluviatilis*, and *Acrocephalus palustris*. *Cygnus cygnus* (autumn max. 130) occurs on passage.

032 Kesonsuo – Juurikkasuo – Piitsonsuo (Pohjois-Karjala)

62°50'N, 30°50'E 4000 ha

Unprotected

A large complex of mires and bogs, together with River Koita.

Perhaps the most important area of bogland for birds in Finland; *c.*2000 pairs of 35 species were recorded nesting in 1964, including *Anser fabalis* and *Grus grus*.

033 Koitilaiskaira (Lappi)

67°40'-67°50'N, 26°50'-27°41'E 34,400 ha Ramsar Site

Strict Nature Reserve

An area south-west of Lake Tekojärvi; 60+ per cent is covered with peatlands interspersed with small streams and pools. The remaining area is forested with subalpine *Betula* stands on higher ground. The area is drained by the River Luiro, tributaries of the Kemijoki, and numerous small channels flowing into Lake Teko.

An important area for breeding waterfowl (5000-6000 pairs of 39 species recorded in 1979) including *Cygnus cygnus*, *Anser fabalis*, *Melanitta nigra*, *M. fusca*, and *Mergus albellus*, plus waders like *Philomachus pugnax*, *Lymnocryptes minimus*, *Tringa erythropus*, *T. glareola*, and *Phalaropus lobatus*.

034 Kiesjärvi, Hautalampi – Jokilampi and Jouhtenuslampi (Pohjois-Karjala)

62°18'N, 29°45'E 475 ha

Unprotected

Hautalampi and Jokilampi are halves of an embayment of Lake Orivesi which is divided into two by a narrow ridge. Jouhtenuslampi is an adjacent area connected with Orivesi by a channel, whilst Kiesjärvi is connected with Jouhtenuslampi by a ditch *c*.5 km in length. Kiesjärvi is the shallowest of the four open-water areas with large beds of *Equisetum* and *Typha*. Jouhtenuslampi is similar but smaller with more floating vegetation. Finally, Hautalampi – Jokilampi is open in character. The water-level of Kiesjärvi was lowered considerably in 1960. Wildfowling is regular in autumn.

An important area for breeding wildfowl and for passage waders.

035 Heinä – Suvanto – Suvantojärvi (Keski-Suomi)

63°08'N, 26°10'E 546 ha

Unprotected

Suvantojärvi is a small lake connected with lake Heinä-Suvanto, which in turn flows into the River Suvanto. Neither lake has much free-flowing water and all commoner water-plant species are to be found in abundance. The lake shores are well forested and the whole site is virtually undisturbed, except for hunting in autumn.

Passage waterfowl include *Cygnus cygnus* (spring av. 150) and *Anser fabalis fabalis* (spring av. 800).

MAIN REFERENCES

IUCN (1987) Directory of wetlands of international importance. Gland, Switzerland, and Cambridge, U.K.: IUCN.

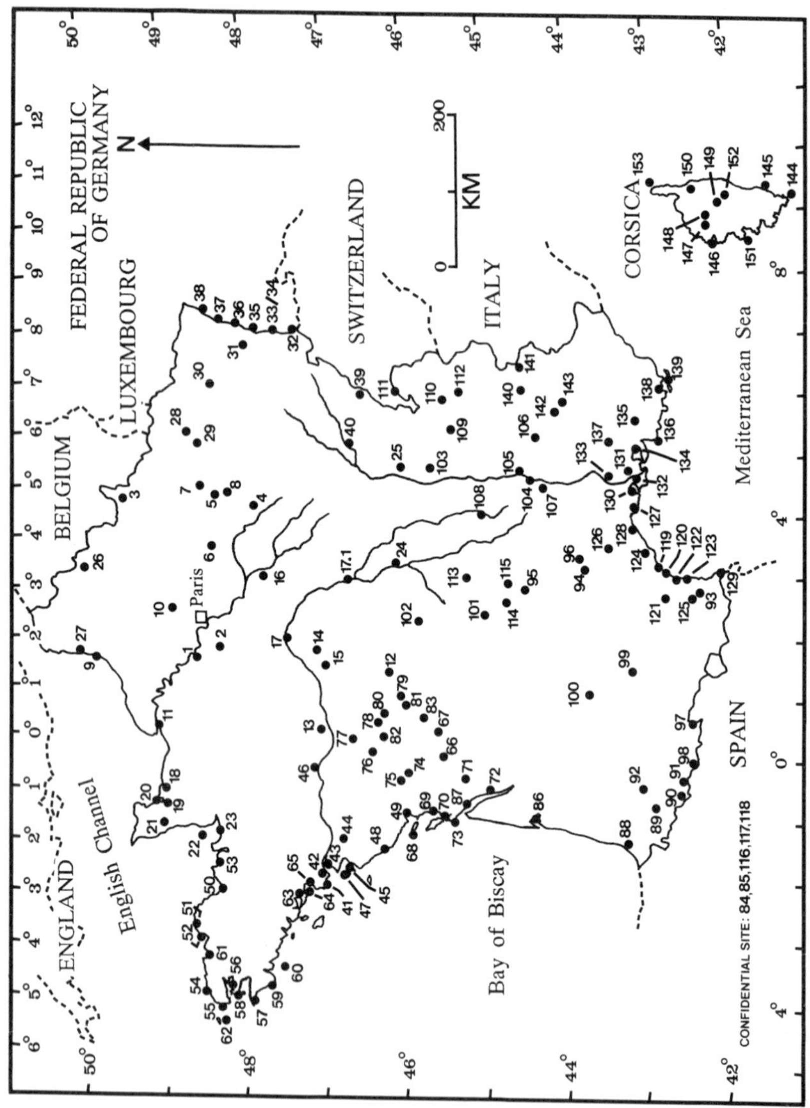

Figure 12: Map showing the location of the sites in France

FRANCE

Calandra Lark *Melanocorypha calandra*

INTRODUCTION

General Information

France is one of the largest countries in Europe, with an area of some 551, 600 sq km. The North Sea, the Channel, the Atlantic Ocean, and the Mediterranean Sea border the country to the north, south, and west, and give it an extensive sandy or rocky coastline.

With 55 million inhabitants, France has a low population density compared with other North-West European countries (an average of 98.5 inhabitants per sq km), but there is considerable variation regionally. For example, some parts such as the valley of the River Seine, the North, the valley of the River Rhone, and the 'Côte d'Azur', have between 100-200 inhabitants per sq km, whilst other regions, such as the Massif Central or the Bourgogne do not have more than 25 inhabitants per sq km.

France has two big sedimentary basins (Bassin Parisien and Bassin Aquitain), two large river systems (catchments of the Rhone and Rhine), two young alpine mountain chains (Pyrenees and Alps), and several older mountain chains (Massif Central, Massif Armoricain, and Vosges).

About 25 per cent of France's territory is woodland, 5-6 per cent are heathland, maquis or garigue, 28-30 per cent are grasslands ('natural' and artificial), and 2.5-3 per cent are wetlands (more than a quarter of the wetlands being on the coast).

In France, four main vegetation zones are recognised:

1. Mountain zone. This has a similar flora to arctic regions and there are numerous boreo-alpine species. Located at the alpine level (in Vosges, Jura, Alps, Pyrenees, Corsica, and in parts of the Massif Central), this zone includes formations with *Pinus uncinata*, alpine grasslands with *Rhododendron* spp. and *Vaccinium uliginosum*, and vegetation associated with snow and ice (*Dryas octopetala*, *Ranunculus glacialis* etc).

2. Mediterranean zone. A floristically rich zone which can be divided into the following sub-zones:

   - Liguro-mediterranean sub-zone. This sub-zone can be distinguished in the departments of Var and Alpes-Maritimes and on Corsica. The climax vegetation is generally formations with *Quercus suber*.

   - Mediterranean sub-zone (*sensu stricto*). This occupies the rest of the Mediterranean zone, where the climax vegetation is generally formations with *Quercus ilex*.

   - Atlantico-mediterranean sub-zone (e.g. in Aquitaine) where the climax vegetation is formations with *Quercus pyrenaica*, *Arbutus unedo*, etc.

   The above-mentioned climax vegetation has generally been replaced by or degraded to: pine forest with *Pinus halepensis*, *P. pinea* or *P. pinaster*, maquis on siliceous soil and garigue on calcareous soil; and calcareous and siliceous grasslands.

   Also within the Mediterranean zone is the Crau with *Asphodelus fistulosus* (the only semi-desert zone in France).

3. Atlantic zone. This is located along the Atlantic coast, and in Normandy it essentially occupies the siliceous zones where there is heathland with *Erica cinerea*, *Genista anglica* etc. In the calcareous zones, there is a northward extension of Mediterranean species as far north as the region of Nantes.

4. Medio-european zone. This occupies the east of France and the Massif Central, and includes montane forests of *Fagus* and *Abies*, and collinean forests of *Quercus* and Carpinus with sub-montane plant species.

Sixty per cent of France is covered by agricultural land or grazing pastures, and all natural habitats are more or less degraded due to human activities. Currently drainage and urbanisation (road networks etc.) are having a major impact on bird habitats, whilst tourism (especially on the coast) and hunting (there are more than 1.5 million hunters) are major factors affecting bird populations.

Ornithological importance

France has more than 250 breeding species with 400 or so species regularly occurring. The country has one endemic species occurring only on the island of Corsica, *Sitta whiteheadi*, and quite a few endemic subspecies including *Luscinia svecica namnetum*. The following habitat-types can be identified:

- Coastal zones with islets, rocky habitat and coastal wetlands. These are important in a European context for their migratory birds, although it is often difficult to estimate the total number of birds occurring. Large numbers of waterfowl use the sites along the north and west coasts on passage and in winter, including *Branta bernicla* (large numbers in winter) and *Platalea leucorodia* (Dutch breeding birds on passage).

  Along the Mediterranean coast there are a number of very important wetland sites, including the Camargue, with its very large breeding populations of Ardeidae and *Phoenicopterus ruber*. The rocky coasts and islands of the Mediterranean also have breeding *Calonectris diomedea* and *Pandion haliaetus*.

- Inland wetlands. These are threatened by drainage and have important populations of Ardeidae including *Botaurus stellaris*. Other important breeding species include *Crex crex* and *Chlidonias hybridus*.

- Woodlands. These are extensive in France and still support important populations of raptors, especially *Pernis apivorus* and *Milvus* spp.

- Agricultural land. In some regions where there is a good diversity of agricultural production, such as the plains of Poitou-Charentes, there are still good populations of *Circus* spp., *Tetrax tetrax*, and *Burhinus oedicnemus*.
- Mountain regions. Especially important are the high ranges of the Pyrenees and the Alps which still hold important populations of raptors such as *Gypaetus barbatus* and gamebirds such as *Lagopus mutus pyrenaicus* and *Alectoris graeca saxatilis*.
- Mediterranean scrub. This is important for Mediterranean species, especially warblers, such as *Sylvia conspicillata*, *S. cantillans*, and *S. melanocephala* (and *S. sarda* on Corsica).

The creation in recent years of different working groups and the coordination of enquiries by 'L'Union Nationale des Associations Ornithologiques' has meant that fairly good population estimates exist for the following species (only those species important in a European context are mentioned): *Ixobrychus minutus* (450+ pairs), *Botaurus stellaris* (320+ pairs), *Nycticorax nycticorax* (3370+ pairs), *Ardea purpurea* (2740+ pairs in 1983), *Phoenicopterus ruber* (*c.*20,000 pairs in Camargue), *Pernis apivorus* (8000-12,000 pairs), *Milvus migrans* (5800-8000 pairs), *M. milvus* (2300-2900 pairs), *Gypaetus barbatus* (20-25 pairs), *Circaetus gallicus* (1000+ pairs), *Circus aeruginosus* (700-1000 pairs), *C. cyaneus* (2800-3800 pairs), *C. pygargus* (3000+ pairs), *Hieraaetus pennatus* (136-239 pairs), *Crex crex* (1750-2500 pairs), *Tetrax tetrax* (7160-8550 males in 1978/79; 5160-6300 males in 1982/83; decline continuing), *Chlidonias hybridus* (1000-2000 pairs) and *Sitta whiteheadi* (2000 pairs). For the following species, information is scant or based on rough estimates: *Burhinus oedicnemus* (4000-5000 pairs), *Lullula arborea* (10,000+ pairs in 1976; but this species is decreasing), *Luscinia svecica* (1000+ pairs in 1976), *Hippolais polyglotta* (less than 100,000 pairs in 1976), *Sylvia undata* (100,000+ pairs in 1976), and *Lanius collurio* (100,000+ pairs in 1976).

France lies on the migratory route for species breeding in northern Europe etc., which are bound for southern Europe or Africa. The diurnal passage of raptors (e.g. *Pernis apivorus, Milvus migrans, M. milvus*) is concentrated at various bottleneck sites in the Massif Central and Pyrenees (e.g. Organbidexka).

The extensive coastal wetlands of France provide an important network of sites for passage waterfowl, especially waders, moving to and from breeding areas. In a European context, these areas are very important too for wintering *Branta bernicla* (e.g. 76,000+ in December 1987), *Recurvirostra avosetta*, *Pluvialis squatarola*, and to a certain extent *Calidris alba* and *Arenaria interpres*. Particularly noteworthy is the passage of *Grus grus*, with 45,000-50,000 birds crossing France and stopping over at three principal sites where some birds also overwinter.

Conservation infrastructure and protected-area system

The two main laws governing conservation of natural habitats are the National Parks Act (1960) and the Nature Conservation Act (1976). There are a number of different types of protected area which can be designated according to these acts (number of sites designated is as on 30 September 1988); the first three categories (high level of protection) cover 0.8 per cent of the territory:

1. Nature Reserve (91 sites covering more than 100,000 ha)
   Established by ministerial decree, Nature Reserves aim at the conservation of the natural environment, its fauna, flora or geological richness. A state or private organisation manages each reserve. Human activities are subject to restrictions.
2. National Parks (6 sites covering 348,500 ha – central zones only)
   Established by a decree issued by Council of State, National Parks include two types of zones:
   - a central zone which is intended to ensure the integrity of the natural environment and where human activities are subject to restrictions.
   - a peripheral zone which must be a buffer between the exterior of the park and the central zone. The peripheral zone has, amongst other things, reception areas and lodging facilities for visitors.

3. 'Arrêté de biotope' (117 sites covering more than 3,500 ha)
   Established by prefectorial decree, the 'arrêtés de biotope' are local conservation measures, which aim at the preservation of protected species' habitats.

4. Conventional reserve
   They are the result of a commitment from state organisations, local authorities or private organisations to safeguard in the long term the richness of the natural environment which is their property. An agreement is signed with the Ministry of Environment or nature conservation organisations.

5. 'Site classé'
   Development is allowed only after ministerial authorization; it is principally a landscape protection instrument.

6. Coastal hunting reserve ('réserve de chasse du Domaine Public Maritime')
   These are created by the Ministry of Environment and are mostly mudflats and open sea; hunting is prohibited.

7. Hunting reserve
   These are created by hunting organisations, and are areas where hunting is prohibited. National Hunting Reserves are created by the Ministry of Environment (31 sites covering 48,800 ha)

The Ministry of Environment is the central administrative authority responsible for nature conservation.

International measures relevant to the conservation of sites

France has ratified the Ramsar Convention, World Heritage Convention, and the Barcelona Convention's Protocol concerning Mediterranean Specially Protected Areas, but not the Bern Convention and Bonn Convention (both signed but not ratified). As a Member State of the European Community, it is also bound by the terms of the EEC Wild Birds Directive. Only one Ramsar Site has been designated (the Camargue) and two natural World Heritage Sites (Baie du Mont-St-Michel and Golfe de Porto et Presqu'île de Scandola) which are all included in this inventory. Forty-one Nature Reserves or Hunting Reserves have been designated as EEC Special Protection Areas (although at least ten of these are not thought to be important bird areas in an EEC context). France has designated ten Mediterranean Specially Protected Areas and a number of Biogenetic Reserves.

Overview of the inventory

One hundred and fifty-two important bird areas are included in the French inventory, with a combined area of over 2,580,000 ha; more than half are wetlands. A large number of them are under threat with problems arising mainly from drainage, agricultural changes, transport developments, hunting and recreational activities. A lot of the areas are wholly or largely unprotected.

The following points should be born in mind when considering the inventory:

1. Although France is important for migratory birds, few sites meet the numerical criteria. This is because the migration of many species is dispersed across France, or because it is difficult to estimate the total numbers of each species occurring during the season at a particular site.

2. Some species, particularly raptors, have large breeding territories and are widely distributed. With regard to the selection of sites, some species have been given particular attention (e.g. *Gypaetus barbatus*, *Gyps fulvus*, and *Hieraaetus fasciatus*), whilst others (e.g. *Pernis apivorus*, *Milvus* spp., and *Hieraaetus pennatus*) have not. Similarly, particular attention was not given to *Burhinus oedicnemus* and most passerines.

3. Some major sites, with large surface areas, have important populations of birds which are distributed heterogeneously, with some sectors richer than others. Despite this, all sectors should be protected from changes that will affect bird populations.

Acknowledgements

The current inventory owes a great deal to the work that was completed in 1981 by the ICBP European Community Working Group (Osieck and Mörzer Bruyns 1981). For France the data was gathered by L. Marion (Université de Rennes), by F. de Beaufort and colleagues at the Muséum National d'Histoire Naturelle (Paris), and by A. Reille and M. Métais (Ligue Française pour la Protection des Oiseaux [LPO]). Also of considerable value was the study completed in 1984 (also by the ICBP European Community Working Group) on important bird areas in the European Community under serious threat (Gammell and Karpowicz 1984), with the data for France gathered by D. Bredin (LPO).

The current inventory, which has updated and added to the above mentioned studies, is based on the report 'Réactualisation des zones françaises de grande importance pour la conservation des oiseaux sauvages dans la Communauté Européenne' (Thauront in press) which has been carried out on behalf of the French section of ICBP and LPO and was financed by the Royal Society for the Protection of Birds (RSPB). This report benefited greatly from advice provided by staff at the Muséum National d'Histoire Naturelle (Paris), and the consultancy firm Ecosphère provided M. Thauront with the time to undertake the work. J.-C. Kovacs and V. Bobe of Ecosphère, and J. Trotignon, G. Jarry, M. Métais, M. Terrasse, and C. Riols also gave much help.

The following organisations and individuals helped with advice and information: Ar Vran, AROMP, CEEP, Centre d'Ecologie Montagnarde de Gabas, CEOA, COA, COCA, C. O. Gard, COL, Conservatoire des Sites Lorrain, CORA, COP, CORIF, CRBPO, CROAP, Espaces et Recherches, FIR, GAEO, G.D.O. Saône et Loire, GEAI, GEPOP, GOAS, GOLA, G. O. Nord, G. O. Normand, GOR, GOT, GOV, GRIVE, Laboratoire d'Evolution des Systèmes Naturels et Modifiés, LPO, Naturalistes de Franche-Comté, Naturalistes de l'Ardèche, Nature-Aveyron, Nature Centre, P. N. R. de Corse, P. N. R. du Marais Poitevin, P. N. R. du Lubéron, SAIAK, SEPOL, SEPNB, SNPN, Sologne-Nature, SPNMP, Station Biologique de Bailleron, Station Biologique de la Tour du Valat, Station de Recherches ONC Chanteloup. The introduction was written by M. Thauront.

INVENTORY

No.	Site name	Region	Criteria used to select site [see p.18]							
			0	1(i)	1(ii)	1(iii)	1(iv)	2	3	4
001	Boucle de Moisson	IF							*	
002	Etangs de Saint Hubert	IF							*	
003	Plateau Ardennais	CA						*	*	
004	Lac de la Forêt d'Orient	CA				*		*	*	
005	Etangs de la Horre	CA				*		*	*	
006	Marais de Saint-Gond	CA							*	
007	Etang de Belval en Argonne	CA						*	*	
008	Lac du Der-Chantecoq et étangs latéraux	CA				*		*	*	
009	Baie de la Somme, Baie de L'Authie et Estuaire de la Canche	NC,PE				*			*	
009-1	Estuaire de la Canche	NC								
009-2	Baie de la Somme	PE								
010	Marais de Sacy	PE							*	
011	Estuaire de la Seine (right bank)	HN				*			*	
012	La Brenne	CE				*			*	
012-1	Etang de la Mer Rouge	CE								
012-2	Etangs de Rochefort, de l'Hardouine et des Bordes	CE							*	
012-3	Réserve naturelle de Chèrine	CE								
013	Lac de Rille	CE							*	
014	Sologne des étangs y compris forêt de Bruadan	CE							*	
015	Etang de l'Arche	CE							*	

No.	Site name	Region	Criteria used to select site [see p.18]							
			0	1(i)	1(ii)	1(iii)	1(iv)	2	3	4
016	Etang de Galetas	CE,BE						*	*	
017	Vallée de la Loire: Feurs – Nantes	PL,CE,BE, RA,AE			*				*	
017-1	La Charité sur Loire	BE,CE								
018	Falaises du Bessin	BN	*							
019	Baie des Veys	BN				*		*	*	
020	Iles Saint-Marcouf	BN			*					
021	Marais de la Sangsurière et des Gorges	BN				*		*	*	
022	Iles Chausey	BN			*					
023	Baie du Mont-St-Michel et île des Landes	BT,BN			*	*			*	
024	Val d'Allier	BE,CE,AE						*	*	
024-1	Mars-sur-Allier	BE,CE								
024-2	Val d'Allier	AE								
025	Bresse et zones inondables du Val de Saône	BE,RA,						*	*	
025-1	La Truchère	BE,RA								
025-2	Cormoranche-sur-Saône	BE,RA								
026	Vallée de la Scarpe	NC							*	
027	Marais de Balançon	NC							*	
028	La Chaussée	LE						*	*	
029	Lac de Madine	LE						*	*	
030	Etang de Lindre	LE				*			*	
031	Ried de Colmar – Selestat	AC						*	*	
032	Rhin et Grand Canal d'Alsace: Village Neuf – Chalampé y compris forêt domaniale de la Harth Sud et forêt domaniale de la Harth Nord	AC				*			*	
033/034	Rhin et Grand Canal d'Alsace: Chalampé – Biesheim	AC				*			*	
035	Rhin et Grand Canal d'Alsace: Schoenau – Daubensand y compris forêt du Rhin Daubensand	AC				*			*	
036	Rhin et Grand Canal d'Alsace: Daubensand – Strasbourg y compris bois de Sommerley	AC				*			*	
037	Rhin: Robertsau – Dalhunden	AC				*			*	
038	Rhin: Dalhunden – Munchhouse y compris bois de Munchhouse	AC				*			*	
039	Bassin du Drugeon: Pontarlier – Frasne	FC							*	
040	Basse vallée du Doubs: Dôle sud	FC						*	*	
041	Traict et marais de Guérande	PL				*			*	
042	Marais de Brière	PL				*			*	
043	Estuaire de la Loire	PL				*		*	*	
044	Lac de Grand-Lieu	PL				*		*	*	
045	Baie et marais de Bourgneuf	PL				*			*	
046	Marais de Basse-Maine et île Saint-Aubin	PL				*		*	*	
047	Marais salants de Noirmoutier	PL				*			*	
048	Marais et forêt d'Olonne	PL				*			*	
049	Marais Poitevin avec Baie de l'Aiguillon, Pointe d'Arçay, Communaux du marais Vendéen et île de Charrouin	PL,PC				*		*	*	
050	Baie de Saint-Brieuc	BT				*				
051	Les Sept-Iles	BT		*	*				*	

No.	Site name	Region	Criteria used to select site [see p.18]							
			0	1(i)	1(ii)	1(iii)	1(iv)	2	3	4
052	Ile de Goulmedec	BT							*	
053	Iles de la Colombière, de la Néllière et des Haches	BT							*	
054	Ilots du Trévors	BT							*	
055	Archipel de Molène	BT							*	
056	Rade de Brest: Baie de Daoulas et Anse du Poulmic	BT							*	
057	Cap Sizun	BT								*
058	Presqu'île de Crozon	BT			*				*	
059	Marais de la Baie d'Audierne	BT						*	*	
060	Archipel des Glénans	BT		*	*				*	
061	Baie de Morlaix et de Carantec	BT				*			*	
062	Ile d'Ouessant	BT			*				*	
063	Golfe du Morbihan, marais de Suscinio et Ile de Meaban	BT				*			*	
064	Etier de Penerf	BT				*			*	
065	Anse de Kervoyal et estuaire de la Vilaine	BT				*			*	
066	Vallée de la Charente	PC						*	*	
067	Plaine de Villefagnan	PC						*	*	
068	Anse du Fiers d'Ars-en-Ré	PC				*			*	
069	Anse de Fouras, baie d'Yves et marais de Rochefort	PC				*		*	*	
070	Ile d'Oléron, marais de Brouage et la Gripperie Saint-Symphorien	PC				*			*	
071	Plaines de Pons-Rouffiac	PC						*	*	
072	Marais du Blayais	PC,AN							*	
073	Bonne Anse	PC				*			*	
074	Plaines de Niort Sud-est	PC						*	*	
075	Plaines de Niort Nord-ouest	PC						*	*	
076	Plaines de Saint-Jouin-de-Marne et d'Assais-les-Jumeaux	PC						*	*	
077	Plaine de Saint-Jean-de-Sauves	PC						*	*	
078	Le Pinail, forêt de Moulière, bois du Défens et de la Roche de Bran	PC							*	
079	Camp de Montmorillon	PC							*	
080	Plateau de Bellefonds	PC				*		*	*	
081	Bois de l'Hospice, étang de Beaufour et environs	PC							*	
082	Plaines de Mirebeau et de Neuville-du-Poitou	PC						*	*	
083	Région de Pressac et étang de Combourg	PC							*	
084	Site name and location confidential					*			*	
085	Site name and location confidential								*	
086	Bassin d'Arcachon et Banc d'Arguin	AN			*	*			*	
087	Pointe de Grave et marais du Verdon/Mer	AN				*			*	
088	Barthes de l'Adour	AN	*							
089	Forêt d'Iraty, massif des Arbailles et pic d'Orhy y compris Organbidexka	AN					*	*	*	
090	Cirque de Lescun, vallée d'Aspe et forêt d'Issaux	AN							*	
091	Vallées d'Ossau, du Bitet et de Soussoueou	AN							*	
092	Barrage d'Artix et Saligue du gave de Pau	AN							*	

No.	Site name	Region	Criteria used to select site [see p.18]							
			0	1(i)	1(ii)	1(iii)	1(iv)	2	3	4
093	Haute vallée de l'Aude et massif des Pyrénées-Orientales	LR,MP					*		*	
094	Gorges de la Dourbie	MP							*	
095	Gorges de la Truyère	AE,MP						*	*	
096	Gorges du Tarn et de la Jonte	LR,MP							*	
097	Vallées du Lis et de la Pique	MP							*	
098	Cirque de Gavarnie et environs	MP							*	
099	Palayre	MP				*			*	
100	Moissac	MP				*			*	
101	Gorges de la Dordogne	LN,AE						*	*	
102	Etang de Landes	LN							*	
103	La Dombes	RA				*			*	
103-1	Etangs de Saint Paul-de-Varax	RA								
103-2	Versailleux-le-Montellier, le Plantay	RA								
104	Val de Drôme: les Ramières	RA							*	
105	Etang de Suze la Rousse	RA							*	
106	Hauts plateaux du Vercors	RA							*	
107	Col de l'Escrinet	RA					*			
108	Etangs du Forez	RA							*	
109	Lac et marais du Bourget	RA							*	
110	Montagne des Frètes et massif environnant	RA							*	
111	Lac Léman	RA				*			*	
112	Les Bauges	RA							*	
113	La Serre	AE					*			
114	Monts et Plomb du Cantal, y compris col du Prat de Bouc	AE					*			
115	Planèze de Saint-Flour	AE							*	
116	Site name and location confidential								*	
117	Site name and location confidential								*	
118	Site name and location confidential								*	
119	Etang de Vendres	LR				*			*	
120	Etang de Pissevache	LR							*	
121	Aérodrome de Lésignan-Corbières	LR						*	*	
122	Etangs de Bages, Sigean, Ayrolle et Campignol	LR				*	*		*	
123	Littoral de l'Aude et des Pyrénées-Orientales, y compris Leucate	LR				*	*		*	
124	Etang de Capestang	LR				*			*	
125	Corbières	LR					*		*	
126	Gorges de la Vis, cirque de Navacelles et causse du Blandas	LR							*	
127	Etangs et salins d'Aigues-Mortes au Petit Rhône	LR			*	*			*	
128	Etangs et salins du Languedoc	LR			*	*			*	
129	Massif des Albères	LR							*	
130	Camargue	PAC			*	*			*	
131	Plaine de la Crau	PAC						*	*	
132	Marais entre Crau et Grand Rhône: Meyranne, Chanoine, Plan de Bourg et salins du Caban	PAC				*			*	
133	Chaîne des Alpilles	PAC							*	
134	Salines de l'étang de Berre	PAC							*	
135	Montagne Sainte Victoire	PAC							*	
136	Iles Marseillaises: Maire, Jarron, Jarre, Calséraigne, Riou et Congloué	PAC							*	
137	Massif du Petit Lubéron	PAC							*	
138	Salins d'Hyères et des Pesquiers	PAC				*			*	

No.	Site name	Region	Criteria used to select site [see p.18]							
			0	1(i)	1(ii)	1(iii)	1(iv)	2	3	4
139	Iles d'Hyères: Porquerolles, Port-Cros, le Levant	PAC							*	
140	Parc national des Ecrins	PAC							*	
141	Bois des Ayes	PAC							*	
142	Bec de Crigne	PAC							*	
143	Vallée et gorges de la Durance	PAC							*	
144	Golfe de Sud Corse: Iles Lavezzi	CS				*			*	
145	Iles Cerbicale	CS						*	*	
146	Golfe de Porto, presqu'île de Scandola et golfe de Galéria	CS							*	
147	Vallée du Fango	CS							*	
148	Vallée d'Asco	CS							*	
149	Vallée de la Restonica	CS							*	
150	Etang de Biguglia	CS				*			*	
151	Iles Sanguinaires	CS							*	
152	Vallée du Verghello	CS							*	
153	Iles Finocchiarola et Côte de Tamarone a Barcaggio	CS		*	*			*	*	

IF=Ile de France CA=Champagne-Ardenne NC=Nord-Pas-de-Calais PE=Picardie HN=Haute Normandie CE=Centre BE=Bourgogne PL=Pays de la Loire RA=Rhône-Alpes AE=Auvergne BN=Basse Normandie BT=Bretagne LE=Lorraine AC=Alsace FC=Franche-Comté PC=Poitou-Charentes AN=Aquitaine LR=Languedoc-Roussillon MP=Midi-Pyrénées LN=Limousin PAC=Provence-Alpes-Côte d'Azur CS=Corse

Comments on the inventory

1. For all sites (unless otherwise stated in the site accounts), all available up to date information (from 1987 and often 1988) has been incorporated.
2. For each site, the site name is followed by the name of the administrative region (NUTS level 2; NUTS level 1 in the case of Ile de France and Nord-Pas-de-Calais) which is given in parentheses.
3. The 'regions' used when applying the site-selection criteria are the regions given in parentheses (NUTS level 2 regions; NUTS level 1 regions in the case of Ile de France and Nord-Pas-de-Calais).
4. Passage counts are in general an estimate of the total number of a species occurring during a season (usually expressed as an average over a number of years or as a range). For some sites, however, passage figures refer to the maximum number that can be seen at the same time.
5. As mentioned above, the information about threats to sites is from 1984. For some sites this information has been brought up to date.
6. All the sites meet the site-selection criteria, except the following which have been included for other reasons (column 0 of above table):
   - 018 has been included because it is the most important site in France for *Fulmarus glacialis* and *Rissa tridactyla*.
   - 088 has been included because it is thought to qualify for several species (which are on Annex I of the EEC Wild Birds Directive), but field surveys have not been carried out.

Glossary

EEC SPA = European Community Special Protection Area. The following French words have been used in the inventory: anse = small bay; archipel = archipelago; baie = bay; barrage = dam, reservoir; cap = cape; col = pass; estuaire = estuary; étang = pond, lagoon; falaise = cliff; forêt = forest; golfe = gulf; gorge = canyon; île = island; îlot = small island; lac = lake; marais = marsh; mont, montagne = mountain; plaine = low plain; plateau = high plain; val, vallée = valley.

---

001 Boucle de Moisson (Ile de France)

49°03'N, 01°38'E 14,000 ha

Partly 'site classé'

Running water and fresh standing water, marshes, woodland, and agricultural land. Human activities include arable farming, tourism and recreation (including boating), and hunting.

Breeding species include *Pernis apivorus* (3-5 pairs), *Milvus migrans* (1 pair), *Burhinus oedicnemus* (6 pairs), and *Caprimulgus europaeus* (2 pairs). Wintering species include *Circus cyaneus* (3-4), *Anas platyrhynchos* (6000; max. 18,000 in 1982), *Mergus merganser* (400-500; max. 1200 in 1979), and *M. albellus* (150 in 1979).

002 Etangs de Saint Hubert (Ile de France)

48°43'N, 01°51'E 660 ha

Partly 'site classé' (225 ha)

Lakes with marshes beside the woodland of Rambouillet (near Paris) and agricultural land. Human activities include hunting, fishing, and agriculture.

Breeding species include *Ixobrychus minutus* (3-4 pairs) and several species of duck. It is an important site for species on passage including *Ixobrychus minutus*, *Pernis apivorus*, *Milvus migrans* (4-5), *Circus aeruginosus* (5-10), *C. cyaneus* (4-5), *Pandion haliaetus* (3-4), *Chlidonias hybridus* (4-5), and *C. niger* (30-50). Wintering species include *Pluvialis apricaria* (1500-2000).

003 Plateau Ardennais (Champagne-Ardenne)

49°51'N, 04°35'E 92,500 ha

Nature Reserve (135 ha)

Running water and fresh, standing water, woodland, bogs and marshes, wet meadows, and rocky habitats. Human activities include forestry, arable farming, hunting and shooting, tourism and recreation.

Breeding species include *Pernis apivorus* (80 pairs), *Milvus migrans* (10 pairs), *M. milvus* (20 pairs), *Circus cyaneus* (10 pairs), *C. pygargus* (5 pairs), *Bonasa bonasia* (200 pairs), *Tetrao tetrix* (15 pairs), *Aegolius funereus* (10 pairs), *Caprimulgus europaeus* (10 pairs), *Alcedo atthis* (50 pairs), *Picus canus* (20 pairs), *Lullula arborea* (30 pairs), and *Lanius collurio* (30 pairs). *Ciconia nigra* possibly breeds. *Circus cyaneus* (20) occurs in winter.

004 Lac de la Forêt d'Orient (Champagne-Ardenne)

48°16'N, 04°21'E 2500 ha

Hunting prohibited

Lake with wet meadows, woodland, hedges and cultivated land, grassland, and arable land. Human activities include agriculture, forestry, stock-raising, hunting, and recreation including sailing. The site is threatened by the creation of an artificial beach and access road with the development of tourist facilities, and the use of powered hang-gliders.

Breeding species include *Pernis apivorus* (2-4 pairs), *Milvus migrans* (15-25 pairs), *M. milvus* (2 pairs), and *Dryocopus martius* (2-3 pairs). Species occurring on passage include *Phalacrocorax carbo* (150-700), *Pernis apivorus* (20-150), *Milvus migrans*, *M. milvus*, *Pandion haliaetus* (5-20), *Falco peregrinus* (1-3), *Grus grus* (500-5000), and *Asio flammeus* (2-5). In winter species occurring include *Podiceps cristatus* (2000),*Anser fabalis* (400-2000), *Milvus milvus* (20-30), *Haliaeetus albicilla* (2-4), *Circus cyaneus* (2-30), *Falco peregrinus* (1-2), *Grus grus* (0-150), and *Asio flammeus* (1-2).

005 Etangs de la Horre (Champagne-Ardenne)

48°30'N, 04°40'E 350 ha

Unprotected

Lake with marshes, surrounded by wet meadows, woodland, grassland, and arable land. Human activities include agriculture, forestry, stock-raising, fishing, and hunting. Threatened by an increase in the area of commercial *Populus* plantations.

Breeding species include *Botaurus stellaris* (2-3 pairs), *Ardea purpurea* (4-6 pairs), *Pernis apivorus* (2-3 pairs), *Milvus migrans* (3-5 pairs), *M. milvus* (1-2 pairs), *Circus aeruginosus* (3-5 pairs), *C. cyaneus* (0-1 pair), and *Dryocopus martius* (1-2 pairs). Species occurring on passage include *Ciconia nigra*, *Pandion haliaetus* (6-7), *Grus grus* (50-2000), *Chlidonias niger* (10-70), and *Asio flammeus* (5-10). *Haliaeetus albicilla* and *Cygnus columbianus* occur in winter.

006 Marais de Saint-Gond (Champagne-Ardenne)

48°49'N, 03°50'E 3000 ha

Unprotected

Marshes and wet meadows. Human activities include hunting. Threatened by the digging of new drainage ditches, peat extraction, and disturbance from tourism.

Breeding species include *Botaurus stellaris*, *Circus aeruginosus*, *C. cyaneus*, *C. pygargus*, *Burhinus oedicnemus*, and *Asio flammeus*. Also *Grus grus* occurs on passage.

007 Etang de Belval en Argonne (Champagne-Ardenne)

48°57'N, 04°59'E 200 ha

Unprotected

Lake with marshes, surrounded by woodland, wet meadows, grassland, and arable land. Human activities include agriculture, forestry, stock-raising, fishing, and hunting. There is disturbance from hunting, fishing, and sailing.

Breeding species include *Botaurus stellaris* (2-3 pairs), *Pernis apivorus* (1-3 pairs), *Milvus migrans* (3-5 pairs), *M. milvus* (1-2 pairs), *Circus aeruginosus* (2-3 pairs), and *Dryocopus martius* (1-2 pairs). Species occurring on passage include *Ciconia nigra* (1-2), *Haliaeetus albicilla* (1), *Pandion haliaetus* (2-5), and *Luscinia svecica* (5-10).

008 Lac du Der-Chantecoq et étangs latéraux (Champagne-Ardenne)

48°34'N, 04°46'E 6000 ha EEC SPA (5000 ha)

Hunting prohibited

Lake with marshes and wet meadows, surrounded by woodland, hedges, and cultivated land, grassland, and arable land. Human activities include agriculture, forestry, stock-raising, fishing, hunting, and recreation including sailing.

Breeding species include *Botaurus stellaris* (1-2 pairs), *Ixobrychus minutus* (2-5 pairs), *Ardea purpurea* (4-6 pairs), *Pernis apivorus* (4-6 pairs), *Milvus migrans* (25-30 pairs), *M. milvus* (4-5 pairs), *Circus aeruginosus* (1-3 pairs), *Alcedo atthis* (3-6 pairs), and *Dryocopus martius* (2-3 pairs). A variety of species occur on passage including *Phalacrocorax carbo* (1300+), *Ciconia nigra* (1-8), *Pandion haliaetus* (25), *Grus grus* (37,000), and *Chlidonias niger* (350+). Wintering species include *Podiceps cristatus* (500-2000), *Cygnus columbianus* (5-20), *Anser fabalis* (700-3000), *Anas strepera* (250-

1200), *Haliaeetus albicilla* (1-3), *Circus cyaneus* (10-35), *Falco peregrinus* (1-3), *Grus grus* (max. 1800), and *Asio flammeus* (max. 25).

009 Baie de la Somme, Baie de L'Authie et Estuaire de la Canche (Nord-Pas-de-Calais, Picardie)

50°11'-50°30'N, 01°36'-01°39'E 22,000 ha

Treated here as two subsites.

009-1 Estuaire de la Canche (Nord-Pas-de-Calais)

50°32'N, 01°40'E 1500 ha EEC SPA (4855 ha)

Nature Reserve (505 ha); Coastal Hunting Reserve (4000 ha)

Estuary of the River Canche seaward of Etaples with mudflats, raised saltmarsh, beaches, sand-dunes, marshes, and wet meadows. Human activities include stock-raising, fishing, tourism, boating and hunting. There is an interchange of birds with Baie de la Somme.

Breeding species include *Caprimulgus europaeus* (10 pairs). Species occurring on passage include *Charadrius hiaticula* (500), *Pluvialis squatarola* (10-200), *Calidris alba* (50-150), and *Limosa lapponica* (50-800). Wintering wildfowl and waders include *Tadorna tadorna* (300-1700), *Haematopus ostralegus* (max. 3000), and *Numenius arquata* (150-400).

009-2 Baie de la Somme (Picardie)

50°13'N, 01°38'E 9000 ha

Coastal Hunting Reserve (7000 ha); Parc Ornithologique du Marquenterre (200 ha); partly unprotected

Large estuary and bay with mudflats and wet meadows; also sand and rocky beaches, woodland, marshes, and agricultural land. Human activities include hunting, fishing, boating, and agriculture; there is also a harbour.

Breeding species include *Botaurus stellaris* (3 pairs), *Egretta garzetta* (1 pair), *Tadorna tadorna* (350 pairs), *Circus aeruginosus* (2 pairs), *C. cyaneus*, *Porzana porzana* (1 pair), *Recurvirostra avosetta* (62-108 pairs), *Charadrius alexandrinus* (20-30 pairs), *Asio flammeus*, *Caprimulgus europaeus* (25 pairs), and *Alcedo atthis*. Species occurring on passage include *Platalea leucorodia* (tens), and *Pandion haliaetus*. Important for wintering wildfowl and waders with *Tadorna tadorna* (450-10,000), *Anas acuta* (165-2400), *Haematopus ostralegus* (3000-7700), *Recurvirostra avosetta* (max. 24), *Calidris alpina* (400-12,000), and *Numenius arquata* (690-1200). *Gavia stellata* (2-30), *G. immer* (0-1), *Platalea leucorodia*, *Circus aeruginosus*, *C. cyaneus*, *Falco peregrinus*, and *Asio flammeus* occur in winter.

010 Marais de Sacy (Picardie)

49°15'N, 02°30'E 1200 ha

Unprotected

Ponds, reedbeds, bogs and marshes. Human activities include hunting. The early shooting of waterfowl (mid-July) when some species are still breeding, and heavy hunting at other times of the year, are problems at the site.

Breeding species include *Botaurus stellaris* (9-13 pairs in 1984/1985), *Ixobrychus minutus*, *Circus aeruginosus*, and possibly *Porzana porzana*, *Chlidonias niger*, *Asio flammeus*, and *Lanius collurio*. An important area for passage migrants; species occurring include *Ciconia ciconia*, *Pandion haliaetus*, and *Crex crex*.

011 Estuaire de la Seine (right bank) (Haute Normandie)

49°28'N, 00°17'E 7800 ha

Coastal Hunting Reserve (7800 ha)

Estuary with mudflats, marshes, and wet meadows. Human activities include stock-raising, fishing, hunting, and sailing, and there are also port facilities (Le Havre) and some industry. Problems include harbour expansion, reclamation of mudflats, sand and gravel extraction, and considerable hunting pressure at night.

Breeding species include *Botaurus stellaris* (2-3 pairs), *Tadorna tadorna* (50 pairs), *Circus aeruginosus* (3-5 pairs), *Crex crex*, *Recurvirostra avosetta* (tens of pairs), *Philomachus pugnax* (1-5 pairs), and occasionally include *Himantopus himantopus*, *Sterna albifrons*, and *Asio flammeus*. Species occurring on passage include *Platalea leucorodia* (140 in spring), *Anser anser* (300), *Recurvirostra avosetta* (5000), *Charadrius hiaticula* (1000), *C. alexandrinus* (100), *Numenius phaeopus* (hundreds), *Tringa totanus* (10,000+), *Sterna sandvicensis* (1500-2000), *S. hirundo* (1500-2000), and *Chlidonias niger* (200). Wintering ducks and waders include *Anas acuta* (700-1200), *Recurvirostra avosetta* (2000), and *Numenius arquata* (1000). Other wintering species include *Gavia stellata* (4-9), *G. arctica* (2-4), *Podiceps cristatus* (340), *P. auritus* (3-4), *Botaurus stellaris*, *Circus aeruginosus*, *C. cyaneus*, *Falco columbarius* (1-2), *Tringa erythropus* (150), and *Asio flammeus* (7).

012 La Brenne (Centre)

46°35'-47°00'N, 01°05'-01°35'E 80,000 ha

Nature Reserve (145 ha); Hunting Reserve (42 ha)

Lakes, marshes, woodland, and wet meadows. Human activities include agriculture, fishing, hunting, and recreation including sailing. Threatened by more intensive fish-farming and considerable disturbance from wind-surfing and sailing.

A very important area for breeding waterfowl. Breeding species include *Podiceps nigricollis* (100 pairs), *Botaurus stellaris* (20-25 pairs), *Ixobrychus minutus* (20-50 pairs), *Nycticorax nycticorax* (25 pairs), *Ardea purpurea* (70-100 pairs), *Anas crecca*, *A. clypeata*, *Aythya ferina*, *A. fuligula*, *Pernis apivorus* (20-40 pairs), *Milvus migrans* (50 pairs), *Circaetus gallicus* (5 pairs), *Circus aeruginosus* (80-100 pairs), *C. cyaneus* (20-30 pairs), *C. pygargus* (10 pairs), *Porzana porzana*, *P. pusilla*, *Tetrax tetrax*, *Himantopus himantopus* (1-3 pairs), *Burhinus oedicnemus* (10-20 pairs), *Chlidonias hybridus* (500 pairs), *C. niger* (15-20 pairs), and *Alcedo atthis* (100 pairs). In addition, wintering wildfowl include *Anas clypeata* (600) and *Aythya ferina* (2000; max. 6160).

012-1 Etang de la Mer Rouge (Centre)

46°42'N, 01°10'E 180 ha

Unprotected

Lake surrounded by marshes. Human activities include forestry, stock-raising, fishing, and hunting.

Breeding species include *Nycticorax nycticorax* (20-30 pairs), *Ardea purpurea* (5-10 pairs), *Pernis apivorus* (1-2 pairs), *Milvus migrans* (1-2 pairs), *Circaetus gallicus* (1 pair), and *Circus aeruginosus* (1-2 pairs). *Chlidonias niger* occurs on passage. *Circus aeruginosus* and *C. cyaneus* occur in winter.

012-2 Etangs de Rochefort, de l'Hardouine et des Bordes (Centre)

46°44'N, 01°10'E 1800 ha

Unprotected

Lake and marshes with hedges, woodland, and plains. Human activities include hunting and fishing.

Breeding species include *Botaurus stellaris* (1 pair), *Ardea purpurea* (10-15 pairs), *Milvus migrans* (2-3 pairs), *Circus aeruginosus* (3-4 pairs), and *Chlidonias hybridus* (10-100 pairs).

012-3 Réserve naturelle de Chèrine (Centre)

46°47'N, 01°12'E 145 ha EEC SPA

Nature Reserve (145 ha)

Lake and marshes, woodland, hedges and cultivated land, uncultivated land, grassland and arable land, and plains. Human activities include agriculture, forestry, stock-raising, fishing, and hunting.

Breeding species include *Botaurus stellaris* (2 pairs), *Ixobrychus minutus* (2-4 pairs), *Ardea purpurea* (15-20 pairs), *Milvus migrans* (1 pair), *Circus aeruginosus* (2 pairs), *Porzana porzana* (0-1 pair), *Chlidonias niger* (2 pairs), *Sylvia undata*, and *Lanius collurio* (3 pairs).

013 Lac de Rille (Centre)

47°27'N, 00°15'E 300 ha

Partly a Hunting Reserve (250 ha)

Lake with reeds, wet meadows, heathland, woodland, and agricultural land. Human activities include agriculture, stock-raising, tourism and recreation.

Breeding birds include *Pernis apivorus* (1 pair), *Milvus migrans* (1-2 pairs), *Circaetus gallicus* (1 pair), and *Circus cyaneus*. Species occurring on passage include *Ciconia nigra* (5), *C. ciconia*, *Milvus milvus*, *Circus aeruginosus*, *Pandion haliaetus*, *Falco columbarius*, *Grus grus* (80), *Chlidonias hybridus*, *C. niger* (30), *Asio flammeus*, and a variety of ducks and waders. Wintering species include *Falco peregrinus* (1-2).

014 Sologne des étangs y compris forêt de Bruadan (Centre)

47°20'-47°40'N, 01°25'-02°03'E 150,000 ha

Partly protected as Hunting Reserves

Lakes, marshes, woodland, grassland, and arable land. Human activities include agriculture, fishing, hunting, and recreation including sailing.

A very important area for breeding species, which include *Botaurus stellaris* (5-20 pairs), *Ixobrychus minutus* (5-30 pairs), *Ardea purpurea* (less than 10 pairs), *Anas crecca* (100-150 pairs), *A. clypeata* (50-100 pairs), *Aythya ferina* (250-300 pairs), *A. fuligula* (40-50 pairs), *Pernis apivorus*, *Circaetus gallicus*, *Circus aeruginosus* (50-70 pairs), *C. cyaneus*, *C. pygargus*, *Hieraaetus pennatus*, *Himantopus himantopus*, *Vanellus vanellus* (20,000 pairs), *Chlidonias hybridus* (20-100 pairs), *C. niger* (0-5 pairs), and *Asio flammeus*.

015 Etang de l'Arche (Centre)

47°20'N, 01°30'E 80 ha

Unprotected

Lake and marshes with woodland and uncultivated land. Human activities include fishing and hunting.

Breeding species include *Podiceps nigricollis* (10-30 pairs), *Botaurus stellaris* (1 pair), *Ixobrychus minutus* (1-3 pairs), *Circus aeruginosus* (2-3 pairs), *Chlidonias hybridus* (5-20 pairs), and *C. niger* (0-10 pairs). *Pandion haliaetus* (irregularly) and *Chlidonias niger* occur on passage.

016 Etang de Galetas (Centre, Bourgogne)

48°07'N, 03°04'E 350 ha

Unprotected

Lake with marshes, woodland, and a wet meadow. Human activities include agriculture, stock-raising, and fishing. There is considerable hunting pressure.

Breeding species include *Milvus migrans* (1 pair) and *Circus aeruginosus* (1 pair). Species occurring on passage include *Botaurus stellaris*, *Ixobrychus minutus* (2), *Milvus migrans* (5-10), *Circus aeruginosus* (5-10), *Chlidonias hybridus* (20-30), *C. niger* (100-200), and *Alcedo atthis* (15-20). *Haliaeetus albicilla* occurs in winter.

017 Vallée de la Loire: Feurs – Nantes (Pays de la Loire, Centre, Bourgogne, Rhône-Alpes, Auvergne)

47°52'N, 02°00'E 43,500 ha (900+ km in length)

Unprotected

The River Loire is the last unaltered and free-flowing large river in Europe. Human activities include arable farming and fishing. This site is threatened by proposed dams and building along the river.

Breeding species include *Burhinus oedicnemus*, *Charadrius dubius* (1000+ pairs), *Sterna hirundo* (hundreds of pairs) and *S. albifrons* (hundreds of pairs). *Ardea purpurea*, *Ciconia nigra*, *C. ciconia*, *Milvus migrans*, *Pandion haliaetus*, *Porzana porzana*, *P. parva*, *P. pusilla*, *Crex crex*, *Chlidonias hybridus*, and *C. niger* have been recorded.

017-1 La Charité sur Loire (Bourgogne, Centre)

47°10'N, 03°00'E 1000 ha

Hunting prohibited; proposed Nature Reserve

Rivers and streams with marshes, woodland, and wet meadows. Human activities include agriculture, fishing, and tourism.

Breeding species include *Sterna hirundo* (40 pairs), *S. albifrons* (30 pairs), *Burhinus oedicnemus* (15 pairs), and *Charadrius dubius* (100 pairs). *Pandion haliaetus* occurs on passage and *Phalacrocorax carbo* (max. 500) occurs in winter.

018 Falaises du Bessin (Basse Normandie)

49°24'N, 00°56'W 270 ha

Conventional Reserve (30 ha of coast)

Rocky coastline and open sea with cliffs, heath, and arable land. There is considerable pressure from tourism.

The most important site in France for *Fulmarus glacialis* (74 pairs) and *Rissa tridactyla* (1300 pairs). Other breeding species include *Sylvia undata*. Wintering species include *Gavia stellata*, *Asio flammeus*, and occasionally *Falco peregrinus*.

019 Baie des Veys (Basse Normandie)

49°24'N, 01°10'W 7000 ha

Unprotected

The valley of the River Douve and Baie des Veys, with mudflats, beaches, sand-dunes, marshes, and wet meadows. Human activities include agriculture, stock-raising, fishing, and hunting. Problems include drainage and night shooting.

Breeding species include *Ciconia ciconia* (1-2 pairs), *Tadorna tadorna* (50 pairs), *Crex crex* (60-100 pairs), *Recurvirostra avosetta* (0-10 pairs), *Limosa limosa* (3-4 pairs), and *Numenius arquata* (20 pairs). Species occurring on passage include *Platalea leucorodia*, *Branta bernicla* (10,000+), *Charadrius hiaticula* (1000+), *Sterna sandvicensis* (1000+), *S. hirundo* (1000+), *S. albifrons* (1000+), and *Chlidonias niger* (1000+). Wintering wildfowl and waders include *Anas crecca* (1000-2000), *A. acuta* (150-400), *Melanitta nigra* (500-1000), *Haematopus ostralegus* (1000-10,000), *Pluvialis squatarola* (500-1000), and *Calidris alpina* (1000-10,000). *Circus cyaneus* (10+), *Falco columbarius*, *F. peregrinus*, and *Asio flammeus* (10+) occur in winter.

020 Iles Saint-Marcouf (Basse Normandie)

49°30'N, 01°09'W 1400 ha

Coastal Hunting Reserve (1400 ha); Conventional Reserve (3 ha) managed by a nature conservation organisation

Small islands in Baie de la Seine with rocky coast. There is considerable disturbance from tourism (boats), and plans exist for the development of tourism and possibly aquacultural projects.

Breeding seabirds include *Phalacrocorax carbo* (500 pairs; the most important site in France), *Larus fuscus* (300 pairs), *L. argentatus* (3500 pairs), and *L. marinus* (88 pairs). Wintering species include *Calidris maritima* (80).

021 Marais de la Sangsurière et des Gorges (Basse Normandie)

49°20'N, 01°31'W 8400 ha

Conventional Reserve (*c*.350 ha); Hunting Reserve (*c*.500 ha)

Marshes and peatbogs. Human activities include hunting. Problems include drainage and water-level regulation, sand and peat extraction, and hunting pressure. In the long term 50-100 per cent damage is predicted.

Breeding species include *Ciconia ciconia* (1 pair), *Anas querquedula* (10+ pairs), *Pernis apivorus* (2-5 pairs), *Circus pygargus* (3-5 pairs), *Crex crex* (100+ pairs), *Vanellus vanellus* (1100 pairs), *Numenius arquata* (30-50 pairs), and *Limosa limosa* (2-8 pairs). Wintering species include *Anas crecca* (1000+), *Circus aeruginosus*, *C. cyaneus*, *Falco columbarius*, *Lymnocryptes minimus* (max. 50), and *Gallinago gallinago* (10,000+).

022 Iles Chausey (Basse Normandie)

48°52'N, 01°50'W 1800 ha EEC SPA

Coastal Hunting Reserve (1800 ha); Conventional Reserve (15 ha) managed by a nature conservation organisation

Islands in the Baie du Mont-St-Michel with rocky coasts and islets, beaches, moorland, scrub, grassland, and arable land. Human activities include agriculture, fishing, and tourism. There is disturbance from tourism and sailing.

Breeding seabirds include *Phalacrocorax carbo* (369 pairs), *P. aristotelis* (400 pairs), *Haematopus ostralegus* (130 pairs), *Larus fuscus* (100 pairs), *L. argentatus* (2500 pairs), *L. marinus* (300 pairs), and *Sterna hirundo* (15-20 pairs). Wintering species include *Gavia arctica*, *Phalacrocorax carbo sinensis* (hundreds), *Falco columbarius*, and *Asio flammeus*.

023 Baie du Mont-St-Michel et île des Landes (Bretagne, Basse Normandie)

48°40'N, 01°40'W 35,000 ha

Two Coastal Hunting Reserves (9900 ha)

A large bay with islands, mudflats (22,000 ha), raised saltmarsh (1000+ ha), grassland and arable land, rocky coast and cliffs. Human activities include agriculture, stock-raising, fishing, hunting, and recreation. Drainage is causing the slow drying out of the whole area.

Breeding species include *Phalacrocorax carbo* (200-300 pairs), *P. aristotelis* (200+ pairs), and *Tadorna tadorna* (max. 40 pairs). *Charadrius hiaticula* (4000), *Pluvialis squatarola* (1000-10,000), *Calidris alpina* (1000-10,000), and *Limosa limosa* (1000-10,000) are very numerous on passage. Important for wintering wildfowl and waders including *Tadorna tadorna* (2000), *Anas penelope* (50-25,000), *Melanitta nigra* (2000-5000), *Haematopus ostralegus* (10,000-20,000), *Pluvialis apricaria* (500-5000), *P. squatarola* (1500-3000), *Calidris canutus* (3000-7000), *C. alpina* (22,000-35,000), *Limosa limosa* (subspecies *islandica*: 1000-2000), and *Numenius arquata* (2000-5000). Other species occurring in winter include *Falco peregrinus*, *Asio flammeus*, and *Alcedo atthis*.

024 Val d'Allier (Bourgogne, Centre, Auvergne)

Valley of the River Allier treated here as two subsites; threatened by proposed dams.

024-1 Mars-sur-Allier (Bourgogne, Centre)

46°53'N, 03°05'E *c*.7500 ha

Hunting prohibited

River (15 km) with woodland, marshes, and arable land. Human activities include fishing and tourism.

Breeding species include *Nycticorax nycticorax* (130 pairs), *Egretta garzetta* (2 pairs), *Ardea cinerea* (320 pairs), *Burhinus oedicnemus* (11 pairs), *Charadrius dubius* (60 pairs), *Sterna hirundo* (7 pairs), and *S. albifrons* (3 pairs). A considerable variety of species occur on passage including *Pandion haliaetus*.

024-2 Val d'Allier (Auvergne)

46°22'N, 03°21'E 8000 ha

'Arrêté de biotope'; hunting prohibited

Fast-flowing river with uncultivated land, lakes, woodland, marshes, hedges, cultivated land, and plains. Human activities include stock-raising, agriculture, recreation, and fishing. Threatened by channelisation and tourism.

Breeding species include *Nycticorax nycticorax* (210-250 pairs), *Egretta garzetta* (10-20 pairs), *Pernis apivorus* (5 pairs), *Milvus migrans* (20-40 pairs), *Circus cyaneus* (5-10 pairs), *C. pygargus* (5-10 pairs), *Burhinus oedicnemus* (50-200 pairs), *Charadrius dubius* (500-1000 pairs), *Sterna hirundo* (50-80 pairs), and *S. albifrons* (20-30 pairs). Species occurring on passage include *Pernis apivorus* (200-500), *Milvus migrans* (200-500), *M. milvus* (200-500), *Circus aeruginosus* (10-50), *Pandion haliaetus* (100-150), *Tetrax tetrax* (10-30), *Burhinus oedicnemus* (500-2000), *Chlidonias niger* (10-40), *C. hybridus* (10-50), and *Asio flammeus* (5-10). *Falco columbarius* (1-5) and *F. peregrinus* (1-2) occur in winter.

025 Bresse et zones inondables du Val de Saône (Bourgogne, Rhône-Alpes)

46°25'-47°20'N, 04°50'-05°30'E 180,000 ha

Hunting prohibited on part of the Rivers Saône and Doubs

Slow-flowing rivers and streams, wet meadows, lakes, marshes, hedges and cultivated land, grassland, and arable land. Human activities include agriculture, fishing, hunting, and recreation including sailing.

An important breeding area for waterfowl with breeding *Botaurus stellaris*, *Ixobrychus minutus*, *Nycticorax nycticorax* (40 pairs), *Anas strepera*, *A. querquedula*, *A. clypeata*, *Netta rufina*, and *Numenius arquata*. Other breeding species include *Milvus migrans*, *Circus aeruginosus*, *C. cyaneus*, and *Crex crex* (200 pairs). Wintering species include *Phalacrocorax carbo* (200) and *Anser anser* (150-180).

025-1 La Truchère (Bourgogne, Rhône-Alpes)

46°30'N, 04°57'E 2500 ha EEC SPA (93 ha)

Partly a Hunting Reserve

Slow-flowing rivers and streams, wet meadows, woodland, and plains.

Breeding species include *Nycticorax nycticorax* (40 pairs), *Ardea cinerea* (150 pairs), *Circus pygargus* (3-5 pairs), *Crex crex* (20-30 pairs), and *Numenius arquata* (100-200 pairs). Wintering species include *Phalacrocorax carbo* (100) and *Falco peregrinus*.

025-2 Cormoranche-sur-Saône (Bourgogne, Rhône-Alpes)

46°16'N, 04°50'E 1800 ha

Partly Hunting Reserve (90 ha on the river)

Slow-flowing rivers and streams, wet meadows, woodland, uncultivated land. Human activities include agriculture, stock-raising, fishing, hunting, and boating.

Breeding species include *Crex crex* (20-30 pairs) and *Numenius arquata* (100-200 pairs). Wintering species include *Falco peregrinus* (1-3) and *Phalacrocorax carbo* (50-100). Many species of duck occur.

026 Vallée de la Scarpe (Nord-Pas-de-Calais)

50°27'N, 03°25'E 12,000 ha

Unprotected

Fresh standing water, bogs and marshes, wet meadows, woodland, and agricultural land. Human activities include arable farming, stock-farming, fishing, tourism and recreation, including hunting and shooting.

Breeding species include *Botaurus stellaris* (3 pairs), *Ixobrychus minutus* (4 pairs), *Pernis apivorus* (5 pairs), *Circus aeruginosus* (3 pairs), *Porzana porzana* (2 pairs), *Caprimulgus europaeus* (10 pairs), *Alcedo atthis* (10 pairs), and *Luscinia svecica* (100 pairs). Passage species include *Circus cyaneus* (100), *Grus grus* (300 in 1987), *Porzana porzana* (10), *Fulica atra* (10,000), *Recurvirostra avosetta* (100), *Philomachus pugnax* (1000), and *Chlidonias niger* (100). Wintering species include *Circus cyaneus* (5).

027 Marais de Balançon (Nord-Pas-de-Calais)

50°28'N, 01°37'E 500 ha

'Site classé'

Marshes with ponds and wet meadows. Human activities include stock-raising, fishing, and hunting.

Breeding species include *Botaurus stellaris* (1 pair), *Circus aeruginosus* (1 pair), *C. cyaneus* (1 pair), *C. pygargus* (3 pairs), *Asio flammeus* (2 pairs), and *Luscinia svecica* (1 pair). Species occurring on passage include *Platalea leucorodia* and several species of ducks and waders. Wintering species include *Circus cyaneus* (15) and *Falco columbarius* (10).

028 La Chaussée (Lorraine)

49°01'N, 05°49'E 500 ha

Conventional Reserve (500 ha)

Lake with reeds, wet meadows, and alluvial forests. The only human activity is fishing.

Breeding species include *Botaurus stellaris* (6 pairs), *Ixobrychus minutus* (2 pairs), *Ardea purpurea* (6-8 pairs), *Milvus migrans*, *M. milvus* (2-3 pairs), *Circus aeruginosus*, *Porzana porzana*, *P. pusilla*, *P. parva*, *Alcedo atthis* (2 pairs), and irregularly *Circus pygargus*. *Circus nigra* occurs in summer. Species occurring on passage include *Pandion haliaetus* (3-5) and *Grus grus* (hundreds). Wintering species include *Circus cyaneus* (20-30), *Falco columbarius*, and irregularly *Haliaeetus albicilla*.

029 Lac de Madine (Lorraine)

48°55'N, 05°45'E 1100 ha

Hunting Reserve (1100 ha)

Lake with reeds and woodland. Human activities include forestry, fishing, tourism, and boating.

Breeding species include *Botaurus stellaris* (1 pair), *Pernis apivorus* (1 pair), *Milvus migrans* (10 pairs), *M. milvus* (7 pairs), *Circus aeruginosus* (1 pair), and *Porzana porzana*. Species occurring on passage include *Ciconia ciconia*, *Milvus milvus* (15), *Haliaeetus albicilla*, *Circus aeruginosus*, *C. pygargus*, *Hieraaetus pennatus*, *Pandion haliaetus* (3-4), *Falco columbiarus*, *F. peregrinus*, and *Grus grus* (200). Wintering species include *Fulica atra* (10,000) and *Circus cyaneus* (15).

030 Etang de Lindre (Lorraine)

48°48'N, 06°46'E 1480 ha

Unprotected; proposed Nature Reserve

Lake and marshes, surrounded by woodland, grassland, and arable land. Human activities include agriculture, forestry, stock-raising, fishing, hunting and sailing. The expansion and intensification of fish-farming is resulting in the construction of new dykes near the proposed nature reserve.

Breeding species include *Podiceps nigricollis* (5-10 pairs), *Botaurus stellaris* (4 pairs), *Ixobrychus minutus* (8 pairs), *Ardea purpurea* (7 pairs), *Milvus milvus*, *Circus aeruginosus*, *Porzana porzana*, and *P. parva*. Non-breeding species include *Anser fabalis* (100-120), *Anas strepera* (250), *A. clypeata* (500), and *Grus grus*.

031 Ried de Colmar – Selestat (Alsace)

48°16'N, 07°28'E 9000 ha

Unprotected

Slow-flowing rivers and streams, dry calcareous grassland, bogs and springs, wet meadows, woodland, grassland, and arable land. Human activities include agriculture, forestry, stock-raising, fishing, and hunting. Threatened by agricultural improvement (ploughing of meadows) and gravel extraction. There is also a motorway planned, which will mean the alteration and dredging of rivers.

Breeding species include *Ciconia ciconia* (3 pairs), *Pernis apivorus*, *Milvus migrans* (5 pairs), *M. milvus* (2 pairs), *Crex crex* (6 pairs), *Alcedo atthis*, and *Dryocopus martius* (5-6 pairs), and possibly *Circus cyaneus* and *Asio flammeus*. Up to 15,000 ducks (mainly *Anas platyrhynchos*) occur in winter; other wintering species include *Cygnus cygnus*, *C. columbianus*, *Anser fabalis*, and *Circus cyaneus*.

032 Rhin et Grand Canal d'Alsace: Village Neuf – Chalampé y compris forêt domaniale de la Harth Sud et forêt domaniale de la Harth Nord (Alsace)

Information is provided by the account for site no. 075 in the Federal Republic of Germany (Haltingen – Neuenburg).

033/034 Rhin et Grand Canal d'Alsace: Chalampé – Biesheim (Alsace)

Information is provided by the account for site no. 074 in the Federal Republic of Germany (Neuenburg – Breisach). The site is adversely affected by disturbance from tourism.

035 Rhin et Grand Canal d'Alsace: Schoenau – Daubensand y compris forêt du Rhin Daubensand (Alsace)

Information is provided by the account for site no. 073 in the Federal Republic of Germany (Weisweil – Nonnenweiher). The site is threatened by forest exploitation and commercial gravel extraction, which will destroy the area.

036 Rhin et Grand Canal d'Alsace: Daubensand – Strasbourg y compris bois de Sommerley (Alsace)

Information is provided by the account for site no. 072 in the Federal Republic of Germany (Nonnenweiher – Goldscheuer). The site is threatened by forestry exploitation and clearance.

037 Rhin: Robertsau – Dalhunden (Alsace)

Information is provided by the account for site no. 071 in the Federal Republic of Germany (Auenheim – Greffern). The site is threatened by gravel extraction.

038 Rhin: Dalhunden – Munchhouse y compris bois de Munchhouse (Alsace)

Information is provided by the account for site no. 070 in the Federal Republic of Germany (Greffern – Murgmündung). The site is threatened by gravel extraction.

039 Bassin du Drugeon: Pontarlier – Frasne (Franche-Comté)

46°54'N, 06°22'E 8000 ha

Partly Nature Reserve (160 ha)

Fresh standing water, bogs and marshes, wet meadows, and woodland. Human activities include arable farming and stock-raising.

Breeding species include *Pernis apivorus*, *Milvus migrans* (40+ pairs), *M. milvus*, *Circus cyaneus* (2 pairs), *Bonasa bonasia* (100 pairs), *Porzana porzana* (2-5 pairs), *Aegolius funereus*, *Caprimulgus europaeus*, and *Dryocopus martius*. Passage species include *Ciconia ciconia* (5-10), *Pandion haliaetus*, *Falco peregrinus*, *Chlidonias hybridus*, and *C. niger*.

040 Basse vallée du Doubs: Dôle sud (Franche-Comté)

47°06'N, 05°30'E 4000 ha

Partly Nature Reserve (95 ha)

Slow-flowing water, wet meadows, marshes, cultivated land, sandbanks, and woodland. Human activities include arable farming and stock-raising.

Breeding species include *Ixobrychus minutus*, *Ardea purpurea* (10-20 pairs), *Milvus migrans*, *Circus aeruginosus* (*c.*5 pairs), *C. cyaneus*, *C. pygargus* (5-10 pairs), *Crex crex* (*c.*10 pairs), *Burhinus oedicnemus* (10 pairs), *Alcedo atthis*, and *Luscinia svecica* (80 pairs).

041 Traict et marais de Guérande (Pays de la Loire)

47°18'N, 02°30'W 2000 ha

Coastal Hunting Reserve (550 ha); Nature Reserve

Bay with saltwater marshes, mudflats, beaches and sand-dunes; also woodland and heathland. Human activities include agriculture, fishing, hunting, and recreation.

Breeding species include *Ardea cinerea* (200 pairs), *Circus aeruginosus* (2 pairs), *Circus pygargus*, *Himantopus himantopus*, *Recurvirostra avosetta*, *Sterna sandvicensis*, *S. hirundo*, *Alcedo atthis*, and *Luscinia svecica*. Wintering waterfowl include *Branta bernicla* (av. 700; max. 1200) and *Recurvirostra avosetta* (av. 300; max. 670).

042 Marais de Brière (Pays de la Loire)

47°20'N, 02°20'W 10,000 ha

Nature Reserve

Marshes and wet meadows. Human activities include stock-raising, fishing, hunting, and recreation including sailing. The Grande Brière is insufficiently inundated during the summer and the salinity level is having a serious effect on the vegetation (as a result of changes to the Estuaire de la Loire). There is also considerable hunting pressure.

Breeding species include *Botaurus stellaris*, *Ardea purpurea*, *Circus aeruginosus*, *C. pygargus*, *Chlidonias niger*, *Alcedo atthis*, *Luscinia svecica*, and *Sylvia undata*. Wintering species include *Circus cyaneus*, *Anas crecca* (2000), and *A. strepera* (av. 190; max. 310).

043 Estuaire de la Loire (Pays de la Loire)

47°18'N, 02°08'W 19,000 ha

Basically unprotected although there are four Hunting Reserves (*c.*5000 ha)

Estuary with mudflats, beaches, and islands; also marshes, wet meadows, and woodland. Human activities include agriculture, stock-raising, fishing, hunting, sailing, and industry. Seriously threatened by hydrological modifications (which have changed the freshwater-saltwater ratios), infilling of saltmarshes, meadows and mudflats, and embankment of the River Loire.

Breeding species include *Botaurus stellaris*, *Ardea cinerea* (200 pairs), *Milvus migrans* (10+ pairs), *M. milvus*, *Circus aeruginosus*, *Crex crex* (450-550 pairs), *Himantopus himantopus* (1-5 pairs), *Recurvirostra avosetta* (irregularly), *Limosa limosa* (10-12 pairs), *C. niger* (10-20 pairs), and *Luscinia svecica* (50 pairs). *Platalea leucorodia* (1-4) oversummers. *Platalea leucorodia*, *Circus cyaneus*, *Gallinago media*, *Chlidonias hybridus*, and *Chlidonias niger* occur on passage, and wintering species include *Botaurus stellaris*, *Tadorna tadorna* (2000), *Anas crecca* (12,500), *A. clypeata* (4000), *Circus aeruginosus*, *C. cyaneus*, and *Recurvirostra avosetta* (3200).

044 Lac de Grand-Lieu (Pays de la Loire)

47°06'N, 01°40'W 6300 ha EEC SPA (2700 ha)

'Site classé' (7500 ha); Nature Reserve (2700 ha)

Lake, marshes and wet meadows, with woodland, hedges and cultivated land. Human activities include agriculture, forestry, stock-raising, fishing, and hunting. The site is experiencing insufficient water exchange with the River Loire, and is drying out.

Breeding species include *Phalacrocorax carbo* (50 pairs), *Botaurus stellaris* (3-10 pairs), *Ixobrychus minutus*, *Nycticorax nycticorax* (40 pairs), *Egretta garzetta* (180 pairs), *Ardea cinerea* (1200 pairs), *A. purpurea* (30 pairs), *Platalea leucorodia* (1-7 pairs), *Pernis apivorus* (2 pairs), *Milvus migrans* (20-25 pairs), *Circus aeruginosus* (18 pairs), *C. pygargus* (1 pair), *Anas strepera* (20 pairs), *Rallus aquaticus* (450 pairs), *Crex crex* (20 pairs), *Porzana porzana*, *Chlidonias hybridus* (0-120 pairs), *C. niger* (0-20 pairs), *Picus canus*, and *Alcedo atthis* (40 pairs). A great variety of species occur on passage including *Platalea leucorodia* (6-12), *Circus aeruginosus* (40-50), *Pandion haliaetus*, and *Philomachus pugnax* (max. 1400). Wintering species include *Anas acuta* (max. 1500), *A. clypeata* (200-2500), *Aythya ferina* (1000-5000), *Circus aeruginosus* (40-50), *Rallus aquaticus* (1000), and *Fulica atra* (5000-10,000).

045 Baie et marais de Bourgneuf (Pays de la Loire)

47°00'N, 02°10'W 8000 ha

Coastal Hunting Reserve (4200 ha)

Bay with saltwater and freshwater lagoons, saltwater marshes, mudflats, and wet meadows. Human activities include agriculture, stock-raising, fishing, and hunting. The site is threatened by drainage and cultivation, marine farming, and digging of ponds.

Breeding species include *Botaurus stellaris* (1-5 pairs), *Ixobrychus minutus* (1-5 pairs), *Tadorna tadorna* (40 pairs), *Anas querquedula* (25-50 pairs), *A. clypeata* (50 pairs), *Circus aeruginosus* (60 pairs), *C. cyaneus* (10+ pairs), *C. pygargus* (50-100 pairs), *Himantopus himantopus* (50-80 pairs), *Recurvirostra avosetta* (100-150 pairs), *Vanellus vanellus* (1000-3000 pairs), *Limosa limosa* (10-30 pairs), *Tringa totanus* (300-500 pairs), *Sterna hirundo* (20-1000 pairs), *Asio flammeus* (20 pairs), and *Luscinia svecica* (several hundred pairs). *Platalea leucorodia* occurs on passage. Wintering species include *Branta bernicla* (3000-5200), *Anas clypeata* (420; max. 850), *Circus aeruginosus*, *C. cyaneus*, *Recurvirostra avosetta* (max. 1900), and *Pluvialis squatarola* (1000-2800).

046 Marais de Basse-Maine et île Saint-Aubin (Pays de la Loire)

47°30'N, 00°27'W 5400 ha

Conventional Reserve (30 ha)

Rivers, streams, and wet meadows. Human activities include stock-raising and hunting. The site is threatened by agricultural improvements and commercial *Populus* plantations. There is considerable hunting pressure.

Breeding species include *Anas querquedula* (15+ pairs), *Porzana porzana* (5-10 pairs), and *Crex crex* (305 pairs in 1984). *Anser anser* (580), *Anas acuta* (3200), *Pluvialis apricaria* (3700), *Vanellus vanellus* (16,600), *Philomachus pugnax* (720), and *Limosa limosa* (17,500) occur on passage.

047 Marais salants de Noirmoutier (Pays de la Loire)

47°01'N, 02°15'W 600 ha

Unprotected

Saltwater marshes and raised saltmarsh. Human activities include fishing and hunting.

Breeding species include *Tadorna tadorna* (40-50 pairs), *Anas clypeata* (20 pairs), *A. querquedula* (5 pairs), *Circus pygargus* (10-30 pairs), *Himantopus himantopus* (30-50 pairs), *Recurvirostra avosetta* (80-100 pairs), *Tringa totanus* (40-50 pairs), *Sterna hirundo* (120 pairs), *Asio flammeus* (max. 5 pairs), and *Luscinia svecica* (25+ pairs).

048 Marais et forêt d'Olonne (Pays de la Loire)

46°35'N, 01°48'W 2200 ha

'Site classé' and Hunting Reserve (400 ha)

Saltwater lagoons, beaches, saltwater marshes, woodland, and arable land. Human activities include agriculture, stock-raising, fishing, hunting, tourism, and recreation. Threatened by the infilling of saltmarsh, and new forest tracks have increased disturbance.

Breeding species include *Milvus migrans* (10+ pairs), *Circus aeruginosus*, *Himantopus himantopus* (10-40 pairs), *Recurvirostra avosetta* (400 pairs), *Caprimulgus europaeus* (10+ pairs), and *Lullula arborea* (10+ pairs). *Platalea leucorodia* (100+), *Anas acuta* (thousands), *A. clypeata* (thousands), *Himantopus himantopus* (100+), *Recurvirostra avosetta* (500+), *Limosa limosa* (thousands), *Numenius phaeopus* (10,000+), and *Larus minutus* (thousands) occur on passage. Wintering waterfowl include *Anas acuta* (400-500), *A. clypeata* (500-700), and *Recurvirostra avosetta* (100).

049 Marais Poitevin avec Baie de l'Aiguillon, Pointe d'Arçay, Communaux du marais Vendéen et île de Charrouin (Pays de la Loire, Poitou-Charentes)

46°22'N, 01°01'E 57,830 ha

Includes two EEC SPAs (Pointe d'Arçais: 212 ha; Saint Denis du Payré: 206 ha)

Partly protected by Nature Reserves (St Denis du Payré and Pointe d'Arçay); National Hunting Reserves (Baie de l'Aiguillon and Parc naturel régional Poitevin)

Includes the two estuaries of the River Sèvre Niortaise and River Lay. Habitats include mudflats and sandflats, saltmarshes, ancient saltpans, sand-dunes with *Pinus* forest, wet meadows, and agricultural land. Human activities include stock and arable farming, oyster and mussel farming, and grazing on reclaimed saltmarshes. The site is seriously threatened by drainage of wet-meadow areas followed by intensive agricultural practices, channelisation of rivers and streams, removal of hedges, scrub and tree-lined channels, drainage of saltmarshes and saltings, and extension of oyster and mussel farming on the mudflats. In addition, the communaux du marais Vendéen is affected by the creation of lakes for wind-surfing.

Breeding species include *Ixobrychus minutus* (7 pairs), *Nycticorax nycticorax* (40 pairs), *Egretta garzetta* (10-50 pairs), *Ardea cinerea* (680 pairs), *A. purpurea* (140 pairs), *Anas querquedula* (10-50 pairs), *Pernis apivorus* (20 pairs), *Milvus migrans* (50 pairs), *Circaetus gallicus* (2 pairs), *Circus aeruginosus* (25 pairs), *C. pygargus* (110 pairs), *Porzana pusilla* (2 pairs), *Crex crex* (20-50 pairs), *Tetrax tetrax* (5 pairs), *Himantopus himantopus* (30 pairs), *Alcedo atthis* (100 pairs), *Calandrella brachydactyla* (10 pairs), and *Luscinia svecica* (150 pairs). A considerable variety of species occurs on passage including *Platalea leucorodia* (50-100), *Anser anser* (2300), *Pandion haliaetus* (10), *Philomachus pugnax* (2000), *Limosa limosa* (50,000), and *Numenius phaeopus* (20,000). Wintering species include *Egretta alba* (2), *Tadorna tadorna* (4000), *Anas penelope* (15,000), *A. crecca* (20,000), *A. platyrhynchos* (20,000), *A. acuta* (6000), *A. clypeata* (5000), *Melanitta nigra* (10,000), *Circus cyaneus* (50), *Falco columbarius* (15), *Recurvirostra avosetta* (6600), *Pluvialis squatarola* (2600), *Vanellus vanellus* (10,000), *Calidris canutus* (4000), *C. alpina* (16,000), *Limosa limosa islandica* (6500), *L. lapponica* (1000), and *Asio flammeus* (200).

050 Baie de Saint-Brieuc (Bretagne)

48°31'N, 02°42'W 650 ha

Coastal Hunting Reserve (650 ha)

A large bay with mudflats. Human activities include fishing, hunting, and boating.

Wintering wildfowl and waders include *Branta bernicla* (2500), *Anas acuta* (900-2000), *Haematopus ostralegus* (2000-4500), and *Charadrius hiaticula* (1200).

051 Les Sept-Iles (Bretagne)

48°54'N, 03°27'W 4300 ha EEC SPA

Coastal Hunting Reserve (4300 ha); Nature Reserve (40 ha)

Several rocky islands.
Breeding species include *Fulmarus glacialis* (48-59 pairs), *Puffinus puffinus* (80-90 pairs), *Hydrobates pelagicus* (10+ pairs), *Sula bassana* (6000-6100 pairs), *Phalacrocorax aristotelis* (206 pairs), *Larus fuscus* (693 pairs), *L. argentatus* (3400-3500 pairs), *L. marinus* (59 pairs), *Rissa tridactyla* (32 pairs), *Uria aalge* (24-26 pairs), *Alca torda* (19-21 pairs), and *Fratercula arctica* (215-225 pairs).

052 Ile de Goulmedec (Bretagne)

48°50'N, 03°33'W 490 ha

Coastal Hunting Reserve (490 ha)

Islets with rocky coast and sand beaches. Human activities include fishing and sailing.
Breeding species include *Sterna sandvicensis* (39-50 pairs), *S. dougallii*, and *S. hirundo*. Numbers of terns are very irregular at this site because birds may use a group of 10-15 other islets away from Ile de Goulmedec.

053 Iles de la Colombière, de la Néllière et des Haches (Bretagne)

48°38'N, 02°12'W 1500 ha

Coastal Hunting Reserve (1500 ha); 'Arrêté de biotope' covering the terrestrial part, which is managed by a nature conservation organisation for the terns.

Several small islets and open sea. Human activities include fishing and boating.
Breeding species include *Phalacrocorax carbo* (*c.*10 pairs), *Tadorna tadorna* (*c.*10 pairs), *Sterna sandvicensis* (350 pairs in 1976; 22 in 1979; 218 in 1986 and 0 in 1987), *S. dougallii* (1-2 pairs), and *S. hirundo* (50-120 pairs).

054 Ilots du Trévors (Bretagne)

48°35'N, 04°38'W 380 ha

Coastal Hunting Reserve (380 ha); Conventional Reserve managed for terns

Open sea and several rocky islets with beaches.
Important for breeding terns in 1979 with *Sterna sandvicensis* (811 pairs), *S. dougallii* (120 pairs), *S. hirundo* (150 pairs), and *S. albifrons* (27 pairs). Since 1983 terns have bred irregularly, with *Sterna sandvicensis* (0 in 1987; 230 in 1988), *S. dougallii* (30-40 pairs in 1987 on a small islet nearby; 10 in 1988), and *S. hirundo* (15 pairs in 1987; 170 in 1988).

055 Archipel de Molène (Bretagne)

48°23'N, 04°55'W 10,000 ha EEC SPA

Coastal Hunting Reserve (10,000 ha); Conventional Reserve (40 ha)

Archipelago of rocky islands with beaches and rocky habitat. Possible disturbance from tourism and sailing.
Breeding species include *Puffinus puffinus* (10 pairs), *Hydrobates pelagicus* (300-400 pairs), *Haematopus ostralegus* (80-100 pairs), *Charadrius hiaticula* (20 pairs), *Larus marinus* (250 pairs), *Sterna hirundo* (20-30 pairs), and *S. albifrons* (30 pairs).

056 Rade de Brest: Baie de Daoulas et Anse du Poulmic (Bretagne)

48°18'N, 04°23'W 6,800 ha

Coastal Hunting Reserve (6800 ha)

Bay with mudflats, rocky coast, and beaches. Human activities include fishing and recreation including sailing; there is a harbour.

Breeding species include *Tadorna tadorna*. Wintering species include *Gavia arctica* (50-100), *Podiceps nigricollis* (800-1000), *Phalacrocorax carbo* (300-500), *Anas penelope* (2000-3000 in 1987), *A. crecca* (1000-1500), *Mergus serrator* (500-1300), and *Alca torda* (100-500).

057 Cap Sizun (Bretagne)

48°06'N, 04°36'W 530 ha

Coastal Hunting Reserve (500 ha); Conventional Reserve (30 ha)

Rocky coastline with cliffs and heath, rocky islets, and open sea. Human activities include agriculture, fishing, and boating.

Breeding species include *Fulmarus glacialis* (10 pairs), *Phalacrocorax aristotelis* (200 pairs), *Larus argentatus* (500 pairs), *Rissa tridactyla* (860 pairs), and *Uria aalge* (60 pairs). In addition, *Hydrobates pelagicus* possibly breeds.

058 Presqu'île de Crozon (Bretagne)

48°16'N, 04°38'W 650 ha

Conventional Reserve covering the islets

Rocky coastline with cliffs, islets and open sea. There is disturbance from tourism and sailing.

Breeding species include *Fulmarus glacialis* (15-20 pairs), *Hydrobates pelagicus* (30-50 pairs), *Phalacrocorax aristotelis* (410 pairs), *Rissa tridactyla* (100 pairs), and *Uria aalge* (40 pairs).

059 Marais de la Baie d'Audierne (Bretagne)

47°53'N, 04°23'W 3000 ha

'Site classé' (700 ha); Conventional Reserve (52 ha)

Saltwater and freshwater lagoons with reedbeds along the coast; also sand-dunes, beaches, rocky coast, wet meadows, agricultural and uncultivated land. Human activities include agriculture, stock-raising, recreation, and hunting.

Breeding species include *Botaurus stellaris* (2-3 pairs), *Ixobrychus minutus*, *Circus aeruginosus* (10-20 pairs), *C. pygargus* (0-1 pair), *Charadrius alexandrinus* (50-100 pairs), and *Limosa limosa* (5-10 pairs). A variety of species occurs on passage including *Ixobrychus minutus*, *Nycticorax nycticorax*, *Egretta garzetta*, *Ardea purpurea*, *Ciconia ciconia*, *Platalea leucorodia*, *Circus aeruginosus*, *Sterna dougallii*, *Chlidonias niger*, *Asio flammeus*, and *Acrocephalus paludicola* (10+ are ringed each year). Wintering species include *Anas crecca* (500-1000), *Circus aeruginosus* (40), *Pluvialis apricaria* (500-1000), and *Calidris alba* (100+).

060 Archipel des Glénans (Bretagne)

47°45'N, 04°00'W 3800 ha

Coastal Hunting Reserve (3800 ha); Conventional Reserve (5 ha); Natural Reserve (12 ha)

Small islands and islets with beaches and rocky habitat surrounded by open sea. Includes Enez ar Razed, Penneg Ern, Castell Bras, Quignenec, Guiriden and Giautec. There is disturbance from sailing. Other human activities include fishing, hunting, and tourism.

Breeding seabirds include *Phalacrocorax aristotelis* (120-130 pairs), *Larus fuscus* (3000-3500 pairs), *L. argentatus* (5500-6000 pairs), *L. marinus* (110-120 pairs), *Sterna sandvicensis* (250 pairs in 1976; 0 in 1987), *S. dougallii* (10 pairs in 1976; 0 in 1987), and *S. hirundo* (50 pairs in 1976; 20 in 1987).

061 Baie de Morlaix et de Carantec (Bretagne)

48°41'N, 03°55'W 5000 ha

Protection status unknown

Estuary and bay with mudflats, beaches, rocky coast and islets. Human activities include fishing, hunting, tourism, and sailing.

Breeding species include *Phalacrocorax aristotelis*, *Sterna sandvicensis*, *S. dougallii*, *S. hirundo*, and *Fratercula arctica*. Wintering species include *Arenaria interpres* (max. 950).

062 Ile d'Ouessant (Bretagne)

48°28'N, 05°05'W 1500 ha partly Biogenetic Reserve

Conventional Reserve (covering 6 islets)

Island and islets, rocky habitat, uncultivated land, marshes, and coastal grassland.

An important site for migratory birds with large numbers of a variety of species occurring. Breeding species include *Fulmarus glacialis* (25 pairs), *Puffinus puffinus*, *Hydrobates pelagicus*, *Phalacrocorax aristotelis* (100 pairs), *Larus marinus* (450-500 pairs), *Rissa tridactyla* (160 pairs), *Fratercula arctica* (10 pairs), and *Pyrrhocorax pyrrhocorax* (12-13 pairs).

063 Golfe du Morbihan, marais de Suscinio et Ile de Meaban (Bretagne)

47°34'N, 02°46'W 15,000 ha

Coastal Hunting Reserves (*c.*3000 ha); Conventional Reserve (2 ha)

Bay with mudflats, saltwater marshes, saltwater lagoons, and raised saltmarsh; also islands, rocky coast, beaches, grassland, and arable land. Human activities include agriculture, stock-raising, fishing, hunting, and recreation including sailing. Wetland areas are threatened by drainage and vegetational encroachment, and there is disturbance of the breeding birds by tourists.

Breeding species include *Egretta garzetta* (50-100 pairs), *Circus aeruginosus* (5-8 pairs), *Tadorna tadorna* (130-160 pairs), *Himantopus himantopus* (20-30 pairs), *Recurvirostra avosetta* (30-50 pairs), *Tringa totanus* (20 pairs), *Sterna hirundo* (50-200 pairs), *S. albifrons*, and *Luscinia svecica*. *Platalea leucorodia* (20-60), *Charadrius hiaticula* (500-1000), *Numenius phaeopus* (500-1000), and *T. nebularia* (100-500) occur on passage. Wintering waterfowl include *Podiceps cristatus* (400-700), *P. nigricollis* (400-700), *Phalacrocorax carbo* (600-1000), *Branta bernicla* (15,000-20,000), *Tadorna tadorna* (1800-2500), *Anas penelope* (7000-25,000), *A. crecca* (2000-4000), *A. acuta* (1000-3500), *A. clypeata* (300-900), *Bucephala clangula* (500-800), *Mergus serrator* (1200-1600), *Recurvirostra avosetta* (400-900), *Pluvialis squatarola* (1500-2500), and *Calidris alpina* (20,000-30,000).

064 Etier de Penerf (Bretagne)

47°32'N, 02°35'W 1500 ha

Unprotected

Estuary with saltwater marshes and mudflats; also beaches. Human activities include fishing and hunting. Threatened by marine farming and limited drainage. Tourism is causing disturbance.

Species on passage include *Calidris alba* (100-500), *C. alpina* (1000-10,000), *Numenius phaeopus* (100-500), *Tringa totanus* (500-1000), and *Arenaria interpres* (100-500). Wintering species include *Egretta garzetta* (20-100), *Branta bernicla* (500-3000), and *Recurvirostra avosetta* (500-800). Also *Pluvialis squatarola* (1500-2500) and *Calidris alpina* (20,000-30,000) that winter at Golfe du Morbihan sometimes use the Etier de Penerf when the tide is very high.

065 Anse de Kervoyal et estuaire de la Vilaine (Bretagne)

47°30'N, 02°32'W 1300 ha

Coastal Hunting Reserve (500 ha)

Estuary with mudflats, beaches, and saltmarshes. Human activities include fishing, hunting, and recreation including sailing.

Breeding species include *Circus pygargus*, *Tadorna tadorna* (10-20 pairs), and *Luscinia svecica*. Species occurring on passage include *Calidris alba* (100-500) and *Arenaria interpres* (100-500). Wintering species include *Podiceps cristatus* (800-1500), *Branta bernicla* (1000-3000), *Tadorna tadorna* (500-1000), *Anas crecca* (max. 1000), *A. acuta* (max. 800), *Aythya ferina* (max. 5000), *A. marila* (1500-2500), and *Recurvirostra avosetta* (100-1000).

066 Vallée de la Charente (Poitou-Charentes)

45°55'N, 00°05'W 8100 ha

Unprotected

Wet meadows, bogs and marshes, and woodland. Human activities include arable farming.

Breeding species includes *Ardea purpurea* (5-15 pairs), *Anas querquedula* (5 pairs), *Pernis apivorus* (5 pairs), *Milvus migrans* (40 pairs), *Circus aeruginosus* (30 pairs), *C. pygargus* (5 pairs), *Porzana porzana* (5-10 pairs), *Crex crex* (100-120 pairs), *Alcedo atthis* (10-20 pairs), and *Lanius collurio* (10-20 pairs).

067 Plaine de Villefagnan (Poitou-Charentes)

45°58'N, 00°20'E 7000 ha

Unprotected

Agricultural land. Human activities include arable farming.

Breeding species include *Circus pygargus* (12 pairs), *Tetrax tetrax* (30 pairs), and *Burhinus oedicnemus* (40 pairs). (Last ornithological survey in 1984)

068 Anse du Fiers d'Ars-en-Ré (Poitou-Charentes)

46°13'N, 01°27'W 2400 ha EEC SPA (1495 ha)

Partly a Nature Reserve (150 ha)

Bay with saltwater lagoons, saltwater marshes, and mudflats. Human activities include fishing and hunting. Problems include disturbance by tourists and aquaculture activities.

Breeding species include *Tadorna tadorna* (100 pairs), *Himantopus himantopus* (20-50 pairs), *Recurvirostra avosetta* (70 pairs) and *Luscinia svecica* (25+ pairs). Species occurring on passage include *Platalea leucorodia* (25). Wintering waterfowl include *Branta bernicla* (10,000-12,000), *Recurvirostra avosetta* (400-600), *Calidris alpina* (8000-12,000), and *Numenius arquata* (2000; max. 2500).

069 Anse de Fouras, baie d'Yves et marais de Rochefort (Poitou-Charentes)

46°02'N, 01°07'W 10,000 ha

Partly a Hunting Reserve and Nature Reserve (194 ha)

A bay, beaches, saltwater lagoons and marshes, mudflats, rivers, lakes, marshes, and wet meadows; also woodland, grassland, and arable land. Human activities include agriculture, fishing, hunting, and recreation including sailing. Threatened by drainage and cultivation.

Breeding species include *Ardea purpurea* (45-100 pairs), *Ciconia ciconia* (2-4 pairs), *Circus aeruginosus* (20-30 pairs), *C. pygargus* (10-30 pairs), *Himantopus himantopus* (100 pairs), *Chlidonias niger* (20-25 pairs), and *Luscinia svecica*. Species occurring on passage include *Limosa limosa* (600-800), *Numenius phaeopus* (200-400), *Chlidonias hybridus* (10-15), and *Acrocephalus paludicola*. Wintering wildfowl include *Branta bernicla* (max.

1200), *Anas acuta* (max. 600), *A. clypeata* (max. 500), and *Calidris alpina* (5000-12,000).

070 Ile d'Oléron, marais de Brouage et la Gripperie Saint-Symphorien (Poitou-Charentes)

45°55'N, 01°10'W 12,000 ha EEC SPA (Réserve naturelle des marais de Moeze)

Nature Reserve (6700 ha)

Bay with saltwater marshes and mudflats; also rivers, lakes, marshes, wet meadows, woodland, grassland, and arable land. Human activities include fishing, hunting, and recreation. Threatened by drainage, cultivation and pressure from tourism.

Breeding species include *Ciconia ciconia* (4-5 pairs), *Egretta garzetta* (50-300 pairs), *Ardea cinerea* (500-1000 pairs), *A. purpurea* (20 pairs), *Milvus migrans* (50 pairs), *Circus aeruginosus* (50 pairs), *C. pygargus* (30-40 pairs), *Himantopus himantopus* (50-100 pairs), *Tringa totanus* (20-25 pairs), *Luscinia svecica* (50-100 pairs), and *Lanius collurio* (15-40 pairs). Species occurring on passage include *Platalea leucorodia* (50-100), *Himantopus himantopus* (200+), and *Chlidonias niger* (200+). Wintering waterfowl include *Branta bernicla* (2000-12,000), *Tadorna tadorna* (3000), *Recurvirostra avosetta* (1000), *Pluvialis squatarola* (400-1000), *Calidris canutus* (3000-5000), and *C. alpina* (10,000-16,000); with total waders max. 49,000.

071 Plaines de Pons-Rouffiac (Poitou-Charentes)

45°35'N, 00°32'W 2000 ha

Unprotected

Agricultural land. Human activities include arable farming.

Breeding species include *Circus pygargus* (10 pairs), *Tetrax tetrax* (60 pairs), and *Burhinus oedicnemus* (30 pairs). (Last ornithological survey in 1984)

072 Marais du Blayais (Poitou-Charentes, Aquitaine)

45°18'N, 00°36'W 6500 ha

Partly a Hunting Reserve

Rivers, streams, marshes and wet meadows, woodland, mudflats, saltmarshes, and peatbogs. Human activities include agriculture, stock-raising, fishing, and hunting.

Breeding species include *Ardea purpurea* (47 pairs), *Ciconia ciconia* (1 pair), *Pernis apivorus* (1 pair), *Milvus migrans* (12-14 pairs), *Circus aeruginosus* (6 pairs), *C. cyaneus* (4 pairs), and *C. pygargus* (23-27 pairs).

073 Bonne Anse (Poitou-Charentes)

45°40'N, 01°20'W 750 ha

Unprotected

Sand-dunes, beaches, and mudflats.

Breeding species include *Anthus campestris* (5-10). An important site for species on passage and in winter, with *Platalea leucorodia* (3-5), *Anser anser* (500-600), *Milvus milvus* (20-30), *Circus aeruginosus* (10), *Pandion haliaetus* (2-5), and *Sterna sandvicensis* (300-400) on passage. Wintering species include *Egretta garzetta* (60), *Branta bernicla* (2000), *Melanitta nigra* (10,000-15,000), *Falco peregrinus* (2), *Pluvialis apricaria* (1500), and *Asio flammeus* (2-5).

074 Plaines de Niort Sud-est (Poitou-Charentes)

46°19'N, 00°27'W 12,000 ha

Unprotected

Agricultural land. Human activities include arable farming.

Important for *Circus pygargus* (30 pairs), *Tetrax tetrax* (100 pairs; 1000 on passage), and *Burhinus oedicnemus* (120 pairs; max. 800 on passage). (Last ornithological survey in 1984)

075 Plaines de Niort Nord-ouest (Poitou-Charentes)

46°23'N, 00°32'W 12,000 ha

Unprotected

Agricultural land. Human activities include arable farming.

Breeding species include *Circus pygargus* (40 pairs), *Tetrax tetrax* (120 pairs), and *Burhinus oedicnemus* (120 pairs). (Last ornithological survey in 1984)

076 Plaines de Saint-Jouin-de-Marne et d'Assais-les-Jumeaux (Poitou-Charentes)

46°48'N, 00°02'W 10,000 ha

Unprotected

Agricultural land. Human activities include arable farming.

Breeding species include *Circus pygargus* (20 pairs), *Tetrax tetrax* (90 pairs), and *Burhinus oedicnemus* (100 pairs). (Last ornithological survey in 1984)

077 Plaine de Saint-Jean-de-Sauves (Poitou-Charentes)

47°01'N, 00°05'E 5000 ha

Unprotected

Agricultural land. Human activities include arable farming.

Breeding species include *Circus pygargus* (20 pairs), *Tetrax tetrax* (70 pairs), and *Burhinus oedicnemus* (80 pairs). (Last ornithological survey in 1984)

078 Le Pinail, forêt de Moulière, bois du Défens et de la Roche de Bran (Poitou-Charentes)

46°41'N, 00°33'E 6000 ha EEC SPA (1500 ha)

Nature Reserve (Pinail: 135 ha)

Woodland, heathland, and ponds. Human activities include forestry and hunting. The site is threatened by forestry exploitation and the felling of ancient woodland and replacement with *Pinus* woodland or with exotic species.

Breeding species include *Pernis apivorus* (3-4 pairs), *Milvus migrans* (1 pair), *Circus cyaneus* (13-20 pairs), *C. pygargus* (9-12 pairs), *Dryocopus martius* (2 pairs), and *Dendrocopos medius* (50-80 pairs). *Circus aeruginosus* and *Pandion haliaetus* occur on passage. Wintering species include *Circus cyaneus* (10-20) and *Falco columbarius* (3-7).

079 Camp de Montmorillon (Poitou-Charentes)

46°26'N, 00°57'E 1350 ha

Unprotected

Woodland, bogs and marshes, ponds, heathland, grassland, uncultivated land, and agricultural land. Human activities include arable farming, stock-raising, and hunting. Owned by the Ministry of Defence.

Breeding species include *Ardea purpurea* (1-4 pairs), *Pernis apivorus* (2 pairs), *Milvus migrans* (1 pair), *Circus cyaneus* (3 pairs), *C. pygargus* (3 pairs), *Burhinus oedicnemus* (5 pairs), *Caprimulgus europaeus* (5 pairs), *Anthus campestris* (2 pairs), *Sylvia undata* (100-200 pairs), and *Lanius collurio* (2 pairs). Wintering species include *Circus cyaneus* (5-10).

080 Plateau de Bellefonds (Poitou-Charentes)

46°34'N, 00°39'E 2000 ha

Unprotected

Bogs and marshes, agricultural land, and wet meadows. Human activities include arable farming, tourism and recreation.

Breeding species include *Pernis apivorus* (2 pairs), *Milvus migrans* (2 pairs), *Circus cyaneus* (3 pairs), *C. pygargus* (5 pairs), *Tetrax tetrax* (20 pairs), *Burhinus oedicnemus* (15 pairs), *Numenius arquata* (3 pairs), *Lanius collurio*, and *Emberiza hortulana*. *Milvus milvus* (5), *Pluvialis apricaria* (*c.*10,000), and *Vanellus vanellus* (*c.*10,000) occur on passage.

081 Bois de l'Hospice, étang de Beaufour et environs (Poitou-Charentes)

46°24'N, 00°52'E 3200 ha

Unprotected

Woodland, moorland, ponds, grassland, uncultivated land, and agricultural land. Human activities include agriculture, forestry, and hunting. Threatened by forestry exploitation and replacement of natural woodland with exotic species; also by the disappearance of moorland.

Breeding species include *Ardea purpurea* (6 pairs), *Pernis apivorus* (1 pair), *Milvus migrans* (1 pair), *Circus aeruginosus* (1 pair), *C. cyaneus* (3 pairs), *C. pygargus* (5 pairs), *Burhinus oedicnemus* (5 pairs), and *Caprimulgus europaeus* (*c.*5 pairs). Passage species include *Grus grus* (1-60), *Burhinus oedicnemus* (150-170), *Pluvialis apricaria* (1000), *Chlidonias niger*, and *C. hybridus*.

082 Plaines de Mirebeau et de Neuville-du-Poitou (Poitou-Charentes)

46°40'N, 00°15'E 8000 ha

Unprotected

Agricultural land. Human activities include arable farming.

Breeding species include *Circus pygargus* (30 pairs), *Tetrax tetrax* (100 pairs), and *Burhinus oedicnemus* (100 pairs). Wintering species include *Pluvialis apricaria* (4000) and *Vanellus vanellus* (30,000).

083 Région de Pressac et étang de Combourg (Poitou-Charentes)

46°08'N, 00°32'E 3800 ha

Unprotected

Woodland, lakes and marshes, cultivated land, and heath. Human activities include fishing and hunting. The site is threatened by drainage and intensification of cereal cultivation.

Breeding species include *Ardea purpurea* (3-6 pairs), *Pernis apivorus* (4 pairs), *Milvus migrans* (3 pairs), *Circus aeruginosus* (1 pair), *C. cyaneus* (3-6 pairs), *Lanius collurio* (20-25 pairs), and irregularly *Circus pygargus* and *Burhinus oedicnemus*. Passage migrants include *Milvus milvus* (1-5) and *Pandion haliaetus* (1-4), also occasionally *Haliaeetus albicilla* occurs in winter.

084 Site name and location confidential

Unprotected

Wet moorland with heath and grassland, arable land, and woodland. Human activities include military use, agriculture, hunting, and recreation. The site is seriously threatened by drainage and the building of access roads.

A traditional migration staging post for *Grus grus* (20,000 on passage; with max. 1700 overwintering). Breeding species include *Circaetus gallicus*, *Circus cyaneus*, *C. pygargus*, and *Numenius arquata* (less than 10 pairs; one of the few breeding sites in south-west France).

085 Site name and location confidential

4.2 ha

Protected by a communal by-law.

Island with cliffs. Human activities include recreation. There is considerable pressure from tourists.

Breeding species include *Hydrobates pelagicus* (32 pairs). Wintering species include *Phalacrocorax carbo* (240).

086 Bassin d'Arcachon et Banc d'Arguin (Aquitaine)

44°40'N, 01°02'W 15,000 ha EEC SPA (2095 ha)

Coastal Hunting Reserve (600 ha); Nature Reserves: Banc d'Arguin (500 ha) and Arès; Parc Ornithologique du Teich (120 ha)

Bay and estuary with islands and sand-dunes, *Zostera* beds, saltwater and freshwater lagoons, wet meadows, marshes, and mudflats. Human activities include fishing, boating, and hunting. Problems include pollution, intensive hunting and tourism.

Breeding species include *Egretta garzetta* (475 pairs), *Ardea cinerea* (275 pairs), *Ciconia ciconia* (1 pair), *Milvus migrans* (20-25 pairs), *Circaetus gallicus, Recurvirostra avosetta, Sterna sandvicensis* (4500 pairs), *Alcedo atthis* (8-10 pairs), and *Luscinia svecica* (120-130 pairs). Species occurring on passage include *Platalea leucorodia* (80-100), *Circus aeruginosus, C. cyaneus, Pandion haliaetus, Himantopus himantopus* (40-50), *Recurvirostra avosetta* (800-1000), *Pluvialis squatarola* (300-1000), *Tringa totanus* (1000-2000), *T. glareola* (50-100), and *Chlidonias niger* (50-100). Wintering species include *Gavia immer* (10-15), *Phalacrocorax carbo* (1000), *Egretta garzetta* (1600), *Platalea leucorodia* (10), *Branta bernicla* (15,000), *Anas acuta* (1000-3000), *Circus aeruginosus* (10), *C. cyaneus* (2-3), *Recurvirostra avosetta* (100-200), *Pluvialis squatarola* (600-1200), *Calidris alpina* (15,000-20,000), and *Numenius arquata* (1200-3200).

087 Pointe de Grave et marais du Verdon/Mer (Aquitaine)

45°33'N, 01°05'E 1900 ha

Unprotected

Woodland, marshes, wet meadow, dunes and beaches, agricultural land, and estuary. Human activities include forestry, agriculture, fishing, hunting and shooting, tourism and recreation. There is considerable pressure from hunting.

Breeding species include *Milvus migrans* (2-5 pairs) and *Circus aeruginosus* (1-2 pairs). Very important site for migratory birds (with a considerable variety of species occurring), including *Ardea purpurea* (30-50), *Platalea leucorodia* (20), *Anser anser* (300), *Pernis apivorus* (100-350), *Milvus migrans* (700), *Circus pygargus* (50-100), *Pandion haliaetus* (5), *Numenius phaeopus* (100-1500), *Chlidonias niger* (hundreds), *Streptopelia turtur* (15,000-40,000), *Apus apus* (50,000; max. 165,000 in 1987) and tens of thousands of hirundines, and other passerines.

088 Barthes de l'Adour (Aquitaine)

43°30'N, 01°36'W 6000 ha

Partly a Hunting Reserve

Marshes, wet meadows, and lakes along the River Adour with woodland, hedges, and arable land. Human activities include agriculture, fishing, and hunting. This site is not well known, but there are certainly several Annex 1 (EEC Wild Birds Directive) species breeding, and field surveys are required.

Breeding species include *Ciconia ciconia* (1 pair) and *Nycticorax nycticorax* (40-50 pairs).

089 Forêt d'Iraty, massif des Arbailles et pic d'Orhy y compris Organbidexka (Aquitaine)

43°20'N, 00°57'W 16,500 ha

Conventional Reserve (2 ha) covering Organbidexka Pass by agreement between Ministry of Environment and a nature conservation organisation (renewable every three years). The rest of the area is unprotected.

Fast-flowing rivers and streams, lakes, forests, and mountains with cliffs and pasture. Human activities include forestry, stock-raising, fishing, hunting and shooting, and recreation. Problems include intensive forestry overgrazing, the opening of new roads and tracks, and the site is over-burdened by tourists and hunters shooting.

Breeding species include *Pernis apivorus* (1 pair), *Milvus milvus*, *Gypaetus barbatus*, *Neophron percnopterus* (3-4 pairs), *Gyps fulvus* (10-12 pairs), *Aquila chrysaetos* (1 pair), *Falco peregrinus* (3 pairs), *Bubo bubo* (1-2 pairs), *Dryocopus martius*, and *Dendrocopos leucotos*. Species occurring on passage at Organbidexka between 1981 and 1987 (seasonal counts) include *Ciconia nigra* (27-128), *C. ciconia* (2-16), *Pernis apivorus* (8604-11,501; max. 17,379 in 1981), *Milvus migrans* (1454-8746), *M. milvus* (2627-3842), *Neophron percnopterus* (50-150), *Circaetus gallicus* (42-90), *Circus aeruginosus* (74-242), *C. cyaneus* (55-127), *C. pygargus* (48-103), *Hieraaetus pennatus* (38-94), *Pandion haliaetus* (45-74), *Falco columbarius* (11-38), *F. peregrinus* (4-19), and *Grus grus* (1443-4816).

090 Cirque de Lescun, vallée d'Aspe et forêt d'Issaux (Aquitaine)

42°55'N, 00°37'W 14,500 ha partly European Diploma Site

Partly included in the Pyrenees National Park (central and peripheral zones)

Fast-flowing rivers and streams, lakes, forests, moorland, grassland and arable land, mountains, and cliffs. Human activities include agriculture, forestry, extensive traditional stock-raising, fishing, hunting, and recreation. Cirque de Lescun is threatened by intensive forestry, new tracks and roads. The area is over-burdened with hunters, tourists, and fishermen.

Breeding species include *Milvus milvus* (1+ pair), *Gypaetus barbatus* (1 pair), *Neophron percnopterus* (1-2 pairs), *Gyps fulvus* (40-50 pairs), *Aquila chrysaetos* (1-2 pairs), *Falco peregrinus* (2 pairs), *Lagopus mutus pyrenaicus* (10+ pairs), *Tetrao urogallus* (10+ pairs), *Perdix perdix hispaniensis* (10+ pairs), *Bubo bubo* (1-3 pairs), *Dryocopus martius* (10+ pairs), *Dendrocopos leucotos* (10+ pairs), and *Pyrrhocorax pyrrhocorax* (10+ pairs).

091 Vallées d'Ossau, du Bitet et de Soussoueou (Aquitaine)

42°55'N, 00°25'W 40,000 ha European Diploma Site

Natural Reserve (82 ha); Pyrenees National Park (central and peripheral zones)

Fast-flowing rivers and streams, lakes, forests, moorland, grassland and arable land, mountains, and cliffs. Human activities include agriculture, forestry, extensive traditional stock-raising, fishing, hunting, and recreation; and there are major roads. Threatened by intensive forestry, new tracks, extension of a ski-station, and urban expansion.

Breeding species include *Gypaetus barbatus* (1 pair), *Neophron percnopterus* (3 pairs), *Gyps fulvus* (50 pairs in 1986), *Milvus migrans* (1-10 pairs), *M. milvus*, *Aquila chrysaetos* (1-2 pairs), *Falco peregrinus* (3-4 pairs), *Lagopus mutus pyrenaicus* (150-200 pairs), *Tetrao urogallus* (100-200 pairs), *Perdix perdix hispaniensis* (10+ pairs), *Bubo bubo* (2-3 pairs), *Dryocopus martius* (50-100 pairs), *Dendrocopos leucotos* (10-50 pairs), and *Pyrrhocorax pyrrhocorax* (10+).

092 Barrage d'Artix et Saligue du gave de Pau (Aquitaine)

43°24'N, 00°34'W 1800 ha

Partly a Hunting Reserve

Reservoir, marshes, and wet forest along the River Pau; also woodland and arable land. Human activities include agriculture, fishing, tourism (including boating), and gravel extraction.

Breeding species include *Nycticorax nycticorax* (70 pairs) and *Egretta garzetta* (20 pairs). *Pandion haliaetus* (4) occurs on passage.

093 Haute vallée de l'Aude et massif des Pyrénées-Orientales (Languedoc-Roussillon, Midi-Pyrénées)

42°48'N, 02°50'E 500,000 ha

Unprotected

Mountains and cliffs, alpine pastures, and deciduous woodland. The area is threatened by development for tourism, forest exploitation, and the abandonment of traditional agricultural practices.

A very important area for *Tetrao urogallus* and *Lagopus mutus*. Other breeding species include *Milvus migrans*, *Neophron percnopterus*, *Circaetus gallicus*, *Circus cyaneus*, *Aquila chrysaetos*, *Hieraaetus pennatus*, *Falco peregrinus*, *Burhinus oedicnemus*, *Charadrius morinellus* (less than 10 pairs), *Bubo bubo*, *Aegolius funereus*, *Alcedo atthis*, *Dryocopus martius*, *Lanius collurio*, and *Pyrrhocorax pyrrhocorax*. In the Cerdagne part of the area there are good sites for passage migrants with 6000-15,000 raptors, *Apus apus* (100,000+), and *Merops apiaster* (1000+) occurring.

094 Gorges de la Dourbie (Midi-Pyrénées)

44°06'N, 03°05'E 12,000 ha

'Site classé'

Rocky habitats, agricultural land, woodland, and garigue. The subsites Causses Noir and du Larzac are threatened by agricultural improvements and cultivation, forestry operations, and tourism; hunting pressure is also high.

Breeding species include *Pernis apivorus* (2 pairs), *Circaetus gallicus* (5 pairs), *Circus cyaneus* (3 pairs), *C. pygargus* (2 pairs), *Aquila chrysaetos* (1 pair), *Falco peregrinus* (2 pairs), *Tetrax tetrax*, *Burhinus oedicnemus*, *Bubo bubo* (8 pairs), *Caprimulgus europaeus* (20+ pairs), *Alcedo atthis*, *Dryocopus martius*, and *Pyrrhocorax pyrrhocorax* (15+ pairs). Species occurring on passage include *Milvus migrans*, *M. milvus*, *Neophron percnopterus*, *Gyps fulvus*, *Hieraaetus pennatus*, and *Pandion haliaetus*. *Falco columbarius* occurs in winter.

095 Gorges de la Truyère (Auvergne, Midi-Pyrénées)

44°52'N, 02°52'E 15,000 ha

Unprotected

Woodland, hedges and cultivated land, grassland, moorland, cliffs, and reservoirs. Human activities include agriculture, forestry, stock-raising, fishing, hunting, and recreation (including boating), and there is a railway. Threatened by forestry exploitation and replacement of natural woodland with exotic species. There is also heavy hunting pressure and disturbance from wind-surfing and sailing.

Breeding species include *Pernis apivorus* (20-30 pairs), *Milvus migrans* (100-120 pairs), *M. milvus* (30-40 pairs), *Circaetus gallicus* (13-18 pairs), *Circus cyaneus* (7-12 pairs), *Hieraaetus pennatus* (15-30 pairs), *Falco peregrinus* (4 pairs), *Bubo bubo* (1-2 pairs), and *Dryocopus martius* (20 pairs). *Pernis apivorus*, *Milvus migrans*, *M. milvus*, and *Pandion haliaetus* occur on passage.

096 Gorges du Tarn et de la Jonte (Languedoc-Roussillon, Midi-Pyrénées)

44°12'N, 03°15'E 7000 ha

Unprotected

Fast-flowing river, woodland, scrub and cliffs. Human activities include agriculture, forestry, fishing, hunting, recreation, and major roads.

Breeding species include *Pernis apivorus*, *Neophron percnopterus* (1 pair), *Gyps fulvus* (18 pairs, with 65 in winter; there was a successful reintroduction project here), *Circaetus gallicus*, *Aquila chrysaetos* (4 pairs), *Falco peregrinus* (3 pairs), *Bubo bubo* (5 pairs), *Dryocopus martius*, and *Pyrrhocorax pyrrhocorax*.

097 Vallées du Lis et de la Pique (Midi-Pyrénées)

42°43'N, 00°38'E 7800 ha

'Site classé' (80 ha); Hunting Reserve (780 ha)

Mountains and cliffs, alpine grassland and arable land, and woodland. Human activities include stock-raising, agriculture, forestry, and hunting. Threatened by the construction of new roads for forestry and tourism. There are also plans to build a new ski-station.

Breeding species include *Pernis apivorus* (3 pairs), *Milvus migrans* (2 pairs), *M. milvus* (1 pair), *Gypaetus barbatus* (1 pair), *Neophron percnopterus* (1 pair), *Aquila chrysaetos* (1 pair), *Falco peregrinus* (1 pair), *Lagopus mutus pyrenaicus* (10+ pairs), *Tetrao urogallus* (10+ pairs), *Perdix perdix hispaniensis* (10+ pairs), *Aegolius funereus* (a few pairs) and *Dendrocopos leucotos* (a few pairs).

098 Cirque de Gavarnie et environs (Midi-Pyrénées)

42°44'N, 00°01'W 6000 ha partly a European Diploma Site

Pyrenees National Park (50 per cent; central and peripheral zones); 'site classé' (100 per cent)

Mountains and cliffs with fast-flowing river and streams, alpine grassland and woodland. Human activities include stock-raising, forestry, tourism and recreation. Threatened by development of tourism, roads, and electric power-lines.

Breeding species include *Gypaetus barbatus* (1 pair), *Neophron percnopterus* (1 pair), *Aquila chrysaetos* (1 pair), *Falco peregrinus* (1 pair), *Lagopus mutus pyrenaicus* (10+ pairs), *Bubo bubo* (1 pair), and *Pyrrhocorax pyrrhocorax* (10 pairs). *Gyps fulvus* occurs in summer.

099 Palayre (Midi-Pyrénées)

43°37'N, 01°27'E 2 ha

'Arrêté de biotope'

Woodland near Garonne, with fresh standing water. The site is threatened by a project to build a track for four-wheel-drive vehicles.

Breeding species include *Egretta garzetta* (7-26 pairs) and *Nycticorax nycticorax* (530-730 pairs). Combined with site 100 this represents one of the largest concentrations in western Europe of *Nycticorax nycticorax* (1270 pairs at both sites in 1987).

100 Moissac (Midi-Pyrénées)

44°06'N, 01°02'E 5 ha

'Arrêté de biotope'

Private park near the confluence of the Rivers Tarn and Garonne.

Breeding species include *Nycticorax nycticorax* (710 pairs) and *Egretta garzetta* (4 pairs).

101 Gorges de la Dordogne (Limousin, Auvergne)

45°22'N, 02°24'E 4862 ha

Unprotected

Fast-flowing river, pools, marshes, woodland, hedges and cultivated land, uncultivated land, moorland, cliffs, and reservoirs. Human activities include agriculture, forestry, stock-raising, mining and quarrying, fishing, hunting, and recreation including sailing. Threatened by forestry exploitation and replacement of natural woodland by exotic species. There is disturbance from sailing.

Breeding species include *Pandion haliaetus*, *Pernis apivorus* (15 pairs), *Milvus migrans* (50 pairs), *M. milvus* (9 pairs), *Circaetus gallicus* (7 pairs), *Circus cyaneus* (1 pair), *Hieraaetus pennatus* (1-3 pairs), *Falco peregrinus* (2 pairs), and *Bubo bubo* (1 pair). *Ardea purpurea*, *Pernis apivorus*, *Milvus migrans*, *Circus aeruginosus*, and *Alcedo atthis* occur on passage.

102 Etang de Landes (Limousin)

46°10'N, 02°20'E 700 ha

Unprotected

Lakes, marshes, and wet meadows, surrounded by woodland, hedges and cultivated land, and plains. Human activities include agriculture, stock-raising, fishing, and hunting.

Breeding species include *Ardea purpurea* (30 pairs), *Porzana porzana*, *Pernis apivorus* (1 pair), *Milvus migrans* (1-4 pairs), and *Circus aeruginosus* (1 pair). A variety of species occurs on passage including *Circus aeruginosus*, *C. cyaneus*, *C. pygargus*, *Pandion haliaetus*, and *Grus grus*.

103 La Dombes (Rhône-Alpes)

45°55'-46°10'N, 04°55'-05°20'E 100,000 ha

Hunting prohibited; partly protected by Réserve de Villars les Dombes (214 ha)

A complex of lakes and marshes, with hedges and cultivated land, and grassland and arable land. Human activities include agriculture, fishing, hunting, and recreation including sailing.

An important breeding area for herons, ducks, and waders. Breeding species include *Podiceps nigricollis* (200 pairs), *Botaurus stellaris* (1-2 pairs), *Ixobrychus minutus*, *Nycticorax nycticorax* (200 pairs), *Egretta garzetta* (0-50 pairs), *Ardea purpurea* (less than 200 pairs), *Anas strepera* (100 pairs), *A. querquedula*, *A. clypeata*, *Netta rufina* (100 pairs), *Aythya ferina*, *Milvus migrans*, *Circus aeruginosus* (10-20 pairs), *C. pygargus*, *Porzana porzana*, *Himantopus himantopus* (0-10 pairs), *Limosa limosa* (0-10 pairs; also thousands on passage), and *Chlidonias hybridus* (300-800 pairs). Wintering waterfowl include *Anas strepera* (max. 300), *A. crecca* (3000), *A. clypeata* (max. 1500), and *Aythya ferina* (max. 4000); concentrations of ducks are irregular according to climatic conditions.

103-1 Etangs de Saint Paul-de-Varax (Rhône-Alpes)

45°05'N, 05°01'E 5000 ha

Unprotected

Lakes, marshes, wet meadows, arable land, and woodland. Human activities include agriculture, forestry, stock-raising, fishing, and hunting.

Breeding species include *Podiceps nigricollis* (10+ pairs), *Ixobrychus minutus* (1-4 pairs), *Ardea purpurea* (20 pairs), *Netta rufina* (10 pairs), *Pernis apivorus* (1-5 pairs), *Milvus migrans* (1-5 pairs), *Circus aeruginosus* (2-4 pairs), *Himantopus himantopus*, *Chlidonias hybridus* (10+ pairs), and *Limosa limosa*. Species occurring on passage include *Nycticorax nycticorax*, *Ardeola ralloides*, *Egretta garzetta*, *Circaetus gallicus*, *Pandion haliaetus*, *Porzana porzana*, *Philomachus pugnax* (700), *Tringa glareola*, *Chlidonias niger*, and *Luscinia svecica*. Wintering wildfowl and waders include *Anas crecca* (300-3000) and *Aythya ferina* (3200-10,000); *Botaurus stellaris* (1-2) and *Egretta alba* (1-2) also occur in winter.

103-2 Versailleux-le-Montellier, le Plantay (Rhône-Alpes)

49°59'N, 05°01'E 6500 ha

Partly a Conventional Reserve

Lakes with marshes, wet meadows, woodland, grassland and arable land. Human activities include agriculture, stock-raising, fishing, and hunting.

Breeding species include *Podiceps nigricollis* (20-40 pairs), *Botaurus stellaris* (1 pair), *Ixobrychus minutus* (2-3 pairs), *Nycticorax nycticorax* (150 pairs), *Egretta garzetta* (30 pairs), *Ardea purpurea*, *Pernis apivorus* (2-3 pairs), *Milvus migrans* (5-6 pairs), *Himantopus himantopus* (2-7 pairs), and *Limosa limosa*. Species occurring on passage include *Platalea leucorodia* (2-3), *Pandion haliaetus* (2-5), *Porzana porzana*, *Limosa limosa* (100-500), *Tringa erythropus*, *T. glareola* (max. 100), and *Chlidonias niger* (40). Wintering species include *Aythya ferina* (max. 6000), *A. fuligula* (max. 4000), and *Falco columbarius* (1-2).

104 Val de Drôme: les Ramières (Rhône-Alpes)

44°46'N, 04°52'E 500 ha EEC SPA (346 ha)

Nature Reserve (350 ha)

Slow and fast-flowing rivers, marshes, with woodland and dry calcareous grassland. Human activities include agriculture, fishing, hunting, and tourism including boating.

Breeding species include *Ixobrychus minutus* (2 pairs), *Nycticorax nycticorax* (40-80 pairs), *Egretta garzetta* (10 pairs), *Pernis apivorus*, *Milvus migrans* (30-40 pairs), *M. milvus* (1-2 pairs), *Circus pygargus* (1 pair), and *Burhinus oedicnemus* (2 pairs). Species occurring on passage include *Phalacrocorax carbo* (1000+; 600 wintering), *Milvus migrans* (1000+), *M. milvus*, and *Pandion haliaetus* (10+).

105 Etang de Suze la Rousse (Rhône-Alpes)

44°50'N, 04°54'E 100 ha

Hunting Reserve (50 ha)

Lake with marshes, woodland, and sclerophyllous scrub. Human activities include agriculture, hunting, tourism, and industry.

Breeding species include *Ixobrychus minutus* (1 pair), *Circaetus gallicus* (1 pair), *Circus pygargus* (2 pairs), *Caprimulgus europaeus* (2 pairs), *Lullula arborea* (5 pairs), *Anthus campestris* (5 pairs), and *Emberiza hortulana*. *Circus cyaneus* (4) occurs in winter.

106 Hauts plateaux du Vercors (Rhône-Alpes)

44°45'N, 05°30'E 16,000 ha EEC SPA (16,662 ha)

Nature Reserve (16,000 ha)

Mountains and cliffs with fast-flowing river and woodland. Human activities include forestry, stock-raising, fishing, and hunting.

Breeding species include *Pernis apivorus*, *Circaetus gallicus*, *Falco peregrinus*, *Tetrao tetrix*, *Bubo bubo*, *Aegolius funereus*, and *Dryocopus martius*.

107 Col de l'Escrinet (Rhône-Alpes)

44°39'N, 04°35'E 15 ha

Unprotected

Mountains and moorland. Human activities include hunting and shooting.

Breeding species include *Pernis apivorus* (1 pair), *Circaetus gallicus* (1 pair), and *Circus pygargus* (2-3 pairs). Large numbers of passage migrants occur including *Phalacrocorax carbo* (800), *Ciconia nigra*, *C. ciconia*, *Pernis apivorus* (5000), *Milvus migrans* (3000-4000), *Circaetus gallicus*, *Circus aeruginosus* (800), *Pandion haliaetus* (150-170), *Columba palumbus* (12,000), and 300,000+ passerines.

108 Etangs du Forez (Rhône-Alpes)

45°07'-45°45'N, 04°00'-04°25'E 50,000 ha

Unprotected

Lakes, marshes, hedges and cultivated land, grassland and arable land. Human activities include agriculture, fishing, hunting, and recreation; there are roads through the area. The site is threatened by a plan to build a motorway, agricultural development, and mineral exploitation. There is considerable disturbance from hunting, shooting, and fishing.

Breeding species include *Podiceps nigricollis* (400 pairs), *Ixobrychus minutus* (0-10 pairs), *Nycticorax nycticorax* (20-30 pairs), *Netta rufina* (50 pairs), *Pernis apivorus*, *Milvus migrans*, *M. milvus*, *Circus aeruginosus*, and *Chlidonias hybridus* (50-100 pairs). Migratory species include *Pandion haliaetus* (10-20), *Grus grus*, and *Chlidonias niger*.

109 Lac et marais du Bourget (Rhône-Alpes)

45°43'N, 05°45'E 5000 ha

Hunting Reserve (700 ha); Arrêté de biotope (132 ha)

Lake, marshes, wet meadows, and agricultural land. Human activities include agriculture, forestry, fishing, hunting, and recreation including sailing.

Breeding species include *Podiceps cristatus* (350 pairs), *Ixobrychus minutus* (2-3 pairs), *Milvus migrans*, *Circus cyaneus* (2 pairs), *Falco peregrinus*, *Numenius arquata*, *Alcedo atthis*, and *Luscinia svecica*. Wintering species include *Podiceps cristatus* (2000-5000).

110 Montagne des Frètes et massif environnant (Rhône-Alpes)

45°50'N, 06°07'E 15,000 ha

Protection status not known

Woodland and agricultural land. Human activities include forestry and agriculture.

Breeding species include *Tetrao tetrix*, *T. urogallus*, and *Dryocopus martius*. (Last ornithological survey in 1984)

111 Lac Léman (Rhône-Alpes)

46°21'N, 06°21'E 23,900 ha

Nature Reserve (147 ha); two Hunting Reserves (1440 ha); hunting prohibited (2200 ha) because of urbanised shoreline

This site is the French part of Lake Geneva (Switzerland); all data are for the French part only. Human activities include fishing, hunting, and recreation (including sailing). The lake is threatened by pollution from heavy metals and eutrophication.

Breeding species include *Mergus merganser* (50 pairs) and *Sterna hirundo* (30-35 pairs). In winter, waterfowl occurring include *Podiceps cristatus* (2860), *P. nigricollis* (538), *Aythya ferina* (1875), *A. fuligula* (10,466), and *Bucephala clangula* (627; max. 1400).

112 Les Bauges (Rhône-Alpes)

45°41'N, 06°20'E 22,000 ha

Protection status not known

Woodland. Human activities include forestry.

Breeding species include *Tetrao tetrix* and *T. urogallus*. (Last ornithological survey in 1984)

113 La Serre (Auvergne)

45°41'N, 03°01'E 3000 ha

Unprotected

Mountains, woodland, uncultivated land, arable land, and rocky habitat. Human activities include agriculture and hunting.

Breeding species include *Milvus migrans*, *Circaetus gallicus*, *Circus pygargus*, *Bubo bubo*, *Caprimulgus europaeus*, and *Lanius collurio*. Large numbers of passage migrants occur (with a lot of resting places) including *Pernis apivorus* (1400-1500), *Milvus migrans* (600-800), *M. milvus* (1200-1400), *Circus aeruginosus* (100-200), *C. cyaneus*, *C.pygargus*, *Pandion haliaetus* (20-40), *Falco peregrinus*, *Columba* spp. (120,000), and 185,000 passerines.

114 Monts et Plomb du Cantal, y compris col du Prat de Bouc (Auvergne)

45°06'N, 02°39'E 4000 ha

Partly 'site classé'

Fast-flowing rivers and streams, peatbog, woodland, uncultivated land, mountains and cliffs. Human activities include forestry, stock-raising, hunting, and recreation. Threatened by extension of existing ski-station and other development projects, and disturbance from trial bikes, four-wheel-drive vehicles, and from hunting activities.

Breeding species include *Falco peregrinus*, *Dryocopus martius*, and *Turdus torquatus*. A migration watchpoint with millions of birds passing. Passage migrants include (av. figures based on Prat de Bouc seasonal counts) *Ciconia nigra* (30), *C. ciconia* (25). *Pernis apivorus* (2000), *Milvus migrans* (1000), *M. milvus* (900), *Circus aeruginosus* (150), *C. cyaneus* (200), *Buteo buteo* (1500), *Pandion haliaetus* (40), *Falco columbarius* (50), and *F. peregrinus* (50).

115 Planèze de Saint-Flour (Auvergne)

45°03'N, 02°56'E 22,000 ha

'Arrêté de biotope' (Lascols Marsh: 70 ha)

Marshes, wet meadows, hedges and cultivated land, grasslands and uncultivated land. Human activities include forestry, stock-raising, fishing, hunting, and recreation; there are villages and major roads. Threatened by drainage, hedge removal, and hunting pressure.

Breeding species include *Milvus migrans* (4-6 pairs), *Circus cyaneus* (2-4 pairs), *C. pygargus* (30-40 pairs in 1970s; irregularly now), *Porzana porzana*, *Crex crex*, and *Asio flammeus* (1-2 pairs; irregularly). Passage migrants include *Milvus migrans* (400-600), *Circus aeruginosus*, *C. cyaneus*, *C. pygargus* (300-500), *Falco columbarius*, *F. peregrinus*, *Grus grus*, *Chlidonias hybridus*, *C. niger*, *Asio flammeus*, and hundreds of thousands of passerines.

116 Site name and location confidential

1000 ha

'Site classé' and 'Arrêté de biotope'

Cliffs and garigue. Human activities include military use, tourism, and shooting. The surrounding areas are affected by considerable disturbance by tourists.

Breeding species include *Neophron percnopterus* (1 pair), *Circaetus gallicus*, *Hieraaetus fasciatus* (2 pairs), and *Bubo bubo* (many pairs).

117 Site name and location confidential

18,000 ha

Unprotected

Garigue and vineyards. Human activities include agriculture, tourism and recreation, and shooting.

Breeding species include *Hieraaetus fasciatus* (1 pair), *Aquila chrysaetos* (2 pairs), and *Bubo bubo* (20 pairs).

118 Site name and location confidential

100,000 ha

Unprotected

Cliffs, river, garigue, and vineyards. Human activities include tourism and recreation, agriculture, and shooting.

Breeding species include *Neophron percnopterus* (1 pair), *Circaetus gallicus* (5-6 pairs), *Hieraaetus fasciatus* (4 pairs), *Bubo bubo* (30+ pairs) and *Pyrrhocorax pyrrhocorax* (20-50 pairs).

119 Etang de Vendres (Languedoc-Roussillon)

43°15'N, 03°14'E 1500 ha

Unprotected

Fresh standing water, reedbeds, and marshes. Human activities include hunting and shooting.

Breeding species include *Botaurus stellaris* (20-30 pairs), *Ixobrychus minutus* (a few pairs), *Ardea purpurea* (100-200 pairs), *Circus aeruginosus* (10+ pairs), *Chlidonias hybridus* (20-50 pairs), and *Acrocephalus melanopogon*.

120 Etang de Pissevache (Languedoc-Roussillon)

43°12'N, 03°13'E 1000 ha

Unprotected

Saltwater lagoon, sand-dunes, marshes, reedbeds, and grassland. Human activities include shooting.

Breeding species include *Himantopus himantopus* (10-40 pairs), *Acrocephalus melanopogon*, and *Lanius minor* (a few pairs). Passage species include *Phoenicopterus ruber* (600+; also 100-400 wintering), *Larus genei* (max. 8), *L. audouinii*, and *Sterna sandvicensis* (100s).

121 Aérodrome de Lésignan-Corbières (Languedoc-Roussillon)

43°13'N, 02°41'E 600 ha

Unprotected

Agricultural land. Human activities include arable farming and there is an airport.

Breeding species include *Tetrax tetrax* (3 pairs), *Burhinus oedicnemus* (6 pairs), *Melanocorypha calandra* (30+ pairs), and *Calandrella brachydactyla*.

122 Etangs de Bages, Sigean, Ayrolle et Campignol (Languedoc-Roussillon)

43°05'N, 03°00'E 13,000 ha

'Site classé' (6000 ha); partly Hunting Reserves (2100 ha) and 'Arrêté de biotope' (13.5 ha)

Beaches, sand-dunes, islands, saltwater lagoons and marshes, mudflats, woodland, maquis, mountains, and cliffs. Human activities include fishing, hunting, and recreation including boating.

Breeding species include *Circaetus gallicus* (2 pairs), *Hieraaetus fasciatus* (1 pair), *Himantopus himantopus* (30-80 pairs), *Recurvirostra avosetta* (0-10 pairs), *Charadrius alexandrinus* (100-200 pairs), *Sterna albifrons* (50-100 pairs), *Bubo bubo*, *Calandrella brachydactyla*, and *Anthus campestris*. Passage species include *Ciconia ciconia* (100-200), *Milvus migrans* (2000-3000), *Circaetus gallicus* (100-500), *Egretta garzetta* (400), *Pernis apivorus* (3000-6000), and *Merops apiaster* (1000-3000). Winter visitors include *Phoenicopterus ruber* (500), *Anas acuta* (max. 500), *A. clypeata* (max. 500), and *Aythya ferina* (max. 2500).

123 Littoral de l'Aude et des Pyrénées-Orientales, y compris Leucate (Languedoc-Roussillon)

42°55'N, 03°00'E 22,000 ha

Partly a 'site classé' and Hunting Reserves

Mudflats, saltmarshes, saltwater lagoon, marshes, sand beaches and dunes, cliffs, rocky islets, garigue, and dry calcareous grassland and agricultural land. Human activities include agriculture, fishing, hunting, and tourism including boating.

Breeding species include *Circus aeruginosus* (10-15 pairs), *Himantopus himantopus* (10-50 pairs), *Recurvirostra avosetta* (10-50 pairs), *Charadrius alexandrinus* (100-200 pairs), *Sterna albifrons* (50-100 pairs), *Bubo bubo*, *Melanocorypha calandra* (4-5 pairs), *Calandrella brachydactyla*, *Galerida theklae*, and *Acrocephalus melanopogon*. Species occurring on passage include *Gavia arctica* (30-50), *Ciconia nigra* (20-50), *Phoenicopterus ruber* (500-1500), *Pernis apivorus* (5000-15,000), *Milvus migrans* (1000-3000), *Circaetus gallicus* (100-500), *Pandion haliaetus* (50-100), and *Larus genei* (50-100). At the Leucate bottleneck area, more than 1700 raptors and 200,000 passerines occur in spring. Wintering species include *Phoenicopterus ruber* (200-500), *Aythya ferina* (2000-7000), and *Fulica atra* (5000-10,000).

124 Etang de Capestang (Languedoc-Roussillon)

43°20'N, 03°20'E 900 ha

Unprotected

Lake and marshes. Human activities include agriculture, fishing, hunting, and tourism. There is night hunting using decoys.

Breeding species include *Botaurus stellaris* (5-10 pairs), *Ixobrychus minutus* (20-50 pairs), *Nycticorax nycticorax* (10-15 pairs), *Ardea purpurea* (50-150 pairs), *Circus aeruginosus* (3-10 pairs), *Coracias garrulus* (5-10 pairs), *Acrocephalus melanopogon*, and *Lanius minor* (2-5 pairs). *Ciconia ciconia* formerly bred.

125 Corbières (Languedoc-Roussillon)

42°46'N, 02°50'E 150,000 ha

Partly 'Site classé'

Maquis, garigue, forest, and cliffs. Human activities include agriculture, vineyards in the valleys, forestry, hunting, fishing, and tourism.

Breeding species include *Pernis apivorus* (*c.*50 pairs), *Milvus migrans* (*c.*10 pairs), *Circaetus gallicus* (20-30 pairs), *Circus cyaneus*, *C. pygargus* (10-50 pairs), *Aquila chrysaetos* (5-10 pairs), *Hieraaetus fasciatus* (3 pairs), *Bubo bubo* (20-50 pairs), *Galerida theklae*, and *Pyrrhocorax pyrrhocorax* (10-100). Passage migrants include *Pernis apivorus* (10,000-20,000), *Milvus migrans* (2000-5000), *M. milvus* (50-200), and *Circaetus gallicus* (100-500).

126 Gorges de la Vis, cirque de Navacelles et causse du Blandas (Languedoc-Roussillon)

43°53'N, 03°31'E 12,700 ha

'Site classé'

Mountains, cliffs, maquis, woodland, agricultural land, marshes, and fast-flowing rivers and streams. Human activities include agriculture, forestry, stock-raising, fishing, hunting, and recreation.

Breeding species include *Circaetus gallicus* (1-5 pairs), *Circus pygargus* (5-10 pairs), *Aquila chrysaetos* (3 pairs), *Bubo bubo*, *Caprimulgus europaeus*, *Lullula arborea*, *Anthus campestris*, *Lanius collurio*, and *Pyrrhocorax pyrrhocorax*.

127 Etangs et salins d'Aigues-Mortes au Petit Rhône (Languedoc-Roussillon)

43°30'N, 04°10'E 32,000 ha

Unprotected

Lakes and saltpans just west of the Camargue with beaches, sand-dunes, islands, saltwater lagoons, marshes, maquis, grassland, and arable land. Human activities include agriculture, stock-raising, fishing, hunting, and recreation.

Breeding species include *Botaurus stellaris* (30 pairs), *Ixobrychus minutus*, *Nycticorax nycticorax* (83 pairs), *Ardeola ralloides* (25 pairs), *Bubulcus ibis* (130 pairs), *Egretta garzetta* (950 pairs), *Ardea purpurea* (600 pairs), *Tadorna tadorna* (250 pairs), *Circus aeruginosus* (20-50 pairs), *Himantopus himantopus* (20 pairs), *Recurvirostra avosetta* (400 pairs), *Burhinus oedicnemus* (1-2 pairs), *Charadrius alexandrinus* (50-100 pairs), *Larus melanocephalus* (5-10 pairs), *Larus genei* (70 pairs), *Gelochelidon nilotica* (150-400 pairs), *Sterna sandvicensis* (200 pairs; irregularly), *S. hirundo* (600-800 pairs), and *S. albifrons* (150-400 pairs). Also some of the *Phoenicopterus ruber* breeding in the Camargue feed at this site. Wintering species include *Phoenicopterus ruber* (5000-10,000), *Tadorna tadorna* (1600), and *Netta rufina*; there is an interchange of birds in winter with the Camargue.

128 Etangs et salins du Languedoc (Languedoc-Roussillon)

43°20'-43°33'N, 03°32'-04°05'E 20,000 ha EEC SPA (Etang de l'Estagnol: 78 ha)

Partly protected by a Nature Reserve (Marais de l'Estagnol: 78 ha); and Coastal Hunting Reserves (Etang de l'Arnel: 220 ha; Etang du Méjean: 463 ha; Etang de Vic: 62 ha; Salins d'Ingril: 46 ha, and Etang de Maugio)

Saltwater lagoons and marshes. Includes the following lakes and saltpan-complexes: Maugio, Pérols, Méjean, du Grec, l'Arnel, Pierre Blanche, Vic and le Peyrade. Human activities include fishing, hunting, and recreation including boating. Adversely affected by seafood gathering at night and night hunting using live decoys. There is also industrial development at Pérols.

Breeding species include *Circus aeruginosus* (10-15 pairs), *Himantopus himantopus* (50-150 pairs), *Recurvirostra avosetta* (100-200 pairs), *Charadrius alexandrinus* (100-200 pairs), *Sterna hirundo* (300-500 pairs), *S. albifrons* (200-300 pairs), *Calandrella brachydactyla* (10-20 pairs), and *Acrocephalus melanopogon* (20-100 pairs). *Limosa limosa* (2000-3000), *Larus genei* (10-100), *Gelochelidon nilotica*, *Chlidonias hybridus* (100-300), and *C. niger* (200-300) occur on passage. An important site for *Phoenicopterus ruber* (3000-10,000 wintering; 10,000-15,000 on passage). In addition, wintering waterfowl include *Phalacrocorax carbo* (500-1000), *Anas crecca* (500-5000), *Anas clypeata* (1000-3000), *Fulica atra* (max. 12,500), and *Recurvirostra avosetta* (400-1000).

129 Massif des Albères (Languedoc-Roussillon)

42°31'N, 03°05'E 13,000 ha

Nature Reserve (Forêt de la Massane: 336 ha)

Maquis, garigue, forest, and cliffs. Human activities include wine growing, forestry, and hunting. The area is threatened by development for tourism and house building.

The only breeding site for *Oenanthe leucura* in France. Other breeding species include *Circaetus gallicus* (1-5 pairs), *Hieraaetus fasciatus* (1 pair), and *Bubo bubo* (5-15 pairs).

130 Camargue (Provence-Alpes-Côte d'Azur)

43°20'-43°35'N, 04°15'04°50'E 76,000 ha

Ramsar Site (85,000 ha) EEC SPA (13,702 ha); Mediterranean Specially Protected Area

Strict Nature Reserve (most of Etang de Vaccarès); Private Nature Reserves and Hunting Reserve

Large delta with beaches, sand-dunes, islands, saltwater lagoons, marshes, and slow-flowing rivers; also woodland, grassland and agricultural land. Human activities include agriculture, fishing, hunting, and recreation including boating. Threatened by development of rice-fields and modifications of water-levels, tourist development, use of toxic chemicals in agriculture, and air pollution.

Breeding species include *Botaurus stellaris* (50 pairs), *Ixobrychus minutus* (10+ pairs), *Nycticorax nycticorax* (300 pairs), *Ardeola ralloides* (50 pairs), *Bubulcus ibis* (50-300 pairs), *Egretta garzetta*, (1000 pairs), *Ardea purpurea* (400 pairs), *Phoenicopterus ruber*

(6,000-13,000 pairs), *Netta rufina* (200-300 pairs), *Circus aeruginosus* (50 pairs), *C. pygargus*, *Himantopus himantopus* (500+ pairs), *Recurvirostra avosetta* (650-800 pairs), *Burhinus oedicnemus*, *Glareola pratincola* (10-20 pairs), *Charadrius alexandrinus* (700 pairs), *Larus melanocephalus* (0-25 pairs), *L. genei* (20-25 pairs), *Gelochelidon nilotica* (120 pairs), *Sterna sandvicensis* (1000 pairs), *S. hirundo* (1500 pairs), *S. albifrons* (350 pairs), *Coracias garrulus*, and *Acrocephalus melanopogon*. Extremely important during the migration period and in winter with *Phalacrocorax carbo* (3000-4000; with 6000 roosting in Nov.), *Bubulcus ibis* (10-1000), *Egretta garzetta* (100-500), *E. alba* (10-20), *Phoenicopterus ruber* (1500-3000 in Jan.), *Anas penelope* (Jan. av. 14,000; max. 23,000), *A. strepera* (Jan. av. 8000; max. 12,000), *A. crecca* (Jan. av. 45,000; max. 55,000), *A. platyrhynchos* (Jan. av. 40,000), *A. acuta* (Jan. av. 3300; max. 6200), *A. clypeata* (Jan. av. 12,000; max. 16,000), *Netta rufina* (Jan. av. 3800; max. 5500), *Aythya ferina* (Jan. av. 13,000), *A. fuligula* (max. 7500), *Fulica atra* (Jan. av. 25,000; max. 41,000), *Recurvirostra avosetta* (300-600), *Charadrius hiaticula* (1500 in autumn), *C. alexandrinus* (3500 in autumn), *Calidris minuta* (1500 in autumn), *Philomachus pugnax* (thousands on passage), *Limosa limosa* (thousands on passage), *Tringa erythropus* (500 in autumn), *T. glareola* (thousands on passage), and *Chlidonias niger* (thousands on passage).

131 Plaine de la Crau (Provence-Alpes-Côte d'Azur)

43°34'N, 04°52'E 15,000 ha

Unprotected

A semi-arid steppe meadow area, mainly dry calcareous grassland with sclerophyllous scrub, with ancient orchards (almond and olive). The area is predominantly used for extensive traditional sheep-farming as well as for growing almonds and olives. The site is seriously threatened by the following activities: cultivation and modification of steppe-meadows, irrigation, felling of old almond and olive orchards and their replacement with commercial groves, the leasing out of military-training areas for agricultural exploitation, disturbance from recreational activities and hunting, and plans to build a motorway. These changes seriously threaten the populations of *Tetrax tetrax*, *Burhinus oedicnemus*, and *Pterocles alchata*.

Breeding species include *Milvus migrans* (50 pairs), *Circus aeruginosus* (2 pairs), *C. pygargus*, *Falco naumanni* (4-6 pairs), *Tetrax tetrax* (700 males in 1980, 400-500 males in 1984; also wintering with a max. of 1100 birds), *Burhinus oedicnemus* (300 pairs), *Pterocles alchata* (max. 170 pairs; also wintering with 400 birds), *Clamator glandarius* (10-50 pairs), *Coracias garrulus* (70 pairs), *Melanocorypha calandra* (50-100 pairs), *Calandrella brachydactyla* (1000 pairs), *Anthus campestris*, and *Lanius minor* (10 pairs). *Charadrius morinellus* (10) occurs on passage, and *Melanocorypha calandra* (200) occurs in winter.

132 Marais entre Crau et Grand Rhône: Meyranne, Chanoine, Plan de Bourg et salins du Caban (Provence-Alpes-Côte d'Azur)

43°30'N, 04°50'E *c.*15,000 ha

Unprotected

Marshes between the steppe of the Crau and the River Rhône alongside the Camargue.

Breeding species include *Botaurus stellaris* (25 pairs), *Nycticorax nycticorax* (80 pairs), *Ardea ralloides* (30 pairs), *Egretta garzetta* (100 pairs), *Ardea purpurea* (200 pairs), *Circus aeruginosus* (20 pairs), *Himantopus himantopus* (10 pairs), *Recurvirostra avosetta* (10 pairs), *Charadrius alexandrinus* (50 pairs), *Sterna albifrons* (30 pairs), *Coracias garrulus* (20 pairs), *Melanocorypha calandra* (15 pairs), and *Acrocephalus melanopogon* (100+ pairs). Species on passage include *Himantopus himantopus* (300) and *Limosa limosa* (3000). Wintering species include *Phoenicopterus ruber* (300), *Egretta alba* (5-10), *Anas strepera* (500), *A. crecca* (4500), *A. clypeata* (1000), and *Circus aeruginosus* (100+). There is an exchange of ducks, waders, and *Phalacrocorax carbo* with the Camargue.

133 Chaîne des Alpilles (Provence-Alpes-Côte d'Azur)

43°47'N, 04°49'E 15,000 ha

Unprotected

Mountains, cliffs, and hills with maquis and woodland. Human activities include agriculture, forestry, stock-raising, hunting, and recreation. Threatened by urban development and forestry operations. Also the construction of new roads and tracks, which will lead to increased disturbance from tourism and hiking.

Breeding species include *Neophron percnopterus* (5 pairs), *Circaetus gallicus* (2 pairs), *Hieraaetus fasciatus* (2 pairs), *Bubo bubo* (45 pairs), *Caprimulgus europaeus* (100 pairs), and *Coracias garrulus* (5 pairs). Large numbers of *Pernis apivorus* (1000+), *Milvus migrans* (500+), *Circaetus gallicus* (100), *Merops apiaster* (1000), *Turdus torquatus* (1000), and *Montifringilla nivalis* (hundreds) occur on passage, and *Aquila chrysaetos* occurs in winter.

134 Salines de l'étang de Berre (Provence-Alpes-Côte d'Azur)

43°28'N, 05°10'E 350 ha

Unprotected

Saltmarshes on the lagoon of Berre. Human activities include hunting.
The site is threatened by urban and industrial development, tourism and hunting pressure.

Breeding species include *Himantopus himantopus* (6 pairs), *Recurvirostra avosetta* (62 pairs), *Larus melanocephalus* (1 pair), *Sterna hirundo* (150 pairs), and *S. albifrons* (40 pairs).

135 Montagne Sainte Victoire (Provence-Alpes-Côte d'Azur)

43°32'N, 05°39'E 10,000 ha

'Site classé' (80 per cent)

Mountains, hills and cliffs, maquis and garigue, dry calcareous grassland, and agricultural land. Human activities include agriculture, forestry, stock-raising, fishing, hunting, and recreation. The site is seriously threatened by the construction of new forest roads, tourist trails and tracks, and there is heavy hunting pressure.

Breeding species include *Circaetus gallicus* (2 pairs), *Aquila chrysaetos* (1 pair), *Hieraaetus fasciatus* (1 pair), *Bubo bubo* (7 pairs), *Caprimulgus europaeus* (50+ pairs), *Lullula arborea* (100+ pairs), *Anthus campestris* (50 pairs), and *Emberiza hortulana* (100 pairs). In addition, *Neophron percnopterus*, *Falco peregrinus*, large numbers of *Turdus torquatus* occur on passage. *Pyrrhocorax pyrrhocorax* (50) occurs in winter.

136 Iles Marseillaises: Maire, Jarron, Jarre, Calséraigne, Riou et Congloué (Provence-Alpes-Côte d'Azur)

43°10'N, 05°23'E 150 ha

Unprotected

An archipelago of islands with rocky coastlines, cliffs, and maquis. Human activities include fishing, hunting, recreation (including boating). There is planned urban development and stray domestic pets are endangering the breeding species.

Breeding species include *Calonectris diomedea* (265-325 pairs), *Puffinus puffinus yelkouan* (10+ pairs), *Hydrobates pelagicus* (10-30 pairs), and *Falco peregrinus* (1-2 pairs).

137 Massif du Petit Lubéron (Provence-Alpes-Côte d'Azur)

43°52'N, 05°25'E 18,000 ha

Conventional Reserve (600 ha); hunting reserve (1100 ha)

Mountains, hills and cliffs with woodland, garigue, grassland, and fast-flowing rivers. Human activities include forestry and agriculture. The site is threatened by forestry activities and replacement of natural forest by exotic species, and by abandonment of agricultural activities.

Breeding species include *Neophron percnopterus* (4-5 pairs), *Circaetus gallicus* (5-6 pairs), *Hieraaetus fasciatus* (1 pair), *Burhinus oedicnemus* (10+ pairs), *Bubo bubo* (20 pairs), *Caprimulgus europaeus* (100+ pairs), *Anthus campestris* (100+ pairs), and *Lanius minor* (less than 10 pairs). Wintering species include *Aquila chrysaetos*, *Circus cyaneus*, and *Falco peregrinus*.

138 Salins d'Hyères et des Pesquiers (Provence-Alpes-Côte d'Azur)

43°05'N, 06°10'W 1000 ha

Unprotected

Saltwater marshes and saltpans. Human activities include recreation (sailing). The site is threatened by urban development; there is a project for a marina, and there is disturbance from tourism.

Breeding species include *Himantopus himantopus* (2-35 pairs), *Recurvirostra avosetta* (15-30 pairs), *Charadrius alexandrinus* (60-100 pairs), and *Sterna albifrons* (20-60 pairs). Wintering species include *Egretta garzetta* (30-100), *Phoenicopterus ruber* (300), and *Charadrius alexandrinus* (80-150). It is a good site for migrants, especially for *Phoenicopterus ruber* (500-2000), *Himantopus himantopus* (70), and *Charadrius alexandrinus* (100-200).

139 Iles d'Hyères: Porquerolles, Port-Cros, le Levant (Provence-Alpes-Côte d'Azur)

43°00'N, 06°25'E 2900 ha EEC SPA (Parc National de Port-Cros: 694 ha)

'Site classé' (1200 ha); National Park (Port-Cros: 685 ha); Conventional Reserve

Archipelago of rocky islands with cliffs, beaches, woodland, and maquis. Human activities include recreation and sailing; and there is a port.

Breeding species include *Calonectris diomedea* (195-245 pairs), *Puffinus puffinus yelkouan* (200-300 pairs), and *Falco peregrinus* (2-3 pairs). Migratory species include *Falco eleonorae* (2-6).

140 Parc national des Ecrins (Provence-Alpes-Côte d'Azur)

44°35'-45°02'N, 05°58'-06°31'E 91,800 ha EEC SPA

National Park

Mountains, cliffs, permanent snow and ice, woodland, and alpine grasslands.

Breeding species include *Pernis apivorus* (5 pairs), *Milvus migrans*, *M. milvus*, *Circaetus gallicus* (4-5 pairs), *Aquila chrysaetos* (24 pairs), *Falco peregrinus* (1 pair), *Bonasa bonasia* (10+ pairs), *Lagopus mutus helveticus*, *Tetrao tetrix* (200+ pairs), *Alectoris graeca saxatilis* (100+ pairs), *Bubo bubo* (2 pairs), *Glaucidium passerinum* (1-2 pairs), *Aegolius funereus* (2-5 pairs), *Dryocopus martius* (40+ pairs), *Lanius collurio*, *Pyrrhocorax pyrrhocorax*, and *Emberiza hortulana*.

141 Bois des Ayes (Provence-Alpes-Côte d'Azur)

44°49'N, 06°40'E 250 ha

Unprotected

Woodland. Human activities include forestry.

Breeding species include *Aquila chrysaetos* (1 pair), *Glaucidium passerinum* (10 pairs), *Aegolius funereus* (4+ pairs), *Dryocopus martius*, *Lullula arborea*, and possibly *Circaetus gallicus* and *Pyrrhocorax pyrrhocorax*.

142 Bec de Crigne (Provence-Alpes-Côte d'Azur)

44°24'N, 05°57'E 400 ha

Proposed 'Arrêté de biotope'

Cliffs, rocky habitats and sclerophyllous scrub. Human activities include stock-raising.

Breeding species include *Pernis apivorus* (1 pair), *Milvus migrans* (2 pairs), *Neophron percnopterus* (1 pair), *Circaetus gallicus* (1 pair), *Circus pygargus* (2 pairs), *Aquila chrysaetos* (1 pair), *Falco peregrinus* (1 pair), *Tetrao tetrix* (less than 10 pairs), *Alectoris graeca saxatilis*, *Bubo bubo* (1-2 pairs), *Lanius collurio*, and *Emberiza hortulana*. Species occurring on passage include *Milvus milvus*, *Circus cyaneus*, and *Falco columbarius* (*c.*10).

143 Vallée et gorges de la Durance (Provence-Alpes-Côte d'Azur)

44°20'N, 06°00'E 1100 ha

River Durance with cliffs and emergent vegetation. Human activities include forestry.

Breeding species include *Ixobrychus minutus* (1 pair), *Milvus migrans*, *Circus pygargus*, *Circaetus gallicus*, *Falco peregrinus* (2 pairs), *Porzana porzana*, *Burhinus oedicnemus* (5+ pairs), *Bubo bubo* (5+ pairs), *Dryocopus martius*, *Anthus campestris*, *Alcedo atthis*, *Lullula arborea*, *Caprimulgus europaeus*, *Lanius collurio*, *L. minor*, and *Emberiza hortulana*. Species occurring on passage include *Egretta garzetta*, *Ardea purpurea*, *Ciconia nigra*, *C. ciconia*, *Milvus milvus*, *Neophron percnopterus*, *Pandion haliaetus* (10+), *Falco columbarius*, *Porzana porzana* (10+), and *P. parva*. Wintering species include *Circus cyaneus*, *Falco peregrinus*, and *Asio flammeus*.

144 Golfe de Sud Corse: Iles Lavezzi (Corse)

41°23'N, 09°15'E 15,000 ha

EEC SPA (5150 ha); Mediterranean Specially Protected Area (Lavezzi Islands)

Nature Reserve for rocky islands (185 ha)

Open sea with rocky islands. Human activities include stock-raising, fishing, and recreation including boating; there were 16,000 visitors on the biggest island in 1986.

Breeding species include *Calonectris diomedea* (250-400 pairs), *Hydrobates pelagicus* (*c.*10 pairs), *Phalacrocorax aristotelis desmarestii* (350-500 pairs), and *Sterna hirundo* (1-2 pairs).

145 Iles Cerbicale (Corse)

41°33'N, 09°22'E 5000 ha EEC SPA; Mediterranean Specially Protected Area

Nature Reserve (36 ha)

Open sea and islands with rocky coast, cliffs and maquis.

Breeding species include *Calonectris diomedea* (85+ pairs), *Hydrobates pelagicus* (hundreds of pairs), *Phalacrocorax aristotelis desmarestii* (120-185 pairs), and *Larus audouinii*

146 Golfe de Porto, presqu'île de Scandola et golfe de Galéria (Corse)

42°20'N, 08°35'E 15,000 ha

EEC SPA (18,150 ha); Mediterranean Specially Protected Area (Scandola)

Natural Reserve (Scandola: 920 ha)

Bays with rocky coast, cliffs, beaches and islets, also woodland and maquis, hills, and mountains. Human activities include stock-raising, fishing, hunting, and recreation (including boating). Threatened by the construction of holiday homes and increased human disturbance.

Breeding species include *Phalacrocorax aristotelis desmarestii* (50-270 pairs), *Pandion haliaetus* (13 pairs), *Falco peregrinus* (10-15 pairs), and *Sylvia sarda*.

147 Vallée du Fango (Corse)

42°23'N, 08°50'E 6500 ha

Biosphere Reserve; Mediterranean Specially Protected Area

Unprotected but there is an agreement for the management of the forest

Fast-flowing rivers and streams with Mediterranean forests and maquis, and mountains with cliffs. Human activities include stock-raising and hunting.

Breeding species include *Gypaetus barbatus* (1 pair), *Accipiter gentilis arrigonii*, *Aquila chrysaetos* (1 pair) and *Sitta whiteheadi* (tens of pairs), and endemic subspecies of *Dendrocopos major*, *Troglodytes troglodytes*, *Muscicapa striata*, *Parus ater*, *P. major*, *Certhia familiaris*, and *Garrulus glandarius*.

148 Vallée d'Asco (Corse)

42°23'N, 08°57'E 3000 ha included in Mediterranean Specially Protected Area

Hunting Reserve

Fast-flowing rivers and streams with forest and maquis, and mountains with cliffs. Human activities include stock-raising.

Breeding species include *Gypaetus barbatus* (1 pair), *Aquila chrysaetos* (1 pair), *Falco peregrinus* (1 pair), *Sitta whiteheadi*, and also endemic subspecies of *Accipiter nisus*, *Dendrocopos major*, *Troglodytes troglodytes*, *Muscicapa striata*, *Parus ater*, *P. major*, *Certhia familiaris*, *Garrulus glandarius*, and *Loxia curvirostra*.

149 Vallée de la Restonica (Corse)

42°15'N, 09°06'E 6000 ha included in Mediterranean Specially Protected Area

'Site classé'

Fast-flowing rivers and streams with woodland and maquis, also mountains and cliffs. Human activities include stock-raising and hunting.

Breeding species include *Gypaetus barbatus* (1 pair), *Aquila chrysaetos* (1 pair), *Falco peregrinus* (1 pair) and *Sitta whiteheadi*, and also endemic subspecies of *Accipiter nisus*, *Dendrocopos major*, *Troglodytes troglodytes*, *Muscicapa striata*, *Parus ater*, *P. major*, *Certhia familiaris*, *Garrulus glandarius*, and *Loxia curvirostra*.

150 Etang de Biguglia (Corse)

42°35'N, 09°28'E 1600 ha

Unprotected

Saltwater lagoon and marshes with beaches, sand-dunes, and maquis. Human activities include fishing and hunting. There is considerable hunting pressure.

Breeding species include *Ixobrychus minutus*, *Ardea purpurea* (1-3 pairs), *Circus aeruginosus* (1-2 pairs), and *C. pygargus* (1-2 pairs). *Oxyura leucocephala* and *Haliaeetus albicilla* formerly bred (in 1960s). An important wintering waterfowl site, with *Anas clypeata* (max. 2000), *Aythya ferina* (500-5000), *A. fuligula* (1500-8000), and *Fulica atra* (4000-24,000). Also important for wintering *Acrocephalus melanopogon*.

151 Iles Sanguinaires (Corse)

41°52'N, 08°35'E 41 ha

Proposed 'Arrêté de biotope'

Rocky islets. Human activities include fishing and boating. Threatened by disturbance from tourism.

Breeding species include *Phalacrocorax aristotelis desmarestii* (80-160 pairs).

152 Vallée du Verghello (Corse)

42°12'N, 09°10'E 4000 ha included in Mediterranean Specially Protected Area

Proposed Nature Reserve; Conventional Reserve

Fast-flowing rivers and streams, woodland, maquis, and rocky habitat. Human activities include stock-raising and some hunting.

Breeding species include *Gypaetus barbatus* (1 pair), *Aquila chrysaetos* (1 pair), *Falco peregrinus* (1 pair), and *Sitta whiteheadi* (10+ pairs), and also endemic subspecies of *Accipiter nisus*, *Dendrocopos major*, *Troglodytes troglodytes*, *Muscicapa striata*, *Parus ater*, *P. major*, *Certhia familiaris*, *Garrulus glandarius*, and *Loxia curvirostra*.

153 Iles Finocchiarola et Côte de Tamarone a Barcaggio (Corse)

43°00'N, 09°28'E 2 ha

Nature reserve

Rocky islets. Human activities include fishing and boating.

Breeding species include *Calonectris diomedea* (30 pairs), *Phalacrocorax aristotelis desmarestii* (10 pairs), *Falco peregrinus* (1 pair), *Larus audouinii* (20-100 pairs), and *Sylvia sarda*.

MAIN REFERENCES

Bournerias, M. (1984) *Guide des groupements végétaux de la région parisienne. 3ième édition, SEDES, Paris.*

Broyer, J. (1985) *Le rale des genêts en France*. SRETIE/UNAO/CORA.

Duhautois, L. (1984) *Hérons paludicoles de France: statut 1983*. Ministère de l'Environnement/ SNPN.

Dubois, P. J. and Maheo, R. (1986) *Limicoles nicheurs de France*. Ministère de l'Environnement/LPO/BIROE.

FIR/UNAO (1984) *Estimation des effectifs de rapaces nicheurs diurnes et non rupestre en France, enquête FIR/UNAO 1979-1982*. Ministère de l'Environnement.

Gammell, A. and Karpowicz, Z. (1984) Important bird areas in the European Community under serious threat. Unpublished report to the Commission of the European Communities.

LPO (1984) *Etude des populations de l'Outarde canepetière dans la CEE*. Commission des Communautés Européennes.

Maheo, R. (1988) *Branta bernicla*: distribution numérique en France, saison 1987-88. IWRB, unpublished report.

Marion, L. (1982) Liste des milieux à protéger en France dans le cadre de la directive du conseil de la CEE sur la conservation des oiseaux sauvages. *Penn ar Bed* 13(106): 97-121.

MIGRANS (1988) Synthèse inter-sites 1986. Unpublished.

Ministère de l'Environnement (1979) *Atlas des réserves d'avifaune aquatique*. Paris.

Osieck, E. R. and Mörzer Bruyns, M. F. (1981) Unpublished report to the Commission of the European Communities.

Piersma, T. (1986) Breeding waders in Europe, a review of population size estimates and a bibliography of information sources. *Wader Study Group Bull.* 48 suppl.

Servan, J. (1980) *Typologie, bilan, problématique des espaces naturels*. Ministère de l'Environnement/Museum National d'Histoire Naturelle de Paris.

SFF (1980) Inventaire des zones de grand intérêt pour la conservation des oiseaux sauvages dans la Communauté européenne, 02-France. Secrétariat de la Faune et de la Flore, Museum National d'Histoire Naturelle de Paris.

SFF (1987) Inventaire des zones de grand intérêt pour la conservation des oiseaux sauvages dans la Communauté européenne, 02-France. Secrétariat de la Faune et de la Flore, Museum National d'Histoire Naturelle de Paris.

SFF (1987) Inventaire des zones de grand intérêt pour la conservation des oiseaux sauvages dans la Communauté européenne. Liste d'attente tous pays. Secrétariat de la Faune et de la Flore, Museum National d'Histoire Naturelle de Paris.

SNPN (1986) *Effets de la vague de froid de Janvier 1985 sur les effectifs reproducteurs de Héron cendré et de l'Aigrette garzette au printemps 1985*. Ministère de l'Environnement.

Thauront, M. (1988) Important bird areas in France. LPO/CIPO. Unpublished.

Thauront, M. (in press) *Réactualisation des zones françaises de grand intérêt pour la conservation des oiseaux sauvages dans la Communauté Européenne. LPO/CIPO.*

Yeatman, L. (1976) *Atlas des oiseaux nicheurs de France*. Société Ornithologique de France.

GERMAN DEMOCRATIC REPUBLIC

Crane *Grus grus* NA

INTRODUCTION

General information

The German Democratic Republic covers about 108,290 sq km, with a human population (in 1983) of 16,701,000 (an average population density of 154 persons/sq km). Around 62,600 sq km (58 per cent) are used for agriculture, of which *c.*47,500 sq km are arable land and *c.*12,330 sq km are grassland and pasture. Forests cover 29,600 sq km (27 per cent) and lakes and rivers cover 2270 sq km (2 per cent). The country is mainly lowland, with upland areas confined to the south (Thüringer Wald and Erzgebirge).

The country is a mosaic of agricultural land, woodland, copses, marshes, fens, and areas of open water. Larger forests are mostly confined to the medium-altitude mountains in the south (coniferous forests, mainly *Picea*) and to the lowlands in the north and east (mostly deciduous and *Pinus*). Most of the forests are exploited by the state forestry department, and (increasingly) species more resistant to pollution are now being planted. Relicts of formerly widespread riverine forests are limited to the flood-plain valleys of the Elbe, Saale, and the Mulde in the south-western part of the country; the most outstanding area being the Steckby-Lödderitzer Forest on the Elbe flood-plain.

The Baltic coastline is generally flat and broken by numerous bays (including the Wismarbucht, Saaler Bodden, Grabow, and Greifswalder Bodden), peninsulas, and islands (the largest being Rügen), with large areas of shallow water and intertidal mudflats. Inland, major wetland areas include the shallow lakes in the fenlands of the north-east, and the complexes of lakes in the vicinity of Waren (including Müritz See), Neustrelitz, and Schwerin. Many of the inland wetlands are of economic importance for fish-farming. Due to increasing eutrophication and growth of emergent vegetation, some waterbird populations are expanding, although others are declining. In addition, many passerines have benefited from these ecological changes.

Ornithological importance

The country is important for birds of water-bodies, marshes, riverine forests and wet meadows; breeding species include *Phalacrocorax carbo sinensis* (2000+ pairs; increasing), *Botaurus stellaris* (*c.*20 per cent of European population, but seriously declining), *Ciconia nigra* (*c.*40 pairs; stable), *Ciconia ciconia* (*c.*2400 pairs; stable population with fluctuations), *Cygnus olor* (decline in the last five years from 2250 pairs to 1870 pairs), *Anser anser* (*c.*3700 pairs; *c.*20 per cent of Baltic population), *Haliaeetus albicilla* (*c.*120 pairs; largest population in central Europe), *Pandion haliaetus* (*c.*120 pairs), and *Grus grus* (1000 pairs; increasing). There has been a decline in the population of a number of duck and wader species breeding in wet meadows, including *Limosa limosa*, *Numenius arquata* and *Tringa totanus*. Very large numbers of *Anser fabalis*, *A. albifrons* (marked increase in recent years), *A. anser* and *Grus grus* (25,000+ at one site on the Baltic coast) occur on passage.

The country has important populations of some raptor species. *Haliaeetus albicilla* and *Pandion haliaetus* have already been mentioned, but other species with populations clearly of European importance are *Milvus migrans* (800 pairs), *M. milvus* (2500 pairs), *Circus aeruginosus* (1500 pairs), and *Aquila pomarina* (*c.*80 pairs). *Circus pygargus* and *C. cyaneus* have drastically declined (only 30-35 pairs each). *Falco peregrinus* has recently recolonised (3-5 pairs) although *F. subbuteo* (400 pairs) is declining. Breeding owls include *Bubo bubo* (60 pairs) and *Glaucidium passerinum* (*c.*100 pairs); *Asio flammeus* is seriously declining.

Other non-passerines include *Tetrao tetrix* (only one population, in the lowlands), *T. urogallus* (isolated population) and *Otis tarda* (460 birds; the largest population in central Europe outside Hungary, although numbers are declining).

GDR is one of the few countries with a breeding population of *Acrocephalus paludicola* (30-40 pairs); a globally threatened species.

Conservation infrastructure and protected-area system

The following categories of protected area have been used in this inventory:

1. Nature Reserve (Naturschutzgebiet)
   These are sites of ecological, scientific, or cultural value, supporting rare plant and/or animal communities, and are designated by the state. There are controls regarding access and the exploitation of natural resources. Total Reserves (Totalreservate) are Nature Reserves where all human activities are barred.

2. Landscape Protection Area (Landschaftsschutzgebiet)
   These are landscape areas of specific cultural or socio-economic value. Changes can only be made in a way which improves or maintains these specific values.

3. Nature Monument (Flächennaturdenkmale)
   These are small (max. 3 ha) areas of ecologically valuable habitats, complementing the network of Nature Reserves.

4. Wetland of National Importance (Feuchtgebiete nationaler Bedeutung)
   These are wetlands designated by the state under national law, but according to criteria developed for identifying wetlands of international importance in the context of the Ramsar Convention.

5. Bustard Protection Area (Trappenschongebiete)
   These are sites, declared by the state, which are managed especially for *Otis tarda*, with restrictions on land-use.

6. Seabird Reserve (Küstenvogelschutzgebiet)
   These are areas designated to protect breeding colonies of coastal species such as terns.

International measures relevant to the conservation of sites

The German Democratic Republic is a party to the Ramsar Convention and has designated eight sites covering 45,387 ha. Two sites have been designated as Biosphere Reserves (covering 18,884 ha) under UNESCO's Man and the Biosphere Programme.

Overview of the inventory

The inventory includes 35 sites covering a total area of just over 164,000 ha; all are protected or at least partly protected. The inventory includes all GDR's Ramsar Sites and, of the two Biosphere Reserves, all Vessertal and part of Middle Elbe are included.

A large proportion of the sites (28 sites) are wetlands (or contain important wetland habitats). Good populations of wetland species are covered by the sites in this inventory; such as passage swans and geese, breeding and passage ducks, breeding waders (of both freshwater and coastal habitats), and breeding terns. Sizeable populations of other species associated with wetlands are also covered, such as *Botaurus stellaris*, *Haliaeetus albicilla*, *Pandion haliaetus*, *Grus grus*, and *Acrocephalus paludicola*. One site (003) is the most important passage area for *Grus grus* in northern and central Europe. Many of the wetland sites have adjacent forests, heathland, and grassland/agricultural land, and are also valuable for their rich variety of non-waterfowl species. The sites in the inventory support good populations of raptors including *Milvus milvus*, *Circus cyaneus* and *C. pygargus*.

The remaining seven sites are woodlands (one with heathland and moorland). These have been included for their populations of *Tetrao* spp., owls and woodpeckers.

Good populations of the country's Red Data Book species are covered by the sites in the inventory. *Milvus milvus* and *Haliaeetus albicilla* have already been mentioned (026 is especially noteworthy for its *Milvus milvus*). Sites 017 and 021 are important for *Otis tarda*, site 024 is important for *Crex crex* and sites 013 and 024 hold the majority of the country's population of *Acrocephalus paludicola*.

Acknowledgements

Professional and amateur wardens, and local ornithological experts provided site information which was coordinated by working groups of the Institute for Landscape Research and Nature Protection (Institut für Landschaftsforschung und Naturschutz) and by the Centre for Waterbirds Research (Zentrale für die Wasservogelforschung der DDR). The introduction was largely written by E. Rutschke and J. Naacke.

INVENTORY

No.	Site name	Region	Criteria used to select site [see p.18]							
			0	1(i)	1(ii)	1(iii)	1(iv)	2	3	4
001	Inseln Langenwerder und Walfisch	RK				*			*	
002	Dambecker Seen	RK,SN				*				
003	Westrügen – Hiddensee – Zingst, (mit Bodden)	RK			*	*		*	*	
004	Inseln Oie und Kirr	RK							*	
005	Greifswalder Bodden	RK				*			*	
006	Gothensee und Thurbruch, Inseln Böhmke und Werder	RK							*	
007	Kuhlrader Moor und Röggeliner See	SN				*		*		
008	Teichgebiet Lewitz	SN				*		*	*	
009	Krakower Obersee	SN						*	*	
010	Ostufer Müritz, Grosser Schwerin und Steinhorn	NG				*		*	*	
011	Serrahn	NG						*	*	
012	Nonnenhof mit Lieps	NG							*	

No.	Site name	Region	Criteria used to select site [see p.18]							
			0	1(i)	1(ii)	1(iii)	1(iv)	2	3	4
013	Peenetalmoor und Anklamer Stadtbruch	NG						*	*	
014	Galenbecker See und Putzarer See	NG				*		*	*	
015	Koblentzer See und Latzig See	NG						*	*	
016	Temmen – Ringenwalde Moränenlandschaft	NG				*		*	*	
017	Steckby-Lödderitzer Forst und Zerbster Ackerland	MG						*	*	
018	Untere Havelniederung, Gülper See und Schollener See	PM,MG				*		*	*	
019	Kremmener Luch	PM				*			*	
020	Rietzer See	PM				*			*	
021	Belziger Landschaftswiesen	PM						*	*	
022	Prierowsee	PM						*	*	
023	Felchowsee	FT						*	*	
024	Unteres Odertal: Polder bei Schwedt	FT				*		*	*	
025	Berga – Kelbra Storage Lake	HE	*							
026	Hakel	HE						*	*	
027	Presseler Heide- und Moorgebiet	LG				*			*	
028	Vessertal	SL,GA							*	
029	Schwarzatal	GA							*	
030	Uhlstädter Heide, Meuraer Heide, Assberg-Hasenleite und Wurzelbergfarmde	SL,GA						*	*	
031	Erzgebirgskamm bei Satzung	KMS							*	
032	Elbsandsteingebirge	DN							*	
033	Teiche bei Königswartha	DN						*	*	
034	Teichgebiet Niederspree	DN						*	*	
035	Teichgebiet Peitz	CS	*							

RK=Rostock SN=Schwerin NG=Neubrandenburg MG=Magdeburg
PM=Potsdam FT=Frankfurt HE=Halle LG=Leipzig SL=Suhl
GA=Gera KMS=Karl-Marx-Stadt DN=Dresden CS=Cottbus

Comments on the inventory

1. The passage figures are total counts during a season, rather than daily figures.
2. The regions, given in parentheses following the site names, are the districts (Bezirke).
3. The whole of GDR has been treated as the 'region' when applying the site-selection criteria (category 3).
4. All of the sites are believed to meet the site-selection criteria except 025 and 035 which have been included because they have been designated as Ramsar Sites.

Glossary

The following German words have been used in the inventory: bei = near; Bodden shallow sea bay; Bucht = bay; Forst = forest; Heide = heath; Insel(n) = island(s); Landschaft = landscape; mit = including; Moor = peatbog; Moräne = moraine; See(n) = lake(s); Stausee = reservoir/storage lake.

---

001 Inseln Langenwerder und Walfisch (Rostock)

54°02'N, 11°30'E 60 ha

Nature Reserve (Langenwerder); Nature Monument (Walfisch); Wetland of National Importance

Two islands in the Wismarbucht (a vast, rather shallow bay of the Baltic Sea), which developed from dunes and quicksand, close to the eastern shore. Walfisch has been artificially enlarged by pumping sand ashore on its eastern side.

Important for breeding waterfowl, with *Tadorna tadorna* (30 pairs), *Mergus serrator* (25 pairs), *Haematopus ostralegus* (50 pairs), *Charadrius hiaticula* (25 pairs), *Larus melanocephalus* (1-3 pairs), *L. canus* (4000-10,000 pairs), *L. argentatus* (100-200 pairs), *Sterna sandvicensis* (300 pairs), *S. hirundo* (100 pairs), *S. paradisaea* (200 pairs), and *S. albifrons* (50 pairs). Also a very important area for non-breeding waterfowl. Wintering species (1981-1986 Jan. av.; 1981-1986 Jan. max.) include *Cygnus olor* (150; 270), *C. cygnus* (80; 220), *Aythya fuligula* (910; 4200), *A. marila* (4520; 7700), *Somateria mollissima* (1120; 2560), *Clangula hyemalis* (100; 140), *Bucephala clangula* (430; 740), and *Fulica atra* (2000; 3900).

002 Dambecker Seen (Rostock, Schwerin)

53°54'N, 11°28'E 204 ha

Nature Reserve; Wetland of National Importance

Two shallow lakes with water-levels maintained to provide suitable habitat for waterfowl. There is fishing on the lakes, and the surrounding areas are used for grazing and agricultural crops. The input of organic matter to the lakes from intensive agriculture is a serious problem.

Breeding species include *Podiceps nigricollis* (*c.*100 pairs; numbers fluctuate), *Circus aeruginosus* (*c.*5 pairs), *Sterna hirundo* (15-20 pairs), *Chlidonias niger* (20-30 pairs), and *Lanius collurio* (2 pairs). Passage wildfowl include *Anser fabalis*, *A. albifrons* (for both species: 3000 in spring; 5000 in autumn), and *A. anser* (300-1000 in spring).

003 Westrügen – Hiddensee – Zingst (mit Bodden) (Rostock)

54°23'-54°36'N, 12°50'-13°16'E 26,250 ha

Includes Ramsar Site (Baltic Sea lagoon waters of Rügen/Hiddensee and eastern part of Zingst Peninsula: 25,800 ha)

Nature Reserves (nine areas)

An extensive coastal area of the southern Baltic Sea, including islands and vast areas of water less than 1 m in depth. The shores include bare outer zones, reedbeds, and saltmarshes, with the hinterland including meadows, forests, and smallholdings. Human activities include fishing and cultivation. Eutrophication is a problem.

Breeding species include *Cygnus olor* (50 pairs), *Anser anser* (20 pairs), *Tadorna tadorna* (100 pairs), *Anas strepera* (120 pairs), *A. crecca* (15 pairs), *A. acuta* (8-10 pairs), *A. clypeata* (120-150 pairs), *Mergus serrator* (180 pairs), *Circus aeruginosus* (5 pairs), *Recurvirostra avosetta* (140 pairs), *Philomachus pugnax* (50 pairs), *Limosa limosa* (80 pairs), *Tringa totanus* (200 pairs), *Sterna caspia* (2 pairs), *S. sandvicensis* (700 pairs), *S. hirundo* (900 pairs), *S. albifrons* (70 pairs), and *Riparia riparia* (2000 pairs). Very important for passage waterfowl with *Phalacrocorax carbo sinensis* (500 in autumn), *Cygnus olor* (2000 in autumn), *C. columbianus* (50 in spring and autumn), *Anser fabalis* (5000 in autumn), *A. albifrons* (20,000 in autumn), *A. anser* (20,000 in autumn), *Branta leucopsis* (200 in autumn), *B. bernicla* (250 in autumn), *Anas crecca* (5000 in spring; 10,000 in autumn), *Aythya fuligula* (15,000 in autumn), *Bucephala clangula* (3000 in autumn), *Grus grus* (10,000 in spring; 25,000 in autumn), *Tringa glareola* (500 in autumn), and *Sterna caspia* (200 in autumn). *Cygnus olor* (1000), *C. cygnus* (250), *Aythya fuligula* (10,000), *Bucephala clangula* (3000), *Mergus albellus* (500), *M. merganser* (2000), *Haliaeetus albicilla* (6), and *Falco peregrinus* (1) occur in winter.

004 Inseln Oie und Kirr (Rostock)

54°26'N, 12°42'E 450 ha

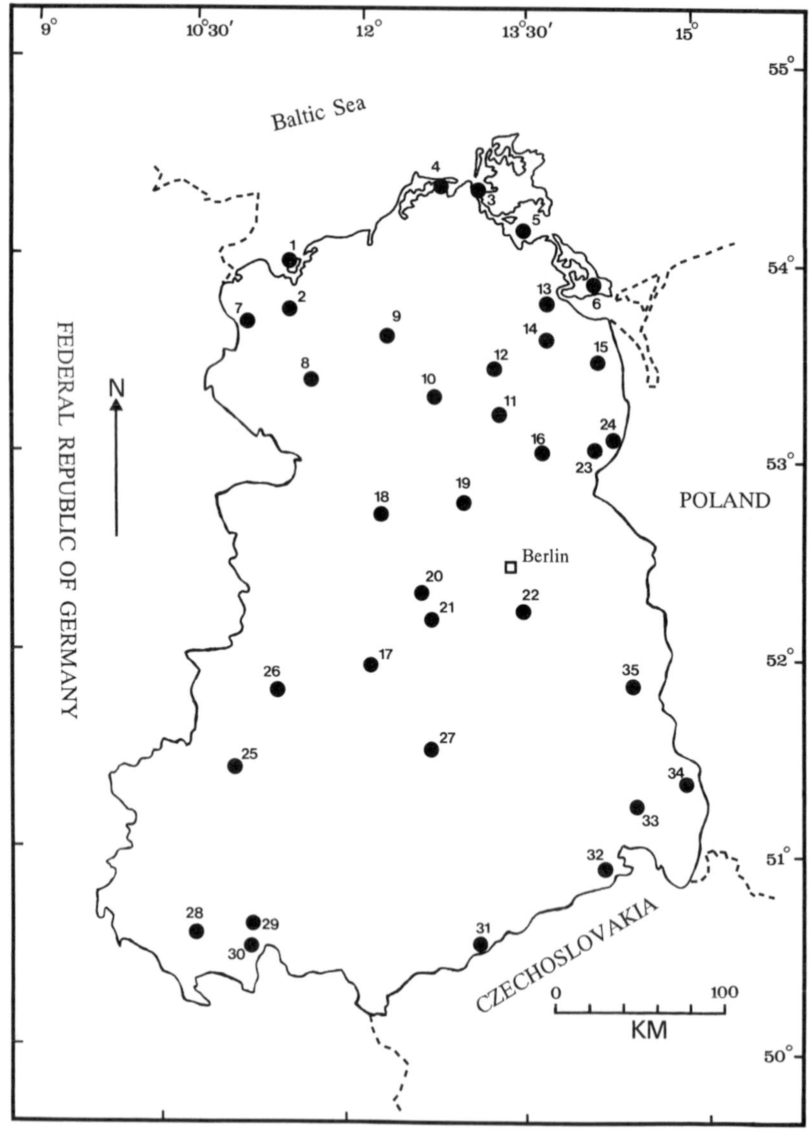

Figure 13: Map showing the location of the sites in the German Democratic Republic

Seabird Reserve

Two islands in the Barther Bodden.

Breeding species include *Recurvirostra avosetta* (2 pairs), *Limosa limosa* (40 pairs), *Tringa totanus* (150 pairs), *Sterna sandvicensis* (350 pairs), and *S. hirundo* (680 pairs).

005 Greifswalder Bodden (Rostock)

54°05'-54°23'N, 13°11'-13°55'E 74,850 ha (6700 ha land)

Nature Reserves (six areas: 2000 ha); partly Landscape Protection Area (Ostrügen); Wetland of National Importance

A bay on the southern shore of the Baltic Sea with large shoals, tidal zones, and saltmarshes. The land areas are used for pasture and haymaking; traditional fishing takes place at sea. A management plan exists for the site. An ice-free water zone near a nuclear power-station has increased the area's importance for wintering waterfowl.

Breeding species include *Phalacrocorax carbo sinensis* (600 pairs), *Recurvirostra avosetta* (12 pairs), *Philomachus pugnax* (12 pairs), *Sterna hirundo* (55 pairs), and *S. albifrons* (40 pairs). *Ciconia ciconia* nests in the surrounding areas. Extremely important for passage waterfowl, with *Phalacrocorax carbo sinensis* (1000 in spring and autumn), *Cygnus olor* (7000 in autumn), *C. columbianus* (600 in spring and autumn), *C. cygnus* (800 in autumn), *Anser fabalis* (8000 in autumn), *A. albifrons* (70,000 in autumn), *A. anser* (10,000 in autumn), *Tadorna tadorna* (1800; summer moult migration), *Anas penelope* (20,000 in autumn), *A. strepera* (3000 in autumn), *A. crecca* (10,000 in autumn), *A. acuta* (2000 in spring and autumn), *Aythya fuligula* (5000 in autumn), *A. marila* (30,000 in spring), *Clangula hyemalis* (50,000 in autumn), *Bucephala clangula* (7000 in autumn), and *Vanellus vanellus* (10,000 in autumn). An important wintering site for *Phalacrocorax carbo sinensis* (1000), *Cygnus olor* (300), and *Mergus merganser* (4000-8000).

006 Gothensee und Thurbruch, Inseln Böhmke und Werder (Rostock)

53°57'N, 14°02'-14°09'E 918 ha

Nature Reserves (Gothensee and Thurbruch: 800 ha; Islands of Böhmke and Werder: 118 ha); partly a Landscape Protection Area

A large shallow eutrophic lake, connected with the sea, with surrounding areas of peatland and reedbeds. Böhmke and Werder are two small islands to the west. Fishing takes place on the lake, and the surrounding meadows are grazed. Human activities also include recreation.

Breeding species include *Botaurus stellaris* (2-3 pairs), *Circus aeruginosus* (4-5 pairs), *Grus grus* (1 pair), *Sterna hirundo* (700 pairs), and *Chlidonias niger* (30-40 pairs).

007 Kuhlrader Moor und Röggeliner See (Schwerin)

53°44'N, 10°58'E 328 ha

Nature Reserve; Wetland of National Importance

A lake with an island and adjacent peatbog (Kuhlrader Moor) with ponds, dams, islets, and bushes (*Alnus*, *Salix*, *Betula*). There is fishing at the lake itself, and the surrounding area outside the peatbog is used for agriculture.

Breeding species include *Botaurus stellaris* (1 pair), *Ciconia ciconia* (2 pairs), *Aythya nyroca* (1 pair), *Circus aeruginosus* (c.5 pairs), *Porzana porzana* (1 pair), *Grus grus* (1 pair), *Sylvia nisoria* (1-2 pairs), and *Lanius collurio* (1-3 pairs). *Anser albifrons* (2000 in spring) occurs on passage, whilst wintering species include a few *Haliaeetus albicilla*.

008 Teichgebiet Lewitz (Schwerin)

53°26'N, 11°37'E 920 ha

Nature Reserve; Wetland of National Importance; part of Lewitz Landscape Protection Area

Part of a large (*c.*10,000 ha) lowland marsh of the River Elde, including several pond complexes and extensive meadowland. The ponds are artificial (for *Cyprinus*-farming) and are generally 20-100 ha in extent and 1 m in depth. The shores are mainly unvegetated, although there are some areas of reedbeds and vegetated islands. The wet meadows hold *Carex* and *Phalaris*, and are dissected by a network of ditches/canals. Intensification of fish-farming has resulted in a decrease in the area of reedbeds.

Breeding species include *Podiceps grisegena* (20-25 pairs), *P. nigricollis* (max. 10 pairs), *Phalacrocorax carbo sinensis* (10 pairs), *Botaurus stellaris* (2-3 pairs), *Aythya nyroca* (0-1 pair), *A. fuligula* (100 pairs), *Milvus migrans* (1 pair), *M. milvus* (2-3 pairs), *Circus aeruginosus* (20-25 pairs), *Pandion haliaetus* (2 pairs), *Porzana porzana* (1-2 pairs), *P. parva* (1-2 pairs), *Grus grus* (1 pair), and *Limosa limosa* (2-4 pairs). Important for passage birds, with *Phalacrocorax carbo sinensis* (200-400 in autumn), *Ciconia ciconia* (max. 150 in autumn), *Cygnus columbianus* (300-800 in spring and autumn), *C. cygnus* (100 in spring and autumn), *Anser albifrons* (4000-8000 in spring and autumn), *Anas clypeata* (1000 in spring and autumn), *Aythya ferina* (3000 in autumn), and *Milvus milvus* (20-30 in spring and autumn). *Cygnus cygnus* (100), *Anser fabalis* (2000), *Mergus merganser* (500), *Haliaeetus albicilla* (4-5), and *Circus cyaneus* (max. 10) occur in winter.

009 Krakower Obersee (Schwerin)

53°35'N, 12°16'E 868 ha Ramsar Site (870 ha)

Nature Reserve

A large coastal lake including eight islands (26 ha) and surrounded by woodland, pastures, and cultivated land. Parts of the islands are grazed; fishing occurs at the lake.

Breeding species include *Botaurus stellaris* (1 pair), *Anser anser* (50-75 pairs), *Anas strepera* (40-60 pairs), *Milvus milvus* (1 pair), *Haliaeetus albicilla* (1 pair), *Circus aeruginosus* (1-3 pairs), *Sterna hirundo* (120-200 pairs), and *Alcedo atthis* (1-3 pairs). *Phalacrocorax carbo sinensis* (300-600), *Aythya fuligula* (6000-9000), and *Haliaeetus albicilla* (4-12) occur on autumn passage. Small numbers of *Haliaeetus albicilla* also occur in winter.

010 Ostufer Müritz, Grosser Schwerin und Steinhorn (Neubrandenburg)

53°22'-53°27'N, 12°40'-12°49'E 5152 ha

Includes Ramsar Site (Eastern shore of Müritz See: 4830 ha)

Nature Reserves (Ostufer der Müritz; Grosser Schwerin and Steinhorn); Wetland of National Importance (Grosser Schwerin and Steinhorn); part of Müritzseen Park Landscape Protection Area

A large freshwater lake with a range of natural, semi-natural and man-made habitats. There are bays and zones of shallow water, with smaller lakes bordering the main lake. There is a rich shoreline vegetation (especially reedbeds and submerged plants). The lake's surroundings contain swamps, beds of *Carex*, dunes, *Juniperus* heaths, and *Pinus*/*Fagus* forest. Human activities include fishing and hunting (not of birds). Intensive agriculture and scrub-invasion are problems at the lake.

Breeding species include *Botaurus stellaris* (*c.*10 pairs), *Anser anser* (80-100 pairs), *Pernis apivorus* (1 pair), *Milvus migrans* (1 pair), *M. milvus* (2-3 pairs), *Haliaeetus albicilla* (1-3 pairs), *Circus aeruginosus* (5 pairs), *Pandion haliaetus* (1-2 pairs), *Porzana porzana* (5-10 pairs), *Grus grus* (5-10 pairs), *Sterna hirundo* (max. 30 pairs), *Dryocopus martius* (3-5 pairs), *Dendrocopos medius* (several pairs), *Sylvia nisoria* (3-5 pairs), *Ficedula parva* (2-5 pairs), and *Lanius collurio* (*c.*30 pairs). Also important for passage birds with *Cygnus cygnus* (100 in autumn), *Anser fabalis*/*A. albifrons* (10,000 in autumn), *A. anser* (2000 in autumn), *Netta rufina* (150 in autumn), *Aythya fuligula* (25,000 in autumn), *Circus cyaneus* (5 in spring), and *Grus grus* (500 in autumn).

011 Serrahn (Neubrandenburg)

53°20'N, 13°11'E 1818 ha

Nature Reserve

A well-forested moraine landscape with stands of *Pinus* and mixed deciduous/coniferous areas. There are scattered lakes with areas of open water, reedbeds, and *Alnus* swamps. Human activities include forestry. Water regulation may affect the area adversely.

Breeding species include *Milvus migrans* (2-3 pairs), *M. milvus* (3-5 pairs), *Haliaeetus albicilla* (1-2 pairs; also up to 10 wintering and on passage), *Pandion haliaetus* (2-3 pairs; 5 on passage), *Grus grus* (2-4 pairs), *Caprimulgus europaeus* (1-2 pairs), *Alcedo atthis* (1-4 pairs), *Dryocopus martius* (5-7 pairs), *Dendrocopos medius* (10-15 pairs), *Lullula arborea* (1-2 pairs), and *Ficedula parva* (40-50 pairs).

012 Nonnenhof mit Lieps (Neubrandenburg)

53°27'N, 13°10'E 700 ha

Nature Reserve

A shallow lake and peninsula with scrub, woodland, reedbeds, moors, and sandy dunes. Increasing pollution by waste water and fertilisers, and the overgrowing of open meadows, are serious problems at the site.

Breeding species include *Milvus migrans* (1 pair), *Circus aeruginosus* (2 pairs), *Porzana porzana* (2-3 pairs), *Grus grus* (2-3 pairs), *Alcedo atthis* (2-3 pairs), *Dryocopus martius* (1 pair), *Sylvia nisoria* (1-2 pairs), and *Lanius collurio* (2-5 pairs). There are also two pairs of *Haliaeetus albicilla* and a single pair of *Ciconia nigra* nesting nearby.

013 Peenetalmoor und Anklamer Stadtbruch (Neubrandenburg)

53°47'-53°53'N, 13°44'-13°54'E 2678 ha

Nature Reserve; Wetland of National Importance

An area of wet peatbog and flood-plains interspersed with reedbeds, *Salix* and *Betula*. Human activities include forestry, reed-cutting, boating, fishing, and hunting (not of birds). The area may be threatened by changing land-use, which has resulted in eutrophication and the increased frequency of flooding.

There is a rich breeding avifauna, with *Botaurus stellaris* (5-10 pairs), *Ixobrychus minutus* (*c.*5 pairs), *Ciconia ciconia* (20 pairs), *Anser anser* (20 pairs), *Anas querquedula* (20 pairs), *A. clypeata* (*c.*10 pairs), *Milvus migrans* (*c.*3 pairs), *M. milvus* (10 pairs), *Haliaeetus albicilla* (3 pairs), *Circus aeruginosus* (20 pairs), *C. cyaneus* (5-8 pairs), *C. pygargus* (6-10 pairs), *Aquila pomarina* (3 pairs), *Porzana porzana* (1-3 pairs), *Crex crex* (1-10 pairs), *Grus grus* (10 pairs), *Gallinago gallinago* (max. 50 pairs), *Limosa limosa* (5 pairs), *Tringa ochropus* (*c.*5 pairs), *Asio flammeus* (1-5 pairs), *Caprimulgus europaeus* (5 pairs), *Alcedo atthis* (*c.*5 pairs), *Dendrocopos medius* (15 pairs), *Lullula arborea* (*c.*20 pairs), *Luscinia svecica cyaneculus* (*c.*20 pairs), *Locustella fluviatilis* (*c.*25 pairs), *L. luscinioides* (*c.*25 pairs), *Acrocephalus paludicola* (1-10 pairs), *Remiz pendulinus* (*c.*15 pairs), and *Carpodacus erythrinus* (10-40 pairs).

014 Galenbecker See und Putzarer See (Neubrandenburg)

53°37'N, 13°40'E 1375 ha

Includes Ramsar Site (Galenbecker See: 1015 ha)

Nature Reserves; Wetland of National Importance (Putzarer See)

Two shallow, eutrophic, freshwater lakes in the drained depressions of former fens. The Galenbecker See has reedbeds, mudbanks, and large vegetated areas which are slowly silting up. The Putzarer See is rather shallower (0.25-0.5 m compared with 0.5-1 m) and also has reedbeds and extensive vegetated areas. Human activities include fishing (notably in the Galenbecker See), with grazing, grass-cutting, and forestry in nearby areas. Eutrophication and drainage adversely affect the site.

The area supports a rich breeding avifauna, with *Botaurus stellaris* (2-3 pairs), *Ciconia nigra* (1 pair), *C. ciconia* (1 pair), *Anas strepera* (10 pairs), *A. querquedula* (5 pairs), *Netta rufina* (2-5 pairs), *A. fuligula* (30-40 pairs), *Milvus migrans* (2 pairs), *M. milvus* (3 pairs), *Haliaeetus albicilla* (1-2 pairs), *Circus aeruginosus* (10 pairs), *C. pygargus* (2 pairs), *Aquila pomarina* (1 pair), *Pandion haliaetus* (2-4 pairs), *Rallus aquaticus* (30+ pairs), *Porzana porzana* (4-10 pairs), *Grus grus* (6-8 pairs), *Asio flammeus* (1-2 pairs), and *Luscinia svecica cyaneculus* (3-5 pairs). Also very important for species on passage, with *Cygnus columbianus* (20-30 in spring; 150 in autumn), *C. cygnus* (120 in autumn), *Anser fabalis* (10,000 in spring; 20,000 in autumn), *A. albifrons* (30,000 in spring; 20,000 in autumn), *Anas strepera* (3000 in autumn), *A. crecca* (1500 in autumn), *A. clypeata* (1500 in autumn), *Aythya ferina* (3500 in autumn), *Mergus albellus* (50-200 in autumn), *Milvus milvus* (20 in spring and autumn) and *Circus cyaneus* (5-10 in spring and autumn). Small numbers of *Cygnus cygnus* and *Circus cyaneus* occur in winter.

015 Koblentzer See und Latzig See (Neubrandenburg)

53°32'N, 14°08'-14°13'E 497 ha

Nature Reserve (Koblentz See: 397 ha); unprotected (Latzig See: 100 ha)

Two shallow lakes with surrounding reeds, *Alnus/Fraxinus* forests and meadows. Human activities include fishing, intensive haymaking, and grazing. There has been a decrease in the area of reedbed in the last ten years.

Breeding species include *Podiceps grisegena* (1-2 pairs), *Botaurus stellaris* (1 pair), *Ciconia ciconia* (3 pairs), *Milvus migrans* (2 pairs), *M. milvus* (2 pairs), *Haliaeetus albicilla* (2 pairs), *Circus aeruginosus* (6 pairs), *C. pygargus* (2 pairs), *Aquila pomarina* (1-2 pairs), *Porzana porzana* (1-3 pairs), *P. parva* (1-2 pairs), *Grus grus* (3 pairs), *Dryocopus martius* (2 pairs), and *Luscinia svecica* (2 pairs). *Ciconia ciconia* (*c.*150 in autumn) and *Grus grus* (*c.*100 in spring and autumn) occur on passage.

016 Moränenlandschaft Temmen – Ringenwalde (Neubrandenburg)

53°05'N, 13°40'E 2100 ha

Nature Reserves (two areas, plus two others proposed); Nature Monuments (five sites); partly a Wetland of National Importance (1700 ha)

A mosaic of morainic lakes, reedbeds, fens, peatbogs, and forests. There is careful use of the woodland by the state forestry service; small-scale agriculture and traditional fishing are practised as part of a management plan for the area. A conservation group manages the area.

Breeding species include *Botaurus stellaris* (2-3 pairs), *Ixobrychus minutus* (1+ pairs), *Ciconia nigra* (2 pairs), *C. ciconia* (4 pairs), *Pernis apivorus* (1-2 pairs), *Milvus migrans* (1 pair), *M. milvus* (2-3 pairs), *Haliaeetus albicilla* (2 pairs), *Circus aeruginosus* (4-5 pairs), *Pandion haliaetus* (1 pair), *Porzana porzana* (1+ pairs), *P. parva* (1+ pairs), *Sterna hirundo* (max. 15 pairs; irregular), *Alcedo atthis* (3+ pairs), *Caprimulgus europaeus*, *Dryocopus medius* (5-6 pairs), *Ficedula parva* (3-5 pairs), *Lanius collurio* (*c.*5-10 pairs), and *Emberiza hortulana* (1+ pairs). *Anser fabalis*, *A. albifrons* (combined max. 17,000 in autumn), and *Grus grus* (500 in autumn) occur on passage.

017 Steckby-Lödderitzer Forst und Zerbster Ackerland (Magdeburg)

51°54'-52°00'N, 12°02'-12°05'E 9000 ha

Included in a Biosphere Reserve (Middle Elbe: 17,500 ha)

Nature Reserve (Steckby-Lödderitzer Forst); Wetland of National Importance (Steckby Lödderitzer Forst); Bustard Protection Area

Part of the Elbe flood-plain, with agricultural land, meadowland, deciduous (*Quercus*) forests, *Salix* scrub, and *Pinus* forests. Human activities include agriculture and forestry.

Breeding species include *Ciconia nigra* (1 pair), *C. ciconia* (8 pairs), *Pernis apivorus* (5 pairs), *Milvus migrans* (5 pairs), *M. milvus* (10 pairs), *Circus aeruginosus* (5 pairs), *C. cyaneus* (1 pair), *C. pygargus* (2 pairs), *Porzana porzana*, *Crex crex*, *Grus grus* (1 pair), *Otis tarda* (20-25 pairs), *Caprimulgus europaeus* (30 pairs), *Alcedo atthis*, *Dendrocopos medius* (30 pairs), and *Lanius excubitor*. Also important for wintering and passage birds, with *Ciconia nigra* (20 in spring and autumn), *C. ciconia* (25 in spring and autumn), *Pandion haliaetus* (10 in spring and autumn), and *Otis tarda* (40 on passage and in winter).

018 Untere Havelniederung, Gülper See und Schollener See (Potsdam, Magdeburg)

52°39'-52°49'N, 12°16'E 6250 ha

Includes Ramsar Site (Lower River Havel and Gülper See: 5792 ha)

Nature Reserves (Gülper See; Stremel-Jäglitz; Schollener See); Landscape Protection Area (Unterhavel)

An extensive river-valley complex with meadows (formerly regularly flooded) and fens interspersed with sandy areas, oxbow lakes, and other shallow water-bodies. The rivers are eutrophic and regulated. The Gülper See and Schollener See (two of the lakes) are shallow and highly eutrophic, with little submerged vegetation but extensive reedbeds and vegetated mud/silt banks with swamp-forest, bushes, and small stands of *Pinus*. Human activities include commercial fishing, angling, grazing, haymaking, hunting (not of birds), and shipping. Intensification of agriculture (with associated drainage, channel regulation and eutrophication) may threaten the area.

Breeding species include *Podiceps cristatus* (50-80 pairs), *Botaurus stellaris* (1-3 pairs), *Ixobrychus minutus* (1-5 pairs), *Ciconia ciconia* (5-10 pairs), *Anser anser* (200 pairs), *Milvus milvus* (1-2 pairs), *Haliaeetus albicilla* (1 pair), *Circus aeruginosus* (10-15 pairs), *Crex crex*, *Limosa limosa* (25 pairs), *Larus ridibundus* (500-1000 pairs), *Sterna hirundo* (20-25 pairs), *Chlidonias niger* (50-100 pairs), *Locustella luscinioides* (50-100 pairs), *Sylvia nisoria* (1-5 pairs), and *Emberiza hortulana* (5-10 pairs). Very important for passage waterfowl, with *Cygnus columbianus* (150 in spring), *C. cygnus* (400 in spring), *Anser fabalis* (50,000+ in autumn), *A. albifrons* (30,000+ in spring), *A. anser* (6500 in autumn), *Grus grus* (5000 in autumn), and *Philomachus pugnax* (1000 in autumn).

019 Kremmener Luch (Potsdam)

52°47'N, 12°59'E 645 ha

Nature Reserve; Wetland of National Importance

A shallow lake with large reedbeds, moorland, sedgebeds, woodlands, and wet meadows. Land-uses include grazing, haymaking, fishing, and recreation. Active management is being carried out to increase habitat diversity.

Breeding species include *Botaurus stellaris* (1-4 pairs), *Ixobrychus minutus* (a few pairs), *Ciconia ciconia* (15-20 pairs nesting nearby), *Pernis apivorus* (1 pair), *Milvus migrans* (2 pairs), *Circus aeruginosus* (5-6 pairs), *C. cyaneus* (1-2 pairs), *C. pygargus* (1 pair), *Grus grus* (4-6 pairs), *Porzana porzana*, *P. parva*, and *Luscinia svecica*. *Anser fabalis*, *A. albifrons* (combined total: 3000) and *Grus grus* (5000-10,000) occur on autumn passage.

020 Rietzer See (Potsdam)

52°22'N, 12°39'E 1000 ha

Nature Reserve (682 ha); Wetland of National Importance

A shallow lake with large reedbeds surrounded by meadows and cultivated land. Land-uses include fishing and agriculture. Unchecked growth of vegetation on land is adversely altering wader breeding habitats.

Breeding species include *Botaurus stellaris* (1-2 pairs), *Ixobrychus minutus* (1-2 pairs), *Ciconia ciconia* (3 pairs), *Anser anser* (40-50 pairs), *Anas querquedula* (2-3 pairs), *Milvus milvus* (1 pair), *Circus aeruginosus* (5-7 pairs), *C. cyaneus* (1-3 pairs), *C. pygargus* (1 pair), *Porzana porzana* (5-7 pairs), *Grus grus* (3-5 pairs), *Limosa limosa* (3-5 pairs), *Sterna hirundo* (3-5 pairs), *Chlidonias niger* (1-2 pairs), *Asio flammeus* (1-3 pairs), *Alcedo atthis* (1-5 pairs), *Dryocopus martius* (1 pair), *Luscinia svecica* (1-3 pairs), *Sylvia nisoria* (1-2 pairs), and *Lanius collurio* (4-5 pairs). Passage species include *Anser fabalis*, *A. albifrons* (combined max. 12,000 in autumn), and *A. anser* (1500 in autumn).

021 Belziger Landschaftswiesen (Potsdam)

52°12'N, 12°40'E 1000 ha

Bustard Protection Area

Part of the flood-plain of the River Baruth with meadows and pastures dissected by ditches. There are a few deciduous trees and bushes. The plain is very intensively cultivated, which has resulted in some adverse ecological changes. A management plan is in preparation.

Breeding species include *Ciconia nigra* (1 pair), *C. ciconia* (3 pairs), *Milvus migrans* (1 pair), *M. milvus* (2-3 pairs), *Circus aeruginosus* (1 pair), *Otis tarda* (18 males, 32 females), *Philomachus pugnax* (1-2 females), *Limosa limosa* (5-8 pairs), and *Emberiza hortulana* (3 pairs). *Anser fabalis* (500), *Circus cyaneus* (max. 20), *Falco columbarius* (1-2), and *Asio flammeus* (5) occur in winter.

022 Prierowsee (Potsdam)

52°14'N, 13°28'E 210 ha

Nature Reserve; partly a Bustard Protection Area

A shallow lake surrounded by reedbeds, moors, bushes, and meadows. The area is managed to ensure protection of diverse habitats.

Breeding species include *Ciconia ciconia* (3 pairs), *Milvus migrans* (1 pair), *M. milvus* (1 pair), *Circus aeruginosus* (6 pairs, decreasing), *C. cyaneus* (1-2 pairs), *C. pygargus* (1-2 pairs), *Porzana porzana* (5 pairs), *Grus grus* (4 pairs), *Otis tarda* (7 females), *Asio flammeus* (1 pair), *Dryocopus martius* (1 pair) and *Lanius collurio* (3 pairs). *Ciconia ciconia* (max. 100 in autumn), *Milvus migrans* (5-10 in spring), *M. milvus* (10-20 in autumn), *Circus aeruginosus* (20-30 in spring), *C. cyaneus* (max. 35 in spring), and *Grus grus* (max. 200 in spring and autumn) occur on passage. *Otis tarda* (4 males, 7 females) occurs in winter and on passage.

023 Felchowsee (Frankfurt)

53°02'N, 14°10'E 305 ha

Nature Reserve; Wetland of National Importance

A lake with a large reedbed and wooded shores, surrounded by ponds, meadows, and cultivated fields. It is intensively used for fish production.

Breeding species include *Botaurus stellaris* (1-3 pairs), *Ixobrychus minutus* (1-2 pairs), *Pernis apivorus* (1 pair), *Milvus milvus* (1 pair), *Circus aeruginosus* (5 pairs), *Porzana porzana* (1-4 pairs), *P. parva* (5-6 pairs), *Grus grus* (1 pair), *Chlidonias niger* (70 pairs), *Dryocopus martius* (1 pair), *Lullula arborea* (1-2 pairs), *Sylvia nisoria* (2-5 pairs), and *Lanius collurio* (15 pairs). Passage species include small numbers of *Pernis apivorus*, *Milvus migrans*, *Haliaeetus albicilla* (also 5-10 in winter), and *Pandion haliaetus*.

024 Unteres Odertal: Polder bei Schwedt (Frankfurt)

52°59'-53°10'N, 14°20'E 5400 ha Ramsar Site (Oder Valley near Schwedt)

Nature Reserve (400 ha)

A large dyked river and shipping canal (Talaue der Oder) flowing south-north through a moraine landscape. The banks are vegetated with reedbeds and herbaceous growth, and the surroundings are polder areas subject to flooding during high tides. Human activities include shipping, intensive grassland cultivation and arable agriculture.

A very important area for breeding species with *Phalacrocorax carbo sinensis* (25 pairs), *Ixobrychus minutus* (1 pair), *Ciconia nigra* (1 pair), *C. ciconia* (3-4 pairs), *Anas querquedula* (10-30 pairs), *A. clypeata* (10-40 pairs), *Pernis apivorus* (1 pair), *Milvus migrans* (1 pair), *M. milvus* (4-5 pairs), *Haliaeetus albicilla* (1-2 pairs), *Circus aeruginosus* (3-5 pairs), *C. cyaneus* (1-2 pairs), *C. pygargus* (1-2 pairs), *Pandion haliaetus* (1 pair), *Porzana porzana* (5-15 pairs), *P. parva* (1-2 pairs), *Crex crex* (60 males), *Grus grus* (1-5 pairs), *Gallinago gallinago* (100 pairs), *Chlidonias niger* (30-60 pairs), *Alcedo atthis* (1-8 pairs), *Dryocopus martius* (4-5 pairs), *Luscinia svecica cyaneculus* (1-5 pairs), *Acrocephalus paludicola* (10-20 pairs), and *Sylvia nisoria* (30-40 pairs). Also very important for passage birds with *Ciconia ciconia* (50 in spring), *Cygnus columbianus* (150 in spring), *C. cygnus* (800 in spring), *Anser fabalis* (15,000 in spring; 10,000 in autumn), *A. albifrons* (35,000 in spring; 4000 in autumn), *Anas penelope* (3500 in spring), *A. crecca* (4000 in spring), *A. platyrhynchos* (15,000 in autumn), *A. acuta* (2500 in spring), *A. querquedula* (1000 in spring), *A. clypeata* (2000 in spring), *Fulica atra* (11,000 in spring), *Vanellus vanellus* (10,000 in spring), *Philomachus pugnax* (1000 in spring), *Gallinago gallinago* (1700 in spring), and *Tringa glareola* (200 in spring). *Cygnus cygnus* (600), *Anser fabalis* (6000), *Mergus merganser* (1000), *Haliaeetus albicilla* (10), and *Falco peregrinus* (1-2) occur in winter.

025 Stausee Berga – Kelbra (Halle)

51°27'N, 11°00'E 1360 ha Ramsar Site

A shallow flood-protection reservoir (constructed in the 1960s) at the foot of the western slopes of the Kyffhäuser Range, between the towns of Nordhausen and Sangerhausen.

Breeding species include small numbers of *Aythya ferina* and other waterfowl. The lake is important as a stop-over for passage ducks, *Fulica atra*, and waders. Forty species of waterfowl occur regularly on both spring and autumn passage.

026 Hakel (Halle)

51°53'N, 11°20'E 1300 ha

Nature Reserves (Grosser Hakel: 290 ha; Kleiner Hakel: 157 ha)

An area of mixed woodland (predominantly *Tilia* and *Quercus* with some *Carpinus*) in the foothills of the Harz mountains. Human activities include forestry.

Breeding birds include *Pernis apivorus* (1 pair), *Milvus migrans* (10 pairs), *M. milvus* (80 pairs), *Aquila pomarina* (2 pairs), *Dryocopus martius*, *Dendrocopos medius*, and *Lanius collurio*.

027 Presseler Heide- und Moorgebiet (Leipzig)

51°34'N, 12°45'E 2500 ha

Nature Reserves (four areas, including a Total Reserve); partly Landscape Protection Area; Wetland of National Importance (Wildenhainer Bruch and Zadlitzbruch)

A mixture of extensive reedbeds, forests, *Alnus/Betula* stands, bushes, fens, and moors. Agriculture and forestry occur within the framework of a management plan for the area, which includes the replacement of *Pinus* plantations with deciduous forests.

Breeding species include *Ciconia nigra* (1 pair), *C. ciconia* (1 pair), *Pernis apivorus* (1 pair), *Milvus migrans* (1 pair), *M. milvus* (2 pairs), *Circus aeruginosus* (5 pairs), *Grus grus* (8 pairs), *Porzana porzana* (5+ pairs), *Caprimulgus europaeus* (5 pairs), *Picus canus* (3 pairs), *Dryocopus martius* (7 pairs), *Lullula arborea* (3-5 pairs), *Sylvia nisoria* (2 pairs), and *Lanius collurio* (10 pairs). In autumn the area serves as a stop-over for passage *Anser fabalis* (max. 2000) and *Grus grus* (200); small numbers of raptors also occur on passage.

028 Vessertal (Suhl, Gera)

50°33'-50°37'N, 10°43'-10°50'E 7464 ha Biosphere Reserve (1384 ha)
Two Nature Reserves; one Total Reserve

A wooded area on the southern slopes of the Thüringer Wald mountains with the valleys of the River Vesser and its tributaries. Rich forests (*Fagus*, *Pinus*, *Abies*), and riverine vegetation create a mosaic of diverse habitats. Forestry is carried out according to a management plan.

Breeding species include *Aegolius funereus* (5-7 pairs), *Picus canus* (5-7 pairs), *Dryocopus martius* (10 pairs), *Lullula arborea* (30 pairs), and *Ficedula parva* (15 pairs).

029 Schwarzatal (Gera)

50°40'N, 11°14'E 600 ha

Nature Reserve, with two Total Reserves

A wooded valley of the River Schwarze within the Thüring schist mountains with steep slopes and a meandering river course. Floristically diverse *Fagus* and *Picea* forests and rocky cliffs create a rich mosaic of habitats. Human activities include forestry and tourism.

Breeding species include *Bubo bubo* (1 pair), *Aegolius funereus* (3-5 pairs), *Picus canus* (10 pairs), and *Dryocopus martius* (3-5 pairs).

030 Uhlstädter Heide, Meuraer Heide, Assberg-Hasenleite and Wurzelbergfarmde (Suhl, Gera)

50°29'-50°42'N, 11°04'-11°27'E 2365 ha

Nature Reserves; part of Thüringer Wald Landscape Protection Area (Meuraer Heide, Assberg-Hasenleite, Wurzelbergfarmde)

A complex of forested areas, with the following subdivisions: Uhlstädter Heide is a forested area of the Saale sandstone plain, between the Saale valley and Orlasenke, dominated by *Pinus sylvestris* interspersed by *Fagus sylvatica*, with a *Vaccinium* or *Pteridium* herbaceous layer and some small areas of *Picea abies*; Meuraer Heide and Assberg-Hasenleite are forest areas in the central Thüringer mountain range, with abundant *Pinus* and smaller areas of *Picea abies* and *Abies alba*; Wurzelbergfarmde is a forest area in the western Thüringer mountains, with *Fagus*, *Picea*, and scattered *Sorbus* and *Betula*. Human activities include forestry and grassland cultivation.

Breeding species include *Ciconia nigra* (occasional), *Pernis apivorus* (occasional), *Milvus milvus* (2-4 pairs), *Tetrao tetrix* (5-8 pairs), *T. urogallus* (20-30 pairs), *Glaucidium passerinum* (7 pairs), *Aegolius funereus* (12-15 pairs), *Caprimulgus europaeus*, *Picus canus*, and *Dryocopus martius* (15 pairs).

031 Erzgebirgskamm bei Satzung (Karl-Marx-Stadt)

50°31'N, 13°11'E 750 ha

Nature Reserve (central part); proposed reserve to protect *Tetrao tetrix*

A high-altitude plain in the Erzgebirge (900 m above sea-level) with *Picea* forests, moors, peatbogs (supporting *Vaccinio/Mugetum* forest), wet meadows, pastures, and cultivated land. The forests are suffering from the affects of acid rain.

Breeding species include *Crex crex* (1-3), *Tetrao tetrix* (2-3 pairs), *Glaucidium passerinum* (1 pair), *Aegolius funereus* (1 pair), *Picus canus* (1 pair), *Dryocopus martius* (1 pair), and *Lanius collurio* (1-2 pairs).

032 Elbsandsteingebirge (Dresden)

50°53'-51°00'N, 14°01'-14°23'E 2000 ha

Nature Reserves (Bastei: 785 ha; Polenztal: 92 ha; Grosser Winterberg und Zschand: 1069 ha; Kirnitzschklamm: 53 ha); part of Sächsische Schweiz Landscape Protection Area

A wooded area (mostly *Pinus* and *Abies*) with narrow canyons, rivers and limestone cliffs (250-560 m above sea-level) within the River Elbe valley. Human activities include forestry and recreation (especially mountain-climbing), which can cause undue disturbance at specific locations.

Breeding species include *Ciconia nigra* (1 pair), *Pernis apivorus* (1 pair), *Bubo bubo* (2 pairs), *Glaucidium passerinum* (5 pairs), *Aegolius funereus* (7 pairs), *Caprimulgus europaeus* (1-2 pairs), *Picus canus* (10 pairs), *Dryocopus martius* (10 pairs), *Lullula arborea* (3 pairs), *Ficedula parva* (max. 3 pairs), and *Lanius collurio* (3 pairs).

033 Teiche bei Königswartha (Dresden)

51°20'N, 14°17'-14°30'E 877 ha

Partly a Nature Reserve; partly a Nature Monument; partly a Landscape Protection Area; Wetland of National Importance

Two groups of fish-ponds near Königswartha, consisting of *c.*30 ponds used for fish-farming (2-50 ha each), large reedbeds, wet meadows, and *Alnus* and *Pinus* woods. Fish-farming, forestry, and hunting are carried out within the framework of a management plan.

Breeding species include *Podiceps grisegena* (1-8 pairs), *Phalacrocorax carbo sinensis* (1-5 pairs), *Aythya ferina*, *A. fuligula* (1000 pairs), *Pernis apivorus* (1 pair), *Milvus migrans* (1 pair), *Haliaeetus albicilla* (2 pairs), *Circus aeruginosus* (8-10 pairs), *Grus grus* (4 pairs), *Porzana porzana* (2 pairs), *Caprimulgus europaeus* (2 pairs), *Alcedo atthis* (1-2 pairs), *Dryocopus martius* (2 pairs), *Lullula arborea* (*c.*3 pairs), and *Lanius collurio* (*c.*5 pairs). *Aythya ferina* (3000), *A. fuligula* (3000), and small numbers of raptors are amongst the birds occurring on passage.

034 Teichgebiet Niederspree (Dresden)

51°24'N, 14°53'E 925 ha

Wetland of National Importance; partly a Nature Reserve (463 ha)

A pond complex near Neisse. The ponds are of various sizes and are highly eutrophic with locally wide reedbeds and zones of siltation with *Alnus* swamps. There are wooded dykes and damp meadows between the ponds. Human activities include fish-farming and forestry. Pond renovations have resulted in the clearance of some reedbeds and other vegetated zones, with a consequently negative impact on breeding birds.

Breeding species include *Podiceps nigricollis* (50-60 pairs), *Botaurus stellaris*, *Ixobrychus minutus*, *Ciconia nigra* (1-2 pairs), *C. ciconia*, *Anser anser* (20-30 pairs), *Anas querquedula*, *A. clypeata*, *Aythya nyroca*, *Haliaeetus albicilla* (1 pair), *Circus aeruginosus*, *Pandion haliaetus* (1 pair), *Tetrao urogallus* (1 pair), *Porzana porzana*, *P. parva*, *Crex crex*, *Grus grus* (3-5 pairs), and *Alcedo atthis*. *Ciconia nigra* (10-15), *Philomachus pugnax* (100), and *Tringa glareola* (100) occur on autumn passage.

035 Teichgebiet Peitz (Cottbus)

51°51'N, 14°25'E 1060 ha Ramsar Site

Fish-ponds north of the town of Cottbus.

Breeding species include *Podiceps cristatus* (50-70 pairs), *P. grisegena* (1-2 pairs), *Anas clypeata* (10-15 pairs), *Aythya ferina* (450-650 pairs; one of the biggest concentrations in central Europe, with 7-8 pairs per ha), *A. fuligula* (350 pairs) and small numbers of *Charadrius dubius*. An important moulting area for *Anas platyrhynchos* (5000-8000 males in June) and *Aythya ferina* (2000 males in June). Waders occur on passage, including *Philomachus pugnax* (100) and *Limosa limosa* (100).

MAIN REFERENCES

Klafs, G. and Stübs, J. (1987) *Die Vogelwelt Mecklenburgs* (Avifauna der DDR, Vol. 1), 3rd ed. Jena, Berlin.

Rutschke, E. (1982) Die Feuchtgebiete von internationaler und nationaler Bedeutung in der DDR. *Beitr. Vogelkd.* 28: 2-15.

Rutschke, E. (Ed.) (1987) *Die Vogelwelt Brandenburgs* (Avifauna der DDR, Vol. 2), 2nd ed. Jena, Berlin.

Weinitschke, H. (Ed.) (1982) *Handbuch der Naturschutzgebiete der DDR*, Vol. 1 and 2, Leipzig, Jena, Berlin.

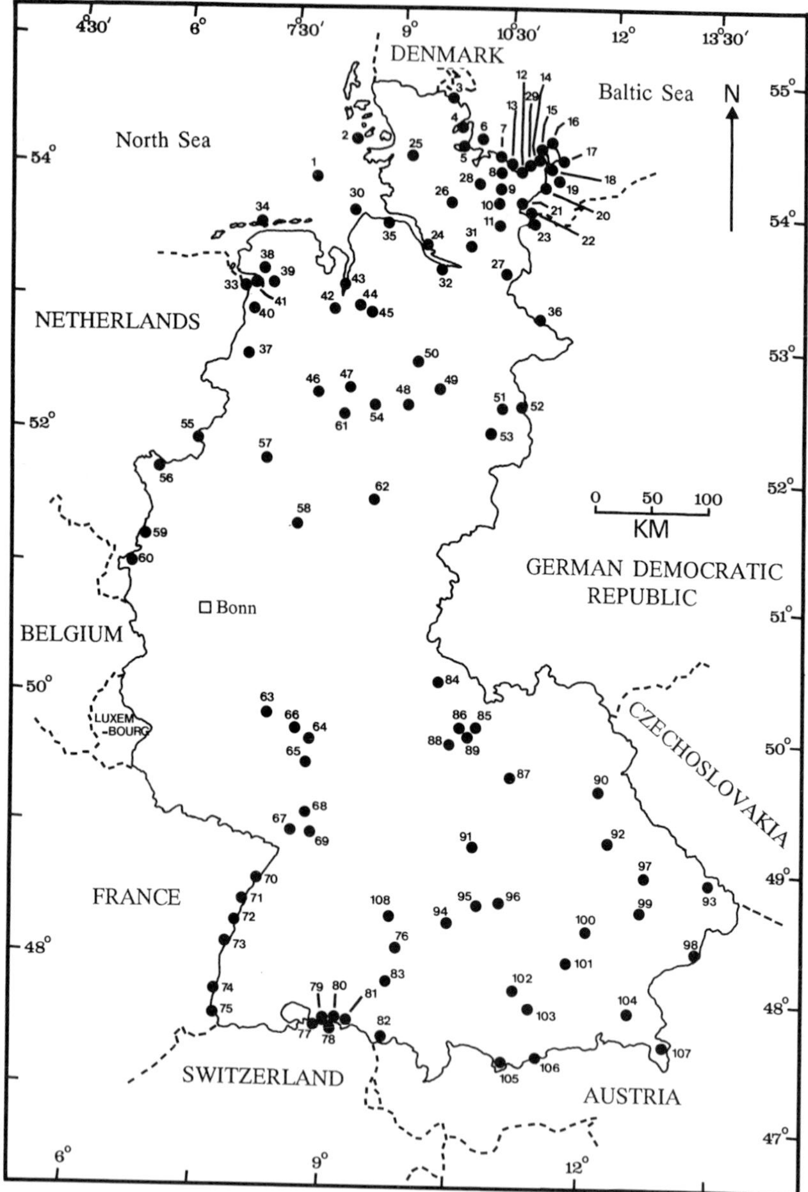

Figure 14: Map showing the location of the sites in the Federal Republic of Germany

FEDERAL REPUBLIC OF GERMANY

Capercaillie *Tetrao urogallus*

INTRODUCTION

General information

The Federal Republic of Germany covers an area of 248,687 sq km and has a population of 61,420,700 (in 1983). This gives the country an average population density of 247 inhabitants per sq km; one of the most densely populated countries in the world, with about 80 per cent of the total population living in cities with more than 100,000 inhabitants. About 57 per cent of the land is used for agriculture (of which about 60 per cent is arable land and 40 per cent is pasture). Forestry is of great economic importance, although in recent years enormous damage has occurred because of acid rain (affecting 34 per cent of forests).

The Federal Republic is landlocked except for its coastline with the North Sea and Baltic Sea in the north. The north-western coast comprises the German section of the Wadden Sea (Wattenmeer) which, together with the Danish and Dutch sectors, is the largest area of intertidal mudflats in Europe, and includes the estuaries of the Elbe, Weser, and Ems and the offshore islands of Ostfriesische Inseln and Nordfriesische Inseln.

The north-eastern coast comprises the Kieler Bucht. South of the North Sea and Baltic lies the Northern German Lowland (Norddeutsches Tiefland), which is characterised by fens, sandy uplands – in their north-western parts with moorland – and natural alluvial plains and marshland. The northern part is separated from the southern part by mountains of medium altitude (Rheinisches Schiefergebirge, Weser- and Leinebergland, Harz, Bayerischer Wald). In the south-western corner is the river plain of the Rhine (Oberrheinische Tiefebene) with the adjacent Black Forest (Schwarzwald) Mountains, which are part of the western and southern mountainous region. The southern German foothill region of the Alps is formed by the Schwäbisch-Bayerische Hochebene with its large lakes (including Ammersee, Starnberger See, and Chiemsee) and the River Danube (Donau) lowlands. The German parts of the Alps (Allgäuer Alpen and Bayerische Alpen), between the Bodensee (Lake Constance) and Bad Reichenhall on the country's southern border with Austria, comprise just a small portion of the Alpine mountain range.

Fagus woodland was the original natural vegetation of the lowland and montane areas (with *Quercus* and *Carpinus* in the centre and south). There is little natural vegetation left due to industry, agriculture, and forestry; with large areas replaced by plantations of *Pinus* and *Picea*.

The north German peatlands are threatened by current exploitation, drainage, and military exercises. These are affecting the last breeding pairs of *Pluvialis apricaria*. Grasslands are being altered through land enclosure, drainage, intensification of agriculture, ploughing, and afforestation; hedges and small woodlands are increasingly being cleared.

Forests, especially in the medium-altitude mountains and Alps, are suffering from the damaging impact of acid rain; riverine and moorland forests are being drained; deciduous and mixed forests are being converted into conifer plantations, and stands of old trees are being continuously removed. Thus important habitats for birds of prey and woodpeckers are being destroyed. Furthermore, rivers and lakes are suffering from increasing recreational activities and the development of shorelines for recreational purposes and weekend facilities.

Ornithological importance

One of the most important habitats for birds is the tidal flats of the Wadden Sea (Wattenmeer), which provides an abundance of food for waterfowl. In spring and autumn this region is certainly among the richest for birds in Europe. The German Wadden Sea holds between 1.4-1.8 million Anseriformes and Charadriformes between August and October; in the Schleswig-Holstein part of the Wadden Sea *Haematopus ostralegus* (max. 80,000), *Calidris canutus* (max. 400,000), *C. alpina* (max. 300,000), *Numenius arquata* (max. 40,000), and *Larus ridibundus* (max. 75,000) occur. A unique phenomenon is the occurrence of large numbers of *Tadorna tadorna*. Up to 100,000 moulting birds are present between mid-July and September in the National Park Schleswig-Holsteinisches Wattenmeer, with birds coming from all of north-western Europe.

Of outstanding importance as a habitat for breeding, passage, and wintering birds are the salt-meadows alongside the tidal mudflats. These meadows are especially important for breeding *Recurvirostra avosetta* (*c*.4700 pairs) and *Tringa totanus*, and are also a favoured feeding site for geese; *Branta leucopsis* (max. 60,000) and *B. bernicla bernicla* (max. 80,000) occur along the coast of Schleswig-Holstein.

As well as being a breeding site for gulls, the salt-meadows and dunes hold many breeding terns, with *Gelochelidon nilotica* (*c*.60 pairs), *Sterna sandvicensis* (*c*.7500 pairs), *S. hirundo* (*c*.9500 pairs), *S. paradisaea* (*c*.6350 pairs), and *S. albifrons* (*c*.500 pairs). Large numbers of *Anser brachyrhynchus*, *A. albifrons*, and *A. fabalis* winter in the coastal regions. The large rivers (e.g. Elbe, Weser, Rhine, Main, Danube, Inn) and the large lakes, mainly in the north and the south of the country, are also important for migrating and wintering waterfowl (including *Cygnus columbianus* and *C. cygnus* in the northern part).

The only seabird cliff colony of the Federal Republic is on the island of Heligoland, which holds, amongst others, *Rissa tridactyla* (*c*.2600 pairs) and *Uria aalge* (*c*.2450 pairs).

The woodland/forests of the upland areas support good populations of a number of species (some largely or entirely restricted in the Federal Republic to the Alps) including *Bonasa bonasia* (1000-3000 pairs), *Tetrao urogallus* (1400-3000 males), *Glaucidium passerinum* (500-1000 pairs), *Aegolius funereus* (900-2400 pairs), *Dendrocopos medius*

(2500-11,000 pairs), *D. leucotos* (100-300 pairs), *Picoides tridactylus* (450-700 pairs), and *Ficedula albicollis*.

Other breeding species in the Federal Republic that are especially worth mentioning are *Ciconia nigra* (*c*.45 pairs), *Milvus milvus* (2000 pairs; one of the largest breeding populations in the world), *Haliaeetus albicilla* (4-5 pairs during the last few years; 6 pairs with 8 young in 1988), *Crex crex* (3000-10,000 pairs), and *Grus grus* (max. *c*.50 pairs, owing to intensive protection measures; the largest breeding population in the European Community).

Conservation infrastructure and protected-area system

The Federal Republic comprises 11 member states or Länder: Schleswig-Holstein, Niedersachsen, Nordrhein-Westfalen, Hessen, Rheinland-Pfalz, Saarland, Baden-Württemberg, Bayern, and the 'city states' of Hamburg, Bremen, and Berlin. Implementation of nature-conservation legislation is primarily the responsibility of the Länder, as is the designation of protected areas (with the local authorities: Kreise and Gemeinden). Although there are differences between the Länder, the recognised categories of protected areas are as follows:

1. Nature Reserves (Naturschutzgebiete [NSG])
   These are used to protect threatened ecosystems, but are usually small areas, and at many sites hunting, fishing, agriculture, and forestry are allowed and are often detrimental. About 1800 sites have been designated, covering less than one per cent of the country.
2. National Parks (Nationalparke)
   These are large areas where there is limited human influence. The aim is to protect the main part of the National Park in the same way as a Nature Reserve, although this does not always happen.
3. Landscape Protection Areas (Landschaftsschutzgebiete [LSG])
   These are protected parts of the countryside which contribute to its beauty and variety, where nature and the landscape features receive more protection than usual, although recreation is often given priority. Unfortunately, negative developments often occur (e.g. exploitation of wetlands), because ongoing agriculture, forestry, and fishing are not considered legally to harm nature and the landscape (Federal Law on Nature Protection: Article 8, para. 7). Landscape Protection Areas tend to include the most important sites covered by the other protected areas categories. There are also protected parts of landscapes (Geschützte Landschaftsbestandteile).
4. Nature Parks (Naturparke)
   These are large areas with more or less the same objectives as Landscape Protection Areas, but are intensively developed for outdoor recreation. The primary purpose is to serve recreational activities and tourism and they are of only limited importance for threatened animal and plant species.
5. Natural Monuments (Naturdenkmale)
   These are very small sites or single features of scientific, historical, or traditional interest.

International measures relevant to the conservation of sites

The Federal Republic is a party to the Ramsar Convention, Bonn Convention, World Heritage Convention, and Bern Convention, and as a member of the European Community it is bound by the terms of the EEC Wild Birds Directive. The country has designated one Biosphere Reserve (Bayerischer Wald: site 093), 20 Ramsar Sites, 387 (many very small) EEC Special Protection Areas (by January 1989), but no World Heritage Sites nor Biogenetic Reserves.

Overview of the inventory

The inventory includes 108 sites, of which 29 are in Schleswig-Holstein, three are in Hamburg, 21 are in Niedersachsen, nine are in Nordrhein-Westfalen, three are in Hessen (one shared with Rheinland-Pfalz), three are in Rheinland-Pfalz (one shared with Hessen),

17 are in Baden-Württemberg, and 24 are in Bayern. The sites cover an area of over 1,220,000; in addition to which there are 455 km of coastline. Of the sites, 90 are at least partly protected (although only a tiny proportion of some), while 18 are without protection. A majority of the sites are wetlands or contain important wetland areas (90+ sites).

Wetland species are therefore covered very well by this inventory; all of the Wadden Sea (and the coastal areas outside the dykes) is included – comprising what is certainly the most important area for birds in the Federal Republic and supporting the entire country's population of some vulnerable species, and the most important concentrations of passage and wintering wildfowl and waders. On the other hand, only a small portion of the total population of other more widely dispersed species (e.g. birds of prey, Tetraonidae, and Picidae) is covered by the inventory.

The Wadden Sea is covered by four sites: IBAs nos. 002 (Schleswig-Holsteinisches Wattenmeer), 030 (Neuwerker and Scharhörner Watt: Hamburger Wattenmeer), 033 (Dollart [Niedersachsen]), and 034 (Nationalpark Niedersächsisches Wattenmeer).

- Site no. 002 (Schleswig-Holsteinisches Wattenmeer), with an area of 305,000 ha, is the largest of all sites; 285,000 ha of it is registered as a National Park, but only 30 per cent of this lies in the mostly unreclaimed zone; an additional 8000 ha are Nature Reserves and *c.*12,000 ha are unprotected. Disturbance factors in this section include: fishing, hunting, tourism, military training, oil, gravel and sand extraction. The recent embankment of parts of the bay of Nordstrand (3400 ha) resulted in the loss of valuable feeding areas for waterfowl and waders. The oil rig 'Trischen' is a potential threat to the mass-moulting area of *Tadorna tadorna*.
- Site no. 030 (Neuwerker and Scharhörner Watt: Hamburger Wattenmeer) consists of two Nature Reserves covering 8193 ha. The planned industrialisation of the area will have a disastrous effect on this habitat.
- Site no. 033 (Dollart) is an area of 5000 ha, out of which 2140 ha are a Nature Reserve. Here disturbance is caused by hunting and tourism. If the planned seaport is built this will have a disastrous impact, and significantly reduce its importance as a stop-over and wintering site for wildfowl and waders.
- Site no. 034 (Nationalpark Niedersächsisches Wattenmeer), covering an area of *c.*240,000 ha, contains three former Important Bird Areas: Ostfriesisches Wattenmeer, Jadebusen und westliche Wesermündung, and Elbe-Weser-Dreieck. The National Park is divided into three zones: I (strict reserve, *c.*130,000 ha); II (intermediate zone, *c.*108,000 ha) and III (recreational zone, *c.*2000 ha). Even in zone I, agriculture, fishing, and hunting (possibility of wildfowl hunting during a restricted season) are allowed with restrictions – this seems to be an intolerable situation within the core zone of a National Park. Serious problems are caused by air and water pollution, and disturbance is caused by boat and air traffic and recreational tourism.

Acknowledgements

The coordination of the data collection was dealt with by R. Berndt on behalf of the ICBP West German section. Dr Rudolf Berndt dedicated himself to this task with perseverance and endurance until his death on 2 June 1987. His work was completed by W. Winkel and M. Frantzen. It would not have been possible without the help of local experts unfortunately too numerous to be cited here. The data-sheets and the introduction were translated into English by T. Salathé at ICBP. The introduction was largely written by W. Winkel.

INVENTORY

No.	Site name	Region	Criteria used to select site [see p.18] 0	1(i)	1(ii)	1(iii)	1(iv)	2	3	4
001	Lummenfelsen Helgoland	SH								*
002	Schleswig-Holsteinisches Wattenmeer	SH			*	*			*	
003	Flensburger Innen- und Aussenförde	SH				*				
004	Schlei	SH				*			*	
005	Südufer der Eckernförder Bucht	SH				*				
006	Stoller Grund, Gabelsflach und Mittelgrund	SH				*				
007	Küste der Probstei: Laboe – Hubertsberg	SH				*				
008	Selenter See	SH				*		*		
009	Lebrader, Lammershagener, Rixdorfer Teiche, Gödfeldteich, Oberwischteich, Rathjensdorfer Teich, und Rummelteich	SH				*		*	*	
010	Grosser Plöner See	SH				*		*	*	
011	Warder See	SH				*		*		
012	Hohwachter Bucht	SH				*				
013	Grosser und Kleiner Binnensee	SH				*				
014	Westbucht des Fehmarnsundes	SH				*			*	
015	Strandseen und Fischteiche im Südwesten Fehmarns	SH				*			*	
016	West- und Nordküste Fehmarns: Krummsteert – Puttgarden	SH				*				
017	Ost- und Südostküste Fehmarns: Puttgarden – Burgtiefe	SH				*				
018	Ostbucht des Fehmarnsundes: Burger Binnensee – Grossenbroder Binnenhafen	SH				*				
019	Sagasbank	SH				*				
020	Ostküste Oldenburgs: Grossenbroder Kai – Pelzerhaken	SH				*				
021	Neustädter Bucht: Pelzerhaken – Niendorf	SH				*				
022	Brodtener Ufer: Niendorf – Travemünde	SH				*				
023	Traveförde und Dassower See	SH				*			*	
024	Pinneberger Elbmarschen	SH				*		*	*	
025	Sorge-Niederung	SH				*		*	*	
026	Naturpark Aukrug	SH						*	*	
027	Naturpark Lauenburgische Seen	SH				*		*	*	
028	Kührener Teich und Lanker See	SH				*				
029	Wesseker See	SH				*				
030	Neuwerker und Scharhörner Watt	HG			*	*			*	
031	Duvenstedter Brook	HG							*	
032	Mühlenberger Loch	HG				*				
033	Dollart	NN				*			*	
034	Nationalpark Niedersächsisches Wattenmeer	NN			*	*			*	
035	Niederelbe: Stade – Otterndorf	NN				*			*	
036	Elbaue: Schnackenburg – Lauenburg	NN				*			*	
037	Tinner und Staverner Dose	NN							*	
038	Ostfriesische Meere	NN							*	
039	Fehntjer Tief	NN							*	
040	Ems-Aussendeichsflächen bei Papenburg	NN				*			*	

No.	Site name	Region	Criteria used to select site [see p.18]							
			0	1(i)	1(ii)	1(iii)	1(iv)	2	3	4
041	Ems-Aussendeichsflächen: Leer – Emden	NN							*	
042	Hunte-Niederung bei Oldenburg	NN							*	
043	Strohauser Plate	NN							*	
044	Hamme-Niederung	NN				*			*	
045	Wümme-Niederung	NN				*			*	
046	Dümmer	NN							*	
047	Diepholzer Moorniederung	NN				*			*	
048	Steinhuder Meer	NN				*			*	
049	Ostenholzer Moor und Meissendorfer Teiche	NN				*			*	
050	Aller-Niederung: Buchholz – Rethem	NN						*	*	
051	Östlicher Barnbruch	NN						*	*	
052	Niedersächsischer Drömling	NN						*	*	
053	Riddagshausen – Weddeler Teichgebiet	NN						*	*	
054	Weserstaustufe Schlüsselburg	NW				*			*	
055	Zwillbrocker Venn und Vredener Wiesen	NW							*	
056	Niederrhein: Wesel/Xanten – Emmerich/Hüthum	NW				*		*		
057	Rieselfelder Münster	NW							*	
058	Möhnetalsperre	NW							*	
059	Krickenbecker Seen im Nettetal	NW							*	
060	Schwalm-Nette-Platte: Grenzwald	NW							*	
061	Bastau-Niederung	NW							*	
062	Weserbergland – Eggegebirge	NW						*	*	
063	Rheinauen: Eltville – Bingen	HN,RP				*				
064	Kühkopf-Knoblauchsaue	HN							*	
065	Lampertheimer Altrhein	HN							*	
066	Gimbsheim-Eicher Altrhein und Fischsee	RP							*	
067	Hördter Rheinaue	RP							*	
068	Insultheimer Hof: Ludwig-See und Im Schacher	BW				*				
069	Wagbachniederung	BW							*	
070	Rhein: Greffern – Murgmündung	BW				*			*	
071	Rhein: Auenheim/Kehl – Greffern	BW				*			*	
072	Rhein: Nonnenweiher – Goldscheuer	BW				*			*	
073	Rhein: Weisweil – Nonnenweiher	BW				*			*	
074	Rhein: Neuenburg – Breisach	BW				*			*	
075	Rhein: Haltingen – Neuenburg	BW				*			*	
076	Öpfinger Donau-Stausee	BW				*				
077	Untersee-Ende: Öhningen – Stein am Rhein	BW				*				
078	Untersee: Hornspitze	BW				*				
079	Untersee: Radolfzeller Aach-Mündung und Mettnau mit Markelfinger Winkel	BW				*				
080	Untersee: Wollmatinger Ried, Ermatinger Becken, Giehrenmoos, und Gnadensee-Ost	BW				*			*	
081	Obersee: Konstanzer Bucht	BW				*				
082	Obersee: Schachener Bucht	BW				*				
083	Federsee	BW						*	*	
084	Lange Rhön	BN						*	*	
085	Main-Tal: Eltmann – Hassfurt	BN						*	*	

No.	Site name	Region	Criteria used to select site [see p.18]							
			0	1(i)	1(ii)	1(iii)	1(iv)	2	3	4
086	Main-Tal bei Schweinfurt	BN							*	
087	Aisch-Regnitz-Grund	BN							*	
088	Main-Tal bei Volkach: Fahr – Dettelbach einschliesslich Klosterforst	BN						*	*	
089	Vogelfreistätte Alter und Neuer See	BN							*	
090	Charlottenhofer Weihergebiet	BN							*	
091	Altmühl-Tal: Ornbau – Gunzenhausen	BN							*	
092	Rötelsee-Weihergebiet einschliesslich Regenaue	BN						*	*	
093	Nationalpark Bayerischer Wald	BN							*	
094	Donau-Auen: Neu-Ulm – Lauingen einschliesslich Faiminger Stausee, Donau-Moos, und Gundelfinger Moos	BN				*		*	*	
095	Donau-Auen und Donau-Ried: Höchstädt – Donauwörth	BN						*	*	
096	Lech-Donau-Winkel: Lechstausee Feldheim und Donaustausee Bertoldsheim	BN						*	*	
097	Donau-Tal: Regensburg-Vilshofen	BN						*	*	
098	Unterer Inn: Haiming – Neuhaus einschliesslich Stauseen Neuhaus, Egglfing, Ering, und Simbach	BN				*			*	
099	Isar-Tal: Gottfrieding – Plattling einschliesslich Isar-Mündungsbereich	BN							*	
100	Mittlere Isar-Stauseen	BN				*			*	
101	Ismaninger Speichersee und Fischteiche	BN				*				
102	Ammersee	BN				*			*	
103	Starnberger See	BN				*				
104	Chiemsee	BN				*			*	
105	Ammergauer Berge	BN							*	
106	Karwendel und Karwendel-Vorgebirge	BN							*	
107	Nationalpark Berchtesgaden	BN							*	
108	Mittleres Vorland der Schwäbischen Alb	BW						*	*	

SH=Schleswig-Holstein HG=Hamburg NN=Niedersachsen NW=Nordrhein-Westfalen
HN=Hessen RP=Rheinland-Pfalz BW=Baden-Württemberg BN=Bayern

Comments on the inventory

1. Most of the numbers of birds given are based on recent data (1987-1988); only for some sites in Niedersachsen has the inventory had to rely on older data.

2. Some sites which are important for *Ciconia ciconia* and *Grus grus* are regarded as confidential and are missing from the inventory; this holds especially for the region Lüneburger Heide (Niedersachsen), which has not been included as a whole.

3. The regions following the site name in parentheses are the Länder. These are the regions (NUTS level 1) which were used when applying the site-selection criteria (category 3).

4. By January 1989, the Federal Republic of Germany had designated 387 EEC Special Protection Areas (SPAs). It has not been possible to thoroughly review the extent to which these SPAs overlap with the important bird areas in this inventory. Where it was clear that an SPA corresponded to an important bird area (partly or completely)

then this has been mentioned. In some cases, however, an SPA may be part of a site in the inventory although this will not be mentioned.

Glossary

EEC SPA = European Community Special Protection Area designated according to the EEC's Wild Birds Directive. The following German words have been used in the inventory: Ost = east; Süd = south; Nord = north; West = west; Aue = river-plain; bei = near; Berg = mountain; Bucht = bay; einschliesslich = including; Fischteich = fish-pond; Küste = coast; See = lake; Speichersee/Stausee = reservoir; Teich = pond, und = and.

---

001 Lummenfelsen Helgoland (Schleswig-Holstein)

54°11'N, 07°53'E 1.1 ha

Nature Reserve

Cliffs with colonies of breeding seabirds on the island of Heligoland. Erosion is affecting the cliffs and there is pressure from tourism. Concern has been expressed about possible oil spills and the accumulation of heavy metals and pesticides.

The only German breeding-seabird cliff with *Fulmarus glacialis* (36 pairs), *Rissa tridactyla* (2633 pairs), *Uria aalge* (2450 pairs), and *Alca torda* (5 pairs, with many wintering birds).

002 Schleswig-Holsteinisches Wattenmeer (Schleswig-Holstein)

53°52'-55°00'N, 08°10'-09°03'E 305,000 ha

National Park (285,000 ha); Nature Reserve (*c.*8000 ha); unprotected (*c.*12,000 ha)

A huge tidal area with mudflats, sandbanks, saltmarshes, estuaries and lagoons, wet meadows, and fresh- and saltwater marshes behind the dams. Intensively used for sheep-grazing, fishing, wildfowl hunting, tourism, military training, and extraction of oil, sand, and gravel. The recent cutting off of the Nordstrand bay (3400 ha) and the installation of the oil platform 'Trischen' has affected waterbirds and especially the moulting area of *Tadorna tadorna*.

A breeding area for *Circus aeruginosus* (15-25 pairs), *Recurvirostra avosetta* (2750 pairs), *Gelochelidon nilotica* (55 pairs), *Sterna sandvicensis* (4500 pairs), *S. hirundo* (3000 pairs), *S. paradisaea* (5000 pairs), and *S. albifrons* (280 pairs). This section of the Wattenmeer is of major importance as a stop-over and refuelling area for many wildfowl and waders, especially (max. daily counts of passage birds unless stated) *Cygnus columbianus* (250), *Anser anser* (800-1000), *Branta leucopsis* (40,000-60,000), *B. bernicla* (60,000-80,000), *Tadorna tadorna* (100,000 moulting, the most important moulting area in north-west Europe; 40,000 wintering), *Anas penelope* (100,000-150,000; 5000 wintering), *A. strepera* (800), *A. crecca* (20,000-25,000), *A. clypeata* (2000), *Somateria mollissima* (100,000; 50,000 wintering), *Haematopus ostralegus* (150,000; 65,000 wintering), *Recurvirostra avosetta* (5000), *Charadrius hiaticula* (10,000), *Pluvialis squatarola* (25,000), *Calidris canutus* (400,000; 8000 wintering), *C. alpina* (400,000), *C. minuta* (1000-1500), *Limosa lapponica* (80,000), *Numenius phaeopus* (2000), *N. arquata* (40,000; 15,000 wintering), *Tringa erythropus* (4000), *T. totanus* (16,000), *T. nebularia* (3000), and *Arenaria interpres* (2000).

003 Flensburger Innen- und Aussenförde (Schleswig-Holstein)

54°47'N, 09°40'E 62 km of coastline

Nature Reserve (Geltinger Birk: 484 ha); Landscape Protection Area (Flensburger Fördeufer: 36 ha); remaining area unprotected

The flat coastline and inshore waters of a sandy bay (up to 1400 m wide). Tourism, boat traffic, and fishing are the main human activities.

The area has small numbers of breeding *Mergus merganser*, *Circus aeruginosus*, *Sterna sandvicensis*, *S. paradisaea*, *S. albifrons*, *Riparia riparia* (200+ pairs), *Saxicola rubetra*, and *Lanius collurio*. Important for passage and wintering waterfowl with *Aythya fuligula* (18,000 in winter), *A. marila* (1500+ in winter; 17,500 on autumn passage), and *Somateria mollissima* (12,000 in winter; 20,000 on autumn passage).

004 Schlei (Schleswig-Holstein)

54°35'N, 09°50'E 135 km of coastline

Nature Reserves (Vogelfreistätte Oehe-Schleimünde: 250 ha and Reesholm/Schlei: 120 ha); small parts are included in two Landscape Protection Areas (3837 ha and 25,505 ha)

A long tidal fjord with saltmarshes and coastal vegetation. Human settlements, industrial plants, harbours, and tourism (boat traffic) are being developed along the shore.

Breeding species include *Mergus merganser*, *Circus aeruginosus* (5-10 pairs), *Recurvirostra avosetta* (52 pairs), *Philomachus pugnax*, *Limosa limosa*, *Larus melanocephalus*, *Sterna paradisaea* (110 pairs), *S. albifrons* (10-12 pairs), *Saxicola rubetra*, and *Locustella luscinioides*. Important winter visitors are *Cygnus cygnus* (220), *Aythya fuligula* (5000+ wintering; 15,000 on autumn passage), and *Mergus merganser* (2000).

005 Südufer der Eckernförder Bucht (Schleswig-Holstein)

54°27'N, 10°04'E 26 km of coastline

Nature Reserve (wooded dune near Noer: 47 ha); partly included in a Landscape Protection Area (25,505 ha); wetland zone unprotected

A flat bay with sandy and stony coast. Tourism (with bathing, camping, and boat traffic) is the main human activities.

Breeding species include *Mergus merganser* (5-10 pairs), *Sterna albifrons* (17 pairs), and *Riparia riparia* (400+ pairs). In winter *Aythya fuligula* (7500), *A. marila* (7600), *Somateria mollissima* (10,000 in winter; max. 28,000 on autumn passage), and *Bucephala clangula* (8000) occur.

006 Stoller Grund, Gabelsflach und Mittelgrund (Schleswig-Holstein)

54°31'N, 10°12'E 2200 ha

Unprotected

Shallow waters with sand and gravel banks in the Baltic Sea. Boat traffic and gravel extraction are destroying this area.

An important site for *Somateria mollissima* (10,000 wintering; 28,000 on autumn passage).

007 Küste der Probstei: Laboe – Hubertsberg (Schleswig-Holstein)

54°25'N, 10°21'E 25 km of coastline

Nature Reserve (Bottsand: 69 ha); parts of the shore are included in a Landscape Protection Area (Kieler Förde and surroundings); the water area is unprotected

A sandy and stony coastal zone (up to 3700 m wide). Tourism (bathing, camping, boat traffic, wind-surfing) and pollution are the main problems.

Breeding species include *Recurvirostra avosetta* (2-4 pairs), *Sterna paradisaea* (2 pairs), *S. albifrons* (26 pairs), *Riparia riparia* (200+ pairs), and *Saxicola rubetra*. Wintering species include *Aythya marila* (20,000), *Somateria mollissima* (40,000), and *Bucephala clangula* (2500).

008 Selenter See (Schleswig-Holstein)

54°18'N, 10°27'E 2141 ha

Nature Reserve (northern part of the lake: 705 ha); Landscape Protection Area (3435 ha)

A slightly eutrophic lake, bordered mainly by natural forest. Increasing pressure from tourism (boat traffic, bathing, settlements) is causing disturbance.

Breeding species include *Phalacrocorax carbo* (*c*.30 pairs; 700 on autumn passage), *Botaurus stellaris*, *Mergus merganser* (*c*.5 pairs), *Haliaeetus albicilla* (1 pair), *Locustella luscinioides*, and *Acrocephalus arundinaceus*. A moulting area for *Anser anser* (800), *Aythya fuligula* (5000; formerly up to 11,000), and *Fulica atra* (25,000).

009 Lebrader, Lammershagener, Rixdorfer Teiche, Gödfeldteich, Oberwischteich, Rathjensdorfer Teich, und Rummelteich (Schleswig-Holstein)

54°14'N, 10°27'E 373 ha

Nature Reserves (Lebrader Teich 146 ha; Rixdorfer Teiche 112 ha)

Fish-ponds with large reedbeds surrounded by an agricultural landscape and small copses. Privately owned wildfowl hunting areas.

Breeding species include *Podiceps nigricollis* (35 pairs), *Botaurus stellaris* (2+ pairs), *Circus aeruginosus* (10+ pairs), *Locustella luscinioides*, and *Acrocephalus arundinaceus*. *Haliaeetus albicilla* (1 pair; breeding nearby) uses the area for hunting. On autumn passage *Anser anser* (1400) and *Anas strepera* (2000) occur.

010 Grosser Plöner See (Schleswig-Holstein)

54°08'N, 10°25'E 3038 ha

Nature Reserve (Ascheberger Warder: 9 ha); the main part is included in a Landscape Protection Area (5430 ha)

An eutrophic lake with reedbeds. Illegal egg collecting, boat traffic, camping, and walking around the shore are the main problems.

Breeding species include *Phalacrocorax carbo* (150 pairs), *Botaurus stellaris* (3-4 pairs), *Haliaeetus albicilla* (1 pair), *Circus aeruginosus* (3-4 pairs), *Larus melanocephalus* (1-2 pairs), *Sterna hirundo* (150 pairs), *Locustella luscinioides*, *Acrocephalus arundinaceus* (15-20 pairs), and *Lanius collurio* (5 pairs). Other species occurring include *Anser anser* (800 in summer) and *Aythya fuligula* (5000 wintering; 11,000 on autumn passage).

011 Warder See (Schleswig-Holstein)

53°58'N, 10°25'E 429 ha

Unprotected

A lake surrounded by an agricultural landscape and small copses. Bathing, wildfowl hunting and agriculture are the main human activities.

Breeding species include *Botaurus stellaris*, *Haliaeetus albicilla* (1 pair), *Circus aeruginosus*, and *Acrocephalus arundinaceus*. On autumn passage *Anser anser* (3000) occurs, and *Mergus merganser* (1500) occurs in winter.

012 Hohwachter Bucht (Schleswig-Holstein)

54°19'N, 10°41'E 38 km of coastline

Nature Reserves inland (Sehlendorfer Binnensee: 214 ha and Wesseker See: 246 ha); coastal area unprotected

A flat bay with a sandy and stony coastline. Tourism (bathing, boat traffic) and military training are the main human activities.

Breeding species include *Riparia riparia* (1900 pairs). Non-breeding visitors include *Aythya marila* (6600 wintering), *Somateria mollissima* (10,000 in winter and on passage), and *Clangula hyemalis* (5000-6000 on spring passage).

013 Grosser und Kleiner Binnensee (Schleswig-Holstein)

54°20'N, 10°38'E 630 ha

Nature Reserve (Kleiner Binnensee: 106 ha); partly included in a Landscape Protection Area; remaining area unprotected

A shallow eutrophic lake and a brackish lake. Land-uses include wildfowl hunting; there is agricultural use of the surrounding areas.

Breeding species include *Mergus merganser* (3-5 pairs), *Circus aeruginosus*, *Recurvirostra avosetta* (7-9 pairs), *Philomachus pugnax*, and *Calidris alpina*. *Anser anser* (1000 on autumn passage) and *Aythya ferina* (2500 moulting) also occur.

014 Westbucht des Fehmarnsundes (Schleswig-Holstein)

54°24'N, 11°05'E 27 km of coastline

Nature Reserves (Graswarder-Heiligenhafen: 81 ha, and parts of Krummsteert-Sulsdorfer Wiek: 298 ha); remaining area unprotected

A flat coast with a sandy and stony shore and a brackish lagoon. Tourism (bathing and boat traffic) is the main human activity.

Breeding species include *Circus aeruginosus* (5 pairs), *Recurvirostra avosetta* (40 pairs), *Sterna sandvicensis* (120 pairs), *S. hirundo* (40 pairs), *S. paradisaea* (180 pairs), and *Riparia riparia*. *Somateria mollissima* (11,000) and *Bucephala clangula* (4000) occur on spring passage, and wintering species include *Cygnus cygnus* (165), *Aythya ferina* (8000), *A. fuligula* (50,000), and *A. marila* (4500).

015 Strandseen und Fischteiche im Südwesten Fehmarns (Schleswig-Holstein)

54°29'N, 11°02'E 360 ha

Nature Reserves (Wallnau/Fehmarn: 297 ha); remaining area unprotected

Fish-ponds, which were originally coastal lakes. There is considerable wildfowl hunting in the unprotected areas.

Breeding species include *Botaurus stellaris*, *Circus aeruginosus*, *Recurvirostra avosetta* (34 pairs), *Limosa limosa*, and *Chlidonias niger* (10-12 pairs). On autumn passage *Anser anser* (1500) and *Anas strepera* (720) regularly occur.

016 West- und Nordküste Fehmarns: Krummsteert – Puttgarden (Schleswig-Holstein)

54°31'N, 11°04'E 27 km of coastline

Nature Reserves (Grüner Brink: 82 ha and Flügger Sand); water area unprotected

A flat sandy coastal zone up to 15 km wide. Tourism and fishing are the main human activities.

Breeding species include *Circus aeruginosus*, *Recurvirostra avosetta* (10-11 pairs), *Sterna hirundo* (5-6 pairs), *S. paradisaea* (2 pairs), and *S. albifrons* (2-4 pairs). *Clangula hyemalis* (25,000-30,000) occurs on spring passage, and winter visitors include *Somateria mollissima* (65,000) and *Bucephala clangula* (3000).

017 Ost- und Südostküste Fehmarns: Puttgarden – Burgtiefe (Schleswig-Holstein)

54°25'N, 11°17'E 20 km of coastline

Unprotected

A flat and sandy coastal zone up to 3.5 km wide. Adversely affected by tourism.

Breeding species include *Recurvirostra avosetta* (2-4 pairs), *Sterna hirundo* (5-6 pairs), and *Riparia riparia*. Wintering species include *Aythya fuligula* (9500).

018 Ostbucht des Fehmarnsundes: Burger Binnensee – Grossenbroder Binnenhafen (Schleswig-Holstein)

54°23'N, 11°08'E 27 km of coastline

Unprotected

A sandy coast and brackish lagoons. Adversely affected by boat traffic and tourism.

Breeding species include *Riparia riparia* (1500 pairs). *Aythya fuligula* (25,000 on autumn passage; 5000+ wintering) and *A. marila* (1600 wintering) occur.

019 Sagasbank (Schleswig-Holstein)

54°18'N, 11°12'E 3000 ha

Unprotected

Shallow waters with banks of sand and gravel in the Baltic Sea. Boat traffic creates some disturbance.

A wintering site for *Somateria mollissima* (19,000) and *Clangula hyemalis* (37,000).

020 Ostküste Oldenburgs: Grossenbroder Kai – Pelzerhaken (Schleswig-Holstein)

54°13'N, 11°06'E 38 km of coastline

Unprotected

A sandy coast with shallow zones. Tourist activities (bathing, camping, boat traffic) adversely affect the site.

Breeding species include *Sterna albifrons* (2-4 pairs) and *Riparia riparia* (2200+ pairs). *Aythya fuligula* (5600), *A. marila* (2000), and *Fulica atra* (14,000) occur in winter.

021 Neustädter Bucht: Pelzerhaken – Niendorf (Schleswig-Holstein)

54°02'N, 10°45'E 22 km of coastline

Nature Reserve (Neustädter Binnenwasser: *c.*200 ha); remaining area unprotected

A shallow sandy bay with some deep-water zones, brackish lagoons (162 ha), small reedbeds, and marshes. Intensive tourist activities including fishing and walking along the shoreline cause disturbance.

Breeding species include *Circus aeruginosus*, *Sterna hirundo* (10 pairs), and *Saxicola rubetra*. In winter *Aythya fuligula* (8500) and *A. marila* (15,000) occur.

022 Brodtener Ufer: Niendorf – Travemünde (Schleswig-Holstein)

53°59'N, 10°52'E 8 km of coastline

Unprotected

A flat sandy coast. Tourism and fishing adversely affect the site.

Breeding species include *Riparia riparia* (2600 pairs). In winter *Aythya fuligula* (21,000), *A. marila* (8400), *Bucephala clangula* (4400), and *Fulica atra* (21,300) are the most numerous species.

023 Traveförde und Dassower See (Schleswig-Holstein)

53°55'N, 10°55'E 1200 ha

Nature Reserve (Dummersdorfer Ufer: 45 ha); eastern coast unprotected but undisturbed (frontier with German Democratic Republic)

A flat and sandy bay (fjord), partly brackish. Human activities include industry, intensive tourism, and boat traffic along the west coast.

A wintering area for *Cygnus cygnus* (400), *Aythya ferina* (5100), *A. fuligula* (11,000), *A. marila* (8500), and *Bucephala clangula* (2000).

024 Pinneberger Elbmarschen (Schleswig-Holstein)

53°49'N, 09°24'E 4200 ha

Nature Reserve (2056 ha); remaining area unprotected

Includes a riverine island (Pagensand) and the edges of the River Elbe, which is tidal, with pastures and agricultural land, riverine forest, and reedbeds. Intensive agriculture, recreational tourism, wildfowl hunting, and fishing are the main activities. Water pollution, the proposed installation of electric power-lines, and the building of a motorway junction threaten the area. In addition the presence of botulism has been confirmed.

Breeding species include *Circus aeruginosus* (5-7 pairs), *C. pygargus* (1 pair), *Porzana porzana* (8 pairs), *Crex crex* (4 pairs), *Recurvirostra avosetta* (15 pairs), *Philomachus pugnax* (20 pairs), *Limosa limosa* (70 pairs), and *Sterna albifrons* (3 pairs). *Cygnus columbianus* (1000 in spring), *Anser albifrons* (*c.*8000 in spring), and *Anas crecca* (10,000 in autumn) occur on passage, *Anser anser* (2000) and *Tadorna tadorna* (2000) occur in winter.

025 Sorge-Niederung (Schleswig-Holstein)

54°22'N, 09°22'E 10,000 ha

Nature Reserve (Tetenhuser Moor: 205 ha); other Nature Reserves and Landscape Protection Areas are planned

A lowland area with wet meadows and moorland, which was regularly flooded in the past but is now drained. Intensification of agricultural use and the promotion of tourism are current problems.

Breeding species include *Botaurus stellaris* (4 pairs), *Ciconia ciconia* (44 pairs), *Pernis apivorus* (3 pairs), *Milvus migrans* (2 pairs), *Circus aeruginosus* (*c.*50 pairs), *C. pygargus* (16 pairs), *Tetrao tetrix* (20 pairs), *Porzana porzana*, *Crex crex* (5 pairs), *Philomachus pugnax* (5 pairs), *Limosa limosa* (220 pairs), *Chlidonias niger* (7 pairs), and *Asio flammeus* (5 pairs). Large numbers of passage *Vanellus vanellus* (20,000) and *Pluvialis apricaria* (10,000) occur in autumn.

026 Naturpark Aukrug (Schleswig-Holstein)

54°06'N, 09°43'E 38,700 ha

Nature Park

A diverse landscape with marshes, patches of woodland, moors, meadows, and agricultural land. Human activities include agriculture, forestry, some tourism, and there are scattered settlements.

Breeding species include *Ciconia nigra* (5 pairs; 75 per cent of the population in Schleswig-Holstein), *Pernis apivorus*, *Milvus migrans*, *M. milvus*, *Circus aeruginosus*, *Alcedo atthis*, *Dryocopus martius*, *Dendrocopos medius*, and *Lanius collurio*.

027 Naturpark Lauenburgische Seen (Schleswig-Holstein)

53°36'N, 10°45'E 45,200 ha

Landscape Protection Area

Lakes surrounded by broadleaved forests (interspersed with moorland) and agricultural land. Human activities include agriculture, forestry, and tourism (walking and camping).

Breeding species include *Phalacrocorax carbo* (170 pairs), *Botaurus stellaris* (10+ pairs), *Ciconia nigra* (1-2 pairs), *Mergus merganser* (10+ pairs), *Pernis apivorus*, *Milvus migrans* (2 pairs), *M. milvus*, *Haliaeetus albicilla* (0-1 pair), *Circus aeruginosus* (10-20 pairs), *Grus grus* (20-25 pairs; 70 per cent of the population in Schleswig-Holstein), *Tringa ochropus* (5-10 pairs), *Caprimulgus europaeus*, *Lullula arborea*, *Anthus campestris*, *Ficedula parva*, and *Lanius collurio*. *Anser anser* (1500) occurs in summer.

028 Kührener Teich und Lanker See (Schleswig-Holstein)

54°13'N, 10°18'E 470 ha

Landscape Protection Area (including 22 ha Nature Reserve)

A shallow eutrophic lake with islands (wooded and under pasture), moorland, and fishponds. Human activities include camping, boat traffic, and fishing.

Breeding species include *Podiceps nigricollis* (3 pairs), *Botaurus stellaris* (3+ pairs), *Circus aeruginosus* (3+ pairs), *Sterna hirundo* (30 pairs), *Locustella luscinioides* (6 pairs), and *Acrocephalus arundinaceus* (6 pairs). *Anser anser* (800) and *Anas strepera* (600 moulting) occur in summer; *Mergus merganser* (3000) occurs in winter.

029 Wesseker See (Schleswig-Holstein)

54°18'N, 10°48'E 250 ha

Nature Reserve

A freshwater marsh with one of the largest reedbeds in Schleswig-Holstein. Land-uses include traditional reed-cutting, hunting, and agricultural use.

Breeding species include *Circus aeruginosus* (3 pairs) and *Saxicola rubetra* (4 pairs). *Anas strepera* (1200) occurs on autumn passage.

030 Neuwerker und Scharhörner Watt (Hamburg)

53°52'-53°57'N, 08°17'-08°34'E 8193 ha

Nature Reserve

The tidal zone (Wadden Sea) in the estuary of the River Elbe including the islands of Scharhörn and Neuwerk. The region is being seriously affected by water pollution, hunting and fishing, boat traffic, and industry.

Breeding species include *Sterna sandvicensis* (2530 pairs), *S. hirundo* (2850), *S. paradisaea* (350 pairs), and *S. albifrons* (25 pairs). The area is very important for passage and wintering waders (20,000+).

031 Duvenstedter Brook (Hamburg)

53°43'N, 10°10'E 780 ha

Nature Reserve

A lowland area with heath, moor, moor and forest, peatbogs, pools of water, brooks, and wet meadows; 140 ha are used for agriculture. Hunting is allowed.

Breeding species include *Grus grus* (1 pair), *Saxicola rubetra* (5 pairs), and *Lanius collurio* (4 pairs).

032 Mühlenberger Loch (Hamburg)

53°31'-53°33'N, 09°46'-09°50'E 675 ha

Landscape Protection Area

A part of the slow-flowing River Elbe with muddy shores.

On passage *Tadorna tadorna* (1250), *Anas crecca* (2000), *A. clypeata* (200), *Aythya ferina* (2500), *A. fuligula* (5000), and *Mergus albellus* (200) occur; daily max. of 10,000+ waterfowl.

033 Dollart (Niedersachsen)

53°14'-53°20'N, 07°04'-07°15'E 5000 ha Ramsar Site (3980 ha); EEC SPA

Nature Reserve (2140 ha); Landscape Protection Area

A tidal area of the North Sea with a maximum width of 1000 m. Current problems include the construction of dykes, tourism, wildfowl hunting, and the planned construction of a large port.

An important area for passage and wintering birds including *Anser fabalis* (1000), *A. albifrons* (5000), *A. anser* (1000), *Anas crecca* (5000), *Recurvirostra avosetta* (19,000), *Pluvialis squatarola* (1000), *Calidris alpina* (50,000), *Limosa limosa* (2500), *L. lapponica* (5000), and *Tringa erythropus* (1000).

034 Nationalpark Niedersächsisches Wattenmeer (Niedersachsen)

53°21'-53°58'N, 06°34'-08°41'E 240,000 ha

Ramsar Sites (Wattenmeer, Elbe-Weser-Dreieck: 38,460 ha; Wattenmeer: Jadebusen and Western Weser Mouth: 49,490 ha; part of Ostfriesisches Wattenmeer and Dollart: 121,620 ha); three EEC SPAs (total area 177,500 ha)

National Park (240,000 ha)

The tidal zone (Wadden Sea) of the North Sea between the estuaries of the Rivers Ems and Elbe including several islands. The region is being seriously affected by water pollution, air pollution, hunting and fishing, air and boat traffic, recreational activities, dyke construction, ports, and industry. The area is extremely important for waterbirds.

Breeding species include *Phalacrocorax carbo* (175 pairs), *Recurvirostra avosetta* (1260 pairs), *Sterna sandvicensis* (350 pairs), *S. hirundo* (2600 pairs), *S. paradisaea* (550), and *S. albifrons* (115 pairs). Passage species (av. max. figures) include *Anser brachyrhynchus* (2000), *A. anser* (1000; occurring on migration and in winter), *Branta leucopsis* (2000), *B. bernicla* (9000), *Tadorna tadorna* (85,000), *Anas penelope* (6000), *A. acuta* (5000), *Somateria mollissima* (20,000), *Haematopus ostralegus* (42,000), *Recurvirostra avosetta* (10,000), *Charadrius hiaticula* (2500), *C. alexandrinus* (500), *Pluvialis squatarola* (17,000), *Calidris canutus* (85,000), *C. alba* (2000), *C. alpina* (120,000), *Limosa limosa* (1000), *L. lapponica* (15,000), *Numenius arquata* (26,000), *Tringa totanus* (7000), and *Arenaria interpres* (800).

035 Niederelbe: Stade – Otterndorf (Niedersachsen)

53°40'-53°52'N, 08°53'-09°30'E 11,760 ha Ramsar Site; EEC SPA (10,500 ha)

Nature Reserve (3000 ha)

The lower reaches of the River Elbe, which is tidal. The region is under serious pressure from industrial development, construction of dykes and power-lines and dredging. Tourism, boat traffic, hunting, and low-flying aircraft (military and civilian) cause considerable disturbance.

Breeding species include *Recurvirostra avosetta* (200 pairs), *Gelochelidon nilotica*, *Sterna hirundo* (250 pairs), and *S. albifrons* (10 pairs). *Cygnus columbianus* (1000), *Anser albifrons* (4000), *A. anser* (2500), and *Branta leucopsis* (6000) use the site on migration.

036 Elbaue: Schnackenburg – Lauenburg (Niedersachsen)

53°00'-53°22'N, 10°33'-11°35'E 7600 ha Ramsar Site (7560 ha); EEC SPA (7500 ha)

Landscape Protection Area (6600 ha); Nature Reserve (240 ha)

Plain of the slow-flowing River Elbe with drying-up oxbow lakes, flooded pastures, and remnant riverine forests. The construction of new dykes will result in reclamation and agricultural improvements. Tourism and hunting pressure are heavy.

Grus grus (3 pairs) is a breeding species and also occurs on passage in large numbers. During winter the flooded plains hold an important number of *Cygnus columbianus* (800), *C. cygnus* (800), *Anser fabalis* (1000), *A. albifrons* (2000), *A. anser* (500), and over 10,000 ducks.

037 Tinner und Staverner Dose (Niedersachsen)

52°48'N, 07°23'E 3200 ha

Nature Reserve

An intact peatbog which is used as a military shooting area.

An important breeding area for *Anas crecca* (25 pairs), *Gallinago gallinago* (50-60 pairs), *Limosa limosa* (10-15 pairs), *Numenius arquata* (35-40 pairs), *Tringa totanus* (30-35 pairs), *Anthus campestris* (10-15 pairs), and *Lanius collurio* (10-22 pairs).

038 Ostfriesische Meere (Niedersachsen)

53°23'-53°28'N, 07°13'-07°22'E 5600 ha EEC SPA

Landscape Protection Area (2580 ha); Nature Reserve (495 ha)

A varied landscape with many freshwater ponds, reedbeds, wet meadows, and large areas of moorland. Water extraction, agricultural development, and disturbance from fishing, hunting, and tourism are problems at the site.

Breeding species include *Botaurus stellaris* (7 pairs), *Circus aeruginosus* (8 pairs), *C. pygargus* (5 pairs), *Asio flammeus* (4 pairs), and *Luscinia svecica*. On migration *Pluvialis apricaria* (550), *Philomachus pugnax* (300), *Limosa limosa* (350), and *Chlidonias niger* (60) occur.

039 Fehntjer Tief (Niedersachsen)

53°20'-53°22'N, 07°24'-07°32'E 1500 ha EEC SPA

Landscape Protection Area (230 ha); Nature Reserve (139 ha)

A polder region with wet meadows, surrounded by dykes. Agricultural intensification, land-use changes, increase in tourism and power-boat use are problems at the site.

Breeding species include *Circus aeruginosus* (6 pairs), *C. pygargus* (3 pairs), *Asio flammeus* (4 pairs), and *Luscinia svecica*.

040 Ems-Aussendeichsflächen bei Papenburg (Niedersachsen)

53°03'-53°06'N, 07°16'-07°21'E *c.*1000 ha EEC SPA (550 ha)

Landscape Protection Area (365 ha); Nature Reserve (185 ha)

Part of the lower Ems, which is tidal, with mudflats, oxbow lakes, reedbeds, sedge-beds, wet meadows, and willow copses. Problems include hunting pressure.

The site is used by *Cygnus columbianus* (500), *C. cygnus* (100), *Pluvialis apricaria* (1100), *Gallinago gallinago* (220), and *Limosa limosa* (1000) on passage.

041 Ems-Aussendeichsflächen: Leer – Emden (Niedersachsen)

53°18'-53°20'N, 07°15'-07°22'E 580 ha EEC SPA

Unprotected

An area of riverine lowland behind the dykes of the River Ems, with reedbeds, mudflats, and intensively used grassland. Boat traffic, fishing, and construction of new dykes are affecting the area.

During migration and in winter the area is used by *Anser fabalis* (54), *A. albifrons* (620), *Branta leucopsis* (55), *Anas penelope* (2500), *A. crecca* (1500), *Mergus merganser* (640), and *Gallinago gallinago* (520).

042 Hunte-Niederung bei Oldenburg (Niedersachsen)

53°09'-53°11'N, 08°16'-08°24'E 1800 ha EEC SPA (1500 ha)

Landscape Protection Area (386 ha); Nature Reserve (99 ha)

Wet meadows alongside the River Hunte surrounded by dykes, which prevent flooding. Regular flooding is needed to maintain the importance of the area for waterfowl.

Breeding species include *Ciconia ciconia* (2 pairs), *Limosa limosa*, and *Gallinago gallinago*. Visiting species include *Cygnus columbianus* (100; declining), *C. cygnus* (30; declining), *Anser brachyrhynchus* (300), *Mergus albellus* (16), and *Pluvialis apricaria* (200).

043 Strohauser Plate (Niedersachsen)

53°21'-53°25'N, 08°27'-08°29'E 1240 ha EEC SPA

Unprotected

The shoreline of the River Weser and island with intensively used agricultural land (840 ha), a river arm, and reedbeds (400 ha). Intensive disturbance is caused by boat traffic and camping activities.

Breeding species include *Circus aeruginosus* (8 pairs), *C. pygargus*, and *Asio flammeus*.

044 Hamme-Niederung (Niedersachsen)

53°11'-53°19'N, 08°45'-08°58'E 6700 ha EEC SPA (1020 ha)

Landscape Protection Area (1770 ha); Nature Reserve (245 ha)

A large intact area of wet meadows and oxbow lakes along the River Hamme. Formerly flooded by spring tides, but this is now inhibited by locks. Disturbance is caused by boat traffic, recreational activities, and hunting.

Breeding species include *Circus aeruginosus* (6 pairs) and *C. pygargus* (3 pairs). Visiting species include (av. max. figures) *Cygnus columbianus* (290), *C. cygnus* (190), *Anser fabalis* (690), *A. brachyrhynchus* (200), *A. anser* (1300), *Anas querquedula* (65), *Pluvialis apricaria* (1070), *Vanellus vanellus* (10,000), *Philomachus pugnax* (320), *Gallinago gallinago* (460), *Limosa limosa* (300), and *Numenius arquata* (120).

045 Wümme-Niederung (Niedersachsen)

53°05'-53°10'N, 08°43'-09°03'E 6300 ha two EEC SPAs (3300 ha; 3000 ha)

Landscape Protection Area (647 ha)

A lowland area in the Wümme valley with wet meadows (flooded by the spring tide), moorland, and the meandering river. Recreational activities such as boating and angling cause disturbance and flooding will be prohibited by the Lesum dyke.

During migration and in winter *Cygnus columbianus* (330) and *C. cygnus* (100) use the area.

046 Dümmer (Niedersachsen)

52°27'-52°32'N, 08°16'-08°22'E 4700 ha

Ramsar Site (3600 ha); EEC SPA (3800 ha)

Landscape Protection Area (3055 ha); Nature Reserve (745 ha)

A eutrophic lake surrounded by pastures and moorland. The eutrophication and drying out of the lake are current problems which could be corrected by periodic flooding. Tourist activities cause serious problems.

Breeding species include *Botaurus stellaris* (2 pairs), *Ciconia ciconia* (2 pairs), *Circus aeruginosus* (7 pairs), *Chlidonias niger* (45 pairs), and *Asio flammeus* (3 pairs). In winter *Anser anser* (500) and more than 10,000 ducks frequent the area.

047 Diepholzer Moorniederung (Niedersachsen)

52°27'-52°37'N, 08°27'-08°54'E 15,060 ha Ramsar Site; EEC SPA (15,900 ha)

Landscape Protection Area (4350 ha); Nature Reserve (2234 ha)

A lowland area with marshes, wet meadows, moor, and peatbogs. Extraction of peat, drainage, training with low-flying helicopters, and disturbance by ornithologists are current problems at the site.

Breeding species include *Circus pygargus* (2 pairs), *Pluvialis apricaria* (10 pairs), and *Asio flammeus* (3 pairs). Up to 500 *Grus grus* stop over during migration.

048 Steinhuder Meer (Niedersachsen)

52°25'-52°30'N, 09°13'-09°26'E 5800 ha Ramsar Site (5730 ha); EEC SPA

Landscape Protection Area (4950 ha); Nature Reserve (814 ha)

A eutrophic lake surrounded by wet meadows, moorland, and peatbogs. Extraction of peat and drainage are altering the moorland. Sport activities on the lake and the building of weekend cottages are serious problems.

Breeding species include *Botaurus stellaris* (2 pairs), *Ciconia ciconia* (1 pair), *Anser anser* (16 pairs), *Anas querquedula* (7 pairs), *Circus aeruginosus* (6-8 pairs), *Porzana*

porzana (17 pairs), *P. parva* (1-6 pairs), *Crex crex* (2 pairs), *Philomachus pugnax*, and *Sylvia nisoria* (4-7 pairs). Visiting species include *Phalacrocorax carbo* (84), *Cygnus columbianus* (15), *C. cygnus* (9), *Mergus albellus* (100), *M. merganser* (1800); with over 10,000 wintering waterfowl.

049 Ostenholzer Moor und Meissendorfer Teiche (Niedersachsen)

52°41'-52°45'N, 09°42'-09°50'E 3200 ha EEC SPA

Unprotected

A large peatbog area with heath, fish-ponds, patches of woodland (*Betula* and *Pinus*), and wet meadows.

Breeding species include *Botaurus stellaris* (4 pairs), *Ciconia nigra*, *Aythya nyroca*, *Circus aeruginosus* (7 pairs), *C. pygargus*, *Asio flammeus* (3 pairs), and *Acrocephalus arundinaceus*. *Grus grus* (*c.*500) stops over during migration.

050 Aller-Niederung: Buchholz – Rethem (Niedersachsen)

52°41'-52°47'N, 09°23'-09°41'E 3000 ha EEC SPA (1280 ha)

Landscape Protection Area (680 ha)

A lowland area of the River Aller including the meandering river, oxbows, wet meadows, and regularly flooded grassland. Tourism, fishing, hunting, and the intensification of agricultural use and drainage are current problems.

Breeding species include *Ardea cinerea* (*c.*50 pairs), *Ciconia ciconia* (5-10 pairs), *Anas querquedula* (5 pairs), *Milvus migrans* (2-3 pairs), *M. milvus* (4 pairs), *Circus aeruginosus* (1-2 pairs), *Alcedo atthis* (3-4 pairs), and *Dryocopus martius* (1 pair).

051 Östliches Barnbruch (Niedersachsen)

52°27'N, 10°40'-10°44'E 1000 ha EEC SPA (243 ha)

Nature Reserve (450 ha); remaining area unprotected

A lowland area of the River Aller with periodically flooded meadows, heath, patches of woodland, and large reedbeds. The extension of the new Wolfburg refuse tip (with subsequent pollution) and increased hunting pressure are current problems affecting the area.

Breeding species include *Podiceps nigricollis* (3-7 pairs), *Botaurus stellaris* (1-3 pairs), *Ixobrychus minutus* (1 pair), *Ciconia ciconia* (2 pairs), *Pernis apivorus* (2 pairs), *Milvus migrans* (2 pairs), *M. milvus* (6-8 pairs), *Circus aeruginosus* (8 pairs), *Porzana porzana* (15 pairs), *P. parva* (1 pair), *Crex crex* (3 pairs), *Limosa limosa* (3 pairs), *Asio flammeus* (1 pair), *Caprimulgus europaeus* (2 pairs), *Alcedo atthis* (2 pairs), *Dryocopus martius* (3 pairs), *Dendrocopos medius* (3 pairs), *Saxicola rubetra* (40 pairs), *Locustella luscinioides* (20 pairs), and *Lanius collurio* (20 pairs).

052 Niedersächsischer Drömling (Niedersachsen)

52°25'-52°33'N, 10°49'-11°00'E 6200 ha EEC SPA

Landscape Protection Area (5750 ha); three Nature Reserves (313 ha)

A large lowland area with regularly flooded meadows, reedbeds, sedge-beds, ditches, hedges, and also the largest area of moorland forest (*Alnus*, *Betula*) in the country (510 ha). The area is threatened by the extension of a domestic refuse tip and the extraction of water. The law enforcement is inadequate especially for the agriculturally used grassland.

Breeding species include *Botaurus stellaris* (1 pair), *Ciconia nigra* (1 pair), *C. ciconia* (8 pairs), *Pernis apivorus* (5 pairs), *Milvus migrans* (5 pairs), *M. milvus* (20 pairs), *Circus aeruginosus* (6 pairs), *C. pygargus* (1 pair), *Porzana porzana* (10 pairs), *Crex crex* (20 pairs), *Grus grus* (3-4 pairs), *Caprimulgus europaeus* (3 pairs), *Alcedo atthis* (2-3 pairs), *Dryocopus martius* (12 pairs), *Dendrocopos medius* (35 pairs), *Saxicola rubetra* (90 pairs),

Sylvia nisoria (70 pairs), and *Lanius collurio* (120 pairs). Up to 500 *Grus grus* stop over on migration, as do many waders.

053 Riddagshausen – Weddeler Teichgebiet (Niedersachsen)

52°17'N, 10°36'E 1800 ha EEC SPA (650 ha)

Landscape Protection Area (partly a Nature Reserve)

A lowland area with approximately 20 ponds surrounded by reedbeds (totalling *c.*120 ha), heath, and wet forests (*Alnus*/*Salix*, *Quercus*/*Carpinus*). It is seriously threatened by a planned motorway (expected to destroy the catchment area of numerous streams and influence water-levels), the demolition of an oil-storage area, and open-cast mining at the edge of the ponds.

Breeding species include *Podiceps grisegena* (3 pairs), *Botaurus stellaris* (2 pairs), *Anser anser* (30 pairs), *Pernis apivorus* (2 pairs), *Milvus milvus* (3 pairs), *Circus aeruginosus* (8 pairs), *Porzana porzana* (5 pairs), *Alcedo atthis* (1 pair), *Picus canus* (2 pairs), *Dryocopus martius* (5 pairs), and *Dendrocopos medius* (5 pairs). Passage waterfowl include with *Anser anser* (300), *Anas clypeata* (600), and *A. crecca* (350).

054 Weserstaustufe Schlüsselburg (Nordrhein-Westfalen)

52°19'-52°25'N, 08°55'-09°00'E 1800 ha Ramsar Site (1550 ha)

Two Nature Reserves (340 ha in the centre); Landscape Protection Area (1450 ha)

Dammed reservoir of the River Weser within a lowland area which is regularly flooded, with cultivated fields and meadows. There is disturbance from intensive sport fishing, aircraft activities throughout the year (army flying school), and water-sports.

Breeding species include *Ciconia ciconia* (5 pairs), *Circus aeruginosus* (1-5 pairs), and *Riparia riparia* (*c.*150 pairs). Wintering waterfowl include *Cygnus cygnus* (*c.*5), *Anser brachyrhynchus* (max. 300), *Anas platyrhynchos* (max. 10,000), *Aythya ferina* (max. 4600), *A. fuligula* (max. 3100), *Mergus merganser* (max. 800), and *Bucephala clangula* (max. 1500).

055 Zwillbrocker Venn und Vredener Wiesen (Nordrhein-Westfalen)

52°02'-52°12'N, 06°42'-07°02'E 2400 ha

Nature Reserves; Landscape Protection Area; partly unprotected

Moors, heath, and wet meadows in the River Berkel basin. Agricultural use is bringing about the increasing drainage of the wet meadows and cultivation of the grasslands.

Breeding species include *Botaurus stellaris* (2 pairs), *Ixobrychus minutus* (1 pair), *Anas crecca* (42 pairs), *A. querquedula* (28 pairs), *A. clypeata* (59 pairs), *Pernis apivorus* (2 pairs), *Milvus migrans* (1 pair), *M. milvus* (1 pair), *Circus aeruginosus* (3 pairs), *Crex crex* (1 pair), *Haematopus ostralegus* (24 pairs), *Gallinago gallinago* (56 pairs), *Limosa limosa* (105 pairs), *Numenius arquata* (48 pairs), *Bubo bubo* (1 pair), *Asio flammeus* (1 pair), *Caprimulgus europaeus* (2-3 pairs), *Alcedo atthis* (5-6 pairs), *Dryocopus martius* (4 pairs), *Lanius collurio* (1 pair), and *Emberiza hortulana* (2 pairs).

056 Niederrhein: Wesel/Xanten – Emmerich/Hüthum (Nordrhein-Westfalen)

51°30'-51°54'N, 05°57'-06°43'E 50,000 ha Ramsar Site (25,000 ha)

Nature Reserve (*c.*2300 ha) and proposed Nature Reserves (*c.*5000 ha)

A large, intact, lowland riverine landscape. Existing threats are many: intensification of agricultural use, extensive extraction of sand and gravel, installation of new industrial and power plants, and recreational activities.

Breeding species include *Phalacrocorax carbo* (15 pairs), *Crex crex* (25 pairs; irregularly), *Actitis hypoleucos* (5-10 pairs), and *Riparia riparia* (60-80 pairs). An important wintering site for *Anser fabalis* (70,000), *A. albifrons* (*c.*100,000), and *Anas acuta* (1000-1500).

057 Rieselfelder Münster (Nordrhein-Westfalen)

52°02'N, 07°39'E 450 ha Ramsar Site (233 ha)

Proposed Nature Reserve

Fields irrigated for water treatment (160 ha), wet meadows (35 ha), cultivated fields, small patches of woodland, and two ponds (5 ha). The major part is managed as a bird reserve.

Breeding species include *Anas querquedula* (max. 30 pairs), *A. clypeata* (max. 50 pairs), *Circus aeruginosus* (5 pairs), *Porzana porzana* (15-40 pairs), *Limosa limosa* (2-5 pairs), *Dryocopus martius* (3 pairs), and *Luscinia svecica* (max. 16 pairs). The irrigated fields are an important stop-over area for *Anas querquedula* (900), *Limosa limosa* (150), *Tringa erythropus* (150), *T. nebularia* (170), *T. glareola* (350), *Actitis hypoleucos* (250), and *Chlidonias niger* (60).

058 Möhnetalsperre (Nordrhein-Westfalen)

51°29'N, 08°05'E 1450 ha EEC SPA (1100 ha)

Landscape Protection Area (water area: *c.*1100 ha) including Nature Reserves (Hevearm der Möhne: 224 ha; Heve und Kleine Schmalenau: 100 ha; Möhneaue Völlinghausen: 22 ha)

A dammed reservoir of the River Ruhr.

Wintering species include *Cygnus cygnus* (10-30), *Anser anser* (60-80), *Anas platyrhynchos* (12,000), *Aythya ferina* (1000), *A. fuligula* (650), *Bucephala clangula* (70), and *Mergus merganser* (350).

059 Krickenbecker Seen im Nettetal (Nordrhein-Westfalen)

51°19'-51°22'N, 06°14'-06°19'E 750 ha

Nature Reserve; Nature Park

A natural wetland with reedbeds, broadleaved forests, and wet meadows. Intensification of agriculture and forestry is continuing, the reedbeds are dying (90 per cent), and disturbance by fishermen is increasing.

Breeding species include *Podiceps cristatus* (90-100 pairs), *Ardea cinerea* (175 pairs), *Caprimulgus europaeus* (1 pair), *Alcedo atthis* (1-2 pairs), *Dryocopus martius* (5-6 pairs), and *Luscinia svecica* (5 pairs). In winter *Circus cyaneus* (3) occurs.

060 Schwalm-Nette-Platte: Grenzwald (Nordrhein-Westfalen)

51°11'-51°20'N, 06°04'-06°10'E 6500 ha

Landscape Protection Area including eight small Nature Reserves

Old dunes with moors, wet meadows, forests, and pine plantations. The largest part is used for forestry.

Breeding species include *Pernis apivorus* (4-5 pairs), *Accipiter gentilis* (10 pairs), *Falco subbuteo* (4 pairs), *Caprimulgus europaeus* (25-30 pairs), *Alcedo atthis* (2-5 pairs), *Dryocopus martius* (10-15 pairs), *Lullula arborea* (30-40 pairs), *Riparia riparia* (100 pairs), *Anthus campestris* (1-2 pairs), *Luscinia svecica* (10-12 pairs), and *Lanius collurio* (2-3 pairs).

061 Bastau-Niederung (Nordrhein-Westfalen)

52°19'-52°21'N, 08°38'-08°51'E 3000 ha

Landscape Protection Area (*c.*2500 ha) including Nature Reserve (*c.*500 ha of peatbog)

The largest remaining peatbog area in Nordrhein-Westfalen. Adjacent meadows are grazed and have recently been turned into maize plantations. Drainage, hunting, and disturbance by tourists have affected the wetland and resulted in the extinction of *Tetrao tetrix*.

Breeding species include *Ciconia ciconia* (1 pair), *Anas crecca* (*c.*30 pairs), *A. clypeata* (2 pairs), *Aythya ferina* (3 pairs), *Circus aeruginosus* (2 pairs), *Tetrao tetrix* (2 pairs; reintroduced), *Limosa limosa* (3 pairs), *Numenius arquata* (20-25 pairs), *Asio flammeus* (min. 5 pairs; irregularly), and *Lanius collurio* (10-20 pairs). On passage *Anser fabalis*, *A. albifrons* (500-1000 each), and *Vanellus vanellus* (*c.*9000) occur.

062 Weserbergland - Eggegebirge (Nordrhein-Westfalen)

51°29'-51°50'N, 09°00'-09°25'E 110,000 ha

Unprotected, but several small nature reserves are proposed

A traditional landscape with a mosaic of copses and agricultural fields. The building of roads and industrial plants is adversely affecting the area.

Breeding species include *Ciconia nigra* (1 pair), *Pernis apivorus* (1 pair), *Milvus migrans* (3-4 pairs), *M. milvus* (*c.*70 pairs), *Circus aeruginosus* (1 pair), *C. pygargus* (1 pair), *Falco peregrinus* (1 pair), *Alcedo atthis* (20 pairs; declining), *Dryocopus martius* (*c.*30 pairs), *Dendrocopos medius* (*c.*10 pairs), and *Riparia riparia* (*c.*100 pairs; increasing).

063 Rheinauen: Eltville - Bingen (Hessen, Rheinland-Pfalz)

49°59'N, 08°02'E 475 ha Ramsar Site

Three Nature Reserves (Mariannenaue, Rüdesheimer Aue, Fulder Aue-Ilmenaue; effective in winter)

Islands and slow-flowing zones of the Rhine with a rich habitat mosaic, including remnant riverine forest, vineyards, orchards, and reedbeds. Waterfowl numbers have been lower in recent years.

Wintering site for *Aythya ferina* (7500), *A. fuligula* (2500), *Mergus albellus* (550), *M. merganser* (800), and *Vanellus vanellus* (3000).

064 Kühkopf-Knoblauchsaue (Hessen)

49°44'N, 08°27'E 2400 ha EEC SPA (2369 ha)

Nature Reserve

Oxbow lakes along the Rhine with riverine forests, wet meadows, and orchards, which are managed according to a conservation plan. Mosquitos were controlled with pesticides in 1988.

Breeding species include *Ixobrychus minutus* (2+ pairs), *Anas querquedula* (1-5 pairs), *Pernis apivorus* (3-4 pairs), *Milvus migrans* (50 pairs), *Alcedo atthis* (2 pairs), *Dryocopus martius* (5 pairs), *Dendrocopos medius* (17-25 pairs), *Luscinia svecica* (*c.*35 pairs), and *Lanius collurio* (*c.*10 pairs). *Phalacrocorax carbo* (200) and *Grus grus* (50-100) occur on passage.

065 Lampertheimer Altrhein (Hessen)

49°36'N, 08°26'E 530 ha EEC SPA (525 ha)

Nature Reserve

An oxbow lake along the Rhine containing shallow-water zones, riverine forest, reedbeds, wet meadows, and cultivated areas. Mosquitos were controlled with pesticides in 1988.

Breeding species include *Podiceps cristatus* (60 pairs), *Phalacrocorax carbo* (20 pairs), *Ixobrychus minutus* (2-3 pairs), *Ardea cinerea* (120-150 pairs), *Milvus migrans* (10 pairs), *Circus aeruginosus* (2 pairs), *Crex crex* (1-2 pairs), *Alcedo atthis* (1-2 pairs), *Picus canus* (3-4), *Dryocopus martius* (1-2 pairs), and *Dendrocopos medius* (3-4 pairs). *Aythya ferina* (max. 4000) and *Pandion haliaetus* (10-20 in a season) occur on autumn passage.

066 Gimbsheim-Eicher Altrhein und Fischsee (Rheinland-Pfalz)

49°48'N, 08°20'E 430 ha EEC SPA (112 ha)

Nature Reserve

An oxbow lake along the Rhine, now partly drained, with moors, large reedbeds, hedges, and small wet meadows. Protection is not very effective, thus extraction of gravel, forestry plantations, oil drilling, construction of dams, extraction of ground water, tourism (bathing, wind-surfing, and fishing), and raptor hunting (illegal) are serious problems.

Breeding species include *Ardea purpurea* (*c.*7 pairs), *Milvus migrans* (1-2 pairs), *Circus aeruginosus* (12 pairs), *Asio flammeus* (1 pair; declined from 10+ pairs), *Alcedo atthis* (1 pair), *Riparia riparia* (*c.*120 pairs), *Luscinia svecica* (*c.*160 pairs), *Locustella luscinioides* (8 pairs), *Acrocephalus arundinaceus* (8 pairs), and *Lanius collurio* (1 pair).

067 Hördter Rheinaue (Rheinland-Pfalz)

49°09'N, 08°21'E 1000 ha

Nature Reserve (812 ha)

An oxbow lake along the Rhine with large riverine forests, sedge-beds, and an open pond. Forestry use, some disturbance by tourism, and the planned construction of polders and catchment areas for water at high tides are serious threats.

Breeding species include *Ixobrychus minutus* (1 pair), *Ardea cinerea* (140 pairs), *Ardea purpurea* (1-2 pairs; sporadically), *Pernis apivorus* (1-2 pairs), *Milvus migrans* (7-9 pairs), *M. milvus* (1-2 pairs), *Alcedo atthis* (2-4 pairs), *Picus canus* (5-10 pairs), *Dryocopus martius* (2-3 pairs), *Dendrocopos medius* (20+ pairs), and *Luscinia svecica* (1-2 pairs). *Aythya ferina* (1000) and *A. fuligula* (1000) occur in winter.

068 Insultheimer Hof: Ludwig-See und Im Schacher (Baden-Württemberg)

49°20'N, 08°30'E 1000 ha

Proposed Landscape Protection Area

Open fields and meadows in the Rhine valley which are used for agriculture. There is disturbance by people and aircraft which use a nearby airfield.

Important wintering area for *Anser fabalis* (max. 1800) in Baden-Württemberg.

069 Wagbachniederung (Baden-Württemberg)

49°15'N, 08°31'E 210 ha

Nature Reserve

A lowland area in the Rhine valley with large reedbeds, mudflats, filter-beds, gravel ponds, wet meadows, and patches of woodland.

Breeding species include *Podiceps nigricollis* (15 pairs), *Ixobrychus minutus* (10 pairs), *Ardea purpurea* (10 pairs), *Milvus migrans* (1 pair), *Circus aeruginosus* (8 pairs), *Porzana porzana* (6 pairs), *Alcedo atthis* (1 pair), *Picus canus* (2 pairs), *Riparia riparia* (330 pairs), *Luscinia svecica* (85 pairs), *Acrocephalus arundinaceus* (34 pairs), and *Lanius collurio* (8 pairs).

070 Rhein: Greffern – Murgmündung (Baden-Württemberg)

48°54'N, 08°09'E 3000 ha

Nature Reserve (Rheinaue Rastatt: 850 ha); remaining area unprotected

Region in the Rhine valley with slow-flowing parts of the main stream (reservoirs), oxbow lakes, and riverine forests. Extraction of gravel and recreational activities (including heavy boat traffic) are serious problems.

Breeding species include *Pernis apivorus* (3 pairs), *Milvus migrans* (10 pairs), *Circus aeruginosus* (1 pair), *Alcedo atthis* (6 pairs), *Picus canus* (20 pairs), *Dryocopus martius* (10 pairs), *Dendrocopos medius* (30 pairs), *Riparia riparia* (200 pairs), and *Lanius collurio* (20 pairs). The site is important for wintering waterfowl with *Podiceps cristatus* (max. 700), *Anser fabalis* (2000), and *Aythya ferina* (7500).

071 Rhein: Auenheim/Kehl – Greffern (Baden-Württemberg)

48°41'N, 07°55'E 2500 ha

Landscape Protection Area (Rheinauenwald Diersheim: 250 ha)

A dammed part of the Rhine with a power-station and a sluice, surrounded by oxbow lakes, artificial ponds, and large riverine forests. Disturbance results from gravel extraction, wildfowl hunting, and boat traffic.

Breeding species include *Ixobrychus minutus* (2 pairs), *Pernis apivorus* (6 pairs), *Milvus migrans* (10 pairs), *Circus aeruginosus* (5 pairs), *C. cyaneus* (1 pair), *Sterna hirundo* (20 pairs), *Alcedo atthis* (5 pairs), *Picus canus* (30 pairs), *Dryocopus martius* (8 pairs), *Dendrocopos medius* (50 pairs), and *Riparia riparia* (300 pairs). In winter the area is important for *Anser fabalis* (max. 2400), *Anas platyrhynchos* (max. 18,600), *Aythya ferina* (max. 18,000), and *A. fuligula* (max. 11,000).

072 Rhein: Nonnenweiher – Goldscheuer (Baden-Württemberg)

48°27'N, 07°45'E 4000 ha

Nature Reserves (Sauscholle: 629 ha)

A dammed part of the Rhine with an artificial lake (700 ha) connected to the river, oxbow lakes, and riverine forests. Extraction of gravel, boat traffic, and wildfowl hunting are current problems at the site.

Breeding species include *Ixobrychus minutus* (2 pairs), *Pernis apivorus* (8 pairs), *Circus aeruginosus* (10 pairs), *C. cyaneus* (1 pair), *Porzana parva* (1 pair), *Alcedo atthis* (12 pairs), *Picus canus* (20+ pairs), *Dryocopus martius* (10 pairs), *Dendrocopos medius* (60 pairs), *Riparia riparia* (200 pairs), and *Acrocephalus arundinaceus* (12 pairs). The most important wintering species are *Podiceps cristatus* (max. 620), *Anas platyrhynchos* (max. 19,200), *A. strepera* (max. 1400), *Aythya ferina* (max. 15,900), *A. fuligula* (max. 13,300), and *Fulica atra* (max. 14,000).

073 Rhein: Weisweil – Nonnenweiher (Baden-Württemberg)

48°18'N, 07°42'E 5000 ha

Nature Reserves (Taubergiessen: 1601 ha; Hechtsgraben); remaining area unprotected

A dammed part of the Rhine and the artificial Rhine canal with extensive riverine forests and numerous meandering side rivers. Forestry, gravel extraction, boat traffic, and hunting are the main human activities. Planned further damming and drainage are serious threats.

Breeding species include *Ixobrychus minutus* (2 pairs), *Pernis apivorus* (10 pairs), *Milvus migrans* (20 pairs), *Circus aeruginosus* (5 pairs), *C. pygargus* (2 pairs), *Alcedo atthis* (30 pairs), *Dryocopus martius* (10 pairs), *Dendrocopos medius* (180 pairs), *Riparia riparia* (200 pairs), *Acrocephalus arundinaceus* (10 pairs), and *Lanius collurio* (50 pairs). An important wintering site for *Tachybaptus ruficollis* (250), *Podiceps cristatus* (330), *Anser fabalis* (800), *Anas strepera* (1100), *A. platyrhynchos* (14,600), and *Mergus albellus* (44).

074 Rhein: Neuenburg – Breisach (Baden-Württemberg)

47°54'N, 07°35'E 5000 ha

Nature Reserves (Rheinwald Neuenburg: 34 ha)

The artificial Rhine canal with two reservoirs and the original course of the Rhine, oxbow lakes, riverine forests (including Rhein-Wald Breisach), and fields (including Feldflur near Müllheim). Agricultural intensification, hunting, the proposed extraction of gravel, and drainage are serious threats.

Breeding species include *Pernis apivorus* (5 pairs), *Milvus migrans* (15 pairs), *Circus pygargus* (2 pairs), *Sterna hirundo* (10 pairs), *Asio flammeus* (1 pair; irregularly), *Caprimulgus europaeus* (10 pairs), *Alcedo atthis* (5 pairs), *Picus canus* (40+ pairs), *Dendrocopos medius* (c.100 pairs), *Riparia riparia* (150+ pairs), *Anthus campestris* (2 pairs), *Saxicola rubetra* (15 pairs), and *Lanius collurio* (50+ pairs). Wintering species include *Tachybaptus ruficollis* (350), *Anser fabalis* (1240), *Anas platyrhynchos* (27,000), *Aythya ferina* (6900), and *Mergus merganser* (260).

075 Rhein: Haltingen – Neuenburg (Baden-Württemberg)

47°42'N, 07°30'E 10,000 ha

Landscape Protection Area (Rheinvorland: 231 ha); remaining area unprotected

The artificial Rhine canal and original course of the Rhine with riverine forests and dry shrubland. Forestry and recreational activities, including canoeing, cause some disturbance.

Breeding species include *Pernis apivorus* (2 pairs), *Milvus migrans* (15 pairs), *Asio flammeus* (1 pair; irregularly), *Caprimulgus europaeus* (15 pairs), *Alcedo atthis* (10 pairs), *Picus canus* (20+ pairs), *Dryocopus martius* (10+ pairs), *Dendrocopos medius* (100+ pairs), *Riparia riparia* (200+ pairs), *Anthus campestris* (3 pairs), *Saxicola rubetra* (50+ pairs), and *Lanius collurio* (100+ pairs). In winter *Anas platyrhynchos* (9000), *Aythya ferina* (6900), and *A. fuligula* (1400) occur.

076 Öpfinger Donau-Stausee (Baden-Württemberg)

48°17'N, 09°48'E 47 ha

Landscape Protection Area

A reservoir connected to the Danube with an electric power-station, small reedbeds, and patches of woodland. The shallow reservoir is heavily polluted (mainly heavy metals) and intensively used for hunting and for boat traffic.

A stop-over site during migration for (av. numbers on passage) *Philomachus pugnax* (55), *Tringa glareola* (60), *T. ochropus* (25), *Actitis hypoleucos* (45), *Chlidonias niger* (135) and *Riparia riparia* (700). In winter *Tachybaptus ruficollis* (520), *Anas crecca* (3700), and *Aythya ferina* (8900) are the most numerous waterfowl.

077 Untersee-Ende: Öhningen – Stein am Rhein (Baden-Württemberg)

47°40'N, 08°52'E 400 ha

Small Nature Reserves

The outlet of Lake Constance (entering the Rhine) with small reedbeds and gravel islands. There is heavy disturbance from bathing, boat traffic, and wildfowl hunting.

The site is important as a wintering locality for *Aythya ferina* (13,000), *A. fuligula* (24,000), *Bucephala clangula* (2500), and *Fulica atra* (17,000).

078 Untersee: Hornspitze (Baden-Württemberg)

47°42'N, 09°01'E 200 ha EEC SPA (26 ha)

Nature Reserve on shoreline

A large reedbed and the shallow eastern edge of Lake Constance. Disturbance from camping and boat traffic are serious problems.

Breeding species are *Ixobrychus minutus* (1 pair) and *Acrocephalus arundinaceus* (15 pairs). It is an important wintering site for *Netta rufina* (max. 600), *Aythya ferina* (max. 10,000), and *A. fuligula* (max. 11,000).

079 Untersee: Radolfzeller Aach-Mündung und Mettnau mit Markelfinger Winkel (Baden-Württemberg)

47°44'N, 08°59'E 550 ha

Nature Reserve

A delta (Radolfzeller Aach) with reedbeds and a peninsula (Mettnau) in Lake Constance, with shallow bays (mudflats exposed when water-level is low), wet meadows, and patches of woodland. Recreational activities (boat traffic, wind-surfing, angling) cause disturbance.

Breeding species include *Ciconia ciconia* (1 pair), *Netta rufina* (40 pairs), *Circus aeruginosus* (1 pair), *Sterna hirundo* (2 pairs), *Saxicola rubetra* (10 pairs), and *Acrocephalus arundinaceus* (12 pairs). Wintering species include *Cygnus cygnus* (50), *Aythya ferina* (10,000), and *A. fuligula* (13,000).

080 Untersee: Wollmatinger Ried, Ermatinger Becken, Giehrenmoos, und Gnadensee-Ost (Baden-Württemberg)

49°41'N, 09°08'E 1050 ha Ramsar Site (1080 ha); EEC SPA (757 ha)

Nature Reserve (Wollmatinger Ried)

Large reedbeds and islands in Lake Constance. The reeds are regularly cut, whilst hunting has been banned.

An important breeding area for *Podiceps cristatus* (300 pairs), *Aythya nyroca* (1 pair), *Circus aeruginosus* (2 pairs), *Porzana parva* (1 pair), *Sterna hirundo* (40 pairs), and *Netta rufina* (50 pairs). An important passage site (autumn counts unless stated) for *Cygnus cygnus* (max. 70 in spring), *Anas strepera* (max. 1750), *A. crecca* (max. 1890), *A. clypeata* (max. 800), *Netta rufina* (max. 1000), *Aythya ferina* (max. 11,680), *A. fuligula* (max. 5000), and *Fulica atra* (max. 11,600).

081 Obersee: Konstanzer Bucht (Baden-Württemberg)

47°40'N, 09°12'E 400 ha

Unprotected

A bay of Lake Constance (which remains unfrozen in winter) where the Rhine leaves the lake. Heavy boat traffic throughout the year causes disturbance.

The bay holds *Aythya ferina* (max. 20,000) and *A. fuligula* (max. 16,000) in winter.

082 Obersee: Schachener Bucht (Baden-Württemberg)

47°33'N, 09°40'E 200 ha

Unprotected

A shallow bay of Lake Constance near Lindau with an artificial shoreline. Boat traffic and wind-surfing cause disturbance.

In autumn and winter *Aythya fuligula* (17,000) is the most numerous waterfowl species; *Somateria mollissima* (100 during autumn and winter) also occurs.

083 Federsee (Baden-Württemberg)

48°05'N, 09°39'E 1410 ha EEC SPA (1400 ha)

Nature Reserve

A shallow lake with large reedbeds, wet meadows and small patches of woodland. A recently built sewage station should improve the quality of the water.

Breeding species include *Ardea purpurea* (1-5 pairs; irregularly), *Ciconia ciconia* (2 pairs), *Pernis apivorus* (1 pair), *Milvus milvus* (1 pair), *Circus aeruginosus* (4-7 pairs), *C. pygargus* (1 pair), *Crex crex* (2 pairs), *Sterna hirundo* (6 pairs), *Asio flammeus* (1-2 pairs; irregularly), *Dryocopus martius* (5 pairs), *Luscinia svecica* (3 pairs), *Saxicola rubetra* (60 pairs), *Locustella luscinioides* (1-3 pairs), and *Panurus biarmicus* (max. 70 pairs). Many species use the site to stop over on migration including *Phalacrocorax carbo* (150), *Philomachus pugnax* (150), *Tringa glareola* (200), and *Chlidonias niger* (150).

084 Lange Rhön (Bayern)

50°30'N, 10°05'E 2657 ha

Nature Reserve

Mountain slopes with forests, peatbogs, and meadows. In places there have been agricultural intensification (use of fertilisers) and development of forestry (pine plantations). The area is also increasingly used by tourists (summer and winter).

Breeding species include *Pernis apivorus* (1 pair), *Milvus migrans* (1 pair), *M. milvus* (1 pair), *Tetrao tetrix* (*c.*40 males; the most important area in West Germany away from the Alps), *Crex crex* (1-2 pairs), *Gallinago gallinago* (45-60 pairs), *Dryocopus martius* (1-2 pairs), *Saxicola rubetra* (*c.*40 pairs), and *Lanius collurio* (5-10 pairs).

085 Main-Tal: Eltmann – Hassfurt (Bayern)

49°57'-50°02'N, 10°31'-10°44'E 560 ha

Nature Reserve; Landscape Protection Area; partly unprotected

Oxbow lakes, wet meadows, sedge-beds, riverine forests, artificial ponds, and wooded slopes in the Main valley. Land-use is diverse, and intense angling, camping, surfing, and bathing create disturbance. The planned construction of a new road is a serious threat.

Breeding species include *Ixobrychus minutus* (2-3 pairs), *Milvus milvus* (2 pairs), *Circus aeruginosus* (3-4 pairs), *Porzana porzana* (1-2 pairs), *Alcedo atthis* (1-2 pairs), *Riparia riparia* (50-150 pairs), *Luscinia svecica* (20-40 pairs), *Saxicola rubetra* (2-5 pairs), and *Lanius collurio* (1-2 pairs).

086 Main-Tal bei Schweinfurt (Bayern)

50°00'N, 10°12'E 1000 ha

Nature Reserve; Landscape Protection Area; partly unprotected

Remnant stretches of the River Main, unique in northern Bavaria, with oxbow lakes, patches of riverine forest, deltas of small rivers, vegetated dunes, and wet meadows. Existing threats are intensification of agricultural (pesticides) and forestry use, construction of new settlements and roads, and tourism (fishing, wind-surfing).

Breeding species include *Botaurus stellaris* (1-2 pairs; irregularly), *Ixobrychus minutus* (5-8 pairs), *Pernis apivorus* (2-3 pairs), *Milvus migrans* (2-3 pairs), *M. milvus* (1 pair), *Circus aeruginosus* (6-10 pairs), *Porzana porzana* (0-1 pair), *P. parva* (1-2 pairs), *Alcedo atthis* (1-3 pairs), *Picus canus* (4-7 pairs), *Dryocopus martius* (2-3 pairs), *Dendrocopos medius* (12-18 pairs), *Riparia riparia* (120-250 pairs), *Anthus campestris* (2-4 pairs), *Luscinia svecica* (25-37 pairs), *Acrocephalus arundinaceus* (6-9 pairs), *Ficedula albicollis* (10-15 pairs), *Lanius collurio* (5 pairs), and *Emberiza hortulana* (15-20 pairs).

087 Aisch-Regnitz-Grund (Bayern)

49°45'N, 10°55'E 68,000 ha

Unprotected (although some small Nature Reserves)

A rich lowland area with about 2000 fish-ponds (total area *c.*2500 ha), which are surrounded by agricultural land, many rivers, and wet meadows. New settlements, power-lines, dykes, agricultural intensification, and tourism are adversely affecting the area.

Breeding species include *Podiceps nigricollis* (*c.*50 pairs), *Botaurus stellaris* (2 pairs), *Ixobrychus minutus* (3 pairs), *Ardea purpurea* (1-2 pairs), *Ciconia ciconia* (10-15 pairs), *Circus aeruginosus* (2-3 pairs), *Limosa limosa* (3 pairs), *Alcedo atthis* (3-6 pairs), *Dryocopus martius* (several pairs), *Luscinia svecica* (8 pairs), and *Acrocephalus arundinaceus* (10-20 pairs).

088 Main-Tal bei Volkach: Fahr – Dettelbach einschliesslich Klosterforst (Bayern)

49°46'-49°57'N, 10°09'-10°15'E 1800 ha

Only partly protected

Part of th

e Main valley with oxbow lakes, ponds, wet meadows, wooded slopes, dry grassland, and sandy heathland. Potential problems include the proposed construction of a water reservoir for the army and intensification of agricultural use.

Breeding species include *Ixobrychus minutus* (1-3 pairs), *Milvus migrans* (1-2 pairs), *M. milvus* (1-2 pairs), *Circus aeruginosus* (1-2 pairs), *Crex crex* (1 pair), *Caprimulgus europaeus* (2 pairs), *Picus canus* (1-2 pairs), *Riparia riparia* (200-300 pairs), *Anthus campestris* (2-3 pairs), *Luscinia svecica* (20-40 pairs), *Saxicola rubetra* (5-10 pairs), *Ficedula albicollis* (2-5 pairs), *Lanius collurio* (15-20 pairs), and *Emberiza hortulana* (15-22 pairs). Important for waterfowl on passage, especially *Aythya ferina* and *A. fuligula*.

089 Vogelfreistätte Alter und Neuer See (Bayern)

49°55'N, 10°21'E 40 ha

Nature Reserve

Two small lakes surrounded by reedbeds, amongst an agricultural landscape. The reserve should be enlarged since the area is currently affected by human disturbance and pollution (pesticides and fertilisers). The lakes are used for fish-farming but bird protection is the main priority.

Breeding species include *Circus aeruginosus* (5-6 pairs), and small numbers of *Botaurus stellaris*, *Ixobrychus minutus*, *Ardea purpurea*, *Porzana parva*, *Crex crex*, *Anthus campestris*, *Luscinia svecica*, *Saxicola rubetra*, *Locustella luscinioides*, *Acrocephalus arundinaceus*, *Lanius collurio*, and *Remiz pendulinus*.

090 Charlottenhofer Weihergebiet (Bayern)

49°20'N, 12°08'E 900 ha

Proposed Nature Reserve

A diverse landscape with many fish-ponds, marshes, and moors. Land-use is unintensive (agriculture, forestry) but hunting pressure is heavy.

Breeding species include *Podiceps nigricollis* (50+ pairs), *Botaurus stellaris* (2+ pairs), *Ixobrychus minutus* (2-3 pairs), *Aythya ferina* (30-40 pairs), *Circus aeruginosus* (1 pair), *Porzana porzana* (1-5 pairs), *P. pusilla* (1 pair; sporadically), *Glaucidium passerinum* (3-5 pairs), *Aegolius funereus* (5+ pairs), *Alcedo atthis* (1-2 pairs), *Dryocopus martius* (2-4), *Lullula arborea* (4-6 pairs), *Luscinia svecica* (*c.*10 pairs), *Locustella luscinioides* (2-3 pairs), and *Acrocephalus arundinaceus* (5-8 pairs).

091 Altmühl-Tal: Ornbau – Gunzenhausen (Bayern)

49°09'N, 10°42'E *c.*1500 ha

Unprotected except for island in reservoir (Altmühlsee)

A river valley (10 km) with large meadows. In its centre lies an artificial reservoir, which is good for breeding birds. Traditional use of meadows benefits the site, but tourism and angling cause some disturbance.

Breeding species include *Ciconia ciconia* (1-3 pairs), *Circus aeruginosus* (1 pair), *Porzana porzana* (*c.*17 pairs), *Vanellus vanellus* (120 pairs), *Charadrius dubius* (16-19 pairs), *Numenius arquata* (40 pairs), and *Limosa limosa* (20-30 pairs).

092 Rötelsee-Weihergebiet einschliesslich Regen-Aue (Bayern)

49°12'N, 12°35'E *c.*500 ha

Nature Reserve

Part of the Regen valley with many fish-ponds and wet meadows. Agricultural intensification and drainage are current problems.

Breeding species include *Podiceps nigricollis* (*c.*120 pairs), *Ciconia ciconia* (1 pair), *Ixobrychus minutus* (1-2 pairs), *Anas clypeata* (2-3 pairs), *Aythya ferina* (75 pairs), *A. fuligula* (50-120 pairs), *Circus aeruginosus* (2-3 pairs), *Porzana porzana* (7-8 pairs), *Crex*

crex (3 pairs), *Gallinago gallinago* (10-20 pairs), *Limosa limosa* (5 pairs), *Numenius arquata* (15-20 pairs), *Asio flammeus* (1 pair), *Dryocopus martius* (1-2 pairs), *Luscinia svecica* (9 pairs), *Saxicola rubetra* (9 pairs), *Locustella luscinioides* (5-10 pairs), and *Acrocephalus arundinaceus* (10-11 pairs).

093 Nationalpark Bayerischer Wald (Bayern)

48°55'N, 13°30'E 13,000 ha Biosphere Reserve

National Park; parts of it are Nature Reserves

A mountain range with ancient and managed forests (*Fagus*, *Acer*, *Abies*, *Picea*), mountain lakes, alpine meadows, peatbogs, cliffs, and ridges. Forestry exploitation and tourism are the main human activities. Construction of new forest roads and skiing facilities are current problems.

Breeding species include *Pernis apivorus* (2-3 pairs), *Bonasa bonasia* (110 pairs), *Tetrao urogallus* (*c.*15 pairs), *Glaucidium passerinum* (40-50 pairs), *Aegolius funereus* (*c.*20 pairs), *Picus canus* (*c.*15 pairs), *Dryocopus martius* (*c.*560 pairs), *Dendrocopos leucotos* (*c.*5 pairs), *Picoides tridactylus* (*c.*70 pairs), *Saxicola rubetra* (*c.*10 pairs), and *Ficedula parva* (20-25 pairs).

094 Donau-Auen: Neu-Ulm – Lauingen einschliesslich Faiminger Stausee, Donau-Moos, und Gundelfinger Moos (Bayern)

48°25'-48°34'N, 10°00'-10°25'E 12,500 ha Ramsar Site (8000 ha)

Nature Reserves (Langenauer Moos, Gundelfinger Moos, Donau-Auen); Landscape Protection Area; partly unprotected

Dammed stretches or reservoirs of the Danube surrounded by riverine forest and meadows. The region is threatened by the extraction of water and gravel, intensification of agriculture, tourism, and construction of a new railway line.

Breeding species include *Aythya fuligula* (160 pairs), *Pernis apivorus* (3-5 pairs), *Milvus migrans* (20-30 pairs), *M. milvus* (*c.*8 pairs), *Circus aeruginosus* (1-2 pairs; irregularly), *C. pygargus* (1-4 pairs; irregularly), *Crex crex* (5-10 pairs; irregularly), *Gallinago gallinago* (30 pairs), *Numenius arquata* (*c.*15 pairs), *Picus canus* (*c.*50 pairs), *Dryocopus martius* (*c.*5 pairs), *Dendrocopos medius* (*c.*30-40 pairs), *Riparia riparia* (500-1000 pairs), and *Ficedula albicollis* (200+ pairs). In winter *Tachybaptus ruficollis* (500), *Anas platyrhynchos* (10,000), *Aythya ferina* (5000), and *A. fuligula* (5000) occur.

095 Donau-Auen und Donau-Ried: Höchstädt – Donauwörth (Bayern)

48°36'-48°44'N, 10°30'-10°48'E *c.*9500 ha

Nature Reserves (Mertinger Hölle: 142 ha; Naturwaldreservat Neugeschüttwöth: 46 ha)

A diverse landscape in the Danube valley with oxbow lakes, wet meadows, moors, and riverine forests. The plain is used for agriculture, gravel extraction, wildfowl hunting, and angling.

Breeding species include *Ixobrychus minutus* (3+ pairs), *Pernis apivorus* (1 pair), *Milvus migrans* (4+ pairs), *M. milvus* (2-3 pairs), *Circus aeruginosus* (4+ pairs), *Numenius arquata* (*c.*25 pairs), *Alcedo atthis* (1 pair), *Picus canus* (3+ pairs), *Dendrocopos medius* (6+ pairs), *Luscinia svecica* (50+ pairs), *Saxicola rubetra* (10 pairs), *Locustella luscinioides* (4+ pairs), *Acrocephalus arundinaceus* (4+ pairs), *Ficedula albicollis* (8+ pairs), and *Lanius collurio* (10+ pairs).

096 Lech-Donau-Winkel: Lechstausee Feldheim und Donaustausee Bertoldsheim (Bayern)

48°43'-48°44'N, 10°54'-11°00'E 239 ha Ramsar Site (230 ha)

Nature Reserve (Lechstausee Feldheim: 91 ha)

Reservoirs of the Danube (Bertoldsheimer Stau) and River Lech (Feldheimer Stau) with shallow zones covered by reedbeds and surrounded by large riverine forests. Intensification of forestry and extraction of water are potential threats, whilst fishing and boat traffic create some disturbance.

Breeding species include *Ixobrychus minutus* (0-3 pairs), *Anas strepera* (5+ pairs), *A. crecca* (5+ pairs), *Milvus migrans* (2-3 pairs), *M. milvus* (2 pairs), *Luscinia svecica* (3 pairs), *Ficedula albicollis* (10+ pairs), and *Lanius collurio* (3 pairs). In winter *Aythya ferina* (3700) and *A. fuligula* (1000) are the most numerous waterfowl.

097 Donau-Tal: Regensburg – Vilshofen (Bayern)

48°39'-49°02'N, 12°08'-13°09'E 15,600 ha

Nature Reserve (400 ha); Landscape Protection Area (2600 ha)

An intact part of the Danube valley with flooded areas, wet meadows, oxbows and riverine forests. The whole landscape is threatened by major alterations affecting the river (construction of dykes to facilitate ship navigation and the installation of electric power-plants) and the surrounding land (agricultural intensification).

The most important breeding species are *Ixobrychus minutus* (30 pairs), *Nycticorax nycticorax* (2 pairs), *Ardea purpurea* (1-2 pairs), *Ciconia ciconia* (1-2 pairs), *Anas querquedula* (30 pairs), *A. clypeata* (25 pairs), *Pernis apivorus* (2 pairs), *Milvus migrans* (4 pairs), *M. milvus* (4 pairs), *Circus aeruginosus* (9 pairs), *Porzana porzana* (15 pairs), *Crex crex* (15 pairs), *Limosa limosa* (60 pairs), *Numenius arquata* (400 pairs), *Tringa totanus* (10 pairs), *Alcedo atthis* (10 pairs), *Picus canus* (30 pairs), *Dryocopus martius* (20 pairs), *Dendrocopos medius*, *Riparia riparia* (200 pairs), *Luscinia svecica* (40-50 pairs), *Saxicola rubetra* (100 pairs), *Locustella luscinioides* (5 pairs), *Acrocephalus arundinaceus* (30 pairs), *Ficedula albicollis* (10 pairs), and *Lanius collurio* (70 pairs). Important for waterfowl in winter, especially *Anas platyrhynchos* and *Bucephala clangula*.

098 Unterer Inn: Haiming – Neuhaus including einschliesslich Stauseen Neuhaus, Egglfing, Ering, und Simbach (Bayern)

48°15'-48°20'N, 12°50'-13°30'E 5000 ha

Ramsar Site (Egglfing and Ering reservoirs: 1955 ha)

Nature Reserve (729 ha)

Four reservoirs on the River Inn with many islands, shallow bays, and inland deltas, with stretches of riverine forest along the river. Uncontrolled fishing and hunting on the Austrian side cause disturbance.

Breeding species include *Ixobrychus minutus* (min. 10 pairs), *Nycticorax nycticorax* (40 pairs), *Ardea purpurea* (1-2 pairs), *Anas acuta* (10 pairs), *Circus aeruginosus* (6 pairs), *Limosa limosa* (2-5 pairs), *Larus melanocephalus* (1 pair), *Bubo bubo* (1 pair), *Alcedo atthis* (5 pairs), *Picus canus* (20 pairs), *Dryocopus martius* (8 pairs), *Riparia riparia* (200 pairs), *Luscinia svecica* (120 pairs), *Locustella luscinioides* (10-15 pairs), *Acrocephalus arundinaceus* (22-30 pairs), and *Lanius collurio* (3-5 pairs). In winter *Anas strepera* (1900), *A. crecca* (4200), *Aythya ferina* (13,000), *A. fuligula* (17,000), and *Larus ridibundus* (30,000) occur.

099 Isar-Tal: Gottfrieding – Plattling einschliesslich Isar-Mündungsbereich (Bayern)

48°39'-48°50'N, 12°32'-12°58'E 8000 ha

Unprotected (some parts are proposed Nature Reserves)

The lower part of the River Isar with many oxbow lakes and riverine forest. The planned development of a hydroelectric power-station (second phase) represents a serious threat.

Breeding species include *Ixobrychus minutus* (1-4 pairs), *Milvus migrans* (1-2 pairs), *Asio flammeus* (1 pair), *Alcedo atthis* (4+ pairs), *Picus canus* (4+ pairs), *Dryocopus martius* (1-2 pairs), *Dendrocopos medius* (1-2 pairs), *Luscinia svecica* (c.200 pairs), *Saxicola rubetra* (20+ pairs), *Ficedula albicollis* (5-8 pairs), and *Emberiza hortulana* (4+ pairs).

100 Mittlere Isar-Stauseen (Bayern)

48°24'N, 12°00'E 500 ha EEC SPA (570 ha)

Nature Reserve

Artificial reservoirs on the River Isar surrounded by reedbeds and remnant riverine forest. The water-level is manipulated by a power-station. Land-uses include wildfowl hunting and fishing.

Breeding species include *Mergus merganser* (10 pairs), *Pernis apivorus* (1-2 pairs), *Milvus migrans* (1-2 pairs), *Sterna hirundo* (30-35 pairs; the largest colony in Bavaria), *Picus canus* (2-3 pairs), *Riparia riparia* (150 pairs in the immediate surroundings), and *Lanius collurio* (1-2 pairs). In autumn *Anas strepera* (750), *A. platyrhynchos* (5400), and *Vanellus vanellus* (4700) occur.

101 Ismaninger Speichersee und Fischteiche (Bayern)

48°13'N, 11°44'E 955 ha Ramsar Site (900 ha)

Unprotected

An artificial reservoir which provides water for Munich. There are small shallow parts and a number of fish-ponds alongside the lake.

Breeding species include *Podiceps nigricollis* (100 pairs), *Phalacrocorax carbo* (65 pairs; increasing), *Nycticorax nycticorax* (c.3 pairs), *Anas strepera* (30+ pairs), *Netta rufina* (c.10 pairs), and *Acrocephalus arundinaceus* (10+ pairs). The reservoir is an important moulting place during late summer and autumn for *Anas strepera* (4000), *A. clypeata* (600), *Netta rufina* (1500), *A. ferina* (20,000), and *Aythya fuligula* (18,000).

102 Ammersee (Bayern)

48°01'N, 11°08'E 6520 ha Ramsar Site (6517 ha)

Two Nature Reserves (Ampermoos: 525 ha; Vogelfreistätte Ammersee Südufer: 499 ha)

A lake with reedbeds and wet meadows, surrounded by riverine forests. Sailing and wind-surfing are causing disturbance throughout the year.

Breeding species include *Netta rufina* (8 pairs), *Crex crex* (2 pairs), *Vanellus vanellus* (48 pairs), *Numenius arquata* (3 pairs), *Sterna hirundo* (30 pairs), *Alcedo atthis* (3 pairs), *Picus canus* (1-2 pairs), *Luscinia svecica* (1 pair), *Saxicola rubetra* (c.18 pairs), *Locustella luscinioides* (2-3 pairs), and *Lanius collurio* (3 pairs). In winter *Anas strepera* (400), *Aythya fuligula* (10,000), *Bucephala clangula* (525), and *Fulica atra* (8000) are the most numerous waterfowl.

103 Starnberger See (Bayern)

47°55'N, 11°18'E 6500 ha Ramsar Site (5720 ha)

Landscape Protection Area

A large lake partly surrounded by reedbeds. At its southern end lies a peatbog (700 ha) (with a number of small ponds: 1-40 ha in size), which is not included in the Ramsar Site. Tourism development (sailing, boat traffic, and bathing) is reducing the area of the reedbeds and is resulting in disturbance. In addition, peat is extracted at the edge of the bog.

Owing to heavy disturbance the breeding of waterbirds is rare, but *Podiceps cristatus* (600), *Aythya ferina* (2250), *A. fuligula* (7000), *Bucephala clangula* (500), *Mergus merganser* (100), and *Fulica atra* (13,500) occur in winter.

104 Chiemsee (Bayern)

47°53'N, 12°27'E 9300 ha Ramsar Site (8660 ha)

Nature Reserve (Tiroler Achen: 730 ha)

A natural lake with a rich delta composed of reedbeds, moorland, wet meadows, and riverine forests (delta of the Tiroler Achen). There is considerable pressure from tourism (boat traffic, bathing, fishing, and hunting).

Breeding species include *Podiceps nigricollis* (15-20 pairs), *Pernis apivorus* (2-3 pairs), *Crex crex* (3-5 pairs; irregularly), *Sterna hirundo* (3-4 pairs; irregularly), *Alcedo atthis* (2-3 pairs) *Picus canus*, *Dryocopus martius*, *Luscinia svecica* (20 pairs), *Saxicola rubetra* (10-15 pairs), *Locustella luscinioides* (c.15 pairs), *Acrocephalus arundinaceus* (20-25 pairs; declining), and *Lanius collurio* (2-3 pairs). Important for waterfowl on passage, especially *Netta rufina*, *Aythya ferina*, *A. fuligula*, and *Bucephala clangula*.

105 Ammergauer Berge (Bayern)

47°30'N, 10°55'E 27,600 ha

Nature Reserve

A calcareous region of the northern Alps (800-2200 m), comprising mountain slopes with mixed forests (*Fagus*, *Abies*, *Picea*) and alpine pastures. Intensification of forestry, water regulation, overgrazing, road construction, and intensive skiing are current problems.

Breeding species include *Aquila chrysaetos* (3-5 pairs), *Falco peregrinus* (4-5 pairs), *Bonasa bonasia*, *Tetrao tetrix*, *T. urogallus*, *Bubo bubo* (3-4 pairs), *Glaucidium passerinum* (20+ pairs), *Aegolius funereus* (20+ pairs), *Picus canus* (30+ pairs), *Dryocopus martius* (80-100 pairs), *Dendrocopos leucotos* (20+ pairs), *Picoides tridactylus* (15+ pairs), *Ptyonoprogne rupestris* (several pairs), *Ficedula parva* (50-80 pairs), *Turdus torquatus* (400+ pairs), *Phylloscopus bonelli* (500+ pairs), *Tichodroma muraria* (5+ pairs), and *Serinus citrinella* (100+ pairs; decreasing).

106 Karwendel und Karwendel-Vorgebirge (Bayern)

47°35'N, 11°25'E 20,000 ha

Mostly a Nature Reserve

A calcareous region of the northern Alps (860-2400 m), comprising mountain slopes with natural forest (*Fagus*, *Acer*, *Abies*, *Picea*), and alpine meadows and rocks above the timberline. Forestry exploitation, overgrazing, road and ski-run construction, military training, and tourism (disturbing the raptors and grouse) are detrimental to the area.

Breeding species include *Aquila chrysaetos* (3 pairs), *Falco peregrinus* (1-2 pairs), *Bonasa bonasia* (20-30 pairs), *Lagopus mutus* (20-30 pairs), *Tetrao tetrix*, *T. urogallus*, *Bubo bubo* (3-4 pairs), *Glaucidium passerinum* (20+ pairs), *Aegolius funereus* (20+ pairs), *Picus canus* (15-30 pairs), *Dryocopus martius* (30+ pairs), *Dendrocopos leucotos* (20+ pairs), *Picoides tridactylus* (30+ pairs), *Turdus torquatus* (300+ pairs), *Phylloscopus bonelli* (500+ pairs), *Ficedula parva* (20-30 pairs), and *Serinus citrinella* (100+ pairs).

107 Nationalpark Berchtesgaden (Bayern)

47°35'N, 12°58'E 20,800 ha

National Park

A mountainous region (480-2700 m) with cliffs, mountain lakes, glaciers, snow-fields, and forests. There is tourism throughout the year (with mountain climbing, skiing, and construction of lifts). Military training (helicopter training) is thought to undermine the area's importance for *Aquila chrysaetos*.

Breeding species include *Pernis apivorus*, *Aquila chrysaetos*, *Falco peregrinus*, *Lagopus mutus*, *Tetrao tetrix*, *T. urogallus*, *Bubo bubo*, *Glaucidium passerinum*, *Aegolius funereus*, *Alcedo atthis*, *Picus canus*, *Dryocopus martius*, *Dendrocopos leucotos*, *Picoides tridactylus*, *Turdus torquatus*, *Phylloscopus bonelli*, *Ficedula parva*, and *Serinus citrinella*.

108 Mittleres Vorland der Schwäbischen Alb (Baden-Württembuerg)

48°35'-41'N, 09°28'-44'E c.15,000 ha

Partly a Landscape Protection Area

A varied landscape with a mosaic of traditionally used orchards, fields, pastures, meadows, and small villages. The rich orchards are insufficiently protected. The recreational activities of visitors from the Stuttgart region are causing increasing disturbance and there is the risk of fires. Some planting of new trees in the orchards is subsidised.

The most important breeding species are *Pernis apivorus* (*c*.5 pairs), *Milvus milvus* (5-10 pairs), *M. migrans* (1 pair), *Falco peregrinus* (2 pairs in cliffs at the edge of the area), *Crex crex* (probably 1 pair), *Alcedo atthis* (1-5 pairs), *Picus canus* (20-50 pairs), *Dryocopus medius* (5-10 pairs), *Dendrocopos medius* (20-50 pairs), *Saxicola rubetra* (1-5 pairs), *Ficedula albicollis* (100+ pairs), *Lanius collurio* (100 pairs), *L. senator* (*c*.15 pairs), and *L. excubitor* (extinct since 1980).

MAIN REFERENCES

Bauer, S. and Thielcke, G. (1982) *Gefährdete Brutvogelarten in der BRD und im Land Berlin.* Kornwestheim.

Berndt, R. (1980) Die Richtlinie vom 2. April 1979 des Rates der Europäischen Gemeinschaften über die Erhaltung der wildlebenden Vogelarten. *Ber. Dt. Skt. ICBP* 20: 113-120.

Berndt, R. (1986) Die Europareservate des Int. Rat für Vogelschutz in der BRD. *Ber. Dt. Skt. ICBP* 26: 61-62.

Busche, G. (1980) *Vogelbestände des Wattenmeeres von Schleswig-Holstein.* Greven.

Haarmann, K. (1984) Feuchtgebiete internationaler Bedeutung und Europareservate in der BRD.

Heckenroth, H. (1985) *Atlas der Brutvögel Niedersachsens 1980* Hannover.

Hölzinger, J. (1987) *Die Vögel Baden-Württembergs, Vol. I: Gefährdung und Schutz.* Stuttgart.

Kottmann, H. J., Schwöppe, W., Willers, T. and Wittig, R. (1985) Heath conservation by sheep grazing: a cost-benefit analysis. *Biol. Conserv.* 31: 1-8.

Mildenberger, H. (1982, 1984) *Die Vögel des Rheinlandes*, 1 and 2. Greven.

Orn. Arbeitsgemeinschaft Bodensee (1983) *Die Vögel des Bodenseegebiets.* Konstanz.

Smit, C. J. and Wolff, W. J. (eds) (1981) *Birds of the Wadden Sea.* Rotterdam.

Winkel, W. and Frantzen, M. (1987) Erfassung von 'Important Bird Areas' der Bundesrepublik Deutschland. *Ber. Dt. Skt. ICBP* 27: 13-58.

Wüst, W. (ed.) (1979, 1986) *Avifauna Bavariae – Die Vogelwelt Bayerns im Wandel der Zeit*, 1 and 2. Munich.

GREECE

Dalmatian Pelican *Pelecanus crispus*

INTRODUCTION

General information

Greece is a large (*c.*132,000 sq km) maritime state composed of part of south-eastern continental Europe, extensive archipelagic waters, including the Ionian islands such as Kerkira (Corfu) and the Aegean islands such as Lesvos (Lesbos), and in the far south, the large island of Kriti (Crete).

The continental mainland is bordered to the north by Albania, Yugoslavia, and Bulgaria, and to the east by Turkey. The southern and western margins are coastal, adjoining the Ionian, Aegean and Mediterranean Seas, with numerous indentations and peninsulas. Peloponnisos (Peloponnese), the southernmost part of the mainland, is connected with the rest of the mainland only by a narrow neck of land (the Isthmus of Corinth).

The human population was estimated in 1985 to be approaching 10 million (9,740,417 million in 1981; an average population density of nearly 74 persons per sq km), with Athinai (Athens) holding over 3 million people. The largest urban areas after Athinai are Thessaloniki in the north and Patrai (Patras) in Peloponnisos. There has been considerable industrial expansion in recent years, but around 25 per cent of the working population remains occupied in agriculture.

Commercially, the most important agricultural products are: tobacco, wheat, cotton, sugar, rice, and fruits (including olives, peaches, grapes, oranges, lemons, figs, and almonds). Industrial activities include mining (e.g. nickel and bauxite); textile, chemical, cement, and glass production and ship-building. Tourism has expanded extremely rapidly in a short time and makes a very important contribution to the Greek economy.

Topographically, Greece is characterised by a mountainous interior intersected by valleys and mountain-basin lakes, and coastal lowlands of varying extent. In the west the mountains are close to the sea, so that any lowland fringe is extremely narrow. In the east and north of the country, however, there are several areas of lowlands associated with the valleys, flood-plains, and deltas of major rivers draining the mountains.

Greece has one of the richest floras in Europe with over a thousand endemic species, with endemism concentrated in the mountains (e.g. Mount Olympos) and islands of the Aegean and Ionian seas (e.g. Crete, with 150 endemic species). Greece was once covered by woodland, but centuries of forest clearance combined with forest fires, cultivation of marginal land, surface mining, and overgrazing by sheep and goats have created large areas of maquis, phrygana, secondary steppe, barren rock, and wastelands; erosion is a serious problem. Forests now cover only 19 per cent of the country, most of them coniferous (13 per cent).

Three main vegetation zones can be distinguished: coastal plains and hills, which were formerly covered with dry evergreen forest, but now evergreen scrub, degraded phrygana or garigue; middle-altitude mountain slopes now mainly cultivated but still supporting large areas of forest and alpine areas above the treeline.

Greece has some of the largest and most important wetlands in the Mediterranean basin. These include: the Evros and Nestos Deltas, the numerous lakes and lagoons in the vicinity of Porto Lagos, Lake Kerkini, and Lake Langada (Koronia) in the north-east; Lakes Mikri Prespa and Megali Prespa in the north; and Amvrakikos Gulf, Mesolongi and Aetoliko Lagoons and Achelos and Evinos Estuaries, along the west coast.

Ornithological importance

Greece supports internationally important populations of a number of globally threatened species, including *Pelecanus crispus* (40-165 pairs at Lake Mikri Prespa, 15-36 pairs at Amvrakikos Gulf; almost certainly the largest breeding population in Europe), *Phalacrocorax pygmeus* (575-750 pairs), *Aegypius monachus* (9-15 pairs), *Aquila heliaca* (2-6 pairs) and *Larus audouinii* (70 pairs). Furthermore, a number of sites in Greece (particularly the Evros Delta and Porto Lagos) are very important for passage *Numenius tenuirostris* and the country's wintering populations of *Anser erythropus* (116 at the Evros Delta in 1988) and *Oxyura leucocephala* (405 at Porto Lagos in Jan. 1988) are also globally significant.

Greece is very important for its breeding waterbirds: 2500-3000 pairs of breeding Ardeidae were censused in 1985-86, including *Egretta garzetta* (1055-1232 pairs), although due to the loss and degradation of wetlands there has been a dramatic decline in the number of breeding *Nycticorax nycticorax* (492-591 pairs; 1100 pairs before 1970), *Ardeola ralloides* (201-377 pairs; 1400 pairs before 1970), and *Ardea purpurea* (105-140 pairs; 600-650 pairs before 1970).

Greece also has important breeding populations of *Plegadis falcinellus* (50-71 pairs; 1840 pairs before 1970) and *Platalea leucorodia* (113-172 pairs; 300 pairs before 1970), but both species continue to decline because of the disappearance of their feeding grounds. The country supports important breeding populations of a number of other waterbirds including: *Pelecanus onocrotalus* (max. 250 pairs), *Aythya nyroca* (400 pairs), *Himantopus himantopus* (1000 pairs), *Recurvirostra avosetta* (700 pairs), *Glareola pratincola* (1900 pairs), *Larus melanocephalus* (max. 7000 pairs), *L. genei*, and *Sterna albifrons* (500-1000 pairs).

Greece has a considerable variety of birds of prey with 26 species, although a high proportion of these are declining because of habitat loss, human disturbance and persecution. The country has particularly important populations of *Gypaetus barbatus* (35 pairs, mainly in Crete), *Neophron percnopterus* (200-250 pairs), *Gyps fulvus* (450 pairs), *Accipiter brevipes* (1000 pairs), *Buteo rufinus* (60 pairs), *Aquila pomarina* (80 pairs), *A. chrysaetos* (220 pairs), *Falco eleonorae* (2800 pairs; the largest population in the world), and *F. biarmicus* (30-50 pairs). There has been a serious decline in the country's population of *Falco naumanni* (2000 pairs estimated in 1980/1981; most colonies reduced to two or three pairs each in 1987). The rocky islands of the Aegean and the Sea of

Crete have large breeding populations of *Calonectris diomedea* (5000 pairs) and *Phalacrocorax aristotelis desmarestii*.

Of the passerines, Greece has very large populations of *Calandrella brachydactyla*, *Lullula arborea*, *Anthus campestris*, *Hippolais olivetorum*, *Sylvia rueppelli*, *Lanius collurio*, *L. nubicus*, *Emberiza hortulana*, and *E. caesia*. Three of these species (*Hippolais olivetorum*, *S. rueppelli*, and *L. nubicus*) have very restricted global distributions.

Pelecanidae, Ciconiidae, Accipitridae, Scolopacidae, Laridae, and Sternidae occur in important numbers on passage.

In winter there are important numbers of *Phalacrocorax carbo sinensis*, *P. pygmeus*, *Pelecanus crispus*, *Egretta alba*, *Larus genei*, *Recurvirostra avosetta*, and various species of Anatidae. The total number of Anatidae wintering in Greece has varied since 1968 from 300,000 to just under one million. The most numerous waterfowl during this period were (av. counts during the period 1982-86 at most important sites): *Anas penelope* (72,700), *A. crecca* (37,000), *A. platyrhynchos* (24,100), *A. acuta* (30,700), *Aythya ferina* (43,100), and *Fulica atra* (67,000); the Evros Delta and Amvrakikos Gulf being the most important sites. Other species wintering in important numbers at Greek wetlands include *Pelecanus crispus*, *Phalacrocorax pygmeus*, and *Egretta alba*.

Conservation infrastructure and protected-areas system

Presidential Decree 996/1971 enables the Greek Forest Service (of the Ministry of Agriculture) to establish National Parks, Aesthetic Forests, and Protected Natural Monuments. Other relevant legislation includes Presidential Decree 61/1980 (concerning the Greek Forest Service), Public Law 860/1976 (Regional Planning and the Environment: laws governing planning protection), Public Law 998/1979 on forests and forest land protection and Public Law 1650/1986 (Protection of the Environment).

Presidential Decree 67/1981 lists some 200 species of fauna (excluding birds) which it is illegal to collect, kill, capture, detain, trade or export. However, there has been little effective enforcement of this legal measure and information/education campaigns are urgently required. Hunting, collecting, capture, detention, trade, and export of birds is now being regulated by the 414985/85 Joint Ministerial Decision, which in fact adopts the 79/409/EEC Wild Birds Directive.

The Greek Forest Service of the Ministry of Agriculture is responsible for National Parks and Aesthetic Forests, whilst the coordinating body for all environmental activities is the Ministry of the Environment, Physical Planning and Public Works.

The following types of protected areas are mentioned in the inventory:

1. National Parks

   National parks are defined, according to the above-mentioned law, as 'mainly forested areas of special conservation interest on account of flora and fauna, geomorphology, subsoil, atmosphere, water and generally their natural environment, the protection of which seems necessary; also on account of the need for the conservation and improvement of their constitution, form and natural beauty, to permit aesthetic, psychic and healthy enjoyment and, moreover, for carrying out special research of any kind'.

   Ten National Parks have been designated covering 68,724 ha, 34,488 ha of which are strictly protected as core zones. The remaining 34,254 ha refer to the peripheral zones of five National Parks. These zones exist for the other National Parks but their areas have not been defined.

2. Aesthetic Forests

   Aesthetic forests are defined, according to the above mentioned law, as 'forests or natural landscapes which possess particular aesthetic, hygienic and touristic significance and which have characteristics that demand the protection of their fauna, flora and natural beauty'. There are 19 Aesthetic Forests that cover a total area of 33,106 ha.

3. Protected Natural Monuments

   These are sites which are important for nature conservation, but are not large or diverse enough to be designated as National Parks or Aesthetic Forests. There are 51 sites which cover more than 16,700 ha, the largest of which is 550 ha.

4. Hunting Reserves

These are areas which have been designated according to the hunting legislation. Five hundred sites have been designated as Game Refuges (covering *c.*800,000 ha), 21 sites have been designated as Game Breeding Stations (covering 13,000+ ha), and 8 sites have been designated as controlled Hunting Areas (covering *c.*120,000 ha).

International measures relevant to the conservation of sites

Greece is a party to the Ramsar Convention, World Heritage Convention, Bern Convention, and Barcelona Convention, and, as a member of the European Community, is bound by the terms of the Wild Birds Directive. Greece has also signed, but not ratified, the Bonn Convention.

As of May 1988, the Greek government had designated 11 Ramsar Sites covering an approximate total area of 107,400 ha; however, the areas of some of the 11 sites remain to be legally defined. A very rough management plan has been drawn up for each site, details of which are deposited with UNESCO and with the Secretariat of the Ramsar Convention.

In addition, Greece has designated two Biosphere Reserves (covering 8840 ha), 16 EEC Special Protection Areas, eight Mediterranean Specially Protected Areas, one Biogenetic Reserve, but no natural World Heritage Sites.

Overview of the inventory

One hundred and thirteen sites are contained in the following inventory. All of the major wetland areas are included (including all the Greek Ramsar Sites) as well as a large number of smaller wetlands, including some on the Greek islands.

The wetland species, mentioned above, are therefore covered extremely well by this inventory. Other, non-wetland species, mentioned above, are not so well covered since their status and distribution are less well known and it has been more difficult to designate sites for widely dispersed species such as birds of prey.

Nevertheless, a good number of sites for birds of prey have been selected – usually mountainous areas containing core areas of importance for nesting (such as areas with gorges and cliffs, ravined foothills, and low-altitude forests) as well as larger buffer zones as feeding areas. In some areas, more fieldwork is needed to identify new sites for birds of prey or more precisely to define existing sites.

The inventory includes all the country's Ramsar Sites, both Biosphere Reserves, and 14 of the 16 EEC Special Protection Areas. Protection at these sites is often very poor. Furthermore, a majority of the sites in this inventory are totally unprotected and many are seriously threatened. As this book goes to press a major study by the Hellenic Ornithological Society has highlighted the serious threats to five important bird areas (site numbers 001, 010, 032, 055, 060) and the potentially damaging impact of the European Community's Integrated Mediterranean Programme.

Acknowledgements

This inventory is based on the work carried out by the ICBP European Community Working Group (compiled by B. Hallmann) in 1982, which was substantially revised by B. Hallmann in 1988, with funding provided by the European Community's CORINE Biotopes Programme. Additional valuable information, and data on new sites, were provided by the Hellenic Ornithological Society (G. Handrinos provided most of the information on Greek wetlands; V. Goutner, M. Gaetlich, G. Kondylis, G. Katsadorakis, G. Mertzanis, K. Papakostantinou, Ph. Pergantis, K. Poitazides, and G. Tsakona also provided information and made comments on the inventory).

INVENTORY

No.	Site name	Region	Criteria used to select site [see p.18] 0	1(i)	1(ii)	1(iii)	1(iv)	2	3	4
001	Delta Evrou (Evros Delta)	ES			*	*		*	*	
002	Vouna Evrou (Evros Mountains)	ES						*	*	
003	Limni Mitrikou (Lake Mitrikou)	RI				*		*	*	
004	Porto Lagos, Limni Vistonis (Lake Vistonis), and coastal lagoons (Lakes of Thrace)	RI,XI				*		*	*	
005	Potamos/Kilada Filiouri (Filiouri River Valley)	RI							*	
006	Kilada Kompsatou (Kompsatos Valley)	RI							*	
007	Delta Nestou (Nestos Delta) including Limnothalassa Gioubournou (Gouboumou Lagoon)	XI,KA				*		*	*	
008	Vouna Limnia (Limnia Hills)	KA							*	
009	Stena Nestou (Nestos Gorge)	KA,XI						*	*	
010	Kentriki Rodopi and Kilada Nestou (Central Rodopi Mountains and Nestos Valley)	DA							*	
011	Kouskouras Oros (Mount Kouskouras)	SS							*	
012	Limni Kerkini (Lake Kerkini)	SS				*		*	*	
013	Oros Beles (Mount Beles or Kerkini)	SS							*	
014	Oros Pangheo (Mount Pangheo)	KA							*	
015	Elos Artzan (Artzan Marshes)	KS				*		*	*	
016	Ekvoli Strymona (Strymon Delta)	SS,KA						*	*	
017	Kroussia Ori (Mount Kroussia or Mavrovouni)	SS						*	*	
018	Axios Potamos (River Axios)	KS,TI				*		*	*	
019	Ekvoles Axiou, Loudias, and Aliakmonas (Axios, Loudias, and Aliakmon Estuaries)	TI,IA,PA			*	*		*	*	
020	Limnothalassa Angelochori (Angelochori Lagoon)	TI				*		*	*	
021	Limnothalassa Epanomis (Epanomi Lagoon)	TI							*	
022	Limni Volvi and Limni Langada (Lake Volvi, and Lake Langada or Lake Koronia)	TI				*		*	*	
023	Stena Rentinas (Rentina Gorge)	TI							*	
024	Ori Cholomontas (Cholomon Mountains)	CI							*	
025	Elos Agiou Mamantou (Agios Mamantos Marsh)	CI				*			*	
026	Oros Itamos (Mount Itamos)	CI							*	
027	Oros Athos (Mount Athos)	CI							*	
028	Oros Tzena (Mount Tzena)	PL							*	
029	Oros Voras (Mount Voras) including Kaimaktsalan and Pinovo	PL,FA						*	*	
030	Stena Apsalou and Moglenitsas (Apsalos and Moglenitsa Gorges)	PL							*	
031	Limni Agra (Lake Agras)	PL							*	
032	Limni Mikri Prespa and Limni Megali Prespa (Lake Mikri Prespa and Lake Megali Prespa)	FA				*		*	*	
033	Limni Vegoritis and Limni Petron (Lake Vegoritis and Lake Petron)	PL,FA,KI				*		*	*	

No.	Site name	Region	Criteria used to select site [see p.18]							
			0	1(i)	1(ii)	1(iii)	1(iv)	2	3	4
034	Limni Kheimaditis and Limni Zazaris (Lake Kheimaditis and Lake Zazaris)	FA				*		*	*	
035	Limni Kastorias (Orestiada) (Lake Kastoria or Orestiada)	KR				*		*	*	
036	Oros Gramos (Mount Gramos)	KR,IN							*	
037	Oros Vourinos (Mount Vourinos)	KI,GA							*	
038	Stena Aliakmona (Aliakmon Gorge)	IA							*	
039	Limnothalassa Alyki Kitros (Alyki Lagoon near Kitros)	PA		*	*	*		*	*	
040	Oros Olympos (Mount Olympos)	PA,LA						*	*	
041	Area of Oriokastrou, Delvinakiou and Meropis, and Kilada Gormou (Gormos Valley)	IN							*	
042	Oros Timfi (Gamila) and Oros Smolikas (Mount Timfi or Gamila, and Mount Smolikas)	IN							*	
043	Central part of Zagori	IN							*	
044	Valia Kalda (Pindos Natural Park)	GA,IN						*	*	
045	Antikhassia Ori (Antikhassia Mountains) and Meteora	TA							*	
046	Kerketio Ori (Kerketion Mountains) (Koziakas)	TA							*	
047	Stena Kalamakiou (Kalamaki Gorge)	LA							*	
048	Kato Olympos/Tembi/Ossa/Delta Piniou	LA						*	*	
049	Ori Mavrovouni (Mavrovouni Mountains)	LA,MA							*	
050	Stena Kalama (Kalamas Gorge)	TT						*	*	
051	Ekvoles Kalama (Kalamas Estuary)	TT				*		*	*	
052	Limni Limnopoula (Lake Limnopoula)	TT							*	
053	Ekvoli and Stena Acherondos (Acheron Gorge and Delta)	PZ,TT							*	
054	Vouna Zalongou (Zalongos Mountains)	PZ							*	
055	Amvrakikos Kolpos (Gulf of Amvrakia or Arta)	PZ,AA,AN			*	*		*	*	
056	Ori Athamanon (Athamanika Mountains)	AA,IN,TA							*	
057	Kilada Akheloou (Achelos Valley)	AA,KT							*	
058	Ori Akarnanika (Akarnanian Mountains)	AN							*	
059	Kalon Oros (Mount Kalon)	KN							*	
060	Limnothalassa Mesolongiou and Aetolikou, Ekvoles Acheloou and Evinou (Mesolongi and Aetoliko Lagoons, and Achelos and Evinos Estuaries)	AN				*		*	*	
061	Oros Vardousia (Mount Vardousia)	FD							*	
062	Oros Ghiona (Mount Ghiona), Kharadra Rekas (Reka Ravines), Lazorema, and Vathia Lakka	FD							*	
063	Southern and eastern part of Parnassos	VA,FD							*	
064	Oros Iti (Mount Iti)	FT							*	
065	Delta Sperchiou (Sperchios Delta)	FT				*			*	
066	Vouna Gouras (Mount Gouras)	MA							*	
067	Ormos Sourpis (Sourpis Bay)	MA							*	

No.	Site name	Region	Criteria used to select site [see p.18]							
			0	1(i)	1(ii)	1(iii)	1(iv)	2	3	4
068	Pilion Oros (Mount Pilion)	MA							*	
069	Limnothalassa Megalo Livari (Megalo Livari Lagoon)	EA							*	
070	Oros Kandili (Kandili Mountain)	EA							*	
071	Oros Dirfis, Xirovouni, Skotini, Mavrovouni, Alokteri, Ortari, and vicinity of Kimi	EA						*	*	
072	Limni Distos (Lake Distos)	EA							*	
073	Oros Ochi (Mount Ochi) and surrounding area	EA							*	
074	Limni Kotichi (Lake Kotichi)	IL				*		*	*	
075	Limnothalassa Kalogrias/Strofilia/ Lamia (Kalogria Lagoon, Strofilia Forest, and Lamia Lakes)	AH,IL							*	
076	Limnothalassa Alyki Aegion (Alyki Lagoon, Aegion)	AH							*	
077	Vouna Barbas/Klokos, Faranghi Selinous (Barbas and Klokos Mountains and Selinous Gorge)	AH							*	
078	Faranghi Vouraikou (Vouraikos Gorge) including Kalavrita	AH							*	
079	Foloi Oros (Foloi Hills)	IL							*	
080	Nissi Strofades (Strofades Islands)	ZS							*	
081	Limni Stymphalia (Lake Stymphalia)	KH							*	
082	Limni Taka (Lake Taka)	AD							*	
083	Central Oros Taigetos (Mount Taigetos)	MN,LN							*	
084	Divari Pilou (Divari Lagoon near Pilos)	MN							*	
085	Notia Mani (Southern Mani), Oros Sanghias (Mount Sanghias), and Akrotirio Tenaro (Cape Tenaro)	LN						*	*	
086	Ekvoles Evrota (Evrotas Delta)	LN				*			*	
087	Ori Ghidovouni, Khionovouni, Gaidourovouni, Korakia, Kalogherovouni, Kouloukhera, and vicinity of Monemvassias	LN							*	
088	Parnitha	AK							*	
089	Koutroulis Oros (Mount Koutroulis)	CA							*	
090	Khersonissos Rodopou (Rodopos Peninsula)	CA							*	
091	Lefka Ori (Lefka Mountains)	CA							*	
092	Limni Kourna, Delta Almyrou, and Paralia Georgioupolis (Lake Kourna, Almiros Delta, and Georgioupolis Beach)	CA							*	
093	Oros Kedros and Kourtaliotiko Faranghi (Mount Kedros and Kourtaliotiko Gorge)	RN							*	
094	Faranghi Prassion (Prassies Gorge)	RN							*	
095	Idi Oros (Mount Idi)	RN,IO							*	
096	Kofinas Oros (Mount Kofinas)	IO							*	
097	Jouchtas Oros (Mount Jouchtas)	IO							*	
098	Nissos Dia (Dia Island)	IO							*	
099	Oros Dikti (Mount Dikti)	IO,LI							*	
100	Ori Thryptis and Ornon (Mount Thryptis and Mount Ornon)	LI							*	
101	Nissi Dionisiades (Dionisiades Islands)	LI						*	*	

No.	Site name	Region	Criteria used to select site [see p.18]							
			0	1(i)	1(ii)	1(iii)	1(iv)	2	3	4
102	Nissos Kasos (Kasos Island)	DS						*	*	
103	Nissos Saria (Saria Island)	DS							*	
104	Northern Sifnos	KL							*	
105	Northern Syros	KL						*	*	
106	Oros Dias, Oros Mavrovouni, Oros Koronos	KL							*	
107	Nissi Kyra-Panaghia/Ghioura/Piperi/ Skantzoura (Vorii Sporades)	MA						*	*	
108	Limni Khortaro and Limni Alyki (Khortaro Lake and Alyki Lake)	LS							*	
109	Kolpos Kallonis (Gulf of Kalloni)	LS				*			*	
110	Oros Kerkis (Mount Kerkis)	SM						*	*	
111	Nissi Fourni (Fourni Islands)	SM							*	
112	Vouno Dikios, Akrotiri Louros, and Limni Psalidi (Mount Dikios, Cape Louros, and Lake Psalidi)	DS							*	
113	Nissos Tilos	DS							*	

ES=Evros RI=Rodopi XI=Xanthi KA=Kavala DA=Drama SS=Serres KS=Kilkis TI=Thessaloniki IA=Imathia PA=Pieria CI=Chalkidiki PL=Pella FA=Florina KI=Kozani KR=Kastoria IN=Ioannina GA=Grevena LA=Larisa TA=Trikala MA=Magnisia TT=Thesprotia PZ=Preveza AA=Arta AN=Aitoloakarnania KT=Karditsa KN=Kefallinia FD=Fokida VA=Voiotia FT=Fthiotida EA=Evvia IL=Ileia AH=Achaia ZS=Zakynthos KH=Korinthia AD=Arkadia MN=Messinia LN=Lakonia AK=Attiki CA=Chania RN=Rethymnon IO=Irakleio LI=Lasithi DS=Dodekanisos KL=Kyklades LS=Lesvos SM=Samos

Comments on the inventory

1. The ornithological data were updated in early 1988. The counts for birds on passage and/or in winter generally refer to the largest number of a species recorded in recent years.

2. The following breeding species have not been mentioned in some site accounts because the Greek compilers felt such data should be treated as confidential (the number of sites where the species breeds but is not mentioned is given in brackets): *Haliaeetus albicilla* (1), *Gypaetus barbatus* (2), *Buteo rufinus* (1), *Hieraaetus fasciatus* (1), *Falco biarmicus* (8), and *Falco peregrinus* (6).

3. The following species which are of interest in a European context are common in Greece and generally have not been mentioned in the site accounts: *Caprimulgus europaeus*, *Calandrella brachydactyla*, *Lullula arborea*, *Anthus campestris*, *Lanius collurio*, *Emberiza caesia*, and *E. hortulana*.

4. Where known, if a site is at least partly protected by a Mediterranean Specially Protected Area, an Aesthetic Forest or a Protected Natural Monument, then this is mentioned. It is possible, however, that some important bird areas may be protected by one or more of the above types of protected area but are currently listed as being unprotected.

5. The site name is first given as a transliteration of the Greek name. This is then followed by the English name in parentheses, and then by the name of the prefecture(s) (Nomoi) where the site is found (also given in parentheses).

6. The regions used when applying the site-selection criteria are the NUTS level 2 regions (component prefectures given in parentheses): Kentriki Kai Dytiki Makedonia (Thessaloniki, Chalkidiki, Kilkis, Pieria, Imathia, Pella, Florina, Kastoria, Kozani, Grevena); Thessalia (Larisa, Magnisia, Trikala, Karditsa); Anatoliki Makedonia

(Kavala, Serres, Drama); Thraki (Rodopi, Xanthi, Evros); Anatoliki Sterea Kai Nisia (Attiki, Voiotia, Fthiotida, Fokida, Evrytania, Evvoia, Kyklades); Peloponnisos Kai Dytiki Sterea Ellada (Korinthia, Argolida, Achaia, Ileia, Messinia, Lakonia, Arkadia, Aitoloakarnania, Zakynthos, Kefallinia); Ipeiros (Ioannina, Arta, Preveza, Thesprotia, Kerkyra, Lefkada); Kriti (Irakleio, Chania, Lasithi, Rethymni); Nisia Anatolikou Aigaiou (Lesvos, Dodekanisos, Samos, Chios).

Glossary

EEC SPA = European Community Special Protection Area

---

001 Delta Evrou (Evros Delta) (Evros)

40°52'N, 26°00'E 10,000 ha Ramsar Site (boundaries not yet precisely defined)

Restrictions on hunting and agriculture (1600 ha)

The delta of the River Evros on the Greek/Turkish border. It holds a diversity of habitats, with sandy offshore islands, sand-dunes, halophytic marshes interspersed with saline lagoons and saltpans, scattered freshwater areas fringed with reed-swamp, and the river (which is bordered by a strip of gallery woodland and *Tamarix* scrub), grassland or seasonal marshy areas. Land-uses include stock-raising, agriculture, commercial fishing, and hunting. A biological station has been established by the Hellenic Society for the Protection of Nature. Current problems include excessive shooting (which seriously affects the use of the delta by wildfowl), overgrazing, and drainage. Gallery woodland along the Greek side of the River Evros has been cleared, and almost all grassland areas (formerly major feeding grounds for wintering geese) have suffered because of poor water-management. Lower water-levels have opened up most of the important bird habitats to grazing cattle, which are degrading the vegetation. Several new access roads will result in an increase of the already high hunting pressure. In May 1987, Drana Lagoon, one of the delta's most important habitats, was drained by farmers because of increasing salination of surrounding agricultural land. The delta's significance for birds has greatly deteriorated, with *Phalacrocorax pygmeus*, *Nycticorax nycticorax*, *Ardeola ralloides*, *Egretta garzetta*, *E. alba*, *Ardea cinerea*, *Plegadis falcinellus,* and *Haliaeetus albicilla* almost certainly no longer nesting, and wintering waterfowl numbers are now much lower.

Breeding species include *Phalacrocorax carbo sinensis* (formerly 100 pairs; now much decreased to *c.*15 pairs), *Ixobrychus minutus* (20+ pairs), *Ardea purpurea* (15 pairs), *Tadorna ferruginea* (1-5 pairs), *Aythya nyroca* (20 pairs), *Himantopus himantopus* (10 pairs), *Recurvirostra avosetta* (5-120 pairs), *Burhinus oedicnemus* (20 pairs), *Glareola pratincola* (200 pairs), *Charadrius alexandrinus* (*c.*50 pairs), *Hoplopterus spinosus* (6 pairs), *Larus melanocephalus* (0-1000 pairs; colony displaced by drainage of Drana Lagoon), *Gelochelidon nilotica* (50-100 pairs), *Sterna hirundo* (400 pairs), and *S. albifrons* (80-450 pairs). In addition, the delta is a valuable feeding area for some raptors breeding in the hills north of the delta. *Phoenicopterus ruber* has been resident since 1983 but has not yet bred. Few of the waders breed successfully. Passage species include *Pelecanus onocrotalus* (max. 1200), *Ciconia ciconia* (max. 7500), *Plegadis falcinellus* (1000), *Platalea leucorodia* (300), *Anser albifrons* (max. 35,000), *A. erythropus* (50-150), and *Numenius tenuirostris* (10-250; regularly recorded in spring; the most important passage site in Greece and possibly the most important in Europe). Still one of the most important localities in Greece for wintering waterfowl; though numbers show great fluctuations, there appears to have been a long-term decline since the 1970s. Mean January maxima (1982-1986) include internationally important numbers of *Anas penelope* (15,000), *A. strepera* (1000), *A. crecca* (35,000), *A. acuta* (36,000), *Cygnus olor* (2105), *Tadorna tadorna* (1220), and *Fulica atra* (25,000). Other wintering species include *Phalacrocorax pygmeus* (500), *Pelecanus crispus* (10), *Egretta alba* (60), *Branta ruficollis* (0-1800), *Circus aeruginosus* (30), *C. cyaneus* (50), *Aquila clanga* (10), and *Recurvirostra avosetta* (1200).

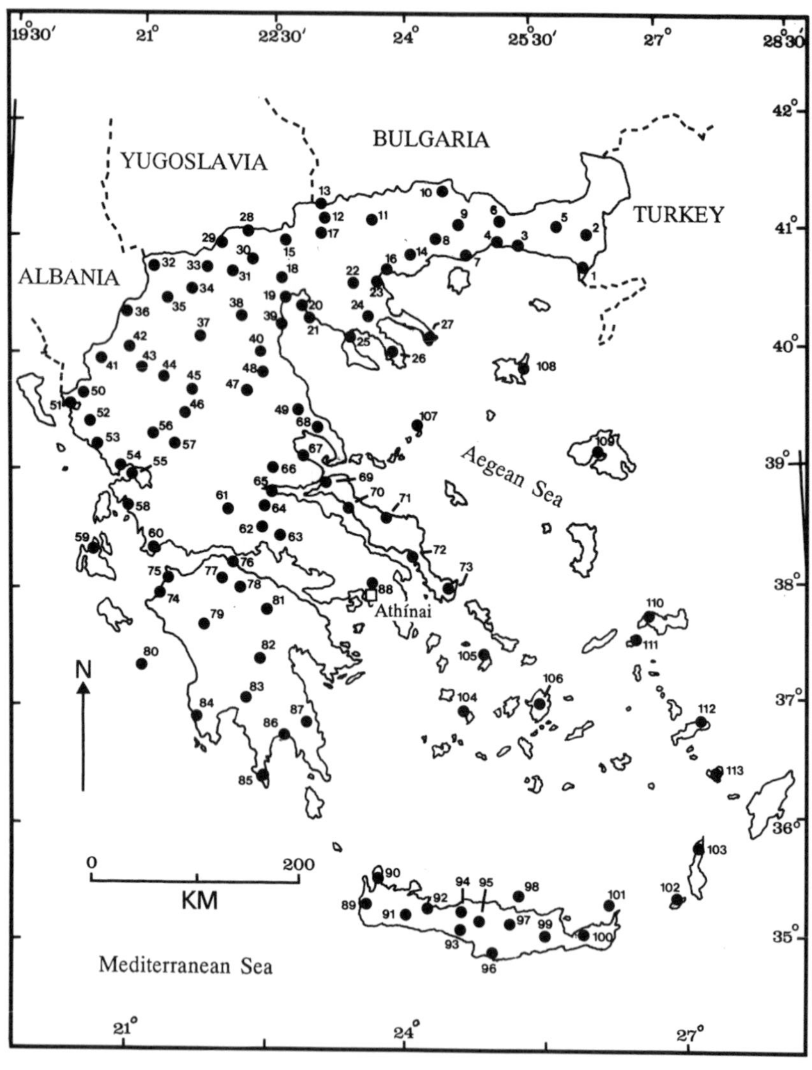

Figure 15: Map showing the location of the sites in Greece

002 Vouna Evrou (Evros Mountains) (Evros)

41°00'N, 26°00'E 90,000 ha EEC SPA (Forest of Dadia-Soufli: 7200 ha)

Reserve (7200 ha) where shooting and forestry are prohibited. There is a proposal for a Biogenetic Reserve of 118,000 ha including the Evros Delta.

The mountains north of Alexandroupolis including the Avas Valley. There are large areas of forest, mostly deciduous, but some *Pinus* with *Quercus* maquis, and alluvial forests along streams. The lower, more eroded hills have rocky outcrops and ravines, with small-scale cultivation (with hedgerows and copses) near villages. Most of the area is grazed. Severe problems include extensive exploitation of natural forests, and hunting.

One of the most important areas for birds of prey in Europe with 24 breeding species including *Pernis apivorus* (12-20 pairs), *Haliaeetus albicilla* (1-3 pairs; also 10 in winter), *Neophron percnopterus* (26-35 pairs), *Gyps fulvus* (5 pairs), *Aegypius monachus* (15 pairs), *Circaetus gallicus* (36-42 pairs), *Accipiter gentilis* (35-45 pairs), *A. brevipes* (10-20 pairs), *Buteo buteo* (75-100 pairs), *B. rufinus* (15 pairs), *Aquila pomarina* (23 pairs), *A. heliaca* (3 pairs), *A. chrysaetos* (12 pairs), *Hieraaetus pennatus* (20+ pairs), *Falco peregrinus* (3 pairs), and *Bubo bubo* (6-10 pairs). Other breeding species include *Ciconia nigra* (12 pairs), *Coracias garrulus*, *Dendrocopos medius*, *Hippolais olivetorum*, *Ficedula semitorquata*, and *Lanius nubicus*.

003 Limni Mitrikou (Lake Mitrikou) (Rodopi)

40°59'N, 25°19'E 5500 ha

Part of Ramsar Site (with Porto Lagos, Limni Vistonis, and adjacent lagoons: 9800 ha; boundaries not yet precisely defined)

The lake is a non-shooting zone, otherwise unprotected

A natural freshwater lake (Limni Mana or Limni Mitrikou; the only freshwater lake with extensive marshes in the Porto Lagos group) where the River Filiouri enters the sea. The lake is surrounded by reedbeds and is covered with floating vegetation in summer, with remnant *Salix* woodland along the river. There is also saltmarsh and agricultural land. Human activities include arable and stock-farming, fishing, and hunting. In recent years negative ecological changes have resulted because of: massive freshwater extraction and subsequent salination; pesticide and fertiliser run-off; and herbicide application to combat floating vegetation which hinders fishing. As a result, populations of herons, *Plegadis falcinellus*, *Platalea leucorodia*, *Chlidonias* terns, and other species have declined markedly.

Breeding species include *Ixobrychus minutus* (20 pairs), *Ardea purpurea* (10 pairs), *Plegadis falcinellus* (0-6 pairs), *Platalea leucorodia* (10-20 pairs), *Tadorna ferruginea*, *Anas strepera*, *Aythya nyroca* (60 pairs), *Himantopus himantopus* (20 pairs), *Recurvirostra avosetta* (possibly 5 pairs), *Glareola pratincola* (formerly 100 pairs), *Hoplopterus spinosus* (2-5 pairs), and *Chlidonias hybridus* (formerly 150 pairs). Numbers of wintering geese have fluctuated according to weather conditions and hunting disturbance (formerly 1200 *Anser albifrons* and 3000 *A. anser*), although *A. erythropus* still occurs (70 in Jan. 1984). Other wintering species include *Phalacrocorax carbo sinensis* (400), *Pelecanus crispus* (10-50), *Anas crecca* (12,000), and *Oxyura leucocephala* (30).

004 Porto Lagos, Limni Vistonis (Lake Vistonis), and coastal lagoons (Lakes of Thrace) (Rodopi, Xanthi)

40°59'-41°05'N, 25°00'-25°11'E 13,000 ha

Ramsar Site (9800 ha; boundaries not yet precisely defined)

Hunting is partly prohibited (6600 ha) and the heronry in Porto Lagos is protected; housing development, commercial fishing, and the water regime are controlled by special measures; proposed National Park

A complex of coastal brackish and freshwater lakes; the largest is Vistonis, which is brackish, fringed by *Phragmites*, and has zones of *Tamarix* scrub, saltmarshes, riverine forest, freshwater pools, and wet meadows. Includes the following lagoons: Porto Lagos,

Lafri, Lafrouda, Xirolimni, Karatza, Messi, Ptelea, and Elos. Vistonis suffers from pollution (from industrial, agricultural, and domestic sources) and the marshes, wet meadows, and riverine forest are threatened by reclamation plans. Limni Mitrikou is adjacent to this site.

Breeding species include *Phalacrocorax pygmeus*, *Nycticorax nycticorax*, *Ardeola ralloides* (5 pairs), *Egretta garzetta* (330 pairs), *Ardea cinerea* (120 pairs), *Aythya nyroca* (20 pairs), *Himantopus himantopus* (100 pairs), *Recurvirostra avosetta* (45 pairs), *Glareola pratincola* (50 pairs), *Hoplopterus spinosus*, *Sterna hirundo* (400 pairs), *S. albifrons* (10 pairs), *Coracias garrulus*, *Melanocorypha calandra*, and *Lanius minor*. Species occurring on migration include *Pelecanus onocrotalus* (100), *Plegadis falcinellus* (400), and *Numenius tenuirostris* (the second most important site in Greece). *Phoenicopterus ruber* is resident (max. 2000). In winter, large numbers of waterfowl occur with *Phalacrocorax carbo sinensis* (4500 in 1984), *P. pygmeus* (4000 in 1986), *Pelecanus crispus* (150), *Egretta alba* (250), *Anser albifrons* (1000), *A. erythropus* (50), *A. anser* (3000+), *Tadorna tadorna*, *T. ferruginea*, *Anas crecca* (11,500), *A. acuta* (3600), *A. clypeata* (1700), *Oxyura leucocephala* (max. 405 in Jan. 1988), *Aythya ferina* (4100), *Fulica atra* (30,500), and *Recurvirostra avosetta* (1500).

005 Potamos/Kilada Filiouri (Filiouri River Valley) (Rodopi)

41°07'N, 25°51'E 22,000 ha

Unprotected

A steep-sided valley with rock-faces, *Quercus* forests, and grazing land. Human activities include agriculture, stock-raising, and hunting, and there is scattered human habitation. Threatened by the planting of terraces of *Pinus* in open *Quercus* forest. Adjacent to Vouna Evrou (site no. 002).

Rich in birds of prey which include *Neophron percnopterus* (6 pairs), *Gyps fulvus* (1 pair), *Circaetus gallicus* (2 pairs), *Aquila pomarina* (2 pairs), *A. chrysaetos* (1 pair), and *Hieraaetus pennatus* (possibly 1 pair). Also the most important feeding area in the region for vultures (all four species). Additional breeding species include *Ciconia nigra* (1 pair), *Dendrocopos medius*, and *Hippolais olivetorum*.

006 Kilada Kompsatou (Kompsatos Valley) (Rodopi)

41°10'N, 25°07'E 9500 ha

Unprotected

The hills north of Iasmos and Amaxades including the steep-sided Kompsatos Valley, with grazed *Quercus* forest and deep valleys containing areas of dense riverine forest. Human activities include stock-raising and hunting, and there is scattered human habitation. Threatened by development and road construction.

Breeding species include *Ciconia nigra* (1+ pair), *Neophron percnopterus*, *Gyps fulvus* (10 pairs), *Circaetus gallicus*, *Accipiter brevipes*, *Buteo rufinus*, *Aquila pomarina*, *A. chrysaetos*, *Hieraaetus pennatus*, *Falco peregrinus*, *Dendrocopos medius*, and *Hippolais olivetorum*.

007 Delta Nestou (Nestos Delta) including Limnothalassa Goubournou (Goubournou Lagoon) (Xanthi, Kavala)

40°56'-40°58'N, 24°30'-24°59'E 13,000 ha

Partly a Ramsar Site (10,593 ha; boundaries not yet precisely defined)

Industrial development prohibited; two non-hunting zones (9500 ha); commercial fishing is regulated; proposed National Park

A large delta, now almost entirely agricultural land, with a series of brackish coastal lagoons separated from the sea by narrow sandy strips. Only patches of the once vast gallery forest remain, and other important habitat-types are also much fragmented, so that areas of freshwater lagoons, saltmarsh, dunes, and scrub are small and isolated. There is also a rocky offshore islet (Thassopoula). Human activities include agriculture, fishing, tourism, and there is a new airport and a U.S. military radio-station next to the lagoons. Negative ecological changes include: intensification of agriculture; a new hydroelectric dam up river which will alter the water regime of the delta considerably; overgrazing; and hunting. Due to extensive land reclamation, the delta has lost much of its former importance for birds.

Breeding species include *Ixobrychus minutus* (15+ pairs), *Nycticorax nycticorax*, *Egretta garzetta* (100+ pairs), *Ardea purpurea* (39 pairs), *Ciconia ciconia*, *Tadorna ferruginea*, *Circus aeruginosus*, *Accipiter brevipes*, *Aquila pomarina*, *Himantopus himantopus* (30 pairs), *Recurvirostra avosetta* (30+ pairs), *Burhinus oedicnemus*, *Glareola pratincola* (20 pairs), *Hoplopterus spinosus*, *Sterna albifrons* (100 pairs), *Coracias garrulus*, *Melanocorypha calandra* (10+ pairs), *Cercotrichas galactotes*, *Lanius minor* (10+ pairs), and *L. nubicus* (10+ pairs). *Phalacrocorax aristotelis desmarestii* nests on Thassopoula. A considerable variety of species occurs on migration; wintering species include *Phalacrocorax carbo sinensis* (2000), *P. pygmeus*, *Pelecanus crispus* (100), *Egretta alba* (150+), *Haliaeetus albicilla*, and *Aquila clanga*.

008 Vouna Limnia (Limnia Hills) (Kavala)

41°03'N, 24°25'E 1300 ha

Unprotected

Hills with cliffs, hedges, cultivated land, and maquis. Human activities include agriculture, stock-raising, and hunting. Marble-quarrying disturbs the area.

Breeding species include *Ciconia ciconia*, *Gyps fulvus*, *Coracias garrulus*, *Hippolais olivetorum*, and *Lanius minor*. *Circaetus gallicus* and *Hieraaetus pennatus* also occur.

009 Stena Nestou (Nestos Gorge) (Kavala, Xanthi)

41°10'N, 24°45'E 5000 ha EEC SPA (Nestos Aesthetic Forest: 2380 ha)

Partly an Aesthetic Forest (2380 ha); hunting is prohibited

A deep gorge of the River Nestos with high cliffs, wooded slopes, riverine forest, and maquis. Human activities include stock-raising, and a railway runs through the area. The hunting restrictions are not enforced.

Breeding species include *Tadorna ferruginea*, *Pernis apivorus*, *Neophron percnopterus*, *Circaetus gallicus*, *Accipiter brevipes*, *Aquila pomarina*, *A. chrysaetos*, *Hieraaetus pennatus*, *Falco peregrinus*, *Bubo bubo*, *Alcedo atthis*, *Hippolais olivetorum*, and sometimes *Ciconia nigra* and *Gyps fulvus*. *Phalacrocorax pygmeus* occurs in winter.

010 Kentriki Rodopi and Kilada Nestou (Central Rodopi Mountains and Nestos Valley) (Drama)

41°20'-41°34'N, 24°20'-24°45'E 35,000 ha EEC SPA (550 ha)

Mainly unprotected, but partly a Protected Natural Monument (Virgin Forest of Central Rodopi: 550 ha)

An extensive forest on the ridge of the Rodopi Mountains between the River Nestos and the Bulgarian border, including the virgin forest of Paranestion, consisting of *Fagus* and *Pinus* forest, with *Quercus* scrub at lower altitude. Human activities include forestry, stock-raising, and hunting. The forest is heavily exploited and recently remote parts have been opened up and deforested. A huge dam and reservoir are being constructed in the Nestos Valley.

An exceptionally rich area with breeding *Ciconia nigra*, *Neophron percnopterus*, *Circaetus gallicus*, *Aquila chrysaetos*, *Hieraaetus pennatus*, *H. fasciatus*, *Falco peregrinus*, *Bonasa bonasia*, *Tetrao urogallus* (one of the very few places in Greece with these two Tetraonidae), *Bubo bubo*, *Aegolius funereus*, *Picus canus*, *Dryocopus martius*, *Dendrocopos medius*, *D. leucotos*, *Picoides tridactylus*, *Ficedula parva*, and possibly *Gypaetus barbatus* and *Gyps fulvus*.

011 Kouskouras Oros (Mount Kouskouras) (Serres)

41°12'N, 23°36'E 6000 ha

Unprotected

The western part of Mount Menikio, with sparsely forested ravines and valleys and *Pinus nigra* at high altitude. Mainly used for grazing.

Important because of its colony of *Gyps fulvus*. Other breeding species include *Neophron percnopterus*, *Aquila chrysaetos*, *Hieraaetus pennatus*, and possibly *Tetrao urogallus*.

012 Limni Kerkini (Lake Kerkini) (Serres)

41°12'N, 23°09'E 12,000 ha

Partly a Ramsar Site (9000 ha; boundaries not yet precisely defined)

Hunting prohibited; restrictions on tree-felling, egg-collecting, reclamation, waste-disposal, commercial fishing, and housing

A freshwater reservoir used for irrigation and flood control, fed by the River Strymonas. Originally a marshy oxbow lake, which was dammed in the 1950s. There are still large marshy areas to the north of the lake and there is extensive floating vegetation. Surrounded by agricultural land, some *Populus* plantations, and hills covered by deciduous forests. Human activities include agriculture, forestry, fishing, and hunting (in places), and there are several towns and villages near the lake. In 1982, the water-level was raised by 4-8 m, which had a serious impact on the shallow marshes and their nesting bird populations (these are now beginning to recover). Dredging and further expansion of deep water may be necessary because of on-going siltation. Negative ecological changes may also result from proposed water-sports development.

One of the most important wetlands in Greece for nesting aquatic birds. Breeding species include *Tachybaptus ruficollis* (240+ pairs), *Podiceps cristatus* (120+ pairs), *Phalacrocorax carbo sinensis* (140 pairs), *P. pygmeus* (50 pairs), *Ixobrychus minutus* (30 pairs), *Nycticorax nycticorax* (100 pairs), *Ardeola ralloides* (85 pairs), *Egretta garzetta* (170+ pairs), *Ardea cinerea* (156 pairs), *A. purpurea* (35 pairs), *Ciconia ciconia* (200 pairs) *Plegadis falcinellus* (40 pairs), *Platalea leucorodia* (30 pairs), *Anser anser* (20+ pairs), *Aythya nyroca* (20 pairs), *Himantopus himantopus* (60 pairs), *Sterna hirundo* (20 pairs), *Chlidonias hybridus* (400 pairs), and *C. niger* (50 pairs). Birds of prey such as *Milvus migrans*, *Circaetus gallicus*, *Accipiter brevipes*, *Aquila pomarina*, and *Hieraaetus pennatus* breed in the nearby forests. Large numbers of *Podiceps cristatus*, *Pelecanus onocrotalus* (100+), *Ardeola ralloides* (1500), *Egretta garzetta* (3500), *Ciconia nigra* (max. 30), *Recurvirostra avosetta* (2900), *Philomachus pugnax* (5000+), and *Limosa limosa* (8000) occur on passage; and in winter, waterfowl occurring (mainly Jan. counts) include *Phalacrocorax carbo sinensis* (2400), *P. pygmeus* (3000), *Pelecanus crispus* (600), *Egretta alba* (1100), *Anser albifrons* (300+), *A. anser* (200+), *Anas crecca* (max. 40,000) and *A. platyrhynchos* (max. 31,000); occasionally *Anser erythropus* (26 in Jan. 1988) and *Grus grus* occur.

013 Oros Beles (Mount Beles or Kerkini) (Serres)

41°20'N, 23°04'E 9000 ha

Border zones protected (permit required); hunting restricted in some areas

A high and remote mountain chain along the border with Yugoslavia and Bulgaria, with bare tops, extensively forested slopes, ravines, and screes. A poorly studied area. *Pinus* plantations and hunting are the main threats.

Breeding species include *Ciconia nigra*, *Pernis apivorus*, *Accipiter brevipes*, *Aquila pomarina* (5 pairs), and *A. chrysaetos* (1 pair). *Haliaeetus albicilla*, *Gyps fulvus*, and *Hieraaetus fasciatus* also occur.

014 Oros Pangheo (Mount Pangheo) (Kavala)

40°55'N, 24°07'E 20,000 ha

Hunting prohibited in part of area

A mountain with extensive high pastures, inland cliffs, streams, and forests. Problems include intensive forestry and marble-quarrying. The important zones still need to be identified.

Breeding species include *Ciconia ciconia*, *Circaetus gallicus* (5-10 pairs), *Aquila chrysaetos* (2-3 pairs), *Hieraaetus pennatus*, *Falco peregrinus*, *Alectoris graeca*, *Bubo bubo*, *Coracias garrulus*, *Picus canus*, *Dryocopus martius*, *Dendrocopos medius*, *Cercotrichas galactotes*, *Hippolais olivetorum*, and *Lanius minor*.

015 Elos Artzan (Artzan Marshes) (Kilkis)

41°02'N, 22°38'E 1700 ha

Unprotected

Freshwater marshes and wet meadows resulting from the drainage of a large lake. The area includes hilly pastureland and some rock-faces. Human activities include agriculture, stock-raising, and hunting. Immediately threatened by complete drainage.

Breeding species include *Ixobrychus minutus* (10-20 pairs), *Ardea purpurea* (max. 5 pairs), *Ciconia ciconia* (40 pairs; also 400 in late summer), *Circaetus gallicus* (1 pair), *Circus aeruginosus* (3 pairs), and *Sterna hirundo* (20 pairs). A very important feeding area for passage migrants including *Pelecanus onocrotalus* (50+), *P. crispus* (50+), *Egretta garzetta* (100), and *Plegadis falcinellus* (30+). *Egretta alba* (20) occurs in winter.

016 Ekvoli Strymona (Strymon Delta) (Serres, Kavala)

40°47'N, 23°49'E 1500 ha

Unprotected

The intact delta of the River Strymon with a large shallow lagoon surrounded by saltmarsh and *Tamarix* scrub. There are also reed marshes along the river, sandy beaches, and coastal heathland. Threatened by industrial development.

Breeding species include *Ciconia ciconia*, *Circus aeruginosus*, *Himantopus himantopus* (4-10 pairs), *Burhinus oedicnemus*, *Glareola pratincola* (15 pairs), *Sterna hirundo* (60 pairs), *S. albifrons* (100 pairs), *Alcedo atthis*, *Melanocorypha calandra*, and *Lanius minor*. Important for passage migrants, particularly waders and gulls. Visitors have included *Phoenicopterus ruber*. Winter visitors include *Egretta alba*, *Haliaeetus albicilla*, and *Circus cyaneus*.

017 Kroussia Ori (Mount Kroussia or Mavrovouni) (Serres)

41°10'N, 23°09'E 10,000 ha

Unprotected

Forested hills bordering the Strymon valley and Kerkini Lake (the marshes are an important feeding area for birds of prey). The forests are mainly *Fagus* at high altitudes, with *Quercus* and scrub at lower levels. Seriously threatened by forestry and hunting.

Breeding species include *Ciconia nigra*, *Pernis apivorus*, *Milvus migrans*, *Neophron percnopterus*, *Accipiter brevipes* (10+ pairs), *Aquila pomarina* (4 pairs), *Aquila chrysaetos* (1 pair), *Hieraaetus pennatus*, *Dryocopus martius*, *Dendrocopos medius*, *Hippolais olivetorum*, and *Lanius minor*. *Aquila heliaca* also occurs.

018 Axios Potamos (River Axios) (Kilkis, Thessaloniki)

40°36'-40°58'N, 22°35'-22°42'E 8500 ha

Unprotected

The River Axios, with strips and islands of riverine forest and pasture, and extensive zones of grazed *Tamarix* scrub. Large sandbanks exposed in spring and summer provide nesting habitat for waders and terns. Human activities include forestry, stock-raising, fishing, hunting, and sand extraction. The heronry is easily disturbed by cattle and visitors, and in 1988 it was completely destroyed by local people.

Breeding species include (although see comments above) *Phalacrocorax pygmeus*, *Nycticorax nycticorax* (300 pairs), *Ardeola ralloides* (93 pairs), *Egretta garzetta* (254 pairs), *E. alba* (2 pairs), *Ardea purpurea* (15 pairs), *Plegadis falcinellus* (30 pairs), *Pernis apivorus*, *Milvus migrans*, *Burhinus oedicnemus*, *Glareola pratincola* and *Sterna hirundo/S. albifrons* (several small colonies). In addition, *Larus melanocephalus* (800) feeds at the site/occurs on passage, and *Phalacrocorax pygmeus* (100+) and *Egretta alba* (50+) occur in winter.

019 Ekvoles Axiou, Loudias, and Aliakmonas (Axios, Loudias, and Aliakmon Estuaries) (Thessaloniki, Imathia, Pieria)

40°30'N, 22°43'E 26,500 ha

Partly a Ramsar Site (11,000 ha; boundaries not yet precisely defined)

Unprotected except for 4000 ha non-hunting zone and limited restrictions on industrial and fishing activities

Delta with brackish lagoons, saltmarsh, and extensive mudflats. Much of the area has been reclaimed for grazing and arable land. The whole length of the River Axios is embanked by retaining dykes. There are also rice-fields. Human activities include agriculture, fishing, and hunting; there is a major road through the area, and several nearby towns and villages. Hunting pressure is intense, and changes in the water regime upstream (e.g. construction of a dam on the River Aliakmon for irrigation) have crucially altered the freshwater and sediment supply to the delta. There are also plans for a sewage-treatment plant at the mouth of the Axios and intensification of both agriculture and fishing is planned.

The site supports some important colonies of herons, waders, and terns with *Ixobrychus minutus* (100+ pairs), *Nycticorax nycticorax* (300 pairs), *Ardeola ralloides* (100+ pairs), *Egretta garzetta* (250+ pairs), *Egretta alba* (2 pairs), *Ardea purpurea* (20 pairs), *Plegadis falcinellus*, *Platalea leucorodia*, *Accipiter brevipes*, *Himantopus himantopus* (60 pairs), *Recurvirostra avosetta* (40 pairs), *Burhinus oedicnemus*, *Glareola pratincola* (100 pairs), *Tringa totanus* (100+ pairs), *Sterna hirundo* (200+ pairs), *S. albifrons* (300+ pairs), and *Melanocorypha calandra*. Large numbers of waders (20,000-50,000) occur on passage including *Calidris ferruginea* (6000), *Philomachus pugnax* (3000), *Limosa limosa* (4000), and *Tringa erythropus* (4000); also *Numenius tenuirostris* (third most important site in Greece) and *Larus melanocephalus*. Wintering wildfowl (formerly reaching 142,000) are much reduced in numbers. Wintering species still include *Phalacrocorax pygmeus*, *Pelecanus crispus* (20+), *Haliaeetus albicilla*, and *Aquila clanga*.

020 Limnothalassa Angelochori (Angelochori Lagoon) (Thessaloniki)

40°29'N, 22°49'E 300 ha

Unprotected

A small coastal lagoon with saltmarshes, and a narrow coastal sandy beach. Human activities include a saltworks (recently expanded), hunting, and tourism.

Breeding species include *Himantopus himantopus*, *Sterna hirundo*, and *S. albifrons*. Important as a passage and feeding area for a variety of wetland species including *Platalea leucorodia* (max. 40), *Recurvirostra avosetta* (max. 150), *Larus melanocephalus* (max. 600), and *L. genei*. *Numenius tenuirostris* has been recently observed twice.

021 Limnothalassa Epanomis (Epanomi Lagoon) (Thessaloniki)

40°20'N, 22°44'E 500 ha

Hunting is prohibited; otherwise unprotected

A small coastal lagoon surrounded by saltmarsh, heathland, a sandy coastal zone, and agricultural land. Human activities include agriculture and tourism. Affected by increasing human pressure, rubbish, etc.

Breeding species include *Himantopus himantopus* (15-50 pairs), *Recurvirostra avosetta*, *Burhinus oedicnemus*, *Glareola pratincola*, *Sterna hirundo*, and *S. albifrons*. Important outside the breeding season for *Egretta garzetta*, *Circus cyaneus*, *Glareola pratincola*, *Philomachus pugnax*, *Larus melanocephalus* (max. 1000), *L. genei*, and *Gelochelidon nilotica*. *Branta ruficollis* (max. 5) has been recorded recently (Jan. 1987).

022 Limni Volvi and Limni Langada (Lake Volvi, and Lake Langada or Lake Koronia) (Thessaloniki)

40°41'N, 23°20'E 10,000 ha

Partly a Ramsar Site (2400 ha; boundaries not yet precisely defined)

Hunting prohibited

Two freshwater lakes fed by numerous creeks and rivulets and connected with each other in winter. Surrounded by arable land and hills with only very narrow marshy fringes and reedbeds. Volvi is deeper and steeper-sided (on north shore) and has relict fragments of gallery forest. Human activities include agriculture, fishing, and (illegal) hunting, and there has been recent industrialisation west of Langada. Changes to the lakes' ecological character stem from: drainage of marshy areas (likely to accelerate); fertiliser run-off; development of tourism (especially connected with water-sports and hot springs); hunting; eutrophication; and sewage effluent from Langada town.

Breeding species include *Ixobrychus minutus* (30 pairs), *Nycticorax nycticorax*, *Egretta garzetta*, *Ardea cinerea* (90 pairs), *A. purpurea*, *Ciconia ciconia* (50 pairs), *Tadorna ferruginea*, *Accipiter brevipes*, *Buteo rufinus*, *Aquila pomarina* (1 pair), *Circus aeruginosus* (3 pairs), *Hieraaetus pennatus*, *Porzana parva*, *Coracias garrulus*, and *Lanius minor*. In addition, *Pelecanus onocrotalus* (550; an important feeding area) occurs in summer and *P. crispus* (50+) occurs on passage. In winter, *Podiceps cristatus* (max. 11,000), *P. nigricollis* (100+), *Aythya ferina* (30,000), *Oxyura leucocephala* (occasional), and *Fulica atra* (20,000) occur.

023 Stena Rentinas (Rentina Gorge) (Thessaloniki)

40°40'N, 23°40'E 5000 ha

Unprotected

Rentina Gorge with cliffs and rocks surrounded by high, dense, and extremely diverse maquis. Human activities include forestry and hunting, and a major road runs through the area. Part of the area is threatened by deforestation.

An important area for birds of prey, which include *Circaetus gallicus* (3+ pairs), *Aquila chrysaetos* (1 pair), *Hieraaetus pennatus*, *Bubo bubo*, and possibly *Neophron percnopterus*. Other breeding species include *Caprimulgus europaeus* and *Hippolais olivetorum*, and perhaps *Ciconia nigra*.

024 Ori Cholomontas (Cholomon Mountains) (Chalkidiki)

40°23'N, 23°30'E 13,000 ha

Unprotected

Forested hills with some steep valleys and rocky gorges. Human activities include agriculture, forestry, stock-raising, and hunting.

An important area for breeding birds of prey, which include *Pernis apivorus*, *Gyps fulvus*, *Circaetus gallicus*, *Aquila chrysaetos*, *Falco peregrinus*, and *Bubo bubo*; *Ciconia nigra* may also breed.

025 Elos Agiou Mamantou (Agios Mamantos Marsh) (Chalkidiki)

40°14'N, 23°20'E 700 ha

Unprotected

A coastal saltmarsh with a brackish lake that dries up in summer; also coastal heathland and low dunes. Grazing and hunting are not very intensive, but the area is vulnerable to disturbance and to tourism. A remarkably intact wetland.

Breeding species include *Circus aeruginosus*, *Tadorna tadorna*, *Himantopus himantopus* (300 pairs), *Recurvirostra avosetta*, *Glareola pratincola* (100 pairs), *Sterna hirundo*, *S. albifrons*, *Burhinus oedicnemus*, *Charadrius alexandrinus*, and *Tringa totanus* (30 pairs). Also likely to be important for passage waders and other waterfowl.

026 Oros Itamos (Mount Itamos) (Chalkidiki)

40°08'N, 23°50'E 8000 ha

Unprotected, partly a non-hunting zone

Forested hills; forests with an open structure. Human activities include stock-raising.

An important area for birds of prey, which include breeding *Circaetus gallicus* (2+ pairs), *Aquila chrysaetos*, *Bubo bubo*, and possibly *Hieraaetus pennatus* and *Falco peregrinus*. *Pernis apivorus*, *Milvus migrans*, *Falco naumanni*, and *F. vespertinus* occur on passage.

027 Oros Athos (Mount Athos) (Chalkidiki)

40°10'N, 24°24'E 12,000 ha

Unprotected; access is controlled

A rugged forested mountain with a bare peak and many gorges.

Breeding species include *Ciconia nigra*, *Circaetus gallicus*, *Aquila chrysaetos*, *Tetrao urogallus*, and *Bubo bubo*.

028 Oros Tzena (Mount Tzena) (Pella)

41°10'N, 22°08'E 5000 ha

No protection except for a military-controlled border zone

A mountain on the border with Yugoslavia with rugged ravines, cliffs, and mountain streams. The main vegetation comprises forests of *Fagus* and of *Pinus*, with bare zones on the upper and lower slopes. Not exploited until recently. Road construction has allowed access for hunting.

Breeding species include *Gypaetus barbatus*, *Circaetus gallicus*, *Aquila chrysaetos*, *Hieraaetus pennatus*, *Falco peregrinus*, *Coracias garrulus*, *Dendrocopos medius*, *D. leucotos*, and *Lanius minor*.

029 Oros Voras (Mount Voras) including Kaimaktsalan and Pinovo (Pella, Florina)

40°55'N, 21°56'E 43,000 ha

Unprotected

A large secluded mountainous area with extensive *Fagus* forest, only recently opened up. The key areas for conservation have still to be identified.

Important for large birds of prey, including vultures. Breeding species include *Neophron percnopterus*, *Circaetus gallicus*, *Aquila chrysaetos*, *Alectoris graeca*, *Dryocopus martius*, *Dendrocopos medius*, and *D. leucotos*. *Gypaetus barbatus* and *Aquila heliaca* also occur.

030 Stena Apsalou and Moglenitsas (Apsalos and Moglenitsa Gorges) (Pella)

40°50'N, 22°10'E 6000 ha

Unprotected

Two gorges and pasture land with *Paliurus* scrub and *Platanus* trees. The River Moglenitsa flows strongly throughout the year. Human activities include agriculture, stock-raising, and hunting.

An important area for birds of prey with breeding *Neophron percnopterus* (2 pairs), *Circaetus gallicus*, and *Falco peregrinus*. Other breeding species include *Coracias garrulus*, *Hippolais olivetorum*, and *Lanius minor*.

031 Limni Agra (Lake Agras) (Pella)

40°47'N, 21°54'E 1300 ha

Hunting prohibited in part of area

An artificial freshwater lake, largely overgrown with emergent vegetation and bordered to the north by cliffs. Surrounded by groves, hedges, and small pastures. Human activities include agriculture, stock-raising, and hunting. Threatened by plans to drain the lake and reclaim the marshes.

Breeding species include *Ixobrychus minutus* (20-30 pairs), *Ardea purpurea* (5-10 pairs), *Ciconia ciconia*, *Aythya nyroca*, *Neophron percnopterus* (1-2 pairs), *Circaetus gallicus* (1 pair), *Alectoris graeca*, *Chlidonias hybridus* (15-20 pairs; one of just a few sites in Greece), *Alcedo atthis*, *Hippolais olivetorum*, and possibly *Chlidonias niger*. Important for migrating waterbirds and birds of prey (including *Buteo rufinus* and *Falco biarmicus*), and also *Grus grus*.

032 Limni Mikri Prespa and Limni Megali Prespa (Lake Mikri Prespa and Lake Megali Prespa) (Florina)

40°45'N, 21°06'E 30,000 ha

Partly a Ramsar Site (8000 ha); EEC SPA (19,470 ha)

Partly a National Park (19,470 ha) with hunting prohibited and restrictions on agriculture, reed-cutting and fishing.

Two large mountain-basin lakes, separated by a narrow strip of land and surrounded by mountains; Limni Mikri Prespa is shared with Albania, Limni Megali Prespa is shared with Albania and Yugoslavia. Mikri Prespa has extensive shallow zones with areas of reedbed and aquatic vegetation, wet meadows, wet woodland, pasture, and agricultural land. The main human activities are agriculture, fishing, and hunting. In 1983 the Greek Government started a pilot development project financed by the EEC aimed at the improvement of agriculture, fish-farming, and road networks. Serious ecological damage resulted, which included felling of remnant gallery forest, dredging of canals previously rich in aquatic vegetation, construction of a fish-farm at a key feeding area for herons, and pollution of the lake from fish-farm effluent.

The only site in Europe (outside the Danube Delta and USSR) where both *Pelecanus onocrotalus* and *P. crispus* breed. In 1984, populations were 116 and 165 pairs respectively and numbers have been relatively stable during the last ten years. Ardeidae populations have fluctuated (some species have declined) and include *Ixobrychus minutus* (50-100 pairs), *Ardeola ralloides* (50-100 pairs), *Egretta garzetta* (less than 100 pairs), *E. alba* (less than 10 pairs), and *Ardea purpurea* (*c.*20 pairs). *Plegadis falcinellus* has ceased breeding. Other breeding species include *Phalacrocorax carbo sinensis* (*c.*450 pairs), *P. pygmeus* (150-200 pairs), *Platalea leucorodia* (5 pairs; formerly max. 200 pairs), *Anser anser* (max. 170 pairs; the main breeding site in Greece), *Aythya nyroca* (10 pairs), *Mergus merganser* (a small population; the southernmost in Europe and only site in Greece), *Neophron percnopterus*, *Circaetus gallicus* (2 pairs), *Circus aeruginosus*, *Aquila chrysaetos* (2 pairs), *Bonasa bonasia* (one of the very few sites for this species in Greece), *Alectoris graeca*, *Chlidonias hybridus*, *Alcedo atthis*, *Dendrocopos medius*, and *Lanius minor*. *Haliaeetus albicilla* possibly still breeds. In winter the lake is usually frozen although several thousand diving ducks have been recorded.

033 Limni Vegoritis and Limni Petron (Lake Vegoritis and Lake Petron) (Pella, Florina, Kozani)

40°45'N, 21°40'E 17,000 ha

Unprotected

Two freshwater lakes between bare mountains. Human activities include agriculture, pisciculture, stock-raising, fishing, and hunting, and there is scattered human habitation. Lake Vegoritis is increasingly affected by industrial pollution and sewage from nearby towns. There are plans for tourist development, which may also have a negative impact on the site. A heronry at Lake Petron with breeding *Nycticorax nycticorax*, *Ardeola ralloides*, *Egretta garzetta*, and *Plegadis falcinellus* still exists, but numbers of nesting birds have seriously declined.

Breeding species include *Ixobrychus minutus* (40 pairs), *Ardea purpurea* (5 pairs), *Phalacrocorax pygmeus* (c.10 pairs), *Neophron percnopterus*, *Circaetus gallicus*, *Circus aeruginosus*, *C. pygargus* (1-3 pairs), *Buteo rufinus* (2+ pairs), *Aquila chrysaetos* (1 pair), and *Sterna hirundo* (5-8 pairs). *Haliaeetus albicilla* also occurs. Wintering waterfowl have included *Podiceps cristatus* (3500), *Netta rufina* (max. 150), and *Fulica atra* (23,000).

034 Limni Kheimaditis and Limni Zazaris (Lake Kheimaditis and Lake Zazaris) (Florina)

40°30'N, 21°35'E 9900 ha

Hunting prohibited

A diversified landscape with woodland and cultivated land around two shallow lakes; Lake Kheimaditis has extensive *Typha* marshes and little open water. Human activities include agriculture, forestry, stock-raising, fishing, and hunting, and there is scattered human habitation. Kheimaditis may be threatened in the near future by drainage. Forest clearance is badly affecting the birds of prey. A priority site for wetland conservation in Greece.

Breeding species include *Ixobrychus minutus* (20 pairs), *Ciconia ciconia* (30 pairs), *Aythya nyroca* (60 pairs; the largest population in Greece), *Pernis apivorus*, *Neophron percnopterus* (2 pairs), *Circus aeruginosus* (3 pairs), *C. pygargus* (1-5 pairs; one of only two nesting sites in Greece), *Accipiter brevipes*, *Buteo rufinus* (1 pair), *Aquila pomarina* (2 pairs), *A. chrysaetos* (1 pair), *Chlidonias hybridus* (50 pairs), *C. niger* (5 pairs), *Alcedo atthis*, *Coracias garrulus*, and *Lanius minor*. *Pelecanus onocrotalus* (75), *P. crispus* (12-20), *Haliaeetus albicilla* (2), and *Gallinago media* also occur; an important feeding site for *Pelecanus* spp.

035 Limni Kastorias (Limni Orestiada) (Lake Kastoria or Orestiada) (Kastoria)

40°30'N, 21°18'E 4000 ha

Unprotected, but hunting is prohibited

A freshwater lake amongst partly forested hills, with wet meadows, reedbeds and marshes, alluvial forest, and hedges. There is intensive agriculture, also plantations of *Populus* at the edge of the lake. Seriously affected by pollution from the city of Kastoria, which is on the lake shore.

Breeding species include *Ixobrychus minutus* (40+ pairs), *Nycticorax nycticorax* (c.60 pairs), *Ardea purpurea*, *Ciconia ciconia*, *Aythya nyroca* (10-30 pairs; one of the best sites in Greece), *Circaetus gallicus*, *Aquila chrysaetos*, *Sterna hirundo*, *Alcedo atthis*, and possibly *Hippolais olivetorum*. *Pelecanus onocrotalus* and *P. crispus* regularly occur and wintering species include *Phalacrocorax carbo sinensis* (500 in Jan. 1987) and *Haliaeetus albicilla*.

036 Oros Gramos (Mount Gramos) (Kastoria, Ioannina)

40°20'N, 20°50'E 27,000 ha

Unprotected

A mountain range on the Albanian border, with rugged valleys, extensive *Fagus* and *Pinus* forests, and grazing pasture at higher altitude. Human activities include forestry, hunting, and stock-raising, and there is scattered human habitation.

Breeding species include *Pernis apivorus*, *Neophron percnopterus*, *Gyps fulvus*, *Circaetus gallicus*, *Aquila chrysaetos*, *Alectoris graeca*, *Picus canus*, *Dendrocopos medius*, *Ficedula semitorquata*, *Pyrrhocorax pyrrhocorax*, and possibly *Bonasa bonasia*, *Tetrao urogallus*, and *Aegolius funereus*.

037 Oros Vourinos (Mount Vourinos) (Kozani, Grevena)

40°12'N, 21°40'E 13,000 ha

Hunting prohibited

A secluded forest in a high enclosed valley in a large bare-mountain area extensively used as pasture. Increased exploitation of the forests is imminent.

Breeding species include *Buteo rufinus*, *Aquila chrysaetos*, *Alectoris graeca*, and *Lanius minor* (30 pairs). *Neophron percnopterus*, *Gyps fulvus*, and *Dendrocopos leucotos* also occur.

038 Stena Aliakmona (Aliakmon Gorge) (Imathia)

40°25'N, 22°14'E 3000 ha

Unprotected

The gorge of the River Aliakmonas. Human activities include stock-raising and hunting. Highly threatened by quarrying and construction works.

Breeding species include *Pernis apivorus*, *Neophron percnopterus*, *Circaetus gallicus*, *Buteo rufinus*, *Hieraaetus pennatus* (1 pair), *Alectoris graeca*, *Sterna hirundo*, and *Coracias garrulus*.

039 Limnothalassa Alyki Kitros (Alyki Lagoon near Kitros) (Pieria)

40°22'N, 22°40'E 1500 ha

Hunting prohibited

A coastal lagoon with islands and extensive saltmarshes enclosed by a coastal zone of sand-dunes and heathland. Part of the lagoon is a complex of saltpans. Human activities include stock-raising, and salt extraction. Seriously threatened by the construction of holiday homes and by an access road.

The most important gull colony in Greece with *Larus melanocephalus* (3000-7000 birds; the largest colony in Europe outside the USSR) and *L. genei* (23 pairs in 1985; the only colony in Greece). Other breeding species include *Ixobrychus minutus* (5 pairs), *Himantopus himantopus* (20 pairs), *Recurvirostra avosetta* (10-50 pairs), *Burhinus oedicnemus* (10-15 pairs), *Glareola pratincola* (100 pairs), *Gelochelidon nilotica* (30-35 pairs), *Sterna hirundo* (30-60 pairs), *S. albifrons* (80+ pairs), *Alcedo atthis*, *Melanocorypha calandra*, *Cercotrichas galactotes*, and *Lanius minor*. A considerable variety of species occur on passage including *Egretta garzetta* (100+), *Platalea leucorodia*, *Phoenicopterus ruber*, *Recurvirostra avosetta*, and *Sterna caspia*. In winter *Egretta alba* (20), *Haliaeetus albicilla*, *Aquila clanga*, and *Falco peregrinus* occur.

040 Oros Olympos (Mount Olympos) (Pieria, Larisa)

40°05'N, 22°20'E 39,000 ha Biosphere Reserve (4000 ha); EEC SPA (4000 ha)

Partly a National Park (core zone: 4000 ha, covering the eastern part of the mountain)

The highest mountain in Greece with rugged peaks and cliffs and well-forested slopes. Human activities include agriculture, forestry, stock-farming, hunting, and recreation, and there is scattered human habitation. The forests at lower altitudes are unprotected and heavily exploited. There are also plans for the construction of roads and ski/tourist resorts, which would threaten the area. Supports many rare and endemic plants and a rare herpetofauna.

An important area for raptors; breeding species include, or probably include, *Pernis apivorus*, *Gypaetus barbatus*, *Neophron percnopterus*, *Aegypius monachus* (with up to 7 birds resident), *Circaetus gallicus*, *Accipiter brevipes*, *Aquila chrysaetos* (3-4 pairs), *Hieraaetus pennatus* (5+ pairs), *Falco biarmicus*, and *F. peregrinus*. *Gyps fulvus* (max. 35 in winter) and *Falco eleonorae* also occur. Other breeding species include *Ciconia ciconia*, *Alectoris graeca*, *Bubo bubo*, *Aegolius funereus*, *Coracias garrulus*, *Picus canus*, *Dryocopus martius*, *Dendrocopos medius*, *D. leucotos*, and *Picoides tridactylus*.

041 Area of Oriokastrou, Delvinakiou and Meropis, and Kilada Gormou (Gormos Valley) (Ioannina)

39°56'N, 20°30'E 2000 ha

Unprotected

The vicinity of Oriokastro, Delvinaki Lake, Meropi Forest and valley of the River Gormos. Habitats include *Quercus* forest with mature trees and small ravines in hilly country. Human activities include agriculture, forestry and stock-raising, and there is scattered human habitation. Problems include the cutting of old trees, and the Gormos Valley north of Parakalamos has recently been subject to a drainage scheme.

Breeding species include *Pernis apivorus*, *Neophron percnopterus*, *Accipiter brevipes*, *Aquila pomarina*, *A. chrysaetos*, *Hieraaetus pennatus*, and *Dendrocopos medius*.

042 Oros Timfi (Gamila) and Oros Smolikas (Mount Timfi or Gamila, and Mount Smolikas) (Ioannina)

40°02'N, 20°50'E 60,000 ha

Partly a National Park (Vikos/Aoos: 12,600 ha; core zone: 3400 ha)

A large and remote mountain range, broken by the River Aoos and River Voidomatis, with extensive forests, rugged peaks and cliffs. Human activities include agriculture, forestry, stock-raising, fishing, hunting, and recreation, and there is scattered human habitation. There are plans to build skiing facilities and roads in Vikos/Aoos National Park, which would be detrimental to this wilderness area.

Breeding species include *Ciconia ciconia*, *Pernis apivorus* (1-5 pairs), *Gypaetus barbatus* (1 pair), *Neophron percnopterus* (10+ pairs), *Circaetus gallicus* (4-10 pairs), *Aquila chrysaetos* (1-4 pairs), *Hieraaetus pennatus*, *Falco biarmicus* (1 pair), *F. peregrinus*, *Alcedo atthis*, *Dryocopus martius*, *Dendrocopos medius*, *D. leucotos*, and *Pyrrhocorax pyrrhocorax*. *Gyps fulvus* (max. 20) is also present.

043 Central part of Zagori (Ioannina)

39°50'N, 20°54'E 20,000 ha

Unprotected

A mosaic of *Quercus*-forested hills, pastures, fields, streams, and small villages. In need of protection from forestry (clear-felling) and shooting.

Breeding species include *Ciconia nigra*, *Pernis apivorus*, *Neophron percnopterus*, *Circaetus gallicus*, *Aquila chrysaetos*, *Dendrocopos medius*, and *Alcedo atthis*.

044 Valia Kalda (Pindos National Park) (Grevena, Ioannina)

39°54'N, 21°06'E 8000 ha EEC SPA (3360 ha)

National Park (6930 ha; core zone: 3390 ha)

A representative part of the Pindos Mountains including Valia Kalda or Pindos National Park, with bare peaks, rocky ridges, and valleys with streams. Densely forested with *Pinus nigra* and *Fagus sylvatica*. There has been much destruction in recent years with the construction of dams, roads, and a hydroelectric plant.

Important for birds of prey including *Neophron percnopterus*, *Gyps fulvus*, *Aquila heliaca* (on passage), *A. chrysaetos*, and *Falco biarmicus*, and for eight woodpecker species including *Dendrocopos medius* and *Picoides tridactylus*.

045 Antikhassia Ori (Antikhassia Mountains) and Meteora (Trikala)

39°48'N, 21°35'E 14,000 ha

Unprotected

Forested hills with spectacular protruding rocks (Meteora) and a river valley with old *Platanus orientalis* forest. Human activities include agriculture, forestry, stock-raising, hunting, and recreation, and there are villages in the area. The *Platanus orientalis* forest is being cut, and there is a need for a safe, artificial feeding site for the vultures.

An exceptionally diverse area, particularly rich in birds of prey. Breeding species include *Ciconia nigra* (2 pairs), *Pernis apivorus*, *Milvus migrans* (10+ pairs), *Neophron percnopterus* (50 pairs; the largest population in Greece, but declining), *Circaetus gallicus* (5+ pairs), *Accipiter brevipes*, *Aquila pomarina* (1 pair), *Hieraaetus pennatus* (3-5 pairs), *Alectoris graeca*, *Bubo bubo*, *Alcedo atthis*, *Coracias garrulus* (10 pairs), and *Dendrocopos medius*.

046 Kerketio Ori (Kerketion Mountains) (Koziakas) (Trikala)

39°35'N, 21°32'E 23,000 ha

There is a controlled hunting area

A partly forested mountain area with many bare and rocky ridges. Human activities include agriculture, forestry, stock-raising, and hunting, and there is scattered human habitation.

An important area for large birds of prey, especially vultures. Breeding species include *Neophron percnopterus*, *Gyps fulvus*, and *Aquila chrysaetos*.

047 Stena Kalamakiou (Kalamaki Gorge) (Larisa)

39°40'N, 22°15'E 1000 ha

Unprotected

A gorge of the River Pinios, with cliffs and riverine woodland, cutting through bare hills. Human activities include stock-raising and hunting.

An important area for birds of prey. Breeding species include *Neophron percnopterus* and *Coracias garrulus*. *Gyps fulvus*, *Buteo rufinus*, and *Aquila chrysaetos* also occur.

048 Kato Olympos/Tembi/Ossa/Delta Piniou (Larisa)

39°55'N, 22°25'E 82,000 ha

Two EEC SPAs (Tembi Valley: 1762 ha; Ossa: 16,900 ha)

Partly a controlled hunting area (Ossa); Aesthetic Forests (Tempi Valley: 1762 ha; Ossa: 16,900 ha)

A large area comprising the foothills of Mount Olympos, Mount Ossa (Kissavos), the Tembi Valley and the delta of the River Pinios. Habitats include extensive pastures, wild and cultivated *Olea* groves, extensive *Abies* and *Fagus* forests, and rugged ravines with old *Castanea* forests (eastern slopes of Mount Ossa). The Pinios Delta has coastal and riverine forests, sandy heathland, and dunes. The riverine forests are subject to uncontrolled cutting, water extraction, and reclamation, and in 1987 there was considerable illegal reclamation of forests and dunes for tourism. A feeding site for vultures has been operating since 1987.

Breeding species include *Ixobrychus minutus*, *Nycticorax nycticorax* (10 pairs), *Ciconia nigra* (1 pair), *C. ciconia* (30+ pairs), *Pernis apivorus*, *Neophron percnopterus* (6-10 pairs), *Gyps fulvus* (10 pairs), *Circaetus gallicus* (6 pairs), *Aquila pomarina* (3 pairs), *A. chrysaetos* (2 pairs), *Hieraaetus pennatus* (4 pairs), *Falco biarmicus*, *F. peregrinus* (2 pairs), *Alectoris graeca*, *Burhinus oedicnemus*, *Bubo bubo*, *Alcedo atthis*, and *Ficedula semitorquata*. Other visitors include *Gypaetus barbatus*, *Aegypius monachus*, *Pandion haliaetus*, and *Falco eleonorae* (max. 200 in summer).

049 Ori Mavrovouni (Mavrovouni Mountains) (Larisa, Magnisia)

39°35'N, 22°49'E 17,000 ha

Unprotected

Forested hills with grazing pastures (creating an open-forest structure), ravines with cliffs, and dense maquis on the seaward side. Human activities include forestry, stock-raising, and hunting, and there is scattered human habitation.

An important area for birds of prey including summering *Falco eleonorae*. Breeding species include *Pernis apivorus* (5+ pairs), *Neophron percnopterus*, *Circaetus gallicus*, *Accipiter brevipes*, *Buteo rufinus* (2+ pairs), *Aquila pomarina*, *Hieraaetus pennatus*, *Falco peregrinus* (2 pairs), *Coracias garrulus*, and *Dendrocopos medius*.

050 Stena Kalama (Kalamas Gorge) (Thesprotia)

39°35'N, 20°14'E 2800 ha

Unprotected

The River Kalamas gorge, with alluvial forest and bushes, and sparsely vegetated cliffs. Human activities include stock-raising and hunting.

Important area for large birds of prey including a colony of *Gyps fulvus*. Breeding species include *Neophron percnopterus*, *Gyps fulvus*, *Circaetus gallicus*, *Aquila chrysaetos*, *Falco naumanni* (in nearby villages), *Alectoris graeca*, *Alcedo atthis*, and *Hippolais olivetorum*.

051 Ekvoles Kalama (Kalamas Estuary) (Thesprotia)

39°32'N, 20°05'E 7000 ha

Hunting prohibited

The River Kalamas estuary comprising a canal with a delta of mudflats and saltmarshes; and an old riverbed, cut off from the sea, with large lagoons and some riverine woodland. The delta includes two hills, with some dense scrub and forest. Much of the area has been reclaimed for arable farming. Now seriously threatened by plans to pump sewage from the town of Ioannina, which would cause pollution of the river and delta.

Breeding species include *Egretta garzetta* (possibly), *Ciconia ciconia*, *Circaetus gallicus*, *Aquila pomarina*, *A. chrysaetos*, *Himantopus himantopus*, *Burhinus oedicnemus*, *Glareola pratincola*, *Sterna hirundo* (30+ pairs), *S. albifrons* (30+ pairs), *Alcedo atthis*, *Calandrella brachydactyla*, and *Hippolais olivetorum*. Passage species include *Plegadis falcinellus* and *Platalea leucorodia* (which may breed), and wintering species include *Pelecanus crispus*, *Phalacrocorax pygmeus* (100+), *Egretta alba*, *Platalea leucorodia*, *Haliaeetus albicilla*, *Circus cyaneus*, *Aquila clanga* (8), *A. heliaca*, and *Larus genei* (250).

052 Limni Limnopoula (Lake Limnopoula) (Thesprotia)

39°28'N, 20°25'E 600 ha

Unprotected

A freshwater lake, which dries out in summer, and permanently wet meadows fed by springs. Human activities include agriculture, stock-raising, hunting, and there is scattered human habitation. There has been recent reclamation of the wet meadows for arable farming, and regulation of water may destroy the site.

Breeding species include *Ciconia ciconia* (20+ pairs), *Circaetus gallicus*, *Aquila pomarina* (2 pairs), and *Hieraaetus pennatus* (1 pair).

053 Ekvoli and Stena Acherondos (Acheron Gorge and Delta) (Preveza, Thesprotia)

39°15'N, 20°30'E 3500 ha

Unprotected

A river delta with brackish marshes, *Tamarix* scrub, sandy heathland and scrub-covered hills at the coast. Inland, the area is largely cultivated, but there is a narrow gorge. Human activities include agriculture, stock-raising, fishing, and hunting, and there is scattered human habitation. The delta is subject to heavy shooting pressure. Currently seriously threatened by complete drainage and tourist development.

Breeding species include *Ciconia ciconia*, *Pernis apivorus*, *Neophron percnopterus* (2 pairs), *Circaetus gallicus*, *Aquila chrysaetos*, *Hieraaetus fasciatus*, *Alectoris graeca*, and *Bubo bubo* (1 pair). *Gyps fulvus* also occurs (max. 6).

054 Vouna Zalongou (Zalongos Mountains) (Preveza)

39°08'N, 20°40'E 2100 ha

Partly a Protected Natural Monument

A small mountain with forests and agricultural land. Human activities include agriculture, forestry, stock-raising, hunting, and recreation, and there is scattered human habitation.

An important area for raptors that feed in the adjacent Amvrakikos wetlands. Breeding species include *Neophron percnopterus*, *Gyps fulvus* (*c.*10 pairs), *Hieraaetus pennatus*, and *Hippolais olivetorum*, and possibly *Accipiter brevipes*. *Hieraaetus fasciatus* also occurs.

055 Amvrakikos Kolpos (Gulf of Amvrakia or Arta) (Preveza, Arta, Aitoloakarnania)

39°00'N, 21°00'E *c.*52,000 ha

Partly a Ramsar Site (25,000 ha; not yet legally defined)

Unprotected except for limited non-hunting zones and some restriction of development

An extensive complex of brackish lagoons, sandy coastal strips, saltmarsh, reedbeds, and mudflats, which has been formed on the northern side of Amvrakikos Gulf by the deltas of the Rivers Louros and Arachtos. The topography is dominated by three rocky hills between the lagoons, and the area is surrounded by hills to the north and east. The upper reaches of the delta are under cultivation, but there are still extensive areas of natural vegetation, including remnant gallery forest and the largest reedbed in Greece. The lagoons are all used as fisheries and other human activities include agriculture, hunting, and tourism. Plans for intensive pisciculture in core areas are progressing quickly, immediately threatening important patches of valuable bird habitat.

One of the most intact European wetlands, particularly important for breeding *Pelecanus crispus* (34 pairs in 1988). Other breeding species include *Ixobrychus minutus* (50+ pairs), *Nycticorax nycticorax* (70+ pairs), *Ardeola ralloides* (120 pairs), *Egretta garzetta* (250+ pairs), *Ardea purpurea* (20+ pairs), *Ciconia ciconia* (80 pairs), *Plegadis falcinellus*, *Platalea leucorodia*, *Aythya nyroca* (100+ pairs), *Circaetus gallicus*, *Circus aeruginosus* (5+ pairs), *Aquila pomarina*, *A. chrysaetos*, *Hieraaetus pennatus*, *Alectoris graeca*, *Himantopus himantopus* (300+ pairs), *Burhinus oedicnemus* (30 pairs), *Glareola pratincola* (150+ pairs), *Sterna sandvicensis* (30 pairs), *S. hirundo*/*S. albifrons* (1000+ pairs), *Chlidonias niger*, *Bubo bubo*, *Alcedo atthis*, *Coracias garrulus*, *Cercotrichas galactotes*, *Hippolais olivetorum*, and *Ficedula semitorquata*. Passage species include *Egretta alba*, *Plegadis falcinellus*, *Platalea leucorodia*, and *Pandion haliaetus*; *Numenius tenuirostris* has recently been recorded on passage. The site holds the largest concentration of wintering waterfowl in Greece with an av. Jan. max. of 145,000 Anatidae and *Fulica atra*. The commonest species in Jan. are *Anas penelope* (av. max. 40,000), *A. crecca* (av. max. 15,300), *A. acuta* (15,500), *Aythya ferina* (18,400), and *Fulica atra* (19,500). Other wintering species include *Pelecanus onocrotalus*, *Egretta alba*, *Circus cyaneus*, *Aquila clanga* (10), and *Larus genei*.

056 Ori Athamanon (Athamanika Mountains) (Arta, Ioannina, Trikala)

39°25'N, 21°10'E 70,000 ha

Unprotected

One of the largest and remotest mountains of the southern Pindos with forested slopes, many streams, and extensive bare areas. Human activities include agriculture, forestry, stock-raising, and hunting, and there is scattered human habitation. A poorly studied area.

An important area for vultures. Breeding species include *Neophron percnopterus*, *Gyps fulvus*, and possibly still *Gypaetus barbatus*. Other breeding species include *Dendrocopos medius* and *Pyrrhocorax pyrrhocorax*.

057 Kilada Akheloou (Achelos Valley) (Arta, Karditsa)

39°18'N, 21°25'E 4000 ha

Unprotected

A steep, partly forested ravine. Human activities include stock-raising and hunting, and there is scattered human habitation. Part of the valley will be dammed to form a water reservoir to irrigate the plains of Thessaly.

The area has a breeding colony of *Gyps fulvus*.

058 Ori Akarnanika (Akarnanian Mountains) (Aitoloakarnania)

38°45'N, 21°00'E 30,000 ha

Unprotected

A large mountain complex, partly forested with *Quercus* (lower slopes) and *Abies cephalonica*, with pastures at higher altitude. Includes a coastal section with cliffs and a small marsh. Human activities include agriculture, stock-raising, and hunting, and there is scattered human habitation.

Breeding species include *Ixobrychus minutus* (5+ pairs), *Gyps fulvus* (30-40 pairs; the largest colony on the Greek mainland), *Aquila chrysaetos* (1-2 pairs), *Falco peregrinus* (2-4 pairs), *Gelochelidon nilotica*, *Bubo bubo*, *Hippolais olivetorum*, and *Lanius minor*.

059 Kalon Oros (Mount Kalon) (Kefallinia)

38°21'N, 20°33'E 600 ha

Unprotected

Evergreen-forest hills and large cliffs.

The only important site for breeding *Gyps fulvus* in Kefallinia (Cephalonia).

060 Limnothalassa Mesolongiou and Aetolikou, Ekvoles Acheloou and Evinou (Mesolongi and Aetoliko Lagoons, and Achelos and Evinos Estuaries) (Aitoloakarnania)

38°20'N, 21°15'E 63,000 ha partly a Ramsar Site (13,900 ha)

Hunting prohibited in part of site (8000 ha); limited restrictions on industry, housing and waste-disposal

An extensive wetland complex which has been created by the Rivers Achelos and Evinos and is dominated by the lagoons of Mesolongi (one of the largest in the Mediterranean) and Aetoliko. Despite land reclamation there are still extensive areas of saltmarsh, sandbanks, and mudflats, and remnant gallery forest along the main river courses. There are rocky hills scattered between the lagoons and rocky islands offshore. Includes the large cliffs of Oros Arakinthos, which are important for breeding raptors. The lagoons are used as fisheries and salinas and the surrounding land is used for agriculture, small-scale industry, and hunting. Serious problems include land reclamation, salina and fishery expansion, the construction of dams on the River Achelos, housing and road construction, overgrazing, and intensive hunting.

Wetland species breeding include *Ixobrychus minutus*, *Ciconia ciconia*, *Himantopus himantopus* (60 pairs), *Recurvirostra avosetta* (30 pairs), *Burhinus oedicnemus* (20 pairs), *Glareola pratincola* (150-200 pairs), *Gelochelidon nilotica* (5 pairs), and *Sterna albifrons* (100 pairs). Other breeding species include *Gyps fulvus* (10 pairs), *Circaetus gallicus* (2 pairs), *Aquila pomarina*, *Bubo bubo*, *Alcedo atthis*, *Melanocorypha calandra*, *Hippolais olivetorum*, and *Lanius minor*. Important for passage herons, *Plegadis falcinellus* (120), waders including occasional *Numenius tenuirostris*, and terns. Wintering waterbirds include *Podiceps nigricollis* (1500), *Phalacrocorax carbo sinensis* (2000), *Pelecanus crispus* (80), *Egretta alba* (150-200), *Anas penelope* (15,600), *Aythya ferina* (20,000), *Fulica atra* (39,000), and *Larus genei* (1500). Also very important for wintering raptors including *Aegypius monachus*, *Circus cyaneus*, *Aquila clanga* (6), *A. heliaca* (5), and *Falco peregrinus* (5).

061 Oros Vardousia (Mount Vardousia) (Fokida)

38°42'N, 22°07'E 23,000 ha

Unprotected

A rugged mountain with large ravines and bare rock, open pastures at high altitude and *Abies cephalonica* at middle altitude. Human activities include agriculture, forestry, stock-raising, hunting, and mining. There is a threat from bauxite mining.

Breeding species include *Pernis apivorus*, *Gypaetus barbatus*, *Neophron percnopterus*, *Circaetus gallicus*, *Aquila chrysaetos*, *Falco peregrinus*, *Dryocopus martius* and *Dendrocopos leucotos*.

062 Oros Ghiona (Mount Ghiona), Kharadra Rekas (Reka Ravines), Lazorema, and Vathia Lakka (Fokida)

38°37'N, 22°15'E 5000 ha

Unprotected

A high mountain with extensive bare areas, alpine grasslands, and a 1300 m high rock-face (Plaka Cliff). Separated from Mt. Vardousia by the deep Mornos Valley. The area is overgrazed and large parts have been damaged by open-cast bauxite mining.

Important for birds of prey with breeding *Gypaetus barbatus*, *Gyps fulvus* (5+ pairs), *Circaetus gallicus*, *Aquila chrysaetos*, and *Falco peregrinus*. Also important for woodpeckers with breeding *Dryocopus martius*, *Dendrocopos medius*, and *D. leucotos*.

063 Southern and eastern part of Parnassos (Voiotia, Fokida)

38°30'N, 22°37'E 10,000 ha EEC SPA (3513 ha)

Partly a National Park (core zone: 3513 ha)

Mount Parnassos with high alpine pastures, bare rocks and scree, and impressive forests of *Abies cephalonica*. Human activities include stock-raising, hunting, recreation, and mining. Increasing human disturbance (skiing and house building), shooting, and large-scale open-cast bauxite mining are affecting the area.

Particularly important for birds of prey, woodpeckers, and alpine birds. Breeding species include *Gypaetus barbatus* (1 pair), *Gyps fulvus* (6-10 pairs), *Neophron percnopterus*, *Circaetus gallicus* (1-3 pairs), *Aquila chrysaetos* (2+ pairs), *Hieraaetus pennatus*, *Alectoris graeca*, *Dryocopus martius*, *Dendrocopos medius*, *D. leucotos*, *Sylvia rueppelli*, *Lanius minor*, and *Pyrrhocorax pyrrhocorax*.

064 Oros Iti (Mount Iti) (Fthiotida)

38°48'N, 22°15'E 13,000 ha EEC SPA (7210 ha)

National Park (Oiti: 7210 ha; core zone: 3010 ha)

Considered to be one of the best National Parks in Greece; a mountain with an open grazed plateau, forested slopes, and steep ravines down to the Sperchios Valley. Wildlife is affected by shooting and poaching.

Breeding species include *Pernis apivorus*, *Circaetus gallicus*, *Aquila chrysaetos*, *Falco peregrinus*, *Alectoris graeca*, *Bubo bubo*, *Picus canus*, *Dryocopus martius*, *Dendrocopos medius*, and *D. leucotos*. Also important for vultures which nest outside the park.

065 Delta Sperchiou (Sperchios Delta) (Fthiotida)

38°53'N, 22°31'E 2600 ha

Partly protected from hunting

An estuary with extensive saltmarshes and islets, which are important for nesting waders and terns. There is rice farming in the delta, which provides important feeding areas. One of the most important wetlands outside northern Greece.

Breeding species include *Ixobrychus minutus*, *Ciconia ciconia* (24+ pairs), *Himantopus himantopus*, *Burhinus oedicnemus*, *Glareola pratincola* (40 pairs), *Sterna hirundo*, and *S. albifrons*. Of particular importance for passage herons, *Plegadis falcinellus*, *Platalea leucorodia*, *Aythya nyroca* (max. 1500), waders, and gulls. Wintering species include *Egretta alba*, *Circus cyaneus*, *Aquila clanga*, and *Recurvirostra avosetta* (max. 1000).

066 Vouna Gouras (Mount Gouras) (Magnisia)

39°07'N, 22°35'E 7000 ha

Unprotected

A ravine area of the western Othrys Mountains including pasture and open forest. Human activities include forestry, stock-raising, and hunting.

Holds an important colony of *Gyps fulvus* (5+ pairs). Other breeding species include *Neophron percnopterus* and *Circaetus gallicus*.

067 Ormos Sourpis (Sourpis Bay) (Magnisia)

39°10'N, 22°50'E 1100 ha

Unprotected

A coastal marsh with reeds, *Salix* and *Tamarix* scrub, and riverine woodland of *Platanus orientalis*. Human activities include agriculture, stock-raising, hunting, and some industry. Threatened by industrial activity and related pollution. There is also heavy hunting pressure.

Breeding species include *Ixobrychus minutus* and *Cercotrichas galactotes*, and possibly *Botaurus stellaris*. Important for migratory herons, ibises, and other waterbirds.

068 Pilion Oros (Mount Pilion) (Magnisia)

39°26'N, 23°03'E 10,000 ha

Protection status uncertain

The higher parts of a large forested mountain chain, with dense maquis and evergreen woods at lower altitudes (north slopes facing the sea), and *Fagus* and *Abies* forest at higher levels.

Breeding species include *Pernis apivorus*, *Circaetus gallicus*, *Hieraaetus pennatus*, and *Dendrocopos medius*. *Neophron percnopterus*, *Buteo rufinus*, *Aquila chrysaetos*, *Falco eleonorae*, *Dendrocopos leucotos*, and *Ficedula semitorquata* also occur.

069 Limnothalassa Megalo Livari (Megalo Livari Lagoon) (Evvia)

39°00'N, 23°08'E 600 ha

Unprotected

A small coastal wetland near Istiea, fed by freshwater springs and streams, with a brackish lagoon, reedbeds, and riverine forest. On the coastal side there are a sandy beach and heathland. The freshwater inflow could easily be disturbed. Shooting is a serious problem.

Breeding species include *Ciconia ciconia* (one of two breeding sites in Evvia) and *Sterna albifrons*. Important for passage migrants including herons, *Plegadis falcinellus*, and *Platalea leucorodia*.

070 Oros Kandili (Kandili Mountain) (Evvia)

38°41'N, 23°28'E 12,000 ha

Unprotected
A low mountain on the southern side of Evvia, with extensive coniferous forests (*Pinus halepensis*, *P. nigra*, *Abies cephalonica*), mixed forests, bare ridges, and pastures; also a few large cliffs on the seaward side. Human activities include arable farming, forestry, stock-farming, hunting, and there is scattered human habitation.

An important area for birds of prey; breeding species include *Pernis apivorus*, *Aquila chrysaetos*, and *Hieraaetus fasciatus*, and possibly *Accipiter brevipes*. *Falco eleonorae* also occurs in summer.

071 Oros Dirfis, Xirovouni, Skotini, Mavrovouni, Alokteri, Ortari, and vicinity of Kimi (Evvia)

38°38'N, 23°45'E 45,000 ha

Unprotected

Mount Dirfis and the peaks of Xirovouni, Skotini, Mavrovouni, Alokteri, Ortari, and the vicinity of Kimi; moist mountains with bare peaks, numerous cliffs (including sea cliffs) and steep slopes, forested with *Castanea* and *Abies* sp. Human activities include agriculture, forestry, stock-raising, and hunting, and there is scattered human habitation.

Breeding species include *Pernis apivorus*, *Gyps fulvus* (5-10 pairs), *Circaetus gallicus*, *Aquila chrysaetos*, *Falco peregrinus*, and *Bubo bubo*. *Hieraaetus fasciatus*, *Falco naumanni*, and *F. eleonorae* also occur.

072 Limni Distos (Lake Distos) (Evvia)

38°21'N, 24°08'E 2600 ha

Unprotected

A eutrophic freshwater lake, largely reed-covered, situated between bare hills. Bordered to the east by a cultivated plain. Human activities include agriculture, stock-raising, and hunting. The lake has been polluted by agricultural run-off of fertilisers and pesticides. More seriously, the lake was dry in 1986 and 1987 due to water extraction for industry and agriculture. Currently threatened by complete drainage.

Breeding species included *Ixobrychus minutus* (5+ pairs), *Nycticorax nycticorax* (10 pairs), *Egretta garzetta* (5-10 pairs), *Ardea purpurea* (5-10 pairs), *Aythya nyroca* (10+ pairs), *Circaetus gallicus*, *Hieraaetus fasciatus* (1 pair), *Alectoris graeca*, *Himantopus himantopus*, *Bubo bubo*, *Sylvia rueppelli*, and *Lanius minor*. In the non-breeding season *Plegadis falcinellus* (max. 35), *Circus aeruginosus* (max. 8), *Falco eleonorae*, and *Philomachus pugnax* (max. 100) have also been recorded.

073 Oros Ochi (Mount Ochi) and surrounding area (Evvia)

38°03'N, 24°27'E 18,000 ha

Unprotected

Poorly forested mountains with extensive scrub, bare uplands, and green valleys with strips of *Platanus* sp.

Breeding species include *Circaetus gallicus*, *Hieraaetus fasciatus*, and *Falco peregrinus*. *Buteo rufinus* and *Falco eleonorae* also occur.

074 Limni Kotichi (Lake Kotichi) (Ileia)

38°00'N, 21°18'E 3700 ha Ramsar Site

Unprotected except for partial prohibition of hunting and limited controls on housing-development, grazing, and tree-felling

A small brackish lagoon, separated from the sea by dunes, fed by several small streams and surrounded by patches of saltmarsh and agricultural land. Human activities include pisciculture, agriculture, tourism (coastal hotels and campsites) and operations associated with the military airbase at Araxos. Negative changes in ecological character are resulting from eutrophication, siltation, development of fisheries, increasing tourism, road construction, and uncontrolled grazing. Shooting is also a serious problem.

There is a low diversity of breeding birds (owing to the negative factors mentioned above) but nesting species include *Himantopus himantopus*, *Burhinus oedicnemus*, *Glareola pratincola*, *Sterna albifrons*, and *Melanocorypha calandra*. A variety of herons, waders, and terns occur on passage. In addition, important numbers of wintering wildfowl occur (although numbers are affected by hunting disturbance) including *Anas clypeata* (max. 1200). Other passage species include *Pelecanus crispus* (30), *Circus aeruginosus*, and *C. cyaneus*.

075 Limnothalassa Kalogrias/Strofilia/Lamia (Kalogria Lagoon, Strofilia Forest, and Lamia Lakes) (Achaia, Ileia)

38°10'N, 21°22'E 7600 ha

The forest is church property and is hardly exploited

An intact coastal ecosystem with a coastal lagoon (Kalogria Lagoon) and saltmarshes, brackish lakes (Lamia Lakes) with extensive reedbeds, sand-dunes, and *Pinus* forest (Strofila). Human activities include agriculture, stock-raising, fishing, hunting, and recreation, and there is scattered human habitation. The shallow lakes can be adversely affected by the manipulation of the water-levels.

Breeding species include *Ixobrychus minutus* (20+ pairs), *Ciconia ciconia* (the only site in the Peloponnisos), *Himantopus himantopus*, *Sterna hirundo*, *Bubo bubo*, and *Alcedo atthis*. Particularly important for passage herons, *Plegadis falcinellus* (200+), waders, and terns. *Circus aeruginosus* and *C. cyaneus* occur in winter.

076 Limnothalassa Alyki Aegion (Alyki Lagoon, Aegion) (Achaia)

38°15'N, 22°06'E 20 ha

Hunting is prohibited; otherwise unprotected

A small coastal lagoon, temporarily drying out in summer, with a few zones of reeds and saltmarsh vegetation. Human activities include tourism (mainly in summer).

Rather small to be important for breeding species, though *Netta rufina* has recently bred (one of the very few sites for this species in Greece). Much more important for species on passage including *Egretta garzetta*, *Ardea purpurea*, *Plegadis falcinellus*, *Platalea leucorodia*, *Phoenicopterus ruber* (5-10), *Himantopus himantopus*, *Philomachus pugnax*, *Tringa glareola* (max. 350), and *Larus melanocephalus* (max. 450).

077 Vouna Barbas/Klokos, Faranghi Selinous (Barbas and Klokos Mountains and Selinous Gorge) (Achaia)

38°10'N, 22°00'E 3600 ha

Unprotected

The eastern section of the Panachaikon Mountains, including the gorge of the River Selinous and adjacent slopes and cliffs, with *Pinus* forests and olive-groves. Human activities include forestry, stock-raising, and hunting.

An important area for *Gyps fulvus* (7 pairs; perhaps the only colony in the Peloponnisos). Other breeding species include *Pernis apivorus*, *Circaetus gallicus*, *Aquila chrysaetos*, *Falco peregrinus*, and possibly *Hieraaetus fasciatus*, *Bubo bubo*, and *Dendrocopos leucotos*.

078 Faranghi Vouraikou (Vouraikos Gorge) including Kalavrita (Achaia)

38°05'N, 22°10'E 3500 ha EEC SPA (Kalavrita: 1750 ha)

Partly an Aesthetic Forest (Kalavryta)

Steep ravine (Vouraikos Gorge) with *Pinus* forest and olive-groves. Human activities include stock-raising and hunting, and a railway runs through the area.

An important area for birds of prey with *Pernis apivorus*, *Gyps fulvus* (5 pairs), and *Circaetus gallicus* (2 pairs). *Dendrocopos leucotos* possibly breeds.

079 Foloi Oros (Foloi Hills) (Ileia)

37°45'N, 21°45'E 10,000 ha

Unprotected

Old groves of *Quercus* and forests of *Pinus*, and *Olea* groves intermingled with cultivated areas and pastures. Human activities include agriculture, forestry, stock-raising, and hunting, and there is scattered human habitation. The area is poorly studied ornithologically.

Breeding species include *Circaetus gallicus*, *Aquila chrysaetos*, *Falco peregrinus*, *Bubo bubo*, *Alcedo atthis*, *Dendrocopos leucotos*, and *Sylvia rueppelli*.

080 Nissi Strofades (Strofades Islands) (Zakynthos)

37°15'N, 21°00'E 500 ha

Owned by the Greek Church; hunting is prohibited

Two small rocky islands with sparse vegetation; uninhabited except by lighthouse keepers.

There is a colony of *Calonectris diomedea*. Very important for migrating passerines and well known for the mass spring migration of *Streptopelia turtur* and other birds.

081 Limni Stymphalia (Lake Stymphalia) (Korinthia)

37°50'N, 22°26'E 2300 ha

Unprotected

A freshwater lake with reedbeds, fed by springs and naturally drained by underground streams. Surrounded by mountains with grazed slopes and numerous bushes and trees. Such lakes are rare in the Peloponnisos and are very important for migratory birds. Human activities include agriculture, stock-raising, and hunting. The area suffers from heavy hunting pressure, and is threatened by plans to divert water to an artificial lake for drinking-water storage and irrigation purposes.

Breeding species include *Ixobrychus minutus*, *Ardea purpurea* (3-10 pairs), *Pernis apivorus* (1 pair), *Circus aeruginosus*, and *Alectoris graeca*. Very important as a stop-over site for migrants, including several species of heron, *Plegadis falcinellus* (max. 35), *Gelochelidon nilotica*, and *Chlidonias niger*. *Nycticorax nycticorax* and *Circus cyaneus* occur in winter.

082 Limni Taka (Lake Taka) (Arkadia)

37°26'N, 22°22'E 1500 ha

Unprotected

A freshwater lake partly fed by springs and naturally drained by underground streams, with some temporary marshes. Surrounded by sparsely vegetated hills with *Olea* groves. Human activities include agriculture, stock-raising, and hunting. The waters of the lake are used for irrigation and in some years it is completely dry. In winter there is very heavy hunting pressure.

Breeding species include *Circaetus gallicus* (2 pairs), *Circus aeruginosus*, *Hieraaetus fasciatus*, and *Alcedo atthis*. Important during spring migration; passage species include *Egretta garzetta* (30+), *Plegadis falcinellus*, and several species of waders and terns.

083 Central Oros Taigetos (Mount Taigetos) (Messinia, Lakonia)

37°03'N, 22°22'E 12,000 ha

Unprotected

A large mountain chain in the southern Peloponnisos with extensive tracts of maquis and partly forested with *Pinus nigra* and *Abies cephalonica*.

Breeding species include *Pernis apivorus*, *Circaetus gallicus*, and *Aquila chrysaetos*.

084 Divari Pilou (Divari Lagoon near Pilos) (Messinia)

36°58'N, 21°40'E 2000 ha

Unprotected

A brackish lake (with marshes), which partly dries up in summer, on the Bay of Navarinos. Human activities include stock-raising, fishing, and hunting. Importance during the breeding season is not well known. Drainage of the surrounding saltmarsh has recently started. Shooting appears to be a major problem.

Breeding species include *Ixobrychus minutus* (20+ pairs), *Circaetus gallicus*, *Circus aeruginosus* (1 pair), *Himantopus himantopus* (max. 5 pairs), *Sterna albifrons*, *Alcedo atthis*, and possibly *Glareola pratincola*. A variety of species occur on passage including *Phoenicopterus ruber*, *Milvus migrans*, *Pandion haliaetus*, and *Grus grus*.

085 Notia Mani (Southern Mani), Oros Sanghias (Mount Sanghias), and Akrotirio Tenaro (Cape Tenaro) (Lakonia)

36°25'N, 22°29'E 22,000 ha

Unprotected

A bare mountainous area with pastures, and many villages and *Olea* groves in the plains. There are some cliffs especially on the coast. Human activities include stock-farming and hunting. The shooting of migratory birds is a major problem.

Breeding species include *Hieraaetus fasciatus*, *Falco peregrinus*, and *Bubo bubo*. *Aquila heliaca* occurs in winter. Cape Tenaro is a resting site for migratory birds.

086 Ekvoles Evrota (Evrotas Delta) (Lakonia)

36°49'N, 22°43'E 3000 ha

Unprotected

A small river delta with coastal marshes, lagoons, heathland, sandy beaches, and *Olea* groves. Human activities include agriculture, stock-raising, fishing, and hunting. Hunting pressure is very high.

An important stop-over site for passage species, which include *Ardeola ralloides*, *Egretta garzetta*, *Plegadis falcinellus* (max. 100), *Pernis apivorus*, *Circaetus gallicus*, and *Falco peregrinus*. *Sterna albifrons* possibly breeds.

087 Ori Ghidovouni, Khionovouni, Gaidourovouni, Korakia, Kalogherovouni, Kouloukhera, and vicinity of Monemvassias (Lakonia)

36°55'N, 22°57'E 32,000 ha

Unprotected

Bare or sparsely forested mountains with many cliffs and abundant scrub. Human activities include stock-raising and hunting, and there is scattered human habitation.

An important area for raptors with breeding *Circaetus gallicus*, *Hieraaetus fasciatus*, *Falco peregrinus*, and possibly *Bubo bubo*. *Falco eleonorae* occurs in summer.

088 Parnitha (Attiki)

38°10'N, 23°43'E 6600 ha EEC SPA (3812 ha)

Partly a National Park (Parnitha; core zone: 3812 ha)

A mountain forested with *Abies cephalonica*, with some bare ravines and pasture land on the higher plateaus. There is considerable disturbance from recreation.

Species occurring include *Gyps fulvus*, *Circaetus gallicus* (breeding), *Aquila chrysaetos*, *Falco peregrinus* (breeding), *Bubo bubo*, and *Sylvia rueppelli*.

089 Koutroulis Oros (Mount Koutroulis) (Chania)

35°23'N, 23°35'E 3200 ha
Unprotected

A bare mountain top with cliffs and evergreen scrub, and *Olea* groves at lower altitude. Human activities include stock-raising and hunting.

An important area for vultures and other birds of prey with breeding *Gypaetus barbatus*, *Gyps fulvus*, and *Aquila chrysaetos*. *Falco peregrinus* possibly breeds. *Pernis apivorus* and *Falco eleonorae* also occur on passage.

090 Khersonissos Rodopou (Rodopos Peninsula) (Chania)

35°35'N, 23°45'E 7000 ha

Unprotected

A largely bare peninsula with a grazed plateau, scrub, grassland, and steep sea cliffs. Human activities include stock-raising and hunting.

Important for cliff-nesting birds of prey with breeding *Hieraaetus fasciatus* and *Falco peregrinus*. *Falco eleonorae* occurs in summer, and the area lies on an important migration route for herons and *Circus* spp.

091 Lefka Ori (Lefka Mountains) (Chania)

35°18'N, 24°00'E 50,000+ ha

Biosphere Reserve (Samaria: 4840 ha); EEC SPA (Samaria: 4850 ha); Mediterranean Specially Protected Area (Samaria)

Partly a National Park (Samaria: 4500 ha); European Diploma site; partly unprotected

A remote area of mountains on the south-west coast of Crete with several spectacular gorges including the Samaria Gorge. The high plateaus are still intensively grazed, and there is little forest except for patches of *Pinus* and evergreen *Quercus* on some slopes. Human activities include stock-raising, hunting, and recreation.

Very important for *Gypaetus barbatus* (2+ pairs). Other breeding species include *Gyps fulvus* (10+ pairs), *Aquila chrysaetos* (1 pair), *Falco peregrinus*, *Alectoris chukar*, *Sylvia rueppelli*, *Pyrrhocorax pyrrhocorax*, and possibly *Hieraaetus fasciatus*.

092 Limni Kourna, Delta Almyrou, and Paralia Georgioupolis (Lake Kourna, Almiros Delta, and Georgioupolis Beach) (Chania)

35°21'N, 24°16'E 1300 ha

Unprotected

One of the very few sites with open fresh water in Crete; a small freshwater lake, stream, and coastal marshland. Threatened by planned construction of holiday homes. Shooting is also a problem.

An important stop-over site for migrants, which include *Ardeola ralloides*, *Ardea purpurea*, *Plegadis falcinellus*, *Porzana parva*, and also raptors.

093 Oros Kedros and Kourtaliotiko Faranghi (Mount Kedros and Kourtaliotiko Gorge) (Rethymnon)

35°12'N, 24°37'E 1500 ha

Unprotected

A bare mountain with many rock-faces and some gorges.

Important for *Gyps fulvus* (breeding), *Gypaetus barbatus*, and *Falco peregrinus* (breeding).

094 Faranghi Prassion (Prassies Gorge) (Rethymnon)

35°20'N, 24°32'E 200 ha

Unprotected

A gorge in the bare hills of Gargani.
Important because of a colony of *Gyps fulvus*. *Hieraaetus fasciatus* also occurs.

095 Idi Oros (Mount Idi) (Rethymnon, Irakleio)

35°15'N, 24°45'E 49,000 ha

Unprotected

A bare mountain in Crete with open stands of *Juniperus* sp. at higher altitudes, and scrub at lower altitudes. Human activities include stock-raising, hunting, and recreation. Uncontrolled tourist development is a possible threat.
Important for birds of prey with breeding *Gypaetus barbatus*, *Gyps fulvus*, *Aquila chrysaetos*, *Hieraaetus fasciatus*, and *Falco peregrinus; Alectoris chukar* and *Pyrrhocorax pyrrhocorax* also breed. *Falco eleonorae* occurs in summer.

096 Kofinas Oros (Mount Kofinas) (Irakleio)

34°58'N, 25°05'E 11,000 ha

Unprotected

A bare, rugged mountain on the southern side of Crete with some *Pinus* and *Ceratonia siliqua* woods on its southern slopes. Human activities include stock-raising and hunting, and there is scattered human habitation.
An important area for raptors with breeding *Gypaetus barbatus*, *Gyps fulvus*, *Aquila chrysaetos*, *Hieraaetus fasciatus*, and *Falco peregrinus*. *Falco eleonorae* occurs in summer.

097 Jouchtas Oros (Mount Jouchtas) (Irakleio)

35°15'N, 25°10'E 1600 ha

Partly protected as an archaeological site.

A hill with cliffs and extensive *Olea* groves. Human activities include stock-raising and hunting.
An important area for *Gyps fulvus*.

098 Nissos Dia (Dia Island) (Irakleio)

35°27'N, 25°13'E 1800 ha

Unprotected

An island with rock stacks and scrub vegetation.
Important for breeding *Hieraaetus fasciatus* and *Falco eleonorae*. Seabirds probably also breed. Important also for Mediterranean Monk Seal *Monachus monachus*.

099 Oros Dikti (Mount Dikti) (Irakleio, Lasithi)

35°10'N, 25°30'E 36,000 ha

Unprotected

A large rugged mountain in the Lasithiotika Mountains with some cultivated plateaus and some *Pinus brutia* forest and areas of *Quercus coccifera*. Human activities include agriculture, forestry, stock-raising, hunting, and tourism, and there is scattered human habitation.
An important area for vultures and other birds of prey; species breeding include *Gypaetus barbatus*, *Gyps fulvus*, *Aquila chrysaetos*, *Hieraaetus fasciatus*, and *Falco peregrinus*.

100 Ori Thryptis and Ornon (Mount Thryptis and Mount Ornon) (Lasithi)

35°05'N, 25°50'E 20,000 ha

Unprotected

A rugged area, with two mountains well-forested with *Pinus* on the southern slopes. Human activities include stock-raising, vine and olive-growing, hunting, and there is scattered human habitation.

An important area for vultures and other birds of prey; species occurring include *Gypaetus barbatus*, *Gyps fulvus*, and *Aquila chrysaetos*.

101 Nissi Dionisiades (Dionisiades Islands) (Lasithi)

35°20'N, 26°10'E 800 ha

Unprotected

Three islands with associated rocky islets. Human activities include stock-raising and fishing. Protection is urgently needed.

Breeding species include *Calonectris diomedea* and *Falco eleonorae* (one of the largest colonies in the world). Other species occurring include *Phalacrocorax aristotelis desmarestii* and *Larus audouinii*. Also important for passage migrants.

102 Nissos Kasos (Kasos Island) (Dodekanisos)

36°24'N, 27°00'E 2000 ha

Unprotected

A large island with hills, maquis, rocky coasts, and cliffs. Human activities include stock-raising, fishing, and hunting, and there is scattered human habitation.

Breeding species include *Calonectris diomedea* (large numbers), *Hydrobates pelagicus*, *Phalacrocorax aristotelis desmarestii*, *Ixobrychus minutus*, *Hieraaetus fasciatus*, *Falco eleonorae*, *F. peregrinus*, *Larus audouinii*, *Coracias garrulus*, *Pyrrhocorax pyrrhocorax*, and possibly *Hieraaetus pennatus*. Also important for Mediterranean Monk Seal *Monachus monachus* and herpetofauna.

103 Nissos Saria (Saria Island) (Dodekanisos)

35°51'N, 27°13'E 2000 ha

Unprotected

Largely bare, rocky island with many sea cliffs, at the northern edge of Karpathos.

Important for breeding *Falco eleonorae*. Other breeding species include *Calonectris diomedea*, *Phalacrocorax aristotelis desmarestii*, *Hieraaetus fasciatus*, *Falco biarmicus*, *F. peregrinus*, *Sylvia rueppelli*, *Lanius minor*, and *Pyrrhocorax pyrrhocorax*.

104 Northern Sifnos (Kyklades)

37°00'N, 24°41'E 3000 ha

Unprotected

A rocky island with abandoned terraced fields (now overgrown), and a marshy valley.

Species breeding, or possibly breeding, include *Calonectris diomedea*, *Hieraaetus fasciatus*, *Falco peregrinus*, and *F. eleonorae*. Also important for passage herons, waders, and other birds.

105 Northern Syros (Kyklades)

37°29'N, 24°56'E 2700 ha

Unprotected

The northern part of the island with a rocky/cliff coastline. Human activities include stock-raising, fishing, hunting, and recreation.

Breeding species include *Calonectris diomedea*, *Phalacrocorax aristotelis desmarestii*, *Hieraaetus fasciatus*, *Falco eleonorae* (18 pairs), *F. peregrinus* (3 pairs), *Larus audouinii*, *Coracias garrulus*, *Sylvia rueppelli*, *Pyrrhocorax pyrrhocorax*, and possibly *Hydrobates pelagicus*. Both species of pelican and many species of raptor occur on passage, and *Larus audouinii* (max. 20) occurs in winter. Also important for Mediterranean Monk Seal *Monachus monachus*.

106 Oros Dias, Oros Mavrovouni, Oros Koronos (Kyklades)

37°00'N, 25°30'E 16,000 ha

Unprotected

Poorly forested mountains (Dias, Mavrovouni, Koronos) on Naxos, with extensive areas of heavily grazed scrub. Also sea cliffs and pebble beaches. Human activities include agriculture, stock-raising, and hunting, and there is scattered human habitation.

Breeding species include *Puffinus puffinus yelkouan*, *Phalacrocorax aristotelis desmarestii*, *Gyps fulvus* (10-20 pairs), *Hieraaetus fasciatus* (3-5 pairs), *Falco eleonorae*, *F. peregrinus* (1-2 pairs), *Sylvia rueppelli*, and possibly *Calonectris diomedea*. A variety of herons and birds of prey occurs on passage.

107 Nissi Kyra-Panaghia/Ghioura/Piperi/Skantzoura (Vorii Sporades) (Magnisia)

39°25'N, 24°20'E 9000 ha

Partly a National Marine Park (Ghioura), although not yet fully declared

A group of small islands in the Northern Sporades with cliffs, caves and offshore rocky islets. The islands are either bare or scrub-covered. Human activities include stock-raising, fishing, and hunting.

Important for breeding *Calonectris diomedea*, *Puffinus puffinus yelkouan*, *Phalacrocorax aristotelis desmarestii* (max. 180 outside the breeding season), *Falco eleonorae*, and *Larus audouinii*. Other breeding species include *Circaetus gallicus* and *Hieraaetus fasciatus*. Mediterranean Monk Seal *Monachus monachus* also occurs.

108 Limni Khortaro and Limni Alyki (Khortaro Lake and Alyki Lake) (Lesvos)

39°50'N, 25°22'E 5300 ha

Unprotected

Brackish and saltwater coastal lakes on Limnos with mudflats, which partly dry up in summer. Human activities include stock-raising, fishing, and hunting, and there is scattered human habitation.

Breeding species include *Tadorna ferruginea*, *Himantopus himantopus*, *Recurvirostra avosetta*, and *Burhinus oedicnemus* The dry mudflats are used by herons, waders, gulls, and other waterbirds.

109 Kolpos Kallonis (Gulf of Kalloni) (Lesvos)

39°10'N, 26°15'E 12,000 ha

Unprotected

A large sea bay with shallow brackish zones, small freshwater marshes, saltmarshes, and saltpans. Also *Olea* groves and *Pinus* forest. Human activities include agriculture, forestry, salt production, stock-raising, fishing, hunting, and recreation, and there is scattered human habitation.

Breeding species include (or possibly include) *Ixobrychus minutus*, *Ciconia ciconia* (5-10 pairs), *Tadorna ferruginea*, *Pernis apivorus*, *Circus aeruginosus*, *Aquila chrysaetos* (1-2 pairs), *Hieraaetus pennatus* (1-5 pairs), *H. fasciatus* (2-4 pairs), *Falco peregrinus*, *Himantopus himantopus*, *Recurvirostra avosetta*, *Burhinus oedicnemus*, *Glareola pratincola*, *Sterna hirundo*, *S. albifrons*, *Bubo bubo*, *Alcedo atthis*, *Dendrocopos medius*, *Sylvia rueppelli*, *Sitta krueperi*, and *Lanius nubicus*. Also very important for passage herons, raptors, waders, gulls, and terns. In winter, visitors include *Botaurus stellaris*, *Egretta alba* (40), *Plegadis falcinellus* (300), *Phoenicopterus ruber*, *Circus cyaneus*, and *Aquila clanga*.

110 Oros Kerkis (Mount Kerkis) (Samos)

37°44'N, 26°37'E 7000 ha

Unprotected

A high mountain with *Cupressus sempervirens* forest and grazing pastures.

Important for birds of prey including *Haliaeetus albicilla*, *Circaetus gallicus*, *Buteo rufinus*, *Aquila chrysaetos*, and *Bubo bubo*, which all breed, or possibly breed. Also (because lying close to the Turkish mainland) very important for passage migrants.

111 Nissi Fourni (Fourni Islands) (Samos)

37°40'N, 26°30'E 10,000 ha

Unprotected

A group of rugged islands between Samos and Ikaria with sea cliffs, bays, and offshore rocky islets. Covered with sparse scrub vegetation. Human activities include stock-raising, fishing, and hunting, and there is scattered human habitation.

Breeding species include (or possibly include) *Calonectris diomedea*, *Phalacrocorax aristotelis desmarestii*, *Circaetus gallicus*, *Hieraaetus fasciatus*, *Falco eleonorae*, *F. peregrinus*, *Alectoris chukar*, and *Lanius minor*. Also important for passage migrants, notably herons and raptors.

112 Vouno Dikios, Akrotiri Louros, and Limni Psalidi (Mount Dikios, Cape Louros, and Lake Psalidi) (Dodekanisos)

36°52'N, 27°16'E 2000 ha

Unprotected

A hill with woodland and scrub on the island of Kos. There is also a small wetland which is unprotected.

Important for breeding *Calonectris diomedea*, *Buteo rufinus*, *Hieraaetus fasciatus*, *Falco eleonorae*, *F. peregrinus*, and *Sylvia rueppelli*. *Haliaeetus albicilla*, *Aquila pomarina*, and *Pandion haliaetus* occur as passage migrants.

113 Nissos Tilos (Tilos Islands) (Dodekanisos)

36°27'N, 27°24'E 5000 ha

Unprotected

Rocky coasts with cliffs, caves, and offshore rocks.

Gyps fulvus and *Falco eleonorae* occur. Also important for Mediterranean Monk Seal *Monachus monachus*.

MAIN REFERENCES

Athanasiou, H. (1987) Past and present importance of the Greek wetlands for wintering waterfowl. Unpublished report by the International Waterfowl Research Bureau.

Crivelli, A. J., Jerrentrup, H. and Hallman, B. (1986) Preliminary results of a complete census of breeding colonial wading birds in Greece, Spring 1985-1986.

Hallman, B. (1982) Important bird areas in the European community: preliminary list of important bird areas in Greece. Unpublished report to the Commission of the European Communities.

Hallman, B. (1982) Status and conservation problems of birds of prey in Greece. Pp. 55-59 in Newton, I. and Chancellor, R. D. eds. *Conservation studies on raptors.* Cambridge: International Council for Bird Preservation, Techn. Publ. No. 5.

Hellenic Ornithological Society (1988) Greek threatened areas project/Integrated Mediterranean Programme monitoring programme. Interim report.

Kassioumis, K. (1988) Protected areas in Greece. *Bull. Hellenic Soc. for the Protection of Nature* 40: 48-56.

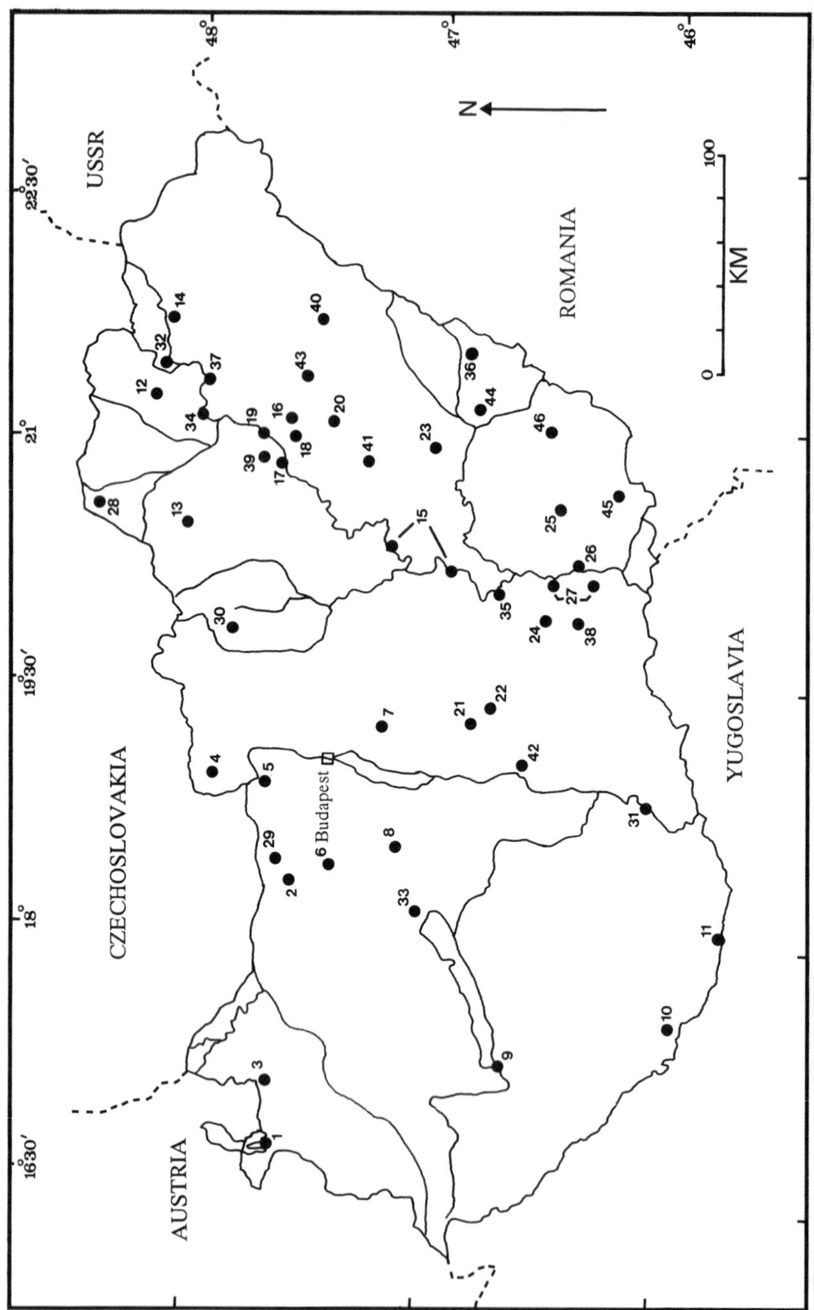

Figure 16: Map showing the location of the sites in Hungary

HUNGARY

Great Bustard *Otis tarda*

INTRODUCTION

General information

Hungary covers an area of 93,030 sq km and has a population of 10,679,000 (in 1984) and an average population density of 115 per sq km. The majority of the country is lowland (Great Hungarian Plain), bisected by the Rivers Danube (Duna) and Tisza, with low mountains in the north (e.g. Bukk, Mátra) reaching a maximum altitude of 1015 m (Kékes). A high proportion of the land surface is used for arable farming (57.7 per cent), with 13.7 per cent forest, 10 per cent grazing land, and 5.4 per cent meadows.

Formerly the natural climax vegetation on the Great Hungarian Plain was steppe-woodland, dominated by *Quercus*, which was drastically cut in the sixteenth and seventeenth centuries during the Hungarian-Turkish war. This has been replaced by steppe-grassland or 'puszta', an alkaline and saline grassland rich in annuals, which is maintained by grazing and is now mostly used as arable farmland. Scattered remnants of steppe--woodland are now present only in the eastern part of the plain and in the Kiskunsági National Park.

Quercus/Carpinus woodland is found between 200 and 700 m, replaced by *Fagus* woodland above 700 m on dry limestone slopes. *Pinus sylvestris* forms extensive stands in western Hungary. Riverine forests of *Alnus*, *Salix/Populus*, although much reduced, are still extensive along the Danube and especially the Tisza and cover an area of

50,000 ha. Although 30,000 ha are protected, the main threat is replacement of native species with fast-growing exotics.

Extensive marshes are an important feature of the lowlands, although much reduced by flood-control measures and drainage. Areas of steppe-grassland often have extensive marshes fed by rain water, and natron (soda) lakes with reedbeds. There are also numerous artificial fish-pond systems (in 1984 there were 26,000 ha of commercial fish-ponds) which are of considerable economic importance.

Ornithological importance

In the Great Hungarian Plain the typical alkaline steppe-grassland and areas of less intensively cultivated farmland support one of the largest populations of *Otis tarda* in Europe (2000 birds; second only to the Spanish population and perhaps that of the USSR). Other important breeding species of the lowlands include *Falco vespertinus*, *Burhinus oedicnemus*, *Coracias garrulus*, *Calandrella brachydactyla* (60 pairs), *Anthus campestris*, and *Lanius minor*. The wetland habitats, typical of the Plain (marshes fed by rain water, natron lakes with reedbeds, fish-ponds, riverine forest with oxbows and wet meadows) and often associated with steppe habitat, support large populations of Ardeidae including *Botaurus stellaris*, *Ixobrychus minutus*, *Nycticorax nycticorax*, *Ardeola ralloides*, *Egretta garzetta*, *E. alba* (400 pairs), and *Ardea purpurea*, and also significant populations of *Platalea leucorodia* (500 pairs), *Haliaeetus albicilla* (15 pairs), *Circus aeruginosus*, *Crex crex*, *Recurvirostra avosetta* (200 pairs), *Glareola pratincola* (40 pairs), *Limosa limosa*, *Chlidonias hybridus*, *C. niger*, *C. leucopterus*, and *Acrocephalus paludicola* (after Poland and probably the USSR, the largest population in the world). Hungary is also important for *Ciconia ciconia* (4500 pairs; 75 per cent of which nest on electricity pylons, where 2500 nesting platforms have been placed). The steppe habitat is important for passage raptors, such as *Buteo rufinus*, *Circus macrourus*, and *Falco peregrinus*, and with the wetlands, for over 50,000 passage and wintering *Anser albifrons* (and small numbers of *A. erythropus*) and 15,000-20,000 *Grus grus*. Also, about 100 *Haliaeetus albicilla* winter at the larger fish-ponds.

Hungary has an extremely effective conservation programme for birds of prey, and breeding raptors include *Aquila pomarina* (50 pairs), *Aquila heliaca* (15 pairs), and *Falco cherrug* (40-50 pairs). The country's woodland also supports good populations of *Ciconia nigra*, *Bonasa bonasia*, *Bubo bubo* (declining), *Picus canus*, *Dryocopus martius*, *Dendrocopos medius*, *D. leucotos*, and *Ficedula albicollis*, some of which are common.

Conservation infrastructure and protected-area system

At the national level, nature conservation is supervised by the Ministry for Environmental Protection and Water Management (KVM), under which operates the Institute for Environment Protection (KVI) and regional inspectorates. The Hungarian Ornithological Society and Hungarian Society of Nature Friends are large voluntary groups which also promote nature conservation.

There are three categories of protected areas suitable for the conservation of areas of national importance: National Park (Nemzeti parkok), Landscape Protection Reserve (Tájvédelmi körzetek) and Nature Conservation Area (Természetvédelmi területek).

1. National Parks

   These are suitable for protecting large areas of land where the landscape, wildlife, and geological formations are of outstanding national importance. The areas are important for education and recreation as well as nature conservation. Within a National Park strictly protected areas may be established where nature conservation is the main objective.

2. Landscape Protection Areas

   These provide protection for medium-sized areas (1000-20,000 ha), and are areas of special scenic value established to protect landscape features and nature.

3. Nature Conservation Areas

   In general these are areas of 500-2000 ha with strict protection for nature. They are sometimes bird sanctuaries.

4. Protection Areas of Local Importance

These are similar to Nature Conservation Areas and are established by provincial councils. They mostly cover small areas (100-500 ha).

International measures relevant to the conservation of sites

Hungary is a party to the Ramsar Convention, World Heritage Convention and Bonn Convention, and has designated eight Ramsar Sites (totalling 29,450 ha). It has not designated any natural World Heritage Sites. Five Biosphere Reserves have been designated (totalling 138,884 ha). All of the Ramsar Sites and Biosphere Reserves are included in this inventory.

Overview of the inventory

Forty-six sites are included in the inventory, covering a total area of 373,000 ha (to nearest 1000 ha), of which 11 (*c.*29,000 ha) are completely unprotected; these are expected to receive legal protection and to become Nature Conservation Areas in the near future. Included in the list are three National Parks and two parts of the fragmented Kiskunsági National Park, 19 Landscape Protection Reserves, and 11 Nature Conservation Areas. The most important areas of steppe-grassland are included in the inventory (Hortobágy: 016; Pusztaszer: 027) and are protected; however, large areas are without protection: sites 035-045 as well as other remnants not included in this inventory. Sites 035-045 require more detailed study and proposals for protection. Extensive areas of agricultural land supporting populations of *Otis tarda* lie outside the sites included in this inventory.

Wetland habitats, including soda and saline lakes, fish-ponds, and riverine forest, are covered well by this inventory. Twenty-four wetland sites, or areas which have important wetlands, are included, covering a large proportion of the waterbird populations discussed above.

Deciduous woodland is also covered well by this inventory; the sites in question hold good populations of birds of prey (such as *Aquila pomarina*, *A. heliaca*), *Bonasa bonasia*, and all the woodpecker species mentioned earlier.

Acknowledgements

The site descriptions were compiled from information provided by F. Márkus (who coordinated the project for ICBP, incorporating material from J. Györy and I. Sterbetz) and from information submitted to IWRB by A. Bankovics and I. Sterbetz. F. Márkus prepared the introduction.

INVENTORY

No.	Site name	Region	Criteria used to select site [see p.18]							
			0	1(i)	1(ii)	1(iii)	1(iv)	2	3	4
001	Fertö-tó	GS				*			*	
002	Tatai Öreg-tó	KM				*				
003	Hanság	GS				*		*	*	
004	Börzsöny	PT,ND						*	*	
005	Pilis	PT							*	
006	Vértes	FR						*	*	
007	Ócsa	PT				*		*	*	
008	Velence and Dinnyés	FR				*			*	
009	Kis-Balaton	ZA				*		*	*	
010	Barcs	SY						*	*	
011	Szaporca-Ó-Dráva	BA						*	*	

No.	Site name	Region	Criteria used to select site [see p.18]							
			0	1(i)	1(ii)	1(iii)	1(iv)	2	3	4
012	Zemplén	BAZ						*	*	
013	Bükk	BAZ,HS						*	*	
014	Tiszatelek-Tiszaberceli ártér	SS							*	
015	Közép-Tisza	SK						*	*	
016	Hortobágy	HB,SK				*		*	*	
017	Tiszafüredi madárrezervátum	HS,SK				*		*	*	
018	Pusztakócsi mocsarak	HB				*		*	*	
019	Ároktö-tiszacsegei hullámtér	BAZ,HB						*	*	
020	Ágota-puszta	HB						*	*	
021	Kiskunsági szikes-tavak	BK				*			*	
022	Kolon-tó	BK				*			*	
023	Dévaványa	BS						*	*	
024	Péteri-tó	BK				*		*	*	
025	Kardoskut Fehér-tó	BS				*		*	*	
026	Mártély	CD						*	*	
027	Pusztaszer and Szeged-Fehértó	CD				*		*	*	
028	Aggtelek	BAZ						*	*	
029	Gerecse	KM						*	*	
030	Mátra	ND,HS						*	*	
031	Gemenc	BK						*	*	
032	Tokaj-Bodrogzug	BAZ				*		*	*	
033	Sárrét	FR						*	*	
034	Tiszadobiártér	SS						*	*	
035	Tiszaalpári rét	BK						*	*	
036	Biharugrai-halastavak	BS				*		*	*	
037	Tiszaluc-Kesznyéten puszta	BAZ,SS						*	*	
038	Müller-szék	CD							*	
039	Mezöség	BAZ						*	*	
040	Hajdusági erdöspuszta	HB							*	
041	Nagykunsági puszta	SK						*	*	
042	Harta-Akasztói puszta	BK						*	*	
043	Nagyszék, Balmazujváros	HB							*	
044	Bélmegyeri puszta	BS							*	
045	Pitvarosi puszta	CD				*		*	*	
046	Szabadkigyósi puszta	BS							*	

GS=Györ-Sopron KM=Komárom PT=Pest ND=Nógrád FR=Fejér ZA=Zala
SY=Somogy BA=Baranya BAZ=Borsod-Abaúj-Zemplén HS=Heves SS=Szabolcs-Szatmár
SK=Szolnok HB=Hajdú-Bihar BK=Bács-Kiskun BS=Békés CD=Csongrád

Comments on the inventory

1. Passage figures (spring and autumn) refer to the total number of birds passing during the season. For security reasons, the presence of four pairs of *Bubo bubo* at one site and one pair of *Aquila chrysaetos* at another site has not been mentioned.
2. Although areas of Ramsar Sites may vary slightly from those given as important bird areas, Ramsar Site names are the same as the site names, unless otherwise stated.
3. The regions given in parentheses following the site names are the counties.

---

001 Fertö-tó (Györ-Sopron)

47°35'-47°38'N, 16°37'-16°40'E 12,542 ha Biosphere Reserve

Landscape Protection Reserve

Part of a shallow, saline lake (Lake Fertö) with reed and sedge vegetation, which represents the southern part of Neusiedler See (Austria). Reed-cutting, fishing, and hunting are the dominant human activities. There are some problems with the shooting of waterfowl within the protected area.

Breeding species include *Podiceps grisegena* (6 pairs), *Botaurus stellaris* (20 pairs), *Egretta alba* (15 pairs), *Ardea purpurea* (15-20 pairs), *Ciconia ciconia* (5 pairs), *Platalea leucorodia* (25 pairs), *Anser anser* (30 pairs), *Anas clypeata* (50 pairs), *Circus aeruginosus* (15 pairs), *Limosa limosa* (10 pairs), *Numenius arquata* (15 pairs), *Luscinia svecica*, *Locustella luscinioides* (*c*.30-40 pairs) and *Acrocephalus arundinaceus* (*c*.80 pairs). Large numbers of *Anser fabalis* (20,000-30,000), *A. albifrons* (2000), and *A. anser* (1500-6000) occur on passage. Other species occurring in autumn include *Egretta alba* (15), *Ciconia ciconia* (30-35), and *Platalea leucorodia* (50-80).

002 Tatai Öreg-tó (Komárom)

47°39'N, 18°18'E 259 ha

Nature Conservation Area

A lake at the southern edge of Tata, with woodland at the southern and south-western end, and small areas of *Phragmites*. Comparatively warm water enters the southern end, which prevents freezing in winter. The lake is used as a fish-pond and for recreation and there is some disturbance from hunting despite regulations. Other problems include increasing eutrophication and disturbance from recreation.

Important for passage and wintering wildfowl with *Anser fabalis* (10,000 in winter; max. 70,000 on spring passage), *A. albifrons* (200-300 on spring and autumn passage), *Anas platyrhynchos* (4000 on spring passage), *A. querquedula* (500-600 on spring passage; 800 on autumn passage), *Aythya ferina* (1500 on spring passage), and *Bucephala clangula* (250 in winter; 400 on spring passage).

003 Hanság (Györ-Sopron)

47°45'N, 17°15'E 6242 ha

Landscape Protection Reserve

Salix and *Alnus* woodland with marshes, fish-ponds and grazing-meadows. Human activities include forestry and stock-raising. Trampling by cattle, damaging the vegetation, is the main problem at the site.

Breeding species include *Botaurus stellaris* (2-3 pairs), *Egretta alba* (7-10 pairs), *Ardea purpurea* (6-8 pairs), *Ciconia nigra* (4 pairs), *Milvus migrans* (3 pairs), *Circus aeruginosus* (6 pairs), *C. pygargus* (10 pairs), *Otis tarda* (5-10 pairs; also 20-25 in winter), *Crex crex* (4-5 pairs), *Limosa limosa* (6 pairs), *Numenius arquata* (10-12 pairs), *Chlidonias niger* (6 pairs), *Asio flammeus* (1-2 pairs), *Coracias garrulus* (2-3 pairs), *Dryocopus martius* (*c*.20 pairs), *Luscinia svecica* (10-15 pairs), *Locustella luscinioides* (*c*.30 pairs), *Acrocephalus melanopogon* (20-30 pairs), *A. arundinaceus* (*c*.30 pairs), *Sylvia nisoria* (100 pairs), and *Lanius collurio* (100-150 pairs). *Haliaeetus albicilla* (1-2) occurs on spring passage, and wintering species include *Egretta alba* (5-6) and *Aquila heliaca* (1-2).

004 Börzsöny (Pest, Nógrád)

47°55'N, 18°55'E 17,897 ha

Landscape Protection Reserve

Hilly country with *Quercus*, *Fraxinus*, and *Fagus* woodland, grassy glades, and rocky slopes.

Important for breeding raptors with *Pernis apivorus* (8-10 pairs), *Milvus migrans* (2-3 pairs), *Circaetus gallicus* (2-3 pairs), *Aquila pomarina* (1-2 pairs), and *A. heliaca* (1 pair). Other breeding species include *Ciconia ciconia* (4-5 pairs), *Bonasa bonasia* (*c*.10-15 pairs), *Picus canus* (common), *Dryocopus martius* (common), *Dendrocopos leucotos* (10-15 pairs), *Lullula arborea* (common), *Sylvia nisoria* (common), and *Lanius collurio* (common). *Ciconia ciconia* (30-40 in autumn) also occurs on spring and autumn passage, and *A. chrysaetos* (1-2) and *Falco peregrinus* (1-2) occur in winter.

005 Pilis (Pest)

47°43'N, 18°54'E 23,323 ha Biosphere Reserve (23,000 ha)

Landscape Protection Reserve

A limestone and dolomite karst region, also with volcanic formations. Includes forests of *Quercus* and *Fagus*, *Quercus* and *Fraxinus*, *Quercus* and *Carpinus*, and valleys with streams and steppe meadows.

Breeding raptors include *Pernis apivorus* (common), *Milvus migrans* (3-4 pairs), *Circaetus gallicus* (3-4 pairs), *Aquila pomarina* (1-2 pairs), *Hieraaetus pennatus* (1 pair), and *Falco cherrug* (1-2 pairs); *Picus canus*, *Dryocopus martius*, *Dendrocopos medius*, *Sylvia nisoria*, and *Lanius collurio* are common. *Aquila heliaca* occurs on spring and autumn passage.

006 Vértes (Fejér)

47°25'N, 18°30'E 13,723 ha

Landscape Protection Reserve

An area of weathered limestone with ridges, clefts, and caves. Predominantly *Quercus* and *Fagus* woodland with shrubs and sub-Mediterranean grasslands.

Breeding raptors include *Pernis apivorus* (common), *Circaetus gallicus* (1-2 pairs), *Aquila heliaca* (2-3 pairs), and *Falco cherrug* (3-4 pairs); *Picus canus*, *Dryocopus martius*, *Dendrocopos medius*, *Lullula arborea*, *Sylvia nisoria*, and *Lanius collurio* are common.

007 Ócsa (Pest)

47°15'N, 19°15'E 3576 ha

Landscape Protection Reserve

A peatbog with wet and mature *Alnus* woodland, meadows, reedbeds, and open water. Problems include drainage of the water in spring, and excessive use of artificial fertilisers in the adjacent arable land.

Breeding species include *Botaurus stellaris* (5-7 pairs), *Ixobrychus minutus* (common), *Nycticorax nycticorax* (4 pairs), *Egretta alba* (8 pairs), *Ciconia nigra* (2 pairs), *C. ciconia* (5 pairs), *Aythya nyroca* (common), *Pernis apivorus* (1-2 pairs), *Circus aeruginosus* (10-12 pairs), *C. pygargus* (4-5 pairs), *Falco cherrug* (1 pair), *Crex crex* (15 pairs), *Burhinus oedicnemus* (2-3 pairs), *Limosa limosa* (10-15 pairs), *Asio flammeus* (2-3 pairs), *Alcedo atthis* (c.10-15 pairs), *Coracias garrulus* (3-5 pairs), *Dryocopus martius* (common), *Lanius collurio* (common), and *L. minor* (common). *Ciconia ciconia* (60-80 in autumn) also occurs on passage, and *Circus cyaneus* (15-20) occurs in winter.

008 Velence and Dinnyés (Fejér)

47°10'N, 18°32'E 965 ha Part of Ramsar Site (1000 ha)

Nature Conservation Areas

The south-western part of Lake Velence and salt-steppe with a salt lake (Dinnyés Fertö) near Dinnyés; part of a 24,000 ha lake and marshland complex. Habitats include extensive reedbeds, wet meadows, and saltmarsh. Economic activities include reed-cutting, with grazing, fish-farming, and cultivation in adjacent areas. Disturbance from aircraft and illegal fishing are problems at the site.

An important breeding site for Ardeidae with *Botaurus stellaris* (c.10 pairs), *Ixobrychus minutus* (c.30 pairs), *Egretta alba* (40 pairs; 10 in winter), and *Ardea purpurea* (20 pairs). Other breeding species include *Ciconia ciconia* (1 pair), *Platalea leucorodia* (50 pairs), *Anser anser* (70-80 pairs), *Aythya nyroca* (30 pairs), *Circus aeruginosus* (10 pairs), *Porzana porzana* (c.30 pairs), *P. parva* (c.10 pairs), *Limosa limosa* (10 pairs), *Chlidonias niger* (50 pairs), *Luscinia svecica* (4-5 pairs), *Acrocephalus melanopogon* (*c.*30 pairs), and *Lanius minor* (2-3 pairs). Large numbers of geese occur on spring and autumn passage with *Anser fabalis* (10,000-20,000; with 5000 in winter), *A. albifrons* (1000-1500; with 100-500 in winter); also *Egretta garzetta* (30 on autumn passage), *Ciconia ciconia* (20-25 on autumn passage), *Philomachus pugnax* (20,000 on spring passage), and *Limosa limosa* (200 on spring passage).

009 Kis-Balaton (Zala)

46°40'N, 17°14'E 14,745 ha Ramsar Site (Kis-Balaton: 1400 ha)

Landscape Protection Reserve

Formerly part of Lake Balaton, but now a freshwater marsh with extensive reedbeds and small eutrophic ponds and stands of *Salix*. Includes the recently established Kis-Balaton water-storage reservoir (Kis-Balaton Tározó). Economic activities include reed-cutting, with grazing and cultivation in surrounding areas. The artificial regulation of the water-level at Kis-Balaton Tározó may adversely affect nesting ducks, waders, gulls, and terns.

Breeding species include *Podiceps nigricollis* (*c.*150-200 pairs), *Phalacrocorax carbo* (400 pairs), *Botaurus stellaris* (10 pairs), *Ixobrychus minutus* (*c.*30 pairs), *Nycticorax nycticorax* (150-200 pairs), *Ardeola ralloides* (24 pairs), *Egretta garzetta* (35 pairs), *E. alba* (130 pairs), *Ardea purpurea* (*c.*40 pairs), *Platalea leucorodia* (35 pairs), *Anser anser* (80 pairs), *Aythya nyroca* (*c.*80 pairs), *Haliaeetus albicilla* (1 pair), *Circus aeruginosus* (*c.*10 pairs), *C. pygargus* (2 pairs), *Porzana porzana* (*c.*20-30 pairs), *P. parva* (*c.*10-20 pairs), *Crex crex* (*c.*2-3 pairs), *Recurvirostra avosetta* (3 pairs), *Sterna hirundo* (*c.*100-150 pairs), *Chlidonias hybridus* (*c.*80-100 pairs), *C. niger* (2 pairs), *Asio flammeus* (2 pairs), *Alcedo atthis* (5 pairs), *Dryocopus martius* (3 pairs), *Luscinia svecica* (*c.*20 pairs), *Acrocephalus melanopogon* (20-25 pairs), and *Lanius collurio* (*c.*15-25 pairs). An important site for birds on autumn (and spring) passage with *Phalacrocorax pygmeus* (3), *Ciconia ciconia* (30-35), *Egretta alba* (400), *Anser anser* (1500), *A. fabalis* (10,000), *Aythya ferina* (10,000 in spring), *Bucephala clangula* (1000), *Pandion haliaetus* (2-3 in spring), and wintering species include *Egretta alba* (15-20) and *Haliaeetus albicilla* (4-5).

010 Barcs (Somogy)

45°58'N, 17°30'E 3417 ha

Landscape Protection Reserve

Hilly country with mixed *Juniperus* and *Betula* woodland with grassland.

Breeding species include *Ciconia nigra* (2-3 pairs), *C. ciconia* (5-7 pairs), *Pernis apivorus* (1-2 pairs), *Haliaeetus albicilla* (1 pair), and *Coracias garrulus* (3-4 pairs); *Dryocopus martius*, *Dendrocopos medius*, *Sylvia nisoria*, *Lanius collurio*, and *L. minor* are common. *Haliaeetus albicilla* (4-5) also occurs in winter.

011 Szaporca-Ó-Dráva (Baranya)

45°50'N, 18°06'E 257 ha Ramsar Site (250 ha)

Nature Conservation Area

An oxbow of the River Dráva which is now almost completely covered in *Phragmites* and *Salix* with just a few open pools remaining. The area is surrounded by arable land and woodland. Economic activities include fishing, which causes some disturbance.

Breeding species include *Nycticorax nycticorax* (10-20 pairs), *Ardeola ralloides* (5-10 pairs), *Egretta garzetta* (10-12 pairs), *Ciconia ciconia* (1-2 pairs), *Aythya nyroca* (5-6 pairs), and *Circus aeruginosus* (1-2 pairs). *Egretta alba* (5-10), *Ciconia nigra* (10-15) and *Aythya nyroca* (100) occur on autumn passage, and *Haliaeetus albicilla* (1-2) and *Circus cyaneus* (10-15) occur in winter.

012 Zemplén (Borsod-Abaúj-Zemplén)

48°14'N, 21°25'E 26,396 ha

Landscape Protection Reserve

A hilly region with volcanic formations and *Quercus* and *Fagus* woodland to 900 m, and valleys with streams and meadows. Also steppe areas with scrub and *Tilia* and *Fraxinus* woodland.

An important area for breeding raptors with *Pernis apivorus* (*c.*20 pairs), *Milvus migrans* (5-7 pairs), *Circaetus gallicus* (7-10 pairs), *Aquila pomarina* (8-10 pairs), *A. heliaca* (6 pairs), *Hieraaetus pennatus* (4-6 pairs), and *Falco cherrug* (7-10 pairs). Other breeding species include *Ciconia nigra* (8-10 pairs), *C. ciconia* (10-12 pairs), *Bonasa bonasia* (*c.*30 pairs), *Bubo bubo* (5-6 pairs), *Strix uralensis* (1-3 pairs), *Picus canus* (common), *Dryocopus martius* (common), *Dendrocopos leucotos* (*c.*10 pairs), *Lullula arborea* (common), *Sylvia nisoria* (common), and *Lanius collurio.*

013 Bükk (Borsod-Abaúj-Zemplén, Heves)

48°10'N, 20°30'E 38,775 ha

National Park

A mountain range with deep valleys and a wide plateau with *Quercus* woodland between 200 and 600 m, and *Fagus* woodland particularly between 700 and 800 m. Also steppe areas with scrub in the southern part.

An important area for breeding raptors with *Pernis apivorus* (*c.*30 pairs), *Circaetus gallicus* (4 pairs), *Aquila pomarina* (9 pairs), *A. heliaca* (2 pairs), *Hieraaetus pennatus* (2 pairs), and *Falco cherrug* (7 pairs). Other breeding species include *Ciconia nigra* (3 pairs), *Bonasa bonasia* (5-10 pairs), *Picus canus* (20-30 pairs), *Dryocopus martius* (common), *Dendrocopos medius* (common), and *D. leucotos* (20-30 pairs).

014 Tiszatelek-Tiszaberceli ártér (Szabolcs-Szatmár)

48°15'N, 21°45'E 718 ha

Nature Conservation Area

A narrow strip of mature *Salix*, *Populus*, and *Fraxinus* riverine forest along the River Tisza, with a rich ground flora, herb layer, and climbers such as wild grape and hop which provide dense cover.

Breeding species include *Chlidonias hybridus* (10-15 pairs), *C. niger* (5-10 pairs), *Alcedo atthis* (common), and *Coracias garrulus* (1-3 pairs). In addition a considerable variety of passerines breed including *Riparia riparia, Luscinia luscinia, L. megarhynchos, Phoenicurus phoenicurus,* and *Locustella fluviatilis*, which are common.

015 Közép-Tisza (Szolnok)

47°10'N, 20°10'E 7670 ha

Landscape Protection Reserve

A meandering and shallow stretch of the River Tisza with rich riverside and submerged vegetation including extensive gallery woodland. The surrounding land is regularly inundated in spring. There is only limited cultivation, and pesticide use and fishing are restricted. Industrial pollution is causing eutrophication and there is some persecution of birds by fishermen.

Breeding species include *Phalacrocorax carbo* (80-90 pairs), *Nycticorax nycticorax* (100-130 pairs), *Ardeola ralloides* (4-5 pairs), *Egretta garzetta* (30-35 pairs), *Ciconia nigra* (2-3 pairs; with 50-60 on autumn passage), *Platalea leucorodia* (4-5 pairs), *Milvus migrans* (2-3 pairs), *Aquila pomarina* (1 pair), *Falco cherrug* (1 pair), *Crex crex* (2-3 pairs), *Limosa limosa* (25-30 pairs), *Coracias garrulus* (2-3 pairs), *Dryocopus martius* (5-6 pairs), *Riparia riparia* (1000-3000 pairs), *Sylvia nisoria* (3-4 pairs), and *Lanius collurio* (5-7 pairs). Also important for *Haliaeetus albicilla* (18-20) and *Aquila heliaca* (3-4) in winter.

016 Hortobágy (Hajdú-Bihar, Szolnok)

47°37'N, 21°05'E 52,000 ha Ramsar Site (15,000 ha); Biosphere Reserve

National Park

Extensive steppe habitat with salt-lakes, water-storage tanks and fish-ponds, reedbeds, marshes and woodland. The Hortobágy-Halastó is a fish-pond system with extensive reedbeds, and the most typical and open steppe remnant is the Zám-Pentezug-Angyalháza area. In some areas there is a complete restriction on use of the land. In other areas traditional stock-raising, reed-cutting, fish-farming, arable farming, and forestry are carried out. There is a demand from agricultural interests to lessen the protection afforded to the Park with a desire to practice more intensive agriculture.

An extremely important site for breeding birds with *Podiceps grisegena* (20-25 pairs), *Botaurus stellaris* (35-45 pairs), *Ixobrychus minutus* (c.60-70 pairs), *Nycticorax nycticorax* (480-500 pairs), *Ardeola ralloides* (40-45 pairs), *Egretta garzetta* (100-110 pairs), *E. alba* (80-90 pairs), *Ardea purpurea* (120-130 pairs), *Ciconia nigra* (2-3 pairs), *C. ciconia* (150-180 pairs), *Plegadis falcinellus* (1-2 pairs), *Platalea leucorodia* (400-450 pairs), *Anser anser* (160-180 pairs), *Aythya nyroca* (c.50-70 pairs), *Circus aeruginosus* (35-40 pairs), *C. pygargus* (3-4 pairs), *Falco cherrug* (1-2 pairs), *F. vespertinus* (360-400 pairs), *Otis tarda* (180-200 pairs), *Porzana pusilla* (8-10 pairs), *Crex crex* (4-5 pairs), *Recurvirostra avosetta* (50-70 pairs), *Burhinus oedicnemus* (10-15 pairs), *Glareola pratincola* (40-45 pairs, decreasing), *Limosa limosa* (150-200 pairs), *Larus melanocephalus* (3-4 pairs), *Sterna hirundo* (20-25 pairs), *Chlidonias hybridus* (300-320 pairs), *C. leucopterus* (180-200 pairs), *Asio flammeus* (1-3 pairs), *Calandrella brachydactyla* (15-20 pairs), *Anthus campestris* (25-35 pairs), *Luscinia svecica* (15-20 pairs), *Acrocephalus melanopogon* (20-25 pairs), *A. paludicola* (200-220 pairs), and *Sylvia nisoria* (5-10 pairs). One of the few stop-over localities in central Europe for *Anser erythropus* (30-40 regularly in autumn; with 450-500 in Nov. 1987), and *Numenius tenuirostris* (1-2 records in most years). Other wildfowl and waders occurring as passage migrants include *Anser fabalis* (1000), *A. albifrons* (600-10,000 in autumn), *A. anser* (800-1500 in autumn), *Anas platyrhynchos* (40,000-60,000), *Charadrius morinellus* (20-30 in autumn), *Philomachus pugnax* (50,000 in spring), and *Limosa limosa* (6000-10,000 in autumn). Other passage species in autumn include *Circaetus gallicus* (4-10), *Buteo rufinus* (30-40), *Falco cherrug* (5-7), and *Grus grus* (2000-3000). Extremely important in winter for *Haliaeetus albicilla* (20-25).

017 Tiszafüredi madárrezervátum (Heves, Szolnok)

47°37'N, 20°46'E 2500 ha Included in Hortobágy Ramsar Site

Nature Conservation Area

Originally an area of riverine forest which was felled to create a reservoir. The resulting habitat is very favourable for birds, with water-levels of varying depths, islets with *Salix* woodland, and extensive beds of *Typha* and *Phragmites*.

Breeding species include *Phalacrocorax carbo* (450-500 pairs), *Nycticorax nycticorax* (15-20 pairs), *Ardeola ralloides* (4-5 pairs), *Egretta alba* (15-20 pairs), *Ciconia nigra* (1 pair), *C. ciconia* (2-3 pairs), *Platalea leucorodia* (100-110 pairs), *Pernis apivorus* (1 pair), *Milvus migrans* (1 pair), *Haliaeetus albicilla* (1 pair), *Falco cherrug* (1 pair), *Sterna hirundo* (15-25 pairs), and *Chlidonias niger* (2-5 pairs). *Ciconia nigra* (20-25), *C. ciconia* (c.50), and *Plegadis falcinellus* (3-5) occur on autumn passage, and *Haliaeetus albicilla* (20-25 birds) and *Falco peregrinus* (1-2) occur in winter.

018 Pusztakócsi mocsarak (Hajdú-Bihar)

47°35'N, 19°58'E 2815 ha Included in Hortobágy Ramsar Site

Nature Conservation Area

An area of wet meadows and marshes with small clumps of *Quercus* woodland with *Falco vespertinus* colonies. Situated close to the Hortobágy National Park.

Breeding species include *Botaurus stellaris* (5-6 pairs), *Egretta alba* (18-20 pairs), *Ardea purpurea* (20-25 pairs), *Ciconia ciconia* (10-12 pairs), *Platalea leucorodia* (18-20 pairs), *Aythya nyroca* (common), *Circus aeruginosus* (12-14 pairs), *C. pygargus* (1 pair), *Falco vespertinus*, *Porzana parva* (2-3 pairs), *Larus melanocephalus* (2 pairs), *Sterna hirundo* (2-3 pairs), and *Acrocephalus melanopogon* (5-6 pairs). *Ciconia ciconia* (c.50) and *Plegadis falcinellus* (5-6) occur on autumn passage, and *Haliaeetus albicilla* (2-3) occurs in winter.

019 Ároktö-tiszacsegei hullámtér (Borsod-Abaúj-Zemplén, Hajdú-Bihar)

47°42'N, 21°00'E 700 ha

Nature Conservation Area

An area of riverine forest along the River Tisza with backwaters. Includes mature *Quercus* woodland (which holds a heronry), mature *Salix/Populus* woodland, mature *Ulmus* and *Quercus* woodland, and meadows. Situated close to the Hortobágy National Park.

Breeding species include *Phalacrocorax carbo* (10-20 pairs), *Nycticorax nycticorax* (150-200 pairs), *Ardeola ralloides* (10-15 pairs), *Egretta garzetta* (50-60 pairs), *Ciconia nigra* (1-2 pairs), *C. ciconia* (2-3 pairs), *Milvus migrans* (1-2 pairs), *Crex crex* (5-10 pairs), *Chlidonias hybridus* (10-15 pairs), and *C. niger* (5-10 pairs). *Ciconia nigra* (10-20) and *C. ciconia* (50) occur on passage, and *Haliaeetus albicilla* (3-5) occurs in winter.

020 Ágota-puszta (Hajdú-Bihar)

47°23'N, 21°05'E 4700 ha

Nature Conservation Area

An area of salt-steppe with shallow marshes, seasonal saltmarshes, *Fraxinus/Ulmus* woodland and grasslands. Situated close to the Hortobágy National Park.

Breeding species include *Ardeola ralloides* (25-30 pairs), *Nycticorax nycticorax* (50-70 pairs), *Egretta garzetta* (30-35 pairs), *Circus aeruginosus* (4-5 pairs), *C. pygargus* (1 pair), *Falco vespertinus* (15-20 pairs), *Crex crex* (2-3 pairs), *Otis tarda* (20-25 pairs), *Burhinus oedicnemus* (2-3 pairs), and *Limosa limosa* (20-25 pairs). *Ciconia ciconia* (30-40) and *Otis tarda* (30-40) occur on autumn passage. *Haliaeetus albicilla* (1-2) occurs in winter.

021 Kiskunsági szikes-tavak (Bács-Kiskun)

46°49'N, 19°15'E 3903 ha

Part of Ramsar Site (4000 ha); included in Biosphere Reserve (22,095 ha).

Included in Kiskunsági National Park (30,636 ha)

Steppe with soda lakes, reedbeds, marshes, and woodland. Only traditional agricultural and grazing methods are allowed and a canal system means that the water-level of the lakes can be changed if needed. There are important salt-lakes, meadows, and pastures lying outside the area (and not included in the National Park) with breeding *Recurvirostra avosetta* and *Limosa limosa*.

Breeding species include *Egretta alba* (4 pairs), *Ardea purpurea* (5 pairs), *Platalea leucorodia* (3 pairs), *Aythya nyroca* (5 pairs), *Circus aeruginosus* (4 pairs), *Burhinus oedicnemus* (2 pairs), *Recurvirostra avosetta* (14 pairs), *Limosa limosa* (40-50 pairs), *Larus melanocephalus* (1 pair), *L. ridibundus* (1500-2000 pairs), *Sterna hirundo* (4 pairs), *Acrocephalus melanopogon* (10-20 pairs), *Lanius collurio* (10-15 pairs), and *L. minor* (5-10 pairs). An important site for birds on spring and autumn passage with *Egretta alba* (25 in autumn), *Anser fabalis* (2000-3000 in spring, 10,000 in autumn), *A. albifrons* (1000-2000 in spring; 5000 in autumn), *Anas platyrhynchos* (10,000 in autumn), *Aythya nyroca* (45 in autumn), *Circus aeruginosus* (15 in autumn), and *Limosa limosa* (200-250 in spring).

022 Kolon-tó (Bács-Kiskun)

46°46'N, 19°20'E 2728 ha Included in Kiskunsági Biosphere Reserve

Included in Kiskunsági National Park

A large lake almost completely covered by *Phragmites* and surrounded by wet meadows and grasslands. Economic activities include reed-cutting and haymaking.

Breeding species include *Nycticorax nycticorax* (120 pairs), *Ardeola ralloides* (20 pairs), *Egretta alba* (10 pairs), *Ardea purpurea* (5 pairs), and *Platalea leucorodia* (10 pairs).

023 Dévaványa (Békés)

40°01'N, 20°58'E 8933 ha

Landscape Protection Reserve (3433 ha); partly unprotected

Secondary grassland with large agricultural fields formed by the drainage of a wetland area. Warm and dry receiving only a small amount of snow. Only land-use compatible with nature conservation is allowed (and every year large fields of rape are sown to provide winter food for *Otis tarda*). Important steppe habitat and arable land supporting *Otis tarda* lies outside the Landscape Protection Reserve and is unprotected. Here, the latter species's nests (in alfalfa and cereal fields) are frequently destroyed during the harvest. Ornithological information below refers to the Reserve only.

An important site for *Otis tarda* (20-25 pairs; 100 in winter and 100-120 in spring). Other breeding species include *Ciconia ciconia* (3-4 pairs), *Falco vespertinus* (20 pairs), *Burhinus oedicnemus* (1-2 pairs), *Limosa limosa* (4-5 pairs), *Coracias garrulus* (1-2 pairs), *Anthus campestris* (15-20 pairs), *Sylvia nisoria* (3-5 pairs), *Lanius collurio* (15 pairs), and *L. minor* (5 pairs). *Grus grus* (100) occurs on autumn passage.

024 Péteri-tó (Bács-Kiskun)

46°37'N, 19°52'E 684 ha

Nature Conservation Area

Originally a soda lake, which was turned into three fish-ponds in the 1920s. Several small soda lakes remain which dry out in summer. The fish-ponds are surrounded by reedbeds and there are grazing-meadows which are occasionally flooded. Economic activities include fish-farming and sheep- and cattle-grazing, and there is some arable land.

Breeding species include *Botaurus stellaris* (5-6 pairs), *Ixobrychus minutus* (common), *Egretta alba* (5-10 pairs), *Ardea purpurea* (10-12 pairs), *Platalea leucorodia* (5-10 pairs), *Aythya nyroca* (common), *Circus aeruginosus* (3-4 pairs), *Porzana parva* (common), *Crex crex* (1-2 pairs), *Recurvirostra avosetta* (5-10 pairs), *Limosa limosa* (10-12 pairs), *Sterna hirundo* (*c.*10-12 pairs), *Alcedo atthis* (common), *Coracias garrulus* (1-2 pairs), *Acrocephalus melanopogon* (10-12 pairs), *Lanius collurio* (common), and *L. minor* (3-4 pairs). In addition *Ciconia ciconia* occurs on autumn passage (*c.*30) and *Haliaeetus albicilla* (3-4) occurs in winter.

025 Kardoskut Fehér-tó (Békés)

46°30'N, 20°28'E 488 ha Part of Ramsar Site (500 ha)

Nature Conservation Area

A shallow soda lake (Fehér-tó) with reedbeds (covering one third of the lake) with salt-steppe and agricultural land. Cultivation and grazing are allowed in the territory. Pollution is caused by the use of artificial fertilisers on the adjacent arable land.

Breeding species include *Botaurus stellaris* (2 pairs), *Circus aeruginosus* (3 pairs), *Recurvirostra avosetta* (20 pairs), and *Limosa limosa* (40-50). Large numbers of geese occur at the site in autumn, mainly *Anser fabalis* (1000), *A. albifrons* (20,000; with 2000-3000 in spring), and also *A. erythropus* (20-50). Other species on passage include *Grus grus* (10,000 in October and November; also 850-1000 in winter) and a variety of waders, including *Numenius tenuirostris* (17 records from 1959 to 1978).

026 Mártély (Csongrád)

46°28'N, 20°12'E 2232 ha part of Ramsar Site (2300 ha)

Landscape Protection Reserve

A meandering stretch of the River Tisza with oxbows, riverine forests of *Salix* and *Populus*, and meadows. Economic activities include fishing, forestry, and grazing, and there are rice fields and arable land in the surrounding area. Occasionally the oxbows are polluted by fertilisers.

Breeding species include *Phalacrocorax carbo* (8-10 pairs), *Nycticorax nycticorax* (4-5 pairs), *Ardeola ralloides* (2-3 pairs), *Egretta garzetta* (1-2 pairs), *Ciconia nigra* (2 pairs), *C. ciconia* (1 pair), *Aythya nyroca* (common), *Milvus migrans* (1 pair), *Haliaeetus albicilla* (1 pair), and *Crex crex* (3-4 pairs). *Ciconia nigra* (10-12 in autumn) and *C. ciconia* (5-10 in autumn) occur on passage, and *Haliaeetus albicilla* (2-3) occurs in winter.

027 Pusztaszer and Szeged-Fehértó (Csongrád)

46°15'N, 20°10'E 22,226 ha Ramsar Site (5000 ha)

Landscape Protection Reserve

The Pusztaszer Landscape Protection Reserve includes four separate wetlands: Szeged-Fehértó, Sasér, Labodár, and Csaj-tó. Szeged-Fehértó was formerly a shallow lake but has been converted to fish-ponds, which are surrounded by dense reedbeds. Csaj-tó is a fish-pond system similar to Szeged-Fehértó. Labodár and Sasér are riverine forests along the River Tisza. There are also extensive areas of puszta and arable land. Grazing is allowed on the puszta to maintain the vegetation, and other economic activities include fish-farming, reed-cutting, and arable farming. It is possible that fertilisers and pesticides are adversely affecting the protected area, also freshwater entering the fish-ponds from the River Tisza is likely to be detrimental to the salt-steppes.

Breeding species include *Phalacrocorax carbo* (150-180 pairs), *Botaurus stellaris* (5-10 pairs), *Ixobrychus minutus* (min. 10-15 pairs), *Nycticorax nycticorax* (150-160 pairs), *Ardeola ralloides* (5-10 pairs), *Egretta garzetta* (45-50 pairs), *E. alba* (20-25 pairs), *Ardea purpurea* (45-50 pairs), *Ciconia ciconia* (10-12 pairs), *Platalea leucorodia* (5-7 pairs), *Aythya nyroca* (min. 10-15 pairs), *Circus aeruginosus* (*c.*10 pairs), *Crex crex* (1-2 pairs), *Himantopus himantopus* (1-2 pairs), *Recurvirostra avosetta* (20-25 pairs), *Burhinus oedicnemus* (2-3 pairs), *Limosa limosa* (40-45 pairs), *Larus melanocephalus* (4-5 pairs), *Sterna hirundo* (50-60 pairs), *Alcedo atthis* (5-10 pairs), *Acrocephalus melanopogon* (min. 10-15 pairs), *Sylvia nisoria* (min. 5-10 pairs), *Lanius collurio* (min. 20-25 pairs), and *Lanius minor* (min. 5-10 pairs). Passage species include *Phalacrocorax carbo* (500-700 in autumn), *Egretta garzetta* (300-350 in autumn), *Ciconia ciconia* (20-30 in spring; 40 in autumn), *C. nigra* (40-45 in autumn), *Anser albifrons* (10,000-15,000 in autumn), *Grus grus* (1000-2000 in autumn), *Limosa limosa* (1000 in spring), and *Philomachus pugnax* (9000 in spring). *Haliaeetus albicilla* (4-5) occurs in winter.

028 Aggtelek (Borsod-Abaúj-Zemplén)

48°27'N, 20°32'E 19,709 ha Biosphere Reserve (19,247 ha)

National Park

A hilly area with wide plateaus and karst landscape with *Fagus*, *Quercus*, *Carpinus*, and *Tilia*/*Fraxinus* woodland, rocky grasslands, and heathlands.

Breeding species include *Ciconia nigra* (2 pairs), *C. ciconia* (5 pairs), *Pernis apivorus* (8-10 pairs), *Circaetus gallicus* (3 pairs), *Aquila pomarina* (2 pairs), *A. heliaca* (1 pair), *Bonasa bonasia* (40-50 pairs), *Crex crex* (2-3 pairs), *Strix uralensis* (2 pairs), *Alcedo atthis* (2-3 pairs), *Picus canus* (3-4 pairs), *Dryocopus martius* (30 pairs), *Dendrocopos medius* (common), *D. leucotos* (8-10 pairs), *Lullula arborea* (common), *Sylvia nisoria* (common), and *Lanius collurio* (common). In addition *Aquila chrysaetos* (1-2) and *Falco peregrinus* (1-2) occur in winter.

029 Gerecse (Komárom)

47°45'N, 18°30'E 8617 ha

Landscape Protection Reserve

A hilly region with interesting red limestone formations. Includes *Quercus*, *Carpinus*/*Fagus*, and *Tilia* woodland, steppe meadows, and rocky grasslands.

Important for breeding raptors with *Pernis apivorus* (3-4 pairs), *Milvus migrans* (2 pairs), *Circaetus gallicus* (1-2 pairs), *Aquila pomarina* (1-2 pairs), *A. heliaca* (1 pair), *Hieraaetus pennatus* (1 pair), and *Falco cherrug* (2-3 pairs). Other breeding species include *Ciconia nigra* (3-4 pairs), *C. ciconia* (1-2 pairs), *Merops apiaster* (50-60 pairs), and *Picus canus* (5-10 pairs); *Dryocopus martius*, *Dendrocopos medius*, *Lullula arborea*, and *Lanius collurio* are common.

030 Mátra (Nógrád, Heves)

47°50'N, 20°00'E 11,863 ha

Landscape Protection Reserve

Hilly country with valleys and streams and *Quercus*/*Fagus* and *Fraxinus* woodland.

Important for breeding raptors with *Pernis apivorus* (12-14 pairs), *Circaetus gallicus* (2-3 pairs), *Aquila pomarina* (2-3 pairs), *A. heliaca* (1 pair), and *Falco cherrug* (2-3 pairs). Other breeding species include *Ciconia nigra* (3-5 pairs), *C. ciconia* (5-7 pairs), *Bonasa bonasia* (25-35 pairs), *Bubo bubo* (2 pairs), *Picus canus* (10-15 pairs), and *Emberiza hortulana* (5-8 pairs); *Dryocopus martius*, *Dendrocopos medius*, *Lullula arborea*, *Sylvia nisoria*, and *Lanius collurio* are common.

031 Gemenc (Bács-Kiskun)

46°07'N, 18°45'E 17,779 ha

Landscape Protection Reserve

Regularly flooded riverine forest of *Salix* and *Populus* along the River Danube, with a rich ground flora.

Important for *Haliaeetus albicilla* (3-4 breeding pairs; 10-12 in winter). Other breeding species include *Nycticorax nycticorax* (50-70 pairs), *Ciconia nigra* (8-10 pairs), *C. ciconia* (5-7 pairs), *Milvus migrans* (5-6 pairs), *Falco cherrug* (3 pairs), *Alcedo atthis* (common), *Coracias garrulus* (3-4 pairs), and *Dryocopus martius* (common).

032 Tokaj-Bodrogzug (Borsod-Abaúj-Zemplén)

48°15'N, 21°25'E 4242 ha

Landscape Protection Reserve

Tokaj is a hill of volcanic origin with *Tilia*/*Fraxinus* woodland. Bodrogzug comprises the flood plain of the Rivers Tisza and Bodrog with regularly flooded meadows and riverine forests of *Salix* and *Populus*. Economic activities include forestry, fishing, and grazing, with some arable land in the surrounding area.

Breeding species include *Phalacrocorax carbo* (20-25 pairs), *Botaurus stellaris* (10-15 pairs), *Nycticorax nycticorax* (50-70 pairs), *Ardeola ralloides* (10-12 pairs), *Egretta garzetta* (25-30 pairs), *E. alba* (20 pairs), *Ardea purpurea* (10-12 pairs), *Ciconia nigra* (4 pairs), *C. ciconia* (30-35 pairs), *Aythya nyroca* (common), *Pernis apivorus* (2-3 pairs), *Milvus migrans* (2 pairs), *Haliaeetus albicilla* (1 pair), *Circaetus gallicus* (2 pairs), *Circus aeruginosus* (10-12 pairs), *C. pygargus* (2-3 pairs), *Porzana porzana* (common), *Crex crex* (common), *Limosa limosa* (10-20 pairs), *Chlidonias hybridus* (25-30 pairs), *C. niger* (10-15 pairs), *Alcedo atthis* (common), *Coracias garrulus* (3-4 pairs), *Lullula arborea* (common), and *Sylvia nisoria* (common). *Ciconia nigra* (200-250 in autumn), *C. ciconia* (200-300 in autumn), and *Grus grus* (400-500 in autumn) occur on spring and autumn passage, and *Haliaeetus albicilla* (2-3) and *Asio flammeus* (2-3) occur in winter.

033 Sárrét (Fejér)

47°08'N, 18°15'E 2211 ha

Landscape Protection Reserve

Grazing-meadows with small ponds and a raised bog with meadows and lakes.

Breeding species include *Circus aeruginosus* (3-4 pairs), *C. pygargus* (1-2 pairs), *Porzana porzana* (4-5 pairs), *Otis tarda* (1-2 pairs), *Limosa limosa* (2-3 pairs), *Asio flammeus* (1-2 pairs), *Anthus campestris* (4-6 pairs), *Lanius collurio* (common), and *L. minor* (2-3 pairs). *Ciconia ciconia* (20-30 in autumn) occurs on spring and autumn passage, and *Circus cyaneus* (10-15), *Otis tarda* (4-6), and *Asio flammeus* (3-4) occur in winter.

034 Tiszadobiártér (Szabolcs-Szatmár)

48°00'N, 21°10'E 1000 ha

Nature Conservation Area

Riverine forest along the River Tisza with meandering backwaters and meadows. Includes mature *Quercus* woodland.

Breeding species include *Nycticorax nycticorax* (30-35 pairs), *Egretta garzetta* (20-25 pairs), *Ardea purpurea* (5-7 pairs), *Aythya nyroca* (common), *Milvus migrans* (2-5 pairs), *Crex crex* (5-10 pairs), *Chlidonias hybridus* (5-10 pairs), *C. niger* (2-3 pairs), and *Coracias garrulus* (1-2 pairs). *Ciconia ciconia* (*c.*30 in autumn) occurs on passage.

035 Tiszaalpári rét (Bács-Kiskun)

46°48'N, 20°00'E 600 ha

Unprotected, but proposed for protection as part of the Kiskunsági National Park

Riverine forest along the River Tisza with backwaters and meadows. Land-uses include grazing and haymaking.

Breeding species include *Nycticorax nycticorax* (25-30 pairs), *Ardeola ralloides* (8-10 pairs), *Egretta garzetta* (20-25 pairs), *E. alba* (5-8 pairs), *Ciconia nigra* (1 pair), *Aythya nyroca* (5-10 pairs), *Milvus migrans* (1-2 pairs), *Circus aeruginosus* (1-2 pairs), *C. pygargus* (1-2 pairs), *Crex crex* (3-5 pairs), *Limosa limosa* (5-10 pairs), and *Coracias garrulus* (1-3 pairs). *Ciconia nigra* (10-20) occurs on autumn passage.

036 Biharugrai-halastavak (Békés)

46°58'N, 21°35'E 5000 ha

Unprotected

A large fish-pond complex on the Romanian border. The fish-ponds are fringed with *Phragmites*, and there are grazing-meadows and steppe. The reedbeds are harvested annually; fish-farming is intensive and there is waterfowl hunting by foreign tourists.

Breeding species include *Botaurus stellaris* (common), *Ixobrychus minutus* (common), *Egretta alba* (5-15 pairs), *Ardea purpurea* (common), *Aythya nyroca* (common), *Circus aeruginosus* (common), *Porzana parva* (common), *Otis tarda* (5-10 pairs), *Recurvirostra avosetta* (10-15 pairs), *Alcedo atthis* (common), and *Acrocephalus melanopogon* (common). *Ciconia ciconia* (25-40) and *Platalea leucorodia* (150-200) occur on autumn passage, and *Haliaeetus albicilla* (3-4) occurs in winter.

037 Tiszaluc-Kesznyéten puszta (Borsod-Abaúj-Zemplén, Szabolcs-Szatmár)

48°02'N, 21°03'E 1700 ha

Unprotected

An area of riverine forest, steppe, and meadows. Further ornithological research is needed to determine its ornithological importance before proposing measures for protection.

The riverine forest has an important heronry with breeding *Nycticorax nycticorax*, *Egretta garzetta*, and *Ardea cinerea*. Other breeding species include *Crex crex* and *Limosa limosa*.

038 Müller-szék (Csongrád)

46°27'N, 19°57'E 200 ha

Unprotected

A characteristic steppe area in the southern part of the Great Hungarian Plain with small temporary soda lakes. Further ornithological research is needed to determine its ornithological importance before proposing measures for protection.

Species regularly occurring include *Himantopus himantopus* and *Recurvirostra avosetta*.

039 Mezöség (Borsod-Abaúj-Zemplén)

47°45'N, 20°48'E 7000 ha

Unprotected

Similar habitat to the Hortobágy, lying on the other side of the River Tisza, east of Mezökövesd. Mainly steppe with sandy loams, wet meadows, and patches of woodland. Further research is needed to determine its ornithological importance before proposing measures for protection.

Breeding species include *Falco vespertinus*, *Otis tarda*, *Burhinus oedicnemus*, and *Glareola pratincola*.

040 Hajdusági erdöspuszta (Hajdú-Bihar)

47°32'N, 21°45'E 5000 ha

Unprotected

Mainly steppe with *Quercus* and *Populus* woodland situated east of Debrecen. Further research is needed to determine its ornithological importance before proposing measures for protection.

An important area for breeding and passage birds of prey; species occurring include *Buteo rufinus*.

041 Nagykunsági puszta (Szolnok)

47°19'N, 20°46'E 3600 ha

Unprotected

Similar habitat to the Hortobágy, lying south of the National Park and east of Karcag.

An area of considerable ornithological importance with breeding *Falco vespertinus*, *Otis tarda*, *Burhinus oedicnemus*, *Glareola pratincola*, *Recurvirostra avosetta*, and *Calandrella brachydactyla* (an extremely rare species in Hungary). Also good for birds of prey and *Grus grus* on passage.

042 Harta-Akasztói puszta (Bács-Kiskun)

46°43'N, 19°07'E 2000 ha

Unprotected

Similar habitat to, and lying south of, Kiskunsági szikes-tavak, situated between the Rivers Duna (Danube) and Tisza. Further research is needed to determine its ornithological importance before proposing measures for protection.

Breeding species include *Circus pygargus*, *Otis tarda*, and *Burhinus oedicnemus*. In addition, it is an important stop-over site for waders.

043 Nagyszék, Balmazujváros (Hajdú-Bihar)

47°36'N, 21°22'E 630 ha

Unprotected

Similar habitat to the Hortobágy, lying to the east of the National Park, with salt-steppe and small soda lakes. Further research is needed to determine its ornithological importance before proposing measures for protection.

An important breeding area for *Recurvirostra avosetta* and *Charadrius alexandrinus*.

044 Bélmegyeri puszta (Békés)

46°54'N, 21°10'E 400 ha

Unprotected

An area of secondary steppe covered with patches of *Quercus* and *Populus* woodland. Further research is needed to determine its ornithological importance before proposing measures for protection.

An important area for breeding *Falco vespertinus* and *Lanius minor*, and a resting and feeding area for birds of prey on migration.

045 Pitvarosi puszta (Csongrád)

46°19'N, 20°43'E 3156 ha

Unprotected

A steppe area with temporary wetland areas and meadows. The area is used for grazing, and the method of grazing (with fencing) is considered to be detrimental to the area.

Otis tarda regularly breeds. Important for passage *Anser albifrons* (10,000), *A. erythropus* (10-100), and *Grus grus* (3000).

046 Szabadkigyósi puszta (Békés)

46°36'N, 21°04'E 3785 ha

Landscape Protection Reserve

An area of steppe with patches of woodland. Further research is needed to determine its ornithological importance.

Falco vespertinus is constantly present during the breeding season and presumably breeds. An important area for gathering and feeding passage birds, particularly *Grus grus*.

MAIN REFERENCES

Haraszthy, L. (1984) *Magyarország fészkelö madarai* (Breeding birds of Hungary). Natura, Budapest.

Janossy, D. Riverine forests in Hungary. Pp. 46-47 in Imboden, E. ed. (1987) *Riverine forests in Europe: status and conservation.* Cambridge: International Council for Bird Preservation.

Polunin, O. and Walters, M. (1985) *A guide to the vegetation of Britain and Europe.* Oxford University Press, Oxford.

Rakonczay, Z. (1987) *Kiskunságtól a Sárrétig Mezögazdasági Kiadó.* Budapest.

Sterbetz, I. (1981) *Protected wetlands of international importance in Hungary.* Mezögazdasági kiadó, Budapest.

Tóth, K. (1979) *Nemzeti Park a Kiskunságban Mezögazdasági Kiadó.* Budapest.

ICELAND

Harlequin Duck *Histrionicus histrionicus*

INTRODUCTION

General information

Iceland is the second largest island in Europe, with an area of some 103,000 sq km. Iceland is close to the northern border of the Atlantic Ocean and is situated on the Mid-Atlantic Ridge. The geographical position is between 63°-66°N and 13°-24°W. The human population is only about 250,000 (an average population density of 2.3 persons per sq km in 1983), about half being concentrated in the south-west.

The bedrock is mostly volcanic basalt. An active volcanic zone with porous bedrock of recent age runs through the country from the south-west to the north-east. This is bordered to the east and west by a Tertiary basalt formation. The volcanic zone is characterised by extensive lava plains with scattered hills and ridges. The Tertiary areas were originally lava plains, that are now cut by rivers and glaciers, forming numerous valleys and fjords separated by mountain ranges. Most (about 70 per cent) of Iceland lies above 300 m altitude, and this is above the limits of human habitation.

Marine life is much influenced by the meeting of warm Atlantic water, brought in by the Irminger branch of the North Atlantic Drift (Gulf Stream) from the south and the cold polar East Greenland current from the north. The boreal seas to the south and west of Iceland vary in temperature between about 6°C in the coldest months (about February) and 10°C in the warmest month (August). The corresponding variation in the subarctic waters off the north and east coasts is 3-8°C. The edge of Arctic pack-ice usually lies some 50-100 nautical miles north-west of Iceland, but in some years drift-ice reaches the northern coasts. Ice frequently forms in sheltered bays, lagoons, and estuaries in winter. Otherwise the seas and coasts around Iceland are typically ice-free in winter.

The original vegetation in the lowlands is thought to have been *Betula pubescens* woodland or scrub. Only small remnants are left of this today and the lowlands are largely occupied by various types of dwarf-shrub heaths, grasslands, and sedge-bogs. A low alpine zone at about 300-600 m above sea-level is characterised by heath vegetation on well-drained sites and extensive poorly drained boggy plateaus with numerous ponds and lakes. Sporadic permafrost occurs in the central parts of the highlands causing palsa formation in the bogs. Above about 600 m altitude a high alpine zone can be distinguished, typically a discontinuous mat of mosses, herbs, and dwarf shrubs, which is much influenced by snow cover. Permanent ice-fields cover about 12,000 sq km. Large areas at all altitudes are covered by lava fields in various early successional stages, glacio-fluvial sand or gravel-plains (especially in the south-east), and gravel-flats where the top soil has blown off.

The vegetation is heavily influenced by man and livestock. Until recently, cutting and burning of scrub (for clearance and fuel) were important activities. Heavy grazing of livestock continues to be a major threat to soils and vegetation. In recent decades, farming has been considerably modernised and large areas of lowland bog have been drained, resulting in a major loss of breeding habitat for wetland birds.

Ornithological importance

Iceland is important as a breeding ground for most boreal Atlantic seabird species and numerous Anatidae and waders, as a wintering area for several coastal and marine Arctic and boreal species, and as a passage area for migratory Arctic geese and waders.

Information on bird populations in Iceland is mainly based on rough estimates, with the exception of certain relatively rare and conspicuous species. The populations of certain seabirds, Anatidae, and raptors are fairly well known. Population estimates of waders and passerines are mostly guesses. Three Nearctic species breed in Iceland but nowhere else in Europe (but see Greenland): *Gavia immer* (*c*.300-500 pairs), *Histrionicus histrionicus*, and *Bucephala islandica* (total *c*.2500 birds). Other breeding species of particular interest in a European context are: *Cygnus cygnus* (autumn total *c*.15,000 birds), *Anser brachyrhynchus*, *Anas penelope*, *Aythya marila*, *Somateria mollissima*, *Haliaeetus albicilla* (30-40 pairs; increasing), *Falco rusticolus* (300+ pairs), very large populations of several waders (*Pluvialis apricaria*, *Calidris maritima*, *C. alpina*, *Gallinago gallinago*, *Limosa limosa*, *Numenius phaeopus*, *Tringa totanus*, *Phalaropus lobatus*), relatively large populations of most North-Atlantic seabirds, including *Sula bassana* (25,000 pairs), *Phalacrocorax carbo* (3500 pairs), *P. aristotelis* (6500 pairs), *Stercorarius skua*, *S. parasiticus*, *Larus hyperboreus*, *Rissa tridactyla*, *Uria aalge* (1.2 million pairs), *U. lomvia* (700,000 pairs), *Alca torda* (450,000 pairs), and *Fratercula arctica*.

Large Greenland and Arctic-Canadian populations of *Anser albifrons*, *Branta leucopsis*, *B. bernicla*, *Calidris canutus*, *C. alba*, and *Arenaria interpres* occur on migration. The most important passage sites for the Arctic waders and *Branta bernicla* are the mudflats on the west coast. *Anser albifrons* occurs on passage in the wetlands of the west and south. *Branta leucopsis* concentrate in the valleys of north Iceland in spring but stop over mainly in the southern highlands in autumn.

Conservation infrastructure and protected-area system

Protected areas are set up and managed by the Nature Conservation Council according to the Nature Conservation Act of 1971. There are certain exceptions to this: one National Park and one Natural Monument are managed by committees appointed by parliament; one protected area, the Mývatn-Laxá, is subject to a separate statutory act. The categories are as follows:

1. National Parks

   Land owned by the state; strict land-use regulations.

2. Nature Reserves

   Can be owned by the state or privately; regulations depend on the purpose of protection.

3. Natural Monuments
   As Nature Reserves, but usually very restricted in area and primarily of aesthetic or geological interest.

4. Public Recreation Areas
   Ownership varies; managed by municipal government.

The Nature Conservation Council moreover maintains a list of sites of conservation interest. Placing a site on such a list is a declaration of intent that has proved of value in preventing encroachment.

Bird protection and bird hunting is governed by an act dating from 1966. Nature conservation as well as bird protection are the responsibility of the Ministry of Culture and Education. The nature-conservation legislation is currently being revised and some major structural changes, some of them overdue, are expected to take place.

International measures relevant to the conservation of sites

Iceland has ratified the Ramsar Convention and has designated one Ramsar Site, 20,000 ha within the Mývatn-Laxá Protected Area. It is not a party to any of the other international conventions covered by this book.

Overview of the inventory

Fifty-three important bird areas are contained in the Icelandic inventory, and they cover a total of 506,000 ha (to nearest 1000 ha). Some form of protection has been established at 13 of these sites which total 64,525 ha. The sites listed fall into three main categories: (1) bird cliffs containing at least one per cent of the Icelandic population of a species; (2) coastal wetlands of international importance; (3) freshwater wetlands of international importance. The seabird colonies are generally not threatened as sites. The most important coastal wetlands are not threatened, although there are some problems with road construction and urban development.

The freshwater wetlands are generally under serious threat, at least in the long run. These sites, which are very limited in area, support high densities of breeding, moulting, and passage Anatidae and waders. Some of these sites are threatened by industry and energy development. Most lowland sites are threatened either directly by drainage or indirectly by siltation and eutrophication. Progress in conserving these areas has been unsatisfactory and many very important sites remain without formal protection. It is important to realise that economic pressure on these sites will continue in the future.

Acknowledgements

The following inventory was prepared from data-sheets compiled by A. Gardarsson and O. K. Nielsen (University of Iceland). A. D. Fox (Wildfowl Trust) provided useful advice. A. Gardarsson prepared the introduction.

INVENTORY

No.	Site name	Criteria used to select site [see p.18]							
		0	1(i)	1(ii)	1(iii)	1(iv)	2	3	4
001	Lónsfjördur				*			*	
002	Skardsfjördur				*				
003	Steinsmýrarflód							*	
004	Veidivötn							*	
005	Thjórsárver				*				
006	Vestmannaeyjar		*	*				*	
007	Skúmsstadavatn				*			*	
008	Oddaflód							*	
009	Safamýri				*			*	

No.	Site name	Criteria used to select site [see p.18]							
		0	1(i)	1(ii)	1(iii)	1(iv)	2	3	4
010	Pollengi							*	
011	Brúará-Laugarvatn				*			*	
012	Stokkseyri							*	
013	Sog				*			*	
014	Ölfusforir				*			*	
015	Krísuvík		*	*					
016	Eldey		*	*				*	
017	Ósar				*			*	
018	Gardskagi				*				
019	Astjörn	*							
020	Álftanes				*				
021	Laxárvogur				*				
022	Leirárvogar				*				
023	Borgarfjördur				*				
024	Ferjubakkaflói-Nordurá				*			*	
025	Hjörsey-Straumfjördur			*	*			*	
026	Löngufjörur				*				
027	Álftafjördur-Hofsstadavogur				*			*	
028	Breidafjördur		*	*	*		*	*	
029	Látrabjarg		*	*				*	
030	Ritur		*	*				*	
031	Hælavíkurbjarg		*	*				*	
032	Hornbjarg		*	*				*	
033	Arnarvatnsheidi-Tvídægra				*			*	
034	Austara Eylendid	*							
035	Eyjavatn	*							
036	Skógar				*			*	
037	Eylendid				*			*	
038	Hörgárósar	*							
039	Höfdavatn	*							
040	Drangey							*	
041	Grímsey		*	*				*	
042	Svarfadardalur				*				
043	Hólmarnir	*							
044	Sandur-Sílalækur				*				
045	Vestmannsvatn				*				
046	Mývatn-Laxá				*			*	
047	Öxarfjördur				*			*	
048	Skoruvík		*	*				*	
049	Langanes		*	*				*	
050	Hjaltastadablá	*							
051	Skrúdur		*	*				*	
052	Papey		*	*					
053	Álftafjördur-Hamarsfjördur				*			*	

Comments on the inventory

1. A number of wetland sites do not meet the criteria but have still been included because of their waterfowl populations (column 0 in above table). It is difficult to select sites for breeding waterfowl, using numerical criteria, because of their dispersed distribution. Furthermore, counts of birds are lacking for several of the passage and moulting sites. Nevertheless, the following such sites are included (and are regarded by the Icelandic contributors to be of international importance): 019, 034, 035, 038, 039, 043, 050.

2. Site 052 is included, despite the lack of numerical data, because of its large *Fratercula arctica* population.
3. The sites have not been assigned to the regions of Iceland (districts). Iceland has been treated as a single 'region' when applying the site-selection criteria (category 3).
4. Sites 042, 044 and 045 are listed as qualifying according to criteria (category 1(iii)) because they hold more than one per cent (200 birds) of the Icelandic flyway population of *Anas penelope* or *Aythya marila*.

---

001 Lónsfjördur

64°25'N, 14°40'W 2700 ha

Unprotected, but listed by NCC as a site with conservation interest

A brackish coastal lagoon (protected from the open sea by a long bar), *c.*30 km north-east of Hornafjördur town, with extensive beds of *Ruppia maritima*, which is the primary food-plant of *Cygnus cygnus*. The area is used for fishing and grazing.

A moulting, passage, and sometimes a wintering site for *Cygnus cygnus* (max. 3000-4000). Also a site for passage Anatidae, notably *Anas penelope*.

002 Skardsfjördur

64°17'N, 15°10'W 1050 ha

Unprotected, but listed by NCC as a site with conservation interest

A coastal brackish lagoon with intertidal mudflats, surrounded mainly by grassland. Infilling at Hornafjördur is a problem at part of the site.

An important passage area for waders including *Charadrius hiaticula* (*c.*1000), *Calidris canutus* (1000+), and *C. alpina* (*c.*10,000).

003 Steinsmýrarflód

63°40'N, 18°00'W 2100 ha

Unprotected, but listed by NCC as a site with conservation interest

Freshwater rivers and streams, with *Carex* marshes. Human activities include stock-grazing and haymaking. Rapid siltation and drainage threaten the site.

Bucephala islandica winters here in small numbers. Also an important passage and wintering area for Anatidae and waders with a wide variety of species occurring, although none present in very high numbers; passage Anatidae do, however, include *Anser albifrons flavirostris*. Formerly the most important site in Iceland for breeding *Rallus aquaticus* (now may no longer nest in Iceland).

004 Veidivötn

64°10'N, 18°50'W 5000 ha

Unprotected, but listed by NCC as a site with conservation interest

Highland freshwater lakes, rivers and streams fed by cold springs. The area is used for sheep-grazing and recreation (including trout-fishing and tourism).

A breeding area for *Gavia immer*, *Cygnus cygnus*, and *Clangula hyemalis*. In addition, *Bucephala islandica* winters in small numbers (*c.*50), and *Aythya marila* moults in the area.

005 Thjórsárver

64°35'N, 18°40'W 37,500 ha

Nature Reserve

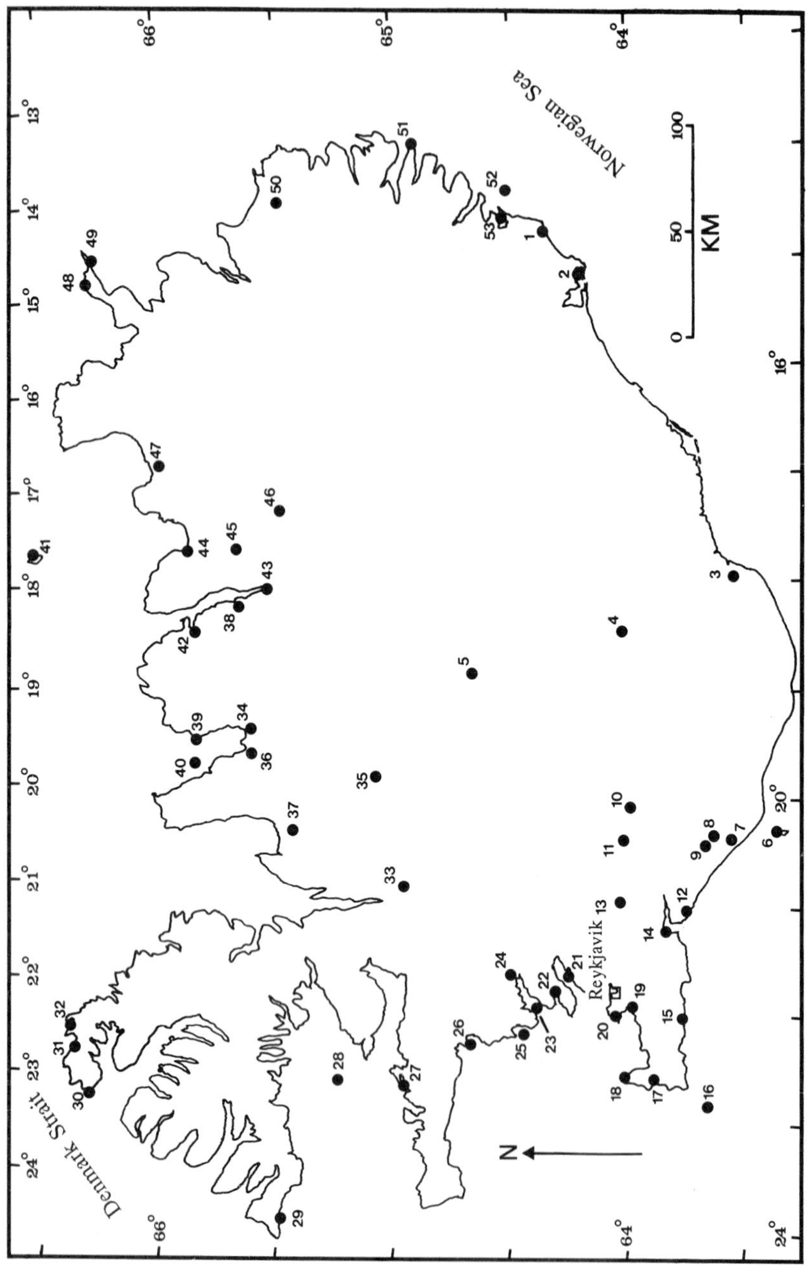

Figure 18: Map showing the location of the sites in Iceland

A tundra complex in the Central Highlands, south of the Hofsjökull glacier, containing rivers, lakes, ponds, and extensive marshy areas. No current land-use or problems, though formerly threatened by a hydroelectric power scheme in the 1970s.

The main breeding site for *Anser brachyrhynchus* (about 10,000 pairs).

006 Vestmannaeyjar

63°25'N, 20°20'W 27,500 ha (including surrounding waters)

Nature Reserve (Surtsey: 200 ha); three other islands are listed by NCC as sites with conservation interest

An archipelago of offshore rocky islands rising to 226 m. The most important sites are Surtsey, Súlnasker, Geldungur, Hellisey, Brandur, Ystiklettur, Heimaklettur, and Ellidaey.

Important for seabird colonies, holding more than one per cent of the Icelandic population of the following breeding species: *Fulmarus glacialis*, *Puffinus puffinus*, *Hydrobates pelagicus*, *Oceanodroma leucorhoa* (thousands of pairs), *Sula bassana* (*c*.9000 nests in 1984), *Rissa tridactyla*, *Uria aalge*, *U. lomvia*, *Cepphus grylle*, and *Fratercula arctica*.

007 Skúmsstadavatn

63°40'N, 20°30'W 800 ha

Unprotected, but listed by NCC as a site with conservation interest

A shallow freshwater lake, ponds, and *Carex* marshes. Human activities include farming. Threatened by drainage, siltation and eutrophication.

Breeding species include *Gavia stellata*, *Cygnus cygnus*, *Calidris alpina*, *Limosa limosa*, *Numenius phaeopus*, *Tringa totanus*, and *Phalaropus lobatus*. A roosting site for *Cygnus cygnus* (max. 200), *Anser albifrons flavirostris* (max. 1000), and other Anatidae.

008 Oddaflód

63°46'N, 20°27'W 700 ha

Unprotected, but listed by NCC as a site with conservation interest

A complex of freshwater rivers, streams, ponds, and extensive *Carex* marshes. Human activities include farming. Threatened by increased drainage for farming purposes.

Important for breeding *Gallinago gallinago*, *Limosa limosa*, *Tringa totanus*, *Phalaropus lobatus*, and possibly also *Rallus aquaticus*. A passage site for *Anser albifrons flavirostris*.

009 Safamýri

63°47'N, 20°35'W 2000 ha

Unprotected, but listed by NCC as a site with conservation interest

A freshwater lake with *Carex* bogs containing ponds. Human activities include farming and hunting. The latter is excessive causing undue disturbance, and the site is also threatened by further drainage.

A roosting and feeding site for *Cygnus cygnus* (200) and *Anser albifrons flavirostris* (max. 4000). Other species include breeding *Limosa limosa* and moulting *Anas penelope*.

010 Pollengi

64°10'N, 20°26'W 1000 ha

Unprotected, but listed by NCC as a site with conservation interest

A large area of rivers, streams, riparian marshes, lakes, and ponds. Farming is the main land-use. Threatened by drainage and siltation.

Breeding species include *Anser anser*, waders, *Larus ridibundus*, and possibly *Rallus aquaticus*. An important area for passage waterfowl, especially for *Cygnus cygnus*, *Anser albifrons flavirostris*, and *Limosa limosa*.

011 Brúará-Laugarvatn

64°10'N, 20°35'W 2000 ha

Unprotected

Freshwater rivers, streams, ponds, and marshy areas. Land-uses include farming and recreation. Threatened by drainage and holiday homes.

One of the very few wintering sites for *Bucephala islandica* (tens) away from the Mývatn-Laxá area. Also a breeding area for *Gavia immer*, *Podiceps auritus*, *Cygnus cygnus*, *Histrionicus histrionicus*, and *Larus ridibundus*.

012 Stokkseyri

63°52'N, 21°07'W 100 ha

Unprotected, but listed by NCC as a site with conservation interest

A small coastal wetland with fresh water and brackish ponds/marshes and an adjacent extensive intertidal area with beaches and flats. Land-use includes farming, urban activities and recreation. The area is threatened by urban development.

A breeding site for *Haematopus ostralegus*, *Charadrius hiaticula*, *Phalaropus fulicarius* (1-5 pairs; max. 20) and *Sterna paradisaea*, and a passage area for *Cygnus cygnus* and waders including large numbers of *Calidris canutus*, *C. alpina*, *Tringa totanus*, and *Arenaria interpres*.

013 Sog

64°10'N, 21°00'W 500 ha

Unprotected, but listed by NCC as a site with conservation interest

A major freshwater river draining Lake Thingvallavatn. Human activities include salmon-fishing, hydroelectric power generation and farming in the surrounding areas.

One of the few wintering sites for *Bucephala islandica* away from the Mývatn-Laxá area, with around 100-150 birds recorded; also wintering *Bucephala clangula* and *Mergus merganser*, and passage *Cygnus cygnus* (several hundred).

014 Ölfusforir

63°57'N, 21°15'W 1000 ha

Unprotected, but listed by NCC as a site with conservation interest

An extensive area of *Carex*-dominated coastal flood-plain, saltmarsh, and shallow freshwater marshes adjacent to land used for intensive agriculture and also peatlands. Human activities include grazing, fishing, and hunting. There are nearby urbanised and industrialised areas. Threatened by industrial activities.

An important breeding area for waterfowl, and wintering species include *Ardea cinerea*, *Cygnus cygnus*, *Anas crecca*, and *A. platyrhynchos*. Of major significance for passage *Cygnus cygnus* and *Anser albifrons flavirostris* (*c*.1000 in spring; 5000+ in autumn).

015 Krísuvík

63°53'N, 22°05'W 1200 ha (40 ha cliff)

Public Recreation Area

The largest sea cliffs in south-west Iceland.

An important seabird colony, with more than one per cent of the Icelandic population of *Rissa tridactyla* (30,000 pairs), *Uria aalge*, and *Alca torda* (10,000 pairs). Other breeding species include *Fulmarus glacialis*, *Uria lomvia*, *Cepphus grylle*, and *Fratercula arctica*. The total auk population is 40,000 pairs.

016 Eldey

63°44'N, 22°58'W 1 ha (island only)

Nature Reserve

A small rocky island (*c.*70 m high) off south-west Iceland, together with the surrounding waters (no area defined).

An important breeding site for *Sula bassana* (14,000 pairs) and other seabirds, including *Rissa tridactyla*, *Uria aalge*, and *U. lomvia*.

017 Ósar

63°57'N, 22°42'W 400 ha

Unprotected, but listed by NCC as a site with conservation interest

A shallow tidal bay just south of Keflavík airport, with rocky and sandy beaches and intertidal flats. The main land-uses are harbour activities and fish-farming. Dredging, pollution, and eutrophication threaten the site and there is the possibility of intensification of harbour operations.

An important wintering area for waterfowl including *Gavia immer*, *Podiceps auritus*, *Aythya marila* (100; the only wintering flock in Iceland), *Histrionicus histrionicus* (100+), and *Clangula hyemalis*.

018 Gardskagi

64°05'N, 22°42'W 600 ha

Unprotected, but listed by NCC as a site with conservation interest

A rich intertidal area with rocky shores, beaches, and estuarine flats; surrounded by a varied landscape including grassland and settlements. Land-uses include recreation and industrial activities. Threatened by urbanisation and infilling.

Important for passage waders (especially *Calidris canutus*, *C. alba*, *C. alpina*, and *Arenaria interpres*). Wintering and passage Anatidae include *Cygnus cygnus*, *Anas platyrhynchos*, and *Somateria mollissima* (max. 40,000).

019 Ástjörn

64°03'N, 21°57'W 25 ha

Nature Reserve

A shallow freshwater lake and associated marshes with extensive *Carex* beds close to Reykjavik. Urbanisation in the surrounding areas is a potential threat.

A breeding site for *Podiceps auritus* (5-10 pairs), *Cygnus cygnus*, waders, and *Larus ridibundus* (70 pairs).

020 Álftanes

64°05'N, 22°00'W 1000 ha

Unprotected, but listed by NCC as a site with conservation interest

A coastal area close to Reykjavik with sea bays, peninsulas, beaches, intertidal flats, brackish lagoons, and marshes. Vegetation includes beds of *Zostera*. Land-uses include urban, industrial, and boating activities. Threatened by dredging and infilling.

An important passage area for *Branta bernicla hrota* and waders, especially *Haematopus ostralegus*, *Calidris canutus*, *C. alpina*, *Tringa totanus*, and *Arenaria interpres*.

021 Laxárvogur

64°20'N, 21°40'W 695 ha

Unprotected, but listed by NCC as a site with conservation interest

A large shallow embayment of Hvalfjördur, including bays and estuarine flats. Human activities include farming.

An important breeding and wintering site for *Somateria mollissima* and passage area for waders (especially *Calidris canutus*).

022 Leirárvogar

64°23'N, 21°55'W 1400 ha

Unprotected, but listed by NCC as a site with conservation interest

A large shallow estuarine bay with small offshore islands and intertidal flats. Farming is the main land-use in the adjoining areas.

Important for passage *Branta bernicla hrota* and waders (especially *Calidris canutus* and *C. alpina*). Other species include breeding *Somateria mollissima*, and wintering *Haematopus ostralegus* and *Calidris maritima*.

023 Borgarfjördur

64°30'N, 22°00'W 7000 ha

Unprotected, but listed by NCC as a site with conservation interest

A large estuary with extensive mussel-beds, mudflats, and adjoining saltmarshes. Human activities include farming, salmon-fishing, and industry. The site is threatened by pollution, dyke construction, and infilling.

A site for moulting *Somateria mollissima* (max. 100,000) and passage waders, notably *Calidris alpina* and *Tringa totanus*.

024 Ferjubakkaflói-Nordurá

64°36'N, 21°40'W 1500 ha

Unprotected, but listed by NCC as a site with conservation interest

River flood-plains containing ponds, marshes, and peatbogs. Parts of the area are used for grazing and haymaking. Drainage for agriculture is a threat; there is also some disturbance from recreation and hunting.

Important concentrations of waterfowl occur on migration, notably *Cygnus cygnus* (max. 1800) and *Anser albifrons flavirostris* (1200).

025 Hjörsey-Straumfjördur

64°32'N, 22°15'W 6000 ha

Unprotected, but listed by NCC as a site with conservation interest

A shallow bay with extensive intertidal flats, numerous islands, coastal saltmarshes, lagoons, freshwater marshes and ponds. There are also extensive *Zostera* beds. The main land-use is stock-rearing.

Important for breeding ducks, waders, and seabirds, notably *Sterna paradisaea* and *Fratercula arctica*. Also important as a moulting site for *Cygnus cygnus* (max. 1300), and for passage *Branta bernicla hrota* (max. 10,000 in autumn) and waders, especially *Calidris canutus*, *C. alpina*, and *Arenaria interpres*.

026 Löngufjörur

64°45'N, 22°30'W 17,000 ha

Unprotected, but listed by NCC as a site with conservation interest

An extensive area of estuarine coast with a variety of habitats including bays, offshore islands, rock/cliff areas, beaches, intertidal flats, brackish lakes and marshes, mussel-beds, and freshwater ponds and marshes. Recreation is the main human activity.

A moulting site for *Somateria mollissima* (max. 80,000) and for waders on passage, notably *Calidris canutus*, *C. alba*, *C. alpina*, *Tringa totanus*, and *Arenaria interpres*. Important numbers of Anatidae, *Haematopus ostralegus*, and *Calidris maritima* occur in winter.

027 Álftafjördur-Hofsstadavogur

65°00'N, 22°40'W 3000 ha

Unprotected, but listed by NCC as a site with conservation interest

A complex of coastal bays, small offshore islands, beaches, and intertidal flats, south of the Breidafjördur area. Vegetation includes *Zostera* beds. Land-use in the adjoining areas includes farming.

A moulting and passage area for *Cygnus cygnus*; also important for passage *Branta bernicla hrota* and waders.

028 Breidafjördur

65°20'N, 23°00'W 270,000 ha

Nature Reserves (Flatey, Hrísey, and Melrakkaey islands: 149 ha; and Vatnsfjördur adjacent to Breidafjördur)

A very large area of coastal waters off western Iceland, containing thousands of islands and islets. The bay is rather shallow and there are extensive intertidal areas adjoining the heavily indented coastline. There are large tracts of *Zostera* in the south. Human activities include harvesting of seaweed (*Ascophyllum nodosum*) and exploitation of fish, *Somateria mollissima*, and seals. The surrounding area has both farmland and urban areas.

A very important breeding area, holding large proportions of the total Icelandic population of some species (denoted by percentages in the following list): *Fulmarus glacialis*, *Phalacrocorax carbo* (1900 pairs; 80 per cent), *P. aristotelis* (*c*.6000 pairs; 90 per cent), *Somateria mollissima* (40,000-50,000 pairs; 25 per cent), *Haliaeetus albicilla* (18 pairs; 70 per cent), *Phalaropus fulicarius* (20 pairs), *Larus hyperboreus* (3000 pairs), *L. marinus*, *Rissa tridactyla*, *Cepphus grylle*, and *Fratercula arctica*. Breidafjördur is also an important passage area for migrating waterfowl, including large numbers of *Branta bernicla hrota* and waders, especially *Calidris canutus* (making particular use of the intertidal zones in spring).

029 Látrabjarg

65°29'N, 24°30'W 2000 ha (360 ha cliff)

Unprotected, but listed by NCC as a site with conservation interest

A sea cliff; half is a sheer precipice (max. 440 m) practically without vegetation, but the upper and more eastern parts are less steep and covered with lush herbaceous vegetation. In several places rockfalls have formed screes.

An important seabird colony including approximately one million pairs of auks, with more than one per cent of the Icelandic population of *Fulmarus glacialis* (100,000+ pairs; largest colony in Iceland), *Uria aalge* (400,000 pairs), *U. lomvia* (150,000 pairs), *Alca torda* (*c*.250,000 pairs; the largest colony in the world and certainly over half of the world population), and *Fratercula arctica* (100,000+ pairs). Other breeding species include *Phalacrocorax aristotelis*, *Rissa tridactyla* (50,000 pairs), and *Cepphus grylle*.

030 Ritur

66°23'N, 23°12'W 700 ha (360 ha cliffs and adjacent area)

Nature Reserve

Sea cliffs in the extreme north-west of mainland Iceland. Recreation is the main human activity; there is no permanent settlement.

An important seabird colony, with more than one per cent of the Icelandic population of *Rissa tridactyla*, *Uria aalge*, *U. lomvia*, and *Alca torda*. Other species include *Fulmarus glacialis* and *Fratercula arctica*. The total auk population is *c*.50,000 pairs.

031 Hælavíkurbjarg

66°28'N, 22°36'W 1000 ha (130 ha cliffs)

Nature Reserve

Mainland sea cliffs, rising to 489 m, in the extreme north-west of Iceland. Recreation is the main human activity; there is no permanent settlement.

An important seabird colony, with more than one per cent of the Icelandic population of *Rissa tridactyla*, *Uria aalge*, *U. lomvia*, and *Alca torda*. Other species include *Fulmarus glacialis* and *Fratercula arctica*. The total auk population is *c*.600,000 pairs.

032 Hornbjarg

66°28'N, 22°24'W 1100 ha (including adjacent waters)

Nature Reserve

Sea cliffs in the extreme north-west of mainland Iceland, rising to 534 m. The adjacent waters are also important. Recreation is the main human activity; there is no permanent settlement.

An important seabird colony, with more than one per cent of the Icelandic population of *Rissa tridactyla*, *Uria aalge*, *U. lomvia*, and *Alca torda*. Other species include *Fratercula arctica*. The total auk population is *c*.400,000 pairs.

033 Arnarvatnsheidi-Tvídægra

65°00'N, 20°30'W 60,000 ha

Unprotected, but listed by NCC as a site with conservation interest

A vast area of river channels, lakes, ponds, and associated marshes. Human activities include fishing.

An important area for breeding *Gavia immer*, *Cygnus cygnus*, *Clangula hyemalis*, *Calidris maritima*, and *C. alpina*.

034 Austara Eylendid

65°45'N, 19°27'W 2500 ha

Unprotected, but listed by NCC as a site with conservation interest

Riparian *Carex* marshes and seasonally flooded meadows; surrounding areas are actively farmed. No actual threats reported, but potentially threatened by drainage and over-grazing.

Important for breeding waterfowl with *Podiceps auritus*, *Anser anser*, *Somateria mollissima* (colony), and waders (especially *Limosa limosa* and *Tringa totanus*).

035 Eyjavatn

65°15'N, 19°42'W 240 ha

Unprotected, but listed by NCC as a site with conservation interest

A shallow eutrophic lake and associated freshwater marshes. The area around the lake is common grazing land. Potentially threatened by nearby hydroelectric development.

There are dense breeding populations of Anatidae, but these have only been surveyed from the air and no detailed information is available.

036 Skógar

65°42'N, 19°35'W 1550 ha

Nature Reserve

A river flood-plain containing a permanent lake and ponds, and seasonally flooded bogs. The surrounding meadowland is used for grazing, whilst the lake is fished. There are plans to enlarge a nearby airport, which would threaten the site.

Important for breeding *Anser anser* (110 pairs), *Anas penelope* (12 pairs), *A. crecca* (12 pairs), *A. platyrhynchos* (25 pairs), *Aythya fuligula* (35 pairs), *A. marila* (20 pairs), *Somateria mollissima* (95 pairs), waders, and *Larus ridibundus* (370 pairs). Also an important moulting ground for *Cygnus cygnus* (150), *Anser anser* (3000), and *Aythya marila* (300).

037 Eylendid

65°32'N, 20°20'W 2550 ha

Unprotected, but listed by NCC as a site with conservation interest

An extensive complex of rivers and associated marshes and grassland. Farming is the principal human activity. Threatened by drainage.

An important passage area for *Branta leucopsis* (10,000-15,000). Also a breeding site for large numbers of waterfowl including *Anser anser*, *Anas penelope*, *A. platyrhynchos*, *Aythya fuligula*, *Calidris alpina*, *Gallinago gallinago,* and *Tringa totanus*.

038 Hörgárósar

65°48'N, 18°12'W 100 ha

Unprotected, but listed by NCC as a site with conservation interest

A shallow estuary surrounded by meadows and bogs. Human activities include stock-raising and cultivation. The area is threatened because it is a potential metal-smelting site.

Important for breeding *Anser anser*, ducks (including *Anas penelope* and *Somateria mollissima*), waders (especially *Calidris alpina*, *Gallinago gallinago*, and *Tringa totanus*), and gulls.

039 Höfdavatn

65°57'N, 19°27'W 800 ha

Unprotected, but listed by NCC as a site with conservation interest

A shallow coastal lagoon with a variable salinity, tending towards fresh water. Human activities include gill-netting.

An important moulting site for *Aythya marila*, *Clangula hyemalis*, and *Mergus serrator*.

040 Drangey

65°57'N, 19°41'W 1500 ha

Unprotected, but listed by NCC as a site with conservation interest

An inshore rocky island with sea cliffs.

An important seabird colony with more than one per cent of the Icelandic populations of *Rissa tridactyla* and *Uria lomvia*. Other breeding species include *Uria aalge* and *Fratercula arctica*.

041 Grímsey

66°33'N, 18°00'W 700 ha (island only)

Unprotected, but listed by NCC as a site with conservation interest

An offshore island with sea cliffs and grassland, together with the surrounding waters. Human activities include fishing and sheep-farming. There is some disturbance by tourists.

An important seabird colony with breeding *Rissa tridactyla* (very large numbers), *Uria aalge*, *U. lomvia*, *Alca torda*, and a relict population of *Alle alle* (1-2 pairs); the combined auk populations exceed 100,000 pairs.

042 Svarfadardalur

65°57'N, 18°32'W 600 ha

Nature Reserve

A complex of river flood-plains, marshes, small lakes, and flood-meadows. Human activities include stock-grazing and haymaking.

An important breeding area for *Anser anser*, *Anas penelope*, *A. crecca*. waders, *Larus ridibundus*, and *L. canus*. Also moulting *A. penelope* (hundreds).

043 Hólmarnir

65°39'N, 18°04'W 700 ha

Unprotected, but listed by NCC as a site with conservation interest

A slow-flowing river and the head of its estuary, with seasonally flooded *Carex* marshes and tidal flats. Land-uses at the site include grazing and an airport. There is urban development in the surrounding area which, is threatening the tidal regime.

An important breeding and passage area for waterfowl including *Anser anser*, *Anas penelope*, *Calidris alpina*, *Gallinago gallinago*, *Limosa limosa*, *Tringa totanus*, *Larus ridibundus*, and *L. canus*.

044 Sandur-Sílalækur

65°58'N, 17°32'W 500 ha

Unprotected, but listed by NCC as a site with conservation interest

Coastal freshwater marshes with rivers, streams, lakes, and ponds. The area is used for grazing and haymaking.

Important for breeding Anatidae, including *Anas penelope*, *A. acuta*, *Aythya fuligula*, *A. marila*, and *Melanitta nigra*; waders, including *Calidris alpina*, *Gallinago gallinago*, and *Tringa totanus*; also *Larus ridibundus* and *Sterna paradisaea*. The area is also important for moulting *Anas penelope*.

045 Vestmannsvatn

65°46'N, 17°20'W 500 ha

Nature Reserve

A complex of shallow riparian lakes including rivers, streams, ponds, and freshwater marshes; surrounded by heath, *Betula* forest and cultivated land. Grazing and fishing are the main human activities.

Important for breeding waterfowl with *Gavia immer* (1 pair), *Cygnus cygnus* (1 pair), *Anser anser*, *Anas penelope*, *A.strepera*, *Aythya fuligula*, and *A. marila*. Also important for moulting *Anas penelope*.

046 Mývatn-Laxá

65°36'N, 17°00'W 20,000 ha (lake: 4000 ha) Ramsar Site

National Park

A shallow eutrophic lake (Mývatn) containing many islands and fed by cold and thermal springs. There are numerous small lakes, ponds, bogs, and marshes in the surrounding area. Laxá is the river draining the lake into the Arctic Ocean. The region is volcanically active. Human activities include farming, fishing, energy production (hydroelectric and geothermal), mining, and tourism. Threatened by a dredging operation for diatomite; fishing and tourism are further disturbances.

An important breeding site particularly for *Bucephala islandica* (2500 birds; at least 95 per cent of the total European breeding population if Greenland is excluded) and *Histrionicus histrionicus* (200 pairs). In addition, the lake supports a large number of other breeding species including *Gavia stellata*, *G. immer*, *Podiceps auritus* (250 pairs), and a variety of ducks (16 species; *c.*10,000 pairs), notably *Anas penelope* (1000 pairs; also an important moulting area for males), *Aythya fuligula* (3500 moulting), *A. marila* (1800 moulting), *Melanitta nigra,* and *Mergus serrator* (250 moulting); also breeding waders, notably *Pluvialis apricaria* and *Phalaropus lobatus* (thousands of pairs). *Falco columbarius* and *F. rusticolus* also occur, and *Cygnus cygnus* (600-700) gathers to moult.

Bucephala islandica remains in the area during the winter (*c.*2000; 86 per cent of the known European wintering population in 1977).

047 Öxarfjördur

66°07'N, 16°45'W 2500 ha
Unprotected, but listed by NCC as a site with conservation interest

An extensive area of rivers fed by cold and thermal springs, freshwater and brackish marshes, streams, lakes, and ponds, bordering the Arctic Ocean. The main land-uses are grazing, fishing, and fish-farming. Intensification of fish-farming is a potential problem.

An important breeding area for large numbers of Anatidae (including *Anas penelope*, *A. crecca*, *A. platyrhynchos*, and *Aythya fuligula*) and waders. Other breeding birds include *Podiceps auritus*. A moulting area for *Cygnus cygnus* and *Anas penelope*.

048 Skoruvík

66°23'N, 14°47'W 1900 ha (including cliff-face)

Unprotected

Sea cliffs in the north-east of mainland Iceland. The only land-use is sheep-farming.

An important seabird colony, with more than one per cent of the Icelandic populations of *Rissa tridactyla*, *Uria aalge*, *U. lomvia*, and *Alca torda*. Other species include *Fulmarus glacialis*, *Sula bassana* (280+ nests in 1984), and *Fratercula arctica*. The total auk population exceeds 50,000 pairs.

049 Langanes

66°23'N, 14°32'W 3400 ha (including cliff and adjoining areas)

Unprotected

A sea cliff in the far north-east of Iceland. The area is used only for sheep-grazing.

An important seabird colony, with more than one per cent of the Icelandic populations of *Rissa tridactyla*, *Uria aalge*, and *Alca torda*. Other species include *Uria lomvia* and *Fratercula arctica*.

050 Hjaltastadablá

65°30'N, 14°20'W 2600 ha

Unprotected, but listed by NCC as a site with conservation interest

Riparian marshes with streams, freshwater ponds, and extensive peatbog areas, dominated by *Carex* and *Eriophorum*. Grazing of livestock is the main land-use. The site is threatened by drainage.

Important for large numbers of breeding Anatidae (including *Anas acuta* and *Clangula hyemalis*) and waders (including *Calidris alpina*, *Numenius phaeopus*, and *Phalaropus lobatus*). Other breeding birds include *Gavia stellata* and *Podiceps auritus*.

051 Skrúdur

64°54'N, 13°38'W 400 ha (island: 22 ha)

Unprotected, but listed by NCC as a site with conservation interest

An offshore rocky island with cliffs rising to 160 m. Uninhabited, although land-uses include some grazing and recreation.

An important seabird colony, with more than one per cent of the Icelandic population of *Sula bassana* (*c.*1100 nests in 1984), *Rissa tridactyla*, *Uria aalge*, and *Fratercula arctica*. Other species include *Fulmarus glacialis* and *Uria lomvia*.

052 Papey

64°36'N, 14°10'W 540 ha (island: 180 ha)

Unprotected, but listed by NCC as a site with conservation interest

A low offshore island with a boggy grassland surface and low cliffs. There are several islets in the surrounding waters. Uninhabited, although land-uses include some grazing and recreational use.

An important seabird colony, with more than one per cent of the Icelandic population of *Fratercula arctica*. There are many other species of breeding seabirds including additional auks.

053 Álftafjördur-Hamarsfjördur

64°34'N, 14°30'W 3500 ha

Unprotected, but listed by NCC as a site with conservation interest

A complex area of shallow coastal bays, brackish lagoons and flats. Farming of the surrounding grassland is the main land-use.

An important moulting and passage area for *Cygnus cygnus* and *Anser anser* (1000-10,000+). Numbers of *Cygnus cygnus* are rather variable from year to year; they may be present in hundreds or over a thousand.

MAIN REFERENCES

Gardarsson, A. (ed.) (1975) Votlendi. Rit Landverndar 4.

Gardarsson, A. (1978) Vatnavernd. Íslensk vatnakerfi og verndun theirra. Náttúruverndarrád. Fjölrit. 4.

Gardarsson, A. (ed.) (1982) Fuglar. Rit Landverndar 8.

Jónasson, P. M. (ed.) (1979) Ecology of eutrophic subarctic Lake Mývatn and the River Laxá. Oikos 32.

Náttúruverndarrád (1984) Náttúruminjaskrá. 4th edition.

Náttúruverndarrád. (1987) Mývatnssveit-Náttúruverndarkort. Náttúruverndarrád Fjölrit 19.

REPUBLIC OF IRELAND

Roseate Tern *Sterna dougallii*

INTRODUCTION

General information

Ireland lies west of Britain and, with the exception of Greenland, Iceland, and the Azores, is the most westerly land mass covered by this project. The island extends from 05°25' to 10°41'W and from 51°23' to 55°27'N, with a total area of 84,421 sq km, 70,282 sq km of which form the Republic of Ireland (Éire). The Republic's coastline, heavily indented in the west, extends over 2700 km. Much of the country's interior is a low-lying plain with limestone bedrock, while the perimeter is often mountainous, with rocks of varied origin, although the highest mountains barely exceed 1000 m in altitude. The River Shannon and its tributaries wind their way through the central plain, draining nearly a quarter of the country and there are many smaller rivers and about 4000 lakes and ponds greater than 1 ha in extent. The climate is heavily influenced by the North Atlantic Drift and Atlantic depressions which give prevailing south-westerly winds. The winters are generally mild with January/February temperatures of (plus) 4° to 7°C.

The Republic's human population numbers approximately 3.25 million people, and about one-third is concentrated in the Greater Dublin conurbation. Overall population density is generally low (an average population density of 49 persons per sq km in 1981), with most of the country being rural in character. A large proportion of land is farmed (generally below the 300 m contour) with the more productive soils and larger farms being mainly in the east and south of the country. Western areas tend to have poorer soils and the majority of farms are under 15 ha in extent. Over 90 per cent of farmland is pasture and the majority of all livestock reared are cattle.

The areas which are neither farmed nor afforested are largely peatlands; both blanket bogs and raised bogs. Afforestation and large-scale mechanical harvesting of peat for fuel and horticulture have greatly reduced or degraded these peatlands. Across Ireland as a whole, some five per cent of the land has been afforested with exotic coniferous trees since the beginning of this century, and much of this planting has been on blanket and raised bogs.

Deciduous woodland was all but cleared by 1700 and today, less than one per cent of the Republic has deciduous woodland. Two types of woodland are dominant: *Quercus* with an under-storey of *Ilex/Betula* on acid soils, and *Fraxinus/Ulmus* on limestone soils. Some of the south-western woodlands are rich in mosses, ferns, and liverworts.

The many rivers, lakes and ponds contain a wide variety of aquatic plants and there is a full range of water regimes from oligotrophic to highly eutrophic (the latter often due to pollution). Many lakes and slow-moving rivers are fringed with *Scirpus lacustris* and *Phragmites*, while the base-rich lakes of the Midlands are often rich in *Charophytes*. Callows – damp riverside meadowlands subject to winter flooding and deposits of alluvium – are particularly notable in the central Shannon basin and on some of its tributaries, such as the Suck and Little Brosna. A band of near-surface limestone, extending from central Clare through east Galway and Roscommon, is noted for its turloughs – shallow basins, usually lined with limestone marl and covered with grasses – which flood in winter.

On the coast there are many areas of saltmarsh and sand-dunes, with associated dune grassland including areas of machair in the west. There are a number of brackish lagoons scattered around the coast, some with abundant *Ruppia* and *Potamogeton*. Many of the sheltered muddy bays and estuaries have *Zostera*, *Spartina* (introduced in 1925), and mats of green algae (e.g. *Enteromorpha*, *Ulva*), whilst parts of the east and south coasts have long shingle beaches. Coastal heathland is now rather rare, much of it having been lost to agriculture.

Ornithological importance

Four hundred bird species have been recorded in Ireland as a whole, but of these, over half (about 225) are irregular, rare or vagrant species. Some 135 species breed regularly; these include both residents and summer visitors. Numbers vary from a few pairs (e.g. *Gavia stellata*, *Phylloscopus sibilatrix*) to hundreds of thousands, and probably over one million. About 35 species are primarily regular winter visitors and five species (e.g. *Numenius phaeopus*) only occur regularly on passage.

Many of the regular species inhabit the low-lying farmland, with its mosaic of fields, hedgerows, and occasional small woodlands. However, those species for which the Republic is most important in an international context (mainly breeding seabirds and wintering waterfowl) tend to concentrate in scarcer habitats, such as inaccessible cliffs, headlands, islands, and larger wetlands.

Several non-seabird/waterfowl species have populations which are of international importance. These include raptors such as *Falco peregrinus*, which has made a remarkable recovery from tens of pairs in the early 1970s to an estimated 278 occupied territories in 1981 and perhaps a larger number now. The breeding populations of *Circus cyaneus*, *Falco columbarius*, *Tyto alba*, and *Asio otus* may also be significant internationally. Parts of the west and the Shannon Callows, where hay-meadows are cut in late summer, are now (together with the Outer Hebrides in Scotland) the stronghold in north-west Europe of the declining *Crex crex*, which is the subject of recent and on-going studies. The most recent estimate of the entire Irish population is 500-600 pairs (1988).

The south, west, and north coasts provide nesting and feeding habitats for a healthy population of *Pyrrhocorax pyrrhocorax* with about 685 pairs in 1982. Apart from small populations in west Scotland, Wales, the Isle of Man, and Brittany these are the only *Pyrrhocorax pyrrhocorax* in north-west Europe.

Ireland has no endemic bird species, such as Scotland's *Loxia scotica*, but some authorities give validity to endemic Irish subspecies of *Lagopus lagopus*, *Cinclus cinclus*, *Parus ater*, and *Garrulus glandarius*.

Breeding numbers of *Sterna dougallii* constitutes over 50 per cent of the European population (excluding the Azores), although the Irish population has decreased from about 3000 pairs in the early 1970s to little over 500 pairs now. Nearly all of the Irish *Sterna dougallii* breed on Rockabill, a tiny island 7 km off the east coast. Ireland's populations of *Sterna albifrons* (*c.*300 pairs) and *S. sandvicensis* (*c.*3500 pairs) are also important internationally.

Hydrobates pelagicus is difficult to census, but it is thought that between half and two-thirds of the world population may breed on coastal islands from west Cork to north-west Donegal. There are several particularly notable colonies, with tens of thousands of birds, concentrated in the south-west (e.g. the Blaskets, Skelligs and Puffin Island). Another nocturnal species, *Puffinus puffinus*, has a colony estimated at up to 20,000 pairs on Puffin Island in the south-west, and a scattering of smaller colonies in suitable habitats around the entire coastline.

There are three major colonies of *Sula bassana* (Little Skellig with 22,000 pairs, Bull Rock with 1500 pairs, and Great Saltee with 800+ pairs) together holding nearly ten per cent of the world population. The Irish population of *Phalacrocorax carbo carbo* has increased greatly in the last decade, probably owing to protective legislation, and now numbers over 4400 pairs; the colony of more than 1000 pairs on Lambay Island is one of the largest in Europe. A large proportion of the southern populations of *Uria aalge* breeds on the Irish coast, with major concentrations at Lambay Island (43,000) and Great Saltee (17,000). The population of *Alca torda* is estimated to be about 34,000, the great majority concentrated in five areas – Horn Head, Cliffs of Moher, Blasket Islands, Saltee Islands and Lambay Island.

Other seabirds which have significant breeding populations include *Fulmarus glacialis* (20,000+ pairs), *Phalacrocorax aristotelis* (4500+ pairs), *Rissa tridactyla* (50,000+ pairs), and *Fratercula arctica* (*c.*25,000 pairs) as well as five Laridae species.

Breeding waders have not been fully censused throughout the country but there is enough information to identify the Shannon Callows, with over 1550 pairs on 34 sq km (mainly *Vanellus vanellus*, *Gallinago gallinago*, *Tringa totanus*, and *Numenius arquata*), as the most important concentration in Ireland. There is a small (*c.*200 pairs) population of *Calidris alpina* mainly concentrated on the machair habitats of the west and north-west coasts.

The Republic of Ireland's wintering populations of three goose species and two swan species are of considerable international importance. *Anser albifrons flavirostris* has a wintering population of about 12,000 (over 50 per cent of the world population), 8000 of which are concentrated on the Wexford Slobs. The remainder are scattered in the midlands and west of the country. The *Branta bernicla hrota* populations breeding in Arctic Canada and Greenland, winter mainly (in Europe) in the bays and estuaries of Ireland. Currently, numbers are high with 21,000-24,000 occurring in the last three winters (1985/6-1987/8). The north-east Greenland breeding population of *Branta leucopsis* winters exclusively in Ireland and western Scotland. A full census in the spring of 1988 revealed 7400 in Ireland and nearly 29,000 in Scotland. Most of the Irish birds winter on islands (and a small number of mainland sites) on the west coast, from north Kerry to north Donegal. The Inishkeas (2300 birds), Lissadell (1700), and Sheskinmore (800) are the most important sites.

A recent census of *Cygnus cygnus* showed over 10,000 wintering in Ireland; over 60 per cent of the Icelandic breeding population. Up to 2000 *Cygnus columbianus* (from Siberia) also occur; over ten per cent of the European wintering population.

Wintering duck species occurring in internationally important concentrations include *Tadorna tadorna*, *Anas penelope*, *A. crecca*, *A. acuta*, *A. clypeata*, *Aythya ferina*, *A. fuligula*, and *A. marila*. Many of the wetlands included in this inventory are recognised as internationally important because they regularly hold significant numbers of one or more of these wildfowl species.

The major wader species occurring in internationally important numbers are *Haematopus ostralegus*, *Pluvialis apricaria*, *P. squatarola*, *Vanellus vanellus*, *Calidris canutus*, *C. alba*, *C. alpina*, *Limosa limosa islandica*, *L. lapponica*, *Numenius arquata*, and *Tringa totanus*. Most of these occur mainly on estuaries and sheltered coastal bays, but *Vanellus vanellus*, *Pluvialis apricaria*, and *Numenius arquata* also occur in very large numbers on damp grassland in the Irish interior. Up to 40,000 *Pluvialis apricaria* and

35,000 *Vanellus vanellus* have been recorded on the Shannon Callows; this area, and the callows of the River Blackwater, are the main inland resorts for *Limosa limosa islandica*. During spring passage hundreds (sometimes more than 1000) of *Numenius phaeopus* have been recorded in Cork Harbour and on the Shannon Callows, presumably en route to Iceland. On the Shannon/Fergus Estuary up to 16,500 *Limosa limosa islandica* have been recorded in spring; these are also assumed to be heading for Iceland.

Wintering numbers (offshore) of *Gavia stellata* and *G. immer* are high (probably several hundreds of each) and may be important in a European context.

Conservation infrastructure and protected-area system

The Wildlife Service (Office of Public Works, Department of Finance) is the principal agency involved in nature conservation. It is responsible for the implementation of the Wildlife Act of 1976 (which is the major piece of conservation legislation), the EEC Wild Birds Directive, and the Ramsar, Bonn, and Bern Conventions.

The main categories of protection afforded to sites in the Republic of Ireland are as follows.

1. No-shooting Area
   No habitat protection; state ownership not necessary.
2. Refuge for Fauna
   Designated where species require special measures to protect their habitat. Land ownership does not affect designation. Various limitations on land-use may be ordered, but there is provision for the payment of compensation. State ownership not necessary.
3. National Nature Reserve
   Section 15 of the 1976 Wildlife Act allows the establishment of a statutory Nature Reserve on 'land' (including foreshore, territorial seas and certain lakes) owned by the state. Section 16 allows the establishment of Nature Reserves in privately owned areas. In the latter case the owner(s) is required to manage the land in accordance with a management plan drawn up with the Wildlife Service. Nature Reserves are established to conserve species, communities, habitats, or ecosystems which are of scientific interest, and which are likely to benefit from the designation.

Finally, there is provision under the 1976 Wildlife Act to prohibit hunting (except under licence) on state-owned foreshore and state-owned lakes.

Furthermore, all known Areas of Scientific Interest in Ireland (ASIs; numbering over 1500), including the bird sites in the inventory, have been listed, mapped, and notified to various land-use agencies and planning authorities. This should help to ensure that no environmentally detrimental development is permitted inadvertently in such areas; although recognition as an ASI does not provide any legal protection.

The Irish Wildbird Conservancy is the principal voluntary organisation concerned with nature conservation. It owns and manages a series of reserves some of which also have National Nature Reserve designation. It is the leading body involved in collecting data on waterfowl and has undertaken a number of single-species surveys to provide baseline information (see reference list).

International measures relevant to the conservation of sites

Ireland is a member of the Council of Europe and European Community, (and is therefore bound by the terms of the Wild Birds Directive), and has also ratified the Ramsar, Bonn, and Bern Conventions. Nine Ramsar Sites, 14 EEC Special Protection Areas and ten Biogenetic Reserves have been designated. Four of the Ramsar Sites and all EEC Special Protection Areas are included in this inventory, although only one Biogenetic Reserve (Pettigo Plateau) is included. Furthermore, Ireland has designated two Biosphere Reserves (under UNESCO's Man and the Biosphere Programme), one of which (North Bull Island) is included in the inventory.

North Bull Island has also been officially linked with Polar Bear Pass on Bathurst Island through the Canadian Wildlife Service's 'Sister Reserves' programme (International Conservation Strategy for Shorebirds and other Long Distance Migrants). Two NNRs

(Wexford Wildfowl Reserve and The Raven) are twinned with similar sites in France, Portugal, and the United Kingdom, as part of the EECs Natural Sites Twinning Programme.

Overview of the inventory

One hundred and ten sites are contained in the following inventory (with a combined area of over 269,000 ha), covering all the major habitats of importance for birds: cliffs, headlands and islands, bays, estuaries and saltmarshes, callows, turloughs, lakes and rivers, agricultural land, etc. The breeding seabirds and wintering/passage waterfowl are well catered for by the sites included in the inventory. However, in the case of some other species, such as *Falco columbarius*, *F. peregrinus*, *Crex crex*, *Pyrrhocorax pyrrhocorax*, which are thinly dispersed over large areas, it has not been possible to identify enough sites of moderate size which are particularly important. It is considered that the conservation of such species cannot be adequately achieved by a sites approach. Perhaps their conservation may best be realised by seeking to preserve a representative selection of boglands, or by introducing to Ireland the European Community's Environmentally Sensitive Areas scheme (this would be the responsibility of the Republic's Department of Agriculture).

Thirty-seven sites in the inventory have received statutory protection (in whole or in part) with more than one protective measure instituted in some cases. Ten sites have been designated National Nature Reserves, (with seven or more under consideration), four as Refuges for Fauna (with several more under consideration), 31 as No Shooting Areas, and one as a Local Authority Bird Sanctuary. Eleven of these sites plus three others have received further recognition either as EEC Special Protection Areas (13), Ramsar Sites (4), Biosphere Reserves (1) or Biogenetic Reserves (1). The Irish Wildbird Conservancy has reserves at nine sites and there are three *de facto* sanctuaries, where the site owners have declared their intention of protecting wildlife (e.g. the Saltee Islands).

Over half of the 63 unprotected sites are (mostly small) uninhabited islands which are largely free of immediate threats. On only one of these are the birds in any way threatened (Inishmaan in the Aran Islands, where the tern colony is beside an aircraft landing strip). A further 18 sites are wholly (or mostly) state-owned, making the introduction of protective measures relatively straightforward. The remaining unprotected sites are privately owned, many of them in multiple private ownership, which often makes habitat protection rather difficult to achieve.

Acknowledgements

This introduction was supplied by O. J. Merne of the Irish Wildlife Service with the assistance of D. Norriss and H. J. Wilson (Wildlife Service); R. Sheppard and R. Nairn (Irish Wildbird Conservancy) also provided data for many of the sites. M. ÓBriain provided information on numbers and distribution of *Branta bernicla hrota*. J. Temple Lang and A. Whilde also provided information and advice.

INVENTORY

No.	Site name	Region	Criteria used to select site [see p.18]							
			0	1(i)	1(ii)	1(iii)	1(iv)	2	3	4
001	Inishtrahull	DL								*
002	Trawbreaga Bay	DL				*			*	
003	River Foyle: St Johnstown – Carrigans	DL				*			*	
004	Lough Swilly including Blanket Nook and Inch Lake	DL				*			*	
005	Greer's Island (Massmount) Mulroy Bay	DL							*	
006	Horn Head Cliffs	DL			*					
007	Tory Island	DL							*	

No.	Site name	Region	Criteria used to select site [see p.18]							
			0	1(i)	1(ii)	1(iii)	1(iv)	2	3	4
008	Inishbofin	DL							*	
009	Inishkeeragh	DL							*	
010	Illancrone	DL							*	
011	Roaninish	DL							*	
012	Sheskinmore Lough	DL				*			*	
013	Rathlin O'Birne	DL							*	
014	Inishduff	DL							*	
015	Durnesh Lough	DL							*	
016	Moors west and north-west of Lough Derg, Brownhall and bogs around Lough Golagh and Dunragh Loughs	DL							*	
017	Inishmurray	NW							*	
018	Lissadell, Drumcliff Bay	NW				*			*	
019	Ardboline Island	NW			*					
020	Cummeen Strand	NW				*				
021	Aughris Head	NW								*
022	Lough Gara	NW,M				*			*	
023	Killala Bay	W,NW				*				
024	Lough Conn and Lough Cullin	W							*	
025	Illaunmaistir (Oilean Maistir)	W		*	*				*	
026	Stags of Broadhaven	W			*				*	
027	Carrowmore Lough	W							*	
028	Broadhaven Bay	W				*				
029	Termoncarragh Lake	W				*			*	
030	Inishglora and Inishkeeragh	W		*	*				*	
031	Inishkea Islands	W				*			*	
032	Duvillaun Islands	W			*	*			*	
033	Blacksod Bay	W				*				
034	Moynish Beg	W							*	
035	Inishraher Islet	W							*	
036	Dorinish Bar	W			*					
037	Clare Island Cliffs	W							*	
038	Cross Lough	W							*	
039	Inishbofin	W								*
040	High Island	W							*	
041	Eeshal Island	W							*	
042	Horse Island	W							*	
043	Hen Island	W							*	
044	Lough Scannive	W			*					
045	Oilean Geabhróg	W							*	
046	Oilean na nGeabhróg	W							*	
047	Duck Island	W							*	
048	Geabhrog Island	W							*	
049	Lough Corrib	W				*			*	
050	Inner Galway Bay	W			*	*			*	
051	Rahasane Turlough	W				*			*	
052	Inishmaan	W							*	
053	Cliffs of Moher	MW			*					
054	Lough Cutra	MW			*					
055	Ballyallia Lake	MW				*				
056	Mutton Island	MW				*			*	
057	Mattle Island	MW							*	
058	Shannon and Fergus Estuary	MW,SW				*			*	
059	Akeragh Lough	SW				*				
060	Magharee Islands	SW				*			*	
061	Lough Gill	SW				*			*	
062	Tralee Bay and Barrow Harbour	SW				*			*	

No.	Site name	Region	Criteria used to select site [see p.18] 0	1(i)	1(ii)	1(iii)	1(iv)	2	3	4
063	Castlemaine Harbour	SW				*				
064	Blasket Islands	SW		*	*				*	
065	Puffin Island	SW		*	*				*	
066	Moylaun Island	SW							*	
067	The Skelligs: Great Skellig and Little Skellig	SW		*	*				*	
068	Bull and Cow Rocks	SW		*	*				*	
069	Whiddy Island	SW							*	
070	Roaringwater Bay Islands	SW							*	
071	Inner Clonakilty Bay	SW				*			*	
072	Sovereign Islands	SW			*					
073	Cork Harbour	SW				*			*	
074	Ballycotton, Ballynamona, and Shanagarry	SW							*	
075	Ballymacoda	SW				*				
076	Blackwater Estuary	SE,SW				*			*	
077	River Blackwater Callows	SE,SW				*			*	
078	Dungarvan Harbour	SE				*			*	
079	Tramore Backstrand	SE				*				
080	Bannow Bay	SE				*				
081	Keeragh Islands	SE			*					
082	The Cull/Killag	SE				*			*	
083	Saltee Islands	SE			*					
084	Tacumshin Lake	SE				*			*	
085	Lady's Island Lake	SE			*				*	
086	Wexford Harbour and Slobs	SE				*			*	
087	Thurles Sugar Factory Lagoons	MW							*	
088	Coast Greystones – Wicklow, including Kilcoole Marshes and Broad Lough	E							*	
089	Dublin Docks (parts)	E							*	
090	North Bull Island	E				*			*	
091	Baldoyle Bay	E				*				
092	Malahide Estuary	E				*				
093	Lambay Island	E			*	*				
094	Rockabill	E			*				*	
095	Rogerstown Estuary	E				*				
096	Church Island, Lough Derg	W			*					
097	River Shannon Callows: Portumna – Athlone	M,W,MW				*		*	*	
098	River Little Brosna Callows: New Bridge – River Shannon	M,SE				*			*	
099	River Suck Callows: Shannon Bridge – Athleague	W,M				*			*	
100	Lough Ennell	M				*			*	
101	Lough Owel	M				*			*	
102	Lough Iron – Glen Lough	M				*			*	
103	Lough Derravaragh	M							*	
104	Castle Forbes Complex	M							*	
105	Lough Oughter	NE				*			*	
106	Stabannan – Braganstown	NE				*			*	
107	Boyne Estuary	NE,E				*			*	
108	Dundalk Bay	NE				*				
109	Carlingford Lough	NE				*				
110	Wicklow Hills and Poulaphouca Reservoir	E							*	

DL=Donegal NW=North West W=West MW=Mid West SW=South West SE=South East E=East M=Midlands NE=North East

Comments on the inventory

1. The species information given for each site has been compiled using data gathered in 1981 and 1984 as well as the new data submitted in 1987 and 1988. A statement at the end of each site account gives an indication of how up to date the information is: 'Information compiled 1987 or 1988' implies all information up to date; 'Major revision 1987' implies most information up to date.; 'Information updated 1987' implies only key information such as internationally important counts up to date.
2. Where possible, new figures for wintering waterfowl are given in the form 'x-yr. av. max':
   - '5-yr. av. max.' refers to 1982/3–86/7.
   - '4-yr. av. max.' refers to 1983/4–86/7.
   - '3-yr. av. max.' refers to 1984/5–86/7.

   Almost all internationally important populations (according to the numerical criteria category 1(iii)) are up-dated in this way, together with *some* other counts. Other figures should be read in the light of the statement at the end of each account and are average winter counts (usually av. Jan. counts, compiled in 1981) unless stated.
3. For each site, the site name is followed by the name of the county, with the name of the Irish planning region given in parentheses (NUTS level 3).
4. When applying the site-selection criteria (categories 3 and 4) the 'region' is the Irish planning region (NUTS level 3). The following are the NUTS level 3 regions (constituent counties given in parentheses): East (Wicklow, Kildare, Dublin, Meath); South West (Kerry, Cork); South East (Waterford, Wexford, Carlow, Kilkenny, Tipperary [South Riding]); North East (Cavan, Monaghan, Louth); Mid West (Clare, Limerick, Tipperary [North Riding]); Donegal (Donegal); Midlands (Laois, Offaly, Westmeath, Longford, Roscommon); West (Galway, Mayo); North West (Sligo, Leitrim).

Glossary

The following abbreviations are used in the statements regarding international and national conservation status, and should be interpreted in conjunction with the section 'Conservation infrastructure and protected area system' contained in the introduction: EEC SPA = European Community Special Protection Area designated according to the EEC's Wild Birds Directive; IWC = Irish Wildbird Conservancy; NNR = National Nature Reserve. Also lough = lake.

---

001 Inishtrahull, Co Donegal (Donegal)

55°26'N, 07°14'W 35 ha

Unprotected

A fairly low (max. height 40 m) marine island, with automated lighthouse, 5 km offshore. Formerly inhabited (early twentieth century).

Most important site in the region for *Phalacrocorax aristotelis* (*c.*300 pairs); also breeding *Fulmarus glacialis* (a few), *Somateria mollissima* (*c.*100 pairs), *Larus canus* (colony), *L. argentatus* (1000+ pairs), and small numbers of terns (*Sterna hirundo* and *S. paradisaea*: *c.*30 pairs). (Information compiled 1987)

002 Trawbreaga Bay, Co Donegal (Donegal)

55°17'N, 07°18'W *c.*880 ha

No-shooting Area

A very sheltered sea bay with a very narrow strait to the open sea at the north end, fed by a number of small streams. There are dunes near the mouth and blocking the western arm of the bay which is *c.*80 per cent exposed at low tide. There is a mixture of mudflats, sandbanks and rocky substrates. Fishing and stock-raising are the main human activities.

Somateria mollissima breed. Important for wintering waterfowl with *Branta leucopsis* (3-yr. av. max. 419), *B. bernicla hrota* (4-yr. av. max. 350; max. 408), *Anas penelope* (180; also max. 2500 in autumn), *Haematopus ostralegus* (200), and *Numenius arquata* (350). (Information compiled 1987)

003 River Foyle: St Johnstown – Carrigans, Co Donegal (Donegal)

54°55'N, 07°27'W 200 ha

Unprotected

A river estuary with saltwater marshes, mudflats, and wet meadows. Human activities include boating, fishing, and stock-grazing.

Wintering waterfowl include *Cygnus cygnus* (100; 350 in autumn), *Anser albifrons flavirostris* (5-yr. av. max. 236; max. 254), *A. anser* (100-180), *Anas crecca* (150-1000), and *A. platyrhynchos* (400-1000). (Information updated 1987)

004 Lough Swilly (including Blanket Nook and Inch Lake), Co Donegal (Donegal)

55°07'N, 07°32'W 17,400 ha

Mainly unprotected; No-shooting Area (Blanket Nook: 48 ha)

A long narrow sea inlet with extensive banks of mud and shingle between Letterkenny and Inch. There is some empoldered land at Big Isle and Blanket Nook; an embanked sea channel, between Inch island and the mainland, is an important brackish roost and feeding area. Surrounded by pasture and tillage. Human activities include stock-raising and mariculture. Heavy hunting pressure and eutrophication from arable-land run-off threaten the area. In addition, in 1984, Inch level was threatened by a drainage scheme.

Wintering waterfowl include *Cygnus columbianus* (40; max. 150), *C. cygnus* (3-yr. av. max. 750), *Anser albifrons flavirostris* (5-yr. av. max. 236; max. 254; the same birds occur at 003), *Branta bernicla hrota* (4-yr. av. max. 272; max. 432), *Anas penelope* (1400; 1600 in autumn), *A. crecca* (1000), *Haematopus ostralegus* (500), *Vanellus vanellus* (800), *Calidris alpina* (2000), *Numenius arquata* (800), and *Tringa totanus* (500). (Information updated 1987)

005 Greer's Island (Massmount), Mulroy Bay, Co Donegal (Donegal)

55°13'N, 07°42'W less than 1.0 ha

Unprotected

A tiny marine island in sheltered water of Mulroy Bay.

Most important colony in the region for *Sterna sandvicensis* (180 pairs in 1984); also *Larus ridibundus* (180 pairs) and *S. paradisaea* (20 pairs in 1984); colony known since 1969. (Information compiled 1987)

006 Horn Head Cliffs, Co Donegal (Donegal)

55°13'N, 07°58'W 8.8 km of vertical cliffs EEC SPA

Refuge for Fauna

A headland with sheer cliffs rising to 200 m.

An important seabird colony with *Fulmarus glacialis* (c.1000 pairs), *Phalacrocorax carbo* (20 pairs), *P. aristotelis* (75-200 pairs), *Uria aalge* (3500-5000 birds), *Alca torda* (4000-6000 birds), *Cepphus grylle* (12-25 pairs), *Fratercula arctica* (max. 100 pairs), and *Rissa tridactyla* (3500-4500 pairs); also breeding *Pyrrhocorax pyrrhocorax*. (Information compiled in 1987)

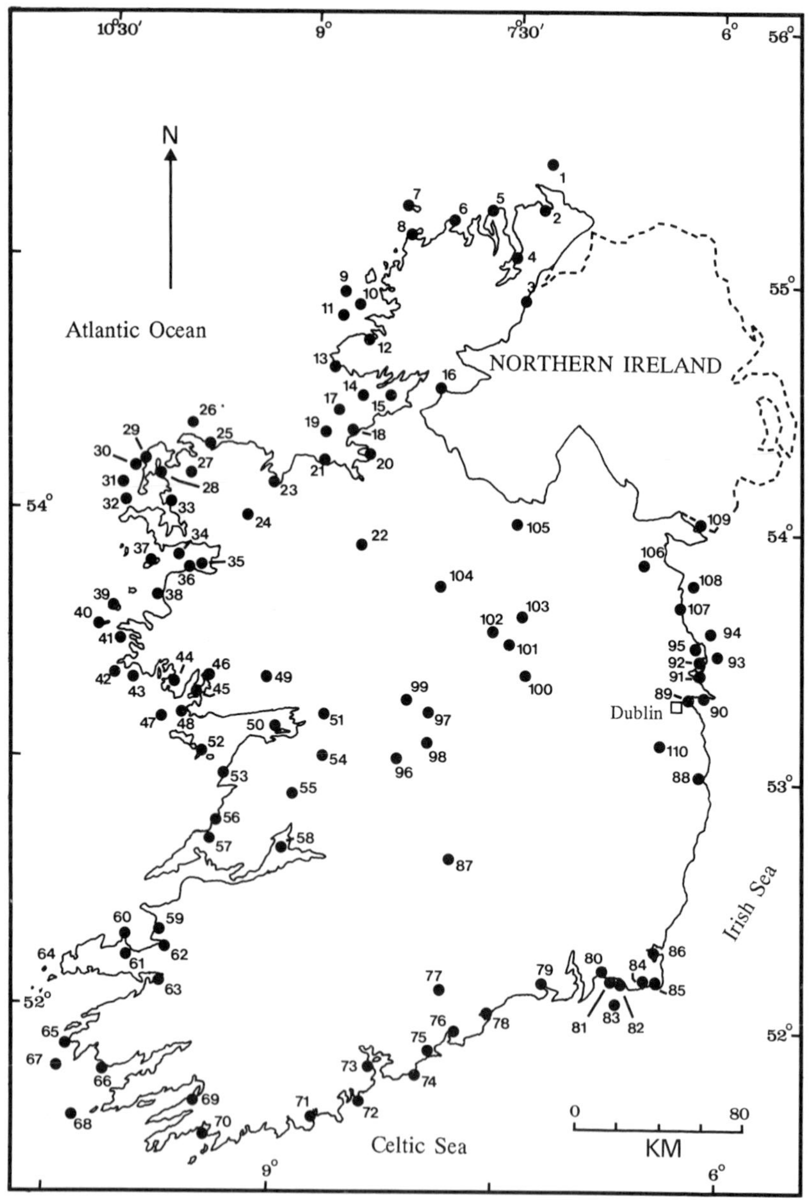

Figure 18: Map showing the location of the sites in the Republic of Ireland

007 Tory Island, Co Donegal (Donegal)

55°16'N, 08°14'W 332 ha

Unprotected

A large inhabited marine island, 11.5 km offshore, mostly low-lying but rising to 90 m at east end.

One of the five (fourth) most important colonies of *Hydrobates pelagicus* in the region; colony small (estimated *c.*20 pairs). Also breeding *Fulmarus glacialis* (*c.*260 pairs), *Rissa tridactyla* (530 pairs), *Uria aalge* (650 birds), *Alca torda* (630 birds), *Fratercula arctica* (700 birds), and *Sterna albifrons* (20 birds). Long history of records of breeding seabirds including *Sterna albifrons* (*c.*40 pairs in 1961). (Information compiled 1987)

008 Inishbofin, Co Donegal (Donegal)

55°11'N, 08°10'W 119 ha

Unprotected

Medium-sized uninhabited marine island, 1.5 km from mainland.

One of the five (second) most important colonies in the region for *Sterna paradisaea* (120 pairs in 1984); also *Sterna hirundo* (25 pairs in 1984) and *Sterna albifrons* (8 pairs in 1984). There is also a small colony (less than 100 pairs) of gulls. (Information compiled 1987)

009 Inishkeeragh, Co Donegal (Donegal)

54°57'N, 08°30'W *c.*20 ha

Unprotected

Medium-sized uninhabited marine island, 2.5 km from mainland.

One of the five (third) most important colonies in the region for *Sterna paradisaea* (77 pairs in 1984); also 270 pairs of gulls including *Larus canus* (150 pairs), and breeding *Sterna sandvicensis*, *S. hirundo*, and *S. albifrons* (9, 7, and 5 pairs respectively in 1984). *Sterna dougallii* (2 pairs) bred in 1969. (Information compiled 1987)

010 Illancrone, Co Donegal (Donegal)

54°56'N, 08°29'W less than 5 ha

Unprotected

A very small marine island on a stony reef, 1.5 km from mainland.

Most important colony in the region for *Sterna paradisaea* (132 pairs in 1984); also breeding *Sterna sandvicensis*, *S. dougallii* and *S. hirundo* (4, 3, and 14 pairs respectively in 1984); colony known since 1954. (Information compiled 1987)

011 Roaninish, Co Donegal (Donegal)

54°52'N, 08°32'W 12 ha

Private bird sanctuary

A tight group of small, low-lying islets and reefs, 3.5 km offshore. Uninhabited.

One of the five most important colonies of *Hydrobates pelagicus* in the region (1000+ pairs). There is also an important colony of *Somateria mollissima*. Small numbers of terns (*Sterna sandvicensis*, *S. hirundo*, *S. paradisaea*, and *S. albifrons*) breed occasionally; tern colony known since 1900. *Branta leucopsis* visits the islands in winter (*c.*250). (Information compiled in 1987)

012 Sheskinmore Lough, Co Donegal (Donegal)

54°48'N, 08°27'-08°30'W 335 ha

No-shooting Area (south and east of Lough); statutory management agreements operate in other parts; IWC Reserve (north-west of Lough)

A shallow, freshwater coastal lagoon formed behind sand-dunes. The dune sand now occupies much of the former lake basin, giving rise to extensive calcareous marshes and machair. Blanket bog overlies basic rocks to the north and east. Grazing of livestock is the main land-use. The area has been threatened by drainage proposals.

Breeding species include *Crex crex*, *Vanellus vanellus*, *Calidris alpina*, *Gallinago gallinago*, and *Tringa totanus*; also an important feeding area for *Pyrrhocorax pyrrhocorax* (50). In winter, a variety of waterfowl occurs including *Cygnus columbianus* (5), *C. cygnus* (20), *Anser albifrons flavirostris* (5-yr. av. max. 299; max. 396), *Branta leucopsis* (1123 in 1981), and *B. bernicla hrota* (50). (Major revision 1987)

013 Rathlin O'Birne, Co Donegal (Donegal)

54°40'N, 08°50'W 38 ha

Unprotected

A fairly small marine island, with automated (since *c.*1980) lighthouse, 2 km offshore.

One of the five most important colonies of *Hydrobates pelagicus* in the region (*c.*1000 pairs; colony known since 1900). Possible breeding site of *Oceanodroma leucorhoa*. Regular wintering area for *Branta leucopsis* (*c.*200). (Information compiled 1987)

014 Inishduff, Co Donegal (Donegal)

54°36'N, 08°33'W 1.8 ha

Unprotected

A very small flat-topped marine island, 2 km offshore. Uninhabited.

One of the five most important colonies of *Hydrobates pelagicus* in the region (*c.*400 pairs); also breeding *Phalacrocorax aristotelis* (116 pairs), *Larus marinus* (*c.*150 pairs) and *Cepphus grylle* (*c.*10 pairs). Small numbers of *Branta leucopsis* occur in winter. (Information compiled 1987)

015 Durnesh Lough, Co Donegal (Donegal)

54°34'N, 08°12'W 365 ha

Unprotected

A shallow, freshwater lake with extensive marshes surrounded by drumlins, and separated from the sea by sand-dunes. Land-uses include some low-intensity grazing. Possibly threatened by drainage, agricultural pollutants, and shooting.

Wintering waterfowl include *Cygnus columbianus* (max. 40), *C. cygnus* (formerly Jan. av. 200; max. 250; numbers now decreased: 3-yr. av. max. 103), and *C. olor* (max. 150). (Information compiled 1987)

016 Moors west and north-west of Lough Derg, Brownhall, and bogs around Lough Golagh and Dunragh Loughs; Co Donegal (Donegal)

54°36'-54°38'N, 07°54'-07°59'W *c.*2600 ha

Includes Ramsar Site (Pettigo Plateau: 900 ha) and Biogenetic Reserve (Pettigo Plateau)

NNR (1400 ha – south-east part of area; extension of NNR is under consideration)

Blanket bog, with numerous lakes and pools, covering an area of low hills and broad basins. Human activities include forestry, turf-exploitation, stock-raising, and wildfowling. Threatened by peat-cutting and afforestation outside NNR.

An important bogland area for wintering *Anser albifrons flavirostris* (Jan. av. 130), numbers dependent on level of disturbance from surrounding areas. *Falco columbarius* is regular in spring. (Information compiled 1987)

017 Inishmurray, Co Sligo (North West)

54°26'N, 08°40'W 95 ha

Unprotected

A medium-sized rather low (20 m), flat marine island, 6 km offshore. Uninhabited since mid-twentieth century.

Most important site in the region for *Phalacrocorax aristotelis* (237 pairs); also the only site in the region for *Hydrobates pelagicus* (100-1000 pairs; probably closer to 1000). Other breeding species include *Somateria mollissima* (important colony) , *Larus marinus* (80+ pairs), *Sterna paradisaea* (60 pairs), and small numbers of other seabirds. *Branta leucopsis* (*c.*250) occurs in winter. (Information compiled 1987)

018 Lissadell, Drumcliff Bay, Co Sligo (North West)

54°21'N, 08°33'W 28 ha EEC SPA

NNR; No-shooting Area

A large pasture field sloping southwards to the shore at Drumcliff Bay. There is a large hollow which holds a pond fed by rain water most of the year, and the area is bordered by woodland to the west.

An important wintering area for *Branta leucopsis* (3-yr. av. max. 600; max. 1700; the largest concentration of this species in mainland Ireland). Other wintering species include *Anas penelope*, *A. crecca* (max. 200), *Haematopus ostralegus*, *Pluvialis apricaria*, *Vanellus vanellus*, *Gallinago gallinago*, *Numenius arquata*, and *Tringa totanus*. (Information compiled 1987)

019 Ardboline Island, Co Sligo (North West)

54°21'N, 08°42'W 13 ha

Unprotected

Rocky island with breeding *Phalacrocorax carbo* (205 pairs in 1985). (Information compiled 1987)

020 Cummeen Strand, Co Sligo (North West)

54°18'N, 08°32'W 1865 ha

Unprotected

The middle one of the three 'arms' forming Sligo Bay, containing the estuary of the River Garavogue with mudflats and extensive sandy flats. Sheltered from the open sea by Coney Island. Human activities include recreation and wildfowling.

Waterfowl occurring include wintering *Branta bernicla hrota* (4-yr. av. max. 621; max. 850; 2000 in autumn) and *Anas penelope* (2000 in autumn), as well as smaller numbers of waders including *Haematopus ostralegus* (700 in autumn), *Charadrius hiaticula* (200), *Calidris alpina* (300), *Limosa lapponica* (180), *Numenius arquata* (300), and *Tringa totanus* (160). (Major revision 1987)

021 Aughris Head, Co Sligo (North West)

54°16'N, 08°45'W *c.*1.5 km of vertical cliff

Unprotected

Stretch of mainland cliff *c.*1.5 km long, horizontally stratified. Land to cliff edge actively farmed.

Most important site in the region for *Alca torda* (250 birds); also breeding *Fulmarus glacialis* (max. 96 pairs), *Rissa tridactyla* (max. 1000 pairs), and *Uria aalge* (max. 1350 birds); colony known since 1891. (Information compiled 1987)

022 Lough Gara, Co Sligo and Co Roscommon (North West, Midlands)

53°57'N, 08°27'W 1100 ha

No-shooting Area (Lower Lough Gara)

A shallow limestone lake divided into two parts, with marshes and wet meadows on the River Boyle up river from Lough Key. Also includes several islands. The shores of the lake and islands have open aspects with little structured vegetation. Fishing and limited shooting are the only land-uses. Peat-cutting in the lake's catchment causes the settling out of detritus which may threaten the area's current ecological character.

There is a large breeding colony of *Larus fuscus*. Wintering waterfowl include *Cygnus cygnus* (140), *Anser albifrons flavirostris* (5-yr. av. max. 369; max. 447), and *Aythya ferina* (900). (Major revision 1987)

023 Killala Bay, Co Mayo and Co Sligo (West, North West)

54°11'-54°16'N, 09°04'-09°14'W *c.*4294 ha

Unprotected

The inner (southern) part of a triangular north-facing bay, which is the estuary of the River Moy and several other small rivers/streams. A long sandy island (Bartragh) separates the south-west side of the bay from open water. Much of the inner part is intertidal, while the northern part shelves to *c.*10 m. The site also includes the estuary of the River Cloonaghmore, in the north-west. Human activities include salmon fishing, wildfowling, recreational boating, and agriculture in the surrounding areas. There are potential sources of pollution at Killala (chemicals plant) and at the town of Ballina (sewage effluent).

Important for wintering *Branta bernicla hrota* (4-yr. av. max. 293; max. 326); also wintering *Anas penelope* (max. 560), and waders. (Information compiled 1987)

024 Lough Conn and Lough Cullin, Co Mayo (West)

53°57'-54°06'N, 09°08'-09°18'W 6100+ ha

No-shooting Area (Lough Conn)

Lough Conn is a large calcareous lake with a shallow stony shoreline, several reefs, and inshore islands. Lough Cullin is smaller, less open, and on metamorphic rocks. The narrow neck of land separating the lakes, and the lakes' shores, are well-wooded grazing areas. Other human activities include fishing. *Anser albifrons flavirostris* is vulnerable to disturbance from agricultural operations.

Breeding waterfowl include *Melanitta nigra* (50 pairs) and *Mergus serrator*. In winter *Cygnus cygnus* (132), *Anser albifrons flavirostris* (5-yr. av. max. 128; max. 169), and *Aythya ferina* (2000) occur. (Information compiled 1987)

025 Illaunmaistir (Oilean Maistir), Co Mayo (West)

54°19'N, 09°38'W 5 ha

IWC Reserve

A small rocky island.

Breeding seabirds include *Fulmarus glacialis* (less than 10 pairs), *Puffinus puffinus* (10-100 pairs), *Hydrobates pelagicus* (7500-10,000 pairs), *Phalacrocorax aristotelis* (less than 10 pairs), *Cepphus grylle* (5 pairs), and *Fratercula arctica* (*c.*2000 pairs). In addition, *Branta leucopsis* (50) occurs in winter. (Information updated 1987)

026 Stags of Broadhaven, Co Mayo (West)

54°23'N, 09°47'W 4 ha

Unprotected

Four precipitous islets.

Breeding seabirds include *Hydrobates pelagicus* and *Oceanodroma leucorhoa* (200 pairs; only known Irish breeding site). (Information compiled 1987)

027 Carrowmore Lough, Co Mayo (West)

54°11'N, 09°48'W 9 ha

No-shooting Area

A small lake island (Derreen's Island) 0.5 km from shore.

Most important colony in the region for *Sterna sandvicensis* (164 pairs in 1984); also *Larus ridibundus* (1500 pairs), *L. canus* (400 pairs), and *Sterna paradisaea* (18 pairs in 1984); colony known since 1898. *Anser albifrons flavirostris* occurs in winter. (Information compiled 1987)

028 Broadhaven Bay, Co Mayo (West)

54°12'-54°18'N, 09°45'-09°59'W *c.*3238 ha

Unprotected

The inner, more sheltered and shallow parts of a large sea bay situated between the north end of the Mullet peninsula and the north-west Mayo coast. There are a number of narrow inlets leading off the main bay. There is one small island (Inishderry) situated near the southern edge of the site. Low-intensity fishing, wildfowling, and stock-raising are the main human activities. There is the possibility of maricultural development in the future.

Inishderry holds an important colony of terns: *Sterna sandvicensis* (114 pairs), *S. hirundo/S. paradisaea* (28 pairs), and *S. albifrons* (6 pairs). There is also nesting *Larus ridibundus*. Important for wintering *Branta bernicla hrota* (4-yr. av. max. 292; max. 363). (Information compiled 1987)

029 Termoncarragh Lake, Co Mayo (West)

54°14'N, 10°05'W 444 ha

Mainly unprotected; IWC Reserves (two small areas)

Coastal lagoon with sand-dunes, sandy beaches, machair, and adjacent marshland. Human activities include intensive stock-grazing. Drainage is a potential, though not immediate threat. Overgrazing, fencing, and fertiliser application are problems on the machair.

Important nesting area for waders including *Phalaropus lobatus* (2 pairs; only regular Irish site; also 30 on passage), *Vanellus vanellus*, *Calidris alpina* (15 pairs), *Gallinago gallinago*, and *Tringa totanus*. Also breeding *Crex crex*. Wintering waterfowl include *Cygnus cygnus* (180), *Branta leucopsis* (3-yr. av. max. 157), *Aythya fuligula*, *Pluvialis apricaria* (3000), and *Numenius arquata* (300). (Major revision 1987)

030 Inishglora and Inishkeeragh, Co Mayo (West)

54°13'N, 10°09'W 43 ha

Unprotected

Two flat, low-lying offshore islands west of the Mullet Peninsula.

Important for breeding seabirds with *Fulmarus glacialis* (10 pairs), *Hydrobates pelagicus* (10,000-20,000 pairs), *Phalacrocorax carbo* (57 pairs), *P. aristotelis* (175 pairs), *Larus canus* (55-65 pairs), *L. fuscus* (20+ pairs), *L. argentatus* (100+ pairs), *L. marinus* (75 pairs), *Sterna paradisaea* (90 pairs), *S. albifrons*, and *Cepphus grylle* (less than 10 pairs). (Information updated 1987)

031 Inishkea Islands, Co Mayo (West)

54°07'N, 10°13'W 389 ha EEC SPA (272 ha)

No-shooting Area

The two largest islands 3-4 km west of the Mullet Peninsula. The northern island is low-lying and dominated by machair, though there is a small lake. The southern island has a low-lying machair-covered north end but a heath-covered hill and ridge extends southwards. Uninhabited, but human activities include stock-raising. Livestock overgrazing could threaten the islands' carrying capacity for geese.

Breeding species include *Sterna hirundo* (20 pairs in 1984), *S. paradisaea* (220 pairs in 1984), *S. albifrons* (41 pairs in 1984), and *Cepphus grylle* (10 pairs). There are also important concentrations of breeding *Haematopus ostralegus, Vanellus vanellus,* and *Calidris alpina*. Important for wintering *Branta leucopsis* (3-yr. av. max. 2608; the main wintering site in Ireland); also wintering *Pluvialis apricaria* (1500), *Calidris alba* (200), *C. maritima* (175), and *Arenaria interpres* (400). (Information compiled 1987)

032 Duvillaun Islands, Co Mayo (West)

54°05'N, 10°12'W 103 ha

Unprotected

A group of five marine islands with outlying reefs. Uninhabited.

A breeding site for *Fulmarus glacialis* (*c.*180 pairs), *Phalacrocorax carbo* (154 pairs in 1985), *P. aristotelis* (25 pairs), *Larus canus* (20-25 pairs), *L. marinus* (210 pairs), and *Cepphus grylle* (80 birds). *Branta leucopsis* occurs in winter (max. 500; interchanging with Inishkea Islands). (Information compiled in 1987)

033 Blacksod Bay, Co Mayo (West)

54°03'-54°13'N, 09°50'-10°05'W *c.*15,770 ha

Unprotected

A large, mostly shallow sea bay sheltered from the Atlantic Ocean by the long Mullet Peninsula. The bay encompasses the estuaries of a number of small rivers entering from the east. The intertidal substrate is rather sandy. Surrounding areas are mainly low-lying grassland. Human activities include low-intensity stock-raising. Development of mariculture is likely in the future.

Sterna albifrons breeds occasionally in small numbers. Important for wintering waterfowl with *Branta bernicla hrota* (4-yr. av. max. 339; max. 401), *Haematopus ostralegus* (several hundred), *Charadrius hiaticula* (3-yr. av. max. 724), *Calidris alba* (3-yr. av. max. 173), *C. alpina* (100-200), *Limosa lapponica* (100-200), *Numenius arquata* (100-200), and *Tringa totanus* (100-200). (Information compiled 1987)

034 Moynish Beg, Co Mayo (West)

53°53'N, 09°43'W 0.7 ha

Unprotected

A very small marine island in the sheltered waters of inner Clew Bay.

One of the five (second) most important colonies in the region for *Sterna hirundo* (76 pairs in 1984); also gulls (143 pairs) and *Sterna albifrons* (4 pairs in 1984); colony known since 1970. (Information compiled 1987)

035 Inishraher Islet, Co Mayo (West)

53°48'N, 09°37'W less than 1.0 ha

Unprotected

A very small marine island in the sheltered waters of inner Clew Bay.

One of the five (fourth) most important colonies in the region for *Sterna hirundo* (69 pairs in 1984). (Information compiled 1987)

036 Dorinish Bar, Co Mayo (West)

53°49'N, 09°40'W *c.*5 ha

Unprotected

A gravel/shingle bar capped with grassy drumlins in the island-studded shelter of inner Clew Bay. Uninhabited.

A breeding site for *Phalacrocorax carbo* (115 pairs in 1985) and *Sterna hirundo* (*c.*30 pairs in 1970). *Sterna paradisaea* has also bred in the past (25 pairs in 1947). (Information compiled in 1987).

037 Clare Island Cliffs, Co Mayo (West)

53°48'N, 10°04'W 8 km of steep cliff

Unprotected

Large inhabited island in Clew Bay, nearly 500 m in height.

Breeding seabirds include *Fulmarus glacialis* (2555 pairs), *Sula bassana* (1-2 pairs), *Phalacrocorax aristotelis* (30 pairs), *Larus argentatus* (500+ pairs), *L. marinus* (30 pairs), *Rissa tridactyla* (*c.*800 pairs), *Uria aalge* (less than 1000 birds), *Alca torda* (200 birds), *Cepphus grylle* (30 pairs), and *Fratercula arctica* (less than 100 pairs). The site also supports an important concentration of *Pyrrhocorax pyrrhocorax*. (Information compiled 1987)

038 Cross Lough, Co Mayo (West)

53°42'N, 09°55'W less than 1.0 ha

Unprotected

A very small island in a brackish coastal lagoon.

One of the five (fifth) most important colonies in the region for *Sterna sandvicensis* (107 pairs in 1984); known as a site for *Sterna sandvicensis* since 1937. There is also a small colony of *Larus ridibundus*. (Information compiled 1987)

039 Inishbofin, Co Galway (West)

53°37'N, 10°13'W 765 ha

Unprotected

A large marine island with several islets and stacks, 5.5 km offshore. Inhabited.

Most important site in the region for *Puffinus puffinus* (several hundred pairs); also breeding *Fulmarus glacialis* (300 pairs), *Hydrobates pelagicus* (numbers unknown), and small numbers of other seabird species; history of seabird data from 1932. *Crex crex* and *Pyrrhocorax pyrrhocorax* breed on the island. Small numbers of *Branta leucopsis* occur in winter. (Information compiled 1987)

040 High Island, Co Galway (West)

53°33'N, 10°17'W 37 ha

Unprotected

A small uninhabited marine island, 3 km offshore.

One of the five most important colonies of *Hydrobates pelagicus* in the region; also breeding *Fulmarus glacialis* (350 pairs), *Puffinus puffinus* (numbers unknown), *Falco peregrinus* (1 pair), *Larus marinus* (200+ pairs), *Cepphus grylle* (11+ pairs), and *Pyrrhocorax pyrrhocorax* (1-3 pairs); seabird colony known since 1896. A small flock of *Branta leucopsis* (*c.*80) winters. (Information compiled 1987)

041 Eeshal Island, Co Galway (West)

53°30'N, 10°09'W 5 ha

Unprotected

A very small marine island, 2 km off mainland.

One of the five (third) most important colonies in the region for *Sterna paradisaea* (100 pairs in 1984); also breeding gulls (250 pairs) and *Sterna hirundo* (12 pairs in 1984). (Information compiled 1987)

042 Horse Island, Co Galway (West)

53°24'N, 10°08'W 6 ha

Unprotected

A very small marine island *c.*1.0 km offshore, east of Slyne Head.

One of the five (second) most important colonies in the region for *Sterna sandvicensis* (150 pairs in 1984); also breeding gulls (130 pairs), *Sterna paradisaea* (39 pairs in 1984), and *S. albifrons* (4 pairs in 1984). (Information compiled 1987)

043 Hen Island, Co Galway (West)

53°23'N, 10°05'W 1.0 ha

Unprotected

A very small marine island, *c.*2.5 km off the mainland south of Ballyconneally.

One of the five (fifth) most important colonies in the region for *Sterna paradisaea* (75 pairs in 1984); colony known since 1969. (Information compiled 1987)

044 Lough Scannive, Co Galway (West)

53°20'N, 09°47'W 83 ha

Unprotected

An oligotrophic lake with rocky islands with trees, surrounded by blanket bog. Uninhabited.

A breeding site for *Phalacrocorax carbo* (218 pairs in 1985); colony known pre-1968. (Information compiled 1987)

045 Oilean Geabhróg, Co Galway (West)

53°19'N, 09°39'W 1.3 ha

Unprotected

A very small marine island in a very sheltered sea bay (Kilkieran Bay).

One of five (fifth) most important colonies in the region for *Sterna hirundo* (60 pairs in 1984); also breeding *Sterna paradisaea* (4 pairs in 1984); history of tern colonies in Kilkieran Bay since 1935. (Information compiled 1987)

046 Oilean na nGeabhróg, Co Galway (West)

53°23'N, 09°35'W less than 1 ha

Unprotected

A tiny marine island in the very sheltered waters of Camus Bay.

One of five (third) most important colonies in the region for *Sterna hirundo* (71 pairs in 1984). There is also a small colony of *Larus ridibundus.* (Information compiled 1987)

047 Duck Island, Co Galway (West)

53°16'N, 09°50'W 3.25 ha

Unprotected

A very small marine island, *c.*1 km offshore.

Most important colony in the region for *Sterna paradisaea* (274 pairs in 1984) and third most important colony for *S. sandvicensis* (120 pairs in 1984); also breeding gulls (56 pairs), *Sterna dougallii* (5 pairs in 1984), and *S. hirundo* (30 pairs in 1984); tern colony known since 1938. (Information compiled 1987)

048 Geabhrog Island, Co Galway (West)

53°17'N, 09°39'W less than 1 ha

Unprotected

A tiny marine islet in the very sheltered waters of Greatman's Bay.

Most important colony in the region for *Sterna hirundo* (210 pairs in 1984); also breeding gulls (very small colony), *Sterna dougallii*, and *S. paradisaea* (1 and 10 pairs respectively in 1984). (Information compiled 1987)

049 Lough Corrib, Co Galway (West)

53°16'-53°33'N, 09°03'-09°31'W 18,240 ha

Unprotected

A very large lake with extensive *Chara* and *Schoenus* fen, in shallow south-east section on limestone; managed to provide material for thatching. Deeper, wider north-west part. Shore mainly karst, bog, and small areas of callow. The surroundings are farmland and holiday-home areas. Uncontrolled discharge of sewage is causing eutrophication and there is heavy shooting and fishing disturbance.

Wintering waterfowl include *Anser albifrons flavirostris* (50; max. 100), *Aythya ferina* (3-yr. av. max. 8660; max. 22,000), *A. fuligula* (800; max. 6000), and *Fulica atra* (max. 12,000 in autumn). (Information updated 1987)

050 Inner Galway Bay, Co Galway (West)

53°07'-53°17'N, 08°55'-09°12'W 11,165 ha

Mainly unprotected; No-shooting Area (Lough Ruisin)

The shallow, more sheltered, eastern part of a large sea bay which is partially protected from the open sea by the Aran Islands. The southern side is fringed by limestone and there are numerous shallow intertidal inlets on the eastern and southern sides. A number of small low islands (including Deer Island) composed of glacial deposits are also located along the east of the bay. The adjacent land is mainly used for low-quality grazing with urban development along the north shore. Galway harbour is a commercial fishing port and other human activities include inshore angling, wildfowling, water-sports, and general recreation. Expansion of urban/industrial areas is a potential threat.

Deer Island supports a large breeding colony of *Phalacrocorax carbo* (200+ pairs). Important for non-breeding waterfowl with the following maxima: *Gavia immer* (50), *Podiceps cristatus* (155), *Phalacrocorax carbo* (338), *P. aristotelis* (638), *Branta bernicla hrota* (4-yr. av. max. 537; max. 567), *Anas penelope* (1855), *A. crecca* (846), *Mergus serrator* (486), *Charadrius hiaticula* (783), *Calidris alpina* (1904), and *Numenius arquata* (1375). (Information compiled in 1987)

051 Rahasane Turlough, Co Galway (West)

53°13'N, 08°47'W 257 ha

Unprotected

The last remaining large-scale turlough (karst lake) with marshes and seasonally flooded wet meadows on the River Dunkellin. Human activities include stock-raising and wildfowling. Arterial drainage, recreational disturbance, and shooting are the main threats. Also, extensive drainage in the catchment is thought to be responsible for higher flood levels and decreased suitability for *Anas* spp. and *Anser albifrons flavirostris*.

Wintering waterfowl include *Cygnus columbianus* (245 in 1985), *C. cygnus* (100; max. 180), *Anser albifrons flavirostris* (5 yr. av. max. 62; max. 71), *Anas penelope* (5100; max. 5400), *A. crecca* (2106 in 1981), *A. acuta* (max. 660), *A. clypeata* (300), *Pluvialis apricaria* (3000; max 10,000-15,000), *Vanellus vanellus* (1500), *Limosa limosa islandica* (100; max. 1100), *Numenius arquata* (600), and *Tringa totanus* (max. 360). (Information updated 1987)

052 Inishmaan (Aran Islands), Co Galway (West)

53°04'N, 09°35'W 908 ha

Unprotected

Island with dry calcareous grassland, bogs and mires and inland limestone cliffs. Human activities include farming and recreation, and there is an airport. Land development and disturbance from tourism threaten the breeding tern colonies.

Breeding terns include *Sterna albifrons* (20 pairs in 1984). (Information compiled 1987)

053 Cliffs of Moher, Co Clare (Mid West)

52°58'N, 09°26'W 7 km of vertifical cliffs EEC SPA

Refuge for Fauna

Sheer cliffs up to 230 m in height.

Breeding seabirds include *Fulmarus glacialis* (3000+ pairs), *Phalacrocorax aristotelis* (50-70 pairs), *Rissa tridactyla* (4300 pairs), *Uria aalge* (12,800 birds), *Alca torda* (2300 birds), and *Fratercula arctica* (700-1000 pairs); also breeding *Falco peregrinus* and *Pyrrhocorax pyrrhocorax*. (Information compiled 1987)

054 Lough Cutra, Co Galway (Mid West)

53°01'N, 08°46'W 390 ha

Unprotected

Human activities include fishing and recreation.

A freshwater lake with breeding *Phalacrocorax carbo* (166 pairs in 1985; max. 300 in winter). (Information compiled 1987)

055 Ballyallia Lake, Co Clare (Mid West)

52°53'N, 08°59'W 33 ha

No-shooting Area

A small shallow lake (occasionally greatly enlarged by winter flooding) on the River Fergus with low-lying rough grazing marshes on the south and west sides. There is some (mainly summer) recreational use; also rough grazing.

Important for *Anas clypeata* (3-yr. av. max. 496; max. 2250); also wintering *A. penelope* (max. 8000), *A. strepera* (max. 180), *A. crecca* (max. 4000), and *Limosa limosa islandica*. (Information compiled 1987).

056 Mutton Island, Co Clare (Mid West)

52°47'N, 09°30'W 75 ha

No-shooting Area

A small rocky island, close to the coast, overlain with glacial drift and covered by maritime grasses (e.g. *Festuca rubra*). Formerly inhabited. There is rough grazing of sheep and cattle (mainly in summer). Surrounding waters used for lobster-potting and fishing.

Important for wintering *Branta leucopsis* (3-yr. av. max. 300; highest numbers occur prior to migration in spring). Also small numbers of breeding seabirds, notably a colony of *Hydrobates pelagicus*. (Information compiled 1987)

057 Mattle Island, Co Clare (Mid West)

52°47'N, 09°32'W *c.*2 ha

Unprotected

A small marine island, 2.5 km offshore. Uninhabited

One of only two colonies in the region of *Hydrobates pelagicus* (numbers unknown); also breeding *Phalacrocorax carbo* (50-90 pairs), *P. aristotelis* (max. 17 pairs), *Larus argentatus* (max. 100 pairs), *L. marinus* (max. 50 pairs), and possibly *Cepphus grylle*; seabird colony known since 1954. (Information compiled 1987)

058 Shannon and Fergus Estuary, Co Clare, Co Limerick and Co Kerry (Mid West, South West)

52°33'-52°49'N, 08°38'-09°45'W 34,000 ha

Mainly unprotected; No-shooting Area (Islandavanna; under consideration as a NNR)

A large estuary complex with islands, saltwater marshes, mudflats (especially in inner half of estuary), raised saltmarsh, and wet meadows. Outer estuary is predominantly narrow and rock-strewn/pebbly. Includes Poulnasherry Bay, Clonderalaw Bay, Aughinish Island, Tarbert Bay, and Ballylongford Bay. Human activities include stock-raising, fishing, industrial shipping, wildfowling, recreation (including boating); there are large centres of human habitation (Limerick, Ennis, Shannon Newtown etc.), and industry. Threatened by industrial development (with consequent reclamation, pollution, and general disturbance), drainage of tributaries, *Spartina* encroachment, and shooting pressure.

Wintering waterfowl include *Cygnus cygnus* (100), *Anser albifrons flavirostris* (80), *A. anser* (100+), *Branta bernicla hrota* (300), *Tadorna tadorna* (1000; max. 1300), *Anas penelope* (3-yr. av. max. 2229), *A. crecca* (3-yr. av. max. 1277), *A. acuta* (250), *A. clypeata* (1000 in 1983), *Aythya marila* (280), *Haematopus ostralegus* (400), *Pluvialis apricaria* (2600), *Vanellus vanellus* (4900), *Calidris canutus* (2500), *C. alpina* (3-yr. av. max. 8635; max. 33,000), *Limosa limosa islandica* (3-yr. av. max. 2205; max. 16,400 on spring passage), *L. lapponica* (900), *Numenius arquata* (3-yr. av. max. 1180), *Tringa totanus* (3-yr. av. max. 1880), and *T. nebularia* (100 on passage). Total waders: max. 50,000. (Major revision 1987)

059 Akeragh Lough, Co Kerry (South West)

52°22'N, 09°50'W 231 ha

Unprotected

Formerly an extensive shallow coastal lagoon separated from the sea by a narrow dune ridge. Rapid siltation has considerably reduced the area of standing water and *c.*95 per cent of the site is now covered with tall marsh vegetation. Human activities include low-intensity stock-raising, hunting, and recreation. Caravan-site development on the western shore of the Lough has resulted in problems with sewage, causing eutrophication, and the open-water area is decreasing owing to unchecked vegetational succession.

Waterfowl occurring include *Anas strepera* (max. 150), *A. crecca* (formerly max. 3500; now much decreased: 3-yr. av. max. 45), *Vanellus vanellus* (10,000), and *Numenius arquata* (max. 4000). Also noteworthy for vagrant American waders. (Major revision 1987)

060 Magharee Islands, Co Kerry (South West)

52°20'N, 10°02'W 45 ha

Unprotected

A group of six marine islands and several additional holms and skerries. Uninhabited.

Most important site in the region for breeding *Phalacrocorax aristotelis* (135 pairs); also breeding *Phalacrocorax carbo* (87-100 pairs), *Larus canus* (20 pairs), *L. fuscus* (32-47 pairs), *L. marinus* (85-100 pairs), *Sterna hirundo* (45-50 pairs), *S. paradisaea* (10 pairs), *and S. albifrons* (22 pairs); tern colony known since 1851. Also wintering *Branta leucopsis* (*c.*300+). (Information compiled 1987)

061 Lough Gill, Co Kerry (South West)

52°16'N, 10°02'W 157 ha EEC SPA

No-shooting Area; under consideration as a NNR

A very shallow coastal freshwater lake, draining into Tralee Bay, bordered by dunes and dune grassland on its north side and by peaty podzolic soils on its south side. The Lough is fringed by *Phragmites* beds along most of its shoreline and it is fed by rainfall/small streams. The lough is a major spawning area for *Bufo calamita*). Human activities include some agriculture, low-intensity stock-raising, and wildfowling. Drainage, eutrophication, and water-sports development may threaten the area.

Wintering waterfowl include *Cygnus olor*, *C. columbianus* (irregular; max. 100), *C. cygnus* (70; 110 on passage), *Anas penelope* (500), *A. strepera* (formerly 100-200 in Jan; none in past 3 yrs), *A. crecca* (formerly 4000; much decreased: 3-yr. av. max. 149), *A. clypeata* (1500), *Aythya ferina* (600), *A. fuligula* (2000), and *Fulica atra* (2000). (Major revision 1987)

062 Tralee Bay and Barrow Harbour, Co Kerry (South West)

52°16'N, 09°48'W 3290 ha

Unprotected; part under consideration as a NNR (south side of Inner Tralee Bay)

Large, shallow sea bay fringed by sandy beaches, protected from the open sea by a sand spit/rocky promontory to the west and with a saltmarsh recurve enclosing mudflats in the sheltered eastern part. Barrow Harbour is a tidal lagoon which almost dries out at low tide and which has extensive *Zostera* beds and algal mats. Human activities include hunting, oyster-farming and low-intensity grazing. Problems may result from pollution, (industrial and domestic) and the spread of *Spartina*.

Wintering waterfowl include *Branta bernicla hrota* (4-yr. av. max. 1430; max. 1707), *Anas penelope* (4500), *A. crecca* (1800), *A. acuta* (formerly 500-800 in Jan; no longer reaches these levels: 3-yr. av. max. 9), *A. clypeata* (200), *Melanitta nigra* (200-300 in Jan.), *Pluvialis apricaria* (3-yr. av. max. 15,000), *Vanellus vanellus* (1000), and *Numenius arquata* (3-yr. av. max. 3000). (Major revision 1987)

063 Castlemaine Harbour, Co Kerry (South West)

52°07'N, 09°55'W 9874 ha

No-shooting Areas (Inch and Rossbeigh; under consideration as a NNR or Refuge for Fauna)

A large, shallow, tidal area at the head of Dingle Bay, sheltered from the open sea by sand and shingle spits on the north and south sides. The area is the estuary of the Rivers Maine and Laune. There are extensive *Zostera* beds. Human activities include stock-raising, fishing, and wildfowling. Increasing pollution of the rivers feeding the estuary, and spread of *Spartina* are the only reported problems.

Wintering waterfowl include *Branta bernicla hrota* (4-yr. av. max. 773; max. 1033), *Anas penelope* (3-yr. av. max. 3409), *A. crecca* (2000), *A. platyrhynchos* (1500), *A. acuta* (3-yr. av. max. 34), *A. clypeata* (formerly max. 1500; virtually none 1984-7), *Melanitta nigra* (100s in Jan.), *Haematopus ostralegus* (2400), *Pluvialis apricaria* (3000), *Calidris canutus* (3000), *C. alba* (less than 50), *C. alpina* (2200), *Limosa lapponica* (3000), *Numenius arquata* (4000), and *Tringa totanus* (300). Total wildfowl: 11,000; total waders: max. 17,000. (Major revision 1987)

064 Blasket Islands: Inishtooskert, Inishvickillaun, Inishnabro, Inishtearaght, and Beginish; Co Kerry (South West)

52°05'N, 10°35'W 287 ha EEC SPA

Unprotected; under consideration as NNRs/Refuges for Fauna

Five exposed rocky islands off Slea Head.

Breeding seabirds include *Fulmarus glacialis* (2200 pairs), *Puffinus puffinus* (2000-5000 pairs), *Hydrobates pelagicus* 40,000+ pairs), *Phalacrocorax aristotelis* (350 pairs), *Larus fuscus* (425 pairs), *L. argentatus* (130 pairs), *L. marinus* (375-425 pairs), *Rissa tridactyla* (750+ pairs), *Sterna paradisaea* (max. 200-225 pairs), *Alca torda* (450 birds), *Uria aalge* (370 birds), *Cepphus grylle* (40 birds), and *Fratercula arctica* (4500-5350 birds). In winter, *Branta leucopsis* (25-50 in Jan.) and *Anser albifrons flavirostris* (*c*.30) occur on Beginish. (Information compiled 1988)

065 Puffin Island, Co Kerry (South West)

51°50'N, 10°24'W 53 ha EEC SPA

NNR; IWC Reserve

Long, narrow and grassy, uninhabited island on the northern side of St Finan's Bay.

Important for breeding seabirds with *Fulmarus glacialis* (700+ pairs), *Puffinus puffinus* (10,000-20,000 pairs), *Hydrobates pelagicus* (4000+ pairs), *Phalacrocorax aristotelis* (35 pairs), *Larus argentatus* (100-150 pairs), *L. marinus* (100-150 pairs), *Uria aalge* (500 birds), *Alca torda* (800 pairs), and *Fratercula arctica* (8000-10,000 pairs). (Information compiled 1987)

066 Moylaun Island, Co Kerry (South West)

51°45'N, 10°11'W 5.4 ha

Unprotected

A small marine island 2 km off the mainland at Lamb's Head.

One of five (third) most important colonies in the region for *Sterna paradisaea* (51 pairs in 1984); colony known since 1969. There is also a gull colony (*c.*150 pairs). (Information compiled 1987)

067 The Skelligs: Great Skellig and Little Skellig, Co Kerry (South West)

51°47'N, 10°31'W 25 ha EEC SPA

NNR; IWC Reserve (Little Skellig)

Two precipitous rocky islets with important *Sula bassana* and *Hydrobates pelagicus* colonies. Human activities include recreation on Great Skellig.

Breeding seabirds include *Fulmarus glacialis* (600 pairs), *Puffinus puffinus* (5000 pairs), *Hydrobates pelagicus* (10,000 pairs), *Sula bassana* (21,900 pairs on Little Skellig), *Rissa tridactyla* (2000 pairs), *Uria aalge* (850 pairs), *Alca torda* (750 pairs), and *Fratercula arctica* (6500 pairs). (Information compiled 1987)

068 Bull and Cow Rocks, Co Cork (South West)

51°35'N, 10°17'W 7 ha

Unprotected

Two tiny rocky islets with breeding *Hydrobates pelagicus* (2000-5000 pairs), *Sula bassana* (1511 pairs in 1985), *Phalacrocorax carbo* (50 pairs), *Rissa tridactyla* (590 pairs), *Uria aalge* (2000 pairs), *Alca torda* (900 pairs), and *Fratercula arctica* (200 pairs). (Information compiled 1987)

069 Whiddy Island, Co Cork (South West)

51°41'N, 09°30'W 300 ha

Unprotected

A medium-sized island at the head of Bantry Bay. The island is a major oil terminal.

Second most important colony in the region for *Sterna paradisaea* (56 pairs in 1984); colony known since 1834. (Information compiled 1987)

070 Roaringwater Bay Islands, Co Cork (South West)

51°32'N, 09°25'W less than 1 ha

Unprotected

Group of three tiny rocky islets in sheltered coastal waters.

One of the five most important colonies in the region for *Sterna hirundo* and *S. paradisaea* (122 pairs combined in 1984); also *S. albifrons* (2 pairs in 1984). (Information compiled 1987)

071 Inner Clonakilty Bay, Co Cork (South West)

51°37'N, 08°52'W *c.*300 ha

Unprotected

A tidal bay in two parts separated by Inchydoney Island. Most of the intertidal area is sandy. There is some recreational use of the sandy beaches and a small number of pleasure-craft use the sheltered parts. Part of the bay beside Clonakilty town is used for refuse disposal.

Important for *Limosa limosa islandica* (3-yr. av. max. 572; max. 1500). Other waders occurring include *Pluvialis apricaria* (max. 2500), *Vanellus vanellus* (max. 3000), *Calidris alpina* (max. 1500), *Limosa lapponica* (max. 300), *Numenius arquata* (max. 4360), and *Tringa totanus* (max. 570). (Information compiled 1987)

072 Sovereign Islands, Co Cork (South West)

51°40'N, 08°27'W *c.*2 ha

Unprotected

Two small flat-topped islands (less than 30 m high), 1.5 km offshore.

Breeding seabirds include *Fulmarus glacialis*, *Phalacrocorax carbo* (100+ pairs), and *Larus marinus*. (Information compiled 1988)

073 Cork Harbour, Co Cork (South West)

51°50'N, 08°17'W 5950 ha

Mainly unprotected; IWC Reserve (Lough Beg; in west of site)

A large and very sheltered sea bay and estuary of several rivers (notably the River Lee), with extensive intertidal mudflats, especially along the north, north-east and north-west shores. Some of these areas also have saltmarsh higher up the shore. Human activities include fishing, wildfowling, and boating, and there are major centres of human habitation (total population *c.*250,000), industry (including an oil refinery) and a harbour. Land reclamation, industrial and urban development, pollution, and the spread of *Spartina* grass threaten the area.

Wintering waterfowl include *Tadorna tadorna* (3-yr. av. max. 1444), *Anas penelope* (1800; max. 2300), *A. crecca* (1400), *A. platyrhynchos* (1300 in Dec.), *Aythya marila* (50), *Bucephala clangula* (50), *Mergus serrator* (300), *Haematopus ostralegus* (1600), *Pluvialis apricaria* (3-yr. av. max. 5124), *Vanellus vanellus* (3-yr. av. max. 14,713), *Calidris alpina* (10,000; max. 17,000), *Limosa limosa islandica* (3-yr. av. max. 1779), *L. lapponica* (500), *Numenius arquata* (2000; max. 2700), and *Tringa totanus* (3-yr. av. max. 2369). Total waders: max. 28,000. Also *Podiceps cristatus* (100, 150 in Nov.) and *Phalacrocorax carbo* (150). (Major revision 1987)

074 Ballycotton, Ballynamona, and Shanagarry, Co Cork (South West)

51°49'N, 08°02'W 200 ha

No-shooting Area

A site notable for its diversity of habitats with freshwater lagoons, saltwater lagoons, saltwater marshes, mudflats, sandflats, dunes and wet meadows. Gravel extraction, development for tourism, drainage, and encroachment of vegetation threaten the area.

Breeding species include *Phalacrocorax carbo* (25-30 pairs on Ballycotton Island), *Sterna hirundo* (10 pairs), and *S. albifrons* (2 pairs). In winter, waterfowl include *Cygnus columbianus* (max. 125), *Pluvialis apricaria* (1000) and *Numenius arquata* (400). In addition, *Limosa limosa islandica* occur on passage (100). Also noteworthy for vagrant American waders. (Information compiled 1987)

075 Ballymacoda, Co Cork (South West)

51°54'N, 07°54'W 602 ha

Unprotected

The estuary of the River Womanagh with a winding channel flanked by marshy fields, saltmarsh and mudflats. The area is sheltered from the open sea by a stabilised shingle bar and extensive sandy beach. Human activities include low-level recreation and wildfowling.

Wintering waterfowl include *Anas penelope* (1000), *Pluvialis apricaria* (3-yr. av. max. 6317), *P. squatarola* (1074 in 1984), *Vanellus vanellus* (4000; max. 8000), *Calidris alpina* (4200), *Limosa limosa islandica* (3-yr. av. max. 399), *L. lapponica* (400), *Numenius arquata* (3-yr. av. max. 1153), and *Tringa totanus* (300). Total waders: 19,000; max. 30,000. (Major revision 1987)

076 Blackwater Estuary, Co Cork and Co Waterford (South East, South West)

51°58'N, 07°50'W *c.*500 ha

Unprotected

A small estuary with a narrow opening to the sea with areas of intertidal mudflats and saltmarsh (mainly on the east side; mostly empoldered on the west side). The main human activities are salmon-netting and pleasure-boating (mainly in summer), with mixed farming and an urban centre in the surrounding area.

Important for wintering *Limosa limosa islandica* (3-yr. av. max. 496; max. 588). Other waterfowl recorded include *Anas penelope* (max. 700), *Pluvialis apricaria* (max. 5200), *Calidris alpina* (max. 1625), and *Numenius arquata* (max. 400). (Information compiled 1987)

077 River Blackwater Callows, Co Waterford and Co Cork (South East, South West)

52°09'N, 07°51'-08°15'W *c.*2000 ha

No-shooting Area (Lismore)

Narrow flood plain of the River Blackwater, hemmed in by parallel sandstone ridges and extending *c.*29 km along the river from Fermoy to Cappoquin. Callows are seasonally flooded riverside grasslands; the Lismore – Ballyduff area is especially prone to flooding. The major land-use is sheep/cattle grazing. There is a sugar-beet factory upstream from the area.

Wintering waterfowl include *Cygnus columbianus* (3-yr. av. max. 95), *C. cygnus* (3-yr. av. max. 212), *Anas penelope* (1000), *A. crecca* (200), *Vanellus vanellus* (1200), *Limosa limosa islandica* (3-yr. av. max. 895), and *Numenius arquata* (500). (Information compiled 1987)

078 Dungarvan Harbour, Co Waterford (South East)

52°04'N, 07°34'W 1300 ha

Unprotected

A large east-facing sea bay sheltered by Helvick Head and Ballynacourty Point, and a north-south shingle spit which almost divides the bay in two, with saltmarshes, mudflats, and *Zostera* beds. A few small rivers flow in from the west. Human activities include low-intensity fishing, wildfowling, and pleasure-boating. There is a built-up area (Dungarvan) at the head of the bay. Threatened by *Spartina* grass encroachment.

Wintering waterfowl include *Branta bernicla hrota* (4-yr. av. max. 694; max. 734), *Tadorna tadorna* (300), *Anas penelope* (600), *Pluvialis apricaria* (1500), *Calidris canutus* (1900), *C. alpina* (1500), *Limosa limosa islandica* (3-yr. av. max. 1329), *L. lapponica* (500), *Numenius arquata* (400), and *Tringa totanus* (400). Total waders: 8600; max. 10,800. (Information updated 1987)

079 Tramore Backstrand, Co Waterford (South East)

52°10'N, 07°06'W *c.*457 ha

Unprotected

Rather small, shallow bay with mudflats, separated from the sea by a sand-dune system. Most of the area is exposed at low tide. Sections of the western part of the bay have been empoldered. There are small areas of saltmarsh in places. Human activities at the site, and in the immediate vicinity, include mixed farming, recreational boating, and wildfowling.

Important for wintering *Branta bernicla hrota* (4-yr. av. max. 485; max. 620); also wintering *Anas penelope* (1500), *Pluvialis squatarola* (200), *Calidris alpina*, and other waders. (Information compiled 1987)

080 Bannow Bay, Co Wexford (South East)

52°13'N, 06°48'W 900 ha

No-shooting Area (parts of the site)

A fairly large sea bay receiving small rivers and streams in the north and south-west. At low tide, up to 75 per cent of the area is exposed mud and sand. There are mudflats in the narrow northern part; also in the south-west and south-east, with saltmarsh at higher levels. The area is otherwise dominated by extensive sandflats and a dune system providing shelter from the open sea. Human activities include wildfowling and fishing. Large-scale maricultural development may occur in the future. Spread of *Spartina* is also a potential threat.

Wintering waterfowl include *Branta bernicla hrota* (4-yr. av. max. 938; max. 1320), *Tadorna tadorna* (300), *Anas penelope* (800; max. 1000), *A. crecca*, *Haematopus ostralegus* (500; max. 700), *Pluvialis apricaria* (max. 12,000), *Vanellus vanellus* (3200), *Calidris canutus* (max. 500), *C. alpina* (2100), *Limosa limosa islandica* (3-yr. av. max. 201), *L. lapponica* (600), *Numenius arquata* (1300; max. 1800), and *Tringa totanus* (800; max. 1000). Total waders: 16,000; max. 20,000. (Major revision 1987)

081 Keeragh Islands, Co Wexford (South East)

52°12'N, 06°44'W 2 ha

IWC Reserve

Two small islands with breeding *Phalacrocorax carbo* (239 pairs in 1987). (Information compiled in 1987)

082 The Cull/Killag, Co Wexford (South East)

52°12'N, 06°39'W *c.*896 ha

NNR (mudflats and dune area; extension under consideration)

The western part is a long narrow inlet/estuary protected from the open sea by a shingle spit with dunes. The eastern part was formerly (pre-1900) tidal with saltmarsh but is now polderland, most of which is intensively farmed grassland and arable land. There may be some disturbance of wintering waterfowl in the eastern sector to discourage feeding on re-seeded grassland.

There is a small breeding colony of *Sterna albifrons* on the shingle spit (*c.*12 pairs). Important for wintering *Cygnus columbianus* (3-yr. av. max. 312; max. 550) and *Branta bernicla hrota* (4-yr. av. max. 915; max. 1015). Also wintering *Tadorna tadorna*, *Anas penelope*, *A. crecca*, *Haematopus ostralegus*, *Charadrius hiaticula*, *Pluvialis apricaria*, *P. squatarola*, *Vanellus vanellus*, *Calidris canutus*, *C. alpina*, *Limosa limosa islandica* (max. 550), *L. lapponica*, *Numenius arquata*, and *Tringa totanus*. (Information compiled in 1987)

083 Saltee Islands, Co Wexford (South East)

52°07'N, 06°36'W 126 ha EEC SPA

Private bird sanctuary

Two islands with rocky coast and cliffs. Great Saltee was formerly a bird observatory and a wide variety of species was recorded.

Breeding seabirds include *Fulmarus glacialis* (325 pairs), *Puffinus puffinus* (50-100 pairs), *Sula bassana* (800+ pairs), *Phalacrocorax carbo* (391 pairs), *P. aristotelis* (550+ pairs), *Larus argentatus* (1000 pairs), *Rissa tridactyla* (3000 pairs), *Uria aalge* (16,329 birds), *Alca torda* (4700 birds), and *Fratercula arctica* (1200 pairs). (Information compiled 1988)

084 Tacumshin Lake, Co Wexford (South East)

52°11'N, 06°29'W 483 ha

No-shooting Area (parts); under consideration as a NNR

Until 1976, a tidal lagoon separated from the open sea by a long shingle bar. Longshore drift closed the connection in 1976, after which the lagoon flooded with freshwater. Local farmers set up a one-way drainage pipe through the bar and now *c.*75 per cent of the lagoon dries out in May-Oct., filling up again in winter. There is some seepage of sea water in summer; however, some excellent areas of freshwater marsh have developed since 1976. Human activities include stock-raising. Potentially threatened by drainage.

Wintering waterfowl include *Cygnus columbianus* (3-yr. av. max. 134), *Branta bernicla hrota* (3-yr av. max. 513), *Anas penelope* (800; 1000 in Oct.), *Aythya marila* (200; 440 in Feb.), *Haematopus ostralegus* (900), *Pluvialis apricaria* (600), *P. squatarola*, *Vanellus vanellus* (900; max. 5000), *Calidris alpina* (900), *Limosa limosa islandica* (100), *L. lapponica* (200), and *Numenius arquata* (2000+). *Sterna dougallii* and *S. hirundo* formerly bred but deserted the area because of disturbance. Also noteworthy for vagrant American waders. (Major revision 1987)

085 Lady's Island Lake, Co Wexford (South East)

52°11'N, 06°24'W 466 ha

Two EEC SPAs (Inish and Sgarbheen: 4 ha; Lady's Island Lake: 356 ha)

Refuge for Fauna

Shallow, coastal lagoon containing a few small islands and separated from the sea by a shingle bank. There are rich marshland areas to the south-east. Human activities include the annual visits of 10,000+ pilgrims to Lady's Island peninsula, wildfowling, fishing, recreation, and stock-raising. Drainage is affected by periodic (usually annual) cutting of a channel through the shingle bar. Drainage and eutrophication may affect the area and there is disturbance of breeding terns by sail-boarding, etc.

Important for breeding terns with *Sterna sandvicensis* (500-700 pairs), *S. dougallii* (less than 10 pairs; max. 300 pairs in early 1980s), *S. hirundo* (200 pairs), and *S. albifrons* (24 pairs). In winter, waterfowl include *Cygnus olor* (600; 300-400 moulting in late summer), *C. columbianus* (3-yr. av. max. 24), *C. cygnus* (20; max. 95), *Anas penelope* (900; max. 5100), *A. crecca* (max. 530), *A. clypeata* (max. 240), *Aythya ferina* (900; max. 1900), *A. fuligula* (800), and *Fulica atra*. (Information updated 1987)

086 Wexford Harbour and Slobs, Co Wexford (South East)

52°19'N, 06°26'W 4000+ ha

Includes two Ramsar Sites (Wexford Wildfowl Reserve: 110 ha; The Raven: 589 ha); EEC SPA (Wexford Wildfowl Reserve: 110 ha)

NNRs (North Slob = Wexford Wildfowl Reserve [part owned by IWC]: 110 ha; The Raven: 589 ha); No-shooting Area (Rosslare Back Strand)

Two areas of empoldered land (each 1000+ ha) on the north and south sides of Wexford Harbour, behind nineteenth century sea-walls. On the seaward side, the partially afforested sand-dunes of The Raven and Rosslare Point partly enclose the harbour. The reclaimed land is a mixture of pasture and arable areas. There are numerous drainage ditches intersecting the area. Human activities include harbour operations, agriculture, stock-raising, wildfowling, and recreation; there is human habitation (including Wexford town; population 15,000).

Important for breeding terns in some years. Important for passage and wintering waterfowl with *Cygnus columbianus* (3-yr. av. max. 168; max. 700), *C. cygnus* (3-yr. av. max. 97), *Anser albifrons flavirostris* (5-yr. av. max. 7581; max. 11,000; most important wintering site in the world), *Branta bernicla hrota* (4-yr. av. max. 1245; max. 2000), *Anas penelope* (3-yr. av. max. 4842), *A. crecca* (3-yr. av. max. 379; max. 1800), *A. platyrhynchos* (2500; 3800 in Sept.), *A. acuta* (900; 1300 in Oct.), *Aythya marila* (300-500 in Jan.), *Bucephala clangula* (300), *Haematopus ostralegus* (1600; 2700 in Aug.), *Pluvialis apricaria* (8400), *Vanellus vanellus* (22,000), *Calidris alpina* (3000; 3800 in May), *Limosa limosa islandica* (3-yr. av. max. 816; max. 2400), *L. lapponica* (1500 in Dec.), *Numenius arquata* (3-yr. av. max. 1601), *Tringa erythropus* (100 in autumn), and *T. totanus* (3-yr. av. max. 607; max. 1500). (Major revision 1987)

087 Thurles Sugar Factory Lagoons, Co Tipperary (Mid West)

52°39'N, 07°50'W 300 ha

No-shooting Area (part of site)

Human activities include wildfowling. Future uncertain due to planned closure of sugar factory.

Lagoons important for passage and wintering waterfowl. *Pluvialis apricaria* (3000), *Philomachus pugnax* (27), *Tringa glareola*, and *Chlidonias niger* occur on passage; *Cygnus columbianus* (120), *C. cygnus* (100), *A. penelope* (less than 1000), *A. crecca* (less than 1500), *Anas platyrhynchos* (less than 3000), and *A. clypeata* (less than 600) occur in winter. (Information compiled 1987)

088 Coast Greystones – Wicklow, including Kilcoole Marshes and Broad Lough, Co Wicklow (East)

52°59'-53°09'N, 06°02'-06°04'W 670 ha (marsh); 18 km (coast)

No-shooting Area (Broad Lough); IWC Reserve (part of Broad Lough)

Shingle ridge with freshwater and brackish marshes and lagoons. The reclamation of marshes threatens the area.

Breeding species include *Sterna hirundo* (2 pairs) and *S. albifrons* (30 pairs; max. 50 pairs). *Larus minutus* (100-200) occurs on passage, and wintering waterfowl include *Cygnus columbianus* (max. 140), *C. cygnus* (50-100), *Anser anser* (350-400), *Anas penelope* (900), *Pluvialis apricaria* (1000), and *Numenius arquata* (700). The only Irish breeding site for *Aegithalos caudatus*. (Information updated 1987)

089 Dublin Docks (parts), Co Dublin (East)

53°21'N, 06°12'W *c.*5 ha

Unprotected

Three sites on industrial wastelands in the dock area of Dublin Port.

One of the five most important colonies in the region for *Sterna hirundo* and *S. paradisaea* (61 and 30 pairs respectively in 1984); also *S. albifrons* (1 pair in 1984). (Information compiled 1987)

090 North Bull Island, Co Dublin (East)

53°22'N, 06°08'W 607 ha Biosphere Reserve; Ramsar Site; EEC SPA (300 ha)

NNR; No-shooting Area; Local Authority Bird Sanctuary

A 5 km-long, 1 km-wide sand-dune system built up over 200 years against a man-made harbour wall. Extensive sandy beaches on exposed south-east side; saltmarshes and mudflats on the sheltered north-west side, between the dunes and the mainland. Surrounding areas mainly urban. Provides a roosting site for birds which feed in Dublin Bay. Human activities include recreation, notably on the two golf courses, which occupy much of the dune system. Domestic refuse-dumping, industrial development and increased siltation from causeway construction threaten the area, as do the spread of *Spartina* and general disturbance.

Breeding species include *Sterna albifrons* (80 pairs in 1987). Wintering waterfowl include *Branta bernicla hrota* (4-yr. av. max. 2222; max. 2874), *Tadorna tadorna* (400; max. 900), *Anas penelope* (2600; max. 4000), *A. crecca* (1200), *A. acuta* (300; max. 450), *A. clypeata* (300; max. 350), *Haematopus ostralegus* (3800), *Pluvialis squatarola*, *Calidris canutus* (3-yr. av. max. 7917), *C. alba* (3-yr. av. max. 178), *C. alpina* (7900), *Limosa limosa islandica* (2300), *L. lapponica*, *Numenius arquata* (3-yr. av. max. 1900), and *Tringa totanus* (2400). Total waders: 30,000; max. 37,000. (Major revision 1987)

091 Baldoyle Bay, Co Dublin (East)

53°24'N, 06°08'W 195 ha

NNR

A tidal bay protected from the open sea by a large sand-dune system. It is the estuary of several small streams and contains a mainly mud substrate. Up to 95 per cent of the bay is uncovered at low tide. There are large areas of *Spartina* in the northern half. The bay is used for low-intensity recreational boating and fishing, whilst human uses of the adjoining areas include farming, golfing, and residential/urban development. Proximity to Dublin may result in applications to reclaim the bay for suburban development; one recent proposal of this kind was refused.

Important for wintering waterfowl with *Branta bernicla hrota* (4-yr. av. max. 331; max. 436), *Tadorna tadorna*, *Anas penelope*, *A. acuta*, and waders including *Calidris alba* (3-yr. av. max. 700). (Information compiled 1987)

092 Malahide Estuary, Co Dublin (East)

53°27'N, 06°09'W 606 ha

Unprotected

Estuary of the River Broadmeadow with saltwater marshes and sand/mudflats almost cut off from the sea by an extensive system of spits and sand-dunes. The western part is heavily used for water-sports and there is a major pleasure-boat anchorage in the east. There are urbanised areas at Swords and Malahide, but the remainder of the surroundings is mixed farmland with a little woodland and parkland. A railway viaduct crosses the site. The spread of *Spartina* and increasing recreation/urbanisation threaten the area.

Wintering waterfowl include *Branta bernicla hrota* (4-yr. av. max. 983; max. 1040), *Bucephala clangula* (150), *Mergus serrator* (100), *Haematopus ostralegus* (600), *Pluvialis apricaria* (1300), *Calidris canutus* (800), *C. alpina* (600), *Numenius arquata* (100), and *Tringa totanus* (400). (Major revision 1987)

093 Lambay Island, Co Dublin (East)

53°29'N, 06°01'W 255 ha

Private Bird Sanctuary

Breeding seabirds include *Fulmarus glacialis* (560 pairs), *Puffinus puffinus* (50-100 pairs), *Phalacrocorax carbo* (1027 pairs in 1985), *P. aristotelis* (1600 pairs), *Rissa tridactyla* (3005 pairs), *Uria aalge* (43,000 birds), *Alca torda* (3500 birds), *Cepphus grylle* (less than 10 pairs), and *Fratercula arctica* (235 pairs). *Anser anser* (800-1000) occurs in winter. (Information compiled 1987)

094 Rockabill, Co Dublin (East)

53°36'N, 06°00'W 1.0 ha EEC SPA

Refuge for Fauna

Two very small granitic islets separated by a *c.*20 m-wide channel. One rock has a lighthouse (manned until 1989) with walled areas of soil and vegetation (dominated by

Lavatera arborea). No cover on the other islet. De-manning of the lighthouse will make wardening of the tern colony necessary. Gulls pose a threat to the breeding terns and control measures are planned.

Breeding species include *Larus argentatus*, *L. marinus*, *Rissa tridactyla* (52 pairs in 1988), *Sterna dougallii* (332 pairs in 1988), *S. hirundo* (119 pairs), and *Cepphus grylle* (9 pairs). (Information compiled 1988)

095 Rogerstown Estuary, Co Dublin (East)

53°30'N, 06°06'W 368 ha

NNR (eastern two-thirds); No-shooting Area

A small estuary separated from the sea by a sand/shingle bar, with saltwater marshes, mudflats/sandflats (95 per cent of area at low tide), raised saltmarsh, and wet meadows. Human activities include stock-raising, horticulture, and recreation (including boating). The site is threatened by the spread of *Spartina* grass and the (local authority) dumping of refuse which has taken place over 40 ha and is due to expand. Apart from direct loss of habitat, this dumping results in silting-up of some areas and eutrophication of the water.

Wintering waterfowl include *Branta bernicla hrota* (4-yr. av. max. 841; max. 1060), *Tadorna tadorna* (3-yr. av. max. 328), *Anas penelope* (1100), *A. crecca* (500-800), *Haematopus ostralegus* (500), *Pluvialis apricaria* (600), *Calidris canutus* (1300), *C. alpina* (1300), *Numenius arquata* (500), and *Tringa totanus* (500). (Major revision 1987)

096 Church Island, Lough Derg, Co Galway (West)

53°04'N, 08°15'W *c.*2 ha

No-shooting Area

A very small lake-island with tall trees, surrounded by shallow waters, reedbeds, and similar islands. Uninhabited.

A breeding site for *Phalacrocorax carbo* (167 pairs in 1988; colony known pre-1977). (Information compiled 1988)

097 River Shannon Callows: Portumna – Athlone; Co Galway, Co Offaly, Co Tipperary, Co Westmeath, and Co Roscommon (Midlands, West, Mid West)

53°05'-53°25'N, 07°56'-08°12'W *c.*8000 ha

Unprotected

Flood plain of the River Shannon with extensive callows (seasonally flooded, semi-natural grassland, either grazed or managed as hay-meadows) and system of surface drains. Once flanked by raised bogs, now largely lost through peat-cutting. Human activities include stock-raising, wildfowling, recreation, and tourism. Threatened by arterial drainage, pollution, shooting pressure, and power-lines across the site.

Supports significant numbers of breeding waders, notably *Vanellus vanellus* (341 pairs), *Gallinago gallinago* (762 pairs), *Numenius arquata* (48 pairs), and *Tringa totanus* (400 pairs). Also breeding *Crex crex* (at least 60 pairs). Wintering waterfowl include *Cygnus columbianus* (200), *C. cygnus* (3-yr. av. max. 211), *Anser albifrons flavirostris* (200-250), *Anas penelope* (3-yr. av. max. 8725), *A. crecca* (2000 in 1982), *Pluvialis apricaria* (8000), *Vanellus vanellus* (7500), *Limosa limosa islandica* (3-yr. av. max. 600), and *Numenius arquata* (1800). (Major revision 1987)

098 River Little Brosna Callows: New Bridge – River Shannon, Co Offaly and Co Tipperary (Midlands, South East)

53°07'-53°09'N, 08°00'-08°06'W 1400 ha

No-shooting Area (one-third of site)

Winter-flooded, semi-natural meadows/marshes (used for grazing or haymaking) along the River Little Brosna, with an extensive system of surface drains. Human activities include stock-raising and hunting. Drainage schemes, agricultural pollution, and wildfowling threaten the area.

The area has an important concentration of breeding waders. Wintering waterfowl include *Cygnus columbianus* (100; max. 250), *C. cygnus* (3-yr. av. max. 201), *Anser albifrons flavirostris* (5-yr. av. max. 346; max. 408), *Anas penelope* (3-yr. av. max. 11,250), *A. crecca* (4600 in 1984), *A. acuta* (max. 1600 in 1983), *A. clypeata* (3-yr. av. max. 150), *Pluvialis apricaria* (3-yr. av. max. 4500), *Vanellus vanellus* (6100; max. 15,000), *Calidris alpina* (1000), *Limosa limosa islandica* (3-yr. av. max. 2375), and Numenius arquata (300). Total wildfowl: max. 16,000; total waders: max. 23,000. (Major revision 1987)

099 River Suck Callows: Shannon Bridge – Athleague, Co Roscommon and Co Galway (West, Midlands)

53°16'-53°33'N, 08°03'-08°17'W 4000+ ha

Mainly unprotected; No-shooting Area (Muckanagh and Cloonloughlin)

Flood plain of the River Suck with callows of semi-natural grassland (either grazed or managed as hay-meadows) and extensive system of surface drains. Flanked by raised bogs, many of which have been converted for agricultural use following peat extraction. Human activities include stock-raising, haymaking, and wildfowling. Arterial drainage, land reclamation, agricultural intensification, and turf exploitation are the main threats to the area.

Wintering waterfowl include *Cygnus columbianus* (180 in 1982), *C. cygnus* (200), *Anser albifrons flavirostris* (5-yr. av. max. 417; max. 483), *Anas penelope* (5400), *A. crecca* (900), *Pluvialis apricaria* (3600), and *Vanellus vanellus* (4600; max. 13,000). (Information updated 1987)

100 Lough Ennell, Co Westmeath (Midlands)

53°26'-53°30'N, 07°22'-07°26'W 388 ha

Unprotected

A large, open, steep-sided but shallow limestone lake with a markedly alkaline pH. There are limited areas of reedbed and scrub, and a number of small wooded islands. Human activities include fishing, wildfowling, boating, wind-surfing, and (in the surrounding area) stock-grazing. Eutrophication, owing to sewage and fertiliser effluent, is a problem. It is thought that the widespread decline of *Chara* (algae) is a result of increased pollution.

Wintering waterfowl include *Cygnus olor* (3-yr. av. max. 424), *Anser albifrons flavirostris* (one of the sites used by the Loughs Iron/Owel flock; see sites 101 and 102), *Aythya ferina* (max. 2600), *A. fuligula* (3-yr. av. max. 720), and *Fulica atra* (3-yr. av. max. 639). (Information compiled 1987)

101 Lough Owel, Co Westmeath (Midlands)

53°34'N, 07°24'W 1008 ha

Unprotected

A shallow limestone lake with relatively unproductive alkaline waters. There are a few small wooded islands near the southern shore. Surrounded by farmland. Fishing, wildfowling, recreation, and mixed farming in the adjacent areas, are the main land-uses.

Wintering waterfowl include *Cygnus cygnus* (10-20 in Jan.), *Anser albifrons flavirostris* (5-yr. av. max 368; max. 445; same flock as site 100), *Anas penelope* (max. 1500), *A. platyrhynchos* (max. 2500), *A. clypeata* (1300; 2000 in autumn), *Aythya ferina* (max. 2000), *A. fuligula* (1100; max. 2000), and *Fulica atra* (2500). (Information updated 1987)

102 Lough Iron – Glen Lough, Co Westmeath (Midlands)

53°37'N, 07°29'W 300 ha

No-shooting Area (Lough Iron and 50 ha of adjacent farmland)

Glen Lough has practically no surface water owing to drainage in the 1960s, and Lough Iron is much reduced and fringed by a broad strip of *Phragmites*, with *Salix* and *Alnus* scrub. Both 'lakes' surrounded by farmland. Human activities include stock-raising. Potentially threatened by further drainage and afforestation.

Important for wintering waterfowl including *Cygnus columbianus* (10-20), *C. cygnus* (3-yr. av. max. 263), *Anser albifrons flavirostris* (5-yr. av. max. 368; max. 445; same flock as site 100 and 101), *Anas platyrhynchos* (1500), *A. clypeata* (3-yr. av. max. 442), and *Aythya ferina* (av. 1300). (Information compiled 1987)

103 Lough Derravaragh, Co Westmeath (Midlands)

53°39'N, 07°20'W 1285 ha

Unprotected

A shallow base-rich lake with a long narrow arm running south-east between steeply sloping ridges. The north-west end is wide and shallow with extensive flats and marshland, with raised bog in the hinterland. The River Inny, a major tributary of the Shannon, flows in and out at the north-west end. Owing to lower lake levels because of drainage, mud/sandbanks are exposed in dry conditions. Angling and wildfowling are the main human activities at the lake, with medium-intensity grazing in the surrounding area. Heavily polluted by pig slurry carried into the Lough by the River Inny; source of pollution is around Lough Sheelin. Restoration and clean-up measures have not been sustained and the numbers of waterfowl have fallen.

Wintering waterfowl include *Cygnus cygnus* (max. 60), *Anas platyrhynchos* (800-1000 in autumn), *Aythya ferina* (formerly 5600 in autumn; now much decreased: 3-yr. av. max. 933), *A. fuligula* (1900; max. 2800), and *Fulica atra* (3000). (Major revision 1987)

104 Castle Forbes Complex, Co Longford (Midlands)

53°46'N, 07°52'W 520 ha

Unprotected

Flood plain of the River Camlin and two adjacent raised bogs. Land-uses include turf-cutting and summer grazing. Potentially threatened by turf-cutting and afforestation of bogs. Nearby Lough Forbes provides a wildfowl roost.

A site for wintering *Anser albifrons flavirostris* (formerly 200-250, now much decreased: 5-yr. av. max 99; max. 110). Probable breeding site for *Falco columbarius*. (Major revision 1987)

105 Lough Oughter, Co Cavan (North East)

54°00'N, 07°28'W 1012 ha

No-shooting Areas (Loughs Derrybrick, Annagh, Derinishbeg, Inchin, Derrygid, and Farnham)

A southward extension of Upper Lough Erne in Northern Ireland, Lough Oughter has numerous partly submerged drumlins whose peaks form complexes of peninsulas and wooded islands.

Wintering species include *Podiceps cristatus* (50-150) and *Cygnus cygnus* (3-yr. av. max. 208). (Information updated 1987)

106 Stabannan – Braganstown, Co. Louth (North East)

53°52'N, 06°26'W *c.*400-500 ha

Unprotected

A small, very flat, alluvial plain adjacent to the River Glyde and bounded to the north and south by rolling hills. The plain was formerly marshland, but is now drained and agriculturally improved, with intensive mixed agriculture (grass, cereals, and root crops).

Important for wintering *Cygnus cygnus* (3-yr. av. max. 170; max. 371). Other waterfowl occurring include *Cygnus columbianus* (max. 26), *Anser anser* (800-1000 in 1986/7 and 1987/8) and occasionally small numbers of *Anser fabalis*, *A. brachyrhynchus*, *A. albifrons flavirostris*, and *Branta leucopsis*. (Information compiled 1987)

107 Boyne Estuary, Co Louth and Co Meath (North East, East)

53°43'N, 06°15'W *c.*250 ha

No-shooting Area (part of estuary)

A rather narrow estuary (*c.*5 km long) opening out near the mouth where there are areas of saltmarsh. Human activities include salmon-netting and some wildfowling. Private dwellings are gradually spreading along the shore of the estuary from Drogheda, and there is a proposal to construct a yachting marina (which will involve the loss of a small area of intertidal mud and perhaps increase disturbance).

There is a colony of *Sterna albifrons* (max. 30 pairs). Important for *Limosa limosa islandica* (3-yr. av. max. 461; max. 563). Other waterfowl occurring include *Haematopus ostralegus* (max. 800), *Pluvialis apricaria* (max. 2850), *Vanellus vanellus* (max. 2000+), *Calidris canutus* (max. 850), *C. alpina* (max. 1764), *Numenius arquata* (max. 625), and *Tringa totanus* (max. 500). (Information compiled 1987)

108 Dundalk Bay, Co Louth (North East)

53°55'N, 06°20'W 4717 ha

No-shooting Areas (Ballymascanlon Bay and Lurgangreen saltmarsh; under consideration as NNRs)

A very extensive sea bay (*c.*20 km north-south) with up to 3 km-wide sand/mudflats at low tide, and two large areas of saltmarsh along the western edge where several small rivers also the bay. The estuary of the River Castletown, in particular, contains a number of sheltered creeks. Human activities include fishing, wildfowling, grazing of livestock, and summer recreation. Problems include the agricultural, sewage, and industrial pollution of the River Castletown, which flows through Dundalk. *Spartina* is spreading and may threaten the quality of feeding for wildfowl.

Important for wintering waterfowl with *Branta bernicla hrota* (4-yr. av. max. 357; max. 550), *Tadorna tadorna* (3-yr. av. max. 358), *Anas penelope* (3-yr. av. max. 601; max. 5000+), *A. crecca* (700), *Haematopus ostralegus* (3-yr. av. max. 12,702; 27,000 on passage), *Pluvialis apricaria* (5400; 26,000 on passage), *Calidris canutus* (3-yr. av. max. 5827; max. 8000), *C. alpina* (12,400; max. 15,000), *Limosa limosa islandica* (3-yr. av. max. 292; max. 525), *L. lapponica* (3-yr. av. max. 5567; 7000 on passage), *Numenius arquata* (4500), and *Tringa totanus* (3700). Total waders: max. 57,000. (Major revision 1987)

109 Carlingford Lough, Co Louth (North East)

54°02'-54°06'N, 06°08'-06°17'W 3662 ha (1478 ha in Republic of Ireland; remainder is in UK)

Unprotected in Republic's sector

A fjord-like, glacier-scoured sea lough with shallow waters near its mouth containing intertidal mudflats and sand/gravel banks. The River Newry flows into the Lough from the north-west. The area is flanked by glacial moraines and mountains. Human activities include recreational boating, low-intensity mariculture, and sheep-grazing and forestry in the surrounding area. No reported threats, though sheltered waters may be attractive for the growth of water-sports.

Branta bernicla hrota (4-yr. av. max. 464; max. 529) occurs in winter. Also wintering *Tadorna tadorna*, *Anas penelope*, *A. crecca*, *A. platyrhynchos*, *Aythya marila* (declined from 2500 in mid-1960s to 500-1000 in mid-1980s), *Haematopus ostralegus*, *Calidris alpina*, *Numenius arquata* and *Tringa totanus*. (Information compiled 1987)

110 Wicklow Hills and Poulaphouca Reservoir, Co Wicklow (East)

53°10'N, 06°24'W 85,000 ha

Mainly unprotected; No-shooting Area (Poulaphouca reservoir)

A large freshwater reservoir, bogs and marshes, rocky habitat, and woodland. Human activities include stock-raising, forestry, peat-cutting, and recreation. Afforestation, turf exploitation, agricultural intensification, and heavy recreational pressure threaten the area.

A breeding area for *Circus cyaneus, Falco columbarius, F. peregrinus* (26 pairs), *Phoenicurus phoenicurus* (50 pairs), *Turdus torquatus* (less than 30 pairs), and *Phylloscopus sibilatrix* (10+ pairs). Also wintering waterfowl include *Cygnus columbianus* (40), *C. cygnus* (46), *Anser anser* (300), *Anas penelope* (900), *A. crecca* (800), and *A. platyrhynchos* (1250). (Information compiled 1987)

MAIN REFERENCES

Anon. (1974) *Report on wetlands of international and national importance in the Republic of Ireland.* Forest and Wildlife Service, Dublin.

Bullock, I. D., Drewett, D. R. and Mickleburgh, S. P. (1983) The Chough in Ireland. *Irish Birds* 2(3): 257-271.

Foras Forbartha (1981) *Areas of scientific interest in Ireland.* Dublin.

Hutchinson, C. (1979) *Ireland's wetlands and their birds.* Irish Wildbird Conservancy, Dublin.

Lloyd, C. S. (1982) *An inventory of seabird breeding colonies in the Republic of Ireland.* Unpublished data and report. Forest and Wildlife Service, Dublin.

Lloyd, C. S. (1984) A method of assessing the relative importance of seabird breeding colonies. *Biological Conservation* 28: 155-172.

Macdonald, R. A. (1987) The breeding population and distribution of the Cormorant in Ireland. *Irish Birds* 3(3): 405-416.

Merne, O. J. (1974) *The birds of Wexford, Ireland.* Bord Failte, Dublin and South East Tourism, Wexford.

Merne, O. J. (1977) The changing status and distribution of the Bewick's Swan in Ireland. *Irish Birds* 1(1):3-15.

Merne, O. J. (1980) Irish seabird islands. *British Birds* 73(2): 80-85.

Merne, O. J. (1986) Greylag Geese in Ireland, March 1986. *Irish Birds* 3(2): 207-214.

Merne, O. J. and Murphy, C. W. (1986) Whooper Swans in Ireland, January 1986. *Irish Birds* 3(2): 199-206.

Mitchell, F. (1986) *The Shell Guide to Reading the Irish Landscape.* Country House, Dublin.

Nairn, R. G. W. (1986) *Spartina anglica* in Ireland and its potential impact on wildfowl and waders – a review. *Irish Birds* 3(2):215-228.

Nairn, R. G. W. and Sheppard, J. R. (1985) Breeding waders of sand dune machair in north-west Ireland. *Irish Birds* 3(1):53-70.

Nairn, R. G. W., Herbert, I. J. and Heery, S. (1988) Breeding waders and other wet grassland birds of the River Shannon Callow, Ireland. *Irish Birds* 3(4): 521-537.

Norriss, D., Wilson, H. J. and Browne, D. (1982) The breeding population of the Peregrine Falcon in Ireland in 1981. *Irish Birds* 2(2): 145-152.

Norriss, D. W. and Wilson, H. J. (1987) Greenland White-fronted Geese in *Ireland 1986/87.* Unpublished report. Wildlife Service, Office of Public Works, Dublin.

Ogilvie, M. A. (1983) The numbers of Greenland Barnacle Geese in Britain and Ireland. *Wildfowl* 34: 77-88.

O'Meara, M. (1979) Distribution and numbers of corncrakes in Ireland in 1978. *Irish Birds* 1(3): 381-405.

Ruttledge, R. F. (1987) The breeding distribution of the Common Scoter in Ireland. *Irish Birds* 3(3): 417-426.

Ruttledge, R. F. and Ogilvie, M. A. (1979) The past and current status of the Greenland White-fronted Goose in Ireland and Britain. *Irish Birds* 1(3): 293-363.

Walsh, A. and Merne, O. J. (1988) Barnacle Geese in Ireland, spring 1988 *Irish Birds* 3(4): 539-550.

Whilde, A. (1985) The 1984 All Ireland Tern Survey. *Irish Birds* 3(1): 1-32.

Whilde, A. (1986) *Computerisation, analysis and application of Irish wetland habitat and bird data.* Corrib Conservation Centre, Rosscahill. ACE Project 6611/84/08-3.

White, J. and Doyle, G. (1982) The vegetation of Ireland: a catalogue raisonné. *J. Life Sciences,* Royal Dublin Society 3: 289-368.

ITALY

Eleonora's Falcon *Falco eleonorae*

INTRODUCTION

General information

Italy covers an area of 301,277 sq km, and in 1983 had a population of 56.9 million (an average population density of 189 per sq km). It includes the large islands of Sardinia (24,090 sq km) to the west and Sicily (25,708 sq km) to the south-west. The climate varies considerably with latitude; in the south it is warm temperate, with almost no rain in the summer months, but the north is cool temperate, often experiencing snow and freezing temperatures in the winter, with rainfall more evenly distributed over the year.

Italy may be divided into four major geographical and vegetational zones: the Alps in the north of the country, the Po valley in the north-east, the Appennines which comprise most of mainland Italy, and the coastal areas. The Alpine area is relatively unspoilt, with coniferous and mixed evergreen forests (as natural stands and plantations), alpine pastures above the tree line that are grazed by sheep, goats, and cattle, and snow-fields and glaciers on the higher peaks. The Po valley is the largest area of lowland in Italy, comprising zones of deciduous forest, and intensive agriculture, notably cereal and rice cultivation and stock-farming, and has many lakes and rivers. Large areas of the Appennine Mountains are still clothed with natural deciduous forest, predominately *Quercus*, *Castanea sativa*, and *Fagus*, although much has been deforestated for agriculture. The coastal areas of Italy are dominated by typical Mediterranean scrub, usually referred to as 'macchia' or when less dense as 'gariga'; *Quercus ilex* scrub is the characteristic climax vegetation-type.

The 5000 km coastline comprises a mixture of sandy beaches with sand dunes, brackish lagoons and marshes, and sections of cliffs and offshore rocky islands. The coastline is broken by a number of major estuaries, including those of the Po, Tiber, and Arno.

Between 1982 and 1984 some 123,030 sq km comprised cropland and 50,140 sq km permanent pasture. In 1980 some 76 per cent of all agricultural holdings were less than 5 ha (representing 16 per cent of the total agricultural area) and only 2 per cent of all agricultural holdings were greater than 50 ha in extent (representing 45 per cent of the total agricultural area). Agricultural methods are still traditional and labour-intensive in some areas, especially the mountain regions, although mechanisation and intensive monoculture have increased appreciably in recent years. Afforestation of marginal land is having a major impact in some areas.

Industrial development is concentrated in the lowland areas and is increasing. Tourism has also expanded appreciably in the last few decades and brings in a large revenue (46.6 million foreigners visited Italy in 1983, for instance, and spent an estimated 13,721,000 million lire).

Agricultural, industrial and touristic developments, aided in recent years by the availability of EEC funding, have destroyed huge areas of natural habitat throughout the country. Some 764,000 ha of wetland existed in Italy in 1865, but this had been reduced to only 190,000 ha by 1972. A large proportion of the steppe areas of southern Italy, mostly on the plains and plateaus of Sardinia, Sicily, and the Apulia region, have been replaced by cultivated fields, mostly cereals, during the last 100 years. The increase in arable land in these regions has been most marked over the last 30 years, expanding from 283,473 ha in 1958 to 1,053,873 ha in 1983. Agricultural modernisation is likely to continue (with an increase in irrigation and land improvement), which, together with increasing industrial and touristic developments, are likely to put further pressure on Italy's avifauna.

Tourism in late spring or summer is having a serious environmental impact along the coast and on many islands, with the result that the natural habitats of some large coastal areas have been almost completely destroyed.

Ornithological importance

The mainland coast and islands are important for their breeding seabirds, notably *Calonectris diomedea* (10,000+ pairs), *Phalacrocorax aristotelis desmarestii* (1000+ pairs, representing approximately 50 per cent of the population of this Mediterranean sub-species, mostly breeding in Sardinia), *Larus audouinii* (450 pairs, around 10 per cent of the world population), and *Sterna albifrons* (5890 pairs, about 30 per cent of the Western Palearctic population, with the region's largest colony of 4000 pairs breeding in the Po Delta and surrounding lagoons).

The Italian populations of *Nycticorax nycticorax* (17,500 pairs), *Egretta garzetta* (6700 pairs), *Neophron percnopterus* (35-45 pairs), *Falco naumanni*, *F. eleonorae* (480-500 pairs), *F. biarmicus* (100 pairs), *F. peregrinus* (450-500 pairs), *Alectoris barbara* (1000-5000 pairs on Sardinia), *Porphyrio porphyrio* (245-285 pairs in Sardinia) and *Larus genei* (1000 pairs) are of European importance.

The following species of passerine that are threatened in major parts of their range in Europe are widely distributed and common in parts of Italy: *Calandrella brachydactyla*, *Anthus campestris*, and *Lanius collurio*.

Many of the major river estuaries and lagoons are important for passage and wintering waterfowl and waders (notable examples including the Delta del Po, Laguna di Venezia, Laghi di Lesina e Varano, Laguna di Grado e Marano and the Valli di Comacchio on the mainland), and there are a number of important heronries (especially important for *Nycticorax nycticorax* and *Egretta garzetta*) along the Rivers Po, Ticino, and Sesia.

The most important habitats for birds include the wetlands, particularly the estuaries and lagoons along the north-west coast of the Adriatic, the offshore islands for breeding seabirds, the forested areas of the Alps and Appennines for birds of prey and forest species, and the cultivated and sheep-grazed plains of Sardinia that support *Tetrax tetrax*.

Conservation infrastructure and protected-area system

The Constitution stipulates that the Republic shall protect the landscape, and general laws dealing with environmental conservation in Italy have recently been approved. Local authorities, regional authorities, and national government all have a role in nature conservation, with the 20 regional governments being perhaps the most important. A presidential decree (616/1977) completed the transfer to the regions of administrative responsibility for, amongst other things, the protection of nature, Nature Reserves, and Natural Parks. More recently some of the responsibility for National Parks has also been devolved. With the establishment of the Ministry of the Environment (Ministero dell'Ambiente) in July 1986 there are hopes for the creation of national laws covering nature conservation and the protection of fauna, flora, and biotopes. The categories of protected areas in Italy referred to in this inventory are outlined below.

1. National Parks (Parchi Nazionali)
   These are created to protect fauna and flora, to preserve geological formations, to safeguard the beauty of the landscape, and, with one exception (Gran Paradiso), to promote tourism. Hunting is prohibited, but commercial activities, including agriculture, forestry, and tourism, are permitted within some areas, although the level of exploitation varies from park to park.

2. Nature Reserves (Riserve Naturali), including WWF Refuges, LIPU Reserves, Wildlife Refuges and Protected Forests
   Most Nature Reserves have been established by the Forestry Agency. Some are privately owned and managed, such as WWF Refuges and LIPU Reserves. In 1987 there were 252, covering an area of 144,391 ha, 127 of which are administered by the State. Control of human activities within these areas is variable, and apart from traditional forms of utilisation, all development may be forbidden.

3. Regional Parks/Natural Parks (Parchi Regionali/Parchi Naturali)
   These are established for conservation, education, and recreational purposes and tend to protect only the most important features and local traditional land-use practices, although some Regional Nature Parks include areas where there are strict rules aimed at wildlife conservation.

Other protected-area categories include Protected Landscapes, Landscape Reserves, Hydrological Reserves and Protected Monuments or natural features. In a number of cases information on the exact protection status afforded to a site was not clear and in these instances 'some national protection status' or 'some other national protection status' has been recorded.

It should be noted that sites that have been designated as EEC Special Protection Areas (sites designated according to the EEC Wild Birds Directive) are not necessarily covered by any other nationally designated protected area.

International relations relevant to the conservation of sites

Italy is a member of the Council of Europe and the European Community, and has ratified the Ramsar Convention, World Heritage Convention, Bern Convention, Barcelona Convention, and Bonn Convention, and is bound by the terms of the European Community's Wild Birds Directive. To date 41 Ramsar Sites, 52 EEC Special Protection Areas, 37 Biogenetic Reserves, ten Mediterranean Specially Protected Areas, and three Biosphere Reserves have been designated, although no natural World Heritage Sites have been designated.

Overview of the inventory

The inventory covers 140 sites (some with a number of subsites), with a combined area of over 3,510,000 ha (to the nearest 10,000 ha). It includes 45 EEC Special Protection Areas, 35 Ramsar Sites, one Biosphere Reserve, two Biogenetic Reserves, five Mediterranean Specially Protected Areas and a large number of sites which have some form of national protection or where hunting is prohibited. Most of the principal wetland and seabird sites (52 and 13 sites respectively) are included in the inventory;

consequently the waterbirds and seabirds are well represented. The forest and other non-wetland sites in the inventory are not so exhaustively covered.

Acknowledgements

The current inventory owes a great deal to the work undertaken on behalf of the ICBP European Community Working Group (Osieck and Mörzer Bruyns 1981). The data for Italy were principally gathered by S. Allavena. Contributors to the Osieck and Mörzer Bruyns report also included V. A. Calandra, S. Frugis, and H. Schenk. Up-to-date information on wetland sites was compiled by A. Agostoni, C. Andrea, E. Arcamoone, N. Baccetti, F. Bergese, S. Berti, G. Boano, G. Bogliani, P. Boldreghini, P. Brichetti, C. Cavallaro, G. Dacunto, A. Farina, P. Gelati, C. Iapichino, M. Lambertini, C. Martignoni, B. Massa, A. Mocci-Demartis, A. Nadalet, M. Palmisani, M. Parisi, P. Pedrini, M. Pellegrini, F. Perco, F. Petretti, W. Pieretti, M. Ravasini, C. Rende, L. Rocco, H. Schenk, F. Spina, R. Tinarelli, F. Visentini, and F. Zanichelli. The introduction was written by N. Varty with useful comments received from P. Galati.

INVENTORY

No.	Site name	Region	Criteria used to select site [see p.18]							
			0	1(i)	1(ii)	1(iii)	1(iv)	2	3	4
001	Media Val d'Ossola (Val Antigorio)	PE							*	
002	Valle Anzasca and Val di Antrona and neighbouring area	PE							*	
003	Mountain area between Lago Maggiore, Val Vigeo and Val Cannobina (Val Grande)	PE							*	
004	Parco Nazionale del Gran Paradiso and Val Soana	PE							*	
005	Heronries in the catchment of the upper Po and Sesia Rivers	PE,LA				*			*	
005-1	Garzaia di Carisio	PE								
005-2	Garzaia di Villarboit	PE								
005-3	Garzaia dell'Isolone di Oldenico	PE								
005-4	Garzaia di Morghengo (Garzaia della Tenuta San Bernardino)	PE								
005-5	Garzaia della Tenuta Baraccone									
005-6	Garzaia di Montarolo and Garzaia del Bosco della Partecipanza	PE								
005-7	Garzaia Isola Langosco	LA								
005-8	Garzaia di Celpenchio	LA								
005-9	Garzaia Cascina San Alessandro	LA								
005-10	Garzaia Cascina Rinalda	LA								
005-11	Lago di Sartirana Lomellina	LA								
005-12	Garzaia della Cascina and Bosco Abbasso	LA								
005-13	Garzaia di Valenza	PE,LA								
005-14	Garzaia Abbazia (Lombardia)									
005-15	Garzaia di Cavo Solero – Villa Biscossi	LA								
005-16	Garzaia di Galliavola	LA								
005-17	Garzaia del Torrente Scrivia	PE								
006	Lago di Candia	PE							*	
007	Area between Val di Susa, Valle del Chisone and Valle del Torrente Pellice	PE							*	
008	Laghetti di Crava-Morozzo	PE	*							
009	Passo del Turchino and surrounding area	PE,LR							*	

No.	Site name	Region	Criteria used to select site [see p.18]							
			0	1(i)	1(ii)	1(iii)	1(iv)	2	3	4
010	Val Maira, area around Vinadio, Valle Gesso, Argentera, Val Varanta	PE							*	
011	Area between Cima Selle Vecchie and Monte Alto	PE,LR							*	
012	Pian di Spagna and Lago di Mezzola	LA							*	
013	Slopes of Valtellina and Alte Valli Brenbara, Seriana and di Scalve	LA							*	
014	Val Solda, Monte di Lenno, Monte di Tremezzo and Monte Tabor	LA							*	
015	Val Camonica	LA							*	
016	Pendici della Grigna facing the Lago di Lecco	LA							*	
017	Campo del Fiori, Valganna, Val Cuvia	LA							*	
018	Palude Brabbia	LA							*	
019	Colline di Salo and area between Lago di Garda and Lago d'Idro	LA							*	
020	Torbiere d'Iseo	LA							*	
021	Bosco Fontana and Valli del Mincio (Lago Superiore di Mantova)	LA							*	
022	La Zerbaglia	LA				*			*	
023	Heronries close to Pavia and the catchment of the Fiume Ticino	LA				*			*	
023-1	Garzaia di Cusago	LA								
023-2	Garzaia di Villarasca	LA								
023-3	Garzaia Cascina Portalupa	LA								
023-4	Garzaia di Bosco Mezzano (La Zelata)	LA								
023-5	Garzaia di San Massimo	LA								
023-6	Garzaia di Cascina Porta Chiossa	LA								
023-7	Garzaia di Vaccarizza	LA								
024	Fiume Po: Lambro – Casalmaggiore	LA,ER				*			*	
024-1	Garzaia di Somaglia	LA								
024-2	Isola de Pinedo	LA,ER								
025	Fiume Po: Viadana – Ostiglia	LA,ER				*			*	
025-1	Garzaia di Pomponesco	LA,ER								
025-2	Palude di Ostiglia (including Palude del Busatello)	LA,VO								
026	Isola Boscone	LA,ER				*			*	
027	Parco Nazionale dello Stelvio and the area adjacent to the Valtellina and Val Camonica	LA,TA							*	
028	Gruppo dell'Adamello and Gruppo del Brenta	TA							*	
029	Catena dei Lagorai and Valli dei Torrenti Maso, Grigno, Vanoi e Cismon	TA,VO							*	
030	Monti Lessini, Monte Pasubio and Monte Piccole Dolomiti	TA,VO							*	
031	Dolomiti Bellunesi from Feltre to the Ospidale di Cadore	VO							*	
032	Lago di Busche and Vincheto di Cellarda	VO	*							
033	Laguna di Caorle	VO				*			*	
034	Laguna di Venezia	VO				*			*	
035	Delta del Po	VO,ER		*	*	*			*	

No.	Site name	Region	Criteria used to select site [see p.18]							
			0	1(i)	1(ii)	1(iii)	1(iv)	2	3	4
035-1	Isola Madonnina	VO								
035-2	Garzaia del Po di Maistra	VO								
035-3	Scanni del Delta del Po	VO								
035-4	Valle Bertuzzi, Lago delle Nazioni, Valle Porticino-Canevié, and Foce del Po di Volano	ER								
036	Area from Val Visdende to Canale di San Pietro	VO,FG							*	
037	Area between Gemona, Valle Resia, Monte Canin and Foresta del Tarvisio	FG							*	
038	Area between Valle del Piave and the Alta Valle del Tagliamento	VO,FG							*	
039	Laguna di Grado e Marano	FG				*			*	
039-1	Foci dello Stella	FG								
039-2	Valle Cavanata	FG								
039-3	Isola dei Belli	FG								
040	Foci dell'Isonzo and 'Isola della Cona	FG							*	
041	Carso Triestino	FG							*	
042	Fiume Taro: Fornovo di Taro-Viarolo	ER							*	
042-1	Garzaia di Ozzano Taro	ER								
043	Vasche dell'Eridania e Oasi LIPU di Torrile	ER							*	
044	Valli di Comacchio, Salina di Comacchio, Mezzano, Vene e Sacca di Bellocchio, Foce del Fiume Reno	ER			*	*			*	
045	Valle Santa and Valle Campotto e Bassarone	ER				*			*	
046	Punte Alberete and Valle della Canna, Pineta San Vitale	ER				*			*	
047	Ortazzo and Ortazzino	ER				*			*	
048	Salina di Cervia	ER			*	*			*	
049	Appennine area from the Passo del Cerreto to S. Marcello Pistoiese	ER,TN							*	
050	Lago and Padule di Massaciuccoli	TN							*	
051	Lame di San Rossore e Migliarino; estuaries of Fiume Arno and Fiume Serchio	TN				*			*	
052	Padule di Fucecchio	TN							*	
053	Ponte Buriano – Lago della Penna (River Arno)	TN							*	
054	Padule di Bolgheri-Renaione	TN	*							
055	Bacino del Fiume Cecina and area of Volterra	TN							*	
056	Arcipelago Toscano (including Isole Capraia, Giglio, Montecristo, d'Elba, and Palmaiola	TN						*	*	
057	Valle del Farma	TN						*	*	
058	Laghi di Montepulciano e Chiusi	TN							*	
059	Padule Diaccia-Botrona (Padule di Castiglione della Pescaia)	TN							*	
060	Stagni della Trappola and Ombrone estuary	TN							*	

No.	Site name	Region	Criteria used to select site [see p.18] 0	1(i)	1(ii)	1(iii)	1(iv)	2	3	4
061	Laguna di Orbetello and Lago di Burano	TN				*			*	
062	Lago Trasimeno	UA							*	
063	Monti Sibillini, Monte Fema, and Monte Cavallo	UA,ME							*	
064	Monti della Laga	UA							*	
065	Lago di Alviano	UA,LO							*	
066	Fiume Fiora	LO							*	
067	Monti Reatini and Val Nerina	UA,LO							*	
068	Lago Lungo and Lago di Pipa Sottile	LO							*	
069	Lago di Vico	LO							*	
070	Lago di Bracciano and Lago di Matignano	LO							*	
071	Monti Lucretili	LO							*	
072	Monti della Tolfa	LO						*	*	
073	Monti Ernici and Simbruini	LO,AO							*	
074	Monti Lepini	LO							*	
075	Laghi Pontini (I Fogliano, Monaci, Caprolace, Sabaudia	LO				*			*	
076	Arcipelago Ponziano (Isole Ventotene, Zannone, Ponza and Palmarola)	LO							*	
077	Gran Sasso d'Italia	AO							*	
078	Monti del Cigolano, Gole di Androdoco, Monte Giano, Monte Cabbia, Val Malito and Piano di Rascino	AO,LO							*	
079	Area of Monte Sirente, Monte Velino and Montagne della Duchessa	AO							*	
080	Massiccio della Maiella, Montagne del Morrone and Monti Pizi	AO							*	
081	Mountains and hills between Capracotta and Rosello	AO,MS						*	*	
082	Parco Nazionale d'Abruzzo, Monte Greco and surrounding area	AO,LO,MS							*	
083	Fiume Biferno and surrounding hills between Ponte Morgia Schiavone and La Strada Larino-Guglionesi	MS						*	*	
084	Monti del Matese	CA,AO						*	*	
085	Isola di Capri	CA	*							
086	Monte Terminio	CA						*	*	
087	Monte Polveracchio	CA							*	
088	Monti Alburni	CA							*	
089	Gole del Fiume Calore	CA						*	*	
090	Monte Cervati and Monte Sacro	CA						*	*	
091	Coast from Marina di Camerota to Policastro Bussentino	CA							*	
092	Isole Tremiti	PA							*	
093	Laghi di Lesina e Varano	PA				*			*	
094	Promontorio del Gargano	PA						*	*	
095	Wetlands along Golfo di Manfredonia	PA			*	*			*	

No.	Site name	Region	Criteria used to select site [see p.18]							
			0	1(i)	1(ii)	1(iii)	1(iv)	2	3	4
095-1	Paludi del Candelaro and Cervaro (including Frattarolo and Daunia Risi)	PA								
095-2	Carapelle – San Floriano	PA								
095-3	Saline di Margherita di Savoia (including Alma Dannata)	PA								
096	Le Murge di Monte Caccia	PA						*	*	
097	Gravina di Laterza	PA							*	
098	Le Cesine	PA							*	
099	Dolomiti di Pietrapertosa	BA						*	*	
100	Complex of the Monte Sirino, Monte Alpi and Monte Raparo Sud	BA							*	
101	Massiccio del Monte Pollino	BA,CR						*	*	
102	Valle del Ferro	CR						*	*	
103	Monte Orsomarso and Monte Verbicaro	CR							*	
104	Area between Torrente Lipuda and Fiume Neto	CR						*	*	
105	Sila Grande e Sila Piccola	CR						*	*	
106	Foce del Fiume Neto	CR							*	
107	Aspromonte	CR						*	*	
108	Arcipelago Maddalena	SA						*	*	
109	Isola Asinara	SA						*	*	
110	North-eastern coast and islands of Sardinia	SA						*	*	
111	Stagno di Pilo and Stagno di Casaraccio	SA				*			*	
112	Campo d'Ozieri and surrounding plains between Torralba, Ardara, Tula, Oschiri, Mores and Campu Giavesu	SA						*		
113	Coasts and islets of north-western Sardinia	SA						*	*	
114	Altopiano di Campeda	SA						*		
115	Inland and coastal area from Bosa to Capo Marargiu and Porto Tangone	SA						*	*	
116	Campidano di Nuraghi Nuradeo	SA						*		
117	Costa di Cuglieri and nearby islets	SA						*	*	
118	Golfo di Orosei, Sopramonte di Oliena e di Orgosolo, Monti del Gennargentu and Entroterra Barbagia di Seulo	SA						*	*	
119	Media Valle del Tirso and l'Altopiano di Abbasanta	SA						*		
120	Wetlands of the Sinis Peninsula and Golfo di Oristano	SA				*			*	
120-1	Stagni di Putzu Idu (Salina Manna and Pauli Marigosa)	SA								
120-2	Sale Porcus	SA								
120-3	Stagno di Cabras and Mari e Pauli	SA								
120-4	Stagno di Mistras	SA								
120-5	Stagno di Santa Giusta	SA								
120-6	Stagno di Pauli Maiori (Stagno di Palmas Arborea)	SA								
120-7	Stagno S'Ena Arrubia	SA								
120-8	Stagno di Corru S'Ittiri	SA								

No.	Site name	Region	Criteria used to select site [see p.18]							
			0	1(i)	1(ii)	1(iii)	1(iv)	2	3	4
121	Area of the Monte Ferru di Tertenía	SA							*	
122	Stagno di Colostrai	SA				*			*	
123	Monte dei Sette Fratelli e Sarrabus	SA							*	
124	Wetlands around Cagliari				*	*			*	
124-1	Saline di Macchiareddu	SA								
124-2	Laguna di Santa Gilla	SA								
124-3	Stagno di Molentargius	SA								
124-4	Saline di Quartu	SA								
125	Islands of southern Sardinia	SA						*	*	
126	South-east Iglesiente (Piscinamanna)	SA							*	
127	Isole Eolie: Lipari, Vulcano, Salina, Panarea, Stromboli, Filicudi and Alicudi	SL							*	
128	Parte dei Monti Peloritani e Monte Ciccia	SL					*	*		
129	Rocche del Crasto and surrounding valley	SL						*	*	
130	Le Montagne delle Madonie	SL						*	*	
131	Area between Piana degli Albanesi, Misilmeri, Ventimiglia di Sicilia e Rocca Busambra	SL						*	*	
132	Area of the Monte Pecoraro, Pizzo Cirina and Raffo Rosso di Capaci	SL						*	*	
133	Area of Monte Cofano, San Vito lo Capo, Capo Puntazza, Monte Sparagio and Monte Inici	SL							*	
134	Isole Egadi (Favignana, Levanzo e Marettimo)	SL							*	
135	Stagnone di Marsala e Saline di Trapani	SL				*			*	
136	Capo Feto	SL							*	
137	Foce del Simeto	SL							*	
138	Gole dell'Anapo between Palazzolo Acreide and Necropoli di Pantalica	SL							*	
139	Pantani di Capo Passero	SL				*		*	*	
140	Pantelleria and Isole Pelagie (Linosa, Lampedusa, Lampione)	SL		*	*				*	

PE=Piemonte LA=Lombardia LR=Liguria ER=Emilia Romagna
TA=Trentino-Alto Adige VO=Veneto FG=Friuli-Venezia Giulia TN=Toscana
UA=Umbria ME=Marche LO=Lazio AO=Abruzzo MS=Molise CA=Campania
PA=Puglia BA=Basilicata CR=Calabria SA=Sardegna SL=Sicilia

Comments on the inventory

1. In general, the site name is given in Italian except where it is a descriptive name when it is given in English. The site name is followed by the name of the Italian Region which is given in parentheses (these are the NUTS level 1 or level 2 regions).
2. The NUTS level 2 regions (level 1 region if there is no NUTS level 2 region) are the 'regions' used when applying the site-selection criteria (category 3).

3. For many of the sites, the information was first compiled in 1981 (see acknowledgements above). This information has been updated for a majority of the wetland sites. Every effort has been made to update the information on the non-wetland sites, but given the limited resources available and in many cases the lack of recent surveys, many of these site accounts are based on comparatively old (pre-1981) data.

4. Nearly all of the sites are believed to meet the site-selection criteria. Sites included for other reasons (column 0) are wetland sites of particular importance nationally for their passage/wintering waterfowl. In addition, 085 has been included because of its importance as a stop-over site for migrating passerines.

5. It has not been possible to standardise the date for passage and wintering waterfowl because of the many different sources of information. For species on passage, some data refer to the total number occurring in a season (spring or autumn), other data refer to a single count or to an average maximum count.

Glossary

EEC SPA = European Community Special Protection Area; alta, alte = upper; altopiano = plateau; arcipelago = archipelago; bacino = basin; bosco = wood/forest; campo = field/-countryside; canale = canal/channel; capo = cape; catera = chain; cima = summit; colline = hills; costa = coast; fiume = river; foce(-i) = mouth(s); foresta = forest; garzaia = heronry; gole = gorge; golfo = gulf; gruppo = group; isola(-e) = island(s); lago (laghi) = lake(s); laguna = lagoon; massiccio = massif; media = middle; monte(-i) = mountain(s); montagne = mountain; ospidale = hospital; palude(-i) = marsh(es); pantano(-i) = bog(s); passo = pass; pendici = slopes; piano = plain; pineta = pinewood; ponte = bridge; promontorio = headland; rocca = fortress; salina(-e) = saltpan(s); stagno(-i) = pond(s); strada = road; torre = castle; torrente = torrent; val, valle(-i) = valley(s).

---

001 Media Val d'Ossola (Val Antigorio) (Piemonte)

46°16'N, 08°18'E 31,900 ha

Nature Reserve; hunting prohibited; partly unprotected

Mountainous area with rivers, streams, woodland and agricultural land. Human activities include arable farming, forestry, stock-farming, fishing, hunting, tourism and leisure.

Breeding species include *Pernis apivorus* (3-5 pairs), *Circaetus gallicus* (1-2 pairs), *Aquila chrysaetos* (3-4 pairs), *Bonasa bonasia*, *Tetrao tetrix*, *Alectoris graeca*, and *Dryocopus martius*.

002 Valle Anzasca and Val di Antrona and neighbouring area (Piemonte)

46°00'N, 08°06'E 42,600 ha

Protected forest area; other national protection; hunting prohibited; partly unprotected

Mountainous area with rivers, streams, woodland, and agricultural land. Human activities include arable farming, forestry, stock-farming, fishing, hunting, tourism and leisure.

Breeding species include *Pernis apivorus* (5-8 pairs), *Circaetus gallicus* (3-5 pairs), *Aquila chrysaetos* (4-6 pairs), *Tetrao tetrix*, *Alectoris graeca*, *Bubo bubo* (3-4 pairs), and *Dryocopus martius*.

003 Mountain area between Lago Maggiore, Val Vigeo and Val Cannobina (Val Grande) (Piemonte)

46°03'N, 08°26'E 29,000 ha

EEC SPA (Riserva Naturale Monte Mottace Val Grande: 3383 ha)

Strict Nature Reserve; hunting prohibited; partly unprotected

Mountainous area with rivers, streams, broadleaved deciduous woodland, native coniferous woodland, agricultural land, exposed bedrock, inland cliffs, and grasslands. Human activities include arable farming, forestry, stock-farming, tourism and leisure, and there are some residential areas.

Breeding species include *Pernis apivorus* (7-8 pairs), *Milvus migrans* (3-4 pairs), *Circaetus gallicus* (2-3 pairs), *Aquila chrysaetos* (3 pairs), *Tetrao tetrix*, *Alectoris graeca*, *Bubo bubo* (2-3 pairs), and *Dryocopus martius*.

004 Parco Nazionale del Gran Paradiso and Val Soana (Piemonte)

45°33'N, 07°16'E 85,000 ha

EEC SPA (Parco Nazionale del Gran Paradiso: 70,000 ha)

National Park; hunting prohibited; partly unprotected

Native coniferous woodland, mixed woodland, agricultural land, inland cliffs, permanent snow and ice, and scree. Human activities include forestry, stock-farming, tourism and leisure, and there is scattered human habitation.

Breeding species include *Aquila chrysaetos* (6-8 pairs), *Tetrao tetrix*, *Alectoris graeca*, *Bubo bubo* (4-6 pairs), *Dryocopus martius*, and *Pyrrhocorax pyrrhocorax*.

005 Heronries in the catchment of the upper Po and Sesia Rivers (Piemonte, Lombardia)

c.45°10'N, 08°25'E

Unprotected

There are many major closely spaced (yet discrete) heronries in this region and for reasons of clarity it has been decided to list them under a general heading. It must be stressed, however, that each heronry (Garzaia) is a separate island of habitat, usually surrounded by agricultural land. Each heronry is therefore an important bird area in its own right. In addition, the list is not to be considered as exhaustive, since there are other heronries, of lesser importance, that have not been included.

005-1 Garzaia di Carisio (Piemonte)

45°26'N, 08°12'E 50 ha

Unprotected; proposed for inclusion in National Park (Lame del Sesia)

A wood of *Robinia pseudacacia* with dry ground and a few bushes in the understorey. The surroundings are cultivated, mainly as rice-fields. The River Elvo is nearby. Many woods in the area have been converted to *Populus* plantations in recent years. Photographers cause some disturbance.

Breeding species (no. of nests in 1986) include *Nycticorax nycticorax* (331), *Egretta garzetta* (59), and *Ardea cinerea* (28).

005-2 Garzaia di Villarboit (Piemonte)

45°07'N, 08°19'E 20 ha

Unprotected

A wood of *Quercus robur* and *Robinia pseudoacacia* with a small area of Alnus glutinosa and *Salix alba*, bordering rivers flowing into the Sesia. The surroundings are intensively cultivated, mainly as rice-fields. The area is also used for pheasant shooting.

Breeding species (no. of nests in 1986) include *Nycticorax nycticorax* (576; declined from 920 in 1981), *Ardeola ralloides* (12), *Egretta garzetta* (421; increased from 350 in 1981), *Ardea cinerea* (99), and *Plegadis falcinellus* (1).

005-3 Garzaia dell'Isolone di Oldenico (Piemonte)

45°24'N, 08°23'E 400 ha

Nature Reserve; included in National Park (Parco Lame Sesia); partly unprotected

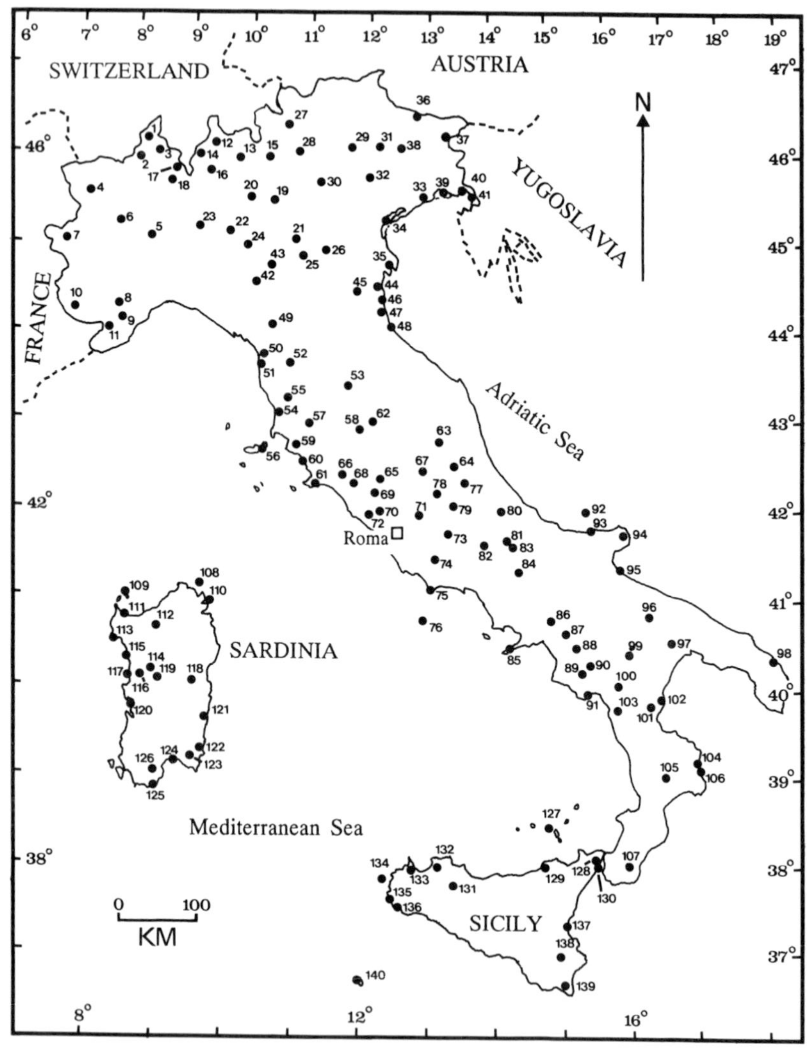

Figure 19: Map showing the location of the sites in Italy

An area of wooded islands in the River Sesia, surrounded by agricultural land. Human activities include fishing and hunting.

Breeding species (in 1981) include *Nycticorax nycticorax* (1200 pairs), *Ardeola ralloides* (5-10 pairs), *Egretta garzetta* (800 pairs), and *Ardea cinerea* (30 pairs).

005-4 Garzaia di Morghengo (Garzaia della Tenuta San Bernardino) (Piemonte)

45°31'N, 08°55'E 6.5 ha

Unprotected

A wood of *Robinia pseudoacacia*, *Quercus robur*, *Picea excelsa*, *Pinus strobus*, and *Tilia cordata*. The surroundings are cultivated, mainly as rice-fields. The wood is used for pheasant shooting.

Breeding species (no. of nests in 1986) include *Nycticorax nycticorax* (851), *Egretta garzetta* (138), and *Ardea cinerea* (161).

005-5 Garzaia della Tenuta Baraccone (Piemonte)

45°11'N, 08°06'E 50 ha

Unprotected

A stand of deciduous woodland with some marshy areas adjacent to the River Po and surrounded by agricultural land. Human activities include arable cultivation, forestry, fishing, and hunting.

Breeding species (in 1981) include *Nycticorax nycticorax* (300 pairs), *Egretta garzetta* (200 pairs), *Ardea cinerea* (60 pairs), and possibly *Plegadis falcinellus* (which has bred in the past).

005-6 Garzaia di Montarolo and Garzaia del Bosco della Partecipanza (Piemonte)

45°13'N, 08°14'E *c.*1000 ha

Hunting prohibited; otherwise unprotected

The heronry at Montarolo (4 km north of the Po) is in a wood of *Robinia pseudacacia*, *Carpinus betulus* and *Corylus avellana*. The trees reach 10 m in height and the ground is dry with gentle undulations. Bosco della Partecipanza is a large semi-natural wood 1 km to the east. The woods are mainly surrounded by rice-fields, and are subject to tree-cutting which may threaten the heronries.

Breeding species (no. of nests in 1985) include *Nycticorax nycticorax* (290; declined from *c.*900 nests in 1981), *Ardeola ralloides* (19), and *Egretta garzetta* (112; declined from 200 in 1981). There are sporadic observations of *Plegadis falcinellus*, which bred in the 1970s.

005-7 Garzaia Isola Langosco (Lombardia)

45°13'N, 08°31'E 100 ha

Unprotected

An island in the River Sesia covered with woodland. The surrounding areas are largely agricultural land. Human activities include arable farming, forestry, stock-raising, fishing, and hunting.

Breeding species (in 1981) include *Nycticorax nycticorax* (600 pairs), *Egretta garzetta* (50 pairs), and *Ardea cinerea* (40 pairs).

005-8 Garzaia di Celpenchio (Lombardia)

45°12'N, 08°37'E 500 ha

Unprotected

An area of woodland and marshes surrounded by agricultural land. Human activities include arable farming, stock-raising, forestry, and hunting.

Breeding species (in 1981) include *Nycticorax nycticorax* (200 pairs), *Egretta garzetta* (100 pairs), and *Ardea purpurea* (30 pairs).

005-9 Garzaia Cascina San Alessandro (Lombardia)

45°12'N, 08°39'E 150 ha

Unprotected

An area of woodland and marshes (some 8 km north-east of the confluence of the Rivers Sesia and Po), surrounded by agricultural land. Human activities include arable farming, stock-raising, forestry, and hunting.

Breeding species (in 1981) include *Nycticorax nycticorax* (150 pairs), *Ardeola ralloides* (4 pairs), *Egretta garzetta* (50 pairs), and *Ardea purpurea* (50 pairs).

005-10 Garzaia Cascina Rinalda (Lombardia)

45°10'N, 08°36'E 150 ha
Unprotected

An area of woodland and marshes surrounded by agricultural land. Human activities include arable farming, stock-raising, forestry, and hunting.

Breeding species (in 1981) include *Nycticorax nycticorax* (520 pairs), *Ardeola ralloides* (10 pairs), and *Egretta garzetta* (60 pairs).

005-11 Lago di Sartirana Lomellina (Lombardia)

45°05'N, 08°40'E 100 ha

Unprotected

An abandoned meander of the Po which has been partially invaded by vegetation. Open water areas are maintained by cutting back of *Phragmites* and *Salix*. The wetland area is surrounded by a wood of *Quercus robur*, *Salix alba*, and *Populus alba*, whilst beyond this the land is mainly cultivated, primarily as rice-fields. Increasing hunting pressure is a problem. There is a very important heronry, which has been censused regularly since 1974.

Breeding species (no. of nests in 1986) include *Nycticorax nycticorax* (many hundreds), *Egretta garzetta* (several hundreds), *Ardeola ralloides* (several tens), and *Ardea purpurea* (80; the largest colony in Italy). Other nesting species include *Circus aeruginosus*, *Locustella luscinioides*, and probably *Botaurus stellaris*. Until 1982, several thousand ducks (mainly *Anas crecca* and *A. platyrhynchos*) occurred in winter. However, hunting pressure is now so great that few birds overwinter.

005-12 Garzaia della Cascina and Bosco Abbasso (Lombardia)

45°06'N, 08°36'E 100 ha

Unprotected

A marshy area with woodland near to the River Po, surrounded by cultivated land. Human activities include arable farming, stock-raising, forestry, fishing, and hunting.

Breeding species (in 1981) include *Nycticorax nycticorax* (120 pairs), *Egretta garzetta* (30 pairs), and *Ardea purpurea* (20 pairs).

005-13 Garzaia di Valenza (Piemonte, Lombardia)

45°02'N, 08°40'E 150 ha

European Diploma Site (designated by the Council of Europe)

Nature Reserve; partly unprotected

A marshy area with woodland adjacent to the River Po, surrounded by cultivated land. Human activities include arable farming, stock-raising, fishing, and hunting.

Breeding species (in 1981) include *Nycticorax nycticorax* (60 pairs), *Egretta garzetta* (30 pairs), and *Ardea purpurea* (40 pairs).

005-14 Garzaia Abbazia (Lombardia)

45°02'N, 08°41'E 100 ha

Unprotected

A heronry a few kilometres north of the River Po, surrounded by agricultural land. The site itself includes running and standing fresh water, and marshy areas. Human activities include agriculture, forestry, fishing, and hunting.

Breeding birds (in 1981) include *Ardea purpurea* (20 pairs).

005-15 Garzaia di Cavo Solero – Villa Biscossi (Lombardia)

45°05'N, 08°47'E 100 ha

Hunting prohibited

A heronry in woodland bordering tributaries of the River Po, surrounded by agricultural land. Human activities include arable farming, stock-raising, and forestry.

Breeding species (in 1981) include *Nycticorax nycticorax* (500 pairs) and *Egretta garzetta* (50 pairs).

005-16 Garzaia di Galliavola (Lombardia)

45°03'N, 08°49'E 10 ha

Unprotected

A wood of *Alnus glutinosa* with scattered *Salix alba*, surrounded by cultivated areas, mostly rice-fields. Human activities include agriculture and pheasant and duck shooting.

Breeding species (no. of nests in 1986) include *Nycticorax nycticorax* (125), *Egretta garzetta* (37), and *Ardea cinerea* (13).

005-17 Garzaia del Torrente Scrivia (Piemonte)

44°46'N, 08°51'E 100 ha

Unprotected

A wooded area on the River Scrivia surrounded by cultivated land. Human activities include arable farming, forestry, and hunting.

Breeding species (in 1981) include *Nycticorax nycticorax* (200 pairs) and *Egretta garzetta* (10 pairs).

006 Lago di Candia (Piemonte)

45°18'N, 07°52'E 687 ha

Hunting prohibited

A permanent freshwater lake fringed with *Phragmites*, with adjacent marshy area, and surrounded by meadows and maize-fields. Human activities include arable farming, fishing, and tourism. Eutrophication, drainage of the adjacent marshes and disturbance from increasing boating, are problems at the lake.

Breeding birds include *Botaurus stellaris* (1 pair) and *Porzana* spp. An important resting area for passage ducks, including *Anas crecca* and *A. platyrhynchos*. *Botaurus stellaris* (5-10) occurs in winter.

007 Area between Val di Susa, Valle del Chisone and Valle del Torrente Pellice (Piemonte)

45°05'N, 06°55'E 8000 ha

Nature Reserve; hunting prohibited; partly unprotected

Rivers, streams, woodland, and agricultural land. Human activities include arable farming, stock-farming, fishing, hunting, tourism and leisure.

Breeding species include *Pernis apivorus* (2-3 pairs), *Circaetus gallicus* (2-4 pairs), *Circus aeruginosus* (7-9 pairs), *Tetrao tetrix, Alectoris graeca, Bubo bubo* (5-6 pairs), *Dryocopus martius, Dendrocopos medius,* and *Pyrrhocorax pyrrhocorax.*

008 Laghetti di Crava-Morozzo (Piemonte)

44°26'N, 07°50'E 300 ha

Regional Park (Alta Valle Pesio); partly unprotected

Bogs, running water, agricultural land, and broadleaved woodland. Human activities include arable farming.

Breeding species include *Falco subbuteo* and *Alcedo atthis.* Important for wintering *Ardea cinerea* (max. 160 in 1986).

009 Passo del Turchino and surrounding area (Piemonte, Liguria)

44°11'N, 08°00'E 38,000 ha

Protected forest area; some other national protection; partly unprotected

Rivers, streams, woodland, and agricultural land. Human activities include arable farming, forestry, stock-farming, fishing, hunting, tourism and leisure.

Important site for migrating raptors. Breeding species include *Pernis apivorus* (6-7 pairs), *Circaetus gallicus* (5-7 pairs), *Aquila chrysaetos* (1 pair), *Accipiter gentilis* (2-3 pairs), and *Bubo bubo.*

010 Val Maira, area around Vinadio, Valle Gesso, Argentera, Val Varanta (Piemonte)

44°18'N, 07°10'E 95,400 ha Biosphere Reserve

Protected Landscape; hunting prohibited; partly unprotected

Mixed woodland, grassland, agricultural land, inland cliffs, and permanent snow and ice. Human activities include forestry, stock-farming, fishing, hunting, tourism and leisure.

Breeding species include *Pernis apivorus* (3-4 pairs), *Circaetus gallicus* (2-3 pairs), *Aquila chrysaetos* (8-10 pairs), *Tetrao tetrix, Alectoris graeca, Bubo bubo* (6-8 pairs), *Dryocopus martius,* and *Pyrrhocorax pyrrhocorax.*

011 Area between Cima Selle Vecchie and Monte Alto (Piemonte, Liguria)

44°03'N, 07°46'E 21,600 ha

Protected forest area; some other national protection; partly unprotected

Mountainous area with rivers, streams, woodland, and agricultural land. Human activities include arable farming, forestry, stock-farming, fishing, hunting, tourism and leisure.

Breeding species include *Pernis apivorus* (2-3 pairs), *Circaetus gallicus* (5 pairs), *Buteo buteo, Aquila chrysaetos* (3 pairs), *Falco peregrinus* (2 pairs), *Accipiter gentilis* (2-3 pairs), *Tetrao tetrix, Alectoris graeca, Bubo bubo* (2-3 pairs), and *Dryocopus martius.*

012 Pian di Spagna and Lago di Mezzola (Lombardia)

46°13'N, 09°27'E 1740 ha Ramsar Site EEC SPA

A lake and associated marshland surrounded by cultivated areas. The lake is connected to Lago di Como by a channel. The marshy area comprises the floodplain of two rivers flowing into Lago di Mezzola.

Breeding species include *Ardea purpurea, Pernis apivorus, Milvus migrans, Circaetus gallicus,* and *Aquila chrysaetos.* The area also supports passage and wintering waterfowl, including *Aythya nyroca* (50 on passage).

013 Slopes of Valtellina and Alte Valli Brenbara, Seriana and di Scalve (Lombardia)

46°03'N, 09°50'E 74,000 ha

Protected forest area; some other national protection; partly unprotected

Mountainous area with rivers, streams, woodland, and agricultural land. Human activities include forestry, stock-farming, fishing, hunting, tourism and leisure.

Breeding species include *Pernis apivorus* (8-10 pairs), *Aquila chrysaetos* (6-8 pairs), *Bonasa bonasia*, *Tetrao tetrix*, *T. urogallus*, *Alectoris graeca*, *Bubo bubo* (4-5 pairs), *Glaucidium passerinum*, and *Aegolius funereus*.

014 Val Solda, Monte di Lenno, Monte di Tremezzo and Monte Tabor (Lombardia)

46°04'N, 09°09'E 28,000 ha

Protected forest area; some other national protection; partly unprotected

Mountainous area with freshwater lakes and reservoirs, woodland, and agricultural land. Human activities include arable farming, forestry, stock-farming, fishing, hunting, tourism and leisure.

Breeding species include *Pernis apivorus* (8-10 pairs), *Milvus migrans* (15-20 pairs), *Aquila chrysaetos* (1 pair), and *Tetrao tetrix*.

015 Val Camonica (Lombardia)

46°03'N, 12°24'E 23,000 ha

Protected forest area; some other national protection; partly unprotected

Mountainous area with rivers, streams, woodland, and agricultural land. Human activities include forestry, stock-farming, fishing, hunting, tourism and leisure.

Important area for birds of prey and other forest species. Breeding species include *Pernis apivorus* (5-8 pairs), *Milvus migrans* (4-5 pairs), *Accipiter gentilis*, *Aquila chrysaetos* (5 pairs), *Bonasa bonasia* (100 pairs), *Lagopus mutus*, *Tetrao tetrix* (100-200 males), *T. urogallus* (10 males), *Alectoris graeca*, *Bubo bubo* (2-3 pairs), *Aegolius funereus*, *Picus canus*, *Dryocopus martius* (10 pairs), and *Tichodroma muraria* (2-3 pairs).

016 Pendici della Grigna facing the Lago di Lecco (Lombardia)

45°57'N, 09°22'E 6500 ha

Protected landscape; protected forest area; some other national protection; partly unprotected

An area with mixed woodland and agricultural land. Human activities include forestry, hunting, tourism and leisure.

Breeding species include *Pernis apivorus* (1-2 pairs), *Milvus migrans* (20-25 pairs), *Circaetus gallicus* (1 pair), *Falco peregrinus* (1 pair), and *Tetrao tetrix*. *Aquila chrysaetos* occurs in winter.

017 Campo del Fiori, Valganna, Val Cuvia (Lombardia)

45°55'N, 08°46'E 24,500 ha

Protected forest area; some other national protection; partly unprotected

An area with rivers, streams, broadleaved deciduous woodland, and agricultural land. Human activities include arable farming, forestry, stock-farming, fishing, hunting, tourism and leisure.

Breeding species include *Nycticorax nycticorax* (20-30 pairs), *Pernis apivorus* (8-10 pairs), *Milvus migrans* (10-15 pairs), and *Circaetus gallicus* (2 pairs).

018 Palude Brabbia (Lombardia)

45°47'N, 08°45'E 459 ha Ramsar Site

Nature Reserve

An area of marshland between Lago di Comabbio and Lago di Varese. The wetland is in a basin surrounded by hills, some of which are settled, others cultivated. There are numerous channels and shallow areas of open water, and the aquatic vegetation is extremely rich.

Breeding species include *Ixobrychus minutus* and *Porzana porzana*. *Ardea purpurea* and *Circus aeruginosus* probably also breed.

019 Colline di Salo and area between Lago di Garda and Lago d'Idro (Lombardia)

45°39'N, 10°28'E 25,900 ha

Unprotected

Mountainous area with cliffs and exposed bedrock, woodland, and agricultural land. Human activities include forestry, stock-farming, fishing, hunting, tourism and leisure.

Breeding species include *Pernis apivorus* (3-5 pairs), *Milvus migrans* (10-15 pairs), *Circaetus gallicus* (1-2 pairs), *Tetrao tetrix*, *T. urogallus*, *Aegolius funereus*, *Alectoris graeca*, and *Sylvia nisoria* (50 pairs).

020 Torbiere d'Iseo (Lombardia)

45°38'N, 10°02'E 325 ha Ramsar Site

A complex of marshland and open-water areas to the south of Lago di Iseo, amongst the foothills of the Alps.

Breeding species include *Ixobrychus minutus*, *Nycticorax nycticorax*, *Ardea purpurea*, *Porzana porzana*, *Circus aeruginosus*, and *Locustella luscinioides*.

021 Bosco Fontana and Valli del Mincio (Lago Superiore di Mantova) (Lombardia)

45°11'N, 10°45'E 2500 ha

Includes Ramsar Site (Valli del Mincio; 1082 ha); EEC SPA (Riserva Naturale del Bosco Fontana: 233 ha)

Nature Reserve

A complex of marshes, canals, reedbeds, and wooded areas in the valley of the River Mincio. Human activities include agriculture, forestry (*Populus* spp.), reed-cutting, and fishing.

Breeding species include *Ixobrychus minutus* (10-30 pairs), *Ardea purpurea* (5-15 pairs), *Anas querquedula* (1-5 pairs), *Circus aeruginosus* (1 pair), *Porzana parva* (1-5 pairs), *Alcedo atthis* (1-2 pairs), *Locustella luscinioides* (30-40 pairs), *Acrocephalus melanopogon*, *A. schoenobaenus*, *A. arundinaceus* (100-150 pairs), and *Panurus biarmicus* (30-50 pairs). Wintering birds include *Phalacrocorax carbo sinensis*, *Botaurus stellaris*, and various Anatidae.

022 La Zerbaglia (Lombardia)

45°16'N, 09°39'E 1100 ha

Natural Park (Adda Sud); hunting prohibited (voluntary measure by owner)

An abandoned meander of the River Adda, now invaded by aquatic vegetation, mainly reedbeds and *Salix*. The water is generally shallow (max. 1 m) but the level fluctuates considerably during the spring and autumn floods. The surrounding area comprises mostly agricultural land with plantations of *Populus* spp.

There is an important heronry with *Nycticorax nycticorax* (190 nests), *Egretta garzetta* (260 nests), and *Ardea purpurea* (30 nests). Several thousand ducks winter in the area, or pass through on migration, notably *Anas crecca* and *A. platyrhynchos*.

023 Heronries close to Pavia and the catchment of the Fiume Ticino (Lombardia)

*c.*45°18'N, 09°10'E

There are many major closely spaced (yet discrete) heronries in this region, and for reasons of clarity it has been decided to list them under a general heading. It must be stressed, however, that each heronry (Garzaia) is a separate island of habitat, usually surrounded by agricultural land. Each heronry is therefore an important bird area in its own right. In addition, the list is not to be considered as exhaustive, since there are other heronries, of less importance, that have not been included.

023-1 Garzaia di Cusago (Lombardia)

45°27'N, 09°04'E 150 ha

Hunting prohibited

A heronry in deciduous woodland. Human activities include forestry.

Breeding species (in 1981) include *Nycticorax nycticorax* (400 pairs) and *Egretta garzetta* (10 pairs).

023-2 Garzaia di Villarasca (Lombardia)

45°18'N, 09°10'E 10 ha

Unprotected

A wood of *Alnus glutinosa* and *Salix caprea* partially submerged by water and surrounded by cultivation. Duck and pheasant shooting occur. The site is threatened by plans to transform the area into a recreation centre.

A very important heronry with (no. of nests in 1986) *Nycticorax nycticorax* (1174) and *Egretta garzetta* (632). There were 23 pairs of *Ardeola ralloides* in 1985 but none in 1986.

023-3 Garzaia Cascina Portalupa (Lombardia)

45°17'N, 09°05'E 150 ha

Nature Reserve; hunting prohibited

An area of woodland, freshwater bodies and marshes, surrounded by agricultural land. Human activities include arable farming, stock-raising, and fishing.

Breeding species (in 1981) include *Nycticorax nycticorax* (300 pairs) and *Egretta garzetta* (10 pairs).

023-4 Garzaia di Bosco Mezzano (La Zelata) (Lombardia)

45°16'N, 08°59'E 390 ha

Nature Reserve; hunting prohibited

An area of woodland, freshwater bodies and marshes, surrounded by agricultural land. Human activities include arable farming, stock-raising, and fishing.

Breeding species (in 1981) include *Ardea cinerea* (35 pairs) and *A. purpurea* (15 pairs).

023-5 Garzaia di San Massimo (Lombardia)

45°12'N, 08°59'E 350 ha

Nature Reserve (part); remainder unprotected

An area of woodland with some marshy ground close to the River Ticino, surrounded by cultivated land. Human activities include pastoral and arable agriculture, forestry, fishing, and hunting.

An important heronry with (in 1981) *Nycticorax nycticorax* (1800 pairs), *Ardeola ralloides* (15 pairs), and *Egretta garzetta* (200 pairs).

023-6 Garzaia di Cascina Porta Chiossa (Lombardia)

45°14'N, 09°14'E 80 ha

Unprotected

A heronry in an area of woodland with marshy ground, adjacent to a tributary of the River Po near Pavia, and surrounded by cultivated land. Human activities include agriculture, forestry, fishing, and hunting.

Breeding species (in 1981) include *Nycticorax nycticorax* (770 pairs) and *Egretta garzetta* (80 pairs).

023-7 Garzaia di Vaccarizza (Lombardia)

45°08'N, 09°16'E 100 ha

Nature Reserve; hunting prohibited

An area of woodland, freshwater bodies and marshes, surrounded by agricultural land. Human activities include arable farming, stock-raising, and fishing.

Breeding herons (in 1981) include *Nycticorax nycticorax* (520 pairs), *Ardeola ralloides* (10 pairs), and *Egretta garzetta* (60 pairs).

024 Fiume Po: Lambro – Casalmaggiore (Lombardia, Emilia Romagna)

*c.*45°05'-44°55'N, 09°35'-10°25'E

The River Po, its islands and banks, between Lambro and Casalmaggiore.

024-1 Garzaia di Somaglia (Lombardia)

45°08'N, 09°39'E 3000 ha

A heronry in wooded marshes adjacent to the Po. Human activities include agriculture, fishing, and hunting.

Breeding species (in 1981) include *Nycticorax nycticorax* (400 pairs) and *Egretta garzetta* (25 pairs).

024-2 Isola de Pinedo (Lombardia, Emilia Romagna)

45°04'N, 09°52'E 100+ ha

Hunting prohibited (part of area)

An island in the River Po covered by a wood of willows (mainly *Salix alba*) with a thick understorey. There are some large reedbeds, whilst the adjacent banks of the Po are mainly *Populus* plantations with some woodland. There is a nuclear power-station nearby. Other human activities include moderate levels of hunting and fishing. Problems include wetland reclamation and felling of woodland.

Breeding herons include *Ixobrychus minutus* (high density), *Nycticorax nycticorax* (20 pairs), *Egretta garzetta* (10 pairs), and *Ardea purpurea* (7 pairs). Other breeding species include *Circus aeruginosus* (1 pair). *Pandion haliaetus* is a regular passage migrant, and small numbers of diving ducks and *Fulica atra* occur in winter.

025 Fiume Po: Viadana – Ostiglia (Lombardia, Emilia Romagna)

44°52'-45°03'N, 10°30'-11°12'E 13,000 ha

The River Po, its islands and banks, between Viadana and Ostiglia.

Breeding species include *Ixobrychus minutus*, *Nycticorax nycticorax*, *Egretta garzetta*, *Ardea purpurea*, *Milvus migrans*, *Circus pygargus*, *Burhinus oedicnemus*, *Sterna hirundo*, and *S. albifrons*.

025-1 Garzaia di Pomponesco (Lombardia, Emilia Romagna)

44°55'N, 10°36'E 20 ha

Nature Reserve

A wood of willows (mainly *Salix alba*) on the floodplain of the River Po, surrounded by cultivated land, and *Populus* plantations. Human activities include forestry and agriculture.

Breeding species (no. of nests in 1986) include *Nycticorax nycticorax* (250; declined from 700 in 1981) and *Egretta garzetta* (50; declined from 80 in 1981).

025-2 Palude di Ostiglia (including Palude del Busatello) (Lombardia, Veneto)

45°05'N, 11°08'E 123 ha Ramsar Site

Nature Reserve

An area of marshland between the Rivers Po and Tione just north of Ostiglia. The marsh itself is approximately 80 ha in extent and is surrounded by an earth dyke (*c*.2 m in height) which separates the wetland from the surrounding flat countryside. Much of the area is occupied by beds of *Phragmites australis* and *Carex elata*.

Nesting species include *Ardea purpurea* (2 pairs), *Circus aeruginosus* (1 pair), and *Panurus biarmicus*. An important site for passage Ardeidae, Anatidae, raptors (including *Milvus migrans*, *Buteo buteo*, *Pandion haliaetus*, and *Asio flammeus*), waders, and passerines.

026 Isola Boscone (Lombardia, Emilia Romagna)

45°02'N, 11°15'E 10 ha

Nature Reserve

An island of the River Po covered by a wood of *Salix alba* with a thick understorey. The surroundings comprise mostly *Populus* plantations. Human activities include angling.

An important heronry with (no. of nests in 1986) *Nycticorax nycticorax* (553), *Ardeola ralloides* (13), and *Egretta garzetta* (49).

027 Parco Nazionale dello Stelvio and the area adjacent to the Valtellina and Val Camonica (Lombardia, Trentino-Alto Adige)

46°30'N, 10°32'E 160,000 ha EEC SPA (Parco Nazionale dello Stelvio: 62,824 ha)

National Park; hunting prohibited

Mountainous area with exposed bedrock, cliffs, areas of permanent snow and ice, running and standing water, bogs and marshes, woodland, agricultural land, and alpine grasslands. Human activities include forestry, stock-farming, fishing, hunting, tourism and leisure.

Important site for raptors and forest birds. Breeding birds include *Pernis apivorus* (1 pair), *Aquila chrysaetos* (22 pairs), *Falco peregrinus* (10 pairs), *Bonasa bonasia* (170 pairs), *Tetrao tetrix* (300 males), *T. urogallus* (72 males), *Alectoris graeca* (280 pairs), *Bubo bubo* (26 pairs), *Glaucidium passerinum* (48 pairs), *Aegolius funereus* (14 pairs), *Picus canus*, and *Picoides tridactylus*.

028 Gruppo dell'Adamello and Gruppo del Brenta (Trentino-Alto Adige)

46°08'N, 10°46'E 79,800 ha

Nature Reserve; protected forest area; some other national protection; hunting prohibited; partly unprotected

Mountainous area with rivers, streams and fresh standing water, native coniferous woodland, agricultural land, inland cliffs, permanent snow and ice. Human activities include agriculture, forestry, stock-farming, fishing, hunting, tourism and leisure.

Breeding species include *Pernis apivorus* (4-6 pairs), *Aquila chrysaetos* (6-8 pairs), *Bonasa bonasia*, *Lagopus mutus*, *Tetrao tetrix*, *T. urogallus*, *Alectoris graeca*, *Bubo bubo* (3-6 pairs), *Glaucidium passerinum*, *Aegolius funereus*, *Picus canus*, *Dryocopus martius*, and *Picoides tridactylus*.

029 Catena dei Lagorai and Valli dei Torrenti Maso, Grigno, Vanoi e Cismon (Trentino-Alto Adige, Veneto)

46°11'N, 11°36'E 57,700 ha

Protected forest area; some other national protection; partly unprotected

Mountainous area with rivers and streams, woodland, and agricultural land. Human activities include forestry, stock-farming, fishing, hunting, tourism and leisure.

Breeding species include *Pernis apivorus* (5-7 pairs), *Aquila chrysaetos* (5-7 pairs), *Falco peregrinus* (2 pairs), *Bonasa bonasia*, *Lagopus mutus*, *Tetrao tetrix*, *T. urogallus*, *Alectoris graeca*, *Bubo bubo* (2-4 pairs), *Glaucidium passerinum*, *Aegolius funereus*, *Picus canus*, and *Picoides tridactylus*.

030 Monti Lessini, Monte Pasubio and Monte Piccole Dolomiti (Trentino-Alto Adige, Veneto)

45°44'N, 11°10'E 39,000 ha

Protected forest area; some other national protection; partly unprotected

Mountainous area of rivers and streams, coniferous and mixed woodland, and agricultural land. Human activities include forestry, stock-farming, fishing, hunting, tourism and leisure.

Breeding species include *Pernis apivorus*, *Circaetus gallicus*, *Aquila chrysaetos* (2 pairs), *Lagopus mutus*, *Tetrao tetrix*, *Alectoris graeca*, and *Bubo bubo* (1-2 pairs).

031 Dolomiti Bellunesi from Feltre to the Ospidale di Cadore (Veneto)

46°13'N, 12°04'E 58,600 ha

Biogenetic Reserve EEC SPA (Riserve Naturali delle Dolomiti Bellunesi: 17,455 ha)

Nature Reserve; hunting prohibited; partly unprotected

Mountainous area with exposed rocks, cliffs, caves, areas of permanent snow and ice, rivers, streams, broadleaved deciduous and coniferous woodland, alpine grasslands, and agricultural land. Human activities include forestry, stock-farming, fishing, hunting, tourism and leisure.

Breeding species include *Pernis apivorus* (1-2 pairs), *Milvus migrans* (5-6 pairs), *Circaetus gallicus*, *Aquila chrysaetos* (5-7 pairs), *Bonasa bonasia*, *Tetrao tetrix*, *T. urogallus*, *Alectoris graeca*, *Bubo bubo* (2-5 pairs), *Glaucidium passerinum*, and *Picus canus*.

032 Lago di Busche and Vincheto di Cellarda (Veneto)

45°50'N, 12°00'E *c.*3500 ha Includes Ramsar Site (Vincheto di Cellarda: 99 ha)

Proposed Nature Reserve; unprotected

A heterogenous wetland along the River Piave that includes the river itself, areas of *Salix* and *Alnus* scrub (Vincheto di Cellarda), a relict continental peatbog (Lipoi), and an artificial lake (Lago di Busche) with some reedbed areas. Human activities include fish-farming, industrial use of the lake's water and recreation. The area is threatened by a planned motorway that will pass close to Vincheto di Cellarda, pollution and urban refuse from nearby towns, and wood-cutting.

Breeding species at Lago di Busche include *Anas platyrhynchos*, *Aythya fuligula* (only site in Italy), *Fulica atra*, *Acrocephalus palustris*, and *A. scirpaceus*. Birds wintering on the lake include *Tachybaptus ruficollis* (250-300), *Egretta alba* (singles), and small numbers of Anatidae.

033 Laguna di Caorle (Veneto)

45°39'N, 12°55'E 2200 ha

Hunting prohibited (Valle Vecchia: 850 ha); mainly unprotected

A lagoon complex between the larger Laguna di Venezia and Laguna di Grado/Marano. The surrounding area comprises large, reclaimed cultivated fields. The wetland is intensively used for fish-farming. Problems include the threat of further drainage, tourism, and hunting.

Breeding species include *Botaurus stellaris* (1 pair), *Nycticorax nycticorax* (200 pairs), *Ardeola ralloides* (10 pairs), *Egretta garzetta* (200 pairs), *Circus aeruginosus*, and *C. pygargus*. Small, but nationally significant, numbers of Anatidae occur in winter (e.g. *Aythya ferina*, 900), together with *Phalacrocorax carbo sinensis* (250) and *Fulica atra* (3500). Geese (*Anser* spp.) have occurred regularly in recent years.

034 Laguna di Venezia (Veneto)

45°11'-45°34'N, 12°18'-12°38'E *c.*55,000 ha

One small WWF Refuge (Valle Averto); largely unprotected

An extensive coastal lagoon between the mouths of the Rivers Brenta and Piave. Three large, open, central waterbodies form the Laguna Viva and there is a chain of smaller peripheral waterbodies ('valli') which have lower salinities. The Laguna Viva is dissected by a number of deep artificial canals which are partly used by large ships moving from the sea to the industrial port of Marghera. The industrial area, the City of Venice, and many small islands are included in the area described. The main waterbodies have *Zostera* beds with *Ruppia* common close to the shore. There are tidal mudflats with *Ulva* and *Enteromorpha* and locally common *Spartina*. The surrounding areas are largely cultivated (notably maize) although there are some wooded parts. Human activities include fish-farming, hunting in most 'valli', mussel farming, fishing in the open lagoon, and industrial operations at Porto Marghera. Tourism and agriculture are also important. The area is threatened by drainage, pollution, excessive disturbance through tourism, hunting, and industrial expansion.

Breeding species include *Nycticorax nycticorax* (100 pairs), *Egretta garzetta* (900 pairs), *Ardea purpurea* (100+ pairs), *Circus aeruginosus*, *C. pygargus*, *Himantopus himantopus* (150 pairs), *Recurvirostra avosetta* (30 pairs), *Tringa totanus* (50+ pairs), *Sterna hirundo*, *S. albifrons*, *Alcedo atthis*, *Sylvia nisoria*, *Panurus biarmicus*, and *Remiz pendulinus*. A very important area for spring passage waterfowl, with *Anas querquedula* (4000+), *Philomachus pugnax* (1000+), *Tringa erythropus* (1000+), and *T. stagnatilis* (20+). Wintering waterfowl ('av.' refers to average of winter counts 1986/87-1987/88) include *Podiceps cristatus* (1000+), *P. nigricollis*, *Phalacrocorax carbo sinensis* (1000), *Egretta alba* (50+), *Ardea cinerea* (*c.*500), *Anas penelope* (av. 1900), *A. strepera* (av. 30), *A. crecca* (av. 2000), *A. platyrhynchos* (av. 3500), *A. acuta* (av. 370), *A. clypeata* (av. 220), *Aythya ferina* (av. 2700), *A. nyroca* (0-42), *Bucephala clangula* (av. 90), *Fulica atra* (20,000+), and *Larus melanocephalus* (1000+). Geese (*Anser* spp.) occur irregularly in cold winters.

035 Delta del Po (Veneto, Emilia Romagna)

*c.*44°56'N, 12°16'E *c.*25,000 ha

Two Ramsar Sites (Valle Bertozzi and adjacent water surfaces: 3100 ha; Valle di Gorino and adjacent territories: 1330 ha); EEC SPA (Riserva Naturale Dune e Isole della Sacca di Gorino: 479 ha)

Two small Nature Reserves; some no-shooting areas; largely unprotected

A vast delta with tidal estuaries, reedbeds, lagoons (mostly used as fish-ponds), sand-dunes, sandy beaches, and agricultural land. Large areas inland have been reclaimed. Human activities include fish-farming, hunting, fishing, bivalve-farming, reed-cutting, and tourism. Problems include pollution of the River Po, eutrophication, beach erosion, heavy poaching, and excessive human disturbance (especially a problem for breeding waders). There is a proposal to establish a National Park.

Breeding species (in 1986) include *Nycticorax nycticorax* (600 pairs), *Egretta garzetta* (600 pairs), *Ardea purpurea* (150 pairs), *Haematopus ostralegus* (20-30 pairs), *Himantopus himantopus* (80 pairs), *Charadrius alexandrinus* (250 pairs), *Sterna hirundo* (800 pairs), and *S. albifrons* (3000 pairs). Large numbers of waterfowl occur in winter with *Phalacrocorax carbo* (500+), *Egretta garzetta* (*c*.1000), *E. alba* (30+), *Anas penelope* (10,000), *A. clypeata* (4000), *Bucephala clangula* (400), and *Fulica atra* (20,000).

035-1 Isola Madonnina (Veneto)

44°57'N, 12°17'E *c*.10 ha

Unprotected

An island covered with *Salix alba* in the lower River Po, surrounded by cultivated land. Human activities include agriculture and fishing. Tree-cutting causes disturbance to the heronry and led to temporary abandonment of the colony in 1986.

Breeding species (no. of nests in 1985) include *Nycticorax nycticorax* (157) and *Egretta garzetta* (293).

035-2 Garzaia del Po di Maistra (Veneto)

44°59'N, 12°21'E *c*.10 ha

Unprotected

An island in a minor branch of the Po Delta. The island is covered by thick bushy vegetation (*Amorpha fruticosa*, *Salix alba*, *Populus nigra*, and *P. alba*) and *Phragmites australis*. The surroundings include extensive areas of cultivation and saltmarshes. Human activities include hunting, fishing, and agriculture.

Breeding species (no. of nests 1986) include *Nycticorax nycticorax* (400), *Ardeola ralloides* (60), *Egretta garzetta* (515), and *Ardea purpurea* (25).

035-3 Scanni del Delta del Po (Veneto)

44°59'N, 12°29'E *c*.3000 ha

Nature Reserve; largely unprotected

The barrier islands at the seaward limit of the Po Delta, connected to the mainland by small bridges. The islands are sandy with dunes and sparse herbaceous vegetation (*Ammophila*). Human activities include fish-farming, angling, agriculture on the surrounding areas, and tourism. The area is immediately threatened by severe disturbance from tourists and the destruction of sand-dunes to form tourist beaches.

The area holds what is possibly the greatest concentration of nesting *Sterna albifrons* in the Western Palearctic with 2400-3000 pairs (around half of the total Italian breeding population). The islands also hold the entire Italian population of nesting *Haematopus ostralegus* (15-30 pairs).

035-4 Valle Bertuzzi, Lago delle Nazioni, Valle Porticino-Canevié, and Foce del Po di Volano (Emilia Romagna)

44°47'N, 12°15'E 2200 ha

Part of a Ramsar Site (Valle Bertuzzi and adjacent water surfaces: 3100 ha); includes 2 EEC SPAs (Riserva Naturale Po di Volano: 220 ha; Riserva Naturale Bassa dei Frassini, Balanzetta e Bosco della Mesola: 1057 ha)

Hunting prohibited (2 areas); partly unprotected

Brackish lagoons with islands and foreshore (very important for breeding herons and waders). The site includes the mouth of the southern branch of the River Po Delta (Po di Volano) with its reedbeds and mudflats. Human activities include arable farming, fishing and fish-farming, boating, and hunting.

Breeding species include *Egretta garzetta* (300 pairs), *Himantopus himantopus* (50 pairs), *Larus melanocephalus* (1000 pairs), *Sterna hirundo* (700 pairs), and *S. albifrons* (150 pairs). Passage and wintering waterfowl include *Phalacrocorax carbo sinensis* (2000), *Egretta alba* (up to 200), many diving ducks including *Netta rufina* (0-5), and *Chlidonias niger* (500+).

036 Area from Val Visdende to Canale di San Pietro (Veneto, Friuli-Venezia Giulia)

46°35'N, 12°50'E 27,800 ha

Protected forest area; some other national protection; partly unprotected

Mountainous area with rivers and streams, woodland, and agricultural land. Human activities include arable farming, forestry, stock-farming, fishing, hunting, tourism and leisure.

Breeding species include *Pernis apivorus* (2-4 pairs), *Aquila chrysaetos* (2-5 pairs), *Bonasa bonasia*, *Tetrao tetrix*, *T. urogallus*, *Alectoris graeca*, *Bubo bubo* (2-4 pairs), *Picus canus*, and *Picoides tridactylus*.

037 Area between Gemona, Valle Resia, Monte Canin and Foresta del Tarvisio (Friuli-Venezia Giulia)

46°25'N, 13°25'E 44,000 ha

EEC SPA (Riserva Naturale della Foresta di Tarvisio: 23,294 ha)

Nature Reserve; hunting prohibited; partly unprotected

Native coniferous woodland, mixed woodland, and agricultural land. Human activities include arable farming, forestry, stock-farming, fishing, hunting, tourism and leisure.

Breeding species include *Pernis apivorus*, *Aquila chrysaetos* (1-4 pairs), *Falco peregrinus*, *Bonasa bonasia*, *Tetrao tetrix*, *T. urogallus*, *Alectoris graeca*, *Bubo bubo* (2 pairs), *Glaucidium passerinum*, *Picus canus*, *Dryocopus martius*, and *Picoides tridactylus*. *Gyps fulvus* occurs in summer.

038 Area between Valle del Piave and the Alta Valle del Tagliamento (Veneto, Friuli-Venezia Giulia)

46°16'N, 12°33'E 63,000 ha

Protected forest area; some other national protection; partly unprotected

Mountainous area with rivers, streams, bogs, marshes, woodland, scrub, grasslands, and agricultural land. Human activities include forestry, stock-farming, fishing, hunting, tourism and leisure.

Breeding species include *Pernis apivorus* (4-5 pairs), *Aquila chrysaetos* (6-8 pairs), *Bonasa bonasia*, *Tetrao tetrix*, *T. urogallus*, *Alectoris graeca*, *Bubo bubo* (2-4 pairs), *Glaucidium passerinum*, *Picus canus*, and *Dryocopus martius*.

039 Laguna di Grado e Marano (Friuli-Venezia Giulia)

45°45'N, 13°04'-13°33'E *c.*2000 ha

Includes 2 Ramsar Sites (Valle Cavanata: 243 ha; Marano Lagunare: 1400 ha)

Regional Park; hunting prohibited (Valle Cavanata; Foci dello Stella)

A tidal lagoon, which is fed by six rivers, 30 km in length and about 5 km in width. There are six major connections with the open sea, with a number of islands and sand-dunes along the coast. The eastern side (Grado) has more emergent land and mudflats than the western part (Marano) because it is the site of an ancient delta of the Isonzo River. The islands in the lagoon are often cultivated or used in fish-farming. The deeper parts of the lagoon are covered with *Zostera* and *Ulva*; the mudflats have *Spartina* and *Ruppia*; permanently exposed banks have *Salicornia* etc.; and the dunes are vegetated by *Agropyron*, *Ammophila*, etc. There are areas of *Scirpus*, *Phragmites*, and *Salix* around the freshwater channels entering the lagoon. Human activities include fish-farming, fishing, shipping, tourism (especially motor boats), agriculture, and hunting. Increased fish-farming activities using EEC funds, enlargement of port facilities, extension of industrial activities, increasing pollution, motor-boating, and channel dredging all threaten the area.

Breeding species include *Egretta garzetta* (300-400 pairs) and *Sterna albifrons* (100-150 pairs). The lagoon is very important for passage and wintering waterfowl (figures from 1986 and 1987 unless otherwise stated) with *Phalacrocorax carbo sinensis* (max. 630), *Egretta garzetta* (500-1300), *E. alba* (max. 15-20), *Anser fabalis* (max. 2000), *A. albifrons albifrons* (max. 2500), *A. anser* (700), *Anas penelope* (max. 7920 in 1983), *A. strepera* (max. 900), *A. platyrhynchos* (max. 10,825 in 1982), *Bucephala clangula* (max. 7390 in 1982), *Mergus serrator* (max. 882 in 1981), *Fulica atra* (max. 24,730 in 1984), *Pluvialis squatarola* (1000 in 1984), and *Chlidonias niger* (av. 2500).

039-1 Foci dello Stella (Friuli-Venezia Giulia)

45°45'N, 13°07'E 1400 ha Ramsar Site (Marano Lagunore)

Hunting prohibited (800 ha) and restricted (remainder); otherwise unprotected

An area of tidal mudflats and a large reedbed at the mouth of the River Stella on the western side of the Laguna di Grado e Marano. Part of the deeper lagoon is included in the Ramsar Site. The site is surrounded by agricultural fields and the remnants of a once-large wood. Human activities include fishing, agriculture, and reed-cutting. Pollution from urban, industrial, and agricultural sources, dredging of channels and excessive disturbance resulting from tourism and hunting all threaten the site.

Breeding species include *Ardea purpurea*, *Cygnus olor*, *Circus aeruginosus*, and *Panurus biarmicus*. A very important area for wintering waterfowl with Anatidae (totalling 10,000+), including *Anas strepera* (500-1000; increasing), *A. crecca* (5000-7000), *Bucephala clangula*, and *Fulica atra* (10,000+). An increasing number of wintering geese (*Anser fabalis*, *A. albifrons albifrons*, and *A. anser*) feed on agricultural land, visiting the lagoon to roost.

039-2 Valle Cavanata (Friuli-Venezia Giulia)

45°45'N, 13°33'E 243 ha Ramsar Site

Hunting prohibited

The area includes a former branch of the ancient River Isonzo Delta (Averto Canal) and a shallow pond surrounded by dykes. There is also a small (10 ha) wood with bushes. Vegetation includes *Zostera*, *Salicornia*, *Aster*, *Typha*, and *Phragmites*. The area is used for fish-farming and collection of water drained from nearby fields. Intensification of pisciculture may threaten the site.

Breeding species include *Circus aeruginosus* (3 pairs) and *Larus argentatus* (350 pairs). An important area for wintering waterfowl with Anatidae (totalling 7500-8000) including *Anser fabalis* (700-800), *A. albifrons albifrons* (700-800), *A. anser* (400-500), and *Anas penelope* (800). Other wintering species include *Phalacrocorax carbo sinensis* (60-80), *Ardea cinerea* (60-70), *Egretta garzetta* (40-70), and *Falco peregrinus*. *Pandion haliaetus* occurs on passage.

039-3 Isola dei Belli (Friuli-Venezia Giulia)

45°43'N, 13°18'E 1 ha

Unprotected

A wood of *Ulmus campestris* with an understorey of *Sambucus nigra* and *Prunus spinosus*, surrounded by wetlands used for fish-farming and hunting.

Breeding species (no. of nests in 1986) include *Nycticorax nycticorax* (111) and *Egretta garzetta* (320).

040 Foci dell'Isonzo and 'Isola della Cona' (Friuli-Venezia Giulia)

45°45'N, 13°34'E *c.*3000 ha

Nature Reserve; proposed Regional Reserve; LIPU Reserve 130 ha; hunting prohibited

The terminal part of the mouth of the River Isonzo, some 30 km west of Trieste. There are sandbanks and mudflats extending east-west, and a large area of emergent mudflats, channels and lagoonal ditches between the embanked branch of the river ('Quarantia') and the river mouth itself. Human activities include fishing, mollusc-collecting, and agriculture. Plans for a dam on the Yugoslavian section of the river (upstream) are likely to affect the area. There is also a threat from uncontrolled development of tourism. However, a programme of wetland restoration and management is to be implemented.

Breeding species include *Ardea purpurea* and *Circus aeruginosus*. An important area for moulting, passage, and wintering waterfowl, with *Gavia stellata*, *G. arctica*, *Podiceps cristatus* (100-200), *P. grisegena*, *P. nigricollis* (400-700), *Phalacrocorax carbo sinensis* (100), *Melanitta nigra*, *M. fusca*, *Bucephala clangula* (max. 500), *Mergus serrator* (max. 200) and *Numenius arquata* (1000-2000 roosting in winter); also one of the few Mediterranean sites where *Somateria mollissima* (30) occurs in summer, and waders during passage periods.

041 Carso Triestino (Friuli-Venezia Giulia)

45°43'N, 13°45'E 9600 ha

Nature Reserve; protected landscape; hunting prohibited,

Woodland, heath and scrub and agricultural land. Human activities include arable farming, forestry, stock-farming, hunting, some industry, and there is a railway.

Breeding species include *Pernis apivorus* (2-3 pairs) and *Falco peregrinus*.

042 Fiume Taro: Fornovo di Taro-Viarolo (Emilia Romagna)

*c.*44°37'-44°43'N, 10°07'-10°09'E *c.*2500 ha

Regional Park; hunting prohibited

The River Taro, its banks and islands. The surrounding areas are largely cultivated. Human activities include arable agriculture, forestry, and fishing.

Breeding species include *Nycticorax nycticorax*, *Ardea purpurea*, *Circus pygargus*, *Burhinus oedicnemus* (10+ pairs), *Sterna hirundo* (200+ pairs), *S. albifrons*, and *Alcedo atthis*.

042-1 Garzaia di Ozzano Taro (Emilia Romagna)

44°43'N, 10°09'E *c.*10 ha

Included in above Regional Park

An area of shingle banks in the River Taro. There are a few wooded stretches with a large wood of *Populus nigra* occupied by a heronry. The region surrounding the Taro at this point is mostly cultivated and urbanised. Human activities include recreation, fishing, and grazing of sheep. There is some deliberate disturbance of the breeding herons by local people, who are entitled to fell the *Populus* wood should the heronry become deserted.

Breeding species (1986 estimates) include *Nycticorax nycticorax* (*c.*100) and *Egretta garzetta* (10). Other nesting species include *Burhinus oedicnemus*, *Sterna hirundo*, and *S. albifrons*.

043 Vasche dell'Eridania e Oasi LIPU di Torrile (Emilia Romagna)

44°56'N, 10°20'E 60 ha

LIPU Reserve (10 ha); access restricted

Ponds, wet grassland and arable farmland. Human activities include arable farming. Waste water from an adjacent sugar factory is discharged into the ponds.

Breeding species include *Himantopus himantopus* (20 pairs). Interesting site for migrating waders, with 50 *Actitis hypoleucos* and 200 *Tringa glareola* on 18/8/86.

044 Valli di Comacchio, Salina di Comacchio, Mezzano, Vene e Sacca di Bellocchio, Foce del Fiume Reno (Emilia Romagna)

44°37'N, 12°10'E 28,570 ha

Includes 2 Ramsar Sites (Valli di Comacchio: 13,500 ha; Sacca di Bellochio: 223 ha); EEC SPA (Riserva Naturale Sacca di Bellocchio I, II e III, Foce Fiume Reno: 369 ha)

Nature Reserves (*c*.350 ha); no shooting areas (80 per cent of site); Landscape Reserve; Hydrological Reserve

The site extends from the River Reno estuary in the east to Agosta dam in the west; and from Comacchio town in the north, south to the banks of the Reno. The Valli di Comacchio are the remnants of a large complex of lagoons/marshes which were drained for agriculture from 1850 onwards. The 'valli' are three basins of a shallow lagoon, partially separated from each other by sandbanks and small islands. Sacca di Bellochio is part of a complex of saltmarshes and basins bordering the Adriatic. Vegetation includes *Salicornia*, *Sueda*, *Agropyon*, *Phragmites*, and submerged *Chara* and *Ruppia*. Mezzano was reclaimed in the 1960s and is now an important pasture area for wintering geese and the canals are a breeding site for *Himantopus himantopus*. Human activities include fishing and fish-farming, salt production, and tourism. Current problems include suspension of salt production in Saline di Comacchio (affecting breeding *Recurvirostra avosetta* and Laridae), eutrophication, disturbance (including that by birdwatchers and photographers), subsidence which is reducing the number and surface area of islets and foreshores, and unfavourable manipulation of water-levels. There are also proposals to develop fisheries in the saltworks.

Breeding species include *Ardea purpurea*, *Tadorna tadorna*, *Anas querquedula*, *A. clypeata*, *Aythya ferina*, *A. nyroca*, *Himantopus himantopus* (100-200 pairs), *Recurvirostra avosetta* (200 pairs), *Glareola pratincola*, *Charadrius alexandrinus* (100 pairs), *Tringa totanus*, *Larus melanocephalus* (157-179 pairs in 1984-86), *L. genei* (11-13 pairs in 1984-86), *Gelochelidon nilotica* (80-107 pairs in 1984-86), *Sterna sandvicensis* (100+ pairs), *S. hirundo* (1513-1820 pairs in 1984-86), *S. albifrons* (950-1208 pairs in 1984-86), and *Panurus biarmicus*. Important for passage and wintering waterfowl with *Phalacrocorax carbo sinensis* (400), *Egretta alba* (15), *Anser fabalis* (*c*.1000), *A. anser* (100+), *Fulica atra* (10,000+), and *Chlidonias niger* (1000-10,000); total Anatidae exceed 10,000.

045 Valle Santa and Valle Campotto e Bassarone (Emilia Romagna)

44°34'-44°35'N, 11°50'-11°51'E 1624 ha

Includes 2 Ramsar Sites (Valle Santa: 261 ha; Valle Campotto e Bassarone: 1363 ha); part of an EEC SPA (Valle Santa e Valle Campotto: 2000 ha)

Provincial Nature Reserve; hunting prohibited; to be included in proposed Regional Park (Po Delta)

A complex of marshes, reedbeds, riverine woods, and cultivated areas between the Rivers Sillaro and Reno. Two large water bodies, Valle Campotto (*c*.450 ha of open water) and Valle Santa (*c*.250 ha of open water) are separated by relict lowland woods and fields crossed by the River Idice. Bassarone is a newly created small permanent water body. Very large reedbeds and vast expanses of water-lillies (*Nymphaea alba*) occur in the area. The surroundings are mainly cultivated, with maize, wheat, and *Populus* plantations. Human activities include extensive fish-farming, angling (part of the year), and silviculture. Pollution from agricultural chemicals is a problem.

Breeding species include *Phalacrocorax carbo sinensis* (61 pairs in 1987; increase from establishment of colony in 1986 when it had 14 pairs), *Botaurus stellaris* (2 pairs), *Ixobrychus minutus* (50+ pairs), *Nycticorax nycticorax* (600-900 pairs), *Ardeola ralloides* (80-100 pairs), *Egretta garzetta* (150-300 pairs), *Ardea purpurea* (80-100 pairs), *Plegadis falcinellus* (1 pair bred at Valle Santa in 1982), *Porzana porzana*, *Chlidonias hybridus* (150-200 pairs; apparently declining sharply), *Locustella luscinioides* (100+ pairs), and *Panurus biarmicus* (hundreds of pairs). An important area for wintering or passage waterfowl with *Anas clypeata* (hundreds), *A. strepera* (300+), *Larus minutus* (500-1000), and *Chlidonias niger* (several thousands). Wintering species include *Egretta alba* (max. 49 in 1985/87).

046 Punte Alberete and Valle della Canna, Pineta San Vitale (Emilia Romagna)

*c.*44°30'N, 12°15'E *c.*6600 ha

Ramsar Site (Punte Alberete: 480 ha); EEC SPA (Punte Alberete e Valle della Canna: 400 ha)

Bird Sanctuary (222 ha); Nature Reserve (part); hunting prohibited

An extensive inland wetland occupying the flood-plain of the River Po system north of Ravenna. The Ramsar Site includes swampy *Populus/Salix* woodland, vegetated relict sand-dunes, extensive reedbeds, areas of *Carex*, and shallow (max. 2 m) open water with *Nymphaea alba*. Human activities include fishing, reed-cutting, recreation, and hunting.

The area supports a rich community of breeding waterfowl with *Egretta garzetta* (700 pairs), *Nycticorax nycticorax* (300 pairs), *Ardeola ralloides* (50 pairs), *Aythya nyroca* (30 pairs), *Himantopus himantopus* (50 pairs), *Sterna albifrons* (100 pairs), and *Chlidonias hybridus* (100 pairs).

047 Ortazzo and Ortazzino (Emilia Romagna)

*c.*44°22'N, 12°24'E 1500 ha Ramsar Site (Ortazzo: 440 ha)

Nature Reserve; hunting prohibited

The area of the confluence of the Rivers Bevano and Ghiaia, including the river mouths, estuarine lagoons, coastal dunes, and some arable land. A *Pinus* wood has been planted behind the dunes. Human activities include arable and pastoral agriculture, fishing, hunting, and tourism.

Breeding species include *Circus aeruginosus* and *Charadrius alexandrinus* (100 pairs). Large numbers of *Chlidonias niger* (1000) occur on passage.

048 Salina di Cervia (Emilia Romagna)

44°15'N, 12°21'E 1000 ha

Ramsar Site (Salina di Cervia: 785 ha); EEC SPA (Riserva Naturale Salina di Cervia: 765 ha)

Nature Reserve (saltpans)

A grid complex of artificially maintained saltpans, which were formerly coastal lagoons but are now isolated from the sea. The area is bounded by the Girondario and Cirondarie canals, and surrounded by agricultural land.

Breeding species include *Himantopus himantopus* (70 pairs), *Recurvirostra avosetta* (100 pairs), *Charadrius alexandrinus* (100 pairs), and *Sterna albifrons* (230 pairs).

049 Appennine area from the Passo del Cerreto to S. Marcello Pistoiese (Emilia Romagna, Toscana)

44°12'N, 10°27'E 45,000 ha

Includes 5 EEC SPAs (Riserva Naturale Orientata Campolino: 98 ha; Riserva Naturale Abetone: 584 ha; Riserva Naturale Pian degli Ontani: 590 ha; Riserva Naturale Orrido di Botri: 192 ha; Riserva Naturale Pania di Corfino: 135 ha)

Strict Nature Reserve; Nature Reserve; hunting prohibited; partly unprotected

Mountainous area with rivers and streams, woodland and agricultural land. Human activities include arable farming, forestry, stock-farming, fishing, hunting, tourism and leisure.

Breeding species include *Pernis apivorus* (10+ pairs), *Accipiter gentilis*, *Aquila chrysaetos* (3 pairs), *Falco peregrinus* (3-4 pairs), and *Bubo bubo* (3-5 pairs).

050 Lago and Palude di Massaciuccoli (Toscana)

43°51'N, 10°20'E 1700 ha

Included in Regional Park (Migliarino-San Rossore); hunting forbidden in 400 ha

A shallow lake, 4 km from the coast, surrounded by reedbeds of variable width, and a large area of marshland bordering the lake to the north. The marsh includes areas of *Cladietum* and scattered pools and canals. There is a rich aquatic flora. The land adjoining the important bird area includes cultivated reclaimed areas and *Pinus* forest. Human activities include sand excavation and hunting. Illegal hunting (the area has one of the highest densities of hunters in Italy), sand excavation, and pollution of the water by agrochemicals all threaten the site. There are proposals to allow access to hunters to part of the park.

Breeding species include *Botaurus stellaris* (1 pair), *Ixobrychus minutus* (50+ pairs), *Ardeola ralloides* (0-5 pairs), *Ardea purpurea* (5-15 pairs), *Himantopus himantopus* (formerly 100 pairs; now *c.*10 pairs), *Glareola pratincola* (0-2 pairs), *Circus aeruginosus* (1-5 pairs), and *Acrocephalus melanopogon* (hundreds of pairs). A very important area for passage ducks, gulls, and terns in spring with *Anas querquedula* (3000+), *Larus minutus* (5000+), *Sterna albifrons* (5000+), *Chlidonias hybridus* (100+), *C. niger* (10,000+), and *C. leucopterus* (500+). The area's importance for wintering wildfowl has been undermined due to the intensity of shooting. *Fulica atra* (av. 1000 birds) and *Remiz pendulinus* are amongst the species occurring in winter.

051 Lame di San Rossore e Migliarino; estuaries of Fiume Arno and Fiume Serchio (Toscana)

43°46'N, 10°16'E *c.*600 ha

Included in Regional Park (Migliarino-San Rossore)

A complex of open and wooded coastal marshes, the estuaries of two large rivers, and the adjacent shallow sea area. There are dunes between the marshes and the sea, and extensive arable/pasture areas at San Rossore. Pollution of the rivers is a very serious problem and the area is disturbed by hunters shooting from boats on the sea.

Breeding species include *Burhinus oedicnemus* (5-15 pairs). An important area for passage waterfowl with *Plegadis falcinellus* (max. 30), *Phoenicopterus ruber* (max. 50), *Anser fabalis* (max. 50), *A. anser* (max. 300), *Anas querquedula* (max. 200), *Aythya nyroca* (max. 30), *Grus grus* (max. of 50 per day), *Chlidonias niger* (5000+), and *C. leucopterus* (200+). *Phalacrocorax carbo sinensis* (150), *Anser anser* (max. 20), *Anas strepera* (max. 200), *A. crecca* (av. 4000; max. 6000), and *Melanitta fusca* (max. 150) occur in winter.

052 Palude di Fucecchio (Toscana)

43°46'N, 10°47'E 2500 ha

Proposed Nature Reserve; LIPU Reserve (50 ha); hunting prohibited; partly unprotected

Marsh with reeds and areas of open water, scattered trees and agricultural land. Human activities include arable farming (drier areas of marsh are cultivated in late spring and summer), fishing, and extraction of water for agricultural use. Problems include hunting, pollution, and burning of reeds.

Breeding species include *Nycticorax nycticorax* (150 pairs), *Ardeola ralloides* (5 pairs), and *Egretta garzetta* (20 pairs). Other nesting species include *Botaurus stellaris*, *Ardea purpurea*, *Circus aeruginosus*, and *Locustella luscinioides*. *Circus aeruginosus* also occurs in winter and *Grus grus* occurs on passage (max. 14 in March 1986).

053 Ponte Buriano – Lago della Penna (River Arno) (Toscana)

43°31'N, 11°45'E 600 ha

Proposed Nature Reserve; hunting prohibited; unprotected

Section of the River Arno, with running and fresh standing water, *Phragmites* beds, and broadleaved deciduous woodland. Human activities include fishing, hunting, and electricity generation. Current problems include hunting, destruction of the reedbeds, reclamation of marshy areas, pollution, and disturbance by fishermen.

Breeding species include *Ardea purpurea* (1 pair) and *Milvus migrans* (2 pairs). *Grus grus* (max. 18 in March 1986) and Anatidae occur on passage.

054 Palude di Bolgheri-Renaione (Toscana)

43°14'N, 10°33'E 562 ha Ramsar Site

Part of Bolgheri Wildlife Refuge (22,000 ha, 500 ha of which is managed by WWF and surrounding area managed as hunting reserves)

An area of coastal marshland, behind a belt of sand-dunes, with scattered ponds, drainage canals, reedbeds and *Juncus* patches. The dunes are covered with Mediterranean maquis. The surroundings include arable land. The Renaione area is managed as a Nature Reserve. Regulation of the water level, for agricultural needs, affects the site adversely. There were recent proposals to construct a tourist harbour at the mouth of the main drainage canal and reclaim marshes outside of the reserve area.

Breeding species include *Podiceps nigricollis* (bred in 1982), *Ardea purpurea*, and *Himantopus himantopus*. Important for passage *Anas querquedula* (daily max. 200), also *Anser fabalis* (max. 50), and *A. anser* (max. 150). Wintering wildfowl include *Anas penelope* (max. 700) and *A. strepera* (max. 50).

055 Bacino del Fiume Cecina and area of Volterra (Toscana)

43°23'N, 10°47'E 58,800 ha

Protected landscape; protected forest area; some other national protection; hunting prohibited; partly unprotected

Cliffs and exposed rock areas, rivers and streams, woodland, grasslands, and agricultural land. Human activities include arable farming, forestry, stock-farming, hunting, and human habitation.

Breeding species include *Pernis apivorus*, *Circaetus gallicus* (5-6 pairs), *Circus pygargus* (3-4 pairs), *Falco biarmicus*, and *Charadrius dubius* (10-15 pairs).

056 Arcipelago Toscano (including Isole Capraia, Giglio, Montecristo, d'Elba, and Palmaiola (Toscana)

*c.*42°48'N, 10°20'E

Isola di Montecristo is a Mediterranean Specially Protected Area

Proposed National Park (Isola di Capraia); Nature Reserve (Isola di Montecristo); unprotected; hunting prohibited (Isola di Montecristo)

Islands with sclerophyllous scrub, garigue, maquis, and sea cliffs, and some have evergreen woodland, grassland, and agricultural land. Human activities include arable and stock-farming, fishing, hunting, boating, tourism and leisure. The seabird colonies suffer heavy disturbance from tourists during late spring and summer; there is also some hunting, burning of vegetation, and housing construction on some islands.

Breeding species include *Puffinus puffinus*, *Calonectris diomedea*, *Phalacrocorax aristotelis* (4-10 pairs), *Falco peregrinus* (15-20 pairs), *Larus audouinii* (50-120 pairs), *Sylvia sarda*, *S. conspicillata*, and *S. undata*. *Pernis apivorus*, *Hieraaetus pennatus*, *H. fasciatus*, and *Pandion haliaetus* occur on passage, and some of the islands are important resting areas for migrating passerines.

057 Valle del Farma (Toscana)

43°04'N, 11°04'E 35,000 ha

Protected forest area; partly unprotected

Large hilly area with woodland, important for birds of prey, and threatened by development to encourage tourism. Human activities include arable farming, forestry, stock-farming, and hunting.

Breeding species include *Pernis apivorus* (2-3 pairs), *Milvus migrans* (6-8 pairs), *M. milvus* (3-4 pairs), *Circaetus gallicus* (4-6 pairs), *Circus pygargus* (5-8 pairs), *Falco biarmicus* (2 pairs), *Bubo bubo* (1-2 pairs), and *Alcedo atthis* (5-7 pairs).

058 Laghi di Montepulciano e Chiusi (Toscana)

43°01'N, 11°58'E 1000 ha

Proposed Natural Park; unprotected

Lakes, marshy areas with *Phragmites*, agricultural land, and broadleaved deciduous woodland. Human activities include arable farming, fishing, and extraction of water for agricultural use. Problems include hunting, pollution, and burning of reedbeds.

Breeding species include *Nycticorax nycticorax* (20 pairs), *Ardeola ralloides*, *Egretta garzetta* (10 pairs), *Ardea purpurea* (2-5 pairs), *Milvus migrans* (2-4 pairs), *Falco subbuteo*, and *Panurus biarmicus*. *Circus aeruginosus* and *Panurus biarmicus* occur in winter, and *Pandion haliaetus* is a regular passage migrant.

059 Palude Diaccia-Botrona (Palude di Castiglione della Pescaia) (Toscana)

42°46'N, 10°55'E 600 ha

Includes one small WWF Refuge (Le Marze); hunting prohibited in part of the area

An area of marshland covered by vast reedbeds with a few ponds and canals. A *Pinus* forest separates the marsh from the sea, and there are extensive areas of cultivated fields on reclaimed land on the site's southern and eastern sides. Human activities include hunting and fish-farming. The former activity causes considerable disturbance, whilst intensification of fish-farming could destroy important habitats.

Breeding species include *Botaurus stellaris* (5-6 pairs), *Egretta garzetta* (20 pairs), *Ardea cinerea* (10-20 pairs), *A. purpurea*, *Circus aeruginosus* (5+ pairs), *Himantopus himantopus*, *Coracias garrulus*, and *Clamator glandarius* (one of the few Italian sites). A very large cormorant and heron colony was destroyed by tree-cutting some 40 years ago and the herons mentioned above occupy a relict colony in reedbeds. *Anas querquedula* occurs on passage (3000+ in spring; up to 350 shot each season). *Numenius tenuirostris* recently occurred on passage. Wintering species include *Egretta alba* (av. 3), *Anas crecca* (max. 1000), *A. acuta* (max. 80), and *A. clypeata* (max. 200).

060 Stagni della Trappola and Ombrone estuary (Toscana)

42°38'N, 11°00'E 700 ha

Included in an EEC SPA (Parco Naturale della Maremma: 9530 ha); Mediterranean Specially Protected Area

Included in Natural Park (Parco Naturale della Maremma); hunting prohibited

La Trappola is a large brackish marsh with very little vegetation (mainly *Salicornia*), bordered by the sea and the River Ombrone. There are also smaller *Juncus* marshes south of the river, scattered among patches of *Pinus pinea*. Human activities include grazing of horses and cattle, and controlled tourism. Overgrazing and beach erosion are serious problems. Pollution of the river has not yet been fully evaluated.

Breeding species include *Burhinus oedicnemus* (5-10 pairs), *Falco subbuteo*, *F. peregrinus*, *Coracias garrulus*, and *Merops apiaster*. *Anser anser* (max. 100), *Anas penelope* (av. 2500), *A. strepera* (av. 70), *A. crecca* (av. 1500), and *A. clypeata* (av. 500) occur in winter, with *A. querquedula* (3000+ in a season; 200 in one day) and *Limosa limosa* (max. 700 daily) amongst the species occurring on migration.

061 Laguna di Orbetello and Lago di Burano (Toscana)

42°22'-42°27'N, 11°15'-11°23'E *c.*4200 ha

Includes 2 Ramsar Sites (Laguna di Orbetello: 887 ha; Lago di Burano: 410 ha); includes 2 EEC SPAs (Laguna di Orbetello: 887 ha; Riserva Naturale di Duna Feniglia: 474 ha); includes 2 Mediterranean Specially Protected Areas (Orbetello and Feniglia, Burano)

WWF Refuges (Laguna di Ponente and Lago di Burano)

The Laguna di Orbetello is divided into two separate areas (Laguna di Levante and Laguna di Ponente) by a dam and by Orbetello town. Two long, forested sandbars separate the lagoons from the sea; there are two narrow channels allowing exchange of water between the lagoons and the sea. Lago di Burano is a freshwater lake, parallel to the coast, and situated south-east of the Laguna di Orbetello. Human activities include fishing, cultivation and industry (chemical factories own parts of the shore of the Laguna di Orbetello). Illegal shooting (especially of cormorants), urbanisation, and expansion of fish-farming are problems occurring at the site.

Breeding species include *Egretta garzetta* (colony established 1988), *Himantopus himantopus* (formerly 50+ pairs; only a few unsuccessful pairs since 1984), *Burhinus oedicnemus* (5-8 pairs), *Clamator glandarius* (irregular), and *Merops apiaster* (large colonies). *Phoenicopterus ruber* (max. 150) is present all year. *Egretta garzetta* (daily max. 800+ in late summer), *Anas querquedula* (seasonal total 3000+), *Limosa limosa* (daily max. 600+), and *Chlidonias niger* (seasonal total 2000+) occur on passage. *Numenius tenuirostris* has also been recorded on passage (one certain record in recent years). Wintering waterfowl include *Podiceps cristatus* (max. 400), *P. nigricollis* (500+), *Phalacrocorax carbo sinensis* (1200), *Egretta garzetta* (max. 100), *E. alba* (max. 15), *Ardea cinerea* (max. 200), *Platalea leucorodia* (max. 10), *Anas crecca* (av. 1500), *A. acuta* (av. 1200), *A. penelope* (av. 500), *A. clypeata* (av. 500), *Aythya ferina* (max. 1600), and *A. nyroca* (av. 15).

062 Lago Trasimeno (Umbria)

43°04'-43°12'N, 12°01'-12°11'E 29,500 ha

Unprotected

The largest lake of peninsular Italy and the fourth largest in the country. The lake is located inland, has three islands and is fringed by an almost continuous belt of reeds of variable width. The south-east corner has the largest reedbeds and numerous ponds and ditches, whilst the south-western part of the lake contains reedbeds with some densely wooded areas. Human activities include hunting, fishing, and agriculture; one of the islands is inhabited. Water pollution derived from agrochemicals, and disturbance from hunters and tourists are the major problems at the lake.

Breeding species include *Podiceps cristatus* (60+ pairs in 1986), *Panurus biarmicus*, and *Remiz pendulinus*. *Chlidonias niger* (seasonal total 1000+) and small numbers of waders occur on passage. High levels of hunting mean that the area is not as important for wintering waterfowl as formerly. Although numbers of grebes (600 *Podiceps cristatus* and 150 *P. nigricollis* in Jan. 1986) appear less affected by hunting disturbance, numbers of Anatidae have decreased markedly and *Fulica atra* (av. 1000; max. 3000) shows considerable decline from former levels (e.g. Jan. av. 18,000).

063 Monti Sibillini, Monte Fema, and Monte Cavallo (Umbria, Marche)

42°56'N, 13°10'E 44,400 ha

Protected landscape; protected forest area; some other national protection; hunting prohibited; partly unprotected

A mountainous area with important woodland. Threatened by road building, intensive forestry, and damage around ski-centres. Human activities include arable farming, forestry, stock-farming, fishing, hunting, tourism and leisure, and there are residential areas.

Breeding species include *Aquila chrysaetos* (2 pairs), *Falco peregrinus* (2-3 pairs), *Alectoris graeca*, *Bubo bubo* (3-4 pairs), *Pyrrhocorax pyrrhocorax* (max. 100 pairs), and possibly *Dendrocopos leucotos*.

064 Monti della Laga (Umbria)

42°40'N, 13°26'E 58,500 ha

Protected landscape; protected forest area; some other national protection; partly unprotected

Mountainous area with broadleaved deciduous woodland, native coniferous woodland, agricultural land and grassland. Human activities include arable farming, forestry, stock-farming, fishing, hunting, tourism and leisure, and there are residential areas. The site is threatened by the building of roads and houses, and hunting is uncontrolled.

Breeding species include *Falco peregrinus* (2-3 pairs), *Alectoris graeca*, *Bubo bubo* (2 pairs), and *Pyrrhocorax pyrrhocorax* (10-100 pairs). *Aquila chrysaetos* possibly breeds.

065 Lago di Alviano (Umbria, Lazio)

42°34'N, 12°15'E 900 ha

Protected by local authority legislation

A lake with associated marshland surrounded by cultivated areas. Human activities include arable and stock-farming and fishing.

Breeding species include *Ixobrychus minutus*, *Nycticorax nycticorax* (5-6 pairs), *Ardea purpurea* (5-6 pairs), *Anas querquedula* (15 pairs), *Milvus migrans*, *Circus aeruginosus* (1-2 pairs), *Alcedo atthis* (10-15 pairs), *Locustella luscinioides*, and *Acrocephalus melanopogon*. *Anas querquedula* (3000), *Aythya nyroca*, and *Pandion haliaetus* (10-15) occur on passage, whilst wintering waterfowl include *Egretta alba* (2-3), *A. penelope* (500), *A. crecca* (2000), *Aythya ferina* (1000+), and *Fulica atra* (5000).

066 Fiume Fiora (Lazio)

42°30'N, 11°34'E 9000 ha

Nature Reserve

Rocky areas, rivers and streams, and woodland. Human activities include forestry, stock-farming, and fishing.

Breeding species include *Pernis apivorus* (2-5 pairs), *Milvus migrans* (5 pairs), *Circaetus gallicus* (2 pairs), *Falco biarmicus* (1 pair), *Bubo bubo*, *Alcedo atthis*, and *Coracias garrulus*.

067 Monti Reatini and Val Nerina (Umbria, Lazio)

42°37'N, 12°57'E 88,600 ha

Protected forest area; some other national protection; hunting prohibited; partly unprotected

A large mountainous area with broadleaved deciduous woodland, agricultural land, and inland cliffs. Human activities include arable farming, forestry, stock-farming, fishing, hunting, tourism and leisure, and there are residential areas. The site is threatened by the development of skiing facilities.

Breeding species include *Aquila chrysaetos* (2 pairs), *Falco peregrinus* (7-8 pairs), *Alectoris graeca*, *Bubo bubo* (2-3 pairs), and *Pyrrhocorax pyrrhocorax*.

068 Lago Lungo and Lago di Pipa Sottile (Lazio)

42°28'N, 11°50'E 2400 ha

Unprotected

An area containing freshwater lakes, marshes, and agricultural land. Human activities include arable cultivation, stock-raising, fishing, and hunting.

Breeding species include *Ixobrychus minutus*, *Ardea purpurea* (5-6 pairs), *Circus aeruginosus* (1 pair), *C. pygargus* (1-2 pairs), and *Alcedo atthis* (2-3 pairs).

069 Lago di Vico (Lazio)

42°20'N, 12°10'E 5000 ha EEC SPA (Riserva Naturale Lago di Vico: 3300 ha)

Hunting prohibited; otherwise unprotected

A freshwater lake with associated marshes, woodland, and agriculture land. Human activities include arable and stock-farming, forestry, hunting, fishing, boating, and tourism.

Breeding species include *Podiceps cristatus* (30-40 pairs), *Ixobrychus minutus*, *Milvus migrans* (2 pairs), *Circus aeruginosus* (1-2 pairs), *Alcedo atthis* (3 pairs), and possibly

Asio flammeus. *Netta rufina* (10), *Aythya ferina* (1000), and *Fulica atra* (5000) occur in winter.

070 Lago di Bracciano and Lago di Matignano (Lazio)

42°08'N, 12°17'E 14,000 ha

Hunting prohibited; otherwise unprotected

An area of lakes with adjacent woodland and agricultural land. Human activities include cultivation, stock-rearing, fishing, hunting, and boating.

Breeding species include *Ixobrychus minutus* and *Milvus migrans* (40 pairs). *Netta rufina* and *Fulica atra* (3000) occur in winter.

071 Monti Lucretili (Lazio)

42°06'N, 12°52'E 21,000 ha EEC SPA (Rifugio Faunistico Monte Pellecchia: 355 ha)

Some national protection; hunting prohibited; partly unprotected

Mountainous area with rivers and streams, woodland, and agricultural land. Human activities include arable farming, forestry, stock-farming, hunting, and human habitation.

Breeding species include *Pernis apivorus* (2-3 pairs), *Milvus migrans* (1-2 pairs), *Buteo buteo*, *Aquila chrysaetos* (1 pair), *Falco peregrinus* (2 pairs), and *Bubo bubo*.

072 Monti della Tolfa (Lazio)

42°08'N, 12°04'E 75,000 ha

Protected forest area; some national protection; partly unprotected

Woodland and agricultural land. Human activities include forestry, stock-farming, hunting, and there are residential areas. The area is threatened by the building of houses and road construction.

Breeding species include *Pernis apivorus* (30 pairs), *Milvus migrans* (20-30 pairs), *M. milvus* (4-5 pairs), *Circaetus gallicus* (6-8 pairs), *Circus pygargus* (2-5 pairs), *Falco biarmicus* (2-3 pairs), *Burhinus oedicnemus*, *Alcedo atthis* (2-5 pairs), and *Coracias garrulus*.

073 Monti Ernici and Simbruini (Lazio, Abruzzo)

41°53'N, 13°19'E 74,000 ha

National Park; protected forest area; some other national protection; hunting prohibited; partly unprotected

A mountainous area with rivers and streams, broadleaved deciduous woodland, grasslands, and agricultural land. Human activities include arable farming, forestry, stock-farming, fishing, hunting, tourism and leisure, and there are residential areas. Threatened by road building and the development of skiing facilities.

Breeding species include *Aquila chrysaetos* (3 pairs), *Falco peregrinus* (4-5 pairs), *Alectoris graeca*, *Bubo bubo* (2-3 pairs), probably *Dendrocopos leucotos*, and *Pyrrhocorax pyrrhocorax*.

074 Monti Lepini (Lazio)

41°36'N, 13°05'E 49,600 ha

Protected forest area; some other national protection; hunting prohibited; partly unprotected

Mountain area with broadleaved deciduous woodland and agricultural land. Human activities include arable farming, forestry, stock-farming, hunting, and there are residential areas. The building of roads, hunting and intensive forestry threaten the area.

Breeding species include *Circaetus gallicus* (2 pairs), *Falco biarmicus* (3-4 pairs), *F. peregrinus* (4-5 pairs), *Bubo bubo* (1-2 pairs), and *Coracias garrulus*. *Neophron percnopterus* (1-2) also occurs but does not breed.

075 Laghi Pontini (I Fogliano, Monaci, Caprolace, Sabaudia) (Lazio)

41°15'-41°24'N, 12°52'-13°02'E *c.*8000 ha

Includes 4 Ramsar Sites (Lago di Fogliano: 395 ha; Lago di Monaci: 94 ha; Lago di Caprolace; 229 ha; Lago di Sabaudia: 1474); included in an EEC SPA (Parco Nazionale del Circeo: 8400 ha); Mediterranean Specially Protected Area

Included in National Park (Parco Nazionale del Circeo)

A group of lakes lying along the coast of Lazio between Roma and Napoli. The lakes are the remains of the reclaimed 'Paludi Pontine', which covered a much larger area (30,000+ ha). All of the lakes (except Monaci) are connected to the sea by narrow channels. The associated marshes and wet meadows/fields dry out in summer. Vegetation includes *Potamogeton*, *Cyperus*, *Carex*, and *Juncus*. There is an important area of seasonally flooded lowland forest (*Quercus*, *Populus*, *Alnus*, *Fraxinus*) adjacent to Lago di Sabaudia. Human activities include fish-farming and cattle-raising. The area is threatened by tourism, house construction, pollution (especially of Lago Monaci), increasing salinity, and poaching.

Breeding species include *Falco peregrinus* and *Coracias garrulus*. There is a large spring passage of *Anas querquedula* and *Philomachus pugnax*. Wintering waterfowl (1983-87) include *Gavia arctica* (av. 20), *Phalacrocorax carbo sinensis* (1500), *Egretta garzetta* (av. 30), *E. alba* (5-10), *Ardea cinerea* (av. 50), *Plegadis falcinellus*, *Platalea leucorodia*, *Anas penelope* (av. 2200), *A. strepera* (max. 130), *A. crecca* (av. 1100), *Aythya ferina* (av. 950), and *A. nyroca* (0-10).

076 Arcipelago Ponziano (Isole Ventotene, Zannone, Ponza and Palmarola) (Lazio)

40°54'N, 12°59'E 108,000 ha

Isole Zannone is included in a National Park (Circeo); protected landscape; hunting prohibited; largely unprotected

Archipelago of islands, islets and rock stacks with sclerophyllous scrub, garigue and maquis. Human activities include stock-farming, fishing, hunting, boating, tourism and leisure. There is intense hunting and, in spring, bird-trapping.

Breeding species include *Calonectris diomedea*, *Puffinus puffinus*, and *Falco peregrinus* (10-15 pairs). Large numbers of birds also stop on migration (*Sylvia communis*, *S. borin*, *S. cantillans*, *Phylloscopus* spp., and *Luscinia megarhynchos* are the commonest species in spring).

077 Gran Sasso d'Italia (Abruzzo)

42°28'N, 13°33'E 42,400 ha Biogenetic Reserve

Protected forest area; some other national protection; hunting prohibited; partly unprotected

A mountainous area with alpine meadows, streams and rivers, woodland, grasslands, agricultural land, exposed bedrock, and inland cliffs. Human activities include arable farming, forestry, stock-farming, fishing, hunting, tourism and leisure, and there are residential areas. The area is threatened by development for winter sports, and hunting is uncontrolled.

Breeding species include *Aquila chrysaetos* (1-2 pairs), *Falco biarmicus* (1 pair), *F. peregrinus* (5 pairs), *Alectoris graeca*, and *Pyrrhocorax pyrrhocorax*.

078 Monti del Cigolano, Gole di Androdoco, Monte Giano, Monte Cabbia, Val Malito and Piano di Rascino (Abruzzo, Lazio)

42°20'N, 13°11'E 42,900 ha

Protected forest area; some national protection; partly unprotected

A mountainous area with extensive broadleaved deciduous woodland and areas of exposed bedrock, inland cliffs, rivers and streams, agricultural land, heath and scrub, and grasslands. Human activities include arable farming, forestry, stock-farming, fishing, hunting, tourism and leisure. The area is threatened by road building and increasing tourism.

Breeding species include *Aquila chrysaetos* (2 pairs), *Falco peregrinus* (6-7 pairs), *Bubo bubo* (3-4 pairs), and possibly *Dendrocopos leucotos*.

079 Area of Monte Sirente, Monte Velino and Montagne della Duchessa (Abruzzo)

42°11'N, 13°27'E 46,800 ha EEC SPA (Riserva Naturale del Monte Velino: 3550 ha)

Nature Reserve; protected forest area; some other national protection; hunting prohibited; partly unprotected

A mountainous area with rivers and streams, broadleaved deciduous woodland, agricultural land, scree, exposed bedrock, inland cliffs, and grasslands. Human activities include arable farming, forestry, stock-farming, fishing, hunting, tourism and leisure, and there are residential areas. Threatened by the building of roads and houses, and the development of skiing facilities.

Breeding species include *Aquila chrysaetos* (2 pairs), *Falco biarmicus* (2 pairs), *F. peregrinus* (4 pairs), *Alectoris graeca*, *Bubo bubo* (1-2 pairs), and *Pyrrhocorax pyrrhocorax*.

080 Massiccio della Maiella, Montagne del Morrone and Monti Pizi (Abruzzo)

42°10'N, 14°12'E 75,000 ha

EEC SPA (Riserva Naturale della Maiella, with Riserva Naturale Quarto Santa Chaira [485 ha]: 9973 ha)

Nature Reserve; protected landscape; hunting prohibited; partly unprotected

A mountainous area with rivers, streams, mixed woodland, agricultural land, and grasslands. Human activities include arable farming, forestry, stock-farming, fishing, hunting, tourism and leisure, and there are residential areas.

Breeding species include *Aquila chrysaetos* (3-4 pairs), *Falco biarmicus* (4 pairs), *F. peregrinus* (10 pairs), *Alectoris graeca*, *Charadrius morinellus* (5 pairs), *Bubo bubo* (2-3 pairs), and *Pyrrhocorax pyrrhocorax* (200 pairs).

081 Mountains and hills between Capracotta and Rosello (Abruzzo, Molise)

41°48'N, 14°15'E 24,000 ha

Nature Reserve; protected forest area; some other national protection; partly unprotected

A mountainous area with rivers and streams, broadleaved deciduous woodland, agricultural land, heath, and scrub. Human activities include arable farming, forestry, stock-farming, and hunting, and there are residential areas.

Breeding species include *Pernis apivorus*, *Milvus migrans* (6-8 pairs), *M. milvus* (4-5 pairs), *Falco biarmicus* (3 pairs), *F. peregrinus* (5 pairs), and possibly *Aquila chrysaetos*.

082 Parco Nazionale d'Abruzzo, Monte Greco and surrounding area (Abruzzo, Lazio, Molise)

41°45'N, 13°51'E 78,000 ha

EEC SPA (Parco Nazionale d'Abruzzo with Riserve Naturali Colle di Licco e Feudo Intramonti: 40,000 ha)

Strict Nature Reserve; National Park (10,000 ha included in Parco Nazionale d'Abruzzo); protected forest area; some other national protection; hunting prohibited; partly unprotected

A mountainous area with rivers and streams, broadleaved deciduous woodland, mixed woodland, agricultural land, exposed bedrock, inland cliffs, and grasslands. Human activities include arable farming, forestry, stock-farming, fishing, hunting, tourism and leisure, and there are residential areas. Threatened by increased tourism and associated development.

Breeding species include *Aquila chrysaetos* (2 pairs), *Falco peregrinus* (4-5 pairs), *Alectoris graeca*, *Bubo bubo* (3-4 pairs), *Alcedo atthis* (3-4 pairs), *Dendrocopos medius*, *D. leucotos* (20-30 pairs), and *Pyrrhocorax pyrrhocorax*.

083 Fiume Biferno and surrounding hills between Ponte Morgia Schiavone and La Strada Larino-Guglionesi (Molise)

41°46'N, 14°47'E 28,000 ha

Protected forest area; some other national protection; partly unprotected

Rivers and streams, woodland, and agricultural land. Human activities include arable farming, forestry, stock-farming, fishing, hunting, and human habitation.

Breeding species includes *Pernis apivorus*, *Milvus migrans* (7-8 pairs), *M. milvus* (4-5 pairs), *Falco peregrinus* (1 pair), and *F. biarmicus*.

084 Monti del Matese (Campania, Abruzzo)

41°27'N, 14°25'E 34,000 ha

Protected landscape; protected forest area; some other national protection; partly unprotected

A mountainous area with rivers and streams, broadleaved deciduous woodland, grasslands, agricultural land, exposed bedrock, and inland cliffs. Human activities include arable farming, forestry, stock-farming, fishing, hunting, tourism and leisure. Threatened by intensive forestry, road construction, and construction of winter sports facilities.

Breeding species include *Pernis apivorus* (2-3 pairs), *Milvus migrans* (2-3 pairs), *M. milvus* (3 pairs), *Aquila chrysaetos* (2 pairs), *Falco peregrinus* (4-5 pairs), *Alectoris graeca*, *Bubo bubo* (1-2 pairs), and *Pyrrhocorax pyrrhocorax*.

085 Isola di Capri (Campania)

40°33'N, 14°15'E 1036 ha

Unprotected

An island with rocky cliffs, sclerophyllous scrub, and maquis. Current problems include heavy shooting and illegal trapping of birds, burning of vegetation, and disturbance from tourists.

Breeding species include *Falco peregrinus*. Important passage site for migrants, particularly passerines. The commonest species captured during a 45-day ringing period in 1987 were *Sylvia borin*, *S. communis*, *Hippolais icterina*, *Phylloscopus trochilus*, *P. sibilatrix*, *Muscicapa striata*, *Ficedula hypoleuca*, *Saxicola rubetra*, and *Oenanthe oenanthe*.

086 Monte Terminio (Campania)

40°51'N, 14°56'E 8000 ha

Unprotected

A mountainous area with rivers and streams, woodland, scrub, grasslands, and agricultural land. Human activities include forestry, stock-farming, and hunting. Threatened by road building and intensive forestry.

Breeding species include *Milvus migrans* (3-4 pairs), *M. milvus* (2 pairs), *Falco peregrinus* (2 pairs), *Bubo bubo* (2 pairs), and *Dryocopus martius*.

087 Monte Polveracchio (Campania)

40°43'N, 15°07'E 30,000 ha

Protected forest area; some national protection; partly unprotected

A mountainous area with rivers and streams, broadleaved deciduous woodland, and agricultural land. Human activities include arable farming, forestry, stock-farming, and hunting. Threatened by the building of roads and tourism.

Breeding species include *Milvus migrans* (5-8 pairs) and *Falco peregrinus* (3-4 pairs).

088 Monti Alburni (Campania)

40°31'N, 15°19'E 16,000 ha

Unprotected

A mountainous area with broadleaved deciduous woodland, agricultural land, and grasslands. Human activities include arable farming, forestry, stock-farming, hunting, and there are residential areas. Threatened by the development of tourism.

Breeding species include *Falco biarmicus* (1 pair), *F. peregrinus* (3 pairs), and *Dryocopus martius*.

089 Gole del Fiume Calore (Campania)

40°19'N, 15°24'E 1650 ha

Unprotected

A river gorge with woodland and rocky areas. Human activities include arable farming, forestry, fishing, and hunting.

Breeding species include *Milvus milvus* (2 pairs), *Accipiter gentilis* (1 pair), *Falco biarmicus* (1 pair), *F. peregrinus* (1 pair), *Bubo bubo*, *Caprimulgus europaeus*, *Alcedo atthis*, and *Coracias garrulus*.

090 Monte Cervati and Monte Sacro (Campania)

40°17'N, 15°29'E 51,000 ha

Protected forest area; some national protection; partly unprotected

A mountainous area with rivers and streams, broadleaved deciduous woodland, and agricultural land. Human activities include arable farming, forestry, stock-farming, hunting, and there are residential areas. Threatened by intensive forestry, road construction and the development of tourism.

Breeding species include *Milvus migrans* (10 pairs), *M. milvus* (10 pairs), *Aquila chrysaetos* (1 pair), *Falco biarmicus*, *F. peregrinus* (5 pairs), *Alectoris graeca*, *Bubo bubo* (1 pair), *Dryocopus martius*, and *Pyrrhocorax pyrrhocorax*.

091 Coast from Marina di Camerota to Policastro Bussentino (Campania)

40°00'N, 15°26'E 2200 ha

Protected monument or natural feature; protected landscape; partly unprotected

Rocky coastline with scrub, grasslands, and agricultural land. Human activities include arable farming, forestry, stock-farming, fishing, and hunting.

Breeding species include *Falco peregrinus* (4 pairs).

092 Isole Tremiti (Puglia)

42°07'N, 15°30'E 360 ha

Unprotected

Islets and rock stacks, scrub, grasslands, and agricultural land. Human activities include arable farming, fishing, hunting, boating, tourism and leisure. Threatened by the development of tourism and illegal hunting.

Breeding species include *Calonectris diomedea*, *Puffinus puffinus*, and *Falco peregrinus* (2-3 pairs).

093 Laghi di Lesina e Varano (Puglia)

41°50'-41°55'N, 15°19'-15°34'E *c*.11,200 ha

EEC SPA (eastern part of Riserva Naturale Lago di Lesina: 930 ha)

Nature Reserve (eastern part of Lesina: 930 ha); remainder unprotected

Two very large, adjacent coastal lakes, both connected to the sea by a few channels. Lesina is relatively narrow, shallow and parallel to the coast; its shores are reed-fringed. Varano is deeper, the banks are mostly artificial (with virtually no reedbeds) and there are steep hills bordering its southern shore. The area immediately offshore is also of importance. There are cultivated fields to the east of Varano and to the south-west of Lesina. Human activities include fishing, hunting and tourism. Holiday housing development (unauthorised) is a problem at Lesina. Hunting is very intense and at Varano flocks of birds are frequently chased by powerful motor-boats.

Wintering waterfowl are severely affected by hunting but the area is nevertheless one of the more important waterfowl sites in Italy with *Phalacrocorax carbo sinensis* (900 in Jan. 1987), *Anas penelope* (2000 in 1986), *A. clypeata* (500 in 1986), *Aythya ferina* (3000+ in 1986), *Mergus serrator* (300), and *Fulica atra* (20,000 in 1986).

094 Promontorio del Gargano (Puglia)

41°50'N, 16°01'E 70,000 ha

Includes 5 EEC SPAs (Riserva Naturale Biogenetica Foresta: 339 ha; Riserva Naturale Biogenetica Ischitella e Carpino: 299 ha; Riserva Naturale Biogenetica Monte Barone: 124 ha; Riserva Naturale Orientata Falascone: 48 ha; Riserva Naturale Integrale Sfilzi: 56 ha)

Nature Reserve; protected landscape; protected forest area; some other national protection; hunting prohibited; partly unprotected

A headland with sea cliffs, agricultural land, broadleaved deciduous woodland, rivers and streams, sclerophyllous scrub, garigue, maquis, coastal sand-dunes, sand beaches, native coniferous woodland, exposed bedrock, and inland cliffs. Human activities include arable farming, forestry, stock-farming, fishing, hunting, tourism and leisure, and there are residential areas. Threatened by road building, intensification of forestry and house building, and illegal hunting occurs.

Breeding species include *Neophron percnopterus* (recent observations), *Pernis apivorus* (5-10 pairs), *Milvus migrans* (10-15 pairs), *M. milvus* (4-5 pairs), *Circaetus gallicus* (3-4 pairs), *Falco peregrinus* (5-10 pairs), *Bubo bubo* (7-8 pairs), *Coracias garrulus*, *Dendrocopos medius*, *D. leucotos*, *Sylvia undata*, and *Lanius minor*.

095 Wetlands along Golfo di Manfredonia (Puglia)

For ease of analysis, information on this area is presented as three subsites:

095-1 Paludi del Candelaro and Cervaro (including Frattarolo and Daunia Risi) (Puglia)

41°32'-41°35'N, 15°50'-15°53'E *c*.1000 ha

EEC SPA (Riserva Naturale Palude di Frattarolo: 257 ha)

Natural Reserve (Frattarolo: 257 ha); hunting reserve (Daunia Risi)

The remains of formerly large wetland areas (Lago Salso and Lago di Diana), now partly drained and partly used as fish-ponds. There are extensive areas of *Salicornia* which dry out in summer (at Frattarolo) and huge reedbeds (Daunia Risi). Human activities include fish-farming, agriculture, and water storage for irrigation. There are proposals to develop Daunia Risi that are likely to affect the site adversely.

Breeding species (in 1986) include *Botaurus stellaris* (1-2 pairs), *Nycticorax nycticorax* (20-25 pairs), *Egretta garzetta* (40 pairs), *Ardeola ralloides* (10-15 pairs), *Ardea purpurea* (10-15 pairs), *Plegadis falcinellus* (1-5 pairs in recent years), and *Panurus biarmicus* (very large numbers). *Plegadis falcinellus*, *Platalea leucorodia*, *Grus grus,* and

Gelochelidon nilotica occur on passage. Waterfowl occurring in winter (1981 information) include *Anas strepera* (300), *A. crecca* (3000), and *Fulica atra* (5000).

095-2 Carapelle and San Floriano (Puglia)

*c.*41°30'N, 15°55'E *c.*800 ha

Private hunting reserves; otherwise unprotected

A complex of wetlands, used for hunting and fish-farming, scattered over an extensive area of (reclaimed) arable land. The most important wetlands are Carapelle and San Floriano. There are large tracts of grassland and saltmarsh (with *Salicornia/Salsola* and flooded only in winter) with some small patches of *Phragmites*. Hunting pressure and water pollution may affect the area adversely.

An important wintering area for waterfowl, with *Phalacrocorax carbo sinensis* (max. 100), *Anas penelope* (5,000-20,000), *A. acuta* (200-500), *A. clypeata* (500+), and *Fulica atra* (1000-2000).

095-3 Saline di Margherita di Savoia (including Alma Dannata) (Puglia)

41°22'-41°27'N, 15°58'-16°09'E 6000 ha

Ramsar Site (Saline di Margherita di Savoia: 3871 ha); EEC SPA (Riserva Naturale Saline di Margherita di Savoia: 3871 ha)

Nature Reserve; hunting prohibited

The largest saltpans in Italy, together with a deeper lagoon to the north (Alma Dannata), saltmarsh (with *Salicornia*), and cultivated land. The area is only 200 m from the open sea, to which it is connected via three canals. The surroundings are mainly cultivated. Human activities include salt extraction and, at Alma Dannata, fish-farming. There is some poaching and general disturbance.

Breeding species include *Himantopus himantopus* (20+ pairs), *Recurvirostra avosetta* (50+ pairs), *Charadrius alexandrinus* (100+ pairs), *Sterna albifrons* (150 pairs), *Melanocorypha calandra*, and *Calandrella brachydactyla*. An important area for passage and wintering waterfowl: *Platalea leucorodia* (30-40) and *Grus grus* (30-40) occur on migration, whilst wintering species include *Egretta garzetta* (200), *Tadorna tadorna* (3000+), *Anas penelope* (10,000+), *Recurvirostra avosetta* (5000), *Numenius arquata* (50-100), and *Larus genei* (100+).

096 Le Murge di Monte Caccia (Puglia)

40°53'N, 16°24'E 12,000 ha

Unprotected

Scrub, grasslands, and agricultural land. Human activities include arable farming, stock-farming, and hunting.

Breeding species include *Milvus milvus* (3 pairs), *Circaetus gallicus* (2 pairs), *Circus pygargus*, *Falco naumanni* (less than 25 pairs), *F. biarmicus* (2-3 pairs), *Burhinus oedicnemus* (less than 40 pairs), *Melanocorypha calandra*, *Calandrella brachydactyla*, and *Lanius minor*.

097 Gravina di Laterza (Puglia)

40°36'N, 16°49'E 1800 ha

Unprotected

Scrub, grassland, and agricultural land. Human activities include arable and stock-farming, hunting and shooting.

Breeding species include *Milvus migrans* (2-3 pairs), *Neophron percnopterus* (1 pair), *Falco biarmicus*, *F. peregrinus* (1-2 pairs), and *Bubo bubo*.

098 Le Cesine (Puglia)

40°21'N, 18°20'E 680 ha

Ramsar Site (Le Cesine: 620 ha)

EEC SPA (Le Cesine with Riserva Naturale Le Cesine: 348 ha; 620 ha)

WWF Refuge

A large pond, in the lee of coastal dunes near Lecce, surrounded by wide zones of *Juncus* marsh. There is a wooded area (*Pinus* with dense understorey) along the landward edge of the marsh. Occasional disturbance of the area occurs from people using the beach. There have been very low numbers of waterfowl in recent years due to the breaching of the sandbar separating the pond from the sea and the invasion of seawater, although the sandbar has now been repaired.

Breeding species include *Himantopus himantopus* and *Gelochelidon nilotica*. *Egretta garzetta*, *Plegadis falcinellus*, *Platalea leucorodia*, and *Grus grus* occur on passage. The status of wintering waterfowl is little known. Species recorded in Jan. 1989 included *Anas crecca* (350) and *Aythya ferina* (400). Irregular winter visitors include *Egretta alba* and *Netta rufina*.

099 Dolomiti di Pietrapertosa (Basilicata)

40°30'N, 16°03'E 2500 ha

Unprotected

A spectacular chain of rocks with exposed bedrock, inland cliffs, agricultural land, and grasslands. Human activities include stock-farming and hunting.

Breeding species include *Milvus milvus* (2-3 pairs), *Neophron percnopterus* (1-2 pairs), *Falco biarmicus* (1-2 pairs), and *F. peregrinus* (2 pairs).

100 Complex of the Monte Sirino, Monte Alpi and Monte Raparo Sud (Basilicata)

40°08'N, 15°55'E 45,000 ha

Protected forest area; some other national protection; partly unprotected

A mountainous area with rivers and streams, fresh standing water, broadleaved deciduous woodland and mixed woodland, grasslands, agricultural land, exposed bedrock, and inland cliffs. Human activities include arable farming, forestry, stock-farming, and hunting. Threatened by the building of roads and houses and development of winter sports.

Breeding species include *Neophron percnopterus* (1-2 pairs), *Aquila chrysaetos* (1-2 pairs), *Falco peregrinus* (5-7 pairs), *Bubo bubo* (3-4 pairs), and *Dryocopus martius*.

101 Massiccio del Monte Pollino (Basilicata, Calabria)

39°54'N, 16°22'E 50,000 ha

Includes 2 EEC SPAs (Riserva Naturale Orientata Rubbio: 211 ha; Riserva Naturale Gole del Raganello: 1600 ha)

Proposed National Park; protected forest area; some other national protection

A mountainous area with rivers and streams, broadleaved deciduous woodland, agricultural land, mixed woodland, scree, exposed bedrock, inland cliffs, heath, and scrub. Human activities include arable farming, forestry, stock-farming, hunting, and there are residential areas. Threatened by intensive forestry, forest fires, road building, the development of winter sports, and increasing human disturbance and illegal hunting occur.

Breeding species include *Milvus migrans* (8-10 pairs), *M. milvus* (8-10 pairs), *Accipiter gentilis* (2 pairs), *Aquila chrysaetos* (1 pair), *Falco biarmicus* (1-2 pairs), *F. peregrinus* (3-4 pairs), *Bubo bubo* (4-5 pairs), *Dryocopus martius* (4 pairs), and *Pyrrhocorax pyrrhocorax*. In addition, *Gypaetus barbatus* is occasionally sighted.

102 Valle del Ferro (Calabria)

39°59'N, 16°32'E 8500 ha

Unprotected

Scrub, grasslands and agricultural land. Human activities include arable farming, forestry, stock-farming and hunting. Threatened by the building of roads and illegal hunting.

An important area for birds of prey with *Milvus migrans* (10-15 pairs), *M. milvus* (3 pairs), *Neophron percnopterus* (1 pair), *Circaetus gallicus* (1 pair), *Falco biarmicus* (1-2 pairs), and *F. peregrinus* (2-3 pairs); *Coracias garrulus* also breeds.

103 Monte Orsomarso and Monte Verbicaro (Calabria)

39°50'N, 15°57'E 48,000 ha

Includes 2 EEC SPAs (Riserva Naturale Valle del Fiume Lao: 5200 ha; Riserva Naturale Valle del Fiume Argentino: 3980 ha)

Unprotected

A mountainous area with rivers and streams, agricultural land, broadleaved deciduous woodland, scrub and grasslands, native coniferous woodland, and mixed woodland. Human activities include arable farming, forestry, stock-farming, and hunting. Threatened by the building of roads and intensive forestry, and there is uncontrolled hunting.

Breeding species include *Milvus migrans* (1-2 pairs), possibly *Hieraaetus fasciatus*, *Falco biarmicus* (4-5 pairs), *Bubo bubo* (2-5 pairs), *Coracias garrulus*, and *Dryocopus martius*.

104 Area between Torrente Lipuda and Fiume Neto (Calabria)

39°15°N, 17°03'E 32,000 ha

Unprotected

Rivers and streams, fresh standing water, bogs and marshes, agricultural land, woodland, scrub, and grasslands. Human activities include arable farming, forestry, stock-farming, and hunting.

Breeding species include *Milvus migrans* (5-6 pairs), *M. milvus* (3 pairs), *Neophron percnopterus* (2 pairs), *Falco biarmicus* (3 pairs), *F. peregrinus* (4 pairs), *Coracias garrulus*, and *Sylvia undata*.

105 Sila Grande e Sila Piccola (Calabria)

39°07'N, 16°35'E 90,000 ha EEC SPA (Parco Nazionale della Calabria: 15,892 ha)

Nature Reserve; National Park; protected forest area; some other national protection; hunting prohibited; partly unprotected

A mountainous area with rivers, streams, and fresh standing water, agricultural land, mixed woodland, and dry calcareous grasslands. Human activities include arable farming, forestry, stock-farming, fishing, and hunting. There is a risk from the development of tourism, building of roads and intensive forestry.

Breeding species include *Pernis apivorus* (1-2 pairs), *Milvus migrans* (7-8 pairs), *M. milvus* (5-6 pairs), *Circaetus gallicus* (1 pair), *Falco biarmicus* (1 pair), *F. peregrinus* (1 pair), *Alcedo atthis* (8-10 pairs), *Dryocopus martius*, *D. medius*, and *Pyrrhocorax pyrrhocorax*.

106 Foce del Fiume Neto (Calabria)

39°12'N, 17°08'E 1500 ha

Hunting prohibited

A tidal river estuary with associated beaches and marshland. There are also areas of cultivated land. Human activities include agriculture and fishing.

Breeding species include *Nycticorax nycticorax*, *Ardeola ralloides*, *Egretta garzetta*, *Aythya nyroca*, *Himantopus himantopus*, and *Burhinus oedicnemus*.

107 Aspromonte (Calabria)

38°07'N, 16°00'E 57,000 ha

Nature Reserve; National Park; protected forest area; some other national protection

Rivers and streams, native coniferous woodland, mixed woodland, scrub, grasslands, and agricultural land. Human activities include arable farming, forestry, stock-farming, and hunting.

Breeding species include *Milvus migrans* (3 pairs), *M. milvus* (3 pairs), *Neophron percnopterus* (1 pair), possibly *Hieraaetus fasciatus*, *Falco biarmicus* (1 pair), *F. peregrinus* (3 pairs), *Burhinus oedicnemus*, *Coracias garrulus*, and *Sylvia undata*.

108 Arcipelago Maddalena (Sardegna)

41°16'N, 09°22'E 800 ha

Unprotected

Sea cliffs, islets and rock stacks, sclerophyllous scrub, garigue and maquis. Human activities include fishing, hunting, boating, tourism and leisure.

Breeding species include *Calonectris diomedea* (100-500 pairs), *Puffinus puffinus*, *Phalacrocorax aristotelis* (150-300), *Falco peregrinus* (1-3 pairs), *Larus audouinii*, *Sterna hirundo*, *Sylvia sarda*, and possibly *Hydrobates pelagicus*.

109 Isola Asinara (Sardegna)

41°01'N, 08°12'E 4800 ha

Some national protection

Islets and rock stacks, sclerophyllous scrub, garigue and maquis, sea cliffs, exposed bedrock, and inland cliffs.

Breeding species include *Hydrobates pelagicus* (possibly), *Phalacrocorax aristotelis*, *Falco peregrinus*, *Larus audouinii*, *Sterna hirundo*, *Sylvia sarda*, and possibly *Calonectris diomedea*.

110 North-eastern coast and islands of Sardinia (Sardegna)

41°00'N, 09°39'E *c.*40,000 ha

Unprotected

Sea cliffs, islets and rock stacks, sclerophyllous scrub, garigue and maquis, coastal sand-dunes and sandy beaches. Human activities include stock-farming, fishing, hunting, boating, tourism and leisure.

Breeding species include *Calonectris diomedea*, *Puffinus puffinus* (600-900 pairs), *Phalacrocorax aristotelis* (400-500 pairs), *Falco peregrinus* (2-4 pairs), *Burhinus oedicnemus* (1 pair), *Larus audouinii*, *Sylvia sarda*, *S. undata*, *Serinus citrinella corsicana*, and possibly *Hydrobates pelagicus*.

111 Stagno di Pilo and Stagno di Casaraccio (Sardegna)

40°51'N, 08°17'E 500 ha

Unprotected

An area of lagoons, marshes, saltpans, sea inlets and agricultural land. Human activities include arable cultivation, fishing, and hunting.

Breeding species include *Ardea purpurea* (2-5 pairs), *Porphyrio porphyrio* (5 pairs), *Burhinus oedicnemus* (3-4 pairs), and *Sterna albifrons* (10-20 pairs). *Phoenicopterus ruber* (max. 500), *Anas crecca*, *Aythya ferina*, and *Fulica atra* (5000) occur in winter. Total wintering waterfowl exceed 10,000.

112 Campo d'Ozieri and surrounding plains between Torralba, Ardara, Tula, Oschiri, Mores and Campu Giavesu (Sardegna)

40°45'N, 08°50'E

Unprotected

Uncultivated land, hedges, and cultivated land. Human activities include agriculture, stock-raising, hunting, and there is scattered human habitation.

An important area for *Tetrax tetrax* (50-100 birds).

113 Coasts and islets of north-western Sardinia (Sardegna)

40°34'N, 08°11'E 3000 ha

Protected landscape

Islets and rock stacks, sea cliffs, sclerophyllous scrub, garigue and maquis. Human activities include fishing, hunting, boating, tourism and leisure.

Breeding species include *Calonectris diomedea* (1500-2000 pairs), *Puffinus puffinus* (possibly), *Hydrobates pelagicus* (possibly), *Phalacrocorax aristotelis* (100 pairs), *Gyps fulvus* (7 pairs), *Falco peregrinus* (8 pairs), *Larus audouinii* (20 pairs), and *Sylvia sarda.*

114 Altopiano di Campeda (Sardegna)

40°18'N, 08°47'E 19,500 ha

Unprotected

Grassland with areas of scattered *Quercus suber* trees. Human activities include arable farming, forestry, stock-farming, and hunting.

Breeding species include *Tetrax tetrax* (35 males), *Burhinus oedicnemus* (a few pairs), *Nycticorax nycticorax*, and *Lullula arborea*. *Gyps fulvus* and *Milvus migrans* feed in the area.

115 Inland and coastal area from Bosa to Capo Marargiu and Porto Tangone (Sardegna)

40°21'N, 08°27'E 8000 ha

Unprotected

Rivers and streams, sea cliffs, sclerophyllous scrub, garigue and maquis, agricultural land, bogs, and marshes. Human activities include arable farming, stock-farming, fishing, hunting, tourism and leisure.

Breeding species include *Milvus milvus* (2 pairs), *Gyps fulvus* (20 pairs), *Hieraaetus fasciatus* (possibly 1 pair), *Falco naumanni*, *F. peregrinus* (5 pairs), *Coracias garrulus,* and *Sylvia sarda.*

116 Campidano di Nuraghi Nuradeo (Sardegna)

40°11'N, 08°34'E 1000 ha

Protection status not known

An area of grassland on basaltic substrate. Potentially threatened by abandonment or modification of traditional livestock-farming.

Breeding species include *Tetrax tetrax* (8-9 males) and *Lullula arborea.*

117 Costa di Cuglieri and nearby islets (Sardegna)

40°10'N, 08°27'E *c.*2800 ha

Unprotected

Islets and rock stacks, sea cliffs, sclerophyllous scrub, garigue and maquis, grassland, and agricultural land. Human activities include arable farming, stock-farming, fishing, hunting, boating, tourism and leisure.

Breeding species include *Puffinus puffinus*, *Phalacrocorax carbo* (30-45 pairs), *P. aristotelis* (50-60 pairs), *Falco peregrinus* (3 pairs), *Larus audouinii* (25-30 pairs), *Coracias garrulus*, *Sylvia sarda*, *S. undata*, and possibly *Calonectris diomedea* and *Hydrobates pelagicus*.

118 Golfo di Orosei, Sopramonte di Oliena e di Orgosolo, Monti del Gennargentu and Entroterra Barbagia di Seulo (Sardegna)

40°10'N, 09°24'E 100,000 ha

Proposed National Park; some national protection, partly unprotected

Sea cliffs, mixed woodland, heath and scrub, agricultural land, broadleaved deciduous woodland, and sea inlets. Human activities include arable farming, forestry, stock-farming, fishing, hunting, boating, tourism and leisure.

Breeding species include *Calonectris diomedea*, *Puffinus puffinus*, *Gyps fulvus* (1 pair), *Accipiter gentilis* (7-10 pairs), *Aquila chrysaetos* (10-12 pairs), *Hieraaetus fasciatus* (2 pairs), *Falco eleonorae* (150 pairs), *F. peregrinus* (20-25 pairs), *Larus audouinii* (10-12 pairs), *Sylvia sarda*, and *Serinus citrinella corsicana*.

119 Media Valle del Tirso and l'Altopiano di Abbasanta (Sardegna)

40°10'N, 08°50'E

Unprotected

Uncultivated land, hedges, and cultivated land. Human activities include agriculture, stock-raising, hunting, and there is scattered human habitation.

An important site for *Tetrax tetrax* (50-70 birds).

120 Wetlands of the Sinis Peninsula and Golfo di Oristano (Sardegna)

39°42'-40°02'N, 08°21'-08°38'E *c*.7500 ha

This important series of wetlands along the central-west coast of Sardinia are treated together under a general heading for reasons of clarity.

120-1 Stagni di Putzu Idu (Salina Manna and Pauli Marigosa) (Sardegna)

40°02'N, 08°23'E 64 ha

Hunting prohibited

Coastal lagoons separated from the sea by a sand-spit which has been used as the base for a road causeway. Salina Manna is the most important part of the wetland. Human activities in the surrounding areas include tourism, fishing, and agriculture. Pollution, general disturbance, building plans, and poaching all threaten the area.

Breeding species include *Recurvirostra avosetta, Himantopus himantopus* (5-8 pairs), and *Charadrius alexandrinus* (15-20 pairs). *Egretta garzetta* (5-10), *Phoenicopterus ruber* (300+), *Charadrius alexandrinus* (50-100), *Calidris minuta* (10-50), and *Larus audouinii* (1-5) occur in winter.

120-2 Sale Porcus (Sardegna)

40°01'N, 08°21'E 325 ha Ramsar Site

LIPU Reserve; hunting prohibited

An inter-dunal saltwater pond, fed only by rainwater, which dries out in most summers. Surrounding areas include *Salicornia* and *Juncus* vegetation. Human activities in the surrounding areas include agriculture, stock-farming, and tourism. Problems include increasing disturbance and building construction related to tourism, increasing levels of agricultural pollutants, and illegal hunting.

Breeding species include *Recurvirostra avosetta*, *Himantopus himantopus*, *Charadrius alexandrinus*, *Larus genei*, *Sterna hirundo*, and *S. albifrons*. *Egretta garzetta*,

Phoenicopterus ruber (max. 7000), *Tadorna tadorna* (50-100), *Anas acuta*, *Charadrius alexandrinus* (100+), *Calidris minuta* (100+), and *C. alpina* (100+) occur in winter.

120-3 Stagno di Cabras and Mari e Pauli (Sardegna)

39°53'N, 08°28'E 3575 ha Ramsar Site

Wildlife Refuge (Mari Pauli); hunting prohibited

The largest natural lake basin in Sardinia, occupying a large portion of the Sinis Peninsula. Winter rains lead to the formation of temporary shallow pools around the lake, the most important of which is Mari e Pauli. The vegetation includes *Ruppia*, *Phragmites*, *Typha*, and *Juncus*, with areas of wheat cultivation and viticulture in the surroundings. Human activities include fishing and tourism. Problems include pollution from agriculture, over-fishing, and illegal hunting.

Breeding species include *Botaurus stellaris* (1-2 pairs), *Ixobrychus minutus*, *Ardea purpurea* (10 pairs), and *Porphyrio porphyrio*. Wintering waterfowl include *Phalacrocorax carbo sinensis* (1000+), *Ardea cinerea*, and Anatidae (1500-4200).

120-4 Stagno di Mistras (Sardegna)

39°52'N, 08°38'E 450 ha

Part of a Ramsar Site (Stagno di Mistras and adjacent territory: 680 ha)

Faunal Reserve; hunting prohibited; fishing restricted

A long, narrow coastal lagoon parallel to the seashore. It is separated from the sea by sandbars, except for a 300 m wide channel, which allows water exchange to take place. Human activities include fishing and agriculture in the surroundings. The construction of an overflow canal for Stagno di Cabras has resulted in the destruction of an important marshland area at Mardini. Other problems include illegal hunting and water pollution.

Breeding species include *Glareola pratincola* (20 pairs), *Charadrius alexandrinus* (abundant), *Sterna hirundo* (max. 20 pairs), and *S. albifrons* (*c*.80 pairs). *Phalacrocorax carbo sinensis* (max. 2000), *Egretta garzetta* (40-70), *Phoenicopterus ruber* (500-2500), Anatidae (1000-6000), and small numbers of waders (wide variety of species) are amongst the wintering waterfowl.

120-5 Stagno di Santa Giusta (Sardegna)

39°51'N, 08°31'E 830 ha

Unprotected

The third largest natural wetland in Sardinia, Santa Giusta is an almost circular lake lying between the towns of Oristano and Santa Giusta. It is separated from the sea by a dune system which is interrupted only by a narrow channel. The adjacent land is mainly cultivated. Human activities include fishing and industry. Pollution arising from increasing industry (including harbour construction) and untreated sewage has caused a dramatic slump in fishing catches, and the value of the area's importance for birds is immediately threatened. Hunting is also a problem.

Breeding species include *Ardea purpurea* (max. 10 pairs) and *Circus aeruginosus* (1-2 pairs). *Glareola pratincola* bred in recent years but the colony was deserted following the harbour construction. Wintering species include *Phalacrocorax carbo sinensis* (500+), Anatidae (now rare), and *Fulica atra* (100-200; compared with thousands in the past).

120-6 Stagno di Pauli Maiori (Stagno di Palmas Arborea) (Sardegna)

39°52'N, 08°37'E 250 ha

Part of a Ramsar Site (Stagno di Pauli Maiori and adjacent territory: 287 ha)

Hunting prohibited

A small pond (50 ha) surrounded by reedbeds and connected with Stagno di Santa Guista by a canal. The wetland is fed by the Fiume de Palmas and by the Rio Arriottu. There is a *Eucalyptus* wood and pastures to the south. Human activities include stock-raising and agriculture.

Breeding species include *Ixobrychus minutus* (max. 10 pairs), *Ardea purpurea* (max. 15 pairs), *Circus aeruginosus* (3-5 pairs), and *Porphyrio porphyrio* (50-80 pairs). *Botaurus stellaris* may breed. Small numbers of Anatidae occur in winter.

120-7 Stagno S'Ena Arrubia (Sardegna)

39°49'N, 08°34'E 300 ha Ramsar Site

Hunting prohibited; construction on nearby beach prohibited

The last remnant of the former Stagno di Sassu, following drainage of the area. Stagno S'Ena Arrubia is a lake separated from the sea by a sandbar. Outflow to the sea is artificially regulated. Vegetation includes *Phragmites*, *Scirpus*, and *Juncus*. The surroundings include cultivated land, *Pinus* forest, and belts of *Eucalyptus*. Human activities include fish-farming. There are problems with illegal hunting and pollution.

Breeding species include *Botaurus stellaris*, *Ixobrychus minutus*, *Ardea purpurea*, *Netta rufina*, *Circus aeruginosus*, and *Porphyrio porphyrio*. *Podiceps nigricollis*, *Phalacrocorax carbo sinensis*, and a variety of ducks (notably *Aythya ferina*) occur in winter.

120-8 Stagno di Corru S'Ittiri (Sardegna)

39°45'N, 08°33'E 250 ha

Part of a Ramsar Site (Corru S'Ittiri Fishery and Stagno di San Giovanni e Marceddi: 2610 ha)

Hunting prohibited

The lagoon of Corru S'Ittiri is a natural coastal inlet, parallel to the shore and bounded to the west by a *Pinus*-wooded sand-spit (Corru Mannu Peninsula). The adjacent land includes cultivated areas and belts of *Eucalyptus*. There is a 70 ha irrigation reservoir to the north. Human activities include tourism, fishing, and agriculture. The site suffers from agricultural pollution and disturbance by tourists, and hunters are trying to open the area to shooting.

Breeding species include *Ixobrychus minutus*, *Ardea purpurea*, *Anas querquedula*, *Rallus aquaticus*, and *Porphyrio porphyrio* (a few pairs). *Phalacrocorax carbo sinensis*, *Ardea cinerea*, *Phoenicopterus ruber* (50+), and small numbers of ducks and waders occur in winter.

121 Area of the Monte Ferru di Tertenia (Sardegna)

39°45'N, 09°37'E 9600 ha

Unprotected

Sea cliffs, scrub, grasslands, and agricultural land. Human activities include arable farming, stock-farming, fishing, hunting, tourism and leisure.

Breeding species include *Aquila chrysaetos* (1 pair), *Falco peregrinus* (3-4 pairs), *Sylvia sarda*, *S. undata*, and *Serinus citrinella corsicana*.

122 Stagno di Colostrai (Sardegna)

39°21'N, 09°35'E 1900 ha

Unprotected

Rivers, streams and fresh standing water, bogs and marshes, scrub, grasslands, and agricultural land.

Breeding species include *Botaurus stellaris*, *Circus aeruginosus* (2 pairs), *Porphyrio porphyrio* (5 pairs), *Himantopus himantopus* (7 pairs), and *Sterna albifrons* (10-15 pairs). *Phalacrocorax carbo* and *Phoenicopterus ruber* (50+) occur in winter.

123 Monte dei Sette Fratelli e Sarrabus (Sardegna)

39°17'N, 09°27'E 64,800 ha

Protected landscape; protected forest area; partly unprotected

Rivers and streams, woodland, scrub, grasslands, and agricultural land. Human activities include arable farming, forestry, stock-farming, hunting, tourism and leisure.

Breeding species include *Accipiter gentilis* (2-3 pairs), *Aquila chrysaetos* (3-4 pairs), *Falco peregrinus* (5-7 pairs), *Sylvia sarda* and *Serinus citrinella corsicana*.

124 Wetlands around Cagliari

39°11'-39°14'N, 09°09'-09°17'E *c.*4800 ha

For ease of analysis information on this area is presented as four subsites.

124-1 Saline di Macchiareddu (Sardegna)

39°11'-39°13'N, 09°12'-09°17'E 1400 ha

Part of Ramsar Site (Stagno di Cagliari: 3466 ha)

Hunting prohibited; access restricted

A salt-extraction complex with evaporation basins (1050 ha) and saltpans (320 ha). The wetland areas are separated from the sea by a sandbar, on which there is a road. There is a freshwater pond (Capoterra) nearby. The area is dominated by halophytic vegetation such as *Salicornia*. Industrial development is occurring in the areas surrounding the site. The area has been degraded by harbour construction, air and water pollution, general disturbance, and road traffic.

Breeding species include *Recurvirostra avosetta* (150-200 pairs), *Larus genei* (800 pairs), *L. argentatus*, *Gelochelidon nilotica* (*c.*80 pairs), and *Sterna albifrons* (60 pairs). *Phoenicopterus ruber* has made nesting attempts, whilst *Egretta garzetta* began nesting (28 pairs) in a colony which was destroyed by construction of the harbour. *Podiceps nigricollis*, *Phalacrocorax carbo sinensis*, *Egretta garzetta*, *Phoenicopterus ruber* (max. 2000), Anatidae, *Recurvirostra avosetta*, and other waders occur in winter.

124-2 Laguna di Santa Gilla (Sardegna)

39°13'N, 09°14'E 2013 ha part of Ramsar Site (Stagno di Cagliari; 3466 ha)

Hunting prohibited

The Laguna di Santa Grilla is the freshwater portion of a larger complex (Stagni di Cagliari) including the Salinas de Macchiareddu and Capoterra ponds. The site is open to the sea and fed by two rivers flowing into the northern part of the area. Human activities in the surrounding areas include chemical industries and agriculture. The construction of a harbour has reduced the size of the wetlands; severe pollution has led to a ban on fishing; there is disturbance from a nearby airport and there are attempts to reopen the area to hunters.

Breeding species include *Egretta garzetta*, *Circus aeruginosus*, *Porphyrio porphyrio*, *Larus genei*, *Gelochelidon nilotica*, *Sterna albifrons*, and *Alcedo atthis*. *Phalacrocorax carbo sinensis*, *Phoenicopterus ruber*, and *Sterna sandvicensis* occur in winter.

124-3 Stagno di Molentargius (Sardegna)

39°14'N, 09°09'E 578 ha

Part of Ramsar Site (Stagno di Molentargius; 1401 ha); part of an EEC SPA (Stagno di Molentargius: 1400 ha)

Partly a Landscape Reserve; hunting prohibited

The Molentargius complex is composed of two parts. The first area (Bella Rosa Maggiore, 460 ha) is a saltpan; the other part (Bella Rosa Minore, 118 ha) is separated from the first by a dyke and holds fresh water. Human activities include agriculture, salt extraction, and other commercial enterprises. Bella Rosa Minore is polluted with sewage and threatened with urban development.

Breeding species include *Ixobrychus minutus*, *Bubulcus ibis*, *Egretta garzetta*, *Ardea purpurea*, *Plegadis falcinellus*, *Circus aeruginosus*, *Porphyrio porphyrio*, *Himantopus himantopus*, *Recurvirostra avosetta*, *Sterna albifrons*, and *Alcedo atthis*. *Phoenicopterus ruber* (*c*.2000), *Tadorna tadorna*, *Netta rufina*, and *Aythya nyroca* occur in winter.

124-4 Saline di Quartu (Sardegna)

39°13'N, 09°10'E 355 ha part of Ramsar Site (Stagno di Molentargius: 1401 ha)

Partly Landscape Reserve; hunting prohibited

A long (3-4 km), narrow (800-1000 m) basin separated from the sea by a strip of land (Poetto's Beach) on which there is a road. The northern shore is separated from the Stagno di Molentargius by a wide strip of land (Is Arenas), which holds a number of houses. Human activities include salt extraction, tourism, and agriculture. The area may be threatened by urbanisation.

Porphyrio porphyrio breeds at the site, whilst *Egretta garzetta*, *Phoenicopterus ruber*, Anatidae, *Himantopus himantopus*, *Recurvirostra avosetta*, and other waders occur in winter.

125 Islands of southern Sardinia (Sardegna)

38°50'-39°10'N, 08°15'-09°40'E *c*.3800 ha

Partly Protected Landscape; partly protected

Islets and rock stacks, sea cliffs, sclerophyllous scrub, garigue and maquis, native coniferous woodland, and agricultural land. Human activities include arable farming, forestry, stock-farming, fishing, hunting, boating, tourism and leisure.

Breeding species include *Calonectris diomedea* (30-50 pairs), *Puffinus puffinus* (100-300 pairs), *Phalacrocorax aristotelis* (50-65 pairs), *Falco eleonorae* (160-180 pairs), *F. peregrinus* (8-10 pairs), *Larus audouinii* (15-20 pairs), and *Sylvia sarda*.

126 South-east Iglesiente (Piscinamanna) (Sardegna)

39°09'N, 08°52'E 44,000 ha

EEC SPA (Riserva Naturale Foresta di Monte Arcosu: 3205 ha)

Protected forest area; some other protection status; hunting prohibited; partly unprotected

Woodland, agricultural land, scrub, and grasslands. Human activities include arable farming, forestry, stock-farming, and hunting.

Breeding species include *Gyps fulvus* (2-3 pairs), *Accipiter gentilis* (3-4 pairs), *Aquila chrysaetos* (2-3 pairs), *Hieraaetus fasciatus* (max. 4 pairs), *Falco peregrinus* (5-6 pairs), *Coracias garrulus*, *Sylvia sarda*, and *Serinus citrinella corsicana*.

127 Isole Eolie: Lipari, Vulcano, Salina, Panarea, Stromboli, Filicudi and Alicudi (Sicilia)

38°30'N, 14°50'E 11,610 ha

Partly Protected Landscape

Islets and rock stacks, sclerophyllous scrub, garigue and maquis, agricultural land, sea cliffs, and grasslands. Human activities include arable farming, stock-farming, fishing, hunting, tourism and leisure.

Breeding species include *Calonectris diomedea* (80-100 pairs), *Falco eleonorae* (20-30 pairs), *F. peregrinus* (8-10 pairs), and *Sylvia undata*.

128 Part of Monti Peloritani and Monte Ciccia (Sicilia)

38°13'N, 15°31'E 17,100 ha

Unprotected

Sclerophyllous scrub, garigue and maquis, broadleaved deciduous woodland, and agricultural land. Human activities include arable farming, stock-farming and fishing, and there are motorways and major roads.

Breeding species include *Milvus milvus* (2-3 pairs). A bottleneck site for migratory birds. Passage totals for the 1987 spring migration were: *Ciconia nigra* (31), *Pernis apivorus* (6032), *Milvus migrans* (137), *Neophron percnopterus* (7), *Circus aeruginosus* (218), *Aquila chrysaetos* (3), *Hieraaetus pennatus* (15), *Falco vespertinus* (507), and *F. subbuteo* (220).

129 Rocche del Crasto and surrounding valley (Sicilia)

38°09'N, 14°42'E 27,000 ha

Unprotected

Broadleaved deciduous woodland, sclerophyllous scrub, garigue and maquis, agricultural land, exposed bedrock, and inland cliffs. Human activities include arable farming, forestry, stock-farming, and hunting.

Breeding species include *Milvus milvus* (4 pairs), *Aquila chrysaetos* (2 pairs), *Falco peregrinus* (6 pairs), *Alectoris graeca*, and *Coracias garrulus*.

130 Le Montagne delle Madonie (Sicilia)

38°12'N, 15°32'E 39,000 ha

Protected forest area; some other national protection

Broadleaved deciduous woodland, sclerophyllous scrub, garigue and maquis, agricultural land, exposed bedrock, and inland cliffs. Human activities include arable farming, forestry, stock-farming, and hunting.

Breeding species include *Milvus milvus* (4-6 pairs), *Neophron percnopterus* (3 pairs), *Aquila chrysaetos* (3 pairs), *Hieraaetus fasciatus* (2 pairs), *Falco peregrinus* (8 pairs), *Alectoris graeca*, and *Pyrrhocorax pyrrhocorax*.

131 Area between Piana degli Albanesi, Misilmeri, Ventimiglia di Sicilia e Rocca Busambra (Sicilia)

37°53'N, 13°27'E 55,000 ha

Protected forest area; some national protection; partly unprotected

Fresh standing water, agricultural land, broadleaved deciduous woodland, sclerophyllous scrub, garigue and maquis. Human activities include arable farming, forestry, stock-farming, and hunting.

Breeding species include *Milvus milvus* (2-3 pairs), *Neophron percnopterus* (3 pairs), *Aquila chrysaetos* (1 pair), *Hieraaetus fasciatus* (1 pair), *Falco biarmicus* (2 pairs), *F. peregrinus* (6 pairs), *Coracias garrulus*, and *Pyrrhocorax pyrrhocorax* (50 pairs).

132 Area of the Monte Pecoraro, Pizzo Cirina and Raffo Rosso di Capaci (Sicilia)

38°09'N, 13°07'E 120,000 ha

Unprotected

Agricultural land, sclerophyllous scrub, broadleaved deciduous woodland, garigue and maquis. Human activities include arable and stock-farming, hunting, and there are major roads and motorways.

Breeding species include *Milvus migrans* (1-2 pairs), *M. milvus* (1-2 pairs), *Neophron percnopterus* (2 pairs), *Aquila chrysaetos* (1 pair), *Falco peregrinus* (4 pairs), *Coracias garrulus*, and *Pyrrhocorax pyrrhocorax*.

133 Area of Monte Cofano, San Vito lo Capo, Capo Puntazza, Monte Sparagio and Monte Inici (Sicilia)

38°03'N, 12°47'E 18,000 ha

Unprotected

Sea cliffs and inlets, stony beaches, coastal sand dunes and sand beaches, agricultural land, sclerophyllous scrub, garigue and maquis. Human activities include arable and stock-farming, fishing, hunting, tourism and leisure.

Breeding species include *Aquila chrysaetos* (1 pair), *Hieraaetus fasciatus* (2 pairs), *Falco peregrinus* (8 pairs), and *Alectoris graeca*.

134 Isole Egadi (Favignana, Levanzo e Marettimo) (Sicilia)

37°59'N, 12°20'E 3700 ha

Unprotected

Sea cliffs, islets and rock stacks, sclerophyllous scrub, garigue and maquis, agricultural land, and broadleaved deciduous woodland. Human activities include arable and stock-farming, fishing, hunting, tourism and leisure.

Breeding species include *Calonectris diomedea* (70-100 pairs), *Puffinus puffinus*, *Hydrobates pelagicus* (200-400 pairs), *Hieraaetus fasciatus* (1 pair), *Falco peregrinus* (6-8 pairs), and *Sylvia undata*.

135 Stagnone di Marsala e Saline di Trapani (Sicilia)

37°40'-37°55'E, 12°28'-12°32'E 3700 ha

Regional Nature Reserve (Stagnone di Marsala and islands: 2400 ha); remainder unprotected.

The Stagnone di Marsala is one of the last remaining lagoons in Sicily and includes saltpans and several islands. It measures 10 km (north-south) by 3 km. The northern area is sheltered from the open sea by the Isola Grande. The other islands are Isola di Santa Maria, Isola di San Pantaleo, and La Scuola. The lagoon has an average depth of 1 m (max. only 2.5 m). Principal vegetation includes *Salicornia* and *Salsola*, whilst the surrounding areas are largely agricultural. The Saline di Trapani are north of the lagoon, just south of Trapani and form a complex of saltpans at the mouth of the River Baiata. Human activities include salt extraction, agriculture, and tourism. Increasing urban development, intensification of agriculture, and growing tourism may cause problems at the site, which is also disturbed by hunting.

Breeding species include *Himantopus himantopus* (50-70 pairs), *Charadrius alexandrinus* (120 pairs), and *Sterna albifrons* (15-40 pairs). Over 21,000 waders pass through the area in spring, whilst numbers of individual migratory species include *Platalea leucorodia* (*c*.120 in spring; *c*.200 in autumn), *Anas querquedula* (*c*.20,000 in spring; daily max. 1500-2000), and *Charadrius alexandrinus* (*c*.3000 in Jul./Aug.; daily max. 500).

136 Capo Feto (Sicilia)

37°40'N, 12°31'E *c*.150 ha

Unprotected; proposed Nature Reserve

Coastal wetlands with sand-dunes and small marshes. Threatened by drainage, infilling from waste dumping, building construction, and illegal shooting.

Breeding species include *Calandrella brachydactyla*. Very important resting and feeding site for migrants including *Anser anser*, *Platalea leucorodia*, and *Phoenicopterus ruber*.

137 Foce del Simeto (Sicilia)

37°22'-37°27'N, 15°06'E *c*.400 ha

Part of Regional Nature Reserve (1600 ha); partly unprotected

The estuary of the River Simeto including the mouth of the river itself, coastal saltpans, an artificial canal, and Gornalunga Lake. The saltpans are about 1 m deep, with Gornalunga having a depth of 3 m, and are flooded from late October to late June.

Vegetation includes *Salsola*, *Agropyron*, *Juncus*, *Phragmites*, and *Scirpus*, and there is a coastal *Pinus* belt between the river mouth and Gornalunga. The surrounding area is largely agricultural. Illegal building is the main threat to the area. Poaching is also a problem.

Breeding species include *Aythya nyroca* (2-3 pairs). An important area for passage waterfowl, with (seasonal totals) *Ardeola ralloides* (50+ in spring), *Egretta garzetta* (200+ in spring), *Plegadis falcinellus* (200+ in spring), *Recurvirostra avosetta* (200+ in autumn), *Larus genei* (200+ in autumn), and *Chlidonias niger* (2000+ in autumn). A wide variety of waders occurs on passage. The area supports small numbers of Anatidae and waders in winter, including a few *Anser anser*.

138 Gole dell'Anapo between Palazzolo Acreide and Necropoli di Pantalica (Sicilia)

37°07'N, 14°59'E 11,700 ha

Unprotected

Scrub, grasslands and agricultural land. Human activities include arable farming, stock-farming, and hunting.

Breeding species include *Hieraaetus fasciatus* (2 pairs), *Falco biarmicus* (5 pairs), and *F. peregrinus* (3 pairs).

139 Pantani di Capo Passero (Sicilia)

36°40'-36°48'N, 14°59'-15°07'E 1385 ha

Part of an EEC SPA (Riserva Naturale Pantani di Vendicari: 1450 ha)

Part of Regional Nature Reserve (Pantani di Vendicari; 1500 ha)

A complex of shallow saltpans, including Pantani di Vendicari (650 ha), Salina Morghello (124 ha), Pantano Cuba – Longarini (444 ha), Pantano Boronello (65 ha), Pantano Bruno (58 ha), and Pantano Auruca (44 ha). The saltpans are virtually dry during July-September. Vegetation includes *Salicornia*, *Juncus*, *Phragmites*, and *Ruppia*. The surroundings are mainly cultivated. Human activities include salt extraction and hunting. Plans to convert the saltpans to marinas have been cancelled but a programme of intensive aquaculture will probably be implemented. Uncontrolled shooting is a problem, as is development of holiday homes in the surrounding areas.

Breeding species include *Himantopus himantopus* (2-25 pairs), *Charadrius alexandrinus* (100 pairs), and *Sterna albifrons* (10-25). A very important area for passage waterfowl, with (seasonal totals unless otherwise stated) *Ardeola ralloides* (200+ in spring), *Egretta garzetta* (400+ in spring), *Plegadis falcinellus* (250 in spring), *Platalea leucorodia* (250 in autumn), *Phoenicopterus ruber* (max. 100), *Anas querquedula* (10,000; daily max. 6000), *Larus genei* (700-1400 in autumn), *L. audouinii* (max. 25, summering), *Gelochelidon nilotica* (100+ in spring), *Sterna caspia* (av. 150 in autumn), *Chlidonias niger* (2500+ in autumn), *Charadrius alexandrinus* (5000 in autumn), *Calidris minuta* (6000 in autumn), *C. ferruginea* (4500 in spring), *Philomachus pugnax* (8000 in spring), *Tringa stagnatilis* (80), and *T. glareola* (3000 in autumn).

140 Pantelleria and Isole Pelagie (Linosa, Lampedusa, Lampione) (Sicilia)

36°45'N, 12°00'E 2445 ha

Unprotected

Islets and rock stacks, sea cliffs, coastal sand-dunes and sandy beaches, sclerophyllous scrub, agricultural land, garigue and maquis. Human activities include arable and stock-farming, fishing, hunting, tourism and leisure.

Breeding species include *Calonectris diomedea* (10,000 pairs), *Puffinus puffinus*, *Hydrobates pelagicus* (100-500 pairs), *Phalacrocorax aristotelis*, *Falco eleonorae* (10 pairs), and *F. peregrinus* (3 pairs).

MAIN REFERENCES

Brichetti, P. (1979-1985) Distribuzione geografica degli uccelli nidificanti in Italia, Corsica e Isole Maltesi, 1-4. *An. Mus. Civ. Sci. Nat. Brescia* 16 ff.

Brichetti, P. (1982-1988) Atlante degli uccelli nidificanti sulle Alpi italiane. *Riv. ital. Orn.* 52-58.

Fasola, M., Barbieri, F., Prigioni, C. and Bogliani, G. (1981) Le garzaie in Italia 1981. *Avocetta* 5: 107-131.

Frugis, S. and Schenk, H. (1981) Red list of Italian birds. *Avocetta* 5: 133-141.

INBS (1987) Distribuzione e populazione dei Laridi e Sternidi nidificanti in Italia. *Suppl. Ric. Biol. Selvaggina* 11(1).

Meschini, E. and Frugis, S. (in press) Progetto Atlante Italiano INBS/CISO. *Suppl. Ric. Biol. Selvaggina*.

Osieck, E. R. and Mörzer Bruyns, M. F. (1981) Important bird areas in Europe. Unpublished report to the Commission of European Communities.

LIECHTENSTEIN

Whinchat *Saxicola rubetra*

INTRODUCTION

General information

The Principality of Liechtenstein, situated between Switzerland and Austria, has an area of 160 sq km and population (in 1983) of 26,512 (an average population density of 166 persons per sq km). One third of the country lies in the Rhine valley and the rest is mountainous; the altitude varies from 430-2599 m. There are three main types of landscape:

1. The alluvial flood-plain of the Rhine which is now used for agriculture and human settlements. There has been a major loss of wetlands as a result of drainage for agriculture, and dry grasslands because of agricultural intensification and urban expansion. In former centuries until at least 1927 much of the valley was often inundated; now only tiny remnants of marshes and wooded swamps remain.
2. The slopes of the Rhine valley, over 40 per cent of which are wooded. Native deciduous woodland formerly dominated; however, coniferous forests now occupy a larger area. The slopes are used mainly for forestry and human settlements.
3. The high mountainous area, which covers a third of the country, and is characterised by north-south running mountain ridges and valleys with forests and alpine pastures. This area is used for livestock grazing (which is highly developed), forestry, and tourism.

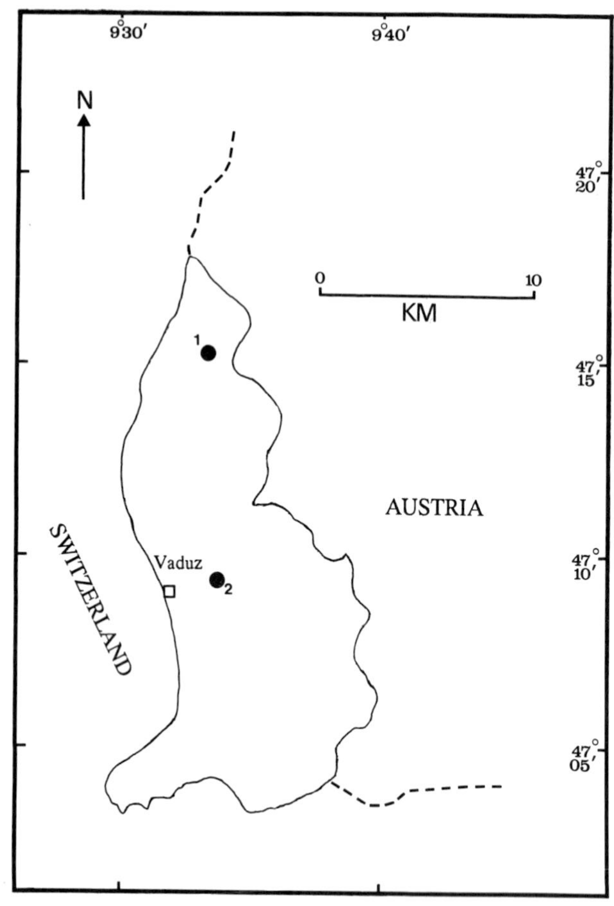

Figure 20: Map showing the location of the sites in Liechtenstein

Ornithological importance

The slopes of the Rhine valley and the high montane areas have noteworthy breeding populations of *Aquila chrysaetos*, *Bonasa bonasia*, *Tetrao tetrix*, *T. urogallus*, *Glaucidium passerinum*, *Aegolius funereus*, *Dendrocopos leucotos*, and *Picoides tridactylus*. In addition, the breeding populations of some lowland species (*Numenius arquata*, *Saxicola rubetra*, and *Locustella naevia*) are important for the Rhine valley. The Rhine valley is also important for migratory birds including ducks and waders.

Conservation infrastructure and protected-area system

There are seven Nature Reserves (Naturschutzgebiet), including Ruggeller Riet where (amongst other things) it is prohibited to intensify agriculture and to leave the paths during the breeding season. The Ministry of Agriculture, Forestry and Environment is responsible for nature conservation.

International measures relevant to the conservation of sites

Liechtenstein has ratified the Bern Convention. The country is not a party to the Ramsar, World Heritage or Bonn Conventions.

Overview of the inventory

Two sites are listed: Ruggeller Riet, which is protected and supports the important lowland species mentioned above, as well as the only population of *Crex crex* in Liechtenstein; and Garselli-Zigerberg, which is an unprotected mountainous area supporting good populations of grouse, owls, and woodpeckers.

Acknowledgements

The following accounts have been compiled from information provided by G. Willi (Botanisch-Zoologische Gesellschaft), who also provided material for the introduction.

INVENTORY

No.	Site name	Region	Criteria used to select site [see p.18]							
			0	1(i)	1(ii)	1(iii)	1(iv)	2	3	4
001	Ruggeller Riet							*	*	
002	Garselli-Zigerberg								*	

Comments on the inventory

1. All information was compiled in 1984 and updated in 1987.
2. When applying the site-selection criteria (category 3) the ‘region’ is Liechtenstein.

---

001 Ruggeller Riet, Talgebiet

47°15'N, 09°33'E 90 ha

Nature Reserve

An area of bog, grassland, and arable land with drainage ditches, scrub, and a small area of open water in the Rhine Valley. The bog is protected and human access is controlled during the breeding season. The main problem is the intensification of agriculture adjacent to the Nature Reserve and to a lesser extent, in spite of protection, within the reserve.

Breeding species include *Coturnix coturnix* (5-15 pairs), *Crex crex* (2-4 pairs), *Numenius arquata* (2-3 pairs), *Saxicola rubetra* (20 pairs), *Locustella naevia* (12 pairs),

Acrocephalus palustris (20 pairs), and *Lanius collurio* (2 pairs). *Circus aeruginosus* (5-10 during the season) and *C. pygargus* occur on spring passage, and *C. cyaneus* occurs in winter.

002 Garselli-Zigerberg, Alpengebiet

47°08'-47°10'N, 09°31'-09°37'E 950 ha

Unprotected

A mountainous area with natural forests and alpine pastures. Human activities include stock-grazing and recreation. The area is threatened by development for tourism and alpine grazing pasture.

An important area for *Bonasa bonasia* (*c.*3 pairs), *Tetrao tetrix* (10-20 pairs), *T. urogallus* (*c.*5 pairs), *Glaucidium passerinum* (2 pairs), *Aegolius funereus* (4 pairs), *Dryocopus martius* (3 pairs), *Dendrocopos leucotos* (1-2 pairs), *Picoides tridactylus* (3 pairs), *Turdus torquatus* (*c.*50 pairs), *Regulus ignicapillus* (*c.*30 pairs), and *Serinus citrinella* (*c.*40 pairs).

MAIN REFERENCES

Willi, G. (1984) *Die Brutögel des liechtensteinischen Alpenraumes.* Naturkdl. Forschung im ürstentum Liechtenstein, Bd. 4. Vaduz.

Willi, G. and Broggi, M. F. (1983, 1985, 1986) Die Vogelwelt des Fürstentums Liechtenstein unter Berücksichtigung der benachbarten Gebiete. Teile I, II, III. *Ber. Bot.-Zool. Ges. Liechtenstein-Sargans-Werdenberg.* 12: 61-117, 14: 103-143, 15: 37-92.

LUXEMBOURG

Red-backed Shrike *Lanius collurio*

INTRODUCTION

General information

Luxembourg is one of Europe's smallest sovereign states, with a surface area of just over 2500 sq km and a population of some 370,000 (an average of 148 persons per sq km); it has a border with Belgium to the west and north, with the Federal Republic of Germany to the east, and with France to the south. It has no mountains, no moorland, and very little standing water. There are four main land divisions:

1. A small area of iron-ore deposits in the south, with a declining but still important iron and steel industry.
2. A large area of lowland farmland in the rest of the south and the centre.
3. A strip of very steep, heavily wooded valleys (part of the Eifel/Ardennes massif).
4. Remnants of marshes and bogs in the north-west on an otherwise cultivated plateau.

Forest covers a third of the land surface (almost entirely modified), and of this area one-third is coniferous, half deciduous, and the rest *Quercus* coppice. A large amount of reafforestation has been carried out in the last 20 years, with *Picea* plantations gaining ground at the expense of native hardwoods. Wetlands, once abundant, have been much reduced by modern agriculture, as have hedgerows.

Agriculture is part pastoral, part arable, with grazing, hay and silage meadows predominating (the main product being milk). Vines are grown for wine along the Moselle and some of its tributaries.

Ornithological importance

Luxembourg supports populations of *Milvus milvus* (a globally threatened species), and populations of *Pernis apivorus, Milvus migrans, Bonasa bonasia, Alcedo atthis, Picus canus, Dryocopus martius, Dendrocopos medius, Lullula arborea, Anthus campestris,* and *Lanius collurio,* which are all on Annex I of the EEC Wild Birds Directive. For some of these species (e.g. *Milvus migrans* and *Picus canus*), Luxembourg lies on the edge of their range. In addition, spring and autumn passage of *Grus grus* is very substantial (11,000 estimated in spring 1988).

The most important bird habitats are the areas of native deciduous woodland and *Quercus* coppice; the fast-flowing, relatively unpolluted streams in the north; and several small wetland areas including Remerschen gravel-pits, the flood-meadows along the Alzette, and the remnant bogs on the Ardennes plateau.

Conservation infrastructure and protected-area system

According to the August 1982 act on the protection of nature and natural resources, it is forbidden to destroy natural environments such as ponds, marshes, reedbeds, hedges, and copses. A declaration of intent, published by the Government in 1981, included an inventory of Natural Areas for designation as protected areas. This included a list of 113 potential nature reserves of which 60 were wetlands, 11 were woodlands, and 11 were dry grasslands. The main problem in these areas results from leisure pursuits (especially fishing and wind-surfing). The first two areas were at last officially designated nature reserves in 1987, but the precise degree of protection has still to be defined.

The other categories of protected area are Natural Parks (Parc Naturel), Protected Recreational Areas and Inter-urban Protected Areas (lists of these were also prepared in 1981). The Natural Parks, which cover 25 per cent of the country, afford virtually no effective habitat protection. The 'Administration des Eaux et Forêts' (Ministry of the Environment) is responsible for nature conservation, including ensuring compliance with the Law of 1982. This is not an altogether satisfactory solution, given the frequent clashes of interest between forestry and conservation.

Private nature reserves are also being established by the Luxembourg Nature Conservation Trust (Fondation 'Hëllef fir d'Natur'), but these tend to be rather small areas.

International measures relevant to the conservation of sites

Luxembourg is a member of the European Community and is therefore bound by the terms of the Wild Birds Directive. One Biogenetic Reserve and two EEC Special Protection Areas (both SPAs included in this inventory) have been designated. It has also ratified the Bern Convention, World Heritage Convention (but has not designated any natural World Heritage Sites), and Bonn Convention.

Overview of the inventory

Three rather large and heterogeneous areas have been identified covering 95,500 ha or 38 per cent of the country. Effective land-use regulations are required for these areas, within which particular subsites will need to be strictly protected.

The most important wetland, the Remerschen gravel-pits along the Moselle, is included (in 003), as are the flood-meadows along the Alzette (in 002), and the remnant bogs on the Ardennes plateau (in 001). The important areas of native deciduous woodland (including one of Europe's most ancient forests, of *Quercus, Fagus,* and *Carpinus,* near Echternach) and *Quercus* coppice, and the unpolluted streams in the north, are also included (in 001). The species mentioned above are covered well by the sites in this inventory.

Acknowledgements

The site accounts were compiled from information provided by J.-P. Schmitz and D. Crowther of LNVL (Lëtzebuerger Natur- a Vulleschutzliga). D. Crowther also provided material for the introduction.

INVENTORY

No.	Site name	Criteria used to select site [see p.18]							
		0	1(i)	1(ii)	1(iii)	1(iv)	2	3	4
001	Haute-Sûre, Eifel and Ardenne Meridionale				*		*	*	
002	Sud-ouest du Luxembourg						*	*	
003	Sud-est du Luxembourg				*		*	*	
003-1	Remerschen/Wintrange								

Comments on the inventory

1. The site information was compiled in 1984 (updated in 1989) or in 1988.
2. When applying the site-selection criteria (category 3) the 'region' is Luxembourg.

Glossary

EEC SPA = European Community Special Protection Area.

---

001 Haute-Sûre, Eifel, and Ardenne Meridionale

50°00'N, 06°00'E 76,000 ha partly an EEC SPA (Pont Misère: 240 ha)

Partly included in the German-Luxembourg Natural Park (Parc naturel Germano-Luxemburgeois) and Belgium-Luxembourg Natural Park (Parc naturel de la Haute-Sûre). In addition, some areas are managed by the Luxembourg Nature Conservation Trust (Fondation 'Hëllef fir d'Natur').

The northern part of Luxembourg with deep, heavily wooded valleys in the south, rising to an agriculturally used plateau in the north. The main habitats are *Quercus* coppice woodland, with agricultural land, marshes, and bogs on the plateau. The main economic activities are forestry and agriculture. *Picea* afforestation, wetland drainage, inadequate management of the traditionally coppiced woodland, and water pollution are the main problems.

Breeding species include *Ciconia nigra* (2 pairs), *Pernis apivorus* (70 pairs), *Milvus migrans* (5 pairs), *M. milvus* (10 pairs), *Circus cyaneus* (1-3 pairs), *Bonasa bonasia* (*c.*100 pairs), *Alcedo atthis* (*c.*40 pairs), *Dryocopus martius* (20-30 pairs), *Dendrocopos medius* (20-30 pairs), *Lullula arborea* (30-60 pairs), and *Lanius collurio* (200+ pairs). Large numbers of *Grus grus* occur on passage (11,000 in spring 1988). Roosts of *Milvus migrans* (30+ birds) also occur on autumn passage.

002 Sud-ouest du Luxembourg

49°30'N, 06°00'E 13,500 ha

Partly a Nature Reserve (Prënzebierg); several areas are managed by private conservation organisations

An area with abandoned open-cast iron-ore mines, small wetland reserves and extensive flood-meadows in the Alzette plain. Existing problems are wetland drainage and use of the old mines for land-fills and the slagheaps for roadstone aggregates.

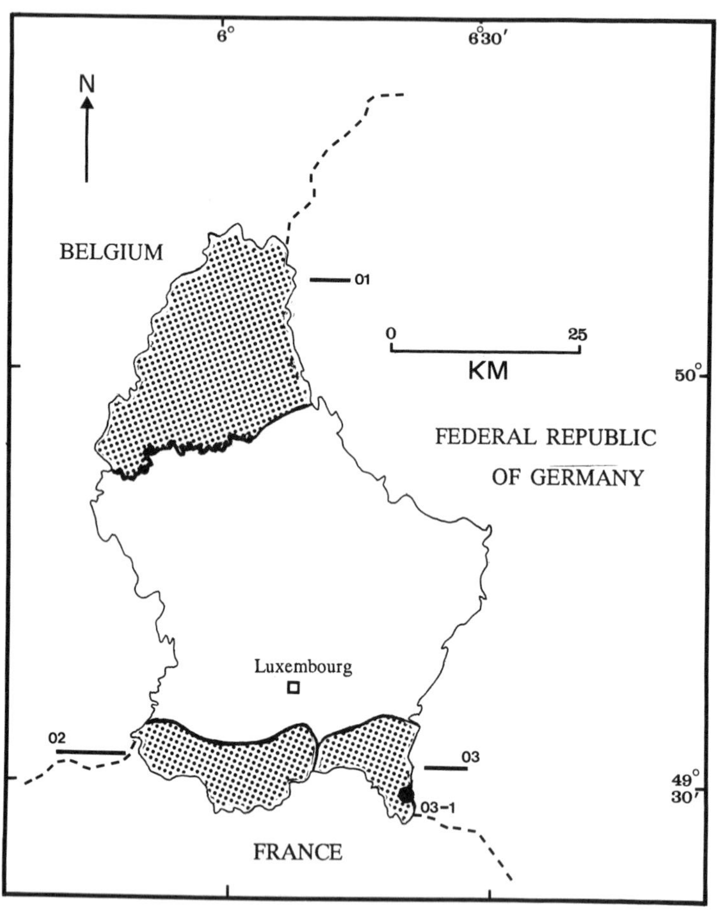

Figure 21: Map showing the location of the sites in Luxembourg

Breeding species include *Pernis apivorus* (10-15 pairs), *Milvus migrans* (1-2 pairs), *M. milvus* (2-3 pairs), *Porzana porzana* (suspected), *Crex crex* (5 pairs), *Dryocopus martius* (10-15 pairs), *Dendrocopos medius* (50-100 pairs), *Lullula arborea* (20-30 pairs), *Anthus campestris* (1-6 pairs), *Oenanthe oenanthe* (5-6 pairs; only breeding site in Luxembourg), and *Lanius collurio* (50-80 pairs).

003 Sud-est du Luxembourg

49°32'N, 06°23'E 6000 ha Partly an EEC SPA (Haff Reimech: 74 ha)

Partly a Nature Reserve (Remerschen/Wintrange) and mostly covered by a Natural Park (Parc naturel de la Moselle)

Agricultural land with gravel-pits (the only major area of standing water in the Grand Duchy). Recreational activities cause disturbance at the gravel-pits.

Breeding species include *Pernis apivorus* (3-5 pairs), *Milvus migrans* (*c.*2 pairs), *M. milvus* (2-3 pairs), *Circus cyaneus* (1 pair), *C. pygargus* (5 pairs), *Bubo bubo* (2-3 pairs), *Picus canus* (15-25 pairs), *Dryocopus martius* (10-15 pairs), *Dendrocopos medius* (20-30 pairs), *Lullula arborea* (20-30 pairs), and *Lanius collurio* (50-80 pairs). *Ixobrychus minutus* would possibly breed if there was proper habitat management (especially less pressure from wind-surfing and fishermen). Large numbers of *Grus grus* occur on passage.

Additional information is provided for the following subsite:

003-1 Remerschen/Wintrange

49°29'N, 06°22'E 315 ha EEC SPA (Haff Reimech: 74 ha)

Partly a Nature Reserve (30 ha of projected 80 ha National Nature Reserve recently established) and small parts owned by Fondation 'Hëllef fir d'Natur'; also included in the Natural Park

A complex of lagoons of differing size, depth and water type adjacent to the Moselle, which are still being worked for sand and gravel; some are intensively used for fishing and wind-surfing. Surrounded by vineyards and woodland. The designation of a Nature Reserve is being contested by fishing interests and there is disturbance from leisure activities. This is undoubtedly Luxembourg's premier wetland site.

Breeding species include *Alcedo atthis* (1-2 pairs), and its populations of *Podiceps cristatus* (10 pairs; only breeding site in Luxembourg), *Cygnus olor* (1-2 pairs), *Acrocephalus scirpaceus* (25 pairs), and *A. arundinaceus* (1-2 pairs; only breeding site in Luxembourg) are nationally important. *Remiz pendulinus* bred for the first time in 1988. Passage species include *Pernis apivorus* (small flocks), *Milvus migrans*, *M. milvus*, *Pandion haliaetus*, *Grus grus* (up to 5000 pass over every year), and *Chlidonias niger*. Wintering species include *Gavia arctica* (1-2), *Circus cyaneus* (1-2), and *Asio flammeus* (1-2).

MALTA

Storm Petrel *Hydrobates pelagicus*

INTRODUCTION

General information

Malta is situated in the centre of the Mediterranean Sea at approximately 36°N, 14°E. The principal islands are Malta (249 sq km), Gozo (70 sq km), and Comino (2.6 sq km), and there are a number of smaller islands of which the most important is Filfla.

Malta is very densely populated with some 340,000 people (an average population density of 1059 persons per sq km) in a seemingly never-ending complex of towns and villages, which are surrounded by fields terracing almost every hillside. The cultivable area totalled 11,491 ha in 1983. In the northern and western parts of Malta, and in Gozo, the landscape comprises steep rocky ridges dividing fertile valleys often choked with vegetation.

Almost all remaining vegetation is semi-natural of which garigue (*Euphorbia*, *Thymus*, *Teucrium*) is dominant in many places. The only woodland of any extent is the coniferous wood at Buskett which runs down to Wied il-Luq, a valley of deciduous trees. Marshy habitats are very scarce, but many valley bottoms have irrigation dams which have standing water for several months.

Ornithological importance

Of the 360 species recorded in the islands, approximately 13 are resident, 5 are summer visitors, 52 are winter visitors, 112 are more-or-less regular migrants, and the rest are rare or irregular migrants or vagrants. Malta is noteworthy for its breeding seabirds, particularly *Calonectris diomedea* and *Hydrobates pelagicus*. Breeding passerines include *Calandrella brachydactyla, Sylvia conspicillata* (which has decreased throughout the islands during the last decade), and *S. melanocephala*. In Malta, more than almost anywhere else, migration dominates the ornithological year. The number of birds occurring is highly variable and is, to a large extent, dependent on the weather. A large proportion of species using the Palearctic-African flyway regularly or occasionally stop over including many species of birds of prey.

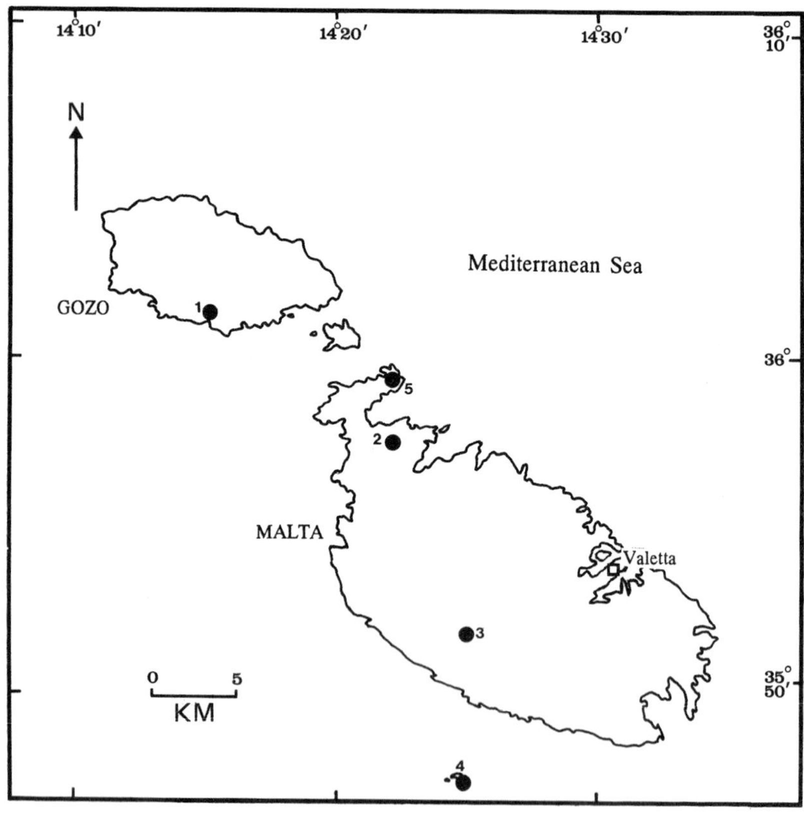

Figure 22: Map showing the location of the sites in Malta

Conservation infrastructure and protected-area system

The Protection of Birds and Wild Rabbits Regulations 1980 totally protected all birds of prey and a large number of migrant species, introduced a close season when no species can be shot or trapped, and listed a number of Bird Sanctuaries where shooting and trapping are totally prohibited. There are also two Nature Reserves. Nature conservation is the responsibility of the Environment Division, Ministry of Education.

International measures relevant to the conservation of sites

Malta is a member of the Council of Europe, although no Biogenetic Reserves have been designated and it has not signed the Bern Convention. It has, however, signed the Ramsar Convention and the World Heritage Convention, and has signed but not ratified the Barcelona Convention's Protocol concerning Mediterranean Specially Protected Areas. One Ramsar Site has been designated, but no natural World Heritage Sites (although three cultural sites have been designated).

Overview of the inventory

Five sites are covered which comprise about 0.15 per cent of the Maltese archipelago. Filfla Islet, Ta'Cenc Cliffs, and Rdum Tal-Madonna support most of the islands' breeding species and a majority of the islands' seabirds; Filfla being one of the largest colonies of *Hydrobates pelagicus* in the Mediterranean. Buskett and Wied il-Luq, and Ghadira Pool are the most important areas for migrants, with Ghadira Pool being the main wetland site. With the exception of Rdum Tal-Madonna, all the important bird areas are listed as Bird Sanctuaries and two are also Nature Reserves, including Filfla where landing without permission is prohibited.

Although these areas are not threatened by development (except Ta'Cenc), the bird-protection laws are not adequately enforced and there is continuous human interference mainly because of bird shooting and catching. The illegal shooting and catching of birds is of international concern and is discussed by Magnin (1986).

Acknowledgements

The following accounts were compiled from information provided by J. Sultana (Malta Ornithological Society), who also provided material for the introduction.

INVENTORY

No.	Site name	Region	Criteria used to select site [see p.18]							
			0	1(i)	1(ii)	1(iii)	1(iv)	2	3	4
001	Ta'Cenc Cliffs, Gozo								*	
002	Ghadira Pool								*	
003	Buskett and Wied il-Luq								*	
004	Filfla Islet			*	*				*	
005	Rdum Tal-Madonna, L-Ahrax								*	

Comments on the inventory

1. When applying the site-selection criteria (category 3) the 'region' is Malta.

---

001 Ta'Cenc Cliffs (Gozo)

36°01'N, 14°15'E

Bird Sanctuary (2.5 ha)

Sheer sea cliffs (135 m high) with profuse vegetation on some ledges. Illegal bird shooting is a problem. Threatened by proposed tourist development.

The area supports the largest colony of *Calonectris diomedea* (800-1000 pairs) in Malta. Other breeding species include *Puffinus puffinus yelkouan* (number of pairs not known), *Calandrella brachydactyla*, *Monticola solitarius* (10 pairs), and *Sylvia conspicillata*, and formerly *Falco peregrinus* (1 pair; exterminated in the last three years).

002 Ghadira Pool

35°57'N, 14°23'E 6 ha Ramsar Site

Nature Reserve and Bird Sanctuary; an important educational area.

A freshwater pool which becomes saline and nearly dries out in summer; surrounded by halophytic vegetation, tamarisks and reeds. The only significant wetland site in Malta. Disturbance from traffic and tourists is a problem.

An important site for migrants, especially waders including *Philomachus pugnax* (up to 100 in spring), and passerines.

003 Buskett and Wied il-Luq

35°52'N, 14°24'E 30 ha

Bird Sanctuary

Coniferous woodland (most extensive on island) and a valley of deciduous woodland (Wied il-Luq). Illegal shooting is a serious problem.

A roosting site for migrants, notably raptors especially *Pernis apivorus*, *Falco subbuteo*, and also *F. eleonorae*. Also an important site for passage and wintering passerines.

004 Filfla Islet

35°47'N, 14°25'E 6 ha

Nature Reserve and Bird Sanctuary

A rocky islet with rising cliffs surrounded by boulders and slopes of rock debris.

Supports one of the largest colonies of *Hydrobates pelagicus* in the Mediterranean (5000-10,000 pairs) as well as breeding *Calonectris diomedea* (200 pairs), *Larus argentatus michahellis* (80-100 pairs), and possibly *Puffinus puffinus yelkouan*.

005 Rdum Tal-Madonna (L-Ahrax)

35°59'N, 14°23'E 4 ha

Protected from development (green area)

A semi-peninsula with sea cliffs (25 m high, 200 m long), with a lot of natural rock debris at the base of the cliffs. Shooting and trapping of birds take place above the cliffs.

The area supports a large colony of *Puffinus puffinus yelkouan* (500 pairs). It is also an important breeding area for *Calandrella brachydactyla*, *Monticola solitarius* (2-3 pairs), and *Sylvia conspicillata*.

MAIN REFERENCES

Magnin, G. (1986) An assessment of illegal shooting and catching of birds in Malta. *ICBP Study Report* No. 13. Cambridge: International Council for Bird Preservation.

Schembri, P.J., Lanfranco, E., Farrugia, P., Schembri, S. and Sultana J. (1987) *Localities with conservation value in the Maltese islands.* Environment Division, Ministry of Education.

Sultana, J. and Gauci, C. (1982) *A new guide to the birds of Malta.* Valletta: Malta Ornithological Society.

NETHERLANDS

Barnacle Goose *Branta leucopsis*

INTRODUCTION

General information

The Netherlands occupies a key position in north-west Europe forming much of the southern North Sea coast of the continent. The human population density is the highest in Europe; nearly 15 million people (1985 estimate) occupy about 37,300 sq km of land (an average population density of over 400 persons per sq km). The country's total area (including coastal and inland waters) is about 41,500 sq km and is divided into 12 provinces. Around 90 per cent of the population is urban, with major cities including 's-Gravenhage (The Hague), Amsterdam (700,000 inhabitants), Rotterdam, Haarlem, Utrecht, Eindhoven, and Arnhem; about 15 per cent of the land surface is built up.

About two-thirds of all land is cultivated (24,000 sq km in 1983), of which half is grazing land and one-third arable land. Thirty per cent of the country (essentially central and western areas) is below sea-level, consisting of embanked polders which have been reclaimed in the past seven centuries. Such areas are drained by dense networks of ditches and pumps, and are protected by large sea-walls or dykes. Water drained from the polders is often stored in the numerous freshwater lakes which are found in these low-lying regions, and pumped to rivers, canals and the IJsselmeer to the sea.

The varied Dutch coastline is dominated in the south-west by the major delta complex of the Rivers Schelde, Maas, and Rijn (Rhine). All the river estuaries were formerly tidal but extensive sea-defence works, carried out following the disastrous storm-surge of

1953, have resulted in the exclusion or restriction of tidal action. Some of the former estuaries (e.g. Haringvliet) are now effectively brackish or freshwater lagoons behind barrages, whilst in the Oosterschelde, for example, a system of sluice-gates ensures that the sea is only shut off when high tides and/or storms are predicted.

Between Hoek van Holland and Den Helder, the coast consists of a narrow continuous belt of dune topography which is above sea-level and seaward of extensive reclaimed land. North-east of Den Helder is the chain of Waddeneilanden – the barrier islands of the Waddenzee – which extend from Texel in the west to Rottumeroog near the border with the Federal Republic of Germany.

The Waddenzee (Wadden Sea) is shared with Denmark and the Federal Republic of Germany and is a very large shallow intertidal sea area between the Waddeneilanden and the mainland. The central Netherlands was once dominated by the Zuiderzee, a large sea embayment. However, major dyke constructions closed off the Zuiderzee in 1932 turning it into a vast freshwater lake – the IJsselmeer – which is being reclaimed (40 per cent of area reclaimed, forming four large polders, totalling 150,000+ ha).

The east and south-east of the Netherlands are characterised by land above sea-level although the landscape is still dominated by wetland features – namely the valleys and tributaries of the major rivers mentioned above and of the IJssel. These upland areas were originally covered with *Quercus* woodland and *Quercus/Fagus* woodland with *Betula*, but only tiny fragments remain, many areas having been cleared in the Middle Ages. Now only 8.5 per cent of the country is covered with woodland; mainly planted in the nineteenth and twentieth centuries. The east and south-east also holds the last remnants of the once quite extensive areas of heathland.

Ornithological importance

From an international point of view, the many wetlands and low-lying grassland areas are of particular importance for migrating and wintering waterfowl as well as for breeding marsh birds including waders and terns. Huge numbers of birds use the Waddenzee, Delta area (south-west Netherlands), IJsselmeer, and the major rivers. Inland grasslands form the main feeding area for swans, geese, *Anas penelope*, and some waders. Important breeding habitats include sandbanks, saltmarsh, wet dune valleys, reedbeds, wooded swamps, and meadows. The significance of meadows for breeding waders is rapidly declining owing to drainage and intensive agricultural methods.

Important breeding populations (maximum numbers of pairs 1983-1987, unless otherwise stated) include *Podiceps cristatus* (9000), *Phalacrocorax carbo sinensis* (13,500), *Botaurus stellaris* (500 males), *Ardea cinerea* (6000-9000), *A. purpurea* (280), *Platalea leucorodia* (400), *Anas clypeata* (12,000), *Circus aeruginosus* (800), *Haematopus ostralegus* (90,000), *Recurvirostra avosetta* (8000), *Vanellus vanellus* (200,000-275,000), *Limosa limosa* (85,000), *Sterna sandvicensis* (10,000-12,000), *S. hirundo* (15,000-19,000), *Chlidonias niger* (1000-1500), *Asio flammeus* (100-200), *Luscinia svecica* (2000-3000), and *Panurus biarmicus* (700-1400).

Important non-breeding waterfowl populations (average maxima and month) include *Podiceps cristatus* (20,000; Aug.), *Cygnus columbianus* (8800), *Anser fabalis* (120,000; Jan.), *A. brachyrhynchus* (17,000; Jan.), *A. albifrons albifrons* (330,000; Jan.), *A. anser* (60,000; Oct./Nov.), *Branta leucopsis* (80,000; Jan.), *B. bernicla bernicla* (50,000-90,000; Apr./May), *Tadorna tadorna* (60,000; Oct.), *Anas penelope* (350,000; Jan.). *Aythya ferina* (110,000; Jan.), *A. fuligula* (150,000; Jan.), *A. marila* (100,000; Feb.), *Mergus albellus* (9000; Jan.), *Haematopus ostralegus* (300,000; Jan.), *Recurvirostra avosetta* (18,000; Sept.), *Pluvialis apricaria* (400,000; Nov.), *P. squatarola* (17,000; May), *Calidris canutus* (100,000; Sept.), *C. alpina* (240,000; Sept.), *Limosa lapponica* (70,000; May), and *Numenius arquata* (100,000; Sept.).

The areas of woodland and heathland also hold noteworthy populations of several species including *Pernis apivorus* (400-500 pairs), *Tetrao tetrix* (rapidly declining), *Caprimulgus europaeus* (500-600 pairs), and *Lullula arborea* (2500-3000 pairs).

Conservation infrastructure and protected-area system

Nature conservation is one of the responsibilities of the Ministry of Agriculture and Fisheries. The Minister is advised by the Nature Conservancy Council and by his own Research Institute for Nature Management (RIN).

About 170,000 ha (including many areas important for birds) of natural and semi-natural habitats are reserves owned by state or private nature conservation organisations. These habitats include saltmarshes, dunes, freshwater lakes and marshland, peatland, heathland, woodland, fens, and meadows. Many of the reserves are at least partly open to the public.

Of the total area of reserves, about 55 per cent are owned and managed by national or regional private bodies, notably Natuurmonumenten (Society for the Preservation of Natural Monuments), the Landschappen ('Landscapes'; one in each of the twelve provinces), and Nederlandse Vereniging tot Bescherming van Vogels (Netherlands Society for the Protection of Birds). State Nature Reserves fall under the responsibility of the National Forest Service, Staatsbosbeheer (SBB), which also cares for the 70,000 ha of state forests.

A small proportion of reserves has been designated under the Nature Conservation Act, and thus receives full legal protection. However, even this does not alter the fact that many of the protected sites are affected by pollution, drainage, and other human influences from surrounding areas. These detrimental effects are often related to agriculture (two thirds of the country is in agricultural use). The above-mentioned figure of 170,000 ha of reserves does not include 150,000 ha of the Waddenzee, which are protected under the Nature Conservation Act.

Management plans are normally drawn up by the body which owns each reserve and in the case of reserves owned by private organisations, the plan needs the approval of the Ministry to qualify for management subsidies provided by the state.

International measures relevant to the conservation of sites

The Netherlands is a member of the Council of Europe and of the European Community (therefore being subject to the terms of the Wild Birds Directive), and has ratified the Ramsar Convention, Bern Convention and Bonn Convention. Nine Ramsar Sites (plus six in Netherlands Antilles) had been designated by June 1988 (two of these are now included in the Waddenzee Ramsar Site) together with 20 Biogenetic Reserves and six EEC Special Protection Areas. The Netherlands has also designated a single Biosphere Reserve (Waddenzee).

Overview of inventory

Seventy sites are included in the inventory and most are at least partially protected. Many Nature Reserves are covered, in addition to all Ramsar Sites (in the European Netherlands).

Coverage of colonially breeding birds is good, with the exception of *Ardea cinerea* which breeds in many colonies scattered over the country. Coverage is also good for three non-colonial species of which the majority of pairs breed in reserves; namely *Asio flammeus*, *Luscinia svecica*, and *Panurus biarmicus*. Approximately 40-50 per cent of breeding *Botaurus stellaris* and *Circus aeruginosus* are thought to be included in the inventory, whilst coverage of other species with dispersed distributions is low, though satisfactory numbers are present in the selected areas.

Non-breeding estuarine species and diving ducks are extremely well covered. Coverage of the agricultural feeding areas of *Cygnus columbianus*, geese, and *Anas penelope* is relatively low, but important roosting sites are mainly within the listed areas. Only small numbers of *Pluvialis apricaria* are covered since this species prefers dry grassland and arable fields.

Acknowledgements

The site accounts have been compiled mainly from data-sheets completed in 1981 by E. R. Osieck (Osieck and Mörzer Bruyns 1981), and in 1987 by J. Rooth (Rijksinstituut voor Natuurbeheer/Research Institute for Nature Management) and J. Vink (Staatsbosbeheer/National Forest Service). Up-to-date supplementary information has also been provided by E. R. Osieck (Nederlandse Vereniging tot Bescherming van Vogels), who also provided material for the introduction. J. A. van der Ven helped to resolve many of the problems that arose when preparing the site accounts.

INVENTORY

No.	Site name	Region	Criteria used to select site [see p.18] 0	1(i)	1(ii)	1(iii)	1(iv)	2	3	4
001	Waddenzee	GN,FD,NH				*			*	
002	Texel	NH			*	*			*	
003	Vlieland	FD			*	*			*	
004	Griend	FD			*	*			*	
005	Terschelling	FD		*	*	*			*	
006	Ameland	FD				*			*	
007	Engelsmanplaat	FD				*				
008	Schiermonnikoog	FD				*			*	
009	Rottumerplaat and Rottumeroog	GN			*	*			*	
010	Groningen buitendijks	GN				*			*	
011	Lauwersmeer	GN,FD				*			*	
012	Friesland buitendijks	FD			*	*			*	
013	Balgzand	NH			*	*			*	
014	Dollard	GN				*			*	
015	Groote Wielen	FD				*			*	
016	Workumerwaard including Makkumerwaard and Kooiwaard	FD			*	*			*	
017	Oudegaasterbrekken, Fluessen, Groote Gaastmeer, and Morra	FD				*			*	
018	Slotermeer	FD				*			*	
019	Steile Bank, Mokkebank, and Sondeler Leyen	FD				*			*	
020	Tjongervallei, Lindevallei, and Rottige Meenthe	FD				*			*	
021	Zwarte en Witte Brekken, Langweerderwielen, Oudhof, and Koevordermeer	FD				*			*	
022	Sneekermeer and Terkaplester Poelen	FD				*			*	
023	Oude Venen and De Deelen	FD				*			*	
024	Van Oordt's Mersken	FD				*			*	
025	Dwingelose and Kraloër Heide	DE				*			*	
026	Bargerveen	DE							*	
027	De Wieden and De Weerribben	OL,DE				*			*	
028	IJsseldelta (including Lower IJssel, Zwarte Meer, and Vossemeer)	OL,FV				*			*	
029	Noordoostpolder-West	FV				*			*	
030	IJsselmeer	NH,FD,FV				*			*	
031	Oostvaardersplassen and Lepelaarsplassen	FV				*			*	
032	Veluwemeer, Harderbroek, and Kievitslanden	GD,FV				*			*	
033	Arkemheen, Zeldert, and Eemmeer	GD,UT				*			*	
034	Oostelijke Vechtplassen	NH,UT							*	
035	Botshol and Ronde Hoep	UT,NH							*	
036	Naardermeer	NH				*			*	
037	Gooimeer	NH,FV				*			*	
038	Zuidelijk Poldergebied, including Eilandspolder, Alkmaardermeer, Wormer- en Jisperveld, Polder Westzaan, Waterland	NH				*			*	
039	Zwanenwater	NH				*			*	
040	Nieuwkoopse Plassen and Kamerikse Nessen	ZH				*			*	
041	Reeuwijkse Plassen	ZH				*			*	

No.	Site name	Region	Criteria used to select site [see p.18]							
			0	1(i)	1(ii)	1(iii)	1(iv)	2	3	4
042	Zouwe and Linge	GD							*	
043	Waal: Nijmegen – Gorinchem (including Hurwenen) and Maas: Hedel – Andel	GD				*				
044	Waal and Rijn: Spijk – Nijmegen – Arnhem (including Oude Rijnstrangen and Ooijpolders)	GD				*			*	
045	Biesbosch	ZH				*			*	
046	Voordelta, Breedewater/ Quackjeswater, and Kwade Hoek	ZH,ZD				*			*	
047	Haringvliet and Hollands Diep (including Oudeland van Strijen)	ZH				*			*	
048	Krammer and Volkerak	ZH,ZD, NB	*							
049	Grevelingen	ZH,ZD			*	*			*	
050	Oosterschelde	ZD,NB			*	*			*	
051	Veerse Meer	ZD			*	*			*	
052	Westerschelde	ZD			*	*			*	
053	Het Zwin	ZD	*							
054	Yersekse Moer	ZD				*				
055	Putting – Groot Eiland	ZD				*				
056	De Peel and Strabrechtse Heide (including Groote Peel)	NB,LG				*			*	
057	De Hamert	LG							*	
058	Meynweg	LG							*	
059	Leekstermeer	GN,DE				*				
060	Fochteloërveen, Esmeer, and Huis ter Heide	FD,DE				*				
061	Zuidlaardermeer	GN,DE	*							
062	Tjeukemeer	FD				*				
063	Engbertsdijkvenen	OL	*							
064	Vennen van Oisterwijk and Kampina, Helvoirtse and Vughtse Gement	NB				*				
065	Maas: Vierlingsbeek – Grave and Ohé – Beesel	NB,LG				*			*	
066	Rijn/Lek: Arnhem – Schoonhoven	GD,UT, ZH	*							
067	IJssel: Westervoort – Zwolle	GD,OL				*			*	
068	Holterberg and Haarlerberg	OL							*	
069	Rechte Heide	NB							*	
070	Oirschotse Heide	NB							*	

GN=Groningen FD=Friesland NH=Noord-Holland DE=Drenthe
OL=Overijssel FV=Flevoland GD=Gelderland UT=Utrecht
ZH=Zuid-Holland NB=Noord-Brabant ZD=Zeeland LG=Limburg

Comments on inventory

1. Where possible, figures for non-breeding birds are averages of annual maxima over a number of (usually 3-5) years, except where a range or maximum figure is given. In general, the ornithological information for a majority of the sites 001-058 is based on the data-sheets compiled in 1981, although many of the site accounts have been brought up to date, and particular attention has been given to incorporating the most significant changes in bird populations.

2. Where 'restrictions on agricultural practices' is noted, farmers can claim compensation for certain voluntary restrictions in farming methods, which are favourable for nature conservation (e.g. late mowing, no use of herbicides etc.).
3. 'Protected by Nature Conservation Act' means that an area has been designated under the act and that it is forbidden 'to perform actions, to have actions performed or to allow actions to be performed, which are detrimental to the scenic beauty or scientific importance of the area, or which disfigure the area' and 'to defile that area, dig out, pick or transport plants, flowers and branches in it, disturb, catch or kill animals in it, or attempt to do such things, or generally damage the area's natural history'.
4. In the inventory, the name of the site is followed by the name of the region, given in parentheses; these are the provinces of the Netherlands.
5. When applying the site-selection criteria (category 3) the whole of the Netherlands has been regarded as a single 'region' (NUTS level 0).
6. All of the sites meet the site-selection criteria except the following:
   - Site 048 was formerly of international importance for non-breeding waterfowl, but has undergone major ecological changes after being closed off from the sea; it is included because it could, if managed appropriately, be developed into an important freshwater ecosystem.
   - Site 053 is included because it is contiguous with an important bird area in neighbouring Belgium.
   - Site 063 is included because it is one of the last remaining large raised bogs in the Netherlands and it supports small numbers of a range of species on Annex I of the EEC Wild Birds Directive.
   - Sites 061 and 066 are wetland sites that are believed to be of international importance, but for which insufficient data were submitted.
7. There is some overlap of sites with regard to the Waddenzee (001) and neighbouring islands and forelands. Thus site 001 includes sites 004, 007, 009, 010, 012, 013, and 014 as well as the forelands of sites 002, 003, 005, 006, and 008.

Glossary

With regard to the information on protected areas, L = provincial Landschap (private bodies for nature conservation; one in each province); NM = Vereniging tot Behoud van Natuurmonumenten in Nederland; SBB = Staatsbosbeheer; VB = Nederlandse Vereniging tot Bescherming van Vogels. EEC SPA = European Community Special Protection Area.

With regard to the site names, the following Dutch words are used: bank = sandbank; broek = marshy land; buitendijks = foreland, gebied = site/area; grote = large; heide = heath; meer = lake; plaat = sandbank; plassen/plas = shallow lakes/shallow lake; vallei = valley; veen = moorland; waard = foreland or land enclosed by rivers; zee = sea.

---

001 Waddenzee (Groningen, Friesland, Noord-Holland)

53°25'N, 06°00'E 250,000 ha Ramsar Site; Biosphere Reserve (260,000 ha)

150,000 ha are protected by Nature Conservation Act

Together with the Danish and German sections, the Waddenzee (Wadden Sea) is the largest intertidal mudflat area in Europe. The Dutch section is bounded by the Waddeneilanden, and it surrounds the island of Griend, and islets such as Engelsmanplaat (see sites 004 and 007). Fishing and water-sports are the main human activities whilst increasing recreational use, proposed reclamation, development of Emden Harbour, military activities (air force), gas exploration, and water pollution (especially from the Rhine) are the more important environmental problems. The site does not include the main islands, but it does include sites 004, 007, 009, 011, 012, 013, and 014 as well as the forelands of sites 002, 003, 005, 006, and 008.

An important foraging area for birds breeding and resting on the Waddeneilanden, such as *Platalea leucorodia*, *Haematopus ostralegus*, *Recurvirostra avosetta*, *Sterna sandvicensis*, *S. hirundo*, and *S. albifrons*. Important for wintering, passage and moulting waterfowl (av. Jan. counts unless stated) including *Branta leucopsis* (max. 50,000), *B. bernicla* (11,000; max. 54,000), *Tadorna tadorna* (35,000; max. 50,000), *Anas penelope* (30,000+; max. 160,000), *A. crecca* (13,000; max. 45,000), *A. platyrhynchos* (26,000), *A. acuta* (3000), *Aythya marila* (11,000; max. 40,000), *Somateria mollissima* (100,000; max. 170,000), *Melanitta nigra* (29,000), *Mergus serrator* (max. 18,000), *M. merganser* (max. 9000), *Haematopus ostralegus* (180,000; max. 290,000), *Recurvirostra avosetta* (17,000 in Jan; max. 10,000), *Charadrius hiaticula* (max. 10,000), *Pluvialis squatarola* (3000; max. 22,000), *Calidris canutus* (40,000; max. 111,000), *C. alba* (2000; max. 5000), *C. ferruginea* (3000 on passage), *Calidris alpina* (150,000; max. 330,000), *Limosa lapponica* (35,000; max. 93,000), *Numenius arquata* (60,000; max. 122,000), *Tringa erythropus* (4000 on passage), *T. totanus* (11,000; max. 45,000), *T. nebularia* (6700 on passage), and *Arenaria interpres* (2000; max. 8100).

002 Texel (Noord-Holland)

53°05'N, 04°48'E 6000 ha foreshore included in Waddenzee Ramsar Site

60 per cent protected with SBB and NM Nature Reserves

Westernmost of the Waddeneilanden. The site comprises the more important parts of Texel, which include: De Muy, De Geul and De Slufter (dunes and lakes); Waal en Burg, Dijksmanshuizen, and De Bol (meadows); De Schorren (saltmarsh); and Zeeburg (farmland managed for *Branta bernicla*). The main bird habitats are beaches, sand-dunes, saltwater lagoons, freshwater marshes, saltwater marshes, raised saltmarsh, wet meadows, grassland, and arable land. Human activities include stock-raising, recreation, tourism, and hunting; there is scattered human habitation.

Breeding species include *Botaurus stellaris* (1 pair), *Platalea leucorodia* (70 pairs; 130 on passage), *Anas clypeata* (65 pairs), *Circus aeruginosus* (10-15 pairs), *C. cyaneus* (5-10 pairs), *Recurvirostra avosetta* (170 pairs), *Limosa limosa* (130 pairs), *Numenius arquata* (120 pairs), *Tringa totanus* (310 pairs), *Philomachus pugnax* (30 pairs), *Larus ridibundus* (12,000 pairs), *Sterna sandvicensis* (750 pairs), *S. hirundo* (300 pairs), *S. paradisaea* (130 pairs), *S. albifrons* (39 pairs), and *Asio flammeus* (14 pairs). Also important for passage and wintering waterfowl; passage species include *Branta bernicla* (6000), *Haematopus ostralegus* (12,000; 9500 in winter), *Recurvirostra avosetta* (1500-2000), *Charadrius alexandrinus* (100), *Pluvialis apricaria* (8000), *P. squatarola* (1500), *Calidris canutus* (5000), *C. alba* (600), *C. alpina* (10,000), *Limosa lapponica* (20,000), *Numenius arquata* (10,000), *Tringa totanus* (1400), and *T. nebularia* (300).

003 Vlieland (Friesland)

53°17'N, 04°59'E 1300 ha foreshore included in Waddenzee Ramsar Site

Largely a Nature Reserve (SBB Reserve)

Parts of the island (including Posthuiswad, Kroonspolders, and part of Vliehors) with beaches, sand-dunes, saltwater lagoons and saltings, mudflats, raised saltmarsh, woodland, and grassland. Human activities include forestry, stock-raising, fishing, military training (airforce) and recreation; there is a village.

Breeding species include *Platalea leucorodia* (24 pairs), *Circus aeruginosus* (5 pairs), *C. cyaneus* (5 pairs), *Rallus aquaticus* (50 pairs), *Recurvirostra avosetta* (22 pairs), *Limosa limosa*, *Numenius arquata* (20 pairs), *Larus argentatus* (10,000 pairs), and *Asio flammeus* (1 pair). Important for passage and wintering waterfowl; passage species include *Branta bernicla* (2000), *Anas penelope* (6000), *Haematopus ostralegus* (10,000; 8000 in winter), *Recurvirostra avosetta* (560), *Calidris canutus* (20,000; 6000 in winter), *C. alpina* (22,000), *Limosa lapponica* (7500), *Numenius arquata* (10,000), *Tringa nebularia* (600), and *Arenaria interpres* (800).

004 Griend (Friesland)

53°15'N, 05°15'E 100 ha Ramsar Site (23 ha)

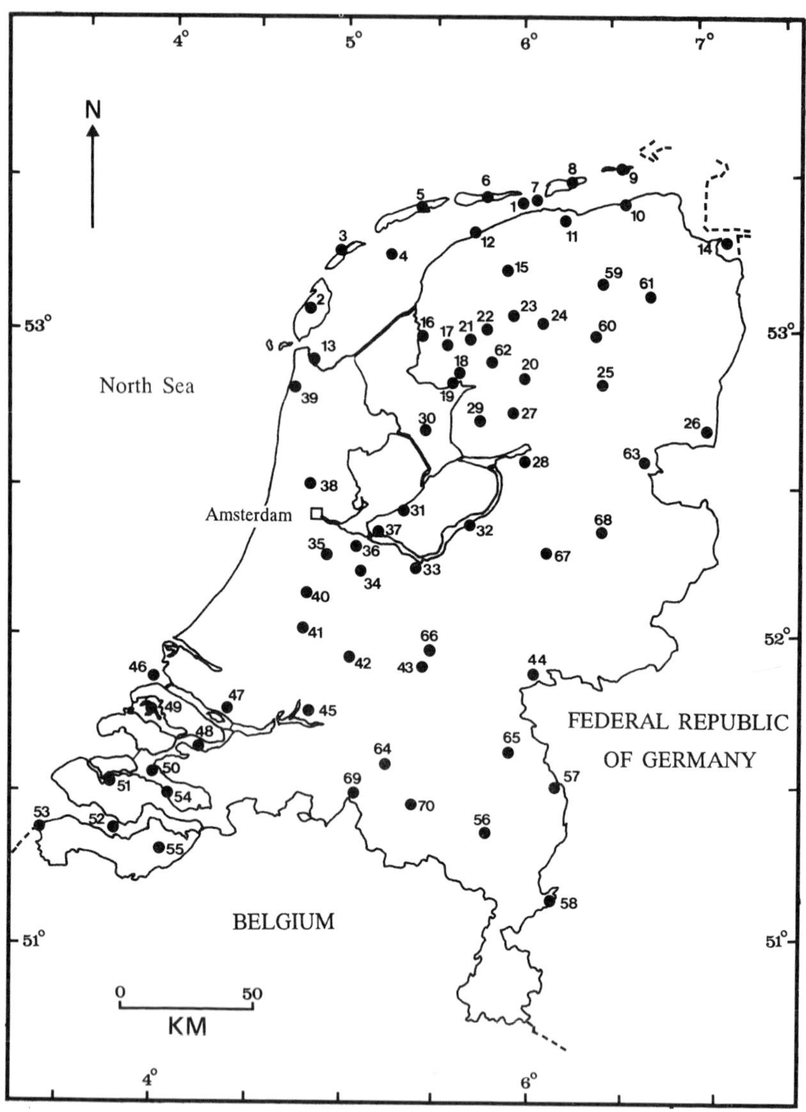

Figure 23: Map showing the location of the sites in the Netherlands

Nature Reserve (NM Reserve)

A small, crescent-shaped island in the Waddenzee with beaches, saltwater marshes, mudflats and raised saltmarsh. Only 16 ha is permanently above water, with the highest part of the island only 1 m above mean high tide. Erosion during storms and spring tides, and subsidence due to nearby gas exploration are problems.

Extremely important for breeding terns with *Sterna sandvicensis* (6000 pairs), *S. hirundo* (1500 pairs), and *S. paradisaea* (500 pairs). Passage waders include *Haematopus ostralegus* (12,000 in winter), *Calidris canutus* (30,000; 15,000 in winter), *C. alpina* (20,000), and *Limosa lapponica* (10,000).

005 Terschelling (Friesland)

53°24'N, 05°22'E *c.*7000 ha

Partly a Ramsar Site (Boschplaat: 4400 ha); European Diploma Site (Boschplaat: 4000 ha)

Mainly Nature Reserve (SBB Reserve); restrictions on agricultural practices

Parts of one of the Waddenzee barrier islands with beaches, sand-dunes, saltwater lagoons and marshes, raised saltmarsh, wet meadows, and grassland. The most important wetland areas are at the east and west extremities of the island; the Boschplaat (4400 ha) and the Noordsvaarder/Kroonpolders area, respectively. Human activities include military training (airforce), stock-raising, hunting, and recreation; there is scattered human habitation.

Breeding species include *Platalea leucorodia* (42 pairs), *Circus aeruginosus* (10-15 pairs), *C. cyaneus* (20-30 pairs), *Porzana porzana* (1-3 pairs), *Recurvirostra avosetta* (80 pairs), *Limosa limosa* (200-250 pairs), *Numenius arquata* (200-300 pairs), *Tringa totanus* (600-800 pairs), *Larus fuscus* (13,000 pairs), *L. argentatus* (21,000 pairs), *S. hirundo* (50-200 pairs), *S. paradisaea* (20-50 pairs), and *Asio flammeus* (10 pairs). Important for passage and wintering waterfowl; passage species include *Anser anser* (800), *Branta bernicla* (20,000), *Tadorna tadorna* (8000), *Anas penelope* (22,000), *Somateria mollissima* (14,000), *Haematopus ostralegus* (20,000; 19,000 in winter), *Recurvirostra avosetta* (400), *Pluvialis squatarola* (2400), *Calidris canutus* (20,000; 8000 in winter), *C. alba* (1600), *C. alpina* (25,000), *Limosa lapponica* (8000), *Numenius arquata* (9000; 7000 in winter), and *Tringa nebularia* (700).

006 Ameland (Friesland)

53°28'N, 05°45'E 4500 ha partly included in Waddenzee Ramsar Site

Partly an SBB Nature Reserve (240 ha); eastern part managed by L (Het Oerd: 750 ha)

Part of the Waddenzee barrier island with beaches, sand-dunes, saltwater lagoons, freshwater marshes, saltwater marshes, raised saltmarsh, wet meadows, and grassland. The reserves are contiguous areas of dunes, saltmarsh, and wet grassland at the eastern end of the island. Human activities include stock-raising, hunting, recreation, drinking water extraction, and gas exploitation; there is scattered human habitation.

Breeding species include *Botaurus stellaris* (4 pairs), *Circus aeruginosus* (14 pairs), *C. cyaneus* (25 pairs), *Recurvirostra avosetta* (60 pairs), *Philomachus pugnax* (40 males), *Limosa limosa* (270-320 pairs), *Numenius arquata* (60 pairs), *Tringa totanus* (230 pairs), *Sterna hirundo* (100 pairs), *S. paradisaea* (100 pairs), *S. albifrons* (10 pairs), and *Asio flammeus* (23 pairs). Important for passage and wintering waterfowl; passage species include *Branta bernicla* (6000), *Tadorna tadorna* (2600), *Anas penelope* (7600), *Haematopus ostralegus* (24,000 in winter), *Recurvirostra avosetta* (600), *Calidris alba* (1000; 600 in winter), *C. alpina* (17,000), *Limosa lapponica* (6800), *Numenius arquata* (17,000; 6000 in winter), *Tringa erythropus* (110), *T. totanus* (3600), and *T. nebularia* (800).

007 Engelsmanplaat (Friesland)

53°27'N, 06°03'E 75 ha included in Waddenzee Ramsar Site

Nature Reserve (SBB Reserve: 40 ha)

An islet in the Waddenzee between Ameland, Schiermonnikoog, and the mainland. Includes intertidal saltmarsh, and mudflat areas.

Breeding species include *Sterna hirundo* (20 pairs). A formerly large tern colony was destroyed in 1982-83 when wind erosion removed the dune nesting area. Passage waders include *Haematopus ostralegus* (8000), *Calidris canutus* (2500), *C. alba* (700), *C. alpina* (8000), and *Numenius arquata* (4500).

008 Schiermonnikoog (Friesland)

53°30'N, 06°15'E *c.*3000 ha partly included in Waddenzee Ramsar Site

80 per cent protected; partly a Nature Reserve (SBB Reserve: 800 ha); restrictions on agricultural practices

Part of the easternmost of the five larger Waddeneilanden, with beaches, sand-dunes, saltwater lagoons, freshwater marshes, saltwater marshes, raised saltmarsh, wet meadows, grassland. Human activities include stock-raising, hunting, and recreation; there is scattered human habitation, but no car traffic.

Breeding species include *Somateria mollissima* (380 pairs), *Circus cyaneus* (7 pairs), *Recurvirostra avosetta* (6 pairs), *Limosa limosa* (30 pairs), *Philomachus pugnax* (5 pairs), *Tringa totanus* (120 pairs), *Sterna hirundo* (8 pairs), *S. paradisaea* (10 pairs), *S. albifrons* (9 pairs), and *Asio flammeus* (2 pairs). Important for passage and wintering waterfowl; passage species include *Branta leucopsis* (10,000; 8300 in winter), *B. bernicla* (4000), *Tadorna tadorna* (5000), *Haematopus ostralegus* (22,000; 20,000 in winter), *Recurvirostra avosetta* (240), *Pluvialis squatarola* (1600), *Calidris canutus* (14,000; 11,000 in winter), *C. alba* (1000), *C. alpina* (31,000), *Limosa lapponica* (4700), *Numenius arquata* (11,000; 4000 in winter), and *Tringa nebularia* (900).

009 Rottumerplaat and Rottumeroog (Groningen)

53°33'N, 06°32'E *c.*1000 ha included in Waddenzee Ramsar Site

Completely protected by Nature Conservation Act; Nature Reserves (SBB Reserves: 200 ha)

Two small uninhabited islands in the Waddenzee, with beaches and sand-dunes, saltwater marshes, and raised saltmarsh. Disturbances include illegal landings by tourists (despite being wardened in breeding season), and military-aircraft activity; there is erosion during storms and high tides.

Breeding species include *Somateria mollissima* (1500 pairs), *Haematopus ostralegus* (250-300 pairs), *Sterna hirundo* (700 pairs), *S. paradisaea* (700 pairs), and *S. albifrons* (50 pairs). In addition, non-breeding waterfowl include *Branta bernicla* (2000), *Haematopus ostralegus* (20,000), *Calidris canutus* (10,000), *C. alpina* (20,000), *Limosa lapponica* (3000), and *Numenius arquata* (6000).

010 Groningen buitendijks (Groningen)

53°26'N, 06°34'E 4000 ha included in Waddenzee Ramsar Site

Protected by Nature Conservation Act

A large area of saltwater marshes, mudflats and raised saltmarsh, seaward of the dykes. Human activities include stock-raising. There is some pollution of the area from industrial sources.

Important for breeding *Recurvirostra avosetta* (140 pairs). Other breeding species include *Sterna hirundo* (90+ pairs) and *S. paradisaea* (16+ pairs). Important for passage and wintering waterfowl (av. Jan. counts unless stated) including *Branta leucopsis* (9000; 20,000 on passage), *B. bernicla* (4000 on passage), *Tadorna tadorna* (9600; 21,000 on passage), *Anas penelope* (12,000 in Nov.), *Anas acuta* (1200 in Nov.), *Haematopus ostralegus* (26,000; 36,000 on passage), *Recurvirostra avosetta* (800; 2600 on passage), *Pluvialis squatarola* (5000 on passage), *Calidris alpina* (27,000 on passage), *Limosa lapponica* (5500), *Numenius arquata* (9400; 11,000 on passage), *Tringa totanus* (5500 on passage), and *T. nebularia* (1100 on passage).

011 Lauwersmeer (Groningen, Friesland)

53°22'N, 06°12'E 11,000 ha

Mainly unprotected; includes two small Nature Reserves (L and NM Reserves: 119 ha); 4300 ha has been designated as a 'Large Nature Unit' (Grote Eenheid Natuurgebied) which provides weak protection

A dammed estuary, formerly part of the Waddenzee (closed off in 1969), which has become freshwater, though the estuary structure remains. The surrounding area is mainly open grassland with some woodland and remnant saltmarsh vegetation. Human activities include recreation, agriculture, and military use. About 2000 ha have been designated as a military-training area, and an ammunition factory has been built in the southern part. Increasingly intensive recreational use of the area is a problem.

Breeding species include *Tadorna tadorna* (450-550 pairs), *Anas strepera* (300 pairs), *A. querquedula* (40-50 pairs), *A. clypeata* (300-350 pairs), *Circus aeruginosus* (80-90 pairs), *C. pygargus* (2 pairs), *Haematopus ostralegus* (1000-1500 pairs), *Recurvirostra avosetta* (400-500 pairs), *Philomachus pugnax* (350-400 pairs), *Limosa limosa* (450-500 pairs), *Tringa totanus* (500 pairs), *Larus minutus* (25-35 pairs), *L. ridibundus* (11,000-13,000 pairs), *Sterna hirundo* (250-275 pairs), *S. paradisaea* (80-90 pairs), and *Asio flammeus* (5-15 pairs). Important for passage waterfowl including *Cygnus columbianus* (max. 4000), *Anser fabalis* (860), *A. anser* (5500), *Branta leucopsis* (formerly 48,000; now decreased: max. 38,000), *Anas penelope* (formerly 60,000; now decreased: max. 41,000), *A. crecca* (formerly 65,000; now decreased: max. 43,000), *A. acuta* (4000 in Sept; max. 7000), and *A. clypeata* (former max. 1500; now increased: max. 4600).

012 Friesland buitendijks (Friesland)

53°20'N, 05°45'E 2500 ha included in Waddenzee Ramsar Site

Partly protected by Nature Conservation Act

An extensive area of mudflats, saltwater marshes, and raised saltmarsh along the Waddenzee coast of Friesland. Human activities include fishing and stock-raising.

Breeding species (1983 data) include *Haematopus ostralegus* (565 pairs), *Recurvirostra avosetta* (2400 pairs), *Tringa totanus* (210 pairs), *Larus ridibundus* (25,100 pairs), *Sterna hirundo* (945 pairs), and *S. paradisaea* (16 pairs). Important for passage waterfowl with *Branta leucopsis* (max. 6500), *B. bernicla* (max. 12,000), *Tadorna tadorna* (max. 3700), *Anas penelope* (max. 31,000), *Haematopus ostralegus* (max. 16,000), *Pluvialis squatarola* (2400), *Calidris alpina* (max. 32,600), *Limosa lapponica* (max. 5800), *Numenius arquata* (max. 16,000), *Tringa erythropus* (max. 600), and *T. totanus* (max. 11,500).

013 Balgzand (Noord-Holland)

52°55'N, 04°46'E 7800 ha included in Waddenzee Ramsar Site

Protected by Nature Conservation Act; includes 50 ha of foreshore managed by VB

A very large area of saltwater marshes, intertidal mudflats, and raised saltmarsh. Human activities include stock-raising. Pollution of the water, increasing recreation pressure, and the industrial activities of gas companies are problems at the site.

Breeding species include *Recurvirostra avosetta* (500 pairs), *Sterna hirundo* (500 pairs), and *S. albifrons* (60 pairs). Passage and wintering species (passage counts unless stated) include *Platalea leucorodia* (100), *Haematopus ostralegus* (18,000 in winter), *Recurvirostra avosetta* (560), *Calidris canutus* (24,000; 12,000 in winter), *C. alpina* (13,000), *Limosa lapponica* (10,000), *Numenius arquata* (3600), *Tringa erythropus* (480), *T. nebularia* (220), *Gelochelidon nilotica* (max. 70), and *Chlidonias niger* (max. 30,000 roosting).

014 Dollard (Groningen)

53°17'N, 07°08'E 6000 ha

Protected by Nature Conservation Act; Nature Reserves (NM and L Reserves: *c.*3600 ha)

Estuary with saltwater marshes, coastal mudflats, and raised saltmarsh. There are plans for harbour development in the adjoining West German sector to provide industrial docking facilities. This would include the building of an island and dam south of Emden which would dramatically change the tidal system. Adjoins site no. 033 in the Federal Republic of Germany.

Breeding species include *Anas clypeata* (40 pairs), *Circus aeruginosus* (7 pairs), *Porzana porzana* (5 pairs), *Recurvirostra avosetta* (900 pairs), *Philomachus pugnax* (32 pairs), *Limosa limosa* (175 pairs), *Tringa totanus* (400 pairs), *Larus ridibundus* (6000-7000 pairs), *S. hirundo* (80 pairs), *S. paradisaea* (30 pairs), and *S.albifrons* (2 pairs). Important for passage and wintering waterfowl (passage counts unless stated) with *Anser fabalis* (1000 in winter), *A. albifrons* (6000 in winter), *A. anser* (800), *Tadorna tadorna* (1600 in Jan.), *Anas penelope* (15,000), *A. crecca* (7,500), *A. acuta* (400), *Recurvirostra avosetta* (6,000), *Pluvialis squatarola* (2800), *Calidris alpina* (30,000), *Limosa lapponica* (7100), *Numenius arquata* (4000), and *Tringa erythropus* (1400).

015 Groote Wielen (Friesland)

53°13'N, 05°52'E 300 ha

Leased and managed by L

Complex of open freshwater, reedbeds, *Alnus/Salix* scrub, and wet meadows. Includes two duck decoys. Human activities include stock-raising, fishing, and recreation (including boating).

Breeding species include *Botaurus stellaris* (1-2 pairs), *Anas strepera* (10-15 pairs), *A. querquedula* (2-4 pairs), *A. clypeata* (25-35 pairs), *Philomachus pugnax* (35-45 pairs), *Gallinago gallinago* (70-100 pairs), *Limosa limosa* (180-210 pairs), *Tringa totanus* (80-120 pairs), and *Sterna hirundo* (15-20 pairs). Non-breeding waterfowl include *Anser albifrons* (av. 27,500), *Branta leucopsis* (av. 1650), and *Anas penelope* (av. 16,500).

016 Workumerwaard (including Makkumerwaard and Kooiwaard) (Friesland)

53°00'N, 05°25'E 3500 ha

1375 ha managed by L with special protection and no public access during the breeding season; restrictions on agriculture (Workumerwaard)

Area in western Friesland, adjoining the IJsselmeer, containing foreshores with shell beaches, wet meadows and reedbeds, and freshwater marshes, with grassland and arable land landward of the dyke. Human activities include agriculture, stock-raising, hunting, and boating; there is scattered human habitation. A particularly important area for wintering geese.

Breeding species include *Anas clypeata* (15 pairs), *Recurvirostra avosetta* (64 pairs), *Charadrius hiaticula* (10 pairs), *Philomachus pugnax* (90 pairs), *Limosa limosa* (320 pairs), *Tringa totanus* (120 pairs), *Sterna hirundo* (2000 pairs), and *S. albifrons* (20 pairs). In addition, non-breeding waterfowl include *Anser brachyrhynchus* (10,000), *A. albifrons* (10,000), *A. anser* (500), *Branta leucopsis* (2000), *Recurvirostra avosetta* (500), *Limosa limosa* (10,000), and *Numenius arquata* (7000).

017 Oudegaasterbrekken, Fluessen, Groote Gaastmeer, and Morra (Friesland)

52°59'N, 05°32'E 4900 ha

Unprotected

An extensive area of marshes and wet meadows with several very large freshwater lakes. Human activities include stock-raising, fishing, hunting, and recreation (including boating); there is some human habitation, and a railway line cuts through the area.

Important for feeding and roosting geese with *Anser brachyrhynchus* (10,000), *A. albifrons* (10,000), and *Branta leucopsis* (7000).

018 Slotermeer (Friesland)

52°55'N, 05°38'E 1200 ha

Nature Reserves (SBB Reserves: 142 ha; L Reserve: 170 ha)

Freshwater lake surrounded by reedbeds, marshes and wet meadows. Human activities include fishing, hunting, and boating; there is scattered human habitation.

Breeding species include *Botaurus stellaris* (4+ pairs), *Circus aeruginosus* (4+ pairs), *Sterna hirundo* (110 pairs), and *Asio flammeus* (1 pair). Particularly important for non-breeding waterfowl with *Anser brachyrhynchus* (5000), *A. albifrons* (10,000), *Branta leucopsis* (3200), and *Anas penelope* (8000).

019 Steile Bank, Mokkebank, and Sondeler Leyen (Friesland)

52°51'N, 05°37'E 3300 ha

Nature Reserve (SBB Reserve: 167 ha); partly managed by L: 1198 ha

An area of lakes, reedbeds, and wet meadows adjoining the IJsselmeer. Steile Bank is a large sandbank in the IJsselmeer and is important as a roosting site. Human activities include stock-raising, fishing, hunting, and boating; there is scattered human habitation.

Breeding species include *Porzana porzana*. A flock of moulting *Podiceps cristatus* at Mokkebank reaches 40,000+ (av. 15,000). Steile bank is important for roosting *Phalacrocorax carbo sinensis* (max. 7000 in summer) and *Chlidonias niger* (max. 20,000). Wintering waterfowl include *Anser brachyrhynchus* (5000), *A. albifrons* (25,000), *A. anser* (5000), and *Branta leucopsis* (15,000).

020 Tjongervallei, Lindevallei, and Rottige Meenthe (Friesland)

52°49'-52°56'N, 05°52'-06°06'E 2700 ha

Nature Reserves (SBB Reserves: 1900 ha; L Reserve: 453 ha)

The site includes marshes along a slow-flowing river (Lindevallei) and an area of wet meadows with two peatbogs (Tjongervallei). Human activities include agriculture, stock-raising, hunting, and recreation (including boating); there is scattered human habitation. Intensive agriculture in the surrounding areas has led to problems with eutrophication and lowering of the water-table.

Breeding species include *Botaurus stellaris* (11+ pairs), *Ardea purpurea* (5 pairs), *Anser anser*, *Circus aeruginosus* (9+ pairs), *Rallus aquaticus* (75 pairs), *Chlidonias niger* (16 pairs), and *Asio flammeus* (1 pair). Waterfowl occurring include *Cygnus columbianus* (300-400), *Anser fabalis* (7500), *A. albifrons* (20,000), and *Anas penelope* (8000).

021 Zwarte en Witte Brekken, Langweerderwielen, Oudhof, and Koevordermeer (Friesland)

53°00'N, 05°41'E 2000 ha

Mainly unprotected but two Nature Reserves (SBB Reserves: 397 ha including 250 ha with no public access); also includes agricultural areas with management agreements

A large lake complex with reedbeds, inlets, marshes, wet meadows, and *Alnus* scrub. Human activities include fishing, stock-raising, hunting, and boating; there is scattered human habitation. Land-reallocation projects in the surrounding areas cause lowering of the water-table. Disturbance from shooting is a further problem.

A breeding site for *Botaurus stellaris* (3 pairs), *Philomachus pugnax*, *Tringa totanus* (50 pairs), and *Sterna hirundo* (200 pairs). Particularly important for roosting and feeding waterfowl in winter with *Anser brachyrhynchus* (12,000), *A. albifrons* (10,000), *Branta leucopsis* (5000), and *Anas penelope* (10,000).

022 Sneekermeer and Terkaplester Poelen (Friesland)

53°01'N, 05°46'E 3500 ha

Nature Reserves (SBB Reserves: 1168 ha)

A large freshwater lake with extensive areas of marsh and wet grassland. Human activities include stock-raising, fishing, hunting, and recreation (including boating); there is scattered human habitation. Increasing recreational pressure is a problem.

Breeding species include *Botaurus stellaris* (2+ pairs), *Circus aeruginosus* (2+ pairs), *Philomachus pugnax*, *Sterna hirundo* (50 pairs), *Chlidonias niger* (50+ pairs), and *Asio flammeus* (1+ pair). Particularly important for roosting and feeding waterfowl in winter with *Anser brachyrhynchus* (750), *A. albifrons* (30,000), *A. anser* (500), *Branta leucopsis* (15,000), and *Anas penelope* (29,000).

023 Oude Venen and De Deelen (Friesland)

53°02'-53°07'N, 05°55'E 4700 ha

Nature Reserves (SBB Reserve: De Deelen, 460 ha; L Reserve: Oude Venen, 1360 ha)

An area of lakes, reedbeds, wet meadows, and woodland. Human activities include stock-raising, fishing, hunting, and recreation (including boating); there is scattered human habitation.

Breeding species include *Phalacrocorax carbo sinensis* (100 pairs), *Botaurus stellaris* (11+ pairs), *Ardea cinerea* (120 pairs), *A. purpurea* (10 pairs), *Anser anser*, *Circus aeruginosus* (16 pairs), *C. pygargus* (1 pair), *Rallus aquaticus* (40 pairs), *Porzana porzana* (7 pairs), *Philomachus pugnax* (20 pairs), *Sterna hirundo* (15 pairs), *Chlidonias niger* (40 pairs), and *Asio flammeus* (2-3 pairs). *A. strepera* (750) moults in the area. Particularly important for roosting and feeding waterfowl in winter with *Anser albifrons* (30,000), *Branta leucopsis* (16,000), and *Anas penelope* (13,000).

024 Van Oordt's Mersken (Friesland)

53°03'N, 06°05'E 1500 ha

Nature Reserve (SBB Reserve: 354 ha); restrictions on agricultural practices

A complex of wet grasslands and marshes along the River Koningsdiep, south-west of Drachten. Human activities include stock-raising, hunting, fishing, and haymaking; there is scattered human habitation.

Breeding species include *Botaurus stellaris*, *Anas querquedula* (30 pairs), *A. clypeata* (100 pairs), *Circus aeruginosus* (1 pair), *Crex crex*, *Philomachus pugnax* (100 pairs), *Gallinago gallinago* (130 pairs), *Limosa limosa* (460 pairs), *Numenius arquata* (30 pairs), *Tringa totanus* (75 pairs), and *Chlidonias niger* (11 pairs). Waterfowl occurring in winter include *Cygnus columbianus* (100-200), *Anser albifrons* (30,000), *Branta leucopsis* (2000), and *Anas penelope* (6000). Roosting waders include *Limosa limosa* and *Numenius phaeopus* (5700).

025 Dwingelose and Kraloër Heide (Drenthe)

52°49'N, 06°23'E 3500 ha

Nature Reserves (NM Reserve: 1130 ha; SBB Reserve: 1111 ha)

An extensive area of heathland and fens containing *c.*40 freshwater bodies of various sizes; surrounded by forest. Human activities include forestry, stock-raising, and recreation.

Breeding species include *Podiceps nigricollis* (6 pairs), *Anas crecca* (130+ pairs), *Circus aeruginosus* (1-2 pairs), *Philomachus pugnax* (1-3 pairs), *Numenius arquata* (65 pairs), *Chlidonias niger* (35 pairs), *Asio flammeus* (0-1 pair), and possibly *Circus cyaneus*. Additional species occurring include wintering *Anser fabalis* (1600), roosting *Limosa limosa* (12,000), and *Numenius phaeopus* (4500).

026 Bargerveen (Drenthe)

52°41'N, 07°02'E 1700 ha

Mainly a Nature Reserve (SBB Reserve)

An area of peatlands which includes one of the last remaining raised bogs in the Netherlands. Most of the area has been used for peat-cutting but there are remnant intact parts near the centre. Human activities include grazing.

Breeding species include *Circus aeruginosus* (2-3 pairs), *C. cyaneus* (2-3 pairs), *Gallinago gallinago* (20 pairs), *Numenius arquata* (20-25 pairs), *Chlidonias niger* (35 pairs), *Asio flammeus* (1 pair), *Caprimulgus europaeus* (5-10 pairs), and *Luscinia svecica* (60 pairs).

027 De Wieden and De Weerribben (Overijssel, Drenthe)

52°47'N, 05°57'E 14,500 ha

Ramsar Site (De Weerribben: 3400 ha); EEC SPA (De Weerribben: 3400 ha)

Nature Reserves (NM Reserve: 4600 ha; SBB Reserves: 3070 ha); restrictions on agricultural practices

Two large nature reserves (plus one small one) consisting of shallow lakes, peat lowlands, woodland, and wet meadows. Human activities include stock-raising, reed-cutting, fishing, hunting, and recreation (including boating); there is scattered human habitation. Increasing disturbance from water-sports, and intensive reed-cutting are current problems.

Breeding species include *Phalacrocorax carbo sinensis* (500 pairs), *Botaurus stellaris* (15-20 pairs), *Ardea cinerea* (300 pairs), *A. purpurea* (60 pairs), *Circus aeruginosus* (30-40 pairs), *C. cyaneus* (0-2 pairs), *Rallus aquaticus* (200-300 pairs), *Porzana porzana* (20-25 pairs), *Gallinago gallinago* (250-300 pairs), *Limosa limosa*, *Numenius arquata* (400-600 pairs), *Chlidonias niger* (100-150 pairs), *Asio flammeus* (0-1 pair), *Locustella naevia* (1000 pairs), and *L. luscinioides* (250-300 pairs). Waterfowl occurring in winter include *Cygnus columbianus* (400-800), *Anser fabalis* (2000-3000), *A. albifrons* (5000), and hundreds of *Mergus albellus* and *M. merganser*.

028 IJsseldelta (including Lower IJssel, Zwarte Meer, and Vossemeer (Overijssel, Flevoland)

52°36'N, 05°50'E 9000 ha

Nature Reserves (SBB Reserve: 850 ha, plus 1500 ha [Zwarte Meer] managed by SBB; 41 ha managed by VB)

This site comprises 21 km of the River IJssel from Zwolle to the river-mouth (adjoining 067), two border lakes separating the Noordoostpolder and Oostelijk Flevoland from the 'old land' (Zwarte Meer and Vossemeer) and an area of low-lying grasslands around Kampen (6000 ha). Human activities include stock-raising, fishing, hunting, reed-cutting boating, and transporting of goods (by barge). The main problems are water pollution, recreation (wind-surfing), hunting, reed-cutting, and intensive agriculture.

Breeding species include *Ardea purpurea* (28 pairs), *Circus aeruginosus* (9-11 pairs), *Limosa limosa* (2000 pairs), *Tringa totanus* (350-400 pairs), *Chlidonias niger* (75 pairs), *Luscinia svecica* (9-13 pairs), and *Acrocephalus arundinaceus* (100 pairs). Non-breeding waterfowl include *Platalea leucorodia* (40), *Cygnus columbianus* (300), *Anser fabalis* (3500), *A. albifrons* (20,400), and *A. anser* (1200).

029 Noordoostpolder-West (Flevoland)

52°45'N, 05°43'E 4400 ha

Unprotected

Grassland and arable land (polderland) bordering the IJsselmeer. Human activities include agriculture, stock-raising, and hunting; there is scattered human habitation.

Wintering waterfowl include *Cygnus columbianus* (1000), *Anser fabalis* (8000), *A. albifrons* (15,000), and *Branta leucopsis* (6000).

030 IJsselmeer (Noord-Holland, Friesland, Flevoland)

52°43'N, 05°27'E 180,000 ha

Unprotected; (although partly managed by L: 3200 ha, including Makkumerwaard and Steile Bank [sites 016 and 019])

Previously the Zuiderzee, the area is now a vast shallow freshwater lake, having been cut off from the sea and partly reclaimed. The original IJsselmeer is bisected by a dyke separating the northern half (Klein IJsselmeer) and the southern half (Markermeer). Human activities include fishing, navigation, hunting, and boating; there are a major road and small harbours. Problems include water pollution (especially PCBs, pesticides, and heavy metals), deepening (sand extraction), intensive fishing, recreation (boating and wind-surfing), and military training. In addition, plans still exist to reclaim part of the Markermeer, although no schemes have yet been financed or dealt with by the Netherlands parliament.

Extremely important for waterfowl especially *Podiceps cristatus* (20,000), *Phalacrocorax carbo sinensis* (30,000+ in July; the main feeding area for birds from the major Dutch colonies), *Anas strepera* (1000), *Aythya ferina* (50,000), *A. fuligula* (115,000), *A. marila* (115,000; regularly 65+ per cent of the western and northern European wintering population), *Bucephala clangula* (10,000), *Mergus albellus* (2500-9000; regularly 50-60 per cent of the western and northern European wintering population), *M. serrator* (9000), *M. merganser* (10,000), *Larus minutus* (2000 in autumn), *Sterna hirundo* (20,000), and *Chlidonias niger* (100,000).

031 Oostvaardersplassen and Lepelaarsplassen (Flevoland)

52°27'N, 05°20'E 7000 ha

Partly protected by the Nature Conservation Act (5600 ha)

Two complexes of shallow lakes, reedbeds and *Salix* woodlands, which have been saved from cultivation on a reclaimed polder (Zuidelijk Flevoland). The area also includes some wet meadows and arable land.

Very important for breeding marsh birds including *Phalacrocorax carbo sinensis* (7000 pairs), *Botaurus stellaris* (5 pairs), *Ardea purpurea* (2 pairs), *Platalea leucorodia* (60 pairs; regularly 300-600 birds), *Anser anser* (150-200 pairs), *Circus aeruginosus* (50 pairs), *C. cyaneus* (5-10 pairs), *Rallus aquaticus* (1000-2000 pairs), *Porzana porzana* (100-200 pairs), *Recurvirostra avosetta* (250-400 pairs; regularly 4000-6000 birds), *Limosa limosa* (10 pairs), *Sterna hirundo* (125 pairs), *A. flammeus* (2-3 pairs), *Luscinia svecica* (100-150 pairs), *Acrocephalus arundinaceus* (20-50 pairs), and *Panurus biarmicus* (500-1000 pairs). Additional passage/wintering species include *Branta leucopsis* (1000-3000), *Anser fabalis* (4000-15,000), *A. albifrons* (25,000-60,000), *A. anser* (20,000-60,000; 30,000 moulting), *Anas strepera* (500-1500), *A. crecca* (5000-15,000), *A. platyrhynchos* (35,000-50,000), *A. acuta* (15,000-30,000), *A. clypeata* (5000-7000), *Aythya fuligula* (5000-10,000), *Mergus albellus* (5000-10,000), *M. merganser* (5000), *Haliaeetus albicilla* (2-5), *Buteo lagopus* (10-20), *Philomachus pugnax* (2000-5000), *Limosa limosa* (5000-10,000), *Chlidonias niger* (30,000), and *Riparia riparia* (tens of thousands).

032 Veluwemeer, Harderbroek, and Kievitslanden (Gelderland, Flevoland)

52°23'N, 05°40'E 7000 ha

Nature Reserve (SBB Reserves, Harderbroek: 182 ha; Kievitslanden: 100 ha; Veluwemeer: 15 ha)

Two border lakes between the new polder and the mainland, and an adjacent marshy area with reedbeds, and bushes (Harderbroek), and wet meadow (Kievitslanden). Human activities include transportation of goods (by barge), stock-raising, fishing, limited hunting, and recreation (including boating); there is scattered human habitation. Eutrophication and recreation pressure are the main problems.

Breeding species include *Podiceps cristatus* (330-400 pairs), *Botaurus stellaris* (3+ pairs), *Anas clypeata* (40 pairs), *Circus aeruginosus*, *Philomachus pugnax* (22 pairs), and *Limosa limosa* (240 pairs). Waterfowl occurring include *Cygnus columbianus* (1500-2000), *Anser albifrons* (16,000), and *Anas clypeata* (2500).

033 Arkemheen, Zeldert, and Eemmeer (Gelderland, Utrecht)

52°15'N, 05°27'E (Arkemheen); 52°12'N, 05°19'E (Zeldert); 52°17'-05°19' (Eemmeer) 3000 ha

Arkemheen and Zeldert: mainly unprotected, although some restrictions on agricultural practices, and small Nature Reserves (SBB Reserves: 150 ha); Eemmeer: protected by Nature Conservation Act

Arkemheen and Zeldert are wet grassland areas adjoining Eemmeer, a remnant lake following the reclamation of Zuidelijk Flevoland. Human activities include stock-raising, fishing, and hunting; there is scattered human habitation. Intensive agriculture in the surrounding area (including lowering of the water-table), and increasing recreation are the main problems.

Breeding species include *Anas clypeata* (52 pairs), *Circus aeruginosus* (1 pair), *Philomachus pugnax* (60 pairs), *Limosa limosa* (610 pairs), *Tringa totanus* (115 pairs), and *Sterna hirundo* (8 pairs). A feeding site for *Platalea leucorodia* (20-30; Eemmeer). Wintering waterfowl include *Cygnus columbianus* (max. 1800), *Anser fabalis*, *A. albifrons*, *Anas penelope*, and *Aythya fuligula* (15,000).

034 Oostelijke Vechtplassen (Noord-Holland, Utrecht)

52°13'N, 05°05'E 7000 ha

Nature Reserves (NM Reserves: 1475 ha; SBB Reserves: 336 ha); restrictions on agricultural practices

A mosaic of fenlands, wet and dry grasslands, swamp-forest, canals, and large lakes. Human activities include stock-raising, fishing, hunting, and water-sports. The water quality is threatened by eutrophication, and there is disturbance from water-sports.

Breeding species include *Botaurus stellaris* (20 pairs), *Ixobrychus minutus* (20+ pairs), *Ardea purpurea* (10 pairs), *Circus aeruginosus* (2+ pairs), *Rallus aquaticus* (50 pairs), *Gallinago gallinago* (40 pairs), *Limosa limosa* (280 pairs), *Sterna hirundo* (45 pairs), *Chlidonias niger* (120 pairs), and *Luscinia svecica* (1-10 pairs). Important for wintering grebes, *Anser fabalis*, *A. albifrons*, *A. anser*, and *Fulica atra*.

035 Botshol and Ronde Hoep (Utrecht, Noord-Holland)

52°16'N, 04°54'E 1415 ha

Nature Reserve (NM Reserve: 256 ha)

An extensive area of wet grassland and peatbog swamps with a variety of open water, swamp-forest, quaking bogs, reedbeds, and scrub. Ronde Hoep is an adjacent polder with wet meadows important for breeding waders and wintering geese. Human activities include stock-raising, fishing, hunting, and boating. The ecosystem, with many submerged plants, has been considerably damaged by pollution (eutrophication).

Breeding species include *Botaurus stellaris* (6 pairs), *Ixobrychus minutus* (0-2 pairs), *Ardea purpurea* (2 pairs), *Anas querquedula* (20 pairs), *A. clypeata* (30-40 pairs), *Aythya nyroca* (1 pair), *Limosa limosa* (210-240 pairs), *Tringa totanus* (60-70 pairs), and *Chlidonias niger* (22 pairs). In addition, *Platalea leucorodia* visits the site to feed. Wintering waterfowl include *Anser fabalis* (1000-1500 roosting), *A. albifrons* (300), and *Anas penelope* (5000 roosting).

036 Naardermeer (Noord-Holland)

52°18'N, 05°07'E 1150 ha partly a Ramsar Site (752 ha); EEC SPA (760 ha)

Nature Reserve (NM Reserve: 901 ha); restrictions on agricultural practices

A freshwater lake with swamp-forest, marshes, canals, and reedbeds; surrounded by grassland. Human activities include stock-raising, fishing and hunting. Potentially threatened by any future reclamation of the Markermeer.

Breeding species include *Phalacrocorax carbo sinensis* (5000 pairs), *Botaurus stellaris* (10 pairs), *Ixobrychus minutus* (1 pair), *Ardea cinerea* (120 pairs), *A. purpurea* (40 pairs),

Platalea leucorodia (100-120 pairs), *Anas querquedula* (20 pairs), *A. clypeata* (10 pairs), *Aythya nyroca* (1 pair), *Circus aeruginosus* (4 pairs), and *Chlidonias niger* (15-20 pairs). *Anser fabalis* occurs in winter.

037 Gooimeer (Noord-Holland)

52°19'N, 05°12'E 750 ha

Nature Reserve (SBB Reserve: 52 ha)

A part of a vast freshwater lake, between the 'mainland' and Flevopolders, with a narrow belt of reeds. Human activities include hunting and recreation.

A site for feeding and roosting *Cygnus columbianus* (460 av. max. 1977-1986).

038 Zuidelijk Poldergebied, including Eilandspolder, Alkmaardermeer, Wormer- en Jisperveld, Polder Westzaan, Waterland (Noord-Holland)

52°31'N, 04°48'E 12,600 ha

Nature Reserves (NM Reserves: 576 ha; L Reserves: 1000 ha; SBB Reserves: 2366 ha; VB Reserve: 100 ha); restrictions on agricultural practices

A vast polder complex of wet grassland dissected by ditches. There are also lakes, reed-swamps, and marshy woodland. Human activities include stock-raising, fishing, hunting, and boating. Recreation, eutrophication and lowering of the water-table are the main problems.

Breeding species include *Botaurus stellaris* (17 pairs), *Anas querquedula* (100 pairs), *A. clypeata* (1000 pairs), *Circus aeruginosus* (10 pairs), *Rallus aquaticus* (100 pairs), *Vanellus vanellus* (4000 pairs), *Philomachus pugnax* (100-200 pairs), *Gallinago gallinago* (150-200 pairs), *Limosa limosa* (4000 pairs), *Tringa totanus* (1000 pairs), *Sterna hirundo*, and *Chlidonias niger* (50 pairs). *Platalea leucorodia* (max. 200) feed in the area, and wintering waterfowl include *Anas penelope* (30,000-70,000) and *Mergus albellus* (2000 roosting).

039 Zwanenwater (Noord-Holland)

52°49'N, 04°42'E 573 ha Ramsar Site; EEC SPA

Nature Reserve (NM Reserve: 573 ha)

An area of sand-dunes, with wet dune-slacks, two dune-lakes, *Salix* scrub, coastal marshes, and woodland. Predation of *Platalea leucorodia* by Fox *Vulpes vulpes* is a problem.

Breeding species include *Botaurus stellaris*, *Platalea leucorodia* (60-90 pairs), *Circus aeruginosus* (1 pair), *Rallus aquaticus* (15 pairs), *Porzana porzana* (1-3 pairs), *Numenius arquata* (23 pairs), and *Asio flammeus* (2 pairs).

040 Nieuwkoopse Plassen and Kamerikse Nessen (Zuid-Holland)

52°09'N, 04°48'E 1850 ha

Partly Nature Reserves (NM Reserves: 1020 ha; L Reserve: 11 ha)

A complex of freshwater lakes with reedbeds, hay/grasslands, small islands and *Betula/-Salix/Alnus* woodland. Surrounded by large expanses of wet grassland. Kamerikse Nessen is a series of peat-fen areas along the River Grecht, just south-east of the main site. Human activities include fishing, reed-cutting, and recreation (including boating). Eutrophication is a problem.

Breeding species include *Phalacrocorax carbo sinensis* (10 pairs), *Botaurus stellaris* (13 pairs), *Ixobrychus minutus* (32 pairs), *Ardea cinerea* (400 pairs), *A. purpurea* (100 pairs), *Anas clypeata* (37 pairs), *Circus aeruginosus* (2 pairs), *Rallus aquaticus* (25+ pairs), *Limosa limosa* (140 pairs), *Sterna hirundo* (40 pairs), and *Chlidonias niger* (130 pairs). *Anser fabalis* (250) and *Anas penelope* (10,000) occur in winter.

041 Reeuwijkse Plassen (Zuid-Holland)

52°03'N, 04°47'E 1560 ha

Nature Reserve (SBB Reserve: 20 ha); mainly unprotected

Large freshwater lake with small islands and reedbeds, surrounded by wet grassland. Human activities include stock-raising, fishing, hunting, reed-cutting, and recreation (including boating); there is scattered human habitation. Eutrophication, hunting, and recreation pressure are the main problems.

Breeding species include *Botaurus stellaris* (2 pairs), *Ixobrychus minutus* (1-2 pairs), *Anas querquedula*, *Limosa limosa* (20 pairs), *Tringa totanus*, *Sterna hirundo* (10 pairs), and *Chlidonias niger* (140 pairs). Other species include non-breeding *Anas penelope* (8000).

042 Zouwe and Linge (Gelderland)

51°52'-51°57'N, 05°00'-05°04'E 1070 ha

Nature Reserves (SBB Reserves: 265 ha; L Reserves: 80 ha)

An area of reedbeds with scattered bushes (Zouwe) and a small river with marshland (Linge). Human activities include stock-raising and recreation; there are scattered settlements and main roads.

Breeding species include *Botaurus stellaris* (8 pairs), *Ixobrychus minutus* (9 pairs), *Ardea purpurea* (55 pairs; the second most important area in the Netherlands in 1985), *Circus aeruginosus* (2 pairs), *Chlidonias niger* (30 pairs), and *Luscinia svecica* (6 pairs).

043 Waal: Nijmegen – Gorinchem (including Hurwenen) and Maas: Hedel – Andel (Gelderland)

51°50'-51°53'N, 05°00'-05°50'E 8000 ha

Nature Reserve (SBB: 215 ha); mainly unprotected

Part of the Rhine system with extensive flood-plains and former meanders containing clay-pits, freshwater marshes, *Salix* scrub, and wet meadows. Human activities include stock-raising, fishing, and hunting; there is scattered human habitation. Threatened by recreation activities, industrial development, urban expansion, intensive farming methods, and (especially) by pollution of the water.

Breeding species include *Botaurus stellaris* (5-10 pairs), *Ixobrychus minutus* (2 pairs), *Circus aeruginosus* (1 pair), *Rallus aquaticus* (30 pairs), *Porzana porzana*, *Crex crex*, *Limosa limosa* (22+ pairs), *Tringa totanus*, *Sterna hirundo* (7 pairs), *Chlidonias niger* (10-25 pairs), and *Luscinia svecica* (4 pairs). Non-breeding species include *Phalacrocorax carbo sinensis*, *Cygnus columbianus* (150), *Anser fabalis* (4000), *A. albifrons* (1000), *A. platyrhynchos* (10,000), *Aythya ferina* (10,000), and *Mergus albellus*.

044 Waal and Rijn: Spijk – Nijmegen – Arnhem (including Oude Rijnstrangen and Ooijpolders) (Gelderland)

51°53'N, 06°02'E 5200 ha

Nature Reserves (SBB Reserves: 570 ha); mainly unprotected

Parts of the Rhine system comprising extensive flood-plains with slow-flowing rivers, marshes, wet meadows, grassland, clay-pits, and arable land. Human activities include stock-raising, fishing, hunting, and recreation (including boating); there is scattered human habitation. Threatened by recreation activities, industrial development, urban expansion, intensive farming methods, and (especially) by pollution of the water. Adjacent to site no. 056, Niederrhein: Wesel/Xanten – Emmerich/Hüthum in the Federal Republic of Germany.

Breeding species include *Phalacrocorax carbo sinensis* (40 pairs), *Botaurus stellaris* (41 pairs), *Anas querquedula* (60 pairs), *A. clypeata* (150 pairs), *Circus aeruginosus* (2 pairs), *Rallus aquaticus* (43 pairs), *Porzana porzana*, *Crex crex*, *Philomachus pugnax* (3 pairs), *Limosa limosa* (320 pairs), *Tringa totanus* (60 pairs), *Sterna hirundo* (27 pairs),

Chlidonias niger (69 pairs), and *Luscinia svecica* (13 pairs). Non-breeding species include *Phalacrocorax carbo sinensis* (500), *Cygnus columbianus* (500), *Anser fabalis* (40,000), *A. albifrons* (8000), *Anas platyrhynchos* (10,000), *Aythya ferina* (10,000), and *Mergus albellus* (100).

045 Biesbosch (Zuid-Holland)

51°43'-51°51'N, 04°37'-04°56'E 18,000 ha includes Ramsar Site (1700 ha)

Nature Reserves (SBB Reserves: 2550 ha; 455 ha managed by VB)

A former tidal estuary of the Rhine/Maas system which was closed off from the sea in 1970; now with only a very slight maritime influence remaining. The land is intersected by many former tidal creeks and consists of polders, marshland, and wooded areas. Industrial pollution of the water and recreation pressure (notably water-sports) are the main problems.

Breeding species include *Phalacrocorax carbo* (160 pairs), *Nycticorax nycticorax* (0-4 pairs), *Anser anser*, *Anas clypeata* (90-100 pairs), *Circus aeruginosus* (40-45 pairs), *C. cyaneus*, *Porzana porzana* (6+ pairs), *Crex crex*, *Recurvirostra avosetta* (20-25 pairs), *Limosa limosa* (200-250 pairs), *Tringa totanus* (70-100 pairs), *Chlidonias niger*, *Alcedo atthis* (1-3 pairs), and *Luscinia svecica* (900-1200 pairs). Important for non-breeding waterfowl including *Phalacrocorax carbo* (500), *Platalea leucorodia* (150-250), *Cygnus columbianus* (150-250), *Anser fabalis* (1500-2500), *A. albifrons* (15,000-20,000), *A. anser* (2000-4000), *Branta leucopsis* (400), *Anas crecca* (3000), and *A. acuta* (3300).

046 Voordelta, Breedewater/Quackjeswater, and Kwade Hoek (Zuid-Holland, Zeeland)

51°52'N, 03°59'E 16,000+ ha

Nature Reserves (L Reserve: 350 ha; NM Reserve: 300 ha); mainly unprotected

The Voordelta is a large area of the North Sea adjoining the closed-off delta area of the Rhine/Maas system. It contains bays with beaches, sand-dunes, coastal mudflats, and raised saltmarsh. Breedewater/Quackjeswater are two lakes in a large dune area (Voornes Duin) with mesotrophic dune-slacks surrounded by *Alnus* woodland and wet dune valleys. It forms part of the coast adjoining the Voordelta, as does Kwade Hoek, which consists of saltmarsh, dunes, and mudflats. Human activities include stock-raising, fishing, and boating; there is scattered human habitation. The area is threatened by pollution of the North Sea (especially heavy metals and pesticides), extension of Rotterdam-Harbour activities, and increasing recreation.

A breeding site for *Phalacrocorax carbo sinensis* (1000 pairs). Non-breeding waterfowl occurring include *Podiceps cristatus* (200), *Branta leucopsis* (500), *Aythya marila* (3000), *Melanitta nigra* (21,500), *Calidris alba* (1100), *C. maritima* (300), and *Arenaria interpres* (1000).

047 Haringvliet and Hollands Diep (including Oudeland van Strijen) (Zuid-Holland)

51°43'-51°50'N, 04°00'-04°37'E 17,900 ha

Nature Reserves (NM: *c.*1100 ha; SBB: 400 ha); restrictions on agricultural practices (Oudeland van Strijen)

One of the former estuaries of the Rhine/Maas system, closed off from the sea in 1970; habitats include mudflats, banks, saltings, marsh, reedbeds, and *Salix* woodland. Surrounding area is mainly agricultural land and Oudeland van Strijen is an important polder area of approximately 2000 ha, 2 km north of Hollands Diep. Human activities include agriculture, stock-raising, fishing, hunting, recreation (including boating), and industry. Recreation and pollution are both problems.

Breeding species include *Circus aeruginosus* (30 pairs), *C. cyaneus* (3 pairs), *Recurvirostra avosetta* (120 pairs), *Philomachus pugnax*, *Limosa limosa* (94 pairs), *Tringa totanus* (115 pairs), *Sterna hirundo* (300 pairs), *S. albifrons* (15 pairs), *Asio flammeus* (3 pairs), and *Luscinia svecica* (4 pairs). Important for non-breeding waterfowl including

Podiceps cristatus (1200), *Phalacrocorax carbo* (1400), *Anser fabalis* (12,000), *A. brachyrhynchus* (1500), *A. albifrons* (max. 24,000), *A. anser* (12,000), *Branta leucopsis* (30,000), *Anas crecca* (8100), and *Aythya ferina* (20,000 in Sept. to Nov.).

048 Krammer and Volkerak (Zuid-Holland, Zeeland, Noord-Brabant)

51°39'N, 04°15'E 6450 ha

Nature Reserves (SBB Reserve: 80 ha; NM Reserves: 50 ha)

Formal tidal estuary of the Rhine/Maas system, now closed off from the sea; includes mudflats and raised saltmarsh. Human activities include fishing, hunting, and boating. A further dam completed in 1988 between St Philipsland and Grevelingen means that the area has effectively become an inland lake, which, if managed properly, could develop into an important freshwater ecosystem.

Breeding species include *Circus aeruginosus*, *Recurvirostra avosetta*, *Limosa limosa*, and *Tringa totanus*. Formerly important for non-breeding waterfowl which included *Haematopus ostralegus* (18,000), *Pluvialis squatarola* (1800), *Numenius arquata* (3000), and *Tringa erythropus* (1000).

049 Grevelingen (Zuid-Holland, Zeeland)

51°40'-51°48'N, 03°49'-04°09'E 14,100 ha

Nature Reserves (SBB Reserves: 3674 ha and 800 ha managed by SBB)

A semi-stagnant saline lake (since the damming of the Grevelingen estuary in 1971), with sand-dunes, islands, and wet meadows. Human activities include grazing, hunting, fishing, and water-sports. Increasing recreation is a problem.

Breeding species include *Mergus serrator* (a few pairs), *Recurvirostra avosetta* (400-500 pairs), *Charadrius hiaticula* (100 pairs), *C. alexandrinus* (175 pairs), *Limosa limosa* (32 pairs), *Tringa totanus* (2700 pairs), *Sterna sandvicensis* (3000-5000 pairs), *S. hirundo* (400 pairs), *S. paradisaea*, and *S. albifrons* (20-30 pairs). Important for wintering and passage waterfowl (av. Jan. counts unless stated) including *Podiceps cristatus* (3600), *Phalacrocorax carbo* (490 in Aug. to Sept.), *Cygnus olor* (1060; 2500 moulting in Aug. to Sept.), *Branta leucopsis* (5000), *B. bernicla* (4000), *Anas penelope* (20,000), *A. crecca* (4500), *A. platyrhynchos* (32,000), *A. acuta* (2400), *Bucephala clangula* (2750), and *Mergus serrator* (1300).

050 Oosterschelde (Zeeland, Noord-Brabant)

51°27'-51°42'N, 03°40'-04°17'E 38,000 ha Ramsar Site

Mainly unprotected; Nature Reserves (SBB Reserve: 367 ha; L Reserve: 50 ha; VB Reserve: 22 ha)

The area was formerly an estuary of the Schelde but has been closed off from the sea since 1986 by a barrage which allows the tidal regime to continue with some restrictions. The sea can be completely shut out during storms or high tides. The eastern part of the area has become a freshwater lake following the construction of a secondary dam. The most important habitats are the intertidal mudflats and creeks. Human activities include grazing, fishing, and hunting. Main problems are increasing erosion, recreation, and fisheries which are affecting the food supply available to birds in the intertidal area.

Breeding species include *Circus aeruginosus* (5 pairs), *C. cyaneus* (6 pairs), *Recurvirostra avosetta* (420 pairs), *Sterna hirundo* (460 pairs), and *S. albifrons*. Important for non-breeding waterfowl including *Branta leucopsis* (2700), *B. bernicla* (7500), *Tadorna tadorna* (7200), *Anas penelope* (18,900), *A. acuta* (6700), *A. clypeata* (2360), *Haematopus ostralegus* (88,000), *Recurvirostra avosetta* (700), *Charadrius hiaticula* (2000), *C. alexandrinus* (1000), *Pluvialis squatarola* (7000), *Calidris canutus* (18,000), *C. alpina* (58,000), *Limosa lapponica* (7000), *Numenius arquata* (10,000), *Tringa erythropus* (1500), *T. totanus* (4000), *T. nebularia* (900), and *Arenaria interpres* (1300).

051 Veerse Meer (Zeeland)

51°32'-51°35'N, 03°38'-03°56'E 4170 ha

Nature Reserves (leased by NM: Middelplaten and Goudplaat, 400 ha)

A brackish lake (formerly part of the Oosterschelde, but closed off in 1961) with sandbanks and small islands, surrounded by woodland, hedges, cultivated land, grassland, and arable land. Human activities include agriculture, forestry, stock-raising, hunting, and fishing. Recreation, including boating and other water sports, is an increasing problem.

Breeding species include *Phalacrocorax carbo sinensis* (40 pairs), *Recurvirostra avosetta* (130 pairs), *Limosa limosa*, *Tringa totanus* (100-120 pairs), *Sterna hirundo* (450 pairs), *S. paradisaea* (4-10 pairs), and *Asio flammeus* (1-2 pairs). Important for non-breeding waterfowl with *Tachybaptus ruficollis* (max. 1400), *Podiceps cristatus* (1250), *Cygnus columbianus* (max. 800), *Anser fabalis* (500-1000), *Branta leucopsis* (max. 1700), *Anas penelope* (max. 16,000), *A. clypeata* (1700), *Bucephala clangula* (2250), *Mergus merganser* (2000-4000), *Fulica atra* (16,000), and *Recurvirostra avosetta* (280).

052 Westerschelde (Zeeland)

51°20'-51°28'N, 03°30'-04°15'E 31,900 ha

Nature Reserves (L Reserve: 2580 ha and 860 ha managed by L)

A tidal estuary of the River Schelde with mudflats, sandbanks and raised saltmarsh - the only estuary in south-west Netherlands which will not be closed from the sea, although the former tidal range has been reduced by a storm-surge barrier. Human activities include grazing, fishing, hunting, and boating; there is industrial/harbour development. In recent years large-scale industrial development has affected the area, including construction of the Baalhoek Canal. Water pollution is a major problem.

Breeding species include *Circus aeruginosus* (5-10 pairs), *Recurvirostra avosetta* (200 pairs), *Philomachus pugnax*, *Larus ridibundus* (25,000 pairs), *Sterna hirundo* (800 pairs), *S. albifrons* (90-180 pairs), and *Asio flammeus* (2 pairs). Important for non-breeding waterfowl with *Anser fabalis* (max. 3000; roosting at night), *A. albifrons* (max. 10,000; roosting at night), *A. anser* (10,000), *Tadorna tadorna* (3600 moulting), *Anas penelope* (19,500), *A. crecca* (3300), *A. acuta* (7500), *Haematopus ostralegus* (17,000), *Recurvirostra avosetta* (750), *Charadrius hiaticula* (1900), *C. alexandrinus* (max. 1200), *Pluvialis squatarola* (max. 5200), *Calidris canutus* (8500), *C. alba* (1500), *C. alpina* (35,000), *Limosa lapponica* (max. 5600), *Numenius arquata* (5000), *Tringa erythropus* (250), *T. totanus* (1000), and *T. nebularia* (200).

053 Het Zwin (Zeeland)

51°23'N, 03°22'E *c.*60 ha
Nature Reserve (L Reserve: 60 ha)

Part of an extensive intertidal area which is mainly in Belgium (site 004). Consists of creeks, sandbanks, mudflats, and dunes. Human activities include shooting. Recreation activities cause disturbance and make the Dutch part of the area less attractive for ground-nesting birds.

Breeding species include *Recurvirostra avosetta* (2-10 pairs) and *Tringa totanus*.

054 Yersekse Moer (Zeeland)

51°30'N, 04°02'E *c.*400 ha

Nature Reserve (L Reserve: 132 ha); restrictions on agricultural practices

An open area of former fenland, with grassland dissected by saltwater ditches. There are some freshwater ponds provided for livestock; stock-raising is the main human activity. The area is threatened by agricultural intensification and land reallocation.

Breeding birds include *Recurvirostra avosetta*, *Philomachus pugnax*, *Limosa limosa*, and *Tringa totanus*. Important for wintering waterfowl, with *Anser fabalis*, *A. albifrons* (4000), *Branta bernicla* (2000), and *Anas penelope*.

055 Putting - Groot Eiland (Zeeland)

51°17'-51°21'N, 04°00'E 56 ha

Nature Reserve (SBB Reserve: 52 ha)

An area containing a network of brackish creeks intersecting damp grassland. Some of the creeks have marshy borders. Human activities include stock-grazing, hunting, and fishing. The site is threatened by agricultural intensification and *Populus* afforestation.

Breeding species include *Anas querquedula*, *Circus aeruginosus*, *Rallus aquaticus*, *Recurvirostra avosetta*, *Gallinago gallinago*, *Limosa limosa*, and *Tringa totanus*. Also important for wintering waterfowl with *Anser fabalis* (150), *A. albifrons* (6000-12,000), *A. anser*, *Branta leucopsis*, and *Anas penelope* (400).

056 De Peel and Strabrechtse Heide (including Groote Peel) (Noord-Brabant, Limburg)

51°23'N, 05°47'E 7500 ha

Ramsar Site (Groote Peel: 900 ha); EEC SPA (Groote Peel: *c.*320 ha)

Nature Reserves (SBB Reserves: 4452 ha; L Reserves: 144 ha); partly unprotected

The area contains remnant fragments of a former raised bog of 30,000 ha, including peatlands, lakes, marshes, heathland, woodland, grassland, and arable land. Human activities include forestry, stock-raising, and recreation. The area is threatened by agricultural intensification, including the drainage of farmland.

Breeding species include *Tachybaptus ruficollis*, *Podiceps grisegena*, *P. nigricollis*, *Botaurus stellaris* (10 pairs), *Circus aeruginosus* (3 pairs), *Limosa limosa* (36 pairs), *Numenius arquata* (100 pairs), *Chlidonias niger* (28-35 pairs), *Asio flammeus* (1 pair), *Alcedo atthis* (4 pairs), and *Luscinia svecica* (60 pairs). Other species occurring include *Anser fabalis rossicus* (4000-5000), *A. fabalis fabalis* (700-1500), and *Grus grus* (200-300).

057 De Hamert (Limburg)

51°31'N, 06°10'E 1100 ha

Partly a Nature Reserve (L Reserve: 800 ha)

An extensive heathland area with scrub, pools, bogs, mires, woodland, hedges, and cultivated land. The Gelderns Canal runs through the area. Human activities include agriculture and recreation. Recreational pressure and intensive agriculture may threaten the area.

Breeding species include *Circus aeruginosus* and *Rallus aquaticus*. A passage site for *Grus grus* (10-250 in autumn; 25-100 in spring). Anatidae occur in winter.

058 Meynweg (Limburg)

51°10'N, 06°08'E 1200 ha

Nature Reserve (SBB Reserve: 1200 ha)

An extensive area of heathland (partly wet) with several pools, two wooded valleys, and woodlands of various types. Shooting and recreation are the main human activities. Threatened by water pollution stemming from coal-mining activities in the Federal Republic of Germany.

Breeding species include *Tachybaptus ruficollis* and *Anas crecca*. An important passage site for *Grus grus* (150-450 in autumn, 50-250 in spring).

059 Leekstermeer (Groningen, Drenthe)

53°11'N, 06°27'E 2250 ha

Nature Reserves (SBB Reserve: 300 ha; L Reserve: 80 ha)

A freshwater lake surrounded by peatbogs, pasture, marsh, and reedbeds. Human activities include cattle-grazing, fishing, hunting, and recreation. Threats include increasing recreational use and the development of surrounding areas under land-reallocation programmes.

Breeding species include *Botaurus stellaris*, *Anas clypeata*, *Circus aeruginosus*, *Vanellus vanellus*, *Philomachus pugnax*, *Gallinago gallinago*, *Limosa limosa*, and *Tringa totanus*. Also important as a moulting ground for *Limosa limosa*. Wintering waterfowl include *Anser fabalis* (max. 1500), *A. albifrons* (max. 26,000), and *Branta leucopsis* (max. 150).

060 Fochteloërveen, Esmeer, and Huis ter Heide (Friesland, Drenthe)

53°00'N, 06°25'E 2575 ha

Nature Reserves (NM Reserve: *c.*1700 ha; SBB Reserve: 60 ha)

An extensive complex of raised bogs with heather moor, open water, large forested areas, sewage-treatment plants, and some wet grasslands. There is a state penal centre on the eastern side of the area; agriculture includes pastoral and arable production.

Breeding species include *Tadorna tadorna* (12 pairs), *Anas crecca* (35 pairs), *A. clypeata* (38 pairs), *Circus aeruginosus* (4 pairs), *C. cyaneus*, *Porzana porzana* (5 pairs), *Crex crex*, *Limosa limosa* (170 pairs), *Numenius arquata* (75 pairs), *Sterna hirundo* (9 pairs), *Chlidonias niger* (14 pairs), *Asio flammeus* (5 pairs), *Caprimulgus europaeus* (1 pair), *Dryocopus martius* (1 pair), *Luscinia svecica* (4 pairs), and *Saxicola rubetra* (18 pairs). Wintering waterfowl include *Anser fabalis* (5000); the area is also important for passage waders, notably *Limosa limosa* (8000) and *Numenius phaeopus* (10,000).

061 Zuidlaardermeer (Groningen, Drenthe)

53°08'N, 06°41'E 900+ ha

Nature Reserve (L Reserve: 165 ha)

A freshwater lake with reedbeds; partly surrounded by wet pasture. Human activities include grazing of livestock and reed-cutting. Water-sports are increasing in the non-reserve parts of the site and in surrounding areas, and agricultural intensification may also be a problem.

The wet pastures are important for breeding and moulting *Limosa limosa*; wintering wildfowl include *Cygnus columbianus*, *Anser fabalis*, and *A. albifrons*.

062 Tjeukemeer (Friesland)

52°55'N, 05°49'E 2000+ ha

Nature Reserve (SBB Reserve: 65 ha)

A large freshwater lake with reedbeds, swamp-forest (especially on the northern side), wet grasslands, and a duck decoy. Agriculture is mainly stock-grazing and haymaking; other human activities include water-sports.

Breeding species include *Botaurus stellaris*, *Circus aeruginosus*, *Philomachus pugnax*, *Limosa limosa* (10-20 pairs), *Tringa totanus* (5 pairs), and *Sterna hirundo* (15 pairs). The area is important for wintering waterfowl with *Anser fabalis* (700), *A. albifrons* (22,000), *Branta leucopsis*, *Anas penelope* (5000), *Aythya ferina* (1500), and *A. fuligula* (2000).

063 Engbertsdijkvenen (Overijssel)

52°35'N, 06°40'E 865 ha

Nature Reserve (SBB Reserve: 865 ha)

One of the last remaining large raised bogs in the Netherlands, although only *c.*10 ha have not been used for peat-cutting. The surrounding areas are arable land. There is pressure from local people to drain the site to prevent large summer hatches of biting insects.

Breeding species include *Podiceps nigricollis* (1 pair), *Anas crecca* (50 pairs), *A. querquedula* (10 pairs), *Aythya nyroca* (1 pair), *Circus aeruginosus* (1 pair), *Numenius arquata* (15 pairs), *Chlidonias niger* (15 pairs), and *Luscinia svecica* (5 pairs). Wintering waterfowl include *Anser fabalis* (700) and *A. albifrons* (100).

064 Vennen van Oisterwijk and Kampina, Helvoirtse and Vughtse Gement (Noord-Brabant)

51°34'-51°37'N, 05°15'E 2000+ ha EEC SPA (Kampina: 1150 ha)

Nature Reserves (NM Reserves: 1532 ha)

A complex of pools surrounded by heathlands, and coniferous and deciduous woodlands. Also includes two areas of wet grassland along the canalised River Oude Ley. Human activities include sheep- and cattle-grazing and hunting. Pollution of the water, from both agricultural and recreational sources, is a problem.

Breeding species include *Anas crecca* (5-10 pairs), *Circus aeruginosus*, *Rallus aquaticus*, *Gallinago gallinago*, *Limosa limosa*, *Numenius arquata*, and *Tringa totanus*. Wintering waterfowl include *Anser fabalis fabalis* (2500), *A. fabalis rossicus* (600), and *A. albifrons* (200).

065 Maas: Vierlingsbeek – Grave and Ohé – Beesel (Limburg, Noord-Brabant)

51°40'N, 05°55'E 4200 ha (Vierlingsbeek – Grave) 51°11'N, 05°55'E 3500 ha (Ohé – Beesel)

Nature Reserve (SBB Reserve: 125 ha)

Two sections of the River Maas including the complex of gravel pits between Ohé and Beesel, with small streams and ponds, some arable land, and considerable tracts of wet grassland where cattle and sheep are grazed. Other human activities include gravel extraction, hunting, and water-sports. The water quality is severely affected by industrial pollution. Other problems include agricultural intensification and increasing recreational use of the area.

Breeding species include *Limosa limosa*. Wintering waterfowl include *Cygnus columbianus* (255), *Anser fabalis* (2000), *A. albifrons* (7000), *Anas platyrhynchos*, *Aythya ferina*, *A. fuligula*, and *Fulica atra*. Other species include increasing numbers of feeding and resting *Phalacrocorax carbo sinensis*.

066 Rijn/Lek: Arnhem – Schoonhoven (Gelderland, Utrecht, Zuid-Holland)

51°57'N, 04°50'-05°55'E 6500+ ha

Nature Reserves (SBB Reserve: *c.*180 ha; L Reserve: 7 ha)

Part of the Rhine system with flood-plains and old meanders containing clay-pits, wet grasslands, and rough marshy vegetation. Human activities include brick-making, stock-grazing, hunting, and fishing. Problems include the high levels of industrial pollutants in the Rhine, industrial expansion, intensification of grassland agriculture, and growing recreation.

Breeding species include *Botaurus stellaris*, *Circus aeruginosus*, *Porzana porzana*, *Crex crex*, *Limosa limosa*, and *Tringa totanus*. Non-breeding waterfowl include *Phalacrocorax carbo sinensis*, *Cygnus columbianus*, *Anser fabalis* (200), *A. albifrons* (500), *Anas acuta*, *Aythya ferina*, *A. fuligula*, and *Mergus albellus*.

067 IJssel: Westervoort – Zwolle (Gelderland, Overijssel)

52°09'-52°24'N, 06°05'-06°10'E 10,700+ ha

Nature Reserves (SBB Reserve: 820 ha; L Reserve: 100 ha)

A large river valley of the Rhine system, together with its flood-plain and former meanders. Includes a number of small lakes surrounded by marshy woodlands and reedbeds. Human activities include stock-grazing and haymaking. Increasing recreation and expansion of agriculture and industry are the main problems.

Breeding species include *Phalacrocorax carbo sinensis*, *Botaurus stellaris*, *Anas querquedula*, *Circus aeruginosus*, *Porzana porzana*, *Crex crex*, *Philomachus pugnax*,

Chlidonias niger, *Acrocephalus arundinaceus*, and *Panurus biarmicus*. Wintering waterfowl include *Cygnus columbianus* (max. 1070), *C. cygnus* (max. 260), *Anser fabalis* (15,000), *A. albifrons* (10,000), *A. brachyrhynchus*, *A. anser*, *Anas penelope* (max. 3700), *Aythya ferina*, *A. fuligula*, *Mergus albellus*, *M. merganser*, and *Fulica atra* (max. 25,000).

068 Holterberg and Haarlerberg (Overijssel)

52°21'N, 06°25'E 2940 ha

Nature Reserves (NM Reserve: 907 ha; SBB Reserve: 450 ha)

Heathland and woodland. Human activities include forestry and recreation.

Stronghold in the Netherlands for *Tetrao tetrix* (32 males in 1986).

069 Rechte Heide (Noord-Brabant)

51°30'N, 05°02'E 250 ha

Unprotected

Heathland with scattered trees. The area is used for military training; at other times open to the public.

One of the last sites in the Netherlands with a population of *Tetrao tetrix* (7 males in 1986).

070 Oirschotse Heide (Noord-Brabant)

51°29'N, 05°21'E 1250 ha

Heathland and woodland. The area is used for military training; at other times open to the public.

One of the last sites in the Netherlands with a population of *Tetrao tetrix* (13 males in 1986).

MAIN REFERENCES

Ebbinge, B. S. *et al.* (1986) Numbers and distribution of wild geese in Netherlands, 1979-1984. *Wildfowl* 37: 28-34.

Osieck, E. R. (1981) Belangrijke waterrijke vogelgebieden in Nederland. *Limosa* 55: 43-55.

Osieck, E. R. (1986) *Bedreigde en karakteristieke vogels in Nederland.* Zeist: Nederlandse Vereniging tot Bescherming van Vogels.

Osieck, E. R. and Mörzer Bruyns, M. F. (1981) Important bird areas in Europe. Unpublished report to the Commission of the European Communities.

Osieck, E. R. and Braakhekke, W. G. (1986) Aanvullingen en verbeteringen op de lijst van belangrijke waterrijke vogelgebieden in Nederland *Limosa* 59: 75-81.

Smit, C. J. and Wolff, W. J. (1981) *Birds of the Wadden Sea.* Rotterdam: Balkema.

SOVON (in press) Nieuwe aantalsschattingen van de Nederlandse broedvogels. *Limosa 61.*

Teixeira, R. M. (1979) *Atlas van de Nederlandse broedvogels.* 's-Graveland: Natuurmonumenten.

NORWAY

Great Snipe *Gallinago media*

INTRODUCTION

General information

The mainland of Norway covers an area of 323,900 sq km, and has an extensive southern and western coastline (bordering the Skagerrak, North Sea, Norwegian Sea, and Arctic Ocean) with numerous fjords and islands (there are 53,789 islands). Norway has one of the lowest population densities in Europe: in 1984, the population numbered only 4.1 million (an average density of 12.6 persons per km). The bulk of human settlement is located on the coast, mainly in the vicinity of Bergen, Stavanger, Trondheim, Oslo, and large parts of Norway are unpopulated or only sparsely populated. The Arctic territories of Svalbard and Jan Mayen are also part of Norway, but are covered by a separate inventory.

Only three per cent of the land area (9500 sq km in 1982) is under cultivation, with the best agricultural land located below 300 m. Areas of productive forests cover about 20 per cent of the land area (66,450 sq km in 1982). Over 70 per cent of the land area is covered by mountains (50 per cent of which is exposed bedrock) or other unproductive ground.

The Langfjellene mountain range divides the country into eastern and western Norway, with the highest mountain peak, Galdhøpiggen, rising to 2469 m. There is little temperature variation from north to south, but there is a significant contrast between the inland and coastal regions. Three main vegetation zones may be defined (Polunin and Walters 1985): Arctic, Boreal, and Atlantic.

Arctic vegetation is found in the northern part of the country and above the forested boreal zone along the central mountain range that bisects the country. The vegetation largely comprises dwarf shrubs, sedges and rushes, mosses and lichens. Palsa mires occur in northern Norway in areas of permafrost where peat accumulates in acidic and moist conditions.

The boreal vegetation zone lies to the west and south of the Arctic vegetation zone, usually at lower altitudes (seldom above 1000 m). Evergreen coniferous forests predominate, mainly *Picea abies* and *Pinus sylvestris*. This vegetation is richest in the south-eastern part of the country, where the deep forests of the major valleys are the basis of the Norwegian lumber industry. Deciduous *Betula* woodlands are well developed in the subalpine zone above the coniferous belt. Mires are extensive in the boreal region.

Atlantic vegetation is confined to the coastal zone of the south-western and western parts of the country. This region was formerly dominated by deciduous forests in the middle of the post-glacial period. The forests have largely been decimated and only remnants remain, having been replaced by cultivated land and grassland.

There are fewer large inland lakes than in Sweden or Finland; freshwater wetland areas cover about 46,100 sq km (14 per cent of the land surface).

Ornithological importance

Mainland Norway's population of *Haliaeetus albicilla* is certainly the largest in Europe (1000 pairs); other Red Data Book species occurring in the country include *Anser erythropus* (breeding population not known, but certainly small) and *Crex crex* (100-200 pairs). Norway has notably large breeding population of the following species: *Gavia stellata* (*c.*1000 pairs), *G. arctica* (1000+ pairs), *Aquila chrysaetos* (600-700 pairs), *Falco rusticolus* (200-500 pairs), *Tetrao tetrix*, *T. urogallus*, *Grus grus* (*c.*1000 pairs), *Charadrius morinellus* (28,000 pairs), *Gallinago media* (1400 pairs), *Pluvialis apricaria*, *Philomachus pugnax*, *Phalaropus lobatus* (9500 pairs), *Uria lomvia* (3000 pairs), *Dendrocopos leucotos* (less than 1000 pairs), and *Picoides tridactylus*. Also of importance is the country's very large populations of a variety of ducks, other waders, and seabirds, including *Phalacrocorax carbo* (20,000 pairs), *P. aristotelis* (15,000 pairs), *Rissa tridactyla* (*c.*500,000 pairs), *Uria aalge* (*c.*40,000 pairs in 1983-86, but suffered a dramatic, greater than 80 per cent, decline in Finnmark in 1986-87, probably as a result of the collapse of the capelin *Mallotus villosus* stocks. There were signs of a recovery in 1988, but numbers were still very low. West of the North Cape numbers have steadily declined since *c.*1970), *Alca torda* (30,000 pairs), *Cepphus grylle* (20,000 pairs), and *Fratercula arctica* (*c.*100,000 pairs). The Norwegian forests are also important for owls including *Surnia ulula*, *Glaucidium passerinum*, *Strix uralensis*, *S. nebulosa*, and *Aegolius funereus*.

The coastal fjords, archipelagic waters, and islands are important for passage and wintering Gaviidae, Podicepidae, Anatidae, and Scolopacidae. All four Palearctic Gaviidae winter in good numbers including *Gavia adamsii*. Passage Anatidae include large concentrations of *Cygnus cygnus*, *Anser brachyrhynchus*, and *Branta leucopsis* (entire Svalbard population). Wintering Anatidae include large concentrations of *Somateria spectabilis* and *Polysticta stelleri* (10,000-12,000 of the latter wintering at Varangerfjord). Wintering waders include large numbers of *Calidris maritima*. A large proportion of the country's *Haliaeetus albicilla* population is resident, with concentrations of 50-100 birds at some localities in winter.

Conservation infrastructure and protected-area system

The central legislation for nature conservation comprises the Nature Conservation Act, the Wildlife Act, and the Open-Air Recreation Act.

The Ministry of the Environment is the government authority responsible for conservation, under which is the Directorate for Nature Management (Direktoratet for Naturforvaltning). At the regional level each county governor's office has an environment-protection section, which is responsible for planning and designation of nature reserves. The following types of protected areas can be designated (no. of sites designated is as on 1 January 1986).

1. National Parks (15 sites; covering 965,200 ha)
   These are mainly designated on state land, and have the double aim of conserving relatively large tracts of land where the impact of human activity is low or non-existent, and preserving areas for non-exploitative recreation.
2. Nature Reserves (632 sites; covering 89,200 ha)
   Creation of Nature Reserves is in accordance with county regional conservation plans developed for the most important types of ecosystem; to date, planning is most advanced with respect to mires, wetlands, deciduous forests, and breeding localities for seabirds. The main reasons for establishing Natures Reserves are to prevent negative environmental changes and to control public access. Nature Reserves can be created on private land, but the restrictions on land-use will normally entitle the owner to compensation.
3. Landscape Protection Areas (53 sites; covering 189,000 ha)
   Landscape Protection Areas are designated to protect large tracts of land, and to gain control over certain economic activities such as forestry and agriculture. In some cases, Landscape Protection Areas are established as buffer zones to Nature Reserves or National Parks where a lesser degree of protection is necessary but where control of certain activities is considered to be essential.

Additional measures are also available to protect areas of value to wildlife. For example, bird protection at coastal sites has been ensured at a large number of state-owned lighthouses and adjacent areas since 1935. Furthermore, single objects such as remarkable trees on geological sites can be protected as Nature Monuments.

International measures relevant to the conservation of sites

Norway is a party to the Ramsar Convention, Bern Convention, Bonn Convention, and World Heritage Convention and has designated nine Ramsar Sites (plus five in Svalbard) but no natural World Heritage Sites. In addition, a single Biosphere Reserve has been designated in Svalbard. Norway also actively contributes to the conservation work of the Nordic Council of Ministers, the Council of Europe (it has designated a number of Biogenetic Reserves), and the Economic Commission for Europe (United Nations).

Overview of the inventory

There are 49 important bird areas in the Norwegian (mainland) inventory, and together they cover a total area of about 781,000 ha (to nearest 1000 ha). Of these, 27 are protected or at least partly protected (for some sites it is only a very small part), with 23 not covered at present by the protected area network (although protection is proposed for at least 12 of these). A majority of the sites are seabird sites or wetlands, and the inventory includes all the mainland's Ramsar Sites.

The coverage of seabird breeding populations, and to a lesser extent sites for passage and wintering waterfowl, is therefore good. However, many bird species (which Norway has important populations of) such as raptors, grouse, owls, and woodpeckers, as well as breeding ducks and waders, tend not to congregate but have scattered distributions. Only a small proportion of their total populations is covered by the inclusion of some representative sites. To conserve these species it is necessary to consider nature conservation in activities such as forestry and agriculture.

Acknowledgements

The inventory was compiled mainly from information provided by J. Sandvik, S. Eldøy (Directorate for Nature Management), and R. Barrett (Tromsø Museum). Additional material has been taken from Carp (1980), Barrett and Vader (1984), and IUCN (1987). S. Eldøy provided helpful background material which was used to compile the introduction and T. Axelsen (Norwegian Ornithological Society) helped by providing final corrections (with new seabird data coming from T. A. Nielsen).

INVENTORY

No.	Site name	Region	Criteria used to select site [see p.18] 0	1(i)	1(ii)	1(iii)	1(iv)	2	3	4
001	Øvre Pasvik	FK						*	*	
002	Neiden and Munkefjord	FK							*	
003	Varangerfjord	FK				*			*	
003-1	Nesseby									
003-2	Vadsøy and Vadsøysundet									
003-3	Ekkerøy									
004	Hornøy and Reinøy	FK			*				*	
005	Syltefjordstauran	FK			*				*	
006	Kongsøy, Helløy and Skarvholmen	FK			*					
007	Tanamunningen	FK				*		*	*	
008	Omgangstauran	FK			*					
009	Sværholtklubben	FK			*					
010	Stabbursneset	FK				*		*		
011	Gjesværstappan	FK		*	*				*	
012	Hjelmsøy	FK		*	*				*	
013	Alta-Kautokeino watercourse	FK							*	
014	Loppa	FK								*
015	Nord Fugløy	TS		*	*			*		
016	Sør Fugløy	TS		*	*				*	
017	Sørkjosen	TS				*			*	
018	Bleiksøy	ND		*	*				*	
019	Skogvoll including Skarvklakken	ND				*				
020	Anda	ND	*							
021	Fuglenyken and Nykvåg	ND		*	*					
022	Grunnfjorden	ND							*	
023	Hovsflesa	ND			*					
024	Værøy	ND		*	*					
025	Røst	ND		*	*				*	
026	Saltstraumen	ND						*		
027	Lovunden	ND		*	*					
028	Svenningen – Risvær	ND						*	*	
029	Vega Archipelago	ND			*	*		*	*	
030	Gjørv,Borgenfjorden	NT				*				
031	Forramyrene	NT							*	
032	Tautra and Svaet	NT						*	*	
033	Ørlandet Wetland System	ST				*		*	*	
034	Froan	ST		*	*	*		*	*	
035	Gaulosen	ST				*			*	
036	Havmyran	ST						*		
037	Smøla Archipelago	MR				*		*	*	
038	Sandblåstvågen/Gaustadvågen	MR				*			*	
039	Runde	MR		*	*			*		
040	Dovrefjell	ST,OD							*	
041	Hardangervidda	BD,TE,HD							*	
042	Jæren Wetland System	RD							*	
043	Ilene and Presterødkilen Wetland System	VD	*							
044	Kurefjorden	OL	*							
045	Øra	OL				*			*	
046	Nordre Øyeren	AS				*			*	
047	Dokkadeltaet	OD	*							
048	Akersvika	HK							*	
049	Lågendeltaet	OD							*	

FK=Finnmark TS=Troms ND=Nordland NT=Nord-Trøndelag ST=Sør-Trøndelag MR=Møre og Romsdal OD=Oppland BD=Buskerud TE=Telemark HD=Hordaland RD=Rogaland VD=Vestfold OL=Østfold AS=Akershus HK=Hedmark

Comments on the inventory

1. Breeding populations of certain species at some sites, have not been published out of a need for confidentiality. This applies in particular to *Haliaeetus albicilla* (with two sites holding over 10 pairs), *Falco peregrinus*, and several species of owl.
2. Almost all the passage figures are daily maxima, with a few exceptional cases (one being the passage figure for *Branta leucopsis* at site 029).
3. All the sites are believed to qualify according to the site-selection criteria except 020 which is included because of its very large *Fratercula arctica* breeding population, and 043, 044 and 047 which are included because they are important passage sites for waterfowl.
4. The regions, given in parentheses following the site names, are the counties (Fylker). The 'region' used when applying the site-selection criteria (categories 3 and 4) is Norway.

---

001 Øvre Pasvik (Finnmark)

69°05'N, 29°00'E *c.*20,000 ha

Partly a National Park (6300 ha), with the rest proposed as an enlargement of the Park

A virgin forest (largest in the country) with a flat landscape (the westernmost limit of the Siberian taiga), dominated by coniferous woodland and bogs. A planned road between Finland and Norway would pass through the site, which may result in extensive forestry and increased tourist traffic.

Breeding species include *Gavia stellata*, *G. arctica*, *Cygnus cygnus*, *Haliaeetus albicilla*, *Buteo lagopus*, *Pandion haliaetus*, *Grus grus*, *Surnia ulula*, *Strix nebulosa*, and *Asio flammeus*. *Gavia arctica* (50) and *Cygnus cygnus* (50) occur on passage.

002 Neiden and Munkefjord (Finnmark)

69°40'N, 29°35'E 1150 ha

Unprotected, but proposed Nature Reserve

Estuaries of the Rivers Neidenelva and Munkelva. There is some boat traffic; other human activities include fishing and bathing.

This area supports one of the largest concentrations of divers in Norway (probably the breeding population from around Lake Enare, with birds waiting for ice-free water in spring), with *Gavia stellata* (100) and *G. arctica* (400; 100 in autumn). Other non-breeding species include *Somateria mollissima* (3000 in winter), *S. spectabilis* (100 in winter), *Clangula hyemalis* (4000 in spring), and *Calidris maritima* (200 in winter).

003 Varangerfjord (Finnmark)

70°05'-70°20'N, 28°35'-31°10'E *c.*60,000 ha

Unprotected, although one small area is proposed for protection and another is a Nature Reserve

An Arctic shoreline with relatively small areas of shallow water. A main road runs along the shore and two towns (Vadsø and Vardø) with harbours lie in the area. The sea is an important fishing zone. A very important area for *Polysticta stelleri*, particularly the harbours, which are very vulnerable to oil pollution.

Important for non-breeding *Somateria mollissima* (5000-6000 in winter), *S. spectabilis* (1500-4000 in winter), and *Polysticta stelleri* (1000 in summer; 10,000-12,000 in winter, 80-90 per cent of the Western Palearctic wintering population). Other non-breeding species include *Clangula hyemalis* (1200 in winter), *Calidris minuta* (1800 in autumn), *C. ferruginea* (1000 in autumn), *C. maritima* (1000 in winter), *C. alpina* (10,000 in autumn), and *Phalaropus lobatus* (500 in spring).

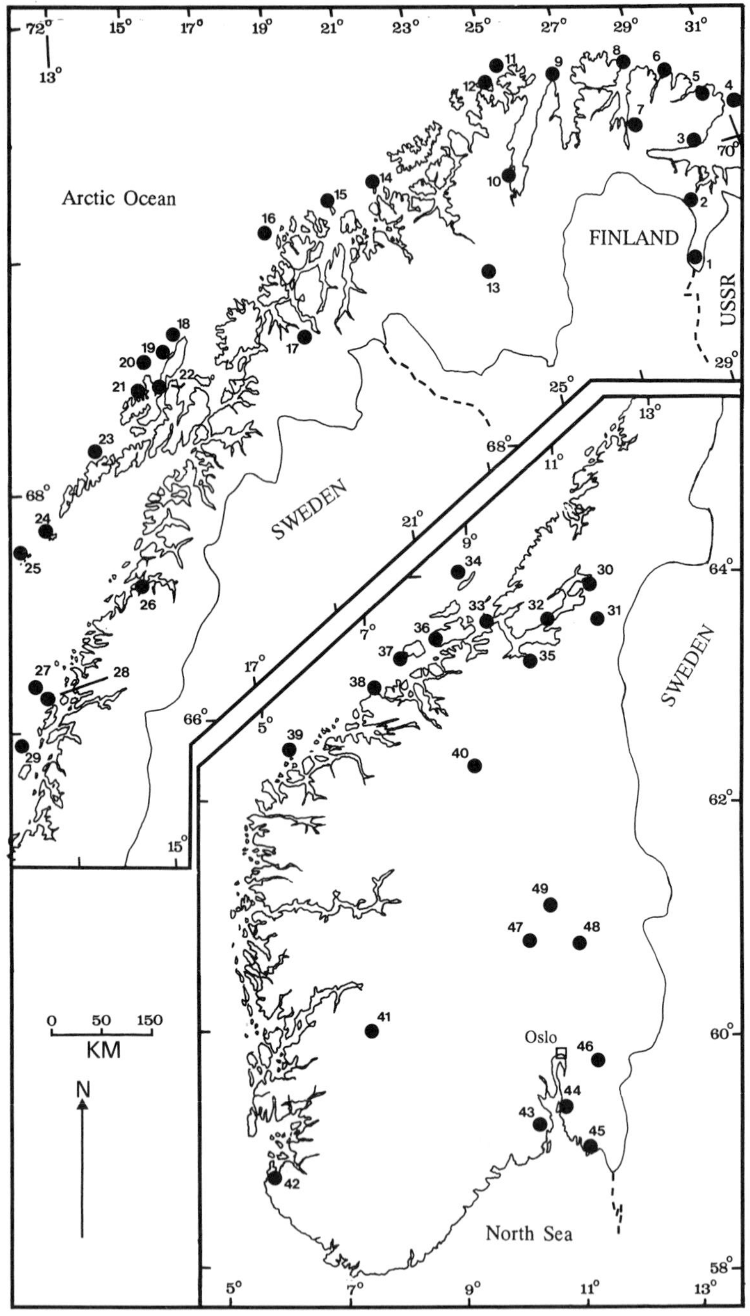

Figure 24: Map showing the location of the sites in Norway

Additional information is provided for the following subsites:

003-1 Nesseby

70°10'N, 28°50'E 74 ha

Unprotected, but proposed Nature Reserve

A broad, tidal bay with shallow water.

Breeding species include *Sterna paradisaea* (200-300 pairs). Non-breeding species include *Polysticta stelleri* (50 in summer and winter), *Calidris minuta* (1400), and *Phalaropus lobatus* (500 in spring).

003-2 Vadsøy and Vadsøysundet

70°05'N, 29°45'E *c.*120 ha

Unprotected

The area consists of the eastern part of Vadsøy island and the bay (with extensive tidal areas and shallow water) between the island and the mainland. There is a plan to fill in a large part of the bay for industrial purposes.

One of the best areas for *Polysticta stelleri* in Varangerfjord with 3500 wintering birds. Other non-breeding species include *Somateria spectabilis* (2500 in winter) and *Phalaropus lobatus* (400 in spring).

003-3 Ekkerøy

70°05'N, 30°10'E 160 ha

Nature Reserve

The southern and eastern half of the Ekkerøy peninsula including a 50 m cliff along the southern coast. There is sheep-grazing and collecting of gull eggs.

The cliffs have a large *Rissa tridactyla* colony (*c.*20,000 pairs).

004 Hornøy and Reinøy (Finnmark)

70°24'N, 31°10'E 200 ha

Nature Reserve

Includes the islands of Hornøy, Reinøy, Prestholmen and Lille-Avløsninga with cliffs and grass-covered slopes. There is a lighthouse on Hornøy and egg collecting (of gulls) is permitted until 14 June.

An important seabird colony with *Phalacrocorax aristotelis* (*c.*150 pairs), *Somateria mollissima* (1000+ pairs), *Larus argentatus* (*c.*50,000 pairs), *Rissa tridactyla* (23,000 pairs), *Uria aalge* (6000 pairs in 1985), *U. lomvia* (400 pairs), *Alca torda* (250 pairs), and *Fratercula arctica* (6000 pairs).

005 Syltefjordstauran (Finnmark)

70°35'N, 30°30'E 11,600 ha

Nature Reserve

Coastline with steep cliffs.

An important seabird colony with *Sula bassana* (300 pairs; the northernmost colony in the world), *Rissa tridactyla* (140,000 pairs; the largest colony in Norway), *Uria aalge* (12,000 pairs in 1985; the largest colony in Norway), *U. lomvia* (1300 pairs), *Alca torda* (1200 pairs), and *Fratercula arctica* (100 pairs).

006 Kongsøy, Helløy and Skarvholmen (Finnmark)

70°44'N, 29°30'E 280 ha

Nature Reserve

Kongsøy is a large, grass-covered island with steep cliffs. Helløy and Skarvholmen are low-lying islands with minimal vegetation.

Three islands with breeding *Phalacrocorax carbo* (600 pairs), *P. aristotelis* (400 pairs), *Rissa tridactyla* (18,000 pairs), *Alca torda* (less than 100 pairs), and *Fratercula arctica* (less than 100 pairs).

007 Tanamunningen (Finnmark)

70°25'-70°35'N, 28°20'-28°35'E *c.*3450 ha

Unprotected, but proposed Nature Reserve

The estuary of the River Tana entering Tanafjord with extensive areas of shallow water and sandbanks. There are plans to dredge between Høgholmen and Lavonjarg, cutting through the eastern part of the area. There are also hunting and disturbance in the area.

An extremely important moulting area for *Mergus merganser* (27,000 males). Other visitors in summer include *Haliaeetus albicilla* and *Falco rusticolus*. Passage species include *Gavia arctica* (40 in autumn), *Mergus serrator* (1500), *Haliaeetus albicilla* (max. 7), and *Phalaropus lobatus* (80 in autumn). Winter visitors include *Somateria mollissima* (4000), *S. spectabilis* (800), and *Clangula hyemalis* (4000).

008 Omgangstauran (Finnmark)

70°55'N, 28°30'E 750 ha

Nature Reserve

Coastline with steep cliffs.

An important seabird colony with *Rissa tridactyla* (74,000 pairs), *Phalacrocorax carbo* (100-1000 pairs), and small numbers of breeding auks.

009 Sværholtklubben (Finnmark)

70°58'N, 26°40'E 220 ha

Nature Reserve

Peninsula with steep cliffs.

An important colony of *Rissa tridactyla* (48,000 pairs), and also small numbers of breeding auks.

010 Stabbursneset (Finnmark)

70°10'N, 24°40'E 1620 ha Ramsar Site

Nature Reserve

Situated on the west coast of Porsangen Fjord. Part of an estuary at the outlet of the Stabburselva. Most of the area consists of shallow water with sandbanks exposed at low tide, and saltmarshes and wet mires inland. There are strict regulations governing human activities.

Breeding species include *Somateria mollissima* (1850 pairs) and *Sterna paradisaea* (100 pairs). One of the most important spring passage sites for *Anser erythropus* in Norway with up to 60 occurring. Other passage species in spring include *Calidris canutus* (31,000). An important moulting area for waterfowl including *Melanitta fusca* (3000) and *Somateria mollissima* (10,000).

011 Gjesværstappan (Finnmark)

71°10'N, 25°20'E 720 ha

Nature Reserve

Three steep-sided, grass-covered islands: Storstappen, Kjerkestappen, and Bukkstappen. The areas of rock-face colonised by cliff-breeding seabirds are mainly on Storstappen.

An important seabird colony with *Phalacrocorax carbo* (70 pairs), *P. aristotelis* (*c.*50 pairs), *Rissa tridactyla* (5000-10,000 pairs), *Uria aalge* (*c.*600 pairs), *U. lomvia* (25 pairs),

Alca torda (2500 pairs), and *Fratercula arctica* (50,000 pairs). *Sula bassana* nests were recorded in 1988.

012 Hjelmsøy (Finnmark)

71°05'N, 24°45'E 430 ha

Nature Reserve

A large island in west Finnmark. The reserve includes two km of vertical cliffs around the northernmost peninsula.

An important seabird colony with *Rissa tridactyla* (50,000 pairs), *Uria aalge* (5000-10,000 pairs in 1986; a significant decline has taken place during the last twenty years, with 111,000 pairs in 1964 and 70,000 pairs in 1974), *U. lomvia* (100-500 pairs), *Alca torda* (7000 pairs; second largest colony in Norway), and *Fratercula arctica* (20,000 pairs).

013 Alta-Kautokeino watercourse (Finnmark)

69°17'-69°50'N, 23°20'-23°55'E *c.*30,000 ha

Unprotected

The site comprises the valley of Alta-Kautokeinoelva which passes through the Sautso Canyon (one of the finest canyons in northern Europe). In the southern part the valley is not so deep and has an area of bogs and lakes. The river is dammed and a lake 20 km long has been created which destroyed a large area of valuable habitat.

The valley has one of the highest breeding densities of raptors in Norway, perhaps in northern Europe. Breeding species include *Buteo lagopus* (50 pairs), *Aquila chrysaetos* (3 pairs), *Accipiter gentilis* (1 pair), *A. nisus* (1 pair), *Falco columbarius* (30 pairs), *Falco rusticolus* (5 pairs), *F. peregrinus* (1 pair), and *F. tinnunculus* (11 pairs).

014 Loppa (Finnmark)

70°22'N, 21°24'E 720 ha

Nature Reserve

Island with cliffs and steep slopes with grassland, bogs, and heath. The reserve includes the steep cliffs on the north-west side.

An important seabird colony with *Stercorarius parasiticus* (50 pairs), *S. skua* (2 pairs), *Rissa tridactyla* (300 pairs), *Uria aalge* (340 pairs), *Alca torda* (2000 pairs), *Cepphus grylle* (20 pairs) and *Fratercula arctica* (14,500 pairs).

015 Nord Fugløy (Troms)

70°17'N, 20°14'E 2130 ha

Nature Reserve

Island with cliffs and steep slopes which rise to a plateau with marshes and small lakes.

An important seabird colony (with the second largest colony of *Fratercula arctica* in Norway), with *Uria aalge* (less than 100 pairs; there has been a significant decline in recent years, with 13,000 pairs in 1964 and 4000 pairs in 1974), *Alca torda* (1000-2000 pairs), and *Fratercula arctica* (200,000+ pairs). The population of *Haliaeetus albicilla* is noteworthy.

016 Sør Fugløy (Troms)

70°07'N, 18°30'E *c.*100 ha

Unprotected, but proposed Nature Reserve

Steep-sided island. Slopes covered in grass with boulder screes at foot.

An important seabird colony with *Hydrobates pelagicus* (breeding confirmed in 1986, although population unknown; perhaps 100-1000 pairs), *Uria aalge* (less than 100 pairs;

after a significant decline in recent years), *Alca torda* (100 pairs), and *Fratercula arctica* (40,000 pairs).

017 Sørkjosen (Troms)

69°15'N, 19°15'E *c.*400 ha

Unprotected

The outlet of two rivers, and large tidal areas of mud, sand, and gravel at the head of Balsfjord. There is industry along the shore, and there are important fishing areas and spawning grounds for herring and capelin. Industry is expanding and threatens the tidal area; also a new highway route is planned through the site.

Breeding species include *Sterna paradisaea* (300 pairs). Important for many species in spring including *Gavia stellata* (10), *G. arctica* (10), *Podiceps auritus* (200), *Clangula hyemalis* (7500), *Melanitta fusca* (2700), and *Calidris canutus* (25,000).

018 Bleiksøy (Nordland)

69°16'N, 15°52'E *c.*20 ha

Unprotected

Steep-sided island. Slopes covered in grass. Boulder screes in gulleys at foot of vertical cliffs. The traditional collecting of eggs of *Phalacrocorax aristotelis*, *Rissa tridactyla* and other gulls is permitted until 1 June.

An important seabird colony with *Hydrobates pelagicus* (breeding confirmed in 1985, although population unknown; perhaps 100-1000 pairs), *Rissa tridactyla* (4000 pairs), *Uria aalge* (100 pairs), *Alca torda* (*c.*100 pairs) and *Fratercula arctica* (80,000 pairs).

019 Skogvoll including Skarvklakken (Nordland)

69°10'N, 15°41'E *c.*300 ha

Nature Reserve

A number of small islands including Skarvklakken, and a tidal zone with extensive tidal mudflats.

Breeding seabirds include *Sula bassana* (800 pairs on Skarvklakken; one of four colonies in Norway) and *Phalacrocorax carbo* (*c.*200-300 pairs on Skarvklakken). Passage species include *Anser brachyrhynchus* (1000+), and *Somateria spectabilis* (350) occurs in winter.

020 Anda (Nordland)

69°10'N, 15°10'E *c.*10 ha

Unprotected

Low-lying, grass-covered island; low, steep cliffs on east side.

An important seabird colony with *Rissa tridactyla* (500 pairs) and *Fratercula arctica* (20,000-25,000 pairs).

021 Fuglenyken and Nykvåg (Nordland)

68°47'N, 14°27'E *c.*20 ha

Unprotected

Fuglenyken is a steep-sided, grass-covered island, nearly vertical on the northern side. Nykvåg is a vertical cliff behind Nykvåg harbour.

An important seabird colony with *Rissa tridactyla* (4000 pairs), *Uria aalge* (350 pairs), *Alca torda* (250 pairs), and *Fratercula arctica* (40,000 pairs).

022 Grunnfjorden (Nordland)

68°55'N, 15°10'E 390 ha

Unprotected, but proposed Natuıe Reserve

A large bog with small streams and small lakes; also large tidal flats and shallow water with a number of islands. New roads are planned through the area and the extraction of peat will destroy the bog. There are also plans for cultivating parts of the area. Probably one of the most important locations for *Podiceps auritus* in Norway.

Important for breeding *Gavia stellata* (5 pairs), *G. arctica* (common) and *Podiceps auritus* (very common; also 100 on autumn passage). *Cygnus cygnus* (100) occurs in winter.

023 Hovsflesa (Nordland)

68°22'N, 14°01'E *c.*0.25 ha

Unprotected

A small, low-lying skerry.

A small island with a *Sula bassana* colony (700 pairs; established in the 1970s); also *Phalacrocorax carbo* (*c.*100-500 pairs).

024 Værøy (Nordland)

67°45'N, 12°45'E *c.*500 ha

Unprotected, but proposed Nature Reserve

A seabird colony on the south-west peninsula of Værøy island; with high vertical cliffs and steep grass-covered slopes.

An important seabird colony with *Rissa tridactyla* (19,000 pairs), *Uria aalge* (1750 pairs), *U. lomvia* (20 pairs), *Alca torda* (800 pairs), and *Fratercula arctica* (70,000 pairs).

025 Røst (Nordland)

67°30'N, 12°00'E 1500-2000 ha

Proposed Nature Reserve; access to the bird cliffs prohibited 15 April-15 August, except for daytime excursions to parts of Vedøy.

An archipelago of numerous islands. Most important are Vedøy, Storfjell, Ellefsnyken, Trenyken, and Hernyken which are steep-sided 92-259 m high and covered in grass.

An important seabird colony with *Fulmarus glacialis* (300-500 pairs), *Hydrobates pelagicus* (*c.*1000 pairs), *Oceanodroma leucorhoa* (*c.*100 pairs), *Phalacrocorax aristotelis* (600-1000 pairs), *Rissa tridactyla* (*c.*17,500 pairs in 1988), *Alca torda* (2000-4000 pairs in 1983), *Uria aalge* (4400 pairs in 1983; declining), *Fratercula arctica* (estimated 700,000 pairs in 1964; the largest colony in Norway, but now declining), and *Cepphus grylle* (1000-1500 pairs).

026 Saltstraumen (Nordland)

67°15'N, 14°35'E *c.*200 ha

Unprotected

A sea inlet with a very strong and fish-rich tidal river. There is considerable tourist traffic along the river, and some boat traffic through the sea inlet. There is some disturbance of the eagles, and plans to expand the tourist traffic may be a problem.

A very important wintering area for *Haliaeetus albicilla* (*c.*25, with 50-100 when food is plentiful).

027 Lovunden (Nordland)

66°21'N, 12°20'E

Unprotected

An important *Fratercula arctica* colony (60,000 pairs).

028 Svenningen - Risvær (Nordland)

66°20'N, 12°30'E *c.*15,000 ha

Unprotected

An archipelago of hundreds of islands (max. size 300 ha), islets, and skerries. The landscape is undulating with a mosaic of rocks and bogs. Parts of the largest islands are cultivated and inhabited. The area is very vulnerable to oil pollution.

A very important area for *Haliaeetus albicilla* (25-30 in winter). Breeding species include *Gavia stellata* (20-25 pairs) and *Bubo bubo*.

029 Vega Archipelago (Nordland)

65°40'-66°00'N, 11°30'-12°00'E *c.*50,000 ha

Unprotected, but proposed National Park

An archipelago of thousands of rocky islands (some very small). Many are covered with heather, but most (especially the outer islands) are grass-covered. Up until 1980, a small number of sheep was kept on the outer islands; the absence of grazing animals and traditional land management on these outer islands has reduced the availability of food for the geese and has forced them to the inner, inhabited islands.

Particularly important for *Haliaeetus albicilla*, and passage *Branta leucopsis* with almost the entire Svalbard population stopping over on spring passage. Breeding species include *Gavia stellata* (5 pairs), *Phalacrocorax carbo* (3500 pairs), *P. aristotelis* (min. 300 pairs), *Anser anser* (250 pairs; with 4000 moulting), *Somateria mollissima* (5000--6000 pairs; with 4500 moulting), *Haliaeetus albicilla*, *Sterna paradisaea* (400 pairs), *Cepphus grylle* (1000 pairs), and *Bubo bubo*. *Branta leucopsis* occurs in spring (10,500 in 1986) and wintering species include *Gavia stellata* (20), *G. immer* (40), *G. adamsii* (15), *Podiceps auritus* (20), *Somateria spectabilis* (300), *Haliaeetus albicilla* (22), and *Calidris maritima* (1100).

030 Gjørv, Borgenfjorden (Nord-Trøndelag)

63°56'N, 11°20'E *c.*200 ha

Unprotected

Tidal mudflats, shallow marine water, and agricultural land at the head of Trondheimsfjord. A large area of tidal mudflats has recently been drained for agricultural purposes and this is now being used as a feeding area by the geese. There is disturbance and the threat of further drainage.

Probably one of the most important passage sites in Norway for the Svalbard population of *Anser brachyrhynchus* (*c.*3000 in spring).

031 Forramyrene (Nord-Trøndelag)

63°35'N, 11°30'E 11,500 ha

Unprotected, but proposed Nature Reserve

Mires in the upper Forra Valley. Possible threat from a hydroelectric power project.

Important breeding area for waterfowl especially *Grus grus*, *Philomachus pugnax*, and *Gallinago media*.

032 Tautra and Svaet (Nord-Trøndelag)

63°35'N, 10°37'E 2054 ha Ramsar Site

Nature Reserve and Bird Sanctuary

A large flat island with (mainly) agricultural land and surrounding shallow seas. The island has been connected to the mainland by a stone pile, which has facilitated access by predators, and nest predation has increased considerably. It has also stopped the current through Svaet and thus adversely affected the availability of food for the seaducks.

Breeding species include *Somateria mollissima* (1600 pairs), *Haematopus ostralegus* (40-50 pairs), *Larus canus* (4000-6000 pairs), and *Sterna paradisaea* (200 pairs). Wintering species include *Gavia stellata* (25), *G. adamsii* (20), *Podiceps auritus* (5-10), small numbers of seaduck, and *Haliaeetus albicilla* (2-3).

033 Ørlandet Wetland System (Sør-Trøndelag)

63°42'N, 09°35'E 2920 ha Ramsar Site

Covered by Grandefjæra Nature Reserve, and Kråkvågsvaet, Innstrandfjæra and Hovsfjæra Bird Sanctuaries

Four areas consisting mainly of tidal mudflats and shallow seas. Inland, formerly extensive meadows and marsh now drained for agriculture. Strict regulations prevent activities such as building, hunting, and drainage.

The most important moulting, passage and wintering area for wetland birds in central Norway. Species occurring include *Gavia immer* (55 in winter), *Podiceps grisegena* (95 in winter), *Somateria mollissima* (6700 moulting; 3900 in winter), *Clangula hyemalis* (1100 in winter), *Melanitta fusca* (7200 moulting; 2750 in winter), and *Calidris maritima* (450 in winter). Small numbers of *Falco rusticolus* and *F. peregrinus* occur on autumn passage and *Haliaeetus albicilla* is regular in winter.

034 Froan (Sør-Trøndelag)

63°50'-64°15'N, 08°40'-09°30'E 73,000 ha

Nature Reserve; Landscape Protection Area and Wildlife Sanctuary

An archipelago with hundreds of islands, islets, and skerries. Most of the islands are low and undulating with rock, moorland, and small bogs. Six of the islands are inhabited and sheep are grazed on some islands. The area is very vulnerable to oil pollution.

Breeding species include *Gavia stellata* (12 pairs), *Phalacrocorax carbo* (2300 pairs), *P. aristotelis* (1100 pairs), *Anser anser* (200 pairs), *Somateria mollissima* (2500 pairs), *Haliaeetus albicilla* (6 pairs), *Sterna paradisaea* (max. 2300 pairs), and *Cepphus grylle* (1000 pairs). Large numbers of moulting wildfowl occur in summer with *Anser anser* (2000-5000), *Somateria mollissima* (30,000), and *Mergus serrator* (2500). Wintering species include *Gavia stellata* (30), *G. immer* (10), *G. adamsii* (30), *Phalacrocorax aristotelis* (5000), *Somateria mollissima* (7500), *Haliaeetus albicilla* (20), *Calidris maritima* (500), *Cepphus grylle* (1700), and *Alle alle* (min. 1500).

035 Gaulosen (Sør-Trøndelag)

63°20'N, 10°13'E 312 ha

Landscape Protection Area and small Nature Reserve

Estuary of the River Gaula with an island and extensive tidal mudflats and coastal shallows.

Passage species include *Gavia stellata* (30) and *Anser brachyrhynchus* (800), and *Falco rusticolus* and *F. peregrinus* are irregular on autumn passage. Winter visitors include *Cygnus cygnus* (60) and *Haliaeetus albicilla*.

036 Havmyran (Sør-Trøndelag)

63°30'N, 08°40'E 3960 ha

Nature Reserve

Open mire landscape with many small freshwater lakes.

A particularly important breeding area for waders, mainly *Pluvialis apricaria*, *Calidris alpina*, and *Numenius phaeopus* (50-100 pairs). Other breeding species include *Gavia stellata*, *G. arctica*, *Haliaeetus albicilla* (1 pair), *Aquila chrysaetos*, *Grus grus* (1-2 pairs), *Tetrao tetrix*, and *T. urogallus*. Up to 35 *Haliaeetus albicilla* occur in winter.

037 Smøla Archipelago (Møre og Romsdal)

63°20'N, 08°00'E *c.*20,000 ha

Currently unprotected, although there is a protection plan which will probably propose a combination of Nature Reserves, Bird Sanctuaries, and areas with special regulations.

An archipelago containing hundreds of islands and numerous islets and skerries, with large areas of continuous shallow water. The main island, Smøla, is dominated by an open mire landscape and heathland, and is cultivated in parts. Current problems include drainage and further cultivation on the largest islands; the archipelago is very vulnerable to oil pollution.

Breeding species include *Gavia stellata*, *Ardea cinerea* (500 pairs; the largest colony in Norway), *Anser anser* (300 pairs; 2000 moulting), *Somateria mollissima* (500 pairs; 1700 moulting), *Haliaeetus albicilla*, *Pluvialis apricaria* (common), *Philomachus pugnax* (50 pairs), *Sterna paradisaea* (900 pairs) and *Cepphus grylle* (250 pairs). Wintering species include *Gavia stellata* (200), *G. immer* (150), *Podiceps grisegena* (600), *P. auritus* (50), *Cygnus cygnus* (335), *Somateria mollissima* (5400), *Clangula hyemalis* (2300), *Melanitta fusca* (2050), *Mergus serrator* (2800), *Haliaeetus albicilla* (50+), *Falco rusticolus*, and *F. peregrinus*.

038 Sandblåstvågen/Gaustadvågen (Møre og Romsdal)

63°00'N, 07°15'-07°20'E 294 ha

Unprotected, but proposed Nature Reserve

An estuary in an undulating coastal area with coastal meadows, surrounded by agricultural land. Two roads cross the site and one has reduced the tidal flow. Plans include the building of a new road and cultivation of parts of the area.

Breeding species include *Pluvialis apricaria* (15 pairs) and *Philomachus pugnax* (15 pairs). A variety of species occurs on passage including *Falco peregrinus* and *Philomachus pugnax* (500). *Cygnus cygnus* (270) occurs in winter.

039 Runde (Møre og Romsdal)

62°24'N, 05°36'E 640 ha

Nature Reserve

Island with cliffs and steep slopes partly covered with boulders, with grassland and heath.

An important seabird colony with *Phalacrocorax aristotelis* (2000 pairs), *Sula bassana* (1100 pairs in 1985), *Stercorarius skua* (min. 8 pairs), *Rissa tridactyla* (50,000 pairs), *Uria aalge* (10,000 pairs), *Alca torda* (3500 pairs), and *Fratercula arctica* (75,000 pairs). *Haliaeetus albicilla* occurs in winter.

040 Dovrefjell (Sør-Trøndelag, Oppland)

62°13'-62°25'N, 09°10'-09°45'E 26,500 ha

National Park and Landscape Protection Area

A typical high-mountain area (900-2290 m) with broad marshy valleys and forests of *Betula*. The park is a major recreation area. Both a railway and road pass through the Landscape Protection Area.

The site has been included because of its population of *Gallinago media* (min. 400 pairs). *Aquila chrysaetos*, *Falco rusticolus*, and *Pluvialis apricaria* (200-400 pairs) also breed.

041 Hardangervidda (Buskerud, Telemark, Hordaland)

59°50'-60°35'N, 06°50'-08°25'E 427,200 ha

National Park (342,200 ha) and Landscape Protection Area (85,000 ha)

The largest mountain plateau in Europe (1000 m - 1500 m), dominated by several large lakes and undulating mountains. A major sheep-grazing area, and there are also reindeer hunting and tourism. Increasing tourism is a potential problem.

Breeding species include *Gavia arctica*, *Aquila chrysaetos*, *Falco columbarius*, *F. rusticolus*, *Charadrius morinellus* (*c.*5000 pairs), *Pluvialis apricaria* (*c.*10,000 pairs), *Gallinago media* (*c.*100 pairs), *Tringa glareola*, and *Nyctea scandiaca*.

042 Jæren Wetland System (Rogaland)

58°50'N, 05°34'E 1000 ha (excluding sea surface) Ramsar Site (400 ha)

Partly a Nature Reserve (Grudevatnet); some other parts covered by strict landscape protection regulations (Kolnes, Revtanger, and Skeie); partly unprotected (Orrevatnet)

Jaeren is one of the main agricultural districts in Norway, with a gently undulating landscape. The site comprises several lakes, shallow sea areas, and sea shores, west and south of Stavanger. The lakes are eutrophic, mainly due to agricultural pollution, with rich aquatic vegetation. The coastline comprises both sand-dune shores and stone/boulder beaches. Pollution is a problem resulting in vegetational succession and blooms of toxic algae.

One of the most important resting and wintering areas for waterfowl in Norway with more than 10,000 occurring in winter. Wintering species in Jan. 1980 included *Gavia stellata* (25), *G. arctica* (6), *G. immer* (20), *G. adamsii* (2), *Podiceps grisegena* (110), and *P. auritus* (55).

043 Ilene and Presterødkilen Wetland System (Vestfold)

59°15'N, 10°20'E 177 ha Ramsar Site

Two Nature Reserves

Two shallow marine bays with mudflats. Ilene has a varied landscape with reed areas, meadows, pastures, and *Picea* forests. Presterødkilen is surrounded by reedbeds and is more urbanised than Ilene.

One of the most important sites for waterbirds along the Oslo Fjord coast, with *Cygnus olor*, *Anas crecca*, *A. platyrhynchos*, *Vanellus vanellus*, *Tringa* spp. including *T. nebularia* (*c.*100), and *Philomachus pugnax* being the most numerous species.

044 Kurefjorden (Østfold)

59°30N, 11°00'E 400 ha Ramsar Site

Nature Reserve

A shallow marine bay (on the Oslo Fjord coast) with mudflats and wet grassland, surrounded by agricultural land. There has been extensive drainage in the surrounding area.

One of the most important sites for passage waterfowl along the Oslo Fjord coast. More than 2000 ducks and 1000 waders occur in autumn, the most numerous species being *Anas crecca*, *A. platyrhynchos*, *Bucephala clangula*, *Calidris alpina*, and *Philomachus pugnax*.

045 Øra (Østfold)

59°10'N, 11°00'E 1560 ha Ramsar Site

Nature Reserve

A large estuary (of the River Glomma at Fredrikstad) with extensive reedbeds. Increased salinity has had a detrimental effect on the site, although measures have been taken to ameliorate this. The estuary is also subjected to pollution from the River Glomma.

Limosa limosa breeds. An important site for non-breeding waterfowl with large numbers of *Cygnus olor* (500), *C. cygnus* (500+), *Anas crecca*, *A. platyrhynchos*, and *Bucephala clangula*. The most numerous waders are *Philomachus pugnax and Calidris alpina*.

046 Nordre Øyeren (Akershus)

59°53'N, 11°09'E 6260 ha Ramsar Site

Nature Reserve

An inland delta (the largest inland delta in Scandinavia, formed by the outlets of Rivers Glomma, Leira, and Nitelva) and shallow lake surrounded by deciduous forest and scrub, grassland, and agricultural land.

Limosa limosa breeds. Waterfowl occurring include *Cygnus cygnus* (1000) as well as large numbers of *Anas penelope*, *A. crecca*, *A. platyrhynchos*, *Bucephala clangula*, and *Mergus merganser*.

047 Dokkadeltaet (Oppland)

60°50'N, 10°10'E *c.*380 ha

Unprotected, but proposed Nature Reserve

A large delta formed by the outlet of the Rivers Etna and Dokka at the northern end of Randsfjorden. Most of the islands were used for grazing which has now ceased. The River Dokka is being regulated to generate electricity, which has reduced the inflow of water, and a major problem is the extraction of large quantities of gravel.

An important site during spring and autumn passage. Species occurring in autumn include *Anser brachyrhynchus* (200), *Philomachus pugnax* (130), and *Tringa glareola* (70).

048 Akersvika (Hedmark)

60°50'N, 11°08'E 415 ha Ramsar Site

Nature Reserve

A shallow bay, on the eastern side of Lake Mjøsa, with wet grassland and *Alnus* and *Salix* scrub. The site is surrounded by urban and industrial areas of the city of Hamar, and agricultural land. The regulation of the water-level exposes large mudflats in spring.

An important site for migrant ducks and waders, being an important part of the eastern flyway for waterfowl in Norway. Species occurring on spring passage include *Gavia arctica* (12), *Pluvialis apricaria* (240), *Philomachus pugnax* (675; 400 in autumn), *Numenius arquata* (300), *Tringa erythropus* (52), and *T. nebularia* (180).

049 Lågendeltaet (Oppland)

61°05'-61°10'N, 10°25'E *c.*860 ha

Unprotected, but proposed Nature Reserve

A large delta formed by the outlet of the Rivers Lågen and Gausa at the northern end of Lake Mjøsa. The delta consists of a large number of islands, channels, meadows, and marshes. There are gravel pits in the delta and the surrounding area is used for agriculture. The main problem is the continued extraction of large quantities of gravel.

An important site during spring and autumn passage. Species occurring include *Gavia arctica* (35 in spring), *Anser brachyrhynchus* (82 in autumn), and *Philomachus pugnax* (100 in spring).

MAIN REFERENCES

Barrett, R. T. and Vader, W. The status and conservation of breeding seabirds in Norway. Pp. 323-333 in Croxall, J. P., Evans, P. G. H. and Schreiber, R. W. (1984) *Status and Conservation of the World's Seabirds*. Cambridge: International Council for Bird Preservation, Techn. Publ. No. 2.

Carp, E. (1980) *Directory of wetlands of international importance in the Western Palearctic.* Nairobi and Gland, Switzerland: UNEP and World Conservation Monitoring Centre.

Direktoratet for Naturforvaltning (1988) *Truede Virveldyr i Norge* Rapport no. 2-1988.

IUCN (1987) *Directory of wetlands of international importance.* Gland, Switzerland: International Union for the Conservation of Nature.

SVALBARD AND JAN MAYEN

INTRODUCTION

General information

The Arctic territory of Svalbard covers an area of 62,049 sq km and includes Spitsbergen, Nordaustlandet, Edgeøya, Kvitøya, Hopen, and Bjørnøya (Bear Island). Jan Mayen, a mountainous island (380 sq km) partly covered by glaciers, is situated between Svalbard, Greenland, and Iceland.

Svalbard is sparsely populated (3000 people), and the main settlement is Longyearbyen. The landscape of much of the archipelago comprises rugged mountains, particularly jagged on the west coast, becoming flatter in the east where there are plateau-type mountains separated by broad valleys. Around the coast is a flat plain (maximum width 8-10 km) which supports most of the fauna and flora. The subsoil is permanently frozen, and the vegetation is mainly grasses, mosses, and lichens.

The main economic activity in Svalbard is coal mining carried out by Norwegian and Russian companies. Other activities include oil exploration (although no worthwhile discoveries have been made), recreation (guided tours, hunting, skidooing), and scientific expeditions.

Ornithological importance

Svalbard is principally important for its huge populations of Alcidae, particularly *Uria aalge*, *U. lomvia*, *Cepphus grylle*, and *Alle alle*, with over 1 million pairs of both *U. lomvia* and *A. alle*. Populations of *Fulmarus glacialis*, *Stercorarius parasiticus*, *Larus hyperboreus*, and *Pagophila eburnea* are also significant. Clearly it is not just the nesting colonies which are important but also the open waters of the fjords and the waters around Svalbard that provide feeding and moulting areas. Jan Mayen also supports sizeable populations of the above seabirds. Breeding populations of *Anser brachyrhynchus*, *Branta leucopsis*, and *B. bernicla hrota* are also extremely important; although their total breeding populations are not known (and many breeding sites presumably remain to be discovered), their wintering populations are estimated to be 25,000, 10,000, and 4000 birds respectively.

Conservation infrastructure and protected-area system

A large part of Svalbard is covered by protected areas, with three National Parks, two Nature Reserves and fifteen Bird Sanctuaries established in 1973.

National Parks and Nature Reserves are protected from all technical interference (including building construction, mining, and oil drilling), the use of cross-country vehicles, and the landing of aircraft. Mammals and birds are completely protected. Moffen Nature Reserve was established in 1983 as a reserve for walrus *Odobenus rosmarus* and has its own regulations for protection.

Bird Sanctuaries are similarly protected from all technical interference; in addition, all traffic (including offshore traffic) is prohibited between 15 May and 15 August. Outside the protected areas all Alcidae can be hunted from 1 September to 31 October (*Uria lomvia* can be hunted from 11 August).

All of Svalbard and Jan Mayen are covered by regulations controlling the interference with nature which apply, amongst other things, to economic activities such as mining and oil drilling.

International measures relevant to the conservation of sites

Svalbard and Jan Mayen are part of Norway. Norway has ratified the Bern Convention, Ramsar Convention, World Heritage Convention, and Bonn Convention, although the Bern Convention only applies to its continental territory (and therefore does not cover Svalbard and Jan Mayen; although the Norwegian Government has declared that Norway will promote policies for Svalbard and Jan Mayen in accordance with the convention). Of the 14 Ramsar Sites designated by Norway, five are in Svalbard (and all are included in this inventory). No natural World Heritage Sites have been designated; however, Northeast Svalbard Nature Reserve is Norway's only Biosphere Reserve designated under UNESCO's Man and the Biosphere programme.

Overview of inventory

The main seabird sites of Svalbard are included in the inventory (including Bjørnøya, Hopen, and Stellingfjellet) as are the main (known) breeding site for geese (Dunøyane, Isøyane, and Forlandsøyane for *Branta leucopsis*; Tusenøyane for *B. bernicla*). The inventory does not adequately cover the inshore feeding areas for seabirds, while geese-breeding areas are still not completely known.

All the sites listed are well protected (although some only by the regulations concerning the conservation of Svalbard and Jan Mayen's natural environment), but if current oil exploration is successful, future oil spills may pose a serious threat to seabirds and *Somateria mollissima*. Furthermore, an expected increase in industrial activities and tourism may cause disturbance to breeding colonies of seabirds and geese and also to flocks of moulting geese.

Acknowledgements

The following accounts were compiled from information provided by P. E. Fjeld, F. Mehlum, and V. Bakken of the Norsk Polarinstitutt (Norwegian Polar Research Institute). P. E. Field provided information which was used to prepare the above introduction.

INVENTORY

No.	Site name	Criteria used to select site [see p.18]							
		0	1(i)	1(ii)	1(iii)	1(iv)	2	3	4
001	North-west Spitsbergen National Park				*			*	
001-1	Guissezholmen Bird Sanctuary								
001-2	Casimir-Perierkammen								
001-3	Kongshamaren								
001-4	Nilsfjellet								
001-5	Knoffberget								
001-6	Moseøya Bird Sanctuary								
001-7	Skorpa Bird Sanctuary								
001-8	South-west Amsterdamøya								
001-9	North Hakluythovden, Amsterdamøya								
001-10	Klovningen								
001-11	Flathuken								
001-12	Hornbækfjellet								
001-13	Austplana								
001-14	Liefdefjorden								
001-15	Moffen Nature Reserve								
001-16	Nissenfjella								
002	Kongsfjorden Bird Sanctuary							*	
003	Hermansenøya Bird Sanctuary							*	
004	Forlandet National Park		*	*	*			*	
004-1	Forlandsøyane Bird Sanctuary								
004-2	Plankeholmane Bird Sanctuary								
004-3	Fuglehuken								

No.	Site name	Criteria used to select site [see p.18] 0	1(i)	1(ii)	1(iii)	1(iv)	2	3	4
005	North-east Svalbard Nature Reserve			*				*	
005-1	Rundisdammen, Kongsøya								
005-2	Retziusfjellet, Kongsøya								
005-3	Sjøgrenfjellet, Kongsøya								
005-4	Hárfagrehaugen, Kongsøya								
005-5	Wahlbergøya (north-east)								
005-6	Alkefjellet								
006	Søuth-east Svalbard Nature Reserve				*			*	
006-1	Negerpynten, Edgeøya								
006-2	Kvalpynten, Edgeøya								
006-3	Tusenøyane, Edgeøya								
007	South Spitsbergen National Park		*	*	*			*	
007-1	Olsholmen Bird Sanctuary								
007-2	Isøyane Bird Sanctuary								
007-3	Dunøyane Bird Sanctuary								
007-4	Sørkapp Bird Sanctuary								
007-5	Stellingfjellet								
007-6	Kovalskifjella								
007-7	Sofiekammen, Gnålberget								
008	Gåsøyane Bird Sanctuary							*	
009	Kongressfjellet							*	
010	Boheman Bird Sanctuary				*			*	
011	Grumant							*	
012	Alkhornet		*	*				*	
013	Daudmansöyra				*			*	
014	Nordenskiöldkysten including Kapp Linné Bird Sanctuary				*			*	
015	Ingeborgfjellet		*	*				*	
016	Hopen		*	*				*	
017	Bjørnøya (Bear Island)		*	*	*			*	
018	Jan Mayen		*	*				*	

Comments on the inventory

1. All population figures, particularly of the seabirds, are estimates.
2. The protection status (National Park, Nature Reserve, Bird Sanctuary) is mentioned as part of the site's name, and this information is not repeated elsewhere in the site account. Sites 009, 011, 012, 013, 015, 016, 017, and 018 are recorded as being 'unprotected' in that they are not covered by any protected areas (but see comments above concerning the regulations protecting the territory's natural environment).
3. Areas (ha) are not given for many of the sites or subsites, because (in most cases) their boundaries have not been determined.
4. Svalbard has been treated as a single 'region' when applying the site-selection criteria (category 3).

---

001 North-west Spitsbergen National Park

79°05'-80°10'N, 10°00'-15°00'E 328,300 ha

The National Park includes Guissezholmen Bird Sanctuary, Skorpa Bird Sanctuary, and Moseøya Bird Sanctuary.

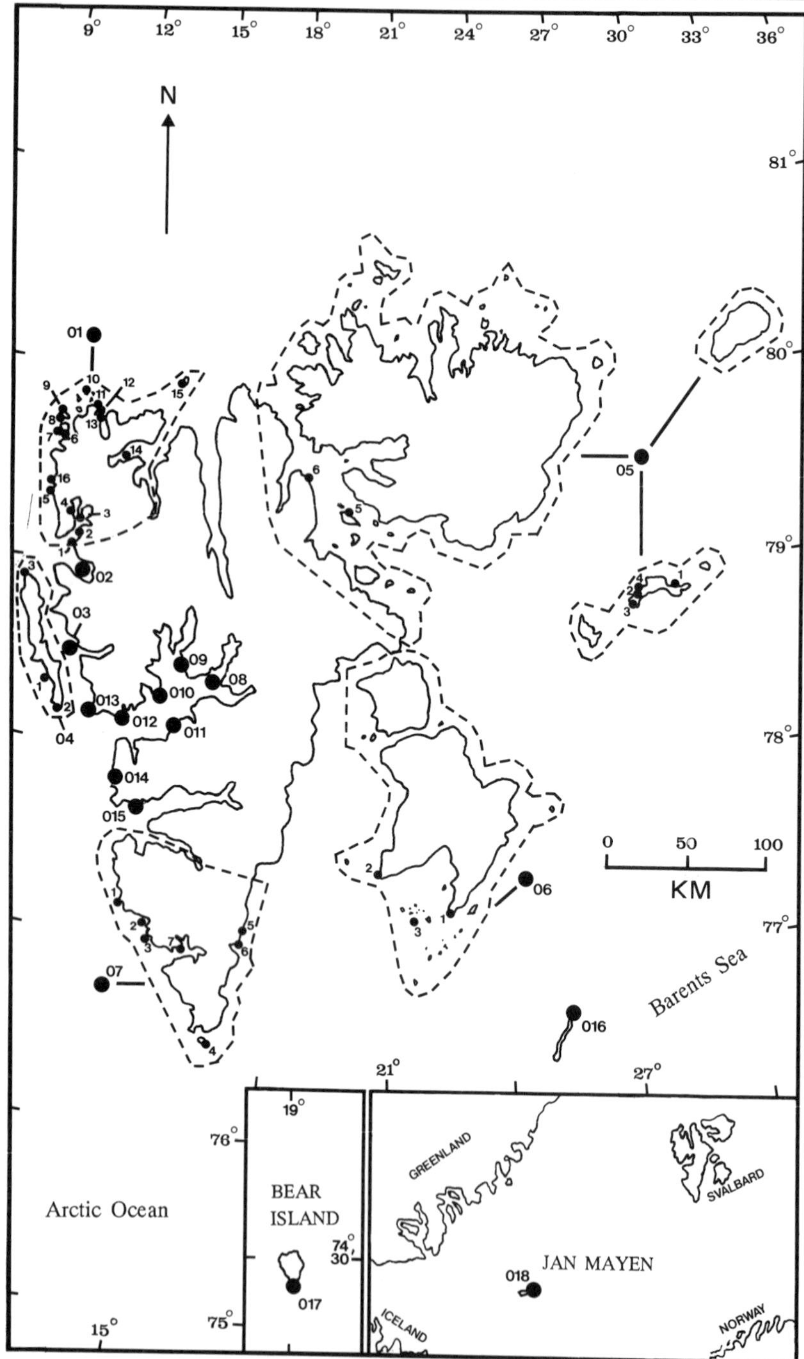

Figure 25: Map showing the location of the sites in Svalbard and Jan Mayen

Information is provided for the following subsites:

001-1 Guissezholmen Bird Sanctuary

79°05N, 11°30'E

Includes the islets near Kapp Guissez.
Breeding species include *Somateria mollissima* (200 pairs).

001-2 Casimir-Perierkammen

79°08'N, 11°52'E

Sea cliffs facing Krossfjorden.
Breeding seabirds include *Rissa tridactyla* (3000 pairs) and *Uria lomvia* (3000 birds).

001-3 Kongshamaren

79°13'N, 11°50'E

A headland with cliffs in Krossfjorden.
Breeding seabirds include *Rissa tridactyla* (1200 pairs) and *Uria lomvia* (2200 birds).

001-4 Nilsfjellet

79°16'N, 11°33'E

Sea cliffs facing Krossfjorden.
Breeding seabirds include *Rissa tridactyla* (1500 pairs) and *Uria lomvia* (3000 birds).

001-5 Knoffberget

79°22'N, 10°52'E

Sea cliffs on the north-west coast of Spitsbergen.
Breeding seabirds include *Uria lomvia* (14,000 birds) and *Cepphus grylle* (130 pairs).

001-6 Moseøya Bird Sanctuary

79°40'N, 11°00'E

Breeding species include *Branta leucopsis* (100-150 pairs) and *Somateria mollissima* (900 pairs).

001-7 Skorpa Bird Sanctuary

79°40N, 11°00'E

Breeding species include *Branta leucopsis* (15-25 pairs) and *Somateria mollissima* (100 pairs).

001-8 South-west Amsterdamøya

79°45'N, 10°45'E

Sea cliffs on Amsterdamøya.
Breeding seabirds include *Uria lomvia* (3500 birds).

001-9 North Hakluythovden, Amsterdamøya

79°47'N, 10°48'E

Sea cliffs on Amsterdamøya.
Breeding seabirds include *Rissa tridactyla* (500 pairs) and *Uria lomvia* (3000 birds).

001-10 Klovningen

79°53'N, 11°30'E

A small island with sea cliffs at the northern tip of Spitsbergen.
Breeding seabirds include *Uria lomvia* (2000-3000 birds).

001-11 Flathuken

79°51'N, 11°50'E

Sea cliffs facing Raudfjorden.
Breeding seabirds include *Uria lomvia* (4000-7000 birds).

001-12 Hornbækfjellet

79°49'N, 11°50'E

Sea cliffs facing Raudfjorden.
Breeding seabirds include *Fulmarus glacialis* (100 pairs) and *Uria lomvia* (4000 birds).

001-13 Austplana

79°47'N, 11°53'E

Sea cliffs facing Raudfjorden.
Breeding seabirds include *Uria lomvia* (16,000 birds).

001-14 Liefdefjorden

79°40'N, 13°00'E

A fjord with numerous small islands.
Breeding species include *Anser brachyrhynchus* (also moulting flocks), *Somateria mollissima* (800-1100 pairs), and *Sterna paradisaea* (500 pairs).

001-15 Moffen Nature Reserve

80°05'N, 12°45'E

Island with lake off the northern coast of Spitsbergen. One of the most important resting places for walrus *Odobenus rosmarus* in Svalbard.
Breeding species include *Somateria mollissima* (400 pairs) and *Sterna paradisaea* (1000 pairs).

001-16 Nissenfjella

79°24'N, 10°51'E

Sea cliffs on the north-west coast of Spitsbergen.
Breeding seabirds include *Rissa tridactyla* (2000 pairs) and *Uria lomvia* (10,000 birds).

002 Kongsfjorden Bird Sanctuary

78°55'N, 12°10'E 140 ha Ramsar Site

Comprises about ten islands, most with rich grassy vegetation; some with small fresh-water ponds. Human activity and increased tourism have had an adverse impact on the breeding population of *Somateria mollissima*.
Small numbers of *Anser brachyrhynchus* (15-20 pairs) and *Branta leucopsis* (10-15 pairs) breed. There is also a dense breeding population of *Somateria mollissima* (2500 pairs), with large numbers resting in the area before the breeding season.

003 Hermansenøya Bird Sanctuary

78°35'N, 12°15'E

Small numbers of *Branta leucopsis* (10-15 pairs) and *Somateria mollissima* (100 pairs) breed.

004 Forlandet National Park

78°10'-78°55'N, 10°00'-12°30'E 56,700 ha

High-Arctic tundra vegetation.

The National Park includes all of Prins Karls Forland. There are two bird sanctuaries within the Park: Plankeholmane and Forlandsøyane.

Information is provided for the following subsites:

004-1 Forlandsøyane Bird Sanctuary

78°20'N, 11°36'E 60 ha Ramsar Site

The reserve covers three islands and a few small skerries; one island is bare, the other two are grassy with small pools.

An important breeding site for *Anser brachyrhynchus* (6 pairs in 1983), *Branta leucopsis* (282-405 pairs in 1983), *B. bernicla* (8-10 pairs in 1983), *Somateria mollissima* (500-1000 pairs; numbers have declined considerably since the beginning of the century, mostly as a result of egg and down collection), and *Sterna paradisaea* (200 pairs).

004-2 Plankeholmane Bird Sanctuary

78°12'N, 12°00'E

Small numbers of *Branta leucopsis* breed (5-10 pairs) and also *Somateria mollissima* (250-300 pairs).

004-3 Fuglehuken

78°53'N, 10°30'E

Sea cliffs at the northern tip of Prins Karls Forland.

Breeding species include *Fulmarus glacialis* (450 pairs), *Anser brachyrhynchus* (40 pairs), *Rissa tridactyla* (3500 pairs), *Uria lomvia* (40,000 birds), *Cepphus grylle* (200 pairs), and *Fratercula arctica* (850 birds).

005 North-east Svalbard Nature Reserve

78°40'-80°50'N - 16°35'-29°00'E 1,555,000 ha Biosphere Reserve

Mainly ice-covered tundra and marsh vegetation, also sea cliffs. The Nature Reserve includes all of Nordaustlandet, Kvitøya, Kong Karls Land, and the north-east coast of Spitsbergen.

Protected mainly because of the importance of Kong Karls Land as a denning area for Polar Bear *Thalassarctos maritimus* and because it has the world's northernmost population of Reindeer *Rangifer tarandus* at Nordaustlandet. There are some important seabird colonies, especially for *Pagophila eburnea* and *Uria lomvia*.

Information is provided for the following subsites:

005-1 Rundisdammen, Kongsøya

78°54'N, 29°06'E

A cliff close to the sea, on Kongsøya, Kong Karls Land.

A breeding site for *Pagophila eburnea* (25 pairs).

005-2 Retziusfjellet, Kongsøya

78°54'N, 28°08'E

A mountain side about 1.5 km from the sea, on Kongsøya, Kong Karls Land.

A breeding site for *Pagophila eburnea* (20-30 pairs).

005-3 Sjøgrenfjellet, Kongsøya

78°52'N, 27°55'E

Sea cliffs on Kongsøya, Kong Karls Land.
A breeding site for *Pagophila eburnea* (10 pairs).

005-4 Hárfagrehaugen, Kongsøya

78°55'N, 28°10'E

Sea cliffs on Kongsøya, Kong Karls Land.
A breeding site for *Pagophila eburnea* (25 pairs).

005-5 Wahlbergøya (north-east)

79°23'N, 19°50'E

Sea cliffs on the island of Wahlbergøya.
A breeding site for *Uria lomvia* (8000 birds).

005-6 Alkefjellet

79°35'N, 18°30'E

Sea cliffs on the north-eastern coast of Spitsbergen.
Breeding seabirds include *Uria lomvia* (45,000-50,000 birds).

006 South-east Svalbard Nature Reserve

76°50'-78°40'N, 20°00'-25°30'E 645,000 ha

High-Arctic tundra vegetation. The Nature Reserve includes all of Barentsøya and Edgeøya.
There are some important seabird colonies with breeding *Fulmarus glacialis*, *Rissa tridactyla*, *Uria lomvia*, and *Cepphus grylle*; it is an important breeding site for *Branta bernicla*.

Information is provided for the following sub-sites:

006-1 Negerpynten, Edgeøya

77°15'N, 22°40'E

Sea cliffs at the south-western tip of Edgeøya.
Breeding species include *Uria lomvia* (2000+ pairs).

006-2 Kvalpynten, Edgeøya

77°27'N, 20°53'E

Sea cliffs at the south-western tip of Edgeøya.
Breeding seabirds include *Uria lomvia* (10,000+ pairs).

006-3 Tusenøyane, Edgeøya

76°50'-77°20'N, 21°00'-23°20'E

Lots of small rocky islands, some with vegetation of grass and moss, in an area of shallow sea, some distance from the south-west coast of Edgeøya. Increasing traffic of small boats is a problem at the site.
A breeding site for *Branta leucopsis* (60-80 pairs) and *B. bernicla* (435-600 pairs).

007 South Spitsbergen National Park

76°20'-77°40N, 13°30'-18°00'E 467,300 ha

High-Arctic tundra vegetation.

The National Park includes Sørkapp Bird Sanctuary, Dunøyane Bird Sanctuary, Isøyane Bird Sanctuary, and Olsholmen Bird Sanctuary. There are also some important seabird colonies with breeding *Fulmarus glacialis*, *Rissa tridactyla*, *Uria lomvia*, *Cepphus grylle*, and *Alle alle*.

Information is provided for the following subsites:

007-1 Olsholmen Bird Sanctuary

77°15'N, 14°15'E

Branta leucopsis breeds here (100 pairs).

007-2 Isøyane Bird Sanctuary

77°08N, 14°48'E 30 ha Ramsar Site

Two islands, one with rich grassy vegetation and small freshwater ponds.

One of the most important breeding localities for *Branta leucopsis* in Spitsbergen (250 pairs); also *Somateria mollissima* (200 pairs).

007-3 Dunøyane Bird Sanctuary

77°04'N, 15°00'E 120 ha Ramsar Site

Islands with rich grassy vegetation and bare islets.

The site is one of the most important breeding and moulting areas for *Branta leucopsis* (600-700 pairs) and *Somateria mollissima* (500 pairs) in Spitsbergen.

007-4 Sørkapp Bird Sanctuary

76°30'N, 16°30'E

Flat islands with numerous freshwater pools and some grassy areas.

Breeding species include *Somateria mollissima* (300 pairs).

007-5 Stellingfjellet

77°06'N, 17°20'E

Sea cliffs on the east coast of Torell Land.

Breeding species include *Rissa tridactyla* (10,500 pairs) and *Uria lomvia* (154,000 birds).

007-6 Kovalskifjella

77°03'N, 17°18'E

Sea cliffs on the east coast of Torell Land.

Breeding seabirds include *Rissa tridactyla* (3200 pairs) and *Uria lomvia* (50,000 birds).

007-7 Sofiekammen, Gnalberget

77°01'N, 15°54'E

Sea cliffs facing Hornsund.

Breeding seabirds include *Rissa tridactyla* (12,200 pairs) and *Uria lomvia* (4500-6000 birds).

008 Gåsøyane Bird Sanctuary

78°25'N, 16°10'E 100 ha Ramsar Site

Three small, partly vegetated islands with freshwater ponds and cliffs. Due to its proximity to Longyearbyen, egg and down collection has been a serious disturbance to the population of *Somateria mollissima*.

The sanctuary has a large breeding population of *Somateria mollissima* (1000 pairs); and also breeding *Branta leucopsis* (6-8 pairs), and *Sterna paradisaea* (400 pairs).

009 Kongressfjellet

78°31'N, 15°20'E

Unprotected

Sea cliffs facing Nordfjorden.
Breeding seabirds include *Uria lomvia* (3000 birds).

010 Boheman Bird Sanctuary

78°22'N, 14°40'E

Breeding species include *Branta leucopsis* (50 pairs) and *Somateria mollissima* (150 pairs).

011 Grumant

78°13'N, 15°15'E

Unprotected

Sea cliffs facing Isfjorden. There is heavy shipping traffic (boats heading for Longyearbyen), although the effect on seabirds has not been investigated.
Breeding seabirds include *Rissa tridactyla* (10,000 pairs) and *Uria lomvia* (20,000 birds).

012 Alkhornet

78°13'N, 13°45'E

Unprotected

Sea cliffs at the entrance of Isfjorden.
Breeding seabirds include *Rissa tridactyla* (5000 pairs) and *Uria lomvia* (10,000-150,000 birds).

013 Daudmansöyra

78°15'N, 13°00'E

Unprotected

A large flat area with bogs and freshwater ponds.
Important for *Anser brachyrhynchus* (moulting flocks of 200-300) and *Branta leucopsis* (50-100 pairs; moulting flocks of 500).

014 Nordenskiöldkysten including Kapp Linné Bird Sanctuary

77°50'N, 13°50'E

Partly a Bird Sanctuary

A large flat area, parts with rich grassy vegetation, with lots of freshwater pools.
Important for breeding and moulting *Branta leucopsis* (400 pairs; 3000 moulting); also *Phalaropus fulicarius* (20 pairs). Kapp Linné Bird Sanctuary, which is situated in the northern part of this area, has breeding *Somateria mollissima* (300 pairs), *S. spectabilis* (0-6 pairs), and *Sterna paradisaea* (100 pairs).

015 Ingeborgfjellet

77°45'N, 14°25'E

Unprotected

Sea cliffs facing Bellsund.

Breeding seabirds include *Uria lomvia* (100,000 pairs in 1976) and *Alle alle* (200,000-300,000 pairs; an old and very approximate estimate).

016 Hopen

76°25'-76°40'N, 24°55'-25°30'E

Unprotected

An elongated island in the Barents Sea. There is a radio station located on the east coast which causes no disturbance.

One of the area's largest seabird colonies, which are mostly located at the northern end of the island. Important for breeding *Rissa tridactyla* (10,000+ pairs) and *Uria lomvia* (500,000 birds).

017 Bjørnøya (Bear Island)

74°30'N, 19°00'E

Unprotected, although there are strict controls on visiting

The northern part of the island is flat with numerous freshwater pools and low cliffs along the coast (max. 20 m). In the southern part where the largest seabird colonies are located there are very high cliffs (max. 400 m). The ground is mainly rocky with thin tundra vegetation, although the vegetation close to the seabird colonies is lush.

Holds extremely important breeding seabird populations including *Fulmarus glacialis* (50,000-60,000 pairs), *Stercorarius parasiticus* (30-50 pairs), *S. skua* (5-10 pairs), *Larus hyperboreus* (2000 pairs), *Rissa tridactyla* (100,000 pairs), *Uria aalge* (245,000 pairs in 1986; although in 1987, 85 per cent of the 1986 breeding population was missing), *U. lomvia* (105,000 pairs in 1986), *Cepphus grylle* (200 pairs), *Alle alle* (10,000 pairs), and *Fratercula arctica* (600 pairs). In addition, the island is a very important staging area for *Branta leucopsis* on autumn migration.

018 Jan Mayen

71°00'N, 07°00'W

Unprotected

A mountain island, partly covered by glaciers, with a rocky landscape and thin tundra vegetation.

Holds extremely important breeding seabird populations including *Fulmarus glacialis* (60,000-100,000 pairs), *Stercorarius parasiticus* (10-100 pairs), *Larus hyperboreus* (100-500 pairs), *Rissa tridactyla* (5000-10,000 pairs), *Sterna paradisaea* (500-1000 pairs), *Uria lomvia* (75,000 pairs), *Cepphus grylle* (100-1000 pairs), *Alle alle* (50,000 pairs), and *Fratercula arctica* (1000-10,000 pairs).

MAIN REFERENCES

Gjaerevoll, O. and Rønning, O. I. (1980) *Flowers of Svalbard.* Universitetsforlaget: Oslo.

Mehlum, F. and Fjeld, P. E. (1987) Catalogue of seabird colonies in Svalbard. *Norwegian Polar Research Institute Report Series* no. 35.

Ministry of Environment (undated) Environmental Regulations for Svalbard and Jan Mayen.

Prestrud, P. and Børset, A. (1984) A status of the goose populations in the bird sanctuaries in Svalbard. *Current research on arctic geese, Norsk Polarinst. skrifter* 1: 129-134.

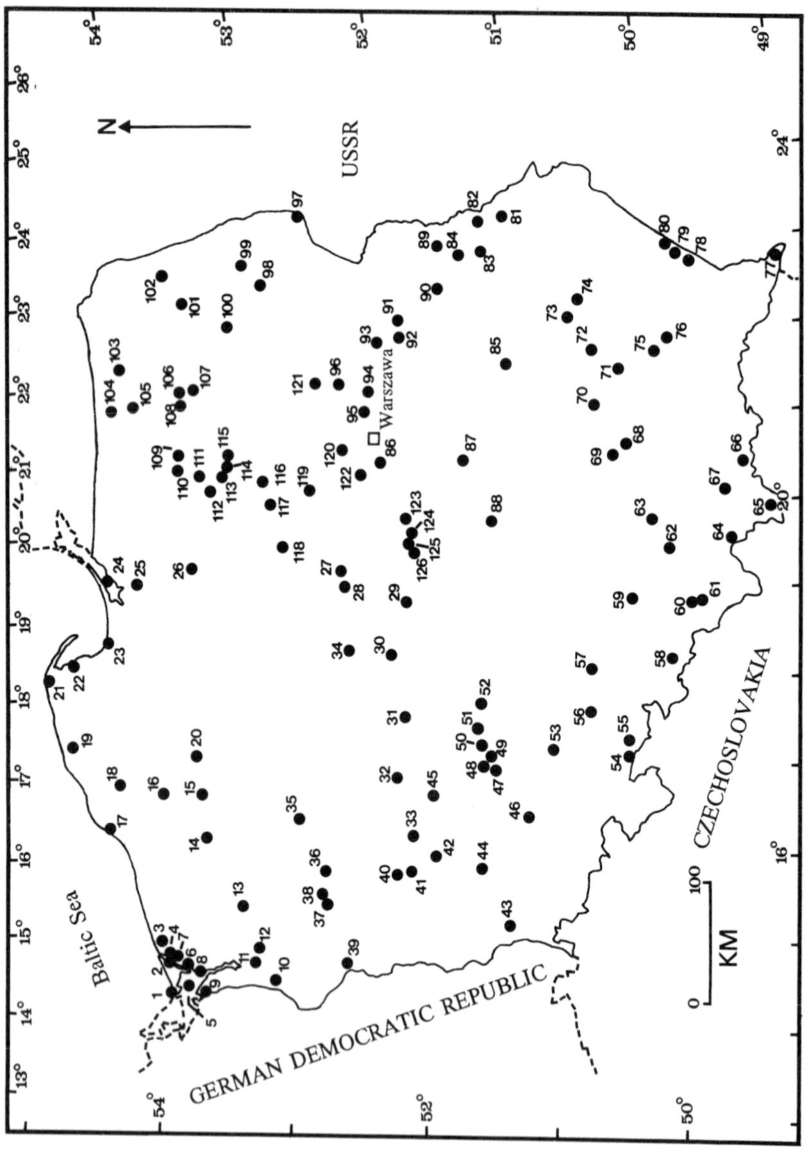

Figure 26: Map showing the location of the sites in Poland

POLAND

Aquatic Warbler *Acrocephalus paludicola*

INTRODUCTION

General information

Poland covers an area of nearly 312,700 sq km and is bordered by the German Democratic Republic, Czechoslovakia and the Soviet Union. The country's northern boundary is formed by the Baltic Sea. The human population numbers over 37 million people, over 1.5 million of whom live in the capital Warszawa (in 1983, the country had an average population density of 116.4 persons per sq km).

Poland is mainly a low-lying country, with only nine per cent of the land surface above 300 m, although in the south there are about 300 sq km of mountains (Beskidy Zachodnie). Areas of water cover about two per cent of Poland's surface; the country is particularly rich in lakes, with nearly 1000 lakes over one hectare in size, mainly in the northern part of the country. The Baltic coast has a number of large coastal lagoons.

Forests cover 27.4 per cent of the country, but consist mainly of young stands; in 1983 it was estimated that two-thirds of all forests were seriously affected by air pollution. In the north-east there are fragments (some large by comparison with other central European countries) of natural forest with *Quercus*, *Tilia* and *Carpinus*, and in the south there are patches of *Fagus*/*Abies* woodland, subalpine *Picea* and alpine *Pinus* forests. There has been extensive reafforestation with *Pinus* and *Picea*, particularly in the mountains of the south. Steppe-grasslands, once extensive, are now reduced to remnants on poor soils and steep slopes. Marshes and peatbogs are still extensive, and peatbogs cover 1.5 million ha (five per cent of the country, with the most extensive areas present in the Szczecin Basin, the valleys of the Rivers Biebrza, Pisa, Warta, Odra, Karwa, Notecka, Wieprza, and Tysmienica, and the Zarnowieckie Marshes).

Poland is an agrarian country, and is characterised by the predominance of independent small farmers (with average private holdings of just over 5 ha and very few exceeding 100 ha; accounting for 75 per cent of all cultivated land). The level of fertiliser application is low by comparison with many other European countries.

In the post-war period, drainage and amelioration projects covered about five million ha of arable land and 2.3 million ha of pasture and meadows. Major projects included 140,000 ha in the Bay of Gdansk, 30,000 ha in the Notec Basin and 25,000 ha in the Odra Basin.

Ornithological importance

Poland includes some exceptional areas holding outstanding bird populations, both in terms of species and absolute numbers. The vast extent of Polish wetlands is reflected in the country's importance for waterfowl, particularly during the breeding and migration season.

Similarly, because there are still relatively large, undisturbed tracts of forest the country supports important populations of, for example, raptors and woodpeckers.

Poland falls within the normal breeding range of five globally threatened species, namely *Milvus milvus* (300 pairs; increasing), *Haliaeetus albicilla* (100-120 pairs), *Crex crex*, *Otis tarda* and *Acrocephalus paludicola*. Of these, *Otis tarda* only has a foothold, with a population of about 16 pairs. Conversely, there are major breeding populations of *Crex crex* (3000-4000 pairs) and *Acrocephalus paludicola* (3000-4000 pairs) with the Biebrza valley being particularly important for both species.

Other species with important breeding populations in Poland include *Botaurus stellaris* (*c.*1000 pairs), *Ciconia nigra* (800-900 pairs), *C. ciconia* (30,000 pairs; probably the most important European population outside USSR), *Pernis apivorus* (2500 pairs), *Circus aeruginosus* (1500-2000 pairs), *C. pygargus* (200-300 pairs), *Aquila clanga* (15-30 pairs), *A. pomarina* (*c.*600 pairs), *Porzana porzana*, *Grus grus* (*c.*1000 pairs), *Philomachus pugnax*, *Gallinago media* (550-600 displaying males), *Limosa limosa* (7000-8000 pairs), *Chlidonias niger*, *Dendrocopos medius*, *Luscinia svecica* and *Ficedula parva*.

The wetlands of Poland are important for passage and moulting waterfowl including *Podiceps cristatus*, *Phalacrocorax carbo sinensis*, *Cygnus olor*, *C. cygnus*, *Anser fabalis*, *A. albifrons*, *A. anser*, *Anas crecca*, *Aythya ferina*, *A. fuligula*, *Bucephala clangula*, *Mergus albellus*, *Fulica atra* and *Grus grus*, The Baltic coast is of particular importance for passage waders, but owing to a very high turnover of birds (as shown by ringing studies), the occurrence of very large numbers at any one time, is unusual.

Important wintering populations are confined to the Baltic coast and associated wetlands which are less liable to freezing than those further inland. Species which occur in significant numbers include grebes, diving ducks and geese.

Conservation infrastructure and protected-area system

The main piece of legislation is the 1949 Law on Nature Conservation which governs the general organisation of nature conservation and introduced three categories of protected areas: National Parks, Nature Reserves, and Natural Monuments. Landscape Parks and Areas of Protected Landscape began to be created in the 1970s. The following are the five categories of protected areas (number of sites as of December 1984):

1. National Park (Park Narodowy) 14 sites

   These are areas that are over 500 ha which have been protected for their unique natural values, for their floral and faunal components and their overall landscape features. The parks have strictly protected areas (where all human activities are prevented) and partially protected areas which allow for conservation management of selected elements. Several National Parks also have buffer zones. The National Park system is managed by the Ministry of Agriculture, Forestry and Food Economy and specifically by its Department of Forestry and National Parks.

2. Nature Reserve (Rezerwat Przyrody) 872 sites
These are areas that are strictly protected and are used for scientific and educational purposes. They are divided into strict reserves (used exclusively for research) and partial reserves (subject to controlled management activities). Nature Reserves are administered by forestry authorities, and management plans are prepared by the administration in each voivodship (regions of Poland). Ornithological Reserves are included in this category.

3. Landscape Park (Park Krajobrazowy) 24 sites
These are areas for nature conservation as well as recreation (also known as Nature Parks). They are created by administrations in the voivodships. A management plan is required which defines levels of tourism, forestry and agricultural exploitation, and the prohibition of mineral exploitation, industrial development and urban construction.

4. Area of Protected Landscape (Obszar chronionego Krajobrazu) 111 sites
These are extensive territories (larger than Landscape Parks) and are designated as major areas for recreation and tourism development. Economic activities such as agriculture, forestry and industry are not subject to serious controls. They are declared and managed by the voivodship authorities.

5. Natural Monument
These are mostly single objects, such as trees, cliffs etc., that are totally protected.

International measures relevant to the conservation of sites

Poland is a party to the Ramsar Convention and, as of September 1988, had designated five Ramsar Sites covering a total of 7102 ha. Four Biosphere Reserves and one natural World Heritage Site (Bialowicza National Park) have also been designated.

Overview of the inventory

The Polish inventory of important bird areas includes details of 126 sites distributed throughout the country and covering a total area exceeding 1 million ha. As foreshadowed in the general information, earlier in this introduction, the majority of the sites are wetlands, whilst nearly all include at least some wetland habitat(s). All of the Polish Ramsar Sites and Biosphere Reserves are included in the inventory.

Poland's globally threatened species (except *Otis tarda*) are well covered by this inventory. A number of sites are outstanding for their populations of *Crex crex* and/or *Acrocephalus paludicola* (e.g. 081, 082, 100, 101, 102). In addition, there is good coverage of many of the other key species listed above under 'ornithological importance' such as *Botaurus stellaris, Circus pygargus, Aquila pomarina, Grus grus, Porzana porzana*, and *Gallinago media*.

Many of the sites described are protected by the national protected-areas system previously outlined. However, at least half of the areas are mainly unprotected or without any protection whatsoever. It is also clear that many very important sites are currently being degraded or are in imminent danger of degradation. Pollution arising from industrial, agricultural and urban/residential sources, drainage, and hunting pressure, appear to be the principal negative forces acting on wetlands, whilst intensive forestry practices may threaten some important non-wetland areas.

Acknowledgements

The inventory was compiled from data-sheets completed by J. Bednorz, D. Bukaciński, S. Chmielewski, A. Dombrowski, M. Goc, W. Górski, W. Grabiński, J. Gromadzka, M. Gromadzki, A. Jermaczek, H. Kot, J. Krogulec, R. Mackowicz, M. Mellin, P. Nawrocki, C. Nitecki, A. Przystalski, M. Rodziewicz, M. Szymkiewicz, K. Walasz, T. Wesołowski, J. Witkowski, Z. Wojciechowski, and P. Zyska; A. Dyrcz assisted with the coordination of the project and the data-sheets were submitted by Z. Krzeminski of the Ministry of Environment Protection and Natural Resources. Z. Karpowicz (WCMC Protected Areas Data Unit) provided very helpful information which was used to prepare the introduction, and the information used to write the section on protected areas was based entirely on material provided by PADU.

INVENTORY

No.	Site name	Region	Criteria used to select site [see p.18]							
			0	1(i)	1(ii)	1(iii)	1(iv)	2	3	4
001	Ujście rzeki Świny (Delta of River Świna)	SN						*	*	
002	Zalew Kamieński (Kamień Bay)	SN				*		*		
003	Jezioro Liwia Łuża (Lake Liwia Łuża)	SN						*		
004	Bagna doliny rzek Świniec i Niemicy (Marshes in the valley of the Rivers Świniec and Niemica)	SN						*		
005	Zalew Szczeciński (Szczecin Bay)	SN				*		*		
006	Łąki Skoszewskie (Skoszewo Meadows)	SN						*	*	
007	Bagna Rozwarowskie (Rozwarowo Marshes)	SN				*		*		
008	Jezioro Karpino (Lake Karpino)	SN						*		
009	Jezioro Świdwie (Lake Świdwie)	SN						*	*	
010	Dolina Odry i jezioro Dąbie (Odra valley and Lake Dąbie)	SN				*		*	*	
011	Obszar wokół miasta Wełtyń (area around Wełtyń town)	SN						*		
012	Jezioro Miedwie (Lake Miedwie)	SN				*		*		
013	Iński Park Krajobrazowy (Iński Landscape Park)	SN						*	*	
014	Drawski Park Krajobrazowy (Drawski Landscape Park)	KL						*	*	
015	Jeziora Szczecineckie (Lakes Szczecineckie)	KL						*	*	
016	Okolice Żydowa-Białego Boru (Żydowo-Biały Bór region)	KL,SK						*	*	
017	Koszaliński i słupski pas nadmorski (coastal areas of Koszalin and Słupsk	KL,SK						*	*	
018	Park Krajobrazowy Dolina Słupi (Słupia Valley Landscape Park)	SK						*	*	
019	Słowiński Park Narodowy (Słowiński National Park)	SK						*	*	
020	Jezior Krępsko/Szczytno (Lakes Krępsko and Szczytno) and surrounding region	SK						*	*	
021	Bielawskie Błota (Bielawskie Bog)	GK				*			*	
022	Łąki Beki i Rewy (Beka and Rewa Meadows)	GK	*							
023	Ujście Wisły (mouth of the River Vistula)	GK							*	
024	Zalew Wiślany (Vistula Lagoon)	EG				*		*	*	
025	Jezioro Drużno (Lake Drużno)	EG				*		*	*	
026	Lasy Iławskie (Iława Forests)	ON,EG				*		*	*	
027	Jezioro Karaś (Lake Karaś)	TN,ON							*	
028	Jezioro Rakutowskie i Olszyny Rakutowskie (Lake Rakutowskie and Rakutowskie Alders)	WK	*							
029	Pradolina Warszawsko-Berlińska (Warsaw-Berlin post-glacial stream valley)	KN,PK,SE				*		*	*	
030	Kramskie Błota (Kramskie Marshes)	KN						*	*	
031	Dolina środkowej Warty (middle River Warta valley)	KN				*		*	*	

No.	Site name	Region	Criteria used to select site [see p.18] 0	1(i)	1(ii)	1(iii)	1(iv)	2	3	4
032	Dolina Warty koło Krajkowa (River Warta valley near Krajkowa)	PN						*		
033	Wielki Łęg Obrzański (Great Obra marshes)	LO,PN						*	*	
034	Jezioro Gopło (Lake Gopło)	BZ						*	*	
035	Dolina Noteci koło Czarnkowa (River Noteć valley near Czarnków)	PA						*	*	
036	Jezioro Wielkie (Lake Wielkie)	GW	*							
037	Dolina Warty koło Santoka (River Warta valley near Santok)	GW							*	
038	Ujście Noteci (Mouth of the River Noteć)	GW						*		
039	Rezerwat Słońsk (Słońsk Reserve)	GW				*		*	*	
040	Dolina Leniwej Obry (Leniwa Obra valley)	GW							*	
041	Jeziora Chobienickie (Chobienickie Lakes)	ZG						*		
042	Pojezierze Sławskie (Sławskie Lakes)	ZG	*							
043	Stawy rybne Darowa (Darowa fish-ponds)	JG						*	*	
044	Stawy rybne Przemków (Przemków fish-ponds)	LA				*		*	*	
045	Zbiornik Wonieść (Wonieść Reservoir)	LO						*	*	
046	Lasy w dolinie Odry: Malczyc i Kaczawy (Forests in the River Odra valley: Malczyce – Kaczawa)	WW						*	*	
047	Stawy rybne w Miliczu – zespół Jamnik (Milicz fish-ponds: Jamnik complex)	WW						*	*	
048	Stawy rybne w Miliczu – zespół Radziądz (Milicz fish-ponds: Radziądz complex)	WW						*	*	
049	Stawy rybne w Miliczu – zespół Ruda Sułowska (Milicz fish-ponds: Ruda Sułowska complex)	WW							*	
050	Stawy rybne w Miliczu – zespół Sławno (Milicz fish-ponds: Sławno complex)	WW						*	*	
051	Stawy rybne w Miliczu – zespół Potasznia (Milicz fish-ponds: Potasznia complex)	WW				*			*	
052	Stawy rybne w Przygodzicach: zespół Dębnica i Trzcielin (Przygodzice fish-ponds: Dębnica and Trzcielin complexes)	KZ	*							
053	Lasy w dolinie Odry: Kotowice i Siechnica (Forests in the River Odra valley: Kotowice and Siechnica)	WW							*	
054	Zbiornik Otmuchowski (Otmuchów Reservoir)	OE	*							
055	Zbiornik Nyski (Nysa Reservoirs)	OE				*				
056	Stawy rybne w Niemodlinie: zespół Dąbrowa (Niemodlin fish-ponds: Dąbrowa complex)	OE	*							

No.	Site name	Region	Criteria used to select site [see p.18]							
			0	1(i)	1(ii)	1(iii)	1(iv)	2	3	4
057	Zbiornik Turawski (Turawa Reservoir)	OE				*				
058	Stawy rybne Łężczak (Łężczak fish-ponds)	KE							*	
059	Zbiornik Świerklaniec (Świerklaniec Reservoir)	KE	*							
060	Zbiornik Goczałkowicki (Goczałkowice Reservoir)	KE							*	
061	Stawy rybne w Ligocie (Ligota fish-ponds)	KE							*	
062	Zespół stawów rybnych w Przerębie i Spytkowicach (Przeręb and Spytkowice fish-pond complex)	BO							*	
063	Ojcowski Park Narodowy (Ojców National Park)	KW	*							
064	Babiogórski Park Narodowy (Babia Góra National Park)	NS							*	
065	Tatrzański Park Narodowy (Tatra National Park)	NS							*	
066	Pieniński Park Narodowy (Pienińy National Park)	NS							*	
067	Gorczański Park Narodowy (Gorce National Park)	NS							*	
068	Zespół stawów w Górkach (Górki fish-pond complex)	KC	*							
069	Zespół stawów rybnych w Młodzowie (Młodzowy fish-pond complex)	KC	*							
070	Zespół stawów rybnych koło Grobli (Fish-pond complex near Grobla)	TG	*							
071	Stawy rybne w Osieczyskach (Osieczyska fish-ponds)	TG	*							
072	Zespół stawów rybnych w Budzie Stalowskiej (Buda Stalowska fish-pond complex)	TG						*	*	
073	Zespół stawów rybnych w Lipie (Lipa fish-pond complex)	TG						*	*	
074	Lasy Janowskie (Janów Forest)	TG							*	
075	Stawy rybne w Porębach Kupieńskich (Poręby Kupieńskie fish-pond)	RW	*							
076	Zbiornik Rzeszowski (Rzeszów Reservoir)	RW	*							
077	Bieszczadzki Park Narodowy (Bieszczady National Park)	KO							*	
078	Zbiornik Przemyski (Przemyśl brick-pits)	PL	*							
079	Starorzecze Sanu koło Hurka (Former bed of River San, near Hurko)	PL	*							
080	Zespół stawów rybnych w Starzowie (Starzawa fish-pond complex)	PL						*		
081	Torfowiska węglanowe koło Chełma (carbonate marshes near Chełm)	CM						*	*	
082	Bagno Bubnów (Bubnów Marshes)	CM						*	*	
083	Jezioro Uściwierz i przyległe torfowiska (Lake Uściwierz and adjacent marshes)	CM						*	*	

No.	Site name	Region	Criteria used to select site [see p.18] 0	1(i)	1(ii)	1(iii)	1(iv)	2	3	4
084	Zespół stawów rybynch w Sosnowicy (Sosnowica fish-pond complex)	CM	*							
085	Wisła (River Vistula)	RM,LN							*	
086	Wisła od Dęblina do Płocka (River Vistula: Dęblin to Płock)	SC,RM,LN, WA,PK				*		*	*	
087	Dolina Pilicy (River Pilica valley)	RM						*	*	
088	Zbiornik Sulejowski (Sulejów Reservoir)	PW	*							
089	Uroczysko Mosty-Zahajki: zbiornik i lasy (Mosty-Zahajki: reservoirs and forest)	BP						*	*	
090	Zespół stawów rybnych w Siemieniu i przyległe bagna (Siemień fish-pond complex and adjacent meadows)	BP							*	
091	Bagno Całownia/lub Biel (Całowanie or Biel Fen)	WA,SC						*		
092	Kompleks leśny Kryńszczak (Kryńszczak forest complex)	SC							*	
093	Zespół stawów rybnych koło Kotunia (fish-pond complex near Kotuń)	SC	*							
094	Dolina Liwca (Valley of the River Liwiec)	SC						*	*	
095	Dolina dolnego Bugu (lower valley of River Bug)	BP,SC,BT, LZ,OA,WA						*	*	
096	Lasy Łochowskie (Łochów forests)	SC,OA							*	
097	Puszcza Białowieska (Białowieża Forest)	BT						*	*	
098	Narwiański Park Krajobrazowy (Narew Landscape Park)	BT						*	*	
099	Puszcza Knyszyńska: część środkowa (Knyszyn Forest: central part)	BT							*	
100	Dolina Biebrzy: basen południowy (Biebrza valley: southern basin)	LZ						*	*	
101	Dolina Biebrzy: basen centralny (Biebrza valley: central basin)	LZ						*	*	
102	Dolina Biebrzy: basen północny (Biebrza valley: northern basin)	SI						*	*	
103	Puszcza Borecka (Borecka Forest)	SI						*	*	
104	Jezioro Oświn (Lake Oświn)	SI						*	*	
105	Jezioro Dobskie (Lake Dobskie)	SI				*			*	
106	Bagna Nietlickie (Nietlickie Marshes)	SI				*			*	
107	Półwysep Czarny Róg (Czarny Róg Peninsula)	SI							*	
108	Jezioro Łuknajno (Lake Łuknajo)	SI				*		*	*	
109	Łąki Dymerskie (Dymerskie Meadows)	ON						*		
110	Bartołty Wielkie	ON						*		
111	Jezioro Kośno (Lake Kośno)	ON						*		
112	Lasy Łańskie (Łańskie Forests)	ON						*		
113	Dolina Czarnej (River Czarna valley)	ON						*	*	
114	Dolina rzeki Omulew (River Omulew valley)	ON							*	

No.	Site name	Region	Criteria used to select site [see p.18]							
			0	1(i)	1(ii)	1(iii)	1(iv)	2	3	4
115	Galwica	ON							*	
116	Dolina rzeki Orzyc: część górna (River Orzyc valley: upper part)	CW						*	*	
117	Dolina Mławki (River Mławka valley)	CW							*	
118	Łąki Raczyny (Raczyny Meadows)	CW	*							
119	Lasy Ościsłowo (Ościsłowo forest complex)	CW	*							
120	Dolina dolnej Narwi i Zalew Zegrzyński (Lower Narew valley and Zegrzyński Reservoir)	CW,WA						*	*	
121	Puszcza Biała (Biała forest complex)	OA						*	*	
122	Kampinoski Park Narodowy (Kampinos National Park)	WA						*	*	
123	Stawy rybne koło Łowicza/stawy Mysłaków (Łowicz and Mysłaków fish-ponds)	SE	*							
124	Stawy rybne Okręt i Rydwan (Okręt and Rydwan fish-ponds)	SE						*	*	
125	Stawy rybne Walewice (Walewice fish-ponds)	SE	*							
126	Stawy rybne Psary (Psary fish-ponds)	SE	*							

SN=Szczecin KL=Koszalin SK=Słupsk GK=Gdańsk EG=Elbląg ON=Olsztyn
TN=Toruń WK=Włocławek KN=Konin PK=Płock SE=Skierniewice PN=Poznań
LO=Leszno BZ=Bydgoszcz PA=Piła GW=Gorzów ZG=Zielona Góra
JG=Jelenia Góra LA=Legnica WW=Wrocław KZ=Kalisz OE=Opole
KE=Katowice BO=Bielsko KW=Kraków NS=Nowy Sącz KC=Kielce TG=Tarnobrzeg
RW=Rzeszów KO=Krosno PL=Przemyśl CM=Chełm RM=Radom LN=Lublin
SC=Siedlce WA=Warszawa PW=Piotrków BP=Biała Podlaska BT=Białystok
LZ=Łomża OA=Ostrołęka SI=Suwałki CW=Ciechanów

Comments on the inventory

1. The site name is in most cases the Polish name which is followed by the English name in parentheses. This is then followed by the name of the region (voivodship) also in parentheses.

2. The whole of Poland has been treated as a single 'region' when applying the site-selection criteria (category 3). The application of the criteria as depicted in the above table is provisional only. A substantial majority of the sites are believed to meet the criteria. Those sites that have been included for other reasons (column 0) include the following:

   –022 has been included because of its important population (for the southern Baltic Coast) of *Calidris alpina*.

   –054 has been included because of its importance for passage waterfowl, although the site does not meet the numerical criteria (see introduction above for comments about the high turn-over of birds at passage sites).

   –063 has been included for its woodland species.

   –078 has been included because it has the only breeding colony of *Merops apiaster* in Poland.

The remaining sites (all fish-pond complexes/lake systems) which have been included for other reasons, each support a diversity of species of considerable interest in a European context.

3. A majority of the sites support one or more globally threatened species (usually *Milvus milvus*, *Haliaeetus albicilla* or *Crex crex*). If a site supports more than one globally threatened species then it is listed as meeting criteria category 2. Sites supporting comparatively small numbers of one such species are not listed as meeting criteria category 2.

4. Many of the sites also support a number of other species which are also of interest in a European context (e.g. *Lullula arborea*, *Anthus campestris*, *Luscinia svecica*, *Sylvia nisoria*, and *Emberiza hortulana*). These species have, in general, not been mentioned due to a shortage of space.

---

001 Ujście rzeki Świny (Delta of River Świna) (Szczecin)

53°52'N, 14°20'E 3000 ha

Unprotected

A delta in the extreme north-west of Poland, containing natural and artificial channels of the River Swina and numerous islands with peatbogs, meadows, reedbeds, and small fields. Some of the islands have *Pinus* or *Alnus* woods. There is some low-intensity grazing on small farms, and other human activities include angling, hunting, and harbour operations. Pollution from industrial/harbour sources is a problem.

Breeding species include *Botaurus stellaris* (3-4 pairs), *Ixobrychus minutus* (1-2 pairs), *Milvus milvus* (2-3 pairs; also a feeding area for other pairs nesting nearby), *Haliaeetus albicilla* (3 pairs; also a feeding area for other pairs nesting nearby), *Circus aeruginosus* (3-4 pairs), *C. cyaneus* (1 pair), *Crex crex* (*c.*5 pairs), *Haematopus ostralegus* (1-2 pairs), *Calidris alpina* (5-7 pairs), *Sterna hirundo* (40-150 pairs), *S. albifrons* (10 pairs), and *Chlidonias niger* (5). In addition, *Pandion haliaetus* (1 pair; nesting nearby) feeds at the site.

002 Zalew Kamieński (Kamień Bay) (Szczecin)

54°00'N, 14°45'E 4000 ha

Unprotected

An estuarine embayment connected with the Baltic Sea by a narrow channel. The area includes the mouth of the Dziwna and three smaller rivers, a medium-sized island (Wyspa Chrząszczewska), and large meadows and peatbogs in the south-east. The shores of the bay are poorly vegetated, mainly by small patches of reeds. Human activities include low-intensity agriculture, commercial fishing, angling, yachting, hunting, and tourism. The area is affected by pollution and eutrophication.

Breeding species include *Botaurus stellaris* (2 pairs), *Ixobrychus minutus* (1 pair), *Tadorna tadorna* (10 pairs), *Milvus milvus* (2 pairs), *Circus aeruginosus* (4-6 pairs), *C. cyaneus* (1-2 pairs), *C. pygargus* (1-2 pairs), *Porzana porzana* (1-2 pairs), *Crex crex* (1-3 pairs), *Grus grus* (2-3 pairs), and *Chlidonias niger* (0-10 pairs). In addition, *Ciconia ciconia* (4 pairs) and *Haliaeetus albicilla* (2 pairs), nesting nearby, use the site for feeding. A site for wintering *Mergus albellus* (200; 200 also occur during passage).

003 Jezioro Liwia Łuża (Lake Liwia Łuża) (Szczecin)

54°05'N, 15°06'E 350 ha

Ornithological Reserve

A eutrophic coastal lake (*c.*220 ha) with marshes, meadows, and reed-fringed shores in the western part of the site. The lake is used as a fishery, whilst the surrounding areas are used for agriculture and tourism (notably the seaside town of Niechorze). Pollution and eutrophication are problems, with sources including sewage from hotels/guest-houses, and agricultural effluent.

Breeding species include *Ciconia ciconia* (2 pairs), *Circus aeruginosus* (2-3 pairs), *Porzana porzana* (1 pair), *Calidris alpina* (0-4 pairs), and *Chlidonias niger* (20-30 pairs). The site is used as a feeding ground by single pairs of *Milvus milvus* and *Haliaeetus albicilla* nesting nearby.

004 Bagna doliny rzek Świniec i Niemicy (Marshes in the valley of the Rivers Świniec and Niemica) (Szczecin)

53°59'N, 14°50'E 1500 ha

Unprotected

The marshy valleys of the Rivers Świniec and Niemica, containing extensive peatbogs with numerous channels and small pools, and *Alnus* thickets. Human activities include haymaking and cattle-grazing. Improvement and exploitation of the peatbogs threaten the site.

Breeding species include *Ciconia nigra* (1 pair), *C. ciconia* (2-3 pairs), *Milvus migrans* (1 pair), *M. milvus* (2 pairs), *Circus aeruginosus* (5-8 pairs), *C. cyaneus* (1 pair), *C. pygargus* (1-3 pairs), *Porzana porzana* (1-3 pairs), and *Crex crex* (3-6 pairs).

005 Zalew Szczeciński (Szczecin Bay) (Szczecin)

53°46'N, 14°28'E 47,900 ha

Unprotected

A very large estuarine embayment containing the lower part of the River Odra. The waters are shallow (mean depth 2-3 m) and extremely productive, with high densities of benthic organisms. Human activities include commercial fishing, yachting, and coastal trade. Agriculture, forestry, industry (chemicals), ship-building, and harbour operations are amongst the land-uses in the areas surrounding the site, which is affected by pollution from industrial, domestic, and agricultural sources. There is also secondary pollution arising from effluent entering the Odra further upstream.

Breeding species include *Circus aeruginosus* (1-3 pairs), *Calidris alpina* (3 pairs), *Sterna hirundo* (0-50 pairs), and *S. albifrons* (1-2 pairs). *Milvus milvus* (10-12 pairs) and *Haliaeetus albicilla* (10 pairs), nesting nearby, use the site as a feeding area. An important site for migrating waterfowl, with *Podiceps cristatus* (400), *Phalacrocorax carbo sinensis* (250), *Aythya ferina* (2000), *A. fuligula* (10,000-15,000), *Bucephala clangula* (10,000), and *Fulica atra* (10,000) during autumn passage. Important wintering populations include *Bucephala clangula* (6000), *Mergus albellus* (2000), *M. merganser* (10,000), *Milvus milvus* (10-15), and *Haliaeetus albicilla* (*c.*60).

006 Łąki Skoszewskie (Skoszewo Meadows) (Szczecin)

53°44'N, 14°37'E 6000 ha

Unprotected

An extensive area of meadows and peatbogs, numerous small channels, *Alnus* and *Pinus* forest (*c.*800 ha), and small areas of *Alnus* woods/scrub. The meadows are used for haymaking and cattle-grazing, with hunting being the only other significant land-use.

Birds breeding in the area include *Botaurus stellaris* (1 pair), *Ciconia ciconia* (4 pairs), *Pernis apivorus* (1 pair), *Milvus milvus* (3-4 pairs), *Haliaeetus albicilla* (2 pairs), *Circus aeruginosus* (5-8 pairs), *C. cyaneus* (1 pair), *Porzana porzana*, *Crex crex*, *Grus grus* (4-6 pairs), *Limosa limosa* (*c.*15 pairs), *Numenius arquata* (*c.*15 pairs), and *Chlidonias niger* (*c.*10 pairs).

007 Bagna Rozwarowskie (Rozwarowo Marshes) (Szczecin)

53°53'N, 14°45'E 1600 ha

Unprotected

The marshy valleys of the Rivers Grzybnica and Wolczenica, containing numerous channels, flooded meadows, extensive peatbogs, scattered *Alnus* woodland, and patches of reeds. The area is used for hunting and cattle-grazing. Agricultural pollution, drainage, and road construction threaten the site.

Breeding species include *Botaurus stellaris* (2 pairs), *Ciconia ciconia* (2 pairs), *Circus aeruginosus* (10-20 pairs), *C. cyaneus* (2-3 pairs), *C. pygargus* (2-5 pairs), *Porzana porzana* (2-5 pairs), *P. parva* (1-2 pairs), and *Grus grus* (2-4 pairs). *Milvus migrans* (1 pair), *M. milvus* (2-3 pairs), and *Haliaeetus albicilla* (1 pair), nesting nearby, use the area for feeding. *Anser fabalis*, *A. albifrons*, and *A. anser* (5000; all species) occur during autumn passage.

008 Jezioro Karpino (Lake Karpino) (Szczecin)

53°38'N, 14°25'E 40 ha

Unprotected; hunting is restricted in some years

A eutrophic lake with peatbogs, meadows, and an area of wet *Alnus* forest. *Pinus* forest predominates in areas surrounding the site. Human activities include angling and haymaking.

The site provides conditions for an avifauna typical of eutrophic lakes. Breeding species include *Larus minutus*, whilst birds using the site as a feeding area include *Haliaeetus albicilla* and *Circaetus gallicus*.

009 Jezioro Świdwie (Lake Świdwie) (Szczecin)

53°33'N, 14°22'E 360 ha (860 ha buffer zone planned) Ramsar Site

Ornithological Reserve

A eutrophic lake with extensive peatbogs, meadows, *Alnus* forest, and large areas of reeds. Conservation is the sole human activity at the site itself, but agriculture in the surrounding areas includes grazing, haymaking, and some arable crops. A proposed buffer zone is expected to be protected from intensive farming and hunting. Drainage of areas surrounding the site is a potential threat, whilst pollution and eutrophication are existing problems.

Breeding species include *Botaurus stellaris* (4-7 pairs), *Ixobrychus minutus* (1-2 pairs), *Ciconia ciconia* (2-3 pairs), *Pernis apivorus* (1-2 pairs), *Milvus migrans* (1 pair), *M. milvus* (1-2 pairs), *Circus aeruginosus* (8-9 pairs), *C. cyaneus* (2-3 pairs), *C. pygargus* (1-2 pairs), *Porzana porzana*, *P. parva* (2-3 pairs), *Crex crex* (1-5 pairs), *Grus grus* (8-12 pairs), *Sterna hirundo* (8-30 pairs), and *Chlidonias niger* (40 pairs). In addition, *Haliaeetus albicilla* (1 pair), *Aquila pomarina* (1 pair), and *Pandion haliaetus* (1 pair), nesting nearby, feed in the area. *Grus grus* (200) occurs on autumn passage.

010 Dolina Odry i jezioro Dąbie (Odra valley and Lake Dąbie) (Szczecin)

52°46'N, 14°40'E 45,600 ha

Ornithological Reserve (small area to protect colony of *Ardea cinerea* at Kurowskie Błota); proposed as a Landscape Park; mainly unprotected

The valley of the River Odra, extending *c.*120 km in length, containing marshy areas with peatbogs, meadows (flooded in spring), oxbow lakes, numerous channels, and *Alnus* woods. Land-uses include cattle-grazing, haymaking, angling, and hunting. Activities in adjacent areas include oil-refining, agriculture, and harbour operations, and there is also a power-station. The site is badly affected by agricultural, industrial, and sewage pollution, and hunting pressure.

Breeding species include *Phalacrocorax carbo sinensis* (200-470 pairs), *Botaurus stellaris* (10-15 pairs), *Ixobrychus minutus* (4-5 pairs), *Ardea cinerea* (200-400 pairs), *Ciconia nigra* (1 pair), *C. ciconia* (40 pairs), *Milvus migrans* (3 pairs), *M. milvus* (*c.*25 pairs), *Haliaeetus albicilla* (4-5 pairs), *Circus aeruginosus* (*c.*20 pairs), *C. cyaneus* (3 pairs), *C. pygargus* (1-2 pairs), *Porzana porzana*, *P. parva*, *Crex crex* (*c.*15 pairs), *Grus grus* (15-20 pairs), *Haematopus ostralegus* (4 pairs), *Philomachus pugnax* (650 birds), *Tringa ochropus* (3 pairs), *Sterna hirundo* (30-40 pairs), *S. albifrons* (5 pairs), and

Chlidonias niger (40-100 pairs). An important site for passage geese, with *Anser fabalis* (15,000 spring; 5000 autumn), *A. albifrons* (5000), *A. anser* (2000 spring; 5000 autumn). Also important for large numbers of wintering waterfowl: *Cygnus cygnus* (550), *Anser fabalis* (2000), *Aythya fuligula* (14,000), *Bucephala clangula* (10,000), *Mergus albellus* (650), and *M. merganser* (10,000). Other species occurring in winter include *Milvus milvus* (3-5) and *Haliaeetus albicilla* (25).

011 Obszar wokół miasta Wełtyń (area around Wełtyń town) (Szczecin)

53°16'N, 14°35'E 4500 ha

Unprotected

A complex of small lakes and reservoirs surrounded by cultivated fields, meadows, and pasture, together with some areas of trees/bushes (notably *Fagus*) and small patches of reeds fringing the shores. Some of the lakes have small islands with bushy vegetation. Drainage and eutrophication are adversely affecting the site.

The area holds a wide range of breeding species, with *Podiceps cristatus* (60 pairs), *P. grisegena* (10 pairs), *Botaurus stellaris* (5-6 pairs), *Ixobrychus minutus* (2 pairs), *Ciconia nigra* (1 pair), *C. ciconia* (6 pairs), *Pernis apivorus* (2 pairs), *Milvus migrans* (2 pairs), *M. milvus* (2-3 pairs), *Circus aeruginosus* (5 pairs), *C. cyaneus* (2 pairs), *C. pygargus* (1 pair), *Aquila pomarina* (2 pairs), *Porzana porzana* (1 pair), *Grus grus* (2-3 pairs), *Chlidonias niger* (25-30 pairs), *Alcedo atthis* (3-5 pairs), *Dryocopus martius* (5 pairs), and *Ficedula parva* (5-6 pairs). In addition, *Haliaeetus albicilla* (1 pair) nesting nearby, feeds in the area.

012 Jezioro Miedwie (Lake Miedwie) (Szczecin)

53°17'N, 14°53'E 3200 ha

Unprotected

A large mesotrophic lake with extensive meadows and peatbogs to the south-west. There is an *Alnus* forest to the east. The lake is a drinking-water reservoir for Szczecin, and it is also used as a fishery. Pollution from agricultural sources is a problem.

Breeding species include *Ciconia nigra* (1 pair), *C. ciconia* (3 pairs), *Circus aeruginosus* (3-5 pairs), *C. pygargus* (2 pairs), and *Chlidonias niger* (*c.*20 pairs). *Pernis apivorus* (1 pair), *Milvus milvus* (2-3 pairs), *Haliaeetus albicilla* (1 pair), and *Aquila pomarina* (1 pair) nest in surrounding areas but feed at the site. Large numbers of geese occur during autumn passage: *Anser fabalis, A. albifrons*, and *A. anser* (a total of 5000-10,000; all species combined).

013 Iński Park Krajobrazowy (Inski Landscape Park) (Szczecin)

53°24'N, 15°30'E 16,563 ha

Landscape Park; fish-ponds near Bytowo proposed as an Ornithological Reserve

The Landscape Park is approx. half (47 per cent) forest and one-third (*c.*31 per cent) agricultural land. The remaining area is composed of open water (9 per cent) and peatbogs (also *c.*9 per cent). Human activities include cultivation, forestry, and fish-farming.

Breeding birds include *Botaurus stellaris* (1 pair), *Ciconia nigra* (2 pairs), *C. ciconia* (25-30 pairs), *Milvus migrans* (2 pairs), *M. milvus* (2-3 pairs), *Haliaeetus albicilla* (3 pairs), *Circus aeruginosus* (10-12 pairs), *Aquila pomarina* (1 pair), *Pandion haliaetus* (1 pair), *Crex crex* (3-5 pairs), *Grus grus* (6-12 pairs), *Sterna hirundo* (10-15 pairs), *Chlidonias niger* (8-12 pairs), *Bubo bubo* (1-2 pairs), and *Dryocopus martius* (10-15 pairs). *Haliaeetus albicilla* (25) and *Grus grus* (300) occur on autumn passage.

014 Drawski Park Krajobrazowy (Drawski Landscape Park) (Koszalin)

53°40'N, 16°10'E 41,430 ha

Landscape Park; Ornithological Reserve (Lake Prosino)

The area contains part of the Drawski complex of lakes with *Pinus* and mixed forest (*c.*10,500 ha), a number of large lakes (Drawsko, Siecino, Prosino, Żerdno, Komorze, and Wilczkowo), meadows, and cultivated fields. Human use of the area includes agriculture, forestry, fish-farming, and tourism.

Breeding species include *Botaurus stellaris* (1-2 pairs), *Ciconia nigra* (1-2 pairs), *C. ciconia* (18-25 pairs), *Pernis apivorus* (1 pair; in neighbouring forest), *Milvus migrans* (1-2 pairs), *M. milvus* (2 pairs), *Haliaeetus albicilla* (1 pair), *Circus aeruginosus* (10-12 pairs), *Crex crex* (2-4 pairs), *Grus grus* (5-8 pairs), *Bubo bubo* (1-2 pairs), *Alcedo atthis* (5-7 pairs), and *Dryocopus martius* (10-15 pairs).

015 Jeziora Szczecineckie (Lakes Szczecineckie) (Koszalin)

53°43'N, 16°45'E 18,000 ha

Area of Protected Landscape

An area containing a number of lakes, the most important of which are: Wielimie, Wierzchowo, Pile, Trzesiecko, and Silnowo. The shoreline vegetation of the lakes is dominated by reeds. The total area of wetland habitats is around 3700 ha; forests cover nearly two-thirds of the site, and other habitats include fields and meadows. Land-uses include agriculture, forestry, tourism, and fish-farming. Wielimie is severely polluted by sewage coming from Szczecineck and the former wetland areas surrounding the lake have been drained. However, no serious change in the breeding avifauna was noted during the period 1981-87.

Breeding species in the area include *Phalacrocorax carbo sinensis* (50-60 pairs), *Botaurus stellaris* (2-3 pairs), *Ciconia nigra* (1 pair), *C. ciconia* (15-20 pairs), *Milvus migrans* (1 pair), *M. milvus* (2-3 pairs), *Haliaeetus albicilla* (1 pair), *Circus aeruginosus* (10-12 pairs), *C. pygargus* (0-1 pair), *Aquila pomarina* (0-1 pair), *Crex crex* (2-4 pairs), *Grus grus* (3-5 pairs), and *Sterna hirundo* (10-25 pairs).

016 Okolice Żydowa-Białego Boru (Żydowo-Biały Bór region) (Koszalin, Słupsk)

54°00'N, 16°45'E 16,000 ha

Three Area of Protected Landscapes

This area is on the border between Koszalin and Słupsk voivodships and is composed of three administratively separate, but physically contiguous, Area of Protected Landscapes. Forests cover over a quarter of the region, whilst the most important lakes for birds are Kwięcko, Bobiecinskie, and Bielsko. All the lakes are deep and mesotrophic with shoreline vegetation. Human activities include farming, forestry, tourism, and fish-farming.

Species breeding in the region include *Ciconia nigra* (1-2 pairs), *C. ciconia* (15-20 pairs), *Milvus migrans* (1 pair), *M. milvus* (2 pairs), *Haliaeetus albicilla* (1 pair), *Circus aeruginosus* (2-3 pairs), *Grus grus* (6-8 pairs), *Bubo bubo* (1-2 pairs), *Alcedo atthis* (4-8 pairs), and *Dryocopus martius* (5-8 pairs).

017 Koszaliński i słupski pas nadmorski (Coastal areas of Koszalin and Słupsk) (Koszalin, Słupsk)

54°10'-54°25'N, 15°25'-16°40'E 55,120 ha (47,600 ha in Koszalin)

Area of Protected Landscape; Ornithological Reserves (Lakes Lubiatowski and Modla); hunting prohibited

The area is composed of a narrow coastal strip of *Pinus* and mixed forests, with five coastal lakes and a eutrophic lake (Lubiatowski) on the southern edge of the region. All the lakes are surrounded by rich shoreline vegetation. Other habitats include meadows and cultivated fields. Human use of the area includes farming, fishing, forestry, and tourism. Some wetland areas around Lake Modla have been drained, and Lake Jamno is polluted by sewage. Wetland areas adjoining Lake Jamno were drained in the 1950s and 1960s. There was a major pollution problem at Lubatowski in the early 1970s.

Breeding species include *Botaurus stellaris* (7-8 pairs), *Ciconia nigra* (3-4 pairs), *C. ciconia* (40-60 pairs), *Milvus migrans* (2-3 pairs), *M. milvus* (5-6 pairs), *Haliaeetus albicilla* (1-2 pairs), *Circus aeruginosus* (18-22 pairs), *C. cyaneus* (0-1 pair), *C. pygargus* (4-5 pairs), *Aquila pomarina* (2-3 pairs), *Crex crex* (8-15 pairs), *Grus grus* (8-10 pairs), *Sterna albifrons* (6-25 pairs), *Chlidonias niger* (20-50 pairs), *Alcedo atthis* (5-7 pairs), *Dryocopus martius* (10-16 pairs), *Anthus campestris* (2-4 pairs), and *Ficedula parva*. Lake Jamno is important for passage wildfowl including *Anser albifrons*, *Aythya ferina*, *Mergus albellus*, and *M. merganser*. The total number of Anatidae and *Fulica atra* reaches 10,000 in autumn.

018 Park Krajobrazowy Dolina Słupi (Słupia Valley Landscape Park) (Słupsk)

54°20'N, 17°15'E 37,040 ha

Landscape Park

Forests cover nearly three-quarters of the area, with fields, meadows, and open water forming the remaining part. The most important lakes are Jasień, Skotawskie, and Głębokie. Human activities include tourism, forestry, farming, and fish-farming.

Breeding species include *Ciconia nigra* (2-4 pairs), *C. ciconia* (40-55 pairs), *Pernis apivorus* (1 pair), *Milvus migrans* (1-2 pairs), *M. milvus* (1-2 pairs), *Haliaeetus albicilla* (1 pair), *Circus aeruginosus* (6-10 pairs), *C. cyaneus* (1 pair), *C. pygargus* (0-1 pair), *Crex crex* (3-5 pairs), *Grus grus* (8-12 pairs), *Alcedo atthis* (6-12 pairs), and *Dryocopus martius* (15-20 pairs).

019 Słowiński Park Narodowy (Słowiński National Park) (Słupsk)

54°37'N, 17°23'E 18,247 ha Biosphere Reserve

National Park; Ornithological Reserves (five, totalling *c.*700 ha)

A unique coastal landscape with mobile sand-dunes, peatbogs, swamps, forests, and lakes (notably Gardno and Łebsko) bordered by extensive areas of reeds. Human activities include forestry, fishing, and tourism. Some wetland areas in the vicinity of the Park have been drained, whilst the cessation of grazing caused a reduction in the breeding populations of some waders.

Breeding species include *Phalacrocorax carbo sinensis* (20 pairs; also 150-200 non-breeding birds), *Botaurus stellaris* (1-2 pairs), *Ciconia nigra* (1 pair), *C. ciconia* (15-20 pairs), *Milvus milvus* (1 pair; in neighbouring forest), *Haliaeetus albicilla* (2 pairs), *Circus aeruginosus* (7-10 pairs), *C. cyaneus* (0-1 pair), *C. pygargus* (2-9 pairs), *Aquila pomarina* (1 pair), *Crex crex* (10-15 pairs), *Grus grus* (10-15 pairs), *Sterna hirundo* (5-25 pairs), *S. albifrons* (3-16 pairs), *Chlidonias niger* (15-45 pairs), *Bubo bubo* (3-5 pairs), and *Aegolius funereus*.

020 Jezior Krępsko/Szczytno (Lakes Krępsko and Szczytno) and surrounding region (Słupsk)

53°47'N, 17°15'E 12,428 ha

Area of Protected Landscape; Ornithological Reserve (Pakotulsko)

The area is centred around the valley of the River Bdra and contains two major lakes: Krępsko and Szczytno. Forests cover about one-third of the site, whilst open water accounts for *c.*7 per cent of the surface area. Land-uses include forestry, fishing, and agriculture. Natural deterioration of old trees, formerly occupied by colonies of *Phalacrocorax carbo sinensis* (max. 426 pairs) and *Ardea cinerea*, resulted in the disappearance of the former species in the early 1980s and greatly reduced numbers of nesting *Ardea cinerea*.

Breeding species in the area include *Botaurus stellaris* (1 pair), *Ciconia nigra* (1-2 pairs), *C. ciconia* (8-12 pairs), *Milvus migrans* (1 pair), *M. milvus* (1 pair), *Haliaeetus albicilla* (1 pair), *Circus aeruginosus* (4-6 pairs), *Tetrao urogallus* (10-20 pairs; in neighbouring forest), *Grus grus* (3-6 pairs), *Bubo bubo* (1 pair), and *Dryocopus martius* (3-6 pairs).

021 Bielawskie Błota (Bielawskie Bog) (Gdańsk)

54°47'-54°49'N, 18°13'-18°16'E 700 ha

Part of Nadmorski Landscape Park; proposed as an Ornithological Reserve

This area is in northernmost Poland close to the Baltic Sea and consists of an Atlantic-type peatbog with shallow dystrophic pools and numerous drainage ditches, surrounded by meadows, arable land, and young *Pinus* forests. The area was heavily exploited for peat over several decades; as a consequence the natural character of the bog was largely destroyed. An extensive restoration project was started in 1985, with several major aims: raising of the water-table, anti-fire precautions, regeneration of plant communities, and regulation of ownership.

Breeding species include *Circus pygargus* (1 pair), *Grus grus* (5-7 pairs), *Tringa glareola* (*c.*10 pairs; only nesting site in Poland), *Asio flammeus* (1 pair), *Caprimulgus europaeus* (4 pairs), *Lullula arborea* (5 pairs), and *Sylvia nisoria* (5-10 pairs). Also an important site for migrating and roosting *Grus grus* (600 on autumn passage; max. 150 non-breeding birds roosting). *Ciconia nigra* and raptors, including *Aquila chrysaetos*, *Falco vespertinus*, and *F. subbuteo*, feed in the area during spring passage.

022 Łąki Beki i Rewy (Beka and Rewa Meadows) (Gdańsk)

54°39'N, 18°30'E (Beka) 54°38'N, 18°30'E (Rewa) 200 ha (100 ha + 100 ha)

Unprotected; proposed as Nature Reserves

Two areas of coastal saltmarshes, partially flooded in autumn and winter, with shallow pools and numerous old drainage ditches and canals. The surrounding areas are drained meadowland and pasture. Land-uses include grazing of livestock and cultivation; there is a power-station ash-dump in the immediate vicinity of the site. Problems affecting the area include the decline of grazing, water pollution by sewage, and air pollution connected with the power-station.

An important breeding area for *Calidris alpina schinzii* (*c.*60 pairs; the largest breeding population on the south Baltic coast). *Haematopus ostralegus* (1 pair; one of the few Polish sites) and *Philomachus pugnax* (4-5 pairs) also breed. One of the most important areas in Poland for passage wildfowl and waders (30 species), in both spring and autumn. Maxima of 3000 resting and feeding waders and 2000 ducks occur in autumn, including *Anas penelope* (1000) and *Pluvialis apricaria* (2000). Ringing and migration studies at Beka/Rewa have shown the turnover of passage waterfowl to be very high, so that the numbers given here tend to underestimate the area's importance.

023 Ujście Wisły (mouth of the River Vistula) (Gdańsk)

54°21'-54°22'N, 18°26'-18°58'E *c.*100 ha

Unprotected; proposed as a Nature Reserve

The shallow estuary of the slow-flowing River Wisła, containing sandy peninsulas, mobile sandflats, small sandy offshore islets, and lagoons, with adjoining dunes and coastal freshwater lakes. In the surrounding areas, dune vegetation merges into *Salix* scrub and young *Pinus* forest. Human activities include fishing, shoreline management (e.g. planting of *Salix*), and dredging of the river mouth. The water is severely polluted by domestic and industrial effluent.

An important site for breeding *Sterna* spp., with *S. sandvicensis* (300 pairs), *S. hirundo* (700 pairs), and *S. albifrons* (160 pairs). Several thousand non-breeding gulls are present in summer, notably *Larus minutus* and *L. canus*. A very important area for passage grebes, ducks, waders, gulls, and terns. The number of ducks may reach a few thousand in autumn, together with a max. of 1000 waders. Around 30 species of waders occur, with *Calidris alpina* being the most numerous. Research has established that the turnover of migrating waders is extremely high; the number given above does not, therefore, reflect the true importance of the area.

024 Zalew Wiślany (Vistula Lagoon) (Elbląg)

54°13'-54°27'N, 19°13'-19°46'E *c.*32,800 ha

Unprotected; adjoins two Landscape Parks (Vistula Spit and Elbląg Hills); proposals for two protected areas

A very large, shallow, brackish lagoon, with significant (*c*.1.5 m), wind-related, daily fluctuations in water-level. There are very extensive belts of reeds along the shore and a rich floating and submerged vegetation. The lagoon is ice-covered from January to mid-April. Human use of the area includes fishing, hunting, recreation, and reed-cutting. The surrounding land includes areas of forestry, grazing, and cultivation. Major problems affecting the avifauna include pollution arising from domestic and industrial effluent, and the mass drowning of waterfowl in fishing nets.

The lagoon supports a rich community of breeding waterfowl and associated species, with *Podiceps cristatus* (200+ pairs), *Phalacrocorax carbo sinensis* (2000+ pairs; colony near Kąty), *Botaurus stellaris* (1-3 pairs), *Ixobrychus minutus*, *Ardea cinerea* (500 pairs; colony near Katy), *Anas strepera* (20 pairs), *A. querquedula* (10-15 pairs), *A. clypeata* (30-50 pairs), *Aythya ferina* (100-150 pairs), *A. nyroca* (1-3 pairs), *A. fuligula* (*c*.100 pairs), *Haliaeetus albicilla* (1 pair), *Circus aeruginosus* (15-20 pairs), *C. pygargus* (2-4 pairs), *Porzana porzana*, *P. parva*, *Crex crex* (4-10 pairs), *Limosa limosa* (7 pairs), *Sterna hirundo* (300-400 pairs), and *S. paradisaea* (1-2 pairs). A very important area for moulting and migrating wildfowl, with *Cygnus olor* (1000-1600 moulting), *C. cygnus* (80 autumn passage; *c*.20 in winter), *Anas strepera* (120 spring passage), *Aythya ferina* (9000 moulting), *A. fuligula* (10,000-12,000 spring and autumn passages), *A. marila* (700 spring and autumn passages), *Bucephala clangula* (1000 spring and autumn passages), and *Mergus albellus* (500 spring passage).

025 Jezioro Drużno (Lake Drużno) (Elbląg)

54°03'-54°07'N, 19°24'-19°30'E 3000 ha

Partly an Ornithological Reserve

A very shallow (av. depth 0.8 m) eutrophic lake, with extensive reedbeds and *Alnus* swamp in the surrounding areas. Human activities include fishing, tourism, and agriculture. The lake is heavily polluted by industrial and agricultural effluent.

Birds nesting at the site include *Podiceps cristatus* (350-400 pairs), *Anser anser* (40-50 pairs), *Anas strepera* (50-70 pairs), *A. querquedula* (10-15 pairs), *A. clypeata* (10-15 pairs), *Aythya ferina* (150-200 pairs), *A. nyroca* (2-3 pairs), *A. fuligula* (100 pairs), *Circus aeruginosus* (10-15 pairs), *C. pygargus* (1-3 pairs), *Porzana porzana* (15-20 pairs), *P. parva* (10-15 pairs), *Crex crex* (2-3 pairs), *Grus grus* (1-2 pairs), *Larus ridibundus* (6000 pairs), *Sterna hirundo* (80-100 pairs), *Chlidonias niger* (100 pairs), and *Luscinia svecica* (10-20 pairs). An important moulting area for geese, ducks, and cranes, with *Anser anser* (300), *Anas strepera* (700), *A. clypeata* (1000), and *Grus grus* (2000).

026 Lasy Iławskie (Iława Forests) (Olsztyn, Elbląg)

53°36'-53°51'N, 19°22'-19°38'E 17,400 ha

Ornithological Reserves (Lakes Gaudy and Czerwica); proposed as a Landscape Park; mainly unprotected

A complex of wooded areas (*c*.60 per cent being over 40 years old), and lakes, with many marshy areas scattered throughout. The lakes range in size from about 0.5 ha to 163 ha and the woods are mainly mixed *Pinus* and Fagus,; although there is some *Alnus* swamp. The area is threatened by the felling of mature trees and by drainage of wet and swampy wooded areas.

Breeding species include *Phalacrocorax carbo sinensis* (140-190 pairs), *Ciconia nigra* (5-8 pairs), *Pernis apivorus* (*c*.15 pairs), *Milvus migrans* (7-9 pairs), *M. milvus* (8 pairs), *Haliaeetus albicilla* (4-5 pairs), *Circus aeruginosus* (3-5 pairs), *Aquila pomarina* (13-15 pairs), *Pandion haliaetus* (4 pairs), *Grus grus* (20-30 pairs), *Porzana porzana*, *P. parva*, *Chlidonias niger* (two colonies; 100-150 pairs and 60 pairs), and *Alcedo atthis* (5-10 pairs), The area is also very important for migrating cranes, with 2000-3000 *Grus grus* on autumn passage.

027 Jezioro Karaś (Lake Karaś) (Torun, Olsztyn)

52°32'-52°34'N, 19°27'-19°30'E 816 ha Ramsar Site

Nature Reserve; Ornithological Reserve

A eutrophic lake (412 ha) with many small islands, broad reedbeds, and an adjacent fen (400 ha) which is sparsely covered with *Betula* and *Alnus*. The lake is surrounded by a 50-100 m wide belt of deciduous trees, and is used as a fishery. Human activities in the surrounding areas include grazing, cultivation, hunting, and forestry. The site is adversely affected by pollution of the Gac (one of the rivers feeding the lake), whilst other major problems include the deterioration of aquatic vegetation (possibly due to acid rain), and afforestation of the adjacent meadows.

Breeding species include *Botaurus stellaris* (3-5 pairs), *Ixobrychus minutus*, *Circus aeruginosus* (3-5 pairs), *Aquila pomarina*, *Porzana porzana*, *Grus grus* (*c.*5 pairs), *Chlidonias niger*, and *Asio flammeus*. The lake is also a summer roost for *Anser anser* and a moulting area for ducks.

028 Jezioro Rakutowskie i Olszyny Rakutowskie (Lake Rakutowskie and Rakutowskie Alders) (Włocławek)

52°32'N, 19°14'E 800 ha

Landscape Park; Nature Reserve; Ornithological Reserve

A rather shallow (av. depth 2.5 m) lake fringed by a broad belt of *Schoenoplectus*, *Typha*, and *Phragmites*, and surrounded by seasonally flooded *Carex* meadows. Human activities include fishing and agriculture. Drainage is a potential threat.

Species breeding at the area include *Botaurus stellaris* (2-3 pairs), *Circus aeruginosus* (3 pairs), *C. pygargus* (1-2 pairs), *Porzana parva* (3 pairs), *Crex crex* (1-2 pairs), *Grus grus* (1-2 pairs), *Limosa limosa* (6-10 pairs), and *Chlidonias niger* (*c.*40 pairs). An important site for passage geese, ducks, coots, and waders; total number exceeds 10,000 in autumn.

029 Pradolina Warszawsko-Berlińska (Warsaw-Berlin post-glacial stream valley) (Konin, Płock, Skierniewice)

52°07'-52°09'N, 18°41'-19°42'E 9000 ha Proposed Ramsar Site

Nature Reserve (small part of area); mainly unprotected

This site is at the end of the 80-km-long Pleistocene valley of the River Vistula. Although varying from 0.5 km to 2.0 km in width, the present valley is only occupied by the small Rivers Ner and Bzura. The valley is overgrown by tall sedges, reeds, and grasses, and around ten per cent is covered with *Salix* thickets. There are numerous small ponds and a number of wooded areas, the largest of which is 60 ha. The surrounding areas are mainly fields with scattered villages. Farming of grasslands is the principal human activity, though Leczyca town occupies part of the valley. Drainage for agricultural purposes threatens the site, and the waters of both the Rivers Ner and Bzura are heavily polluted.

Birds nesting in the valley include *Botaurus stellaris* (14 pairs), *Ixobrychus minutus* (3 pairs), *Ciconia nigra* (2 pairs), *C. ciconia* (40 pairs), *Circus aeruginosus* (64 pairs), *C. pygargus* (9 pairs), *Aquila pomarina* (1 pair), *Porzana porzana* (100 pairs), *P. parva*, *Crex crex* (80 pairs), *Grus grus* (8-9 pairs), *Philomachus pugnax* (0-15 females), *Limosa limosa* (250 pairs), *Chlidonias niger* (120 pairs), *C. leucopterus* (0-7 pairs), *Asio flammeus* (0-8 pairs), *Anthus campestris* (15 pairs), *Luscinia svecica cyaneculus* (8-9 pairs), *Acrocephalus paludicola* (0-5 pairs), *Sylvia nisoria* (25-30 pairs), and *Emberiza hortulana* (30 pairs). An important area for migrating *Grus grus* (2000 on spring passage). Wintering species include *Falco columbarius* (2-4).

030 Kramskie Błota (Kramskie Marshes) (Konin)

52°16'N, 18°28'E 3700 ha

Unprotected; proposed for protected status

The eastern part of the area contains mainly hay-meadows, pasture, and many peaty ponds, whilst the western part is dominated by open peatbogs partly overgrown with shrubs and scattered trees. The grasslands are actively farmed. Drainage and scrub clearance was carried out some years ago in the western sector.

Breeding species in the area include *Botaurus stellaris* (6 pairs), *Ixobrychus minutus* (1-2 pairs), *Ciconia ciconia* (8-10 pairs), *Circus aeruginosus* (13 pairs), *C. cyaneus* (1 pair), *C. pygargus* (3-4 pairs), *Porzana porzana* (5-10 pairs), *P. parva* (1-2 pairs), *Crex crex* (10-12 pairs), *Grus grus* (5-7 pairs), *Limosa limosa* (26 pairs), *Chlidonias niger* (15-20 pairs), *C. leucopterus* (11 pairs), *Asio flammeus* (1 pair), *Acrocephalus paludicola* (6-12 pairs), and *Emberiza hortulana* (many).

031 Dolina środkowej Warty (middle River Warta valley) (Konin)

52°09'-52°15'N, 17°39'-18°43'E 35,000 ha

Unprotected; proposed for protected status

A river flood-plain. The principal habitats are pastures, meadows, small fragments of peatbogs, marshy woods, and sand-dunes. Owing to periodic flooding, agriculture is low-intensity. The area is only partly drained and further drainage work has been suspended.

The area supports a rich community of breeding birds, with *Botaurus stellaris* (25-30 pairs), *Ixobrychus minutus* (8-10 pairs), *Nycticorax nycticorax* (3-5 pairs), *Ciconia ciconia* (60-70 pairs), *Anas acuta* (10-15 pairs), *A. querquedula* (250 pairs), *A. clypeata* (170-200 pairs), *Aythya nyroca* (2-5 pairs), *Circus aeruginosus* (40-50 pairs), *C. pygargus* (1-2 pairs), *Porzana porzana* (20-50 pairs), *P. parva* (7-10 pairs), *Crex crex* (50-60 pairs), *Grus grus* (1-2 pairs), *Philomachus pugnax* (20-25 females), *Gallinago media* (2 pairs), *Limosa limosa* (600-700 pairs), *Tringa totanus* (250 pairs), *Sterna hirundo* (*c.*25 pairs), *S. albifrons* (35 pairs), *Chlidonias niger* (*c.*100 pairs), *Coracias garrulus* (3-4 pairs), *Lullula arborea* (40-50 pairs), *Anthus campestris* (20-25 pairs), *Luscinia svecica cyaneculus* (40-50 pairs), *Sylvia nisoria* (30-40 pairs), and *Emberiza hortulana* (many). A very important area for passage waterfowl, with flocks of *Anser fabalis* and *A. anser* reaching 15,000, and flocks of *Anas crecca* and *A. platyrhynchos* reaching 20,000. Other migrating waterfowl include *Philomachus pugnax* (max. 3000) and *Limosa limosa* (3000-4000).

032 Dolina Warty koło Krajkowa (River Warta valley near Krajkowa) (Poznań)

52°12'N, 16°54'E 1290 ha

Nature Reserve (Krajkowo: 160 ha); mainly unprotected

A meandering stretch of the River Warta's middle course near Poznań. There are two major habitats: open flood-meadows and pasture with scattered, single, very old *Quercus* trees and semi-natural marshy woodland. The grasslands are intensively farmed. Part of the site (northern grasslands) was drained some years ago and the area is threatened by further drainage.

Breeding species include *Ciconia nigra* (1 pair), *C. ciconia* (8-11 pairs), *Milvus migrans* (3 pairs), *M. milvus* (2 pairs), *Circus aeruginosus* (1 pair), *Porzana porzana* (4-6 pairs), *P. parva* (1-2 pairs), *Crex crex* (3-6 pairs), *Grus grus* (2 pairs), *Limosa limosa* (6-7 pairs), and *Chlidonias niger* (12-25 pairs).

033 Wielki Łęg Obrzański (Great Obra marshes) (Leszno, Poznań)

52°01'-52°07'N, 16°10'-16°30'E 15,880 ha

Unprotected; proposed for protected status

The widest part of a river valley, containing the three branches of the Obra which dissect the area east-west. The principal habitats are meadowland, marsh, marshy woods, ditches, peaty hollows, and mixed *Pinus* forest on the higher sandy ground. Except for the marshy ground, the area is intensively cultivated. Drainage is the most serious threat to the future of the site.

Species breeding in the area include *Botaurus stellaris* (3-4 pairs), *Ciconia nigra* (3-4 pairs), *C. ciconia* (*c.*43 pairs), *Pernis apivorus* (1-2 pairs), *Milvus migrans* (2-3 pairs), *M. milvus* (2-3 pairs), *Circus aeruginosus* (5-7 pairs), *Aquila pomarina* (1 pair), *Porzana porzana* (5-6 pairs), *P. parva* (2-5 pairs), *Grus grus* (15 pairs), *Limosa limosa* (5-6 pairs), *Dryocopus martius* (8-10), *Anthus campestris* (many pairs), and *Sylvia nisoria* (*c.*20 pairs).

034 Jezioro Gopło (Lake Gopło) (Bydgoszcz)

52°29'-52°40'N, 18°24'E 2180 ha

Landscape Park (part of area); Ornithological Reserves (two small areas: Potrzymionek Island and the tip of Potrzymiech Peninsula)

A 25-km-long post-glacial lake with flat open banks fringed by wide reedbeds. There are some islets (total 25 ha) which are overgrown with reeds. The surrounding areas are mainly wet meadows, fields, and small woods. Human activities include fishing and yachting. Drainage and the use of fertilisers in the surrounding areas have resulted in lower water-levels and eutrophication.

Breeding birds include *Botaurus stellaris* (7-10 pairs), *Ixobrychus minutus* (3-5 pairs), *Ciconia ciconia* (5-7 pairs), *Milvus migrans* (3-4 pairs), *M. milvus* (1-2 pairs), *Circus aeruginosus* (*c.*40 pairs), *C. pygargus* (2-3 pairs), *Porzana porzana* (7-10 pairs), *P. parva* (2-3 pairs), *Crex crex* (many pairs), *Grus grus* (4-5 pairs), *Limosa limosa* (40-60 pairs), *Sterna hirundo* (15-100 pairs), *Chlidonias niger* (*c.*50 pairs), *Coracias garrulus* (1 pair), and *Emberiza hortulana* (many pairs).

035 Dolina Noteci koło Czarnkowa (River Noteć valley near Czarnków) (Piła)

52°53'-53°04'N, 16°15'-16°36'E 9860 ha

Unprotected; proposed for protected status

A part of the Noteć river valley between Wrzeszczyna and Biała. The principal habitats are flood-meadows, low-lying peatbogs with many channels, ditches, former river-bed areas, and water-filled peaty hollows. Parts of the area are overgrown with bushes and trees. The main land-use is intensive farming of meadowland. The site is potentially threatened by drainage and clearance of trees/bushes.

Breeding birds include *Botaurus stellaris* (9-10 pairs), *Ciconia ciconia* (30-40 pairs), *Milvus migrans* (1 pair), *M. milvus* (1-3 pairs), *Haliaeetus albicilla* (feeding area for one pair nesting in nearby forest), *Circus aeruginosus* (12-16 pairs), *C. pygargus* (0-2 pairs), *Porzana porzana* (8-9 pairs), *P. parva* (1-2 pairs), *Crex crex* (47-50 pairs), *Grus grus* (3-4 pairs), *Limosa limosa* (66-70 pairs), *Numenius arquata* (48-50 pairs), *Chlidonias niger* (17-25 pairs), and *Luscinia svecica cyaneculus* (66 pairs).

036 Jezioro Wielkie (Lake Wielkie) (Gorzów)

52°48'N, 15°52'E 400 ha

Unprotected; proposed as an Ornithological Reserve

The area of the lake itself is 377 ha, with an average depth of 2.1 m (max. = 3.9 m). The lake is eutrophic, contains two small islands (total area *c.*10 ha), and is surrounded by forests and meadows. Human activities include fishing and hunting. General disturbance in the breeding season, and hunting during the autumn, adversely affect the site's avifauna.

Breeding birds include *Botaurus stellaris* (2 pairs), *Ixobrychus minutus* (1 pair), *Pernis apivorus* (1 pair), *Milvus migrans* (1-2 pairs), *M. milvus* (1 pair), and *Circus aeruginosus* (2-3 pairs).

037 Dolina Warty koło Santoka (River Warta valley near Santok) (Gorzów)

52°36'N, 15°25'E 850 ha

Unprotected

A part of the Warta flood-plains south-west of Santok, including meadows/pastures, fields, and old drainage channels. The meadows are flooded annually between March and May. Human activities include hay-making and cultivation. Drainage and agricultural intensification are potential threats.

Birds breeding in the area include *Botaurus stellaris* (1 pair), *Ciconia nigra* (feeding area for one pair nesting nearby), *C. ciconia* (1-2 pairs), *Circus aeruginosus* (2-3 pairs),

Crex crex (1 pair), *Philomachus pugnax* (120-150 males in spring), *Limosa limosa* (5-10 pairs), and *Chlidonias niger* (20-30 pairs).

038 Ujście Noteci (Mouth of the River Noteć) (Gorzów)

52°46'N, 15°30'E 3530 ha

Unprotected

The lower section/mouth of the River Noteć, north-east of Santok. The river is channelled between two artificial raised embankments but there are associated wet meadows, drainage channels, former river-bed areas, and marshes with scrub and small woods. Human activities include fishing and grassland cultivation. There is considerable disturbance from anglers.

Birds breeding in the area include *Botaurus stellaris* (2-3 pairs), *Ciconia ciconia* (2 pairs), *Milvus migrans* (2-3 pairs), *M. milvus* (1 pair), *Circus aeruginosus* (6 pairs), *Porzana porzana* (3-4 pairs), *Crex crex* (2-3 pairs), *Grus grus* (1-2 pairs), *Chlidonias niger* (10-35 pairs), *Asio flammeus* (1 pair), and *Luscinia svecica cyaneculus* (15 pairs).

039 Rezerwat Słońsk (Słońsk Reserve) (Gorzów)

52°34'N, 14°43'E 4166 ha Ramsar Site

Ornithological Reserve (3066 ha partial reserve; 1100 ha strict reserve)

The reserve includes the flood-plain of the River Warta where it joins the Odra, and the River Postomia. There is a combination of natural stretches of river and man-made storage reservoirs, with numerous old drainage channels, meadows, and pastures. The reserve is flooded for about eight months of the year. There are frequent large fluctuations in the water-level between March and July. The meadows are used for haymaking and grazing. Overgrazing and intensive haymaking in some areas may threaten breeding waterfowl.

Breeding birds include *Podiceps grisegena* (30-160 pairs), *P. nigricollis* (100-180 pairs), *Phalacrocorax carbo sinensis* (450-500 pairs), *Botaurus stellaris* (4-7 pairs), *Ixobrychus minutus* (0-6 pairs), *Ciconia nigra* (feeding area for 1-2 pairs nesting nearby), *Anas strepera* (30-120 pairs), *Milvus milvus* (0-1 pair), *Haliaeetus albicilla* (0-1 pair), *Circus aeruginosus* (10-40 pairs), *C. pygargus* (0-1 pair), *Porzana porzana* (10-20 pairs), *Crex crex* (2-30 pairs), *Grus grus* (0-1 pair; also 20-30 non-breeding birds), *Philomachus pugnax* (10-30 pairs), *Limosa limosa* (20-160 pairs), *Sterna hirundo* (6-180 pairs), *Chlidonias niger* (150-410 pairs), and *Acrocephalus paludicola* (0-50 pairs). A very important site, in both spring and autumn, for passage waterfowl, with (maxima): *Cygnus olor*, *C. columbianus*, and *C. cygnus* (spring 760; autumn 480); geese (spring 3000; autumn 36,000; 70-95 per cent *Anser fabalis*); ducks, including *Anas strepera*, *A. crecca*, *A. querquedula*, *A. clypeata*, *Aythya ferina* and *A. fuligula* (spring 33,000; autumn 72,000), and *Fulica atra* (spring 32,000; autumn 70,000). Large numbers of wildfowl also occur in winter, with (maxima): swans (900), geese (49,000), ducks (49,000), and *Fulica atra* (15,000).

040 Dolina Leniwej Obry (Leniwa Obra valley) (Gorzów)

52°15'N, 15°45'E 1300 ha

Mainly unprotected; Forest Reserves (three small reserves totalling 95 ha)

The valley was drained in the nineteenth century and is now a mosaic of dry, open and scrub-covered meadows/pastures, with *Fraxinus/Alnus* and *Quercus/Carpinus* forests (20-100 years old). Human uses of the area include haymaking and grazing of cattle. There are some serious problems owing to felling operations in the forests, and the digging of over-deep drainage channels.

Birds nesting in the valley include *Ciconia ciconia* (1-2 pairs), *Circus cyaneus* (1 pair), *Aquila pomarina* (3 pairs), *Crex crex* (1 pair), *Grus grus* (6-8 pairs), *Dendrocopos medius* (10-15 pairs), *Sylvia nisoria* (5-10 pairs), and *Emberiza hortulana* (5-10 pairs).

041 Jeziora Chobienickie (Chobienickie Lakes) (Zielona Góra)

52°08'N, 15°54'E 420 ha

Mainly unprotected; Ornithological Reserve (26 ha); whole area projected as Ornithological Reserve

A complex of three eutrophic lakes surrounded by forest: Chobienicki (230 ha), Wielkowiejskie (78 ha), and Kopanickie (*c.*70 ha). The average water depth is 1.8 m (max. 2.6 m) and the total area of reeds associated with the lakes is *c.*35 ha. There are three islands (*c.*30 ha) in Lake Chobienicki. Human activities include fishing, farming, hunting, and recreation. The site's avifauna is adversely affected by high levels of general disturbance during the breeding season, and by hunting during the autumn migration period.

Breeding birds include *Botaurus stellaris* (2-3 pairs), *Ixobrychus minutus* (1 pair), *Milvus migrans* (1-2 pairs), *M. milvus* (1-2 pairs), *Circus aeruginosus* (3-4 pairs), *Porzana porzana* (1 pair), *Crex crex* (1 pair), and *Grus grus* (1 pair).

042 Pojezierze Sławskie (Sławskie Lakes) (Zielona Góra)

51°51'-51°56'N, 15°57'-16°04'E 1065 ha (lakes only)

Mainly unprotected; Nature Reserves (Swięte: 17 ha; Mesze: 3ha)

A lake complex surrounded by *Pinus* forests and fields. The lakes range in size from two ha to 817 ha and between six and 37 per cent of their surface areas are covered with *Phragmites* and *Typha*. This vegetation type also covers large parts of the lakes' shores. Three of the large lakes are used for recreation.

Species breeding in the area include *Botaurus stellaris* (4 males), *Ixobrychus minutus* (4 pairs), *Ciconia nigra* (1 pair), *Milvus migrans* (2 pairs), *M. milvus* (1 pair), *Circus aeruginosus* (8 pairs), *Porzana parva* (1 pair), *Grus grus* (1 pair), *Dryocopus martius* (common), and *Lanius excubitor* (1-2 pairs).

043 Stawy rybne Darowa (Darowa fish-ponds) (Jelenia Góra)

51°18'-51°21'N, 15°12'-15°17'E 460 ha

Unprotected

A complex of fish-ponds surrounded by forest. The three central ponds are almost natural, with large areas of *Phragmites* and *Typha*, but the other ponds have been heavily altered by man. The area also includes 50 ha of wet meadows lying between some of the ponds. Fish-farming is the principal human activity.

Birds nesting at the complex include *Botaurus stellaris* (4 males), *Ciconia nigra* (2-3 pairs), *Milvus milvus* (1 pair), *Haliaeetus albicilla* (1 pair), *Circus aeruginosus* (4 pairs), *Tetrao tetrix* (2-3 males, 6 females), *Grus grus* (2 pairs), *Dryocopus martius* (13 pairs), and *Sylvia nisoria* (10-15 pairs).

044 Stawy rybne Przemków (Przemków fish-ponds) (Legnica)

51°33'-51°36'N, 15°45'-15°53'E 948 ha

Nature Reserve

A pond complex, parts of which are overgrown by *Phragmites* and *Typha*. There are 75 ha of woodland and extensive wet meadows in the north-east. Fish-farming is the principal human activity.

Birds breeding in the area include *Podiceps nigricollis* (200 pairs), *Botaurus stellaris* (6-9 males), *Ixobrychus minutus* (1 pair), *Ciconia nigra* (1 pair), *C. ciconia* (13 pairs), *Anser anser* (14 pairs), *Aythya nyroca* (2-4 pairs), *Pernis apivorus* (1 pair), *Milvus migrans* (1 pair), *Haliaeetus albicilla* (1 pair), *Circus aeruginosus* (11-16 pairs), *Tetrao tetrix* (6-13 males), *Porzana porzana* (1-7 males), *P. parva* (1 pair), *Crex crex* (1 pair), *Grus grus* (2-3 pairs), and *Limosa limosa* (20 pairs). An important area for passage Anatidae, with (maxima) *Anser fabalis* (2500), *Anas crecca* (1400), *A. platyrhynchos*

(10,000), *Aythya ferina* (9000), and *A. fuligula* (2600); also large numbers of passage *Fulica atra* (max. 11,600).

045 Zbiornik Wonieść (Wonieść Reservoir) (Leszno)

51°59'N, 16°43'E 1970 ha

Unprotected; proposed for protected status

A reservoir (900 ha) formed in the rather narrow Wonieść valley, in the area formerly occupied by five lakes. The adjoining areas are composed of woodland, fields, and meadows. The fields and meadows are intensively cultivated. Marshy woodland and reedbeds were lost when the valley was flooded (some years ago).

Breeding birds include *Botaurus stellaris* (11 pairs), *Ciconia ciconia* (4-5 pairs), *Ixobrychus minutus* (3-4 pairs), *Aythya nyroca* (3-4 pairs), *Milvus migrans* (1 pair), *M. milvus* (1 pair), *Circus aeruginosus* (*c.*15 pairs), *Porzana porzana* (7-10 pairs), *P. parva* (1-2 pairs), *Crex crex* (1 pair), *Grus grus* (4-5 pairs), *Sterna hirundo* (*c.*20 pairs), *Chlidonias niger* (30-50 pairs), *Anthus campestris* (many pairs), *Sylvia nisoria* (many pairs), and *Emberiza hortulana* (many pairs).

046 Lasy w dolinie Odry: Malczyc i Kaczawy (Forests in the River Odra valley: Malczyce – Kaczawa) (Wrocław)

51°13'-51°18'N, 16°25'-16°32'E 1500 ha

Unprotected

An area of *Fraxinus/Ulmus* carr and *Quercus/Carpinus* forest on alluvial soil, alongside the River Odra, between Malczyce town and the mouth of the River Kaczawa. The area is intensively exploited.

Breeding species include *Ciconia nigra* (2 pairs), *Pernis apivorus* (3 pairs), *Milvus migrans* (3-4 pairs), *M. milvus* (2 pairs), *Haliaeetus albicilla* (1 pair probably breeding), *Circus aeruginosus* (1-2 pairs), *Grus grus* (2-3 pairs), *Picus canus* (2-4 pairs), and *Dendrocopos medius* (common; 80-100 pairs).

047 Stawy rybne w Miliczu – zespół Jamnik (Milicz fish-ponds: Jamnik complex) (Wrocław)

51°27'-51°29'N, 17°00'-17°03'E 300 ha

Nature Reserves

The complex consists of four ponds, varying in size from 35-129 ha. All four are filled from the River Barycz; three have artificially created islets, and two have fairly extensive areas of reeds. The ponds are used extensively for pisciculture (principally *Cyprinus*) and the fish-farmers seek control of fish-eating birds (notably *Phalacrocorax carbo sinensis* and *Ardea cinerea*) and financial compensation for food eaten by ducks and coots. All species of birds are protected, at least in the breeding season, although environmental changes to the ponds are allowed if they are deemed necessary for fish-farming interests. Three of the ponds have apparently been seriously altered in recent years, but details are lacking.

Breeding species in the area include *Botaurus stellaris* (1-2 males), *Ciconia nigra* (feeding area for one pair nesting nearby), *C. ciconia* (4-5 pairs), *Aythya nyroca* (*c.*15 pairs), *Milvus migrans* (1 pair), *Haliaeetus albicilla* (feeding area for one pair nesting nearby), *Circus aeruginosus* (5-6 pairs), and *Porzana parva* (0-2 pairs). *Haliaeetus albicilla* (2-5) occurs on passage.

048 Stawy rybne w Miliczu – zespół Radziądz (Milicz fish-ponds: Radziądz complex) (Wrocław)

51°29'-51°33'N, 16°58'-17°05'E *c.*750 ha

Nature Reserve (western group of ponds only)

A complex of 12 ponds: six in the west and six in the east. The ponds in the western part of the area have not been significantly 'improved' and many areas are therefore covered with reeds. Two of these ponds also merge into *Alnus* swamp and one has natural islets with *Quercus/Alnus*. The eastern section has been highly modified and areas of reeds are scarce, although there are artificial islands suitable for breeding ducks and *Larus ridibundus*. Pisciculture and hunting (in eastern part) are the principal human activities. Fish-eating birds are controlled, and the fish-farmers are seeking compensation for food eaten by ducks and coots.

Birds breeding in the area include *Phalacrocorax carbo sinensis* (3-12 pairs; also on passage: 80 spring; 500 autumn), *Botaurus stellaris* (9-12 males), *Ixobrychus minutus* (1-2 pairs), *Ciconia nigra* (feeding area for two pairs nesting in nearby forest), *C. ciconia* (5-7 pairs), *Milvus milvus* (0-1 pair), *Haliaeetus albicilla* (feeding area for one pair nesting in nearby forest), *Circus aeruginosus* (23-32 pairs), *Porzana parva* (4-8 pairs), *Grus grus* (3 pairs), *Chlidonias niger* (0-15 pairs), and *Alcedo atthis* (3-10 pairs). The total post-breeding/autumn passage population of Anatidae exceeds 10,000 birds. *Haliaeetus albicilla* (*c*.10) occurs on autumn passage.

049 Stawy rybne w Miliczu – zespół Ruda Sułowska (Milicz fish-ponds: Ruda Sułowska complex) (Wrocław)

51°28'-52°33'N, 17°05'-17°08'E 800 ha

Nature Reserve

A complex of 34 ponds, almost all of which have been heavily modified. Most areas of reeds have been bulldozed and piled up to form small artificial islands. However, the largest pond (283 ha) is largely unchanged, with 40 ha overgrown by *Phragmites* and *Typha*. The ponds are surrounded by fields and forest. Intensive pisciculture is carried out and some fish-eating birds are controlled outside the breeding season. Fish-farmers want to extend such measures to include breeding birds and to receive compensation for food taken by ducks and coots.

Breeding birds include *Botaurus stellaris* (7-9 males), *Ixobrychus minutus* (1-3 pairs), *Ciconia nigra* (feeding area for 2 pairs nesting in nearby forest), *C. ciconia* (9-12 pairs), Anatidae (1000+, including *Aythya nyroca* 10-35 pairs), *Haliaeetus albicilla* (feeding area for one pair nesting in nearby forest), *Circus aeruginosus* (18-25 pairs), *Porzana parva* (6-11 pairs), and *Grus grus* (0-1 pair). The total number of Anatidae in the post-breeding/autumn passage period exceeds 10,000 birds. Other species occurring on passage include *Phalacrocorax carbo sinensis* (40 spring; 150 autumn) and *Haliaeetus albicilla*.

050 Stawy rybne w Miliczu – zespół Sławno (Milicz fish-ponds: Sławno complex) (Wrocław)

51°31'-51°34'N, 17°18'-17°25'E 2400 ha

Nature Reserve

A fish-farming estate consisting of 31 ponds (total area *c*.1730 ha), most of which are partly (max. 20 per cent) overgrown with *Phragmites* and *Typha*, and basically resemble natural eutrophic lakes. The most important ponds are Grabownica, Henryk, and Słoneczny. Surrounding habitats include woods, fields, and meadows. Fish-farmers want to remove as much as possible of the reeds fringing banks and islands, and to control fish-eating birds; currently, all species are protected during the breeding season.

Birds breeding in the area include *Botaurus stellaris* (16-20 males), *Ixobrychus minutus* (3-6 pairs), *Ciconia nigra* (feeding area for 2 pairs nesting nearby), *C. ciconia* (3-5 pairs), Anatidae (3000; including *Aythya nyroca*: 33-53 pairs), *Milvus migrans* (1 pair), *Haliaeetus albicilla* (feeding area for one pair nesting nearby), *Circus aeruginosus* (40-50 pairs), *Porzana parva* (6-9 pairs), *Grus grus* (2-5 pairs), *Sterna hirundo* (50-100 pairs), *Chlidonias niger* (0-25 pairs), *Alcedo atthis* (3-14 pairs), and *Riparia riparia* (500-1800 pairs). The total number of post-breeding/autumn passage Anatidae exceeds 10,000. *Phalacrocorax carbo sinensis* occurs during both spring and autumn passage periods (spring 80; autumn 500). *Haliaeetus albicilla* occurs during autumn passage (5-8) and in winter (2-3).

051 Stawy rybne w Miliczu – zespół Potasznia (Milicz fish-ponds: Potasznia complex) (Wrocław)

51°31'-51°34'N, 17°28'-17°32'E 750 ha

Nature Reserve (southern group; 322 ha)

The complex consists of three groups of ponds. Most of the ponds were highly modified during the period 1956-1970, when areas of reeds were cleared and artificial islands were formed. Many of the islands are now covered with *Alnus*. The most important ponds for breeding birds are Jan, Górnik, and Wrocławicki (latter two are unprotected). Jan merges into *Alnus* swamp, and there are some restricted areas of reeds remaining. The surrounding areas include *Alnus* forests, *Pinus* forests, meadows, and arable fields. The area is used for pisciculture and hunting. Fish-farmers control fish-eating birds.

Breeding birds include *Phalacrocorax carbo sinensis* (240 pairs), *Botaurus stellaris* (3-6 males), *Ardea cinerea* (60 pairs), *Ciconia nigra* (feeding area for 2 pairs nesting nearby), *C. ciconia* (3-5 pairs), *Anser anser* (90 pairs), *Aythya nyroca* (3-11 pairs), *Milvus migrans* (1 pair), *Haliaeetus albicilla* (feeding area for one pair nesting nearby), *Circus aeruginosus* (18-22 pairs), *Porzana parva* (0-2 pairs), and *Grus grus* (2-4 pairs). The total number of post-breeding/autumn passage Anatidae exceeds 10,000.

052 Stawy rybne w Przygodzicach: zespół Dębnica i Trzcielin (Przygodzice fish-ponds: Dębnica and Trzcielin complexes) (Kalisz)

51°31'-51°35'N 17°47'-17°50'E 700 ha

Unprotected

A complex of fish-ponds, many of which have been heavily modified in the last ten years. Parts of some ponds are overgrown with *Salix*, forming an important habitat for breeding birds.

Breeding birds include *Botaurus stellaris*, *Ciconia nigra* (feeding area for 1-2 pairs nesting nearby), *C. ciconia* (4-6 pairs), *Aythya nyroca* (1-3 pairs), *Pernis apivorus* (1 pair), *Haliaeetus albicilla* (feeding area for one pair nesting in nearby forest), *Circus aeruginosus* (5 pairs), *Grus grus* (2 pairs), and *Chlidonias niger* (5-24 pairs).

053 Lasy w dolinie Odry: Kotowice i Siechnica (Forests in the River Odra valley: Kotowice and Siechnica) (Wrocław)

51°01'-51°03'N, 17°10'-17°13'E 620 ha

Unprotected

A forested area on alluvial soil between the settlements of Siechnica and Kotowice. There are large stands of *Fraxinus* and *Ulmus* carr, together with *Quercus/Carpinus* forest. The area also includes numerous streams and former parts of the Odra riverbed. The area is intensively exploited.

Breeding birds include *Ciconia nigra* (1 pair), *Pernis apivorus* (1-2 pairs), *Milvus migrans* (2 pairs), *M. milvus* (1 pair), *Circus aeruginosus* (1-2 pairs), *Picus canus* (2-3 pairs), *Dendrocopos medius* (1.3-1.7 pairs per 10 ha), *Sylvia nisoria* (200-260 pairs), *Ficedula parva* (1-2 pairs), and *F. albicollis* (1.0-2.7 pairs per 10 ha).

054 Zbiornik Otmuchowski (Otmuchów Reservoir) (Opole)

50°27'-50°29'N, 17°05'-17°10'E 2300 ha

Unprotected

A large storage reservoir situated amongst hills on the River Nysa Kłodzka and surrounded by fields and meadows. There are considerable fluctuations in water-level and although some parts of the shores consist of shingle, the bottom of the reservoir is generally muddy. The eastern part is embanked with stones, but the western shores have a more natural character.

An important area for migrating birds, especially during the autumn when the total number of Anatidae exceeds 15,000. Species include (maxima) *Anser* spp. (2000), *Anas crecca* (1200), and *A. platyrhynchos* (13,500). The reservoir is also important for passage waders.

055 Zbiornik Nyski (Nysa Reservoirs) (Opole)

50°26'-50°28'N, 17°12'-17°18'E 2000 ha

Unprotected

The reservoir is situated in lowlands and surrounded by fields and meadows. The water-level fluctuates considerably and extensive areas of mud may be exposed when the level is low. The shoreline is varied, with many bays, islets, and shallows. The reservoir is used to control water flow for navigation purposes on the River Odra, and is also used for fish-farming.

Breeding birds include *Ixobrychus minutus* (1 pair), *Circus aeruginosus* (1 pair) and *Sterna hirundo* (5-7 pairs). An important site for passage Anatidae (total number exceeds 25,000). Species include (maxima) *Anser fabalis* (6000), *Anas crecca* (1700), *A. platyrhynchos* (16,000), *A. querquedula* (600), and *Aythya ferina* (1000). There is also a significant passage of waders in autumn, with (maxima) *Vanellus vanellus* (6000), *Calidris minuta* (500), *C. alpina* (800), *Philomachus pugnax* (600), *Tringa glareola* (480), and *Actitis hypoleucos* (420).

056 Stawy rybne w Niemodlinie: zespół Dąbrowa (Niemodlin fish-ponds: Dąbrowa complex) (Opole)

50°40'-50°43'N, 17°37'-17°42'E 360 ha

Unprotected; proposed Nature Reserve

The complex consists of seven ponds (varying from 6 ha to 160 ha in size), most of which were heavily modified in the period 1970-1974. Only the largest pond still has an extensive area of reeds, but three ponds have artificial islands. The whole area is surrounded by forests. Fish-farming is the principal human activity.

Breeding birds include *Botaurus stellaris* (3-4 males), *Ixobrychus minutus* (1 pair), *Ciconia nigra* (1-2 pairs), *C. ciconia* (1 pair), *Pernis apivorus* (1-2 pairs), *Milvus migrans* (1 pair), *M. milvus* (0-1 pair), *Circus aeruginosus* (8-10 pairs), *Grus grus* (1-2 pairs), *Picus canus* (2-3 pairs), and *Dryocopus martius* (3 pairs).

057 Zbiornik Turawski (Turawa Reservoir) (Opole)

50°42'-50°43'N, 18°05'-18°11'E 2000 ha

Unprotected

A storage reservoir situated in lowland and surrounded mainly with forests. There are considerable fluctuations in water-level, and large areas of sand may be exposed; the bottom substrate is sandy rather than muddy.

Breeding birds include *Limosa limosa* (1-4 pairs), *Sterna hirundo* (1-5 pairs), and *Chlidonias niger*. The reservoir is an important locality for migrating waterfowl: the total number of passage Anatidae may exceed 20,000 including *Anas crecca* (3300), *A. platyrhynchos* (18,500), and *Aythya ferina* (1000). Waders on autumn passage include *Calidris minuta* (400), *C. alpina* (400), *Gallinago gallinago* (max. 1100), and *Tringa glareola* (350 pairs).

058 Stawy rybne Łężczak (Łężczak fish-ponds) (Katowice)

50°07'-50°09'N, 18°16'-18°17'E 225 ha

Nature Reserve

A complex of nine ponds (166 ha), most of which are at least 20 per cent overgrown with *Phragmites* and *Typha*. The remainder of the area is woodland and meadows. The principal human activity is fish-farming.

Breeding birds include *Botaurus stellaris* (1-2 males), *Ixobrychus minutus* (1 pair), *Ciconia nigra* (1 pair), *Aythya nyroca* (3-7 pairs), *Pernis apivorus* (1 pair), *Milvus migrans* (1 pair), *M. milvus* (1 pair), *Circus aeruginosus* (4-5 pairs), *Picus canus* (4-7 pairs), and *Dendrocopos medius* (4-8 pairs).

059 Zbiornik Świerklaniec (Świerklaniec Reservoir) (Katowice)

50°25'-50°27'N, 18°58'-19°00'E 500 ha

Unprotected

A reservoir surrounded mainly by forests, with wet meadows to the south and east. There are also small islands with reeds. Water-level fluctuations are not very great.

Breeding birds include *Botaurus stellaris* (1 pair), *Ixobrychus minutus* (2 pairs), *Aythya nyroca* (1 pair), *Circus aeruginosus* (1 pair), *Porzana porzana* (1 pair), *Crex crex* (1 pair), *Limosa limosa* (2-4 pairs), and *Chlidonias niger* (1-2 pairs).

060 Zbiornik Goczałkowicki (Goczałkowice Reservoir) (Katowice)

49°54'-49°57'N, 18°48'-18°56'E 32,000 ha

Unprotected (although status as drinking-water reservoir means that boats are forbidden)

A very large drinking-water reservoir bordered to the north and west by wet meadows, and to the south and east by extensive areas of *Glyceria maxima* and *Typha* sp. There are seasonal fluctuations in water-level, and the reservoir is also used for fish-farming.

Breeding birds include *Phalacrocorax carbo sinensis* (21 pairs), *Botaurus stellaris* (2 males), *Ixobrychus minutus* (3 pairs), *Ciconia ciconia* (10-15 pairs), *Aythya nyroca* (6 pairs), *Circus aeruginosus* (2 pairs), *Grus grus* (1 pair), *Limosa limosa* (9-12 pairs), *Sterna hirundo* (90-100 pairs), *Chlidonias niger* (90-105 pairs), and *C. leucopterus* (1 pair).

061 Stawy rybne w Ligocie (Ligota fish-ponds) (Katowice)

49°53'N, 18°57'E 150 ha

Unprotected

A complex of ponds, all of which have been heavily modified for fish-farming purposes. The area is also used for hunting.

Breeding birds include *Botaurus stellaris* (1 pair), *Nycticorax nycticorax* (55-60 pairs; the main colony in Poland), *Circus aeruginosus* (1 pair), and *Alcedo atthis* (2 pairs).

062 Zespół stawów rybnych w Przerębie i Spytkowicach (Przeręb and Spytkowice fish-pond complex) (Bielsko)

50°01'N, 19°24'-19°29'E 746 ha (Przeręb: 396 ha; Spytkowice: 350 ha)

Unprotected; proposed Nature Reserve (parts of both complexes)

An area containing two large complexes of fish-ponds, which are separated by the valley of the River Skawa. There are 80 ha of mixed forest adjacent to Przeręb and some of the ponds are partially covered (max. 50 per cent) with *Phragmites*. Reed-cutting during the breeding season may threaten nesting species, whilst fish-eating birds such as grebes, *Ardea cinerea*, and *Larus ridibundus* are controlled.

Breeding species include *Podiceps grisegena*, *P. nigricollis*, *Botaurus stellaris* (3 pairs), *Ixobrychus minutus* (5 pairs), *Nycticorax nycticorax* (8 pairs), *Ciconia ciconia* (5-6 pairs), *Circus aeruginosus* (4 pairs), *Porzana porzana* (1 pair), *Limosa limosa* (16 pairs), *Sterna hirundo* (22 pairs), *Chlidonias niger* (10 pairs), and *Picus canus* (2 pairs).

063 Ojcowski Park Narodowy (Ojców National Park) (Kraków)

50°12'N, 19°50'E 1570 ha

National Park

The southern margins of the Kraków-Częstochowa uplands, consisting of limestone hills with numerous gorges, valleys, and caves, and the River Prądnik/Sąspówka valleys. The park area is covered with mixed *Fagus* and *Quercus/Carpinus* forest, with alpine vegetation in many rocky areas. There are some small villages within the park boundaries. There are several major problems threatening the site's future; situated between two major industrial centres (Kraków and Katowice), the park suffers from severe atmospheric pollution, and very high concentrations of sulphur dioxide are killing coniferous trees. In addition, the freshwater resources of the area are over-exploited, and there is severe pressure from tourism.

Breeding birds include *Alcedo atthis*, *Picus canus*, *Dryocopus martius*, *Ficedula parva*, *F. albicollis*, and *Emberiza hortulana*.

064 Babiogórski Park Narodowy (Babia Góra National Park) (Nowy Sącz)

49°32'N, 19°32'E 1727 ha Biosphere Reserve

National Park

A part of the Babia Góra mountain range, between 700 m and 1725 m above sea-level. Vegetation shows altitudinal variation, with forests of *Picea/Fagus* or *Abies/Fagus* at lower altitudes, and *Abies* forest on higher areas. *Pinus mugo* and alpine meadows occur above the tree-line. Human activities include tourism and forestry. Excessive development of tourism around Zawoja could threaten the site.

Breeding species include *Bonasa bonasia*, *Tetrao urogallus*, *Bubo bubo*, *Strix uralensis*, *Picus canus*, *Dryocopus martius*, *Picoides tridactylus*, *Prunella collaris*, *Turdus torquatus*, and *Ficedula parva*.

065 Tatrzański Park Narodowy (Tatra National Park) (Nowy Sącz)

49°15'N, 19°56'E 21,400 ha

National Park

The park covers all of the Polish section of the Tatras range and, lying at 800-2499 m above sea-level, includes the highest mountain region in Poland. *Picea/Abies* forests are found at lower altitudes, with *Picea* forest on the upper slopes merging into *Pinus mugo*, alpine meadows, and bare rock with permanent snow-cover. Fifty-seven per cent of the park's area consists of strict reserves where no economic activities are carried out, whilst around 30 per cent has limited forestry taking place. The area is managed for tourism, and used by scientific institutions for research/teaching. The park is severely threatened by excessive tourist development (*c*.3.5 million visitors per year), and there is illegal trade in the feathers of *Aquila chrysaetos*, which form part of the traditional local folk-costume.

Breeding birds include *Aquila chrysaetos*, *Falco peregrinus*, *Bonasa bonasia*, *Tetrao tetrix*, *T. urogallus*, *Crex crex*, *Bubo bubo*, *Aegolius funereus*, *Picus canus*, *Dryocopus martius*, *Picoides tridactylus*, *Luscinia svecica svecica*, *Turdus torquatus*, and *Tichodroma muraria*.

066 Pieniński Park Narodowy (Pieniňy National Park) (Nowy Sącz)

49°25'N, 20°24'E 2312 ha

National Park

A small group of mountains in the Carpathian range, between 420 m and 928 m above sea-level, and dominated by the peak of Trzy Korony. The rocks are mainly limestone and sandstone/shale, and are dissected by the River Dunajec. Vegetation includes *Fagus* forest, meadows, and alpine grassland. The flora and fauna of the river gorge are threatened by the construction of a hydroelectric complex on the Dunajec (only a few hectares of park will be affected).

Breeding birds include *Ciconia nigra*, *Bonasa bonasia*, *Crex crex*, *Bubo bubo*, *Aegolius funereus*, *Alcedo atthis*, *Picus canus*, *Dryocopus martius*, *Picoides tridactylus*, and *Turdus torquatus*.

067 Gorczański Park Narodowy(Gorce National Park) (Nowy Sącz)

49°32'N, 20°10'E 5908 ha

National Park

The park occupies part of the Gorce Mountains in the Beskidy range, 10 km north of the town of Nowy Targ. The altitude of the area varies from 700 m to 1228 m above sea-level and the vegetation is dominated by *Quercus/Carpinus* and *Fagus* forests, with *Abies* and *Abies/Picea* forest at higher levels. Meadow/herbaceous vegetation is scattered over the whole area and was intensively grazed until recently. Problems include plagues of destructive insects, which are threatening stands of trees, and strong grazing pressure.

Breeding species include *Ciconia nigra*, *Bonasa bonasia*, *Tetrao urogallus*, *Bubo bubo*, *Aegolius funereus*, *Picus canus*, *Dryocopus martius*, *Dendrocopos leucotos*, *Lullula arborea*, and *Turdus torquatus*.

068 Zespół stawów w Górkach (Górki fish-pond complex) (Kielce)

50°21'N, 20°44'E 350 ha

Unprotected

A large pond complex on the extensive Niecka Solecka plain, west of the Nida Valley. Meadows to the south are periodically flooded by the Vistula. Most of the ponds have extensive reedbeds, covering (on average) 30 per cent of the ponds' surface areas. The complex is used for *Cyprinus* farming. The ponds are in a high water-deficit area and are fed only by a few small ditches, which are polluted with sewage from Busko-Zdrój.

Breeding species include *Botaurus stellaris* (3 pairs), *Ixobrychus minutus* (4 pairs), *Ciconia ciconia* (4 pairs), *Aythya nyroca* (1 pair), *Circus aeruginosus* (4 pairs), *Porzana parva* (1 pair), *Limosa limosa* (10 pairs), and *Chlidonias niger* (30 pairs).

069 Zespół stawów rybnych w Młodzowie (Młodzowy fish-pond complex) (Kielce)

50°27'N, 20°32'E 115 ha

Unprotected

A compact pond complex south of Pińczów, near the River Nida; 20 ha of riverside forest border the site to the west. Some of the ponds have abundant *Phragmites* growth. The ponds are used for *Cyprinus* farming.

Breeding species include *Podiceps grisegena*, *P. nigricollis* (45 pairs), *Botaurus stellaris*, *Ixobrychus minutus*, *Anas querquedula*, *Circus aeruginosus*, *Porzana parva*, *Limosa limosa*, *Sterna hirundo*, *Chlidonias niger*, and *Luscinia svecica cyaneculus*.

070 Zespół stawów rybnych koło Grobli (Fish-pond complex near Grobla) (Tarnobrzeg)

50°31'N, 21°11'E 250 ha

Unprotected

A fish-pond complex located in the valley of the River Czarna, among mixed forest dominated by *Pinus*. Some of the ponds are covered by rushes to a considerable extent. The area is used for *Cyprinus* farming. Pollution from sewage arising from Staszów and a nearby canal, carrying waste-water from a deep-shaft sulphur mine, may threaten the site. Other problems include cutting back of reeds and shooting of grebes, herons, and raptors.

Breeding birds include *Botaurus stellaris* (1 pair), *Ixobrychus minutus* (1 pair), *Ciconia ciconia* (2 pairs), *Circus aeruginosus*, *Porzana parva*, *Sterna hirundo*, *Chlidonias niger*, and *Alcedo atthis*.

071 Stawy rybne w Osieczyskach (Osieczyska fish-ponds) (Tarnobrzeg)

50°23'N, 21°34'E 120 ha

Unprotected

A complex of ponds which are surrounded by mixed forest, except to the north-west where they are bordered by meadowland. Some of the ponds are overgrown with *Phragmites*. The ponds are used for *Cyprinus* farming. Breeding birds are disturbed by frequent reed-cutting.

Breeding species include *Podiceps grisegena*, *Ciconia ciconia*, *Bucephala clangula*, *Circus aeruginosus*, and *Sterna hirundo*.

072 Zespół stawów rybnych w Budzie Stalowskiej (Buda Stalowska fish-pond complex) (Tarnobrzeg)

50°30'N, 21°47'E 724 ha

Unprotected

The complex lies between the villages of Buda Stalowska and Grzybowe Bardo and is bordered to the south by Sandomierz Forest. The remaining parts are surrounded by wet meadows. Some ponds are densely overgrown, whilst others have islands which are important for nesting birds. The ponds are used for *Cyprinus* farming. Shooting and reed-cutting disturb birds in the breeding season.

Breeding species include *Botaurus stellaris* (5 pairs), *Ixobrychus minutus* (5 pairs), *Ciconia ciconia* (4 pairs), *Aythya nyroca* (11 pairs), *Pernis apivorus* (1 pair), *Milvus migrans*, *Haliaeetus albicilla* (feeding area for one pair nesting nearby), *Circus aeruginosus*, *C. pygargus*, *Porzana porzana*, *P. parva*, *Crex crex* (2 pairs), *Limosa limosa* (6 pairs), *Sterna hirundo* (25 pairs), *Chlidonias niger* (7 pairs), *Caprimulgus europaeus*, *Picus canus*, *Dryocopus martius*, and *Sylvia nisoria* (1 pair).

073 Zespół stawów rybnych w Lipie (Lipa fish-pond complex) (Tarnobrzeg)

50°45'N, 22°10'E 18,500 ha

Nature Reserves (several small areas); proposed Landscape Protection Area

The area consists of extensive mixed forest with *Pinus*/*Vaccinium* forest on sandy elevations and *Pinus*/moss forest with peatbogs at lower levels. There are eight groups of small fish-ponds, totalling *c.*150 ponds in all. Reed-cutting and killing of fish-eating birds are the main problems.

Breeding species include *Botaurus stellaris* (4-6 males), *Ciconia nigra* (10 pairs), *C. ciconia* (6-10 pairs), *Aythya nyroca* (2-3 pairs), *Pernis apivorus* (5+ pairs), *Milvus milvus* (1 pair), *Haliaeetus albicilla* (1 pair), *Circaetus gallicus* (2-3 pairs), *Circus aeruginosus* (12-16 pairs), *Aquila pomarina* (5 pairs), *Pandion haliaetus* (1-2 pairs), *Bonasa bonasia*, *Tetrao tetrix*, *T. urogallus*, *Porzana porzana* (6+ pairs), *P. parva*, *Crex crex*, *Grus grus* (5 pairs), *Limosa limosa* (2 pairs), *Picus canus*, and *Dryocopus martius*.

074 Lasy Janowskie (Janów Forest) (Tarnobrzeg)

50°40'N, 22°30'E 14,000 ha

Landscape Park (part); proposed area of Protected Landscape

Extensive forest, with *Pinus*/*Vaccinium* on sandy elevations, and *Pinus*/moss with peatbogs at lower levels. There are two complexes of fish-ponds in the area, totalling 180 ha. The principal human activities are forestry and fish-farming. Tree-felling and reed-cutting may adversely affect nesting birds.

Breeding species include *Ciconia nigra* (12 pairs), *C. ciconia*, *Circus aeruginosus* (1 pair), *Milvus migrans* (1 pair), *M. milvus* (1 pair), *Aquila pomarina* (5 pairs), *Bonasa bonasia* (30 pairs), *Tetrao tetrix*, *T. urogallus* (30+ males), *Grus grus* (5+ pairs), *Limosa limosa*, *Caprimulgus europaeus*, *Dryocopus martius*, *Dendrocopos medius*, *Ficedula parva*, and *Emberiza hortulana*.

075 Stawy rybne w Porębach Kupieńskich (Poręby Kupieńskie fish-pond) (Rzeszów)

50°09'N, 21°49'E 50 ha

Unprotected

A compact complex of fish-ponds, mainly small in size, and invaded by rushes to a considerable extent. The area has recently been abandoned as a site for *Cyprinus* farming, and the ponds are therefore becoming overgrown.

Breeding birds include *Podiceps grisegena*, *Anas querquedula*, *Aythya nyroca*, *Circus aeruginosus*, and *Porzana porzana*. The ponds are also used as a feeding area by *Ciconia nigra*, *Aquila pomarina* and *Pandion haliaetus*.

076 Zbiornik Rzeszowski (Rzeszów Reservoir) (Rzeszów)

50°00'N, 21°59'E 90 ha

Unprotected

A reservoir surrounded by arable fields and scattered buildings. Continuous siltation has created favourable nesting conditions for waterfowl, especially by the formation of islands. There is some disturbance from boating.

Breeding birds include *Podiceps grisegena*, *Ixobrychus minutus*, *Anas querquedula*, *Crex crex*, *Sterna hirundo*, *S. albifrons*, *Chlidonias niger*, and *Alcedo atthis*. The reservoir is also important for migrating and wintering waterfowl. Wintering Anatidae may exceed 10,000 in total.

077 Bieszczadzki Park Narodowy (Bieszczady National Park) (Krosno)

49°05'N, 22°44'E 5726 ha

National Park

The westernmost part of the Eastern Carpathians, in the region of the Bieszczady uplands, at an altitude of 750 m to 1346 m above sea-level. The mountain forests are dominated by *Fagus*, whilst *Abies*, *Picea*, and alpine meadows are found around the peaks of Tarnica, Halicz, Krzemien, and the Bukowaka/Caryńska meadows. Human activities include limited forestry. Atmospheric pollution originating in Czechoslovakia is a problem, and excess tourist development is a potential threat.

Breeding species include *Ciconia nigra*, *Pernis apivorus*, *Circaetus gallicus*, *Aquila pomarina*, *A. clanga*, *A. chrysaetos*, *Hieraaetus pennatus*, *Bonasa bonasia*, *Crex crex*, *Bubo bubo*, *Strix uralensis*, *Picus canus*, *Dendrocopos medius*, *D. leucotos*, *Picoides tridactylus*, *Turdus torquatus*, *Ficedula parva*, and *F. albicollis*.

078 Zbiornik Przemyski (Przemyśl brick-pits) (Przemyśl)

49°48'N, 22°47'E 66 ha

Unprotected; proposed Nature Reserve

The area of the proposed reserve (confirmation awaited), is mainly a working brickworks surrounded by arable fields, orchards, meadows, and private gardens. There is some general disturbance of the site, which is only 6 km from the centre of Przemyśl.

The only permanent nesting site in Poland of *Merops apiaster* (12 pairs).

079 Starorzecze Sanu koło Hurka (Former bed of River San, near Hurko) (Przemyśl)

49°47'N, 22°53'E 30 ha

Unprotected; proposed Floristic Reserve

A part of the flood-plain of the River San, containing a section of former riverbed. A 7 ha open-water area is surrounded by dense *Phragmites* and *Salix*. The area is immediately threatened by nearby gravel extraction, which will cause dramatic lowering of the water-table in the area of the old riverbed.

Breeding species include *Ixobrychus minutus*, *Anas querquedula*, *Aythya nyroca*, *Circus aeruginosus*, *Porzana porzana*, *Sterna hirundo*, *Chlidonias hybridus*, and *Alcedo atthis*.

080 Zespół stawów rybnych w Starzowie (Starzawa fish-pond complex) (Przemyśl)

49°52'N, 23°00'E 700 ha

Unprotected

A pond complex on the south-eastern margins of the Sandomierz Basin. Some of the ponds have up to 50 per cent *Phragmites* cover, and the complex is adjacent to a small riverside wood. The ponds are used for *Cyprinus* farming. Reed-cutting is frequently carried out during the nesting season.

Breeding species include *Botaurus stellaris* (1 pair), *Ixobrychus minutus* (4 pairs), *Ciconia nigra* (1 pair), *C. ciconia* (4 pairs), *Pernis apivorus* (1 pair), *Milvus migrans* (1-3 pairs), *Haliaeetus albicilla* (1 pair), *Circus aeruginosus* (2-3 pairs), *Crex crex* (2-3 pairs), *Limosa limosa* (3 pairs), *Picus canus* (1 pair), *Dendrocopos medius* (2-3 pairs), and *Luscinia svecica cyaneculus* (6-7 pairs). The area is also important for passage waterfowl, with a max. of 14,000 birds.

081 Torfowiska węglanowe koło Chełma (carbonate marshes near Chełm) (Chełm)

51°10'N, 23°30'E 1500 ha

Nature Reserves (two of four marshes); proposed Nature Reserves (remaining areas)

A complex of four carbonate marshes dominated by *Cladium mariscus* and partly overgrown with *Salix* and *Betula*. Parts of the area are used for hay production, and some of the site is threatened by drainage proposals.

Breeding birds include *Botaurus stellaris* (5 pairs), *Ixobrychus minutus* (1 pair), *Ciconia ciconia* (feeding area for 10 pairs nesting in nearby villages), *Milvus migrans* (feeding area for one pair nesting nearby), *Circus aeruginosus* (35-40 pairs), *C. pygargus* (40-45 pairs), *Tetrao tetrix* (1 pair), *Porzana porzana* (5 pairs), *P. parva* (5 pairs), *Crex crex* (3 pairs), *Grus grus* (1 pair), *Gallinago media* (5 pairs), *Limosa limosa* (70 pairs), *Chlidonias leucopterus* (5 pairs), *Asio flammeus* (1 pair), *Luscinia svecica cyaneculus* (5 pairs), and *Acrocephalus paludicola* (300-350 singing males). *Circus cyaneus* occurs on passage (4-5 roosting).

082 Bagno Bubnów (Bubnów Marshes) (Chełm)

51°20'N, 23°30'E 1000 ha

Unprotected; proposed Nature Reserve

A large area of marshes with a mosaic of thick *Salix/Betula* scrub and open *Cladium mariscus* fens. Some parts of the area are mown for hay, and the marshes are threatened by drainage proposals.

Breeding birds include *Botaurus stellaris* (1 pair), *Ciconia ciconia* (feeding area for 5 pairs nesting in nearby villages), *Circus aeruginosus* (3-5 pairs), *C. pygargus* (6-10 pairs), *Tetrao tetrix*, *Porzana porzana*, *P. parva*, *Crex crex* (3 pairs), *Gallinago media*, *Limosa limosa* (10+ pairs), *Asio flammeus* (2 pairs), and *Acrocephalus paludicola* (200 pairs).

083 Jezioro Uściwierz i przyległe torfowiska (Lake Uściwierz and adjacent marshes) (Chełm)

51°20'N, 23°05'E 600 ha

Unprotected; proposed Nature Reserve (parts of site)

A large lake (284 ha) with extensive reedbeds surrounded by a mosaic of dense *Salix/Betula* and open sedge fens. Some parts of the lake are used for recreation, which results in some disturbance of nesting birds by tourists and fishermen.

Breeding species include *Botaurus stellaris* (3-4 pairs), *Ixobrychus minutus*, *Ciconia ciconia* (5 pairs), *Milvus migrans* (hunting area for one pair nesting in nearby forest), *Circus aeruginosus* (2-4 pairs), *C. pygargus* (5 pairs), *Tetrao tetrix* (10-15 pairs), *Crex*

crex (3 pairs), *Gallinago media* (1+ pairs), *Limosa limosa* (10 pairs), *Asio flammeus* (1 pair), and *Acrocephalus paludicola* (10-30 pairs).

084 Zespół stawów rybynch w Sosnowicy (Sosnowica fish-pond complex) (Chełm)

51°30'N, 23°05'E 500 ha (not including surrounding forest)

Unprotected; proposed Ornithological Reserve

A fish-farming estate consisting of four large ponds and 60 smaller ones; most are overgrown with *Phragmites* and *Typha*. Other habitats include *Pinus* and *Fraxinus/Alnus* forest and peatbogs. Reed-cutting and control of fish-eating birds are carried out by the fish-farmers, whilst the felling of mature stands may affect birds nesting in the forest.

Breeding species include *Botaurus stellaris* (6 males), *Ciconia nigra* (1 pair nesting in the forest), *C. ciconia* (3 pairs at the fish-farm; 12 pairs in nearby villages), *Aythya nyroca* (2-3 pairs), *Pernis apivorus* (1-2 pairs), *Milvus migrans* (1 pair), *Haliaeetus albicilla* (hunting area of one pair breeding in nearby forest), *Circus aeruginosus* (9-11 pairs), *Aquila pomarina* (hunting area of one pair), *Porzana porzana* (1+ pair), *P. parva* (1+ pairs), *Grus grus* (1 pair), and *Bubo bubo* (1 pair).

085 Wisła (River Vistula) (Radom, Lublin)

51°08'-51°18'N, 21°47'-21°53'E 1300 ha

Unprotected

The channel of the Wisla (Vistula) with meanders, high banks, and numerous islands. These islands vary in character from low, bare, sandy islets to high areas overgrown with *Salix*. The banks of the river are overgrown with *Salix* thickets and stands of *Salix/-Populus*. The river itself is extensively used for navigation purposes, whilst adjacent areas are used for mowing and grazing. Damming, artificial channelling, and water pollution threaten the river and, in particular, the islands which provide the most important bird habitats.

Breeding species include *Charadrius hiaticula*, *Limosa limosa* (50 pairs), *Sterna hirundo* (200 pairs), *S. albifrons* (40 pairs), *Locustella fluviatilis*, *Remiz pendulinus*, and *Carpodacus erythrinus*. *Crex crex* probably also occurs.

086 Wisła od Dęblina do Płocka (River Vistula: Dęblin to Płock) (Siedlce, Radom, Lublin, Warszawa, Płock)

51°34'-52°32'N, 19°40'-21°36'E *c.*18,000 ha

Area of Protected Landscape (Nadwiślański; proposed for upgrading to Landscape Park); proposed Ornithological Reserves (to be within proposed Landscape Park)

A largely unregulated stretch of the Wisla with numerous islands of various types, from sandbars to well-raised vegetated areas. The river banks are largely covered with *Salix* thickets with some remnant stands of *Salix/Populus*. There is extensive grazing of sheep and cattle along some sections, with locally intensive exploitation of osier beds. The area is threatened by planned regulation of the riverbed (involving narrowing of the channel by installation of groynes). There are longer-term plans to convert the river section into a chain of reservoirs.

Breeding species include *Ixobrychus minutus* (1 pair), *Ciconia nigra* (feeding area of 5-6 pairs), *Circus aeruginosus* (feeding area of 5-6 pairs), *Crex crex* (5 pairs), *Burhinus oedicnemus* (2-3 pairs), *Charadrius dubius* (124-146 pairs), *C. hiaticula* (50-53 pairs), *Vanellus vanellus* (48 pairs), *Limosa limosa* (12-14 pairs), *Actitis hypoleucos* (40-54 pairs), *Larus melanocephalus* (3-4 pairs), *L. canus* (2825-3045 pairs), *Sterna hirundo* (1576-1690 pairs), *S. albifrons* (431-455 pairs), *Alcedo atthis* (43-52 pairs), *Luscinia svecica* (31 pairs), *Sylvia nisoria* (30 pairs), and *Lanius collurio* (15 pairs). An important area for wintering waterfowl, including (max. counts 1984-1986) *Ardea cinerea* (414), *Cygnus olor* (115), *Anas platyrhynchos* (20,071), *Bucephala clangula* (825), *Mergus albellus* (52), and *M. merganser* (1518).

087 Dolina Pilicy (River Pilica valley) (Radom)

51°36'-51°40'N, 20°35'-20°57'E 6800 ha

Included in Area of Protected Landscape

A section of the channel and flood-plain of the River Pilica, including many meanders, high banks, and some islands. The flood-plain is partially drained. The islands' characteristics are very variable with low, bare areas as well as substantial *Salix*-covered areas. The adjoining land consists of a mosaic of grass/other herbaceous plants in higher areas, and sedge/reedbed communities on lower-lying land. There are also former riverbed sections, *Salix* thickets, *Salix/Populus* stands, *Alnus* forests, and a small fish-pond complex. Human activities include grass-cutting, grazing, recreation, and *Cyprinus* farming. Planned channelling of the riverbed, drainage of wet flood-plain areas, and lower water-levels (due to dam-construction upstream) threaten the site.

Breeding species include *Botaurus stellaris* (1 pair), *Ixobrychus minutus* (2 pairs), *Ciconia nigra* (feeding area of 2 pairs), *Pernis apivorus* (feeding area of one pair), *Circus aeruginosus* (3 pairs), *C. pygargus* (2 pairs), *Porzana porzana* (2-3 pairs), *P. parva* (1 pair), *Crex crex* (10 pairs), *Limosa limosa* (100 pairs), *Sterna hirundo* (16 pairs), *S. albifrons* (13 pairs), *Chlidonias niger* (15-18 pairs), *Alcedo atthis* (max. 14 pairs), *Luscinia svecica* (12 pairs), and *Sylvia nisoria* (18-23 pairs).

088 Zbiornik Sulejowski (Sulejów Reservoir) (Piotrków)

51°21'-51°28'N, 19°52'-20°00'E 2000 ha

Included in Area of Protected Landscape

A section of the River Pilica flood-plain, which was inundated by the construction of a dam near Tomaszów. There are a number of islands, some of which have reedbed and sedge communities, and others which are partially overgrown with dry *Pinus* forest. The reservoir supplies water to the city of Lódź, and is also used for angling. Islands of importance for birds may be threatened by raising the water-level.

Breeding species include *Podiceps grisegena* (17-30 pairs), *P. nigricollis* (42 pairs), *Botaurus stellaris* (2 pairs), *Ixobrychus minutus* (2 pairs), *Circus aeruginosus* (2 pairs), *Porzana porzana* (2 pairs), *Limosa limosa* (5-8 pairs), *Sterna hirundo* (10-20 pairs), *S. albifrons* (5 pairs), *Chlidonias niger* (10 pairs), and *Coracias garrulus* (2 pairs).

089 Uroczysko Mosty-Zahajki: zbiornik i lasy (Mosty-Zahajki: reservoirs and forest) (Biała Podlaska)

51°40'N, 23°15'E 760 ha

Unprotected; proposed Nature Reserve

Two adjacent shallow storage reservoirs (390 ha and 240 ha), surrounded by mixed forest and some *Alnus* swamp (totalling 130 ha). The reservoirs are used for fish-farming, whilst the surrounding areas (beyond the forest) are used mainly as arable and grazing land. There is some disturbance of the area by hunters and fishermen.

Breeding species include *Podiceps cristatus* (70-120 pairs), *P. grisegena* (90-160 pairs), *P. nigricollis* (*c*.70 pairs), *Botaurus stellaris* (4-5 pairs), *Ixobrychus minutus* (2-4 pairs), *Ciconia nigra* (feeding area for 2 pairs), *C. ciconia* (feeding area for 10 pairs nesting in nearby villages), *Anas querquedula* (15-25 pairs), *Aythya nyroca* (4-6 pairs), *Milvus migrans* (hunting area for 1-2 pairs), *Circus aeruginosus* (25-28 pairs), *Aquila pomarina* (hunting area for 1 pair), *Porzana parva* (3-6 pairs), *Crex crex* (5-10 pairs), *Chlidonias hybridus* (8 pairs), *C. niger* (0-110 pairs), *C. leucopterus* (4 pairs), *Bubo bubo* (1 pair), *Caprimulgus europaeus* (4-8 pairs), *Luscinia svecica cyaneculus* (10-15 pairs), and *Ficedula parva* (4-5 pairs). *Pandion haliaetus* (3-4 birds) and *Philomachus pugnax* (max. 1000 birds) occur on passage, whilst *Haliaeetus albicilla* (1-2 birds) winters in the area.

090 Zespół stawów rybnych w Siemieniu i przyległe bagna (Siemień fish-pond complex and adjacent meadows) (Biała Podlaska)

51°40'N, 22°50'E 600 ha

Unprotected; proposed Ornithological Reserve

A fish-farming estate consisting of two large ponds and ten smaller ones, most of which are overgrown with *Phragmites* and *Typha*. The fish-farmers want to clear as much of the vegetation as possible, and to control fish-eating birds.

Breeding birds include *Botaurus stellaris* (8-10 males), *Ixobrychus minutus* (1 pair), *Ciconia ciconia* (3-5 pairs), *Aythya nyroca* (5-10 pairs), *Haliaeetus albicilla* (hunting area for 1 pair nesting in nearby forest), *Circus aeruginosus* (10-15 pairs), *Porzana parva* (5 pairs), *Limosa limosa* (5-10 pairs), *Sterna hirundo* (25-20 pairs), and *Chlidonias leucopterus* (0-5 pairs).

091 Bagno Całownia/lub Biel (Całowanie or Biel Fen) (Warszawa, Siedlce)

52°00'N, 21°25'E 2900 ha

Landscape Park (Mazowiecki); Area of Protected Landscape

An area of hay meadows on drained fens alongside the fully regulated River Jagodzianka. There are some marshy-fen fragments in the northern part of the valley, whilst extensive areas of meadow are overgrown by *Salix* bushes, with *Alnus* and *Alnus/Fraxinus* forest in northern/central parts. There are also several peaty hollows and dunes in the central areas. Human activities include grazing of horses and cattle, and haymaking. There is large-scale peat exploitation of the sector in Warszawa voivodship.

Breeding birds include *Ciconia nigra* (1 pair), *C. ciconia* (4 pairs), *Circus aeruginosus* (feeding area of 1-2 pairs), *C. pygargus* (2-3 pairs), *Aquila pomarina* (feeding area of 1-2 pairs), *Tetrao tetrix* (formerly bred; now extinct), *Crex crex* (6-8 pairs), *Limosa limosa* (8-10 pairs), and *Coracias garrulus* (1 pair).

092 Kompleks leśny Kryńszczak (Kryńszczak forest complex) (Siedlce)

52°00'N, 22°15'E 2400 ha

Nature Reserves (Jata: *c.*335 ha; Topór: *c.*57 ha)

A forested area dominated by *Pinus*, with both dry and wet parts. *Quercus/Carpinus*, *Alnus*, and *Fraxinus/Alnus* woodlands also occur. There are small fragments of open meadows, fields, and marshes. There are intensive forestry operations which may threaten the nesting area of some birds.

Breeding species include *Ciconia nigra* (2-3 pairs), *C. ciconia* (5-10 pairs; nesting in nearby villages), *Pernis apivorus* (2-4 pairs), *Tetrao tetrix* (3-6 pairs), *Grus grus* (1-2 pairs), *Aegolius funereus* (1 pair), *Coracias garrulus* (1-2 pairs), and *Emberiza hortulana* (12+ pairs).

093 Zespół stawów rybnych koło Kotunia (fish-pond complex near Kotuń) (Siedlce)

52°11'N, 22°09'E 380 ha

Nature Reserves (some ponds)

A complex of ponds largely overgrown with *Carex*, *Typha*, *Phragmites*, and *Salix*. The area is surrounded by meadows, arable fields, forests, and urban development. Excessive scrub-invasion may adversely affect breeding waterfowl.

Nesting species include *Botaurus stellaris* (1-2 pairs), *Ciconia nigra* (feeding area for 1-2 birds), *C. ciconia* (feeding area for 3-5 pairs), *Milvus migrans* (feeding area for 1 pair), *Circus aeruginosus* (5 pairs), *Crex crex* (1-2 pairs), *Limosa limosa* (2-4 pairs), and *Chlidonias niger* (0-24 pairs).

094 Dolina Liwca (Valley of the River Liwiec) (Siedlce)

52°00'-52°30'N, 21°32'-22°35'E 11,800 ha

Areas of Protected Landscape (Siedlce-Wegrów; River Łochów mouth)

A 140-km-long stretch of river valley, with meadows and flooded pastures on reclaimed fens and mineral soils. There are also some local areas of secondary marsh, two small

(48 ha and 70 ha) fish-pond complexes, *Alnus* carrs, fragments of *Fraxinus/Alnus* riverine woods, and *Pinus* forests along the valley sides. Human activities include grazing of cattle and haymaking. There is localised but intensive use of fertilisers, and there are plans to drain secondary marshland.

Breeding species include *Botaurus stellaris* (2 pairs), *Ciconia nigra* (feeding area of 5-6 pairs), *C. ciconia* (57 pairs), *Circus aeruginosus* (5-7 pairs), *Aquila pomarina* (1-2 pairs), *Porzana porzana* (1 pair), *Crex crex* (51 pairs), *Grus grus* (2 pairs), *Vanellus vanellus* (471-525 pairs), *Gallinago gallinago* (107-122 pairs), *G. media* (1 pair), *Limosa limosa* (195-225 pairs), *Actitis hypoleucos* (23-35 pairs), *Chlidonias niger* (24-30 pairs), *C. leucopterus* (1 pair), *Alcedo atthis* (11-13 pairs), *Coracias garrulus* (2 pairs), *Dryocopus martius* (4-7 pairs), *Lullula arborea* (12 pairs), *Anthus campestris* (14 pairs), *Luscinia svecica* (5-6 pairs), *Sylvia nisoria* (20-28 pairs), and *Emberiza hortulana* (40 pairs).

095 Dolina dolnego Bugu (lower valley of River Bug) (Biała Podlaska, Siedlce, Białystok, Łomża, Ostrołęka, Warszawa)

52°06'-52°33'N, 21°13'-23°30'E 50,000 ha

Area of Protected Landscape; proposed Landscape Park

Extensive dry pastures dominate the area; fens are mostly situated at the river mouths of tributaries to the River Bug, and around fragments of former riverbeds. The bed of the Bug is largely unaltered by man and there are numerous sandy islets, some bare, and others overgrown with *Salix* bushes. There are local remnants of *Salix/Populus* riverside forest, and well-developed *Salix* bushes alongside the Bug. The area is mainly used for grazing, and some meadows are intensively fertilised. The main threat to the more important bird habitats is higher embankment construction, which could cut off former riverbed areas from annual flood water. There are also plans to drain some of these areas. In the western part of the region, intensification of recreation (especially involving the building of holiday homes) is a problem.

Breeding birds include *Botaurus stellaris* (1 pair), *Ixobrychus minutus* (5-6 pairs), *Ciconia nigra* (1 pair; also feeding area of 8-10 pairs), *C. ciconia* (211 pairs), *Pernis apivorus* (2 pairs), *Milvus migrans* (2 pairs), *Circaetus gallicus* (1 pair), *Circus aeruginosus* (4-6 pairs), *C. pygargus* (1-3 pairs), *Aquila pomarina* (5-6 pairs), *Porzana porzana* (1-2 pairs), *P. parva* (2-3 pairs), *Crex crex* (numerous; 100+ pairs), *Grus grus* (3 pairs), *Burhinus oedicnemus* (4-5 pairs), *Charadrius dubius* (128-145 pairs), *C. hiaticula* (86-106 pairs), *Vanellus vanellus* (1198-1348 pairs), *Gallinago gallinago* (216-248 pairs), *G. media* (56 birds; 13 sites), *Limosa limosa* (488-563 pairs), *Tringa totanus* (195-228 pairs), *T. ochropus* (15 pairs), *Actitis hypoleucos* (67-84 pairs), *Sterna hirundo* (140-170 pairs), *S. albifrons* (90-100 pairs), *Chlidonias niger* (350 pairs), *Alcedo atthis* (55-65 pairs), *Coracias garrulus* (5-8 pairs), *Dryocopus martius* (7-10 pairs), *Luscinia svecica* (23-26 pairs), *Sylvia nisoria* (common in eastern part of site), and *Lanius minor* (1-2 pairs).

096 Lasy Łochowskie (Łochów Forests) (Siedlce, Ostrołeka)

52°30'N, 21°42'E 20,000 ha

Area of Protected Landscape; Nature Reserves (Jagiel: 18.5 ha; Czaplowizna: 213.2 ha; Šlize: 44.3 ha)

A fragmented forest complex in the vicinity of the Bug valley. Dry *Pinus* stands are dominant; mainly in the form of single-species plantations. There are many small river valleys and other small depressions which are covered with swampy stands of deciduous trees – e.g. *Fraxinus/Alnus* woods and *Alnus* carrs. The area is used for intensive forestry operations, which, together with increasing tourism (notably building of summer cottages), may threaten important nesting areas for birds.

Breeding species include *Ciconia nigra* (5-6 pairs), *Pernis apivorus* (1 pair), *Grus grus* (6-7 pairs), *Lullula arborea* (40-50 pairs), *Anthus campestris* (10-14 pairs), *Sylvia nisoria* (10 pairs), *Ficedula parva* (4-5 pairs), and *Emberiza hortulana* (common).

097 Puszcza Białowieska (Białowieża Forest) (Białystok)

52°40'N, 23°50'E 58,000 ha Biosphere Reserve (4700 ha); World Heritage Site

National Park (4700 ha); Nature Reserves

A forest complex with substantial swampy, deciduous stands; some of the best-preserved primary temperate forest existing in Europe. There is intensive forestry outside the protected areas, which may threaten tree-nesting birds and other species feeding in the forest.

Breeding birds include *Ciconia nigra* (23 pairs), *C. ciconia* (40 pairs), *Pernis apivorus* (50 pairs), *Circaetus gallicus* (2 pairs), *Circus pygargus* (1 pair), *Aquila pomarina* (50 pairs), *Hieraaetus pennatus* (3 pairs), *Bonasa bonasia* (common), *Tetrao tetrix*, *T. urogallus*, *Crex crex*, *Grus grus*, *Glaucidium passerinum*, *Aegolius funereus* (10 pairs), *Caprimulgus europaeus*, *Picus canus*, *Dryocopus martius* (common), *Dendrocopos medius* (numerous), *D. leucotos* (*c*.30 pairs), *Picoides tridactylus* (*c*.30 pairs), *Lullula arborea*, *Sylvia nisoria*, *Ficedula parva* (common in mature stands), and *F. albicollis* (dominant in mature stands).

098 Narwiański Park Krajobrazowy (Narew Landscape Park) (Białystok)

c.53°00'N, 23°00'E 8000+ ha

Landscape Park

A natural, permanently flooded lowland river valley transected by a complex network of meandering channels. The vegetation is dominated by mixed stands of *Glyceria* and *Phalaris*, *Carex* meadows, and reedbeds/*Salix* thickets. Human activities include cattle-grazing, haymaking, angling, and hunting. Construction of storage reservoirs upstream, and water pollution may adversely affect the area.

Breeding birds include *Botaurus stellaris* (40 pairs), *Ixobrychus minutus*, *Ciconia nigra*, *C. ciconia* (nesting nearby), *Aythya nyroca*, *Circus aeruginosus* (150-200 pairs), *C. pygargus*, *Tetrao tetrix*, *Rallus aquaticus* (300-450 pairs), *Porzana porzana* (200-450 pairs), *P. parva* (80-250 pairs), *Crex crex*, *Grus grus*, *Philomachus pugnax* (several tens of females), *Gallinago media*, *Limosa limosa* (380 pairs), *Tringa totanus* (120 pairs), *Sterna hirundo*, *Chlidonias niger* (700-1000 pairs), *Alcedo atthis*, *Luscinia svecica cyaneculus* (100 pairs), *Locustella luscinioides* (1500-2000 pairs), and *Acrocephalus paludicola*. An important area for passage waders in spring, notably for *Philomachus pugnax* (max. 4000).

099 Puszcza Knyszyńska: część środkowa (Knyszyn Forest: central part) (Białystok)

53°10'N, 23°15'E 45,000 ha

Unprotected

A forest complex, *c*.80 per cent of which are *Pinus*/*Picea*, with *c*.20 per cent deciduous and swampy stands. The area is used for intensive forestry. Excessive tree-felling, removal of mature stands, and reclamation of swampy areas threaten the site.

Breeding species include *Ciconia nigra* (5-6 pairs), *Aquila pomarina* (15-16 pairs), *Bonasa bonasia* (100+ pairs), *Grus grus* (2 pairs), *Alcedo atthis* (6 pairs), *Dryocopus martius* (21 pairs), *Dendrocopos medius* (5 pairs), *D. leucotos* (2 pairs), and *Picoides tridactylus* (2 pairs).

100 Dolina Biebrzy: basen południowy (Biebrza valley: southern basin) (Łomża)

53°14'-53°30'N, 22°25'-22°39'E *c*.30,000 ha

Unprotected; proposed Nature Reserves; proposed as part of National Park

A river valley containing fens preserved in a natural state, which form an area 30 km long and 5-12 km wide. There are also wide belts of alluvial plains with numerous oxbow lakes. Vegetation is dominated by tall sedges, with riverside reedbeds merging into moss/sedge fens, and areas overgrown with bushes. Less than ten per cent of the area is used as pasture/hay-meadows. Other human activities include hunting. Scrub invasion may threaten nesting habitats for waders.

Breeding species include *Botaurus stellaris* (14 males), *Ixobrychus minutus* (10-25 pairs), *Ciconia nigra* (4-5 pairs), *C. ciconia* (*c.*60 pairs), *Cygnus cygnus* (1 pair), *Anas querquedula*, *A. clypeata*, *Aythya nyroca* (1-3 pairs), *A. ferina* (total nesting Anatidae exceeds 5000 pairs), *Pernis apivorus* (2-3 pairs), *Haliaeetus albicilla* (1-2 pairs), *Circaetus gallicus* (1 pair), *Circus aeruginosus* (*c.*50 pairs), *C. cyaneus* (*c.*5 pairs), *C. pygargus* (25-30 pairs), *Aquila pomarina* (4-5 pairs), *A. clanga* (1-2 pairs), *Tetrao tetrix* (*c.*30 displaying males), *Porzana porzana* (*c.*700 males holding territory), *P. parva* (5-10 pairs), *Crex crex* (*c.*800 males holding territory), *Grus grus* (5-13 pairs), *Philomachus pugnax* (*c.*70 females), *Lymnocryptes minimus*, *Gallinago media* (*c.*150 displaying males), *Limosa limosa* (380 pairs), *Sterna hirundo* (10-20 pairs), *Chlidonias niger* (400-800 pairs), *C. leucopterus* (170-350 pairs), *Bubo bubo* (2-3 pairs), *Asio flammeus* (2-5 pairs), *Coracias garrulus* (2 pairs), *Dendrocopos leucotos* (2-5 pairs), *Luscinia svecica* (15-20 pairs), *Saxicola rubetra* (*c.*800 pairs), *Acrocephalus paludicola* (*c.*650 pairs), *Sylvia nisoria* (50+ pairs), and *Ficedula parva* (2-5 pairs).

101 Dolina Biebrzy: basen centralny (Biebrza valley: central basin) (Łomża)

53°30'-53°42'N, 22°26'-23°09'E 40,000 ha

Mainly unprotected; Nature Reserves (Grzędy; Czerwone Bagno); proposed National Park

A mosaic of open and scrub-covered sedge fens and grassland occupying the central part of the Biebrza valley, which was partially drained in the nineteenth century. There are two extensive areas of wet *Betula* forest, together with fragments of *Alnus/Picea* forest and *Pinus* bog forest. A number of areas next to the river are subject to spring floods. Human activities include hay production and grazing of livestock. Cessation of grassland cultivation would threaten breeding waders.

Breeding birds include *Botaurus stellaris* (4-7 males), *Ixobrychus minutus* (10-25 pairs), *Ciconia nigra* (6-10 pairs), *C. ciconia* (*c.*25 pairs), Anatidae (*c.*3000 pairs), *Pernis apivorus* (1-2 pairs), *Haliaeetus albicilla* (1 pair), *Circaetus gallicus* (0-1 pair), *Circus aeruginosus* (*c.*25 pairs), *C. cyaneus* (*c.*10 pairs), *C. pygargus* (*c.*30 pairs), *Aquila pomarina* (4-5 pairs), *Tetrao tetrix* (*c.*50 displaying males), *Porzana porzana* (*c.*700 males holding territory), *P. parva* (5-10 pairs), *Crex crex* (*c.*1000 males holding territory), *Grus grus* (11-17 pairs), *Philomachus pugnax* (*c.*150 females), *Gallinago media* (*c.*150 displaying males), *Limosa limosa* (*c.*180 pairs), *Sterna hirundo* (10-15 pairs), *Chlidonias niger* (100-150 pairs), *C. leucopterus* (65-300 pairs), *Bubo bubo* (2 pairs), *Asio flammeus* (2-5 pairs), *Coracias garrulus* (2 pairs), *Dendrocopos leucotos* (2-3 pairs), *Luscinia svecica* (10+ pairs), *Saxicola rubetra* (*c.*100 pairs), *Acrocephalus paludicola* (*c.*300 pairs), *Sylvia nisoria* (50+ pairs), and *Ficedula parva* (5-10 pairs). An important area for passage Anatidae (max. 10,000+) in spring.

102 Dolina Biebrzy: basen północny (Biebrza valley: northern basin) (Suwałki)

53°42'-53°45'N, 23°01'-23°20'E *c.*9000 ha

Unprotected

The upper course of the River Biebrza, cutting through peat deposits. The area was partially drained many years ago and presently consists of moss fens and sedge/moss fens with (on the drained parts) pasture and riverine hay-meadows. The grasslands are intensively cultivated. There is an immediate threat of further drainage, proposed by local inhabitants. Illegal fires are set by landowners almost every year.

Breeding species include *Ixobrychus minutus* (2-5 pairs), *Ciconia nigra* (2-3 pairs), *C. ciconia* (10 pairs), *Pernis apivorus* (1 pairs), *Circus aeruginosus* (5 pairs), *C. cyaneus* (3 pairs), *C. pygargus* (12 pairs), *Aquila pomarina* (1-2 pairs), *Tetrao tetrix* (*c.*20 displaying males), *Porzana porzana* (*c.*100 males holding territory), *Crex crex* (*c.*300 males holding territory), *Grus grus* (2 pairs), *Philomachus pugnax* (*c.*80 females), *Gallinago media* (*c.*70 displaying birds), *Limosa limosa* (*c.*430 pairs), *Luscinia svecica* (5+ pairs), *Acrocephalus paludicola* (*c.*80 pairs), and *Sylvia nisoria* (*c.*40 pairs).

103 Puszcza Borecka (Borecka Forest) (Suwałki)

54°02'-54°12'N, 22°00'-22°16'E 23,000 ha

Mainly unprotected; Forest Reserves (four, totalling *c.*800 ha)

A complex of largely deciduous forest with a significant admixture of *Picea*. Important bird habitats include rivulets, lakes and ponds, swampy forest areas, numerous wet grasslands scattered amongst the forest, and fragments of remnant natural forest. The whole area is used for intensive forestry which may adversely affect birds nesting in mature stands.

Breeding birds include *Ciconia nigra* (*c.*8 pairs), *Pernis apivorus*, *Haliaeetus albicilla* (2 pairs), *Aquila pomarina* (*c.*20 pairs), *Bonasa bonasia* (numerous), *Grus grus* (20-30 pairs), *Sterna hirundo*, *Bubo bubo* (probably), *Glaucidium passerinum* (probably), *Dryocopus martius*, *Dendrocopos medius*, *D. leucotos*, *Lullula arborea*, *Sylvia nisoria*, *Ficedula parva*, and *F. albicollis*.

104 Jezioro Oświn (Lake Oświn) (Suwałki)

54°18'N, 21°35'E *c.*1500 ha Ramsar Site

Nature Reserve (Jezioro Siedmiu Wysp)

A lake with vast reedbeds and many islands, surrounded by swampy *Alnus* forest and *Salix* thickets.

Breeding birds include *Botaurus stellaris* (6-7 pairs), *Milvus migrans* (1 pair), *Haliaeetus albicilla* (1 pair), *Circus aeruginosus* (20-25 pairs), *Porzana porzana* (max. 6 pairs), *P. parva* (40-45 pairs), *Crex crex* (1-3 pairs), *Grus grus* (6-7 pairs), *Sterna hirundo* (max. 10 pairs), *Chlidonias niger* (max. 50 pairs), *and Luscinia svecica* (*c.*20 pairs).

105 Jezioro Dobskie (Lake Dobskie) (Suwałki)

54°06'N, 21°37'E 1776 ha

Nature Reserve

A large freshwater lake with four islands, set in a moraine landscape. The islands are covered with deciduous woods, whilst the lake shores are bordered by meadows and fields, except to the south, where there is more woodland. Human activities include fishing. Nesting herons and cormorants have destroyed tree stands.

Breeding species include *Phalacrocorax carbo sinensis* (371 pairs in 1987), *Botaurus stellaris* (1 pair), *Milvus migrans* (2 pairs), *Circus aeruginosus* (2 pairs), *Aquila pomarina* (1 pair), *Crex crex* (2 pairs), *Grus grus* (2 pairs), and *Chlidonias niger*. *Haliaeetus albicilla* may occur throughout the year. The area is an important migration stop-over for geese (mainly *Anser albifrons*) in autumn.

106 Bagna Nietlickie (Nietlickie Marshes) (Suwałki)

53°21'-53°54'N, 21°45'-21°52'E *c.*1200 ha

Unprotected

A fen area (result of drainage of former lake) with a system of drainage canals, surrounded by wet *Betula* forest, *Alnus* swamp-forest, and meadows which are extensively used for grazing and haymaking. Other human activities include hunting. Intensive drainage at the site margins is an immediate threat.

Breeding species include *Circus aeruginosus* (7-8 pairs), *C. pygargus* (1-2 pairs), *Aquila pomarina* (3 pairs), *Tetrao tetrix*, *Porzana porzana*, *Grus grus* (*c.*10 pairs), *Chlidonias niger* (25-30 pairs), and *Luscinia svecica*. The area is used in summer/autumn by moulting Anatidae (1500) and *Grus grus* (max. 3000) occurs on autumn passage.

107 Półwysep Czarny Róg (Czarny Róg Peninsula) (Suwałki)

53°41'N, 21°49'E 600-800 ha

Unprotected

A wooded peninsula projecting into Lake Rós, with surrounding meadows and *Salix* thickets. Vegetation is dominated by coniferous forest, but some areas are covered with *Alnus* swamp forest and other deciduous forest. Human activities include agriculture, forestry, and hunting. There are plans to drain part of the site.

Breeding species include *Botaurus stellaris* (2 males), *Haliaeetus albicilla* (1 pair), *Circus aeruginosus* (2-3 pairs), *C. pygargus* (1-2 pairs), *Tetrao tetrix* (4 males), *Grus grus* (3-4 pairs), *Dryocopus martius* (3-4 pairs), and *Ficedula parva*.

108 Jezioro Łuknajno (Lake Łuknajno) (Suwałki)

53°48'-53°49'N, 21°36'-21°37'E 680 ha Biosphere Reserve; Ramsar Site

Ornithological Reserve

A very shallow eutrophic lake (av. depth 0.6 m; max. 3.0 m); *c.*75 per cent of the lake bottom is covered with *Chara* meadows. The surrounding areas include *Salix* scrub, reedbeds, and swampy *Alnus* forest. There are problems with siltation and water pollution.

Breeding birds include *Podiceps cristatus* (200 pairs), *Phalacrocorax carbo sinensis*, *Botaurus stellaris* (16-21 pairs), *Ixobrychus minutus* (2-4 pairs), *Ciconia ciconia* (2-3 pairs), Anatidae (including 5 pairs of *Netta rufina*), *Pernis apivorus* (1 pair), *Milvus migrans* (1 pair), *M. milvus* (1 pair), *Haliaeetus albicilla* (2 pairs), *Circus aeruginosus* (9-11 pairs), *C. cyaneus* (1 pair), *Aquila pomarina* (1 pair), *Pandion haliaetus* (2 pairs), *Porzana porzana* (4-7 pairs), *P. parva* (12-18 pairs), *Crex crex* (2-3 pairs), *Sterna hirundo* (5-10 pairs), *Lanius collurio* (6-10 pairs), and *Emberiza hortulana* (5-8 pairs). An important area for moulting and autumn passage wildfowl with *Cygnus olor* (max. 1500 moulting; 2200 on passage), Anatidae (10,000+ on autumn passage; including 900 *Netta rufina*), and *Fulica atra* (18,000 on autumn passage). *Grus grus* (max. 40) also occurs on autumn passage.

109 Łąki Dymerskie (Dymerskie Meadows) (Olsztyn)

53°46'-53°48'N, 20°59'-21°02'E *c.*300 ha

Unprotected

A meadow area remaining after the drainage of a lake in the 1930s, with a system of drainage canals/ditches and partially covered with reedbeds and *Salix* thickets. The surroundings are extensive arable fields. Part of the area is cultivated and attempts have been made to drain the site further.

Breeding birds include *Botaurus stellaris* (2 males), *Ciconia ciconia* (5-6 pairs), *Circus aeruginosus* (4-5 pairs), *C. pygargus* (1-2 pairs), *Porzana porzana* (6-7 pairs), *Crex crex* (7-10 pairs), and *Grus grus* (2-3 pairs). In addition, *Grus grus* (200-300) occurs on autumn passage.

110 Bartołty Wielkie (Olsztyn)

53°45'-53°48'N, 20°47'-20°51'E *c.*1400 ha

Unprotected

A moraine landscape including forested hills (conifers dominant) with scattered lakes, fish-ponds, meadows, and peatbogs. Human activities include fishing and forestry; the latter operations may adversely affect species nesting in mature stands.

Breeding birds include *Ciconia nigra* (2 pairs), *C. ciconia* (3-4 pairs), *Pernis apivorus* (2 pairs), *Milvus milvus* (1-2 pairs), *Haliaeetus albicilla* (1-2 pairs; also max. 10 wintering birds), *Circus aeruginosus* (2-3 pairs), *Aquila pomarina* (2 pairs), and *Grus grus* (3-4 pairs).

111 Jezioro Kośno (Lake Kośno) (Olsztyn)

53°37'-53°41'N, 20°39'-20°43'E *c.*1500 ha

Partly protected (1200 ha)

A freshwater lake surrounded by intensively exploited forest areas.

Breeding species include *Ciconia nigra* (1-2 pairs), *Pernis apivorus* (1-2 pairs), *Milvus migrans* (2 pairs), *Haliaeetus albicilla* (1 pair; also 6-8 wintering birds), *Circus aeruginosus* (1-2 pairs), *Aquila pomarina* (1-2 pairs), *Crex crex* (6-8 pairs), *Bubo bubo* (1 pair), *Caprimulgus europaeus*, *Dryocopus martius*, *Dendrocopos medius* (2-3 pairs), *Alcedo atthis* (1-2 pairs), and *Ficedula parva*.

112 Lasy Łańskie (Łańskie Forests) (Olsztyn)

53°33'-53°41'N, 20°27'-20°33'E *c.*4200 ha

Nature Reserve (Las Warmiński; *c.*1680 ha)

An area of mainly coniferous woodland (some deciduous) with scattered meadows and lakes. The largest lake is Łańskie (*c.*1100 ha). Human activities include forestry and hunting.

Breeding species include *Ciconia nigra* (3-4 pairs), *Pernis apivorus* (2-3 pairs), *Milvus migrans* (2-3 pairs), *Haliaeetus albicilla* (1-2 pairs), *Aquila pomarina* (1-2 pairs), *Crex crex* (6-10 pairs), *Grus grus* (4-6 pairs), *Bubo bubo* (1-2 pairs), *Alcedo atthis* (3-4 pairs), *Dryocopus martius* (common), *Dendrocopos medius* (8-10 pairs), *Lullula arborea*, and *Ficedula parva* (fairly common).

113 Dolina Czarnej (River Czarna valley) (Olsztyn)

53°30'-53°32'N, 20°36'-20°40'E *c.*700 ha

Nature Reserve (34 ha)

A river flowing through swampy *Alnus* forest, sedge-fens, wet meadows, and fragments of old *Pinus* stands. The area is intensively used for forestry.

Breeding birds include *Ciconia nigra* (2 pairs), *Pernis apivorus* (1-2 pairs), *Milvus migrans* (1-2 pairs), *M. milvus* (1 pair), *Haliaeetus albicilla* (1 pair), *Aquila pomarina* (2 pairs), *Pandion haliaetus* (2 pairs), *Tetrao tetrix* (4 males), *Grus grus* (2-3 pairs), and *Coracias garrulus* (1 pair).

114 Dolina rzeki Omulew (River Omulew valley) (Olsztyn)

53°27'-53°30'N, 20°43'-20°46'E *c.*1000 ha

Unprotected; proposed Landscape Park (part of area)

A river valley containing fens, wet meadows, and fields. Human activities include agriculture and forestry. Drainage may threaten the site.

Breeding species include *Milvus migrans* (1 pair), *Circaetus gallicus* (1 pair), *Circus aeruginosus* (2-3 pairs), *C. pygargus* (1 pair), *Aquila pomarina* (2-3 pairs), *Tetrao tetrix* (10 males), *Porzana porzana* (5-6 pairs), *Grus grus* (3-4 pairs), and *Coracias garrulus* (2-3 pairs).

115 Galwica (Olsztyn)

53°29'-53°32'N, 20°49'-20°58'E *c.*3500 ha

Nature Reserve (90 ha; proposed for extension); proposed Landscape Park

An area of mostly coniferous forest, with some patches of *Betula* and wet *Alnus* woods. Human activities include agriculture and forestry. Lake Sasek Mały is polluted with sewage, whilst intensive forestry (including afforestation of bogs and wet meadows) also threatens the area.

Breeding birds include *Ciconia ciconia* (6 pairs), *Milvus migrans* (2 pairs), *Haliaeetus albicilla* (1 pair), *Circus aeruginosus* (5 pairs), *C. pygargus* (1 pair), *Aquila pomarina* (8 pairs), *Tetrao tetrix* (10 males), *Grus grus* (10 pairs), and *Aegolius funereus* (2 males).

116 Dolina rzeki Orzyc: część górna (River Orzyc valley: upper part) (Ciechanów)

53°07'-53°15'N, 20°37'E 7000 ha

Area of Protected Landscape; proposed Ornithological Reserves (three areas)

A river valley containing marshy meadows, areas overgrown with *Salix*, numerous peat hollows, fragments of *Alnus* forest, and reedbeds. Part of the area is used for grazing/haymaking. Drainage of the marshes is the main problem.

Breeding birds include *Ciconia nigra* (feeding area for one pair), *C. ciconia* (12-15 pairs), *Pernis apivorus* (feeding area for 1-2 pairs), *Circus aeruginosus* (2-3 pairs), *C. pygargus* (2 pairs), *Aquila pomarina* (feeding area for one pair), *Tetrao tetrix* (4-8 pairs), *Crex crex* (5-10 pairs), *Grus grus* (2-3 pairs), and *Sylvia nisoria* (20-30 pairs).

117 Dolina Mławki (River Mławka valley) (Ciechanów)

53°05'N, 20°14'E 6500 ha

Included in Area of Protected Landscape; proposed Ornithological Reserve (*c.*70 ha)

The river valley is dominated by hay-meadows, some of which are partly overgrown with bushes. There is also a complex of fishponds (90 ha) and some *Alnus* and *Quercus/Carpinus* afforestation. The surrounding areas include arable fields and some settlement. Human activities include *Cyprinus* farming, grazing, and haymaking. Drainage may threaten the site.

Breeding species include *Botaurus stellaris* (1 pair), *Ciconia nigra* (1 pair), *C. ciconia* (19 pairs), *Pernis apivorus* (1 pair), *Circaetus gallicus* (1 pair), *Circus aeruginosus* (2 pairs), *C. pygargus* (1 pair), *Aquila pomarina* (0-1 pair), *Crex crex* (2 pairs), *Grus grus* (2 pairs), *Limosa limosa* (4-5 pairs), and *Lanius minor* (1 pair).

118 Łąki Raczyny (Raczyny Meadows) (Ciechanów)

53°02'N, 19°44'-19°48'E *c.*150 ha

Unprotected; protection proposed

An area of wet meadows and pastures, with *Salix* thickets and hollows left after peat-cutting. Human activities include agriculture, grazing and haymaking. Scrub invasion may threaten birds nesting in open areas.

Breeding species include *Circus aeruginosus* (1-2 pairs), *C. cyaneus* (1 pair), *C. pygargus* (2-3 pairs), *Crex crex* (1 pair), *Grus grus* (1 pair), *Limosa limosa* (8 pairs), and *Sylvia nisoria* (2 pairs).

119 Lasy Ościsłowo (Ościsłowo forest complex) (Ciechanów)

52°50'N, 20°25'E 1500 ha

Unprotected; proposed Nature Reserves (130 ha and 303 ha)

A forested area containing mature *Alnus*, *Quercus/Carpinus*, and *Pinus* stands. There is intensive forestry and the *Alnus* woods are threatened by drainage.

Breeding birds include *Ciconia nigra* (1 pair), *Pernis apivorus* (1-2 pairs), *Aquila pomarina* (0-1 pair), *Grus grus* (2 pairs), *Dryocopus martius* (4-5 pairs), *Dendrocopos medius* (2 pairs), *Lullula arborea* (5-6 pairs), *Sylvia nisoria* (3-5 pairs), and *Ficedula parva* (2 pairs).

120 Dolina dolnej Narwi i Zalew Zegrzyński (Lower Narew valley and Zegrzyński Reservoir) (Ciechanów, Warszawa)

52°25'-52°50'N, 20°47'-21°06'E *c.*12,000 ha

Included in Area of Protected Landscape; proposed for inclusion in Landscape Park

A 40-km length of the River Narew and a 30-km-long dam. The northern and western river banks are high, covered mainly with human habitation. To the south and east, embankments separate the river from meadows on its former flood-plain. The meadows are intensively farmed. Important bird habitats include oxbow lakes, *Salix* thickets, and several islands, which are used by breeding waterfowl. The banks of the dam are overgrown with emergent vegetation. Human activities include tourism and fishing, which may cause some disturbance.

Breeding birds include *Phalacrocorax carbo sinensis* (10-12 pairs), *Ixobrychus minutus* (10-12 pairs), *Ciconia nigra* (1 pair), *C. ciconia* (23 pairs), *Milvus migrans* (1 pair), *Circus aeruginosus* (4 pairs), *C. pygargus* (2 pairs), *Porzana porzana*, *Crex crex* (25+ pairs), *Limosa limosa* (50-60 pairs), *Sterna hirundo* (50 pairs), *S. albifrons* (1-2 pairs), *Chlidonias niger* (90-100 pairs), *Coracias garrulus* (1 pair), *Lullula arborea* (5-8 pairs), *Anthus campestris* (4-8 pairs), *Luscinia svecica* (2-4 pairs), and *Sylvia nisoria* (5-10 pairs). Important for wintering and passage Anatidae (maxima: 6800 winter; 11,200 spring passage; 18,200 autumn passage).

121 Puszcza Biała (Biała forest complex) (Ostrołęka)

52°35'-52°45'N, 21°30'-22°00'E 57,000 ha

Proposed for inclusion in Landscape Park

An area dominated by dry, medium-age *Pinus* stands, with locally distributed mixed *Quercus/Carpinus*, *Fraxinus/Alnus*, and *Alnus* stands. There are also meadows and *Salix* thickets in stream valleys, and two small fish-pond complexes. Exploitation for forestry is degrading the nesting habitat of larger birds.

Breeding species include *Ciconia nigra* (4-5 pairs), *C. ciconia* (15-20 pairs), *Pernis apivorus* (3-4 pairs), *Aquila pomarina* (1 pair), *Crex crex* (2+ pairs), *Grus grus* (5-7 pairs), *Chlidonias niger* (0-6 pairs), *Caprimulgus europaeus* (12+ pairs), *Coracias garrulus* (7-9 pairs), *Dendrocopos medius* (several), and *Lullula arborea* (fairly numerous).

122 Kampinoski Park Narodowy (Kampinos National Park) (Warszawa)

52°22'N, 20°20'-20°50'E 34,000 ha

National Park; Nature Reserves (ten, totalling 2029 ha)

An area dominated by dry *Pinus* stands, with some *Quercus/Carpinus* and *Alnus*. There is also a long range of dunes (up to 20 m in height). Open areas include meadows, fields, and fens. Air pollution, increasing tourism, and destruction of raptor nests by local inhabitants are problems in the area.

Breeding species include *Ciconia nigra* (8-11 pairs), *C. ciconia* (*c.*20 pairs), *Pernis apivorus* (8 pairs), *Circus aeruginosus* (2+ pairs), *C. pygargus* (1+ pairs), *Aquila pomarina* (1-3 pairs), *Crex crex* (max. 50 pairs; rapidly decreasing), *Grus grus* (5-6 pairs), *Dryocopus martius* (11-15 pairs), *Dendrocopos medius* (*c.*5 pairs), *Lullula arborea* (*c.*25 pairs), *Anthus campestris*, *Sylvia nisoria*, *Ficedula parva* (10-15 pairs), and *Emberiza hortulana* (5+ pairs).

123 Stawy rybne koło Łowicza/stawy Mysłaków (Łowicz and Mysłaków fish-ponds) (Skierniewice)

52°06'N, 20°00'E 100 ha

Unprotected

A complex of six ponds surrounded by meadows and the town of Łowicz. On average, about ten per cent of each pond is reed-covered. The complex is used for *Cyprinus* farming, and fish-eating birds are shot. Ducks are also hunted.

Breeding species include *Botaurus stellaris* (1 pair), *Ixobrychus minutus* (0-2 pairs), *Ciconia ciconia* (feeding area of 2-3 pairs), *Circus aeruginosus* (3 pairs), *Porzana porzana* (2 pairs), *P. parva* (3 pairs), *Crex crex* (1 pair), *Limosa limosa* (3 pairs), *Sterna hirundo* (5-10 pairs), and *Chlidonias niger* (15-20 pairs).

124 Stawy rybne Okręt i Rydwan (Okręt and Rydwan fish-ponds) (Skierniewice)

52°02'-52°04'N, 19°49'-19°51'E 285 ha

Unprotected; proposed Ornithological Reserve

A complex of five ponds surrounded by *Pinus* woods, fields, and meadows. The ponds have a total area of 270 ha and have between 10 and 50 per cent reed coverage. The complex is used for *Cyprinus* farming and intensive duck hunting. Fish-farmers want to reduce the areas of reeds, and fish-eating birds are shot.

Breeding species include *Botaurus stellaris* (2-3 pairs), *Ixobrychus minutus* (5 pairs), *Ciconia nigra* (feeding area for 1 pair), *C. ciconia* (3 pairs), *Circus aeruginosus* (8-10 pairs), *Porzana porzana* (2 pairs), *P. parva* (6 pairs), *Crex crex* (4 pairs), *Limosa limosa* (2 pairs), *Sterna hirundo* (0-6 pairs), *Chlidonias niger* (10-30 pairs), and *Anthus campestris* (10 pairs). In addition, a few *Haliaeetus albicilla* occur on passage.

125 Stawy rybne Walewice (Walewice fish-ponds) (Skierniewice)

52°06'N, 19°42'E 260 ha

Unprotected; proposed Ornithological Reserve

A complex of ten ponds surrounded by *Alnus* and *Pinus* forest and fields/meadows. On average, reeds cover ten per cent of the pond areas. The complex is used for *Cyprinus* farming and hunting. Fish-farmers shoot some species of fish-eating birds.

Breeding species include *Botaurus stellaris* (1 pair), *Ixobrychus minutus* (0-2 pairs), *Ciconia ciconia* (3 pairs), *Aythya nyroca* (0-3 pairs), *Circus aeruginosus* (3 pairs), *Porzana porzana* (1 pair), *P. parva* (4 pairs), *Crex crex* (2 pairs), *Sterna hirundo* (5 pairs), and *Chlidonias niger* (0-12 pairs). Also an important area for passage waders.

126 Stawy rybne Psary (Psary fish-ponds) (Skierniewice)

52°02'N, 19°39'E 120 ha

Unprotected

A complex of eight ponds, surrounded by meadows, pastures, and fields. There is a large area (1500 ha) of old forest close to the ponds; the latter are all partly (5-40 per cent) covered with reeds. The complex is used for *Cyprinus* farming and duck-hunting. Fish-farmers want to reduce the areas of reeds and to control fish-eating birds.

Breeding birds include *Botaurus stellaris* (1-2 pairs), *Ciconia nigra* (feeding area for 1 pair), *C. ciconia* (4-5 pairs), *Aythya nyroca* (2 pairs), *Circus aeruginosus* (5 pairs), *Porzana porzana* (2 pairs), *P. parva* (5 pairs), *Crex crex* (3 pairs), *Sterna hirundo* (15-20 pairs), and *Chlidonias niger* (max. 30 pairs).

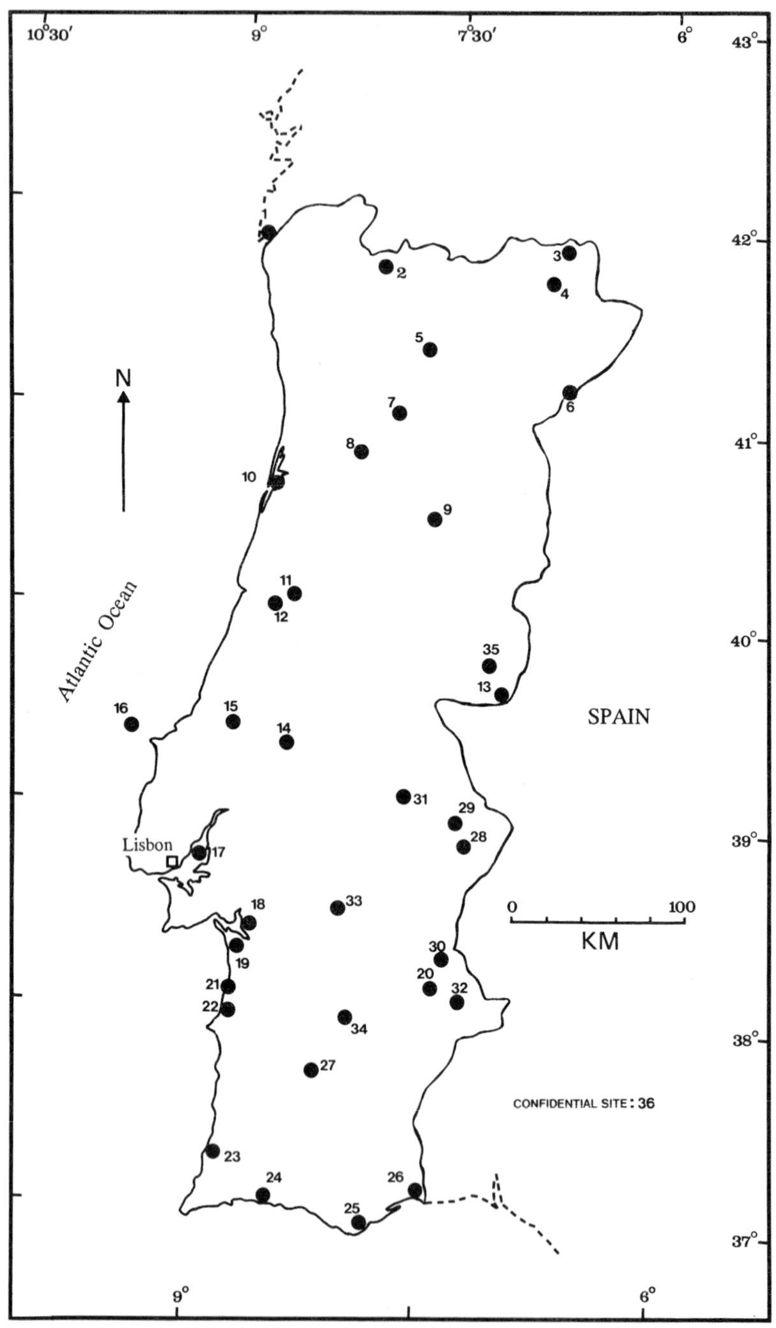

Figure 27: Map showing the location of the sites in Portugal

PORTUGAL

Little Bustard *Tetrax tetrax*

INTRODUCTION

General information

Portugal covers an area of 91,971 sq km and in 1978 had a population of 9,778,000 (an average population density of 106 persons per sq km). The original cover of deciduous and evergreen forest has been largely cleared for agriculture or converted to maquis and garigue. Topography and exposure to the Atlantic winds are highly variable, creating a remarkable abundance and diversity of climatic types.

The River Tejo may be said to divide Portugal: the country to the north is rather mountainous with some original *Quercus* forest, ericaceous heathland and plenty of *Pinus* plantations and other coniferous cover; the country to the south is best described as a succession of undulating plains cultivated with cereals, grazed with sheep, goats and cattle, or covered with Mediterranean forest, particularly *Quercus suber* (abundant as natural stands or in extensive plantations).

The long Portuguese coastline runs in a north-south and east-west direction and is largely sandy with sand-dunes and marshes, although there are stretches of cliffs and offshore rocky islands. The coastline is broken by a number of major estuaries.

There is a wide variation in the size of agricultural properties. Small family plots, intensively cultivated, predominate in well-irrigated and fertile soils in the north-west and around the major river basins, while extensive farming, forestry, and cattle-raising in vast properties still dominate in areas of poor dry soils in central and eastern Portugal. Agriculture in many areas is still traditional and labour-intensive, and mechanisation and intensive monoculture of cash crops have not been widely introduced. Afforestation of poor farmland and wasteland is having a major impact on the landscape. In 1982, a five-year programme included the planting of 910 sq km with *Pinus* and 450 sq km with *Eucalyptus*. Portugal has a thriving pulp-mill industry which has prompted the marked increase in areas of *Eucalyptus*.

Although industrialisation is not developed compared with central Europe, tourism has expanded considerably in the last few decades and is becoming increasingly important. Thus house building and tourism-orientated land speculation have been particularly intensive in the southernmost region of Algarve, threatening the local wetland systems and causing disturbance.

There is a national urge to develop fast which has accelerated since Portugal joined the European Community in 1986. The recent availability of EEC funding now ensures the feasibility of many agricultural, industrial, and other large-scale development projects that could never have been attempted previously. Agriculture is certain to modernise (with an increase in irrigation and land improvement, including improvement of meadows and grasslands), with forestry replacing marginal land. This is likely to have a major impact on Portugal's avifauna.

Ornithological importance

The coast of mainland Portugal is interesting for its breeding seabirds including *Calonectris diomedea* (100+ pairs), *Oceanodroma castro* (50 pairs on the Berlengas Islands; the only breeding site in continental Europe), *Sterna albifrons* (100+ pairs) and the drastically declining *Uria aalge ibericus* (70 pairs; over 50 per cent of the world population).

The Portuguese populations of *Ciconia nigra* (35-50 pairs) and *C. ciconia* (2000-5000 pairs) are of European importance, as are its populations of *Elanus caeruleus* (150-200 pairs), *Neophron percnopterus* (40-60 pairs), *Gyps fulvus* (100-150 pairs), *Circus pygargus* (1000-1300 pairs), *Hieraaetus fasciatus*, and *Falco naumanni* (300-500 pairs). Excluding the USSR, Portugal is with Spain the European stronghold for *Tetrax tetrax* and its population of *Otis tarda* (1015 birds) is, after Spain, Hungary and perhaps Turkey, the largest in Europe.

Of the passerines, the following species (threatened in parts of their range in Europe) are, in parts of Portugal, widely distributed and common: *Calandrella brachydactyla*, *Galerida theklae*, *Lullula arborea*, *Anthus campestris*, and *Sylvia undata*.

The major river estuaries and lagoons are important for passage and wintering waders, especially *Recurvirostra avosetta* (with very large numbers wintering on the Tejo Estuary), and for large numbers of migrant passerines, especially *Acrocephalus* warblers. Other especially noteworthy wintering species are *Phoenicopterus ruber* and *Pandion haliaetus*.

The most important bird habitats therefore are the estuaries and lagoons along both the west and south coasts, with their extensive areas of mudflats and reedbeds; the small freshwater marshes such as that at Paúl do Boquilobo and along the River Guadiana (with their large colonies of breeding Ardeidae); the upper Douro Valley, and the *Quercus suber* woodlands (particularly in the lowlands of the western half of Alentejo) for birds of prey; and the undulating and extensively cultivated or sheep-grazed plains in the central and eastern part of southern Portugal.

Conservation infrastructure and protected-area system

The Portuguese protected-area system includes the following categories of protected areas which are referred to in this inventory:

1. National/Natural Parks (Parques Nacional/Natural)
   These tend to be very large areas in remote parts of the country (normally mountain zones) where human settlement is at a relatively low density and where human activities (such as agriculture, house building and craftwork) are characteristically traditional. In such regions, which may include outstanding landscape or important fauna/flora, human communities have been managing ecosystems in the same way for long periods of time.

2. Natural Reserve (Reserve Natural)
   These are smaller areas with almost no human occupation, but with outstanding faunal and/or floral values (e.g. major roosting and breeding areas for birds).

The system also includes Protected Landscapes and Protected Monuments or Natural Features.

Ornithologists from CEMPA started a national survey in 1986 to census and monitor important bird habitats and other areas of great ornithological importance. A genuine interest in nature conservation has been growing steadily in Portugal, and spreading through the media; it has now reached most areas in the country.

International measures relevant to the conservation of sites

Portugal is a member of the European Community, has ratified the Ramsar Convention, World Heritage Convention, Bern Convention, and Bonn Convention, and is bound by the terms of the European Community's Wild Birds Directive. To date, two Ramsar Sites, 17 EEC Special Protection Areas (plus one in Madeira) and one Biosphere Reserve have been designated (all included in this inventory), as well as two Biogenetic Reserves. No natural World Heritage Sites have been designated.

Overview of the inventory

A total of 36 sites are included in the inventory covering an area of 532,000+ ha (to nearest 1000 ha). The inventory provides excellent coverage of the country's wetland sites (13 sites), of which three coastal sites (Ria de Aveiro, Tejo Estuary, and Sado Estuary) and two inland wetlands (Paúl do Boquilobo and River Guadiana) are particularly important. The main seabird site is included, and all seabirds and wetland species are therefore covered extremely well by the sites in this inventory. All of these sites are protected, except for the River Guadiana valley, either by EEC Special Protection Areas or other nationally designated protected areas.

Ten of the sites have been selected, at least partly, because they are especially important for breeding birds of prey; *Neophron percnopterus*, *Gyps fulvus*, *Circus cyaneus*, *Hieraaetus fasciatus*, and *Pandion haliaetus* are well covered (breeding sites at least) by this inventory. An additional ten sites have been selected because of their bustard populations (and for other birds of extensively cultivated/grazed land). None of these is protected at present, and it is these types of sites which are likely to be threatened by changes in agriculture, and afforestation, which will be encouraged by Portugal's membership of the European Community. Castro Verde plains (18,000 ha) are of particular significance.

The following species for which Portugal is especially important are not very well covered by this inventory: *Ciconia ciconia*, *Circus pygargus*, *Tetrax tetrax*, and *Falco naumanni*. There is also an urgent need to identify and protect the remaining large stands of *Quercus suber* woodland, which are not covered very well by this inventory, but which are important for birds of prey.

Acknowledgements

Data-sheets for all of the sites listed below were compiled at CEMPA (Centro de Estudos de Migrações e Protecção de Aves), Serviço Nacional de Parques, Reservas e Conservação da Natureza, by A. Araújo, R. Neves, M. Pinto, and R. Rufino, under the supervision of A. M. Teixeira. Additional information was provided by A. R. Johnson (Tour du Valat, France), P. D. Goriup, and N. J. Collar (ICBP Bustard Group), and R. Filipe. A. M. Teixeira provided material for the introduction.

INVENTORY

No.	Site name	Region	Criteria used to select site [see p.18]							
			0	1(i)	1(ii)	1(iii)	1(iv)	2	3	4
001	Minho and Coura Estuaries	NE							*	
002	Gerês Mountain	NE							*	
003	Montesinho Mountain	NE							*	

No.	Site name	Region	Criteria used to select site [see p.18]							
			0	1(i)	1(ii)	1(iii)	1(iv)	2	3	4
004	Nogueira Mountain	NE							*	
005	Alvão Mountain	NE							*	
006	Upper River Douro including Rivers Sabor and Águeda	NE						*	*	
007	Montemuro Mountain	NE,CO							*	
008	Arada and Freita Mountains	NE,CO							*	
009	Estrela Mountain	CO							*	
010	Ria de Aveiro	CO				*			*	
011	Paúl de Arzila	CO							*	
012	Paúl de Madriz	CO							*	
013	Upper River Tejo	CO						*	*	
014	Paúl do Boquilobo	OE				*			*	
015	Candeeiros Mountain	LA e VT							*	
016	Berlengas Islands	LA e VT							*	
017	Tejo Estuary	LA e VT				*		*	*	
018	Sado Estuary	AO				*			*	
019	Murta Dam	AO				*			*	
020	River Guadiana	AO				*		*	*	
020-1	Moinho das Fazendas	AO								
020-2	Moinho da Abóboda	AO								
021	Santo André Lagoon	AO							*	
022	Sancha Lagoon	AO							*	
023	South-west coast of Portugal	AO,AE						*	*	
024	Leixão da Gaivota	AE							*	
025	Ria Formosa (Faro Lagoon)	AE				*			*	
026	Castro Marim	AE				*		*	*	
027	Castro Verde plains	AO						*	*	
028	Elvas plains	AO						*	*	
029	Monforte plains	AO						*	*	
030	Mourão	AO						*	*	
031	Alter do Chão	AO						*	*	
032	Moura – Safara	AO						*	*	
033	Évora	AO						*	*	
034	Vidigueira – Beja	AO						*	*	
035	Idanha-a-Nova	CO						*	*	
036	Name and location confidential	AO						*	*	

NE=Norte CO=Centro OE=Oeste
LA e VT=Lisboa e Vale do Tejo AO=Alentejo AE=Algarve

Comments on the inventory

1. The material was compiled in 1987 and updated in 1988; maximum figures from the winter 1987/1988 are included for some wetland sites. Estimates of migrants on passage and wintering birds refer to average counts, except where otherwise stated.
2. The bustard populations for sites 027-036 refer to numbers of birds present at the lekking grounds, which are included in the important bird areas, where birds concentrate to perform their breeding displays; not all of these birds will actually breed within the site, for after displaying some will disperse beyond the site boundaries.
3. The site name is followed by the NUTS level 2 region, which is given in parentheses. When applying the site-selection criteria (category 3) the 'region' is this NUTS level 2 region.

Glossary

EEC SPA = European Community Special Protection Area.

001 Minho and Coura Estuaries (Norte)

41°55'N, 08°50'W 5000 ha EEC SPA

Hunting and shooting prohibited in part of area

A river estuary which forms the border with Spain, with mud- and sandflats, saltmarsh, islands, reedbeds, riparian woodland, and irrigated arable land. Human activities include agriculture, stock-farming, fishing, hunting, yachting, and tourism.

Important for warbler migration, with considerable numbers of *Acrocephalus schoenobaenus*, *A. scirpaceus*, *A. arundinaceus*, and *Phylloscopus trochilus* occurring in autumn. Winter visitors include *Phalacrocorax carbo* (100+), *Egretta garzetta*, *Cygnus columbianus* (less than 5), and *Recurvirostra avosetta*.

002 Gerês Mountain (Norte)

41°49'N, 08°07'W 80,000 ha EEC SPA

National Park (5 per cent of the area is outside the National Park)

A complex of mountains (serras) including Gerês, Amarela, Soajo, and Peneda, with altitudes up to 1500 m; some ranges running north to south and others east to west, which results in a great variation in the vegetation. The area is covered with oak (*Quercus robur*, *Q. pyrenaica*) and pine (*Pinus pinaster*, *P. sylvestris*) woodland, heathland, upland pasture, and agricultural land. Some of the mountains (mainly Gerês) have steep cliffs. Within the area there are three dams for electricity production (Vilarinho das Furna, Paradela, and Tourém). Human activities include agriculture, forestry, stock-farming, fishing; there is scattered human habitation.

Important for breeding raptors with *Pernis apivorus* (5 pairs), *Circus cyaneus* (less than 10 pairs), *C. pygargus*, *Aquila chrysaetos* (3+ pairs), *Hieraaetus pennatus*, *Falco naumanni*, *F. peregrinus*, and *Bubo bubo*. The area supports the majority of Portugal's breeding population of *Lanius collurio* as well as populations of several species which are on the south-western edge of their range including *Saxicola rubetra*, *Ficedula hypoleuca*, *Pyrrhula pyrrhula*, and *Emberiza citrinella*.

003 Montesinho Mountain (Norte)

41°55'N, 06°50'W 35,000 ha EEC SPA

Natural Park

The site includes Montesinho and Corôa mountains and reaches an altitude of 1470 m. The vegetation cover includes *Quercus pyrenaica* and pine (*Pinus pinaster*, *P. sylvestris*) woodland, *Castanea sativa* plantations, heathland, upland pasture, and agricultural land generally with a good network of hedgerows (dominated by *Fraxinus* sp. and *Ulmus* sp.). Montesinho mountain and some of the valleys have steep cliffs. Human activities include agriculture, forestry, stock-farming, hunting, and tourism. The increasing planting of heathland and pasture with conifers (mainly *Pseudotsuga* sp.) is reducing the hunting areas for large raptors, and is affecting the upland passerine community.

Important for breeding raptors including *Circaetus gallicus*, *Circus pygargus*, *Aquila chrysaetos* (2-3 pairs), *Falco peregrinus* (1-2 pairs) and possibly *Circus cyaneus*. *Caprimulgus ruficollis* possibly breeds, and it is an important area for *Anthus campestris* and *Emberiza hortulana*.

004 Nogueira Mountain (Norte)

41°42'N, 06°50'W 20,000 ha

State Managed Forest

A mountainous area (max. 1300 m) with the largest area of *Quercus pyrenaica* woodland in Portugal. The area also includes agricultural land (with hedgerows), *Castanea sativa* plantations, and heathland. Human activities include agriculture, forestry, stock-farming, and hunting.

Breeding species include *Circus pygargus*. The area of *Quercus* woodland, provided it received appropriate management, could hold good populations of *Phoenicurus phoenicurus*, *Sylvia borin*, and *Ficedula hypoleuca*, which are on the edge of their range in Portugal.

005 Alvão Mountain (Norte)

41°22'N, 07°46'W 30,000 ha

Natural Park

A mountainous area (max. 1340 m), rather flat on higher ground, and fairly steep with cliffs on the north-western and western sides. The landscape is dominated by upland pastures, heathland, agricultural land, and deciduous, coniferous and mixed woodland. On the southern side there is a reservoir for water storage. Human activities include agriculture, forestry, stock-farming, fishing, hunting; there is scattered human habitation.

A species-rich site with breeding *Circus pygargus* and *Aquila chrysaetos* (2 pairs). One of the most important areas in Portugal for *Anthus campestris* and *Emberiza hortulana*.

006 Upper River Douro including Rivers Sabor and Águeda (Norte)

41°10'N, 06°45'W 40,000 ha

Unprotected; hunting and shooting prohibited in part of area

Major river valleys which are rocky (schist and granite) and steep, with sclerophyllous scrub, evergreen woodland (*Quercus rotundifolia*, *Q. suber*, *Juniperus oxycedrus*), cliffs and agricultural land. Along the Douro itself there are five large dams for electricity production. Human activities include agriculture, stock-farming, fishing, hunting, boating, and tourism.

Breeding species include *Ciconia nigra* (15+ pairs), *Milvus migrans*, *M. milvus*, *Neophron percnopterus* (40 pairs), *Gyps fulvus* (100+ pairs; majority of Portuguese population), *Circaetus gallicus* (5+ pairs), *Aquila chrysaetos* (5+ pairs), *Hieraaetus pennatus* (5 pairs), *H. fasciatus* (5+ pairs), *Falco naumanni* (25+ pairs), *F. peregrinus* (5+ pairs), *Bubo bubo*, *Caprimulgus ruficollis*, *Coracias garrulus*, *Galerida theklae*, *Oenanthe leucura*, *Cyanopica cyana*, and *Pyrrhocorax pyrrhocorax*.

007 Montemuro Mountain (Norte, Centro)

41°01'N, 08°00'W 24,000 ha

Unprotected

A mountainous area (max. 1380 m) with gentle slopes. Landscape features include upland pasture, heathland, wet grasslands, oak woodland (*Quercus pyrenaica*), and agricultural land with a good network of hedgerows. Human activities include agriculture, stock-farming, hunting; there is scattered human habitation.

A species-rich site with breeding *Circus pygargus*; also one of the most important areas in Portugal for *Anthus campestris* and *Emberiza hortulana*.

008 Arada and Freita Mountains (Norte, Centro)

40°52'N, 08°08'W 15,000 ha

Unprotected

A mountainous area (max. 1120 m) with sclerophyllous scrub, heathland, upland pastures, coniferous and broadleaved woodland, cliffs, and agricultural land. Human activities include agriculture, forestry, stock-farming, and hunting. The area is being increasingly covered with coniferous plantations, and large-scale mineral mining exploitation is planned for the area.

Breeding species include *Circus pygargus* and *Hieraaetus fasciatus* (1-2 pairs). Also an important area for *Anthus campestris* and *Emberiza hortulana*.

009 Estrela Mountain (Centro)

40°25'N, 07°35'W 40,000 ha

Natural Park

Portugal's highest mountain (max. 2000 m) with upland pastures, heathland, deciduous, coniferous and mixed woodland, cliffs, and agricultural land. Human activities include agriculture, forestry, stock-farming, fishing, hunting, tourism; there is scattered human habitation. An effort is being made to maintain the grazing of the pastures by vast herds of sheep.

Breeding species include *Circaetus gallicus*, *Circus cyaneus*, *C. pygargus* (possibly), *Anthus campestris*, *Pyrrhocorax pyrrhocorax*, and *Emberiza hortulana*.

010 Ria de Aveiro (Centro)

40°40'N, 08°40'W 30,000 ha EEC SPA

Small Natural Reserve at São Jacinto

Estuary with extensive mud- and sandflats, islands, saltmarshes, reedbeds, saltpans (partially abandoned), and fish-ponds; bordered by agricultural land, human settlements, sand-dunes, deciduous woodland, and pine plantations. Human activities include salt extraction, agriculture, forestry, stock-farming, fishing, hunting, yachting, tourism; there is human habitation, also a port. Chemical plants and pulp-mill industries are causing severe pollution upstream and the enlargement of the dockyards, industrial development, and transformation of the saltpans for intensive fish-farming may adversely affect the area.

Breeding species include *Ixobrychus minutus*, *Ardea purpurea*, *Milvus migrans*, *Circus aeruginosus*, *Himantopus himantopus* (max. 100 pairs), *Sterna albifrons*, *Locustella luscinioides*, *Acrocephalus scirpaceus*, and *A. arundinaceus*. *Pandion haliaetus* and *Falco columbarius* occur in winter, and large numbers of passerine migrants occur in the reedbeds in autumn. An important wintering site for waders including *Recurvirostra avosetta* (1000; max. 1800), *Pluvialis squatarola* (1200; max. 1400), and *Limosa limosa* (4000; max. 4500). Wintering Anatidae have included *Anas clypeata* (700) and *Melanitta nigra* (4000).

011 Paúl de Arzila (Centro)

40°10'N, 08°33'W 300 ha EEC SPA

Natural Reserve

Freshwater marsh.

Breeding species include *Ixobrychus minutus*, *Ardea purpurea*, *Locustella luscinioides*, *Acrocephalus scirpaceus*, and *A. arundinaceus*. Considerable numbers of *Acrocephalus schoenobaenus*, *A. scirpaceus*, *A. arundinaceus*, and *Phylloscopus trochilus* occur on autumn migration. *Falco peregrinus* occurs in winter.

012 Paúl de Madriz (Centro)

40°08'N, 08°38'W 50 ha EEC SPA

Hunting and shooting prohibited

Freshwater marsh.

Breeding species include *Alcedo atthis*, *Acrocephalus scirpaceus*, *A. arundinaceus*; *Ixobrychus minutus*, *Ardea purpurea*, and *Circus aeruginosus* possibly breed. Considerable numbers of *Acrocephalus schoenobaenus*, *A. scirpaceus*, *A. arundinaceus*, and *Phylloscopus trochilus* occur on autumn migration.

013 Upper River Tejo (Centro)

39°40'N, 07°15'W 18,000 ha

Unprotected

Major, rocky (schist), steep-sided river valley, which forms the border with Spain, with sclerophyllous scrub, broadleaved evergreen woodland, and cliffs. Human activities include forestry, stock-farming, fishing, and hunting. The planting of exotic trees (*Eucalyptus* sp.) and human disturbance are problems at the site.

Very important for breeding *Ciconia nigra* (10+ pairs), *Neophron percnopterus* (10+ pairs), *Gyps fulvus* (10+ pairs), *Circaetus gallicus*, *Hieraaetus pennatus*, *H. fasciatus* (3 pairs), *Falco naumanni*, *Bubo bubo*, *Caprimulgus ruficollis*, *Galerida theklae*, *Cercotrichas galactotes*, and *Oenanthe leucura*.

014 Paúl do Boquilobo (Oeste)

39°23'N, 08°32'W 500 ha Biosphere Reserve; EEC SPA

Natural Reserve

Freshwater marshes (almost permanently flooded) with riparian woodland mainly of *Salix* sp., with agricultural land which is flooded in winter. Human activities include agriculture, stock-farming, fishing, and hunting. There is a conflict with agricultural interests, and polluted waters around the reserve represent a problem.

The area has an important heronry with breeding *Ixobrychus minutus*, *Nycticorax nycticorax* (100 pairs), *Ardeola ralloides* (max. 5 pairs), *Bubulcus ibis* (1500 pairs), *Egretta garzetta* (500 pairs), and *Ardea purpurea*. Other breeding species include *Milvus migrans*, *Chlidonias hybridus*, *Caprimulgus ruficollis*, and *Acrocephalus arundinaceus*. Wintering Anatidae include *Anas acuta* (700; max. 2000), *A. clypeata* (max. 750), and *Aythya ferina* (2000; max. 6000). *Pandion haliaetus* occurs in winter.

015 Candeeiros Mountain (Lisboa e Vale do Tejo)

39°30'N, 08°52'W 1000 ha

Natural Park

Low mountainous area (max. 487 m) with exposed bedrock (limestone), inland cliffs and caves, dry calcareous grasslands, and scrub. Human activities include stock-farming, hunting, tourism; there is scattered human habitation.

The site has an isolated population of *Pyrrhocorax pyrrhocorax* (30-40 pairs) which are breeding in unusual conditions (in natural vertical caves called 'algares'). Other breeding species include *Anthus campestris*.

016 Berlengas Islands (Lisboa e Vale do Tejo)

39°25'N, 09°37'W 400 ha EEC SPA

Natural Reserve (10 per cent of the area is outside the Natural Reserve)

Includes the Estelas and Farilhões. Islands with sea cliffs, islets, and rock stacks. Human activities include fishing and tourism. Egg-collecting, fishing techniques, and human disturbance and predation have affected the seabird colonies.

The most important locality for breeding seabirds in mainland Portugal with *Calonectris diomedea* (100+ pairs), *Oceanodroma castro* (50 pairs on Farilhão Grande; the only breeding site in continental Europe), *Phalacrocorax aristotelis* (70 pairs), *Larus fuscus* (5+ pairs), *Larus argentatus* (5000+ pairs), and *Uria aalge ibericus* (70 pairs; although the population has declined considerably from 6000 pairs in 1939). *Falco peregrinus* (1 pair) also breeds sporadically; *Rissa tridactyla* became extinct in 1983.

017 Tejo Estuary (Lisboa e Vale do Tejo)

38°45'N, 09°05'W 40,000 ha Ramsar Site (14,563 ha); EEC SPA

Mainly a Natural Reserve

Estuary with vast expanses of mudflats, saltmarshes and reedbeds. Human activities include stock-farming, fishing, hunting, fish-farming, and salt extraction. The estuary also has three large cultivated islands and is surrounded by two cities, several towns, and industry.

Breeding species include *Ixobrychus minutus*, *Ardea purpurea* (*c.*20 pairs), *Circus aeruginosus* (10 pairs), *C. pygargus* (5-10 pairs), *Porzana pusilla* (possibly), *Tetrax tetrax*, *Himantopus himantopus* (200+ pairs), *Glareola pratincola* (100+ pairs), *Sterna albifrons*, *Melanocorypha calandra*, *Acrocephalus scirpaceus*, and *A. arundinaceus*. Very important for passage and wintering waterfowl (winter data unless stated) including *Phoenicopterus ruber* (200-300; sometimes 500 with max. 800 on passage), *Anser anser* (400; max. 800), *Anas crecca* (4000; max. 6350), *A. clypeata* (1500), *Recurvirostra avosetta* (9000; max. 18,000), *Pluvialis squatarola* (5000; max. 9000), *C. alpina* (30,000), *Calidris ferruginea* (1000 on passage), *Limosa limosa* (7000; max. 12,200) and *Tringa totanus* (3000; 5000 on passage). Other species occurring include *Aquila adalberti* and *Falco peregrinus* on passage, and *Ciconia ciconia* (50), *Elanus caeruleus*, *Circus cyaneus*, and *Tetrax tetrax* (500) in winter.

018 Sado Estuary (Alentejo)

38°32'N, 08°50'W 20,000 ha EEC SPA

Natural Reserve

Estuary with vast expanses of mud- and sandflats and saltmarshes, also saltpans and fish-ponds. It is flanked by one of Portugal's main industrial areas and cultivated land. Human activities include agriculture, stock-farming, fishing, and hunting.

Breeding species include *Ixobrychus minutus*, *Ardea purpurea* (*c.*15 pairs), *Ciconia ciconia*, *Circus aeruginosus*, *C. pygargus*, *Himantopus himantopus* (60-80 pairs), *Recurvirostra avosetta* (irregular breeder), and *Glareola pratincola*. Wintering waders include *Recurvirostra avosetta* (1200; max. 2200) and *Pluvialis squatarola* (900; max. 1800). Other wintering species include *Egretta garzetta* (*c.*1000), *Pandion haliaetus*, and *Anas clypeata* (max. 1200). Otter *Lutra lutra* and Bottle-nosed Dolphin *Tursiops truncatus* occur.

019 Murta Dam (Alentejo)

38°25'N, 08°43'W 45 ha EEC SPA

A small reservoir close to the Sado Estuary with two small islets and abundant aquatic vegetation. Human activities include fishing.

Important heronry with breeding *Ixobrychus minutus*, *Bubulcus ibis* (1500 pairs), *Egretta garzetta* (500 pairs), and *Ardea purpurea* (*c.*10 pairs).

020 River Guadiana including Moinho das Fazendas and da Abóboda (Alentejo)

38°13'N, 07°28'W 25,000 ha

Unprotected

A long steep-sided river valley with flooded margins, with sclerophyllous scrub, alluvial forest, broadleaved evergreen woodland, cliffs, and agricultural land. Human activities include agriculture, stock-farming, fishing, hunting; there is scattered human habitation. A large dam is planned which, if built, will flood just over 50 per cent of the area and will affect the vegetation and fish communities downstream.

Breeding species include *Ixobrychus minutus*, *Nycticorax nycticorax* (150 pairs), *Bubulcus ibis* (8000+ pairs), *Egretta garzetta* (500+ pairs), *Ardea purpurea*, *Ciconia nigra* (2-5 pairs), *C. ciconia*, *Milvus migrans*, *Neophron percnopterus* (5 pairs), *Circaetus gallicus*, *Hieraaetus pennatus*, *H. fasciatus* (2 pairs), *Bubo bubo*, *Caprimulgus ruficollis*, *Galerida theklae*, and *Cercotrichas galactotes*. *Aegypius monachus* occurs as a non-breeder.

020-1 Moinho das Fazendas

38°05'N, 07°39'W 5 ha

Unprotected

A tract of the River Guadiana near Pedrógão with an island covered by *Salix*. Commercial and sport fishing take place.

An important heron colony with breeding *Nycticorax nycticorax*, *Bubulcus ibis*, *Egretta garzetta*, and *Ardea purpurea*.

020-2 Moinho da Abóboda

38°40'N, 07°16'W 5 ha

Unprotected

A tract of the River Guadiana near Alandroal with small islands (of *Salix* and *Tamarix*) and small temporary ponds. Commercial and sport fishing take place.

An important heron colony with breeding *Nycticorax nycticorax*, *Bubulcus ibis*, and *Egretta garzetta*.

021 Santo André Lagoon (Alentejo)

38°06'N, 08°49'W 900 ha EEC SPA

Brackish coastal lagoon with vast expanses of reedbeds, surrounded by sand-dunes, *Pinus* and *Quercus suber* woodland, and some farmland. There is a connection with the sea which is opened once a year. Human activities include cattle-rearing, fishing, hunting, agriculture, tourism; there is scattered human habitation. Parts of the reed- and sedge-beds are cut and burnt for pasture. There is pollution from urban effluents and over-intensive fishing.

Breeding species include *Ixobrychus minutus*, *Ardea purpurea*, *Circus aeruginosus*, *Elanus caeruleus*, *Porzana pusilla* (possibly), *Himantopus himantopus*, *Sterna albifrons*, *Caprimulgus ruficollis*, *Locustella luscinioides*, *Acrocephalus scirpaceus*, and *A. arundinaceus*. A variety of species occurs on passage, with considerable numbers of *Acrocephalus schoenobaenus*, *A. scirpaceus*, *A. arundinaceus*, and *Phylloscopus trochilus* on autumn migration.

022 Sancha Lagoon (Alentejo)

38°01'N, 08°50'W 50 ha EEC SPA

Brackish lagoons with reedbeds amongst sand-dunes, north of Sines. Human activities include stock-farming, fishing, and hunting.

Breeding species include *Ixobrychus minutus*, *Ardea purpurea*, *Circus aeruginosus* (2 pairs), *Himantopus himantopus*, and *Acrocephalus arundinaceus*. Large numbers of passerine migrants use the reedbeds, and *Luscinia svecica* occurs on passage and in winter.

023 South-west coast of Portugal (Alentejo, Algarve)

37°27'N, 08°48'W 30,000 ha EEC SPA

Proposed Natural Reserve; Protected Landscape

A stretch of coast comprising mainly sea cliffs, islets and rock stacks; also tidal rivers, sand-dunes, mud- and sandflats, saltmarsh, sclerophyllous scrub, and agricultural land. Human activities include agriculture, stock-farming, fishing, hunting, tourism; there is scattered human habitation.

Breeding species include *Phalacrocorax aristotelis* (50 pairs), *Egretta garzetta*, *Ciconia ciconia*, *Circaetus gallicus*, *Circus pygargus*, *Hieraaetus fasciatus* (5+ pairs), *Pandion haliaetus* (2-3 pairs; the only Portuguese breeding population), *Falco naumanni*, *F. peregrinus* (5+ pairs), *Tetrax tetrax*, *Himantopus himantopus*, *Burhinus oedicnemus*, *Caprimulgus ruficollis*, *Galerida theklae*, and *Pyrrhocorax pyrrhocorax* (20+ pairs). *Uria aalge* used to breed, but is probably now extinct.

024 Leixão da Gaivota (Algarve)

37°05'N, 08°30'W 2 ha EEC SPA

A small coastal islet, the top covered in scrub, close to the mouth of the Arade Estuary. Negligible human activity.

An important breeding colony of *Bubulcus ibis* (250+ pairs) and *Egretta garzetta* (250+ pairs), with birds feeding in the Arade Estuary.

025 Ria Formosa (Faro Lagoon) (Algarve)

37°00'N, 07°55'W 16,000 ha Ramsar Site; EEC SPA

Natural Park

A complex of coastal lagoons, vast areas of mud- and sandflats, saltmarshes, sand islands, and saltpans; partly enclosed by a belt of sand-dunes. There are also a freshwater marsh and agricultural land. Human activities include bivalve exploitation and farming, boating, fishing, hunting, tourism, intensive agriculture, and stock-farming; there are also industrial and urban areas, while Faro Airport borders the site. Possible changes include reclamation of the saltmarshes to develop Faro Airport and building of recreational facilities.

Breeding species include *Ixobrychus minutus*, *Egretta garzetta* (300 pairs), *Ardea purpurea*, *Ciconia ciconia* (10-15 pairs), *Circus pygargus* (3-5 pairs), *Porphyrio porphyrio* (15 pairs), *Himantopus himantopus* (100+ pairs), *Recurvirostra avosetta* (20+ pairs), *Glareola pratincola* (50 pairs), *Charadrius alexandrinus* (100+ pairs), *Sterna albifrons* (100+ pairs), *Caprimulgus ruficollis*, and *Acrocephalus arundinaceus*. Important for passage and wintering waders (20,000+ wintering), with *Calidris canutus* (4500), *C. alba* (500) and *Arenaria interpres* (700) on spring passage, and *Recurvirostra avosetta* (500) and *Pluvialis squatarola* (1500) in winter. In addition *Platalea leucorodia* (50), *Pandion haliaetus*, *Falco peregrinus* (1-2), *Anas clypeata* (max. 425), and *Asio flammeus* occur in winter.

026 Castro Marim (Algarve)

37°12'N, 07°26'W 2000 ha EEC SPA

Natural Reserve

A complex of saltpans, reclaimed saltmarshes, ditches, and a small area of tidal mudflats at the mouth of the River Guadiana. Human activities include salt extraction, sheep- and cattle-raising, tourism, fishing, and hunting, with agriculture in the surrounding area.

Breeding species include *Ciconia ciconia* (5-10; 15-20 pairs if nearby areas are included), *Circus pygargus*, *Falco naumanni* (formerly 10-20 pairs; the present population is smaller), *Tetrax tetrax* (10 pairs), *Himantopus himantopus* (max. 200 pairs), *Recurvirostra avosetta* (50+ pairs), *Glareola pratincola* (15-20 pairs), *Charadrius alexandrinus* (100+ pairs), *Gelochelidon nilotica* (possibly), *Sterna albifrons* (50+ pairs), *Melanocorypha calandra*, *Calandrella rufescens* (actual breeding not yet confirmed, but strongly suspected), and *Cercotrichas galactotes*. *Platalea leucorodia* (100+; max. 250) and *Phoenicopterus ruber* (50+; max. 450) occur on passage, and in winter *Recurvirostra avosetta* (100+) occurs.

027 Castro Verde plains (Alentejo)

37°40'N, 08°05'W 18,000 ha

Unprotected; hunting and shooting prohibited in part of area (50 per cent)

Agricultural fields and dry pasture. Human activities include agriculture and stock-farming; there is scattered human habitation.

Breeding species include *Ciconia ciconia*, *Milvus migrans*, *Circus pygargus*, *Tetrax tetrax* (300 pairs), *Otis tarda* (500 birds), *Burhinus oedicnemus*, *Pterocles orientalis*, *Melanocorypha calandra*, and *Galerida theklae*. *Grus grus* (120) occurs in winter.

028 Elvas plains (Alentejo)

38°55'N, 07°19'W 3000 ha

Game Reserve

Wheatfields and dry pasture. Human activities include agriculture and stock-farming; there is scattered human habitation.

Breeding species include *Ciconia ciconia* (4 pairs), *Elanus caeruleus* (3 pairs), *Milvus migrans* (2 pairs), *Circus pygargus* (15 pairs), *Falco naumanni* (10 pairs), *Tetrax tetrax* (200 pairs), *Otis tarda* (100 birds), *Burhinus oedicnemus* (15 pairs), *Pterocles orientalis*, *Coracias garrulus*, *Melanocorypha calandra*, and *Galerida theklae*. Just north of Elvas is a reservoir (Bge. do Caia), which holds small numbers of waterfowl in winter including *Netta rufina* (max. 140).

029 Monforte plains (Alentejo)

39°03'N, 07°26'W 4000 ha

Unprotected; hunting and shooting prohibited in part of area (50 per cent)

Wheatfields and dry pasture. Human activities include agriculture and stock-farming.

Breeding species include *Ciconia ciconia* (1 pair), *Elanus caeruleus*, *Circus pygargus*, *Tetrax tetrax* (50 pairs), *Otis tarda* (30 birds), *Burhinus oedicnemus*, *Melanocorypha calandra*, and *Galerida theklae*.

030 Mourão (Alentejo)

38°18'N, 07°20'W 7000 ha

Unprotected; hunting and shooting prohibited in part of area

Wheatfields and dry pasture. Human activities include agriculture and stock-farming.

Breeding species include *Elanus caeruleus*, *Milvus migrans*, *Circus pygargus*, *Tetrax tetrax*, *Otis tarda* (40 birds; also max. 200 in winter), *Pterocles orientalis*, *Melanocorypha calandra*, and *Galerida theklae*. *Grus grus* (400) occurs in winter.

031 Alter do Chão (Alentejo)

39°12'N, 07°40'W 4000 ha

Unprotected; hunting and shooting prohibited in part of area

Wheatfields and dry pasture. Human activities include agriculture and stock-farming.

Breeding species include *Circus pygargus*, *Tetrax tetrax*, *Otis tarda* (40 birds), *Burhinus oedicnemus*, *Melanocorypha calandra*, and *Galerida theklae*.

032 Moura – Safara (Alentejo)

38°09'N, 07°25'W 4000 ha

Unprotected; hunting and shooting prohibited in part of area

Wheatfields and dry pasture. Human activities include agriculture and stock-farming.

Breeding species include *Ciconia ciconia*, *Elanus caeruleus*, *Circus pygargus*, *Tetrax tetrax*, *Otis tarda* (10 birds), *Burhinus oedicnemus*, *Melanocorypha calandra*, and *Galerida theklae*. *Grus grus* (max. 120) occurs in winter.

033 Évora (Alentejo)

38°34'N, 07°54'W 10,000 ha

Unprotected; hunting and shooting prohibited in part of area

Wheatfields and dry pasture. Human activities include agriculture and stock-farming.

Breeding species include *Ciconia ciconia*, *Elanus caeruleus*, *Circus pygargus*, *Falco naumanni*, *Tetrax tetrax*, *Otis tarda* (50 birds), *Burhinus oedicnemus*, *Melanocorypha calandra*, and *Galerida theklae*. *Grus grus* (max. 200) occurs in winter.

034 Vidigueira – Beja (Alentejo)

38°12'N, 07°50'W 3000 ha

Unprotected; hunting and shooting prohibited in part of area

Wheatfields and dry pasture. Human activities include agriculture and stock-farming. Recent changes in agricultural practices are thought to have caused the disappearance of *Otis tarda*.

Breeding species include *Circus pygargus*, *Falco naumanni*, *Tetrax tetrax*, *Burhinus oedicnemus*, *Melanocorypha calandra*, and *Galerida theklae*. *Otis tarda* formerly bred, but was not present in 1987 and is thought to have moved to suitable areas nearby.

035 Idanha-a-Nova (Centro)

39°55'N, 07°15'W 5000 ha

Unprotected; hunting and shooting prohibited in part of area

Wheatfields and dry pasture. Human activities include agriculture and stock-farming.

Breeding species include *Milvus migrans*, *M. milvus*, *Circus pygargus*, *Otis tarda* (30 birds), *Burhinus oedicnemus*, *Melanocorypha calandra*, and *Galerida theklae*.

036 Name and location confidential

*c.*1000 ha

Unprotected, except some restrictions on hunting

Rolling grasslands with scattered *Quercus suber*, olive-groves and *Eucalyptus* plantations. Unintensively farmed, with stock-raising and agriculture. A road bisects the site.

An important lek for *Otis tarda*, with up to 150 present in spring, plus high breeding densities of *Tetrax tetrax*. Other breeding species include *Ciconia ciconia* (several pairs), *Elanus caeruleus* (1-2 pairs), *Circus pygargus* 1-2 pairs), *Falco naumanni* (small colony), *Burhinus oedicnemus*, *Pterocles orientalis*, *Clamator glandarius*, *Melanocorypha calandra*, *Lullula arborea*, and *Anthus campestris*.

MAIN REFERENCES

Bárcena, F., Teixeira, A. M. and Bermejo, A. Breeding seabird populations in the Atlantic sector of the Iberian Peninsula. Pp. 335-346 in Croxall, J. P., Evans, P. G. H. and Schreiber, R. W. (1984) *Status and conservation of the world's seabirds*. Cambridge, U.K.: International Council for Bird Preservation, Techn. Publ. No. 2.

Candeias, D. (1981) *As colónias de garças em Portugal*. CEMPA and SEA, Lisboa.

Candeias, D. and Araújo, A. (in press) The White Stork in Portugal. International Stork Conservation Symposium, ICBP/Vogelpark Walsrode 1985.

Fernandez-Cruz, M. and Araújo, J. eds. (1985) *Situación de la avifauna de la Peninsula Ibérica, Baleares and Macaronesia*. Sociedad Española de Ornitología, Madrid.

Grimmett, R. and Gammell, A. (1987) *Preliminary inventory of important bird areas in Spain and Portugal*. Unpublished report to the Commission of the European Communities.

Palma, L. The present situation of birds of prey in Portugal. Pp. 3-14 in Newton, I. and Chancellor, R. D. (1985) *Conservation studies on raptors*. Cambridge, U. K.: International Council for Bird Preservation, Techn. Publ. No. 5.

Rufino, R., Miranda, P. S., Pina, J. P. and Araújo, A. (1984) Límicolas invernantes na Ria de Faro: dados sobre a sua distribuição e disponibilidades alimentares. Actas do Colóquio Nacional para a Conservação das Zonas Ribeirinhas. *Bol. LPN* 18 (3a): 207-223.

Rufino, R., Araújo, A. and Abreu, M. V. Breeding raptors in Portugal: distribution and population estimates. Pp. 15-28 in Newton, I. and Chancellor, R. D. (1985) *Conservation studies on raptors*. Cambridge, U.K.: International Council for Bird Preservation, Techn. Publ. No. 5.

Rufino, R. and Araújo, A. (in press) Seasonal variation in wader numbers and distribution at the 'Ria de Faro'. WSG Bull.

Teixeira, A. M. (1984) Aves marinhas nidificantes no litoral português. Actas do Colóquio nacional para a conservação das zonas Ribeirinhas. *Bol. LPN* 18(3a): 105-115.

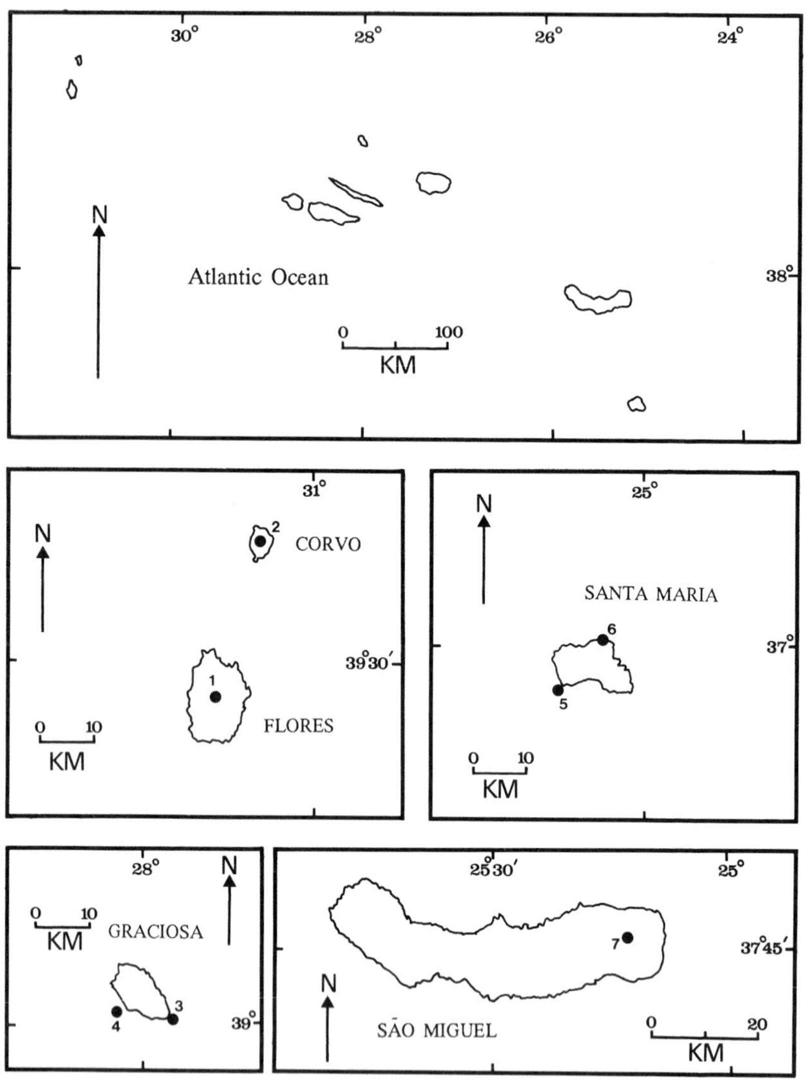

Figure 28: Map showing the location of the sites in the Azores

AZORES

Cory's Shearwater *Calonectris diomedea*

INTRODUCTION

General information

The volcanic Atlantic archipelago of the Azores (Arquipélago dos Açores) comprises nine main islands (Flores, Corvo, Terceira, São Jorge, Pico, Faial, Graciosa, São Miguel, and Santa Maria) and is situated 1420-1563 km from Europe. It occupies an area of 2344 sq km with a population of 250,000 in 1981, and reaches a maximum height of 2381 km on Pico. On the main islands there is a cultivated zone along the coast, above which the land is used mainly for grazing and forestry.

The native vegetation has been considerably altered by human activity and more than half of the islands' vascular plants are exotic, some of which are extremely competitive and invasive (e.g. *Pittosporum undulatum*, *Hedychium gardnerianun*, *Clethra arborea*, and *Gunnera* sp.). Forests have been cleared to create pastures and have been replaced by exotic plantations (principally *Acacia* spp. and *Cryptomeria japonica*), and the native laurel forest now covers only two per cent of the islands, with important remnants on São Miguel (Pico da Vara), Pico, Faial, and São Jorge.

Ornithological importance

The Azores are of considerable importance for their breeding seabirds, particularly *Calonectris diomedea* (c.500,000 pairs; perhaps 80+ per cent of the world population) which breeds on all islands and islets (although is known to have declined in some areas) and *Sterna dougallii* (600+ pairs in 1984, mainly on Flores and Graciosa; a larger population than that in either France, United Kingdom or Ireland). Other breeding seabirds include *Bulweria bulwerii, Puffinus assimilis* and *Oceanodroma castro.* The total population of all of these seabirds is poorly known (except perhaps *Sterna dougallii*).

Unlike Madeira and the Canary Islands, there are no endemic species, although a laurel-forest pigeon has become extinct in historical times (G. Le Grand pers. comm. 1987). There are a number of distinct subspecies including *Columba palumbus azorica* and *Pyrrhula pyrrhula murina* (thought by some experts to be a full species, and likely to be added to Annex I of the EEC Wild Bird Directive when it is next amended), both of which have declined dramatically.

Conservation infrastructure and protected-area system

The protected-area system is poorly developed compared with Madeira, with only three Nature/Scientific Reserves according to the Council of Europe (1987). In 1987, the Regional Forestry Service in Ponta Delgada had plans to create Forestry Reserves on a number of islands including one at Pico da Vara. It is not clear which agency is responsible for the protection of seabird sites. The tern population is probably erratic in its use of sites (sites which do not seem to be important one year may be favoured the next) and this calls for vigilance over a variety of alternative sites (E. Dunn pers. comm. 1988).

International measures relevant to the conservation of sites

The Azores is an integral part of Portugal but has its own autonomous government. Portugal is a member of the European Community, has ratified the Ramsar Convention, World Heritage Convention, Bern Convention, and Bonn Convention, and is bound by the terms of the European Community's Wild Birds Directive. These measures also apply to the Azores. To date, no Biogenetic Reserves, Special Protection Areas, Ramsar Sites, or natural World Heritage Sites have been designated in the Azores (although there is a cultural World Heritage Site).

Overview of the inventory

Seven sites have been listed; none on Terceira, São Jorge, Pico, and Faial. Six of them are seabird sites, covering some very important populations of *Calonectris diomedea* and *Sterna dougallii,* although legal protection of these is extremely poor with some of the tern colonies being especially vulnerable. Considering the importance of the Azores, especially for *Calonectris diomedea,* more seabird sites need to be protected and new sites identified; the latter requiring a full survey. Only one area of laurel forest is covered; probably the most important in the archipelago and almost certainly supporting the entire population of *Pyrrhula pyrrhula murina,* as well as all terrestrial bird species except *Coturnix coturnix* and *Passer domesticus* (an alien pest species), and probably *Scolopax rusticola.* Additional areas of laurel forest, especially those important for the pigeon, also need to be identified.

Acknowledgements

The following accounts were compiled from data-sheets submitted by G. Le Grand. Additional information was provided by D. Furtado, M. Avery (RSPB), and E. Dunn.

INVENTORY

No.	Site name	Region	Criteria used to select site [see p.18]							
			0	1(i)	1(ii)	1(iii)	1(iv)	2	3	4
001	Coast of Flores, Flores			*	*				*	
002	Coast of Corvo, Corvo			*	*				*	

No.	Site name	Region	Criteria used to select site [see p.18] 0	1(i)	1(ii)	1(iii)	1(iv)	2	3	4
003	Ilhéu de Baixo, Graciosa				*				*	
004	Ilhéu da Praia, Graciosa				*				*	
005	Ilhéu da Vila do Porto, Santa Maria				*				*	
006	Lagoinhas, Santa Maria				*				*	
007	Pico de Vara, São Miguel								*	

Comments on the inventory

1. The site name is followed by the name of the island where the site can be found. The Azores have been treated as a single 'region' when applying the site-selection criteria (category 3).

Glossary

The following Portuguese words have been used in the inventory: ilhéu = islet; pico = peak; ponta = point/peak; ribeira = river valley.

---

001 Coast of Flores, Flores

39°25'N, 31°12'W

Unprotected

Rocky coastline with cliffs, numerous islets, and stacks. Human activities include fishing, private yachting, and tourism. The tern colonies are affected by disturbance and vandalism.

Supports the richest concentration of seabirds in the Azores and the largest breeding population of *Sterna dougallii* anywhere in the eastern Atlantic. Breeding petrels and shearwaters include *Bulweria bulwerii* (less than 50 pairs), *Calonectris diomedea* (probably more than 25,000 pairs in the vicinity of Ponta do Albarnaz, Ilhéu da Gadelha, and Ilhéu de Monchique), *Puffinus assimilis* (less than 100 pairs), and possibly *P. puffinus* and *Oceanodroma castro*. Breeding terns include *Sterna dougallii* (300+ pairs, with 220 pairs between Santa Cruz and Ponta Delgada, including 110 pairs on Baixa do Moinho) and *S. hirundo* (300 pairs).

002 Coast of Corvo, Corvo

39°50'N, 31°07'W

Unprotected

Coastline with sea cliffs

Breeding seabirds include *Bulweria bulwerii* (50+ pairs), *Calonectris diomedea* (10,000+ pairs), *Puffinus assimilis* (100+ pairs), *Oceanodroma castro* (present at 2 sites), and *S. hirundo*.

003 Ilhéu de Baixo, Graciosa

39°00'N, 27°56'W 30-40 ha

Unprotected

Rocky island (basalt with an overlay of basalt boulders and ash) with a mixture of steep cliffs and sloping foreshore. Sparsely vegetated on top, mostly with tussock grass. Uninhabited but visited by fishermen, and in June 1984 there was considerable evidence of killing of seabirds for fishing bait.

Breeding seabirds include *Puffinus assimilis* (450 pairs), *Oceanodroma castro* (300 pairs), and *Sterna hirundo* (3 pairs).

004 Ilhéu da Praia, Graciosa

39°04'N, 28°04'W

Unprotected

A small island off the south-west coast of Graciosa. The island is mainly grass-covered, with rocky boulder shores.

In 1988 *Sterna dougallii* (125 pairs) and *S. hirundo* (20 pairs) were breeding.

005 Ilhéu da Vila do Porto, Santa Maria

36°56'N, 25°10'W 30-40 ha

Nature Reserve

An island surrounded by cliffs of basalt, boulders, and frothy ash. On top, a rich maritime flora including four endemic plants. Cats and possibly rats threaten the seabird colony and there are six goats present which are said to eat tern eggs.

Breeding seabirds include *Bulweria bulwerii* (less than 50 pairs), *Puffinus assimilis* (150 pairs), and *Oceanodroma castro* (100+ pairs). In 1987, 300 pairs of terns were thought to be breeding of which 75 per cent were *Sterna dougallii*. In 1988 fewer terns were present, with 20 pairs of *Sterna hirundo* and 20 pairs of *S. dougallii* estimated.

006 Lagoinhas, Santa Maria

37°00'N, 25°05'W

Unprotected; but difficult access from land

Rocky foreshore at foot of cliff on the north coast of Santa Maria.

An important breeding site for *Sterna dougallii* (*c.*100 pairs in 1988); also *S. hirundo* (*c.*25 pairs).

007 Pico da Vara, São Miguel

37°48'N, 25°15'W 400 ha

Unprotected; proposed Forestry Reserve

The Pico da Vara area includes the peaks of Pico da Vara (1110 m) and Pico Verde (931 m), and the valley of Ribeira do Guilherme. One of the few remaining areas of native laurel forest, with numerous plant species which are endemic to the Azores, or Azores and Madeira. The area is severely encroached upon by commercial forestry and invaded by exotic plants.

The area supports the only known population of *Pyrrhula pyrrhula murina* (population unknown, but approximately 40-80 pairs). Other breeding birds include *Buteo buteo rothschildi*, *Scolopax rusticola* (probably), *Columba palumbus azorica*, *Motacilla cinerea patriciae*, *Turdus merula azorensis*, *Regulus regulus azoricus*, and *Fringilla coelebs moreletti*, all of which are endemic to the Azores.

MAIN REFERENCES

Council of Europe (1987) Management of Europe's natural heritage: twenty-five years of activity. Environment Protection and Management Division, Council of Europe, Strasbourg.

Grimmett, R. and Gammell, A. (1987) *Preliminary inventory of important bird areas in Spain and Portugal*. Unpublished report to the Commission of the European Communities.

Le Grand, G., Sjogren, E. and Furtado, D. S. (1982) Pico da Vara: uma zona de valor internacional a preservar.

Le Grand, G., Emmerson, K. and Martin, A. The status and conservation of seabirds in the Macaronesian Islands. Pp. 377-391 in Croxall, J. P., Evans, P. G. H. and Schreiber, R. W. (1984) *Status and conservation of the world's seabirds*. Cambridge, U.K.: International council for Bird Preservation, Techn. Publ. No. 2.

MADEIRA

Madeira Laurel Pigeon *Columba trocaz*

INTRODUCTION

General information

The volcanic Atlantic archipelago of Madeira comprises the main island of Madeira and the islands of Porto Santo, Desertas, and Selvagens. Madeira lies 600 km from the continent of Africa (Morocco). Madeira and Porto Santo are inhabited with a population of 265,000 (in 1975) with 80 per cent of Madeira's population on the south coast; the archipelago covers an area of 798 sq km.

Madeira was almost totally covered by forest and other Macaronesian flora when first discovered in 1419. At present, 40.1 per cent of the island is forested, which comprises indigenous vegetation (13.6 per cent of island) and cultivated forest (26.5 per cent of island). The island is precipitous (max. altitude 1861 m), and the northern part, which is less suitable for human habitation, supports important areas of indigenous laurisilva (laurel forest). The land is cultivated up to *c.*1200 m (accounting for 27.1 per cent of the island), with the south coast and slopes particularly heavily cultivated.

Porto Santo, Desertas, and Selvagens are quite different, being much drier and arid with sparse vegetation. The archipelago is extremely important for its endemic and threatened invertebrate fauna, especially its land molluscs (171 endemic species), many of which have extremely restricted distributions, and its endemic flora with 145 species endemic to Madeira. An endemic subspecies of bird, *Columba palumbus maderensis*, has become extinct since 1600.

Ornithological importance

The archipelago is particularly important for its breeding seabirds. Madeira supports the only known breeding population of *Pterodroma madeira* (probably less than 30 pairs), and the Desertas support the only European population of *P. feae* (70 pairs). Both species are in the ICBP/IUCN Red Data Book. Other breeding species which are noteworthy in a European context include *Bulweria bulwerii* (3500+ pairs), *Calonectris diomedea* (15,000-30,000 pairs), *Puffinus assimilis* (5000+ pairs), *Pelagodroma marina* (20,000-30,000 pairs; the only population in Europe), *Oceanodroma castro* (2000-3000 pairs), and *Sterna dougallii* (10+ pairs). Madeira supports the endemic pigeon, *Columba trocaz* (2700+ birds), which is distributed throughout the laurel forest. Three species endemic to the Macaronesian islands, *Apus unicolor*, *Anthus berthelotii*, and *Serinus canaria*, are widely distributed in the archipelago, and are fairly common on Madeira.

The most important bird habitats therefore are the laurel forests, which are now the largest and best examples of this habitat in the world and support the endemic *Columba trocaz*, and the rocky or precipitous islands of Porto Santo, the Desertas, and Selvagens.

Conservation infrastructure and protected-area system

The Parque Natural da Madeira covers almost two-thirds of the island of Madeira and virtually all of the laurisilva. The following types of protected areas exist (which also provide stricter protection within the Natural Park) and are referred to in this inventory.

1. Strict Nature Reserve (Reserva Natural Integral)
   These are areas of total protection. Access only allowed for study/scientific purposes; cattle-grazing and hunting are prohibited.
2. Partial Nature Reserve (Reserva Natural Parcial)
   These are areas of special protection. Access is restricted; cattle-grazing is prohibited; hunting, tree-cutting, and construction are restricted.
3. Geological and high-altitude Vegetation Reserve (Geológica e de Vegetação de Altitude)
   These are all areas above 1400 m. There is full protection of flora and fauna; hunting, construction, and cattle-grazing are restricted.
4. Zone of Silence and Rest (Zona de Repouso e Silêncio)
   These are recreation areas where noise and motorised vehicles are restricted/forbidden.

The protected areas are administered by the Parque Natural da Madeira and Direção de Serviços Florestais.

International measures relevant to the conservation of sites

The archipelago of Madeira is an integral part of Portugal but has its own autonomous government. Portugal is a member of the European Community, has ratified the Ramsar Convention, World Heritage Convention, Bern Convention, and Bonn Convention, and is bound by the terms of the European Community's Wild Birds Directive. These measures also apply to Madeira. To date, there have been no Ramsar Sites or natural World Heritage Sites designated for Madeira. A single EEC Special Protection Area has, however, been designated: Ilhas Selvagens (covering 30,400 ha).

Overview of the inventory

A total of 13 sites have been listed covering an area of about 12,057 ha or 15 per cent of the archipelago. Of these 13 sites, seven are on Madeira and are covered entirely by the Parque Natural da Madeira (although the legislation regarding grazing, forestry, and forest fires is inadequately enforced) as well as being individually protected by Strict Nature Reserves and Partial Nature Reserves, etc. The inventory covers a large proportion of the laurel forest and therefore important populations of *Columba trocaz* (450+ pairs), *Accipiter nisus granti* and other subspecies endemic to the Macaronesian Islands. The most important seabird sites are completely covered; however, the islands off Porto Santo and the three Desertas islands (which are threatened and their seabird populations exploited) are still unprotected.

Acknowledgements

Data-sheets for all of the sites listed below were compiled by M. J. Biscoito (Museu Municipal do Funchal) and F. Zino (ICBP Representative for Madeira). Valuable supplementary information was provided by P. Jepson and M. Jones of Manchester University (United Kingdom). M. J. Biscoito, F. Zino and T. H. Johnson provided material for the introduction.

INVENTORY

No.	Site name	Region	Criteria used to select site [see p.18]							
			0	1(i)	1(ii)	1(iii)	1(iv)	2	3	4
001	Vale da Ribeira da Janela, Fanal and Ribeira Funda, Madeira							*	*	
002	Rabaças and Folhadal, Madeira							*	*	
003	Montado dos Pessegueiros, Cabeceira da Ribeira do Seixal and Lombo Barbinhas, Madeira							*	*	
004	Caldeirão Verde, Moquinhas, Pico Casado and Tis Amarelos, Madeira							*	*	
005	Confidential			*	*			*		
006	Fajã da Nogueira and Ribeiro Frio, Madeira							*	*	
007	Ponta da São Lourenço, Madeira								*	
008	Ilhéu de Cima, Porto Santo								*	
009	Ilhéu de Baixo and Ilhéu de Ferro, Porto Santo								*	
010	Ilhéu do Bugio, Desertas			*	*			*	*	
011	Ilhéu Chão and Deserta Grande, Desertas								*	
012	Selvagem Grande, Selvagens			*	*				*	
013	Selvagem Pequena and Ilhéu de Fora, Selvagens				*				*	

Comments on the inventory

1. The site name is followed by the name of the island where the site can be found. The archipelago of Madeira has been treated as a single 'region' when applying the site-selection criteria (category 3).
2. The table at the end of this inventory provides further information about the species and subspecies occurring at the sites.

Glossary

The following Portuguese words have been used in the inventory: ilhéu = islet; pico = peak; ponta = point/peak; ribeira = river valley; vale = valley, EEC SPA = European Community Special Protection Area.

---

001 Vale da Ribeira da Janela, Fanal, and Ribeira Funda, Madeira

32°47'N, 17°09'W 3490 ha

Partial Nature Reserve (Ribeira da Janela and Ribeira Funda); Zone of Silence and Rest (Fanal).
A steep-sided valley covered in laurel forest with many large trees in valley bottom. There is grazing by goats, pigs, horses, sheep, and cows, as well as fishing and hunting. There is also scattered human habitation.

An important area for *Columba trocaz* (100+ pairs; perhaps the densest population on the island). Other breeding species include *Puffinus puffinus* and *Accipiter nisus granti*. *Regulus ignicapillus madeirensis* and *Fringilla coelebs madeirensis*, two birds dependent on laurel forest, are very common.

002 Rabaças and Folhadal, Madeira

32°44'N, 17°03'W 702 ha

Partial Nature Reserve

Mainly laurel forest. Human activities include goat-herding and hunting. Goat-herding is carried out on a large scale and is a serious threat to the native vegetation (there is no new tree growth because of serious overgrazing).

An important area for *Columba trocaz* (50+ pairs). Other breeding species include *Puffinus puffinus* and *Accipiter nisus granti*.

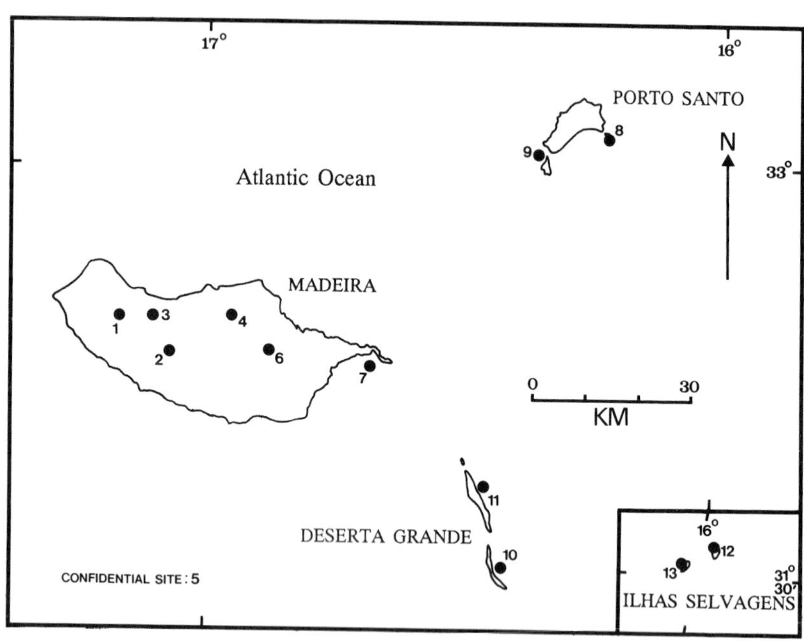

Figure 29: Map showing the location of the sites in Madeira

003 Montado dos Pessegueiros, Cabeceira da Ribeira do Seixal, and Lombo Barbinhas, Madeira

32°47'N, 17°07'W 1357 ha

Strict Nature Reserve (Montado dos Pessegueiros and Lombo Barbinhas); Partial Nature Reserve (Cabeceira da Ribeira do Seixal)

The best-preserved area of laurel forest on Madeira; there has been little human encroachment and it is almost free of livestock. Human activities include fishing.

An important area for *Columba trocaz* (125+ pairs). Other breeding species include *Calonectris diomedea* (on maritime cliffs), *Puffinus puffinus*, and *Accipiter nisus granti*.

004 Caldeirão Verde, Moquinhas, Pico Casado, and Tis Amarelos, Madeira

32°46'N, 16°58'W 1773 ha

Strict Nature Reserve (Caldeirão Verde and Pico Casado); Partial Nature Reserve (Moquinhas and Tis Amarelos)

Steep-sided valleys with dense laurel forest, high-altitude grasslands and large areas of exposed cliffs. Human activities include goat-herding, fishing, and hunting. Some parts of the area are heavily overgrazed by goats and pigs despite being strictly protected.

An important area for *Columba trocaz* (100+ pairs) and *Accipiter nisus granti*. *Regulus ignicapillus madeirensis* and *Fringilla coelebs madeirensis* are common in the forested areas.

005 Confidential

*c.*1900 ha

Geological and high-altitude Vegetation Reserve

A precipitous mountainous area with cliffs and ridges partly covered in scrub and grassland. The area is severely overgrazed, resulting in erosion. Supports a high-altitude, indigenous flora with several endemic species.

Supports the only known breeding site of *Pterodroma madeira* in the world with less than 10 pairs attempting, but failing, to breed in 1985 and 1986. In 1987, 2-3 pairs almost certainly bred successfully. Other breeding species include *Buteo buteo harterti*.

006 Fajã da Nogueira and Ribeiro Frio, Madeira

32°44'N, 16°53'W 693 ha

Strict Nature Reserve (Fajã da Nogueira); Partial Nature Reserve (Ribeiro Frio)

Mainly laurel forest (with some of the biggest trees on Madeira). Human activities include agriculture, forestry, fishing, hunting, tourism; there is scattered human habitation.

An important area for *Columba trocaz* (75+ pairs). Other breeding species include *Puffinus puffinus* and *Accipiter nisus granti*. *Regulus ignicapillus madeirensis* and *Fringilla coelebs madeirensis* are common.

007 Ponta de São Lourenço, Madeira

32°44'N, 16°42'W 281 ha

Partial Nature Reserve (Ponta de São Lourenço); Strict Nature Reserve (Ilhéu dos Desembarcadouros)

A rocky peninsula and islands that comprise the eastern tip of Madeira, with sea cliffs, mainly covered by scrub and grassland. Human activities include cattle-grazing, hunting, tourism (it is a very popular area during summer), and there is scattered human habitation. The main problems are overgrazing, predation of seabirds by fishermen, and illegal sand extraction. The area contains one of the most important fossil beds on the island and Ilhéu dos Desembarcadouros is an important area for plants because it is separated from the mainland and therefore not grazed.

Breeding species include *Bulweria bulwerii*, *Calonectris diomedea*, *Puffinus assimilis*, *Oceanodroma castro*, and *Sterna hirundo* (10+ pairs). It is one of the best sites on the island for *Petronia petronia madeirensis* and *Sylvia conspicillata bella*. *Sterna dougallii* occurs on passage (and possibly breeds) and the area is important for passerine migrants.

008 Ilhéu de Cima, Porto Santo

33°03'N, 16°16'W 29 ha

Unprotected

Island off Porto Santo. Introduced rabbits have caused considerable destruction to the vegetation, and now the lighthouse is no longer manned the nesting seabirds are subject to human persecution.

An important site for breeding seabirds including *Bulweria bulwerii*, *Calonectris diomedea*, *Puffinus assimilis*, *Oceanodroma castro*, and *Sterna hirundo*. *Sterna dougallii* occurs on passage.

009 Ilhéu de Baixo and Ilhéu de Ferro, Porto Santo

33°01'N, 16°23'W 145 ha

Unprotected

Two islands off the south-east corner of Porto Santo. Human activities include fishing. The seabird colonies, still exploited by local fishermen, are subject to human disturbance, and grazing by rabbits on Ilhéu de Baixo is causing serious erosion. Ilhéu de Baixo has important fossil beds, including corals.

An important site for breeding seabirds including *Bulweria bulwerii*, *Calonectris diomedea*, *Puffinus assimilis*, *Oceanodroma castro*, and *Sterna hirundo*. *Sterna dougallii* occurs on passage.

010 Ilhéu do Bugio, Desertas

32°25'N, 16°26'W 333 ha

Unprotected

An elongated island of precipitous basalt rock which is overgrazed by introduced goats and rabbits (resulting in soil and vegetation loss). There are two plateaus of relatively flat grassland with a good depth of earth; the northern plateau has comparatively little vegetation. Annual illegal expeditions are mounted by fishermen to collect seabirds (originally aimed at collecting juvenile *Calonectris diomedea*, they have become progressively indiscriminate) and there has been an increase in the number of private yachts visiting the Desertas resulting in greater human disturbance. There have been frequent calls to include this island in a national park but it is still unprotected. In the last year, permanent wardens have been stationed on the island and this has apparently reduced human disturbance and persecution of the seabirds.

An extremely important site for breeding seabirds, particularly for *Pterodroma feae* (70+ pairs; of a world population of only a few hundred pairs, so that protection of the grassy plateau where the species burrows and breeds is particularly urgent). Other breeding seabirds include *Bulweria bulwerii* (150+ pairs), *Calonectris diomedea* (150+ pairs), *Puffinus assimilis*, and *Oceanodroma castro* (200+ pairs).

011 Ilhéu Chão and Deserta Grande, Desertas

32°32'N, 16°31'W 1089 ha

Unprotected

Two islands with introduced goats and rabbits (Deserta Grande only). Fishermen illegally kill large numbers of seabirds. The Mediterranean Monk Seal *Monachus monachus* breeds on Deserta Grande but has almost been exterminated by the use of fishing nets and dynamite.

Important for breeding seabirds including *Bulweria bulwerii*, *Calonectris diomedea*, *Puffinus assimilis*, *Oceanodroma castro*, and *Sterna hirundo*. *Sterna dougallii* occurs on passage.

012 Selvagem Grande, Selvagens

30°09'N, 15°52'W 245 ha Part of EEC SPA (Ilhas Selvagens: 30,400 ha)

Strict Nature Reserve

Rocky island. Despite being permanently wardened, a certain amount of human predation of *Calonectris diomedea* takes place.

This is one of the most important Procellariidae colonies in the North Atlantic with *Bulweria bulwerii* (500+ pairs), *Calonectris diomedea* (10,000+ pairs), *Puffinus assimilis* (1000+ pairs), *Oceanodroma castro* (500+ pairs), *Pelagodroma marina* (9000+ pairs). *Asio flammeus* (less than 10) occurs in winter.

013 Selvagem Pequena and Ilhéu de Fora, Selvagens

30°02'N, 16°02'W 20 ha Part of EEC SPA (Ilhas Selvagens: 30,400 ha)

Strict Nature Reserve

Islands with rock stacks and sand-dunes. There are no rabbits and the vegetation is in a natural state, with at least two endemic plant species. *Calonectris diomedea* is systematically killed each year.

Very important for breeding seabirds with *Bulweria bulwerii*, *Calonectris diomedea* (50 pairs), *Oceanodroma castro*, *Pelagodroma marina* (10,000+ pairs; with site no. 12 the only breeding site in Europe), *Sterna dougallii* (5+ pairs), and *S. hirundo*; *S. fuscata* has been observed on several occasions and has bred.

Macaronesian bird species present at sites in Madeira.

Species	Site Number												
	1	2	3	4	5	6	7	8	9	10	11	12	13
Pterodroma madeira					*								
Pterodroma feae										*			
Columba trocaz	*	*	*	*		*							
Apus unicolor	*	*	*	*	*		*	*	*		*		
Anthus berthelotii	*	*	*	*	*		*	*	*	*	*	*	
Serinus canaria		*	*				*		*	*	*		

Macaronesian bird subspecies present at sites in Madeira.

Species	Site Number												
	1	2	3	4	5	6	7	8	9	10	11	12	13
Accipiter nisus granti	*	*	*	*		*							
Buteo buteo harterti	*	*	*	*	*	*	*		*	*	*		
Falco tinnunculus canariensis	*	*	*	*	*	*	*	*	*	*	*	*	
Coturnix coturnix confisa		*		*									
Columba livia atlantis	*	*	*				*	*	*		*		
Tyto alba schmitzi	*	*	*			*				*	*		
Motacilla cinerea schmitzi	*	*	*	*		*							
Turdus merula cabreae	*	*	*	*	*	*							
Sylvia conspicillata bella							*						
Sylvia atricapilla heineken	*		*	*		*							
Regulus ignicapillus madeirensis	*	*	*	*		*							
Fringilla coelebs madeirensis	*		*	*		*							
Carduelis carduelis parva			*			*	*						
Carduelis cannabina nana			*				*						
Petronia petronia madeirensis							*						

MAIN REFERENCES

Bannerman, D. A. and Bannerman, W. A. (1965) *Birds of the Atlantic Islands, Vol. II. A history of the birds of Madeira, the Desertas and the Porto Santo Islands*. Oliver and Boyd, Edinburgh.

Bernström, J. (1951) Checklist of the breeding birds of the archipelago of Madeira. *Biol. Mus. Funchal* 5(14): 64-82.

Collar, N. J. and Stuart, S. N. (1985) *Threatened birds of Africa and related islands. The ICBP/IUCN Red Data Book, Part 1.* Cambridge, U.K.: International Council for Bird Preservation and World Conservation Monitoring Centre.

Fernandez-Cruz, M. and Araújo, J. eds. (1985) *Situación de la avifauna de la Peninsula Ibérica, Baleares and Macaronesia*. Sociedad Española de Ornitología, Madrid.

Grimmett, R. and Gammell, A. (1987) *Preliminary inventory of important bird areas in Spain and Portugal.* Unpublished report to the Commission of the European Communities.

Johnson, T. H. (in prep.) *Biodiversity and conservation in the Atlantic Ocean*. Cambridge, U.K.: International Council for Bird Preservation, ICBP Monograph.

Jones, M. J. *et al.* (1986) A survey of the distribution, density and habitat preferences of the Long-toed Pigeon Columba trocaz *on Madeira*. Unpublished report, pp. 117

Le Grand, G., Emmerson, K. and Martin, A. The status and conservation of seabirds in the Macaronesian Islands. Pp. 377-391 in Croxall, J. P., Evans, P. G. H. and Schreiber, R. W. (1984) *Status and conservation of the world's seabirds*. Cambridge, U.K.: International Council for Bird Preservation, Techn. Publ. No. 2.

Mougin, J.-L. and Stahl, J.-C. (1982) Essai de dénombrement des Puffins Cendrés *Calonectris diomedea borealis* de l'Ile Selvagem Grande (30°09'N, 15°52'W) en 1980. *Bocagiana* 63: 1-17.

Mougin, J.-L., Roux, F., Stahl, J.-C. and Jouanin, Chr. (1984) L'évolution des effectifs des Puffins Cendrés *Calonectris diomedea borealis* de l'Ile Selvagem Grande (30°09'N, 15°52'W) de 1980 à 1983. *Bocagiana* 75: 1-8.

Mougin, J.-L., Jouanin, Chr., Roux, F. and Stahl, J.-C., (1984) Démographie du Puffin Cendré de l'Ile Selvagem Grande. *La Vie des Sciences, Comptes Rendus, ser. gén.* 1(5): 351-366.

Zino, F. and Zino, P. A. (1986) An account of the habitat, feeding habits, density, breeding and need of protection of the Long-toed Wood Pigeon, *Columba trocaz Bocagiana* 97: 1-16.

Zino, P. A. (1969) Observations sur *Columba trocaz. Oiseaux et R.F.O.* 39: 261-264.

Zino, P. A. and Zino, F. (1986) Contribution to the study of the petrels of the genus *Pterodroma* in the archipelago of Madeira. *Bol. Mus. Mun. Funchal* 38(180): 141-165.

ROMANIA

Red-breasted Goose *Branta ruficollis*

INTRODUCTION

General information

Romania covers an area of 237,500 sq km and in 1988 had a population of 23 million (an average population density of 97 persons per sq km). Thirty-one per cent of the country is occupied by mountains (above 800 m), 36 per cent by hills and plateaus (200-800 m), and 33 per cent by plains (under 200 m). In the centre of the country lies the Transylvanian Plateau which is surrounded by the Carpathian Mountains that reach a maximum altitude of 2544 m (Moldoveanu). Beyond the Carpathians are the sub-Carpathian hills and then the plains which reach the Danube to the south and Black Sea to the east.

Agricultural land covers 149,800 sq km (63 per cent of the land surface), of which 99,040 sq km is arable land and 44,260 sq km is meadows and pastures. Forests, mostly deciduous, cover 63,400 sq km (26.7 per cent of the land surface). Alpine and subalpine vegetation occurs in the high mountains above 1600-1700 m; it comprises mainly herbaceous species with areas of *Pinus mugo*, *Juniperus*, and *Salix*. The montane vegetation, partly cleared for pasture, comprises three zones: a *Picea* and *Abies* zone at high altitude; an intermediate zone of mixed woodland; and a *Fagus* zone at lower altitude. The natural vegetation of the hills and plateaus is mainly *Fagus* and *Quercus*, but these regions are now partly covered with secondary grasslands and extensive areas of agricultural land.

The plains are predominantly agricultural land with remnant areas of *Quercus* woodland, steppe-woodland, and steppe (particularly in the south-east). There are important areas of wet meadows and riverine forests of *Salix*, *Populus*, and *Quercus* along the main rivers.

There are many wetlands along the Danube (Dunărea), which forms the southern border of the country and then flows north entering the Black Sea via a huge delta (one of the least-developed major deltas in Europe). Extensive drainage has been carried out, mainly in the Danube valley, since 1945. For example, the extensive area of lakes and marshes between Brăila and Hîrşova, and the string of lakes between Hîrşova and Călăraşi have been drained and converted to farmland. Furthermore, drainage has significantly reduced the size of Lake Suhaia (Balta Suhaia) and Lake Brateş (Lacul Brateş) near Galati. Lake Greaca (Balta Greaca) and Lake Potelu (Balta Potelu) have now disappeared, and Lake Călăraşi (Lacul Călăraşi) has been converted to fish-ponds. In addition, a major programme to develop the Danube Delta is currently being implemented which aims to reclaim *c.*97,000 ha of the Delta, mainly for agriculture. By 1987, some 50,000 ha of agricultural land had been created.

The loss of such wetland habitats has been partly compensated for by the construction of water reservoirs and fish-ponds. These newly created areas are important for passage migrants and winter visitors, but not as breeding habitats (although, owing to their silting and to the development of aquatic vegetation, several have become suitable for breeding birds).

Ornithological importance

In the Carpathians important breeding species include *Charadrius morinellus* (2-4 pairs) and *Eremophila alpestris* (20 pairs), which breed on the high alpine plateaus and are of considerable biogeographical interest. Other species breeding in the Carpathians include *Aquila chrysaetos* (*c.*25 pairs), *Tetrao tetrix* (150 birds), *T. urogallus* (12,000 birds), *Glaucidium passerinum*, *Strix uralensis*, *Aegolius funereus* (very scarce), *Dendrocopos leucotos*, and *Picoides tridactylus*.

Areas of steppe and unimproved grassland have been much reduced; breeding species include *Circus macrourus*, *Otis tarda* (100 birds; declining steadily since World War Two), *Burhinus oedicnemus*, *Melanocorypha calandra*, *Calandrella brachydactyla*, and *Oenanthe pleschanka*.

Raptor populations have declined greatly, although breeding species still include *Haliaeetus albicilla* (6-8 pairs), *Accipiter brevipes*, *Aquila pomarina*, *A. heliaca* (*c.*60 pairs), *Falco naumanni* (120-130 pairs) and *Falco cherrug*, as well as those species mentioned above.

Romania has particularly important breeding populations of wetland species including *Pelecanus onocrotalus* (2500 pairs; the largest breeding population in Europe), *P. crispus* (perhaps now only 25-40 pairs; the Danube Delta population having seriously declined), *Phalacrocorax carbo sinensis* (3000 pairs), *P. pygmeus* (3500 pairs), *Egretta garzetta* (1600 pairs), *Nycticorax nycticorax* (3000+ pairs), *Plegadis falcinellus* (1500 pairs), *Platalea leucorodia* (75 pairs), *Ardeola ralloides* (2000+ pairs), *Grus grus* (2-3 pairs), *Tadorna ferruginea* (small numbers), *Recurvirostra avosetta* (200 pairs), *Glareola pratincola*, *G. nordmanni*, *Larus melanocephalus*, and *Sterna sandvicensis* (1700 pairs).

The wetlands and surrounding agricultural land of the Danube Delta and Dobrogea support very large numbers of wintering wildfowl, including especially large numbers of *Anser albifrons*, *Branta ruficollis* (max. 25,000), *Anas crecca*, *A. platyrhynchos*, *A. acuta*, *A. clypeata*, *Netta rufina*, *Aythya ferina*, and *A. nyroca*. Small numbers of *Anser erythropus* and *Oxyura leucocephala* also occur in winter. The delta and lakes along the Black Sea coast are also of major importance for migrants in spring and autumn.

A number of Mediterranean species have recently expanded their range into Romania including *Oenanthe isabellina*, *Hippolais olivetorum*, and *Sylvia rueppellii*.

Conservation infrastructure and protected-area system

The Commission for Protection of Natural Monuments is responsible for designating and administering protected areas, and has subcommissions in Cluj-Napoca, Timisoara, Craiova, and Iaşi. Within each county (judeţ) there are local committees responsible for environmental conservation. There is also a National Council for Environmental Protection (part of the Romanian Government), which has a coordinating role.

Protected areas are classified either as National Parks or Nature Reserves. At present, there is only one National Park (Retezat), which is divided into two sections: a strictly protected area and a protected area. There are, however, plans to create a national-park system with at least 12 parks.

Nature Reserves are divided into a number of categories, which include botanical, zoological, ornithological and speleological, etc. There are also some ornithological reserves/sanctuaries. Several of the Nature Reserves have strictly protected areas or scientific-research zones. By 1986 there were 420 Nature Reserves which, with the one National Park, covered 222,545 ha (one per cent of the country's surface).

Furthermore, about 36 per cent of Romania's forests are classified as Protected Forest, where there are restrictions on forestry and where one of the objectives (amongst many others) is to protect rare fauna. There are also proposals to create an extensive network of regional parks for landscape-protection purposes.

International measures relevant to the conservation of sites

Romania has not signed any of the major international wildlife conventions, but is involved in UNESCO's Man and the Biosphere Programme and has designated three Biosphere Reserves (all of which are included in this inventory).

Overview of the inventory

This inventory includes 24 sites covering 515,000 ha (to nearest 1000 ha), which comprise a representative selection of important bird areas in Romania. Knowledge of the status and distribution of birds in Romania is still limited because of the small number of Romanian ornithologists. The inventory includes 14 wetland sites, by far the most important of which is the Danube Delta. Only a small portion of the Delta is protected and much of it is threatened by a major reclamation programme. Of the other wetland sites included only two are protected. A number of lakes along the Danube, not listed in this inventory, are known to be ornithologically important including: Bistreţ, Suhaia, Boianu, Călăraşi, Bugeac (Gîrlita), Crapina, and Jijila.

Four of the sites are canyons or gorges and two are high mountainous areas. Further survey work is needed to identify more sites for non-wetland species.

Acknowledgements

The inventory was compiled from information provided by A. Kiss, S. Kohl, A. Libuş, D. Munteanu, R. Poliş, J. Szabó, N. Toniac, and P. Weber; with the project coordinated by D. Munteanu. All of the information on the reclamation of the Danube Delta was provided by sources based in Western Europe. D. Munteanu provided material for the introduction.

INVENTORY

No.	Site name	Region	Criteria used to select site [see p.18]							
			0	1(i)	1(ii)	1(iii)	1(iv)	2	3	4
001	Delta Dunarii (Danube Delta) and Razelm-Sinoie complex	TA,CA			*	*	*		*	
001-1	Roşca-Buhaiova-Hrecisca Nature Reserve	TA								
001-2	Perişor-Zătoane-Sacalin Nature Reserve	TA								
001-3	Periteaşca-Leahova-Gura Portiţei Nature Reserve	TA								
001-4	Razelm-Sinoie complex	TA,CA								

No.	Site name	Region	Criteria used to select site [see p.18]							
			0	1(i)	1(ii)	1(iii)	1(iv)	2	3	4
001-5	Lacul Istria, Lacul Nuntaşi and southern Lacul Sinoie	CA								
001-6	Pădurea Letea (Letea Forest)	TA								
002	Pădurea Niculiţel-Babadag (Niculiţel and Babadag Forest)	TA						*	*	
003	Lacul Taşaul	CA				*		*	*	
004	Lacul Siutghiol	CA							*	
005	Lacul Techirghiol	CA				*		*		
006	Pădurea Hagieni (Hagieni Forest)	CA						*	*	
007	Canaraua Fetii	CA						*	*	
008	Lacul Dunăreni	CA				*		*	*	
009	Lacul Balta Albă, Lacul Amara, and Lacul Jirlău	BU,BA				*		*	*	
010	Eleşteele Sînpaul (Sînpaul Ponds)	HA							*	
011	Cheile Bicazului and Lacul Roşu (Bicaz Gorge and Lake Roşu)	NT,HA						*	*	
012	Lacul Bicaz (Izvoru Muntelui)	NT						*	*	
013	Pietrosul Rodnei Mountain	MS							*	
014	Fărăgău – Glodeni Fish-ponds	MR				*		*	*	
015	Cheile Ţurzii (Turda Gorge)	CJ							*	
016	Cheile Întregalde and Cheile Rîmeţi (Întregalde and Rîmeţi Gorges)	AA							*	
017	Iezerele Cindrelului (Cindrel Lakes)	SU							*	
018	Cefa Fish-ponds and Rădvani Wood	BR				*			*	
019	Lunca Mureşului: Ceala, Pecica, and Bezdin	AD						*	*	
020	Satchinez Reserve	TS							*	
021	Retezat National Park	HR							*	
022	Domogled Mountain	CS						*	*	
023	Zona Mostiştea (Mostiştea wetlands)	CI,IA							*	
024	Lacul Snagov	BI							*	

TA=Tulcea CA=Constanţa BU=Buzău BA=Brăila HA=Harghita NT=Neamţ MS=Maramureş MR=Mureş CJ=Cluj AA=Alba SU=Sibiu BR=Bihor AD=Arad TS=Timiş HR=Hunedoara CS=Caraş-Severin CI=Calaraşi IA=Ialomiţa BI=Bucureşti

Comments on the inventory

1. The site names are the Romanian site names where this is known (lacul = lake). For some sites this is followed by an English translation of the site name. In all cases the name of the county (judeţ) is given in parentheses.
2. The whole of Romania has been treated as a single 'region' when applying the site-selection criteria (category 3).
3. The figures for birds on passage are the total number occurring in a season (spring or autumn) rather than maximum daily counts.

---

001 Delta Dunarii (Danube Delta) and Razelm-Sinoie complex (Tulcea, Constanţa)

44°25'-45°28'N, 28°45'-29°40'E 442,000 ha

Biosphere Reserve (Roşca-Letea: 18,145 ha)

Nature Reserves (Roşca-Buhaiova-Hrecisca: 15,600 ha; Perişor-Zătoane-Sacalin: 15,400 ha; Periteaşca-Leahova-Gura Portiţei: 3900 ha; Istria: 8000 ha; Popina: 90 ha; Sărăturile: 100 ha; Haşmacul Mare: 700 ha).

The Delta of the Danube (including Rivers Chilia, Sulina, and Sfîntu Gheorghe) and the Razelm-Sinoie complex (including Lakes Razelm, Sinoie, Zmeica, and Golovita). An extensive delta with numerous freshwater lakes interconnected by narrow channels with huge expanses of *Phragmites*, *Scirpus* and *Typha*. Most of the reedbeds grow on a floating mass of decaying vegetation ('plaur'). Higher ground supports stands of *Salix*, *Populus*, *Alnus*, and *Quercus*. The Razelm-Sinoie complex to the south consists of several large brackish lagoons separated from the sea by a sandbar.

A major programme to develop the delta is currently being implemented. This involves the reclamation of *c*.97,000 ha of the Delta for irrigated agricultural crop production by the construction of polders. Other developments include the improvement of reed production, construction of fish-ponds and extension of forests. By 1987, some 50,000 ha of agricultural land had been created (with very poor agricultural production in places) and an additional 47,000 was still to be reclaimed, much of it from the central and ecologically most important part of the delta (despite being considered totally unsuitable for agriculture by authorities both inside and outside Romania).

Another project includes the re-routing of the River Sfîntu-Gheorghe by cutting a straight canal through the numerous meanders, which will speed up the flow of water and radically alter the pattern of alluvial deposition.

Over 160 species of birds breed, the most important being (1986 population estimates): *Phalacrocorax carbo sinensis* (3000 pairs), *P. pygmeus* (2500 pairs; one of the most important sites in the world), *Pelecanus onocrotalus* (2500 pairs), *P. crispus* (estimated until recently at 150 pairs, perhaps now only 25-40 pairs), *Nycticorax nycticorax* (2100 pairs), *Ardeola ralloides* (2150 pairs), *Egretta alba* (700 pairs), *E. garzetta* (1400 pairs), *Ardea purpurea* (1250 pairs), *Plegadis falcinellus* (1500 pairs), *Ciconia ciconia* (many pairs), *Cygnus olor* (500 pairs), *Haliaeetus albicilla* (*c*.5 pairs), *Circus aeruginosus* (300+ pairs), *Pandion haliaetus* (3 pairs), *Falco cherrug* (1-2 pairs), *F. vespertinus* (150 pairs), *Sterna sandvicensis* (1700 pairs), *S. hirundo* (20,000+ pairs), *Chlidonias hybridus* (20,000+ pairs), and *C. niger* (10,000-20,000 pairs). *Oxyura leucocephala* possibly still breeds. *Numenius tenuirostris* occurs on autumn passage (28 in 1971). In winter, huge numbers of Anatidae occur, including (counts from 1968 unless stated) *Anser albifrons* (500,000; 64,000-77,500 in 1982), *A. erythropus* (2 in 1982; other counts include max. 500), *Branta ruficollis* (25,000; 12,130 in 1982), *Anas crecca* (150,000), *A. platyrhynchos* (200,000), *A. acuta* (14,000), *A. clypeata* (40,000), *Netta rufina* (32,400), *A. ferina* (970,000), *A. nyroca* (13,000), and *Mergus albellus* (1500 in 1982). *Haliaeetus albicilla* also occurs in winter (30-40 in 1969, but fewer since). Additional ornithological information is given for the following subsites.

001-1 Roşca-Buhaiova-Hrecisca Nature Reserve (Tulcea)

45°22'N, 29°25'E 15,600 ha

Nature Reserve and part of the Roşca-Letea Biosphere Reserve

Extensive reedbeds and marshes, several shallow lakes (Poliacova, Argintiu, and Roşca) and narrow channels bordered by *Salix*. Almost unaltered by man owing to shallow water which renders access difficult.

Breeding species include *Phalacrocorax carbo sinensis*, *P. pygmeus*, *Pelecanus onocrotalus* (2500 pairs), *P. crispus* (*c*.25 pairs), *Botaurus stellaris*, *Ixobrychus minutus*, *Ardeola ralloides*, *Egretta alba*, *E. garzetta*, *A. purpurea*, *Plegadis falcinellus*, *Platalea leucorodia*, *Aythya nyroca*, *C. aeruginosus*, *Porzana porzana*, *P. parva*, *P. pusilla*, *Chlidonias hybridus*, *C. niger*, and *C. leucopterus*.

001-2 Perişor-Zătoane-Sacalin Nature Reserve (Tulcea)

44°50'N, 29°25'E 15,400 ha

Nature Reserve

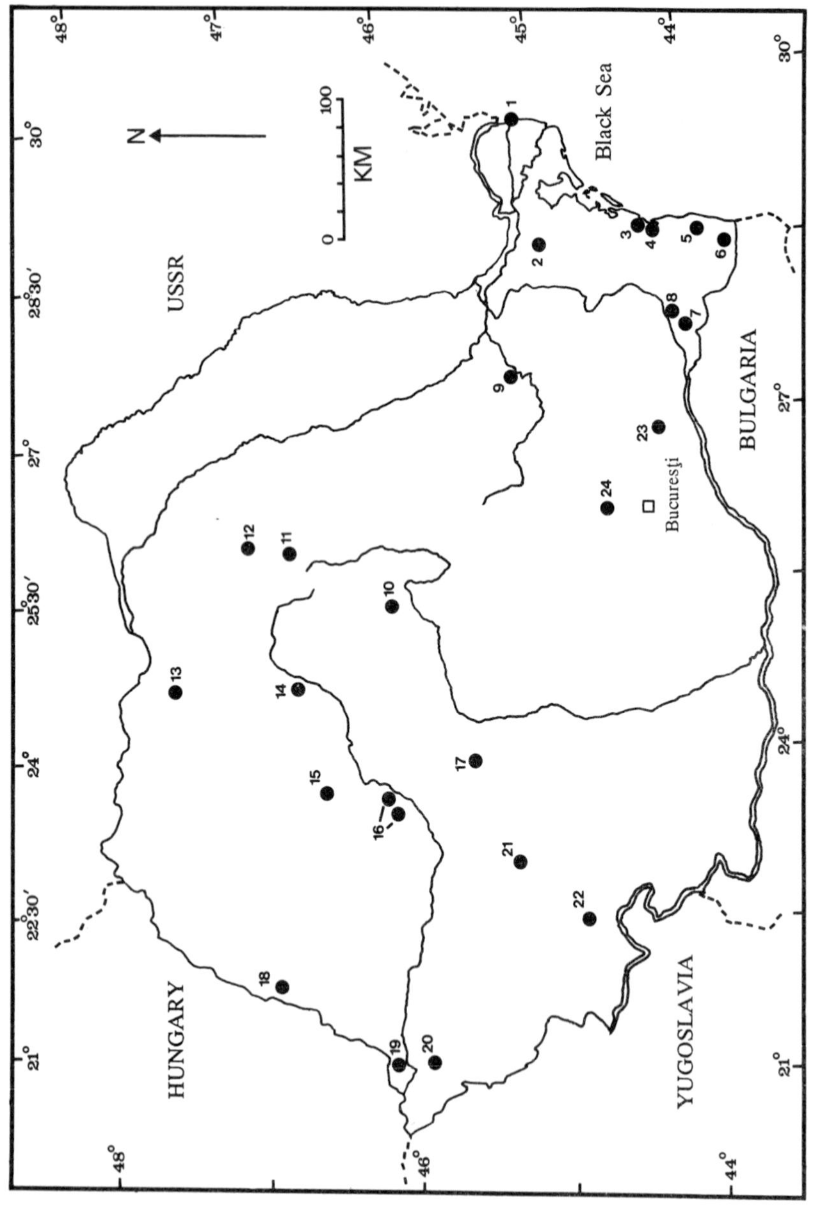

Figure 30: Map showing the location of the sites in Romania

Lakes and ponds with wide reedbeds amongst parallel strips of sand dunes ('grinduri'). Sacalin Island is made up of alluvial deposits with sand dunes and small patches of reed and *Tamarix*. Sacalin Island is adversely affected by illegal grazing (with the animals destroying the eggs and chicks) and the basin between the island and the mainland is silting up.

Breeding species are similar to Roşca-Buhaiova-Hrecisca (except *Pelecanus onocrotalus*) including *P. crispus* (0-20 pairs). Additional breeding species include *Aquila pomarina*, *Grus grus* (2-3 pairs), *Recurvirostra avosetta* (10-40 pairs), *Himantopus himantopus*, *Glareola pratincola*, *Tringa stagnatilis*, *Sterna sandvicensis* (1200-2500 pairs), *S. hirundo* (1000 pairs; 15,000 pairs in 1968-1970), and *S. albifrons* (100 pairs). Sacalin Island is an important site for passage migrants. *Haliaeetus albicilla* (2-6) occurs in winter.

001-3 Periteaşca-Leahova-Gura Portiţei Nature Reserve (Tulcea)

44°45'N, 29°05'E 3900 ha

Nature Reserve

Narrow sandy strips, reedbeds, marshes, ponds, and shallow lakes, with an uninterrupted sandy strip along the coast. Fishing takes place, and there is a small tourist camp on the eastern edge.

Breeding species include *Botaurus stellaris*, *Ixobrychus minutus*, *Nycticorax nycticorax*, *Ardeola ralloides*, *Egretta garzetta*, *Ardea purpurea*, *Aythya nyroca*, *Chlidonias hybridus*, *C. niger*, *C. leucopterus*, and *Coracias garrulus*.

001-4 Razelm-Sinoie complex (Tulcea, Constanţa)

44°50'N, 29°00'E 73,000 ha

Unprotected (except Popina Island: 90 ha)

Consists of four large brackish lakes (Razelm, Golovita, Zmeica, and Sinoie) completely separated from the sea by natural sandbanks or short artificial sea walls. The area is used for fishing and hunting, and is surrounded by fish-ponds, agricultural land, and grazing pastures.

Breeding species are few, but include *Tadorna ferruginea* (*c*.6 pairs on Popina Island) and several species of gulls and waders. An important feeding area for birds breeding in the delta and for migrants in spring and autumn. Large numbers of geese and ducks occur in autumn and winter (with important roosting and feeding areas near Sinoie and Sarinasuf villages) notably *Anser albifrons* (64,000-77,500), *Branta ruficollis* (max. 25,000), and *Mergus albellus* (15,000).

001-5 Lacul Istria, Lacul Nuntaşi and southern Lacul Sinoie (Constanţa)

44°33'N, 28°44'E 8000 ha

Unprotected except Istria Bird Sanctuary

Three main lakes (and other small ponds) with mud and sand shores, surrounded by steppe and agricultural land. Istria has emergent freshwater vegetation including *Phragmites* beds. The surrounding land is used for farming and grazing, Istria is used as a fish-pond, and there is a small health resort on the western shore of Nuntaşi. The intensification of grazing and the inflow of fresh water (from irrigation schemes) are adversely affecting the area.

Breeding species include *Botaurus stellaris* (6-8 pairs), *Ixobrychus minutus* (50-60 pairs), *Tadorna ferruginea* (1-2 pairs), *Aythya nyroca* (20-40 pairs), *Circus aeruginosus* (4-5 pairs), *Himantopus himantopus* (60 pairs), *Recurvirostra avosetta* (100 pairs), *Burhinus oedicnemus* (4-5 pairs), *Glareola pratincola* (50-80 pairs), *G. nordmanni* (possibly 4-5 pairs), *Sterna hirundo* (50-80 pairs), and *S. albifrons* (50-100 pairs). Important during spring and autumn passage with (seasonal totals) *Pelecanus onocrotalus* (500 in spring; 2000 in autumn), *P. crispus* (20 in spring; 10 in autumn), *Egretta garzetta* (2000 in autumn), *Ciconia nigra* (10-15 in spring), *Plegadis falcinellus* (1000 in autumn), *Platalea leucorodia* (150 in spring; 300 in autumn), and *Aythya nyroca* (100 in spring). Wintering species include *Gavia arctica* (50-100), *Cygnus cygnus* (2000), *Anser erythropus* (max. 500), *Branta ruficollis* (max. 5000), *Haliaeetus albicilla* (5-6), and *Falco peregrinus* (2-4).

001-6 Pădurea Letea (Letea Forest) (Tulcea)

45°17'N, 29°33'E 5700 ha Partly included in Roşca-Letea Biosphere Reserve

Partly a Nature Reserve (Haşmacul Mare: 700 ha)

A forest consisting mainly of *Populus* and *Quercus* with many mature trees; belts of trees (2-10 km long and 300-500 m wide) alternate with strips of steppe vegetation and sand dunes. Land-uses include agriculture, grazing, and forestry. Problems include the replacement of open areas by plantations. A detailed ornithological study is required.

Breeding species include *Pernis apivorus* (2-4 pairs), *Haliaeetus albicilla* (1 pair), *Circaetus gallicus* (1-2 pairs), *Falco cherrug* (1 pair), *Burhinus oedicnemus* (4-6 pairs), *Bubo bubo* (3-6 pairs), *Caprimulgus europaeus* (50 pairs), *Coracias garrulus* (20-30 pairs), *Lanius collurio* (150 pairs), and *L. minor* (120 pairs). *Falco peregrinus* (2-4) occurs in winter.

002 Pădurea Niculiţel-Babadag (Niculiţel and Babadag Forest) (Tulcea)

45°00'N, 28°25'E *c.*10,000 ha

Unprotected

A hilly area (Niculiţel Hills and Babadag Plateau) with deciduous woodland interspersed with grassland and steppe; the only forested area in the northern Dobrogea. There are extensive agricultural areas in the valleys. Land-uses include forestry, agriculture, grazing, and apiculture, and there are some villages and roads. Forestry operations (felling and tree-planting) and cultivation of natural grasslands are having an adverse effect on the area.

Of particular importance for breeding raptors with *Circaetus gallicus* (8-12 pairs), *Accipiter brevipes*, *Buteo rufinus*, *Aquila heliaca* (4-6 pairs), *Hieraaetus pennatus* (6-8 pairs), *Falco naumanni*, and *F. cherrug* (2-4 pairs); although several species are declining and *Gyps fulvus* and *Aegypius monachus* no longer breed. There are isolated relict populations of *Dryocopus martius* and *Dendrocopos leucotos lilfordi*, whilst other breeding species include *Bubo bubo* (8-10 pairs), *Caprimulgus europaeus* (200-400 pairs), *Coracias garrulus* (50-70 pairs), and *Emberiza hortulana* (*c.*1000 pairs). *Aquila pomarina* (200) occurs on autumn passage.

003 Lacul Taşaul (Constanţa)

44°21'N, 28°35'E 1830 ha

Unprotected

A large, slightly brackish lake (supplied by the River Casimcea) with barren shores, and some marshes in the north-western corner. Human activities include fishing. The south-eastern part of the lake is affected by the Năvodari industrial plant.

There are little ornithological data and the breeding bird fauna has not been studied (but is likely to be poor). Breeding species documented in 1965 included *Ixobrychus minutus* and *Aythya nyroca*. The lake is an important place for roosting and feeding passage migrants in spring and autumn. Passage species in autumn documented in 1970 included *Recurvirostra avosetta* (4-25), *Philomachus pugnax* (100-400), *Sterna caspia* (22), *Chlidonias niger* (35-130) and *C. leucopterus* (4-12). Wintering species are better known and counts have included *Branta ruficollis* (400), *Anser albifrons* (3000), and *Aythya ferina* (10,000).

004 Lacul Siutghiol (Constanţa)

44°16'N, 28°36'E 2100 ha

Unprotected

Formerly a marine lagoon, now a freshwater lake separated from the sea by a narrow (200-500 m) sandbank. The shore is flat at the eastern edge, abrupt at the western edge. There are narrow belts of *Phragmites*, interrupted by sandy shores. The water freezes in winter. About half of the shore-line is covered by villages and holiday resorts (included Mamaia holiday resort) and there is some industry. In summer tourism and aquatic sports cause some disturbance.

Breeding species include *Ixobrychus minutus* and *Aythya nyroca*. The lake is particularly important for passage migrants and for oversummering immature birds. *Larus melanocephalus* (immatures) occur in summer, and passage species include *Egretta garzetta*, *Ciconia ciconia*, *Chlidonias hybridus*, *C. niger*, and *C. leucopterus*. Wintering species include *Podiceps cristatus* (300), *P. nigricollis* (75), and *Aythya ferina* (2000).

005 Lacul Techirghiol (Constanţa)

44°01'N, 28°29'E 1170 ha

Unprotected

Formerly a coastal bay, now separated from the sea by a 200 m wide sandbar. A saline lake, not freezing in winter, with abrupt and barren shores except for marsh vegetation in the vicinity of several freshwater streams. There are bathing resorts which use the mud from the lake bottom (for therapeutic purposes) on the northern and eastern shores. A decrease in salinity has been recorded at the lake in recent years, because of irrigation in the surrounding areas.

Not important for breeding species except *Tadorna tadorna* (6-8 pairs). Large numbers of *Podiceps nigricollis* (700-1000; max. 5000-6000) and *Larus minutus* (1000-2000; max. 21,000) occur in summer and early autumn. In autumn and winter *Oxyura leucocephala* has been recorded (max. 218), together with many other migratory species.

006 Pădurea Hagieni (Hagieni Forest) (Constanţa)

43°48'N, 28°27'E 600 ha

Forest Reserve and Nature Reserve (208 ha)

The most important woodland area remaining in southern Dobrogea; mainly *Quercus* on undulating ground interspersed with numerous small clearings and patches of wet grassland. The replacement of open areas by plantations, introduction of feral *Phasianus colchicus* and irrigation of the surrounding land are adversely affecting the area.

Particularly important for breeding and passage passerines. Breeding species include *Ixobrychus minutus* (6 pairs), *Aythya nyroca* (4 pairs), *Pernis apivorus* (1 pair), *Circaetus gallicus* (1 pair), *Circus aeruginosus*, *Porzana porzana*, *P. pusilla*, *Crex crex* (4-6 pairs), *Bubo bubo*, *Caprimulgus europaeus* (15 pairs), *Coracias garrulus*, *Dendrocopos syriacus* (10 pairs), *D. medius* (5 pairs), *Sylvia nisoria* (8 pairs), *Ficedula albicollis* (8 pairs), *Lanius collurio* (50 pairs), *L. minor* (12 pairs), and *Emberiza hortulana* (30 pairs).

007 Canaraua Fetii (Constanţa)

44°05'N, 27°39'E 550 ha

Nature Reserve (234 ha)

A canyon with abrupt barren slopes and deciduous woodland and luxuriant herbaceous vegetation in the valley bottom. Some agriculture and grazing takes place in the canyon; also reafforestation.

Breeding species include *Pernis apivorus* (4 pairs), *Neophron percnopterus* (1 pair), *Circaetus gallicus* (3-4 pairs), *Accipiter brevipes* (2-3 pairs), *Buteo rufinus* (2-4 pairs), *Aquila heliaca* (2 pairs), *Hieraaetus pennatus* (4-6 pairs), *Bubo bubo* (2 pairs), *Caprimulgus europaeus* (40 pairs), *Coracias garrulus* (15 pairs), *Dendrocopos medius* (6-8 pairs), *Sylvia nisoria* (5 pairs), *Lanius collurio* (50 pairs), *L. minor*, and *Emberiza hortulana*.

008 Lacul Dunăreni (Constanţa)

44°11'N, 27°46'E 600 ha

Unprotected

A large shallow lake in the Danube valley with reedbeds and a few *Salix* trees along the shore. There are villages and roads along the eastern and southern shores; vineyards, pastures, and some agricultural land along the northern and western shores. Human activities include reed-cutting and private fishing.

The lake holds the most important *Platalea leucorodia* colony in Romania (60 pairs). Other breeding species include *Ixobrychus minutus*, *Plegadis falcinellus*, *Aythya nyroca*, and *Chlidonias niger*. Passage species include *Phalacrocorax pygmeus* and *Ciconia ciconia*.

009 Lacul Balta Albă, Lacul Amara, and Lacul Jirlău (Buzău, Brăila)

45°15'N, 27°15'E Balta Albă (1050 ha); Amara (700 ha); and Jirlău (1100 ha)

Unprotected

Three brackish lakes along the River Buzău with extensive muddy shores and halophytic vegetation (*Suaeda maritima*, *Salicornia herbacea*, *Statice gmelini*, *Juncus gerardii*) with small patches of emergent freshwater vegetation. There is a bathing resort on the northern shore of Balta Albă, with grazing and agriculture in the surrounding area.

Breeding species include *Botaurus stellaris*, *Ixobrychus minutus*, *Ardeola ralloides*, *Ardea purpurea*, *Ciconia ciconia*, *Platalea leucorodia*, *Aythya nyroca*, *Circus aeruginosus*, *Porzana porzana*, and *Recurvirostra avosetta*. Additional passage species include *Pelecanus onocrotalus*, *P. crispus*, *Plegadis falcinellus*, *Pandion haliaetus*, *Porzana porzana*, *Charadrius morinellus*, *Sterna caspia*, *Chlidonias hybridus*, *C. niger*, and *C. leucopterus*.

010 Eleşteele Sînpaul (Sînpaul Ponds) (Harghita)

46°11'N, 25°23'E 100 ha

Ornithological Reserve

Fish-ponds (created recently by the slight modification of some natural lakes and marshes) along the Homorodul Mare. There are extensive areas of *Phragmites* and other aquatic plants, with grassland in places near the ponds. Surrounded by meadows, agricultural land, *Quercus* and *Fagus* woodland and *Pinus* plantations. Illegal hunting takes place.

Breeding species include *Botaurus stellaris* (1 pair), *Ixobrychus minutus* (4 pairs), *Ciconia ciconia* (14 pairs), *Aythya nyroca* (4 pairs), *Circus aeruginosus* (1 pair), *Porzana porzana* (6 pairs), *P. parva* (3 pairs), and *Crex crex* (2 pairs). *Aquila pomarina* feeds in the area. An important site for passage birds which include (seasonal totals) *Ciconia ciconia* (150 in autumn), *C. nigra* (10 in autumn), *Platalea leucorodia* (5 in spring), *Circus cyaneus* (25 in autumn), *Pandion haliaetus* (4 in spring and autumn), *Falco peregrinus* (4-6 in spring), *Tringa stagnatilis* (20 in spring), *T. glareola* (800 in spring), *Chlidonias niger* (400-600 in spring), and *C. leucopterus* (200 in spring).

011 Cheile Bicazului and Lacul Roşu (Bicaz Gorge and Lake Roşu) (Neamţ, Harghita)

46°48'N, 25°51'E *c.*2200 ha

Nature Reserve

A deep gorge through the calcareous Haşmaş (Hăghimas) Mountains. Roşu is a natural lake. The slopes are covered by dense forests (mainly *Picea*, also *Fagus*, and mixed) with some pastures. Land-uses include intensive tourism, livestock grazing, quarrying, and hay cultivation; there is a popular health resort at Lake Roşu.

Breeding species include *Aquila heliaca* (1-2 pairs), *A. chrysaetos* (1-2 pairs), *Bonasa bonasia* (20-40 pairs), *Tetrao urogallus* (5-12 pairs), *Bubo bubo* (4-6 pairs), *Strix uralensis*, *Aegolius funereus*, *Dryocopus martius* (15 pairs), *Dendrocopos leucotos*, *Ficedula parva*, *F. albicollis*, and *Turdus torquatus*. *Falco peregrinus* possibly breeds.

012 Lacul Bicaz (Izvoru Muntelui) (Neamţ)

47°00'N, 26°04'E 4000 ha (open water = 3300 ha)

Unprotected

A large freshwater reservoir in the Bistriţa valley. Surrounded by *Fagus* and *Picea* forests, scrub, pastures, and some villages. There is intensive tourism, with angling and sailing.

Breeding species include *Crex crex* (4 pairs), *Actitis hypoleucos* (8 pairs), *Picus canus*, *Dryocopus martius*, *Dendrocopos leucotos*, *Ficedula parva*, *Lanius collurio*, and *Emberiza hortulana* (2 pairs). Numerous species occur on passage including *Ciconia ciconia* (30 in spring), *Aythya nyroca*, and *Chlidonias niger* (30 in spring). *Gavia arctica* (10) occurs in winter.

013 Pietrosul Rodnei Mountain (Maramureş)

47°35'N, 24°37'E 2700 ha Biosphere Reserve

Nature Reserve

Mountainous area in the south-east Carpathians (700-2305 m) with *Fagus* forest, *Picea* forest, *Pinus mugo* shrub, alpine meadows and *Rhododendron kotschyi*. There is a small glacial lake. Human activities are limited, with some grazing and controlled tourism.

Breeding species include *Aquila pomarina*, *Bonasa bonasia*, *Tetrao urogallus*, *Dryocopus martius*, *Dendrocopos leucotos*, *Picoides tridactylus*, and *Turdus torquatus*. *Aquila chrysaetos* and *Falco peregrinus* possibly breed.

014 Fărăgău – Glodeni Fish-ponds (Mureş)

46°40'N, 24°32'E 180 ha

Unprotected

Fărăgău is a natural lake which has recently been modified to create fish-ponds; the site also includes six additional fish-ponds, situated along the River Şar between Fărăgău and Glodeni village, which were created in about 1980. Some of the fish-ponds have well-developed reedbeds. Human activities include pisciculture and reed-cutting, and there is agriculture in the surrounding area.

Breeding species include *Podiceps grisegena*. An important site for passage species which include *Phalacrocorax pygmeus*, *Ciconia nigra*, *C. ciconia*, *Aythya nyroca*, *Tringa glareola*, *Gelochelidon nilotica*, and *Chlidonias niger*. *Pandion haliaetus* feeds at the site during summer and *Haliaeetus albicilla* is a winter visitor.

015 Cheile Turzii (Turda Gorge) (Cluj)

46°31'N, 23°40'E 200 ha

Nature Reserve

A deep gorge through the calcareous Trascău Mountains with impressive rock formations and a rich and interesting vegetation and invertebrate fauna. Land-uses include tourism and rock-climbing; there are grassland and agricultural areas in the surrounding hills.

Breeding species include *Aquila chrysaetos* (1 pair), *Bubo bubo* (1-2 pairs), *Picus canus*, *Dryocopus martius*, *Dendrocopos syriacus*, *Lullula arborea*, *Sylvia nisoria*, *Ficedula parva*, *Lanius collurio*, and possibly *Pernis apivorus*.

016 Cheile Întregalde and Cheile Rîmeţi (Întregalde and Rîmeţi Gorges) (Alba)

46°15'N, 23°24'E (Întregalde) and 46°20'N, 23°30'E (Rîmeţi); 4000 ha (including surrounding area)

Nature Reserves

Two narrow gorges through the calcareous Trascău Mountains; surrounded by *Fagus* forest, *Quercus* forest, extensive meadows, and some agricultural land. Land-uses include rock-climbing (with no serious impact), with grazing, arable agriculture, and hay cultivation in the surrounding area.

Breeding species include *Pernis apivorus, Circaetus gallicus, Aquila pomarina* (4 pairs), *A. chrysaetos* (5 pairs), *Hieraaetus pennatus* (2 pairs), *Bonasa bonasia, Bubo bubo, Caprimulgus europaeus, Dendrocopos medius, Lullula arborea, Ficedula parva*, and *Lanius collurio*. *Falco peregrinus* (1-2) occurs in winter.

017 Iezerele Cindrelului (Cindrel Lakes) (Sibiu)

45°35'N, 23°48'E *c.*1000 ha

Nature Reserve (450 ha)

Extensive alpine meadows, areas of rocks and stones, *Pinus mugo* woodland, and two small glacial lakes (Iezerul Mare and Iezerul Mic) on the Diavolului Plateau (2100 m). There is *Picea* forest below 1900 m. Human activities include grazing and tourism; the vegetation and terrestrial birds are adversely affected by sheep and cattle.

Of considerable biogeographical importance for *Charadrius morinellus* (a small population, never more than 4 pairs, since at least the mid-nineteenth century) and *Eremophila alpestris balcanica*. Other breeding species include *Tetrao urogallus* (10-12 pairs), *Bonasa bonasia, Strix uralensis, Dryocopus martius, Picoides tridactylus*, and *Turdus torquatus*.

018 Cefa Fish-ponds and Rădvani Wood (Bihor)

46°55'N, 21°41'E 1000 ha

Unprotected (fish-ponds), Zoological Reserve (Rădvani Wood)

Fish-ponds with barren or reed-fringed shores (the vegetation is periodically burnt) with *Quercus* and *Ulmus* woodland. Surrounded by grazing pasture and agricultural land. Intensive fish-farming with no hunting and minimal human disturbance.

Breeding species include *Podiceps grisegena* (1-2 pairs), *Botaurus stellaris* (4-6 pairs), *Ixobrychus minutus, Nycticorax nycticorax* (60 pairs), *Ardeola ralloides* (15 pairs), *Egretta garzetta* (2-4 pairs), *Ardea purpurea* (1-2 pairs), *Anser anser* (2-3 pairs), *Aythya nyroca, Circus aeruginosus* (1-2 pairs), *Porzana porzana*, and *Chlidonias niger* (4-6 pairs). A stop-over site for migrants, including (seasonal totals) *Platalea leucorodia* (10-30 in spring), *Anser albifrons* (3000-5000 in autumn), and *Tringa erythropus* (100-500 in autumn).

019 Lunca Mureşului: Ceala, Pecica, and Bezdin (Arad)

46°09'N, 21°05'E 6000 ha

Unprotected, except Bezdin Lake and Wood (County Reserve: 60 ha)

An extensive area of wet meadows and riverine woodland ('lunca') along the River Mureş, which floods part of the area in spring. The dominant vegetation is *Salix* and *Populus* in the wet areas; *Quercus, Ulmus*, and *Fraxinus* in the drier areas. Only 14 per cent of the woodland is natural with many mature trees; the rest is plantations. Within the woodland there are clearings, pastures, and permanent marshes and lakes. Land-uses include forestry, and there are proposals to drain the wet areas.

Breeding species include *Ixobrychus minutus* (10 pairs), *Nycticorax nycticorax* (20-45 pairs), *Egretta garzetta* (5-12 pairs), *Ciconia ciconia* (10 pairs), *Aythya nyroca* (5 pairs), *Pernis apivorus* (1-2 pairs), *Milvus migrans* (4 pairs), *Aquila pomarina* (4-6 pairs), *Circus aeruginosus* (1-3 pairs), *Caprimulgus europaeus* (20-30 pairs), *Alcedo atthis* (4-5 pairs), *Coracias garrulus* (6 pairs), *Dryocopus martius* (10 pairs), *Anthus campestris* (1-2 pairs), and *Lanius minor* (5-10 pairs). *Crex crex* has disappeared as a breeding species in recent years. Passage species include *Ciconia nigra, Pandion haliaetus, Circus cyaneus, Falco peregrinus*, *Grus grus*, and *Chlidonias niger*. Wintering species include *Haliaeetus albicilla*, *Aquila heliaca*, *Falco columbarius*, and *Asio flammeus*.

020 Satchinez Reserve (Timiş)

45°58'N, 21°04'E 101 ha

Ornithological Reserve

A remnant of the once-extensive marshes which covered Banat (south-western corner of Romania). An earth dam maintains the water level and there are numerous small pools, extensive reedbeds and clusters of *Salix*. Surrounded by meadows and agricultural land. The heron populations have declined in recent years because of a recently established *Corvus frugilegus* colony.

Breeding species include *Botaurus stellaris* (7-8 pairs), *Ixobrychus minutus*, *Ardeola ralloides* (4-6 pairs), *Nycticorax nycticorax* (80-100 pairs), *Egretta garzetta* (8-10 pairs), *Ardea purpurea* (5-7 pairs), *Aythya nyroca*, *Circus aeruginosus* (7-8 pairs), *Crex crex*, and possibly *Porzana porzana*, *P. parva*, *Chlidonias niger*, and *Luscinia svecica*.

021 Retezat National Park (Hunedoara)

45°22'N, 22°41'E 20,000 ha Biosphere Reserve

National Park; includes scientific area (no human activity permitted: 1800 ha)

Mountainous area (700-2509 m) in the south-eastern Carpathians (including 20 summits over 2,300 m) with *Fagus* forest, *Picea* forest, extensive areas of *Pinus mugo* and *P. cembra*, and alpine meadows. There are several glacial lakes. Supports an extremely rich and varied flora with many endemic species (including 34 endemic *Hieracium*). Land-uses include tourism and limited grazing, although these activities are forbidden in the scientific area. The only National Park in Romania.

Breeding species include *Aquila pomarina* (6-8 pairs), *A. chrysaetos* (2 pairs), *Bonasa bonasia*, *Tetrao urogallus*, *Bubo bubo*, *Glaucidium passerinum*, *Strix uralensis*, *Picus canus*, *Dryocopus martius*, *Dendrocopos leucotos*, *Picoides tridactylus*, *Turdus torquatus*, *Ficedula parva*, and *F. albicollis*. *Falco peregrinus* and *Aegolius funereus* possibly breed, but *Gypaetus barbatus*, *Gyps fulvus*, *Aegypius monachus*, and *Tetrao tetrix* have become extinct this century.

022 Domogled Mountain (Caraş-Severin)

44°52'N, 22°27'E 1000 ha

Nature Reserve

A mountain (max. 1105 m), part of the Mehedinţ Mountains in the southern Carpathians, with deciduous (*Fagus*, *Carpinus*, *Corylus*) and coniferous (*Pinus*) woodland, grassland at high altitude and abrupt barren limestone slopes. The mountain is famous for its flora, which includes many scarce or interesting Mediterranean species, and for its invertebrate fauna, especially butterflies. Land-uses include tourism. The Nature Reserve is one of the oldest in Romania (established in 1932).

Breeding species include *Pernis apivorus*, *Circaetus gallicus*, *Aquila pomarina*, *A. heliaca*, *A. chrysaetos*, *Bonasa bonasia*, *Caprimulgus europaeus*, *Dryocopus martius*, *Dendrocopos leucotos*, and *Lanius collurio*.

023 Zona Mostiştea (Mostiştea wetlands) (Calaraşi, Ialomiţa)

44°20'N, 26°48'E 10,000 ha

Unprotected

An extensive and interesting wetland area along the River Mostiştea. There are two large lakes (Mostiştea: 2000 ha; Frimu: 800 ha) and several small lakes (Frăsinet; Cocorilor: 125 ha; Siliştea: 62 ha; Codreni: 54 ha), and many swamps and marshes. Several of the lakes have been converted to fish-ponds or reservoirs. There is rich aquatic vegetation in areas with shallow water.

Breeding species include *Botaurus stellaris*, *Ixobrychus minutus*, *Nycticorax nycticorax*, *Ardeola ralloides*, *Egretta garzetta*, *Ardea purpurea*, *Ciconia ciconia*, *Aythya nyroca*, *Circus aeruginosus*, *Porzana porzana*, *P. parva*, and *Dendrocopos medius*. *Plegadis falcinellus* and *Sterna hirundo* possibly breed.

024 Lacul Snagov (Bucureşti)

44°43'N, 26°09'E 600 ha

Unprotected

A long narrow freshwater lake in the Ialomita valley (between Bălteni and Căldăruşani Lakes), with rich aquatic vegetation including *Phragmites*, *Juncus*, *Typha*, and abundant *Salix*, *Populus*, and *Alnus*. In the vicinity of the lake there is agricultural land, and also an important forest (Snagov Forest), which is a remnant of the extensive forests that once covered the plains of Romania. The lake is used for tourism, aquatic sports, and angling; the northern part is less affected by human activities.

Breeding species include *Botaurus stellaris*, *Ixobrychus minutus*, *Nycticorax nycticorax*, *Ardeola ralloides*, *Egretta garzetta*, *Ardea purpurea*, *Ciconia ciconia*, *Aythya nyroca*, *Circus aeruginosus*, *Porzana porzana*, *P. parva*, *Crex crex*, and *Chlidonias hybridus*.

MAIN REFERENCE

Carp, E. ed. (1980) Directory of wetlands of international importance in the Western Palearctic. Gland, Switzerland: IUCN-UNEP.

SPAIN

Dupont's Lark *Chersophilus duponti*

INTRODUCTION

General Information

Spain is one of the largest states in Europe. Most of the country (97.5 per cent; some 492,463 sq km) lies within the Iberian peninsula; this inventory also covers the Balearic Islands (5014 sq km), but the Canary Islands, also belonging to Spain, are dealt with in a separate section.

After Switzerland, Spain has the highest average altitude (660 m) of any European country. However, the wide central plateaus (mesetas) contribute more to this figure than do the major mountain areas. The most important mountains are: the Pyrenees, which separate the Iberian peninsula from France and extend 435 km with a maximum height of 3404 m; the Cantabrian Mountains (western extension of the Pyrenees), and the Sierra Nevada (in the south-east, maximum height: Mulhacen, 3482 m). Other mountainous areas above 2000 m include the León Mountains, Iberian System, Central System (Sierra de Gredos, 2592 m), and Cazorla-Segura ranges. Sizeable areas below 300 m are to be found only in the usually narrow coastal fringe, the tectonic depressions of the Rivers Ebro and Guadalquivir, and the Balearic Islands.

The Spanish coast extends for 3904 km in the peninsula and 910 km in the Balearic Islands, and is generally rocky, but there are straight sandy stretches in the south-west (Atlantic coast of Andalucía) and east (coasts of Valencia and southern Catalonia). There are comparatively few islands or islets along the coast, with the exception of the

Balearics. These comprise three major islands (Mallorca: 3640 sq km, Menorca: 701 sq km, and Ibiza: 521 sq km) and several smaller islands. Mallorca is mostly flat but has a mountain range along the north-western coast that peaks at 1445 m. The climate is very varied, especially with regard to rainfall which gradually decreases from north to south and from west to east. There is an extensive fringe along the northern seaboard, including the Cantabrian Mountains and the Pyrenees, where annual precipitation averages more than 1000 mm, whilst in the hinterland rainfall usually ranges between 400 and 600 mm per year. In the centre of the Ebro Valley and in the south-east (Almería and Murcia) it rarely exceeds 300 mm. Much of Spain is dry, almost semi-arid, and this is reflected in a paucity of big rivers or lakes, although there are some important wetlands in the coastal zone, particularly the Ebro Delta, the Albufera de Valencia, and the Marismas del Guadalquivir. Winters are mild and rainy along the coast, especially in the south, but dry and quite cold in the mesetas. During the summer there is virtually no rain and temperatures can be extremely high.

The natural vegetation, like the climate, is quite varied, being of Euro-Siberian type in the north and some of the mountains (*Fagus sylvatica*, *Quercus robur*, and *Q. petraea* woods), and Mediterranean in the rest of the country (with Quercus ilex/*Q. ilex/-rotundifolia* as the dominant species). Conifers are frequent in mountain and hilly areas (mostly *Pinus pinaster* and *P. sylvestris*), in the highest plateaus (*Juniperus thurifera*), and on the eastern seaboard (*Pinus halepensis*), with extensive plantations in other areas.

Cultivation also reflects the variable climatic conditions: corn and potatoes are important in the north, olive-trees and vines in the centre and south, and citrus fruits in the extreme south and eastern coastal regions. Cereal fields cover most of the plateaus and big depressions, which are almost devoid of trees. Some 40 per cent of Spanish territory is cultivated (17 million ha unirrigated and 3 million ha irrigated) whilst 30 per cent is wooded (about half of which is actually exploitable for timber) and 13 per cent is pasture. Cattle-rearing (some 5 million cows) is an important activity only in the mountainous areas, on the northern seaboard, and in some areas of the west and south-west, whilst sheep-grazing (approximately 17 million sheep) is quite widespread. During recent decades, irrigated areas have considerably increased, many cultivated mountain areas have been abandoned, and extensive stock-raising has declined. Also, although enormous areas (some 3 million ha) have been reafforested with *Pinus* spp. and *Eucalyptus*, natural woods, especially alluvial woods, have still suffered very significant losses. In the near future, partly as a result of Spanish entry to the EEC, massive land-use changes are expected (e.g. reduction of vine and olive areas, and large-scale replacement of pasture land by *Eucalyptus* plantations along the humid northern fringe).

The human population of Spain, some 37 million inhabitants if the Canary Islands are excluded (another 1.4 million), is very unevenly distributed, being largely concentrated in the coastal areas and around Madrid in the centre of the peninsula. So, while the overall population density is 74 inhabitants per sq km – rather low by European standards – there are only 25 inhabitants per sq km in interior regions such as Aragón, Extremadura, and most of Castile. During recent decades there has been a marked population shift from these interior areas to the big cities (Madrid and along the coast). At present, some 60 per cent of Spaniards live in towns holding more than 20,000 inhabitants. In rural areas in the northern half of the country, small villages close to one another predominate, while in the south populations tend to be concentrated in scattered big towns. Urban areas amount to 3.7 per cent of the Spanish territory, but there is wide regional variation, being as low as 0.9 per cent in Extremadura.

Although the industrial development of Spain is already considerable, most of the industrial activity takes place in the heavily populated areas of the coast or around Madrid. Tourism is of paramount economic importance (some 45 million foreign visitors in 1986), but again it is very concentrated, mainly along the Mediterranean coast, and on the Balearic Islands, where urbanisation has severely affected many biotopes that were previously of interest and has destroyed others, including wetlands.

Ornithological importance

Accurate population estimates for breeding or wintering birds in Spain are not yet available, except for some groups such as herons, storks, vultures, gulls etc. For some species only rough estimates can be made, and even estimates are lacking for most passerines and other small birds. The figures given below must therefore be interpreted with caution; accuracy will certainly improve rapidly in the future, as an interest in birds continues to increase in Spain.

Spain is of outstanding importance in Europe and the Western Palearctic for its remaining large populations of birds of prey, now apparently recovering from past persecution and poisoning. It is especially interesting for its populations of *Elanus caeruleus* (100+ pairs), *Milvus migrans, M. milvus* (one of the most important populations in Europe), *Gypaetus barbatus* (45 pairs), *Neophron percnopterus* (1000+ pairs), *Gyps fulvus* (4000+ pairs), *Aegypius monachus* (365 pairs), *Circaetus gallicus* (1000+ pairs), *Circus pygargus, Aquila adalberti* (104 pairs; accepted by ICBP as a separate Iberian-endemic species), *A. chrysaetos* (800-900+ pairs), *Hieraaetus pennatus* (5000+ pairs), *H. fasciatus* (700+ pairs), *Falco naumanni* (almost certainly the most important population in Europe), *F. peregrinus* (1600 pairs), and *Bubo bubo*. Their strongholds coincide with the thinly populated areas of the Spanish mountains and interior (Aragón, Extremadura, etc.), where extensive stock-raising, forestry, and hunting are still the main economic activities. These are also important areas for *Ciconia nigra* (150 pairs) and, during the winter, for the western population of *Grus grus* (40,000-50,000 birds).

The Spanish avifauna associated with steppe-like areas is also of great importance, and is presently at risk. There are globally important populations of *Tetrax tetrax* (50,000+ birds) and *Otis tarda* (8000+ birds). Some species, such as *Pterocles orientalis, Chersophilus duponti, Calandrella rufescens*, and *Bucanetes githagineus*, are found within Europe only in Spain, or Turkey and Spain. There are also large populations of *Burhinus oedicnemus, Pterocles alchata, Anthus campestris, Oenanthe hispanica*, and *Sylvia conspicillata*.

The few remaining extensive wetlands in Spain, many of them still under heavy pressure, are important for a very large number of waterbirds including several species which are unique or very rare in Europe. The most important region for them is Andalucía (including Marismas del Guadalquivir and nearby lagoons). Important species are *Ardeola ralloides* (200-300 pairs), *Egretta garzetta* (2250-2500 pairs), *Ardea purpurea* (500-800 pairs), *Platalea leucorodia* (400-500 pairs), *Phoenicopterus ruber* (2000-8000 pairs; variable), *Marmaronetta angustirostris* (100-200 pairs), *Oxyura leucocephala* (counts of max. 200 birds), *Porphyrio porphyrio* (several hundreds), *Fulica cristata* (very few pairs), *Himantopus himantopus* (4000-6000 pairs), *Recurvirostra avosetta* (1000-2000 pairs), *Glareola pratincola* (1000+ pairs), *Larus genei* (300 pairs), *Gelochelidon nilotica* (800-1000 pairs), *Sterna albifrons* (3000+ pairs), and *Chlidonias hybridus* (5000+ pairs). These areas are also notable for wintering and/or passage species, among them *Anser anser* (60,000+ birds) and *Limosa limosa* (20,000+ birds).

The northern mountain ranges (Pyrenees and the Cantabrian Mountains) hold important populations of *Lagopus mutus pyrenaicus* (100-500 pairs), *Tetrao urogallus* (1000+ birds), *Perdix perdix hispaniensis* (1000+ pairs), *Dendrocopos medius*, and *D. leucotos lilfordi*.

The Mediterranean islands (Balearics, Columbretes, and Chafarinas) hold important populations of *Calonectris diomedea* (10,000+ pairs), *Puffinus puffinus mauretanicus* (1000-5000 pairs), *Phalacrocorax aristotelis desmarestii* (*c.*1500 pairs), and *Larus audouinii* (5000+ pairs in the whole of Spain; the largest population in the world). In addition to seabirds, the Balearics are important for *Pandion haliaetus* (9 pairs) and *Falco eleonorae* (450 pairs). On the Atlantic coast of the north-western corner of the peninsula (Galicia) there is a relict population of *Uria aalge ibericus* (max. 40 pairs).

Other species which are relatively common and widely distributed in Spain, but rare in Europe as a whole, include *Bubulcus ibis* (25,000+ pairs), *Ciconia ciconia* (7000 pairs), *Clamator glandarius, Caprimulgus ruficollis, Coracias garrulus, Melanocorypha calandra, Galerida theklae, Sylvia cantillans, Lanius senator, Cyanopica cyana, Pyrrhocorax pyrrhocorax*, and *Sturnus unicolor*. Less common and mostly restricted to southern areas are *Apus caffer, Cercotrichas galactotes, Oenanthe leucura, Acrocephalus melanopogon*, and *Sylvia sarda* (only in the Balearics).

Conservation infrastructure and protected-area system

Interest in wildlife conservation is growing steadily in Spain, but there is an urgent need for revised legislation, as well as for more public funding (presently just 0.2 per cent of the general budget of the state). Most bird species are totally protected (Reales Decretos

3181/1980 and 1497/1986), but enforcement must be considerably improved. There were 1,274,706 hunting licenses in 1986.

Wildlife conservation is the responsibility of the 17 Autonomous Regions, with a central body – ICONA (Instituto para la Conservación de la Naturaleza) – which mostly provides coordination and advice. The protected-area system, regulated by the acts 'Ley de Caza' (1970) and 'Ley de Espacios Naturales Protegidos' (1975), included in early 1988:

1. National Parks (Parques Nacionales)
   Although the first two parks were established in Spain in 1918, the network has developed little over peninsular Spain (five parks) or the Balearic Islands (none). Existing parks are found either in the northern mountains (Covadonga, Ordesa, Aigües Tortes) or covering the Ramsar wetlands (Doñana and Daimiel), and total just 95,337 ha (0.19 per cent of the peninsula's territory). The last park was created in 1973 and there seem to be no immediate plans for more. Their regulation – which is controlled by ICONA – appears too permissive, in terms of both land-use and maximum visitor numbers.
2. Natural Parks (Parques Naturales)
   In recent years there has been a very promising upsurge: between 1978 and 1988, up to 30 Natural Parks were established, covering some 450,000 ha; several more will be designated soon.
3. Natural Reserves (Reservas Naturales)
   Several categories can be regarded as nature reserves or wildlife sanctuaries, including Natural Reserves (Reservas Naturales) (51 sites), Integral Reserves of Scientific Interest (Reservas Integrales de Interés Científico) (16; some of them included in National or Natural Parks), Ornithological Reserves, Game Refuges (Refugios de Caza) (five; some non-governmental) and National Game Refuges (Refugios Nacionales de Caza) (six). Most are of small size.
4. Natural Monuments (Sitios o Parajes de Interés Nacional)
   An outmoded category, scarcely enforced, with some ten sites.

In all, the protected-areas system presently covers some 600,000 ha (1.2 per cent of the total Spanish territory). In addition, National Game Reserves (Cotos o Reservas Nacionales de Caza) cover 1,679,424 ha (3.4 per cent of the territory) and can afford some protection to certain bird species. There are 46 National Game Reserves, mainly in mountain areas. There are also three Areas of Special Natural Interest (Area Natural de Interés Especial) in the Balearics, where urbanisation is prohibited.

International measures relevant to the conservation of sites

Spain is a member of the European Community (and is therefore bound by the terms of the Wild Birds Directive), and has ratified the Ramsar Convention, World Heritage Convention, Bern Convention and Bonn Convention. Three Ramsar Sites, ten Biosphere Reserves (one in the Canary Islands), and 44 EEC Special Protection Areas (35 in the peninsula; two in the Balearic Islands; one in the Chafarinas Islands; six in the Canary Islands) have been designated to date. The only designated World Heritage Site is in the Canary Islands.

Overview of the inventory

A total of 288 sites has been included in the inventory (269 in the Iberian peninsula, 18 in the Balearic Islands, and one off the North African coast). The sites can be classified by habitats as follows:

- Marine sites (islands or coastal cliffs): 23 sites covering 26,130 ha (0.3 per cent of the total area included in the inventory). Most are in the Balearic Islands or in north-west Galicia). Only two are fully protected.
- Wetlands: 55 sites (including four subsites) covering 577,864 ha (6.2 per cent of the total area included in the inventory). Mainly concentrated in the south (Andalucía) and east (Valencia and Catalonia coasts). The most important areas are already protected, but some serious problems remain.

- 'Euro-Siberian' mountains (Atlantic woodland and high-mountain landscapes): 25 sites covering 1,054,700 ha (11.2 per cent of the total area included in the inventory) within the Cantabrian and Pyrenean Mountains. They include three National Parks and many National Game Reserves, but protection afforded to woodland is totally unsatisfactory.
- Mediterranean mountains: 103 sites covering 4,517,300 ha (48.2 per cent of the total area included in the inventory). The typical Iberian landscape, but without a single National Park and with very few Natural Parks or Reserves. In several areas there are still large expanses of important semi-natural habitat that should be protected.
- Mediterranean wooded plains: 23 sites covering 809,600 ha (8.6 per cent of the total area included in the inventory). Mostly concentrated in the central-west (most important region is Extremadura); this is a vulnerable habitat, indispensable for birds such as *Aquila adalberti*. At present there are no protected areas covering this habitat-type.
- Steppe-like habitats: 63 sites covering 2,388,425 ha (25.5 per cent of the total area included in the inventory). The second most extensive habitat-type represented in the Spanish inventory but quite rare in Western Europe as a whole. Most important regions are Extremadura, Castile, Aragón, and the south-east. Only two sites, covering some 2000 ha, are fully protected.

The size of the areas differs markedly depending on the habitat-type involved: for marine sites the average figure is only 1136 ha, and for wetlands 10,507 ha; whereas for the other habitat-types it is around 40,000 ha. If strict protection is required, this probably represents rather a large average area, but in most cases it is thought that the need for habitat preservation, which often tolerates or even requires (e.g. steppelike habitats) traditional land-uses, should be stressed. As much as possible, the inventory incorporates discrete areas (different in character from the surrounding land) which are empty of villages or roads.

The inventory covers 9,374,019 ha in all, some 18.8 per cent of Spanish territory, both in the Iberian peninsula and in the Balearic Islands. This high figure must be judged in relation to the large territory of Spain, its relatively low population density, and the remaining healthy level of habitat preservation. However, there are large differences in the proportion of each region's territory which is covered by the inventory, this variation reflecting the land-use and population density in each region. For example, in Galicia the ten sites described represent only 0.8 per cent of the region, while the 42 sites in Extremadura represent 33.4 per cent of the region.

Most of the regions, habitat-types and species are thought to be covered adequately, but it is important to stress that the inventory should be considered as only a first step; much fieldwork is still required.

Acknowledgements

Data-sheets for all the sites listed below were compiled at SEO (Sociedad Española de Ornitología) by E. de Juana, L. M. Carrascal, and C. Sáez-Royuela; E. de Juana prepared the introduction. Information for wetlands had previously been compiled, also at SEO, by M. Fernández-Cruz, R. Martí, A. Martínez Abraín, and J. Monreal, under a contract from ICONA. A previous report of Important Bird Areas in Spain, which has been widely used in this inventory, was prepared in 1984 by SEO (J. L. Tellería and L. M. Carrascal) for CODA-ICBP Spain. ICONA gave encouragement and some data on threatened species (L. M. González). Over 80 individuals and organisations contributed data to SEO for the Inventory of Important Bird Areas, among them: ADENEX, J. A. Aja, Amigos de la Malvasía, A. Aragüés, J. Araújo, B. Arroyo, C. Atencia, R. Balada, L. F. Basanta, A. Bermejo, F. Bernis, J. Caballero, M. Cabrera, F. Campos, J. Canut, H. Castro, P. Chozas, L. Costa, Departamento de Biología y Ecología de la Universidad de Murcia, Diputación General de Aragón (Servicio de Conservación del Medio Natural), J. Elósegui, V. Ena, E. Errando, J. Escorsa, Estación Ornitológica de la Albufera, F. Ferrer, J. C. Finlayson, A. Galarza, D. García, V. Garza, J. Garzón, GLEDAS, D. Gómez, J. A. Gómez, A. Gómez Manzaneque, N. González, J. M. González Cachinero, Grupo Zaragoza de Ornitología, J. Guiral, J. Guitián, T. Gullick, B. Heredia, F. Hernández, M. A. Hernández, J. A. Izquierdo, F. de Juana, O. del Junco, J. L. Lagares, F. de Lope, G.

López, J. López Pardo, L. Lopo, A. J. Lucio, A. Madero, J. Manrique, E. Martín, A. Martínez, F. Martínez, A. Martínez-Vilalta, J. Mayol, S. Moreno, Ll. Motge, J. Muntaner, J. Muñoz-Cobo, R. Muñoz Pulido, J. Nadal, M. Navarro, A. Noval, C. Palacín, R. Pardo, E. Pelayo, J. L. Pérez Chiscano, E. Pérez de la Fuente, S. J. Peris, J. M. Pleguezuelos, F. J. Purroy, R. F. Ramón, J. A. Román, M. A. Sánchez, J. Sanpietro, C. San Segundo, T. Santos, SECONA, Servicio de Medio Ambiente Natural de Pontevedra (Xunta de Galicia), M. Soler, F. Suárez Cardona, F. Tejedor, J. A. Torres, and V. Urios.

INVENTORY

No.	Site name	Region	Criteria used to select site [see p.18]							
			0	1(i)	1(ii)	1(iii)	1(iv)	2	3	4
001	Islas Cíes	GA			*				*	
002	Islas Ons y Onza	GA								*
003	Ría de Arosa (O Grove)	GA				*				
004	Cabo Finisterre – Costa de Touriñán	GA								*
005	Cabo Vilán	GA							*	
006	Islas Sisargas y Acantilados de Corme – Malpica	GA							*	
007	Ría de Ortigueira	GA				*				
008	Ría de Ribadeo	GA,AS				*				
009	Cabo Torres – Cabo Busto	AS							*	
010	La Limia	GA						*		
011	Sierra de los Ancares	GA,CL							*	
012	Muniellos	AS							*	
013	Degaña	AS,CL							*	
014	Somiedo	AS,CL							*	
015	Sierras de Gistreo y Coto	CL							*	
016	Piedrafita – San Isidro	AS,CL							*	
017	Sierras del Crespón y Mermeja	AS							*	
018	Reres – Mampodre	AS,CL							*	
019	Riaño	AS,CL							*	
020	Picos de Europa	AS,CL							*	
021	Fuentes Carrionas	CL,CA							*	
022	Sierras de Peña Labra y del Cordel	CL,CA							*	
023	Embalse del Ebro	CA,CL				*			*	
024	Marismas de Santoña	CA				*			*	
025	Ría de Guernica – Cabo de Ogoño	EI				*			*	
026	Sierra de la Cabrera	CL,GA							*	
027	Montes Aquilanos	CL							*	
028	Humada – Peña Amaya	CL							*	
029	Páramo de la Lora	CL							*	
030	Hoces del Alto Ebro y Rudrón	CL							*	
031	Páramo de Masa	CL							*	
032	Sierras de Oña y de la Tesla	CL							*	
033	La Losa – Orduña (Sierra Salvada)	CL,EI							*	
034	Hoz de Sobrón	CL,EI							*	
035	Montes Obarenes	CL,LR							*	
036	Los Oteros	CL						*	*	
037	Tierra de Campos	CL						*	*	
038	Villafáfila – Embalse del Esla	CL				*		*	*	
038-1	Salinas de Villafáfila									
038-2	Embalse del Esla									
039	Villalpando – Villardefrades	CL						*		
040	Tordesillas – Mota del Marqués	CL						*	*	
041	Castronuño – Pollos	CL							*	
042	Alaejos – Nava del Rey	CL						*		
043	Madrigal – Peñaranda	CL						*	*	

No.	Site name	Region	Criteria used to select site [see p.18]							
			0	1(i)	1(ii)	1(iii)	1(iv)	2	3	4
044	Gallegos del Pan	CL						*		
045	Peleas de Abajo	CL						*		
046	Arribes del Duero – Fermoselle	CL							*	
047	Río Huebra – Arribes del Duero	CL							*	
048	Ledesma – Río Tormes	CL							*	
049	Peña de Francia	CL,EA						*	*	
050	Sierra de Gredos	CL,EA						*	*	
051	Río Moros	CL						*	*	
052	Riofrío – Segovia	CL							*	
053	Cañón del Duratón	CL							*	
054	Montejo de la Vega	CL							*	
055	Tiermes – Caracena	CL							*	
056	Altos de Barahona	CL						*	*	
057	Cañón del Río Lobos	CL							*	
058	Valle del Arlanza – Silos	CL							*	
059	Páramos del Cerrato	CL						*	*	
060	Río Carrión en Husillos	CL							*	
061	El Escorial – San Martín de Valdeiglesias	CM,CL						*	*	
062	Sierra de Guadarrama	CL,CM						*	*	
063	El Pardo – Viñuelas	CM						*	*	
064	Talamanca – Camarma	CM						*	*	
065	Cortados del Jarama	CM						*	*	
066	Sierra de Ayllón	CLM,CL,CM							*	
067	Puebla de Beleña	CLM				*			*	
068	Entrepeñas – Buendía	CLM				*			*	
068-1	Embalse de Buendía									
069	Alto Tajo	CLM							*	
070	Parameras de Maranchón – Layna	CLM,CL						*	*	
071	Paramera de Embid – Molina	CLM						*	*	
072	Serranía de Cuenca	CLM							*	
073	Valeria	CLM						*	*	
074	Carboneras de Guadazaón	CLM							*	
075	Moya	CLM							*	
076	Hoces del Cabriel Medio	CLM							*	
077	Pétrola – Almansa – Yecla	CLM,MA						*	*	
078	Hoces del Río Mundo	CLM							*	
079	Hoces del Río Segura	CLM							*	
080	Campo de Montiel	CLM						*	*	
081	San Clemente – Villarrobledo	CLM						*		
082	Complejo lagunar de Pedro Muñoz – Manjavacas	CLM			*	*		*	*	
083	Tarancón – El Hito – Corral de Almaguer	CLM				*		*		
083-1	El Hito									
084	Dehesa de Monreal	CLM			*	*			*	
085	Llanos de Tembleque – La Guardia	CLM						*	*	
086	Complejo lagunar de Alcázar de San Juan – Quero	CLM			*	*		*	*	
087	Tablas de Daimiel, Embalses del Vicario y Gasset y Navas de Malagón	CLM				*		*	*	
088	Valle y Sierra de Alcudia	CLM						*	*	
089	Sierra de los Canalizos (Saceruela)	CLM						*		
090	Sierra del Chorito (Cabañeros)	CLM						*	*	
091	Montes de Toledo	CLM						*	*	
092	Embalse de Castrejón	CLM				*			*	
093	Torrijos	CLM						*		
094	Embalse de Azután	CLM				*			*	

No.	Site name	Region	Criteria used to select site [see p.18]							
			0	1(i)	1(ii)	1(iii)	1(iv)	2	3	4
095	Llanos de Oropesa	CLM						*	*	
096	Valle del Tiétar y Embalses de Rosarito y Navalcán	CL,CLM				*		*	*	
097	Sierra de Gata	EA,CL						*	*	
098	Embalse de Gabriel y Galán	EA				*			*	
099	Embalse del Borbollón	EA				*		*	*	
100	Sierras de Coria	EA						*	*	
101	Embalse de Alcántara	EA				*		*	*	
102	Cuatro Lugares	EA				*		*	*	
103	Monfragüe	EA						*	*	
104	Campo Arañuelo	EA,CLM				*		*	*	
105	Embalse de Valdecañas	EA				*			*	
106	Sierras de las Villuercas	EA						*	*	
107	Embalse de Cijara	CLM,EA							*	
108	Embalse de Puerto Peña – Valdecaballeros	EA				*		*	*	
109	Sierra de Pela y Embalse de Orellana	EA				*			*	
110	Zorita – Madrigalejo	EA				*		*	*	
111	Trujillo – Torrecillas de la Tiesa	EA				*		*	*	
112	Llanos entre Cáceres y Trujillo	EA				*		*	*	
113	Cáceres – Sierra de Fuentes	EA						*	*	
114	Malpartida de Cáceres – Arroyo de la Luz	EA				*		*	*	
115	Brozas – Membrío	EA						*	*	
116	Embalse del Cedillo	EA							*	
117	Sierra de San Pedro	EA						*	*	
118	Aldea del Cano – Casas de Don Antonio	EA						*	*	
119	Embalse del Salor	EA				*		*	*	
120	Sierra de Montánchez – Embalse de Cornalvo	EA							*	
121	Lácara	EA				*		*	*	
122	Mérida – Embalse de Montijo	EA				*		*	*	
123	Morante	EA				*				
124	Botoa – Villar del Rey	EA						*	*	
125	El Membrío – La Albuera	EA						*	*	
126	Albalá – Malpica	EA						*		
127	Valongo	EA				*			*	
128	Cheles – Villanueva del Fresno – Barcarrota	EA				*		*	*	
129	Dehesas de Jerez de los Caballeros	EA							*	
130	Embalse de Valuengo	EA				*			*	
131	Fuente de Cantos – Montemolín	EA						*	*	
132	Bienvenida – Usagre	EA				*		*	*	
133	Sierra Grande de Hornachos	EA						*	*	
134	Granja de Torrehermosa – Llerena	EA				*		*	*	
135	Peraleda de Zaucejo – Campillo de Llerena	EA				*		*	*	
136	Puerto de Mejoral – Almorchón – Cabeza del Buey	EA				*			*	
137	La Serena	EA				*		*	*	
138	Siruela – Agudo	EA,CLM				*			*	
139	Sierra de la Demanda	CL,LR							*	
140	Sierras de Urbión y Cebollera	CL,LR							*	
141	Hoces del Iregua, el Leza y el Jubera	LR							*	
142	Arnedillo – Peña Isasa	LR							*	

No.	Site name	Region	Criteria used to select site [see p.18]							
			0	1(i)	1(ii)	1(iii)	1(iv)	2	3	4
143	Sierra de Alcarama y Rio Alhama	LR,CL							*	
144	Laguna de las Cañas	NA							*	
145	Bardenas Reales	NA,AN						*	*	
146	Gallipienzo – Sierra de la Peña	NA							*	
147	Peña Izaga	NA							*	
148	Peñas de Echauri	NA							*	
149	Sierras de Zariquieta y Archuba	NA							*	
150	Sierras de Leyre, Orba e Illón	NA							*	
151	Monte Gorramendi – Peñas de Itxusi	NA								*
152	Roncesvalles – Irati – Sierra de Abodi	NA							*	
153	Belagua – Ansó – Hecho	AN,NA							*	
154	Collarada – Telera	AN							*	
155	Panticosa – Viñamala – Tendeñera	AN							*	
156	Ordesa – Bielsa	AN							*	
157	Gistaín – Cotiella	AN							*	
158	Posets – La Madaleta – Entecada	AN,CN							*	
159	San Mauricio – Bohí – Beret	CN							*	
160	Monteixo – L'Orri – Tornafort	CN							*	
161	Cerdaña	CN							*	
162	Fresser – Setcases	CN							*	
163	Foces de Biniés y Fago	AN							*	
164	San Juan de la Peña – Peña Oroel	AN							*	
165	Santo Domingo – Riglos – Gratal	AN						*	*	
166	Sierra de Guara	AN						*	*	
167	Oturia – Canciás	AN							*	
168	Turbón – Espés – Sis	AN							*	
169	Sierra de Sant Gervás	CN							*	
170	Sierra del Boumort	CN							*	
171	Sierra del Cadí	CN							*	
172	Sierras del Montsech y Mongay	CN,AN							*	
173	Embalse de Tormos (La Sotonera)	AN				*			*	
174	Montes de Zuera	AN							*	
175	Sierra de Alcubierre	AN							*	
176	Bajo Alcanadre	AN							*	
177	El Saso (Osera)	AN							*	
178	Los Monegros (Pina – Bujaraloz)	AN						*	*	
179	Ballobar	AN							*	
180	Almacelles – Gimenells	CN,AN						*	*	
181	Cogull – Alfés	CN						*	*	
182	Río Ebro (La Alfranca – Pina de Ebro)	AN							*	
183	Sierras de Valdurrios – Serreta Negra y Los Rincones	AN							*	
183-1	Embalse de Caspe o de Mequinenza									
184	Urrea de Jalón	AN							*	
185	Bajo Huerva	AN							*	
186	Belchite – Mediana	AN						*	*	
187	Saladas de Alcañiz	AN							*	
188	Sierra del Moncayo	AN,CL							*	
189	Río Manubles	AN							*	
190	Hoces del Jalón – Sierra de Algairén	AN							*	
191	Cortados del Río Mesa	AN,CLM							*	
192	Gallocanta	AN				*			*	
193	Blancas – Torralba de los Sisones	AN						*	*	
194	Visiedo	AN							*	
195	Río Martín	AN							*	
196	Sierra de Arcos	AN							*	

No.	Site name	Region	Criteria used to select site [see p.18] 0	1(i)	1(ii)	1(iii)	1(iv)	2	3	4
197	Río Guadalope	AN							*	
198	Sierra de Albarracín	AN							*	
199	Los Alberes – Cabo de Creus – Aiguamolls	CN							*	
200	Islas Medas	CN			*				*	
201	Sierra del Montsant	CN							*	
202	Delta del Ebro	CN		*	*	*		*	*	
203	Puertos de Beceite – Monte Turmell	CN,AN,PV							*	
204	Els Ports de Morella	AN,PV							*	
205	Peñagolosa	PV,AN							*	
206	Sierra de Espadán	PV							*	
207	Hoces del Turia y Sierra de Tejo	PV							*	
208	Hoces del Cabriel y del Júcar	PV,CLM							*	
209	Sierras del Norte de Alicante	PV							*	
210	Islas Columbretes	PV		*	*			*	*	
211	Prat de Cabanes – Torreblanca	PV				*			*	
212	Desembocadura del Río Mijares	PV							*	
213	Estanys y Marjal de Almenara	PV				*				
214	Albufera de Valencia	PV				*			*	
215	Embalse del Hondo	PV				*		*	*	
216	Salinas de Santa Pola	PV			*	*		*	*	
217	Salinas de la Mata y Torrevieja	PV				*			*	
218	Mar Menor	MA				*			*	
219	Islotes litorales de Murcia y Almería	MA,AA							*	
220	Sierra de Moratalla	MA,CLM							*	
221	Cagitán – Armorchón	MA						*	*	
222	Valle del Guadalentín	MA						*	*	
223	Topares – El Moral – Puebla de Don Fadrique	MA,AA						*	*	
224	Hoya de Baza	AA						*	*	
225	Depresión de Guadix	AA						*	*	
226	Sierra del Cabo de Gata	AA							*	
227	Salinas del Cabo de Gata – estepa litoral	AA				*		*	*	
228	Sierra Alhamilla – Campo de Níjar	AA							*	
229	Desierto de Tabernas	AA							*	
230	Punta Entinas – Punta del Sabinar – Salinas de Cerrillos	AA				*			*	
231	Picos de Aroche	AA						*		
232	Sierra Morena de Sevilla	AA							*	
233	Sierra Morena de Córdoba	AA						*	*	
234	Los Blázquez – La Granjuela – Fuenteovejuna	AA				*		*	*	
235	Hinojosa del Duque – El Viso	AA				*		*	*	
236	Sierra Madrona – Sierra Morena de Jaén	AA,CLM						*	*	
237	Aldeaquemada – Dañador	AA,CLM						*	*	
238	Sierras de Cazorla y Segura	AA,CLM,MA							*	
239	Embalses del Tramo medio del Guadalquivir	AA				*			*	
240	Embalse de Marmolejo	AA				*			*	
241	Sierras al sur de Jaén	AA							*	
242	Sierras de Cabra Luque, Priego y Rute	AA							*	
243	Zonas húmedas del sur de Córdoba	AA				*		*	*	
244	Campiña de Carmona	AA						*	*	
245	Marismas de Isla Cristina y Ayamonte	AA				*				

No.	Site name	Region	Criteria used to select site [see p.18]							
			0	1(i)	1(ii)	1(iii)	1(iv)	2	3	4
246	Ría de Huelva	AA			*	*			*	
247	Marismas del Guadalquivir	AA			*	*		*	*	
248	Coria del Río	AA				*			*	
249	Lagunas de Espera	AA				*		*	*	
250	Lagunas de Terry	AA				*		*	*	
251	Bahía de Cádiz	AA			*	*			*	
252	Laguna de Medina	AA				*		*	*	
253	Lagunas de Puerto Real	AA				*			*	
254	Embalse de Bornos	AA				*				
255	Medina-Sidonia	AA				*			*	
256	Tajo de Barbate	AA			*	*			*	
257	La Janda	AA				*	*	*	*	
258	Sierra de la Plata	AA							*	
259	Tarifa	AA				*	*	*	*	
260	Sierras del Bujeo, Ojén, del Niño y Blanquilla	AA							*	
261	Sierras de las Cabras, del Aljibe y de Montecoche	AA						*	*	
262	Sierras de Ubrique y Grazalema	AA							*	
263	Sierra de Líjar – Peñón de Zaframagón	AA							*	
264	Sierras Bermeja y Crestellina	AA							*	
265	Serranía de Ronda	AA							*	
266	Sierra de Antequera – El Chorro	AA							*	
267	Lagunas de Fuente de Piedra, Gosque y Campillos	AA				*			*	
268	Sierras de Tejeda y Almijara	AA							*	
269	Sierra Nevada	AA							*	
270	Islas Chafarinas	ML		*	*			*	*	
271	Islas Vedrá y Vedranell	BS		*	*			*	*	
272	Cabo Nono – Isla Murada	BS							*	
273	Isla de Tagomago	BS							*	
274	Islas de los Freus	BS		*	*			*	*	
275	Salinas de Formentera	BS	*							
276	La Mola de Formentera	BS							*	
277	Isla Dragonera	BS		*	*			*	*	
278	Acantilados del noroeste de Mallorca y Sierra de Alfabia	BS						*	*	
279	Cabo Pinar	BS							*	
280	Albufera de Alcudia	BS							*	
281	Cabo del Freu – Cabo Farruch	BS						*	*	
282	Cabo d'es Piná	BS							*	
283	Lagunas de Salobrar de Campos	BS				*			*	
284	Acantilados entre Cap Enderrocat y Cala Pí	BS							*	
285	Acantilados costeros Islas Malgrats – Isla del Sech	BS		*	*			*	*	
286	Archipiélago de Cabrera	BS		*	*			*	*	
287	Costa Norte de Menorca	BS						*	*	
288	Sierras Interiores de Menorca	BS						*	*	

GA=Galicia AS=Asturias CL=Castilla y León CA=Cantabria
EI=Euskadi LR=La Rioja EA=Extremadura CM=Comunidad de Madrid
CLM=Castilla-La Mancha MA=Murcia NA=Navarra AN=Aragón CN=Cataluña
PV=País Valenciano AA=Andalucía ML=Melilla BS=Baleares

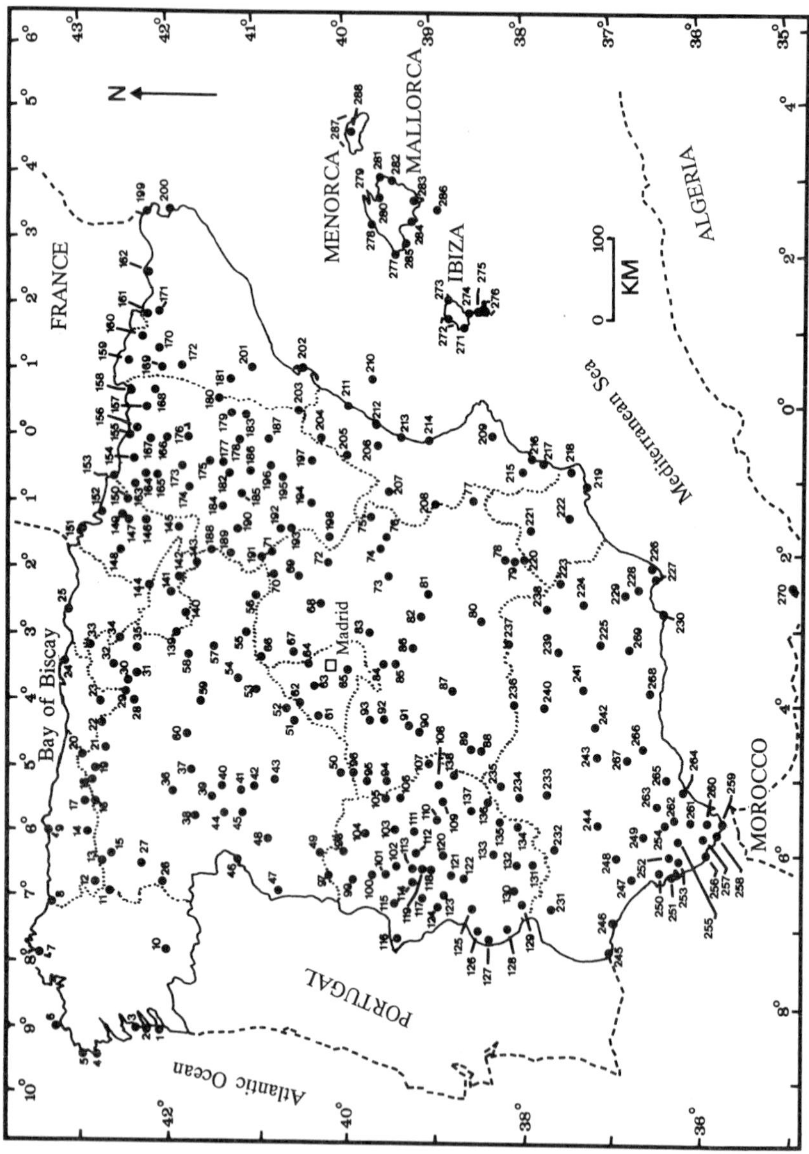

Figure 31: Map showing the location of the sites in Spain

Comments on the inventory

1. All the sites are beleived to meet the site-selection criteria except site 275 which has been included because of its large wintering population of *Podiceps nigricollis* (would certainly qualify as an internationally important wetland if a numerical criterion for this species was determined).

2. The regions, given in parentheses following the site name, are the autonomous provinces. The regions used when applying the site-selection criteria (Category 3) are the NUTS level 1 regions. These are (component autonomous provinces given in parentheses): Noroeste (Galicia, Asturias, Cantabria); Noreste (Euskadi, Navarra, La Rioja, Aragón); Madrid; Centro (Castilla y León, Castilla-La Mancha, Extremadura); Este (Cataluña, País Valenciano, Baleares); Sur (Andalucía, Murcia, Melilla).

Glossary

The following Spanish words are used in the inventory: acantillado = sheer coast; altos = highland; bahía = bay; cabo = cape; cañón = canyon; costa = coast; dehesa = grazed savanna (with many scattered *Quercus*); desembocadura = river mouth; embalse = reservoir; estepa = steppe; fuente(s) = fountain(s), spring(s); hoz, hoces = bottle-neck, narrow valley; isla(s) = island(s); islote(s) = small island(s); laguna(s) = lagoon(s), lake(s); llanos = plains; montes = mountains; páramo(s) = open mountain top(s); pico(s) = peak(s); puerto = mountain pass; punta = spit of land; ría = river mouth; río = river; salinas = saltpans, salines; sierra(s) = mountain chain(s); valle = valley.

---

001 Islas Cíes (Galicia)

42°13'N, 08°55'W 650 ha EEC SPA (433 ha)

Natural Park (433 ha)

Two long offshore islands with steep slopes in front of the Ría de Vigo estuary. There are cliffs, some densely covered by grass, with scrub and some tree plantations (*Pinus pinaster*, *Eucalyptus* sp.) in the interior. Occasionally inhabited by fishermen and, during summer, by tourists. Used for military manoeuvres.

Important for breeding seabirds with *Phalacrocorax aristotelis* (*c.*400 pairs), *Larus argentatus cachinnans* (12,000 pairs), and *Uria aalge ibericus* (1-2 pairs).

002 Islas Ons y Onza (Galicia)

42°23'N, 08°57'W 500 ha

Game Refuge

Two small coastal islands in front of the Ría de Pontevedra estuary, with some cliffs, covered mostly by scrub and grasslands. The islands are uninhabited.

Important for colonies of *Phalacrocorax aristotelis* (300 pairs).

003 Ría de Arosa (O Grove) (Galicia)

42°28'N, 08°51'W 1000 ha

Partly a Game Refuge

A small harbour (Ensenada de O Grove) in the south of the Ría de Arosa, separated from the open sea by a large sandbar with some dunes, with wide intertidal mud areas and sandbanks. Human activities include fishing, mollusc collecting, and trawling; problems include an industrial dump, residential areas, and sand extraction. There is a small ornithological observatory.

An important passage and wintering area for waders including *Pluvialis squatarola* (max. 1047 in winter), gulls, and terns.

004 Cabo Finisterre – Costa de Touriñán (Galicia)

42°52'N, 09°16'W 800 ha

Unprotected

A coastal section with cliffs broken by beaches between the Ría de Camariñas and the Ría de Corcubión (estuaries). The area includes two small rocky islets in the Ría de Corcubión (Islas Lobeiras). There are human settlements and three lighthouses.

Important for *Phalacrocorax aristotelis* (*c.*100 pairs).

005 Cabo Vilán (Galicia)

43°08'N, 09°12'W 10 ha

Natural Monument

A rocky cape and two small stacks (Vilán de Terra and Vilán de Fora) with difficult access. There is a lighthouse on the cape.

The area supports the best colony of *Uria aalge ibericus* (30-40 pairs) in Spain (around one-third of the world population), and other seabird colonies with *Phalacrocorax aristotelis* (*c.*30 pairs).

006 Islas Sisargas y Acantilados de Corme – Malpica (Galicia)

43°20'N, 08°52'W 900 ha

Partly a Game Refuge

A rugged and rocky section of coast with three small offshore islets (Islas Sisargas). The vegetation consists of grass and *Ulex* scrub. There is coastal fishing.

Important for seabirds, particularly *Phalacrocorax aristotelis* (65 pairs) and *Uria aalge ibericus* (5-8 pairs). The site is the most important in Spain for *Larus fuscus* (200 pairs) and *Rissa tridactyla* (200 pairs).

007 Ría de Ortigueira (Galicia)

43°40'N, 07°52'W 2000 ha

Unprotected

An estuary between Cape Ortegal and the Estaca de Bares cape, with wide intertidal mud areas, a halophytic vegetation belt, and some islets. There is intense mollusc collecting. The cutting of marsh vegetation, building, and poaching are current problems.

The estuary supports large numbers of a variety of wintering duck species, including *Anas penelope* (max. 7500), and waders (an important resting site for passage birds).

008 Ría de Ribadeo (Galicia, Asturias)

43°30'N, 07°04'W 1500 ha

Partly a Game Refuge

The Eo River estuary, which is narrow and long, with intertidal mudflats and sandbanks. There is a large saltmarsh in the inner part. Economic activities include fishing and mollusc collecting. Poaching, building, and uncontrolled dumping are problems at the site.

An important passage and wintering area for ducks and waders, particularly for *Anas acuta* (max. 1000) and *Calidris alba* (min. 500).

009 Cabo Torres – Cabo Busto (Asturias)

43°40'N, 06°00'W 1000 ha

Unprotected

A rocky stretch of coast, 65 km long, immediately to the west of Gijón, with cliffs and scattered steep islets close to the shore. Of special interest are the cliffs of Novellana,

the isle of Deva, and the small islets close to the capes of Peñas and Torres. Generally well preserved, but fishing pressure and pollution cause concern. Also, an increasing *Larus argentatus cachinnans* population could pose problems for other seabirds.
Important because of its populations of *Hydrobates pelagicus* (possibly 150+ pairs) and *Phalacrocorax aristotelis* (min. 80 pairs).

010 La Limia (Galicia)

42°10'N, 07°40'W 20,000 ha

Unprotected

A plain along the upper River Limia in southern Orense province; formerly the wide lagoon of Antela, now drained. There are potato fields and some small villages.
The most north-westerly breeding area for *Ciconia ciconia* in Spain (4 pairs; decreasing). Also interesting for *Tetrax tetrax* (750-800 birds).

011 Sierra de los Ancares (Galicia, Castilla y León)

42°50'N, 06°50'W 50,000 ha

National Game Reserve (46,000 ha)

A mountain massif (max. 1969 m). A rugged area with many valleys, covered by deciduous woodland (mainly *Quercus robur*), scrub, and grasslands. Only sparsely populated; human activities include cattle-grazing and big-game hunting.
Important for *Tetrao urogallus* (min. 20 males) and *Perdix perdix hispaniensis* (min. 50 pairs); also abundant birds of prey, especially *Circaetus gallicus* (min. 5 pairs).

012 Muniellos (Asturias)

43°05'N, 06°44'W 4700 ha EEC SPA (Bosque de Muniellos: 2975 ha)

Integral Reserve (695 ha)

An unpopulated area (Sierra de Rañadoiro: max. 1680 m) in the Cantabrian Mountains (Cordillera Cantábrica), densely covered by deciduous woodlands (mainly *Quercus robur*, *Q. petraea*, *Fagus sylvatica*). The Muniellos Forest (3000 ha), probably the best preserved in the Cordillera Cantábrica, is located within the area.
Important because it supports good populations of species typical of the Cantabrian woods including *Tetrao urogallus*, *Dryocopus martius*, and *Dendrocopos medius*.

013 Degaña (Asturias, Castilla y León)

42°55'N, 06°30'W 27,000 ha

National Game Reserve (8657 ha)

A mountainous area (max. 2007 m) in the Cordillera Cantábrica with large deciduous woods especially of *Fagus sylvatica* (including Monasterio de Hermo: 1500 ha). Wolf *Canis lupus* and Brown Bear *Ursus arctos* are present. The area is used for big-game hunting and cattle-grazing.
Important for *Tetrao urogallus* (50 males) and *Perdix perdix hispaniensis* (min. 50 pairs) and other species typical of the Cordillera Cantábrica.

014 Somiedo (Asturias, Castilla y León)

43°10'N, 06°00'W 90,000 ha

National Game Reserve (87,918 ha)

A very large and well-preserved mountainous area (800-2417 m) in the Cordillera Cantábrica, with narrow valleys, many small villages, and some cultivation. Covered by good deciduous woods (*Fagus*, *Quercus*, *Betula*), scrub, and grasslands, with rocks and subalpine grasslands in the highest areas. Brown Bear *Ursus arctos* (best population in Spain) and *Canis lupus* are present. The area is used for cattle-grazing, big-game hunting, forestry and tourism.

Important for *Circaetus gallicus*, *Tetrao urogallus* (120 males), *Perdix perdix hispaniensis* (min. 50 pairs), *Dryocopus martius*, and *Dendrocopos medius*. Other birds of prey include *Pernis apivorus* and *Aquila chrysaetos*.

015 Sierras de Gistreo y Coto (Castilla y León)

42°50'N, 06°20'W 40,000 ha

Unprotected

A mountainous area (1200-2117 m) in the southern part of the Cordillera Cantábrica, with slopes covered by scrub, grassland, and woods (*Quercus robur*, *Q. pyrenaica*, *Betula celtiberica*, *Fagus sylvatica*). Land-uses include grazing by cattle and sheep, big-game hunting, and tourism; there is a threat of human settlement.

Breeding species include *Circaetus gallicus* (min. 15 pairs), *Tetrao urogallus* (25-30 males), and *Perdix perdix* (min. 100 pairs).

016 Piedrafita – San Isidro (Asturias, Castilla y León)

43°00'N, 05°30'W 45,000 ha

Unprotected

A mountainous area (800-2189 m) in the Cordillera Cantábrica with deep valleys and deciduous woods (mainly *Fagus sylvatica*); also scrub, grasslands, and rocks at higher altitude. The area is grazed by cattle.

An important area for *Perdix perdix hispaniensis* (min. 50 pairs), with a small population of *Tetrao urogallus* (4-5 males).

017 Sierras del Crespón y Mermeja (Asturias)

43°10'N, 05°30'W 15,000 ha

Unprotected

A mountainous area (max. 1862 m) in the Cordillera Cantábrica to the north of Piedrafita - San Isidro. It comprises two small ranges and the narrow valley between them, with deciduous woodland (*Quercus* spp., *Fagus sylvatica*) and humid scrub. There are small villages with pastures and cultivation.

An interesting area for *Tetrao urogallus*, *Perdix perdix hispaniensis*, *Dryocopus martius*, and *Dendrocopos medius*.

018 Reres – Mampodre (Asturias, Castilla y León)

43°05'N, 05°15'W 20,000 ha

Two National Game Reserves (Reres: 14,225 ha; Mampodre: 29,238 ha)

A 28-km-long section of the Cordillera Cantábrica (800-2190 m), including the Puerto de Tarna mountain pass, which comprises an area of rocks, scrub, mountain grasslands, and deciduous woods (mainly *Fagus sylvatica*). Wolf *Canis lupus* and Brown Bear *Ursus arctos* are present. The area is used for big-game hunting and sheep- and cattle-grazing.

An interesting area for *Tetrao urogallus* (min. 10 males), *Perdix perdix hispaniensis*, *Dryocopus martius*, and *Dendrocopos medius*.

019 Riaño (Asturias, Castilla y León)

43°05'N, 05°00'W 35,000 ha

Included in a National Game Reserve (Riaño: 73,000 ha)

A mountainous area (800-2140 m) in the Cordillera Cantábrica with steep slopes covered by scrub and grasslands, interesting woods (*Quercus robur*, *Q. pyrenaica*, *Q. petraea*, *Fagus sylvatica*), and limestone cliffs at high altitude. The summer pastures are grazed by sheep and cattle and there is big-game hunting. Brown Bear *Ursus arctos* is present. A reservoir (on the River Esla) is being filled, and deforestation to create new pastures (replacing those covered by water) is a potential threat.

Very important for breeding *Tetrao urogallus* (min. 180 males) and *Perdix perdix hispaniensis* (*c.*50 pairs). There is a rich forest-bird community, including *Circaetus gallicus* (min. 10 pairs), *Dryocopus martius* (min. 15 pairs), and *Dendrocopos medius* (10-15 pairs).

020 Picos de Europa (Asturias, Castilla y León)

43°10'N, 04°50'W 60,000 ha EEC SPA (Montaña de Covadonga: 16,925 ha)

National Park (Montañas de Covadonga: 16,925 ha); National Game Reserve (Picos de Europa: 7600 ha)

A very rugged massif (500-2648 m); a limestone karst landscape, with expanses of rocks, cliffs (many of them very high), two deep gorges (Cares and La Hermida), and two small mountain lakes (Enol and Ercina). Grasslands predominate, but in the lower areas woods (*Fagus sylvatica*, *Quercus robur*, etc.) are extensive. There are some small villages; human activities include tourism, sheep- and cattle-grazing, and big-game hunting.

The most important area for high-mountain birds in the Cordillera Cantábrica, with numerous pairs of *Tichodroma muraria*, *Pyrrhocorax graculus*, *P. pyrrhocorax*, and *Montifringilla nivalis*. Breeding birds of prey include *Gyps fulvus*, *Circaetus gallicus*, *Aquila chrysaetos* (min. 5 pairs), *Falco peregrinus*, and *Bubo bubo*. There is a good population of *Perdix perdix hispaniensis*, and *Tetrao urogallus*, *Dryocopus martius* and *Dendrocopos medius* are common in the woods.

021 Fuentes Carrionas (Castilla y León, Cantabria)

42°55'N, 04°40'W 60,000 ha

National Game Reserve (Fuentes Carrionas: 47,000 ha)

A mountainous area (800-2500 m) in the Cordillera Cantábrica with great limestone cliffs, woods of *Quercus robur* and *Fagus sylvatica* on the northern slopes and *Quercus pyrenaica* on the southern slopes, and alpine grasslands grazed by cattle. Brown Bear *Ursus arctos* and Wolf *Canis lupus* are present. There is heavy pressure from tourism and the potential threat of urbanisation.

The area supports good populations of *Tetrao urogallus* (*c.*30 males) and *Perdix perdix hispaniensis*; in addition, breeding birds of prey include *Gyps fulvus*, *Circaetus gallicus*, and *Aquila chrysaetos*.

022 Sierras de Peña Labra y del Cordel (Castilla y León, Cantabria)

43°00'N, 04°20'W 40,000 ha

Included in a National Game Reserve (Saja: 177,086 ha)

A mountainous area (600-2175 m) in the Cordillera Cantábrica, with limestone rocks, extensive scrub and grassland areas, and some deciduous woods (*Fagus sylvatica*, *Quercus petraea*, *Q. robur*). Human activities include hiking, skiing, big-game hunting, and cattle-grazing.

Important for *Tetrao urogallus* (min. 10 males), *Perdix perdix hispaniensis* (min. 50 pairs), and for breeding birds of prey including *Circaetus gallicus* and *Circus cyaneus*.

023 Embalse del Ebro (Castilla y León, Cantabria)

43°00'N, 04°00'W 6000 ha

Unprotected

A wide, generally shallow reservoir (20 km in length) with open banks, on the River Ebro. Reinosa town and some small villages are close to the area, and human activities include agriculture and cattle- and sheep-grazing. The area is affected by pollution, sand extraction, and poaching; the transfer of water from the River Ebro to the River Besaya is reducing the water-level of the reservoir and having an impact on the aquatic vegetation.

The area holds the only significant population of *Ciconia ciconia* in the northernmost part of Spain (10-15 pairs, decreasing); there are also good numbers of breeding *Podiceps cristatus* and *Anas strepera*. It is an important moulting site for *Netta rufina* (max. 2100 in July); wintering ducks and coots (av. Jan. 5000+) also occur.

024 Marismas de Santoña (Cantabria)

43°30'N, 03°30'W 2000 ha

Game Refuge; proposed Natural Park

A coastal marsh with sand-dunes at the mouth of several estuaries, with extensive intertidal mudflats and halophytic pastures. The area is used for fishing and mollusc collecting, with many villages nearby. There are numerous current and potential threats that include: proposals for industrial development with infilling, a road project, marine farming projects, urban and industrial dumping, intense poaching, and tourism.

The best wetland along the northern coast of Spain, important for passage *Platalea leucorodia* (max. 56), and for passage and wintering ducks and waders including *Anas penelope* (max. 5000), *Numenius arquata* (max. 700), and *N. phaeopus* (max. 350).

025 Ría de Guernica – Cabo de Ogoño (Euskadi)

43°22'N, 02°40'W 800 ha Included in a Biosphere Reserve (Urdaibai: 22,500 ha)

Game Refuge (1900 ha)

A deep estuary with some remnant brackish marshes, extensive mudflats and sandbanks. There is a small rocky islet covered by grass (Isla de Izaro) at the estuary mouth and a large coastal cliff in the west of the area. Heavily populated, with pressure from tourists, intense mollusc collecting, and trawling. Hunting is forbidden.

There is a colony of *Phalacrocorax aristotelis*. An important passage site for *Platalea leucorodia* (max. 100) and for waders.

026 Sierra de la Cabrera (Castilla y León, Galicia)

42°15'N, 06°45'W 40,000 ha

Unprotected

A mountainous area (1200-2122 m) in the western Cordillera Cantábrica, with extensive areas of scrub (*Cytisus*, *Ulex*, *Calluna*), patches of *Quercus pyrenaica*, plantations of *Pinus sylvestris*, and mountain grasslands grazed by sheep and cows. Sparsely populated.

The area supports a very important population of *Perdix perdix hispaniensis* (min. 100 pairs) and an interesting population of birds of prey.

027 Montes Aquilanos (Castilla y León)

42°25'N, 06°30'W 30,000 ha

Unprotected

A mountainous area (1200-2185 m) comprising the Montes Aquilanos and the Sierra del Teleno ranges, with woods and scrub of *Quercus pyrenaica*, *Picus sylvestris* plantations, and alpine grasslands grazed in summer by numerous cattle and sheep. Almost unpopulated.

The area supports a good population of *Perdix perdix hispaniensis* (min. 50 pairs) and many birds of prey including *Circaetus gallicus* (15-20 pairs).

028 Humada – Peña Amaya (Castilla y León)

42°40'N, 04°00'W 20,000 ha

Unprotected

A mountainous area (800-1362 m) with many cliffs, slopes with maquis (*Quercus faginea*, *Q. rotundifolia*, *Q. pyrenaica*), and plantations of *Pinus sylvestris*. The area is used for sheep-grazing, some cereal cultivation, and hunting. Sparsely populated.

Important for *Neophron percnopterus* (min. 5 pairs), *Gyps fulvus* (27 pairs), *Aquila chrysaetos* (min. 5 pairs), and *Falco peregrinus* (min. 7 pairs).

029 Páramo de la Lora (Castilla y León)

42°45'N, 03°55'W 5000 ha

Unprotected

High plateaus covered by grassland and low heath, with small depressions which are used for cereal cultivation. The area is also used for sheep-grazing; there are also some small pine plantations (mainly *Pinus sylvestris*) and oil wells.

An important area for breeding *Chersophilus duponti* (min. 10 pairs).

030 Hoces del Alto Ebro y Rudrón (Castilla y León)

42°45'N, 03°35'W 10,000 ha

Unprotected

The area comprises the small canyons of the Rivers Ebro and Rudrón with high limestone cliffs. The vegetation is diverse at the base of the cliffs (*Quercus rotundifolia*, *Q. faginea*, *Q. pyrenaica*, *Fagus sylvatica)*, and low open scrub (*Thymus*, *Erica*) grazed by sheep from the nearby plateaus. The area could be damaged by a road and a viaduct project.

The area holds a rich population of birds of prey including *Neophron percnopterus*, *Gyps fulvus* (min. 40 pairs), *Aquila chrysaetos*, *Falco peregrinus*, and *Bubo bubo.*

031 Páramo de Masa (Castilla y León)

42°40'N, 03°40'W 20,000 ha

Unprotected

A high plateau with poor, stony ground (limestone bedrock) and scrub of heath and thyme. Areas are being reafforested with *Pinus sylvestris,* and small depressions are used for cereal cultivation. The area is grazed by sheep. There is a project to build a road.

Important for *Circus pygargus* (min. 10 pairs) and *Chersophilus duponti* (min. 30 pairs).

032 Sierras de Oña y de la Tesla (Castilla y León)

42°50'N, 03°30'W 11,000 ha

Unprotected

A 30-km-long mountain range (750-1300 m) with numerous cliffs, two small gorges (Rivers Ebro and Oca), slopes covered by scrub (*Buxus*, *Genista*), pine plantations (*Pinus sylvestris*, *P. pinaster*), and small woods of *Quercus* spp. and *Fagus sylvatica.* The area is used for sheep- and cattle-grazing and forestry.

Important for cliff-nesting birds of prey including *Gyps fulvus* (min. 30 pairs) and several pairs of *Neophron percnopterus*, *Aquila chrysaetos*, *Falco peregrinus*, and *Bubo bubo.*

033 La Losa – Orduña (Sierra Salvada) (Castilla y León, Euskadi)

43°03'N, 03°11'W 20,000 ha

Unprotected

A 40-km-long mountain range (700-1200 m), with great cliffs, large expanses of scrub and grassland, a few woods of *Fagus sylvatica* and *Quercus* sp., and plantations of *Pinus sylvestris.* The area is used for sheep- and cattle-grazing, and hunting.

Important for breeding birds of prey particularly *Neophron percnopterus* (min. 5 pairs), *Gyps fulvus* (29 pairs), *Circaetus gallicus* (min. 5 pairs), and *Falco peregrinus* (min. 10 pairs). *Pyrrhocorax pyrrhocorax* is numerous and there is an isolated breeding population of *P. graculus.*

034 Hoz de Sobrón (Castilla y León, Euskadi)

42°45'N, 03°05'W 2000 ha

Unprotected

The area comprises the gorges of the River Ebro, with great cliffs and slopes covered by woodland (*Quercus rotundifolia*, *Q. faginea*, *Fagus sylvatica*), scrub (*Buxus sempervirens*), and plantations of *Pinus sylvestris*.

Important for breeding *Gyps fulvus* (min. 95 pairs).

035 Montes Obarenes (Castilla y León, La Rioja)

42°40'N, 03°15'W 10,000 ha

Unprotected

A low range (700-1200 m) to the west of Miranda de Ebro, which includes many cliffs and a small gorge (Desfiladero de Pancorbo); with grasslands, scrub (*Quercus rotundifolia*, *Buxus*, *Lavandula*), and woodland areas (*Quercus faginea* and some *Fagus sylvatica*). The area is used for sheep- and cattle-grazing, and hunting; there are agricultural villages at the edge of the area.

Interesting for birds of prey including *Neophron percnopterus* (min. 5 pairs), *Gyps fulvus* (min. 25 pairs), *Aquila chrysaetos* (min. 4 pairs), *Falco peregrinus*, and *Bubo bubo*; *Pyrrhocorax pyrrhocorax* (min. 200 pairs) is numerous.

036 Los Oteros (Castilla y León)

42°15'N, 05°25'W 80,000 ha

Unprotected

Wide plains between the Rivers Esla and Cea, comprising cereal cultivation alternating with grasslands and lucerne fields. There is also sheep-grazing.

An important area for breeding steppe birds including *Circus pygargus* (min. 10 pairs), *Otis tarda* (200 birds), *Tetrax tetrax* (min. 200 birds), and *Pterocles alchata* (min. 50 pairs).

037 Tierra de Campos (Castilla y León)

42°00'N, 05°00'W 270,000 ha

Unprotected

Large plains used mainly for dry cereal cultivation (barley, wheat, oats) with some grasslands. Irrigated fields have been introduced (corn, beetroot, lucerne) recently. The area is used for extensive sheep-grazing and hunting; there are many villages. An increase in irrigated agriculture would be detrimental to the avifauna.

A very important area for breeding steppe birds, particularly *Otis tarda* (*c.*2000 birds); other species include *Circus pygargus*, *Tetrax tetrax*, *Pterocles orientalis*, and *P. alchata*.

038 Villafáfila – Embalse del Esla (Castilla y León)

41°50'N, 05°40'W 45,000 ha EEC SPA (32,682 ha)

National Game Reserve (Villafáfila: 32,682 ha)

An extensive, semi-arid, treeless plain typical of the Meseta Norte. An endorreic area, with some seasonal and brackish lagoons (Salinas de Villafáfila). Mainly dry cultivation (wheat, barley, lucerne) with grasslands between cultivated fields, in depressions, and surrounding the lagoons. The area is also used for extensive sheep-grazing and hunting; there are some villages.

Very important for steppe birds, being one of the best area in the Iberian peninsula for *Otis tarda* (*c.*1000 birds); also *Tetrax tetrax* (min. 200 pairs) and *Pterocles orientalis* (min. 50 pairs) breed.

Additional information is provided for the following subsites:

038-1 Salinas de Villafáfila

Three seasonal brackish and shallow lagoons close to the village of Villafáfila, surrounded by marshes and wet pastures. In immediate danger of natural infilling because of sedimentation.

A regular site for migrating *Platalea leucorodia*; also wintering ducks and geese, being particularly important for *Anser anser* (max. 5500 in Jan.).

038-2 Embalse del Esla

A long narrow vegetation-free reservoir on the River Esla.

A roosting site for the only wintering population of *Anser fabalis* in Spain (max. 2800 in Jan. 1981; decreasing).

039 Villalpando – Villardefrades (Castilla y León)

41°45'N, 05°25'W 22,000 ha

Unprotected

The plains to the west of Villafáfila, mainly covered by dry cereal cultivation with small areas of scrub and grasslands. There are some small villages.

A breeding area for steppe birds including *Otis tarda* (min. 200 birds).

040 Tordesillas – Mota del Marqués (Castilla y León)

41°40'N, 05°15'W 40,000 ha

Unprotected

Plains between Tordesillas and the border with Zamora province with extensive wheat and barley cultivation broken by small pinewoods (*Pinus pinea*). The area is also grazed by sheep.

A rich area for steppe birds with *Otis tarda* (min. 100 birds), *Tetrax tetrax* (min. 50-100 birds), and *Pterocles orientalis* (min. 50 birds). In addition, a good variety of birds of prey breeds in the pinewoods.

041 Castronuño – Pollos (Castilla y León)

41°25'N, 05°15'W 9000 ha

Unprotected

The River Duero between Pollos (Valladolid) and Toro (Zamora) with alluvial woodland (*Salix*, *Populus*, *Ulmus*). A dammed part (Embalse de San José) has abundant marshy vegetation. There is dry and irrigated cultivation nearby (cereal, beetroot).

The site holds the best heronries in Castilla y León: *Nycticorax nycticorax* (81 pairs), *Egretta garzetta* (2 pairs), and *Ardea cinerea* (143 pairs).

042 Alaejos – Nava del Rey (Castilla y León)

41°18'N, 05°15'W 30,000 ha

Unprotected

A wide plain to the south-west of Valladolid used for dry cereal cultivation (wheat, barley) and sheep-grazing. There are some small villages.

An important area for breeding steppe birds with *Otis tarda* (min. 200 birds).

043 Madrigal – Peñaranda (Castilla y León)

41°00'N, 05°05'W 60,000 ha

Unprotected

A plain immediately to the south of the previous area which is used for dry cereal cultivation and sheep-grazing.

Important for steppe birds including *Otis tarda* (min. 400 birds), *Tetrax tetrax* (min. 200 birds), *Burhinus oedicnemus*, *Pterocles orientalis*, and *P. alchata*.

044 Gallegos del Pan (Castilla y León)

41°40'N, 05°35'W 10,000 ha

Unprotected

A small plain used mainly for dry cereal cultivation (wheat, barley), with some sheep-grazing. There are several villages.

An important area for breeding *Otis tarda* (min. 200 birds).

045 Peleas de Abajo (Castilla y León)

41°25'N, 05°35'W 12,000 ha

Unprotected

A plain to the south-east of Zamora, used mainly for dry cereal cultivation (wheat, barley) and as sheep pasture.

An important area for breeding *Otis tarda* (min. 200 birds).

046 Arribes del Duero – Fermoselle (Castilla y León)

41°25'N, 06°15'W 10,000 ha

Unprotected

Granite cliffs along the River Duero between Zamora province and Portugal, with slopes covered in *Quercus rotundifolia*, sclerophyllous scrub, and grassland. The area is used for sheep- and cattle-grazing, barley and wheat cultivation; there are also vineyards, some small villages, and small dams for electric-power generation.

Very important for breeding birds of prey with *Neophron percnopterus* (25-30 pairs), *Gyps fulvus* (min. 40 pairs), *Aquila chrysaetos* (8-13 pairs), *Hieraaetus fasciatus* (5-7 pairs), *Falco peregrinus* (max. 10 pairs), and *Bubo bubo* (min. 15 pairs). *Ciconia nigra* (4-6 pairs) also breeds.

047 Río Huebra – Arribes del Duero (Castilla y León)

40°50'N, 06°45'W 30,000 ha

Unprotected

A group of granite cliffs carved by the River Duero and its tributaries, the Huebra and Agueda, immediately to the south of the previous area, with scrub of *Quercus rotundifolia*, *Cistus*, and *Juniperus* on the slopes. The area is used for sheep- and cattle-grazing; hydroelectric dams are proposed along the River Huebra. Sparsely populated.

Extremely important for breeding *Ciconia nigra* (min. 10 pairs), *Neophron percnopterus* (min. 50 pairs), *Gyps fulvus* (min. 120 pairs), *Circaetus gallicus* (min. 7 pairs), *Hieraaetus fasciatus* (min. 7 pairs), *Falco peregrinus* (min. 10 pairs), *Bubo bubo* (8-10 pairs), and *Pyrrhocorax pyrrhocorax* (100-160 pairs).

048 Ledesma – Río Tormes (Castilla y León)

41°05'N, 06°00'W 3000 ha

Unprotected

A small area with granite cliffs in the River Tormes basin, with *Salix*, *Ulmus*, and *Populus* zones, and 'dehesa'-like woods (*Quercus rotundifolia*, *Q. pyrenaica*). The area is grazed by cattle.

A breeding area for *Ciconia nigra* (min. 2 pairs).

049 Peña de Francia (Castilla y León, Extremadura)

40°30'N, 06°10'W 60,000 ha

Includes 2 EEC SPAs (Las Batuecas: 21,500; Arca y Buitrera: 2200 ha)

National Game Reserve (Las Batuecas: 20,796 ha)

A mountainous area (650-1730 m) in the western spurs of the Sistema Central, with slopes covered by woodland of *Quercus rotundifolia* and *Q. pyrenaica*, and *Cytisus* scrub; also *Castanea sativa* woodland and a few pine plantations (*Pinus sylvestris*). The area is used for sheep- and cattle-grazing and big-game hunting. Problems include the building of roads, afforestation, and uncontrolled human access. Lynx *Lynx lynx* is present.

An important area for *Aegypius monachus* (25-30 pairs); also breeding *Ciconia nigra* (1 pair), *Aquila adalberti* (min. 1 pair), and *Gyps fulvus* (20-25 pairs).

050 Sierra de Gredos (Castilla y León, Extremadura)

40°16'N, 05°00'W 200,000 ha

National Game Reserve (Sierra de Gredos: 27,000 ha)

A mountain range (500-2592 m), *c.*115 km long, in the Sistema Central, with woodland (*Quercus pyrenaica*), pine plantations (*Pinus pinaster*, *P. sylvestris*), large areas of scrub (*Genista*, *Cytisus*), alpine grassland, and rocks. Human activities include forestry, cattle-grazing (summer pastures), big-game hunting, and tourism. Building, an increase in the number of roads, inappropriate forestry management, and scrub burning are problems in the area.

Very important for breeding birds of prey with *Pernis apivorus* (min. 10 pairs), *Milvus migrans* (min. 100 pairs), *M. milvus* (min 100 pairs), *Gyps fulvus* (20-25 pairs), *Aegypius monachus* (50 pairs), *Aquila adalberti* (5 pairs), *A. chrysaetos* (20 pairs), and *Hieraaetus pennatus* (min. 50 pairs). Also interesting for breeding passerines, which include *Luscinia svecica* (the best population in Iberia) and *Prunella collaris*.

051 Río Moros (Castilla y León)

40°55'N, 04°22'W 5000 ha

Unprotected

Coniferous woodland (*Pinus pinaster*, *P. pinea*) along the River Moros, with some alluvial vegetation (*Fraxinus*, *Ulmus*), and grasslands. The area is used for sheep-grazing, and there is dry cereal cultivation (barley, wheat) in the surrounding area.

Important for breeding *Ciconia ciconia* (*c.*40 pairs), *Milvus migrans* (min. 50 pairs), and *M. milvus* (min. 20 pairs).

052 Riofrío – Segovia (Castilla y León)

40°58'N, 04°08'W 7000 ha

Unprotected

This area comprises the surroundings of Segovia and the Riofrío park (belonging to the Spanish Royal Family); a former royal hunting ground with good *Quercus rotundifolia* woodland and some small limestone cliffs. The area is extensively settled and there are some hazardous power-lines.

An important breeding area for *Ciconia ciconia* (min. 25 pairs), *Milvus migrans* (min. 50 pairs), other birds of prey and *Pyrrhocorax pyrrhocorax* (min. 100 pairs).

053 Cañón del Duratón (Castilla y León)

41°20'N, 03°50'W 15,000 ha

Unprotected

A limestone canyon, carved by the River Duratón and its tributaries, downstream from Sepúlveda, with *Populus* plantations and *Salix* and *Ulmus* along the river; low open scrub (*Thymus*, *Lavandula*), xerophytic grasslands, and some small patches of *Juniperus thurifera* and *Quercus rotundifolia* on the sides of the canyon. The area is grazed by sheep.

The canyon holds important populations of cliff-nesting birds of prey with *Neophron percnopterus* (15 pairs), *Gyps fulvus* (170-180 pairs), and *Falco peregrinus* (12 pairs); also *Pyrrhocorax pyrrhocorax* (min. 200 pairs), and *Chersophilus duponti* (min. 50 pairs) in areas of wasteland.

054 Montejo de la Vega (Castilla y León)

41°30'N, 03°40'W 7000 ha EEC SPA (2100 ha)

Game Refuge (managed by ADENA – WWF)

A limestone canyon, carved by the River Riaza, with *Populus* plantations, small woods of *Quercus rotundifolia* and *Juniperus thurifera*, open scrub (*Thymus*, *Lavandula*), grasslands, and dry cultivation (wheat, barley) in surrounding areas. There is also sheep-grazing. The area is affected by a railway, hazardous power-lines, and many visitors.

Important for cliff-nesting birds of prey, especially *Neophron percnopterus* (15 pairs) and *Gyps fulvus* (*c.*150 pairs). *Pterocles orientalis* and *Chersophilus duponti* (min. 80 pairs) breed in nearby wastelands.

055 Tiermes – Caracena (Castilla y León)

41°25'N, 03°00'W 38,000 ha

Unprotected

A rugged landscape with many small gorges, small woods of *Juniperus thurifera* and *Quercus rotundifolia*, wastelands (*Thymus*, *Lavandula*), and dry cereal cultivation. The area is used for sheep-grazing, and there are many small villages.

Important for cliff-nesting birds of prey including *Neophron percnopterus* (min. 15 pairs), *Gyps fulvus* (108 pairs), *Aquila chrysaetos* (5 pairs), *Falco peregrinus*, and *Bubo bubo*.

056 Altos de Barahona (Castilla y León)

41°20'N, 02°30'W 50,000 ha

Unprotected

A deforested, high, stony, limestone plateau in southern Soria (with small cliffs along rivers and streams), mainly covered by dry cereal cultivation, which is broken by fringes of low scrub (*Thymus*, *Lavandula*, *Genista scorpius*) and dry grassland. The area is used for sheep-grazing, and there are some small villages.

Very interesting for steppe birds including *Tetrax tetrax*, *Pterocles orientalis* (min. 30 pairs), and especially *Chersophilus duponti* (min. 2000-3000 pairs; the most important population in Spain). There are also many birds of prey.

057 Cañón del Río Lobos (Castilla y León)

41°40'N, 03°07'W 8000 ha EEC SPA (9580 ha)

Natural Park (9580 ha)

A limestone canyon carved by the River Lobos and its tributaries in the Sierra de Nafría. The slopes are covered by pinewoods (*Pinus sylvestris*, *P. pinaster*), maquis (*Quercus rotundifolia*, *Juniperus thurifera*), scrub, and grasslands. The area is used for forestry and sheep-grazing. Problems include massive tourism and sand extraction from the river.

Interesting for cliff-nesting birds of prey: *Neophron percnopterus* (5 pairs) and *Gyps fulvus* (min. 35 pairs).

058 Valle del Arlanza – Silos (Castilla y León)

42°03'N, 03°24'W 10,000 ha

Unprotected

A group of limestone cliffs carved by the Rivers Arlanza and Mataviejas, in the southern spurs of the Sistema Ibérico Norte. The slopes and plateaus are covered by low woods

(*Juniperus thurifera*, *Quercus rotundifolia*) and scrub (*Juniperus communi*, *Cistus laurifolius*. The area is used for cereal cultivation (wheat, oats; in the valleys) and sheep-grazing.

There is a rich population of birds of prey with breeding *Neophron percnopterus* (min. 10 pairs), *Gyps fulvus* (min. 115 pairs), *Aquila chrysaetos*, *Hieraaetus fasciatus*, *Falco peregrinus*, and *Bubo bubo*.

059 Páramos del Cerrato (Castilla y León)

41°55'N, 04°00'W 40,000 ha

Unprotected

A wide high plateau, mainly used for cereal cultivation (wheat, barley), with small areas of scrub (*Thymus*, *Lavandula*), and a few areas of maquis (*Quercus rotundifolia*, *Q. faginea*). The area is used for sheep-grazing and hunting; there are some small villages.

An important area for breeding *Otis tarda* (min. 100 birds) and *Tetrax tetrax* (min. 100 birds); also *Circus pygargus* (min. 10 pairs).

060 Río Carrión en Husillos (Castilla y León)

42°05'N, 04°31'W 150 ha

Unprotected

An alluvial plain with woodland of *Alnus glutinosa* and *Populus nigra*. There is human disturbance to the heron colony.

Holds the most important breeding colony of *Nycticorax nycticorax* (165 pairs) in the Duero valley.

061 El Escorial – San Martín de Valdeiglesias (Castilla y León, Comunidad de Madrid)

40°30'N, 04°10'W 150,000 ha

Unprotected

Ranges of the Sistema Central between the Puerto de Guadarrama and Gredos, including the upper basins of the Rivers Guadarrama, Perales and Alberche. Vegetation includes 'dehesa' woodland (*Quercus rotundifolia*), large grassland or scrub areas, and, in the mountains, small woods of *Quercus pyrenaica* and *Pinus* spp. (*Pinus pinaster*, *P. pinea*, *P. sylvestris*). The area is used for cereal cultivation, cattle-grazing and forestry. Close to Madrid with conurbations in many places; problems include massive tourism, hazardous power-lines, rubbish-dumps, and egg-collecting.

Very important for *Aquila adalberti* (min. 10 pairs). Other birds of prey are generally abundant including *Milvus migrans*, *Aegypius monachus*, *Aquila chrysaetos*, *Hieraaetus fasciatus*, *H. pennatus*, and *Bubo bubo*. Also breeding *Ciconia nigra* (min. 2 pairs).

062 Sierra de Guadarrama (Castilla y León, Comunidad de Madrid)

40°50'N, 04°00'W 54,000 ha

Includes 2 EEC SPAs (El Espinar: 4792 ha; Pinar de Valsain: 10,472 ha)

Regional Natural Park (Cuenca Alta del Manzanares: 35,829 ha); two controlled hunting areas are included (Lozoya and Guadarrama)

A mountain range (900-2430 m) in the Sistema Central with woodland of *Quercus pyrenaica* and *Pinus sylvestris*, and *Q. rotundifolia* below 1000 m; also large areas of degraded *Cistus* and *Lavandula* scrub, with *Cytisus* and *Juniperus* scrub and alpine grasslands above 1800 m. The area is used for cattle-grazing, big-game hunting, and skiing. There is pressure from tourism and building development.

An important nesting area for birds of prey including *Gyps fulvus* (*c.*30 pairs), *Aegypius monachus* (30 pairs), *Aquila adalberti* (min. 3 pairs), *A. chrysaetos* (7 pairs), and *Hieraaetus pennatus* (min. 20 pairs).

063 El Pardo – Viñuelas (Comunidad de Madrid)

40°35'N, 03°45'W 40,000 ha

Includes 2 EEC SPAs (Monte del Pardo: 14,777 ha; Soto de Viñuelas: 4252 ha)

Unprotected

An undulating area in the foothills of the Sistema Central, immediately to the north of Madrid. Sandy ground, with 'dehesa'-like oak woodland (*Quercus rotundifolia*) and grasslands. The El Pardo dam on the River Manzanares is included. The largest estate (El Pardo, a former royal hunting park) belongs to the Spanish Royal Family. The nearby conurbations are constantly expanding, and there is uncontrolled access and egg-collecting.

An extremely important area for nesting birds of prey with *Aegypius monachus* (min. 6 pairs), *Aquila adalberti* (min. 7 pairs), and *Bubo bubo* (min. 10 pairs). The dam supports abundant wintering *Fulica atra* and ducks, and is a resting site for *Ciconia nigra*.

064 Talamanca – Camarma (Comunidad de Madrid)

40°40'N, 03°25'W 17,000 ha

Unprotected

An area of plains and hillocks with extensive cereal croplands (wheat, barley) and small patches of wasteland (*Thymus*, *Lavandula*). The area is used for sheep-grazing. Problems include house building (mostly illegal) due to its proximity to Madrid, intense hunting, and hazardous power-lines.

An important area for breeding steppe birds including *Circus pygargus*, *Burhinus oedicnemus* (min. 100 pairs), *Otis tarda* (120 birds), and *Tetrax tetrax* (min. 300 birds).

065 Cortados del Jarama (Comunidad de Madrid)

40°15'N, 03°30'W 4000 ha

Unprotected

The River Jarama and River Manzanares, with chalk cliffs, to the south-east of Madrid. Several river sections have patches of *Salix*, *Populus*, and *Fraxinus*. In certain areas, gravel and sand extraction have produced many small lagoons which are partially covered by reeds. Human activities include cereal cultivation and livestock-grazing, and there are major centres of human habitation. The rivers are very polluted, and other problems include refuse dumping, uncontrolled hunting, and hazardous power-lines.

Holds interesting populations of *Ciconia ciconia* (min. 40 pairs), *Milvus migrans* (min. 50 pairs), *Falco naumanni* (*c.*40 pairs), and *F. peregrinus* (min. 10 pairs).

066 Sierra de Ayllón (Castilla-La Mancha, Castilla y León, Comunidad de Madrid)

41°15'N, 03°20'W 150,000 ha

National Game Reserve (Sonsaz: 68,000 ha); Natural Park (Hayedo de Tejera Negra: 1641 ha)

A wide massif (1000-2262 m) at the eastern end of the Sistema Central mountains. A very eroded area with sclerophyllous scrub (*Cistus* sp.) predominating; also small woods (*Quercus pyrenaica*, *Fagus sylvatica*), and recent extensive pine plantations (*Pinus sylvestris*). Almost unpopulated, with many abandoned small villages, and only a small amount of livestock-grazing.

Very important for *Aquila chrysaetos* (18 pairs); other birds of prey include *Pernis apivorus* (5+ pairs), *Gyps fulvus* (5 pairs), *Hieraaetus fasciatus* (3 pairs), *Falco peregrinus* (5+ pairs), and *Bubo bubo* (5+ pairs).

067 Puebla de Beleña (Castilla-La Mancha)

40°51'N, 04°14'W 400 ha

Unprotected

Two small, shallow lagoons (sometimes totally dry) surrounded by meadows. The surrounding areas are devoted to cereal crops and sheep-grazing. There is intense human pressure due to hunting, building on the banks, nearby army installations, and water exploitation.

An important resting site for *Grus grus* (frequently 500+ birds) lying between the Laguna de Gallocanta and the wintering areas in Extremadura.

068 Entrepeñas – Buendía (Castilla-La Mancha)

40°30'N, 02°40'W 25,000 ha

Unprotected

A small range (800-1189 m) crossed by the Rivers Tajo and Guadiela, with numerous limestone cliffs, maquis of *Quercus rotundifolia* and *Q. faginea*, pinewoods of *Pinus halepensis*, and sclerophyllous scrub. The area is used for goat- and sheep-grazing, tourism, and recreation; there are also some hydroelectric power-stations and residential areas.

Important for cliff-nesting birds of prey including *Aquila chrysaetos* (7 pairs), *Hieraaetus fasciatus* (6 pairs), *Falco peregrinus* (5 pairs), and *Bubo bubo* (min. 5 pairs).

Includes the following subsite:

068-1 Embalse de Buendía

Unprotected

A wide reservoir on the River Guadiela to the east of the mountain range. Activities include water-sports and hunting.

An important resting site for *Grus grus* (used by thousands of birds) lying between the Laguna de Gallocanta and the wintering areas in Extremadura.

069 Alto Tajo (Castilla-La Mancha)

40°48'N, 02°15'W 60,000 ha

Unprotected

An almost continuous limestone canyon along the upper River Tajo, *c.*80 km long. Vegetation includes pinewoods (*Pinus nigra*, *P. sylvestris*), garigue, and grassland areas. Sparsely populated, with forestry and some sheep-grazing. There is the risk of hydro-electric development (a dam is already proposed).

Very important for cliff-nesting birds of prey such as *Neophron percnopterus* (12 pairs), *Gyps fulvus* (min. 100 pairs), *Hieraaetus fasciatus* (5 pairs), *Falco peregrinus* (min. 20 pairs), and *Bubo bubo* (min. 20 pairs).

070 Parameras de Maranchón – Layna (Castilla-La Mancha, Castilla y León)

41°00'N, 02°15'W 20,000 ha

Unprotected

A highland 'páramo' area at 1200 m with poor vegetation, comprising scrub and grasslands, and some small open woods of *Juniperus thurifera* and *Quercus faginea*. The area is used for sheep-grazing and some dry cereal cultivation. Potential threats include agricultural transformation and afforestation.

Interesting for its steppe-bird populations including *Tetrax tetrax*, *Burhinus oedicnemus*, *Pterocles orientalis*, and *Chersophilus duponti* (min. 500 pairs).

071 Paramera de Embid – Molina (Castilla-La Mancha)

41°00'N, 01°55'W 15,000 ha

Unprotected

Treeless flat highlands at 1000-1200 m with dry cereal crops and patches of cushion-shaped scrub (*Genista pumila*, *Lavandula* sp.), and grasslands; grazed by sheep. There is a risk of afforestation.

Interesting for its steppe-bird populations including *Tetrax tetrax*, *Pterocles orientalis*, and *Chersophilus duponti* (min. 400 pairs).

072 Serranía de Cuenca (Castilla-La Mancha)

40°25'N, 02°00'W 75,000 ha

National Game Reserve (25,000 ha); Natural Monument (Ciudad Encantada)

Flat-topped mountains (1200-1600 m) to the north of Cuenca with abundant gorges, cliffs, and eroded karstic forms, almost completely covered by pinewoods (*Pinus nigra*, *P. pinaster*). Used mainly for forestry, with a proposed residential park at El Cambrón.

Important for birds of prey including *Neophron percnopterus* (min. 10 pairs), *Gyps fulvus* (70 pairs), *Circaetus gallicus* (min. 10 pairs), *Aquila chrysaetos* (12 pairs), *Hieraaetus pennatus* (min. 5 pairs), *H. fasciatus* (4 pairs), *Falco peregrinus* (min. 15 pairs), and *Bubo bubo* (min. 5 pairs).

073 Valeria (Castilla-La Mancha)

39°50'N, 02°10'W 300 ha

Unprotected

Small area of scrub (*Genista*, *Thymus*, *Lavandula*) on a plateau (1100 m) mostly devoted to dry cereal crops.

Important for *Chersophilus duponti* (min. 100 pairs); also holds *Tetrax tetrax*, *Burhinus oedicnemus*, and *Pterocles orientalis*.

074 Carboneras de Guadazaón (Castilla-La Mancha)

39°55'N, 01°50'W 500 ha

Unprotected

A small area of plateau (1000 m) covered with scrub (*Genista*, *Thymus*), situated amongst some dry cereal croplands.

Important for *Chersophilus duponti* (min. 50 pairs).

075 Moya (Castilla-La Mancha)

40°00'N, 01°20'W 2000 ha

Unprotected

Plains devoted to dry cereal cultivation with interspersed patches of scrub; grazed by sheep.

Important for *Chersophilus duponti* (min. 100 pairs).

076 Hoces del Cabriel Medio (Castilla-La Mancha)

39°50'N, 01°40'W 40,000 ha

Unprotected

The gorges of the River Cabriel and its tributaries upstream of the Contreras Dam with many cliffs. Vegetation comprises open pinewoods (*Pinus nigra*, *P. halepensis*), *Quercus rotundifolia*, *Juniperus thurifera*, and Mediterranean scrub and grassland areas. Sparsely populated, with forestry and some sheep-grazing.

Very important for birds of prey including *Neophron percnopterus* (min. 5 pairs), *Circaetus gallicus* (min. 10 pairs), *Aquila chrysaetos* (6 pairs), *Hieraaetus pennatus*, *H. fasciatus* (7 pairs), *Falco peregrinus* (min. 15 pairs), and *Bubo bubo* (min. 5 pairs).

077 Pétrola – Almansa – Yecla (Castilla-La Mancha, Murcia)

38°45'N, 01°20'W 80,000 ha

Unprotected

An undulating plain; croplands (cereal, vineyards) alternate with dry grasslands and mat-weed areas (*Stipa tenacissima*), maquis (*Quercus rotundifolia*) and a few pines (*Pinus halepensis*). Also endorreic areas with lagoons. The area is used for sheep-grazing, and there is poaching.

Important for steppe birds including *Otis tarda* (min. 100 birds), *Tetrax tetrax* (possibly 100+ birds), *Burhinus oedicnemus* (numerous), and *Pterocles orientalis* (min. 50 pairs).

078 Hoces del Río Mundo (Castilla-La Mancha)

38°30'N, 02°00'W 12,000 ha

Unprotected

Limestone gorges and cliffs carved by the Mundo River, with pinewoods (*Pinus halepensis*, *P. nigra*) in some areas. The area is used for sheep-grazing. Roads cross the area and there are some scattered villages.

An important area for cliff-nesting birds, especially birds of prey, with breeding *Neophron percnopterus*, *Aquila chrysaetos*, *Hieraaetus fasciatus* (4 pairs), *Falco peregrinus*, *Bubo bubo* (6 pairs), and *Pyrrhocorax pyrrhocorax* (min. 100 pairs).

079 Hoces del Río Segura (Castilla-La Mancha)

38°20'N, 02°00'W 25,000 ha

Unprotected

A stretch of the River Segura valley, with two dams (Fuensanta and El Cenajo), limestone cliffs, woods (mainly *Pinus halepensis*), and Mediterranean scrub. Sparsely populated, with sheep-grazing.

An important area for birds of prey with *Aquila chrysaetos* (7 pairs), *Hieraaetus fasciatus* (4 pairs), *Falco peregrinus* (min. 10 pairs), and *Bubo bubo* (min. 5 pairs).

080 Campo de Montiel (Castilla-La Mancha)

38°40'N, 02°50'W 130,000 ha

Unprotected

An undulating stony plain; dry croplands (barley, wheat, sunflower) alternate with patches of wasteland (garigue and grasslands) and small woods (*Juniperus thurifera*, *Quercus rotundifolia*). Sparsely populated. The area is used for sheep-grazing, and recently large areas have been irrigated (for corn).

Of great importance for steppe birds including *Otis tarda* (130 birds in the Albacete zone), *Tetrax tetrax*, *Burhinus oedicnemus*, *Pterocles orientalis* and *P. alchata* (all relatively numerous), and *Chersophilus duponti* (min. 30 pairs).

081 San Clemente – Villarrobledo (Castilla-La Mancha)

39°20'N, 02°30'W 120,000 ha

Unprotected

An area of cultivated plains with dry cereal croplands and vineyards, with a few woods of *Quercus rotundifolia*. There are some irrigation schemes.

Important for *Otis tarda* (min. 100 birds).

082 Complejo lagunar de Pedro Muñoz – Manjavacas (Castilla-La Mancha)

39°25'N, 02°45'W 50,000 ha

Some lagoons are Game Refuges

A group of lagoons of different sizes (most important being those at Pedro Muñoz and Manjavacas) and the small Embalse de los Muleteros (reservoir) on the River Záncara; surrounded by agricultural land, either dry (mainly cereals and vineyards) or irrigated (sunflowers). Problems include drought and over-exploitation of underground water-supplies. Densely populated.

The lagoons support variable numbers of breeding *Podiceps nigricollis* (max. 100+ pairs), *Circus aeruginosus* (5+ pairs), *Glareola pratincola* (25+ pairs), *Recurvirostra avosetta* (50+ pairs), *Himantopus himantopus* (150+ pairs), and *Gelochelidon nilotica* (190+ pairs). *Otis tarda*, *Tetrax tetrax*, *Burhinus oedicnemus*, and many *Pterocles alchata* occur in the surrounding agricultural land.

083 Tarancón – El Hito – Corral de Almaguer (Castilla-La Mancha)

40°00'N, 03°00'W 150,000 ha

Unprotected

A mainly cultivated plain (cereal, sunflowers, legumes, vineyards) but with patches of grassland and *Quercus rotundifolia*. The area is also grazed by sheep. Poaching is a problem.

Important for *Otis tarda* (min. 240 birds).

Includes the following subsite:

083-1 El Hito

Unprotected

A seasonal lagoon (875 ha) of varying importance depending on the rainfall. Surrounded by cereal croplands.

In good years, *Grus grus* occurs on migration and in winter (max. 1000).

084 Dehesa de Monreal (Castilla-La Mancha)

39°47'N, 03°29'W 180 ha

Unprotected

A small group of artificial lagoons fed by a seasonal creek, with abundant islands and marshy zones. There is moderate hunting. Threatened by drainage.

Holds an important breeding colony of *Gelochelidon nilotica* (min. 25 pairs), with post-nuptial concentrations of several hundred birds. Also breeding *Circus aeruginosus* (min. 3 pairs) and wintering *Netta rufina* (max. 400).

085 Llanos de Tembleque – La Guardia (Castilla-La Mancha)

39°40'N, 03°30'W 60,000 ha

Unprotected

A cultivated area in the plains of La Mancha covered mainly with dry cereal croplands and some vineyards. Endorreic in parts with seasonal lagoons and salt pastures with *Tamarix* sp. The area is used for sheep-grazing, and there are some medium-sized villages. Poaching is a problem.

One of the most important areas for *Otis tarda* in Castilla-La Mancha (several hundred birds). *Tetrax tetrax* and *Pterocles alchata* are also abundant.

086 Complejo lagunar de Alcázar de San Juan – Quero (Castilla-La Mancha)

39°30'N, 03°10'W 44,000 ha

Some of the lagoons are Game Refuges

An extensive agricultural area (cereal, vineyards) with several natural and some artificial lagoons. Severe problems include drying out and pollution of the lagoons, and hunting. Densely populated.

The lagoons are important for breeding *Podiceps nigricollis* (min. 30 pairs), *Nycticorax nycticorax*, *Egretta garzetta*, *Netta rufina* (several hundred pairs), *Circus aeruginosus* (min. 5 pairs), *Glareola pratincola* (min. 25 pairs), and *Gelochelidon nilotica* (min. 300 pairs). The surrounding fields are interesting for breeding *Otis tarda*, *Tetrax tetrax*, *Burhinus oedicnemus*, and *Pterocles alchata* (common). Important concentrations of *Grus grus* (500+), *Netta rufina* (min. 800) and other ducks occur on migration and in winter.

087 Tablas de Daimiel, Embalses del Vicario y Gasset y Navas de Malagón (Castilla-La Mancha)

39°00'N, 03°45'W 26,000 ha

Ramsar Site (1812 ha); Biosphere Reserve (La Mancha Humeda: 25,000 ha); EEC SPA (Tablas de Daimiel: 1928 ha)

National Park (Tablas de Daimiel: 2232 ha)

A group of wetlands to the north of Ciudad Real, comprising the wide flood-plains of the River Guadiana (Tablas de Daimiel), two reservoirs (Vicario and Gasset), and two small endorreic lagoons (Navas de Malagón). There are important marshy areas, especially in the Tablas de Daimiel, where large expanses of *Cladium mariscus* occur. The surrounding area is cultivated; formerly dry cultivation (olive, cereal, vine) but now irrigated (corn). The exploitation of underground water-supplies has caused the drying up of the Tablas de Daimiel during recent years, and it has declined in importance. Other problems include overhunting and human disturbance.

With good water-levels, it is important as a breeding area for *Ixobrychus minutus*, *Ardea purpurea*, *Netta rufina*, and *Circus aeruginosus* (min. 5 pairs). Steppe birds are abundant in the surrounding fields, especially *Otis tarda*, *Tetrax tetrax*, *Burhinus oedicnemus*, and *Pterocles alchata*. Interesting for wintering ducks (10,000+), particularly *Anas strepera* (min. 1000) and *Netta rufina* (min. 700).

088 Valle y Sierra de Alcudia (Castilla-La Mancha)

38°40'N, 04°30'W 70,000 ha

Unprotected

A wide valley almost completely devoted to sheep-farming (winter pastures); mostly treeless, although 'dehesa' zones (*Quercus rotundifolia*) exist. Also a mountain range to the south, reaching 1000-1100 m, with cliffs, expanses of *Cistus ladanifer*, and patches of maquis with oaks (*Quercus rotundifolia*, *Q. faginea*). There are lead mines (many abandoned) and the area is sparsely populated.

The valley is interesting for steppe birds with *Circus pygargus* (min. 10 pairs), *Tetrax tetrax* (min. 100 pairs), *Burhinus oedicnemus* (min. 100 pairs), *Pterocles orientalis* (min. 50 pairs), and *P. alchata* (min. 50 pairs); also many *Ciconia ciconia* (min. 50 pairs). In the mountains, breeding species include *Ciconia nigra* (min. 10 pairs) and many birds of prey, notably *Elanus caeruleus* (min. 5 pairs), *Aegypius monachus* (5 pairs), *Aquila adalberti*, *A. chrysaetos* (min. 5 pairs), and *Bubo bubo* (min. 10 pairs).

089 Sierra de los Canalizos (Saceruela) (Castilla-La Mancha)

38°50'N, 04°30'W 50,000 ha

Unprotected

A wide 'dehesa' plain, with small isolated ranges rising to 884 m. Vegetation comprises Mediterranean scrub and woodland (*Quercus rotundifolia*, *Q. suber*) in the hills, and 'dehesas' and wide grasslands in the plain. Sparsely populated, with sheep- and cattle-grazing. Lynx *Lynx lynx* is present. Problems include reafforestation.

Important for birds of prey including *Aegypius monachus* (min. 20 pairs), *Aquila adalberti* (min. 3 pairs), and *A. chrysaetos* (min. 3 pairs). Also breeding *Ciconia nigra* and *C. ciconia* (min. 20 pairs).

090 Sierra del Chorito (Cabañeros) (Castilla-La Mancha)

39°25'N, 04°20'W 70,000 ha

Proposed Natural Park

The southern part of the Montes de Toledo, extremely well preserved, especially the 'Cabañeros' estate. In the plains there are extensive 'dehesas' (*Quercus rotundifolia*) and grasslands, with Mediterranean scrub and woods (*Q. rotundifolia*, *Q. faginea*, *Q. suber*) in the mountains. The area is used for sheep-grazing. Lynx *Lynx lynx* and Mongoose *Herpestes ichneumon* are present. Divided into large estates; one of them, 'Cabañeros', is owned by the Defence Ministry and may become an air force training area.

Very important for *Aegypius monachus* (min. 70 pairs; the second-largest breeding colony in Spain). Other interesting species are *Ciconia nigra* (min. 3 pairs), *C. ciconia* (min. 25 pairs), *Elanus caeruleus* (min. 3 pairs), *Aquila adalberti* (min. 3 pairs), *A. chrysaetos* (min. 5 pairs), and *Bubo bubo* (min. 5 pairs).

091 Montes de Toledo (Castilla-La Mancha)

39°30'N, 04°20'W 130,000 ha

Unprotected

A mountain range (800-1447 m) between Los Yébenes and Sevilleja de la Jara, about 95 km in length. Vegetation comprises large expanses of sclerophyllous scrub (mostly *Cistus ladanifer*), dense maquis areas (with *Arbutus unedo*), and small woods (*Quercus rotundifolia*, *Q. faginea*, *Q. suber*, *Q. pyrenaica*). Almost unpopulated and only a small amount of cattle-grazing. Owned in large estates, with big-game hunting. Lynx *Lynx lynx* is present.

Very important for birds of prey including *Aegypius monachus*, *Aquila adalberti* (min. 3 pairs), *A. chrysaetos* (min. 15 pairs), and *Bubo bubo* (min. 20 pairs). Also breeding *Ciconia nigra*.

092 Embalse de Castrejón (Castilla-La Mancha)

39°48'N, 04°20'W 750 ha

Unprotected

An irrigation reservoir with steep banks on the River Tajo, with sections of marshy vegetation, alluvial woodland (*Tamarix*, *Salix*, *Populus alba*), and several islets. Some parts at the end of the reservoir are being filled by sedimentation.

Holds an important breeding colony of *Nycticorax nycticorax* (144 pairs), *Bubulcus ibis* (70 pairs), and *Egretta garzetta* (10+ pairs). Also breeding *Circus aeruginosus*. A good wintering area for waterfowl including *Phalacrocorax carbo* (min. 738).

093 Torrijos (Castilla-La Mancha)

40°00'N, 04°15'W 40,000 ha

Unprotected

Plains to the north-west of Toledo, with dry cereal croplands (wheat, barley). The area is used for sheep-grazing and small-game hunting, and there are several villages.

Important for *Otis tarda* (probably 150+ birds).

094 Embalse de Azután (Castilla-La Mancha)

39°50'N, 05°10'W 1000 ha

Unprotected

A very long reservoir on the River Tajo and the River Gevalo, with steep banks in many sections, including some partially flooded islets with vegetation (*Tamarix*, *Salix*, *Populus alba*). The area is used for grazing and hunting.

Holds important colonies of *Nycticorax nycticorax* (80 pairs) and *Bubulcus ibis* (2000 pairs). Good in winter for *Phalacrocorax carbo* and ducks.

095 Llanos de Oropesa (Castilla-La Mancha)

40°00'N, 05°10'W 40,000 ha

Unprotected

Plains in the Tajo Valley to the west of Talavera de la Reina. Mainly grassland and dry cereal cultivation with 'dehesa' zones (*Quercus rotundifolia*), and irrigated croplands by the River Tajo. Sparsely populated, with sheep-grazing and hunting.

Important for steppe birds including *Circus pygargus* (min. 20 pairs), *Otis tarda* (min. 60 birds), and *Tetrax tetrax* (many hundreds). Also breeding *Ciconia ciconia* (min. 40 pairs) and an important colony of *Passer hispaniolensis*. Large numbers of wintering *Pluvialis apricaria* occur.

096 Valle del Tiétar y Embalses de Rosarito y Navalcán (Castilla y León, Castilla-La Mancha)

40°10'N, 05°00'W 90,000 ha

Unprotected

The River Tiétar valley between Santa María del Tiétar and the Rosarito Dam (*c.*70 km). A steep-banked river and two great reservoirs, surrounded by large expanses of 'dehesa' (*Quercus rotundifolia*, *Q. suber*, *Q. pyrenaica*), grassland, and scrub (*Cistus*, *Lavandula*). There is some dry cereal cultivation, and sheep and cattle are grazed. Threatened by a huge dam project.

A well-preserved area (with a diverse avifauna), which is very important for birds of prey including *Elanus caeruleus*, *Milvus migrans* (numerous), *Circaetus gallicus*, *Aquila adalberti* (min. 5 pairs), and *Hieraaetus pennatus*. Also *Ciconia nigra* (min. 4 pairs, and post-nuptial concentrations) and *C. ciconia* colonies. *Phalacrocorax carbo* (*c.*2000) and *Grus grus* (min. 500) occur in winter.

097 Sierra de Gata (Extremadura, Castilla y León)

40°20'N, 06°35'W 50,000 ha

Unprotected

A mountain range (max. 1367 m) largely in northern Extremadura near Portugal. Diverse vegetation, mostly pine plantations (*Pinus pinaster*), also scrub, grasslands, and small woods of *Quercus pyrenaica*, *Q. rotundifolia*, and *Castanea sativa*. There is some agricultural land-use (olive-groves, orchards) and forestry; sheep and goats are grazed. Sparsely populated. Lynx *Lynx lynx* is present. Forest fires are a problem.

Important for breeding birds of prey including *Pernis apivorus* (min. 6 pairs), *Aegypius monachus* (8-10 pairs), *Aquila adalberti*, and *Hieraaetus pennatus* (min. 25 pairs). *Ciconia nigra* also breeds (min. 3 pairs).

098 Embalse de Gabriel y Galán (Extremadura)

40°16'N, 06°16'W 25,000 ha

Unprotected

A reservoir for irrigation and electric power on the River Alagón, surrounded by 'dehesas' (*Quercus rotundifolia*, *Q. suber*, *Q. pyrenaica*), plantations of *Pinus pinaster*, grasslands, and dry and irrigated croplands. The area is also used for sheep- and cattle-grazing and hunting. Lynx *Lynx lynx* is present. The planting of *Eucalyptus* and an increase in the area of irrigated agriculture are detrimental to the site.

A breeding site for *Ciconia nigra* (perhaps 3 pairs). *Grus grus* (min. 600) and *Pluvialis apricaria* (numerous) occur in winter.

099 Embalse del Borbollón (Extremadura)

40°10'N, 06°35'W 16,000 ha

Small Ornithological Reserve

This site comprises a reservoir on the River Arrago and the surrounding territory, with 'dehesa', extensive dry cereal croplands, grasslands, and irrigated areas downstream from the dam. There is a wooded island in the reservoir where many birds breed; this is managed as an Ornithological Reserve. Future irrigation schemes would result in the island disappearing and the destruction of some 'dehesa'. The area is used for sheep- and cattle-grazing and hunting; there is only one village and some farms.

The island holds a colony of *Bubulcus ibis* (1236 pairs) and other herons, and numerous *Milvus migrans* (min. 50 pairs). Breeding species in the surrounding area include *Ciconia nigra* (min. 1 pair), *Elanus caeruleus* (min. 5 pairs), *Circus pygargus* (min. 10 pairs), *Otis tarda* (50 birds), *Burhinus oedicnemus*, and *Pterocles orientalis* (min. 50 pairs). Also passage and wintering *Grus grus* (min. 600) and *Limosa limosa* (several thousands).

100 Sierras de Coria (Extremadura)

39°50'N, 06°30'W 50,000 ha

Unprotected

A plain to the south-east of Coria crossed by a small range of hills, with cliffs particularly along the River Alagón. Most of the land is 'dehesa' (*Quercus rotundifolia*); also areas of dry cereal cultivation, scrub, grassland, woods (*Quercus suber*), and some pine (*Pinus pinea*) and *Eucalyptus* plantations. The area is grazed by sheep and cattle. Problems include reafforestation, irrigated cultivation (Rivera de Fresnedosa), and hazardous power-lines.

Important for many woodland- and cliff-nesting birds of prey such as *Elanus caeruleus*, *Milvus migrans* (min. 50 pairs), *Neophron percnopterus* (min. 5 pairs), *Gyps fulvus* (*c.*100 pairs), *Aegypius monachus* (1 pair), *Aquila adalberti* (2 pairs), and *Hieraaetus pennatus* (min. 20 pairs). *Ciconia nigra* also breeds (min. 4 pairs).

101 Embalse de Alcántara (Extremadura)

39°45'N, 06°30'W 110,000 ha

Unprotected

A huge reservoir with rugged banks on the River Tajo and its affluent, the River Almonte, and the surrounding land. Vegetation includes xerophytic grasslands, sclerophyllous scrub (*Cistus ladanifer*), 'dehesa' (*Quercus rotundifolia*), some olive-groves and cereal croplands, and some old plantations of *Pinus pinea* (Garrovillas). Human activities include sheep-grazing, hunting, sailing, and pleasure boating. There are some irrigation schemes.

The area supports breeding *Ciconia nigra* (min. 10 pairs) and a high density of *C. ciconia* (min. 160 pairs). Also many birds of prey including *Milvus migrans* (min. 100 pairs), *Circus pygargus* (min. 25 pairs), *Hieraaetus pennatus* (min. 50 pairs), and *Falco naumanni* (min. 150 pairs). Interesting for steppe birds, especially *Tetrax tetrax* (min. 200 birds) and *Burhinus oedicnemus* (min. 100 pairs). Also a wintering area for *Phalacrocorax carbo* (500) and *Grus grus* (min. 500).

102 Cuatro Lugares (Extremadura)

39°40'N, 06°20'W 20,000 ha

Unprotected

Plains to the north of the city of Cáceres, between the Rivers Tajo and Almonte, adjacent to the Alcántara Dam. Xerophytic grasslands alternate with dry cereal cultivation and 'dehesas' (*Quercus rotundifolia*). There are several villages and the area is grazed by sheep.

Very interesting for steppe birds, which include *Otis tarda* (*c.*200 birds) and *Tetrax tetrax* (*c.*2000 birds). Also wintering *Grus grus* (1200 birds).

103 Monfragüe (Extremadura)

39°40'N, 05°45'W 50,000 ha EEC SPA (17,852 ha)

Natural Park (Monfragüe: 17,852 ha)

A range of hills with many cliffs and gullies broken by the Rivers Tajo and Tiétar, which have steep sides and are dammed at two places (Torrejón Dam and Alcántara Dam). Well-preserved vegetation with extensive, dense sclerophyllous scrub (*Erica*, *Arbutus*, *Phillyrea*, *Olea*, *Cistus*), small woods of *Quercus suber*, *Q. rotundifolia*, and *Q. faginea*, and excellent 'dehesas' nearby. There are some *Eucalyptus* plantations on the northern side. Sheep and cattle are grazed, but the site is far from any villages. Lynx *Lynx lynx* and Mongoose *Herpestes ichneumon* are present.

An area of exceptional ornithological importance and probably the best area in the world for *Aegypius monachus* (min. 120 pairs). Important for other birds of prey, including *Elanus caeruleus*, *Milvus migrans* (many), *M. milvus*, *Neophron percnopterus* (10 pairs), *Gyps fulvus* (165 pairs), *Circaetus gallicus*, *Aquila adalberti* (min. 8 pairs), *A. chrysaetos* (4 pairs), *Hieraaetus pennatus* (many), *H. fasciatus* (4 pairs), *Falco peregrinus*, and *Bubo bubo* (*c.*20 pairs). Also *Ciconia nigra* (10 pairs, the best area in Spain) and a very high density of *Cyanopica cyana*.

104 Campo Arañuelo (Extremadura, Castilla-La Mancha)

40°00'N, 05°50'W 100,000 ha

Unprotected

A wide, clay and sandy plain to the south of the River Tiétar. There are many creeks and small ponds for cattle-watering, extensive 'dehesas' (mainly of *Quercus rotundifolia* but also *Q. suber* and *Q. pyrenaica*), grasslands, and dry cereal croplands. Goats and sheep are grazed. To the north, by the River Tiétar, there are plans to extend the existing area of irrigated agricultural land. There is a nuclear power-station (Almaraz) and hazardous power-lines.

Important because of its colonies of *Nycticorax nycticorax* (*c.*50 pairs), *Bubulcus ibis* (450 pairs), and *Egretta garzetta*, and a high density of *Ciconia nigra* (min. 6 pairs), and *C. ciconia* (min. 170 pairs). Also supports large numbers of birds of prey including *Elanus caeruleus* (min. 10 pairs; one of the highest densities in Spain) and *Aquila adalberti*, and a high density of *Cyanopica cyana*. Also an important wintering area for *Grus grus* (min. 1000), *Vanellus vanellus*, and *Columba palumbus*.

105 Embalse de Valdecañas (Extremadura)

39°50'N, 05°25'W 20,000 ha

Unprotected

A large reservoir on the River Tajo, surrounded by croplands (cereal and irrigated cultivation), wastelands, and 'dehesas'. The area is used for cattle-grazing and hunting. Threats include an expansion of irrigated agriculture, hazardous power-lines (close to Almaraz Nuclear Power-station) and water pollution.

Breeding species include *Ciconia nigra* (5 pairs), *C. ciconia* (55 pairs), *Circus pygargus* (min. 10 pairs), and *Passer hispaniolensis* (a very large colony). Important for wintering *Phalacrocorax carbo* (1140+).

106 Sierras de las Villuercas (Extremadura)

39°40'N, 05°25'W 100,000 ha

Unprotected

A dense group of parallel mountain ranges with steep-sloping valleys. Dense vegetation with *Quercus rotundifolia*, *Q. suber*, *Q. faginea*, *Q. pyrenaica*, and *Castanea sativa*, pine plantations (*Pinus pinaster*), and wide scrub areas. There is agricultural land around the villages, with olive-groves, irrigated fields, and small, dry cultivated areas (cereal). Lynx

Lynx lynx is present. The area is used for goat- and sheep-grazing and big-game hunting; there are some villages and many roads.

Important for birds of prey such as *Milvus migrans* (min. 50 pairs), *M. milvus* (min. 20 pairs), *Neophron percnopterus* (min. 10 pairs), *Gyps fulvus* (70 pairs), *Aegypius monachus* (2 pairs), *Aquila adalberti* (min. 3 pairs), *A. chrysaetos* (min. 5 pairs), *Hieraaetus pennatus* (min. 20 pairs), *Falco peregrinus* (min. 10 pairs), and *Bubo bubo* (min. 20 pairs). *Ciconia nigra* (min. 10 pairs) also breeds.

107 Embalse de Cijara (Castilla-La Mancha, Extremadura)

39°20'N, 04°50'W 30,000 ha

National Game Reserve (25,000 ha)

A wide reservoir on the River Guadiana and surrounding territory. Rough country, with stony plains ('rañas'), sclerophyllous scrub (*Cistus ladanifer*), woodland zones (*Quercus rotundifolia*), pine plantations (*Pinus pinaster*, *P. pinea*), 'dehesa', pasture, and dry cereal cultivation. The area is also used for sheep- and cattle-grazing, and hunting. Sparsely populated.

Breeding species include *Ciconia nigra* (2-3 pairs), *Gyps fulvus* (15 pairs), *Neophron percnopterus* (3 pairs), *Aquila chrysaetos* (min. 5 pairs), and *Bubo bubo* (min. 3 pairs).

108 Embalse de Puerto Peña – Valdecaballeros (Extremadura)

39°15'N, 05°10'W 50,000 ha

Unprotected

A wide reservoir on the River Guadiana and surrounding land. Vegetation comprises woods of *Quercus rotundifolia* and some *Q. suber*, sclerophyllous scrub (*Cistus ladanifer*), and plantations (*Pinus pinaster*, *P. pinea*, and *Eucalyptus* sp.) in the mountains; with 'dehesa' (*Q. rotundifolia*), pasture, and dry cereal cultivation (barley) in the plains. The area is used for sheep- and goat-grazing, hunting and forestry; there is also a nuclear power-station (Valdecaballeros). Problems include inappropriate forestry management. Sparsely populated.

Good for birds of prey with *Elanus caeruleus*, *Milvus milvus* (min. 20 pairs), *Gyps fulvus* (*c.* 35 pairs), *Circaetus gallicus* (min. 5 pairs), *Hieraaetus pennatus* (min. 20 pairs), *Bubo bubo* (min. 5 pairs). *Ciconia nigra* (min. 8 pairs; max. 40 birds after breeding) and *C. ciconia* (min. 30 pairs) also breed. *Grus grus* (500-1000) winters in the 'dehesa' and elsewhere in the lowlands.

109 Sierra de Pela y Embalse de Orellana (Extremadura)

39°05'N, 05°25'W 22,000 ha

Unprotected

An isolated mountain range (Sierra de Pela) with sclerophyllous scrub (*Cistus ladanifer*), a dam on the River Guadiana, and plains with extensive 'dehesas' (*Quercus rotundifolia*), pastures, olive-groves, and dry cereal cultivation. Sheep are grazed.

Breeding species include *Bubulcus ibis* (1500 pairs), *Egretta garzetta* (60 pairs), *Ciconia nigra* (also post-breeding concentrations of 30+ birds), *C. ciconia* (*c.*50 pairs), and several species of birds of prey. *Grus grus* (min. 3000) and many wildfowl occur in winter.

110 Zorita – Madrigalejo (Extremadura)

39°10'N, 05°40'W 30,000 ha

Unprotected

Undulating country of extensive grasslands with 'dehesas' (*Quercus rotundifolia*), and irrigated and cereal croplands. The area is used for sheep- and cattle-grazing and hunting; there are also several large villages.

The area supports colonies of *Bubulcus ibis* (3500 pairs), and a high density of birds of prey including *Elanus caeruleus* (min. 3 pairs), *Milvus migrans* (min. 5 pairs), *M. milvus*, *Circaetus gallicus* (min. 50 pairs), *Circus pygargus* (min. 100 pairs), *Hieraaetus pennatus*, and *Falco naumanni* (min. 25 pairs). Other steppe birds include *Otis tarda* (perhaps 300+), *Tetrax tetrax* (min. 200 birds), *Burhinus oedicnemus* (min. 100 pairs), *Glareola pratincola*, and *Pterocles alchata*. Also a wintering area for *Grus grus* (1000+).

111 Trujillo – Torrecillas de la Tiesa (Extremadura)

39°30'N, 05°50'W 50,000 ha

Unprotected

A wide undulating plain around Trujillo with granite outcrops. 'Dehesas' (*Quercus rotundifolia*) and grasslands predominate, although there is dry cereal cultivation. The area is used for sheep- and cattle-grazing and hunting, and is also crossed by a major road and power-lines.

Very important for its breeding storks, with *Ciconia nigra* (min. 3 pairs) and *C. ciconia* (min. 160 pairs), colonies of *Bubulcus ibis* (max. 5000 pairs in some years), and abundant birds of prey, especially *Elanus caeruleus* (min. 3 pairs), *Milvus migrans* (min. 50 pairs), *M. milvus*, *Circaetus gallicus* (min. 5 pairs), *Circus pygargus* (min. 100 pairs), *Hieraaetus pennatus* (min. 20 pairs), and *Falco naumanni* (min. 110 pairs, most of them in Trujillo). Large numbers of steppe birds occur including *Otis tarda* (min. 90 birds), *Tetrax tetrax* (500+ birds), *Burhinus oedicnemus* (100+ pairs), *Pterocles orientalis* (min. 50 pairs), and *P. alchata* (50+ pairs). There is a high density of *Cyanopica cyana*. Also a wintering area for *Grus grus* (350 birds).

112 Llanos entre Cáceres y Trujillo (Extremadura)

39°25'N, 06°10'W 25,000 ha

Unprotected

Undulating plains and some steep-sided rivers, with grasslands, garigue areas (*Lavandula*), dry cereal cultivation, and patches of 'dehesa' (*Quercus rotundifolia*). The area is used for sheep- and cattle-grazing and small-game hunting; there are also some abandoned mines.

Important for steppe birds with *Circus pygargus* (min. 80 pairs), *Otis tarda* (800-1000 birds), *Tetrax tetrax* (min. 2000 birds), *Burhinus oedicnemus* (min. 100 pairs), *Pterocles orientalis* (min. 50 pairs), *P. alchata* (min. 50 pairs), and *Coracias garrulus* (min. 100 pairs). Also breeding *Bubulcus ibis* (min. 500 pairs), *Ciconia nigra* (at least 3 pairs), and abundant *C. ciconia* (100+ pairs). Also a wintering area for *Grus grus* (200 birds).

113 Cáceres – Sierra de Fuentes (Extremadura)

39°25'N, 06°20'W 500 ha

Unprotected

The town of Cáceres, and a small granite range (644 m) to the south-east of the town partly covered by *Quercus rotundifolia* and *Pinus pinea*.

Breeding species include *Ciconia nigra* (1 pair), *C. ciconia* (min. 30 pairs), *Milvus migrans* (min. 50 pairs), *Circaetus gallicus* (min. 5 pairs), *Hieraaetus pennatus* (min. 10 pairs), and *Falco naumanni* (min. 100 pairs; mostly in Cáceres).

114 Malpartida de Cáceres – Arroyo de la Luz (Extremadura)

39°25'N, 06°30'W 45,000 ha

Unprotected

A wide, undulating plain with granite hillocks, numerous ponds and small old dams, 'dehesa' (*Quercus rotundifolia*) mixed with grasslands and cereal cultivation, and some patches of pine (*Pinus pinea*). Some villages are within the area. The area is extensively grazed by sheep. Agricultural transformation (irrigation) would be detrimental to the area.

The area supports a diversity of species including *Bubulcus ibis* (min. 2000 pairs), *Egretta garzetta* (min. 40 pairs), *Ardea cinerea* (min. 60 pairs), *Ciconia nigra* (2 pairs; max. 40 in post-nuptial concentrations), *C. ciconia* (min. 200 pairs; including a colony of 20 pairs on rocks), *Milvus migrans* (min. 50 pairs), *Circus pygargus* (min. 50 pairs), *Hieraaetus pennatus* (min. 20 pairs), *Falco naumanni* (min. 120 pairs; most of them in Cáceres), *Tetrax tetrax* (200+ birds), *Burhinus oedicnemus* (min. 100 pairs), *Pterocles orientalis* (min. 50 pairs), and *P. alchata* (min. 50 pairs).

115 Brozas – Membrío (Extremadura)

39°40'N, 06°50'W 85,000 ha

Unprotected

A wide plain between the River Tajo and the Sierra de San Pedro. A greater part is endorreic, with many ponds. Vegetation includes extensive grasslands with occasional dry cereal cultivation (wheat, barley), and large 'dehesas' (*Quercus rotundifolia*) in the River Salor basin. The area is used for sheep- and cattle-grazing and hunting. Sparsely populated.

Exceptionally interesting for steppe birds including *Circus pygargus* (min. 50 pairs), *Otis tarda* (800-1000 birds), *Burhinus oedicnemus* (probably 1000+ pairs), *Pterocles orientalis* (500+ pairs), and *P. alchata* (min. 500 pairs). Also breeding *Ardea cinerea* (*c.*85 pairs), *Ciconia nigra* (*c.*5 pairs) and *C. ciconia* (min. 60 pairs). *Grus grus* (200) occurs in winter.

116 Embalse del Cedillo (Extremadura)

39°40'N, 07°20'W 20,000 ha

Unprotected

A reservoir on the River Tajo and surrounding areas. The banks of the reservoir are very steep with occasional cliffs. Vegetation comprises Mediterranean scrub (*Cistus ladanifer*, *Quercus coccifera*), woodland (*Q. suber*, *Q. rotundifolia*), 'dehesas', and some olive-groves. The area is used for sheep- and cattle-grazing.

Very important for *Ciconia nigra* (10 pairs). Also many birds of prey breed including *Neophron percnopterus* (min. 5 pairs), *Gyps fulvus* (min. 40 pairs), *Hieraaetus fasciatus* (4 pairs) and *Bubo bubo* (min. 10 pairs).

117 Sierra de San Pedro (Extremadura)

39°20'N, 06°45'W 100,000 ha

Unprotected

A large mountainous area, almost 70 km in length, on the Portuguese border. Well-preserved Mediterranean vegetation, with *Quercus rotundifolia* and *Q. suber* woodland, 'dehesas', grassland, scrub, and maquis (*Cistus ladanifer*, *Lavandula pedunculata*, *Arbutus unedo*). The area is used for grazing (cattle, pigs, sheep, goats), big-game hunting, and cork exploitation. Lynx *Lynx lynx* is still present. Sparsely populated.

One of the best-preserved wild areas in Spain, with excellent bird of prey populations including *Elanus caeruleus*, *Milvus migrans* (min. 100 pairs), *Neophron percnopterus* (min. 10 pairs), *Aegypius monachus* (min. 60 pairs), *Aquila adalberti* (min. 8 pairs), *A. chrysaetos*, *Hieraaetus pennatus* (min. 50 pairs), *H. fasciatus* (min. 2 pairs), and *Bubo bubo* (min. 25 pairs). *Ciconia nigra* also breeds (min. 5 pairs; with post-breeding concentrations of 30+ birds).

118 Aldea del Cano – Casas de Don Antonio (Extremadura)

39°15'N, 06°20'W 17,000 ha

Unprotected

Plains adjacent to the Sierra de San Pedro with grasslands, dry cereal croplands, and some *Quercus rotundifolia*. The area is used for sheep- and cattle-grazing, and hunting; there are also two small villages, a road, and railway.

Important for steppe birds with *Circus pygargus* (min. 30 pairs), *Otis tarda* (100-150 birds), *Tetrax tetrax* (3000 birds), and *Pterocles alchata* (min. 50 pairs). Also a high density of *Ciconia ciconia* (min. 40 pairs) and remarkable concentrations of *Cyanopica cyana*. *Grus grus* (min. 400 birds) occurs in winter.

119 Embalse del Salor (Extremadura)

39°20'N, 06°20'W 3200 ha

Unprotected

An irrigation reservoir on the River Salor, surrounded by 'dehesas' and dry and irrigated croplands. There is a project to remove all the oaks in the 'dehesas'. The best-preserved area is the southern part, with large private estates. The northern part is suffering from uncontrolled and increasing human pressure (disturbance, residential areas, hunting).

Breeding species include *Ardea cinerea* (40 pairs), *Ciconia nigra*, *C. ciconia* (70+ pairs), *Elanus caeruleus*, *Milvus migrans*, *Hieraaetus pennatus* and *Glareola pratincola* (25-30 pairs). Also interesting for its steppe birds including *Tetrax tetrax* (300+ birds in winter) and *Pterocles orientalis*.

120 Sierra de Montánchez – Embalse de Cornalvo (Extremadura)

39°10'N, 06°10'W 30,000 ha

Unprotected

An undulating landscape along the River Aljucén to the north-east of Mérida, reaching 984 m (Sierra de Montánchez), with extensive 'dehesa' areas (*Quercus rotundifolia*, *Q. suber*), grasslands, scrub, granite outcrops, and a small reservoir. It includes two villages and several cultivated areas (vineyards, fig trees, olive-groves). The area is used for grazing (cattle, sheep, goats) and small-game hunting.

Ciconia nigra breeds (2 pairs; and post-breeding concentrations of 20 birds) as well as many pairs of *C. ciconia*. Breeding raptors include *Elanus caeruleus* (5 pairs) and *Circus pygargus* (min. 20 pairs). *Grus grus* (*c.*150) occurs in winter.

121 Lácara (Extremadura)

39°00'N, 06°25'W 5000 ha

Unprotected

Plains to the north of Mérida, mainly covered by 'dehesa' (*Quercus rotundifolia*, *Q. suber*, *Fraxinus angustifolia* alternating with extensive grasslands. The area is grazed by sheep and cattle.

Breeding species include *Ciconia nigra* (1 pair), *Elanus caeruleus* (min. 5 pairs), and *Otis tarda* (75 birds). Also a wintering area for *Grus grus* (500 birds).

122 Mérida – Embalse de Montijo (Extremadura)

38°55'N, 06°25'W 500 ha

Unprotected

The site comprises Mérida town, surrounding area, and nearby reservoirs in the River Guadiana valley. Habitats are diverse, with dry cereal cultivation, irrigated cultivation, olive-groves, 'dehesa' and *Quercus* woods, and alluvial vegetation. The area is used for grazing (cattle, sheep, pigs) and hunting.

Breeding species include *Nycticorax nycticorax*, *Bubulcus ibis* (1500 pairs), *Egretta garzetta*, *Ciconia ciconia* (min. 35 pairs), and *Falco naumanni* (min. 50 pairs, most of them in Mérida). A resting area for migrating *Grus grus* (min. 290).

123 Morante (Extremadura)

39°05'N, 06°40'W 2400 ha

Unprotected

A small expanse of dry cereal cultivation in an area occupied mainly by 'dehesas' and oak woods (*Quercus rotundifolia*, *Q. suber*), with some irrigation ponds. The area is grazed by sheep and pigs.

Breeding species include *Bubulcus ibis* (800 pairs).

124 Botoa – Villar del Rey (Extremadura)

39°10'N, 06°50'W 10,000 ha

Unprotected

Plains along the Portuguese border to the north of Badajoz, with dry cereal cultivation, grasslands, and 'dehesas' of *Quercus rotundifolia*. The area is grazed by sheep.

Supports a high density of steppe birds including *Circus pygargus*, *Otis tarda* (min. 100+ birds), *Tetrax tetrax* (several hundred birds), *Burhinus oedicnemus*, and *Pterocles alchata*. Also wintering *Grus grus* (min. 400).

125 El Membrío – La Albuera (Extremadura)

38°50'N, 06°50'W 8000 ha

Unprotected

Plains to the south-east of Badajoz with grasslands, 'dehesas' (*Quercus rotundifolia*), and some dry cereal cultivation. The area is used for sheep-grazing and hunting.

Important for breeding *Elanus caeruleus*, *Circus pygargus* (min. 10 pairs), *Otis tarda* (min. 500 birds), *Tetrax tetrax* (min. 200 pairs), *Burhinus oedicnemus*, *Pterocles orientalis*, and *P. alchata*. *Grus grus* (250) occurs in winter.

126 Albalá – Malpica (Extremadura)

38°48'N, 07°08'W 1500 ha

Unprotected

Plains along the River Guadiana to the border with Portugal; used for dry cereal cultivation (wheat) and sheep-grazing.

Supports a high density of steppe birds, particularly *Tetrax tetrax* (min. 200 birds in summer and 3000 birds in winter).

127 Valongo (Extremadura)

38°40'N, 07°15'W 7000 ha

Unprotected

The River Guadiana with patches of alluvial woodland along the border with Portugal. Surrounded by extensive oak 'dehesas' and cereal croplands with some recent orange-groves. The area is devoted mainly to sheep- and cattle-grazing. There is a dam project (to be built in Portugal) that would flood the area.

Holds the biggest colony of *Bubulcus ibis* in Spain (min. 5300 pairs), with some *Nycticorax nycticorax* (35 pairs) and *Egretta garzetta* (25 pairs). Also important populations of *Ciconia ciconia*.

128 Cheles – Villanueva del Fresno – Barcarrota (Extremadura)

38°20'N, 07°10'W 40,000 ha

Unprotected

An undulating territory along the Portuguese border to the west of Badajoz, with open 'dehesas' (*Quercus rotundifolia*) alternating with grasslands and dry cereal cultivation. There are a few olive-groves, and sheep, cattle, and pigs are grazed.

Breeding species include *Bubulcus ibis* (400 pairs) and *Ciconia ciconia* (min. 60 pairs; a high density). Also interesting for steppe birds including *Otis tarda* (250 birds), *Tetrax tetrax*, *Burhinus oedicnemus*, *Glareola pratincola*, *Pterocles orientalis*, and *P. alchata*, and as a wintering area for *Grus grus* (2000 birds).

129 Dehesas de Jerez de los Caballeros (Extremadura)

38°15'N, 06°50'W 50,000 ha

Unprotected

Undulating territory covered by wide expanses of *Quercus rotundifolia* and *Q. suber* 'dehesas' which in some areas constitute dense and mature woods. Land-uses include grazing (pigs, sheep, cattle).

Important for birds of prey including *Milvus migrans* (min. 200 pairs), *Circaetus gallicus* (min. 25 pairs), and *Hieraaetus pennatus* (min. 50 pairs). *Ciconia nigra* also breeds (min. 10 pairs).

130 Embalse de Valuengo (Extremadura)

38°20'N, 06°40'W 500 ha

Unprotected

A reservoir along the River Ardila, close to Jerez de los Caballeros, surrounded by 'dehesas' of *Quercus rotundifolia*.

Important because of its breeding colony of *Bubulcus ibis* (*c.*1500 pairs); also holds important post-breeding concentrations of *Ciconia nigra* (100+ birds).

131 Fuente de Cantos – Montemolín (Extremadura)

38°10'N, 06°15'W 15,000 ha

Unprotected

An undulating territory with dry cereal cultivation and grasslands, surrounded by wide 'dehesas'. The area is grazed by sheep.

Important for steppe birds with *Circus pygargus* (min. 50 pairs), *Otis tarda* (min. 100 birds), *Tetrax tetrax*, *Pterocles orientalis*, *P. alchata*, and *Burhinus oedicnemus*.

132 Bienvenida – Usagre (Extremadura)

38°20'N, 06°15'W 30,000 ha

Unprotected

A plain to the east of Zafra with dry cereal cultivation, grasslands, and 'dehesas' (*Quercus rotundifolia*); also some vineyards and olive-groves. The area is used for sheep-grazing and hunting. High-voltage power-lines are a problem.

Important for steppe birds with breeding *Circus pygargus*, *Otis tarda* (100+ birds), *Tetrax tetrax*, *Burhinus oedicnemus*, *Pterocles orientalis*, and *P. alchata*. *Grus grus* (min. 550) occurs in winter.

133 Sierra Grande de Hornachos (Extremadura)

38°35'N, 06°05'W 6000 ha

Unprotected

An isolated mountain with high cliffs, extensive areas of low scrub (*Cistus ladanifer* and, on the northern side, *Quercus rotundifolia* and *Q. suber*). The area is used for grazing (cattle, sheep, goats, pigs).

The area supports very interesting bird of prey populations, which include *Neophron percnopterus* (min. 4 pairs), *Gyps fulvus* (min. 10 pairs), *Aquila adalberti* (1 pair), *A.*

chrysaetos (2 pairs), and *Hieraaetus fasciatus* (4 pairs). Also breeding *Ciconia nigra* (1 pair).

134 Granja de Torrehermosa – Llerena (Extremadura)

38°20'N, 05°40'W 45,000 ha

Unprotected

Situated to the south of the previous area, with wide, dry, cultivated plains, grasslands and small patches of oak woodland. The area is used for sheep-grazing, hunting, and mining, and is close to several big villages.

An important area for steppe birds including *Circus pygargus*, *Otis tarda* (min. 600 birds), *Tetrax tetrax* (min. 2000 birds), *Burhinus oedicnemus*, *Pterocles orientalis*, and *P. alchata*. Also breeding are *Elanus caeruleus* and numerous *Ciconia ciconia*. *Grus grus* (min. 3000) occurs in winter.

135 Peraleda de Zaucejo – Campillo de Llerena (Extremadura)

38°30'N, 05°40'W 22,000 ha

Unprotected

An undulating territory. Dry cereal cultivation predominates, although there are grasslands and some oaks (*Quercus rotundifolia*). The area is grazed by sheep. Sparsely populated.

Interesting for steppe birds including *Circus pygargus* (*c.*60 pairs), *Otis tarda* (200 birds), *Tetrax tetrax*, *Burhinus oedicnemus*, and *Pterocles alchata*. *Grus grus* (min. 500) occurs in winter.

136 Puerto de Mejoral – Almorchón – Cabeza del Buey (Extremadura)

38°40'N, 05°15'W 60,000 ha

Unprotected

The mountain ranges and 'dehesas' immediately to the south of La Serena. Mostly sclerophyllous scrub (*Cistus ladanifer*) in the mountains; to the south of the range is the River Zújar valley with wide 'dehesas' (*Quercus rotundifolia*), olive-groves, and dry cereal cultivation. The area is used for grazing (sheep, goats, pigs), and hunting.

Breeding species include *Ciconia nigra* and a diversity of birds of prey. Very important for wintering *Grus grus* (min. 2000).

137 La Serena (Extremadura)

38°50'N, 05°30'W 90,000-100,000 ha

Unprotected

huge area of xerophytic grassland on undulating ground, with frequent slate outcrops. Practically treeless and with occasional dry cereal cultivation. The area is used for hunting and extensive sheep-grazing, with some villages in the outer part and only a few farms in the interior. There are also abandoned mines and two large dams (Ovellana and Zújar), with another one being built (La Serena: 14,000 ha).

Of exceptional importance for steppe birds (probably the most important area in Spain) with breeding *Circus pygargus* (min. 200 pairs), *Otis tarda* (min. 500 birds), *Tetrax tetrax* (*c.*20,000 birds), *Burhinus oedicnemus* (thousands), *Glareola pratincola* (small colonies), *Pterocles orientalis* (hundreds), and *P. alchata* (thousands). Wintering species include *Grus grus* (min. 2000), *Pluvialis apricaria*, and *Vanellus vanellus* (tens of thousands). A hunting area for many birds of prey. Post-nuptial concentrations of *Ciconia nigra* (max. 50+ at Zújar Dam) and *C. ciconia* (hundreds) occur.

138 Siruela – Agudo (Extremadura, Castilla-La Mancha)

39°00'N, 05°00'W 12,000 ha

Unprotected

Situated to the north of the Sierra de Siruela. Undulating territory covered mostly by 'dehesa' (*Quercus rotundifolia*), with grasslands and some dry cereal cultivation (barley, wheat). There is also cattle-grazing. Sparsely populated.

Breeding species include *Ciconia nigra* (with post-breeding concentrations of 50), *C. ciconia* (min. 55 pairs, a high density), and *Elanus caeruleus*. *Grus grus* (1200) occurs in winter.

139 Sierra de la Demanda (Castilla y León, La Rioja)

42°15'N, 03°00'W 100,000 ha

Two National Game Reserves (La Demanda: 73,819; Ezcaray: 18,300 ha)

A mountainous area (800-2271 m) which comprises a large part of the Sistema Ibérico Norte. Severely deforested; scrub (*Genista*, *Erica*) and alpine grasslands predominate, although there are some woods (*Quercus pyrenaica*, *Fagus sylvatica*) and extensive and increasing plantations of *Pinus sylvestris*. The area is used for sheep- and cattle-grazing, big-game hunting, and as a ski station. The forestry programme is detrimental to the area.

Important for breeding birds of prey including *Pernis apivorus* (min. 10 pairs), *Circaetus gallicus* (min. 10 pairs), *Circus cyaneus* (min. 10 pairs), and *Hieraaetus pennatus* (min. 15-20 pairs). Also isolated populations of *Perdix perdix hispaniensis* (probably min. 150 pairs), *Scolopax rusticola*, *Certhia familiaris*, and *Parus palustris*.

140 Sierras de Urbión y Cebollera (Castilla y León – La Rioja)

42°05'N, 02°45'W 100,000 ha

Partly a National Game Reserve (Urbión: 99,000 ha)

The central mountains (1000-2278 m) of the Sistema Ibérico Norte with large pinewoods (*Pinus sylvestris*), some oakwoods (*Quercus pyrenaica*) and beechwoods (*Fagus sylvatica*), and extensive grassland and scrub areas. The area is used for forestry, sheep- and cattle-grazing, hiking; there are also several villages (many abandoned).

Supports an isolated population of *Perdix perdix hispaniensis* (min. 100 pairs) and other species which are at the south-westernmost limit of their range. Birds of prey include *Pernis apivorus* (min. 10 pairs), *Circaetus gallicus* (min. 20 pairs), *Circus cyaneus* (min. 10 pairs), *Aquila chrysaetos* (min. 10 pairs), and *Hieraaetus pennatus* (min. 20 pairs). There are some mountain passes (Santa Inés, Sancho Leza) where large numbers of *Columba palumbus* and passerines converge during autumn migration.

141 Hoces del Iregua, el Leza y el Jubera (La Rioja)

42°17'N, 02°20'W 10,000 ha

Unprotected

The Sistema Ibérico Norte along the River Ebro valley with abundant cliffs and three small gorges. Vegetation includes extensive scrub (*Cistus laurifolius*, *Genista scorpius*, *Buxus sempervirens*), grassland, and some small woods. The area is grazed by cattle. Sparsely populated, with some abandoned villages.

Interesting for birds of prey including *Gyps fulvus* (min. 50 pairs), *Aquila chrysaetos* (4-5 pairs), *Falco peregrinus* (10-12 pairs), and *Bubo bubo* (8-9 pairs).

142 Arnedillo – Peña Isasa (La Rioja)

42°10'N, 02°10'W 4000 ha

Unprotected

Limestone cliffs along a spur of the Sistema Ibérico Norte (700-1475 m) in the Rioja Baja, with slopes covered by scrub (*Genista*, *Buxus*, *Quercus rotundifolia*) and grassland. The area is grazed by sheep.

Important for *Gyps fulvus* (80-85 pairs).

143 Sierra de Alcarama y Rio Alhama (La Rioja, Castilla y León)

41°55'N, 02°00'W 20,000 ha

Unprotected

A mountainous area (600-1300 m) in the Sistema Ibérico Norte, including the River Alhama valley; comprises limestone rocks with cliffs, deforested slopes with open scrub, dry grassland and occasional patches of *Quercus rotundifolia*, and also small areas of cereal cultivation, olive-groves and orchards. The area is used for cattle-grazing and there are some small villages.

An interesting area for birds of prey with *Neophron percnopterus* (min. 10 pairs), *Gyps fulvus* (min. 80 pairs), *Hieraaetus fasciatus* (min. 3 pairs), *Falco peregrinus* (min. 7 pairs), and *Bubo bubo* (min. 7 pairs).

144 Laguna de las Cañas (Navarra)

42°25'N, 02°23'W 75 ha

Natural Reserve

An irrigation pond on the River Ebro close to Logroño, with good marshy vegetation (*Typha*, *Phragmites*) and small patches of *Tamarix*. The surrounding areas are used for vine and cereal cultivation, and there is an industrial zone. There is human disturbance.

Holds a breeding colony of *Ardea purpurea* (min. 25 pairs) and *Nycticorax nycticorax* (65-70 pairs).

145 Bardenas Reales (Navarra, Aragón)

42°10'N, 01°30'W 60,000 ha

Unprotected

One of the most interesting steppe areas in the River Ebro valley. Very eroded gypsum, marl, and clay ground, with plateaus ('mesas'), many gullies, and small cliffs. Dry cereal cultivation alternates with dry grassland and scrub (*Lygeum spartum*, *Rosmarinus*, *Thymus*, *Quercus coccifera*). There are some small woods (*Pinus halepensis*). Sparsely populated but used as an air force firing range.

Important for steppe birds especially *Pterocles orientalis* (min. 50 pairs), *P. alchata* (min. 50 pairs), *Chersophilus duponti* (min. 500 pairs), and *Calandrella rufescens* (min. 1000 pairs), with smaller populations of *Otis tarda*, *Tetrax tetrax*, and *Burhinus oedicnemus*. Also, numerous birds of prey including *Neophron percnopterus* (min. 10 pairs), *Aquila chrysaetos*, and *Bubo bubo*.

146 Gallipienzo – Sierra de la Peña (Navarra)

42°35'N, 01°25'W 10,000 ha

Natural Reserve (Gallipienzo)

A 15 km range (400-1062 m) with rocky cliffs partly carved by the River Aragón. There are woodland (*Quercus rotundifolia*, *Q. faginea*, *Pinus halepensis*) and scrub areas, mainly on abandoned cultivation. Sparsely populated, with sheep-grazing.

Interesting for cliff-nesting birds of prey including *Neophron percnopterus*, *Gyps fulvus* (min. 20 pairs), *Aquila chrysaetos*, *Hieraaetus fasciatus*, and *Bubo bubo*.

147 Peña Izaga (Navarra)

42°45'N, 01°25'W 800 ha

Unprotected

A small range (700-1353 m) to the south-east of Pamplona, with limestone cliffs, woods (*Quercus faginea*, *Fagus sylvatica*), scrub and pine plantations. The area is grazed by sheep.

Important for *Gyps fulvus* (min. 20 pairs) and other cliff-nesting birds of prey.

148 Peñas de Echauri (Navarra)

42°48'N, 01°50'W 2000 ha

Unprotected

A small range (800-1132 m) with high limestone cliffs, scrub, and woodland (*Quercus rotundifolia*). There are many small agricultural villages close by; land-uses include agriculture and sheep-grazing.

An important area for *Gyps fulvus* (min. 20 pairs).

149 Sierras de Zariquieta y Archuba (Navarra)

42°47'N, 01°22'W 6000 ha

Natural Reserve

Two small rocky ranges (600-1055 m) to the east of Pamplona, with limestone cliffs, pinewoods (*Pinus sylvestris*), grassland, and scrub. Used predominantly for sheep-grazing.

Important for cliff-nesting birds of prey including *Gyps fulvus* (min. 20 pairs).

150 Sierras de Leyre, Orba e Illón (Navarra)

42°48'N, 01°05'W 20,000 ha

Partly a Natural Reserve

Part of the pre-Pyrenean range (700-1420 m). Limestone rocks, with abundant cliffs and several great gorges carved by the Rivers Salazar and Esca. Diverse vegetation with grassland and scrub, woods (*Quercus rotundifolia*, *Q. faginea*) and, on the shady slopes, *Pinus sylvestris* and *Fagus sylvatica*. The area is used for forestry, sheep-grazing, and there are a few small villages.

Very important for cliff-nesting birds including *Gypaetus barbatus*, *Neophron percnopterus* (min. 10 pairs), *Gyps fulvus* (*c.*700 pairs), *Aquila chrysaetos* (several pairs), *Falco peregrinus*, *Bubo bubo*, and *Pyrrhocorax pyrrhocorax*.

151 Monte Gorramendi – Peñas de Itxusi (Navarra)

43°10'N, 01°30'W 10,000 ha

Natural Reserve

A mountainous area (200-1081 m) along the French border, with some cliffs and high rocks. Wet grasslands alternate with small woods of *Fagus sylvatica*. The area is used for sheep- and goat-grazing and there are some scattered farms.

Important for *Gyps fulvus* (min. 40 pairs) and other birds of prey.

152 Roncesvalles – Irati – Sierra de Abodi (Navarra)

43°00'N, 01°15'W 30,000 ha

Partly a Natural Reserve

A mountainous area (700-2021 m) along the French border with extensive woods (*Fagus sylvatica*, *Abies alba*) that include the Monte de la Cuestión in Irati (largest *Fagus sylvatica* forest in Spain). The area is used for forestry and livestock-grazing. Sparsely populated.

Very important for woodland birds including *Dryocopus martius* (min. 5 pairs) and *Dendrocopos leucotos* (min. 20 pairs).

153 Belagua – Ansó – Hecho (Aragón, Navarra)

42°50'N, 00°45'W 35,000 ha

National Game Reserve (Los Valles); partly a Natural Reserve

A Pyrenean high-mountain zone (1000-2670 m), with well-preserved *Fagus sylvatica* and *Abies alba* woods (Larra, Zuriza, Oza) and woods of *Pinus sylvestris* and *P. uncinata*.

Land-uses include forestry, sheep-grazing in summer, hiking, and skiing. Brown Bear *Ursus arctos* occasionally occurs.

Breeding species include *Gypaetus barbatus* (several pairs), *Aquila chrysaetos* (min. 5 pairs), *Tetrao urogallus* (min. 20 males), *Dryocopus martius* (min. 5 pairs), and *Dendrocopos leucotos*; *Pyrrhocorax pyrrhocorax* and *P. graculus* are abundant. Also the western limit in the Pyrenees for several species, such as *Lagopus mutus*, *Turdus torquatus*, and *Montifringilla nivalis*.

154 Collarada – Telera (Aragón)

42°40'N, 00°25'E 25,000 ha

Unprotected

A high-mountain zone (1500-2886 m) between the Aragón and Gállego valleys, with big limestone rocks and alpine grasslands. The area is used for sheep- and cattle-grazing in summer and skiing.

Supports a typical Pyrenean avifauna including *Gypaetus barbatus* (2 pairs), *Aquila chrysaetos* (several pairs), and *Lagopus mutus pyrenaicus* (min. 5 pairs).

155 Panticosa – Viñamala – Tendeñera (Aragón)

42°45'N, 00°10'W 30,000 ha included in a Biosphere Reserve (Ordesa – Viñamala)

National Game Reserve (Viñamala: 50,000 ha)

A high-mountain zone (1500-3300 m) in the Pyrenees, with limestone and granite rocks, numerous small glacial lakes ('ibones'), and coniferous woodlands (*Pinus uncinata*). The area is used for sheep- and cattle-grazing in summer, big-game hunting, hiking, and skiing.

Supports a typical Pyrenean avifauna including *Gypaetus barbatus* (several pairs), *Aquila chrysaetos* (min. 5 pairs), *Lagopus mutus pyrenaicus* (min. 5 pairs), *Perdix perdix hispaniensis*, and *Dryocopus martius* (min. 5 pairs).

156 Ordesa – Bielsa (Aragón)

42°40'N, 00°00' 35,000 ha

Included in a Biosphere Reserve (Ordesa – Viñamala); EEC SPA (Ordesa y Monte Perdido: 15,608 ha)

National Park (Ordesa: 15,709 ha); National Game Reserve (Los Circos: 22,800 ha)

Comprises some of the most spectacular and best-known areas in the central Pyrenees, from 1200-3355 m (Monte Perdido), with many peaks over 3000 m. Basically limestone bedrock with huge rock-faces (Añisclo and Arazas canyons) and woodlands of *Pinus sylvestris*, *P. uncinata*, and *Fagus sylvatica*. It is the only place in the Pyrenees where Ibex *Capra pyrenaica* survives and Chamois *Rupicapra rupicapra* is abundant. Human activities include tourism.

Important for *Gypaetus barbatus* (several pairs), *Aquila chrysaetos* (min. 5 pairs), *Lagopus mutus pyrenaicus* (min. 10 pairs), *Tetrao urogallus* (min. 10 males), *Perdix perdix hispaniensis* (perhaps 50+ pairs), *Dryocopus martius* (min. 5 pairs), and *Dendrocopos leucotos*.

157 Gistaín – Cotiella (Aragón)

42°35'N, 00°25'E 45,000 ha

Unprotected

The Gistaín Valley (River Cinqueta) and the northern and southern massifs of the central Pyrenees, between 1000 and 3177 m (Bachimala peak). There are spectacular cliffs in the southern part. Includes some important woods, predominantly coniferous (*Pinus sylvestris*, *P. uncinata*). Sparsely populated. Area is used for cattle-grazing, forestry, and some hydroelectric dams.

Supports a typical Pyrenean avifauna including *Gypaetus barbatus*, *Lagopus mutus pyrenaicus* (min. 5 pairs), *Tetrao urogallus* (min. 10 males), *Perdix perdix hispaniensis* (perhaps 50+ pairs), and *Dryocopus martius* (min. 5 pairs).

158 Posets – La Madaleta – Entecada (Aragón, Cataluña)

42°40'N, 00°30'E 50,000 ha

National Game Reserve (Benasque: 50,000 ha)

A high-altitude region of the Pyrenees with large areas over 3000 m and the highest peak at 3404 m (Aneto), with a few small glaciers, numerous small mountain lakes, and many rocky areas. There are woodlands of *Pinus sylvestris*, *Abies alba*, and *Fagus sylvatica*, including the remarkable forests of Vallibierna and Artiga de Lin - Portillón where the Brown Bear *Ursus arctos* occurs. The area is used for cattle-grazing in summer, hiking, and skiing.

Supports a good high-mountain avifauna including *Gypaetus barbatus*, *Aquila chrysaetos* (min. 5 pairs), *Lagopus mutus pyrenaicus* (min. 12 pairs), and *Perdix perdix hispaniensis* (min. 30 pairs). In the forests, *Tetrao urogallus* (min. 40 males), *Dryocopus martius* (min. 20 pairs), and *Aegolius funereus* occur.

159 San Mauricio – Bohí – Beret (Cataluña)

42°40'N, 01°00'E 120,000 ha

EEC SPA (Aigües Tortes y Lago San Mauricio: 10,230 ha)

National Park (Aigües Tortes y Lago de San Mauricio: 22,369 ha); partly a National Game Reserve (Alto Pallars – Arán: 94,231 ha)

A high-altitude mountain area (1500-2951 m) in the Pyrenees with many peaks over 2500 m. Comprises great rocks and cliffs, numerous small mountain lakes ('estanys'), and good woodland of *Pinus uncinata* and *Abies alba* (Valencia de Aneu is particularly important), although alpine grasslands predominate. The area is used for forestry, stock-grazing in summer, tourism, skiing, and there are some hydroelectric dams. Forestry is possibly detrimental to the Valencia de Aneu woodland.

One of the best areas in Spain for Pyrenean avifauna; birds of prey include *Gypaetus barbatus* (3 pairs), *Circaetus gallicus* (min. 10 pairs), and *Aquila chrysaetos* (min. 18 pairs); galliformes include *Lagopus mutus pyrenaicus* (min. 70 pairs), *Tetrao urogallus* (min. 215 males; possibly the best area in the Spanish Pyrenees), and *Perdix perdix hispaniensis* (min. 150 pairs). *Dryocopus martius* is common in the forest (min. 90 pairs) and *Aegolius funereus* (min. 7 pairs) also occurs. *Pyrrhocorax graculus* and *P. pyrrhocorax* (min. 300 pairs) are numerous.

160 Monteixo – L'Orri – Tornafort (Cataluña)

42°30'N, 01°20'E 80,000 ha

Partly a National Game Reserve (Alto Pallars – Arán: 94,231 ha)

An extensive area in the Pyrenees mainly between 1500 and 2500 m, but up to 3143 m (Pica d'Estats). Large woods (mainly *Pinus sylvestris*, *P. uncinata*, and some *Betula* areas), with scrub, pasture, and alpine-grassland zones. Sparsely populated; the area is used for forestry, stock-grazing, hiking, and skiing. Forestry is too intensive in some subalpine woods of *Pinus uncinata*, and some skiing pistes at Portainé are destructive.

Very interesting for birds of high-mountain woodlands, especially *Tetrao urogallus* (min. 187 males) and *Aegolius funereus* (min. 3 pairs). Other breeding species include *Pernis apivorus* (min. 10 pairs), *Gypaetus barbatus* (1 pair), *Circaetus gallicus* (10 pairs), *Aquila chrysaetos* (min. 11 pairs), *Falco peregrinus* (5 pairs), *Lagopus mutus pyrenaicus* (min. 30 pairs), and *Perdix perdix hispaniensis* (min. 50-100 pairs).

161 Cerdaña (Cataluña)

42°30'N, 01°45'E 23,000 ha

National Game Reserve (La Cerdaña: 19,437 ha)

A high-mountain area (1600-2900 m) on the border with Andorra, with large pine woodlands (*Pinus sylvestris, P. uncinata*), pastures, grasslands, and rocks. The area is used for stock-farming (cattle), big-game hunting, hiking, and skiing.

Mountain birds include *Circaetus gallicus* (5 pairs), *Lagopus mutus pyrenaicus* (*c.*20 pairs; declining), *Tetrao urogallus* (39-45 males), and *Perdix perdix hispaniensis. Charadrius morinellus* has bred in the area (only place in Spain).

162 Fresser – Setcases (Cataluña)

42°25'N, 02°20'E 25,000 ha

National Game Reserve (Fresser y Setcases: 18,000 ha)

The easternmost high-mountain area (1800-2909 m) in the Pyrenees, with large coniferous woods (*Pinus uncinata, P. sylvestris*, some *Abies alba*), scrub, grasslands, and rocks. The area is used for big-game hunting, forestry, stock-farming, and hiking.

Supports a typical Pyrenean avifauna, which includes *Lagopus mutus pyrenaica* (30-40 pairs; declining), *Tetrao urogallus* (31-41 males), *Perdix perdix hispaniensis* (50 pairs), and *Aegolius funereus* (3-4 pairs).

163 Foces de Biniés y Fago (Aragón)

42°40'N, 00°50'W 12,000 ha

Unprotected

Two gorges crossing the Sierra de los Dos Ríos range with limestone cliffs, dense maquis (*Quercus faginea, Q. rotundifolia*), and pinewoods (*Pinus sylvestris*).

Important for *Gyps fulvus* (min. 30 pairs) and other birds of prey including *Gypaetus barbatus* (1 pair).

164 San Juan de la Peña – Peña Oroel (Aragón)

42°30'N, 00°45'W 17,000 ha

Natural Monument (San Juan de la Peña: 310 ha)

A part of the pre-Pyrenean range about 30 km long, reaching 1769 m; comprises cliffs, large pine plantations (*Pinus sylvestris*) and scrub and maquis areas with *Buxus sempervirens* and *Quercus faginea*. The area is used for forestry and big-game hunting.

Supports a remarkable diversity of birds of prey including *Gypaetus barbatus* and colonies of *Gyps fulvus* (min. 20 pairs). Also *Dryocopus martius* breeds.

165 Santo Domingo – Riglos – Gratal (Aragón)

42°25'N, 00°40'W 40,000 ha

Unprotected

A mountain range about 50 km long with many cliffs, in the southern limit of the Pyrenees (max. 1500-1600 m) immediately to the west of the Sierra de Guara. Vegetation includes maquis of *Quercus faginea* and *Q. rotundifolia*, with pine plantations (*Pinus uncinata, P. sylvestris*), and extensive scrub and grassland areas. The area is used for sheep-grazing and rock-climbing. Sparsely populated.

Excellent for birds of prey including *Pernis apivorus, Milvus milvus* (min. 20 pairs), *Gypaetus barbatus, Neophron percnopterus* (min. 10 pairs), *Gyps fulvus* (min. 50 pairs), *Aquila chrysaetos* (min. 5 pairs), *Hieraaetus fasciatus*, and *Bubo bubo* (min. 5 pairs). There is also an interesting population of *Perdix perdix hispaniensis*.

166 Sierra de Guara (Aragón)

42°20'N, 00°10'W 70,000 ha EEC SPA (Sierra y Cañones de Guara: 81,350 ha)

Proposed Natural Park

An impressive massif (600-2077 m) at the southern edge of the Pyrenees; the biggest of the pre-Pyrenean ranges. Limestone bedrock with large walls and deep gorges (San Martín, Vadiello, Mascún, Vero), extensive areas of scrub and grassland, with some maquis (*Quercus rotundifolia*, *Q. faginea*), and pine plantations (*Pinus sylvestris*). The area is used for sheep- and cattle-grazing, forestry, trekking, and big-game hunting. Sparsely populated, with many abandoned small villages.

Extremely important for birds of prey with *Pernis apivorus*, *Milvus milvus* (min. 20 pairs), *Gypaetus barbatus* (several pairs), *Neophron percnopterus* (min. 10 pairs), *Gyps fulvus* (min. 200 pairs), *Circaetus gallicus* (min. 5 pairs), *Aquila chrysaetos* (min. 5 pairs), *Falco peregrinus* (min. 10 pairs), and *Bubo bubo* (min. 5 pairs).

167 Oturia – Canciás (Aragón)

42°30'N, 00°10'W 20,000 ha

Unprotected

The pre-Pyrenean mountain ranges (100-1928 m) between Sabiñánigo and Boltaña, to the north of the Sierra de Guara area, with cliffs, woodland (*Quercus faginea*, *Pinus sylvestris*), and scrublands. Almost unpopulated.

Important for birds of prey including *Gypaetus barbatus* (2 pairs), *Circaetus gallicus*, and *Aquila chrysaetos*.

168 Turbón – Espés – Sis (Aragón)

42°25'N, 00°35'E 40,000 ha

Unprotected

A group of pre-Pyrenean mountain ranges (800-2492 m) with big cliffs and gorges (of the Rivers Esera and Isábena), extensive pinewoods (*Pinus sylvestris*), scrub, and grasslands. Sparsely populated; land-uses include forestry and sheep-grazing.

Important for many birds of prey including *Gypaetus barbatus*; *Tetrao urogallus* (min. 10 pairs) and *Dryocopus martius* (min. 5 pairs) occur in the forests.

169 Sierra de Sant Gervás (Cataluña)

42°20'N, 00°55'E 15,000 ha

Unprotected

A mountain range (800-1800 m) in the interior pre-Pyrenees with abundant cliffs, scrub, and grasslands (with some small woods of *Quercus* and *Fagus sylvatica*). There is a dam for electric-power generation. The area is used for sheep-grazing.

Interesting for birds of prey including *Neophron percnopterus* (5 pairs), *Gypaetus barbatus* (2 pairs), and *Gyps fulvus* (25 pairs). Also many *Pyrrhocorax pyrrhocorax* (c. 300 pairs).

170 Sierra del Boumort (Cataluña)

42°20'N, 01°10'E 30,000 ha

Unprotected

A mountain range (600-2076 m) in the interior of the pre-Pyrenees. A rugged landscape with big limestone rocks and a narrow gorge. Mainly pine woodland (*Pinus nigra*, *P. sylvestris*, some *P. uncinata*), scrub, and mountain grasslands. The area is used for big-game hunting, forestry, and some stock-farming. Sparsely populated. Forest fires are a problem.

Very interesting for birds of prey including *Gypaetus barbatus* (1 pair), *Gyps fulvus* (25 pairs; the biggest colony in Cataluña), *Neophron percnopterus* (5 pairs), *Aquila chrysaetos* (8 pairs), *Falco peregrinus* (6 pairs), and *Bubo bubo* (min. 6 pairs). Interesting for Pyrenean bird populations, this being the southern limit of their distribution, with *Tetrao urogallus* (c.50 males), *Perdix perdix hispaniensis* (15-20 pairs), *Dryocopus martius* (min. 10 pairs), *Aegolius funereus* (min. 1 pair), and many *Pyrrhocorax pyrrhocorax* (min. 400 pairs).

171 Sierra del Cadí (Cataluña)

42°20'N, 01°40'E 60,000 ha EEC SPA (Sierra del Cadí-Moixeró: 41,342 ha)

Natural Park (Cadí-Moixeró: 41,342 ha); National Game Reserve (Cadí: 27,202 ha)

A mountain range (1500-2647 m), *c.*50 km long, in the pre-Pyrenees. Limestone rock with frequent high cliffs and extensive woodlands, mainly coniferous (*Pinus sylvestris*, *P. nigra*, *P. uncinata*, *Abies alba*) but also deciduous. The area is used for big-game hunting, forestry, stock-farming, hiking, and skiing.

The mountain avifauna includes *Gypaetus barbatus* (1 pair), *Circaetus gallicus* (min. 5 pairs), *Aquila chrysaetos* (5-6 pairs), *Falco peregrinus* (min. 6 pairs), *Tetrao urogallus* (50 males), *Perdix perdix hispaniensis* (min. 50 pairs), *Dryocopus martius* (min. 15 pairs), *Aegolius funereus* (min. 5 pairs), and *Pyrrhocorax pyrrhocorax* (min. 100 pairs).

172 Sierras del Montsech y Mongay (Cataluña, Aragón)

42°05'N, 00°55'E 40,000 ha

Unprotected

The outer range of the pre-Pyrenees (400-1678 m), with limestone rocks, big cliffs, and two deep gorges (Terradets and Montrebei). Sclerophyllous shrub (*Quercus coccifera*, *Buxus sempervirens*, *Genista scorpius*) predominates, with some scattered woods (*Quercus rotundifolia*, *Q. pubescens*), and croplands (olive-trees, vineyards, cereal) which are mainly abandoned. A sparsely populated area with limited stock-farming. There are some hydroelectric dams, and also roads. A plan to build a road through the Montrebei gorge is a threat to the area.

Interesting for its breeding birds of prey which include *Gypaetus barbatus*, *Neophron percnopterus* (min. 10 pairs), *Gyps fulvus* (12 pairs), *Circaetus gallicus* (min. 30 pairs), *Aquila chrysaetos* (min. 8 pairs), *Hieraaetus fasciatus*, *Falco peregrinus* (min. 10 pairs), and *Bubo bubo* (min. 10 pairs). Also many *Pyrrhocorax pyrrhocorax* (*c.*400 pairs).

173 Embalse de Tormos (La Sotonera) (Aragón)

42°05'N, 00°39'W 3000 ha

Unprotected

A reservoir (for irrigation) with a strongly fluctuating water-level in the pre-Pyrenees. There is marsh vegetation along some of the banks. Surrounded by cereal croplands. Problems include poaching, yachting and pleasure-boating, and hazardous power-lines.

Important for *Grus grus* (max. 7200) during spring migration.

174 Montes de Zuera (Aragón)

42°00'N, 00°55'W 30,000 ha
Unprotected

Hills in the centre of the River Ebro depression, to the north of Zaragoza, and covered with *Pinus halepensis*, *Quercus rotundifolia*, and sclerophyllous scrub. Sparsely populated.

Important for birds of prey including *Circaetus gallicus* (min. 5 pairs), *Aquila chrysaetos*, *Hieraaetus pennatus* (min. 20 pairs), and *Bubo bubo*. Also *Chersophilus duponti* (min. 20 pairs) breeds.

175 Sierra de Alcubierre (Aragón)

41°40'N, 00°30'W 40,000 ha

Unprotected

An eroded range of hills (500-820 m), 50 km long, in the central area of the River Ebro depression. Vegetation comprises sclerophyllous scrub and xerophytic grassland, with *Juniperus thurifera* and large pine woods of *Pinus halepensis*. Sparsely populated; sheep are grazed.

One of the richest areas for birds of prey in Aragón and particularly important for *Milvus migrans* (many pairs), *Neophron percnopterus*, *Circaetus gallicus* (min. 5 pairs), *Aquila chrysaetos* (min. 5 pairs), and *Bubo bubo*.

176 Bajo Alcanadre (Aragón)

42°00'N, 00°05'W 30,000 ha

Unprotected

A large semi-arid plain with eroded limestone plateaus ('muelas'), and many gullies and cliffs, especially along the River Alcanadre. There are dry cereal croplands (barley, wheat), low sclerophyllous scrub, and unploughed pastures for sheep-grazing.

Supports a high density of birds of prey including *Neophron percnopterus* (min. 10 pairs) and *Bubo bubo* (min. 10 pairs). Also important for steppe birds with *Burhinus oedicnemus*, *Pterocles orientalis*, and *P. alchata*.

177 El Saso (Osera) (Aragón)

41°35'N, 00°35'W 2500 ha

Unprotected

A small steppe area to the west of Los Monegros. Agricultural transformation is a possible threat.

Supports an interesting community of steppe birds, including *Pterocles alchata*, *Chersophilus duponti* (min. 30 pairs), and *Calandrella rufescens* (min. 100 pairs).

178 Los Monegros (Pina – Bujaraloz) (Aragón)

41°25'N, 00°15'W 70,000 ha

Unprotected

The most famous of the Aragón 'desert' territories. Extensive endorreic plains with some seasonal brackish lagoons ('saladas') and interesting steppe vegetation, which surrounds the best patches of *Juniperus thurifera* in the Ebro Valley. The area is used for dry cereal agriculture (barley) and sheep-grazing (now decreasing). Threatened by huge irrigation schemes.

The last stronghold for *Otis tarda* in the Ebro Valley (max. 32 in 1986). However, there are significant populations of other steppe birds with tens or hundreds of pairs of *Burhinus oedicnemus*, *Pterocles orientalis*, *P. alchata*, *Chersophilus duponti*, and *Calandrella rufescens*, and interesting populations of *Circus pygargus* (10 pairs) and *Falco naumanni* (50 pairs).

179 Ballobar (Aragón)

41°37'N, 00°12'E 500 ha

Unprotected

A small area of well-preserved steppe vegetation in the semi-arid Los Monegros territory. Agricultural transformation is a possible threat.

Important for its steppe avifauna, which includes *Chersophilus duponti* (min. 50 pairs).

180 Almacelles – Gimenells (Cataluña, Aragón)

41°40'N, 00°25'E 25,000 ha

Unprotected

Undulating plains to the west of Lérida (Lleida) with wide croplands, which are being changed from cereals (wheat, barley) to irrigated fields, and a few areas of sclerophyllous scrub (garigue) and grassland. There are two villages and some farms. Sheep-grazing is declining and the area is severely endangered by agricultural intensification.

Important for steppe birds including *Circus pygargus* (5 pairs), *Tetrax tetrax* (perhaps 20 pairs, and concentrations of 200 birds in winter), *Burhinus oedicnemus* (min. 50 pairs),

Pterocles orientalis (50 birds), *P. alchata* (50 birds), and *Lanius minor* (min. 5 pairs). Its ornithological importance is steadily decreasing: *Chersophilus duponti* seems to have disappeared in recent years, and *Pterocles alchata* and *P. orientalis* may soon do so.

181 Cogull – Alfés (Cataluña)

41°30'N, 00°40'E 14,000 ha EEC SPA (Mas de Melons: 1140 ha)

Partly a Natural Reserve (Mas de Melons: 1140 ha)

The only steppe area in Cataluña which is acceptably preserved, comprising undulating plains to the south of Lérida with dry cereal croplands (barley, wheat) mixed with garigue-like low scrub (*Rosmarinus*, *Thymus*, *Artemisia*, *Salsola*) and almond trees. There are some small villages and farms. Sheep-grazing is declining and a large part of the original area has already been affected by an irrigation project.

Of great importance in Cataluña for steppe birds, with *Circus pygargus* (5 pairs), *Tetrax tetrax* (60 birds), *Burhinus oedicnemus* (30 pairs), *Pterocles orientalis* (15 birds), *P. alchata* (180-200 birds), *Chersophilus duponti* (min. 60 pairs), *Calandrella rufescens*, and *Lanius minor* (min. 10 pairs).

182 Río Ebro (La Alfranca – Pina de Ebro) (Aragón)

41°30'N, 00°45'W 6000 ha

Unprotected

A 25 km stretch of the River Ebro downstream from Zaragoza. Although much damaged, alluvial woods, ponds, and small areas of marsh vegetation remain. An intensively cultivated and heavily populated area. Major problems include a lack of water, afforestation with *Populus*, sand and gravel exploitation, and hunting.

Supports relict populations of herons with *Botaurus stellaris* (*c.*2-3 pairs), *Ixobrychus minutus* (max. 5 pairs), *Nycticorax nycticorax* (40 pairs), *Egretta garzetta* (min. 6 pairs), and *Ardea purpurea* (3 pairs). Also an important roosting area for wintering and migrating passerines.

183 Sierras de Valdurrios – Serreta Negra y Los Rincones (Aragón)

41°20'N, 00°10'E 45,000 ha

Unprotected

A group of low hills, crossed by the River Ebro, with some cliffs, pinewoods (*Pinus halepensis*), scrub (*Quercus coccifera*, *Rosmarinus*, *Thymus*), wasteland, and grasslands. The area is used for sheep-grazing, and there is a dam for electric-power generation and residential areas.

Breeding birds of prey include *Circaetus gallicus* (min. 5 pairs), *Aquila chrysaetos* (min. 5 pairs), and *Bubo bubo* (min. 5 pairs).

Includes the following subsite:

183-1 Embalse de Caspe o de Mequinenza

Unprotected

A very long reservoir (6000 ha) on the River Ebro with alluvial vegetation, including woodland, and islets (some wooded). Problems include aquatic sports and uncontrolled tree-felling.

Supports the most important breeding colony of *Nycticorax nycticorax* in Spain (*c.*250 pairs).

184 Urrea de Jalón (Aragón)

41°40'N, 01°11'W 2000 ha

Unprotected

Plains to the west of the city of Zaragoza, mostly dry cereal croplands, with patches of xerophytic scrub (*Lygeum spartum*). The area is grazed by sheep and there is a risk of agricultural transformation.

Important for steppe birds including *Chersophilus duponti* (min. 100 pairs) and *Calandrella rufescens* (min. 200 pairs).

185 Bajo Huerva (Aragón)

41°25'N, 01°00'W 40,000 ha

Unprotected

Adjacent to the Belchite area. Plains and hillocks with a few gullies and cliffs, and dry agricultural land mixed with areas of steppe vegetation and pinewoods (*Pinus halepensis*). The area is used for sheep-grazing and hunting.

Important for birds of prey including *Circaetus gallicus* (min. 5 pairs), *Aquila chrysaetos* (min. 5 pairs), and *Bubo bubo* (min. 5 pairs).

186 Belchite – Mediana (Aragón)

41°20'N, 00°45'W 40,000 ha

Partly a Natural Reserve; proposed Ornithological Reserve

One of the best-preserved steppe areas in the River Ebro basin, very near to Zaragoza. Plains with some hills reaching 700 m with sparse xerophytic vegetation. Land-uses include dry agriculture (barley) and sheep-grazing. Threatened by agricultural transformation (irrigation schemes).

Of great importance for steppe birds including *Burhinus oedicnemus* (*c.*150 pairs), *Pterocles orientalis* (800-1000 pairs), *Chersophilus duponti* (min. 800 pairs; the most important area in the Ebro Valley), and *Calandrella rufescens* (1400-2000 pairs). *Otis tarda* (max. 15 birds) is occasionally present. Also a resting area for *Charadrius morinellus* during migration (max. 200).

187 Saladas de Alcañiz (Aragón)

41°03'N, 00°16'W 6000 ha

Unprotected

An endorreic depression with some small seasonal lagoons and interesting halophytic vegetation. The area may be destroyed by an irrigation project which is now under way.

Interesting because of its breeding steppe birds, with *Chersophilus duponti* and *Calandrella rufescens* (80-90 pairs).

188 Sierra del Moncayo (Aragón, Castilla y León)

41°45'N, 01°50'W 45,000 ha

Natural Park (Dehesa del Moncayo: 1389 ha)

An isolated massif (800-2316 m) which has some large limestone gullies. Largely deforested, although there are relict woods on the northern slopes (*Quercus pyrenaica*, *Pinus sylvestris*, *Fagus sylvatica*), which constitute the Natural Park. Used predominantly for sheep-grazing. Sparsely populated.

Important for *Gyps fulvus* (min. 100 pairs), *Aquila chrysaetos* (min. 5 pairs), *Bubo bubo* (min. 5 pairs), *Pyrrhocorax pyrrhocorax*, and *Apus melba*. Also interesting isolated populations of *Pernis apivorus* (several pairs), *Perdix perdix hispaniensis*, and *Scolopax rusticola*.

189 Río Manubles (Aragón)

41°30'N 01°55'W 12,000 ha

Unprotected

Limestone cliffs along the River Manubles with maquis of *Quercus rotundifolia* and grasslands. Land-uses include dry agriculture and sheep-grazing; there are some small villages.

Important for *Gyps fulvus* (min. 20 pairs) and other birds of rocky habitat.

190 Hoces del Jalón – Sierra de Algairén (Aragón)

41°30'N, 01°30'W 40,000 ha

Unprotected

The central part of the Iberian Range (Sierra de la Virgen, Sierra de Vicor and Sierra de Algairén) with frequent cliffs, scrub, garigue (*Quercus rotundifolia*), grasslands, and some pines (*Pinus pinaster*). Sparsely populated with limited agricultural land (orchards) along rivers. The area is also used for sheep- and goat-grazing.

Important because of its *Gyps fulvus* colonies (min. 30 pairs) and *Bubo bubo* (min. 5 pairs).

191 Cortados del Río Mesa (Aragón, Castilla-La Mancha)

41°11'N, 01°54'W 6000 ha

Unprotected

A steep-sloped valley (20 km long), with many limestone cliffs, maquis of *Quercus rotundifolia*, and grazing pasture. Land-uses include dry agriculture and sheep-grazing, and there are some small villages.

Important for colonies of *Gyps fulvus* (min. 34 pairs).

192 Gallocanta (Aragón)

40°56'N, 01°30'W 7000 ha EEC SPA (6720 ha)

National Game Refuge

A large brackish lagoon in an endorreic basin, with marsh vegetation in some places and many islets; subject to drought, and refilling every 12-13 years. Surrounded by cereal croplands, where feeding *Grus grus* cause damage.

One of the most important passage sites in Europe for *Grus grus* (max. 12,100 in autumn and 22,000 in spring). Important for wintering waterfowl (av. Jan. counts) with *Anas strepera* (1017), *Netta rufina* (8318), *Aythya ferina* (22,392), and *Fulica atra* (12,241).

193 Blancas – Torralba de los Sisones (Aragón)

40°50'N, 01°30'W 2500 ha

Unprotected

Flat highlands (1100 m) to the south-east of Gallocanta lagoon, covered by scrub (*Genista pumila*, *Thymus*); also small areas of dry cereal cultivation, many abandoned. The area is grazed by sheep.

Interesting for steppe birds including *Tetrax tetrax*, *Burhinus oedicnemus*, *Pterocles orientalis*, and especially *Chersophilus duponti* (min. 400 pairs).

194 Visiedo (Aragón)

40°40'N, 01°05'W 2500 ha

Unprotected

Flat highlands (1200 m) covered by scrub (*Erinacea anthyllis*, *Thymus*, *Genista*) and surrounded by dry cereal croplands. The area is used for sheep-grazing.

Important for *Chersophilus duponti* (min. 200 pairs).

195 Río Martín (Aragón)

40°55'N, 00°45'W 30,000 ha

Unprotected

Cliffs along some 40 km of the River Martín in the northern foothills of the Sistema Ibérico range. Many limestone cliffs with Mediterranean scrub and dry pastures. The area is used for sheep-grazing and some agriculture; there are several small villages and mines in nearby areas. Problems include the illegal use of poisoned baits by game-keepers.

Important for cliff-nesting birds of prey including *Neophron percnopterus* (min. 10 pairs), *Gyps fulvus* (perhaps 100+ pairs), *Aquila chrysaetos* (min. 5 pairs), *Hieraaetus fasciatus* (min. 5 pairs), and *Bubo bubo* (min. 5 pairs).

196 Sierra de Arcos (Aragón)

41°05'N, 00°35'W 5000 ha

Unprotected

Limestone cliffs along the River Martín in the Sierra de Arcos range, with scrub and xerophytic grasslands, maquis with *Quercus rotundifolia*, and a few pinewoods (*Pinus halepensis*). Land-uses include sheep-grazing and dry agriculture; there is a thermic power-station nearby.

Important for colonies of *Gyps fulvus* (min. 70 pairs).

197 Río Guadalope (Aragón)

40°40'N, 00°35'W 25,000 ha

Unprotected

The gorges along some 40 km of the River Guadalope in the northern foothills of the Sistema Ibérico range. Limestone cliffs with *Pinus nigra*, scrub, and grassland areas. Land-uses include sheep-grazing. Problems include illegal use of poisoned baits for game-keeping.

Important for colonies of *Gyps fulvus* (min. 40 pairs) and other birds of prey.

198 Sierra de Albarracín (Aragón)

40°25'N, 01°40'W 100,000 ha

National Game Reserve (Montes Universales: 59,260 ha)

A mountainous area (1100-1900 m) next to the Alto Tajo area. Large pinewoods (mainly *Pinus sylvestris*) predominate, although there are zones of maquis (*Quercus rotundifolia*, *Q. pyrenaica*), scrub, and pasture. The area is used for forestry and sheep-grazing, and there are some small villages with orchards and small cereal fields.

Important for birds of prey including *Aquila chrysaetos* (min. 10 pairs), *Hieraaetus pennatus* (min. 20 pairs), and *Bubo bubo* (min. 5 pairs).

199 Los Alberes – Cabo de Creus – Aiguamolls (Cataluña)

42°20'N, 03°10'E 40,000 ha EEC SPA (Aguamolls del Empordá: 867 ha)

Unprotected

A coastal strip with low coastal mountains (max. 1180 m). In Rosas Bay there are a sandy shore and small saltmarshes (Aiguamolls del Empordá). Vegetation includes open sclerophyllous scrub (garigue) and xerophytic grasslands, with small woods of *Quercus suber* and *Q. rotundifolia*. The area is used for sheep-grazing, arable farming, and there are a few fishing villages with considerable tourist development.

The best area in the Iberian peninsula for *Lanius minor* (min. 30 pairs). In the Aiguamolls, *Botaurus stellaris* (3 pairs) and other marsh species breed.

200 Islas Medas (Cataluña)

42°02'N, 03°13'E 20 ha

Hunting prohibited

Small scrub-covered island (Meda Gran: 15 ha) and several islets, 1 km off Cape Estartit, on the Costa Brava. The islands are uninhibited and there is a lighthouse.

Breeding seabirds include *Hydrobates pelagicus melitensis* (min. 5 pairs), *Phalacrocorax carbo* (1-2 pairs; only site in Spain), *P. aristotelis desmarestii* (a few pairs), and *Larus argentatus cachinnans* (min. 8000 pairs; one of the biggest colonies in the Mediterranean). There is also a recently established heronry with *Nycticorax nycticorax* (10 pairs), *Egretta garzetta* (10 pairs in 1986), and *Bubulcus ibis* (5 pairs).

201 Sierra del Montsant (Cataluña)

41°20'N, 00°50'E 40,000 ha

Unprotected

Perhaps the most interesting area in the Cataluña coastal range, comprising low mountains (400-1200 m) of sandstone and conglomerate rock, with many cliffs, extensive pine woodlands (*Pinus halepensis*, *P. nigra*, *P. sylvestris*), and large scrub areas (*Quercus rotundifolia*, *Pistacia lentiscus*). The area is used for hunting, forestry, agriculture (olive-groves, vineyards, orchards), and there are some small villages and many roads.

Breeding birds of prey include *Circaetus gallicus*, *Aquila chrysaetos*, *Hieraaetus fasciatus* (min. 5 pairs), *Falco peregrinus*, and *Bubo bubo* (min. 5 pairs).

202 Delta del Ebro (Cataluña)

40°43'N, 00°44'E 35,000 ha EEC SPA (7736 ha)

Natural Park (5900 ha); National Game Reserve (1227 ha)

A large delta that protrudes into the Mediterranean Sea forming a complex of shallow brackish lagoons, saltmarshes, salt-lakes, sea bays, and sandy beaches with dunes. Includes *c.*1500 ha of paddy fields that provide freshwater areas. The area is used for hunting, fishing, reed-cutting, agriculture and cattle-grazing. Problems include disturbance by tourists at waterbird colonies (waders, gulls and terns), hunting pressure, chemical pollution (pesticides), and a decline in sedimentation caused by dams along the River Ebro.

Extremely important for breeding gulls, waders, and terns with *Haematopus ostralegus* (23 pairs), *Himantopus himantopus* (min. 1000 pairs), *Recurvirostra avosetta* (400 pairs), *Glareola pratincola* (100 pairs), *Charadrius alexandrinus* (min. 1000 pairs), *Larus genei* (280 pairs), *L. audouinii* (2200 pairs), *Gelochelidon nilotica* (min. 100 pairs), *Sterna sandvicensis* (*c.*250 pairs), *S. hirundo* (2300 pairs), *S. albifrons* (650 pairs), and *Chlidonias hybridus* (600 pairs). Breeding herons include *Ixobrychus minutus* (150 pairs), *Ardeola ralloides* (195 pairs), *Bubulcus ibis* (1729 pairs), *Egretta garzetta* (563 pairs), and *Ardea purpurea* (294 pairs). The second most important Spanish wetland for wintering wildfowl, which include (av. Jan. counts unless stated) *Anas penelope* (7100), *A. strepera* (1700), *A. crecca* (max. 12,800), *A. platyrhynchos* (max. 42,600), *A. clypeata* (8100), and *Netta rufina* (1100; also 1500 breeding pairs). Also wintering *Phalacrocorax carbo* (1300) and *Phoenicopterus ruber* (2000).

203 Puertos de Beceite – Monte Turmell (Cataluña, Aragón, País Valenciano)

40°50'N, 00°15'E 100,000 ha

National Game Reserve (Puertos de Tortosa y Beceite: 29,234 ha)

A mountainous area (400-1400 m), 50 km long, comprising limestone and conglomerate bedrock, with many cliffs and gullies. Vegetation includes extensive pine woodlands (mainly *Pinus sylvestris*), maquis areas (*Quercus rotundifolia*, *Q. faginea*), and large areas of scrub. The area is used for forestry, stock-grazing, and hunting. Problems include the use of poisoned baits and woodland fires.

Interesting for birds of prey including *Gyps fulvus* (*c.*60 pairs), *Circaetus gallicus* (min. 10 pairs), *Aquila chrysaetos* (min. 8 pairs), *Hieraaetus fasciatus* (*c.*5 pairs), *Falco peregrinus* (min. 10 pairs), and *Bubo bubo* (min. 5 pairs). Also many *Pyrrhocorax pyrrhocorax* (several hundred pairs) and other birds of rocky habitat.

204 Els Ports de Morella (Aragón, País Valenciano)

40°35'N, 00°10'W 40,000 ha

Unprotected

A low mountain range (700-1400 m) with abundant cliffs, pinewoods (*Pinus halepensis*), small oak woods (*Quercus rotundifolia*, *Q. faginea*), and large expanses of Mediterranean scrub. The area is used for forestry, sheep-grazing, and there are also roads and scattered villages.

Important for birds of prey including *Gyps fulvus* (min. 20 pairs) and *Hieraaetus fasciatus* (min. 5 pairs).

205 Peñagolosa (País Valenciano, Aragón)

40°15'N, 00°25'W 45,000 ha

Unprotected

A group of limestone mountain ranges (500-1813 m), crossed by deep valleys and with many cliffs. Predominantly covered by pinewoods (*Pinus halepensis*, *P. nigra*, *P. pinaster*), with some oak woods (*Quercus ilex*), and Mediterranean scrub. The area is used for forestry and some sheep-grazing. Sparsely populated.

Important for birds of prey with *Circaetus gallicus* (5 pairs), *Aquila chrysaetos* (3 pairs), *Hieraaetus fasciatus* (3 pairs), *Falco peregrinus*, and *Bubo bubo*. Also colonies of *Pyrrhocorax pyrrhocorax* (min. 100 pairs).

206 Sierra de Espadán (País Valenciano)

39°50'N, 00°20'W 30,000 ha

Unprotected

A small mountain massif (200-1041 m) with limestone cliffs, covered by pinewoods (*Pinus halepensis*) and Mediterranean scrub. A populated area, crossed by several roads. The area is used for forestry, sheep-grazing and hunting. Problems include forest fires.

An important zone for birds of prey; populations of *Hieraaetus fasciatus* (5 pairs), *Falco peregrinus* (4 pairs), and *Bubo bubo* (5 pairs).

207 Hoces del Turia y Sierra de Tejo (País Valenciano)

39°45'N, 01°00'W 100,000 ha

Unprotected

A mountainous area (300-1300 m) with abundant cliffs (especially along the River Turia and its tributaries), large pinewoods (*Pinus halepensis*, *P. pinaster*), and scrub areas (*Quercus coccifera*, *Rosmarinus officinalis*). The area is used for forestry and cultivation (wheat, almond, vineyards). There are some villages, roads, and three hydroelectric dams. Problems include forest fires, hazardous power-lines, and hunting.

Important for birds of prey with *Gyps fulvus* (20 pairs), *Circaetus gallicus* (min. 5 pairs), *Aquila chrysaetos* (5 pairs), and *Hieraaetus fasciatus* (9 pairs).

208 Hoces del Cabriel y del Júcar (País Valenciano, Castilla-La Mancha)

39°20'N, 01°08'W 90,000 ha

Partly a National Game Reserve (Muela de Cortes: 36,000 ha)

A large mountainous area (200-1100 m) crossed by the steep valleys of the Rivers Cabriel and Júcar, with abundant cliffs, pinewoods (mainly *Pinus halepensis*), and scrub.

The area is used for forestry, sheep-grazing, and there are some electricity dams. Subject to large forest fires.

Important for its high densities of *Circaetus gallicus* (16 pairs), *Aquila chrysaetos* (14 pairs), *Hieraaetus fasciatus* (13 pairs), *Falco peregrinus* (17 pairs), *Bubo bubo* (6 pairs), and *Pyrrhocorax pyrrhocorax* (min. 100 pairs).

209 Sierras del Norte de Alicante (País Valenciano)

38°40'N, 00°15'W 70,000 ha

Unprotected

A mountainous area (400-1588 m) with many small ranges (Sierra Aitana), abundant cliffs, pinewoods (*Pinus halepensis*), and Mediterranean scrub. The area is used for forestry and cultivation (olive, almond, fruit, vineyards); there are also many roads and small villages.

Breeding birds include *Aquila chrysaetos* (min. 5 pairs), *Hieraaetus fasciatus* (min. 10 pairs), *Falco peregrinus* (min. 5 pairs), *Bubo bubo* (min. 5 pairs), and *Pyrrhocorax pyrrhocorax* (min. 100 pairs).

210 Islas Columbretes (País Valenciano)

39°55'N, 00°40'E 2500 ha

Natural Park

An archipelago some 70 km from the Castellón coast, comprising a long curved island and other minor islets, which have some grassland, scrub zones, and steep cliffs. Until recently it was used as an air force firing range. A lighthouse exists on the larger island. There are uncontrolled visits by yachts.

Important because of its seabird colonies with *Calonectris diomedea* (200+ pairs), *Hydrobates pelagicus melitensis* (several pairs), and *Larus audouinii* (375 pairs). Also *Falco eleonorae* (17+ pairs).

211 Prat de Cabanes – Torreblanca (País Valenciano)

40°14'N, 00°12'E 900 ha

Unprotected

A well-preserved, unpolluted, coastal marsh, flooded only in winter, with emergent vegetation (*Phragmites*, *Typha*, *Cladium*), salty meadows with rushes and halophytic vegetation, and a well-preserved gravel-dune range. The main disturbances are caused by cattle-grazing and peat extraction (which produced the lagoons). There is the threat of house building along 1 km of the coast, while eel fishing and overgrazing are additional current problems.

Included because of its colony of *Glareola pratincola* (min. 40 pairs). Also *Circus aeruginosus* breeds.

212 Desembocadura del Río Mijares (País Valenciano)

39°57'N, 00°01'W 375 ha

Game Reserve

A river mouth with a stony bed and small shallow lagoons with considerable expanses of *Typha* and other marsh plants. The water comes mainly from nearby villages and is purified before reaching the sea. There was intense hunting until it became a Game Reserve. A clay-pigeon shooting field.

Included because of its breeding colony of *Himantopus himantopus* (60 pairs). Also an interesting passage area for *Phoenicopterus ruber*, herons, ducks, and waders.

213 Estanys y Marjal de Almenara (País Valenciano)

39°46'N, 00°14'W 1500 ha

Unprotected

A former marsh now with only a few small lagoons. The area is devoted to agriculture and in winter is flooded and baited to attract ducks. Problems include intense winter hunting, urban development, and dumping.

Important for its winter concentrations of *Netta rufina* (max. 700) and other ducks, and as a roosting area for *Hirundo rustica* on autumn passage.

214 Albufera de Valencia (País Valenciano)

39°20'N, 00°15'W 21,000 ha EEC SPA

Natural Park

A freshwater coastal lagoon with abundant emergent vegetation and several islands, connected to the sea. The area also includes some 14,000 ha of paddyfields (flooded most of the year), sand beaches, dunes, and a wide coastal pinewood (*Pinus halepensis*). Human activities include rice cultivation, fishing, hunting, and leisure activities. There is intense pollution (agricultural, industrial and urban), illegal drying of paddyfields and over-hunting.

An important breeding area for herons with *Nycticorax nycticorax* (75 pairs), *Bubulcus ibis* (1450 pairs), *Egretta garzetta* (650 pairs), and *Ardea purpurea* (91 pairs). Also *Netta rufina* (200 pairs), *Himantopus himantopus* (100 pairs), *Glareola pratincola* (100+ birds after the breeding season), *Charadrius alexandrinus* (100 pairs), and *Sterna hirundo* (150 pairs). The third most important area in Spain for wintering wildfowl, with *Anas clypeata* (av. Jan. 8700; max. 24,500) and *Netta rufina* (av. Jan. 5600; max 12,200).

215 Embalse del Hondo (País Valenciano)

38°20'N, 00°42'W 2200 ha

Unprotected

Two irrigation reservoirs (formerly a natural marsh) with a covering of reed (*Phragmites*) and emergent vegetation and surrounded by small brackish and freshwater lagoons. The area is used for hunting and fishing. There is a project to increase the water-level which would destroy the vegetation. A study has been carried out in order to assist the appeal for its protection.

Very important for breeding *Ardea purpurea* (35 pairs), *Marmaronetta angustirostris* (max. 15 pairs), *Netta rufina* (max. 500 pairs), *Himantopus himantopus* (80-100 pairs), *Sterna albifrons* (100 pairs), and *Chlidonias hybridus* (110 pairs). Important also for passage and wintering *Netta rufina* (av. 700+; max. 1500+).

216 Salinas de Santa Pola (País Valenciano)

38°13'N, 00°35'W 2700 ha

Unprotected

Saltworks which have replaced a natural coastal lagoon, surrounded by artificial freshwater and brackish ponds with dense plant cover. There is great hunting pressure, a road crosses the middle of the area resulting in bird mortality, and the beach zone is subject to property development.

An important area for breeding *Marmaronetta angustirostris* (3 pairs), *Netta rufina* (60-120 pairs), *Himantopus himantopus* (200-250 pairs), *Recurvirostra avosetta* (500+ pairs), *Charadrius alexandrinus* (150+ pairs), *Sterna hirundo* (100 pairs), and *S. albifrons* (400 pairs). An important wintering area for *Recurvirostra avosetta* (av. 440), and *Phoenicopterus ruber* occurs in variable numbers with breeding attempted.

217 Salinas de la Mata y Torrevieja (País Valenciano)

38°03'N, 00°40'W 2200 ha

Unprotected

Two wide coastal lagoons which have been transformed for salt extraction, with a permanent saltwater supply from the sea. There is a narrow belt of reeds and halophytic vegetation. Problems include building nearby, water pollution, and human disturbance.

Important for breeding *Tadorna tadorna* (max. 4 pairs), *Himantopus himantopus* (60 pairs), *Charadrius alexandrinus* (100 pairs), and *S. albifrons* (70 pairs). Also outstanding concentrations in winter or during passage of *Podiceps nigricollis* (winter: av. 797; max. 3500), *Phoenicopterus ruber* (1000-2000 on passage), and *Netta rufina* (2000-3000 in winter).

218 Mar Menor (Murcia)

37°45'N, 00°45'W 16,000 ha

Unprotected, although in some zones building is not allowed

A hyper-saline coastal lagoon with two islands. In several places there are saltpans surrounded by reeds and sandy areas or saltmarshes. Land-uses include salt extraction, tourism, and fishing. Problems include pollution, infilling, building, and hunting.

An important breeding area for *Tadorna tadorna* (several pairs) and *Charadrius alexandrinus* (290 pairs), and passage and wintering area for *Phoenicopterus ruber* (700). Also wintering *Podiceps nigricollis* (200+), *Tadorna tadorna* (200+), and *Mergus serrator* (160+).

219 Islotes litorales de Murcia y Almería (Murcia, Andalucía)

37°35'N, 01°00'W *c.*50 ha

Unprotected

Small, rocky, sparsely vegetated islets, close to the Spanish coast. The area is affected by tourism and an army detachment on Isla Grosa. Rats are probably present, threatening the seabird colonies.

Important for breeding *Hydrobates pelagicus melitensis* (a small population, undoubtedly threatened, with 25-30 pairs on Hormigas). Also breeding *Calonectris diomedea* and *Larus argentatus cachinnans.*

220 Sierra de Moratalla (Murcia, Castilla-La Mancha)

38°15'N, 02°00'W 50,000 ha

Unprotected

A group of limestone ranges (500-1475 m) crossed by deep valleys. There is cultivation in the valleys; mixed woods (mostly *Pinus halepensis, P. nigra*), some oakwoods (*Quercus rotundifolia*), and Mediterranean scrub in the mountains. The area is used for stock-grazing, and there are some scattered small villages.

Important for birds of prey particularly *Aquila chrysaetos* (7 pairs), *Hieraaetus fasciatus* (5 pairs), *Falco peregrinus* (18 pairs), and *Bubo bubo* (16-20 pairs). There are also several colonies of *Pyrrhocorax pyrrhocorax* (min. 100 pairs).

221 Cagitán – Armorchón (Murcia)

38°15'N, 01°40'W 30,000 ha

Unprotected

An area of low semi-arid hills with some scrub (*Stipa tenacissima*); also some reedbeds around a reservoir (Quípar). Mainly used for cereal farming (some almond-groves), sheep- and goat-grazing, and hunting.

Perhaps the best area for steppe birds in Murcia province with *Circus pygargus* (min. 6 pairs), *Tetrax tetrax* (common), *Burhinus oedicnemus* (very common; min. 100 pairs), and *Pterocles orientalis* (common).

222 Valle del Guadalentín (Murcia)

37°45'N, 01°25'W 15,000 ha

Unprotected

Wide plains both sides of the River Guadalentín (Sangonera) with ravines and small expanses of unploughed saline ground. There are orchards, cereal croplands, and almond groves.

Important for steppe birds including *Circus pygargus* (several pairs), *Tetrax tetrax* (very scarce in Murcia), *Pterocles orientalis*, and *Calandrella rufescens* (min. 300 pairs).

223 Topares – El Moral – Puebla de Don Fadrique (Murcia, Andalucía)

37°50'N, 02°20'W 80,000 ha

Unprotected

A high plateau (1000-1200 m) with extensive dry cereal cultivation alternating with matweed (*Stipa tenacissima*) and other sclerophyllous scrub (*Quercus coccifera*) areas. There are some small woods of *Quercus rotundifolia* and *Pinus halepensis*. Sparsely populated; sheep are grazed.

Important for steppe birds including *Circus pygargus*, *Tetrax tetrax*, *Burhinus oedicnemus* (min. 100 pairs), *Pterocles orientalis* (min. 50 pairs), and *P. alchata*.

224 Hoya de Baza (Andalucía)

37°35'N, 02°41'W 30,000 ha

Unprotected

A semi-arid depression (700-1000 m) mostly devoted to dry cereal croplands with interspersed expanses of scrub (*Stipa tenacissima*; also *Suaeda* in salty areas). There is an immediate risk of agricultural transformation.

Important for steppe birds including *Tetrax tetrax*, *Burhinus oedicnemus* (min. 100 pairs), *Pterocles orientalis* (min. 20-30 pairs), *Chersophilus duponti* (min. 10 pairs; isolated population), and *Calandrella rufescens* (min. 200 pairs).

225 Depresión de Guadix (Andalucía)

37°25'N, 03°10'W 30,000 ha

Unprotected

A semi-arid depression (900-1000 m) to the north of Sierra Nevada; gypsum ground with many ravines. There are dry cereal croplands (wheat, rye), some oak (*Quercus rotundifolia*) areas with scattered trees resembling a savanna, extensive areas of low scrub (*Stipa tenacissima*), and xerophytic grasslands. Sparsely populated; there is some sheep-grazing.

One of the best areas for steppe birds in Andalucía with *Tetrax tetrax* (min. 100 birds), *Burhinus oedicnemus* (100-150 pairs), and *Pterocles orientalis* (min. 80 pairs). A number of birds of prey breed including *Circus pygargus*, *Falco peregrinus* (min. 6 pairs), *F. subbuteo* (min. 9 pairs), *Bubo bubo* (min. 6 pairs), and *Asio otus* (min. 5 pairs). In addition, there is a large population of *Pyrrhocorax pyrrhocorax* (min. 500 pairs).

226 Sierra del Cabo de Gata (Andalucía)

36°50'N, 02°05'W 40,000 ha

Partly a Natural Park (Cabo de Gata: 26,000 ha)

Coastal mountains, and a very rugged coast with a few beaches and frequent cliffs, with xerophytic vegetation of great interest. Sparsely populated, with abandoned mines and coastal fishing. Tourism is being developed with residential areas and roads being built.

Supports an interesting bird community typical of semi-desert habitat including *Bucanetes githagineus* (min. 50 pairs). Also breeding *Hieraaetus fasciatus* (min. 4 pairs), *Bubo bubo* (min. 3 pairs), *Larus argentatus cachinnans*, and possibly *Phalacrocorax aristotelis desmarestii*.

227 Salinas del Cabo de Gata – Estepa Litoral (Andalucía)

36°43'N, 02°15'W 3000 ha

Included in a Natural Park (Cabo de Gata: 26,000 ha)

A coastal strip, *c.*15 km long, in the Bahía de Almería, with a wide depression occupied by saltpans. Supports interesting steppe vegetation, with clumps of *Tamarix* sp. and *Zyzyphus lotus*, and expanses of *Salicornia*. Threats include sand extraction, building, and tourism.

The saltpans support *Phoenicopterus ruber* (max. 2000 birds with nesting attempted), *Himantopus himantopus*, and *Recurvirostra avosetta* (max. 450 wintering), as well as passage waders and *Larus audouinii*. In the steppe areas, *Tetrax tetrax*, *Burhinus oedicnemus*, *Pterocles orientalis*, and *Calandrella rufescens* (hundreds of pairs) occur.

228 Sierra Alhamilla – Campo de Níjar (Andalucía)

37°00'N, 02°20'W 50,000 ha

Unprotected

A 25 km range (100-1387 m) including the southern foothills close to Almería, with deep (usually dry) gullies, wasteland and plains. Vegetation comprises small woods of *Quercus rotundifolia* in the highest zones; otherwise scrub (mostly *Stipa tenacissima*) and bare, stony ground. Sparsely populated with some abandoned small villages. The area is almost unused for cattle-grazing or agriculture, but military manoeuvres take place.

The most important area for *Bucanetes githagineus* (min. 200 pairs) in continental Europe. Other birds of steppe or semi-desert habitats occurring include *Tetrax tetrax* (scarce), *Burhinus oedicnemus* (min. 100 pairs), *Pterocles orientalis* (min. 30 pairs), *Galerida theklae* (very common), *Chersophilus duponti* (min. 150 pairs), and *Oenanthe leucura* (very common). In the mountains *Hieraaetus fasciatus* (min. 5 pairs) and *Bubo bubo* (min. 3 pairs) occur.

229 Desierto de Tabernas (Andalucía)

37°05'N, 02°30'W 18,000 ha

Unprotected

A depression between the Sierra de los Filabres and the Sierra Alhamilla, to the north of Almería. Perhaps the most spectacular arid zone in the Iberian peninsula, with seasonal rivers and creeks (usually dry) and relatively high cliffs. Very sparse vegetation and mainly bare ground, with *Nerium oleander* and *Tamarix* along river courses. Used by the film industry, and for tourism, and there are roads and railways.

Interesting for birds of semi-arid habitats including *Burhinus oedicnemus*, *Bubo bubo*, *Pterocles orientalis*, *Coracias garrulus*, *Apus melba*, *Galerida theklae*, *Monticola solitarius*, *Oenanthe leucura*, *Sylvia conspicillata*, and *Bucanetes githagineus*.

230 Punta Entinas – Punta del Sabinar – Salinas de Cerrillos (Andalucía)

36°40'N, 02°40'W 5000 ha

Unprotected

A coastal strip 15 km long, to the south of Roquetas de Mar (Almería), with a sandy beach, a small range of sandhills, a long depression with saltpans (450 ha), and large seasonal lagoons with sparse halophytic vegetation and reed belts. Interesting botanical communities including high scrub of *Juniperus phoenicea* and *Pistacia lentiscus*. Close to residential areas, golf-courses, and plastic-covered cultivation. Problems include sand extraction, massive tourism, and over-exploitation of ground water.

Burhinus oedicnemus (probably 100+ pairs) and *Calandrella rufescens* (min. 200 pairs) are abundant, and *Phoenicopterus ruber* use the saltpans (max. 1000 birds congregate after breeding). The area is also a resting site for passerines on migration.

231 Picos de Aroche (Andalucía)

37°50'N, 07°05'W 100,000 ha

Unprotected

A mountain range (100-800 m) in the western Sierra Morena along the Portuguese border, with cliffs and slopes covered by scrub (*Cistus*), and woodland (*Quercus suber*, *Q. rotundifolia*) frequently occurring as 'dehesa'. The area is used for livestock-grazing.
Important for breeding *Aegypius monachus* (max. 30 pairs; the best area in Andalucía) and *Aquila adalberti* (1 pair).

232 Sierra Morena de Sevilla (Andalucía)

37°50'N, 06°00'W 53,000 ha

Unprotected

A rugged mountainous area (75-906 m) to the north of Sevilla, with steep-sided valleys (River Viar). Vegetation comprises Mediterranean scrub and woodland, mostly 'dehesa' (*Quercus rotundifolia*, *Q. suber*), and a few olive-groves. The area is used for sheep- and cattle-grazing.
Rich in birds of prey with *Gyps fulvus* (min. 7 pairs and many wintering birds).

233 Sierra Morena de Córdoba (Andalucía)

38°00'N, 05°15'W 100,000 ha

Unprotected; proposed Natural Park (Hornachuelos)

A low range (200-693 m) in the central section of the Sierra Morena, with Mediterranean scrub (*Cistus ladanifer*, *Pistacia lentiscus*), 'dehesa' (*Quercus rotundifolia* and *Q. suber*) and a few olive-groves. The area is used for stock-grazing and big-game hunting. Sparsely populated.
A very important area for breeding birds of prey with *Gyps fulvus* (75 pairs), *Aegypius monachus* (min. 22 pairs), *Aquila chrysaetos* (min. 12 pairs), and *Hieraaetus fasciatus* (7 pairs).

234 Los Blázquez – La Granjuela – Fuenteovejuna (Andalucía)

38°20'N, 05°20'W 11,000 ha

Unprotected

An undulating area covered by grasslands and 'dehesa'-like oakwoods (*Quercus rotundifolia*), olive-groves and cereal croplands. The area is used for sheep-grazing. Problems include intense hunting and destructive cutting of oaks.
An important area for *Grus grus* during winter (min. 470) and on passage (200). Also breeding *Otis tarda* (min. 20 birds) and other steppe birds.

235 Hinojosa del Duque – El Viso (Andalucía)

38°30'N, 05°10'W 18,000 ha

Unprotected

An undulating area, with 'dehesa' (*Quercus rotundifolia*), olive-groves, grasslands, and cereal croplands (wheat, barley). The area is used for sheep-grazing and hunting. Close to several large villages.
Important for *Grus grus* (min. 100 birds in winter; max. 750 during spring passage) and steppe birds including *Tetrax tetrax* (numerous).

236 Sierra Madrona – Sierra Morena de Jaén (Andalucía, Castilla-La Mancha)

38°20'N, 04°00'W 200,000 ha

Unprotected

An extensive mountain range, 75 km long, in the Sierra Morena system, including large foothill areas to the south, with steep river gorges and some cliffs. Vegetation comprises Mediterranean scrub (*Cistus ladanifer*, *Pistacia lentiscus*, *Olea europaea*) and 'dehesa' (*Quercus rotundifolia*, *Q. faginea*, *Q. pyrenaica*), with some pine plantations (*Pinus pinaster*) and small croplands (cereal and olive). The area is used for sheep- and cattle-grazing, big-game hunting, and forestry (which is destructive). Lynx *Lynx lynx* is present.

A very important area for breeding birds of prey with *Aegypius monachus* (min. 2 pairs), *Aquila chrysaetos* (min. 15 pairs), *Hieraaetus fasciatus* (min. 10 pairs), and *Bubo bubo* (many pairs). *Ciconia nigra* (min. 5 pairs) also breeds.

237 Aldeaquemada – Dañador (Andalucía, Castilla-La Mancha)

38°25'N, 03°10'W 35,000 ha

Unprotected

A mountainous area (500-960 m) in Sierra Morena. Vegetation comprises Mediterranean woodland of *Quercus faginea* and *Q. rotundifolia*, 'dehesa', and extensive scrub areas (*Cistus*). Sparsely populated, with big-game hunting, livestock-grazing, and a dam (Dañador). Lynx *Lynx lynx* is present.

Birds of prey are numerous, including *Aquila adalberti*, *A. chrysaetos* (several pairs), and *Bubo bubo* (several pairs). *Ciconia nigra* also breeds.

238 Sierras de Cazorla y Segura (Andalucía, Castilla-La Mancha, Murcia)

38°00'N, 02°40'W 140,000 ha Biosphere Reserve (190,000 ha)

Included in a Natural Park (214,000 ha); National Game Reserve (Cazorla: 76,000 ha)

A group of mountain ranges (800-2383 m) with many high cliffs, extensive pinewoods (*Pinus pinaster*, *P. nigra*, *P. halepensis*), small oak woods (*Quercus rotundifolia*, *Q. faginea*), grasslands, and expanses of scrub. The area is used for big-game hunting, forestry, sheep-grazing, tourism, and there is also a dam on the River Guadalquivir.

Important for birds of prey including *Gypaetus barbatus* (the only breeding locality in Spain outside the Pyrenees), *Gyps fulvus* (min. 40 pairs), *Aquila chrysaetos* (min. 5 pairs), *Hieraaetus pennatus* (min. 20 pairs), *Falco peregrinus* (min. 5 pairs), and *Bubo bubo* (min. 5 pairs). Also *Pyrrhocorax pyrrhocorax* (several hundred).

239 Embalses del Tramo medio del Guadalquivir (Andalucía)

37°55'N, 03°21'W 700 ha

EEC SPA (Sierra de Cazorla, Segura y las Villas: 214,300 ha)

Unprotected

A group of three shallow reservoirs (Doña Aldonza, Pedro Marín, and Puente de la Cerrada) on the River Guadalquivir in Jaén province, with a constant water-level and abundant emergent vegetation. Surrounded by croplands and olive-groves. Problems include poaching, vegetation burning, and infilling.

Important for breeding *Porphyrio porphyrio* (min. 62 birds) and marsh passerines.

240 Embalse de Marmolejo (Andalucía)

38°02'N, 04°03'W 600 ha

Unprotected

A narrow reservoir (6 km long) on the River Guadalquivir in Jaén province, with abundant emergent vegetation on two central islands and along some bank sections. The area is used for agriculture and cattle-grazing. Problems include urban and industrial dumping, infilling, and periodic fires.

Important for breeding *Porphyrio porphyrio* (min. 6 pairs). Also breeding *Ixobrychus minutus* and *Ardea purpurea*.

241 Sierras al sur de Jaén (Andalucía)

37°35'N, 03°50'W 95,000 ha

Unprotected

A mountainous area (600-1872 m) immediately to the south of Jaén with frequent cliffs, Mediterranean scrub (*Quercus rotundifolia*), and olive-tree covered slopes. The area is used for stock-grazing and hunting; there are also some large villages.

An interesting area for cliff-nesting birds including *Hieraaetus fasciatus* (min. 10 pairs), *Falco peregrinus* (min. 10 pairs), and *Pyrrhocorax pyrrhocorax* (min. 100 pairs).

242 Sierras de Cabra Luque, Priego y Rute (Andalucía)

37°25'N, 04°20'W 50,000 ha

Unprotected

A mountainous area with many cliffs (600-1570 m) in the northern spurs of the Sistema Bético. The slopes are covered with Mediterranean scrub, with some oaks (*Quercus rotundifolia*), and croplands (mainly olive, also cereal and some orchards). The area is used for sheep-grazing and hunting. Densely populated.

An interesting area for *Falco peregrinus* (min. 15 pairs) and *Pyrrhocorax pyrrhocorax* (min. 100 pairs). Other birds nesting in the area include *Neophron percnopterus*, *Gyps fulvus* (min. 8 pairs), *Aquila chrysaetos*, and *Hieraaetus fasciatus*.

243 Zonas húmedas del sur de Córdoba (Andalucía)

37°25'N, 04°45'W 500 ha

EEC SPA (Lagunas de Zoñar, Amarga y Rincón: 1107 ha)

Integral Reserve of Scientific Interest: most of the lagoons are protected, and hunting and visiting are forbidden at the reservoirs.

A complex of brackish lagoons, some permanent (Zoñar, Amarga and Rincón), others seasonal (Salobral, Tiscar, Jarales), and two small reservoirs (Malpasillo, Cordobilla); generally with wide belts of emergent vegetation, and olive-groves and dry cereal cultivation in the surrounding areas.

The main breeding area for *Oxyura leucocephala* in Spain (min. 45 pairs; with winter concentrations of 100+ birds). Also breeding *Ardea purpurea*, *Porphyrio porphyrio*, and other interesting waterbirds.

244 Campiña de Carmona (Andalucía)

37°25'N, 05°40'W 30,000 ha

Unprotected

An undulating area (in the Guadalquivir valley) with extensive cereal croplands (wheat), some sunflower fields and olive-groves. The area is used for sheep- and cattle-grazing and hunting. Densely populated.

One of the few interesting areas for steppe birds in the River Guadalquivir valley, with relict populations of *Circus pygargus*, *Otis tarda*, and *Tetrax tetrax*.

245 Marismas de Isla Cristina y Ayamonte (Andalucía)

37°13'N, 07°25'W 700 ha

Unprotected

Coastal marshes at the mouth of River Guadiana with sand beaches and numerous abandoned saltpans. The area is used for halophytic-scrub collecting, trawling, and tourism. Problems result from uncontrolled building, irrigation schemes, and marine farming.

A passage and wintering area for waders, gulls and terns, and of particular importance for *Charadrius alexandrinus* (av. 346 in Jan.).

246 Ría de Huelva (Andalucía)

37°15'N, 06°50'W 11,700 ha

Biosphere Reserve (8728 ha); EEC SPA (Marismas del Odiel: 7150 ha)

Natural Park with 2 Integral Reserves of Scientific Interest

A large area of tidal coastal marshes at the mouths of the Rivers Tinto and Odiel with extensive areas of mud and halophytic scrub and some saltpans. The area is used for fishing, mollusc collecting, and tourism. Problems include industrial pollution, uncontrolled visits, and occasional egg-collecting.

Very important for breeding *Egretta garzetta* (400 pairs), *Ardea purpurea* (80 pairs), *A. cinerea* (80 pairs), *Platalea leucorodia* (300 pairs), and *Sterna albifrons* (300 pairs). It is also important as a breeding, passage, and wintering area for waders including *Himantopus himantopus* (100 pairs), *Recurvirostra avosetta* (1550 on passage), and *Calidris alba* (620 in winter). Also post-nuptial concentrations of *Phoenicopterus ruber* (1000+ birds).

247 Marismas del Guadalquivir (Andalucía)

37°00'N, 06°25'W 180,000 ha

Ramsar Site; Biosphere Reserve (Doñana: 77,260 ha); EEC SPA (Parque Nacional de Doñana: 50,720 ha)

National Park (Doñana: 77,260 ha)

One of the largest and best-known wetlands in Europe comprising the marshes at the mouth of the River Guadalquivir. Large areas have been transformed especially to the north and east, being replaced by rice paddies, irrigated cultivation, fish-farms, saltworks (those in Bonanza are important for birds), and expanses of halophytic scrub. Marshes, Mediterranean scrub, woodland, and dunes occur to the south. The marshes are flooded only seasonally (there are some permanent rivers and lagoons), with expanses of *Salicornia*, *Scirpus*, *Typha*, and *Phragmites*. In the outer zones, Mediterranean scrub (Halimium, *Cistus*) and woodland (patches of *Quercus suber*) predominate. The dunes are located in a wide coastal belt, being covered mainly by pinewoods (*Pinus pinea*) and scrub. Lynx *Lynx lynx* and Mongoose *Herpestes ichneumon* are present. Land-uses include agriculture, cattle-grazing, hunting, fishing, fish-farming and tourism. There are numerous and severe problems caused mainly by agricultural activities, with an expansion of agricultural areas, uncontrolled use of pesticides (massive bird poisoning has occurred), over-exploitation of ground water (a strong decrease in the water-levels of the marshes may soon occur), changes in the natural inundation and drought cycles, intensive poaching (especially in the northern periphery of the National Park), intensive crayfish fishing (introduced *Procambarus clarkii*), increase in fish-farming, river pollution, expansion of residential areas (especially at Matalascañas beach), and uncontrolled tourism.

This area is extraordinarily important. There are major colonies of *Egretta garzetta* (some 400 pairs), *Ardea purpurea* (several hundred pairs) and *Platalea leucorodia* (350 pairs), and large numbers of *Phoenicopterus ruber* (*c.*10,000 birds in winter, with occasional breeding of 300 pairs). Among the nesting waterfowl, *Marmaronetta angustirostris* (max. 175 pairs), *Oxyura leucocephala* (irregular), *Porphyrio porphyrio* (hundreds of pairs), and *Fulica cristata* are especially noteworthy, and there are very important breeding populations of *Himantopus himantopus* (min. 1000 pairs), *Recurvirostra avosetta* (min. 350 pairs), *Glareola pratincola* (several hundred pairs), *Charadrius alexandrinus* (min. 500 pairs), *Larus genei* (19 pairs), *Gelochelidon nilotica* (min. 500 pairs), *Sterna albifrons* (min. 400 pairs), and *Chlidonias hybridus* (many hundreds of pairs). Many birds of prey are found in the dry zones; especially important are *Aquila adalberti* (min. 16 pairs), *Milvus migrans* and *M. milvus*; there are also steppe birds with *Pterocles alchata* and *Calandrella rufescens*. It is the most important wetland for wintering ducks in Spain, including (all max. Jan. counts) *Anser anser* (69,200), *Tadorna tadorna* (4200), *Anas strepera* (8700), *A. crecca* (126,200), *A. acuta* (39,900), *A.*

clypeata (86,000), and *Netta rufina* (5000). Wintering and passage waders include *Limosa limosa* (max. 20,000).

248 Coria del Río (Andalucía)

37°15'N, 06°04'W 11,000 ha

Unprotected

A riverine island connected to the bank by a wall, at the northern edge of the Marismas del Guadalquivir. There is alluvial vegetation (*Tamarix*, *Populus*, *Typha latifolia*, *Phragmites australis*) as well as cereal crops on the island, with irrigated cultivation and rice-fields nearby. Problems include urban and industrial dumping, ship-cleaning and intense shipping traffic, uncontrolled visits, hunting, and pesticide use.

Supports an old and important breeding colony of herons, with *Nycticorax nycticorax* (50+ birds), *Ardeola ralloides* (min. 25 pairs), *Bubulcus ibis* (450+ pairs), and *Egretta garzetta* (min. 300 pairs); a roosting site during winter.

249 Lagunas de Espera (Andalucía)

36°53'N, 06°47'W 1100 ha EEC SPA (438 ha)

Integral Reserve of Scientific Interest (covering 30 per cent with only the three most important lagoons protected)

A complex of nine main lagoons and several minor ponds, mostly surrounded by dense emergent vegetation. The area is seriously disturbed by cattle, uncontrolled visits, hunting, and harvesting during the breeding season.

Oxyura leucocephala and *Fulica cristata* are present throughout the year and may breed.

250 Lagunas de Terry (Andalucía)

36°38'N, 06°14'W 62 ha EEC SPA (63 ha)

Integral Reserve of Scientific Interest

Three small lagoons to the north of Puerto de Santa María. One of them has good plant cover and receives water from an irrigation channel. Surrounded by cereal croplands, irrigated fields, and grassland, with some farms. There is human disturbance.

A regular nesting site for *Ixobrychus minutus*, *Porphyrio porphyrio* (several pairs), and *Fulica cristata*. *Marmaronetta angustirostris* and *Oxyura leucocephala* (max. 76 birds) occur outside the breeding season.

251 Bahía de Cádiz (Andalucía)

36°35'N, 06°20'W 12,000 ha

Unprotected

A shallow bay with a wide intertidal zone and a large saltpan complex (some abandoned), with small lagoons, rivers ('caños'), artificial channels ('esteros'), and expanses of halophytic scrub (*Salicornia*). There are many severe problems, which include major transformation of the lagoons and saltpans for marine farming (this means dredging and the destruction of islands and other breeding areas for waders and gulls), intensive poaching, military manoeuvres, building (with a project for a huge tourist and sports complex), and urban and industrial pollution.

Very important as a breeding area for *Sterna albifrons* (best area in Spain), *Himantopus himantopus*, *Recurvirostra avosetta*, and *Charadrius alexandrinus*, with several hundred pairs of each species. Also very important for post-nuptial concentrations of *Phoenicopterus ruber* (max. 1200), and wintering *Anas penelope* (av. 5000+), *Recurvirostra avosetta* (max. 600), *Charadrius hiaticula* (1700), and *C. alexandrinus* (1820).

252 Laguna de Medina (Andalucía)

36°37'N, 06°03'W 362 ha EEC SPA (121 ha)

Integral Reserve of Scientific Interest

An endorreic lagoon close to Jerez de la Frontera with a variable water-level and sometimes dry in summer. There is a dense belt of *Tamarix*, *Juncus* and *Phragmites* in several sections, with cereal croplands and hillocks covered by scrub and grassland in the surrounding area. A stone quarry and concrete factory are close to the lagoon. A part of the water-supply is now used for irrigation.

Large numbers of waterfowl occur, especially *Fulica atra* (sometimes 25,000+ from the nearby Marismas del Guadalquivir); also *Phoenicopterus ruber* (max. 800), *Marmaronetta angustirostris* (max. 110 in autumn), *Oxyura leucocephala* (max. 122 in the 1985-1986 winter), and *Fulica cristata* (also breeding). There is also a small number of breeding *Porphyrio porphyrio*, and during autumn passage it is a roosting site for huge numbers of *Hirundo rustica* and other hirundines (hundreds of thousands of birds).

253 Lagunas de Puerto Real (Andalucía)

36°32'N, 06°11'W 800 ha EEC SPA (300 ha)

Integral Reserve of Scientific Interest

A complex of three main lagoons (Taraje, San Antonio, Comisario) and some minor ponds, fringed with *Phragmites*, *Juncus*, and *Typha* and surrounded by grasslands and cereal croplands. Sewage water runs into one of the lagoons (San Antonio).

A breeding site for *Porphyrio porphyrio* (*c.*15 pairs) and *Fulica cristata*.

254 Embalse de Bornos (Andalucía)

36°45'N, 05°34'W 4000 ha

Unprotected

A reservoir on the River Guadalete surrounded by hillocks with maquis (*Pistacia lentiscus*, *Olea europaea*), grasslands, dry cereal cultivation, and irrigated fields. At the end of the reservoir there is a large and dense expanse of *Tamarix*. The main threats are rapid infilling with sediments, and pesticide use in the fields.

There is an important *Bubulcus ibis* colony (*c.*1000 pairs) with some pairs of *Nycticorax nycticorax*, *Egretta garzetta*, and *Ardea purpurea*. Wintering birds include *Phalacrocorax carbo* (max. 300) and *Podiceps cristatus* (max. 450).

255 Medina-Sidonia (Andalucía)

36°30'N, 05°55'W 20,000 ha

Unprotected

An undulating area around Medina-Sidonia, with grasslands and wheat cultivation and a few irrigated fields. There are creeks with dense vegetation (*Tamarix*, *Salix*) and some ponds. Used predominantly for sheep- and cattle-grazing.

The area holds a large breeding colony of *Bubulcus ibis* (min. 1000 pairs) and supports important post-nuptial concentrations of *Ciconia ciconia* (several hundred birds).

256 Tajo de Barbate (Andalucía)

36°12'N, 06°00'W 10,000 ha

Unprotected

The coastal cliffs between Cabo Trafalgar and Barbate, including an inland plateau covered by a large pinewood (*Pinus pinea*), scrub, and grasslands. The area is used for sheep- and cattle-grazing, and there are some residential areas. Fires are a problem.

Holds a very important colony of *Bubulcus ibis* (min. 2600 pairs), with *Egretta garzetta* (min. 50 pairs) and *Larus argentatus cachinnans* (min. 700 pairs).

257 La Janda (Andalucía)

36°15'N, 05°51'W 20,000 ha

Unprotected

Formerly an important freshwater lagoon, drained in the 1950s, that was rich in marsh vegetation and birds including *Ardeola ralloides*, *Ardea purpurea*, *Porphyrio porphyrio*, *Grus grus* (then the last breeding population in southern Europe), and *Chlidonias hybridus*. Presently it is a large expanse of land devoted to agriculture and cattle-ranching, with large drainage channels that retain some aquatic vegetation, although there are areas regularly flooded in winter.

Breeding species include *Ciconia ciconia* (*c.*35 pairs), *Bubulcus ibis* (2200 pairs; one colony), *Circus pygargus* (min. 20 pairs), *Otis tarda* (max. 12 birds), *Tetrax tetrax* and *Glareola pratincola*. Important stop-over place for many migrants, because of its proximity to the Straits of Gibraltar, including *Ciconia ciconia* (3000+) and *Circus pygargus* (400+). Wintering species include *Grus grus* (max. 500) and *Pluvialis apricaria* (max. 5000). Also important as a feeding ground for birds of prey breeding in the adjacent range including *Gyps fulvus* and *Hieraaetus fasciatus*.

258 Sierra de la Plata (Andalucía)

36°05'N, 05°45'W 3000 ha

Unprotected

A small range with some high cliffs ('lajas' of La Zarga and Ranchiles). A Mediterranean scrub-covered zone, with some patches of *Quercus suber* and *Eucalyptus* plantations. Includes a military base and a residential area. Fires are a problem.

Breeding species include *Gyps fulvus* (min. 35 pairs) and *Apus caffer*.

259 Tarifa (Andalucía)

36°05'N, 05°35'W 10,000 ha

Partly an Ornithological Reserve (Los Lances: 400 ha)

A coastal area around Tarifa bordering the Straits of Gibraltar. The site includes the plains and hillocks surrounding the Santuario Valley (River Jara), covered by Mediterranean scrub (*Pistacia lentiscus*, *Chamaerops humilis*) or grasslands, with some creeks with dense scrub vegetation. Also a long sandy beach.

A major passage site for migratory birds crossing the Straits of Gibraltar. Especially important as a passage/resting site for *Ciconia ciconia* (min. 30,000 birds; many stopping over when the weather is bad), birds of prey including *Milvus migrans* (min. 39,000 birds), and many passerines. The beach is important for breeding *Charadrius alexandrinus* (min. 50 pairs), and for passage and wintering waders and gulls including *Larus audouinii* (200+) and *Calidris alba* (max. 400).

260 Sierras del Bujeo, Ojén, del Niño y Blanquilla (Andalucía)

36°10'N, 05°35'W 25,000 ha

Unprotected

A chain of limestone hills with many rocky outcrops, about 30 km long, to the west of Algeciras. Covered by woodland (*Quercus suber*, *Q. canariensis*), with very dense and interesting vegetation along some creeks (*Laurus nobilis*, Rhododendron baeticum. Sparsely populated, with cattle- and goat-grazing and cork exploitation.

Very interesting for nesting birds of prey including *Gyps fulvus* (several colonies; min. 120 pairs), *Circaetus gallicus*, *Hieraaetus fasciatus*, *H. pennatus*, and *Bubo bubo*; also holds a rich cork-oak woodland passerine community, and *Apus caffer* breeds (several pairs).

261 Sierras de las Cabras, del Aljibe y de Montecoche (Andalucía)

36°25'N, 05°35'W 60,000 ha

Unprotected

A range of hills/mountains (100-1091 m), 45 km long, to the east of Alcalá de los Gazules. Limestone rocks with some cliffs, deep gullies, large oakwoods (*Quercus suber*, *Q. faginea*), and scrub areas. Sparsely populated, with cattle-grazing and cork exploitation.

Very interesting for birds of prey including *Gyps fulvus* (min. 75 pairs), *Aquila adalberti* (1 pair), *Circaetus gallicus*, *Hieraaetus fasciatus* (min. 5 pairs), *H. pennatus*, and *Bubo bubo* (min. 10 pairs). Also *Apus caffer* breeds (min. 6 pairs). Good passerine communities in the cork oak woodlands.

262 Sierras de Ubrique y Grazalema (Andalucía)

36°40'N, 05°25'W 25,000 ha

Biosphere Reserve (32,210 ha); EEC SPA (Sierra de Grazalema)

Natural Park (Sierra de Grazalema: 47,120 ha)

A mountain massif (400-1655 m) with many high limestone cliffs. Vegetation comprises scrub, grasslands, oakwoods (*Quercus faginea*, *Q. rotundifolia*), and fir woods (*Abies pinsapo*) of great interest (Pinar de Grazalema). The area is used for sheep- and goat-grazing and tourism.

Breeding species include *Gyps fulvus* (min. 100 pairs), *Aquila chrysaetos*, *Hieraaetus fasciatus* (min. 5 pairs), *Bubo bubo* (min. 10 pairs), *Apus caffer*, and *Pyrrhocorax pyrrhocorax*.

263 Sierra de Líjar – Peñón de Zaframagón (Andalucía)

36°52'N, 05°23'W 6000 ha

Unprotected

A small mountain area (400-1051 m) with limestone cliffs (some very high). Vegetation comprises scrub, grasslands, and woodland (*Quercus rotundifolia*).

Very interesting for *Gyps fulvus* (min. 120 pairs) and other cliff-nesting birds of prey such as *Neophron percnopterus*, *Hieraaetus fasciatus*, and *Bubo bubo*.

264 Sierras Bermeja y Crestellina (Andalucía)

36°30'N, 05°12'W 6000 ha

Unprotected

Small mountains (300-1449 m) with limestone rocks and abundant cliffs. Mainly scrub-covered, although small woods (*Quercus rotundifolia*, *Q. suber*, *Abies pinsapo*) occur. The area is grazed by sheep and goats.

Important for *Gyps fulvus* (min. 30 pairs), *Hieraaetus fasciatus*, and other cliff-nesting birds.

265 Serranía de Ronda (Andalucía)

36°40'N, 05°00'W 30,000 ha

Proposed Natural Park (Sierra de las Nieves: 17,000 ha); partly a National Game Reserve (Ronda: 21,300 ha)

A limestone massif including Sierra de las Nieves (1918 m) and some other smaller ranges, to the south-east of Ronda. Large areas of exposed rock with many cliffs alternate with upland pastures and expanses of scrub, maquis, and woodland (*Quercus rotundifolia*, *Q. suber*, *Pinus pinaster*, *P. halepensis*, *Abies pinsapo*). The area is grazed by sheep and goats and there is big-game hunting.

Important for its diversity of birds of prey including *Hieraaetus pennatus*, *H. fasciatus*, and *Falco peregrinus*, which are relatively common. Also it holds rich passerine communities, especially at higher altitudes.

266 Sierra de Antequera – El Chorro (Andalucía)

36°55'N, 04°35'W 20,000 ha EEC SPA (El Torcal de Antequera: 1710 ha)

Natural Park (El Torcal de Antequera: 1200 ha)

A range (300-1369 m) to the north of Málaga (30 km long), with a large gorge (Los Gaitanes). Very deforested, with some patches of *Quercus rotundifolia* and *Pinus halepensis*. The slopes are heavily cultivated (olive- and almond-groves, vineyards, orchards). The area is also used for goat- and sheep-grazing, stone quarrying, and tourism.

Important because of a *Gyps fulvus* colony (16-18 pairs) which is relatively isolated and vulnerable. Also interesting because it supports numerous *Apus melba*, *Columba livia*, *Monticola solitarius*, and *Pyrrhocorax pyrrhocorax* (min. 100 pairs).

267 Lagunas de Fuente de Piedra, Gosque y Campillos (Andalucía)

37°10'N, 04°45'W 15,000 ha

Ramsar Site; EEC SPA (Laguna de Fuentepiedra: 1364 ha)

Integral Reserve of Scientific Interest (Fuente de Piedra: 2000 ha)

A wetlands complex comprising a main lagoon (Fuente de Piedra) and nine minor lagoons. The lagoons are endorreic, shallow, and seasonal (frequent drought periods) with brackish water, and are surrounded by croplands (wheat, olive-trees). Problems include serious pollution from villages and oil mills ('alperchines' – waste produced by olive-oil extraction), and a decrease in the water supply (the groundwater supply may be over exploited).

Holds the only permanent colony of *Phoenicopterus ruber* in Spain (max. 12,000 pairs in 1988). In addition, *Larus genei* and *Gelochelidon nilotica* breed in small numbers (only occasionally in recent years), and *Circus pygargus* (min. 20 pairs) and *Burhinus oedicnemus* (common) breed in the nearby fields. It is also an isolated wintering area for *Grus grus* (min. 250).

268 Sierras de Tejeda y Almijara (Andalucía)

36°50'N, 03°50'W 35,000 ha

National Game Reserve (20,000 ha)

A mountain range (800-2065 m) 25 km long, along the Mediterranean coast. Vegetation comprises sclerophyllous scrub and expanses of grassland, pine plantations (*Pinus pinaster*, *P. nigra*, *P. halepensis*) damaged by frequent fires, and patches of natural woods (mainly *Quercus rotundifolia*). The area is used for goat-grazing and big-game hunting.

Important for birds of prey including *Hieraaetus fasciatus* (min. 8 pairs), *Falco peregrinus* (min. 5 pairs), and *Bubo bubo* (min. 10 pairs).

269 Sierra Nevada (Andalucía)

37°05'N, 03°10'W 120,000 ha Biosphere Reserve

National Game Reserve (35,430 ha)

A mountain range (1000-3481 m) 70 km long, very deforested, vegetation dominated by scrub and grassland, partly alpine. Also pine plantations with some indigenous patches (*Pinus sylvestris*, *P. pinaster*) and a few broadleaved trees (*Quercus rotundifolia*, *Q. pyrenaica*, *Castanea sativa*). The area is used for cattle- and sheep-grazing, big-game hunting, hiking, skiing and residential development.

Breeding birds of prey include *Aquila chrysaetos* (10 pairs), *Hieraaetus fasciatus* (min. 8 pairs), *Falco peregrinus* (min. 11 pairs), and *Bubo bubo* (min. 13 pairs). *Pyrrhocorax pyrrhocorax* is common (min. 150 pairs) and *Prunella collaris* is present (only breeding site in the southern half of Spain).

270 Islas Chafarinas (Melilla)

35°11'N, 02°26'W 50 ha EEC SPA

National Hunting Refuge

Three small islands close to the north-eastern Moroccan coast (3.5 km off Ras Quebdana), with volcanic rocks, some cliffs, xerophytic and halophytic scrub, and bare ground. The central island (Isabel II) is occupied by a small army detachment, the other two (Congreso and Rey) are uninhabited. Problems include uncontrolled visiting, egg-collecting, and an expanding *Larus argentatus cachinnans* colony, which are all detrimental to the *Larus audouinii* colony. The Mediterranean Monk Seal *Monachus monachus* is regularly present.

Exceptionally important for marine birds and one of the best sites in the Mediterranean, with the largest colony of *Larus audouinii* in the world (2800 pairs in 1987). Other species occurring include *Calonectris diomedea* (several thousand birds), *Phalacrocorax aristotelis desmarestii* (some birds regularly present), *Pandion haliaetus* (1 pair), and *Larus argentatus cachinnans* (4000-5000 pairs).

271 Islas Vedrá y Vedranell (Baleares)

38°52'N, 01°14'E 200 ha

Unprotected

Two rocky limestone islets, very steep in places, close to Ibiza's south-western coast.

Important for its colonies of *Puffinus puffinus mauretanicus*, *Falco eleonorae* (30-40 pairs in 1986), and *Larus audouinii* (*c.*150 pairs).

272 Cabo Nono – Isla Murada (Baleares)

39°05'N, 01°22'E 900 ha

Unprotected

Limestone cliffs and small islets along Ibiza's north-western coast, covered mainly by pinewoods (*Pinus halepensis*). The area is affected by tourism and residential use.

Important for breeding *Hydrobates pelagicus*, *Phalacrocorax aristotelis desmarestii* (min. 50 pairs), and *Falco eleonorae* (*c.*70 pairs).

273 Isla de Tagomago (Baleares)

39°02'N, 01°40'E 100 ha

Unprotected

A steep limestone islet close to Ibiza's north-east coast.

Holds a breeding colony of *Falco eleonorae* (min. 17 pairs in 1986).

274 Islas de los Freus (Baleares)

38°49'N, 01°28'E 250 ha

Area of Special Natural Interest

Several small low rocky islets between Ibiza and Formentera.

Important for its seabird colonies with *Calonectris diomedea*, *Puffinus puffinus mauretanicus*, and *Larus audouinii* (135 pairs in 1982).

275 Salinas de Formentera (Baleares)

38°40'N, 01°30'E 35 ha

Area of Special Natural Interest

Several old saltpans and two big ponds (Estany des Peix and Estany Pudent) at the northern end of Formentera. Saline or hyper-saline water with small *Salicornia* scrub areas. Problems include uncontrolled hunting and tourism. There is also a plan to urbanise the area (covering 80 per cent of the site, excluding the Estany des Peix), and fish-farming is a possible future use.

Important for its winter concentrations of *Podiceps nigricollis* (max. 3900).

276 La Mola de Formentera (Baleares)

38°40'N, 01°28'E 200 ha

Unprotected

Several high, coastal limestone cliffs on Formentera.

Important for *Puffinus puffinus mauretanicus* (best area in the Balearics) and *Phalacrocorax aristotelis desmarestii* (64 pairs).

277 Isla Dragonera (Baleares)

39°35'N, 02°18'E 1000 ha

Unprotected; a Natural Park is proposed

An island very close to Mallorca's western tip, with very high limestone cliffs and Mediterranean scrub. Also includes the rocky cape of Mallorca (Andraitx) and some small rocky islets (Isla de Pantaleu).

An important area for breeding seabirds including *Calonectris diomedea*, *Puffinus puffinus mauretanicus* (min. 15 pairs), *Phalacrocorax aristotelis desmarestii* (min. 50 pairs), and *Larus audouinii* (60 pairs in 1983). *Pandion haliaetus* (1 pair) and *Falco eleonorae* also breed in this area.

278 Acantilados del noroeste de Mallorca y Sierra de Alfabia (Baleares)

39°50'N, 02°45'E 48,000 ha

Unprotected

The north-western coast of Mallorca, with limestone cliffs, islets, and small beaches; and the Sierra de Alfabia (max. 1436 m), covered by Mediterranean scrub and woodland (*Pinus halepensis*, *Quercus ilex*). A very rugged and unpopulated area, partially controlled by the army. The area is used for sheep- and goat-grazing and tourism.

Very important because of its threatened and isolated population of *Aegypius monachus* (20 birds and two breeding pairs). Also good populations of coastal birds of prey with *Pandion haliaetus* (4-5 pairs) and *Falco eleonorae* (200-250 pairs), and breeding *Phalacrocorax aristotelis desmarestii* (min. 50 pairs).

279 Cabo Pinar (Baleares)

39°52'N, 03°10'E 2500 ha

Unprotected

A small rocky peninsula in northern Mallorca with limestone cliffs and a small range of hills, with Mediterranean scrub and pinewoods (*Pinus halepensis*). Land-uses include tourism.

An important breeding area for *Phalacrocorax aristotelis desmarestii* (min. 50 pairs).

280 Albufera de Alcudia (Baleares)

39°47'N, 03°06'E 1700 ha EEC SPA (Albufera de Mallorca: 2584 ha)

Natural Park (S'Albufera de Mallorca: 1700 ha)

A large coastal lagoon connected to the sea in northern Mallorca. The water varies from saline to fresh, with extensive vegetation (*Phragmites*, *Scirpus*, *Cladium mariscus*) and a few areas of open water. There is an area of abandoned saltpans; also a range of sand hills, with Mediterranean scrub and pines (*Pinus halepensis*), lies between the lagoon and the sea. The area is used for some fishing and much tourism; there is also a thermic power-station close to the area. Nearby residential areas are continuously expanding.

Important for *Ixobrychus minutus* (several hundred), *Ardea purpurea* (min. 50 pairs), *Acrocephalus arundinaceus* (abundant), and *A. melanopogon* (hundreds of pairs). Ducks and *Fulica atra* winter.

281 Cabo del Freu – Cabo Farruch (Baleares)

39°45'N, 03°26'E 800 ha

Unprotected

A rocky section of coast at the north-eastern tip of Mallorca with high limestone cliffs and Mediterranean scrub.

Holds a colony of *Phalacrocorax aristotelis desmarestii* (40 pairs) and several pairs of *Larus audouinii.*

282 Cabo d'es Piná (Baleares)

39°39'N, 03°25'E 200 ha

Unprotected

A small section of coast with limestone cliffs in eastern Mallorca. A road goes along the top of the cliff and the area is used for tourism.

Supports a colony of *Phalacrocorax aristotelis desmarestii* (min. 50 pairs).

283 Lagunas de Salobrar de Campos (Baleares)

39°19'N, 03°05'E 200 ha

EEC SPA (Lagunas de Salobrar de Campos – Playa des Trenc: 200 ha)

Area of Special Natural Interest

A plain at Mallorca's southern tip occupied by small natural lagoons and some larger saltpans surrounded by Mediterranean scrub. There are roads and residential areas.

Important for colonies of *Himantopus himantopus* (min. 100 pairs).

284 Acantilados entre Cap Enderrocat y Cala Pí (Baleares)

39°30'N, 02°45'E 900 ha

Unprotected

Limestone cliffs along the southern coast of Mallorca. A road goes along the top crossing a scrub-covered plain. There is increasing tourism and residential development.

Holds the biggest colony of *Phalacrocorax aristotelis desmarestii* in the Mediterranean (*c.*250 pairs).

285 Acantilados costeros Islas Malgrats – Isla del Sech (Baleares)

39°30'N, 02°30'E 600 ha

Unprotected

Limestone cliffs and several offshore rocky islets (Islas Malgrats, Isla del Toro, Isla del Sech) in south-eastern Mallorca.

Important for breeding seabirds with *Calonectris diomedea* (50 pairs), *Puffinus puffinus mauretanicus* (min. 50 pairs), *Hydrobates pelagicus melitensis*, *Phalacrocorax aristotelis desmarestii* (min. 50 pairs), and *Larus audouinii* (variable in numbers; 62 pairs in 1983).

286 Archipiélago de Cabrera (Baleares)

39°09'N, 02°55'E 2000 ha

Unprotected; a National Park is proposed

A small archipelago to the south-east of Mallorca, formed by two main islands (Cabrera and Conejera) and many small rocky islets, with rocky limestone ground and high cliffs. Mediterranean scrub and small pinewoods occur on the largest islands. There is a small military garrison on Cabrera, and manoeuvres can have an adverse affect on the seabird colonies.

A very important area for Mediterranean seabirds and coastal birds of prey with *Calonectris diomedea* (300 pairs), *Puffinus puffinus mauretanicus* (min. 50 pairs), *Hydrobates pelagicus melitensis* (min. 50 pairs), *Phalacrocorax aristotelis desmarestii* (min. 95 pairs), *Pandion haliaetus* (1 pair), *Falco eleonorae* (20 pairs), and *Larus audouinii* (100 pairs).

287 Costa Norte de Menorca (Baleares)

40°03'N, 04°00'E 10,000 ha

Albufera de Es Grao is protected

Limestone cliffs interrupted by rocky beaches and harbours, including the Albufera de Es Grao, an interesting coastal lagoon with emergent vegetation. The vegetation is mainly garigue and maquis, with *Quercus ilex* and *Pinus halepensis*. Many roads and paths go to the cliff-tops and to some beaches, and there are residential areas. The site can be divided into six zones of major importance, very close to one another: Cap de Banyos – Falconera; Islas Bledas – Cap de Caballería; Fornells; Islas d'Addaya S'Albufera; La Mola; and Na Girada – Isla del Aire. Threats include mass tourism and building.

A very important area for breeding seabirds with colonies of *Calonectris diomedea* (min. 1500 pairs), *Phalacrocorax aristotelis desmarestii* (84 pairs) and *Larus audouinii* (15 pairs). It is also important for *Pandion haliaetus* (3 pairs) and *Falco peregrinus*. Albufera de Es Grao is interesting for breeding and wintering waterfowl.

288 Sierras Interiores de Menorca (Baleares)

40°00'N, 04°05'E 25,000 ha

Unprotected

An area in the centre of Menorca including Monte Toro (230 m) and Santa Agueda (260 m), and the southern coast with some cliffs. There are limestone cliffs along ravines, pinewoods (*Pinus halepensis*), garigue, and some cultivation. The area is crossed by roads and includes some residential areas especially by the shore. Includes the Marismas de Son Bou with interesting emergent vegetation. Land-uses include tourism.

Important populations of birds of prey occur in the inland areas, with *Milvus milvus* (min. 20 pairs), *Neophron percnopterus* (min. 10 pairs), and *Hieraaetus pennatus* (min. 20 pairs). *Phalacrocorax aristotelis desmarestii* breeds in the coastal zone, and there is an isolated population of *Acrocephalus melanopogon* (min. 40 pairs) at Marismas de Son Bou.

MAIN REFERENCES

Alvarez, J., Bea, A., Faus, J. M., Castién, E. and Mendiola, I. (1985) *Atlas de los Vertebrados Continentales de Alava, Vizcaya y Guipúzcoa*. Bilbao: Gobierno Vasco.

Bárcena, F., Teixeira, A. M. and Bermejo, A. (1984) *Breeding seabird populations in the Atlantic sector of the Iberian peninsula*. In Croxall, J. P., Evans, P. G. H. and Schreiber, R. W. (eds.) Status and Conservation of the World's Seabirds. *Cambridge, U.K: International Council for Bird Preservation, Techn. Publ. No. 2.*

Bernis, F. (1966-1971) *Aves Migradoras Ibéricas*. (fascículos 1-8). Madrid: Sociedad Española de Ornitología.

Chozas, P. (1982) Estudio general sobre la dinámica de la población de la Cigüeña Blanca *Ciconia ciconia* (L.) en España. Madrid: Editorial de la Universidad Complutense.

de Juana, E. (1980) *Atlas Ornitológico de La Rioja*. Logroño: Instituto de Estudios Riojanos.

de Juana, E. (1984) *The status and conservation of seabirds in the Spanish Mediterranean*. Cambridge, U.K.: International Council for Bird Preservation, Techn. Publ. No. 2. Pp. 347-361.

de Juana, E., Santos, T., Suárez, F. and Tellería, J. L. (1988) *Status and conservation of steppe birds and their habitats in Spain*. Cambridge, U.K.: International Council for Bird Preservation, Techn. Publ. No. 7. Pp. 113-123.

Elósegui, J. (1985) *Atlas de las Aves Nidificantes de Navarra*. Pamplona: Caja de Ahorros de Navarra.

Ena, V. (ed.) (1987) *I. Congreso Internacional de Aves Esteparias*. León: Junta de Castilla y León.

Ena, V. and Purroy, F. J. (1982) Censos invernales de aves acuáticas en España (enero 1978, 79 y 80). Madrid: ICONA, Ministerio de Agricultura, Pesca y Alimentación.

Fernández-Cruz, M. (1975) Revisión de las actuales colonias de Ardeidas en España. *Ardeola* 21: 65-126.

Fernández-Cruz, M. (ed.) (1981) La migración e invernada de la Grulla Común (*Grus grus*) en España. Resultados del Proyecto Grus (Crane Project). *Ardeola*, 26-27: 3-164.

Fernández-Cruz, M. and Araújo, J. (eds.) (1985) *Situación de la Avifauna de la Península Ibérica, Baleares y Macaronesia*. Madrid: Coordinadora para la Defensa de las Aves/Sociedad Española de Ornitología.

González, L. M., González, J. L., Garzón, J. and Heredia, B. (1987) Censo y distribución del Aguila Imperial Ibérica *Aquila (heliaca) adalberti* Brehm 1961, en España durante el período 1981-1986. *Boletín de la Estación Central de Ecología*, 31: 99-109.

ICONA (1986) *Lista Roja de los Vertebrados de España*. Madrid: Ministerio de Agricultura, Pesca y Alimentación.

Mayol, J. (1977) Estudios sobre el Halcón de Eleonor en las Islas Baleares. *Ardeola*, 23: 103-136.

Mayol, J. (1981) Evolución de las colonias mallorquinas del Halcón de Eleonor (*Falco eleonorae* Gene, 1839) durante el verano de 1981. *Boletín de la Estación Central de Ecología*, 20: 21-25.

Sociedad Española de Ornitología (1981) Primer Censo de Buitreras (1979). *Ardeola*, 26-27: 165-312.

Tellería, J. L. (1984) Areas importantes para las aves en España. Informe preliminar. *La Garcilla*, 63: 9-20.

Tellería, J. L. (ed.) (1987) *Invernada de Aves en la Península Ibérica*. Madrid: Sociedad Española de Ornitología.

Tellería, J. L. and Carrascal, L. M. (1986). Informe sobre la realización del "Catálogo Abierto" de las Areas Importantes para las Aves en España. *La Garcilla*, 66: 7-13.

CANARY ISLANDS

Fuerteventura Stonechat *Saxicola dacotiae*

INTRODUCTION

General information

The Canary Islands (Islas Canarias) are situated between 27°37'-29°25'N and 13°20'-18°10'W off the north-west coast of Africa (southern Morocco) and south of the archipelago of Madeira. The seven main islands are Lanzarote (796 sq km), Fuerteventura (1725 sq km), Gran Canaria (1532 sq km), Tenerife (2058 sq km), La Palma (730 sq km), La Gomera (380 sq km), and El Hierro (278 sq km); the archipelago has a population of about 1.3 million people.

The islands are all mountainous (with Pico del Teide reaching 3718 m, the highest elevation in Spain), and are characterised by deep ravines, cliffs, and precipices.

The islands are extremely varied. The eastern islands of Lanzarote and Fuerteventura are arid and rocky, and covered mostly in xerophytic scrub, with extensive sand-dunes, rocky barrancos (ravines), and vast lava flows (covering over 25 per cent of Lanzarote). The western islands are more humid and some still have extensive laurel and coniferous forests. Bramwell and Bramwell (1974) have listed six vegetational types: semi-desert succulent scrub (0-700 m), juniper scrub (400-600 m, southern slopes), tree heath and evergreen forest (the latter is the species-rich laurisilva forest) (400-1300 m), savanna of *Pinus canariensis* (800-1900 m), montane scrub (1900-2500 m), and subalpine scrub (*c.*2600 m, only on Tenerife).

Environmental changes have taken place on a huge scale since the end of the fifteenth century, and now more than half of the island's land surface has been cultivated at one time or another, mainly with tomatoes, bananas, potatoes, and cereals (maize, wheat, barley). The laurel forests have been devastated by humans (on Gran Canaria it now covers less than one per cent of the original area, and on Tenerife only about 10 per cent of the original area), with the main relicts on La Palma, La Gomera (where it is especially magnificent), and Tenerife. None of the destroyed laurel forests has ever been replanted.

The islands support a remarkably rich flora with about 470 endemic species, including 19 endemic genera.

Ornithological importance

Of the 29 globally threatened species occurring in Europe, six are (or were) resident in the Canary Islands: *Chlamydotis undulata*, of the distinctive endemic race *fuertaventurae*, occurs only on Fuerteventura and Lanzarote; *Haematopus meadewaldoi* is almost certainly extinct, having been known with certainty only from the Canary Islands; *Columba bollii* and *C. junoniae* are known only from the laurel forest on Tenerife, La Palma, and La Gomera, with *Columba bollii* also occurring on El Hierro but having become extinct on Gran Canaria; *Saxicola dacotiae* occurs only on Fuerteventura; *Fringilla teydea* is confined to the pine forests on Tenerife and Gran Canaria. Conservation of these species' habitats is therefore a priority of global proportions.

The islands are also important for subspecies either endemic to the Canary Islands or confined to the Macronesian Islands (see tables on pp.672-677). The islands also have breeding *Puffinus assimilis*, *Bulweria bulwerii*, and *Oceanodroma castro* (which breed elsewhere in Europe only on the Atlantic islands of Portugal), and important populations of *Falco eleonorae* (the most southerly breeding population) and *F. pelegrinoides* (only European population).

Conservation infrastructure and protected-area system

Administratively, the islands belong to Spain, but have their own regional government. The responsibility for nature conservation is primarily the concern of the local autonomous government authorities (Dirección General de Medio Ambiente and the Cabildos Insulares). However, in the case of National Parks and international conventions, the central Spanish Government is the authority concerned.

At the present time, there exist in the archipelago four National Parks and a recently created network of Natural Parks, in the broadest sense (Parques Naturales), and Protected Landscapes (Parajes Naturales). In addition, every year a few areas are designated as Hunting Refuges, which indirectly protect the avifauna. Forests can also be designated as Protected Forest Areas.

International measures relevant to the conservation of sites

Spain is a member of the European Community, has ratified the Ramsar Convention, World Heritage Convention, Bern Convention and Bonn Convention, and is bound by the terms of the European Community's Wild Birds Directive. The Canary Islands are covered by the above measures. There is one World Heritage Site (Garajonay National Park on La Gomera, Spain's only natural World Heritage Site), one Biosphere Reserve (Canal y Los Tiles), and six EEC Special Protection Areas in the Canary Islands.

Overview of the inventory

A total of 64 sites have been listed, 11 on Lanzarote, 15 on Fuerteventura, 14 on Tenerife, six on Gran Canaria, five on La Gomera, five on La Palma, seven on El Hierro; one site is confidential.

The inventory is believed to provide very good coverage of the archipelago's birdlife, including its endemic and threatened species.

Acknowledgements

The following site accounts were compiled from information provided by G. Delgado, K. Emmerson, A. Martín, M. Nogales, and V. Quilis of the Grupo Ornitológico Canario, with the data-gathering coordinated by K. Emmerson and A. Martín. Additional information was provided by B. N. Phillips.

INVENTORY

No.	Site name	Region	Criteria used to select site [see p.18] 0	1(i)	1(ii)	1(iii)	1(iv)	2	3	4
001	Los islotes de Lanzarote	LE			*				*	
002	Riscos de Famara	LE							*	
003	Salinas de Janubio	LE	*							
004	Haría – Tabayesco	LE	*							
005	Litoral de Arrecife	LE	*							
006	Llanos de Famara	LE						*		
007	Llanos de La Corona – Las Honduras	LE						*		
008	El Mojón	LE							*	
009	Llanos de la Mareta – Hoya de la Yegua	LE						*		
010	Barranco de Teneguime	LE	*							
011	Costa Punta Lima – Playa de Matagorda	LE	*							
012	Jable Istmo de Jandía	FA						*	*	
013	Jable de Lajares	FA						*	*	
014	Costa de Corralejo – Tostón	FA							*	
015	Morro Tabaiba y Morro de los Rincones – Vallebrón	FA						*		
016	Barranco de Ajuí – Betancuria	FA						*		
017	Barranco de Los Molinos – Llano de La Laguna	FA						*		
018	Costa de Esquinzo – Puertito de Los Molinos	FA							*	
019	Macizo Tarajalejo – Gran Tarajal	FA						*		
020	Cuchillete de Buenavista – Barranco de La Torre	FA						*		
021	Península de Jandía	FA						*	*	
022	Macizo de Pozo Negro Vigán	FA						*	*	
023	Isla de Lobos	FA							*	
024	Jable de Corralejo	FA						*	*	
025	Playa de Sotavento – Jandía	FA	*							
026	Barranco de Río Cabras	FA							*	
027	Barranco de Tágara	TE						*	*	
028	Acantilados de Los Gigantes	TE							*	
029	Roques de Anaga	TE							*	
030	Roque de Garachico	TE							*	
031	Roque de la Playa	TE							*	
032	Monte de Las Vueltas, Aguas Negras y Quebradas	TE						*	*	
033	Ladera de Tigaiga	TE						*	*	
034	Monte de 'San Andrés, Pijaral y Anaga'	TE						*	*	
035	Montes de 'Las Mercedes, Mina y Yedra', 'Aguirre', 'La Goleta y Pedro Alvarez'	TE						*	*	
036	Monte del Agua, Barranco de los Cochinos y Barranco de Cuevas Negras	TE						*	*	
037	'Monte Verde' de Santa Ursula y La Victoria	TE						*	*	
038	Pinar de Arico	TE						*	*	

No.	Site name	Region	Criteria used to select site [see p.18]							
			0	1(i)	1(ii)	1(iii)	1(iv)	2	3	4
039	Pinar de Vilaflor	TE						*	*	
040	Los Rodeos – La Esperanza	TE							*	
041	Costa de Arinaga – Castillo del Romeral	GC	*							
042	Roque Partido	GC							*	
043	Pinar de Tamadaba	GC						*	*	
044	Pinares de Pajonales, Ojeda, Inagua y la Data	GC						*	*	
045	Pinar de Tauro	GC						*	*	
046	Pinar de Tirajana	GC						*	*	
047	Costa de Majona	LG							*	
048	Costa meridional de La Gomera	LG							*	
049	Costa de Vallehermoso	LG							*	
050	Riscos de Hermigua y Agulo	LG						*	*	
051	Parque Nacional de Garajonay	LG						*	*	
052	'Monte Verde' de La Palma	LP						*	*	
053	Roques de Garafía	LP							*	
054	Roque Negro	LP							*	
055	Parque Nacional de La Caldera de Taburiente	LP							*	
056	El Canal y Los Tiles	LP						*	*	
057	La Dehesa	EL							*	
058	Cordillera de Ventejís	EL							*	
059	'Monte Verde' de Frontera	EL						*	*	
060	Bahía de Naos – Hoya de Tacorón	EL							*	
061	Costa occidental de El Hierro	EL							*	
062	Roques de Salmor	EL							*	
063	Llanos de Nizdafe	EL							*	
064	Name and location confidential								*	

LE=Lanzarote FA=Fuerteventura TE=Tenerife GC=Gran Canaria
LG=La Gomera LP=La Palma EH=El Hierro

Comments on the inventory

1. All sites included meet the criteria, except 003, 005, 011, 025, and 041, which are the most important areas for migrant waders and other waterbirds in the Canary Islands, and 004 and 010 which are especially important for two endemic subspecies.
2. 064 is confidential because of its breeding population of *Sterna dougallii.*
3. For each site, the site name is followed by the name of the main island, which is given in parentheses. The 'region' used when applying the site-selection criteria (category 3) is the Canary Islands.
4. The area (ha) is not given for many of the sites because in most cases the site boundaries have not been accurately determined.

Glossary

The following Spanish words are used in the inventory: barranco = gully/gorge; cordillera = mountain chain; ladera = hillside/mountain slope; jable = sandy plain; litoral = coastal zone; macizo = mountainous zone; pinar = pine forest; playa = beach; risco = rock/cliff; roque = rocky islet. See also the glossary for Spain.

001 Los islotes de Lanzarote (Lanzarote)

29°18'N, 13°30'W 1134 ha EEC SPA (1722 ha, with Riscos de Famara)

Natural Park

Four rocky islands: Montaña Clara (29°17'N, 13°32'W), Alegranza (29°23'N, 13°30'W), Roque del Oeste (29°18'N, 13°31'W), and Roque del Este (29°16'N, 13°20'W). The most important area in the archipelago for *Calonectris diomedea*, *Hydrobates pelagicus*, *Pandion haliaetus*, and *Falco eleonorae*.

Breeding species include *Bulweria bulwerii* (100 pairs on Montaña Clara), *Calonectris diomedea* (several thousand pairs on Alegranza; the largest colony in the Canaries), *Puffinus assimilis*, *Hydrobates pelagicus*, *Oceanodroma castro*, *Neophron percnopterus*, *Pandion haliaetus*, *Falco eleonorae* (60+ pairs), *F. pelegrinoides*, *Burhinus oedicnemus*, *Tyto alba gracilirostris*, *Calandrella rufescens*, and *Bucanetes githagineus*.

002 Riscos de Famara (Lanzarote)

29°11'N, 13°30'W 1800 ha EEC SPA (1722 ha, with Los islotes de Lanzarote)

Natural Park

An impressive area of sea cliffs with an accumulation of landslide/erosion material at the base in many sectors. The area is very rich botanically with many endemic plants.

Breeding species include *Calonectris diomedea*, *Neophron percnopterus*, *Pandion haliaetus*, *Falco pelegrinoides*, *Tyto alba gracilirostris*, *Bucanetes githagineus*, and possibly *Falco eleonorae*.

003 Salinas de Janubio (Lanzarote)

28°55'N, 13°50'W 160 ha

Protected Landscape

An area of saltpans and lagoons with a sand and shingle beach. One of the most important areas in the Canary Islands for migrant waders.

Breeding species include *Calandrella rufescens* and *Bucanetes githagineus*.

004 Haría – Tabayesco (Lanzarote)

29°08'N, 13°31'W

Unprotected

An area of scrub, grasslands, and agricultural land. Human activities include agriculture, stock-farming, hunting, and tourism, and there is a major road.

Breeding species include *Tyto alba gracilirostris* and *Parus caeruleus degener*. Also important for migrant passerines.

005 Litoral de Arrecife (Lanzarote)

28°57'N, 13°32'W

Unprotected

A stretch of coast with sea inlets and shingle beaches. Human activities include fishing, yachting, tourism, and there are human habitations, industry, and a port.

One of the most important sites in the archipelago for passage herons, waders, gulls, and terns.

006 Llanos de Famara (Lanzarote)

29°06'N, 13°36'W

Included in a Natural Park

Scrub, grassland, and rocky habitat. Human activities include stock-farming and tourism, and there is a major road.

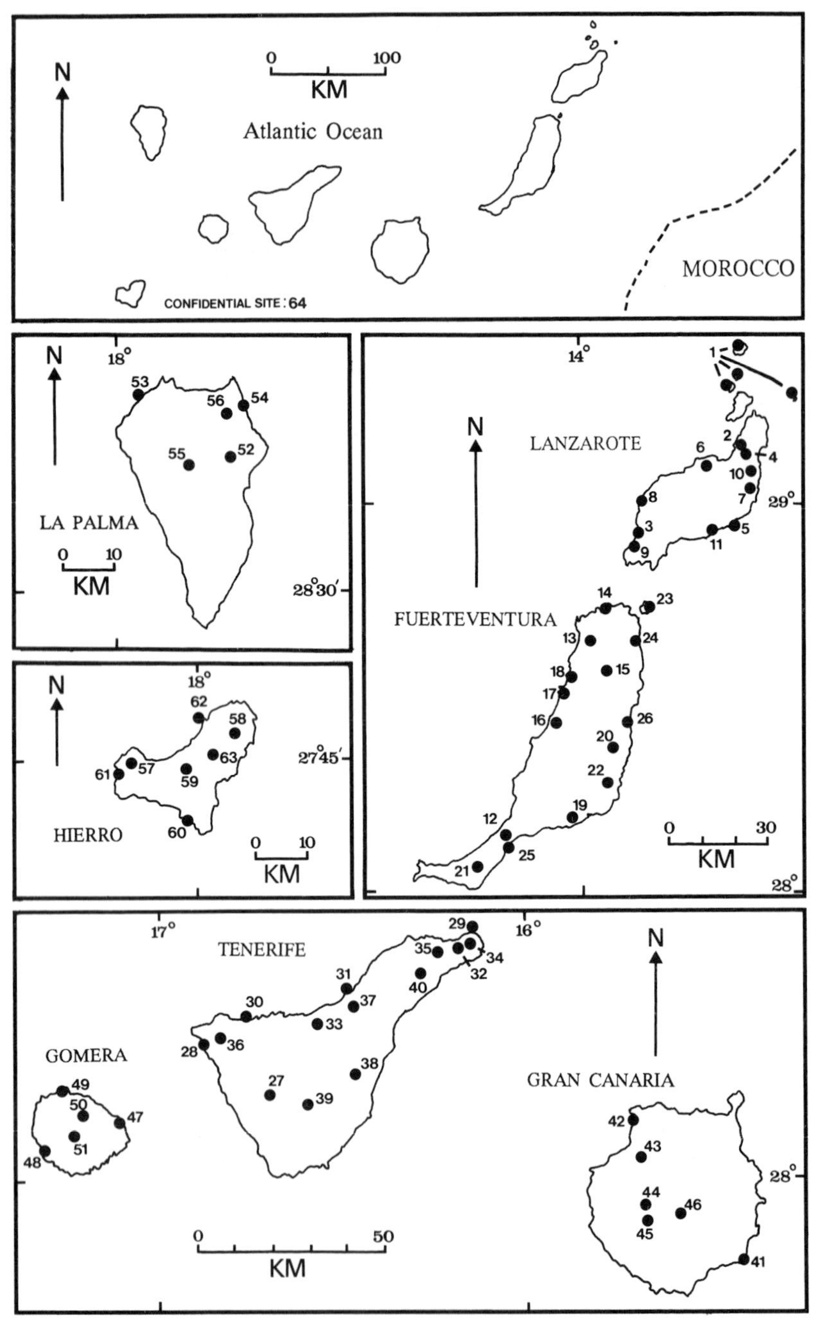

Figure 32: Map showing the location of the sites in the Canary Islands

Breeding species include *Chlamydotis undulata*, *Burhinus oedicnemus*, and *Calandrella rufescens*.

007 Llanos de La Corona – Las Honduras (Lanzarote)

29°02'N, 13°30'W

Unprotected

An area of scrub and grasslands. Human activities include stock-farming, hunting, and tourism.

Breeding species include *Chlamydotis undulata*, *Burhinus oedicnemus*, and *Calandrella rufescens*.

008 El Mojón (Lanzarote)

29°00'N, 13°48'W

National Park

Sea cliffs and lava fields ('malpais'). Human activities include fishing.

Breeding species include *Calonectris diomedea* and possibly *Bulweria bulwerii*, and *Tyto alba gracilirostris*.

009 Llanos de la Mareta – Hoya de La Yegua (Lanzarote)

28°54'N, 13°50'W

Unprotected

An area of scrub and grasslands. Human activities include stock-farming, hunting, and tourism.

Breeding species include *Chlamydotis undulata*, *Burhinus oedicnemus*, *Cursorius cursor*, and possibly *Pterocles orientalis*.

010 Barranco de Teneguime (Lanzarote)

29°05'N, 13°29'W

Protected Landscape

A valley with scrub and grasslands, exposed bedrock, and inland cliffs. Human activities include agriculture, stock-farming, and hunting.

Breeding species include *Calonectris diomedea*, *Tyto alba gracilirostris*, and *Parus caeruleus degener*.

011 Costa Punta Lima – Playa de Matagorda (Lanzarote)

28°56'N, 13°37'W

Unprotected

Sandy beaches, mudflats, and sandflats. Human activities include fishing, yachting, and tourism.

An important feeding area for waders. The most frequent waders are: *Charadrius hiaticula*, *C. alexandrinus*, *Pluvialis squatarola*, *Calidris alba*, *C. alpina*, *Limosa lapponica*, *Numenius phaeopus*, *Tringa totanus*, and *Arenaria interpres*.

012 Jable Istmo de Jandía (Fuerteventura)

28°09'N, 14°16'W 2754 ha EEC SPA

Hunting Refuge (hunting forbidden)

An extensive sandy plain with halophytic and xerophytic scrub vegetation. Goats are grazed over the area. In addition, the development of tourism and the use of four-wheel-drive vehicles are, if uncontrolled, a threat to the area.

Breeding species include *Chlamydotis undulata, Burhinus oedicnemus, Cursorius cursor, Pterocles orientalis, Calandrella rufescens*, and *Bucanetes githagineus.*

013 Jable de Lajares (Fuerteventura)

28°39'N, 13°59'W 2700 ha

Hunting Refuge (hunting forbidden)

An extensive sandy plain with halophytic and xerophytic scrub vegetation. Goats are grazed over the area.

Breeding species include *Chlamydotis undulata* (one of the most important areas on the island for this species), *Burhinus oedicnemus, Cursorius cursor, Pterocles orientalis, Calandrella rufescens*, and *Bucanetes githagineus. Neophron percnopterus* and *Buteo buteo insularum* also occur.

014 Costa de Corralejo – Tostón (Fuerteventura)

28°45'N, 13°55'W

Unprotected

Sand-dunes and sand beaches along the northern coast of Fuerteventura including Caleta del Barco, Playa de Majanicho, and Caleta La Seba. Human activities include fishing, boating, and tourism.

Breeding species include *Burhinus oedicnemus* and *Sterna hirundo.* An important area for migrant waders.

015 Morro Tabaiba y Morro de los Rincones – Vallebrón (Fuerteventura)

28°34'N, 13°52'W

Unprotected

A mountainous area (max. 527 m) with scrub and grasslands. Human activities include agriculture, stock-farming, and hunting. Vallebrón (2400 ha) is a large valley with steep slopes and terracing in places; the upper slopes are sparsely vegetated with low scrub, and there is some subsistence farming and goat-herding in the valley bottom.

Breeding species include *Neophron percnopterus, Burhinus oedicnemus, Saxicola dacotiae*, and *Bucanetes githagineus.* Vallebrón is one of the best areas on the island for *Saxicola dacotiae* (1+ males per 100 ha over much of the area).

016 Barranco de Ajuí – Betancuria (Fuerteventura)

28°23'N, 14°10'W 16,000 ha

Most of the area is included in a Hunting Refuge (hunting forbidden)

A valley (with running water), scrub, grasslands, and agricultural land. Human activities include agriculture, stock-farming, and hunting. Betancuria is a semi-arid mountainous area with sparse scrub.

Breeding species include *Neophron percnopterus, Burhinus oedicnemus, Calandrella rufescens, Saxicola dacotiae*, and *Bucanetes githagineus.* The area is also important for many small passerine migrants. Betancuria is one of the best areas on the island for *Saxicola dacotiae* (1+ males per 100 ha over much of the area).

017 Barranco de Los Molinos – Llano de La Laguna (Fuerteventura)

28°32'N, 14°05'W

Protected Landscape

A valley with running water (Barranco de Los Molinos) and stony plain (Llano de La Laguna). Human activities include agriculture, stock-farming, and hunting.

Breeding species include *Neophron percnopterus, Burhinus oedicnemus, Cursorius cursor, Pterocles orientalis, Saxicola dacotiae*, and *Bucanetes githagineus.* Llano de La

Laguna is a very good area for *Chlamydotis undulata*, *Cursorius cursor*, and *Calandrella rufescens*. The area is also important for many small passerine migrants.

018 Costa de Esquinzo – Puertito de Los Molinos (Fuerteventura)

28°35'N, 14°05'W

Unprotected

Sea cliffs (to 50 m) along the western coast. Human activities include fishing and hunting.

Breeding species include *Calonectris diomedea*, *Neophron percnopterus* and *Bucanetes githagineus*.

019 Macizo Tarajalejo – Gran Tarajal (Fuerteventura)

28°12'N, 14°05'W

Unprotected

A mountainous area (max. 464 m) with scrub, inland cliffs and exposed bedrock, with cliffs at the coast. Human activities include stock-farming and tourism.

Breeding species include *Calonectris diomedea*, *Neophron percnopterus*, *Saxicola dacotiae*, and *Bucanetes githagineus*.

020 Cuchillete de Buenavista – Barranco de La Torre (Fuerteventura)

28°22'N, 13°50'W

Unprotected

A mountainous area (max. 416 m) with scrub and grasslands, rocky habitat, and agricultural land. Human activities include agriculture, stock-farming, and hunting.

Breeding species include *Neophron percnopterus*, *Burhinus oedicnemus*, *Tyto alba gracilirostris*, *Saxicola dacotiae*, *Calandrella rufescens*, and *Bucanetes githagineus*.

021 Península de Jandía (Fuerteventura)

28°05'N, 14°20'E 16,000 ha

Natural Park

A rugged semi-arid massif which includes the highest peak on the island, Pico de la Zarza (807 m). The vegetation is sparse and includes several unique associations, including stands of *Euphorbia canariensis*. Rare, endemic plants occur, including *Euphorbia handiensis*. There are some subsistence farming, tourism, fishing, boating, hunting, stock-farming, and residential areas. An increase in the number of goats would represent a serious threat to the remaining natural vegetation.

One of the best areas on the island for *Saxicola dacotiae* (1+ males per 100 ha over much of the area). Other breeding species include *Calonectris diomedea*, *Neophron percnopterus*, *Falco pelegrinoides*, *Chlamydotis undulata*, *Burhinus oedicnemus*, *Cursorius cursor*, *Pterocles orientalis*, *Calandrella rufescens*, and *Bucanetes githagineus*.

022 Macizo de Pozo Negro – Vigán (Fuerteventura)

28°18'N, 13°55'W

Protected Landscape

Coastal areas from Gran Tarajal to Playa de Leandro, and rocky habitats (max. altitude 462 m) inland to Morro de los Halcones. Human activities include stock-farming, fishing, hunting, boating, and tourism.

Breeding species include *Calonectris diomedea*, *Neophron percnopterus*, *Falco pelegrinoides*, *Burhinus oedicnemus*, *Calandrella rufescens*, *Saxicola dacotiae*, and *Bucanetes githagineus*.

023 Isla de Lobos (Fuerteventura)

28°45'N, 13°45'W EEC SPA (2482 ha with Dunas de Corralejo)

Included in a Natural Park (Parque Natural de Corralejo)

An island off the north-east coast. Human activities include fishing and tourism, and there is some human habitation.

Breeding species include *Bulweria bulwerii*, *Calonectris diomedea*, *Puffinus assimilis*, *Hydrobates pelagicus*, *Oceanodroma castro*, *Sterna hirundo*, *Tyto alba gracilirostris*, and *Bucanetes githagineus*.

024 Jable de Corralejo (Fuerteventura)

28°41'N, 13°48'W EEC SPA (2482 ha: Dunas de Corralejo and Isla de Lobos)

Included in a Natural Park (Parque Natural de Corralejo)

Sand-dunes and sand beaches on the north-east coast. Human activities include fishing, boating, tourism; there is also a major road.

Breeding species include *Chlamydotis undulata*, *Burhinus oedicnemus*, *Cursorius cursor*, *Sterna hirundo*, *Pterocles orientalis*, *Calandrella rufescens*, and *Bucanetes githagineus*.

025 Playa de Sotavento (Jandía) (Fuerteventura)

28°08'N, 14°14'N

Natural Park (50 per cent of site)

A stretch of sandy beach and line of sandy, offshore islands. Human activities include tourism and recreation, and there is scattered human habitation.

This site is one of the best in the archipelago for waders. The commonest species are *Charadrius hiaticula*, *C. alexandrinus*, *Pluvialis squatarola*, *Calidris alba*, *C. alpina*, *Limosa lapponica*, and *Numenius phaeopus*.

026 Barranco de Río Cabras (Fuerteventura)

28°28'N, 13°54'W

Unprotected

A rocky valley with running water. Human activities include stock-farming and hunting.

A very important drinking site for resident birds and attractive to good numbers of migrant species on passage. Species occurring include *Neophron percnopterus*, *Calandrella rufescens*, *Saxicola dacotiae*, and *Bucanetes githagineus*.

027 Barranco de Tágara (Tenerife)

28°13'N, 16°43'W

Protected Landscape

An area of pine forest *Pinus canariensis* (max. altitude 1800 m). Human activities include hunting.

Breeding species include *Accipiter nisus granti*, *Dendrocopos major canariensis*, and *Fringilla teydea teydea*.

028 Acantilados de Los Gigantes (Tenerife)

28°17'N, 16°53'W

Natural Park

Sea cliffs. Human activities include fishing and boating.

Breeding species include *Calonectris diomedea* and *Pandion haliaetus*.

029 Roques de Anaga (Tenerife)

28°36'N, 16°10'W 12 ha

Unprotected

Two rock islets (Roque de Fuera and Roque de Dentro). Human activities include fishing, hunting, and sailing.

One of the most important areas in the archipelago for seabirds with breeding *Bulweria bulwerii*, *Calonectris diomedea*, *Puffinus assimilis*, *Hydrobates pelagicus*, and *Oceanodroma castro*.

030 Roque de Garachico (Tenerife)

28°23'N, 16°46'W 5 ha

Unprotected

A rock islet. Human activities include fishing, hunting, and sailing.

Important for breeding seabirds including *Bulweria bulwerii*, *Calonectris diomedea*, and possibly *Oceanodroma castro*.

031 Roque de la Playa (Tenerife)

28°26'N, 16°29'W less than 1 ha

Unprotected

A rock stack. Human activities include fishing.

A breeding site for *Bulweria bulwerii*.

032 Monte de Las Vueltas, Aguas Negras y Quebradas (Tenerife)

28°32'N, 16°12'W 150 ha

Protected Forest Area

Laurel forest, mainly with a well-developed tree canopy. Human activities include forestry and hunting.

Breeding species include *Accipiter nisus granti* and *Columba bollii*.

033 Ladera de Tigaiga (Tenerife)

28°22'N, 16°35'W 200 ha

Mainly a Protected Forest Area

The greater part of the area is laurel forest growing on steep slopes and cliffs, with *Pinus radiata* interspersed amongst laurisilva at higher altitude, and copses of *Castanea sativa* and exotic conifers at lower altitude. Human activities include forestry and hunting.

Breeding species include *Accipiter nisus granti*, *Columba bollii*, and *C. junoniae*.

034 Monte de 'San Andrés, Pijaral y Anaga' (Tenerife)

28°34'N, 16°10'W 350 ha

Partly a Protected Forest Area

Laurel forest ranging from degraded and exploited areas to areas with a well-developed tree canopy. Human activities include forestry, hunting, and tourism.

Breeding species include *Accipiter nisus granti* and *Columba bollii*.

035 Montes de 'Las Mercedes, Mina y Yedra', 'Aguirre', 'La Goleta y Pedro Alvarez' (Tenerife)

28°32'N, 16°18'W 900 ha

Mainly a Protected Forest Area

Laurel forest ranging from degraded and exploited areas to areas with a well-developed tree canopy. Human activities include forestry, hunting, and tourism.

Breeding species include *Accipiter nisus granti*, *Columba bollii* (a very important site for this species), and *C. junoniae*.

036 Monte del Agua, Barranco de los Cochinos y Barranco de Cuevas Negras (Tenerife)

28°20'N, 16°49'W 800 ha

Mainly a Protected Forest Area

Mainly laurel forest (trees and scrub); also virtually abandoned cultivation invaded by scrub and fruit groves, and vertical cliffs with characteristic vegetation. Human activities include agriculture, forestry, hunting, and tourism. A very important area for the two endemic pigeons and other laurel-forest birds.

Breeding species include *Accipiter nisus granti*, *Columba bollii*, and *C. junoniae*.

037 'Monte Verde' de Santa Ursula y La Victoria (Tenerife)

28°24'N, 16°27'W 500 ha

Mainly a Protected Forest Area

Laurel forest which has been heavily exploited and is now regenerating with *Pinus canariensis* forest at higher altitude, bordered by patches of terraced cultivation and *Castanea* coppices. Human activities include agriculture, forestry, and hunting.

Breeding species include *Accipiter nisus granti*, *Columba bollii*, and *C. junoniae*.

038 Pinar de Arico (Tenerife)

28°13'N, 16°32'W 2667 ha

Protected Forest Area

Forest of *Pinus canariensis* with high mountain scrub dominated by *Spartocytisus supranubius* and *Adenocarpus viscosus* at higher altitude. Human activities include forestry.

Breeding species include *Accipiter nisus granti*, *Dendrocopos major canariensis*, and *Fringilla teydea teydea*.

039 Pinar de Vilaflor (Tenerife)

28°11'N, 16°39'W 900 ha

Protected Forest Area

Forest of *Pinus canariensis* with high mountain scrub dominated by *Spartocytisus supranubius* and *Adenocarpus viscosus* at higher altitude. Human activities include forestry.

Breeding species include *Accipiter nisus granti*, *Dendrocopos major canariensis*, and *Fringilla teydea teydea*.

040 Los Rodeos – La Esperanza (Tenerife)

28°28'N, 16°21'W

Unprotected

An area of grassland, scrub, and agricultural land. Human activities include agriculture, stock-farming and hunting, and there are residential areas and an airport.

This is the best site on the island for grassland birds (*Coturnix coturnix*, *Calandrella rufescens*, *Carduelis cannabina*, *Miliaria calandra*). Other species occurring include *Circus aeruginosus* (1-2 in winter), *C. pygargus* (occasionally on passage), and *Asio flammeus* (1-2 occasionally in winter).

041 Costa de Arinaga – Castillo del Romeral (Gran Canaria)

27°48'N, 15°25'W

Protected Landscape (30 per cent of the site); Hunting Refuge (hunting forbidden; 30 per cent of the site)

A stretch of coast with mudflats and sandflats, sand and shingle beaches, and brackish standing water. Human activities include fishing, tourism, and recreation; and there is scattered human habitation.

Breeding species include *Charadrius alexandrinus* and *Calandrella rufescens*. The site is one of the best in the archipelago for passage herons and waders. The most frequent species are *Egretta garzetta, Ardea cinerea, Charadrius hiaticula, Pluvialis squatarola, Calidris alba, C. minuta, C. alpina, Numenius phaeopus, Tringa totanus, T. nebularia, Actitis hypoleucos*, and *Arenaria interpres*.

042 Roque Partido (Gran Canaria)

28°06'N, 15°42'W

Unprotected

Islet off the north-west coast. Human activities include fishing and boating.

A breeding site for *Sterna hirundo*.

043 Pinar de Tamadaba (Gran Canaria)

28°03'N, 15°41'W 2085 ha

Protected Forest Area

An example of *Pinus canariensis* forest. Human activities include forestry and hunting.

Breeding species include *Dendrocopos major thanneri* and *Fringilla teydea polatzeki*.

044 Pinares de Pajonales, Ojeda, Inagua y la Data (Gran Canaria)

27°56'N, 15°41'W 4000 ha EEC SPA (3734 ha)

Protected Forest Area

A fine example of arid *Pinus canariensis* forest. Human activities include forestry.

Breeding species include *Dendrocopos major thanneri* and *Fringilla teydea polatzeki*. This is the most important area on Gran Canaria for these two species.

045 Pinar de Tauro (Gran Canaria)

27°54'N, 15°41'W 600 ha

Protected Forest Area

An area of arid *Pinus canariensis* forest. Human activities include hunting.

Breeding species include *Dendrocopos major thanneri* and *Fringilla teydea polatzeki*.

046 Pinar de Tirajana (Gran Canaria)

27°55'N, 15°35'W 2990 ha

Protected Forest Area

Arid *Pinus canariensis* forest. Human activities include forestry and hunting.

Breeding species include *Dendrocopos major thanneri* and possibly *Fringilla teydea polatzeki*.

047 Costa de Majona (La Gomera)

28°08'N, 17°06'W

Protected Landscape

Sea cliffs and rock stacks along the north-east coast. Human activities include stock-farming, fishing, and hunting.

Breeding species include *Calonectris diomedea, Pandion haliaetus, Falco pelegrinoides*, and *Sterna hirundo*.

048 Costa meridional de La Gomera (La Gomera)

28°06'N, 17°21'W – 28°01'N, 17°12'W

Protected Landscape

Sea cliffs and rock stacks between Punta de la Calera and Playa de Santiago. Human activities include fishing and hunting.

Breeding species include *Bulweria bulwerii*, *Calonectris diomedea*, *Puffinus assimilis*, *Hydrobates pelagicus*, *Pandion haliaetus*, *Sterna hirundo*, and *Bucanetes githagineus*.

049 Costa de Vallehermoso (La Gomera)

28°13'N, 17°16'W

Protected Landscape

Sea cliffs and rock stacks along the northern coast. Human activities include fishing.

Breeding species include *Pandion haliaetus* and *Sterna hirundo*.

050 Riscos de Hermigua y Agulo (La Gomera)

28°10'N, 17°12'W 450 ha

Unprotected

Scarp face and valley (with running water) with heath and scrub, exposed bedrock, inland cliffs, and laurel forest. Adjacent to Parque Nacional de Garajonay. Human activities include forestry and hunting.

Breeding species include *Accipiter nisus granti*, *Columba bollii*, and *C. junoniae* (a very important area for this species).

051 Parque Nacional de Garajonay (La Gomera)

28°07'N, 17°13'W 3984 ha World Heritage Site EEC SPA

National Park

The largest continuous expanse of laurel forest in the Canary Islands (max. 1487 m). Other habitats include heath and scrub, and exotic coniferous woodland. Human activities include tourism.

Breeding species include *Accipiter nisus granti*, *Columba bollii* (a very important area for this species), and *C. junoniae*. Also the site supports one of the most important populations of *Scolopax rusticola* in the archipelago.

052 'Monte Verde' de La Palma (La Palma)

28°44'N, 17°49'W

Protected Landscape

A mountainous area (max. 2200 m) with laurel forest, coniferous forest, scrub, grasslands, and agricultural land, with exposed bedrock and cliffs. Human activities include agriculture, forestry, stock-farming and hunting, and there is scattered human habitation.

Breeding species include *Puffinus puffinus*, *Accipiter nisus granti*, *Columba bollii*, *C. junoniae*, and *Pyrrhocorax pyrrhocorax*.

053 Roques de Garafía (La Palma)

28°50'N, 17°58'W

Unprotected

Islets and rock stacks. Human activities include fishing.

Breeding species include *Bulweria bulwerii*, *Calonectris diomedea*, *Sterna hirundo*, and *Pyrrhocorax pyrrhocorax*.

054 Roque Negro (La Palma)

28°49'N, 17°46'W

Unprotected

Sea cliffs and rock stacks.
Breeding species include *Bulweria bulwerii.*

055 Parque Nacional de La Caldera de Taburiente (La Palma)

28°43'N, 17°52'W EEC SPA (4690 ha)

National Park

A mountainous area (max. 2366 m) with coniferous woodland. Human activities include stock-farming and tourism.
Breeding species include *Accipiter nisus granti* and *Pyrrhocorax pyrrhocorax.*

056 El Canal y Los Tiles (La Palma)

28°47'N, 17°45'W 511 ha Biosphere Reserve

Protected Forest Area with hunting prohibited

A valley with laurel forest, mixed and coniferous woodland, exposed bedrock, and cliffs.
Breeding species include *Puffinus puffinus*, *Accipiter nisus granti*, *Columba bollii*, and *C. junoniae* (a very important area for the two pigeons).

057 La Dehesa (El Hierro)

27°44'N, 18°08'W

Protected Landscape

A grassland area. Human activities include agriculture, stock-farming, and hunting.
Breeding species include *Calonectris diomedea* and *Burhinus oedicnemus.*

058 Cordillera de Ventejís (El Hierro)

27°47'N, 17°55'W

Protected Landscape

An area of scrub, heaths, and grasslands. Human activities include agriculture, forestry, stock-farming, and hunting.
Breeding species include *Accipiter nisus granti.*

059 'Monte Verde' de Frontera (El Hierro)

27°44'N, 18°01'W

The northern part of the area is a Protected Landscape, whilst the southern sector is enclosed within a Natural Park

An area of heath, scrub, and laurel forest with exposed bedrock and inland cliffs (max. altitude 1500 m). Human activities include forestry, stock-farming, and hunting.
Breeding species include *Calonectris diomedea*, *Accipiter nisus granti*, *Pandion haliaetus*, and *Columba bollii.*

060 Bahía de Naos – Hoya de Tacorón (El Hierro)

27°39'N, 18°01'W

Natural Park (50 per cent)

A stretch of coastline facing south-west with sea cliffs and rock stacks. Human activities include fishing, hunting, and sailing.
Breeding species include *Calonectris diomedea*, *Puffinus assimilis*, *Pandion haliaetus*, and *Sterna hirundo.*

061 Costa occidental de El Hierro (El Hierro)

27°44'N, 18°09'W

Natural Park

A stretch of sea cliffs and rock stacks along the west coast. Human activities include fishing and hunting.

Breeding species include *Bulweria bulwerii*, *Calonectris diomedea*, *Puffinus assimilis*, *Hydrobates pelagicus*, *Pandion haliaetus*, and *Sterna hirundo*.

062 Roques de Salmor (El Hierro)

27°49'N, 18°00'W

Natural Park

Islets and rock stacks. Human activities include fishing.

An important seabird colony with *Bulweria bulwerii*, *Calonectris diomedea*, *Puffinus assimilis*, *Hydrobates pelagicus*, *Oceanodroma castro*, and *Sterna hirundo*; also *Pandion haliaetus* is present.

063 Llanos de Nizdafe (El Hierro)

27°46'N, 17°58'W

Unprotected

An area of scrub, grasslands and agricultural land. Human activities include agriculture and stock-farming, and there are several major roads.

Breeding species include *Accipiter nisus granti* and *Burhinus oedicnemus*.

064 Name and location of site confidential

Unprotected

Rock stacks. Human activities include fishing.

Important for breeding *Sterna dougallii* (the only site in the Canary Islands); also breeding *S. hirundo*.

Macaronesian bird species present at sites on Lanzarote and Fuerteventura.

Species	Lanzarote site number										Fuerteventura site number															
	1	2	3	4	5	6	7	8	9	10	11	12	13	14	15	16	17	18	19	20	21	22	23	24	25	26
Columba bollii																										
Columba junoniae																										
Apus unicolor		*		*				*		*						*	*	*	*	*	*	*	*			*
Anthus berthelotii	*	*	*	*		*	*	*	*	*		*	*	*	*	*	*	*	*	*	*	*	*	*		*
Saxicola dacotiae														*	*	*	*		*	*	*	*				*
Fringilla teydea																										
Serinus canaria																										

Macaronesian bird subspecies present at sites on Lanzarote and Fuerteventura.

Species	Lanzarote site number										Fuerteventura site number															
	1	2	3	4	5	6	7	8	9	10	11	12	13	14	15	16	17	18	19	20	21	22	23	24	25	26
Accipiter nisus granti																										
Buteo buteo insularum													*		*				*	*	*	*				
Falco tinnunculus dacotiae	*	*	*	*		*	*	*	*	*		*	*		*	*	*	*	*	*	*	*	*	*		*
Falco tinnunculus canariensis																										
Alectoris barbara koenigi	*	*		*								*	*		*	*	*				*	*	*	*		
Coturnix coturnix confisa																										
Chlamydotis undulata fuertaventurae						*	*		*			*	*				*				*			*		
Larus argentatus atlantis	*	*																			*		*			
Columba livia canariensis	*	*		*				*		*		*			*	*	*	*	*	*	*	*	*			
Tyto alba gracilirostris	*	*		*				*		*						*	*		*	*		*	*			
Asio otus canariensis																										
Dendrocopos major canariensis																										
Dendrocopos major thanneri																										
Motacilla cinerea canariensis																										
Erithacus rubecula superbus																										
Erithacus rubecula microrhynchos																										
Turdus merula cabreae																										
Sylvia conspicillata orbitalis	*	*		*		*	*		*	*		*	*	*	*	*	*		*	*	*	*	*	*		
Sylvia melanocephala leucogastra																										
Sylvia atricapilla heineken																										
Phylloscopus collybitus canariensis																										
Regulus (ignicapillus) regulus teneriffae																										
Parus caeruleus teneriffae																										
Parus caeruleus degener		*		*						*					*	*	*			*	*					
Parus caeruleus palmensis																										

continued

Species	Lanzarote site number										Fuerteventura site number															
	1	2	3	4	5	6	7	8	9	10	11	12	13	14	15	16	17	18	19	20	21	22	23	24	25	26
Parus caeruleus ombriosus																										
Lanius excubitor koenigi	*		*	*		*	*		*			*	*	*	*	*	*		*	*	*	*	*	*		
Pyrrhocorax pyrrhocorax barbarus																										
Corvus corax tingitanus	*	*		*						*			*		*	*	*		*	*	*	*	*			
Fringilla coelebs tintillon																										
Fringilla coelebs palmae																										
Fringilla coelebs ombriosa																										
Carduelis carduelis parva															*	*										
Carduelis cannabina harterti	*	*	*	*								*	*		*	*				*						
Carduelis cannabina meadewaldoi																										

Macaronesian bird species present at sites on Tenerife, Gran Canaria and La Gomera.

Species	Tenerife site number														Gran Canaria site number						La Gomera site number				
	27	28	29	30	31	32	33	34	35	36	37	38	39	40	41	42	43	44	45	46	47	48	49	50	51
Columba bollii						*	*	*	*	*	*													*	*
Columba junoniae							*		*	*	*													*	*
Apus unicolor	*	*	*	*		*	*	*	*	*	*	*	*	*			*	*	*	*	*	*	*	*	*
Anthus berthelotii	*	*	*							*		*	*	*	*		*	*	*	*	*	*	*		*
Fringilla teydea	*											*	*				*	*	*	*					
Serinus canaria	*	*	*			*	*	*	*	*	*	*	*				*	*	*	*	*		*	*	*

Macaronesian bird subspecies present at sites on Tenerife, Gran Canaria and La Gomera.

Species	Tenerife site number														Gran Canaria site number						La Gomera site number				
	27	28	29	30	31	32	33	34	35	36	37	38	39	40	41	42	43	44	45	46	47	48	49	50	51
Accipiter nisus granti	*					*	*	*	*	*	*	*	*											*	*
Buteo buteo insularum	*	*				*	*	*	*	*	*	*	*				*	*	*	*	*			*	*
Falco tinnunculus dacotiae																									
Falco tinnunculus canariensis	*	*	*				*	*	*	*		*	*				*	*	*	*	*	*	*	*	*
Alectoris barbara koenigi	*											*	*								*				*
Coturnix coturnix confisa																									
Chlamydotis undulata fuertaventurae																									
Larus argentatus atlantis		*	*	*												*					*	*	*		
Columba livia canariensis	*	*	*	*		*	*			*		*	*				*	*	*	*	*	*	*	*	*
Tyto alba gracilirostris																									
Asio otus canariensis						*	*	*	*	*	*							*						*	*
Dendrocopos major canariensis	*											*	*												
Dendrocopos major thanneri																	*	*	*	*					
Motacilla cinerea canariensis		*					*	*	*	*	*						*							*	
Erithacus rubecula superbus						*	*	*	*	*	*	*	*					*							
Erithacus rubecula microrhynchus																								*	*
Turdus merula cabreae						*	*	*	*	*	*	*	*				*	*						*	*
Sylvia conspicillata orbitalis										*		*	*					*			*	*	*		*
Sylvia melanocephala leucogastra						*	*	*	*	*	*							*						*	*
Sylvia atricapilla heineken						*	*	*	*	*	*							*						*	*
Phylloscopus collybitus canariensis	*					*	*	*	*	*	*	*	*				*	*	*	*				*	*
Regulus (ignicapillus) regulus teneriffae						*	*	*	*	*	*	*	*											*	*
Parus caeruleus teneriffae	*					*	*	*	*	*	*	*	*				*	*	*	*				*	*

continued

Species	Tenerife site number														Gran Canaria site number						La Gomera site number				
	27	28	29	30	31	32	33	34	35	36	37	38	39	40	41	42	43	44	45	46	47	48	49	50	51
Parus caeruleus degener																									
Parus caeruleus palmensis																									
Parus caeruleus ombriosus																									
Lanius excubitor koenigi													*						*	*					
Pyrrhocorax pyrrhocorax barbarus																									
Corvus corax tingitanus	*	*				*	*	*	*	*		*	*				*	*	*	*		*		*	*
Fringilla coelebs tintillon						*	*	*	*	*	*													*	*
Fringilla coelebs palmae																									
Fringilla coelebs ombriosa																									
Carduelis carduelis parva							*		*																
Carduelis cannabina harterti																									
Carduelis cannabina meadewaldoi										*				*										*	*

Macaronesian bird species present at sites on La Palma and El Hierro.

	Palma site number					El Hierro site number							
	52	53	54	55	56	57	58	59	60	61	62	63	64
Columba bollii	*				*			*					
Columba junoniae	*			*	*								
Apus unicolor	*	*	*	*	*	*	*	*	*	*		*	*
Anthus berthelotii	*			*		*	*	*	*	*			*
Saxicola dacotiae													
Fringilla teydea													
Serinus canaria	*			*	*	*	*	*					*

Macaronesian bird subspecies present at sites on La Palma and El Hierro.

	Palma site number					El Hierro site number							
	52	53	54	55	56	57	58	59	60	61	62	63	64
Accipiter nisus granti	*			*	*	*	*	*				*	
Buteo buteo insularum	*		*	*	*		*	*		*		*	
Falco tinnunculus dacotiae													
Falco tinnunculus canariensis	*			*		*	*	*	*	*		*	
Alectoris barbara koenigi													
Coturnix coturnix confisa	*						*					*	
Chlamydotis undulata fuertaventurae													
Larus argentatus atlantis		*							*	*	*		*
Columba livia canariensis	*			*	*	*	*	*	*	*	*		
Tyto alba gracilirostris													
Asio otus canariensis	*		*		*	*	*	*				*	
Dendrocopos major canariensis													
Dendrocopos major thanneri													
Motacilla cinerea canariensis	*			*									
Erithacus rubecula superbus													
Erithacus rubecula microrhynchus	*			*	*	*	*	*				*	
Turdus merula cabreae	*			*	*	*	*	*				*	
Sylvia conspicillata orbitalis						*						*	
Sylvia melanocephala leucogastra	*			*	*	*	*	*		*			
Sylvia atricapilla heineken	*				*		*	*				*	
Phylloscopus collybitus canariensis	*			*	*	*	*	*		*		*	
Regulus (ignicapillus) regulus teneriffae	*			*	*		*	*				*	
Parus caeruleus teneriffae					*								
Parus caeruleus degener													
Parus caeruleus palmensis	*			*	*								
Parus caeruleus ombriosus						*	*	*				*	
Lanius excubitor koenigi													
Pyrrhocorax pyrrhocorax barbarus	*			*	*								
Corvus corax tingitanus	*			*	*	*	*	*	*	*		*	
Fringilla coelebs tintillon													
Fringilla coelebs palmae	*			*	*								
Fringilla coelebs ombriosa						*	*	*				*	
Carduelis carduelis parva													
Carduelis cannabina harterti													
Carduelis cannabina meadewaldoi	*					*	*	*				*	

MAIN REFERENCES

Bramwell, D. and Bramwell, Z. I. (1974) *Wild Flowers of the Canary Islands.* London: Stanley Thornes.

Collar, N. J. and Goriup, P. D. (eds.) (1983) Report of the ICBP Fuerteventura Houbara Expedition, 1979. *Bustard Studies* 1: 1-92.

Collar, N. J. and Stuart, S. N. (1985) *Threatened Birds of Africa and Related Islands. The ICBP/IUCN Red Data Book, Part I.* Cambridge, U.K.: International Council for Bird Preservation and Conservation Monitoring Centre.

Delgado, G. *et al.* (1988) *Censo de aves rapaces del Archipiélago Canario.* Dirección General de Medio Ambiente, Gobierno Autónomo de Canarias.

Dominguez, F. and Díaz, G. (1985) *Plan de Recuperación de la Hubara Canaria.* Instituto Nacional para la Conservación de la Naturaleza, Spain.

Emmerson, K. W. (1985) *Estudio de la biología y ecología de la Paloma Turqué (Columba bollii) y la Paloma Rabiche (C. junoniae) con vistas a su conservación. Volumen Dos,* ICONA. Unpublished report: 355 pp.

Emmerson, K. W. (1988) *Estudio para la catalogación y valoración ecológica de las principales areas del litoral canario como base para un futuro programa de conservación,* Dirección General de Medio Ambiente, Gobierno Autónomo de Canarias. Unpublished report.

Le Grand, G., Emmerson, K. and Martín, A. The status and conservation of seabirds in the Macaronesian Islands. Pp. 377-392 in Croxall, J. P., Evans, P. G. H. and Schreiber, R. W. (1985) *Status and Conservation of the World's Seabirds.* Cambridge, U.K.: International Council for Bird Preservation.

Martín, A. (1987) *Atlas de las Aves Nidificantes en la isla de Tenerife.* Instituto de Estudios Canarios. Monografía XXXII, Tenerife: 272 pp.

Martín, A., Nogales, M., Quilis, V., Delgado, G., Hernandez, E., Trujillo, O. and Santana, F. (1987) *Distribución y status de las aves marinas nidificantes en el Archipiélago Canario con vista a su conservación,* Dirección General de Medio Ambiente, Gobierno Autónomo de Canarias. Unpublished report, 583 pp.

SWEDEN

Lesser White-fronted Goose *Anser erythropus*

INTRODUCTION

General information

Sweden is the largest of the three Scandinavian countries and, with an area of some 450,000 sq km, it is also one of the bigger states in Europe. The Baltic Sea, the Gulf of Bothnia, and the Kattegat-Skaggerak area form Sweden's extensive and complex southern and eastern coastline.

Despite the country's great size, the human population is both disproportionately small and very unevenly distributed. The total population numbers approximately 8.3 million (with an average population density of 18.5 persons per sq km), nearly 85 per cent of which are urban dwellers, with over one-third concentrated into three densely settled areas in the south of the country: Stockholm, Göteborg (Gothenburg) – Norwegian border, and Malmö – Helsingborg. This reflects – amongst other factors – Sweden's northerly latitude (between 55°N and 69°N) and the extensive mountainous terrain of the north and interior; the northern half of the country holds less than ten per cent of the whole population.

In geomorphological terms, most of Sweden is underlain by the Fennoscandian shield, of Precambrian origin, which gives relative long-term tectonic stability to the region. Areas of younger rocks are very limited in extent and distribution. The north-west is dominated by the Caledonian mountain chain, with numerous valleys oriented north-west to south-east, with lowland areas being restricted to the south and to the coastal fringes.

The primary factor responsible for Sweden's present landscape has been the cycle of glacial and inter-glacial stages during the Quaternary (i.e. the last 2 million years). The most recent glaciation, which ended only in the past few thousand years, resulted in the characteristic land forms of today, including areas denuded of soil-cover, ground-down mountain peaks, U-shaped valleys, vast expanses of deep glacial drift, drumlin fields, ribbon lakes and extensive moraines.

About nine per cent of Sweden's territory is open water (including over 90,000 lakes, notably Lakes Vänern, Vättern and Hjälmaren), but if other wetland types are considered this figure increases to as much as 25 per cent.

The vegetation is naturally closely linked to the physical factors summarised above and in many areas this is indeed the case, although elsewhere it has been greatly modified by human activities. Four principal zones, running approximately south-north may be defined (T. Larsson pers. comm.), namely: Nemoral, Boreonemoral, Boreal, and Alpine.

The first is restricted to the south-west coastal fringe and contains vegetation strongly influenced by oceanic effects – notably tree species unable to survive in the less ambient conditions further north, such as *Fagus sylvatica*. However, much of the area which would naturally be Atlantic deciduous forest, is *Calluna vulgaris* heath or cultivated land resulting from deforestation to create areas suitable for settlement and agriculture.

The second zone is one of transition between the Nemoral and the Boreal zone which is dominated by extensive coniferous forests of *Pinus sylvestris* and *Picea abies*. This Boreonemoral zone covers most of southern Sweden, (extending to the counties of Göteborg och Bohus, southern Värmland, and Uppsala). It is typified by mixed forest (although up to 75 per cent of trees are conifers) containing deciduous species which are rare or absent in the Boreal zone, such as *Quercus* sp. and *Corylus avellana*.

The Boreal zone covers most of the remaining parts of Sweden and is effectively a western extension of the Eurasian taiga with vast expanses of coniferous forest containing low species-diversity, interspersed with *Sphagnum* bogs and fenlands. The latter are relatively species-rich owing to locally improved nutrient supply.

The Alpine zone is restricted to the Caledonian mountains, where the harsh physical environment has produced vegetation characterised by Arctic-Alpine species.

Only about nine per cent of Sweden is agricultural land, and the areas this represents are largely used for stock-raising and haymaking. A further three per cent of the country is urbanised, with major urban-industrial centres restricted to the south. Almost all the remaining land is mountain, forest or wetland, with human land-use at a low level or absent. The major exception to this is the timber industry (timber-derived products feature prominently in Sweden's economy) centred in the boreal forests.

The virgin coniferous forests are under considerable pressure from forestry (new roads, new felling and replanting techniques, and planting of non-indigenous species). Furthermore, Sweden's forests and (especially) lakes are being affected by acid rain.

Ornithological importance

Several principal bird habitat-types can be identified, as follows:

(i) Extensive and uninterrupted mountain/forest zones; size and lack of disturbance of crucial importance for breeding owls and raptors. The bogs found scattered in the forest zones are also important for breeding waders such as *Calidris temminckii*.

(ii) Lakes and associated bogs/fenlands; very important breeding and passage sites for large numbers of waterfowl ranging from Gaviidae and Podicipedidae to Gruidae and Scolopacidae.

(iii) Coastal areas with islands, beaches, lagoons, and adjacent coastal marshland, grassland or scrub/woodland; important for breeding and migrating waders and some Anatidae (e.g. *Somateria mollissima*), also for migrant passerines and, at certain sites, raptors.

Information available on bird populations in Sweden is currently either scant or based on rough estimates, although work is progressing towards the production of more accurate and comprehensive data (T. Larsson pers. comm.). However, there are known to be very important breeding populations (in a European context) of the following species (all figures, except for *Branta leucopsis*, *Haliaeetus albicilla*, and *Sterna albifrons*, are rough estimates): *Gavia stellata, G. arctica, Podiceps auritus, Cygnus cygnus, Anser erythropus* (less than 50 pairs), *Branta leucopsis* (700+ pairs; of great biogeographic interest, lying well south of the Arctic populations of Greenland, Svalbard and USSR), *Pernis apivorus* (8000 pairs), *Haliaeetus albicilla* (75-100 pairs; numbers fluctuating). *Circus cyaneus* (1000-2000 pairs), *Pandion haliaetus* (at least 2000 pairs; largest population in Europe except perhaps European USSR), *Falco columbarius* (5000 pairs), *F. rusticolus* (less than 100 pairs), *Bonasa bonasia* (common), *Tetrao tetrix* (common), *T. urogallus* (common), *Crex crex* (250-500 pairs), *Porzana porzana* (500 pairs), *Sterna caspia* (500 pairs), and very sizeable populations of eight species of owl including *Surnia ulula* (10,000 pairs) and *Strix uralensis* (3000 pairs). To this should be added the large species-rich populations of ducks and waders including *Gallinago media* (100+ pairs), *Limicola falcinellus* (5000 pairs), and very large populations of *Pluvialis apricaria, Philomachus pugnax, Tringa glareola*, and *Phalaropus lobatus*.

The extensive wetlands of Sweden provide an important network of sites for passage waterfowl moving to and from breeding areas, both within the country, and elsewhere in northern Eurasia. The south of Sweden is a natural collecting point for migrants breeding throughout Fennoscandia. This is most clearly manifested by the diurnal passage of raptors (e.g. *Pernis apivorus*) which gather in large numbers at bottleneck sites such as Falsterbo in order to make the shortest possible sea-crossing over the Baltic. The southern coastal areas are also important feeding and resting grounds for Fennoscandian migrant passerines and waders.

Owing to the country's northerly location, its importance for wintering species is relatively low in comparison with the very significant breeding/passage populations. However, there are some important concentrations of wildfowl in the south, such as *Anser fabalis* around Lake Krankesjön in Malmöhus, and Lake Tåkern. There are also several key concentrations of moulting wildfowl in late summer, including *Anser anser* on Gotland.

Conservation infrastructure and protected-area system

There is a clear structure to statutory (Nature Conservancy Act 1964, amended 1973 and 1975) protected areas in Sweden, as follows (no. of sites designated is as on 1.7.87).

1. National Parks (20 sites; covering 618,000 ha)
   Crown land only, strict land-use regulations. Managed by authority appointed by the National Environmental Protection Board.

2. Nature Reserves (1265 sites; covering 1,164,000 ha)
   Regulations dependent on purpose of protection. Compensation available for landowners where land-use restrictions imposed. Designated by county authorities, as is the case with the following categories.

3. Nature Conservation Areas (71 sites; covering 106,000 ha)
   Regulations less strict. No compensation available for landowners but state supports management activities.

4. Wildlife Sanctuaries (607 sites; covering 59,000 ha)
   Access normally restricted for part of the year. No land-use restrictions. This category includes Bird Sanctuaries which are referred to in the inventory.

5. Natural Monuments (1314 sites; covering 700 ha)
   Outmoded category of protection, including sites of less than one ha.

Further relevant legislation includes the Hunting Act (1987), Fishing Act (1950), Hunting Statute (1987), and the Deciduous Forest Law (1983). The National Environmental Protection Board (Statens Naturvårdsverk SNV) is the central administrative authority responsible for nature conservation.

International measures relevant to the conservation of sites

Sweden has ratified the Ramsar Convention, World Heritage Convention, Bonn Convention and Bern Convention, and has designated 20 Ramsar Sites (totalling 270,075 ha) but no natural World Heritage Sites. In addition, one Biosphere Reserve has been designated under UNESCO's Man and the Biosphere Programme, and Sweden has designated a number of Biogenetic Reserves.

Overview of the inventory

There are 33 important bird areas in the Swedish inventory, and together they cover a total area of just over 978,000 ha. None is under serious threat, although there are some limited problems arising mainly from agricultural change, eutrophication, recreational activities, transport developments, and the decreasing pH recorded at many Fennoscandian wetlands in recent years. Only four of the areas are wholly or largely unprotected. The remainder are mostly Nature Reserves (in whole or in part), with some additional Nature Conservation Areas and Bird Sanctuaries (Wildlife Sanctuaries as defined above), whilst all 20 Swedish Ramsar Sites are included.

The sites listed here provide a representative cross-section of the most important Swedish bird habitats and species. The following points should be born in mind when considering the inventory:

1. Vast areas are covered by continuous habitats, e.g. coniferous forests, mountainous areas and tundra. To designate sites within these tracts is difficult and may even be misleading since it is their very size rather than a specific part of it that constitutes the conservation value.
2. There is no doubt that Fennoscandia is of great importance in Europe for breeding geese, ducks and waders. However, this is mainly due to the fact that a very large number of small and scattered wetlands, lakes and rivers hold populations of these birds. The number of sites with an outstanding number of birds is relatively few.
3. Many bird species in Fennoscandia tend not to congregate but have scattered distributions. This is especially true during the breeding season. This fact makes it more difficult to designate particular sites.
4. Since there may be a risk of focusing too much interest on site protection, it is necessary to stress the need for general consideration of nature conservation in different forms of land-use such as forestry and agriculture, for these activities affect much larger areas. It is also important to consider the need for protection or the proper management of certain diminishing types of habitat or ecosystem such as virgin coniferous forest, certain types of deciduous forest in southern Sweden, and natural meadows (both open and sparsely wooded).
5. It is, therefore, important that the 33 listed sites should not in any way be regarded as the total number of sites/areas that deserve protection in Sweden, but rather as important examples.

Acknowledgements

Data-sheets for the following sites were compiled by T. Larsson and H. Lindahl of the Swedish Environmental Protection Board. T. Larsson provided helpful background material which was used to compile the above introduction.

INVENTORY

No.	Site name	Region	Criteria used to select site [see p.18]							
			0	1(i)	1(ii)	1(iii)	1(iv)	2	3	4
001	Falsterbo – Bay of Foteviken	MS					*		*	
002	River Klingavälsån – Lake Krankesjön	MS				*		*		
003	River Helgeån	KD				*		*	*	
004	Ottenby	KR							*	
005	Coastal areas of Isle of Öland	KR							*	

No.	Site name	Region	Criteria used to select site [see p.18]							
			0	1(i)	1(ii)	1(iii)	1(iv)	2	3	4
006	Lake Åsnen	KG							*	
007	Getterön	HD				*		*	*	
008	Lake Kävsjön – Store Mosse	JG	*							
009	Coastal areas around Isle of Gotland	GD				*			*	
010	Islands of Karlsö	GD								*
011	Fjord of Stigfjorden	GB				*				
012	Archipelago of St Anna	OD							*	
013	Lake Tåkern	OD				*			*	
014	Lake Hornborgasjön	SG				*			*	
015	Dättern – Södra Brandfjorden (Lake Vänern)	AG,SG							*	
016	Lake Östen	SG				*			*	
017	Bay of Kilsviken	VD,SG							*	
018	Former Lake Kvismaren	OO				*				
019	Archipelagic areas of Stockholm	SM								*
020	Lake Hjälstaviken	UA	*							
021	River Svartån	VN	*							
022	River Dalälven: Färnebofjärden	VN,GR				*			*	
023	River Dalälven: Hovran	KR				*			*	
024	Lake Ånnsjön	JD	*							
025	River Umeälven Delta	VT	*							
026	Mountains of Vindelfjällen	VT	*							
027	Lake Tjålmejaure – Laisdalen Valley	NN	*							
028	Lake Gammelstadsviken	NN	*							
029	Lake Persöfjärden	NN	*							
030	Lake Laidaure	NN	*							
031	Sjaunja	NN	*							
032	Påkketan	NN	*							
033	Taavavuoma	NN	*							

MS=Malmöhus KD=Kristianstad KR=Kalmar KG=Kronoberg HD=Halland JG=Jönköping GT=Gotland GB=Göteborg och Bohus OD=Östergötland SG=Skaraborg AG=Älvsborg VD=Värmland OO=Örebro SM=Stockholm UA=Uppsala VN=Västmanland GR=Gävleborg KR=Kopparberg JD=Jämtland VT=Västerbotten NN=Norrbotten

Comments on the inventory

1. Some information about breeding areas for rare and/or sensitive birds has been omitted out of a need for confidentiality. However, when estimating the value of different sites, the existence of such species has been considered.

2. It has not been possible to carry out any field investigations in connection with this project. Thus information concerning the avifauna does not necessarily represent the situation in 1987 (when the data-sheets were compiled), but rather reflects the situation during the last few years.

3. Sweden has been treated as a single 'region' when applying the site-selection criteria (category 3). For reasons discussed in the introduction it has not been possible to follow the criteria completely; some sites have, therefore, been selected because of their overall species-diversity (column 0 of above table).

4. For certain wintering species the figures refer to totals during a season; this is indicated where appropriate.

5. All passage figures refer to numbers of birds that can be seen at the same time (i.e. maximum daily totals).

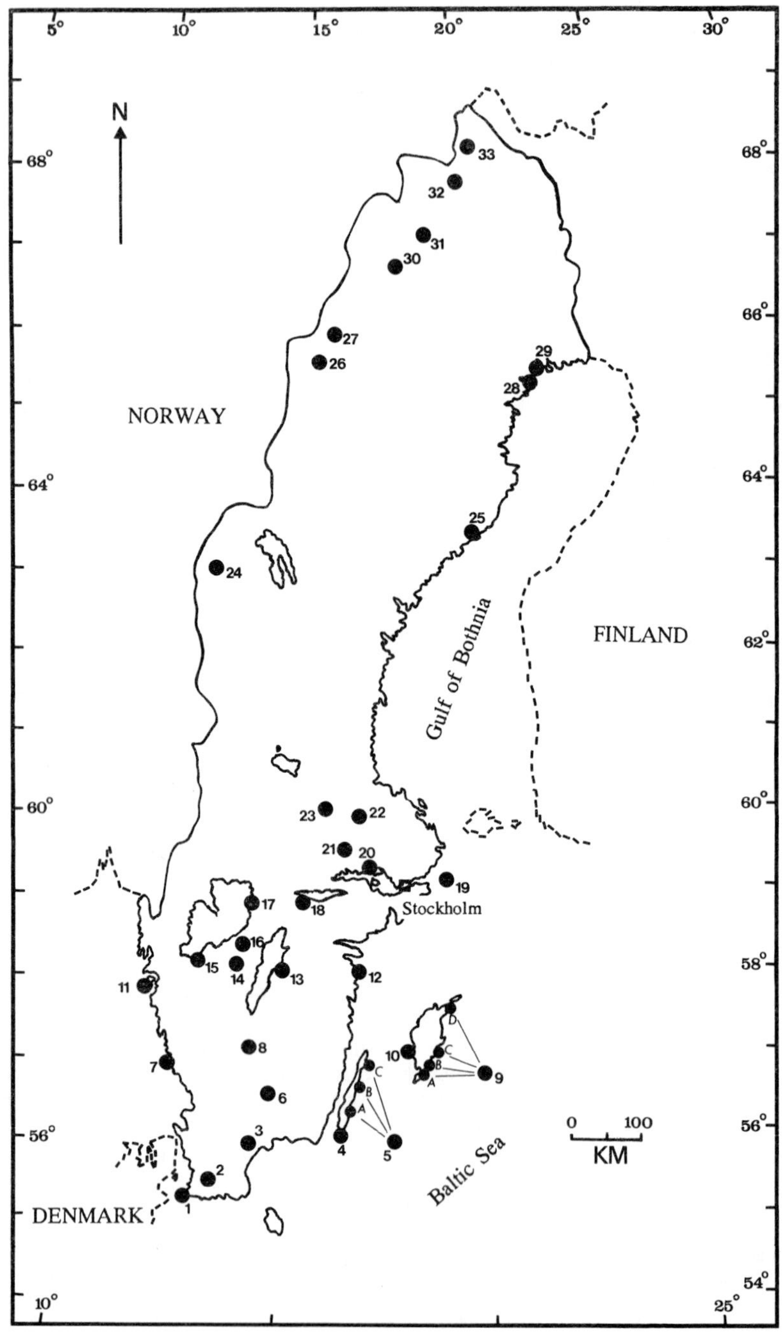

Figure 33: Map showing the location of the sites in Sweden

001 Falsterbo – Bay of Foteviken (Malmöhus)

55°25'N, 12°55'E 7450 ha Ramsar Site (7150 ha)

Four Nature Reserves (*c.*2070 ha)

An area of shallow coastal waters containing lagoons, sandbanks, and sand/shingle beaches. Also included are coastal grasslands, marshland, heather (*Calluna*) moorland, wet heaths, and some cultivated land. Human activities include the grazing of cattle and horses, recreation and the operation of an important bird observatory. The only reported problems are disturbance resulting from recreational activities, and a lack of grazing in some grassland areas allowing vegetational change. Coastal processes of erosion and deposition result in a coastline with a constantly changing form.

Breeding species include *Tadorna tadorna, Somateria mollissima, Mergus serrator, Porzana porzana, Haematopus ostralegus, Recurvirostra avosetta, Charadrius hiaticula, C. alexandrinus, Calidris alpina, Sterna sandvicensis, S. paradisaea, S. albifrons,* and *Saxicola rubetra.* Wildfowl outside the breeding season include important numbers of *Cygnus olor, Mergus serrator* and *M. merganser.* This site is most notable for its very large concentrations of passage migrants, mainly birds of prey (including *Pernis apivorus*: max. 20,900 and *Buteo buteo*: max. 36,700) and waders; in this respect it is one of the most important bird areas in Europe.

002 River Klingavälsån – Lake Krankesjön (Malmöhus)

55°37'N, 13°38'E 3975 ha Ramsar Site

Two Nature Reserves (2181 ha)

The area contains shallow eutrophic lakes, meandering streams, reedbeds, riverside meadows (flooded annually), marshland, *Alnus* forests, and thickets of *Salix.* Large parts of the site are used to graze cattle and for haymaking, whilst further human activities include fishing, bathing, and other recreation and military exercises. Drainage has impoverished the fauna and flora of some of the meadowland, and recently the widespread disappearance of aquatic plants has resulted in large reductions of waterfowl populations. Lack of grazing in some parts has had an adverse effect on waders.

Breeding birds include *Podiceps nigricollis, Botaurus stellaris, Tadorna tadorna, Anas crecca, A. querquedula, A. clypeata, Aythya ferina, A. fuligula, Circus aeruginosus* (1 pair), *Crex crex* (1 pair), *Vanellus vanellus, Calidris alpina, Gallinago gallinago, Limosa limosa, Numenius arquata, Tringa totanus, Acrocephalus arundinaceus,* and *Remiz pendulinus.* Passage birds are present in significant numbers in both spring and autumn, including *Cygnus cygnus* (several hundred), *Anser albifrons* (several hundred in autumn), *Philomachus pugnax, Tringa erythropus, T. nebularia,* and *T. glareola.* The area is very important for wintering *Anser fabalis* with smaller numbers of *A. albifrons,* and is also a winter locality for raptors, with *Milvus milvus, Haliaeetus albicilla* (5-10), *Circus cyaneus, Buteo lagopus,* and *Aquila chrysaetos* all occurring.

003 River Helgeån (Kristianstad)

56°00'-56°03'N, 14°07'-14°12'E 5300 ha Ramsar Site (4600 ha)

Nature Reserve (166 ha next to Lake Hammarsjön)

This area, part of the Helga valley, is divided into two halves by the city of Kristianstad: to the north-west there are 1150 ha including Lake Araslövsjön; to the south-east, 4150 ha including Lake Hammarsjön and the former Lakes Svarta Sjo and Egeside. The Helga flows through a flat valley surrounded largely by arable land. Many of the lakes formerly occupying the valley have been drained but those which remain (such as Araslövsjön) have extensive reedbeds, shallow eutrophic waters, and are bordered in places by scrub and wet pasture. Agriculture is the principal human activity. Proximity to Kristianstad makes the site liable to disturbance, whilst encroachment of vegetation into the lakes and drainage are also potential problems. Several wader populations have shown a negative trend during recent years.

Breeding birds include *Botaurus stellaris* (5 pairs), *Circus aeruginosus* (25-30 pairs), *C. pygargus* (1 pair occasionally), *Porzana porzana, Crex crex, Calidris alpina schinzii* (10 pairs), *Philomachus pugnax* (50 females), *Limosa limosa* (*c.*50 pairs), *Chlidonias niger* (*c.*100 pairs), and *Remiz pendulinus* (10 pairs). Very important for migrating birds especially geese, ducks and waders, including *Cygnus cygnus* (max. 1200 in spring) and *Anser fabalis* (*c.*5000 in both spring and autumn), together with thousands of ducks. Migrant passerines include *Locustella naevia*, *L. fluviatilis*, *L. luscinioides* and *Carpodacus erythrinus*. Wintering species include *Cygnus cygnus*, *Anser fabalis*, *Haliaeetus albicilla* (3-10), and *Circus cyaneus*.

004 Ottenby (Kalmar)

56°12'N, 16°24'E 1600 ha Ramsar Site

Nature Reserve (995 ha)

This site forms the southernmost tip of the island of Öland and consists of deciduous woodland with *Betula*, *Quercus*, and *Populus tremula*, open grazing-land, scrub, sand/pebble beaches, sandbanks, and small bays. There are also extensive shallows and seaweed-covered beaches. The dominant human activity is stock-raising and there is also a bird observatory. Loss of breeding waders owing to low grazing density has required increased stocking levels. No other problems reported.

An important breeding site with species including *Anas strepera* (7 pairs), *Recurvirostra avosetta* (80 pairs), *Charadrius hiaticula* (25 pairs), *Vanellus vanellus* (90 pairs), *Calidris alpina schinzii* (20 pairs), *Philomachus pugnax* (50 females), *Gallinago gallinago* (60 pairs), *Limosa limosa* (1 pair), *Numenius arquata* (25 pairs), *Tringa totanus* (60 pairs), *Arenaria interpres* (10 pairs), *Hippolais icterina* (dense population), *Sylvia nisoria*, *Ficedula parva*, *Oriolus oriolus*, and *Carpodacus erythrinus*. Very important site for many migratory species, with birds passing through virtually throughout the year. Species stopping over for some time include *Branta leucopsis* and *B. bernicla*, as well as waders such as *Calidris alpina*.

005 Coastal areas around Island of Öland (Kalmar)

a) 56°19'-56°32'N, 16°35'E; b) 56°50'N, 16°50'E; c) 57°02'N, 16°55'E
10,190 ha Ramsar Site: Södviken (790 ha)

Bird Sanctuaries – 130 ha in area (a) and 300 ha in area (c) – with hunting forbidden and access restricted in breeding season

Öland is a long, narrow island close to the south-east coast of mainland Sweden. These three sites are located on the low-lying east coast of Öland along a major migration route for birds moving to/from north-east Scandinavia and north-west USSR. The main habitat consists of grazed coastal meadows with marshy areas and scrub. The shores are sandy beaches or low chalk cliffs and the shallow offshore waters contain many sandbanks. Apart from grazing, arable agriculture in some parts is the only significant land-use.

An important group of breeding sites for species such as *Anas strepera* (20-30 pairs), *Aythya marila* (20-30 pairs), *Somateria mollissima* (major nesting ground), *Recurvirostra avosetta* (40-50 pairs), *Calidris alpina schinzii*, *Limosa limosa*, *Larus minutus*, *Sterna sandvicensis*, *S. albifrons* (50-100 pairs), *Chlidonias niger*, and *Sylvia nisoria*. These areas are very important resting places for migrants, especially during the autumn, when several thousand waders of many species pass through, together with a large passage of raptors. Wintering raptors include *Haliaeetus albicilla* and *Aquila chrysaetos*, both in small numbers.

006 Lake Åsnen (Kronoberg)

56°33'-56°47'N, 14°35'-14°49'E 13,500 ha

Nature Reserves (*c.*1200 ha) and Bird Sanctuaries

A large oligotrophic lake with many small bays, peninsulas, and islands, surrounded by mainly coniferous forest (especially *Picea*). There is some deciduous woodland, particularly on the islands, which is important because of its great age. Further wetland habitats are found all round the lake including grazed wet meadows. Apart from grazing, human activities include regulation of the lake water-level, forestry, and boating. There is a potential threat to species such as *Gavia arctica* from the inflow of nutrients used in agricultural fertilisers, which is causing eutrophication. There is disturbance from boating and clear-felling in some areas.

The lake holds one of the densest breeding populations in Europe of both *Gavia arctica* (*c.*70 pairs) and *Pandion haliaetus* (*c.*45 pairs). Other nesting species include *Circus aeruginosus* (1-2 pairs), *Falco subbuteo* (8-10 pairs), *Porzana porzana*, *Crex crex* (occasional), and *Motacilla flava* (30-35 pairs).

007 Getterön (Halland)

57°08'N, 12°14'E 340 ha Ramsar Site

Nature Reserve

Formerly an island, the area has been joined with the mainland by the construction of an artificial embankment and roadway, which also resulted in the partial enclosure and desalinisation of Farehammarsviken Bay (the main part of the reserve). The bay is shallow and brackish with a freshwater inflow. It contains areas of marshy vegetation and is surrounded by grazed coastal meadows. Apart from agricultural activities, the area is used as a bird observatory. Water quality is threatened by eutrophication of the freshwater flowing into Farehammarsviken Bay and by seepage from refuse dumps near the town of Varberg. Some meadows and shallow-water areas are being invaded by tall macrophytes.

Breeding birds include *Anas penelope*, *A. strepera*, *A. crecca*, *A. clypeata*, *Somateria mollissima*, *Porzana porzana*, *Recurvirostra avosetta*, *Calidris alpina schinzii* (11 pairs), *Philomachus pugnax* (9 pairs), *Limosa limosa* (7 pairs), *Tringa totanus* (22 pairs), and *Motacilla flava*. Other species occurring include *Gavia stellata*, *G. arctica*, *Podiceps auritus*, *Botaurus stellaris*, *Cygnus columbianus* (*c.*100 wintering), *C. cygnus* (*c.*150 wintering; 200 on passage), *Anser albifrons* (small numbers), *A. anser* (1000 wintering), *Branta canadensis* (2000-3000 wintering), *Branta bernicla* (large numbers wintering), *Pernis apivorus* (regular), *Haliaeetus albicilla* (2-5 wintering), *Circus aeruginosus* (*c.*15), *C. cyaneus*, *Pandion haliaetus*, *Falco peregrinus* (*c.*4 during the winter season; max. 10 daily on passage), *Crex crex* (occasional on passage), and *Asio flammeus*.

008 Lake Kävsjön and Store Mosse (Jönköping)

57°18'N, 13°57'E 7450 ha Ramsar Site

National Park

A freshwater lake and the largest bog in Sweden south of Lapland. Kävsjön was formerly much larger but drainage in the nineteenth century reduced the area considerably. However, this led to the creation of important damp grasslands on the reclaimed land and these areas are now being managed for birds, after a period of neglect. Store Mosse contains fens and raised bogs with scattered sandy ridges (which are covered by *Pinus*) and sand/gravel/rock moraines. The only land-uses are conservation and grazing, and the only reported problem is that of scrub invasion in some areas.

Very important populations of breeding birds including *Gavia stellata*, *G. arctica*, *Podiceps grisegena*, *P. auritus*, *Cygnus cygnus*, *Anas penelope*, *A. crecca*, *A. acuta*, *A. querquedula*, *A. clypeata*, *Aythya ferina*, *A. fuligula*, *Bucephala clangula*, *Rallus aquaticus*, *Porzana porzana*, *Grus grus* (5-10 pairs), *Pluvialis apricaria* (many pairs), *Calidris alpina*, *Philomachus pugnax*, *Lymnocryptes minimus*, *Tringa totanus*, *T. glareola*, and *Asio flammeus*. Kävsjön is important as a resting site for migrating waterfowl, including large numbers of *Cygnus cygnus* and *Anser fabalis*. Other non-breeders include *Haliaeetus albicilla*.

009 Coastal areas around Island of Gotland (Gotland)

(a)	Faludden	57°00'N, 18°22'E	1810 ha
(b)	Grötlingboholme	57°07'N, 18°30'E	1050 ha
(c)	Lausholmar	57°18'N, 18°45'E	540 ha
(d)	Skenholmen	57°48'N, 19°03'E	700 ha

Ramsar Site (Grötlingboholme, Lausholmar and Skenholmen: 2290 ha)

Nature Reserves (Grötlingboholme: 340 ha; Lausholmar: 500 ha) with access restricted; miliary use of Skenholmen means access is also restricted there.

All four areas are on the eastern coast of Gotland and consist of very low-lying peninsulas and/or islands with a gravel-covered limestone foundation. Essentially treeless and mainly covered by short grassy vegetation used for grazing livestock. Faludden is a narrow peninsula next to a shallow bay, almost cut off from the sea. Grötlingboholme is a small island with a long series of ridged beaches. Lausholmar is a flat grass-covered island used for military target practice outside the most important time for birds. No reported problems.

Breeding species include *Anser anser*, *Branta leucopsis* (700 pairs), *Somateria mollissima*, *Recurvirostra avosetta*, *Charadrius hiaticula*, *Calidris alpina schinzii*, *Philomachus pugnax*, *Limosa limosa*, *Numenius arquata*, *Arenaria interpres*, *Larus minutus*, *Sterna caspia*, *S. sandvicensis*, and *S. albifrons*. A very important area for migrating swans and geese with *Cygnus columbianus* (50-100), *Anser anser* (Grötlingboholme is the most important Baltic moulting ground for this species), *Branta leucopsis* (7000-10,000), and *B. bernicla*.

010 Islands of Karlsö (Gotland)

57°16'-57°19'N, 17°57'-18°05'E 4570 ha

Nature Reserve with restricted access

Two islands with cliffs off south-west Gotland. The tops of the islands have flat areas with *Juniperus* and a few copses. Sheep-grazing is the only land-use. No problems reported.

Breeding birds include *Uria aalge* (9000 pairs), *Alca torda* (2400 pairs), *Cepphus grylle* (30 pairs), and *Carpodacus erythrinus*.

011 Fjord of Stigfjorden (Göteborg och Bohus)

58°05'N, 11°37'E 8500 ha

Four Nature Reserves (*c*.1515 ha); remainder is a Nature Conservation Area

A fjord between two rather large islands off the west Swedish coast, with extensive shallow waters and a *Zostera*-covered clay sea-floor. The islands have well-managed coastal meadows with a saltmarsh character and some, mostly deciduous, forest dominated by *Quercus*. Of great interest botanically, with a number of rare species. Human activities include boating, swimming, fishing, and grazing for conservation purposes. No reported problems.

An important area for large numbers of migrating birds, as well as for breeding and wintering species, notably wildfowl and waders. Breeding species include *Calidris alpina* and *Bubo bubo*, whilst *Cygnus cygnus* (a few hundred) is amongst the species using the area on passage.

012 Archipelago of St Anna (Östergötland)

58°17'-58°27'N, 17°00'E 5690 ha

Nature Reserves (850 ha); Bird Sanctuaries (1800 ha)

An archipelago off the Swedish east coast containing many small islands. The surrounding shallow waters have a rich flora of algae. Most of the islands are treeless but a few have maritime *Betula* forests with rich floras. Large parts of the area are uninhabited, but intensive recreational use (especially boating) in summer causes disturbance.

Breeding birds include *Somateria mollissima* (many pairs), *Melanitta fusca* (many pairs), *Haliaeetus albicilla*, *Stercorarius parasiticus*, *Sterna caspia*, and *Bubo bubo*.

013 Lake Tåkern (Östergötland)

58°21'N, 14°49'E 5600 ha Ramsar Site

Nature Reserve (5420 ha)

A shallow eutrophic lake which was partly drained in the nineteenth century allowing the development of extensive reedbeds, which presently cover about one third of the total area. The shallow waters (average depth = 0.8 m) are rich in aquatic flora with *Myriophyllum, Chara,* and *Potamogeton.* The surrounding land is mainly grazed grassland, but there are also some arable areas. Some meadow areas have become overgrown, due to under-grazing, with a consequent adverse effect on waders. Mechanical methods (mowing etc.) are being used to simulate the effects of grazing.

Breeding species include *Podiceps cristatus* (200 pairs), *P. grisegena* (100 pairs), *P. auritus* (30 pairs), *P. nigricollis* (5-10 pairs), *Botaurus stellaris* (30-40 pairs), ten species of duck, *Circus aeruginosus* (30-40 pairs), *Crex crex* (occasional), *Haematopus ostralegus, Calidris alpina, Philomachus pugnax, Tringa totanus, Larus ridibundus* (largest Swedish colony), *Chlidonias niger* (25-35 pairs), *Acrocephalus arundinaceus, Panurus biarmicus,* and *Emberiza hortulana.* The area is important for moulting *Cygnus olor* (2000-3000) and *Anser anser,* whilst passage species (max. daily totals) include *Cygnus cygnus* (200-300), *Anser fabalis* (25,000-40,000), *A. albifrons* (less than 100), *Anas penelope, A. crecca,* and *Mergus merganser.*

014 Lake Hornborgasjön (Skaraborg)

58°19'N, 13°33'E 6350 ha Ramsar Site

Nature Reserve (9 ha) and restricted access to large parts of the area in spring

A shallow calcareous lake, formerly 3 m deep with extensive open water. Drainage projects lowered the water-level five times between 1802 and 1933, with canalisation in 1933. The lake basin used to dry up completely in summer following these changes and it became overgrown by *Phragmites, Carex,* and *Salix.* In the 1960s and 1970s experimental restoration of the lake was carried out in some areas and open water has increased in recent years as a consequence of vegetation removal. If plans submitted to the legal system in 1988-89 are accepted, final measures for the lake's restoration (including raising of the water-level) will be ready by 1993. The lake's surroundings are mainly cultivated or grazed by cattle, although there are some forested areas. Human activities, other than agriculture, include the running of a Bird Station and Information Centre. The ecological value of the area will increase if restoration proposals are approved.

The lake holds increasingly important breeding populations of many wetland species. *Calidris alpina, Philomachus pugnax, Larus minutus,* and *Chlidonias niger* have commenced nesting since the start of the lake's restoration. Also breeding are *Podiceps grisegena* (less than 5 pairs), *P. auritus* (10+ pairs), *P. nigricollis* (5 pairs), *Botaurus stellaris* (5 pairs), *Cygnus cygnus* (1-2 pairs), *Anser anser, Anas strepera, A. crecca, A. querquedula, A. clypeata, Aythya ferina, A. fuligula, Pernis apivorus* (less than 5 pairs), *Circus aeruginosus* (15-20 pairs), *C. cyaneus* (1-2 pairs), *Rallus aquaticus, Porzana porzana, Crex crex* (1-3 pairs), *Grus grus* (10 pairs), *Vanellus vanellus, Tringa totanus, T. ochropus, T. glareola, Larus ridibundus* (8000 pairs), *Locustella naevia, Carpodacus erythrinus* (several pairs), and *Emberiza hortulana* (5 pairs). Also very important for migratory birds with many wildfowl, raptors, and (to a lesser extent) waders, including (max. daily totals) *Cygnus cygnus* (100-200 in spring), *Circus aeruginosus, C. cyaneus, Pandion haliaetus, Grus grus* (3000-4000 in spring; 1000-2000 in autumn), and *Philomachus pugnax* (max. 3000).

015 Dättern – Södra Brandfjorden (Älvsborg, Skaraborg)

58°22'-58°25'N, 12°32'-12°39'E 3320 ha

Unprotected; potential future Ramsar Site

Dättern is an almost enclosed bay of Lake Vänern with a *Phragmites* dominated shoreline. Large areas of sand and clay are exposed when the water-level is low, forming important resting areas for waders. The sound connecting Dättern with the main lake becomes ice-free early in the spring. The area is surrounded by grazed meadows.

There are approximately 45 wetland bird species which have been recorded breeding at this site including *Botaurus stellaris* (7 males), *Circus aeruginosus*, *Pandion haliaetus*, *Rallus aquaticus*, *Charadrius dubius*, *Limosa limosa* (occasional), and *Panurus biarmicus*. Wintering and passage birds include *Cygnus cygnus*, *Haliaeetus albicilla*, and *Circus cyaneus*.

016 Lake Östen (Skaraborg)

58°33'-58°37'N, 13°52'-13°56'E 1020 ha

Mainly unprotected; small part (less than 25 ha) included in Odensåker Nature Reserve

A shallow eutrophic lake in a generally flat landscape, except for a few higher parts which are covered by coniferous forest. The lake was lowered three times by drainage projects in the nineteenth century and the reclaimed land, now grazed water-meadows, form an important wader habitat. The rapid water exchange in the lake means that the period of ice-cover is quite short. Grazing of livestock is the main land-use. The only reported problem is the invasion of scrub in some areas where there is a lack of grazing.

The site is very important for migrants including *Podiceps auritus*, *Botaurus stellaris* (occasional), *Cygnus cygnus* (1000+ in spring), *Anser fabalis* (3000-5000), *A. erythropus* (occasional), *Branta leucopsis* (occasional), *Porzana porzana* (probably also breeds), *Crex crex*, *Philomachus pugnax* (150-1000), *Gallinago media* (occasional), and *Sterna caspia* (rare).

017 Bay of Kilsviken (Värmland, Skaraborg)

59°03'N, 14°04'E 7900 ha

Nature Reserve (60 ha); Nature Conservation Area (*c.*2400 ha)

Kilsviken is a eutrophic bay off Lake Vänern, surrounded by agricultural areas. The shoreline is largely made up of reedbeds and water-meadows and there is a rich sub-aquatic vegetation. Associated with Kilsviken is Kolstrandsviken Bay, which is less eutrophic with mudflats, and Åråsviken Bay, which contains many small islands some of which are wooded. The northern part of Åråsviken is characterised by extensive areas of *Phragmites*, and islands with grazing meadows and damp forests. Human activities include recreation and agriculture. Canoeing and other recreational activities may endanger important breeding areas and the bays' sediments still contain mercury (Hg) from a former paper factory.

Breeding birds include *Gavia stellata* (5-7 pairs), *G. arctica*, *Botaurus stellaris* (5-8 pairs), *Circus aeruginosus* (5-8 pairs), *Pandion haliaetus* (10 pairs), and *Porzana porzana* (1-3 pairs). *Podiceps auritus*, *Cygnus cygnus*, *Haliaeetus albicilla* (2-4), and *Circus cyaneus* are amongst the birds passing through in spring and autumn. *Haliaeetus albicilla* also occurs in winter.

018 Former Lake Kvismaren (Örebro)

59°10'N, 15°23'E 800 ha Ramsar Site

Nature Reserve (558 ha)

Kvismaren is a valley containing a rather flat fertile agricultural landscape. Up to the mid-nineteenth century there were extensive marshy areas surrounding two lakes, but following drainage programmes in the 1880s the lakes disappeared. They have now been replaced by extensive reedbeds and *Salix* thickets surrounded by marshy meadows, low-lying pasture and arable land. There are also some more densely wooded areas. The main wetland area is enclosed by embankments and canals to protect the nearby arable land from flooding. Other than the canals, there are now three areas of open water, covering *c.*230 ha, which have recently been restored as shallow lakes or water-meadows. In addition to agricultural activities, there is also an important ornithological station. Further drainage is a potential threat to the area, but measures are currently being taken to improve the ecological quality of the wetland.

Breeding birds include *Podiceps grisegena* (1-2 pairs), *P. auritus*, *P. nigricollis* (6 pairs), *Botaurus stellaris* (2-4 pairs), *Anser anser* (30 pairs), *Anas strepera* (10-15 pairs),

A. querquedula (3-5 pairs), *A. clypeata* (2-5 pairs), *Circus aeruginosus* (7-8 pairs), *Porzana porzana* (3-5 pairs), *Crex crex* (rare), *Limosa limosa* (1-3 pairs), *Luscinia luscinia*, *Locustella naevia* (100 pairs), and *Carpodacus erythrinus*. Amongst birds passing through the area in spring and autumn are many waders and Anatidae including *Anser fabalis* (1000-2000); also *Circus cyaneus, Porzana parva, Larus minutus, Chlidonias niger, Asio flammeus*, and *Locustella fluviatilis*. Wintering species include *Aquila chrysaetos* (2-4).

019 Archipelago areas off Stockholm (Stockholm)

59°22'-59°28'N, 19°09'-19°32'E 9100 ha

Nature Reserve (3400 ha); large parts are also Bird Sanctuaries

The main area of interest belongs to the outer part of the Stockholm archipelago and it can be divided into four groups of islands:

(a) Stora Nassa – *c.*400 closely spaced rocky islets with little or no vegetation. The largest island has maritime *Betula* forest whilst a few others have *Juniperus*. Wet grasslands are also present on some islands.

(b) Lilla Nassa – smaller area than Stora Nassa but with islands more spread out and with very little vegetation.

(c) Gillöga – very flat islands in shallow waters with abundant cover and offshore submerged reefs.

(d) Svenska Högarna – a flat island with *Juniperus*, Graminae and *Calluna*.

The archipelago is largely uninhabited but during the summer it is a very popular leisure (boating) area, which has the potential risk of disturbing breeding birds.

An important breeding area, especially for seabirds, with *Somateria mollissima* (3000 pairs), *Melanitta fusca* (700 pairs), *Arenaria interpres* (100 pairs), *Stercorarius parasiticus* (a few pairs), *Uria aalge* (a few pairs), *Alca torda* (300 pairs), *Cepphus grylle* (600 pairs), and *Asio flammeus*.

020 Lake Hjälstaviken (Uppsala)

59°40'N, 17°23'E 790 ha Ramsar Site

Nature Reserve

Shallow (average depth = 1 m), almost enclosed bay of Lake Mälaren, surrounded by wet, tussocky meadows which merge into drier pasture and fields. A couple of deciduous copses overlook the bay and there is a conifer-covered hill with some bare rock outcrops along the eastern edge. Only 30 ha of open water remain, the rest being choked by invasive *Phragmites*, *Scirpus* and *Typha*. The submerged vegetation has been greatly impoverished in recent years and this, together with the decreasing open water area, has resulted in the decline of some bird species, notably ducks.

Approximately 100 species nest in the area including *Botaurus stellaris*, *Cygnus olor* (colonised Sweden from this base), *Anas strepera, A. crecca, A. querquedula, Aythya ferina, A. fuligula, Circus aeruginosus* (4 pairs), *Porzana porzana, Crex crex* (rare), and *Locustella naevia*. Passage species include *Podiceps auritus, Anser fabalis, Mergus merganser, Circus pygargus, Pandion haliaetus, Porzana parva, Grus grus, Gallinago media, Limosa limosa*, and *Carpodacus erythrinus*. *Buteo lagopus* and *Aquila chrysaetos* occur in winter.

021 River Svartån (Västmanland)

59°50'-59°57'N, 16°20'-16°22'E 1870 ha

Unprotected

This area contains three eutrophic lakes: Fläcksjön, Gussjön and Gorgen, all connected by the River Svartån and surrounded by low-lying water-meadows. Associated vegetation includes areas of *Phragmites australis* and *Scirpus lacustris*, as well as wet *Betula* forest. The land is used for stock-grazing and hay-making and is one of the largest areas remaining in Sweden where mowing still takes place. Leaching of fertilisers into the wetland areas has accelerated growth of reeds and rushes (especially in Lake Fläcksjön). Mowing and grazing must be maintained if the area is not to be overgrown by *Salix* scrub. There has recently been a threat from proposed dyke construction for agricultural purposes.

Breeding birds include *Podiceps auritus* (10 pairs), *Anas querquedula* (8-10 pairs), *A. clypeata* (10 pairs), *Circus aeruginosus* (1 pair), *Porzana porzana*, *Crex crex* (1 pair), *Pluvialis apricaria*, *Larus minutus*, and *Chlidonias niger*. *Gavia arctica* and *Cygnus cygnus* are amongst the wintering and passage species. The latter also include *Porzana porzana* and *Pluvialis apricaria*.

022 River Dalälven: Färnebofjärden (Västmanland, Gävleborg)

60°13'N, 16°47'E 11,200 ha

Nature Reserve (4640 ha)

An extensive lake and associated wetland complex along the River Dalälven. Much of the area is regularly flooded and contains freshwater marsh, peatbogs etc. The surrounding forests of both coniferous and deciduous species are largely old and undisturbed. Commercial forestry is, however, carried out in some areas. Locally, concentrations of visitors may cause disturbance in the breeding season. The site is situated on the 'limes norlandicus' where flora and fauna of both northern and southern aspects meet.

Breeding birds include *Gavia arctica* (5-10 pairs), *Pandion haliaetus* (30 pairs), *Strix uralensis* (20-25 pairs), *Picus canus* (a few pairs), *Dendrocopos leucotos* (10-15 pairs), *Picoides tridactylus* (a few pairs), *Ficedula parva* (a few pairs), and *Emberiza hortulana* (5-10 pairs). *Haliaeetus albicilla* and *Aquila chrysaetos* occur in winter, with several hundred *Cygnus cygnus* on passage.

023 River Dalälven: Hovran (Kopparberg)

60°11'-60°25'N, 16°03'E 5030 ha

Unprotected except for a Nature Reserve (40 ha)

This site includes some broader stretches of the River Dalälven, notably 'Lake' Hovran (in fact, effectively part of the river) and some smaller lagoons alongside. It is surrounded by arable land, coniferous and deciduous forests, and there are also open areas around the lakes with *Salix*/*Phragmites* vegetation. The only problem at the site is that of dramatic water-level fluctuations which result in destruction of nests.

A total of 230 bird species has been recorded with the following amongst the breeders: *Gavia arctica*, *Podiceps auritus*, *Cygnus cygnus* (1 pair), *Pandion haliaetus* (10 pairs), *Crex crex* (occasional), and *Dendrocopos leucotos*. Passage migrants include *Gavia stellata*, *G. arctica*, *Botaurus stellaris* (occasional), *Cygnus cygnus* (1000-1500), *Phalaropus lobatus* (irregular), *Calidris ferruginea* (regular), *Tringa erythropus* (250), and *Sterna caspia* (irregular; 1-5).

024 Lake Ånnsjön (Jämtland)

63°16'N, 12°33'E 11,300 ha Ramsar Site

Nature Conservation Area; Bird Sanctuary (275 ha)

A very shallow oligotrophic lake in the upper part of the River Indal system, partly surrounded by marshy areas with a sandy ridge along one 2 km stretch of shoreline. The confluence of two rivers at the western end of the site has formed the Handol Delta and there are other delta areas to the north-west and south-east. The lower River Handolan contains rapids, waterfalls, and gorges; there is extensive forest nearby. There are no reported problems.

Over 90 species breed regularly, with *Gavia stellata*, *Anser fabalis* (occasionally), 10 species of duck (including *Anas penelope*, *A. acuta*, *Clangula hyemalis*, *Melanitta nigra*, and *M. fusca*), and 14 species of wader (including *Calidris temminckii*, *Limicola falcinellus*, *Numenius arquata*, and *Phalaropus lobatus*). Formerly, *Anser erythropus* bred at this site. An important staging area for migrant species.

025 River Umeälven Delta (Västerbotten)

63°45'N, 20°20'E 1150 ha

Nature Reserve (120 ha)

The delta of a river system flowing into the Gulf of Bothnia in north-east Sweden. The form of the delta is constantly changing, owing to the deposition of sediment, while the water-level is very variable according to the flow of the river and tidal/sea-level factors. Much of the delta shoreline is surrounded by water-meadows but there is also deciduous forest with a few conifers. *Phragmites* is scarce. The area is used for commercial and leisure shipping, general recreation, and forestry, which cause some disturbance.

Breeding species include *Larus minutus* (*c.*10 pairs) and possibly *Limosa limosa*. An important staging area for migrants, especially waterfowl with the following species using the site: *Gavia stellata*, *G. arctica*, *Cygnus cygnus*, *Anser albifrons*, *Mergus albellus* (10-15), *Haliaeetus albicilla*, *Calidris temminckii* (125), *Philomachus pugnax* (1200), *Lymnocryptes minimus*, *Limosa limosa*, *Numenius phaeopus*, *Tringa erythropus* (150) *Phalaropus lobatus* (20), and *Larus minutus* (10).

026 Mountains of Vindelfjällen (including Lake Tärnasjön) (Västerbotten)

65°27'-66°22'N, 15°26'-16°30'E 550,000 ha

Ramsar Site: Lake Tärnasjön (11,800 ha)

Nature Reserve (virtually whole area; largest Nature Reserve in Sweden)

A very extensive mountainous area with virgin *Picea* forests, mountain *Betula* forests, creeks, and marshes. There is a mosaic-like landscape of mires, lakes and valleys containing rivers, deltas, and lake systems. The Ramsar Site (Lake Tärnasjön) is composed of a large lake with a delta formed by the River Tärna at its northern end. It is surrounded by seasonally flooded marshland. This site is generally very rich botanically, whilst threatened mammals present include *Ursus arctos*, *Gulo gulo* and *Lutra lutra*. There is also considerable geological interest. The whole area is used for reindeer grazing, hunting, fishing, and hiking. No reported threats, although a proposed road through the site may have some adverse effects.

Important for breeding birds with *Cygnus cygnus*, about ten species of duck (including *Aythya marila*), *Haliaeetus albicilla* (possibly), *Aquila chrysaetos*, *Falco rusticolus*, ten species of wader (including *Calidris maritima*, *Philomachus pugnax*, *Gallinago gallinago*, *G. media*, and *Phalaropus lobatus*), *Bubo bubo*, *Strix nebulosa*, and *Phylloscopus borealis*.

027 Lake Tjålmejaure – Laisdalen Valley (Norrbotten)

66°17'-66°19'N, 15°54'-16°37'E 22,200 ha

Ramsar Site: Tjålmejaure – Laisdalen (13,400 ha)

Nature Reserve (500 ha); extensive Bird Sanctuary

Two converging valleys in the mountains of northern Sweden, containing small rivers and their deltas. The southern valley has a large lake system with flat shores, which form an important breeding and nesting habitat for waterfowl. The narrower northern valley contains the River Laisälven which is bordered by a strip of marshland and surrounded by *Betula* forest, with some *Pinus*. Mammals include *Ursus arctos*, *Martes martes*, and *Gulo gulo*. No reported problems.

Important for breeding birds with *Gavia stellata* (several pairs), *G. arctica* (several pairs), *Cygnus cygnus* (a few pairs), *Anser erythropus* (a few pairs), ten species of duck, *Circus cyaneus*, *Buteo lagopus*, *Aquila chrysaetos*, *Pandion haliaetus*, *Falco columbarius*, *F. rusticolus*, *F. peregrinus* (seen occasionally in breeding season), *Lagopus lagopus*, *Tetrao urogallus* (strong population), *Calidris maritima*, *Limicola falcinellus*, *Gallinago media*, *Tringa erythropus*, *Phalaropus lobatus*, *Stercorarius longicaudus*, *Nyctea scandiaca*, *Strix uralensis*, *Anthus cervinus*, *Bombycilla garrulus*, and *Perisoreus infaustus*. The site is also one of the final staging areas for northward-moving migrants in spring.

028 Lake Gammelstadsviken (Norrbotten)

65°38'N, 22°00'E 440 ha Ramsar Site

Nature Reserve with access to central islands prohibited 1 May to 31 July

A shallow (1-4 m) eutrophic lake at the head of the Gulf of Bothnia, formed when rising land isolated a bay from the sea. The lake floor is covered by fine marine sediments with an increasing overlying thickness of mud. Water exchange is low owing to the small inflow entering the lake. Large parts of the shoreline are marshy, with *Phragmites, Typha, Equisetum* etc. and the lake itself has floating vegetation. A road was built across the northern part of the lake some years ago and further disturbance may result from proximity with the town of Lulea. Owing to its position as a very northerly (but coastal) eutrophic lake, the area has become an outpost for a variety of southern flora and fauna as well as holding those with a more northerly aspect.

Breeding species include *Podiceps grisegena, P. auritus, Anas penelope, A. crecca, A. querquedula, A. clypeata, Aythya ferina, Bucephala clangula, Circus aeruginosus, Philomachus pugnax, Gallinago gallinago, Tringa totanus, T. glareola* (probable), *Phalaropus lobatus*, and *Larus minutus*. Spring and autumn passage migrants include *Mergus albellus, Circus cyaneus, Pandion haliaetus, Grus grus, Calidris ferruginea, Limicola falcinellus, Limosa limosa, L. lapponica*, and *Tringa erythropus*.

029 Lake Persöfjärden (Norrbotten)

65°47'N, 22°08'E 3350 ha Ramsar Site

No additional protective status

A lake, *c.*15 km long, which was isolated from the Gulf of Bothnia by land elevation. It is characterised by shallowness (partly due to drainage in 1957) and flat shores which are regularly flooded. The shallow waters have favoured the spread of *Scirpus* and *Phragmites*, which almost divide the lake into two at one point. Floating vegetation is also extensive and parts of the south-west have been invaded by *Salix* scrub. Plans for further drainage have been considered, but current discussions are concentrating on conservation aspects. A decrease in pH has been recorded at the lake in recent years.

Breeding birds include *Podiceps grisegena, P. auritus, Circus aeruginosus, Philomachus pugnax, Phalaropus lobatus*, and *Larus minutus*. The area is most important as a resting area for geese (e.g. *Anser fabalis*), ducks, raptors and waders.

030 Lake Laidaure (Norrbotten)

67°07'N, 17°45'E 4150 ha Ramsar Site

National Park (300 ha; part of Sarek National Park)

This site consists of the delta of the River Rapaälvens and Lake Laidaure, into which the delta is gradually expanding from the west. To the south is Sarek National Park, and to the north a zone of coniferous forest. No current land-use. There is some disturbance in the summer months from canoeists.

The delta region is important for breeding *Anas penelope, A. crecca, A. acuta, Aythya fuligula, A. marila*, and *Bucephala clangula*, as well as numerous passerines in the scrub-covered parts. Both delta and shorelines are important for breeding waders with *Tringa glareola, Actitis hypoleucos*, and *Phalaropus lobatus*. The delta area becomes ice-free early in the spring and is consequently an important staging area for migrants, including *Cygnus cygnus*.

031 Sjaunja (Norrbotten)

67°06'-67°40'N, 18°42'-20°07'E 208,000 ha

Ramsar Site: Sjaunja-Kaitum (176,000 ha); proposed World Heritage Site

Nature Reserve

An extensive, largely untouched wilderness area with a wide range of habitats dominated by wetlands but including forest to the east and mountainous territory to the west. The main wetlands are open marshes, shallow lakes, and wet *Betula* forests. There are also 44,000 ha of virgin *Picea* and *Pinus* forests in the drier areas. At least 25 mammal species have been recorded, including *Ursus arctos*, *Gulo gulo*, *Lutra lutra*, and *Lynx lynx*. The only human activities are reindeer farming and restricted hunting/fishing. There is some disturbance from snowmobiles in spring.

About 100 species have been recorded nesting including *Cygnus cygnus*, *Haliaeetus albicilla* (1-4 pairs), *Aquila chrysaetos* (1-3 pairs), *Falco rusticolus* (1-2 pairs), *Limicola falcinellus*, *Lymnocryptes minimus*, *Tringa erythropus*, *Phalaropus lobatus*, *Asio flammeus*, *Anthus cervinus*, *Emberiza rustica*, and *E. pusilla*.

032 Påkketan (Norrbotten)

67°57'-68°14'N, 20°00'-20°45'E 24,000 ha

Nature Reserve (5000 ha)

Part of the mountainous area in the north of Sweden, including a valley containing lakes and marshes. About 60 per cent of the total area is covered by coniferous forest, most of which is very old but there are some parts with very young trees as a result of several forest fires.

Breeding birds include *Haliaeetus albicilla*, *Aquila chrysaetos*, *Falco rusticolus*, and *Tetrao urogallus*.

033 Taavavuoma (Norrbotten)

68°24'-68°37'N, 20°30'-20°55'E 28,400 ha Ramsar Site (8900 ha)

Certain industries and other technical development prohibited without parliamentary sanctions.

A mosaic of marshes, watercourses, lakes, and pools lying in a depression of one of the most northerly Lapland plateaux at an altitude of 900-1000 m. The area is part of the River Lainio's catchment. The vegetation is strongly influenced by permafrost and the Arctic and sub-Arctic peatlands and lakes are of considerable botanical interest. The only land-use is reindeer farming and there are no reported problems.

Approximately 80 bird species are found nesting in the area, with *Podiceps auritus*, *Cygnus cygnus*, *Anser erythropus* (possibly; seen in the breeding season), *Anas crecca*, *A. acuta*, *Clangula hyemalis*, *Mergus albellus*, *Haliaeetus albicilla*, *Circus cyaneus* (possibly; seen in the breeding season), *Aquila chrysaetos*, *Falco rusticolus*, *F. peregrinus*, *Charadrius hiaticula*, *Pluvialis apricaria*, *Calidris alpina*, *Limicola falcinellus*, *Philomachus pugnax*, *Lymnocryptes minimus*, *Limosa lapponica*, *Tringa erythropus*, *Phalaropus lobatus*, *Stercorarius longicaudus*, *Anthus cervinus*, *Carduelis hornemanni*, and *Calcarius lapponicus*.

MAIN REFERENCES

IUCN (1987) *Directory of wetlands of international importance*. Gland, Switzerland and Cambridge, U.K.: Conservation Monitoring Centre.

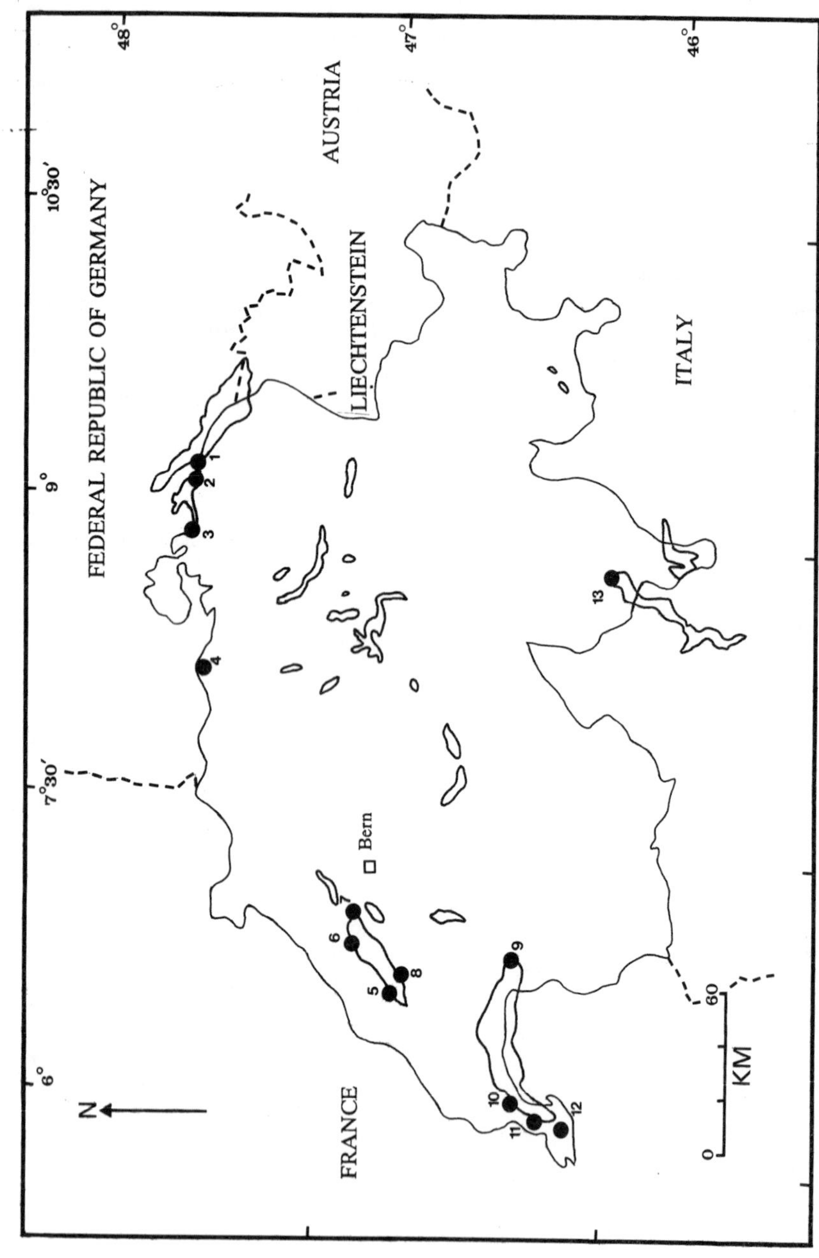

Figure 34: Map showing the location of the sites in Switzerland

SWITZERLAND

Pochard *Aythya ferina* and Tufted Duck *A. fuligula*

INTRODUCTION

General information

Switzerland covers an area of 41,293 sq km and has a total population of 6,298,000 (in 1978), with an average density of 152.52 persons per sq km. Because of the terrain there are considerable differences in population density between the mountain regions of the Alps and the Jura, and the flatter rolling lowlands.

Switzerland may be divided into three main regions: the mountains of the Alps (covering roughly 60 per cent), the Jura mountains (10 per cent), and the Mittelland plateau (30 per cent) between the two mountainous regions. These zones divide the country into three large belts running from south-west to north-east.

The Alps have an important climatic and hydrographic influence on the rest of the country. High mountains are separated by deep valleys, which create a great diversity in relief and fauna. The Alps are not geologically uniform, but may be divided into three main parts: the northern and the southern lower Alps, and the central high mountains with peaks higher than 4000 m. Owing to its difficult topography, the landscape in the Alps is less altered by man than in the Jura and Mittelland. However, the timberline was lowered centuries ago to increase the area of pasture land.

The Mittelland plateau is a strip of 40-50 km extending from Lake Geneva (Lac Léman) in the south-west to Lake Constance (Bodensee) in the north-east, forming a plain slightly bent towards the east. The River Aare drains most of the smaller waters along the southern border of the Jura into the Rhine, which forms the border between Switzerland and the Federal Republic of Germany in the north. The Mittelland valleys lie at 400-500 m and the bordering hillsides rarely exceed altitudes of 700 m. The border to the southernmost steep Jura mountain chain in the north-west is well marked. By contrast, the southern limit of the Mittelland towards the northern Alps is gradual. A large number of lakes remaining from the Pleistocene characterise the region. However, their shores have been altered to a large extent for agricultural purposes, building of houses, roads, and railways; marshes and moors have mostly been drained for agricultural use. Most of the remaining river courses are now artificial and only minute parts of the original riverine forests remain. The Mittelland plateau is mostly used for agriculture and is densely populated. The very patchy forest area covers 25 per cent of the Mittelland; a great deal of the original deciduous trees have been replaced by plantations of *Picea abies*.

The Jura mountains attain altitudes up to 1700 m in the south-west and up to 900 m in the north-east. The water generally drains subterraneously into the calcareous ground. Thus, most of the mountain chains are rather dry and only a few rivers flow in the valleys. Some basins on loamy soil retain water, leading to the formation of peatbogs. Cold air captured above such basins create a local climate similar to that in northern latitudes.

There are five altitudinal zones with characteristic vegetation types: colline zone, montane zone, subalpine zone, alpine zone, and nivale zone.

The colline zone reaches up to 600 m in the Mittelland and Jura, and up to 700 m in the central Alps and up to 800 m on their southern slopes. At these altitudes the annual mean temperature varies between 8° and 12°C. Climax vegetation consists of diverse deciduous forests, mainly *Fagus sylvatica* forests, often with *Quercus* sp., *Quercus/Betula*, and *Q. pubescens* communities, and *Castanea* sp. stands at special localities. The typical crops include maize, tobacco and wine; orchards and extensive cereal fields characterise the landscape.

The montane zone situated above the former reaches up to 1200 m in the Jura and the northern slopes of the Alps, up to 1400 m in the central Alps and up to 1700 m on their southern slopes. Its annual mean temperature varies between 5° and 8°C. Forests of *Fagus sylvatica*, mixed with *Abies alba* dominate the zone. In drier parts, especially of the central Alps, *Pinus sylvestris* replaces *Fagus sylvatica*. At these sites traditional crops include some cereals. In general potatoes are a typical crop of this zone.

The subalpine zone includes the summits above 1200 m in the Jura and reaches from 1400 m up to 1800 m and 2400 m in the northern and central Alps respectively. In the southern Alps this zone is limited to 1700 m up to 1900 m. Mean annual temperatures vary from 0° to 5°C. Coniferous forests are dominant with *Picea abies* the most abundant species. *Picea abies* is replaced to a large extent by *Pinus sylvestris*, *P. montana*, *P. cembra*, and *Larix decidua* in the dry valleys of the central Alps. The steep slopes, regularly affected by avalanches, are characterised by *Alnus viridis*. The main human activity is forestry and only exceptionally some crops are cultivated. The upper limit of this zone is formed by the timberline, which lies higher in the central Alps than on the outer slopes. However, extensive wood exploitation and grazing have lowered the timberline well below its original altitude. Shrubs are found above the timberline where grazing pressure is low.

The alpine zone begins above the timberline and reaches up to the mountain tops. It consists of grazed grasslands which, with increasing altitude, become sparse and patchy and are gradually replaced by boulders and rocks. Cattle graze the lower parts while sheep can also use the steeper slopes of the zone. In the uppermost, nivale zone, most of the area is covered with snow and ice continuously throughout the year; nevertheless, sparse patches of vegetation are found up to over 4000 m at microclimatically favourable places.

About three-quarters of Switzerland is productive land. This part is used for agriculture as arable land, grassland, orchards, and vineyards (38 per cent), pasture (28 per cent), and for forestry (34 per cent). During the last decades, the diverse traditional landscape has been modified to a large extent. Since 1850 more than 90 per cent of the marshes and peatbogs have been drained. In the last 20 years, a third of the hedges in the Mittelland have been eliminated. Some ten million fruit trees have been cut since the fifties. Between 1942 and 1967 an area of 1000 sq km has been built over. This trend still continues. Even in those parts of the country where the traditional land-use remains heavy machines and increasing amounts of fertilisers and pesticides are used in modern agriculture. This has contributed to an increasing loss of habitats and biological diversity. Nevertheless, there are still large areas of natural and semi-natural habitats where rich and diverse bird communities exist. Federal and additional cantonal laws urge in general, and occasionally in specific terms, for conservation measures to be taken; however, more has to be done to implement this legislation.

Ornithological importance

A third (65 species) of all 192 breeding species (in 1972) live predominantly in forests, 54 (28 per cent) in cultivated land, 50 (26 per cent) in wetlands, 13 (7 per cent) above the timberline, and 10 (5 per cent) in various habitats. The proportion of declining or vulnerable species (in a Swiss context) frequenting forests is the lowest (14 per cent), followed by wetland species (22 per cent). Vulnerability is highest in species living in cultivated land, where over one third of the species (37 per cent) are threatened.

The most important bird habitats can be summarised as the following:

1. Large freshwater lakes
   The conservation of lakes (including water quality) and their shores is regulated by Federal laws (nos. 3, 4, 5, 6, 8, 9; see below) and further Cantonal acts that provide stronger protection status depending on the Cantons (this is the case for all the following habitats). These lakes support large numbers of waterfowl in winter, particularly *Anas strepera* (6000, 7 per cent of the Western-Palearctic breeding population), *Aythya ferina* (67,000, 4 per cent), *A. fuligula* (162,000, 12 per cent), *Bucephala clangula* (10,000, 3 per cent), *Mergus merganser* (3700, 3 per cent), and *Fulica atra* (111,000, 3 per cent).

2. Reedbeds, oxbow lakes and natural river courses in the Swiss lowlands
   The conservation of this habitat is regulated by Federal laws (nos. 1, 4, 5, 6, 7, 9). The few remaining natural wetlands provide habitat for *Ixobrychus minutus* (max. 50 pairs [1979] in reedbeds in the Mittelland, Ticino, and Valais), and *Alcedo atthis* (some 200 pairs [1978] along rivers, with banks suitable for digging nest holes, throughout the lower parts of the country; problems are disturbance by tourists, anglers, and fish-farming).

3. Traditionally cultivated landscape with forest patches and hedges
   The conservation of this habitat is regulated by Federal laws (nos. 1, 4, 7, 9, 10). This landscape provides habitat for *Milvus migrans* (presently *c.*1500 pairs; mostly near lakes and rivers throughout the lower parts of the country; especially in western Switzerland the species breeds in higher numbers than anywhere else in Central Europe with densities locally up to 30 pairs/1.8 sq km), *M. milvus* (235-300 pairs [1987]; increasing in the Jura and lower Mittelland), and *Lanius collurio* (declining; now largely confined to regions moderately affected by intensive agriculture above 600 m, in the Alps and the Jura, locally up to 1700 m).

4. Highly structured mixed forests in montane and subalpine regions
   The conservation of this habitat is regulated by Federal laws (nos. 1, 2, 4, 7, 9). These are forests with old trees and open parts which are not heavily exploited or disturbed, that provide habitat for *Bonasa bonasia* (total population unknown) and *Tetrao urogallus* (total spring population 550-650 males [1985]; steeply declining).

5. Sunny alpine slopes in the central and southern Alps
   The conservation of this habitat is regulated by Federal laws (nos. 4, 7, 9). The steep slopes and boulders with rocks, where snow melts early in spring, provide habitat for *Alectoris graeca saxatilis* (total population unknown).

6. Sunny open forest and bushland
   The conservation of this habitat is regulated by Federal laws (nos. 1, 2, 4, 7, 9, 10). The open woods, bushland, and shrubs in climatically favourable sites at lower altitudes, provide habitat for *Caprimulgus europaeus* (declining) and *Hippolais polyglotta* (expanding).

7. *Quercus/Carpinus* forests
   The conservation of this habitat is regulated by Federal laws (nos. 1, 2, 4, 7, 9). These deciduous forests with stands of old *Quercus* and a high species-diversity in the Mittelland and the low regions of the Jura, provide habitat for *Dendrocopos medius* (total population 320 pairs in 1984).

8. Dry slopes in the Jura and the central valleys of the Alps
   The conservation of this habitat is regulated by Federal laws (nos. 4, 7, 9, 10). The open slopes facing south with bushes and dry meadows provide habitat for *Lullula arborea* (270 pairs [1979]); declining: Jura, Valais, and Grisons) and *Emberiza hortulana* (240 pairs [1979]; declining, mostly in Valais and near Geneva).

9. Open woods of *Castanea sativa* in the lower valleys south of the Alps
   The conservation of this habitat is regulated by Federal laws (nos. 2, 4, 9); endangered by the parasitic fungus *Endothia parasiticus*. These are traditionally used forests (with old trees, mostly in Ticino) that provide habitat for *Ficedula albicollis* (very small population).

Conservation infrastructure and protected-area system

There are general and specific provisions in the Swiss Federal legislation for the conservation of landscapes and particular habitats as well as for protected areas (the most important acts are outlined below), but the conservation of nature is largely the responsibility of the Cantons (of which there are 26). There is one National Park situated in the eastern Alps and administered by a Federal act. Nature Reserves and other types of protected areas are established by the Federal Government, the Cantons, and by non-governmental organisations, such as the Swiss League for Nature Protection and several ornithological societies.

The degree of management and the regulations regardings the use of protected areas vary from one reserve to another. In most there is a strict prohibition on collecting plants and animals, and some are closed to the public. The restrictions on land-use vary considerably.

The most important provisions significant for nature conservation, which are written in to the Swiss legislation, are (from Zbinden, Imhof and Pfister 1987, and Marti 1987):

1. Federal Constitution (1884, 1971), particularly paragraphs on agriculture, heath and boglands.
2. Federal Laws and accompanying guidelines on forestry (1902, 1965, 1959/63), where it is defined in particular that the woodland area has to be maintained.
3. Federal Law on hunting and protection of wild living birds and mammals (1986), notably protecting waterfowl wintering sites of international importance.
4. Federal Law and accompanying guidelines on protection of natural and cultural sites, habitats and monuments (1966, 1983), protecting particularly vulnerable and ecologically valuable habitats.
5. Federal Law and accompanying guidelines to protect water resources from pollution (1971).
6. Federal Law on Fishery (1973).
7. Federal Guidelines accompanying the Inventory of Landscapes and Natural Monuments (1977).
8. Federal Guidelines on ship and boat traffic on Swiss waters (1978).
9. Federal Law and accompanying guidelines on landscape planning (1979, 1986).
10. Federal Law and accompanying guidelines regulating subsidies to agriculture (1979, 1980).

International measures relevant to the conservation of sites

Switzerland has ratified the Bern Convention, Ramsar Convention, and World Heritage Convention, and has designated two Ramsar Sites (both included), nine Biogenetic

Reserves but no natural World Heritage Sites. In addition, one Biosphere Reserve has been designated as part of UNESCO's Man and the Biosphere Programme.

Overview of the inventory

Switzerland supports breeding populations of one Red Data Book species (*Milvus milvus*), 21 vulnerable species and subspecies as defined by this study (*Ixobrychus minutus*, *Milvus migrans*, *Aquila chrysaetos*, *Bonasa bonasia*, *Lagopus mutus helveticus*, *Tetrao tetrix*, *T. urogallus*, *Alectoris graeca saxatilis*, *Bubo bubo*, *Glaucidium passerinum*, *Aegolius funereus*, *Caprimulgus europaeus*, *Alcedo atthis*, *Picus canus*, *Dryocopus martius*, *Dendrocopos medius*, *Picoides tridactylus*, *Lullula arborea*, *Ficedula albicollis*, *Lanius collurio*, and *Emberiza hortulana* [plus four irregular species]). None of these species is concentrated at a restricted number of specific sites as their typical habitats are usually scattered over larger areas; for some species existing knowledge is at present not sufficient to identify the most important sites.

The important habitats for birds other than wetlands, outlined above, are therefore not covered by this inventory. Studies in progress and future investigations will provide the data needed to design the most important areas for some of these species. The vulnerable species not mentioned in the habitat accounts above are still regularly distributed within their suitable habitats in Switzerland.

Switzerland has a number of internationally important wetlands for wintering waterfowl. These are included as sites 001–012 and cover a total area of 5840 ha. Site 013 has been designated as a Ramsar Site but does not qualify as internationally important for its numbers of waterfowl. These 13 sites and their specific protection status are described in Marti and Schifferli (1987) and Marti (1987).

Acknowledgements

The introduction was written by N. Zbinden, C. Marti, L. Schifferli, O. Biber (all Swiss Institute of Ornithology), and T. Salathé. The following site descriptions were compiled by S. Bräger from Marti and Schifferli (1987) and Marti (1987).

INVENTORY

No.	Site name	Region	Criteria used to select site [see p.18]							
			0	1(i)	1(ii)	1(iii)	1(iv)	2	3	4
001	Bodensee: Konstanzer Bucht	TG				*				
002	Untersee (Bodensee): Ermatinger Becken	TG				*			*	
003	Untersee-Ende and Rhein up to Bibermühle	TG,SH				*				
004	Aarestau Klingnau	AG				*				
005	Lac de Neuchâtel: Corcelettes-Vaumarcus	VD				*				
006	Lac de Neuchâtel: Colombier – Canal de la Thielle	NE				*				
007	Lac de Neuchâtel: Fanel and Chablais de Cudrefin	BE,NE,VD				*				
008	Lac de Neuchâtel: Estavayer – Yvonand	FR,VD				*				
009	Lac Léman: St Gingolph – Rivaz	VS,VD				*				
010	Lac Léman: Rolle – Céligny	VD,GE				*				
011	Lac Léman: Versoix – Genève	GE				*				
012	Rhône: Genève – Barrage de Verbois	GE				*				
013	Lago Maggiore: Bolle di Magadino	TI	*							

TG=Thurgau SH=Schaffhausen AG=Aargau VD=Vaud NE=Neuchâtel
BE=Bern FR=Fribourg VS=Valais GE=Genève TI=Ticino

Comments on the inventory

1. Following Szijj (1972), who considered Switzerland as part of the Baltic-North Sea flyway, Leuzinger (1976) adopted the criterion of one per cent of the numbers of wintering ducks in this biogeographic region. Atkinson-Willes (1976) considered Switzerland as part of the Black Sea-Mediterranean region. However, ringing data of *Aythya ferina* and *A. fuligula* show that Switzerland's wintering birds come from both biogeographic populations. To account for this the mean figure of these two flyways has been used. A site is considered as internationally important if it holds one per cent of the mean population of the Baltic-North Sea and the Black Sea-Mediterranean region (i.e. at least: 400 *Anas strepera*, 250 *Netta rufina*, 8000 *Aythya ferina*, 6800 *A. fuligula*, and 1500 *Bucephala clangula*).

2. Site 013 is included because it is a Ramsar Site with valuable breeding bird populations, although this does not qualify according to the quantitative criteria.

3. The site name is followed by the name of the Canton, given in parentheses, where the site can be found.

Glossary

Lac/see/lago = lake.

---

001 Bodensee: Konstanzer Bucht (Thurgau)

47°39'N, 09°12'E 400 ha

Reserve and no-hunting area (Konstanzer Trichter)

A shallow bay of the Lake Constance (Bodensee) with the outflow of the Rhine (Rhein). Due to the strong current there is no total ice-cover even in cold winters. There are considerable variations in water-level with gravel-banks appearing when the level is low. It has a mainly artificial shoreline with walkways/public footpaths, parks, bathing sites, and a small campsite. In the north-west there is the city of Konstanz with its harbour. Overlaps with site no. 081 in Federal Republic of Germany.

Important for wintering ducks although the numbers have decreased considerably since the early 1970s: *Anas strepera* (Nov. av. 52; max. 153), *Netta rufina* (max. 84), *Aythya ferina* (Nov. av. 6790; max. 13,105), *A. fuligula* (Jan. av. 5320; max. 11,443), and *Bucephala clangula* (Dec. av. 381; max. 547). Regularly supports 10,000+ waterfowl.

002 Untersee (Bodensee): Ermatinger Becken (Thurgau)

47°41'N, 09°06'E 900 ha

Hunting is only allowed from the shoreline; no-hunting area on German side since 1986

A large, shallow lake basin connected to the Bodensee with a narrow, deep-cut underwater gully of the Rhine running through it. On the German side there are extensive reedbeds (300 ha), with a shallow-water area (3 m deep) at the edge of the reedbeds rich in waterplants. On the Swiss side there is a fairly natural lake shore, 3 km long, with reedbeds (100 ha). Extensive mudflats covered with *Enteromorpha* appear when the water-level is low. Many of these usually freeze up in winter, but even in cold winters the gully of the Rhine and parts of the shallow-water area stay ice-free. Overlaps with IBA site no. 080 in Federal Republic of Germany.

Important for breeding, moulting, migrating, and wintering waterfowl: *Anas strepera* (Sept. av. 758; max. 1810 in Nov.), *Netta rufina* (Sept. av. 223 moulting; max. 666), *Aythya ferina* (Oct. av. 9659; max. 20,271), and *A. fuligula* (Oct. av. 4918; max. 14,185 in Nov). Also, the only significant wintering site of *Cygnus cygnus* and *Numenius arquata* in this region. Regularly supports 20,000+ waterfowl in late autumn (max. 28,000+ in Oct./Nov.).

003 Untersee-Ende and Rhein up to Bibermühle (Thurgau, Schaffhausen)

47°40'N, 08°51'E 450 ha

Includes several small Nature Reserves; no hunting on open water

A basin at the end of the Untersee and the uncontrolled outflow of the River Rhine with reedbeds and adjacent natural surroundings. Large areas of limestone support a rich invertebrate fauna at the bottom of the river. Some bays (like the Eschenzer Bucht) and some islands (like the Werd) have large reedbeds. There are considerable changes in the water-level; in autumn and in winter, sand- and gravel-banks, as well as muddy or sandy shores, appear. On the peninsula a small swamp-forest has developed.

This part of the Untersee and the Rhine is the most important Swiss wintering site for *Aythya ferina* and *A. fuligula*. Wintering waterfowl include *Netta rufina* (April av. 30; max. 64 in March; also breeding), *Aythya ferina* (Dec. av. 14,416; max. 27,481), *A. fuligula* (Jan. av. 24,430; max. 42,159), and *Bucephala clangula* (Jan. av. 1724; max. 2262). In February there are also major concentrations of *Tachybaptus ruficollis*, *Anas platyrhynchos*, and *A. crecca*. The total waterfowl (Dec. av.) exceeds 40,000; with a max. of 70,000+ in Dec./Jan.

004 Aarestau Klingnau (Aargau)

47°35'N, 08°15'E 170 ha

Nature Reserve next to site; no hunting

The dammed River Aare with a relatively constant water-level (daily fluctuations about 10 cm) and periodically large mudflats. Artificial dams surround the lake on all sides. The gully of the river is separated from the south-western shallow-water zone by a peninsula and small islands. Small reedbeds surround the islands and there are large mudbanks in the shallow water. A small swamp-forest has developed on the peninsula.

This artificial lake supports a high diversity of wintering waterfowl species and considerable numbers of dabbling ducks and waders during migration: *Anas strepera* (Nov. av. 200; max. 401 in March), *Aythya ferina* (Nov. av. 582; max. 1671), *A. fuligula* (march av. 557; max. 1103 in Jan.), and *Bucephala clangula* (Feb. av. 121; max. 269).

005 Lac de Neuchâtel: Corcelettes-Vaumarcus (Vaud)

46°50'N, 06°43'E 240 ha

Hunting is partly restricted; one small Nature Reserve

A flat, fairly natural lake margin with extensive reedbeds and marshes including some rather rare types of swampy meadows as well as some large areas of swamp-forest. The shallow-water zone stretches several hundred metres into the lake.

An important wintering site for *Aythya fuligula* since the Zebra Mussel *Dreissena polymorpha* appeared in 1967. Wintering waterfowl include *Aythya ferina* (Jan. av. 470; max. 1881) and *A. fuligula* (Jan. av. 6128; max. 21,350).

006 Lac de Neuchâtel: Colombier – Canal de la Thielle (Neuchâtel)

47°00'N, 06°56'E 480 ha

Includes some Landscape Protection Areas

The lake bottom consists of sand or gravel, and the shoreline is covered with buildings, streets and the harbour of Neuchâtel. Considerable amounts of earth are being deposited. Remaining parts of natural shore vegetation can still be found between the campsite of Colombier and the harbour of Auvernier, and near Champréveyres (Hauterive). An extensive swamp-forest covers the area between the harbour of St Blaise and the campsite at La Tène (Marin) at the mouth of the Zihlkana.

An important site for wintering diving ducks: *Aythya ferina* (Jan. av. 979; max. 2259) and *A. fuligula* (Jan. av. 12,109; max. 41,525). Regularly supports 10,000+ waterfowl (Jan. max. *c.*50,000).

007 Lac de Neuchâtel: Fanel and Chablais de Cudrefin (Bern, Neuchâtel, Vaud)

46°59'N, 07°03'E 1155 ha Ramsar Site (Fanel Bay and Le Chablais)

Cantonal Nature Reserve

The Ramsar Site comprises 630 ha of lake surface, 125 ha of reedbed and marshland, 325 ha of woodland, and 75 ha of meadows. The lake area is eutrophic and maintained at a fairly constant level. There are two artificial islands of 120 m length and 40 m width, which are important nesting sites for birds. They were constructed to compensate for the damage caused by a water-level change. The extensive reedbeds are fringed by deciduous woodland. The extensive marsh vegetation comprises bog-rush *Schoenus* sp., moorgrass *Molina* sp., Marsh Helleborine *Epipactis palustris*, and the marsh gentian *Gentiana pneumonanthe*; also supports an interesting and varied insect population.

An important wintering site for diving ducks: *Aythya ferina* (Jan. av. 775; max. 5050) and *A. fuligula* (Jan. av. 6935; max. 20,000); regularly 10,000+ wintering waterfowl. This site also has a high diversity of rare habitats which function as breeding and wintering sites for many bird species.

008 Lac de Neuchâtel: Estavayer – Yvonand (Fribourg, Vaud)

46°50'N, 06°47'E 315 ha

Large Nature Reserve with a no-hunting area for birds (hunting of mammals allowed)

Mostly a natural lake margin with extensive reedbeds and meadows. There are some weekend cottage areas near Estavayer, Font, and Cheyres.

An important wintering site for diving ducks: *Aythya ferina* (Jan. av. 350; max. 724) and *A. fuligula* (Jan. av. 3868; max. 11,800).

009 Lac Léman: St Gingolph – Rivaz (Valais, Vaud)

46°26'N, 06°52'E 830 ha

Includes Nature Reserves with some small no-hunting areas

The shoreline of Lake Geneva (Lac Léman) from St Gingolph to Bouveret, adjacent to the Rhone delta (Villeneuve) with several canals, oxbow lakes, and a natural lake shore with reedbeds. From Villeneuve to Rivaz the shore is a rather artificial cliff with many buildings. There are some bays and deep-water areas (max. 70 m), with a stony lake bottom.

An important wintering site for diving ducks due to the appearance of *Dreissena polymorpha* in 1962: *Aythya ferina* (Jan. av. 680; max. 1375), *A. fuligula* (Jan. av. 5593; max. 12,210), and *Bucephala clangula* (Jan. av. 112; max. 141); regularly 10,000+ wintering waterfowl. Also significant as a moulting site for ducks, stop-over site for migrating waders and breeding site in general.

010 Lac Léman: Rolle – Céligny (Vaud, Genève)

46°24'N, 06°16'E 510 ha

No hunting over most of the area

Partly a very quiet and natural lake margin with narrow sandy beaches (Fleur d'Eau – Pointe de Promenthoux). Other parts are densely populated (city of Nyon) and there are some negative effects as a consequence of the considerable volume of boat traffic.

An important wintering site for diving ducks, although the numbers have declined in the last decade: *Aythya ferina* (Jan. av. 1244; max. 4872), *A. fuligula* (Jan. av. 3904; max. 9743), and *Bucephala clangula* (Jan. av. 955; max. 1457).

011 Lac Léman: Versoix – Genève (Genève)

46°14'N, 06°10'E 210 ha

Hunting totally prohibited

A considerably built-up area; the depth of the freshwater lake varies considerably and its bottom consists of gravel or rock. There are disturbances as a result of boating and wind-surfing.

An important wintering site for diving ducks especially because of the prohibition of hunting: *Netta rufina* (Jan. av. 15; max. 58), *Aythya ferina* (Jan. av. 4663; max. 8517) and *Bucephala clangula* (Jan. av. 318; max. 593). Regularly supports 10,000+ wintering waterfowl (max. *c.*20,000).

012 Rhône: Genève – Barrage de Verbois (Genève)

46°12'N, 06°04'E 180 ha

Hunting totally prohibited

The controlled outflow of the River Rhone (total stretch of river: 12 km) from Lac Léman. Along the upper 8.5 km the river flows through a valley with steep forested slopes and through the city of Genève. The lower 3.5 km are dammed producing a lake up to 350 m wide and max. 22.5 m deep with small reedbeds along part of the shoreline. The water-level occasionally fluctuates up to 1.55 m. Only a few disturbances occur.

An important wintering site for diving ducks entirely due to the prohibition of hunting: *Aythya ferina* (Jan. av. 2258; max. 5278) and *A. fuligula* (Jan. av. 6240; max. 12,178). Regularly supports 10,000+ waterfowl (max. 16,000).

013 Lago Maggiore: Bolle di Magadino (Ticino)

46°10'N, 08°52'E 661 ha Ramsar Site

Undisturbed virgin water's-edge and reedbed vegetation along the shores of Lago Maggiore with a wide variety of marsh and aquatic plant associations. It is an important ornithological site for migrant and nesting reed and wetland species. The lake provides a favourable environment for breeding amphibians and fish populations. The area is one of the few intact river deltas in Switzerland. Vegetation includes a number of plant species unique in Switzerland.

Some threatened bird species are known to breed.

MAIN REFERENCES

Atkinson-Willes, G. L. (1976) The numerical distribution of ducks, swans and coots as a guide in assessing the importance of wetlands in midwinter. *Proc. Int. Conf. Conserv. Wetlands and Waterfowl, Heiligenhafen 1974*: 199-254.

Biber, O. (1984) Bestandesaufnahmen von elf gefährdeten Vogelarten in der Schweiz. *Orn. Beob.* 81: 1-28.

Bossert, A. (1988) Die Reservate der Ala. *Orn. Beob.* Beih. 7.

Bruderer, B. and Thönen, W. (1977) *Rote Liste der gefährdeten und seltenen Vogelarten der Schweiz.* Schweizerisches Landeskomitee für Vogelschutz (SLKV)/Schweizerische Vogelwarte Sempach.

Burckhardt, D. (1986) Wild, Wald und Mensch. *Schweizer Naturschutz*, Sonderheft 3/1986, Basel.

Fuchs, E. (1970) Bestand, Biotop und Verbreitung des Rotmilans *Milvus milvus* in der Schweiz. *Orn. Beob.* 67: 221-230.

Géroudet, P. (1987) *Les oiseaux du Lac Léman.* Neuchâtel.

Glutz von Blotzheim, U. N. (1962) *Die Brutvögel der Schweiz.* Aargauer Tagblatt, Aarau.

Glutz von Blotzheim, U. N., Bauer, K. M. and Bezzel, E. (1971) *Handbuch der Vögel Mitteleuropas*, Band 4. Akademische Verlagsgesellschaft, Frankfurt a.M.

Glutz von Blotzheim, U.N., Bauer, K. M. and Bezzel, E. (1973) *Handbuch der Vögel Mitteleuropas*, Band 5. Akademische Verlagsgesellschaft, Frankfurt a.M.

Glutz von Blotzheim, U.N. and Bauer, K. M. (1980) *Handbuch der Vögel Mitteleuropas*, Band 9. Akademische Verlagsgesellschaft, Wiesbaden.

Juillard, M. (1977) Répartition et densité de la population des Milans royaux *Milvus milvus* (L.) dans le Jura septentrional. *Actes de la Société Jurassienne d'Emulation* 80: 259-263.

Leuzinger, H. (1976) Inventar der Schweizer Wasservogelgebiete von internationaler und nationaler Bedeutung. *Orn. Beob.* 73: 147-194.

Marti, C. (1986) Verbreitung und Bestand des Auerhuhns *Tetrao urogallus* in der Schweiz. *Orn. Beob.* 83: 67-70.

Marti, C. (1987) *Schweizer Wasservogelgebiete von internationaler Bedeutung.* Schweizerische Vogelwarte, Sempach.

Marti, C. and Schifferli, L. (1987) Inventar der Schweizer Wasservogelgebiete von internationaler Bedeutung – Erste Revision 1986. *Orn. Beob.* 84: 11-48.

Maurizio, R. (1987) Beobachtungen am Halsbandschnäpper *Ficedula albicollis* im Bergell, Südostschweiz. *Orn. Beob.* 84: 207-217.

Mosimann, P. and Juillard, M. (1988) Brutbestand und Winterverbreitung des Rotmilans *Milvus milvus* in der Schweiz. *Orn. Beob.* 85: 199-208.

Müller, W. and Pfister, H. P. (1982) *Vogelschutz in der Schweiz.* Schweizerisches Landeskomitee für Vogelschutz.

Pfister, H. P., Zbinden, N. and Marti, C. (1987) *Lebensraum für unsere Vögel.* Schweizerische Vogelwarte, Sempach.

Schifferli, A., Géroudet, P. and Winkler, R. (1980) *Verbreitungsatlas der Brutvögel der Schweiz.* Schweizerische Vogelwarte, Sempach.

Schuster, S. *et. al.* (1983) *Die Vögel des Bodenseegebietes.* Orn. Arbgem. Bodensee, Konstanz.

Szijj, J. (1972) Some suggested criteria for determining the international importance of wetlands in the Western Palearctic. *Proc. Int. Conf. Wetlands and Waterfowl,* Ramsar 1971: 111-124.

Winkler, R. (1984) Avifauna der Schweiz, eine kommentierte Artenliste. I. Passeriformes. *Orn. Beob.* Beih. 5

Winkler, R., Luder, R. and Mosimann, P. (1987) Avifauna der Schweiz, eine kommentierte Artenliste. II. Non-Passeriformes. *Orn. Beob.* Beih. 6.

Zbinden, N., Imhof, T. and Pfister, H. P. (1987) *Ornithologische Merkblätter für die Raumplanung.* Schweizerische Vogelwarte, Sempach.

TURKEY

White-headed Duck *Oxyura leucocephala*

INTRODUCTION

General information

Turkey covers an area of 779,452 sq km, of which 23,764 sq km are in continental Europe (Trakya or Thrace) and 755,855 sq km are in the Middle East or Asia Minor (Anadolu or Anatolia). It is the largest country in the region covered by this project apart from the USSR, being a third larger than either Spain or France. It shares extensive borders with three countries outside the region: Syria, Iraq, and Iran. The human population is 48 million, with large parts of the country very sparsely populated. Agricultural land covers 36 per cent of the country, meadows and grasslands cover 28 per cent, and forests cover 26 per cent (of which over half is unproductive forest). The country can be divided into seven natural regions with distinct geological, climatic, and faunistic characteristics (Erol 1982).

The Marmara region comprises the parts of Turkey in continental Europe as well as the area south of the Sea of Marmara (Marmara Denizi). *Quercus pubescens*, now much degraded, is the climax vegetation in Thrace. This has largely been replaced by steppe which is now almost completely cultivated. In the Black Sea coastal zone and along the southern coast of the Sea of Marmara, there are forests of *Quercus*, *Fagus*, and *Abies*. The region includes the flood-plain and delta of the Meriç and the lakes of Manyas and Apolyont.

The Aegean region includes the western end of the Toros Dağları (Taurus Mountains), with a few peaks which rise above 2000 m, and the meandering river valleys of the Gediz and Büyük Menderes. The vegetation is predominantly maquis. The coastline is irregular with many coastal promontories and islands (some adjacent to the Aegean Islands of Greece).

The Mediterranean region is dominated by the Taurus Mountains, which reach an altitude of 3734 m in the Ala Dağlar and 3585 m in the Bolkar Dağları. The main vegetation consists of *Pinus nigra pallasiana* on the northern side, and *Pinus brutia* and *Quercus coccifera* on the southern side, below 1700 m; *Cedrus libani* and *Abies cilicica* between 1700 and 2200 m; and *Juniperus* between 2200 m and the treeline. The Mediterranean region includes the comparatively recently formed deltas of the Rivers Seyhan, Ceyhan, and Göksu, as well as the south-western part of the Anatolian 'lake district' including Burdur Gölü and Eğirdir Gölü. There are very few coastal islands.

The Black Sea region is dominated by the Kuzeydoğu Karadeniz Dağları (Pontic Mountains), which run almost parallel (and close) to the coast and form a climatic barrier, rising to many points over 3000 m; with high levels of precipitation on the northern side and low levels on the southern side. There are almost no islands offshore. There is a strip of maquis along the coast, with deciduous forests of *Castanea sativa*, *Carpinus orientalis*, and *C. betulus* at lower altitudes, and *Pinus nigra*, *P. sylvestris*, *Picea orientalis*, *Fagus orientalis*, and *Abies nordmanni* at higher altitudes. Turkey's productive forests (for their timber) are located mainly in this region. Open areas, including those above the treeline, are usually covered with *Rhododendron* scrub. Tea and hazelnuts are typical crops. The region includes the large deltas of the Kızılırmak and Yeşilırmak (the latter is intensively cultivated and has lost much of its importance) which comprise, along with the lower valley of the Fılyos, the only extensive coastal plains along the north coast.

The Inner Anatolian region has a mountainous landscape with many plateaux. Due to overgrazing and human exploitation the native plant cover has suffered extensive damage, and the forests have been entirely lost (although there has been some reafforestation). A greater part of the region is covered by steppe, much of which has been converted into agricultural land (mainly wheat). There are many important wetlands (some of which are surrounded by large areas of steppe), which include Tuz Gölü (a large, in many places inaccessible, salt lake), Ereğli sazlığı and Sultansazlığı.

The East Anatolian region is highly mountainous (reaching 5122 m in Ağrı Dağı or Mount Ararat) intersected with plains and deep valleys. The great differences in altitude result in a richly structured vegetation. There are many wetlands around the large soda lake, Van Gölü, which are comparatively untouched by drainage programmes.

The South-eastern Anatolian region is a low plateau to the south of the eastern Taurus Mountains. Human activities have removed the forests and turned them into vast steppes, large parts of which are now cultivated. The region is hot and dry and lies on the edge of the Syrian Desert. The region is divided by the River Fırat (Euphrates).

Many of Turkey's wetlands have been altered by drainage/irrigation programmes. Large parts of the major deltas (Büyük Menderes, Seyhan, Ceyhan, Kızılırmak, and Yeşilırmak) have been converted to agricultural land, as have parts of many of the important inland wetlands, such as Sultansazlığı. Furthermore, some sites have been completely drained, such as Amik Gölü (which was once one of the most important wetlands in Turkey with breeding *Anhinga melanogaster*, *Pelecanus onocrotalus*, and *Porphyrio porphyrio*), Karagöl, Avlan Gölü, Suğla Gölü, and the Alanya wetlands.

Ornithological importance

Turkey is amongst the richest countries in Europe for birds, because of its geographical position, situated at the junction of the Asian, European, and African continents, and its considerable diversity of habitats.

The wetlands of Turkey are of global importance for *Phalacrocorax pygmeus*, *Pelecanus crispus* (at least five breeding sites; very important numbers occurring in winter), *Marmaronetta angustirostris*, and *Oxyura leucocephala* (180+ pairs; max. 8990 at Burdur Gölü in winter, the largest wintering concentration in the world). Turkey has the largest breeding populations of these two Anatidae in Europe. Other wetland species which are threatened in a European context and have significant breeding populations in

Turkey include several species of Ardeidae, *Plegadis falcinellus*, *Platalea leucorodia*, *Phoenicopterus ruber* (max. 5000 pairs in 1970 at Tuz Gölü), *Tadorna ferruginea*, *Porphyrio porphyrio* (20+ pairs), *Recurvirostra avosetta*, *Glareola pratincola*, *Hoplopterus spinosus*, *Larus genei*, *Gelochelidon nilotica*, *Sterna caspia*, *S. albifrons*, *Halcyon smyrnensis*, and *Ceryle rudis* – the last two kingfishers occur nowhere else in Europe and are at the north-westernmost limits of their ranges.

Huge concentrations of waterfowl occur on passage and in winter, including particularly large numbers of *Podiceps nigricollis*, *Anser albifrons*, *A. anser*, *Tadorna ferruginea*, *Anas crecca*, *A. acuta*, *A. clypeata*, *Aythya ferina*, and *Fulica atra*.

Turkey lies on the migration route for many species, but particularly for the large soaring birds, such as pelicans, storks, and numerous species of Accipitridae, with most birds bound for wintering quarters in Africa. Three major bottleneck areas have been studied: Bosphorus, Borçka-Arhavi, and Belen Geçidi. Migratory species recorded on autumn passage include *Ciconia ciconia* (315,000) at the Bosphorus, and 380,000 raptors including *Pernis apivorus* (138,000) and *Buteo buteo* (205,000) at Borçka-Arhavi. Turkey's breeding populations of a number of raptors are of European importance, for example *Gypaetus barbatus*, *Neophron percnopterus*, *Gyps fulvus*, *Aegypius monachus*, *Buteo rufinus*, *Aquila heliaca*, *Falco naumanni*, and *F. cherrug*.

Other non-passerines which have significant breeding populations in a European context include *Ciconia ciconia*, *Grus grus*, *Anthropoides virgo*, *Otis tarda*, *Tetraogallus caspius*, *Francolinus francolinus*, *Charadrius leschenaultii*, and *Pterocles orientalis*. Furthermore, Turkey has the only European breeding population (although now very small) of the globally endangered *Geronticus eremita*, which breeds elsewhere only in Morocco.

Of the passerines, a number of species which are threatened in many parts of Europe are amongst the commonest species in Turkey, notably *Melanocorypha calandra*, *Calandrella brachydactyla*, and *C. rufescens*, and the country has good populations of other such species, notably *Lullula arborea*, *Lanius collurio*, and *L. minor*. Although the country has no endemic birds (*Emberiza cineracea* is nearly so), a number of species with restricted global ranges have a major part of their range in Turkey, including *Prunella ocularis*, *Irania gutturalis*, *Hippolais olivetorum*, *Sylvia rueppelli*, *Sitta krueperi*, *Lanius nubicus*, and *Emberiza cineracea*.

Conservation infrastructure and protected-area system

Responsibility for the management of the main protected areas in the country lies with the Ministry of Agriculture, Forestry and Rural Affairs. The principles governing the selection and designation of protected areas were set out in the National Park Law (No. 2873), which was enacted in 1983 and defined the four main types of protected areas: National Park (Milli Parkı), Nature Park (Tabiat Parkı), Natural Monument (Tabiat Anıtı), and Nature Reserve (Tabiatı Koruma Alanı).

1. NATIONAL PARK

   A National Park is principally an area of state-owned land of at least 500 ha (although Bandırma-Kuş Cenneti National Park only covers 64 ha) in which wood-gathering, timber-cutting, mining, and hunting are prohibited. They are areas which are considered to be of national and international importance for science, education, and recreation, and also aesthetically. Parts of a National Park are protected against all usage except scientific research. Current management of the parks has tended to be biased towards the development of tourism. There are currently 19 National Parks covering almost 285,100 ha.

2. NATURE PARK

   A Nature Park is a natural area containing characteristic vegetation and wildlife that is also suitable for recreational activities. By 1987, two sites had been designated.

3. NATURAL MONUMENT

   A Natural Monument is a natural area of scientific value and should be protected in the same way as National Parks. No sites appear to have been designated under this category.

4. Nature Reserve
   A Nature Reserve is a natural area (which holds a threatened ecosystem or species or is an outstanding natural landscape or geological feature) which should only be used for scientific and educational purposes. By September 1988, 80 sites had been listed for designation. Of these 16 had been established, five had been designated, and a further two were in the process of being approved by the Ministry.

In addition, National Forests are established partly to preserve nature, and the Central Hunting Commission can establish areas in which hunting is forbidden (which has to be renewed for every site each year). The latter category provides no habitat protection, but some sites are wardened. There are currently 107 hunting reserves, of which 13 relate to important bird areas. Three sites in this inventory (Burdur Gölü, Eber Gölü, and Karamik Sazlığı) have lost their status as hunting reserves in recent years.

Regional hunting commissions can also forbid hunting in an area for a maximum of two years: Manyas Gölü and the Göksu Delta are currently protected in this way, although hunting at Göksu has been allowed for the 1988-89 winter.

International measures relevant to the conservation of sites

Turkey is a party to the World Heritage Convention, Bern Convention, and Barcelona Convention (and has ratified the Protocol concerning Mediterranean Specially Protected Areas). To date it has designated a single natural World Heritage Site, and three Mediterranean Specially Protected Areas.

Overview of the inventory

A total of 79 sites are included in this inventory covering an area of over 1,500,000 ha (excluding the Bosphorus and Belen Geçidi). Of these sites, three are bottleneck sites for soaring migratory birds, eight are mountain or forest areas, five are rocky islands (four coastal), and one is an area of steppe and dry agricultural land. The remaining 62 sites are wetlands.

Fifteen of the sites receive protection (or are at least partly or temporarily protected) from hunting. Six sites are (or are covered at least partly by) National Parks. A total of 50 sites are totally without protection.

Wetlands and the waterfowl species mentioned above are covered very well by the sites in this inventory, although important areas of flood-meadow along the rivers in the Eastern Anatolian region have been more difficult to select, and only a few such sites have been included.

Only one steppe site has been included, although some important areas of steppe have been included as part of a number of wetland sites, such as Akşehir and Eber Gölü, Tuz Gölü, Kulu Gölü, Seyfe Gölü, Hotamış Gölü, Ereğli Sazlığı, and Sultansazlığı.

Mountain and forest sites are also poorly represented and certain bird species (e.g. raptors) are poorly covered by this inventory. Several sites have been included as examples – these tend to be more easily accessible and therefore their ornithological importance is better known.

Acknowledgements

The following accounts were compiled by M. Kasparek, A. Kiliç-Kasparek, and A. Ertan (Doğal Hayati Koruma Derneği); their review was made possible by financial support from the World Wide Fund for Nature, Ornithological Society of the Middle East, and Royal Society for the Protection of Birds (Bedford Members Group). C. Bilgin provided some useful comments on a draft of the inventory. M. Kasparek, A. Kiliç-Kasparek and Doğal Hayati Koruma Derneği provided material for the introduction.

INVENTORY

No.	Site name	Region	Criteria used to select site [see p.18] 0	1(i)	1(ii)	1(iii)	1(iv)	2	3	4
001	Apolyont Gölü (Uluabat or Ulubat Gölü)	BA				*		*	*	
002	Büyük Çekmece Gölü	IL				*			*	
003	Bosphorus	IL					*			
004	İznik Gölü	BA	*							
005	Kocaçay Deltası (Kocasu Deltası or Nilüfer Deltası)	BA				*		*	*	
006	Manyas Gölü (Kuş Gölü) including Bandırma – Kuş Cenneti Milli Parki	BR				*		*	*	
007	Saros Körfezi (Kavak Deltası)	CE				*			*	
008	Meriç Deltası	EE				*		*	*	
009	Terkos Gölü (Durusu Gölü or Durugöl)	IL							*	
010	Uludağ	BA							*	
011	Çam Burnu	OU							*	
012	Ilgaz Dağları	CI,KU						*		
013	Kaçkar Dağları	AT,EM,RE						*	*	
014	Kızılcahamam including Soğuksu National Park	AA						*	*	
015	Kızılırmak Deltası	SN				*		*	*	
016	North-east Turkey	AT,RE					*			
017	Yeniçağa Gölü	BU						*	*	
018	Yeşilırmak Deltası	SN							*	
019	Akşehir Gölü	KA,AF				*		*	*	
020	Bolluk Gölü (Bulak Gölü)	KA			*	*			*	
021	Çavuşçu Gölü	KA				*		*	*	
022	Eber Gölü	AF				*		*		
023	Ereğli Sazlığı	KA				*		*	*	
024	Hotamış Sazlığı including Bataklık Gölü	KA				*		*	*	
025	Karapınar Ovası	KA				*		*	*	
026	Krater Gölü and Meketuzlası	KA	*							
027	Kulu Gölü (Küçük Göl or Düden Gölü)	KA			*	*		*	*	
028	Mogan Gölü (Gölbaşı Gölü or Gökçe Gölü)	AA	*							
029	Seyfe Gölü	KR			*	*		*	*	
030	Sultansazlığı (Sultan Marshes)	KI			*	*		*	*	
031	Tödürge Gölü (Demiryurt Gölü)	SS						*	*	
032	Tuz Gölü	AY,AA,KA				*		*	*	
033	Tuzla Gölü	KI							*	
034	Bafa Gölü	AD,MA				*		*	*	
035	Büyük Menderes Deltası	AD				*		*	*	
036	Çamaltı Tuzlası	IR				*		*	*	
037	Güllük Bataklığı (Güllük Marshes)	MA							*	
038	Işıklı Gölü (Çivril Gölü)	DI				*		*	*	
039	Karamık Bataklığı (Karamık Marshes)	AF				*		*	*	
040	Küçük Menderes Deltası	IR							*	
041	Marmara Gölü	MS				*		*	*	
042	Samsun Dağı	AD							*	
043	Acıgöl (Acıtuz Gölü, Tuz Gölü or Çardak Gölü) and Çaltı Gölü	AF,DI				*		*	*	
044	Aksaz Adası	MI							*	
045	Aladağlar (including Demirkazık Tepesi and Karanfil Dağı)	AN,NE							*	
046	Beyşehir Gölü	KA,IA				*		*	*	

No.	Site name	Region	Criteria used to select site [see p.18] 0	1(i)	1(ii)	1(iii)	1(iv)	2	3	4
047	Burdur Gölü	BD,IA				*		*	*	
048	Büyük and Küçük Ada	MI						*		
049	Çorak Gölü (Akgöl or Bayındır Gölü)	BD				*		*		
050	Çukurova including Ceyhan, Seyhan and Tarsus Deltas	AN,MI				*		*	*	
051	Eğirdir Gölü and Hoyran Gölü	IA				*		*	*	
052	Göksu Deltası including Paradeniz Gölü and Akgöl	MI				*		*	*	
053	Karataş Gölü	BD				*		*	*	
054	Kovada Gölü	IA	*							
055	Köyceğiz Gölü including Dalyan Deltası, Sülüngür Gölü and İztuzu Gölü	ML							*	
056	Salda Gölü (Yeşilova Gölü)	BD							*	
057	Yarışlı Gölü	BD				*		*		
058	Yılanlı Ada	MI							*	
059	Belen Geçidi (Topboğazı Geçidi)	HY					*			
060	Ceylanpınar	UA,MN						*	*	
061	Fırat (Euphrates) at Birecik	UA						*		
062	Fırat (Euphrates) at Kargamış	UA				*		*	*	
063	Fırat (Euphrates) at Rumkale	GP,UA							*	
064	Ağrı Ovası	AI							*	
065	Ahtamar Adası	VN	*							
066	Balık Gölü	AI	*							
067	Bendimahi Deltası	VN				*		*	*	
068	Çaldıran Sazlığı	VN				*		*		
069	Çelebibağ Sazlığı	VN				*		*	*	
070	Edremit Sazlığı	VN				*		*		
071	Erçek Gölü	VN				*		*	*	
072	Horkum Gölü	VN				*		*		
073	Upper Murat Vadisi near Yoncalı	MU			*	*		*	*	
074	Nemrut Dağı	BS	*							
075	Saz Gölü (Doğubayazıt Sazlığı)	AI							*	
076	Sodalı Göl (Arın Gölü)	BS				*		*	*	
077	Van Sazlığı (marshes near Van Kalesi or Van İskelesi or Van Lagoon)	VN				*		*		
078	Yüksekova	HI						*	*	
079	Sarikum Gölü	SP				*				

BA=Bursa IL=İstanbul BR=Balıkesır CE=Çanakkale EE=Edirne OU=Ordu
CI=Çankırı KU=Kastamonu AT=Artvin EM=Erzurum RE=Rize AA=Ankara
SN=Samsun BU=Bolu KA=Konya AF=Afyon KR=Kırşehir KI=Kayseri
SS=Sivas AY=Aksaray AD=Aydın IR=İzmir MA=Muğla DI=Denizli
MS=Manisa MI=Mersin (İçel) AN=Adana NE=Niğde IA=Isparta
HY=Hatay UA=Urfa MN=Mardin GP=Gaziantep AI=Ağrı VN=Van
BD=Burdur MU=Muş BS=Bitlis HI=Hakkari SP=Sinop

Comments on the inventory

1. Information has been extracted from numerous published and unpublished reports held by the compilers (M. Kasparek, A. Kiliç-Kasparek, and A. Ertan). Figures for breeding birds are either the most recent (for some sites only) estimates, or where old information is included a year is given. Figures for passage and wintering birds generally refer to maximum counts.

2. The area (ha) given for some of the wetland sites refers only to the lake, and any protected area would need to be expanded to include surrounding habitat where it is of ornithological importance.
3. There are certain to be a large number of other important bird areas; only those sites that are known to be important, because of recent surveys, have been included in this inventory. Many additional sites are thought likely to support important bird populations such as Sultan Dağı (Afyon), Beynam Ormanı (Ankara), Eften Gölü (Bolu), Aladağ Yaylası (Bolu), Amik Orası (Hatay), and Sarıkum Gölü (Sinop).
4. The presence of a breeding pair of *Falco cherrug* at one site has been kept confidential.
5. The site name is generally given in Turkish, and is usually followed by an alternative Turkish name in parentheses. The name of the province is given in parentheses following the site name.
6. The whole of Turkey has been treated as a single 'region' when applying the site-selection criteria (category 3). The application of the criteria is provisional only. A substantial majority of the sites are believed to meet the criteria. The following sites have been included for other reasons (column 0):
   - 004 has been included, despite the paucity of recent data, because of its former importance and the lack of recent surveys.
   - 026, 028 and 054 almost certainly do not meet the criteria, but each site supports an interesting variety of species which are threatened in a European context.
   - 065 has been included because of its breeding population of *Larus argentatus armenicus*.
   - 066 and 074 have been included because of their breeding populations of *Melanitta fuscus*, which are of considerable biogeographical interest.

Glossary

The following Turkish words have been used in inventory: ada = island; adalar = islands; batuklığı = marshes; cayı/deresi = river; dağ/dağı and dağlar/dağları = mountain(s); deltası = delta; geçidi = pass; göl and gölü = lake; körfezi = gulf or bay; nehri = river; ova/ovasi = plain; sazlığı = marshes; vadisi = valley; and yarımadası = peninsula.

---

001 Apolyont Gölü (Uluabat or Ulubat Gölü) (Bursa)

40°12'N, 28°40'E 13,400 ha

Unprotected; although studies have been started by the National Parks Department to establish a protected area

A large lake, with several small islands, fed by the Mustafakemalpaşsa River and with an outflow connected to the Sea of Marmara (Marmara Denizi) via the Kocaçay. The water-level of the lake can be regulated by sluices at the outflow. The south-western side has large wet meadows, reedbeds, and beds of water-lilies. The other shores are surrounded by agricultural land, with some marsh vegetation in a few places. Along the River Mustafakemalpasşa and around its mouth there are extensive areas of *Tamarix*. Apolyont Gölü was rich in crayfish *Astacus leptodactylus*, which have recently disappeared, probably because of pollution. Hunting pressure is extremely high.

Breeding species include *Podiceps cristatus* (30+ pairs), *Ixobrychus minutus*, *Nycticorax nycticorax*, *Ardeola ralloides*, *Egretta garzetta*, *Ardea purpurea*, *Anser anser*, *Circus aeruginosus*, *C. pygargus*, *Glareola pratincola*, *Hoplopterus spinosus* (55 pairs), *Chlidonias hybridus* (150 pairs) and *C. niger* (100 pairs). *Phalacrocorax pygmeus*, *Plegadis falcinellus*, *Platalea leucorodia*, and *Aquila pomarina* possibly breed. During winter, large numbers of waterfowl occur, notably *Podiceps cristatus* (max. 2780),

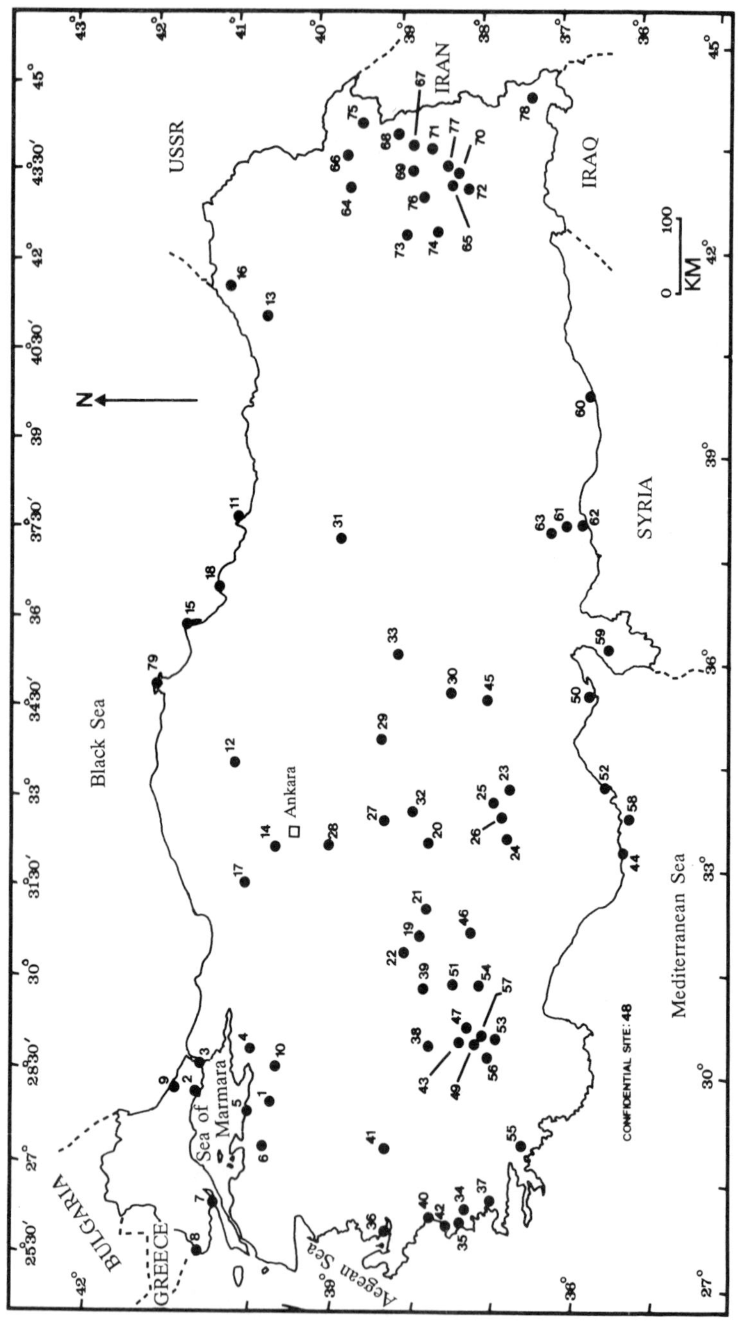

Figure 35: *Map showing the location of the sites in Turkey*

Phalacrocorax pygmeus (max. 840), *Pelecanus onocrotalus* (max. 1310), *P. crispus* (max. 35), *Anas acuta* (max. 1000), *Aythya ferina* (max. 20,100), *A. fuligula* (max. 2190), and *Fulica atra* (max. 5800).

002 Büyük Çekmece Gölü (İstanbul)

41°02'N, 28°32'E 1100 ha

Unprotected

A slightly saline lagoon connected to the Sea of Marmara, with reedbeds along the northern and western edge. Much of the lake is surrounded by agricultural fields, industrial areas, and human settlements. The lagoon has been deepened and enlarged to provide drinking water for İstanbul. Hunting pressure is extremely high.

The lake holds large numbers of non-breeding waterfowl including *Podiceps cristatus* (max. 880 in March), *Anser albifrons* (max. 1000 in December), *Anas clypeata* (max. 980 in March), *Aythya ferina* (max. 2800 in Jan.), *A. fuligula* (max. 2350 in March), and *Fulica atra* (max. 24,000 in Oct.). Large numbers of *Larus melanocephalus* (max. 3320) occur in autumn.

003 Bosphorus (İstanbul)

41°00'N, 29°00'E

Unprotected

The Bosphorus is a classic bottleneck area for migrants passing from Europe to the Middle East. Büyük and Küçük Çamlıca (two hills on the Asiatic side of the Bosphorus), Adalar (Prince Islands) in the Sea of Marmara, and Sarıyer (the latter only during spring) are well-known observation points for migration, but principally all of the Bosphorus and its surroundings have to be treated as part of the migration corridor. Studies covering the whole migration season (or even a major part of it) are rare, so that data on phenology and population changes are only badly known. As the Bosphorus area is now more or less covered by the city of İstanbul, hunting is no longer a problem. However, the extreme pollution of the air above İstanbul has probably affected the migration routes. The catching of birds of prey and passerines such as *Carduelis carduelis* is common in the surrounding countryside.

The main migrants are (the figures are the maximum numbers recorded for a single migration period since the beginning of the 1960s): *Ciconia nigra* (7200), *C. ciconia* (315,000), *Pernis apivorus* (25,700), *Milvus migrans* (2600), *Neophron percnopterus* (550), *Circaetus gallicus* (2300), *Accipiter brevipes* (5300), *Aquila pomarina* (18,800), *Hieraaetus pennatus* (520), and an impressive number of other rarer species. Although exact figures are lacking, it has become evident that many species have decreased drastically, especially between 1870 and 1930.

004 İznik Gölü (Bursa)

40°27'N, 29°33'E 30,800 ha

Unprotected

A eutrophic to oligotrophic freshwater lake with gravel and sand shores and many small reedbeds, especially where streams enter the lake. Arable land is the main habitat surrounding the lake with extensive olive-groves along the southern shore. The eastern side of the lake (İznik and its environs) is developing rapidly as a recreation centre for people, especially from İstanbul. On the lake, fishing and hunting are practised. İznik Gölü appears to have declined in importance since the 1950s, although there is a lack of recent information.

Breeding species have included *Phalacrocorax carbo* (hundreds of birds in June 1959, 60-100 pairs in 1963; none in 1967), *Pelecanus crispus* (probably breeding in 1959), *Ixobrychus minutus* (35 pairs in 1966), *Nycticorax nycticorax* (150 pairs in 1959; 40 pairs in 1967), *Ardeola ralloides* (50 pairs in 1959), *Egretta garzetta* (50 pairs in 1959), *Ardea cinerea* (a large colony in 1959; 25-30 pairs in 1967), and *Plegadis falcinellus* (probably

10-15 pairs in 1959). *Ardea purpurea*, *Tadorna ferruginea*, *Netta rufina*, and *Circaetus gallicus* still breed.

005 Kocaçay Deltası (Kocasu Deltası or Nilüfer Deltası) (Bursa)

40°22'N, 28°30'E 10,000 ha

Dalyan Gölü and Poyraz Gölü are protected from hunting

The delta of the Rivers Kocaçay and Nilüfer including Dalyan Gölü and Poyraz Gölü (on the western side), and Arapçiftliği Gölü (on the eastern side). The delta has a considerable variety of habitats, including Mediterranean maquis, deciduous forests (mainly *Populus*, *Quercus*, and *Fraxinus*), pastures, lakes, dunes, coastal areas, and agricultural land. The mixed deciduous and pine forests in the surrounding hills are also a very important habitat. Replacement of natural forests by *Populus* plantations, reed-burning, illegal hunting, and development of tourism are the main conservation problems. Also the extreme pollution of the Sea of Marmara probably has some effect on bird life.

Breeding species include *Himantopus himantopus* (15 pairs), *Tadorna ferruginea*, *Circaetus gallicus*, *Haliaeetus albicilla* (1-2 pairs), *Circus aeruginosus* (several pairs), *Burhinus oedicnemus* (7 pairs), *Glareola pratincola* (30-40 pairs), *Chlidonias hybridus* (12 pairs), *Dendrocopos leucotos*, *Cercotrichas galactotes*, and probably *Gelochelidon nilotica*. *Pelecanus crispus*, *Phalacrocorax carbo*, *P. pygmeus*, *Ixobrychus minutus*, *Ardeola ralloides*, *Egretta garzetta*, *Ciconia nigra*, *Plegadis falcinellus*, *Platalea leucorodia*, and *Pernis apivorus* are regularly seen during the breeding season and some presumably breed. *Pelecanus onocrotalus* occurs on migration (max. 400).

006 Manyas Gölü (Kuş Gölü) including Bandırma – Kuş Cenneti Milli Parki (Balıkesır)

40°10'N, 28°00'E 16,800 ha

European Diploma Site (designated by the Council of Europe)

Bandırma – Kuş Cenneti National Park (64 ha), with a Hunting Reserve as a buffer zone (eastern and north-eastern shore); also hunting is temporarily prohibited over the whole lake

The lake is surrounded by agricultural fields which reach the shore in most places. There is a small wood (mainly *Salix* sp.) at the mouth of the River Sigirci on the eastern shore, and reeds along the southern shore at the mouth of the Kocaçay. The use of water for irrigation (construction of canals), pollution in places (from factories), and illegal hunting (which recent controls have reduced) are serious problems at the lake, and moth larvae of the genus *Hyponomenta* are damaging the nesting trees within the National Park. Bandırma – Kuş Cenneti is Turkey's only ornithological National Park, but comprises less than 0.4 per cent of the whole lake.

The National Park has a mixed colony of *Pelecanus crispus* (max. 30 pairs), *Phalacrocorax carbo* (300 pairs in the 1950s and 1970s; 700 pairs in the 1960s), *P. pygmeus* (100-150 pairs), *Botaurus stellaris* (possibly 1 pair), *Nycticorax nycticorax* (30-500 pairs), *Ardeola ralloides* (100-175 pairs), *Egretta garzetta* (200-350 pairs), *Ardea cinerea* (300-600 pairs), *A. purpurea* (40-55 pairs), *Plegadis falcinellus* (150-300 pairs; 400+ pairs in 1975), and *Platalea leucorodia* (400-835 pairs). Outside Bandırma - Kuş Cenneti, breeding species have included *Circus aeruginosus* (3 pairs), *Burhinus oedicnemus* (4 pairs), *Hoplopterus spinosus* (11 pairs), and *Sterna hirundo* (500 pairs). There seem to be other breeding colonies at the mouth of the Kocaçay, but no detailed information is available. During the migration period, species occurring include *Pelecanus onocrotalus* (max. 3400 in Sept.). The lake has some importance as a wintering area, with *Anas crecca* (max. 3500), *A. platyrhynchos* (max. 42,000 in 1968; although max. 3500 recently), and *A. clypeata* (max. 2500).

007 Saros Körfezi (Kavak Deltası) (Çanakkale)

40°37'N, 26°51'E 300-1000 ha

Unprotected

A small delta of the River Kavak which enters Saros Bay. There is a small lagoon with halophytic vegetation and *Scirpus* beds north of the delta. The marshes are replaced inland by wet meadows and agricultural fields. There is considerable hunting pressure because of its proximity to İstanbul. Grazing of livestock is also a conservation problem.

Breeding species include *Glareola pratincola* (*c.*100 pairs), *Charadrius alexandrinus* (*c.*20 pairs), *Sterna hirundo* (3 pairs), and *S. albifrons* (6 pairs). Counts of waterfowl have included *Tadorna ferruginea* (70 in Jan. 1968), *Anas penelope* (10,200 in Jan. 1968), and *Tringa stagnatilis* (60 in April 1987).

008 Meriç Deltası (Edirne)

40°45'N, 26°08'E 48,000 ha (whole delta including the inundated areas)

Unprotected

The Meriç Delta includes Enez Gölü (Dalyan Gölü) and Gala Gölü (Çeltik Gölü), as well as a number of smaller lakes such as Pamuklu Gölü, Sığırcı Gölü, Domuz Gölü, Küçük Gala Gölü, Hüzmene Gölü, Taşaltı Gölü, and Küçük Göl

The River Meriç forms the border between Greece and Turkey, and large parts of the delta are in Greece (Evros Delta). To the south-east of the river there is a *c.*4000 ha reedbed interspersed with *Salix* and *Tamarix*. There were large gallery forests in the centre and western part of the delta until the 1940s, but these have been reduced considerably in size. The Meriç Delta has lost a good deal of its original character due to intensive agricultural development. In particular its bird life has suffered from the spread of rice cultivation and also from increasing hunting pressure. Gala Gölü is experiencing eutrophication because of the use of fertilisers in the surrounding area.

Species breeding in or near the delta include (or have included) *Pelecanus crispus* (no breeding records since the 1960s), *Phalacrocorax carbo* (140 pairs in 1966; 70-90 pairs in 1967), *P. pygmeus* (probably), *Botaurus stellaris* (probably, although no record since 1973), *Ixobrychus minutus*, *Nycticorax nycticorax* (80-100 pairs in 1967), *Ardeola ralloides* (100 pairs in 1967), *Egretta garzetta* (200-250 pairs in 1967), *Ardea purpurea* (100-120 pairs in the whole delta in 1966-1967), *Plegadis falcinellus* (700-800 pairs in 1967), *Cygnus olor*, *Anser anser*, *Aythya nyroca*, *Haliaeetus albicilla* (12 pairs in the whole delta in 1965), *Aquila heliaca* (probably 1 pair), *A. pomarina*, *Himantopus himantopus* (100 pairs), *Recurvirostra avosetta*, *Chlidonias niger* (10-15 pairs), and *C. hybridus* (150-180 pairs). Winter counts have included *Phalacrocorax pygmeus* (max. 420), *Anser anser* (max. 1565), *Anas crecca* (max. 10,580), *A. platyrhynchos* (max. 11,870), *Aythya ferina* (max. 2950), *Aquila clanga* (max. 10), and *Fulica atra* (max. 81,400).

009 Terkos Gölü (Durusu Gölü or Durugöl) (İstanbul)

41°19'N, 28°32'E 5850 ha

Unprotected

A lake (2500 ha) of low salinity (originally a bay of the Black Sea, now connected only by a small channel) with some reedbeds along the shore. Between the lake and the sea, large dunes with some woodland and scrub cover about 3350 ha. Prevailing winds blow sand into the lake (filling up 75,000-80,000 sq m of the lake each year). The lake provides much of Istanbul's drinking water and efforts to prevent infilling include afforestation of the dunes. Hunting is a great problem for the waterfowl.

Pandion haliaetus, which bred at least in 1984, might still do so. Other species which are presumed to breed include *Botaurus stellaris*, *Ixobrychus minutus*, *Nycticorax nycticorax*, *Ardeola ralloides*, *Ardea purpurea*, *Circus aeruginosus*, *Burhinus oedicnemus*, and *Chlidonias leucopterus*. There is no information on wintering geese and ducks. Situated north-west of the Bosphorus, Terkos Gölü lies on a major migration route for raptors and storks, and thousands of birds pass over twice a year and some stop over to feed.

010 Uludağ (Bursa)

40°04'N, 29°11'E 11,388 ha

National Park

The Uludağ massif represents the highest elevation in western Anatolia (from almost sea-level to over 2500 m). There are four main vegetation belts: Mediterranean maquis including *Olea*, *Laurus* etc; mixed deciduous with *Corylus*, *Quercus*, *Tilia* etc; *Fagus orientalis*; and *Abies bornmuelleriana*; above which lie alpine meadows. The summit is the most important winter-sports centre in Anatolia. Several luxury hotels and other tourist installations (with a bed capacity of 5,000+) are currently being developed, with negative consequences including the complete use of spring water, and litter. Other conservation problems include livestock-grazing and deforestation (to provide ski slopes). Areas important for conservation currently lie outside the National Park. A relict population of the butterfly *Parnassius apollo graslini* is threatened by collectors.

The most outstanding breeding species is *Gypaetus barbatus* (1+ pairs). *Neophron percnopterus*, *Aegypius monachus*, *Circaetus gallicus*, *Accipiter gentilis*, *Aquila pomarina*, *A. chrysaetos*, *Falco peregrinus*, and *Aegolius funereus* (one of the two known sites in Turkey) presumably breed. *Sitta krueperi* and *Serinus pusillus* breed and reach the westernmost limit of their range at Uludağ.

011 Çam Burnu (Ordu)

41°07'N, 37°47'E less than 10 ha

Unprotected

Rocky cliff and small offshore island along the Black Sea coast.

A breeding site for *Phalacrocorax carbo* (20-25 pairs), *P. aristotelis* (2-4 pairs), and *Larus argentatus* (300 pairs in 1973).

012 İlgaz Dağları (Çankırı, Kastamonu)

41°00'N, 33°40'E 25,000+ ha

National Park (1090 ha)

A large mountain ridge which reaches its highest altitude to the north of İlgaz (including Yayla Tepesi, Emirgazi Tepesi, Küçük and Büyük Hacet Tepesi, and Tosya Dağı, which are all mountain peaks). Large areas are covered by *Pinus* and *Abies* forests with dense undergrowth, interspersed with meadows (rich in orchids) and agricultural fields, and there are a number of villages within the area. There is a plan to enlarge the National Park (founded in 1976) to 4600 ha. Several hotels and tourist facilities are under construction or are planned.

The İlgaz Mountains are especially important for raptors, and *Milvus migrans*, *Neophron percnopterus*, *Aegypius monachus*, *Circaetus gallicus*, *Accipiter gentilis*, *Buteo rufinus*, *Aquila chrysaetos*, *Hieraaetus pennatus*, and probably *Gyps fulvus* and *Aquila heliaca* are among the breeding species. Other species of interest occurring are *Tadorna ferruginea*, *Dryocopus martius*, *Anthus campestris*, *Irania gutturalis* (an isolated breeding population), *Sitta krueperi*, and *Serinus pusillus*.

013 Kaçkar Dağları (Artvin, Erzurum, Rize)

40°35'-41°10'E, 40°42'-41°35'E *c.*80,000 ha

Partly a Hunting Reserve

A section of the eastern Black Sea mountain range, which includes the highest mountains of the Kaçkar massif: Demir Dağı (3354 m), Kaçkar Dağı (3932 m), and Gül Dağı (3131 m); geologically and biogeographically linked to the Caucasus in the USSR. There are extensive forests mainly of *Abies nordmanni*, *Picea orientalis*, and *Fagus orientalis*, with large areas of *Rhododendron ponticum* in the forest zone and *R. caucasicum* above the treeline. Above the treeline there are also mountain pastures (which are used by semi-nomadic people) and rubble fields. The area is only thinly populated. The mountains also support populations of Brown Bear *Ursus arctos*, Wild Goat *Capra aegagrus* and Caucasian Chamois *Rupicapra rupicapra*.

These mountains are the only known breeding area for *Tetrao mlokosiewiczi* in Europe outside the USSR. Its occurrence is known from at least two sites, but it is presumably distributed over the whole mountain ridge. Other breeding species include *Gypaetus barbatus*, *Gyps fulvus*, *Neophron percnopterus*, *Accipiter gentilis*, *Aquila chrysaetos*, *Hieraaetus pennatus*, *Tetraogallus caspius*, and *Grus grus* (breeding at 2100 m). *Aegypius monachus* and *Falco peregrinus* are presumed breeders. Other mountain species breeding include *Phylloscopus sindianus lorenzii*, *Sitta krueperi*, *Serinus pusillus*, *Rhodopechys sanguinea* and *Pyrrhocorax pyrrhocorax*.

014 Kızılcahamam including Soğuksu National Park (Ankara)

40°28'N, 32°29'E 1050+ ha

Includes Soğuksu National Park (1050 ha)

Kızılcahamam is a forested hillside mainly consisting of *Pinus nigra* with *Pinus sylvestris* at higher altitudes. Valleys and open areas with scrub provide a diversity of habitats. The geographic situation (between the vast forests of the Black Sea coastlands and the steppes of Central Anatolia) results in an abundance of raptors. The construction of new roads within the National Park (even to hitherto remote places) is causing much disturbance.

Very important for breeding raptors with *Gypaetus barbatus* (1-2 pairs), *Neophron percnopterus* (10-15+ pairs), *Gyps fulvus* (*c*.5 pairs), *Aegypius monachus* (3 pairs), *Circaetus gallicus*, *Buteo rufinus*, *Hieraaetus pennatus*, and *Falco naumanni*. *Ciconia nigra* (5+ pairs), *C. ciconia* (9+ pairs), *Tadorna ferruginea* (a few pairs), *Aegolius funereus* (one of only two known sites in Turkey), *Picus canus*, *Hippolais olivetorum*, and *Sitta krueperi* also breed.

015 Kızılırmak Deltası (Samsun)

41°40'N, 36°00'E 50,000 ha (lakes and marshes: *c*.5000 ha)

Hunting Reserve (Çernek Gölü only); only a rather small and unimportant part of the area is protected from hunting

The largest wetland along the Turkish Black Sea coast. Most of the land is under agricultural use; however, there are several lakes situated along the coast in the eastern delta, the largest of which are Balık Gölü (828 ha), Uzungöl (294 ha), Çernek Gölü (369 ha), and Liman Gölü (175 ha). Balık Gölü and Uzungöl have extensive reedbeds, and vast areas of the delta are covered by almost inaccessible *Scirpus* beds. Between the lakes and the sea, a forest of about 1400 ha provides an excellent breeding habitat, especially for raptors.

Breeding species include *Pelecanus crispus* (25 pairs in 1966, 60-70 pairs in 1970-73; possibly now breeding only irregularly in smaller numbers), *Botaurus stellaris* (2-3+ pairs), *Ixobrychus minutus*, *Ardeola ralloides* (10+ pairs), *Egretta garzetta* (130-150 pairs), *Ciconia nigra* (12-20 pairs), *C. ciconia* (30 pairs), *Haliaeetus albicilla* (2-4 pairs; but probably not breeding since 1977), *Circus aeruginosus* (30+ pairs), *Aquila pomarina* (1 pair presumed), *Pandion haliaetus*, *Falco subbuteo* (12 pairs), *Anas querquedula* (20 pairs), *Aythya nyroca*, *Grus grus* (10-15 pairs), *Himantopus himantopus* (15 pairs), *Burhinus oedicnemus* (8 pairs), *Glareola pratincola*, *Dendrocopos medius*, *Acrocephalus melanopogon*, and *Sylvia nisoria*. During autumn large numbers of *Tringa nebularia* (max. 200) and *Chlidonias leucopterus* (max. 200-300) have been recorded. In winter large numbers of waterfowl occur including *Gavia arctica* (max. 1500, but usually less than 100), *Podiceps nigricollis* (max. 600), *Egretta alba* (max. 100-200), *Anser anser* (max. 5000), *Anas strepera* (max. 740), *A. crecca* (max. 16,750), *A. platyrhynchos* (max. 40,000), *A. acuta* (max. 4360), *A. clypeata* (max. 8000), *Oxyura leucocephala* (max. 59), and *Fulica atra* (max. 15,300). Important also for wintering raptors especially *Aquila clanga* and *Circus aeruginosus* (max. 30-50).

016 North-east Turkey (Artvin, Rize)

41°20'N, 41°30'E *c.*100,000 ha

Unprotected

North-east Turkey, especially the Black Sea coastal region extending from Ardeşen eastwards to the Soviet border, is an area where huge numbers of raptors concentrate on migration. The main area is located on the northern side of the Kuzeydoğu Karadeniz Dağları (Pontic Mountains). The coastal strip is densely populated, with tea, corn, and hazelnuts being the main crops. Further inland the forests (both coniferous and deciduous) dominate and are considered to be amongst the most productive forests of Turkey. In the higher parts, areas with alpine vegetation occur (cf. Kaçkar Dağları as a separate site). Of special importance for migrating raptors is the Çoruh Valley. Several other valleys extend from the Black Sea coast inland and cause considerable convergence of raptors. After raptors have passed the mountain range, the migration front widens.

Falconry, using *Accipiter nisus*, has a long tradition. *Lanius collurio* is caught and serves as a fluttering decoy to attract migrating *Accipiter nisus*, which are subsequently trained to catch migrating *Coturnix coturnix*. Thousands of raptors are trapped and shot annually, half of which are other species of raptor (especially falcons and harriers) which are killed to be fed to the decoy birds.

The most complete count of migrating raptors in 1976 yielded some 380,000 birds, including *Pernis apivorus* (138,000), *Milvus migrans* (5775), *Buteo buteo vulpinus* (205,000), and smaller numbers of *Haliaeetus albicilla*, *Neophron percnopterus*, *Gyps fulvus*, *Circaetus gallicus*, *Circus aeruginosus*, *C. cyaneus*, *C. macrourus*, *Accipiter gentilis*, *A. nisus*, *A. brevipes*, *Buteo rufinus*, *Aquila pomarina*, *A. clanga*, *A. rapax nipalensis*, *A. heliaca*, *A. chrysaetos*, *Hieraaetus pennatus*, *Falco naumanni*, *F. tinnunculus*, *F. vespertinus*, *F. subbuteo*, *F. cherrug*, and *F. peregrinus*. Illustrative of the magnitude of the passage in the region is the staggering total of raptors migrating over Borçka on 28 Sept. 1976, when more than 137,000 were counted. Hardly anything is known about spring migration through the area. Since the best censusing points are not thought to have been evaluated, the actual numbers of migrating raptors may be even higher.

017 Yeniçağa Gölü (Bolu)

40°47'N, 32°02'E 1800 ha

Unprotected

A freshwater lake with reedbeds which are dense in parts but almost absent along the southern shore. There are wet meadows to the east, north, and west of the lake which are flooded when the water-level is high, and *Populus* plantations and *Salix* around the lake. The grazing of cattle in the marshes and pollution from the town of Yeniçaga (which discharges its sewage into the lake) are serious problems.

Breeding species include *Ixobrychus minutus* (1-5 pairs), *Ardea purpurea* (1-5 pairs), *Tadorna ferruginea* (5-10 pairs), *Circus aeruginosus* (1-2 pairs), and *Grus grus* (8 pairs). *Haliaeetus albicilla* and *Pandion haliaetus* presumably breed. During migration, the area is especially important for raptors which use the area for resting and feeding (as it lies on the migration route to and from the Bosphorus); 25 species of raptors have been recorded so far.

018 Yeşilırmak Deltası (Samsun)

41°17'N, 36°50'E 60,000 ha

Hunting Reserve (Simenlik Gölü); a small area is a breeding station for *Phasianus colchicus*

A large alluvial plain of the River Yesilırmak with a series of small lakes and lagoons along the coast. Recently, large parts of the delta have been drained and the lakes have been reduced in size. Simenlik Gölü is the largest of the lakes (about 150 ha), has reedbeds, and is bordered by forest. *Populus* plantations and fields bordered by *Salix* characterise the delta.

A native population of *Phasianus colchicus* has survived in the delta and has been enlarged by releases from a breeding station which is situated in the delta. *Botaurus stellaris*, *Nycticorax nycticorax*, *Ardeola ralloides*, *Egretta garzetta*, *Circus aeruginosus*, *Grus grus*, *Himantopus himantopus*, and *Locustella luscinioides* are presumed to breed. Winter counts (1967-70) have included *Anas penelope* (max. 2200), *A. crecca* (max. 2500), *A. platyrhynchos* (max. 12,000), *A. acuta* (max. 900), and *Aythya fuligula* (max. 2000).

019 Akşehir Gölü (Konya, Afyon)

38°30'N, 31°28'E 35,300 ha

Unprotected

A eutrophic freshwater lake with a shoreline almost completely covered by reedbeds (from 1-8 km in width). The open water is covered by water-lilies. The water-level is subject to considerable long-term fluctuations. Barren hills on the north side, orchards on the southern side, and arable land on the western and eastern side surround the lake. There is pollution from the town of Akşehir (which sends its sewage directly into the lake) and from factories (via Eber Gölü, which has an outflow to Akşehir Gölü) resulting in eutrophication. Hunting is excessive, and reed-cutting (for the paper mill at Çay) is continued into the breeding season and causes much disturbance.

Breeding species include *Podiceps cristatus* (at least 150 pairs), *P. grisegena*, *P. nigricollis*, *Phalacrocorax pygmeus* (7+ pairs), *Botaurus stellaris* (2+ pairs), *Ixobrychus minutus* (probably 100+ pairs), *Nycticorax nycticorax*, *Ardeola ralloides*, *Egretta garzetta*, *E. alba*, *Ardea purpurea*, *Plegadis falcinellus*, *Circus aeruginosus*, *Tringa totanus*, *Gelochelidon nilotica*, *Sterna hirundo* (50+ pairs), *Chlidonias hybridus* (25+ pairs), *C. niger*, and *C. leucopterus*. *Haliaeetus albicilla* formerly bred but is currently only a winter visitor. The lake freezes in most years, and because the open water is difficult to observe there are no reliable waterfowl counts available, although important numbers of *Pelecanus onocrotalus* (max. 900 in Nov.), *Anser albifrons* (max. 29,580 in Jan.), *A. anser* (max. 10,000 in Nov.), and *Anas acuta* (max. 2850 in Jan.) have been recorded.

020 Bolluk Gölü (Bulak Gölü) (Konya)

38°32'N, 32°56'E 1150 ha

Unprotected

A highly saline lake which is rich in sodium phosphate and sodium chloride. Some springs north of the lake provide warm sulphurous water. There is halophytic vegetation (*Salicornia* sp.), and some freshwater marshes develop in winter after heavy rainfall between Ağabeyli and Kırkışla. A sodium-phosphate factory is being built on the northern shore of the lake.

The lake is an important breeding site for waders, gulls and terns with *Haematopus ostralegus* (1 pair presumed), *Recurvirostra avosetta* (30 pairs in 1973; 200 pairs in 1982), *Larus melanocephalus* (50 pairs in 1973; 300 pairs in 1982), *Larus ridibundus* (300 pairs in 1982), *L. genei* (470 pairs in 1973; 100 pairs in 1982), and *Gelochelidon nilotica* (450 pairs in 1973; 250 pairs in 1982). Passage species have included *Pluvialis apricaria* (max. 1000 in March).

021 Çavuşçu Gölü (Konya)

38°21'N, 31°53'E *c.*1000 ha

Unprotected

A shallow freshwater lake fed by the River Battal from the south. Until about 30 years ago, the lake had large reedbeds and a maximum size of 5100 ha. A drainage project significantly reduced the size of the lake and flooded its large reedbeds, and at present the northern and southern shores are embanked and the water of the River Battal is controlled by sluices. Lakeside vegetation is now very sparse, with only a few scattered reedbeds (none of them exceeding 1 ha) and a few *Scirpus* beds. There are practically no trees around the lake and the surrounding area comprises arid, sparsely vegetated hills, except for the south where there is some irrigated arable land (former bed of the lake). There is considerable disturbance from a quarry, which is located on the north-eastern edge of the lake.

The number of breeding birds is low but includes *Podiceps cristatus*, *Ciconia ciconia*, *Tadorna ferruginea*, and *Sterna hirundo*. *Gelochelidon nilotica*, *Chlidonias hybridus*, *C. niger*, and *C. leucopterus* probably breed, and *Otis tarda* has survived in the surrounding area. Visitors include *Podiceps nigricollis* (max. 150), *Egretta garzetta* (max. 300 in Aug.), *Plegadis falcinellus* (max. 250 in Aug.), *Platalea leucorodia* (max. 120 in Aug.), *Anser anser* (max. 300 in Aug.), *Anas crecca* (max. 3090 in Dec.), *A. clypeata* (max. 2570 in Dec.), *Netta rufina* (max. 1610 in Feb.), *Aythya ferina* (max. 3120 in Dec.), *A.fuligula* (max. 5000 in Jan.), *Oxyura leucocephala* (max. 430 in Feb.), *Fulica atra* (max. 70,000 in Jan. 1969; but much lower numbers since), *Calidris minuta* (max. 900 in Aug.), and *Philomachus pugnax* (max. 1100 in April). *Aquila heliaca* and probably *Aegypius monachus* overwinter.

022 Eber Gölü (Afyon)

38°38'N, 31°10'E 5200-17,600 ha

Formerly a Hunting Reserve, now unprotected

A natural freshwater lake, almost entirely overgrown with *Phragmites* and *Typha*, but with a few hundred hectares of open water and numerous channels through the dense vegetation kept open by fishermen. The lake is highly eutrophic, but has a rich aquatic fauna and flora. Fish (mainly Carp *Cyprinus carpio* and Pontian Crayfish *Astacus leptodactylus*) are abundant and are used economically. Eber Gölü has an outflow to Akşehir Gölü, which is 7 km away. The lake is subject to excessive pollution by the paper factory at Çay and sewage from Afyon and Bolvadin. Reed-cutting (reed is used at the paper factory) and hunting are other serious conservation problems.

The lake is almost inaccessible and its ornithological importance is not fully understood. Breeding species (or presumed breeders) include *Phalacrocorax pygmeus*, *Ixobrychus minutus*, *Nycticorax nycticorax*, *Ardeola ralloides*, *Egretta garzetta*, *Ardea purpurea*, *Plegadis falcinellus*, *Anas querquedula*, *A. clypeata*, *Aythya nyroca*, *Oxyura leucocephala*, *Circus aeruginosus*, *Himantopus himantopus*, and *Burhinus oedicnemus*. Wintering waterfowl include *Anser albifrons* (max. 2700), *Anas penelope* (max. 10,000), *A. crecca* (max. 2580), and *A. acuta* (max. 1420), although fewer waterfowl have been recorded in recent years because of a lower water-level. *Aquila clanga* overwinters.

023 Ereğli Sazlığı (Konya)

37°30'N, 33°44'E 5900 ha

Unprotected

Includes Akgöl, which is the western half of the marshes, and Düden Gölü south of the marshes. Until the 1960s the Ereğli Marshes were covered by impenetrable reedbeds with open water in just a few small areas. After canals were constructed to drain water into the marshes, the water-level rose and the dense reedbeds were flooded and new, less thick reedbeds grew. However, as a consequence of recent hydraulic works (mainly the construction of the İvriz Dam) and drought, the water-level has fallen continuously since 1982. At present, the greater part of the lake consists of open water with interspersed reedbeds of varying sizes and a great number of sand and mud islands. The marshes are bordered (except in the south) by huge alluvial plains, partly steppe (*Artemisia* steppe) and partly agricultural land. The huge marshes around Sazgeçidi (Hortu) were drained in the 1960s (one of the reasons for the rise of the water-level at that time). Drainage is the greatest threat to the marshes, and another problem is reed-burning even during the breeding season. Hunters, including foreigners, are present in huge numbers during winter.

The marshes provide a breeding habitat for many threatened species and a recent study (1987) confirmed results from the early 1970s, with *Podiceps cristatus* (60-100 pairs), *P.*

grisegena (1-2 pairs), *P. nigricollis* (50 pairs in 1971), *Phalacrocorax carbo* (30-35 pairs in 1968-73; 2-3 pairs in 1987), *P. pygmeus* (breeding since about 1970 and increasing, with 500-600 pairs in 1987), *Pelecanus crispus* (50-70 pairs 1968-71; 20 pairs 1973; 3 pairs 1987), *Ixobrychus minutus*, *Nycticorax nycticorax* (20 pairs), *Ardeola ralloides* (5-10 pairs), *Egretta garzetta* (35 pairs), *E. alba* (*c*.5 pairs), *Ardea purpurea* (15-20 pairs), *Plegadis falcinellus* (30-40 pairs), *Platalea leucorodia* (200-250 pairs), *Phoenicopterus ruber* (35-40 pairs in 1986), *Cygnus olor* (8-11 pairs), *Anser anser* (25-30 pairs in 1987; 120 in 1970), *Tadorna ferruginea* (20 pairs), *T. tadorna* (less than 10 pairs), *Marmaronetta angustirostris* (2-3 pairs), *Netta rufina* (150+ pairs), *Oxyura leucocephala* (35 pairs), *Neophron percnopterus* (1 pair), *Circaetus gallicus* (1 pair), *Circus aeruginosus* (30 pairs), *Grus grus* (2 pairs), *Himantopus himantopus* (200 pairs), *Recurvirostra avosetta* (300 pairs in 1970; 13 pairs in 1987), *Burhinus oedicnemus* (5-10 pairs), *Glareola pratincola* (20-40 pairs), *Hoplopterus spinosus* (40-100 pairs), *Charadrius leschenaultii* (less than 10 pairs), *Larus genei* (20-100 pairs), *Gelochelidon nilotica* (10-200 pairs), *Sterna albifrons* (10-60 pairs), *Chlidonias hybridus* (40 pairs), and *C. niger*. *Pelecanus onocrotalus* (max. 2000 pairs in the 1960s and 1970s), *Bubulcus ibis* (max. 30 pairs in the 1960s), *Falco cherrug* and *Bubo bubo* have disappeared as breeding species. Passage and wintering waterfowl include *Podiceps cristatus* (max. 260), *Tachybaptus ruficollis* (max. 690), *Egretta alba* (max. 140), *Anser albifrons* (max. 3100), *A. anser* (max. 6000), *Tadorna ferruginea* (max. 8000), *Anas crecca* (max. 17,320), *A.acuta* (max. 3000), *Aythya ferina* (max. 2400), *Oxyura leucocephala* (max. 98), *Fulica atra* (max. 55,000), *Grus grus* (max. 530), *Calidris minuta* (max. 8000), and *Limosa limosa* (max. 2270).

024 Hotamış Sazlığı including Bataklık Gölü (Konya)

37°35'N, 33°03'E 12,600 ha

Unprotected

An extensive freshwater marsh, almost completely overgrown by reeds, *Scirpus*, and *Typha*. A greater part of the marshes has dried up in recent years, with a 20-km-long strip now without water. However, flooded reedbeds are still present principally in the west. The marshes are dependent on an irrigation project which brings water from Beyşehir Gölü (150 km away) to the Konya plain, although the area now receives less water because the irrigation channels have been continued to the north. In addition, drought in recent years has contributed to the drying-up of the marshes.

The area is almost impossible to survey and population estimates are minimum figures only. Breeding species include *Phalacrocorax pygmeus* (2000 birds in July 1981), *Pelecanus onocrotalus*, *P. crispus*, *Botaurus stellaris*, *Ixobrychus minutus*, *Nycticorax nycticorax*, *Ardeola ralloides*, *Egretta garzetta*, *E. alba*, *Ardea purpurea*, *Plegadis falcinellus*, *Platalea leucorodia*, *Anser anser*, *Tadorna ferruginea*, *T. tadorna*, *Anas strepera*, *A. crecca*, *A. acuta*, *A. querquedula*, *Marmaronetta angustirostris* (at least 3-4 pairs), *Netta rufina*, *Aythya nyroca*, *Oxyura leucocephala* (20+ pairs presumed), *Circus aeruginosus*, *C. pygargus*, *Grus grus* (1+ pair), *Himantopus himantopus* (100+ pairs), *Burhinus oedicnemus*, *Glareola pratincola* (30 pairs in 1987), *Charadrius leschenaultii*, *Chettusia leucura*, *Hoplopterus spinosus* (15+ pairs in 1987), *Sterna albifrons*, *Chlidonias hybridus*, *C. leucopterus*, and *Pterocles orientalis*. Large numbers of waterfowl have occurred on passage and in winter (although few in 1986 and 1987 when the water-level was too low), including *Anser albifrons* (max. 27,100), *A. anser* (max. 1500), *Tadorna ferruginea* (max. 1010), *Anas penelope* (max. 5030), *A. strepera* (max. 2490), *A. crecca* (max. *c*.10,000 in 1981), *A. acuta* (max. 3110), *A. clypeata* (max. 1660), *Netta rufina* (max. 790), *Marmaronetta angustirostris* (max. 53), *Fulica atra* (max. 57,140), *Recurvirostra avosetta* (max. 750), *Calidris minuta* (max. 1000), *Philomachus pugnax* (max. 6860 in Feb. 1974), *Limosa limosa* (max. 1200), *Tringa erythropus* (max. 800), and *T. stagnatilis* (max. 54).

025 Karapınar Ovası (Konya)

37°48'N, 33°40'E *c*.19,000 ha: whole plain

Unprotected

Karapınar Ovası is a huge plain with a vegetation-free saltpan at its centre. The water-level is lower than half a metre in winter and the saltpan often dries up in summer. The lake is surrounded by *Salicornia* steppe for some distance, and at a few places fresh water enters and grass and *Scirpus* sp. are found. The adhesive mud makes large parts of the area practically inaccessible.

Phoenicopterus ruber bred at least in 1977 (30-100? pairs) and it is a possible breeding site for *Marmaronetta angustirostris*. Other notable breeding species are *Anser anser* (5-15 pairs), *Tadorna ferruginea* (10+ pairs), *T. tadorna* (less than 10 pairs), *Grus grus* (1-2 pairs), *Himantopus himantopus* (120 pairs in 1971; fewer since), *Recurvirostra avosetta* (200 pairs in 1971; 40 pairs in 1987), *Burhinus oedicnemus*, *Glareola pratincola* (15 pairs), *Charadrius leschenaultii* (less than 10 pairs), *Tringa totanus* (less than 10 pairs), *Larus genei* (1000 pairs in 1971, 700 pairs in 1972; apparently none since), and *Gelochelidon nilotica* (80 pairs in 1971; 5-15 pairs in 1987). Important also for wintering *Anser albifrons* (max. 5100), and for passage *Pelecanus onocrotalus* (max. 190) and *Tadorna ferruginea* (max. 740).

026 Krater Gölü and Meketuzlası (Konya)

37°42'N, 33°38'E *c.*3000 ha

Unprotected

Two small saline volcanic lakes embedded in volcanic ashes. Krater Gölü is a classic crater lake with funnel-shaped steep shores. The other lake, just a few kilometres to the south of Krater Gölü, is completely different in shape, being ring-shaped with a cone-shaped mountain in its centre. Since the ashes absorb light, the microclimate is warmer than that in the surrounding area. The warm ashes provide an isolated site for the Syrian Agama *Agama ruderata*, Hardun *Agama stellio*, and the Skink *Mabuya aurata*.

The area has a comparatively poor, but interesting avifauna. Breeding birds include or have included *Anser anser* (1+ pair), *Tadorna ferruginea* (15+ pairs), *T. tadorna* (5-10 pairs), *Neophron percnopterus* (5-6 pairs in the 1960s; currently one pair), *Buteo rufinus* (1-2 pairs), *Aquila chrysaetos* (1 pair until 1964; none since then), *Falco naumanni* (common until about 1970; none at present), *F. cherrug* (breeding 1964-70 and probably in 1976; has disappeared since), *Himantopus himantopus* (3 pairs), and *Bubo bubo* (1 pair). *Melanocorypha bimaculata* is the most frequent lark species and *Rhodopechys sanguinea* breeds on the slopes.

027 Kulu Gölü (Küçük Göl or Düden Gölü) (Konya)

39°05'N, 33°09'E 800 ha

Unprotected

An almost vegetationless steppe lake with some small islands which serve as a breeding place for gulls and terns. Reeds are found at only a few places. The surroundings are under agricultural use, although there is some remnant steppe to the east of the lake. The replacement of steppe by agricultural fields and hunting on an enormous scale (some illegal) are the main conservation problems.

Kulu Gölü is one of the most important sites in the world for *Oxyura leucocephala* (*c.*30 pairs breed and max. 500 occur as moulting flocks). Other breeding species include *Podiceps nigricollis* (220 pairs), *Tadorna ferruginea* (50 pairs), *Haematopus ostralegus* (10 pairs), *Recurvirostra avosetta* (200-400 pairs), *Himantopus himantopus* (100 pairs), *Charadrius leschenaultii* (5 pairs), *Larus melanocephalus* (389 pairs), *L. genei* (100 pairs), and *Gelochelidon nilotica* (200 pairs). In addition, *Otis tarda* breeds around the lake. Impressive numbers of waterfowl have occurred, especially in summer and autumn, with *Phoenicopterus ruber* (max. 3000), *Anser anser* (max. 800), *Tadorna ferruginea* (max. 10,000), *Anas querquedula* (max. 2000), *Aythya nyroca* (max. 100), *Himantopus himantopus* (max. 700), *Recurvirostra avosetta* (max. 640), *Burhinus oedicnemus* (max. 75), *Charadrius alexandrinus* (max. 250), *Calidris minuta* (max. 500), *C. temminckii* (max. 300), *Larus genei* (max. 550), and *Chlidonias leucopterus* (max. 300); other visitors include *Pterocles orientalis* (max. 200). As the lake often freezes, it does not usually hold important numbers of waterfowl in winter, although *Anas clypeata* (6000) and

Aythya ferina (45,000) have been recorded in Nov., and *Anser albifrons* (max. 19,000) has occurred around the lake in winter.

028 Mogan Gölü (Gölbaşı Gölü or Gökçe Gölü) (Ankara)

39°47'N, 32°50'E 600 ha

Unprotected

A freshwater lake with some reedbeds along its northern shore, close to the town of Gölbaşı. Agricultural land borders the eastern, western and southern shores. Being close to Ankara, the lake has now been developed for industry and recreation; especially the eastern shore, which is becoming increasingly covered by buildings. These developments have undermined the importance of the lake in recent years.

Breeding species include *Podiceps cristatus* (25+ pairs), *Ixobrychus minutus* (10 pairs), *Nycticorax nycticorax* (10+ pairs), *Ardea purpurea*, *Tadorna tadorna*, *Netta rufina*, and possibly *Ardeola ralloides*.

029 Seyfe Gölü (Kırşehir)

39°12'N, 34°25'E 1545-7000 ha

Unprotected but designated for protection as a Strict Nature Reserve

Seyfe Gölü is a typical shallow, brackish, steppe lake with extensive vegetation only to the south, where a stream has given rise to freshwater marshes before entering the lake. Several channels, a small water reservoir, gardens, marshes, fields and *Populus* plantations form a richly structured biotope. A drainage project, which had been proposed by the State Hydraulic Works, has been cancelled, but hunting pressure is enormous.

Breeding species include *Ciconia ciconia* (3+ pairs), *Tadorna ferruginea*, *T. tadorna* (less than 10 pairs), *Netta rufina* (*c.*30 pairs), *Grus grus* (less than 10 pairs), *Glareola pratincola* (*c.*30 pairs), *Tringa totanus* (*c.*10 pairs), and *Sterna albifrons* (60 pairs). *Otis tarda* apparently breeds in the surrounding area, with up to 61 birds in winter. In addition, *Phoenicopterus ruber* bred in 1971. *Recurvirostra avosetta* (300 pairs in 1971), *Larus genei* (2100 pairs in 1971), and *Gelochelidon nilotica* (1000 pairs in 1971) seem not to have bred in recent years, but detailed surveys are lacking. During autumn and winter the lake holds significant numbers of waterfowl, and counts have included *Phoenicopterus ruber* (10,000+), *Tadorna ferruginea* (1625 in Nov.), *T. tadorna* (1358 in Jan.), *Anas crecca* (16,500 in Sept.), *Aythya ferina* (9042 in Dec.), *Fulica atra* (max. 152,380 in winter 1969-70, but usually considerably fewer), *Himantopus himantopus* (max. 780 in July), *Recurvirostra avosetta* (max. 1490 in July), *Tringa totanus* (max. 980 in July), *Sterna hirundo* (max. 1840 in July), *S. albifrons* (max. 1460 in July), and *Chlidonias leucopterus* (max. 11,800 in Aug.).

030 Sultansazlığı (Sultan Marshes) (Kayseri)

38°20'N, 35°15'E *c.*20,000 ha (lakes and marshes) and *c.*100,000 ha (whole plain)

Strict Nature Reserve; Hunting Reserve controlled by wardens (covering 47,000 ha)

Includes Çöl Gölü (İncesu saltpans) and Yay Gölü ('Kurbağa Gölü' has often wrongly been used as a name for the whole area or for parts of it; the whole plain is called Develi Ovası). Yay Gölü is a brackish lake with islands. To the north and south, large freshwater marshes border the lake with immense reedbeds, and the southern marshes have large floating reed islands. Çöl Gölü is a saltpan to the north of the plain which dries out in summer and is surrounded by expanses of steppe. A large-scale drainage project which opened the closed basin to the River Kızılırmak has undermined the importance of the area in recent years and some breeding species have declined. Other problems are heavy grazing, disturbance by local people and foreign visitors, reed-cutting, and illegal hunting.

Breeding species include *Phalacrocorax pygmeus* (200 pairs), *Pelecanus onocrotalus* (probably), *Ixobrychus minutus* (350 pairs), *Nycticorax nycticorax* (50 pairs), *Ardeola ralloides* (50 pairs), *Egretta garzetta* (200 pairs), *Ardea purpurea* (50 pairs), *Ciconia ciconia* (50 pairs), *Plegadis falcinellus* (150-200 pairs in 1979; currently 25-30 pairs),

Phoenicopterus ruber (only once, with 1500 pairs in 1971), *Anser anser* (20-30 pairs), *Anas strepera* (30-40 pairs), *Marmaronetta angustirostris* (2 pairs in 1972), *Netta rufina* (50 pairs), *Aythya nyroca* (5 pairs), *Oxyura leucocephala* (less than 20 pairs), *Circus pygargus* (a few pairs), *Grus grus* (50 pairs in 1970; currently 20 pairs), *Otis tarda* (probably a few pairs), *Himantopus himantopus* (200-250 pairs), *Recurvirostra avosetta* (300 pairs in 1970; currently 13 pairs), *Glareola pratincola* (40 pairs), *Charadrius leschenaultii* (15 pairs), *Hoplopterus spinosus* (20 pairs), *Larus melanocephalus* (less than 10 pairs), *L. genei* (100 pairs), *Gelochelidon nilotica* (100 pairs), *Sterna hirundo* (50 pairs), *S. albifrons* (40 pairs), and *Pterocles orientalis* (25-30 pairs). Observations of waterbirds in the post-breeding period and in winter have included *Phoenicopterus ruber* (max. 52,000), *Anser albifrons* (max. 3280), *A. anser* (12,000; usually considerably less), *Tadorna ferruginea* (max. 11,000), *Anas crecca* (max. 200,000-600,000 in 1971), *A. acuta* (max. 15,000), *A. querquedula* (max. 1500), *A. clypeata* (max. 9000), *Marmaronetta angustirostris* (max. 150), *Netta rufina* (max. 17,000), *Aythya ferina* (max. 41,000), *Oxyura leucocephala* (max. 40), *Grus grus* (max. 1400), *Fulica atra* (max. 300,000; usually much less), *Recurvirostra avosetta* (max. 1500), *Tringa erythropus* (max. 1350), *Calidris minuta* (max. 1750), and *Limosa limosa* (max. 1710). Up to 1000 *Pelecanus onocrotalus* regularly occur throughout the year.

031 Tödürge Gölü (Demiryurt Gölü) (Sivas)

39°53'N, 37°36'E 330 ha

Unprotected

A circular freshwater lake in the upper Kızılırmak area. The shores are covered with beds of *Juncus*, *Carex*, and some *Phragmites*, and the lake is surrounded by meadows and agricultural land. The Sivas – Erzincan highway passes through the area.

Breeding species include *Podiceps cristatus* (5-10 pairs), *P. grisegena* (probably 1 pair), *Phalacrocorax pygmeus* (possibly), *Ciconia ciconia* (*c.*25 pairs at Hafik, which is part of the site), *Tadorna ferruginea*, *Anas acuta*, *Milvus migrans*, *Haliaeetus albicilla* (1 pair present during the breeding season in 1975), *Circus aeruginosus*, *Grus grus* (4 pairs around the lake and a further 1-2 pairs towards Hafik), *Himantopus himantopus*, *Tringa totanus*, *Sterna hirundo* (6 pairs), and probably *S. albifrons*. *Grus grus* (max. 250-280) occurs in autumn.

032 Tuz Gölü (Aksaray, Ankara, Konya)

38°43'N, 33°22'E 200,000+ ha

Unprotected

Includes Tersakan Gölü (Gez Gölü) and smaller lakes like Köpek Gölü, Acıgöl, and Akgöl. Tuz Gölü is a huge shallow lake (*c.*110,000 ha) with a high salinity, which makes the water intolerable to most organisms. Salt crystalises under water and produces a thick layer (up to 30 cm) on the lake bottom. Apart from an area south of Şerefli Koçhisar, Tuz Gölü dries up completely during summer. Especially on the south-western side some small freshwater springs give rise to lakes and marshes, with a salinity which is lower than that of Tuz Gölü, of which Tersakan Gölü (*c.*6400 ha) is the largest. Within the zone around Tuz Gölü, halophytic vegetation grows, with xeromorphic shrubs and enclosed salt-meadows (which are often flooded) to the south and south-west. The surroundings of the lake are thinly populated and much of it is inaccessible. There is commercial salt extraction in places and also some agricultural land.

The most outstanding ornithological feature at Tuz Gölü is the breeding colony of *Phoenicopterus ruber*, with up to 5000 pairs in 1970. However, because of a lack of surveys breeding has not been confirmed for almost 15 years. The environs of the lake support a population of *Otis tarda*, probably the largest in Turkey. Other breeding species include *Tadorna ferruginea*, *T. tadorna*, *Anas acuta*, *A. querquedula*, *Circus pygargus*, *Aquila heliaca*, *Falco cherrug*, *Glareola pratincola*, *Charadrius alexandrinus*, *C. leschenaultii*, *Larus argentatus* (600 pairs), and *Sterna caspia* (max. 25 pairs). An important site for wintering waterfowl (Nov. figures unless stated) including *Anser albifrons* (max. 57,000), *A. anser* (max. 1400 in April), *Tadorna ferruginea* (max. 2160),

T. tadorna (max. 1240), and *Anas crecca* (max. 57,000). Other notable species occurring on passage include *Aquila heliaca*, *Grus grus* (max. 8000 in Oct.), *Charadrius morinellus* (max. 800-1000 in April), *Philomachus pugnax* (max. 1000 in April), and *Calidris minuta* (max. 1000 in Oct.).

033 Tuzla Gölü (Kayseri)

39°01'N, 35°49'E 2300 ha

Unprotected

A small saline steppe lake situated close to the River Kızılırmak. The shores are almost without vegetation. To the east, an extensive basin has been entirely converted to agricultural fields. Grazing of livestock seems to prohibit vegetation growth. There seem to be plans to drain the lake using the River Kızılırmak.

One waterfowl count in autumn 1985 demonstrated the lake's ornithological importance, with *Tadorna ferruginea* (2930; with 770 in Jan. 1986) and *Grus grus* (730).

034 Bafa Gölü (Aydın, Muğla)

37°31'N, 27°27'E 7000 ha

Unprotected

A slightly saline lake (originally a bay of the sea) with rocky shores on the northern and southern sides and alluvial plains to the east and west, with extensive areas of *Tamarix*. The River Menderes passes 1-2 km away. A dyke between the lake and the river was finished in 1985 and has lead to a fall in the water-level, and the drying out of the *Tamarix* areas and marshes. As a consequence, important breeding and feeding areas were lost. A planned road to the remote northern side of the lake will cause much disturbance, and hunting is also a problem.

Of particular importance for breeding *Phalacrocorax pygmeus* (*c.*10 pairs), *Ciconia ciconia* (25+ pairs), *Haliaeetus albicilla* (2-3 pairs), and *Falco peregrinus* (1-2 pairs). Other important breeding species are *Ixobrychus minutus* (10 pairs), *Nycticorax nycticorax* (10-20 pairs), *Ardeola ralloides* (5-10 pairs), *Egretta garzetta* (100 pairs), *Ardea purpurea* (5-10 pairs), *Tadorna ferruginea* (20-30 pairs), *Circaetus gallicus* (less than 5 pairs), *Circus aeruginosus* (1-2 pairs), *Buteo rufinus* (more than 5 pairs), *Falco naumanni* (25+ pairs), *Himantopus himantopus* (less than 10 pairs), *Halcyon smyrnensis* (1-2 pairs; in recent years only at the River Menderes), and *Ceryle rudis* (1-2 pairs at the River Menderes). *Plegadis falcinellus*, *Platalea leucorodia*, and *Hieraaetus fasciatus* perhaps breed. Wintering waterfowl have included *Podiceps cristatus* (max. 2820), *Phalacrocorax carbo* (max. 400), *Pelecanus crispus* (max. 185), *Egretta alba* (max. 27), *Anas strepera* (max. 1200), and *Recurvirostra avosetta* (max. 780). The number of *Podiceps cristatus* has declined considerably during the last decade, whereas the number of *Fulica atra* has increased (400,000+ in Jan. 1986).

035 Büyük Menderes Deltası (Aydın)

37°34'N, 27°13'E *c.*13,000 ha (no discrete borders)

Unprotected

The delta consists of a large lagoon (Karine Gölü or Dil Gölü: *c.*2100 ha) to the north of the mouth of the River Menderes and several smaller lagoons (Derin Göl, Mavi Göl, Karagöl) between the river mouth and the old mouth of the River Menderes. The coastal zone is a mixture of *Salicornia*, bare soil, and sand. The freshwater vegetation along the River Menderes is mainly composed of *Typha*, *Phragmites*, *Juncus*, and *Tamarix*. The salinity of the soil decreases away from the sea and most of the hinterland is under cultivation. The extension of arable land (cotton fields) by washing the saline soil (flooding with freshwater) is diminishing the size of the *Salicornia* steppe. The delta is a famous hunting area and disturbance of breeding colonies by fishermen is considerable.

Pelecanus crispus breeds in the delta (16 nests in 1980; 62 birds at a colony in 1981). Other noteworthy breeding species include *Ixobrychus minutus*, *Nycticorax nycticorax*, *Ardeola ralloides*, *Egretta garzetta*, *Ardea purpurea*, *Tadorna ferruginea*, *Haliaeetus albicilla* (1 pair), *Circaetus gallicus, Porzana parva, Haematopus ostralegus* (a few pairs), *Himantopus himantopus, Recurvirostra avosetta, Burhinus oedicnemus, Glareola pratincola* (40-50 pairs), *Hoplopterus spinosus, Larus melanocephalus, Gelochelidon nilotica* (less than 10 pairs), *Sterna caspia, S. albifrons, Chlidonias niger, Halcyon smyrnensis*, and *Ceryle rudis*. From December to early spring, the delta and the inundated cotton fields are a major wintering and passage area for waterfowl with *Pelecanus crispus* (max. 225), *Egretta alba* (max. 200), *Plegadis falcinellus* (max. 230 in April), *Phoenicopterus ruber* (max. 7000-8000), *Anser albifrons* (max. 420), *Anas penelope* (max. 13,220), *A. strepera* (max. 1000), *A. crecca* (max. 33,000), *A. acuta* (max. 6740), *A. clypeata* (max. 2600), *Limosa limosa* (max. 720), *Numenius arquata* (max. 1250), and *Tringa stagnatilis* (max. 100+ in April).

036 Çamaltı Tuzlası (İzmir)

38°27'N, 26°52'E 8000 ha

Hunting Reserve (controlled by wardens)

An extensive coastal area of bays, saltmarshes, and numerous saltpans, with three lagoons (Çilazmak, Homa, Kırdeniz Dalyanı) and extensive reedbeds between the delta of the River Gediz and the lagoons. Problems include drainage (for the extension of the saltpans), illegal hunting, disturbance and even destruction of the breeding colonies by local fishermen.

Species breeding regularly include *Pelecanus crispus* (10 pairs), *Phoenicopterus ruber* (100-150 pairs), *Egretta garzetta* (100 pairs), *Tadorna ferruginea* (100 pairs), *Himantopus himantopus, Recurvirostra avosetta* (150-200 pairs), *Hoplopterus spinosus*, and *Sterna caspia*. Passage species include *Phalacrocorax carbo* (max. 500) and *Anser anser* (max. 100); wintering species are insufficiently known, although they have included *Phoenicopterus ruber* (3000) and *Calidris minuta* (970).

037 Güllük Bataklığı (Güllük Marshes) (Muğla)

37°15'N, 27°38'E *c.*1200 ha

Unprotected

The marshes lie at the head of Güllük Körfezi (Güllük Bay) and have originated from the alluvial deposits of the River Değirmen. In its lower course, this river is winding with dense *Tamarix* scrub; *Phragmites* and *Salicornia* vegetation is also present in places. The mouth of the river is a relatively narrow gorge and the greatest part of the upper course is canalised. In 1987 new canals were opened for drainage and the wet areas (mainly the halophytic plant communities) were reduced in size. The cutting and burning of reed is another environmental problem.

Hoplopterus spinosus, Himantopus himantopus, Halcyon smyrnensis, and *Ceryle rudis* breed, as well as numerous *Merops apiaster* and *Remiz pendulinus*. Passage species include *Plegadis falcinellus* (max. 40).

038 Işıklı Gölü (Çivril Gölü) (Denizli)

38°14'N, 29°55'E *c.*3500 ha (lake only)

Unprotected

A freshwater lake at the spring of the River Büyük Menderes, embanked at the western, southern, and eastern sides. Includes Gökgöl. Water flows into the lake from the eastern side, where there are many dykes and canals. The lake itself is almost totally overgrown with *Phragmites*, which is interspersed with muddy islands and open water. Sluices control the outflow of the lake to the River Büyük Menderes. Barren hills and agricultural land surround the lake. Fishing (including fishing for crayfish *Astacus leptodactylus*) and hunting cause much disturbance.

Species probably breeding include *Ixobrychus minutus, Ardeola ralloides, Egretta garzetta, E. alba, Ardea purpurea, Plegadis falcinellus, Anser anser, Tadorna ferruginea, Aythya nyroca, Haliaeetus albicilla, Circus aeruginosus, Buteo rufinus, Himantopus*

himantopus, *Gelochelidon nilotica*, *Chlidonias hybridus*, *C. leucopterus*, and *Anthus campestris*. Winter waterfowl counts have included *Podiceps nigricollis* (max. 1100), *Phalacrocorax pygmeus* (max. 390), *Egretta alba* (max. 140), *Anser albifrons* (max. 3100), *A. anser* (max. 920), *Anas crecca* (max. 5025), *A. acuta* (max. 7800), *A. clypeata* (max. 750), and *Limosa limosa* (max. 1080). Other wintering species include *Haliaeetus albicilla*, *Gypaetus barbatus*, *Circus cyaneus*, *Aquila clanga* (max. 16), *A. heliaca*, *Falco biarmicus*, and *F. cherrug*. *Gyps fulvus*, *Aquila chrysaetos*, and *Serinus pusillus* are thought to breed in the surrounding area. *Plegadis falcinellus* (200) occurs on spring migration.

039 Karamık Bataklığı (Karamık Marshes) (Afyon)

38°26'N, 30°50'E 4100 ha

Formerly a Hunting Reserve, now unprotected

A freshwater swamp mainly overgrown with *Phragmites*, *Typha,* and other aquatic vegetation. There is an exchange of water with underground springs which can be partly regulated by sluices. The marshes are surrounded by wet meadows, arable land and rocky steppe (towards the mountains on the eastern side). Some northern parts of the marshes have been drained; reed-cutting for the paper factory at Çay is a major disturbance, and hunting is intensive.

Since the mountains are very close to the marshes, many mountain species occur. Among the breeding species are *Podiceps nigricollis* (7 pairs), *Phalacrocorax pygmeus*, *Ixobrychus minutus*, *Nycticorax nycticorax*, *Ardeola ralloides*, *Egretta garzetta*, *Ardea purpurea*, *Plegadis falcinellus*, *Cygnus olor*, *Anser anser*, *Tadorna ferruginea*, *Anas strepera*, *Aythya ferina*, *A. nyroca*, *Oxyura leucocephala* (10+ pairs), *Neophron percnopterus*, *Circus aeruginosus*, *Buteo rufinus*, *Aquila chrysaetos*, *Grus grus* (2-3 pairs), *Himantopus himantopus*, *Tringa totanus*, *Sterna hirundo*, *Chlidonias hybridus*, *C. niger*, *C. leucopterus*, *Bubo bubo*, *Irania gutturalis*, and *Pyrrhocorax pyrrhocorax*. Counts of wintering waterfowl have included *Tadorna ferruginea* (max. 760), *Anas acuta* (max. 4000; usually less than 600), *A. clypeata* (max. 2030), *Netta rufina* (max. 910), *Aythya fuligula* (max. 7110), and *Fulica atra* (max. 61,040). *Haliaeetus albicilla*, *Aquila clanga*, and *A. heliaca* are wintering species.

040 Küçük Menderes Deltası (İzmir)

37°58'N, 27°17'E *c.*1500 ha

Hunting Reserve (core area)

The marshes of the delta are situated to the north of the River Küçük Menderes and include Alaman Gölü, Gebekirse Gölü, and Akgöl as well as other smaller lakes. The agricultural area in the delta (mainly cotton) has been enlarged considerably by drainage. Tourism development (the ancient sites of Ephesus and Selçuk are situated within the delta) is a threat to the area. Illegal hunting is frequent. The area has not been studied in detail and further information is required.

Breeding species include *Ixobrychus minutus*, *Ardeola ralloides*, *Egretta garzetta*, *Ardea purpurea*, *Plegadis falcinellus*, *Anas querquedula*, *Circus aeruginosus*, *Porzana parva*, and *Glareola pratincola*.

041 Marmara Gölü (Manisa)

38°41'N, 28°00'E 3400 ha

Unprotected

A shallow lake with wet meadows and reedbeds, with thick vegetation especially on the northern shore near inflowing streams. Densely vegetated ditches around the lake enrich the area. An embankment cuts off the lake from the River Gediz and sluices control the water-level. Hunting is a serious problem.

Pelecanus crispus has often been presumed to breed but this has not been proven. However, up to 210 have occurred in winter and the lake is one of the most important wintering areas for this species. Other breeding birds include *Podiceps cristatus*, *Cygnus olor*, *Tadorna ferruginea*, *Aythya nyroca*, *Circaetus gallicus*, *Himantopus himantopus* (15+ pairs in 1987), *Hoplopterus spinosus*, *Tringa totanus* (50+ pairs), and perhaps *Gelochelidon nilotica*. *Ceryle rudis* has its northernmost breeding site at the River Gediz. In winter, it is an important site for *Podiceps nigricollis* (max. 250), *Phalacrocorax carbo* (max. 325), *Anas crecca* (max. 35,000 in 1969, max. 8000 since), *Aythya ferina* (max. 11,700), and *Fulica atra* (max. 8720). *Haliaeetus albicilla* is a winter visitor.

042 Samsun Dağı (Dilek Yarımadası) (Aydın)

37°40'N, 27°10'E 10,985 ha (protected area)

National Park

Samsun Dağı is a peninsula to the north of the Büyük Menderes Delta, with a mountain ridge running from east to west. There are high peaks, steep slopes, deep canyons, and plains grading into rocky coastlines with bays of sand and gravel. Most of the area is covered by Mediterranean vegetation: about two-thirds by maquis and one-third by mixed *Pinus* woodland. *Pinus brutia* is the common tree at lower altitudes, being replaced by *P. nigra* at higher altitudes. The construction of forest roads has caused much disturbance and perhaps was one of the reasons for the recent (1970s) disappearance of the Anatolian Leopard *Panthera pardus tulliana*. The touristic pressure (the National Park is close to the tourist centre of Kuşadası and close to the ancient sites of Milet, Didyma, and Ephesus) is confined to some parts along the coast in the north-east of the Park.

Hieraaetus pennatus is probably a breeding bird of the Park. Several pairs of *Falco peregrinus* breed, and *F. eleonorae* can be seen regularly outside the breeding season. Other species of interest include *Sylvia conspicillata* and *Sitta krueperi*. A colony of *Gyps fulvus* had existed before 1920 but has disappeared.

043 Acıgöl (Acıtuz Gölü, Tuz Gölü or Çardak Gölü) and Çaltı Gölü (Afyon, Denizli)

37°49'N, 29°52'E 16,000 ha (lake only)

Hunting Reserve (Çaltı Gölü)

Apart from Tuz Gölü, Acıgöl is the most saline lake in Turkey. During the summer, the greater part of the surface area is covered by an inaccessible salt-swamp. Springs at the edge of the lake give rise to some freshwater marshes. Çaltı Gölü (Beylemli Gölü or Kurugöl) is a satellite lake of Acıgöl, but has fresh water. Acigöl is surrounded by steppe, which is most extensive in the west. The north-eastern side is under agricultural use, the south-east and north-western sides are flanked by mountains. In 1981 Çaltı Gölü was reduced in size (from several hundred to 35 ha) by drainage. On the plain to the south-west of Acigöl, a military airport is under construction and planes will fly over the lake.

Phoenicopterus ruber is regularly observed throughout the year and may breed irregularly. Breeding species include *Tadorna ferruginea*, *T. tadorna*, *Grus grus* (15+ pairs), *Otis tarda* (possibly 10+ pairs), *Himantopus himantopus* (tens of pairs), *Recurvirostra avosetta* (50+ pairs), and *Gelochelidon nilotica* (probably a colony of several hundred pairs). In addition, *Bubo bubo* and *Irania gutturalis* breed on the mountain slopes, and *Neophron percnopterus*, *Gyps fulvus*, *Aegypius monachus*, and *Gypaetus barbatus* possibly do so. An important site for non-breeding species, with *Podiceps nigricollis* (max. 1800 in July; but usually much less), *Tadorna ferruginea* (max. 450 in June), *Recurvirostra avosetta* (max. 6000 in Oct.), *Calidris minuta* (max. 1700 in Aug.), and *Larus genei* (max. 1000 in Oct.). Winter counts (mainly at Çaltı Gölü) have included *Anser albifrons* (max. 660), *A. anser* (max. 200), *Anas clypeata* (max. 2100), *Netta rufina* (max. 3230), *Aythya ferina* (max. 70,000), and *Fulica atra* (max. 40,000).

044 Aksaz Adası (Mersin [Içel])

36°06'N, 33°09'E less than 1 ha

Unprotected

A small rocky island.

Phalacrocorax aristotelis desmarestii (a few pairs) and *Larus argentatus cachinnans* (40+ pairs in 1973) breed.

045 Aladağlar (including Demirkazık Tepesi and Karanfil Dağı) (Adana, Niğde)

37°50'N, 35°10'E *c.*85,000 ha

Partly a Hunting Reserve

A large mountainous area (1300-3756 m) and valleys (River Ecemiş and its tributaries) with villages and orchards, as well as a high alpine zone above 3000 m. The forests mainly consist of *Abies cilicia*, *Cedrus libani* and *Juniperus excelsa*. The subalpine region is characterised by thorn-cushion vegetation, above which alpine grassland and rubble fields are found.

The mountains are rich in raptors: *Milvus migrans*, *Neophron percnopterus*, *Gypaetus barbatus*, *Gyps fulvus*, *Circaetus gallicus*, *Buteo rufinus*, *Aquila chrysaetos*, *Hieraaetus pennatus*, and *Falco cherrug* are breeding species. *Tetraogallus caspius* occurs at higher altitudes. Other breeding species include *Eremophila alpestris*, *Anthus campestris*, *Prunella ocularis*, *Irania gutturalis*, *Sitta krueperi*, *Pyrrhocorax pyrrhocorax*, *Serinus pusillus*, and *Rhodopechys sanguinea*.

046 Beyşehir Gölü (Konya, Isparta)

37°45'N, 31°36'E 65,600 ha

Unprotected

The largest freshwater lake in Turkey, which is used for the irrigation of the Konya plain. The shores are steep and rocky in many parts and are covered by forests and arable land, and there are more than 20 islands. Some marshes are situated in the south-west corner and there are smaller marshy areas at other places around the lake.

Several pairs of *Haliaeetus albicilla* seem to have bred until the 1960s; but it is probably only a winter visitor in recent years. Also in the 1960s, there were important breeding colonies on the islands (figures mainly from 1964) of *Pelecanus crispus* (83 pairs), *Phalacrocorax carbo* (50 pairs), *Nycticorax nycticorax* (50 pairs in 1962, 60 pairs in 1964; possibly 6 pairs in 1987), and *Egretta garzetta* (50 pairs in 1964; 5 pairs in 1978). There is almost no information on these species since then, perhaps because there have not been any comprehensive surveys. Recent breeding species include *Phalacrocorax pygmeus*, *Ardea purpurea*, and *Sterna hirundo*. Usually the number of wintering waterfowl is low; however, exceptionally *Podiceps nigricollis* (300), *Egretta alba* (120), *Anas penelope* (9000) and *Fulica atra* (30,000) have been recorded.

047 Burdur Gölü (Burdur, Isparta)

37°43'N, 30°15'E 19,400 ha

Formerly a Hunting Reserve, now unprotected

A highly saline lake which allows only specialised organisms to live, including *Arctodioptomus burduricus* (a zooplankton) and the fish *Aphanius burduricus*, both of which are endemic. Most of the shoreline is steep, although the southern side has some shallow edges. Hunting and apparently pollution are serious conservation problems.

Breeding species include *Podiceps cristatus*, *Tadorna ferruginea*, *T. tadorna*, *Himantopus himantopus* and *Hoplopterus spinosus*, and in June, up to 4000-5000 *Tadorna ferruginea* have been counted. Burdur Gölü would appear to be the most important wintering site for *Oxyura leucocephala* in the world. The species is present in considerable numbers from Sept. to April with the highest numbers in Dec. and Jan. Several thousand are regularly present and the max. count is 8990 in Jan. 1973. Other notable wintering species include *Podiceps cristatus* (max. 1950, but usually much less), *P. nigricollis* (max. 18,660), *Anser albifrons* (max. 3000), *Netta rufina* (max. 2600), *Aythya ferina* (max. 54,300), *A. fuligula* (max. 11,210), and *Fulica atra* (max. 120,690). *Haliaeetus albicilla* also overwinters.

048 Büyük and Küçük Ada (Mersin, [İçel])

Exact location is confidential a few hectares

Unprotected

Two small rocky islands (almost vegetationless) off the Mediterranean coast. Gulls eggs are collected for food by local fishermen.

The islands are a breeding site for *Larus audouinii*. At least one pair bred there in 1971; 25 pairs in 1973; 28 pairs in 1974; 6 pairs in 1978, and about 30 pairs in 1987. *Larus cachinnans* also breeds (about 400 pairs in 1971; 90 pairs in 1973 and 1974; and 150-200 pairs in 1987).

049 Çorak Gölü (Akgöl or Bayındır Gölü) (Burdur)

37°41'N, 29°45'E 1150 ha

Unprotected

A shallow freshwater lake enclosed by mountains, with meadows and some arable land on the western side. A stream which entered the lake on the eastern side is now being held back by a dam, and this and drought have resulted in an extremely low water-level during recent years.

No information on breeding birds is available, although April observations of *Gypaetus barbatus*, *Gyps fulvus*, and *Aquila heliaca* are an indication that they might breed in the mountains to the north of the lake. In winter, the lake is especially important for *Oxyura leucocephala* (max. 930). The composition of the wintering waterfowl has changed because of a lower water-level, from predominantly *Aythya* spp. and *Podiceps* spp. in the 1960s and 1970s to predominantly dabbling ducks in recent years, with smaller numbers of *Oxyura leucocephala*. Counts have included *Podiceps cristatus* (max. 3500 in 1963-1973), *P. nigricollis* (max. 3615 in 1969-1973), *Anas crecca* (max. 20,200 in 1986-1987), *A. acuta* (max. 6600 in 1986-1987), and *Aythya ferina* (max. 40,000 in 1969-1973).

050 Çukurova including Ceyhan, Seyhan and Tarsus Deltas (Adana, Mersin [İçel])

36°45'N, 35°25'E 62,500 ha (lakes, marshes, beaches, dunes, and *Eucalyptus* plantations)

About 6,000 ha (including Akyatan Gölü) are a Hunting Reserve; a large area including Akyatan Gölü is soon to become a Strict Nature Reserve.

The Çukurova area comprises the Ceyhan, Seyhan and Tarsus (Berdan) river deltas; the larger lakes – Akyatan Gölü, Akyayan Gölü, and Tuzla Gölü; the smaller lakes – Ömer Gölü, Yapı Gölü, Dipsiz Göl, and Aynaz Gölü (the latter now drained); these are mainly surrounded by saltmarshes. Towards the sea, extensive dunes, varying from 100 to 5000 m in width and *c.*100 km in length, are found. The major towns of Yumurtalık and Karatas lie within the area, which also includes the *Eucalyptus* plantations near Tarsus. Çukurova is one of the main agricultural areas of Turkey with cotton being the main crop. The use of large amounts of fertiliser and pesticide (including DDT) will undoubtedly have crucial long-term effects. Overgrazing, drainage, industrial (Yumurtalık) and touristic (Karataş) development, and hunting are other serious problems.

Recent studies (mainly in 1987) have demonstrated the importance of the area as a resting place for migrants and as a breeding area. Breeding birds include *Tadorna ferruginea* (2-5 pairs), *Marmaronetta angustirostris* (*c.*32 pairs in 1987; with 50-100 pairs estimated), *Aythya nyroca* (2-5 pairs), *Oxyura leucocephala* (2 pairs), *Circaetus gallicus* (1 pair), *Circus aeruginosus* (10+ pairs), *Francolinus francolinus* (126 calling males; 300-450 pairs estimated), *Himantopus himantopus*, *Burhinus oedicnemus* (25 pairs), *Glareola pratincola*, *Charadrius alexandrinus* (3000 pairs), *Hoplopterus spinosus* (36 pairs; 40-50 pairs estimated), *Sterna albifrons* (50 pairs in 1981), *Halcyon smyrnensis* (45-50 pairs), *Riparia riparia* (*c.*3000 pairs), *Lanius nubicus* (common), and *Passer moabiticus* (common). Migrants and winter visitors include (counts from spring 1987 unless stated) *Pelecanus onocrotalus* (max. 7000 passing over during the survey), *Egretta garzetta* (max. 280), *E. alba* (max. 95), *Ciconia ciconia* (max. 4000 passing over during the survey),

Plegadis falcinellus (max. 300 in April), *Phoenicopterus ruber* (max. 19,000 in Jan.), *Anas penelope* (max. 39,125 in Jan.), *A. querquedula* (max. 1100), *A. crecca* (max. 252,500 in Jan.), *A. acuta* (max. 19,700 in Jan.), *A. clypeata* (max. 1200 in Jan.), *Aythya ferina* (max. 6750 in Jan.), *Oxyura leucocephala* (max. 175 in Jan.), *Fulica atra* (max. 100,000 in Jan.), *Recurvirostra avosetta* (max. 2100), *Charadrius leschenaultii* (max. 80), *Calidris minuta* (max. 10,000), *C. ferruginea* (max. 2000), *C. alpina* (max. 10,000), *Limicola falcinellus* (max. 125), *Philomachus pugnax* (max. 2500), *Limosa limosa* (max. 1100), and *Larus genei* (max. 1300).

051 Eğirdir Gölü and Hoyran Gölü (Isparta)

38°00'N, 30°54'E 44,200-48,100 ha (dependent on water-level)

Unprotected

One of the largest lakes in south-west Anatolia. An oligotrophic freshwater lake that narrows considerably in the middle. Hoyran Gölü, to the north of this bottleneck, is shallower and richer in nutrients than the southern part. Apart from one place on the eastern shore south of the bottleneck, extensive marshes and reedbeds are found only at Hoyran Gölü, and only this part is of international ornithological importance. Fishing is of major economic importance for the surrounding villages; mainly for *Stizostedion lucioperca* (which was introduced in 1955) and crayfish *Astacus leptodactylus* (the latter have been seriously affected by a disease, causing problems for the fishing industry). A large irrigation project is under construction in the north-eastern corner of Hoyran Gölü.

Breeding species are thought to include *Phalacrocorax pygmeus*, *Ixobrychus minutus*, *Ardeola ralloides*, *Egretta garzetta*, *Tadorna ferruginea*, *Circus aeruginosus*, *Porzana parva*, *Himantopus himantopus*, and *Chlidonias hybridus*. Breeding species in the area surrounding the lake include *Neophron percnopterus*, *Gyps fulvus*, *Circaetus gallicus*, *Buteo rufinus*, *Aquila chrysaetos*, *Irania gutturalis*, and probably *Otis tarda* (although only winter records are available, with max. 15). During winter, the lake holds populations of *Anser albifrons* (max. 985), *Tadorna ferruginea* (max. 530), *Anas crecca* (max. 12,000 but usually much less), *Netta rufina* (max. 1300), *Aythya ferina* (max. 9400), *A. fuligula* (max. 4420), and *Fulica atra* (max. 25,400).

052 Göksu Deltası including Paradeniz Gölü and Akgöl (Mersin [İçel])

36°20'N, 33°59'E *c.*13,000 ha

Hunting temporarily prohibited

The Göksu Delta is one of the most important bird areas in Europe and the Middle East. Paradeniz Gölü and Akgöl are two shallow brackish lagoons, situated to the west of the River Göksu. Paradeniz, which has a connection with the sea, has no extensive reedbeds and its shores are covered mainly with *Salicornia* salt-steppe; vegetationless sand-dunes divide the lagoon from the sea. Akgöl has a lower salinity and is fringed with reedbeds, which vary from 50-200 m in width, on the western shore. Large sand-dunes between the Akgöl and the sea are densely covered with scrub, mainly *Genistra* sp., and provide an important habitat for migrants. Part of the salt-steppe is inundated in winter and spring, but is dry in summer. The area north of the lagoons and the eastern half of the delta are almost completely intensively cultivated. The extension of a holiday village on the dunes between Akgöl and the sea is a serious threat to the area. Hunting is intensive and *Porphyrio porphyrio* is especially persecuted.

About 310 bird species have been recorded in the delta. Breeding *Marmaronetta angustirostris* (30+ pairs; one of the largest populations in Turkey) and *Porphyrio porphyrio* (20+ pairs; the only site in Turkey) are particularly noteworthy. Other breeding species include *Phalacrocorax pygmeus*, *Pelecanus onocrotalus* (presumed), *P. crispus* (possibly), *Botaurus stellaris* (possibly), *Ixobrychus minutus*, *Nycticorax nycticorax* (50 pairs in 1971), *Ardeola ralloides* (230+ pairs in 1971), *Egretta garzetta*, *E. alba*, *Ardea purpurea* (50 pairs in 1971), *Plegadis falcinellus*, *Platalea leucorodia*, *Tadorna ferruginea* (15+ pairs), *Aythya nyroca*, *Circus aeruginosus*, *Falco naumanni*, *Francolinus francolinus* (5+ pairs), *Porzana parva*, *Himantopus himantopus* (50+ pairs), *Recurvirostra avosetta*, *Burhinus oedicnemus*, *Glareola pratincola* (30+ pairs), *Hoplopterus spinosus*

(40+ pairs), *Gelochelidon nilotica* (presumed), *Sterna caspia* (possibly), *S. albifrons* (100+ pairs), *Chlidonias hybridus*, *C. niger*, *C. leucopterus*, *Halcyon smyrnensis*, *Ceryle rudis*, and *Acrocephalus melanopogon*. Counts of waterfowl have included *Podiceps cristatus* (max. 435), *Egretta alba* (max. 125), *Phoenicopterus ruber* (max. 3950 in Sept.), *Anser albifrons* (max. 1000), *A. anser* (max. 1200), *Anas penelope* (max. 38,950), *A. crecca* (max. 14,000), *A. acuta* (max. 2400), *A. querquedula* (max. 1500 in Oct.), *A. clypeata* (max. 2800 in Feb.), *Marmaronetta angustirostris* (max. 150 in Sept.), *Aythya ferina* (max. 37,500), and *Fulica atra* (max. 54,350). The delta is also a very important resting place for migrants and for wintering species such as *Haliaeetus albicilla*, *Gyps fulvus* (max. 60), *Circus aeruginosus* (max. 50 in winter), *C. cyaneus* (10+ in winter), *Aquila clanga*, *Falco peregrinus*, *Grus grus* (150-200 in winter), *Calidris minuta* (max. 1550 in Jan.), *Philomachus pugnax* (max. 3000 in April), and *Tringa stagnatilis* (max. 70 in Sept.).

053 Karataş Gölü (Burdur)

37°23'N, 29°58'E 800 ha

Unprotected

A shallow freshwater lake with some reedbeds along the western shore, and arable land bordering its other shores. The water of the lake is used for irrigation. The construction of dams at the southern end has resulted in an increase in arable land, an increase in the water-level and a decrease in the size of the reedbeds. Fishing (including fishing for crayfish *Astacus leptodactylus*) causes considerable disturbance.

Ixobrychus minutus and *Chlidonias hybridus* probably breed in the reedy fringes, and *Otis tarda* probably breeds in the surrounding area. The lake is important as a wintering area for waterfowl, and counts have included *Anser albifrons* (max. 550), *A. anser* (max. 780), *Tadorna ferruginea* (max. 200), and *Anas crecca* (max. 2200). *Haliaeetus albicilla* and *Aquila chrysaetos* overwinter.

054 Kovada Gölü (Isparta)

37°38'N, 30°53'E 1100 ha (lake only)

Included in a National Park (6534 ha) and Hunting Reserve

The lake is surrounded by forests, mainly deciduous (predominantly *Platanus orientalis*). The lake has steep shores and no marshes, and is connected with Eğirdir Gölü by a 2-km-long canal, which brings in water. There is a small marsh situated close to the canal towards the town of Eğirdir.

The ornithological importance is not fully understood; however, *Gyps fulvus* and *Aquila chrysaetos* are regularly observed. Other breeding species are *Dendrocopos medius* and *Phylloscopus bonelli*.

055 Köyceğiz Gölü including Dalyan Deltası, Sülüngür Gölü, and İztuzu Gölü (Muğla)

36°55'N, 28°40'E 5200 ha (Köyceğiz Gölü) and *c.*1150 ha (Dalyan Delta)

Partly a Mediterranean Specially Protected Area

Special Preservation Area (area between Gökova Körfezi and Antalya including Dalyan Deltası); protection provided by this category of protected area not yet determined

A rich variety of habitats are found around Dalyan – Köyceğiz in a rather small area, including a river, freshwater lake, marshes, freshwater canal, brackish delta with many reed-fringed channels, amber forest, which is flooded throughout the year (*Liquidamber orientalis* is endemic to south-west Anatolia, with the largest stands around Köyceğiz Gölü), sand-dunes, coastal habitats, *Pinus* forests, and Mediterranean maquis. The development of tourism is likely to affect the area adversely. It is also a breeding site for the threatened Loggerhead Turtle *Caretta caretta*, Nile Soft-shelled Turtle *Trionyx triungius*, and small numbers of Green Turtle *Chelonia mydas*.

The delta is an important breeding site for *Halcyon smyrnensis* (2-3 pairs) and *Ceryle rudis* (*c.*5 pairs). Other notable species are *Ixobrychus minutus*, *Nycticorax nycticorax*, *Ardea purpurea*, and *Gelochelidon nilotica* (2 pairs).

056 Salda Gölü (Yeşilova Gölü) (Burdur)

37°33'N, 29°40'E 4100 ha

Unprotected

A slightly saline, deep lake (deepest in Turkey) surrounded by wooded mountains (mainly *Pinus* forests). At the south-west corner a stream flows into the lake, with some wet meadows. There are buildings for recreation (hotel, picnic places), especially on the southern side.

The lake is of some importance for a few wintering species, such as *Tadorna ferruginea* (max. 190), *Aythya ferina* (max. 2700), and *Fulica atra* (max. 9740).

057 Yarışlı Gölü (Burdur)

37°34'N, 29°58'E 1500 ha

Unprotected

A saline lake (sodium phosphate and sodium chloride being the most abundant salts) without emergent vegetation. Meadows and arable land reach the water's edge on the northern and eastern shores, while the other shores are rather steep. The lake is regularly visited by hunters.

Important for wintering *Oxyura leucocephala* (max. 420). Other notable wintering species are *Podiceps nigricollis* (max. 800+), *Anas crecca* (max. 6400), and *A. clypeata* (max. 1920).

058 Yılanlı Ada (Mersin [İçel])

36°07'N, 33°23'E less than 1 ha

Unprotected

A small rocky island along the Mediterranean coast.

The island holds a few pairs of *Phalacrocorax aristotelis desmarestii* and a colony of *Larus cachinnans* (110 pairs in 1973 and 1974).

059 Belen Geçidi (Topboğazı Geçidi) (Hatay)

36°30'N, 36°12'E

Unprotected

The Amanos Dağları (Amanus Mountains) form a biogeographical barrier in the southernmost part of Turkey, dividing the Mediterranean region from the Syrian plateau. Migrants which have passed the Bosphorus and have crossed Anatolia in a south-easterly direction cross the western chain of the Amanos Dağları and then migrate south, and many birds are forced to cross the Belen Pass. However, gliding migrants must use other, as yet undiscovered, places to cross the mountain chain.

Large numbers of raptors, storks, pelicans, and spoonbills occur on passage. Eighty-three thousand *Ciconia ciconia* have been counted (this and all other figures refer to a four-week count in autumn 1976, which is the most complete so far). Other migrants which have been recorded in important numbers are *Pelecanus onocrotalus* (6200), *Ciconia nigra* (3300), *Platalea leucorodia* (590), *Pernis apivorus* (16,000), *Milvus migrans* (500), *Neophron percnopterus* (870), *Circaetus gallicus* (730), *Accipiter brevipes* (2950), and *Hieraaetus pennatus* (590). Spring migration has never been studied.

060 Ceylanpınar (Urfa, Mardin)

36°51'N, 40°03'E 150,000+ ha

260 ha are a breeding station for the Goitred Gazelle *Gazella subgutturosa*

Ceylanpınar is situated in a vast plain which stretches along the Turkish – Syrian border. Originally steppe/semi-desert, many areas are currently under agricultural use, with remnant habitat confined to just a few places. Around the Ceylanpınar state farm many trees have been planted, and trees and scrub are also found along the River Chabur (Arslanbaba Deresi), which carries water during the winter and spring. The most serious problem is the cultivation of steppe habitat, and the excessive use of fertilisers and insecticides is also of concern. The area supports a relict population of Goitred Gazelle *Gazella subgutturosa* and there is a breeding station at the state farm. This is also one of the few sites for Varan *Varanus griseus* in Turkey.

The enormous size of the plain and difficult access (border area) make it practically impossible to survey. However, the plain seems still to be a very good area for *Otis tarda* and even *Tetrax tetrax* (although the most recent record of the latter species is from 1981). *Neophron percnopterus, Circaetus gallicus, Buteo rufinus, Aquila chrysaetos, Ammoperdix griseogularis, Burhinus oedicnemus*, and *Pterocles alchata* (over 500 have been observed at drinking places) are typical breeding species. Especially along the River Chabur, *Ixobrychus minutus, Ardea purpurea, Anas acuta, A. querquedula, Circus aeruginosus, C. macrourus, C. pygargus*, and *Grus grus* occur during the breeding season and probably breed. Other species of interest include *Merops superciliosus, Cercotrichas galactotes, Petronia brachydactyla*, and *Passer moabiticus*.

061 Fırat (Euphrates) at Birecik (Urfa)

37°02'N, 38°00'E *c.*1500 ha

A few hectares around the Bald Ibis breeding station are a Hunting Reserve

Birecik is situated where the River Fırat enters the Syrian plateau. The west bank of the river is flat and under agricultural use, as is the area below the town on both sides of the river. There are many sandbanks in the Fırat (mainly thickly covered with *Tamarix* scrub), a tree nursery (below the town), and a gravel-pit. The barren limestone plateau, up-river from the town, is cut by valleys with steep walls, which carry water after heavy rainfall.

Birecik is the only breeding site for *Geronticus eremita* in Turkey, but by 1987 there were only four pairs (half of them captive bred birds). Other breeding birds in the Birecik area are *Neophron percnopterus, Buteo rufinus, Falco naumanni, Ammoperdix griseogularis, Burhinus oedicnemus, Hoplopterus spinosus, Pterocles alchata* (up to 2000 at drinking places), *Bubo bubo, Otus brucei, Ceryle rudis, Merops superciliosus, Ammomanes deserti* (the only known site in Turkey), *Hippolais pallida, Sylvia mystacea, Petronia xanthocollis, Passer moabiticus*, and *Rhodopechys obsoleta*. The Euphrates represents an important route for passage raptors.

062 Fırat (Euphrates) at Kargamış (Urfa)

36°51'N, 38°00'E 1000 ha

Unprotected

A lake in the old bed of the River Fırat on the border with Syria, with scrub consisting mainly of *Tamarix* covering the river banks and islands. Parts of the area are mined and access is restricted, and its ornithological importance is poorly known.

The breeding birds probably include *Phalacrocorax pygmeus* (5+ pairs in 1987), *Nycticorax nycticorax* (20+ pairs), *Ixobrychus minutus* (20+ pairs), *Porzana parva, Halcyon smyrnensis, Ceryle rudis*, and *Remiz pendulinus*.

063 Fırat (Euphrates) at Rumkale (Gaziantep, Urfa)

37°16'N, 37°50'E 2000 ha

Unprotected

A stretch of the River Fırat (including the settlements at Halfeti and Savaşan Köyü) with steep cliffs on both sides of the river, hills with pistachio trees, rocky fields and low scrub, a sand bank with dense *Tamarix* scrub, and a narrow valley with a fast-running stream and *Salix* in places.

Breeding species include *Neophron percnopterus* (1 pair), *Circaetus gallicus, Buteo rufinus, Hieraaetus fasciatus* (1 pair), *Ammoperdix griseogularis, Otus brucei, Apus affinis, Ceryle rudis, Oenanthe xanthoprymna* (presumed), *Hippolais languida, Sylvia mystacea, Sitta tephronota, Passer moabiticus, Petronia brachydactyla, Rhodopechys obsoleta,* and *Emberiza cineracea.*

064 Ağrı Ovası (Ağrı)

39°45'N, 43°00'E *c.*125,000 ha

Unprotected

A huge plain surrounding the town of Ağrı and including numerous villages (Eleşkirt, Hamur, Aşkale, Cumaçay, Goncali). The upper Murat, which passes Ağrı, has many tributaries. Along all rivers and streams, more or less original grassland is found, which is inundated in spring and is cut only once a year without machines. A gravel-pit provides an additional habitat. Intensification of agriculture is a continuous threat to the crane population and human disturbance is considerable.

Ağrı Ovası is a breeding site for a few pairs of *Anthropoides virgo* and a somewhat higher number of *Grus grus.* Other breeding species include *Haematopus ostralegus* and *Sterna hirundo.*

065 Ahtamar Adası (Van)

38°21'N, 43°02'E 2 ha

Unprotected

A small rocky island (alternatively spelt Ahdamar, Aktamar and Achtamar) in Van Gölü with low scrub and scattered trees. The place is very popular with tourists and is also frequently used for picnics by people from Van and Tatvan.

Breeding species include *Nycticorax nycticorax* (20-40 pairs), *Tadorna ferruginea* (*c.*5 pairs), and *Larus argentatus armenicus* (50-80 pairs).

066 Balık Gölü (Ağrı)

39°47'N, 43°33'E 3400 ha

Unprotected

Balık Gölü is one of Turkey's highest lakes and lies in a field of geologically rather young lava. Its shores are muddy and have small reedy fringes, and it is surrounded by meadows, agricultural land, and mountain slopes.

Apart from Nemrut Gölü this is the only breeding site for the relict population of *Melanitta fusca* in Turkey.

067 Bendimahi Deltası (Van)

38°56'N, 43°39'E 230 ha

Unprotected

A freshwater marsh where the River Bendimahi enters Van Gölü. The lower Bendimahi is winding and has many wet meadows and *Typha* and *Phragmites* beds along its bends. Van Gölü has several inlets with *Phragmites* and muddy banks. The wet meadows are cut once a year without machines, and arable land borders the meadows. Large parts of the area are used for cattle-grazing, which damages the vegetation and results in disturbance.

Breeding species include *Podiceps cristatus* (30 pairs), *P. nigricollis* (probably), *Phalacrocorax pygmeus* (5 pairs), *Nycticorax nycticorax, Ardeola ralloides, Ardea purpurea, Anser anser, Tadorna ferruginea, Anas penelope, A. strepera, A. crecca, A. acuta, A. clypeata, Marmaronetta angustirostris* (presumed), *Aythya ferina, A. nyroca, Oxyura leucocephala* (11 pairs), *Circus aeruginosus* (1-3 pairs), *C. pygargus* (4 pairs), *Porzana porzana* (probably), *P. parva* (possibly), *Grus grus* (5-10 pairs), *Haematopus ostralegus* (a few pairs), *Himantopus himantopus* (20-25 pairs), *Recurvirostra avosetta,*

Burhinus oedicnemus, *Tringa totanus* (50+ pairs), *Gelochelidon nilotica* (5-10 pairs), *Sterna caspia* (max. 40 birds during the breeding season), *S. albifrons* (25 pairs), *Chlidonias hybridus*, *C. leucopterus*, and *Acrocephalus melanopogon*. In the surrounding area *Falco peregrinus*, *Bubo bubo*, and *Irania gutturalis* breed. During the breeding season *Pelecanus onocrotalus* is regularly observed (max. 2000).

068 Çaldıran Sazlığı (Van)

39°09'N, 43°56'E *c.*2000 ha

Unprotected

Wet meadows situated at the foot of Tendürek Dağı, in an original state and rich in orchids, inundated for several months by the upper River Bendimahi. The meadows are only cut once a year without machines. Apart from the complex of wet meadows near Çaldıran, there are several other similar, but smaller, areas at Çaldıran Ovası.

Noteworthy breeding species (or probable breeding species) are *Phalacrocorax pygmeus*, *Egretta alba*, *Botaurus stellaris*, *Ardea purpurea*, *Anser anser*, *Anas strepera*, *A. crecca*, *Circus pygargus*, *Grus grus*, *Himantopus himantopus*, *Chlidonias hybridus*, and *C. leucopterus*.

069 Çelebibağ Sazlığı (Van)

38°58'N, 43°20'E 350 ha

Unprotected

Mainly salt marshes, where the River Ilıca (also called Druç Deresi or İncesu Çayı) enters Van Gölü, with some small *Phragmites* beds at freshwater inflows. The area is heavily disturbed by grazing cattle, herdsmen and children, and the livestock prevents the regeneration of the meadows.

Pelecanus onocrotalus occurs regularly. *Egretta garzetta*, *Tadorna ferruginea* (max. 300 in July), *T. tadorna*, *Marmaronetta angustirostris*, *Aythya ferina*, *A. nyroca*, *Himantopus himantopus*, *Recurvirostra avosetta* (max. 200 in July), *Tringa totanus*, *Gelochelidon nilotica*, *Sterna caspia*, *S. hirundo*, *S. albifrons*, and *Chlidonias leucopterus* are summer visitors and most are presumed to breed.

070 Edremit Sazlığı (Van)

38°24'N, 43°18'E 5 ha

Unprotected

A shallow lake separated from Van Gölü by a narrow sandy ridge. The only aquatic vegetation is a 5 m wide stretch of *Phragmites* along part of the inland shore. Disturbance by herdsmen and especially at weekends by bathers, and the construction of buildings, are problems in the area.

The lagoon is a breeding site for *Oxyura leucocephala* (*c.*20 pairs). Other breeding species include *Podiceps grisegena* (1 pair), *P. cristatus* (1 pair), *Tadorna ferruginea* (3-4 pairs), *Aythya nyroca* (5 pairs), *Tringa totanus* (9+ pairs), *Himantopus himantopus* (20+ pairs), *Chlidonias hybridus* (5+ pairs), and *Sterna albifrons* (1 pair).

071 Erçek Gölü (Van)

38°39'N, 43°33'E 9800 ha

Unprotected

Erçek Gölü is a brackish lake with steep and rocky shores on the northern and western sides, and shallow shores on the southern and eastern sides where some saline mudflats border the lake. Apart from some meadows there is almost no vegetation along the shore, although around the River Memedik, which feeds the lake, some small reedbeds are found.

The area is an important breeding site for *Tadorna ferruginea* (100 pairs), *T. tadorna* (50 pairs), *Haematopus ostralegus*, *Himantopus himantopus* (50+ pairs), *Recurvirostra avosetta*, *Burhinus oedicnemus*, *Tringa totanus* (400+ pairs), and *Sterna hirundo*. *Branta ruficollis* apparently bred in 1982 (a remarkable record), but probably not since. *Grus grus* and *Otis tarda* bred in the plain to the east of the lake. Erçek Gölü is a site of major importance for moulting and migrating waterfowl and waders (Sept. figures unless stated) with *Tachybaptus ruficollis* (max. 1000), *Podiceps nigricollis* (max. 3000), *Tadorna ferruginea* (max. 9000 in July), *T. tadorna* (max. 2500), *Recurvirostra avosetta* (max. 2000), and *Phalaropus lobatus* (max. 900 in May). *Phoenicopterus ruber* (apparently from the Iranian breeding population) occurs regularly (max. 900).

072 Horkum Gölü (marshes between Balaban and Gevaş) (Van)

38°20'N, 42°56'E 8 ha

Unprotected

A small lagoon on the southern shore of Van Gölü, and separated from it by a narrow strip of gravel and sand. The lagoon has relatively large reed- and sedge-beds in a few places, and to the south and south-west there are wet meadows and pastures.

About 10 pairs of *Oxyura leucocephala* breed on the lake (also max. 170 in autumn). Other notable breeding species include *Podiceps grisegena* (10+ pairs), *Ixobrychus minutus* (1-2 pairs), *Tadorna ferruginea* (5+ pairs), *T. tadorna* (presumed), *Anas crecca*, *A. querquedula*, *Aythya nyroca*, *Himantopus himantopus* (5-20 pairs), and *Tringa totanus* (20+ pairs).

073 Upper Murat Vadigi near Yoncalı (Muş)

39°10'N, 42°19'E *c.*2000 ha

Unprotected

A river valley in an enclosed basin with a gorge at the western end. There is a lower flood-plain with some areas of wet grassland. The plain is covered mainly by arable land with many winding irrigation channels. The river itself has islands and gravelly spits.

An important site for breeding *Anthropoides virgo* (2 pairs). Other species are *Grus grus* (3-10 pairs; also max. 100 in July and max. 260 in Oct.), *Phalacrocorax pygmeus* (probably 2+ pairs), *Anser anser*, *Tadorna ferruginea* (10+ pairs; also max. 1420 in Oct.), *Anas strepera*, *Circus pygargus* (9+ pairs), *Haematopus ostralegus* (15+ pairs), *Himantopus himantopus* (10-20 pairs), *Tringa totanus* (10-25 pairs), *Gelochelidon nilotica* (200 pairs on an island), and *Sterna albifrons* (1-2 pairs).

074 Nemrut Dağı (Bitlis)

38°37'N, 42°13'E *c.*25,000 ha

A National Park is planned for the area and designation has started

Nemrut Dağı (2935 m) is a sparsely vegetated volcano which has closed the basin of Van (and is responsible for the existence of Van Gölü). The volcano was still active until 1441, and the crater is one of the largest in the world and has two small lakes. The more important, Ilıgöl (*c.*30 ha), has hot springs and reedbeds. The crater lake itself is surrounded by low scrub and barren rocks at higher altitudes. Rocky cliffs form the crater walls which reach up to 690 m above the lake. The edge of the volcano is subject to heavy erosion, particularly because of snow melt.

The crater lake is a breeding site for a relict population of *Melanitta fusca*: up to 39 birds have been counted during the breeding season and breeding has been confirmed several times. Other breeding species include *Neophron percnopterus*, *Gyps fulvus*, *Circus pygargus*, *Aquila chrysaetos*, *Hieraaetus pennatus*, *Falco biarmicus*, *Bubo bubo*, *Anthus campestris*, *Prunella ocularis*, *Luscinia svecica*, *Irania gutturalis*, *Monticola saxatilis*, *Serinus pusillus* (common), and *Bucanetes githagineus* (presumed).

075 Saz Gölü (Doğubayazıt Sazlığı) (Ağrı)

39°45'N, 44°03'E *c.*1000 ha

Unprotected

Saz Gölü is at the foot of Ararat Dağ and is almost completely covered by reeds, with very little open water. In 1987 the marshes were almost dry probably because of drought.

Anthropoides virgo apparently bred in 1971, but has not been found since. *Botaurus stellaris*, *Himantopus himantopus*, and *Motacilla citreola* are still known to breed.

076 Sodalı Göl (Arın Gölü) (Bitlis)

38°49'N, 42°59'E 1100 ha

Unprotected

A saline lake without aquatic vegetation, mostly surrounded by arable land. There is a separate lagoon with marshes between the lake and Göldüzü village. Extensive grazing of cattle in the wet meadows results in disturbance to some breeding species.

Breeding species at the lake include *Podiceps nigricollis* (50+ pairs presumed), *Tadorna ferruginea*, *T. tadorna* (at least 4 pairs), *Anas strepera*, *A. acuta*, *A. querquedula*, *A. clypeata*, *Oxyura leucocephala* (20-25+ pairs), *Haematopus ostralegus* (a few pairs), *Himantopus himantopus* (200 pairs), *Recurvirostra avosetta*, *Burhinus oedicnemus*, *Tringa totanus* (250+ pairs), *Sterna caspia* (10 pairs), *S. hirundo*, *S. albifrons*, *Chlidonias leucopterus* (300 pairs), and *C. hybridus* (10 pairs). *Otis tarda* breeds in the environs of the lake (up to 10 birds during the breeding season) as do *Falco cherrug*, *F. peregrinus*, and *Bubo bubo*. The lake is also of great importance as a moulting and passage site for many species, including *Podiceps nigricollis* (max. 4000-5000 in July), *Oxyura leucocephala* (max. 300), *Tadorna ferruginea* (max. 6000-8000 in July), *Tringa totanus* (max. 2000), *Himantopus himantopus* (max. 1000), *Calidris minuta* (2000-3000) and *Chlidonias leucopterus* (max. 1650).

077 Van Sazlığı (marshes near Van Kalesi or Van İskelesi or Van Lagoon) (Van)

38°29'N, 43°19'E 80 ha

Unprotected

A complex of some small lagoons alongside Van Gölü (separated from it by a narrow strip of sand), partly covered by extensive reedbeds. The area includes Van Kalesi (Van Castle). Wet meadows are found around the marshes and towards the castle. Disturbance by grazing cattle, tourists (visiting the castle), bathing (on the sandy ridge between the lagoon and the lake), reed-cutting, and shooting are serious conservation problems.

Breeding species include or probably include *Podiceps grisegena* (1-2 pairs), *Ixobrychus minutus*, *Nycticorax nycticorax*, *Ardeola ralloides* (presumed), *Ardea purpurea* (1+ pair), *Tadorna ferruginea* (5+ pairs), *T. tadorna*, *Anas strepera*, *A. crecca*, *A. clypeata*, *Aythya ferina*, *A. nyroca* (8-11 pairs), *Marmaronetta angustirostris* (4 pairs in 1986), *Oxyura leucocephala* (10-15 pairs), *Milvus migrans*, *Neophron percnopterus*, *Circus aeruginosus*, *Falco naumanni* (10 pairs at castle), *Grus grus* (1 pair until 1985), *Himantopus himantopus* (20 pairs), *Recurvirostra avosetta* (15 pairs), *Tringa totanus* (15 pairs), *Gelochelidon nilotica* (probably 2 pairs), *Sterna hirundo* (3-4 pairs), *Chlidonias leucopterus*, *Bubo bubo* (1 pair at castle), *Locustella luscinioides*, *Acrocephalus melanopogon*, and *Motacilla citreola*. Recent records of *Acrocephalus agricola* might indicate breeding (only site in Turkey).

078 Yüksekova (Hakkari)

37°33'N, 44°15'E 28,000 ha

Unprotected

A large plain at high altitude (about 2000 m), which is crossed by the River Nehil. This winding river is in an original state, with marshes and wet meadows (with many orchids) along its bends. A change in agricultural use might quickly destroy the habitats.

Ardea purpurea, Circus aeruginosus, C. pygargus (15+ pairs), *Grus grus* (less than 5 pairs), *Otis tarda* (less than 5 pairs), and *Tringa totanus* breed, and *Gyps fulvus, Circaetus gallicus, Accipiter brevipes, Aquila pomarina, A. chrysaetos, Hieraaetus pennatus, Falco peregrinus*, and *Bubo bubo* occur in the surrounding area.

079 Sarikum Gölü (Sinop)

42°01'N, 34°51'E 100 ha

Nature Reserve

A coastal lake, connected to the sea by a small river. On the south side of the lake there is a forest of *Fraxinus excelsior*. There is afforestation around the lake. The site is poorly known ornithologically.

In Oct. 1987, *c.*100,000 birds were present at the lake including *Podiceps cristatus, Tachybaptus ruficollis, Phalacrocorax carbo, Ardea cinerea, Egretta garzetta, E. alba, Anser albifrons, A. anser, Anas platyrhynchos, Netta rufina, Aythya ferina, A. nyroca, A. fuligula, Fulica atra*, and *Vanellus vanellus*.

MAIN REFERENCES

Bariş, S., Akcakaya, R. and Bilgin (1984) *Birds of Turkey 3: Kızılcahamam.* Heidelburg.

Beaman, M., Porter, R. F. and Vittery, A. (1975) *The Ornithological Society of Turkey Bird Report 1970-73.* Ornithological Society of Turkey, Sandy.

Beaman, M. (eds.) (1986) Turkey Bird Report 1976-81 *Sandgrouse* 8: 1-41.

Carp, E. (1980) *A directory of Western Palearctic wetlands.* Gland: IUCN-UNEP.

Dijksen, L. and Kasparek, M. (1985) *Birds of Turkey 4: Kızılirmak Deltası.* Heidelburg.

Erol, O. (1982): Die naturräumliche Gliederung der Türkei. Beih. Tübinger Atlas d. Vorderen Orients, Reihe A. (Naturwiss.). No. 13. Pp. 245. Heidelburg.

Husband, C. and Kasparek, M. (1984) *Birds of Turkey, 2: Seyfe Gölü.* Heidelburg.

Kasparek, M. and Vander Ven, J. (1983) *Birds of Turkey, 1: Erçek Gölü.* Heidelburg.

Kasparek, M. (1985) Die Sultanssümpfe. Naturgeschichte eines Vogelparadieses in Anatolien. Heidelberg.

Kasparek, M. (1988) Bafasee: Natur und Geschichte in der turkischen Ägäis. Heidelberg.

Merkez Av Komisyonu (1987) 1987-1988 Av Mevsimi Merkez Av Komisyonu Karari. T. C. Tarum Orman ve Köyişleri Bakanliği, Orman Genel Müdürlüğü. Ankara.

Molu, M. and Gürpinar, T. (1972) Wetlands and Waterfowl in Turkey. *Proceedings of the International Conference on Conservation of Wetlands and Waterfowl. Ramsar 1971.* P. 251-254. Slimbridge.

Porter, R., Squire, J. E. and Vittery, A. (1972) *The Ornithological Society of Turkey Bird Report 1968-1969.* Ornithological Society of Turkey, Sandy.

Savage, C. D. W., Porter, R. F. and Wilkinson, W. H. N. (1968) A provisional check-list of Turkish wetlands. *Proceedings of a technical meeting on wetland conservation.* IUCN Publ. new ser. 12: 94-96.

Turan, N. and Gürpınar, T. (1976) Turkey National Report. *Proceedings of the International Conference on Conservation of wetlands and waterfowl. Heiligenhafen 1974.* Pp. 158-163. Slimbridge.

van der Berk, V., van der Berk, N., Bijlsma, R. G. and de Roder, F. E. (1983) *The importance of some wetlands in Turkey as transient and wintering areas for waterbirds.* Zeist: Stichting WIWO.

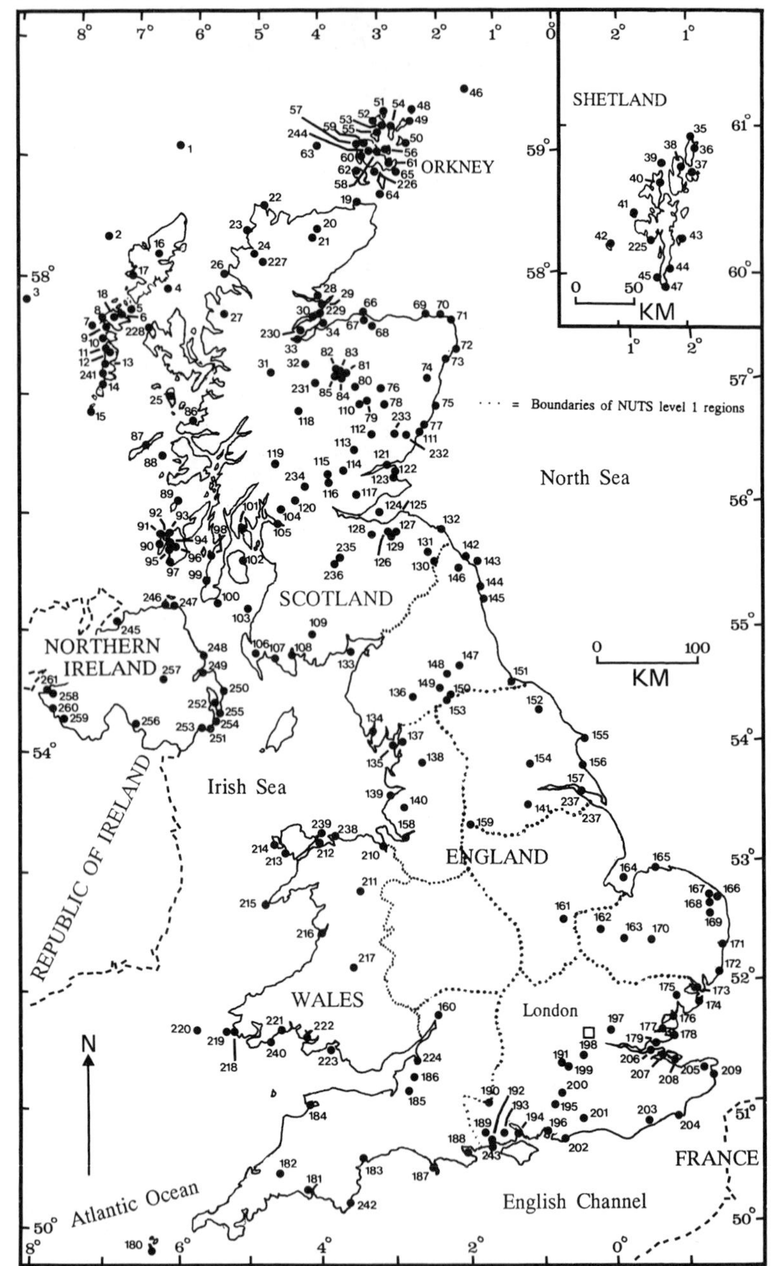

Figure 36: Map showing the location of the sites in the United Kingdom

UNITED KINGDOM

Bar-tailed Godwit *Limosa lapponica*, Dunlin *Calidris alpina*, and Grey Plover *Pluvialis squatarola*

INTRODUCTION

General information

The United Kingdom is made up of England, Scotland, Wales, and Northern Ireland. All are governed by the national parliament in London, but each has different degrees of administrative independence. While the U.K. has responsibility for defence and, in general, the international relations of the Isle of Man, Channel Islands, and Gibraltar, these are self-governing Crown Dependencies and are given separate entries in this book. The U.K. shares a common border with the Republic of Ireland.

The U.K. extends from 07°40'W (with an outlying island at 13°41'W) to 01°46'E, and from 49°52' to 60°51'N. Its area of 244,100 sq km is inhabited by a relatively stable population of 56.5 million (an average population density of 230 persons per sq km), 80 per cent of whom live in urban areas. It is a crowded and industrialised country with diverse landscapes, over 85 per cent of which are used for agriculture or forestry. Maritime influences are prominent, no part of the country being further than 115 km from tidal waters. The climate is warmer and wetter than at the same latitudes in central Europe. Soils are varied and resilient. The highest point (in Scotland) is 1344 m above sea level.

The U.K. does not suffer from problems of desertification, large-scale deforestation or widespread soil erosion, and is a net importer of many raw materials. However, since the Second World War there has been a dramatic intensification of land-use, particularly for agriculture. High agricultural subsidies have made the country 75 per cent self-sufficient in temperate foodstuffs, but are now contributing to over-production. Exploitation of mineral resources (primarily coal, limestone, aggregates, oil, gas), establishment of forest plantations, and the expansion of industrial development and agriculture have altered irrevocably the land surface of this small country. Very few truly natural habitats exist.

Nevertheless, there are natural or semi-natural biological features of outstanding interest. For example, the sheer diversity of habitats in a restricted area is due to unusual variations in geology and climate; the country's wetlands hold huge numbers of waterfowl in winter; humid deciduous woodlands in the west have a rich bryophyte flora; the wide range and extent of heathlands include types which are restricted to the U.K.; extensive peatland 'flows' exist in northern Scotland; and unique machair habitats are found on some western Scottish coasts.

Threats and pressures continue, as figures for England and Wales illustrate. Some 30-50 per cent of ancient lowland broadleaved woodland have been lost since 1945, mostly by conversion to farmland or to conifer plantations. Woodlands in total cover 9 per cent of the land surface, with largely alien conifer plantations accounting for about half of these. Ninety-five per cent of lowland neutral grasslands and 50 per cent of lowland fens and mires have been damaged or destroyed by agricultural intensification in the same period. 240,000+ km of hedgerows, 30 per cent of upland grasslands, heath, and bog, and 40 per cent of southern heathlands have been lost, while 97 per cent of limestone pavements have suffered damage. Industry, roads, housing and mineral extraction consume 15,000 ha of land each year in England, and possibly twice this area in the country as a whole. About 40 U.K. estuaries of international importance are significantly threatened by development, while at current rates of loss lowland dry heath outside a few protected areas is likely to disappear before the end of the century.

The pace of loss and fragmentation of habitats have put a number of wildlife populations at risk. Species currently classed as 'endangered' or 'vulnerable' in the U.K. include 33 per cent of reptiles and amphibians, 24 per cent of terrestrial mammals, and 8 per cent of flowering plants. In the case of birds, nearly one-third are the subject of significant concern for the future of their populations, for reasons other than extreme rarity *per se*.

Set against this is the existence in the U.K. of one of the oldest and strongest non-governmental conservation movements in the world, with over three million members subscribing to organisations involved in this field. Government conservation agencies suffer from poor funding, and operate as part of a highly complex and incompletely integrated system of land-use planning; but they are relatively sophisticated and have been pioneers in a number of areas. Nature conservation is now receiving increasing attention at a political level.

Ornithological importance

The U.K. has just over 200 bird species which breed regularly, with about 25 more which have bred sporadically this century. There are a further 52 winter visitors. Forty-eight species are on Annex I of EEC Directive 79/409 on the Conservation of Wild Birds.

There is only one endemic species, namely *Loxia scotica*. There are in addition several endemic passerine subspecies.

Three types of U.K. bird community and habitat can be highlighted as of special international importance:

1. Estuaries

   Almost one and a half million wading birds winter on U.K. estuaries, comprising 40 per cent of the European total. Many others use these sites as stop-over refuges on migration. Wildfowl numbers on estuaries may reach 500,000. U.K. estuaries support more than one-third of the north-west European wintering population of six species of wader and five species of wildfowl: overall 13 wildfowl and ten wader species winter in internationally significant numbers. Twenty-eight sites hold over 20,000 waders and/or 10,000 wildfowl. The special importance of U.K. estuaries for birds in a European context derives from a number of factors: they are numerous, their tidal range is large, and the winter climate is relatively mild, with tidal waters rarely freezing. Many sites have been damaged or are threatened, and large declines have been noted in populations of *Calidris alpina*, *C. canutus*, and *Tringa totanus*.

2. Peatlands and heather moorland
Eight species of bird whose breeding populations are largely dependent on moorland habitats in the U.K. breed in numbers which constitute a significant proportion of European or world totals: *Aquila chrysaetos* (425 pairs; representing 20 per cent of the west European population), *Circus cyaneus* (400 pairs; representing 10 per cent of the European population), *Falco columbarius* (550-600 pairs in Great Britain; representing 5-7 per cent of the European population, but virtually 100 per cent of the EEC's population), *Lagopus lagopus* (300,000 pairs in Great Britain; representing 60 per cent of the EEC's population), *Pluvialis apricaria* (22,600 pairs; representing 96 per cent of the EEC's total). The biggest area of peatlands, the so-called 'Flow Country' of north-east Scotland, is one of the world's outstanding examples of this ecosystem. Large reductions in the extent of these habitats have occurred with consequent reductions in bird populations.

3. Seabirds
Britain and Ireland together hold one of the outstanding assemblages of North Atlantic breeding seabirds. Important colonies are found on small islands, and on sea cliffs: *Hydrobates pelagicus* (20,000 pairs; representing 30 per cent of the world total), *Sula bassana* (161,000 pairs; 61 per cent of the world population), *Alca torda* (145,000 pairs; at least 20 per cent of the world total, possibly much higher since the Icelandic population is not known), and the races *Uria aalge aalge*, *U. a. albionis*, *Larus fuscus graellsii*, *Stercorarius skua skua*, and *Puffinus puffinus puffinus*. Up to 95 per cent of the EEC's *Larus marinus* population breed in the U.K. Approximately 12 per cent of the west European population (or 25 per cent excluding the Azores) of *Sterna dougallii* breed in the U.K., and this species is in serious decline.

There are three globally threatened species that breed in the U.K.: *Milvus milvus* (200-600 birds; of which 50 pairs breed), *Haliaeetus albicilla* (recently reintroduced to the U.K. from Norway; currently over 40 birds known to be surviving, of which six pairs are breeding or attempting to breed), and *Crex crex* (estimated 450 breeding pairs, representing 10 per cent of the west European population). At the time of writing, a new bird Red Data Book for Great Britain is in preparation, due for publication in 1989 by NCC/RSPB. This is organised on a different basis from the ICBP/IUCN Red Data Books. One hundred and nineteen species are included for their rarity, declining populations, localised populations, severe habitat threat, or international population significance. In the case of 26 species, the only threat to their continued presence is their extreme rarity in the U.K. context.

Examples of other species for which the U.K. is particularly important include *Anser brachyrhynchus* (134,000 birds in winter, representing 80 per cent of the world population), *Anser albifrons flavirostris* (11,000 birds in winter, representing 50 per cent of the world population), and *Branta leucopsis* (34,000 birds in winter).

Conservation infrastructure and protected-area system

The basis for conservation legislation in the United Kingdom was the National Parks and Access to the Countryside Act 1949, and the Protection of Birds Acts 1954-67. The principal statute now is the Wildlife and Countryside Act 1981, which was amended by the Wildlife and Countryside (Amendment) Act 1985, and the Wildlife and Countryside (Service of Notices) Act 1985. These apply to England, Scotland and Wales, and are mirrored closely in Northern Ireland by the Conservation and Amenity Lands (Northern Ireland) Orders 1985-89, and the Wildlife (Northern Ireland) Order 1985. These statutes are the means by which the U.K. is able to implement relevant parts of the (Ramsar) Convention on Wetlands of International Importance, and EEC Directive 79/409 on the

Conservation of Wild Birds; indeed the latter was one of the principal reasons for their inception.

Other legislation which addresses conservation includes the Countryside (Scotland) Act 1967, the Forestry Act 1967, the Countryside Act 1968, the Water Act 1973, and the Control of Pollution Act 1974. A sophisticated system for authorising development projects derives mainly from the Town and Country Planning Act 1971; but this does not cover agriculture, forestry, and most port operations, and it can override the Wildlife and Countryside Acts. Most protective mechanisms do not apply to maritime areas below the littoral zone and thus do not cover the requirements of the EEC Directive. Northern Ireland generally, and Scotland often, have separate but similar systems to England and Wales.

The principal statutory agency concerned with nature conservation is the Nature Conservancy Council (NCC). It establishes and manages reserves, identifies other important sites, carries out research, disseminates information, and advises government on all aspects of conservation. Although funded by the Department of the Environment it determines its policy independently. In Northern Ireland these functions are carried out by the Department of the Environment (Northern Ireland), advised by the Commission for Nature Conservation. The Countryside Commission (CC) and Countryside Commission for Scotland (CCS) are responsible for the conservation and enhancement of natural beauty and amenity of the countryside, and securing access for recreation. In Northern Ireland the Department of the Environment (Northern Ireland) fulfils this role. Other relevant statutory authorities include District, Borough, County, Regional, and Island Councils; Water Authorities; River Purification Boards; the Forestry Commission; and the four Agriculture Departments.

The voluntary conservation sector is well developed, and land is owned and managed by, *inter alia*, the National Trust, National Trust for Scotland, Royal Society for the Protection of Birds, the County Trusts for Nature Conservation, Scottish Wildlife Trust, Ulster Trust for Nature Conservation, and Woodland Trust. These non-governmental nature conservation organisations have significant landholdings managed as nature reserves.

The main categories of protected area in the U.K. are as follows:

1. National Nature Reserve (234 Great Britain; 45 Northern Ireland)
   Usually managed by NCC (Great Britain) or by agreement with the Department of Environment (Northern Ireland), for the conservation of flora, fauna, geological or physiographical features. There is a Marine Nature Reserve equivalent for marine sites: only one of these has so far been established.

2. Site of Special Scientific Interest (*c.*5000 Great Britain, *c.*60 Northern Ireland, where they are termed 'Areas of Scientific Interest' and are being converted under new legislation to 'Areas of Special Scientific Interest'). SSSIs/ASIs/ASSIs are the backbone of statutory site protection in the U.K. They are mostly in private ownership, and are selected and notified by NCC (or Department of Environment [NI] for Northern Ireland) on scientific grounds relating to flora, fauna, geological or physiographical interest. Special consultation arrangements apply to land-use operations on these sites but, despite a legal requirement for owners of SSSIs not to damage the interest, adequate protection depends on voluntary cooperation by owners and occupiers.

3. Local Nature Reserve (154)
   LNRs are established by local planning authorities, are often but not always owned by them, and are regulated by by-laws for (e.g.) control of access and protection of wildlife.

4. National Park (10; England and Wales only)
   Generally in upland areas, these were designated in the 1950s for landscape and amenity purposes. They are inhabited, and entail no special state ownership. There are some special planning constraints and consultative arrangements, administered by a National Park Authority for each Park. General promotion of the Parks is undertaken by the Countryside Commission for England and Wales. In addition to the ten

designated parks, two other areas in England are accorded a status which has some similarities.

5. Area of Outstanding Natural Beauty (40 England and Wales; 8 Northern Ireland). AONBs are established for the conservation of natural beauty, by the Countryside Commission (or Department of Environment in Northern Ireland). Special planning restrictions apply.

6. National Scenic Area (40, Scotland only)
These replaced the five former National Park Direction Areas in Scotland, and are designated on landscape grounds. Special consultation arrangements between planning authorities and the Countryside Commission for Scotland apply.

Other important designations include Green Belts; Heritage Coasts; Environmentally Sensitive Areas; Areas of Special Protection (Bird Sanctuaries; not to be confused with EEC Special Protection Areas); Areas of Great Landscape Value; Tree Preservation Orders; Country Parks; Forest Nature Reserves; and a variety of local nature-conservation designations made by local planning authorities.

International measures relevant to the conservation of sites

The U.K. is a member of the Council of Europe and the European Community, and is bound by the latter's Directive 79/409 on the Conservation of Wild Birds. It has ratified the Ramsar, Bern, Bonn, and World Heritage Conventions. By February 1989, 33 Special Protection Areas and 40 Ramsar Sites (Wetlands of International Importance) had been declared. These are designated by central government under the terms of EEC Directive 79/409 on the Conservation of Wild Birds, and the Ramsar Convention, respectively. Their statutory protection is by means of notification as SSSI/ASSI, and no extra statutory protection is provided over and above the SSSI/ASSI procedures. However, designation of SPAs does bind the U.K. government to particular actions. A significant number of additional sites still await designation.

There are 27 Biosphere Reserves (UNESCO/MAB), and two natural World Heritage Sites (World Heritage Convention); but no Biogenetic Reserves as yet.

Overview of the inventory

There are 261 sites in the U.K. inventory of which 147 are in Scotland (one shared with England), 82 in England (one shared with Scotland, two with Wales), 18 in Wales (two shared with England), and 17 in Northern Ireland. Of these, 23 per cent (60 sites) have been included principally because of their breeding seabirds (rocky coasts, cliffs, beaches), 41 per cent (106 sites) have been included principally because of their wintering wildfowl and waders (estuaries, reservoirs, inland and coastal marshes, meadows, and rocky coasts), and 14 per cent have been included principally because of their breeding wildfowl and waders (inland wetlands and uplands). The inventory also includes a small number of woodland sites and lowland heath sites (including the Brecks) (less than 10 of each).

Over 90 per cent of the sites are protected (or at least partly protected) usually as SSSIs. It should be stressed that large parts of some sites are unprotected. Of the 244 sites in Scotland, England and Wales, the U.K. government has accepted that 224 qualify for designation (or have been designated) as EEC Special Protection Areas and/or Ramsar Sites: 133 in Scotland (one shared with England), 79 in England (one shared with Scotland, two with Wales), and 15 in Wales (two shared with England).

Understandably, populations of species that breed at low densities (particularly birds of prey) are less well covered by the sites in this inventory than are seabirds and waterfowl. One species on Annex I of the EEC Wild Birds Directive stands out, however, as being particularly poorly covered by the inventory: *Milvus milvus* (a globally threatened species).

As mentioned above, about 40 estuaries of international importance are threatened with development (all included in this inventory). A large number of the other sites lack the protection needed if the bird populations they support are to be maintained. One of the most seriously threatened (most important and least protected) sites in the inventory is the Peatlands of Caithness and Sutherland, which is being irreparably damaged by commercial afforestation.

Acknowledgements

At an early stage, it was agreed that the inventory (for England, Scotland and Wales) should be based on the Nature Conservancy Council (NCC)'s list of sites qualifying for designation as EEC Special Protection Areas and/or Ramsar Sites prepared in 1987 and updated in 1988 (e.g. Hansard: 11 May 1987 and 20 December 1988) by the Chief Scientists' Directorate of the NCC. C. A. Galbraith (NCC) was of considerable help in providing ornithological information for a large proportion of the sites, with seabird data being provided by M. L. Tasker and C. Lloyd (NCC Aberdeen/Seabird Group). Additional help was forthcoming from L. Butler and C. Monk. The NCC's contribution to the project was coordinated by M. W. Pienkowski and L. Batten with some last-minute information coming direct from I. Davies, D. Kite, and S. Tolhurst.

Data for wildfowl and waders were largely provided by D. Salmon (Wildfowl Trust; published and unpublished data from the NCC-funded National Waterfowl Counts) and British Trust for Ornithology (data from the BTO/NCC/RSPB-funded Birds of Estuaries Enquiry). D. E. Pritchard coordinated RSPB's contribution to the project and D. Allen, R. Broad, A. Bunten, T. Cleeves, C. Crooke, M. Davies, D. Dick, C. Durdin, A. Farrar, R. Lovegrove, E. Meek, J. O'Sullivan, A. Prater, D. Radford, D. Sexton, J. Stevenson, S. Tyler, J. Waldon, G. Williams, and R. Wynde of RSPB's outposted staff were extremely helpful in providing last-minute information on a number of sites. L. Campbell and I. Dawson at RSPB headquarters also provided assistance. D. E. Pritchard and A. Gammell provided advice on many occasions, and D. Bashford at the final stages. D. E. Pritchard provided the introduction for the U.K. H. Welch gathered a great deal of information, and filled many gaps in the final weeks prior to publication.

Acknowledgement should also be given to D. A. Scott, I. Prestt, R. F. Porter, K. T. Standring, T. J. Stowe, and G. J. Thomas, who jointly compiled information for the first inventory of important bird areas (Osieck and Mörzer Bruyns 1981) which was used extensively to prepare the current text, and to D. E. Pritchard who has provided ICBP with information on sites since 1983.

Data for Northern Ireland were provided largely by C. J. Murphy with comments on a final draft provided by J. K. Partridge (both of RSPB's Northern Ireland office).

INVENTORY

No.	Site name	Region	Criteria used to select site [see p.18]							
			0	1(i)	1(ii)	1(iii)	1(iv)	2	3	4
001	North Rona and Sula Sgeir	SD		*	*				*	
002	Flannan Isles	SD			*				*	
003	St Kilda	SD		*	*				*	
004	Shiant Isles	SD		*	*	*			*	
005	West Sound of Harris	SD				*			*	
006	Loch An Duin	SD				*				
007	Monach Islands	SD				*			*	
008	Balranald	SD				*		*		
009	Baleshare and Kirkibost	SD				*			*	
010	Bagh Nam Foailean to Ardivachar	SD				*				
011	Iochdair and Geirinish Machair and Loch Bee	SD							*	
012	Na Meadhoinean Iar (including Loch Druidibeg)	SD				*				
013	Machair Lochs (including Lochs Hallan and Kilpheder), South Uist	SD						*		
014	West Sound of Barra	SD				*			*	
015	Mingulay and Berneray	SD		*	*					
016	Lewis peatlands	SD							*	
017	North Harris Mountains	SD							*	
018	Loch Scadavay	SD							*	

No.	Site name	Region	Criteria used to select site [see p.18] 0	1(i)	1(ii)	1(iii)	1(iv)	2	3	4
019	Caithness Cliffs	SD		*	*					
020	Caithness Lochs	SD							*	
021	The Peatlands of Caithness and Sutherland	SD				*			*	
022	Cape Wrath – Aodann Mhor	SD			*					
023	Handa	SD		*	*					
024	Loch Assynt, Loch Urigill and nearby lochs	SD							*	
025	Rhum	SD		*	*			*	*	
026	Priest Island	SD		*	*				*	
027	Loch Maree	SD							*	
028	Lower Dornoch Firth (including Morrich More)	SD				*				
029	Loch Eye	SD				*			*	
030	Cromarty Firth	SD				*			*	
031	Affric-Cannich Hills and Glens	SD							*	
032	Lochs Ashie and Ruthven	SD							*	
033	Beauly Firth	SD				*			*	
034	Moray Firth: Munlochy Bay to Findhorn Bay	SD				*				
035	Hermaness and Saxa Vord	SD		*	*					
036	Croussa Field and the Heogs	SD	*							
037	Fetlar	SD			*	*			*	
038	Blackpark, Yell	SD							*	
039	Ramna Stacks and Gruney	SD							*	
040	North Roe	SD		*	*				*	
041	Papa Stour	SD			*				*	
042	Foula	SD		*	*				*	
043	Noss	SD		*	*					
044	Mousa (part)	SD		*	*				*	
045	Loch Spiggie	SD							*	
046	Fair Isle	SD		*	*				*	
047	Sumburgh Head	SD			*					
048	North Ronaldsay Coast	SD	*							
049	East Sanday	SD				*			*	
050	South-eastern Stronsay	SD	*							
051	Papa Westray (North Hill and Holm)	SD			*				*	
052	West Westray	SD			*				*	
053	South Westray Coast	SD				*				
054	Eday	SD			*					
055	Rousay (part)	SD			*				*	
056	Mill Dam, Shapinsay	SD							*	
057	Marwick Head	SD			*					
058	North Mainland Coast	SD				*				
059	West Mainland Moors	SD							*	
060	Lochs of Harray and Stenness	SD	*							
061	Orphir and Stenness Hills	SD							*	
062	Hoy	SD		*	*				*	
063	Sule Skerry and Stack Skerry	SD		*	*				*	
064	Pentland Firth Islands	SD			*				*	
065	Copinsay	SD			*					
066	Moray Firth: Burghead and Spey Bays	SD				*				
067	Loch Spynie	SD				*				
068	Loch Oire	SD							*	
069	Troup, Pennan, and Lion Heads	SD			*					

No.	Site name	Region	Criteria used to select site [see p.18]							
			0	1(i)	1(ii)	1(iii)	1(iv)	2	3	4
070	Quarry Head to Fraserburgh Coast	SD				*				
071	Loch of Strathbeg	SD			*	*			*	
072	Bullers of Buchan and Whinnyfold	SD			*					
073	Ythan Estuary, Sands of Forvie, and Meikle Lochs	SD			*	*			*	
074	Loch of Skene	SD				*				
075	Fowlsheugh	SD			*					
076	Muir of Dinnet	SD	*							
077	St Cyrus	SD							*	
078	Glen Tanar	SD							*	
079	Lochnagar	SD							*	
080	Cairngorms	SD							*	
081	Abernethy Forest	SD							*	
082	Kinveachy	SD							*	
083	Loch Vaa	SD							*	
084	Loch Alvie	SD							*	
085	River Spey – Insh Marshes	SD							*	
086	Kentra Moss	SD							*	
087	Tiree and Coll	SD				*		*	*	
088	Treshnish Islands	SD		*	*	*			*	
089	North Colonsay and Western Cliffs	SD			*				*	
090	Islay: Rinns	SD				*		*	*	
091	Islay: Glac na Criche	SD							*	
092	Islay: Feur Lochain	SD				*			*	
093	Islay: Loch Gruinart	SD				*			*	
094	Islay: Bridgend Flats	SD				*			*	
095	Islay: Laggan	SD				*			*	
096	Islay: Eilean na Muice Dubh (Duich Moss)	SD				*			*	
097	Islay: The Oa	SD				*			*	
098	Rhunahaorine	SD				*			*	
099	Machrihanish and Tangy Loch	SD				*			*	
100	Sanda	SD		*	*				*	
101	North end of Bute	SD							*	
102	North Arran Mountains	SD							*	
103	Ailsa Craig	SD		*	*					
104	Loch Lomond	SD				*			*	
105	Inner Clyde Estuary	SD				*				
106	Lochinch (White Loch) and Torrs Warren	SD				*			*	
107	Mochrum and Castle Lochs	SD				*				
108	Wigtown Bay	SD				*			*	
109	Loch Ken and Dee Marshes	SD				*			*	
110	Caenlochan	SD							*	
111	Montrose Basin	SD				*				
112	Loch of Lintrathen	SD				*				
113	Tay – Isla Valley	SD				*				
114	Dupplin Lochs	SD				*				
115	Drummond Lochs	SD				*				
116	Carsebreck and Rhynd Lochs	SD				*				
117	Loch Leven	SD				*			*	
118	Drumochter Hills	SD							*	
119	Ben Dubhchraig	SD	*							
120	Flanders Moss and Lake of Menteith	SD				*				
121	Firth of Tay	SD				*				

No.	Site name	Region	Criteria used to select site [see p.18]							
			0	1(i)	1(ii)	1(iii)	1(iv)	2	3	4
122	Eden Estuary, Tentsmuir Point, and Abertay Sands	SD	*							
123	Cameron Reservoir	SD				*				
124	Inner Firth of Forth and Outer Firth of Forth	SD				*				
125	Forth Islands	SD		*	*				*	
126	Gladhouse Reservoir	SD				*				
127	Fala Flow	SD				*				
128	Westwater	SD				*				
129	Moorfoot Hills	SD							*	
130	Hoselaw Loch	SD				*				
131	Greenlaw Moor and Hule Moss	SD				*				
132	St Abb's Head – Fast Castle	SD			*					
133	Upper Solway Flats and Marshes	SD,N				*			*	
134	Duddon Estuary	N				*				
135	Morecambe Bay	N,NW		*	*	*			*	
136	Shap Fells	N							*	
137	Leighton Moss	NW							*	
138	Bowland Fells	NW							*	
139	Ribble and Alt Estuaries	NW				*			*	
140	Martin Mere	NW				*			*	
141	Thorne and Hatfield Moors	YH							*	
142	Lindisfarne	N				*			*	
143	Farne Islands	N		*	*				*	
144	Northumberland Coast	N							*	
145	Coquet Island	N			*				*	
146	Holburn Moss	N	*							
147	Muggleswick, Stanhope and Wolsingham Commons	N							*	
148	Bollihope and Middleton Commons	N							*	
149	Upper Teesdale and Moor House	N,YH							*	
150	Bowes Moor	N							*	
151	Teesmouth and Cleveland Coast	N			*	*			*	
152	Spaunton, Wheeldale, Egton, and Glaisdale Moors	YH							*	
153	Abbotside, Askrigg, and Mallerstang Commons	N,YH							*	
154	Derwent Ings	YH							*	
155	Flamborough Head and Bempton Cliffs	YH		*	*					
156	Hornsea Mere	YH				*				
157	Humber Flats, Marshes, and Coast	YH,EA				*			*	
158	Mersey Estuary	NW				*				
159	Peak District Moors	YH,EM							*	
160	Walmore Common	SW							*	
161	Rutland Water	EM				*				
162	Nene Washes	EA				*			*	
163	Ouse Washes	EA				*			*	
164	The Wash	EM,EA				*			*	
165	North Norfolk Coast	EA			*	*			*	
166	Upper Thurne Broads and Marshes	EA				*			*	
167	Ant Broads and Marshes	EA							*	
168	Bure Broads and Marshes	EA							*	
169	Yare Broads and Marshes	EA				*				
170	Breckland Heaths	EA							*	
171	Minsmere – Walberswick	EA				*			*	
172	Orfordness – Havergate	EA				*			*	

No.	Site name	Region	Criteria used to select site [see p.18] 0	1(i)	1(ii)	1(iii)	1(iv)	2	3	4
173	Stour and Orwell Estuary	EA,SE				*			*	
174	Hamford Water	SE				*			*	
175	Abberton Reservoir	SE				*				
176	Blackwater, Colne and Dengie	SE				*			*	
177	River Crouch Marshes	SE				*				
178	Foulness and Maplin Sands	SE				*			*	
179	Benfleet and Southend Marshes	SE				*				
180	Isles of Scilly Coastal Habitats	SW		*	*	*			*	
181	Tamar Complex	SW							*	
182	Bodmin Moor	SW							*	
183	Exe Estuary	SW				*			*	
184	Taw and Torridge Estuary	SW	*							
185	Somerset Levels and Moors	SW							*	
186	Chew Valley Lake	SW				*				
187	Chesil Beach and The Fleet	SW							*	
188	Poole Basin	SW				*			*	
189	Horton Common and Holt Heath	SW							*	
190	Porton Down	SE,SW							*	
191	Windsor Forest and Great Park	SE	*							
192	Avon Valley	SE				*			*	
193	New Forest	SE							*	
194	West Solent Marshes and Southampton Water	SE				*			*	
195	Woolmer Forest	SE							*	
196	Chichester and Langstone Harbours	SE				*			*	
197	Lee Valley	SE	*							
198	South-west London Reservoirs and Gravel Pits	SE	*							
199	Chobham to Yateley Commons	SE							*	
200	Thursley, Hankley and Frensham Commons	SE							*	
201	Amberley	SE							*	
202	Pagham Harbour	SE				*			*	
203	Pevensey Levels	SE	*							
204	Dungeness to Pett Levels	SE							*	
205	Stodmarsh	SE							*	
206	South Thames Marshes	SE				*				
207	Medway Estuary and Marshes	SE				*				
208	The Swale and South Sheppey	SE				*			*	
209	Thanet Coast	SE				*				
210	Dee Estuary	WS,NW				*			*	
211	Berwyn	WS							*	
212	Traeth Lafan (Lavan Sands)	WS				*				
213	Anglesey Islands and Cemlyn Bay	WS			*				*	
214	Holy Island Coast	WS								*
215	Bardsey Island and Aberdaron Coast	WS		*	*				*	
216	Cors Fochno and Dyfi	WS						*	*	
217	Elenydd – Mallaen	WS							*	
218	Pembrokeshire Cliffs	WS			*				*	
219	Skokholm and Skomer	WS		*	*				*	
220	Grassholm	WS		*	*					
221	Carmarthen Bay	WS				*				
222	Burry Inlet	WS				*				
223	Swansea Bay – Blackpill	WS				*				
224	Severn Estuary	SW,WS				*			*	

No.	Site name	Region	Criteria used to select site [see p.18]							
			0	1(i)	1(ii)	1(iii)	1(iv)	2	3	4
225	Clett Stacks	SD			*					
226	Scapa Flow	SD							*	
227	Inchnadamph	SD							*	
228	Isay	SD				*			*	
229	North Sutor of Cromarty	SD			*					
230	Black Isle sites	SD				*				
231	Monadhliath	SD							*	
232	Forfar, Rescobie, and Balgavies Lochs	SD				*				
233	Loch of Kinnordy	SD				*				
234	Loch Mahaick	SD				*				
235	Haughs of Clyde	SD				*				
236	Loch Lyoch and Cleuch Reservoirs	SD				*				
237	Tetney Marshes	EM							*	
238	Great and Little Orme	WS			*					
239	Puffin Island	WS			*					
240	St Margaret's Island	WS			*					
241	Kilpheder to Smerclate	SD						*		
242	Slapton Ley	SW	*							
243	Christchurch Harbour	SW	*							
244	Loch of Banks	SD							*	
245	Lough Foyle	NI				*			*	
246	Sheep Island	NI			*					
247	Rathlin Island	NI		*	*				*	
248	Larne Lough and Swan Island	NI			*	*			*	
249	Belfast Lough	NI				*				
250	Outer Ards Peninsula	NI				*				
251	Killough Harbour, Coney Island Bay and Strand Lough	NI				*				
252	Strangford Lough and islands	NI			*	*			*	
253	Dundrum Inner Bay	NI				*				
254	Carlingford Lough including Green Island	NI			*	*			*	
255	Sandy Island including Gun's Island	NI							*	
256	Annaghroe, Blackwater River	NI							*	
257	Lough Neagh and Lough Beg	NI				*			*	
258	Lower Lough Erne	NI							*	
259	Upper Lough Erne	NI				*		*	*	
260	Lower Lough McNean	NI							*	
261	Pettigoe Plateau	NI							*	

SD=Scotland N=North NW=North West YH=Yorkshire and Humberside
EA=East Anglia EM=East Midlands SW=South West SE=South East
WS=Wales NE=North East NI=Northern Ireland

Comments on the inventory

1. *Branta bernicla* is *B. b. bernicla*, *Anser albifrons* is *A. a. albifrons*, and *Limosa limosa* is *L. l. limosa*, unless stated otherwise.
2. The inventory of sites for Scotland, England and Wales (001 – 224) is arranged as closely as possible so as to follow the NCC's list of sites qualifying for designation as Special Protection Areas and/or Ramsar Sites. This is followed by a number of sites (225 – 244) which are not on this list, but which NGOs agree are worthy of designation as Special Protection Areas and/or Ramsar Sites (for some of these sites

the data were compiled in 1981 and have not been updated), and by the inventory for Northern Ireland (245 – 261). As mentioned above, the Channel Islands, Isle of Man and Gibraltar are treated separately in this book.

3. It is widely agreed that the above-mentioned NCC list needs further attention to determine the exact boundaries of many of the sites and the full extent of their bird interest (the list comprises sites considered, according to NCC criteria, to be of international importance for at least one species). The area (ha) of the site given is in most cases approximate, and further investigations may demonstrate that it should be smaller or larger, and also that the site is of greater ornithological importance than previously thought. The area (ha) has either been calculated from component SSSI schedule(s), or it has been taken from the studies of important bird areas carried out by the European Community Working Group of ICBP in 1981 (Osieck and Mörzer Bruyns 1981) and 1984, and has not been reassessed. In some cases only the area of part of the site is known and in a few cases the area has been suggested by an appropriate expert. No area is given for some sites, where it was felt unwise to make a statement about the extent of the bird interest before the necessary studies have been undertaken.

4. The figures given for wildfowl and waders are normally the average winter maximum (denoted as 'av. max.') or the absolute winter maximum (denoted as 'max.') based on the seasons 1982/83-1986/87 in the case of waders, and 1983/84-1986/87 in the case of wildfowl. In some cases, spring and/or autumn passage figures are given instead (or in addition), but this is always made clear. It should be noted that a number of sites have some data-gaps during the period 1982-1987, and in a few such cases data from before 1982/83 were included; this has not been identified in the following accounts. There are some other waterfowl data where the above qualifying comments do not apply, in cases where data have been received from other sources. The figures given are mainly those which qualify under the one per cent criteria for international importance. Lower figures may be included, either when they approach the one per cent levels (which are very tentative in the case of waders) or when they refer to sites which are important in terms of species diversity.

5. Almost all other population figures were provided by the Chief Scientists' Directorate of the NCC as a result of the data collection exercise in connection with the international designation of sites. This collection draws on information supplied by Regional Staff as well as numerous volunteers. Most of the data for seabirds derive from information largely gathered in 1985-1987 for the NCC/Seabird Group Seabird Colony Register.

6. The site name is followed by the county in England and Wales, the district and region (or just region) or island district in Scotland, and the county in Northern Ireland. This is followed by the NUTS region (NUTS level 1), which is given in parentheses.

7. The 'regions' used when applying the site-selection criteria (category 3) are the NUTS level 1 regions. The approximate boundaries of these regions are shown on the map for the U.K.

8. Two points need to be considered when interpreting the information on national protection status. Firstly, a small proportion of the SSSIs have not been renotified following the Wildlife and Countryside Act 1981, although this process is continuing. Secondly, where it says SSSI, NNR, RSPB Reserve etc., this indicates that the site is covered by one or more of these protected areas. For some sites, such designations may overlap, but for many sites they will not provide complete coverage (in which case a proportion, sometimes large, will be unprotected). It has not been possible to ensure that the listing for LNR, CCT, NT, NTS, and SWT sites is complete.

9. The coordinates given for each site are generally the central point. Thus in cases where two or more widely separated areas are included in one site, the coordinates may mark a point which is not actually part of the IBA.

10. The presence of certain bird species (e.g. *Gavia arctica*, *Podiceps auritus*, and various species of birds of prey) has not been mentioned in the site accounts because of a need for confidentiality.

11. The majority of the sites are believed to meet the site-selection criteria. Those that appear not to meet the criteria (column 0) have been included because the U.K. government has accepted that they qualify for designation as EEC Special Protection Areas and/or Ramsar Sites (except for two sites, 242 and 243, which have been included because of their importance for passerine migrants). It is important to note that the justification given here for inclusion of a site in the inventory may be different to the reason why a site is a proposed EEC Special Protection Area and/or Ramsar Site.

Glossary

The following abbreviations have been used to denote international and national categories of protection: EEC SPA = European Community Special Protection Area designated according to the EEC Directive 79/409; NNR = National Nature Reserve; SSSI = Site of Special Scientific Interest (in some cases these have not yet been renotified under the terms of the Wildlife and Countryside Act 1981); NP = National Park; AONB = Area of Outstanding Natural Beauty; LNR = Local Nature Reserve; RSPB = Royal Society for the Protection of Birds Reserve; CCT = County Conservation Trust (or equivalent) Reserve; NT = National Trust property; NTS = National Trust for Scotland property; SWT = Scottish Wildlife Trust Reserve; ESA = Environmentally Sensitive Area; ASI = Area of Scientific Interest; ASSI = Area of Special Scientific Interest.

---

001 North Rona and Sula Sgeir; Western Isles (Scotland)

59°07'N, 06°00'W 130 ha

NNR; SSSI

Two islands: North Rona is about 70 km north of Lewis; Sula Sgeir is 15 km west of North Rona.

Breeding species include *Fulmarus glacialis* (10,300 pairs), *Hydrobates pelagicus*, *Oceanodroma leucorhoa* (a large colony), *Sula bassana* (9100 pairs), *Phalacrocorax aristotelis* (140 pairs), *Stercorarius skua* (15 pairs), *Larus marinus* (740 pairs), *Rissa tridactyla* (5000 pairs), *Uria aalge* (42,000 breeding birds), *Alca torda* (1600 breeding birds), *Cepphus grylle* (55 breeding birds), and *Fratercula arctica* (6000 pairs).

002 Flannan Isles; Western Isles (Scotland)

58°17'N, 07°36'W 80 ha

SSSI

A remote cluster of six rocky islands with important seabird colonies, west of the Isle of Lewis.

Breeding species include *Fulmarus glacialis* (4700 pairs), *Hydrobates pelagicus*, *Oceanodroma leucorhoa*, *Sula bassana* (410 pairs), *Phalacrocorax aristotelis* (340 pairs), *Larus marinus* (168 pairs), *Rissa tridactyla* (2800 pairs), *Uria aalge* (22,000 breeding birds), *Alca torda* (3200 breeding birds), and *Fratercula arctica* (*c.*4000 pairs).

003 St Kilda; Western Isles (Scotland)

57°50'N, 08°30'W 853 ha Biosphere Reserve; World Heritage Site

NNR; SSSI; NSA; NTS

An isolated group of islands, 80 km west of the Sound of Harris, with high cliffs and immense seabird colonies (one of the largest concentrations in the North Atlantic).

Breeding species include *Fulmarus glacialis* (63,000 pairs), *Puffinus puffinus* (1000+ pairs), *Hydrobates pelagicus* (10,000+ pairs), *Oceanodroma leucorhoa* (10,000+ pairs), *Sula bassana* (50,000 pairs), *Phalacrocorax aristotelis* (50 pairs), *Stercorarius skua* (55 pairs), *Larus fuscus* (150 pairs), *Rissa tridactyla* (7800 pairs), *Uria aalge* (breeding birds), *Alca torda* (3800 breeding birds), *Cepphus grylle* (17 breeding birds), and *Fratercula arctica* (230,500 pairs). The island also has an endemic subspecies, *Troglodytes troglodytes hirtensis*.

004 Shiant Isles; Western Isles (Scotland)

57°54'N, 06°21'W 200 ha

SSSI

An archipelago of small islands situated in the Minch with important seabird colonies and a wintering flock of *Branta leucopsis*.

Breeding species include *Fulmarus glacialis* (6800 pairs), *Phalacrocorax aristotelis* (1800 pairs), *Stercorarius skua* (6 pairs), *Larus fuscus* (50 pairs), *L. argentatus* (160 pairs), *L. marinus* (130 pairs), *Rissa tridactyla* (1900 pairs), *Uria aalge* (18,400 breeding birds), *Alca torda* (10,900 breeding birds), and *Fratercula arctica* (77,000 pairs). *Branta leucopsis* occurs in winter and spring (530 in March 1988).

005 West Sound of Harris; Western Isles (Scotland)

57°43'N, 07°03'W 900 ha

SSSI

Islands (Berneray, Pabbay, and Boreray), and Machairs Robach and Newton with dune-slacks and wet and uncultivated machair.

A site for wintering *Branta leucopsis* (1007 in March 1988).

006 Loch An Duin; Western Isles (Scotland)

57°40'N, 07°11'W 3600 ha

SSSI; NSA

A complex of freshwater, brackish, and sea lochs, and tidal channels. Also included in the site is a stretch of the North Uist coast and adjacent islands and skerries.

An important breeding site for *Anser anser* (50 pairs). A variety of other wildfowl, raptors, and waders feed, rest, and overwinter within the site.

007 Monach Islands; Western Isles (Scotland)

57°31'N, 07°38'W 577 ha

NNR; SSSI

A small archipelago of low islands with outstanding shell-sand habitat and uncultivated machair. Important for *Branta leucopsis* and breeding waders and seabirds.

Breeding species include *Fulmarus glacialis* (250 pairs), *Phalacrocorax carbo carbo* (13 pairs), *P. aristotelis* (25 pairs), *Somateria mollissima*, *Haematopus ostralegus*, *Charadrius hiaticula*, *Calidris alpina*, *Sterna sandvicensis* (72 pairs), *S. hirundo* (194 pairs), *S. paradisaea* (122 pairs), *S. albifrons* (26 pairs), and *Cepphus grylle* (850 breeding birds in 1988). There is a regular wintering flock of *Branta leucopsis* (715 in Mar. 1988).

008 Balranald; Western Isles (Scotland)

57°35'N, 07°31'W 840 ha

SSSI; RSPB Reserve

The site comprises the intertidal flats, estuary, and saltmarsh of Loch Paible, coastal dunes backed by machair, and marshes and lochs (including Loch Nam Feithean).

Important for breeding waders and *Crex crex* (7 pairs). Breeding waders include *Haematopus ostralegus* (220 pairs), *Charadrius hiaticula* (121 pairs), *Vanellus vanellus* (342 pairs), *Calidris alpina* (105 pairs), *Gallinago gallinago* (30 pairs), and *Tringa totanus* (129 pairs). Wintering waders include *Charadrius hiaticula* (366) and *Calidris alba* (210).

009 Baleshare and Kirkibost; Western Isles (Scotland)

57°31'N, 07°22'W 1465 ha

SSSI

Two islands with freshwater lochs, fens and marshes, machair, extensive sand-dune systems, and intertidal flats and saltmarshes.

Important for breeding waders including *Haematopus ostralegus* (234 pairs), *Charadrius hiaticula* (330 pairs), *Vanellus vanellus* (232 pairs), *Calidris alpina* (122 pairs), *Gallinago gallinago* (37 pairs), and *Tringa totanus* (125 pairs). Wintering geese include *Anser anser* (900) and *Branta leucopsis* (600).

010 Bagh Nam Foailean to Ardivachar; Western Isles (Scotland)

57°25'N, 07°23'W

Unprotected

An extensive intertidal area between Benbecula and South Uist.

Wintering waders include *Charadrius hiaticula* (500), *Calidris alba* (440), *C. maritima* (260), *Limosa lapponica* (1020), and *Arenaria interpres* (450).

011 Iochdair and Geirinish Machair and Loch Bee; Western Isles (Scotland)

57°21'N, 07°23'W 1172 ha (Loch Bee only)

SSSI

Loch Bee is the largest, shallow, brackish-water loch in the Western Isles, and is surrounded by rocky grassland, acid moorland, and machair.

Breeding waders include *Haematopus ostralegus* (178 pairs) and *Calidris alpina* (nesting here in very high densities). Wintering waterfowl include *Cygnus olor* (200) and *Anser albifrons flavirostris* (51).

012 Na Meadhoinean Iar (including Loch Druidibeg); Western Isles (Scotland)

57°18'N, 07°20'W 2730 ha Ramsar Site; EEC SPA; Biosphere Reserve

NNR; SSSI

The site comprises Loch Druidibeg, Howmore Estuary, and Bornish and Ormiclate Machairs. Part of the largest machair systems in the British Isles.

An important breeding area for *Anser anser* (40 pairs). Other breeding species include *Haematopus ostralegus* (245 pairs), *Charadrius hiaticula* (450 pairs), *Vanellus vanellus* (500 pairs), *Calidris alpina* (80 pairs), *Gallinago gallinago* (40 pairs), *Tringa totanus*, and *Sterna paradisaea*.

013 Machair Lochs (including Lochs Hallan and Kilpheder), South Uist; Western Isles (Scotland)

57°10'N, 07°24'W 500 ha

SSSI; NSA

Loch Hallan is a shallow machair loch with extensive reedbeds; it is surrounded by marshes and machair.

Breeding species include *Crex crex* (10 pairs), *Haematopus ostralegus* (70 pairs), *Charadrius hiaticula* (40 pairs), *Vanellus vanellus* (90 pairs), *Calidris alpina* (110 pairs), *Gallinago gallinago* (80 pairs), and *Tringa totanus* (120 pairs). A wintering area for *Anser albifrons flavirostris* (31 in Mar. 1987).

014 West Sound of Barra; Western Isles (Scotland)

57°03'N, 07°25'W

SSSI

Islands including Eoligarry, Fuday, Fiaray, and Lingay.
Wintering area for *Branta leucopsis* (340 in Mar. 1988).

015 Mingulay and Berneray; Western Isles (Scotland)

56°48'N, 07°39'W 820 ha

SSSI

Two small, rocky islands with lowland grassland, peatland and sea cliffs.
Breeding species include *Fulmarus glacialis* (10,500 pairs), *Phalacrocorax aristotelis* (720 pairs), *Larus fuscus* (95 pairs), *Rissa tridactyla* (8600 pairs), *Uria aalge* (21,600 pairs), *Alca torda* (11,800 pairs), and *Fratercula arctica* (11,800 pairs).

016 Lewis peatlands; Western Isles (Scotland)

58°10'N, 06°37'W

NSA

An extensive area of peatland covering the greater part of the island. Largely vegetated with grazed, poor quality grassland, replaced by heather on coasts and interspersed with boggy areas and lochans.
Important breeding populations of *Gavia stellata*, *Aquila chrysaetos* (15 pairs), *Falco columbarius* (20+ pairs), *Pluvialis apricaria*, *Calidris alpina*, and *Tringa nebularia*. Smaller numbers of *Stercorarius parasiticus* and *S. skua*.

017 North Harris Mountains; Western Isles (Scotland)

57°59'N, 06°57'W 12,700 ha

NSA

An extensive area of montane grassland and moorland.
Supports one of the densest populations of *Aquila chrysaetos* (9 pairs) in Britain, also *Falco columbarius*.

018 Loch Scadavay; Western Isles (Scotland)

57°35'N, 07°15'W 526 ha

SSSI

A large nutrient-poor loch in North Uist.
A site for *Gavia stellata* and *Anser anser*.

019 Caithness Cliffs; Caithness, Highland (Scotland)

58°40'N, 03°23'W 822 ha

SSSI

Cliffs and open sea. Includes Duncansby Head, Castle of Old Wick to Craig Hammell, Craig Hammell to Dunbeath, Berriedale Cliffs, Dunnet Head, and Red Point Coast.
Breeding species include *Fulmarus glacialis* (27,200 pairs), *Phalacrocorax carbo carbo* (320 pairs), *P. aristotelis* (2500 pairs), *Larus argentatus* (9500 pairs), *L. marinus* (820 pairs), *Rissa tridactyla* (40,800 pairs), *Sterna paradisaea*, *Uria aalge* (127,700 breeding birds), *Alca torda* (16,600 breeding birds), *Cepphus grylle* (1075 breeding birds), and *Fratercula arctica* (2200 breeding birds).

020 Caithness Lochs; Caithness, Highland (Scotland)

58°30'N, 03°35'W 600+ ha

SSSI

Lochs, marshes, wet meadows, grassland, and arable land. Includes Lochs Heilen, Mey, Scarmclate, Winless, Wester, Meadie, and A'cherigol. Human activities include stock-raising and hunting

Wintering waterfowl include *Cygnus cygnus* (av. max. 90), *Anser albifrons flavirostris* (144 counted in Loch Heilen area, Mar. 1987), *A. anser*, and *Bucephala clangula*.

021 The Peatlands of Caithness and Sutherland; Highland (Scotland)

58°19'N, 04°03'W 270,000 ha

SSSI

Largely ancient, undisturbed peatland, covered by a mixture of rushes, sedges, rough grasses and heather. Numerous permanently waterlogged areas with bog mosses, and the entire area interspersed with thousands of small pools.

Of considerable importance for its breeding birds which include *Gavia stellata* (200 pairs), *Anser anser* (200 pairs), *Anas penelope* (80 pairs), *Melanitta nigra* (60 pairs), *Circus cyaneus*, *Pluvialis apricaria* (5340 pairs), *Calidris alpina* (2680 pairs), *Tringa nebularia* (1030 pairs), and *Stercorarius parasiticus* (60 pairs).

022 Cape Wrath – Aodann Mhor; Sutherland, Highland (Scotland)

58°36'N, 04°54'W 3296 ha

SSSI

Coastal cliffs.

Breeding seabirds include *Fulmarus glacialis* (2300 pairs), *Rissa tridactyla* (10,300 pairs), *Uria aalge* (14,600 breeding birds), *Alca torda* (2000 breeding birds), and *Fratercula arctica* (5900 breeding birds).

023 Handa; Sutherland, Highland (Scotland)

58°22'N, 05°13'W 360 ha

NNR; SSSI; NSA; RSPB

Sandstone island with sea cliffs and important seabird colonies.

Breeding species including *Fulmarus glacialis* (3500 pairs), *Phalacrocorax aristotelis* (260 pairs), *Pluvialis apricaria*, *Stercorarius parasiticus* (30 pairs), *S. skua* (65 pairs), *Rissa tridactyla* (10,700 pairs), *Uria aalge* (99,000 breeding birds), *Alca torda* (16,400 breeding birds), and *Fratercula arctica* (800 breeding birds).

024 Loch Assynt, Loch Urigill and nearby lochs; Sutherland, Highland (Scotland)

58°11'N, 05°04'W 1200 ha

NSA

Two upland water-bodies, surrounded by moorland. Half of the open moorland, largely blanket bog, surrounding Loch Urigill is now covered by forestry.

An important site for a variety of waterbirds.

025 Rhum; Lochaber, Highland (Scotland)

57°00'N, 06°30'W 10,795 ha Biosphere Reserve; EEC SPA

NNR; SSSI; NSA

A large island with a rocky coastline, with burns and lochs and a mountainous interior supporting montane and submontane grassland, dwarf-shrub heath, and mire communities.

Breeding species include *Gavia stellata*, *Fulmarus glacialis* (580 pairs), *Puffinus puffinus* (100,000+ pairs), *Crex crex*, *Pluvialis apricaria* (a high density), *Rissa tridactyla* (2200 pairs), *Uria aalge* (3600 breeding birds), *Alca torda* (470 breeding birds), *Fratercula arctica* (50 pairs), and *Aquila chrysaetos* (3-4 pairs).

026 Priest Island; Ross and Cromarty, Highland (Scotland)

57°58'N, 05°30'W 137 ha EEC SPA

SSSI; RSPB

The outermost and most exposed of the Summer Isles. Habitats include a range of water bodies, small woodland areas, heath, and coastal-cliff communities.

The island supports a major colony of *Hydrobates pelagicus* (10,000+ pairs). Other breeding species include moorland birds, seabirds, wildfowl, and waders. *Anser anser* and *Branta leucopsis* occur in winter.

027 Loch Maree; Ross and Cromarty, Highland (Scotland)

57°45'N, 05°34'W – 57°38'N, 05°20'W 3100 ha

NNR; SSSI; NSA; large proportions of loch unprotected

A large upland water-body. The islands and sections of the bank support some of the best remaining fragments of *Pinus sylvestris* in Scotland.

An important site for a variety of waterbirds.

028 Lower Dornoch Firth (including Morrich More); Ross and Cromarty, Highland (Scotland)

57°49'-57°52'N, 03°59'-04°11'W 6550 ha

SSSI; NSA

The Dornoch Firth has extensive intertidal mudflats and saltmarsh. Morrich More is an outstanding coastal site with sand-dunes, brackish pools and heath land. The site, unlike nearby Cromarty Firth, is virtually unaffected by industrial development as yet, but there is the possibility of new industrial centres in the Dornoch Firth itself.

Breeding species include *Charadrius hiaticula, Sterna sandvicensis, S. hirundo*, and *S. paradisaea*. Wintering waterfowl include *Anas penelope* (av. max. 11,719; max. 15,029), *A. crecca* (av. max. 1741), *Melanitta nigra* and small numbers of waders. The av. winter max. for wildfowl is 16,000. The area provides a roosting site for *Anser brachyrhynchus* and *A. anser* (av. max. 3920) on spring passage.

029 Loch Eye; Ross and Cromarty, Highland (Scotland)

57°48'N, 03°56'W 195 ha Ramsar Site; EEC SPA

SSSI

A shallow, nutrient-rich loch with a profuse growth of aquatic plants. The loch is surrounded mainly by a narrow fringe of trees or fen, except at the eastern end, where there is a diverse swamp and *Salix* carr.

Wintering waterfowl include *Cygnus olor* (200 in Oct. 1987), *C. cygnus* (av. max. 218; max. 461; a roosting site, with birds feeding at Cromarty Firth), *Anser albifrons flavirostris* (small numbers), and *A. anser* (av. max. 10,667; max. 12,000). The av. winter max. for wildfowl is 11,800.

030 Cromarty Firth; Ross and Cromarty, Highland (Scotland)

57°39'-57°45'N, 04°01'-04°10'W 8550 ha

NNR; SSSI

A large estuary with saltmarshes and extensive sand- and mudflats. Key areas largely intact but under considerable threat from further industrial development.

Wintering waterfowl include internationally important populations of *Cygnus cygnus* (av. max. 404; max. 500), *Anser anser* (av. max. 2899; max. 4213), *Anas penelope* (av. max. 9876; max. 12,364), and *Mergus serrator* (av. max. 586; max. 615), and nationally important numbers of *Aythya marila* (av. max. 134; max. 155), *Bucephala clangula* (av. max. 304; max. 445), *Mergus merganser* (av. max. 105; max. 238), *Numenius arquata* (av. max. 1018; max. 1120), *Limosa lapponica* (av. max. 778; max. 1434), and *Tringa totanus* (av. max. 1941; max. 2450). (Source RSPB coordinated wildfowl and wader counts 1985/86-87/88)

031 Affric-Cannich Hills and Glens; Inverness, Highland (Scotland)

57°18'N. 05°00'W 23,330 ha

SSSI

The Affric-Cannich Hills are a range of high hills with heath and blanket mire on the lower slopes, and montane dwarf heather at higher altitude. Includes Glen Affric and Glen Strathfarrar that contain one of the largest stands of native *Pinus sylvestris* remaining in Scotland.

Breeding species include *Aquila chrysaetos* and *Falco columbarius*.

032 Lochs Ashie and Ruthven; Inverness, Highland (Scotland)

57°23'N, 04°17'W (Loch Ashie); 57°19'N, 04°17'W (Loch Ruthven)

RSPB

Two freshwater lochs with marginal emergent vegetation.

Lochs important for breeding waterfowl.

033 Beauly Firth; Inverness, Highland (Scotland)

57°29'N, 04°20'W 2060 ha

SSSI

A shallow tidal estuarine lagoon with extensive areas of saltmarsh and sand- and mudflats.

Wildfowl and waders occurring in winter include *Cygnus cygnus* (av. max. 113), *Anser anser* (av. max. 4985; max. 5890), *Mergus serrator* (av. max. 1589; max. 3063), *M. merganser* (av. max. 1754; max. 2400), *Limosa lapponica*, and *Tringa totanus*.

034 Moray Firth: Munlochy Bay to Findhorn Bay; Grampian, Highland (Scotland)

57°40'N, 03°40'W 5500+ ha

SSSI; RSPB

Estuary and bay with saltwater marshes and mudflats.

Wintering species include *Gavia immer*, *Anser brachyrhynchus* (av. max. 6338), *A. anser* (av. max. 2580; max. 3200), *Clangula hyemalis* (av. max. 8310), *Melanitta nigra* (av. max. 4176), *Haematopus ostralegus* (Findhorn Bay: av. max. 3908; max. 5123), with smaller numbers of *Calidris canutus*, *Limosa lapponica*, *Numenius arquata*, and *Tringa totanus*.

035 Hermaness and Saxa Vord, Unst; Shetland (Scotland)

60°50'N, 00°53'W 1000 ha

NNR; SSSI; NSA

The peninsula of Hermaness with acid grassland, blanket mire/heathland, with sea cliffs, islets (including Muckle Flugga), and rocky coast. Includes the cliffs of Saxa Vord. An important seabird colony especially for *Stercorarius skua*.

Breeding species (data for Hermaness only) include *Gavia stellata*, *Fulmarus glacialis* (13,600 pairs), *Sula bassana* (9900 pairs), *Phalacrocorax aristotelis* (940 pairs), *Numenius phaeopus*, *Stercorarius parasiticus* (16 pairs), *S. skua* (600 pairs), *Rissa tridactyla* (2000 pairs), *Uria aalge* (14,300 breeding birds), *Alca torda* (940 breeding birds), *Cepphus grylle* (17 breeding birds), and *Fratercula arctica* (25,500 pairs).

036 Croussa Field and the Heogs; Shetland (Scotland)

60°46'N, 00°52'W 495 ha

SSSI

An area of herb-rich heathland. Parts of the area have been extensively affected by (former) industrial chromate workings.

The site holds more than 150 pairs of waders including relatively high numbers of breeding *Numenius phaeopus*. Also good numbers and high density of *Stercorarius parasiticus*.

037 Fetlar; Shetland (Scotland)

60°37'N, 00°57'W 2640 ha

SSSI; RSPB

The site comprises the peninsula of Lamb Hoga, and the northern and eastern parts of the island. Habitats include heather moorland, grass-heaths, freshwater lochs and marshes (including sedge-mires), with rocky coastlines, cliffs, islets, and beaches. An important area for breeding waders and seabirds. Formerly, the only breeding site for *Nyctea scandiaca* in the European Community.

A breeding site for *Gavia stellata* (14 pairs at RSPB Reserve in 1987), *Fulmarus glacialis* (9000 pairs), *Puffinus puffinus* (largest colony in Shetland), *Hydrobates pelagicus* (largest colony in Shetland), *Phalacrocorax aristotelis* (80 pairs), *Pluvialis apricaria*, *Numenius phaeopus* (70 pairs), *Phalaropus lobatus* (15 pairs), *Stercorarius parasiticus* (180 pairs), *S. skua* (290 pairs), *Sterna hirundo* (40 pairs), *S. paradisaea* (140 pairs; 3200 pairs in recent years), *Uria aalge* (230 breeding birds), *Alca torda* (130 breeding birds), *Cepphus grylle* (720 breeding birds), and *Fratercula arctica* (400 breeding birds). *Nyctea scandiaca* is resident (1 pair bred 1967-75).

038 Blackpark, Yell; Shetland (Scotland)

60°40'N, 01°01'W

RSPB

An area of blanket bog.

Important for breeding *Gavia stellata, Pluvialis apricaria, Numenius phaeopus*, and *Stercorarius parasiticus*.

039 Ramna Stacks and Gruney; Shetland (Scotland)

60°40'N, 01°20'W 12 ha

SSSI; RSPB

A small island with rocky coast and cliffs.

Breeding seabirds include *Oceanodroma leucorhoa* (less than 50 pairs), *Hydrobates pelagicus, Larus marinus* (150 pairs), *Rissa tridactyla* (1200 pairs), *Uria aalge* (4400 breeding birds), *Alca torda* (90 breeding birds), and *Fratercula arctica* (100 pairs).

040 North Roe, Mainland; Shetland (Scotland)

60°32'N, 01°25'W 4900 ha

SSSI

Includes Ronas Hill which supports mire communities and heather moorland; north of Ronas Hill are several lochs.

The site has a dense breeding population of *Gavia stellata* (40 pairs), and a rich community of breeding moorland birds including *Stercorarius parasiticus* (80 pairs), *S. skua* (115 pairs), and *Pluvialis apricaria* (95 pairs).

041 Papa Stour; Shetland (Scotland)

60°20'N, 01°42'W 590 ha

SSSI

The site comprises the northern and western part of the island, which is covered mainly by lichen-rich heathland.

Breeding species include *Fulmarus glacialis* (2700 pairs), *Phalacrocorax aristotelis* (195 pairs), *Stercorarius parasiticus* (90 pairs), *S. skua* (14 pairs), *Rissa tridactyla* (1100 pairs), *Sterna paradisaea* (5900 pairs), *Uria aalge* (2500 pairs), *Alca torda* (95 pairs), and *Cepphus grylle* (240 pairs).

042 Foula; Shetland (Scotland)

60°08'N, 02°04'W 1325 ha

SSSI; NSA

Large island with high cliffs, rocky coast, beaches, moorland, lakes, marshes, and peatbogs. The island supports a very important seabird colony.

Breeding species include *Fulmarus glacialis* (46,800 pairs), *Puffinus puffinus*, *Hydrobates pelagicus*, *Oceanodroma leucorhoa*, *Sula bassana* (125 pairs), *Phalacrocorax aristotelis* (2400 pairs), *Stercorarius parasiticus* (170 pairs), *S. skua* (2500 pairs), *Rissa tridactyla* (4350 pairs), *Sterna paradisaea* (300 pairs), *Uria aalge* (37,500 pairs), *Alca torda* (6200 pairs), *Cepphus grylle*, and *Fratercula arctica* (48,000 pairs).

043 Noss; Shetland (Scotland)

60°08'N, 01°01'W 310 ha

NNR; SSSI

A small island adjoining Bressay with high cliffs and moorland. Supports a spectacular seabird colony.

Breeding species include *Fulmarus glacialis* (6300 pairs), *Sula bassana* (5200 pairs), *Phalacrocorax aristotelis* (100 pairs), *Stercorarius parasiticus* (18 pairs), *S. skua* (390 pairs), *Rissa tridactyla* (9400 pairs), *Sterna paradisaea*, *Uria aalge* (37,700 breeding birds), *Alca torda* (1000 breeding birds), *Cepphus grylle* (150 breeding birds), and *Fratercula arctica* (1900 breeding birds).

044 Mousa (part); Shetland (Scotland)

59°60'N, 01°11'W 210 ha (whole island)

SSSI

A low grassy island with shallow tidal lagoons.

Mousa has one of the largest breeding concentrations of *Cepphus grylle* (620 breeding birds) in Shetland. Also many thousands of breeding *Hydrobates pelagicus*, and *Stercorarius parasiticus* (20 pairs).

045 Loch Spiggie; Shetland (Scotland)

59°56'N, 01°20'W 154 ha

SSSI; NSA; RSPB

The site comprises Lochs Spiggie and Brow, which are the largest eutrophic lochs in Shetland and have extensive marshes.

A wintering site for *Cygnus cygnus* (147).

046 Fair Isle; Shetland (Scotland)

59°32'N, 01°38'W 590 ha

SSSI; NSA; NTS

Large island with grassland and heather moorland. Supports important seabird colonies and has a bird migration observatory (Fair Isle Bird Observatory).

Breeding species include *Fulmarus glacialis* (27,000 pairs), *Hydrobates pelagicus, Sula bassana* (260 pairs), *Phalacrocorax aristotelis* (1100 pairs), *Stercorarius parasiticus* (115 pairs), *S. skua* (85 pairs), *Larus argentatus* (260 pairs), *L. marinus* (110 pairs), *Rissa tridactyla* (9100 pairs), *Sterna hirundo* (25 pairs), *S. paradisaea* (80 pairs), *Uria aalge* (35,200 breeding birds), *Alca torda* (3950 breeding birds), *Cepphus grylle* (380 breeding birds), and *Fratercula arctica* (20,200 breeding birds). The island has an endemic subspecies, *Troglodytes troglodytes fridariensis.*

047 Sumburgh Head; Shetland (Scotland)

59°52'N, 01°16'W 41 ha

SSSI

A section of the Sumburgh Head cliffs and the boulder-strewn area of the Looss Laward.

Breeding seabirds include *Fulmarus glacialis* (1800 pairs), *Phalacrocorax aristotelis* (490 pairs), *Rissa tridactyla* (2500 pairs), *Uria aalge* (14,800 breeding birds), *Alca torda* (800 breeding birds), *Fratercula arctica* (5000 breeding birds), and *Sterna paradisaea.*

048 North Ronaldsay Coast; Orkney (Scotland)

59°24'N, 02°23'W 20 km of coast

Unprotected

Low-lying rocky coast, interspersed with sandy bays.

Breeding species include *Cepphus grylle* (120 pairs). Important for wintering *Calidris maritima* (250).

049 East Sanday; Orkney (Scotland)

59°17'N, 02°25'W

SSSI; coastal section unprotected

A stretch of rocky and sandy coast (*c.*50 km long) with extensive areas of intertidal sand. The SSSI inland is a wetland area with open water and marshes.

Breeding species include *Stercorarius parasiticus* (3 pairs), *S. skua* (1 pair), *Larus canus* (200 pairs), *Sterna sandvicensis* (60 pairs) and *S. paradisaea* (430 pairs). Important as a wintering site for *Cygnus cygnus* (150), *Calidris alba* (420), *C. maritima* (710), and *Arenaria interpres* (760).

050 South-eastern Stronsay; Orkney (Scotland)

59°05'N, 02°34'W 15 km of coast

Unprotected

Low-lying rocky coast, interspersed with sandy bays.

Breeding species include *Cepphus grylle* (120 breeding birds). Important for wintering *Calidris maritima* (300).

051 Papa Westray (North Hill and Holm); Orkney (Scotland)

59°22'N, 02°53'W 250 ha

SSSI; RSPB

The northern part of Papa Westray (North Hill) with maritime heathland, and the low, grassy island, Holm of Papa.

Breeding species (figures for North Hill only) include *Gavia stellata, Stercorarius parasiticus* (125 pairs), *Larus marinus* (500 pairs), *Rissa tridactyla* (2100 pairs), *Sterna paradisaea* (1800 pairs), *Uria aalge* (1300 breeding birds), and *Alca torda* (120 pairs). The Holm of Papa holds the largest recorded colony of *Cepphus grylle* (650 breeding birds in Britain). *Calidris maritima* occurs in winter.

052 West Westray; Orkney (Scotland)

59°18'N, 03°01'W 372 ha

SSSI

An 8 km stretch of cliffs and sections of the Westray Hills with maritime grassland and sedge-heath.
Breeding species include *Fulmarus glacialis* (3000 pairs), *Phalacrocorax aristotelis* (20 pairs), *Stercorarius parasiticus* (20 pairs), *Rissa tridactyla* (31,200 pairs), *Sterna paradisaea* (1500 pairs), *Uria aalge* (61,000 breeding birds), *Alca torda* (1800 breeding birds), and *Cepphus grylle* (310 breeding birds).

053 South Westray Coast; Orkney (Scotland)

59°17'N, 02°56'W 20 km of coast

Unprotected

Low-lying rocky coast, interspersed with sandy bays.
Wintering waders include *Calidris alba* (180), *C. maritima* (640), and *Arenaria interpres* (350).

054 Eday; Orkney (Scotland)

59°14'N, 02°44'W 475 ha

SSSI

Two islands including the Calf of Eday with rocky coasts. Human activities include agriculture.
Calf of Eday supports a large colony of *Phalacrocorax carbo carbo* (223 pairs in 1985). *Calidris maritima* (250) occurs in winter.

055 Rousay (part); Orkney (Scotland)

59°10'N, 03°02'W *c.*2000 ha

RSPB

Part of Rousay Island with marshes, peatbogs, moorland, rocky coast and beaches.
Breeding species (at RSPB Reserve in 1987) include *Gavia stellata* (1 pair), *Circus cyaneus* (2 pairs), *Falco columbarius* (1 pair), *Pluvialis apricaria* (2 pairs), *Numenius arquata* (18 pairs), *Stercorarius parasiticus* (1 pair), and *S. skua* (1 pair). *Calidris maritima* (270) occur in winter. A breeding site for *Sterna paradisaea* (1470 pairs in 1980).

056 Mill Dam, Shapinsay; Orkney (Scotland)

59°03'N, 02°54'W 10 ha

Unprotected

An artificial dam now encroached by vegetation, with open water especially after heavy rains.
Breeding species include *Anas acuta*. Wintering waterfowl include *Cygnus cygnus* (117).

057 Marwick Head; Orkney (Scotland)

59°07'N, 03°21'W 9 ha

SSSI; RSPB Reserve

Cliffs and open sea. Very important seabird cliffs.
Breeding birds include *Fulmarus glacialis* (1200 pairs), *Rissa tridactyla* (4700 pairs), *Uria aalge* (25,000 breeding birds), *Alca torda* (900 breeding birds), and *Fratercula arctica*.

058 North Mainland Coast; Orkney (Scotland)

59°04'N, 03°01'W 50 km of coast

Unprotected

Low-lying rocky coast, interspersed with sandy bays.
Wintering waders include *Charadrius hiaticula* (120), *Calidris maritima* (200), *Numenius arquata* (3200), *Tringa totanus* (770), and *Arenaria interpres* (510).

059 West Mainland Moors; Orkney (Scotland)

59°04'N, 03°08'W 4400 ha

SSSI; RSPB

Important moorland areas, including Milldoe, Starling Hill, and Keelying Hill. Also of interest is Waulkmill Bay.
Breeding species include *Gavia stellata* (15 pairs), *Circus cyaneus* (53 pairs; also wintering), *Falco columbarius* (7 pairs), *Pluvialis apricaria*, *Calidris alpina*, *Stercorarius parasiticus* (25 pairs), *S. skua*, and *Asio flammeus* (24 pairs).

060 Lochs of Harray and Stenness; Orkney (Scotland)

59°00'N, 03°14'W 1930 ha

SSSI; NSA

Two lochs, one almost saltwater (Loch Stenness) and the other (Loch Harray) is fresh and eutrophic.
Wintering waterfowl include (data for Harray only) *Cygnus olor* (av. max. 221), *C. cygnus* (av. max. 65), *Aythya ferina* (av. max. 2664; max. 4500), and *A. fuligula* (av. max. 1493; max. 2279).

061 Orphir and Stenness Hills; Orkney (Scotland)

58°57'N, 03°09'W 1250 ha

SSSI

A compact cluster of hills with moorland.
Breeding species include *Circus cyaneus* (25 pairs), *Falco columbarius* (2 pairs), *Pluvialis apricaria*, and *Asio flammeus*.

062 Hoy; Orkney (Scotland)

58°54'N, 03°22'W 8186 ha

SSSI; NSA; RSPB

Hoy has an extremely diverse vegetation including dwarf-shrub heaths, which occur here at low altitudes. Other habitats include marshes and freshwater lakes, rocky coast, islets, and cliffs. The site includes the most northerly natural wood in the U.K. Important seabird colonies in northern part of Hoy.
Breeding species include *Gavia stellata* (21 pairs at RSPB Reserve), *Fulmarus glacialis* (28,000 pairs), *Puffinus puffinus* (50 pairs), *Phalacrocorax aristotelis* (100 pairs), *Stercorarius parasiticus* (190 pairs), *S. skua* (990 pairs), *Larus canus* (290 pairs), *L. marinus* (1200 pairs), *Rissa tridactyla* (1700 pairs), *Sterna hirundo* (30 pairs), *Uria aalge* (7800 breeding birds), *Alca torda* (850 breeding birds), *Cepphus grylle* (170 breeding birds), and *Fratercula arctica* (1000 pairs).

063 Sule Skerry and Stack Skerry; Orkney (Scotland)

59°01'N, 04°30'W (Stack Skerry); 59°05'N, 04°24'W (Sule Skerry) 20 ha

SSSI

Two islets.

Breeding species include *Fulmarus glacialis* (250 pairs), *Hydrobates pelagicus* (1000+ pairs), *Sula bassana* (5900 pairs), *Phalacrocorax aristotelis* (870 pairs), *Rissa tridactyla* (970 pairs), *Sterna paradisaea* (50 pairs), *Uria aalge* (9400 breeding birds), *Alca torda* (90 breeding birds), and *Fratercula arctica* (45,000 pairs).

064 Pentland Firth Islands; Orkney (Scotland)

58°41'N, 03°07'W (Stroma); 58°44'N, 03°03'W (Swona); 58°40'N, 03°00'W (Pentland Skerries)

SSSI; Swona and Pentland Skerries are unprotected

Two islands and a small group of rocky islets in the Pentland Firth.

Breeding seabirds include (combined totals for three sites) *Fulmarus glacialis* (1870 pairs), *Hydrobates pelagicus*, *Phalacrocorax aristotelis* (115 pairs), *Larus canus* (200 pairs), *L. marinus* (260 pairs), *Rissa tridactyla* (2600 pairs), *Sterna sandvicensis* (300 pairs), *S. hirundo* (65 pairs), *S. paradisaea* (3600 pairs), *Uria aalge* (13,700 breeding birds), *Alca torda* (350 breeding birds), *Cepphus grylle* (240 breeding birds), and *Fratercula arctica* (430 breeding birds).

065 Copinsay; Orkney (Scotland)

58°55'N, 02°40'W 152 ha

SSSI; RSPB

Island.

Breeding species include *Fulmarus glacialis* (1600 pairs), *Phalacrocorax aristotelis* (70 pairs), *Larus marinus* (620 pairs), *Rissa tridactyla* (9550 pairs), *Sterna paradisaea* (35 pairs), *Uria aalge* (29,450 breeding birds), *Alca torda* (180 breeding birds), and *Cepphus grylle* (165 breeding birds).

066 Moray Firth: Burghead and Spey Bays; Grampian, Highland (Scotland)

57°43'N, 03°24'W

SSSI (Spey Bay - 492 ha)

Two bays with shellfish beds providing important inshore feeding areas.

Important for wintering *Clangula hyemalis* (12,000), *Melanitta nigra* (5000), and *M. fusca* (4600).

067 Loch Spynie; Moray, Grampian (Scotland)

57°41'N, 03°17'W 93 ha

SSSI

A large eutrophic loch with well-developed areas of *Alnus* and *Salix* carr, reedbeds and fens.

An important wintering area for *Anser anser* (av. max. 4212; max. 7750).

068 Loch Oire; Moray, Grampian (Scotland)

57°38'N, 03°12'W 9 ha

SSSI

A mesotrophic loch with sedge-fen and marginal carr woodland.

Important for a variety of waterfowl.

069 Troup, Pennan and Lion Heads; Banff and Buchan, Grampian (Scotland)

57°42'N, 02°18'W 322 ha

SSSI

Extensive sea cliffs.

Breeding seabirds include *Larus argentatus* (2200 pairs), *Rissa tridactyla* (15,000 pairs), *Uria aalge* (16,100 breeding birds), and *Alca torda* (1200 breeding birds).

070 Quarry Head to Fraserburgh Coast; Banff and Buchan, Grampian (Scotland)

57°41'N, 02°09'W – 57°42'N, 02°00'W 235 ha

SSSI

A stretch of rocky coastline with sea cliffs.
Important for wintering *Calidris maritima* (350) and *Arenaria interpres* (640).

071 Loch of Strathbeg; Banff and Buchan, Grampian (Scotland)

56°37'N, 01°52'W 913 ha

SSSI; RSPB

A shallow, eutrophic lake with freshwater marshes, reeds, and *Alnus*, and *Salix* carr. Includes nearby dunes and dune-slacks that are rich in flora.
Breeding species include *Sterna sandvicensis* (490 pairs), *S. hirundo* (78 pairs), and *S. paradisaea* (130 pairs). Very important for passage and wintering waterfowl with *Cygnus olor* (av. max. 252; max. 352), *C. cygnus* (av. max. 432; max. 633), *Anser brachyrhynchus* (av. max. 18,300; max. 29,800), and *A. anser* (av. max. 6970; max. 9600). The av. winter max. for wildfowl is 25,400.

072 Bullers of Buchan and Whinnyfold; Banff and Buchan, Gordon; Grampian (Scotland)

57°28'N, 01°46'W – 57°23'N, 01°52'W 212 ha

SSSI

A section of coastline with cliffs and offshore stacks.
Breeding seabirds include *Fulmarus glacialis* (1600 pairs), *Phalacrocorax aristotelis* (440 pairs), *Larus argentatus* (3600 pairs), *Rissa tridactyla* (19,100 pairs), *Uria aalge* (12,900 breeding birds), and *Alca torda* (1000 breeding birds).

073 Ythan Estuary, Sands of Forvie and Meikle Lochs; Gordon, Grampian (Scotland)

57°21'N, 02°00'W 1050 ha

NNR; SSSI

The Sands of Forvie is one of the largest and least disturbed sand-dune systems in the U.K. The Ythan Estuary is one of the least modified estuaries in Scotland and has intertidal mudflats, saltmarshes, and reedbeds. Meikle Loch is small and eutrophic with some aquatic vegetation.
Breeding species include *Somateria mollissima* (2000 pairs), *Larus ridibundus* (570 pairs), *L. argentatus* (1000 pairs), *Sterna sandvicensis* (1080 pairs), *S. hirundo* (160 pairs), *S. paradisaea* (50 pairs), and *S. albifrons* (27 pairs). Also important for wintering and passage waterfowl with *Anser brachyrhynchus* (av. max. 12,038; max. 17,400), *A. anser* (av. max. 1959), and small numbers of waders.

074 Loch of Skene; Gordon, Grampian (Scotland)

57°09'N,02°20'W 125 ha Ramsar Site; EEC SPA

SSSI

A shallow loch with fringing reedbed and *Betula/Salix* carr.
Breeding species include *Aythya fuligula* (100 pairs). An important wintering site for *Anser anser* (av. max. 5272; max. 8500). Other wintering Anatidae include *Bucephala clangula* and *Mergus merganser*. Also a major autumn roost site for *Larus canus* (max. 45,000).

075 Fowlsheugh; Kincardine and Deeside, Grampian (Scotland)

56°55'N, 02°10'W 7 ha

SSSI; RSPB

A stretch of coastline with sheer cliffs and important seabird colonies.

Breeding species include *Fulmarus glacialis* (300 pairs), *Phalacrocorax aristotelis*, *Rissa tridactyla* (22,000 pairs), *Uria aalge* (52,400 breeding birds), *Alca torda* (4500 breeding birds), and *Fratercula arctica* (10 pairs).

076 Muir of Dinnet; Kincardine and Deeside, Grampian (Scotland)

57°05'N, 02°56'W 1610 ha

SSSI

A complex of habitats including herb-rich heather moor, *Betula* scrub, fen carr, and open water.

Important wintering site for *Anser anser*.

077 St Cyrus; Kincardine and Deeside, Grampian (Scotland)

56°46'N, 02°25'W 312 ha

NNR; SSSI

A coastal sand-dune system with lichen-rich dune heathland, foreshore, river estuary, saltmarsh and cliff.

An important site for breeding *Sterna albifrons* with up to 60 pairs in recent years.

078 Glen Tanar; Kincardine and Deeside, Grampian (Scotland)

57°02'N, 02°53'W 4185 ha

SSSI

Glen Tanar comprises the third largest area of native *Pinus sylvestris* in the U.K., which is well protected from grazing deer.

The site holds important populations of *Tetrao tetrix* and *T. urogallus*, and is probably the most important locality in the world for *Loxia scotica*.

079 Lochnagar; Kincardine and Deeside, Grampian (Scotland)

56°57'N, 03°14'W 4300 ha

SSSI; NSA

A rich upland area with Arctic/subarctic flora, moorland and marshes.

The area supports a variety of breeding waders including a high density of *Pluvialis apricaria*.

080 Cairngorms; Grampian, Highland (Scotland)

57°05'N, 03°35'W 49,200 ha Ramsar Site; EEC SPA

NNR; SSSI; NSA; RSPB

An important site with extensive upland habitat areas with high plateaus and snow-bed habitat, lochs, marshes and peatbogs, moorland, and streams. Includes one of the largest tracts of native *Pinus sylvestris* woodland in the U.K. (Rothiemurchus Pinewood). Human activities include recreation. The further development of skiing facilities continues to threaten this area.

Breeding species include *Aquila chrysaetos*, *Falco columbarius*, *F. peregrinus*, *Lagopus mutus*, *Charadrius morinellus*, *Pluvialis apricaria*, *Turdus torquatus*, and *Plectrophenax nivalis*. Rothiemurchus is one of the most important areas in the world for *Loxia scotica*.

081 Abernethy Forest; Badenoch and Strathspey, Highland (Scotland)

03°47'W, 57°14'N 5795 ha (SSSI only)

NNR; SSSI; RSPB

Habitats include *Pinus* woodland, moorland, marshes, slow- and fast-flowing rivers and streams. Important habitats for birds extend beyond the SSSI. Human activities include forestry and recreation.

Breeding species include *Anas penelope, A. crecca, Aythya fuligula, Bucephala clangula, Aquila chrysaetos, Pandion haliaetus, Lagopus lagopus, Tetrao tetrix, T. urogallus, Pluvialis apricaria, Numenius arquata, Actitis hypoleucos, Asio otus, A. flammeus,* and *Loxia scotica* (90 pairs).

082 Kinveachy; Badenoch and Strathspey, Highland (Scotland)

57°14'N, 03°54'W 5335 ha

SSSI

An important area of Caledonian Pine forest and moorland.

The site holds more than 15 per cent of the world population of *Loxia scotica* (50 pairs). Other breeding species include *Tetrao urogallus,* and the moorland supports several species of raptor.

083 Loch Vaa; Badenoch and Strathspey, Highland (Scotland)

57°14'N, 03°48'W 20 ha

Unprotected

An upland water body surrounded by native *Pinus* woods and *Betula.*

An important site for a variety of waterfowl.

084 Loch Alvie; Badenoch and Strathspey, Highland (Scotland)

57°09'N, 03°51'W 340 ha

SSSI

A large *Betula* wood (with areas of *Quercus* and *Pinus sylvestris*) along the River Spey, and a shallow mesotrophic loch.

An important site for a variety of waterbirds.

085 River Spey – Insh Marshes; Badenoch and Strathspey, Highland (Scotland)

57°07'N, 03°56'W 1177 ha

SSSI; NSA; RSPB

A section of the River Spey, comprising Loch Insh and the Insh Marshes and representing one of the largest areas of freshwater fen in Britain.

Breeding species include *Bucephala clangula, Mergus merganser,* and *Porzana porzana* (possibly). *Anser brachyrhynchus* and *A. anser* occur on passage. Wintering waterfowl include *Cygnus cygnus* (av. max. 132).

086 Kentra Moss; Lochaber, Highland (Scotland)

56°45'N, 05°50'W 1630 ha Ramsar Site; EEC SPA; Biosphere Reserve

SSSI; NSA

Marshes and peatbog.

Anser albifrons flavirostris feeds in the mosses between the Loch Shiel and the sea.

087 Tiree and Coll; Argyll and Bute, Strathclyde (Scotland)

56°35'N, 06°40'W 16,000 ha

SSSI

Islands with marshes, moorland, grassland, and arable land.

Breeding species include *Phalacrocorax aristotelis*, *Crex crex* (75-100 males), *Stercorarius parasiticus*, *Sterna hirundo*, *S. paradisaea*, and *S. albifrons*. In winter, important for *Anser albifrons flavirostris* (Coll: max. 405 in Feb. 1987; Tiree: max. 760 in Nov. 1986), *Branta leucopsis* (av. max. 497) and waders, especially *Charadrius hiaticula* (Tiree: av. max. 805; max. 987), *Calidris alba* (Tiree: av. max. 353; max. 402), *C. maritima* (max. 160+), and *Arenaria interpres* (av. max. 1008; max. 1196).

088 Treshnish Islands; Argyll and Bute, Strathclyde (Scotland)

56°30'N, 06°24'W 208 ha

SSSI

An archipelago of small islands with maritime grassland, heathland, and peatland.

Breeding seabirds include *Fulmarus glacialis* (330 pairs), *Puffinus puffinus* (200+ pairs), *Hydrobates pelagicus* (2000 birds), *Phalacrocorax aristotelis* (140 pairs), *Uria aalge* (5177 birds), *Alca torda* (300 pairs), *Cepphus grylle*, and *Fratercula arctica* (850 birds). *Branta leucopsis* winters on the islands (378 in Mar. 1988).

089 North Colonsay and Western Cliffs; Argyll and Bute, Strathclyde (Scotland)

56°06'N, 06°09'W 850 ha

SSSI

An area of coastal *Quercus* woods, sand-dunes, craggy terrain with dry and wet heathlands, and rocky coast and near-vertical cliffs.

The sites support breeding *Fulmarus glacialis* (450 pairs), *Hydrobates pelagicus*, *Phalacrocorax aristotelis* (90 pairs), *Rissa tridactyla* (5400 pairs), *Uria aalge* (13,000 breeding birds), and *Alca torda* (1400 breeding birds). *Pyrrhocorax pyrrhocorax* (7 pairs) also breeds.

090 Islay: Rinns; Argyll and Bute, Strathclyde (Scotland)

55°46'N, 06°23'W 8312 ha

SSSI

Much of the Rinns is covered by blanket peat, and there are coastal grasslands, dunes, ancient woodlands, and rough pasture.

Breeding species include *Melanitta nigra*, *Circus cyaneus*, *Aquila chrysaetos*, *Falco columbarius*, *F. peregrinus*, *Crex crex*, *Asio flammeus*, and *Pyrrhocorax pyrrhocorax*. *Cygnus cygnus* (140) occurs on passage and *Anser albifrons flavirostris* (1100) occurs in winter.

091 Islay: Glac na Criche; Argyll and Bute, Strathclyde (Scotland)

55°51'N, 06°27'W 265 ha

SSSI

An area of blanket mire, with sea cliffs that have breeding seabirds.

A wintering site for *Anser albifrons flavirostris* (150).

092 Islay: Feur Lochain; Argyll and Bute, Strathclyde (Scotland)

55°50'N, 06°21'W 384 ha

SSSI

An extensive area of blanket peat with numerous lochans and pools.

An important roosting and night feeding area for *Anser albifrons flavirostris* (600 in winter; 1100 on passage).

093 Islay: Loch Gruinart; Argyll and Bute, Strathclyde (Scotland)

55°49'N, 06°18'W 3170 ha Ramsar Site; EEC SPA

SSSI; RSPB

The area includes a wide range of coastal and intertidal habitats, raised shorelines, and low-level blanket peat and marsh.

Important for roosting and feeding *Anser albifrons flavirostris* (500), *Branta leucopsis* (av. 8600), and *B. bernicla hrota* (av. 300) in winter. Other non-breeding species include wintering *Cygnus cygnus* (70) and passage *Charadrius hiaticula* (300).

094 Islay: Bridgend Flats; Argyll and Bute, Strathclyde (Scotland)

*c.*55°46 N, 06°14'W 331 ha Ramsar Site; EEC SPA

SSSI

Saltmarsh and intertidal flats of sand and silt. Some agricultural land is included in the site.

Important for wintering *Branta leucopsis* (av. 6700 roosting; av. 900 feeding). Other wintering species include smaller numbers of *Cygnus cygnus* and *Anser albifrons flavirostris*. *Falco peregrinus* occurs.

095 Islay: Laggan; Argyll and Bute, Strathclyde (Scotland)

55°42'N, 06°17'W 1270 ha EEC SPA

SSSI

An area of peatland and dune swards. Includes Laggan Bay, which has extensive sand-dunes.

Breeding species include *Falco peregrinus* (1 pair) and *Pyrrhocorax pyrrhocorax* (3 pairs; 20 in winter). Wintering species include *Anser albifrons* (300) and *Branta leucopsis* (1800).

096 Islay: Eilean na Muice Dubh (Duich Moss); Argyll and Bute, Strathclyde (Scotland)

*c.*55°44'N, 06°14'W 574 ha Ramsar Site; EEC SPA

SSSI

An area of low-level blanket mire, with scattered peaty pools and lochans. Hummocks of *Sphagnum* spp., and *Rhynchospora alba* are frequent on the extensive areas of level bog.

Breeding species include *Gavia stellata*, *Calidris alpina*, *Tringa totanus*, *Larus canus*, *L. fuscus*, *L. argentatus*, and possibly *Pluvialis apricaria*. *Falco columbarius* uses the area as a hunting ground in summer. Important for wintering (roosting and feeding) *Anser albifrons flavirostris* (600). Other non-breeding species include *Cygnus cygnus*, *Circus cyaneus*, *Falco peregrinus*, and *Asio flammeus*.

097 Islay: The Oa; Argyll and Bute, Strathclyde (Scotland)

55°37'N, 06°18'W *c.*2000 ha

Unprotected

An extensive area of coastal moorland.

Breeding species include *Gavia stellata* (1 pair), *Aquila chrysaetos* (1 pair), *Falco peregrinus* (2 pairs), and *Pyrrhocorax pyrrhocorax* (16 pairs). Important for wintering *Anser albifrons flavirostris* (840).

098 Rhunahaorine; Argyll and Bute, Strathclyde (Scotland)

55°40'N, 05°39'W 325 ha

SSSI; SWT

An area of heathland and vegetated shingle ridges.
A wintering site for *Anser albifrons flavirostris* (825).

099 Machrihanish and Tangy Loch; Argyll and Bute, Strathclyde (Scotland)

55°26'N, 05°43'W 750 ha

SSSI

The site comprises the dunes of Machrihanish and Tangy Loch.
An important wintering area for *Anser albifrons flavirostris* (528), which feeds at Machrihanish and roosts at Tangy Loch.

100 Sanda; Argyll and Bute, Strathclyde (Scotland)

55°16'N, 05°34'W

Unprotected

Offshore island with associated islets, cliffs and coastal grassland.
Breeding seabirds include *Puffinus puffinus* (70 pairs), *Hydrobates pelagicus* (less than 100 pairs), *Phalacrocorax aristotelis* (950 pairs), *Larus argentatus* (800 pairs), *L. fuscus* (50 pairs), *Uria aalge* (1500 breeding birds), and *Alca torda* (800 breeding birds).

101 North end of Bute; Argyll and Bute, Strathclyde (Scotland)

55°54'N, 05°12'W 624 ha

SSSI

An area of *Quercus* woodland, *Betula* woodland, and open moorland.
Breeding species include *Gavia stellata, Circus cyaneus, Falco columbarius, F. peregrinus,* and *Asio flammeus. Aquila chrysaetos* frequently hunts near the area.

102 North Arran Mountains; Cunninghame, Strathclyde (Scotland)

55°38'N, 05°13'W 10,200 ha

NNR; SSSI; NSA; NTS

An upland area with typical plant communities; also excellent examples of corries, aretes, and horns.
Important for divers and birds of prey.

103 Ailsa Craig; Kyle and Carrick, Strathclyde (Scotland)

55°14'N, 05°07'W 105 ha

SSSI

A small rocky island with steep cliffs and important seabird colonies.
Seabirds breeding include *Fulmarus glacialis* (190 pairs), *Sula bassana* (22,800 pairs), *Larus fuscus* (1800 pairs), *L. argentatus* (2350 pairs), *Rissa tridactyla* (3100 pairs), *Uria aalge* (5000 breeding birds), and *Alca torda* (1000 breeding birds).

104 Loch Lomond; Strathclyde, Central (Scotland)

56°04'N, 04°31'W 451 ha Ramsar Site; EEC SPA

NNR; SSSI; NSA; ESA; Loch Lomond Regional Park

Loch with islands; with marshes, wet meadows, woodland, and farmland. Increasing pressure from recreation, and there remains a possibility of a proposed pump-storage hydroelectric scheme.
Wintering waterfowl include *Cygnus cygnus, Anser albifrons flavirostris* (*c.*250), and *A. anser* (up to 2000). Also supports a small and declining breeding population of *Melanitta nigra.*

105 Inner Clyde Estuary; Dumbarton, Strathclyde (Scotland)

55°57'N, 04°37'W 1000+ ha

SSSI; RSPB

An area of saltmarsh and tidal mudflats on the inner Clyde important for passage and wintering wildfowl.

Species occurring in winter include *Somateria mollissima* (av. max. 2585; max. 3501), *Bucephala clangula* (av. max. 471; max. 706), *Mergus serrator* (av. max. 111), *Haematopus ostralegus* (av. max. 4423; max. 4929), and *Tringa totanus* (av. max. 2821; max. 3169). The av. winter max. for waders is 12,729.

106 Lochinch (White Loch) and Torrs Warren; Wigtown, Dumfries and Galloway (Scotland)

54°54'N, 04°57'W 2470 ha

SSSI

Lochinch is a shallow, eutrophic lake. Torrs Warren is a large acid dune system (the largest in southern Scotland).

An important wintering site for geese, especially *Anser albifrons flavirostris* (av. max. 266), which feed on nearby farmland and roost either on the loch or at sea. Also large numbers of *Anser anser* (av. max. 1467; though about half are of feral origin).

107 Mochrum and Castle Lochs; Annandale and Eskdale, Dumfries (Scotland)

54°51'N, 04°40'W 109 ha

SSSI

Castle Loch is a shallow and eutrophic loch with extensive areas of emergent vegetation.

Important for wintering *Anser brachyrhynchus* (av. max. 7090; max. 13,400) and *A. anser* (av. max. 2320; max. 3100). The av. winter max. for wildfowl is 11,000.

108 Wigtown Bay; Wigtown, Dumfries and Galloway (Scotland)

54°51'N, 04°26'W 3456 ha (Cree Estuary SSSI only)

SSSI

An extensive and continuous stretch of grazed saltmarsh, mudflats, and open water.

Wintering waterfowl include *Cygnus cygnus* (210), *Anser brachyrhynchus* (9200), and *Haematopus ostralegus* (3100).

109 Loch Ken and Dee Marshes; Stewartry, Dumfries and Galloway (Scotland)

55°02'N, 04°06'W 980 ha

SSSI; RSPB

A wetland system with extensive fens, marshy grassland, rivers, and lochs (including Loch Ken and Carlingwark Loch). Recreation and boating are problems at the site.

A wintering site for *Anser albifrons flavirostris* (av. max. 288) and *A. anser* (av. max. 1059).

110 Caenlochan; Angus/Perth and Kinross, Tayside; Kincardine and Deeside, Grampian (Scotland)

56°53'N, 03°17'W 5040 ha

NNR; SSSI

An outstanding upland area with tundra vegetation, moorland, and marshes. The development of skiing facilities and increased access continue to threaten this site.

Species include a dense breeding population of *Pluvialis apricaria*. One of the most important sites in Scotland for *Charadrius morinellus*.

111 Montrose Basin; Angus, Tayside (Scotland)

56°43'N, 02°30'W 920 ha

SSSI; SWT

An estuarine basin with extensive mudflats and saltmarshes. The site includes Dun's Dish, which is a eutrophic lowland loch with rich fen and carr plant communities.

Dun's Dish supports a high number of breeding birds including a variety of *Anas* spp. and a colony of *Sterna hirundo*. Wintering (and passage) waterfowl at Montrose Basin include *Cygnus olor* (av. max. 216; max. 245), *Anser brachyrhynchus* (av. max. 9931; max. 12,600), *A. anser* (av. max. 1290), *Anas penelope* (av. max. 4401), *Haematopus ostralegus* (av. max. 3469), *Tringa totanus* (av. max. 1631; max. 3000), and *Calidris canutus* (av. max. 4000; max. 10,000). The av. winter max. for wildfowl is 18,600 and for waders 11,146.

112 Loch of Lintrathen; Angus, Tayside (Scotland)

56°41'N, 03°11'W 189 ha Ramsar Site; EEC SPA

SSSI; SWT Reserve

A eutrophic loch, now used as a reservoir.

Important for wintering *Anser anser* (av. max. 2800; max. 6200).

113 Tay – Isla Valley; Perth and Kinross, Tayside (Scotland)

56°35'N, 03°22'W 412 ha

SSSI

A number of shallow lochs; other habitats include extensive areas of rich fen vegetation and unimproved lowland pastures. Includes Lochs Clunie and Marlee, the Meikleour stretch of the River Tay, and Hare Myre, Monk Myre, and Stormont Loch.

Very important feeding and roosting area for *Anser anser* (av. max. 7144; max. 18,295).

114 Dupplin Lochs; Perth and Kinross, Tayside (Scotland)

56°22'N, 03°34'W 124 ha

SSSI

A small group of lochs.

An important area for breeding ducks and for roosting *Anser brachyrhynchus* (av. max. 6413; max. 8448) and *A. anser* (av. max. 1686) in winter.

115 Drummond Lochs; Perth and Kinross, Tayside (Scotland)

56°20'N, 03°51'W 130 ha

SSSI

Two small lochs with interesting emergent vegetation.

An important wintering area for *Anser anser* (av. max. 4952; max. 7500).

116 Carsebreck and Rhynd Lochs; Perth and Kinross; Tayside (Scotland)

56°16'N, 03°51'W 224 ha

SSSI

A group of artificial lochs with a comparatively large raised mire.

Important for wintering wildfowl with *Anser brachyrhynchus* (av. max. 4260; max. 7200) and *A. anser* (av. max. 3326; max. 4450).

117 Loch Leven; Perth and Kinross, Tayside (Scotland)

56°12'N, 03°22'W 1612 ha Ramsar Site; EEC SPA

NNR; SSSI; RSPB

A large eutrophic loch surrounded by unimproved pasture. Human activities include fishing and hunting. Problems include eutrophication from agricultural, industrial and domestic effluent, and shoreline erosion.

Breeding species (breeding wildfowl figures compiled in 1981) include *Anas penelope* (35 pairs), *A. strepera* (50-60 pairs), *A. platyrhynchos* (400-600 pairs), *A. clypeata* (6 pairs), *Aythya ferina*, *A. fuligula* (500-600 pairs), *Larus ridibundus* (8000 pairs), and *Sterna hirundo* (320 pairs). Large numbers of waterfowl occur in autumn and winter including *Podiceps cristatus* (av. max. 104), *Cygnus cygnus* (av. max. 110), *Anser brachyrhynchus* (av. max. 11,334; max. 12,670), *A. anser* (av. max. 2060; max. 3000), *Anas strepera* (av. max. 208; max. 250), *A. clypeata* (av. max. 444; max. 780), and *Aythya fuligula* (av. max. 2972; max. 4830). The av. winter max. for wildfowl is 17,000.

118 Drumochter Hills; Highland, Tayside (Scotland)

56°52'N, 04°15'W 9690 ha

SSSI

A rich upland area with a varied moorland including an extensive blanket mire. Development of part of the area for skiing has been approved which may result in further proposals and diminish the value of the site.

The area holds important numbers of breeding waders including *Charadrius morinellus*, *Pluvialis apricaria*, *Calidris alpina*, and *Tringa nebularia*.

119 Ben Dubhchraig; Stirling, Central (Scotland)

56°24'N, 04°44'W

NNR

Upland heather moorland, peatbog and pools.

Upland breeding species.

120 Flanders Moss and Lake of Menteith; Stirling, Central (Scotland)

56°08'N, 04°20'W 245 ha (Flanders Moss only)

NNR; SSSI; SWT

Flanders Moss is one of the largest remaining raised mires in the U.K.

An important winter roost for *Anser brachyrhynchus* (av. max. 4506; max. 8700) and *A. anser* (av. max. 1363).

121 Firth of Tay; Tayside, Fife (Scotland)

56°26'N, 03°01'W 5610 ha

SSSI

The site comprises the Inner Tay Estuary and Monifieth Bay with extensive mudflats, salt marshes, and extensive *Phragmites* beds (one of the most extensive continuous stands in the U.K.)

Important for wintering and passage waterfowl, with a major roosting area on Mugdrum Island. Species include *Anser brachyrhynchus* (1120), *Somateria mollissima* (14,000 in outer Firth 1983/84) and waders, including *Tringa totanus* (av. max. 1346), and *Calidris alba* (av. max. 595; max. 750). The av. winter max. for waders is 12,965.

122 Eden Estuary, Tentsmuir Point, and Abertay Sands; Fife, Tayside (Scotland)

56°27'N, 02°49'W 2250+ ha

SSSI; NNR

A small estuary with mudflats, saltmarsh, and shingle areas (Eden Estuary); coastal mudflats and sand-dune system of great botanical interest (Tentsmuir Point and Abertay Sands).

Important for passage and wintering waterfowl including *Tadorna tadorna*, *Melanitta nigra*, *Haematopus ostralegus* (av. max. 3702; max. 4130), *Charadrius hiaticula* (spring passage max. 580), and *Pluvialis squatarola* (av. max. 453; max. 576). The av. winter max. for waders is 12,356.

123 Cameron Reservoir; North-east Fife, Fife (Scotland)

56°17'N, 02°51'W 64 ha

SSSI

Reservoir.

An important autumn and winter roost for wildfowl particularly *Anser brachyrhynchus* (av. max. 6100; max. 8000) and *A. anser* (av. max. 1030).

124 Inner Firth of Forth and Outer Firth of Forth; Fife, Lothian, Central (Scotland)

56°03'N, 03°00'W 2750 ha

SSSI; LNR; RSPB

Large estuary, bay and open sea, with beaches, saltwater marshes, mudflats, and sand-dunes.

Breeding species include *Sterna hirundo*, *S. paradisaea* and *S. albifrons*. In winter, the site supports very important concentrations of waterfowl with *Podiceps cristatus* (av. max. 412; max. 759), *Anser brachyrhynchus* (av. max. 5797; max. 12,500), *Tadorna tadorna* (av. max. 2245), *Aythya marila* (av. max. 1699), *Bucephala clangula* (av. max. 1604; max. 2017), *Haematopus ostralegus* (av. max. 8537; max. 8807), *Limosa lapponica* (av. max. 3910; max. 5787), *Tringa totanus* (av. max. 2820; max. 3067), *Calidris canutus* (av. max. 8096; max. 11,419), and *Arenaria interpres* (av. max. 1066; max. 1815). The av. winter max. for wildfowl is 14,000 and for waders 36,415.

125 Forth Islands; Lothian, Fife (Scotland)

56°03'N, 03°00'W 88 ha

SSSI; RSPB

Small islands in the Firth of Forth: Inchmickery, Fidra, Eyebroughty, the Lamb, Craigleith, Isle of May, and Bass Rock.

Breeding species include *Fulmarus glacialis* (1000 pairs), *Sula bassana* (21,590 pairs), *Phalacrocorax carbo* (200 pairs), *Phalacrocorax aristotelis* (2500 pairs), *Somateria mollissima* (159 pairs), *Larus fuscus* (3400 pairs), *L. argentatus* (9500 pairs), *Rissa tridactyla* (9300 pairs), *Sterna sandvicensis* (650 pairs), *S. dougallii* (21 pairs), *S. hirundo* (280 pairs), *Uria aalge* (25,800 breeding birds), *Alca torda* (2100 breeding birds), and *Fratercula arctica* (*c.* 15,000 pairs).

126 Gladhouse Reservoir; Midlothian, Lothian (Scotland)

55°46'N, 03°07'W 186 ha Ramsar Site; EEC SPA

SSSI; LNR

An artificial, mesotrophic freshwater body with limited development of aquatic and emergent vegetation.

The reservoir provides an important roosting site for *Anser brachyrhynchus* (av. max. 7040; max. 13,700).

127 Fala Flow; Midlothian, Lothian (Scotland)

55°49'N, 02°54'W 323 ha

SSSI

An area of relatively undisturbed blanket bog.
A roosting site for *Anser brachyrhynchus* (av. max. 3740; max. 6548).

128 Westwater; Tweeddale, Borders (Scotland)

55°46'N, 03°24'W 51 ha

SSSI

An upland reservoir.
Sterna hirundo breeds and large numbers of *Anser brachyrhynchus* (av. max. 15,434; max. 24,610) occur in winter.

129 Moorfoot Hills; Tweeddale, Borders (Scotland)

55°45'N, 03°05'W 8125 ha

SSSI

Rich upland area with marshes and moorland.
One of the richest areas in the U.K. for breeding upland waders, especially for *Pluvialis apricaria*, also breeding *Calidris alpina*, *Gallinago gallinago*, and *Numenius arquata*.

130 Hoselaw Loch; Roxburgh, Borders (Scotland)

55°35'N, 02°18'W 46 ha Ramsar Site; EEC SPA

SSSI; SWT

A mid-altitude loch with associated fen and raised bog.
An important winter roost for *Anser brachyrhynchus* (av. max. 3120; max. 4100) and *A. anser*.

131 Greenlaw Moor and Hule Moss; Berwick, Borders (Scotland)

55°44'N, 02°28'W 1175 ha

SSSI

Habitats include a confined raised mire, extensive heather moor, and an area of secondary woodland.
An important winter roost for *Anser brachyrhynchus* (av. max. 4780; max. 5550).

132 St Abb's Head – Fast Castle; Berwick, Borders (Scotland)

55°55'N, 02°08'W 257 ha

NNR; SSSI; SWT: NTS

A fine series of sea cliffs; also of considerable botanical interest.
A large seabird breeding colony with *Fulmarus glacialis* (750 pairs), *Phalacrocorax carbo* (40 pairs), *Phalacrocorax aristotelis* (650 pairs), *Larus argentatus* (1500 pairs), *Rissa tridactyla* (21,400 pairs), *Uria aalge* (28,900 breeding birds), *Alca torda* (1850 breeding birds), and *Fratercula arctica* (100 breeding birds).

133 Upper Solway Flats and Marshes; Cumbria, Dumfries and Galloway (Scotland, North)

54°52'N, 03°30'W 29,300 ha EEC SPA; Biosphere Reserve

NNR; SSSI; AONB; NSA; RSPB; CCT; NTS; Wildfowl Trust Reserve

Estuary with saltwater marshes and mudflats, raised saltmarsh, and grassland and arable land. Human activities include agriculture, stock-raising, and wildfowling.
Breeding species include *Tadorna tadorna* (40 pairs), *Haematopus ostralegus* (180 pairs), and *Tringa totanus* (90 pairs). Very important for wintering waterfowl, supporting

the entire Svalbard breeding population of *Branta leucopsis* (av. max. 9417; 1986/87 max. 10,500) in addition to *Cygnus cygnus* (av. max. 172; max. 220), *Anser brachyrhynchus* (av. max. 15,112; max. 27,000), *A. anser* (av. max. 1237), *Anas acuta* (max. 1000), *Aythya marila* (av. max. 1387; max. 1709), *Haematopus ostralegus* (av. max. 26,574; max. 40,396; smaller numbers wintering in outer Solway), *Charadrius hiaticula* (av. max. 227; autumn passage max. 713; spring passage max. 2075), *Calidris canutus* (av. max. 7039; max. 8189), *C. alba* (small numbers wintering; autumn passage max. 425; spring passage max. 1708; also important numbers in outer Solway), *Limosa lapponica* (av. max. 3366; max. 4185, both figures exclude outer Solway which holds important numbers), *Numenius arquata* (av. max. 5150; max. 6663), *Tringa totanus* (av. max. 1949; max. 2655), and *Arenaria interpres* (av. max. 412; max. 654). The av. winter max. for wildfowl is 34,100 and for waders 70,028.

134 Duddon Estuary; Cumbria (North)

54°13'N, 03°14'W 5120 ha

SSSI; RSPB

An extensive intertidal tract of sand, saltmarsh, and coastal dunes, and a large coastal lagoon (Hodbarrow Lagoon). The area is under pressure from recreation and derelict land reclamation.

A breeding site for *Sterna albifrons* (*c.*25 pairs in 1988). Also important for wintering waterfowl with *Tadorna tadorna*, *Anas crecca*, *A. acuta* (max. 560), *Mergus serrator*, *Haematopus ostralegus* (av. max. 6886; max. 10,665), *Calidris canutus* (av. max. 3662; max. 12,000), *C. alba* (av. max. 340; max. 606), *C. alpina*, and *Numenius arquata* (av. max. 2268). Passage waders include *Charadrius hiaticula* (autumn passage max. 512). The av. winter max. for waders is 21,628.

135 Morecambe Bay; Cumbria, Lancashire (North, North West)

54°07'N, 02°59'W 39,100 ha

SSSI; AONB; RSPB; LNR

A large bay with mudflats, saltwater marshes, raised saltmarsh, and beaches. Includes the two low sandy islands of Walney and Foulney. Human activities include stock-raising, fishing, hunting, recreation including boating, and there are a town and harbour.

Breeding species include *Tadorna tadorna* (95 pairs), *Somateria mollissima*, *Haematopus ostralegus* (80 pairs), *Tringa totanus* (150 pairs), *Larus fuscus* (27,500 pairs), *L. argentatus* (27,000 pairs), *Sterna sandvicensis* (550 pairs), *S. hirundo* (200 pairs), *S. paradisaea* (145 pairs), and *S. albifrons* (55 pairs). A very important site for non-breeding waterfowl with (winter counts, unless otherwise stated) *Tadorna tadorna* (av. max. 3100; max. 4236), *A. platyrhynchos* (av. max. 4282; max. 4463), *A. acuta* (av. max. 2610; max. 2889), *Melanitta nigra* (av. Jan. 1000), *Haematopus ostralegus* (av. max. 48,913; max. 61,833), *Charadrius hiaticula* (max. 348; spring passage max. 833), *Pluvialis squatarola* (av. max. 1045; max. 1846), *Vanellus vanellus* (av. max. 13,162; max. 15,692), *Calidris canutus* (av. max. 24,661; max. 28,087), *C. alba* (max. 348; spring passage max. 4191), *C. alpina* (av. max. 35,313; max. 50,211), *Limosa lapponica* (av. max. 4857; max. 5752), *Numenius arquata* (av. max. 8603; max. 10,979), *Tringa totanus* (av. max. 5575; max. 7802), and *Arenaria interpres* (av. max. 1267; max. 1703). The av. winter max. for wildfowl is 16,700 and for waders 143,552.

136 Shap Fells; Cumbria (North)

54°28'N, 02°39'W 2107 ha

SSSI; NP

Exclusive upland fells with heather-dominated blanket bog and widespread wet flushes.

The site supports the largest and most diverse upland breeding bird population in West Cumbria, with *Falco columbarius*, *F. peregrinus*, *Lagopus lagopus*, *Pluvialis apricaria*, *Vanellus vanellus*, *Calidris alpina*, *Gallinago gallinago*, *Numenius arquata*, *Tringa totanus*, *Asio flammeus*, *Corvus corax*, and *Carduelis flavirostris*.

137 Leighton Moss; Lancashire (North West)

54°10'N, 02°47'W 125 ha Ramsar Site; EEC SPA

SSSI; AONB; RSPB

A complex of base-rich shallow meres, extensive *Phragmites* beds (the largest area of *Phragmites* in north-west England), *Salix* scrub, mixed fen vegetation, and woodland.

Important breeding site for *Botaurus stellaris* (6-7 males in 1987); also breeding *Circus aeruginosus* (first bred in 1987; 1 pair) and *Panurus biarmicus* (*c.*15 pairs in 1987). Wintering wildfowl include *Anas crecca* (1800).

138 Bowland Fells; Lancashire (North West)

53°56'N, 02°37'W 10,090 ha

SSSI; AONB

Extensive upland area of acid moorland (with continuous large areas of blanket peat). Includes several valleys with remnants of the original *Quercus-Betula-Sorbus* woodlands.

Holds a characteristic assemblage of upland birds including important populations of *Circus cyaneus* and *Falco columbarius*, and a very large inland gull colony, mainly *Larus fuscus*.

139 Ribble and Alt Estuaries; Lancashire, Merseyside (North West)

53°41'N, 03°00'W 13,000 ha Ramsar Site; EEC SPA

NNR; SSSI

Two estuaries with saltwater marshes, raised saltmarsh, mudflats, and wet meadows. Threats from agricultural development, industrial development (on the Alt), marina proposals and sand winning.

The Ribble Estuary is a very important area for passage and wintering waterfowl including *Cygnus columbianus* (av. max. 206), *C. cygnus* (av. max. 163), *Anser brachyrhynchus* (av. max. 10,003), *Tadorna tadorna* (av. max. 3023; max. 5055), *Anas penelope* (av. max. 18,338; max. 24,462), *A. crecca* (4670; max. 4808), *A. acuta* (av. max. 501), *Haematopus ostralegus* (av. max. 7990; max. 10,963), *Charadrius hiaticula* (small numbers wintering; spring passage av. max. 2380), *P. squatarola* (av. max. 1945; max. 2177), *Vanellus vanellus* (av. max. 10,940; max. 15,482), *Calidris canutus* (av. max. 16,753; max. 27,007), *C. alba* (av. max. 1608; max. 2038; spring passage av. max. 5458), *C. alpina* (av. max. 15,270; max. 18,612), *Limosa limosa islandica* (av. max. 1106; max. 2110), and *L. lapponica* (av. max. 9830; max. 13,880). The av. winter max. for wildfowl is 38,000 and for waders 72,438. The Alt Estuary is also important for wintering and passage waders with *Pluvialis squatarola* (av. max. 660; max. 1023), *Calidris canutus* (av. max. 35,261; max. 46,000), *C. alba* (av. max. 538; max. 727; spring passage max. 2234), and *Limosa lapponica* (av. max. 7078; max. 11,310).

140 Martin Mere; Lancashire (North West)

53°37'N, 02°53'W 119 ha Ramsar Site; EEC SPA

SSSI; Wildfowl Trust Reserve

A low-lying wetland complex of open water, marsh, and grassland habitats overlying peat. The present wetland is a product of drainage of what was formerly the largest lake in Lancashire.

Breeding species include *Anser anser*, *Anas strepera*, and *Gallinago gallinago*. Wintering wildfowl include *Cygnus columbianus* (av. max. 220; max. 350), *C. cygnus* (av. max. 219; max. 475), *Anser brachyrhynchus* (av. max. 6280), *Anas strepera* (av. max. 159), *A. crecca* (av. max. 3400; max. 4000), *A. platyrhynchos* (av. max. 3480; max. 4600), and *A. acuta* (av. max. 1884; max. 3700). The av. winter max. for wildfowl is 12,200.

141 Thorne and Hatfield Moors; South Yorkshire, Humberside (Yorkshire and Humberside)

53°38'N, 00°54'W (Thorne Moor); 53°33'N, 00°55'W (Hatfield Moor) 2117 ha

SSSI

Moorland with marshes and slow-flowing rivers and streams. Thorne Moor comprises the largest extent of lowland raised mire in England.

Breeding species include *Anas crecca*, *A. clypeata*, *Aythya fuligula*, *Gallinago gallinago*, *Numenius arquata*, *Asio otus*, *A. flammeus*, and nationally important for *Caprimulgus europaeus*.

142 Lindisfarne; Northumberland (North)

55°41'N, 01°48'W 3640 ha Ramsar Site; EEC SPA

NNR; AONB; Heritage Coast

Large island (Lindisfarne) with rocky coast, cliffs, beaches, sand-dunes, grassland, and arable land; separated from the mainland by mudflats and saltwater marshes. Includes Ross Links and Budle Bay. Human activities include stock-raising, fishing, hunting, and recreation. Threat from encroachment of *Spartina*, particularly on the mainland side of the causeway.

Breeding species include *Sterna dougallii* (4 pairs), *S. paradisaea* (35 pairs), and *S. albifrons* (25 pairs). In winter, large numbers of wildfowl and waders occur, including *Cygnus cygnus* (av. max. 92), *Anser anser* (av. max. 3402), *Branta bernicla hrota* (av. max. 2120; 3000 in 1986/87, 75 per cent of the Svalbard breeding population), *Anas penelope* (av. max. 22,299; max. 41,000), *Somateria mollissima* (av. max. 3824), *Charadrius hiaticula* (av. max. 386; max. 716; spring passage max. 1912), *Pluvialis squatarola* (av. max. 856; max. 2100), *C. maritima* (max. 314), *C. alpina* (av. max. 12,636; max. 23,000), *Limosa lapponica* (av. max. 6277; max. 9600), and *Tringa totanus* (av. max. 3033; max. 4041). The av. winter max. for wildfowl is 23,000 and for waders 31,587.

143 Farne Islands; Northumberland (North)

55°38'N, 01°37'W 97 ha EEC SPA

SSSI; NT

A group of low rocky islets with pioneer vegetation.

Breeding species include *Fulmarus glacialis* (215 pairs), *Phalacrocorax carbo* (266 pairs), *P. aristotelis* (1390 pairs), *Somateria mollissima* (1740 pairs), *Larus fuscus* (1260 pairs), *Rissa tridactyla* (5680 pairs), *Sterna sandvicensis* (3400 pairs), *S. dougallii* (21 pairs), *S. hirundo* (350 pairs), *S. paradisaea* (3350 pairs), *Uria aalge* (13,770 pairs), and *Fratercula arctica* (20,730 pairs in 1984).

144 Northumberland Coast; Northumberland (North)

55°25'N, 01°35'W

SSSI; AONB; Heritage Coast

Series of geological SSSIs and hard rock outcrops plus soft shore habitats running from the Scottish border to Tynemouth.

Wintering species include nationally important populations of *Pluvialis apricaria*, *Calidris alba*, *C. maritima*, *Limosa lapponica*, and *Arenaria interpres*. The area also supports nationally important numbers of breeding *Sterna albifrons*, and migrant *Sterna* sp. in autumn.

145 Coquet Island; Northumberland (North)

55°20'N, 01°32'W 2 ha EEC SPA

SSSI; RSPB

A small, low rocky island.

Breeding species include *Fulmarus glacialis, Somateria mollissima* (460 pairs), *Larus ridibundus* (4000 pairs), *Sterna sandvicensis* (1600 pairs; one of the most important colonies in Britain), *S. dougallii* (17 pairs), *S. hirundo* (700 pairs; the largest colony in Britain), *S. paradisaea* (500 pairs), and *Fratercula arctica* (3300 pairs).

146 Holburn Moss; Northumberland (North)

55°37'N, 01°55'W 22 ha Ramsar Site; EEC SPA

SSSI

An area of peat mire to the east of an artificial lake (Holburn Lake, created by damming in 1934).

Large numbers of *Anser anser* roost in winter.

147 Muggleswick, Stanhope and Wolsingham Commons; Durham (North)

54°47'N, 02°00'W

AONB

Managed *Calluna* moorland with underlying peat and associated wet flushes. Grazing on moorland edge. Improved valley sides with *Pteridium* slopes.

An important breeding site for upland moorland species which include *Falco columbarius, Lagopus lagopus, Pluvialis apricaria* (70 pairs), *Calidris alpina, Gallinago gallinago, Numenius arquata* (40 pairs), *Tringa totanus, Asio flammeus, Saxicola rubetra, Oenanthe oenanthe,* and *Turdus torquatus.*

148 Bollihope and Middleton Commons; Durham (North)

54°04'N, 02°03'W

AONB

Managed *Calluna* moorland with underlying peat and associated wet flushes. Grazing on moorland edge. Improved valleys sides with *Pteridium* slopes.

An important breeding site for upland moorland species which include *Falco columbarius, Lagopus lagopus, Pluvialis apricaria* (60 pairs), *Calidris alpina, Gallinago gallinago* (10 pairs), *Numenius arquata* (35 pairs), *Tringa totanus, Asio flammeus, Saxicola rubetra, Oenanthe oenanthe,* and *Turdus torquatus.*

149 Upper Teesdale and Moor House; Durham, Cumbria, North Yorkshire, (North, Yorkshire and Humberside)

54°39'N, 02°18'W 39,400 ha EEC SPA; Biosphere Reserve

NNR; AONB

An extensive block of Pennine upland with moorland, blanket bog, meadows, and woodland.

The area has some of the highest upland wader breeding densities in northern England with a max. of 13 pairs per sq km. Breeding species include *Haematopus ostralegus, Pluvialis apricaria* (in densities as high as any other surveyed site in Britain), *Vanellus vanellus,* and *Calidris alpina. Gallinago gallinago, Numenius arquata, Tringa totanus,* and *Actitis hypoleucos* breed in numbers of national importance. Contains the highest number of *Tetrao tetrix* at any English site.

150 Bowes Moor; Durham (North)

54°29'N, 02°07'W

AONB

Managed *Calluna* moorland with underlying peat and associated wet flushes. Grazing on moorland edge. Improved valley sides with *Pteridium* slopes.

An important breeding site for upland moorland species which include *Falco columbarius*, *Lagopus lagopus*, *Pluvalis apricaria* (40 pairs), *Calidris alpina*, *Gallinago gallinago*, *Numenius arquata* (50 pairs), *Tringa totanus* (10 pairs), and *Actitis hypoleucos* (4 pairs). *Lagopus lagopus*, *Asio flammeus*, and *Turdus torquatus* also breed.

151 Teesmouth and Cleveland Coast; Cleveland (North)

54°38'N, 01°09'W 900 ha

SSSI

An extensive area of intertidal mudflats; also sand-dunes and saltmarshes. Includes five SSSI sites: Seal Sands; Seaton Dunes and Common; South Gare, Bran Sands; Coatham Sands; Cowpen Marsh; Redcar Rocks. A long-term nature reserve agreement (between the Secretary of State, NCC, Crown Estate and industry) has recently (1989) been reached, with regard to Seal Sands SSSI and part of Seaton Dunes and Common SSSI. However, there remains some conflict between the needs of industry and nature conservation, and pressure from recreation.

Each year the area holds more than 20,000 waterfowl including *Tadorna tadorna* (av. max. 1708), *Anas crecca* (av. max. 2086; max. 4400), *Calidris canutus* (av. max. 5783; max. 6462), *C. alba* (av. max. 444; max. 800), and *Tringa totanus* (av. max. 1485; max. 1912 on autumn passage). *Charadrius hiaticula* occurs on passage (av. max. 347; max. 464), together with other waders e.g. *Tringa nebularia*. The av. winter max. for waders is 16,640. The area also supports internationally important numbers of *Sterna sandvicensis* and a nationally important breeding colony of *S. albifrons*.

152 Spaunton, Wheeldale, Egton and Glaisdale Moors; North Yorkshire (Yorkshire and Humberside)

54°23'N, 00°52'W 5800 ha

NP

Many high grade areas of managed *Calluna* moorland and associated habitats currently without SSSI protection.

Breeding species include *Anas crecca*, *Falco columbarius*, *Lagopus lagopus*, *Pluvialis apricaria*, *Calidris alpina*, *Gallinago gallinago*, and *Numenius arquata*.

153 Abbotside, Askrigg and Mallerstang Commons; Cumbria, North Yorkshire, (North, Yorkshire and Humberside)

54°22'N, 02°14'W 2174 ha (Mallerstang to Swalehead SSSI only)

SSSI; NP

Managed *Calluna* moorland with underlying peat and associated wet flushes. Grazing on moorland edge. Improved valley sides with *Pteridium* slopes.

An important breeding site for waders, which include *Pluvialis apricaria* (235 pairs), *Calidris alpina* (20 pairs), *Gallinago gallinago* (50 pairs), *Numenius arquata* (100 pairs), and *Tringa totanus* (10 pairs). *Lagopus lagopus*, *Asio flammeus*, and *Turdus torquatus* also breed.

154 Derwent Ings; North Yorkshire, Humberside (Yorkshire and Humberside)

53°48'-53°55'N, 00°56'W 783 ha Ramsar Site; EEC SPA

SSSI; LNR; CCT

An area of neutral alluvial grassland which is regularly inundated by the River Derwent during winter. The vegetation composition is variable, according to the extent of winter flooding. Drainage plans formerly threatened the area (rejected by Ministry of Agriculture in 1984).

Breeding species include *Tadorna tadorna*, *Anas crecca*, *A. clypeata* (100 pairs), *Aythya fuligula*, *Vanellus vanellus*, *Gallinago gallinago*, *Numenius arquata*, and *Tringa totanus*, together with small numbers of *Anas querquedula*, *Haematopus ostralegus*,

Charadrius dubius, and *Actitis hypoleucos*. Wildfowl occurring in winter include *Cygnus columbianus* (av. max. 116), *Anas penelope* (av. max. 6348; max. 8000), *A. crecca* (av. max. 2252; max. 3620), *A. platyrhynchos* (av. max. 2800; max. 5240), and *Aythya ferina* (av. max. 917; max. 2250). The av. winter max. for wildfowl is 13,500.

155 Flamborough Head and Bempton Cliffs; Humberside (Yorkshire and Humberside)

54°08'N, 00°08'W 340 ha

SSSI; RSPB; Heritage Coast

A stretch of coast between Reighton and Sewerby, of great geological interest, with sea cliffs. Holds the only mainland breeding population of *Sula bassana* in the U.K.

Breeding species include *Fulmarus glacialis* (900 pairs), *Sula bassana* (780 pairs), *Phalacrocorax aristotelis* (60 pairs), *Rissa tridactyla* (85,000 pairs), *Uria aalge* (32,600 breeding birds), *Alca torda* (7700 breeding birds), and *Fratercula arctica* (7000 breeding birds).

156 Hornsea Mere; Humberside (Yorkshire and Humberside)

53°54'N, 00°11'W 230 ha

RSPB

A large shallow eutrophic lake with *Phragmites* beds and fen and carr woodland.

Breeding species include *Anas strepera*, *A. clypeata*, and *Acrocephalus scirpaceus* (800 pairs). *Larus minutus* (max. 50) occur in summer. Wintering waterfowl include *Anser anser* (450), *A. strepera* (180), and *Bucephala clangula* (180).

157 Humber Flats, Marshes, and Coast; Humberside, Lincolnshire (Yorkshire and Humberside, East Midlands)

53°43'N, 00°15'W 15,750+ ha

SSSI; CCT; RSPB

Extensive intertidal mud- and sandflats of the River Humber, with saltmarshes, associated freshwater pools, and sand-dune systems. Includes the marshes along the north Lincolnshire coast. There has been a proposal to dump waste on the mudflats. There are also proposals for a tidal barrage and dock expansion: pollution levels in the river are a continual cause for concern.

Large numbers of wildfowl and waders use the area, especially in winter including *Tadorna tadorna* (av. max. 4229; max. 6495), *Charadrius hiaticula* (av. max. 445; spring passage max. 1481), *Pluvialis apricaria* (av. max. 9124; max. 10,233), *P. squatarola* (av. max. 863; max. 1031), *Calidris canutus* (av. max. 29,206; max. 33,054), *C. alba* (av. max. 393; autumn passage max. 979), *C. alpina* (av. max. 26,493; max. 32,026), *Numenius arquata* (av. max. 2984; max. 3943), *Tringa totanus* (av. max. 3995; max. 5719 on autumn passage), and *Arenaria interpres* (av. max. 507). The av. winter max. for wildfowl is 15,500 and for waders 83,127.

158 Mersey Estuary; Merseyside, Cheshire (North West)

53°19'N, 02°50'W 6700 ha

SSSI; CCT; Merseyside Naturalists' Association Reserve

An extensive area of intertidal sand- and mudflats; also reclaimed marshland, saltmarshes, and brackish marshes. A barrage across the Mersey has been proposed as has an industrial reclamation scheme, which would seriously threaten the site.

Important for wildfowl and waders including *Tadorna tadorna* (av. max. 5574; max. 7605), *Anas penelope* (av. max. 9560; max. 12,000), *A. crecca* (av. max. 11,670; max. 26,100), *A. acuta* (av. max. 10,550; max. 16,000), *Calidris alpina* (av. max. 25,960; max. 34,700), and *Tringa totanus* (av. max. 1739; max. 3300). The av. winter max. for wildfowl is 28,800 and for waders 33,699.

159 Peak District Moors; Derbyshire, South Yorkshire, Staffordshire (Yorkshire and Humberside, East Midlands)

53°22'N, 01°51'W 11,750 ha

SSSI; NP

An upland area with moorland, grassland and arable land, fast-flowing rivers and streams, lakes, marshes. Increased recreational pressure is possibly affecting the *Pluvialis apricaria* population.

The site holds high densities of breeding waders including *Pluvialis apricaria*, *Calidris alpina*, and *Numenius arquata*.

160 Walmore Common; Gloucestershire (South West)

51°50'N, 02°23'W 58 ha

SSSI

A low-lying area of unimproved and improved grassland, marshy grassland and ditches.

Important for wintering *Cygnus columbianus* (135).

161 Rutland Water; Leicestershire (East Midlands)

52°39'N, 00°40'W 1540 ha

SSSI

A large recently created reservoir with extensive areas of open water and lakeside habitats including lagoons, islands, mudflats, *Phragmites* beds, meadows, scrub, and woodland. One of the richest reservoirs for wintering and passage wildfowl in the U.K.

Important for wintering waterfowl, which include *Podiceps cristatus* (545), *Anas penelope* (4480), *A. strepera* (900), *A. crecca* (1460), *A. clypeata* (530), *Aythya fuligula* (2500), *Bucephala clangula* (230), and *Mergus merganser* (70).

162 Nene Washes; Cambridgeshire (East Anglia)

52°34'N, 00°05'W 1310 ha

SSSI; RSPB

A mosaic of rough grassland and wet pasture. The area is used for the seasonal storage of flood-waters, and cattle-grazing in the summer. Besides its own wintering populations, the area also holds wildfowl from the nearby Ouse Washes when flooding there prevents feeding.

Breeding species include *Anas strepera* (25 pairs), *A. querquedula* (5 pairs), *A. clypeata* (46 pairs), *Vanellus vanellus* (50 pairs), *Gallinago gallinago* (120 drumming birds in 1988), and *Tringa totanus* (80 pairs); figures given relate to populations on the RSPB Reserve only. Wintering Anatidae include *Cygnus columbianus* (av. max. 555; max. 937), *Anas penelope* (av. max. 2858), *A. crecca* (av. max.* 1253), and *A. acuta* (av. max.* 482).

163 Ouse Washes; Cambridgeshire, Norfolk (East Anglia)

52°30'N, 00°13'E 2400 ha Ramsar Site; EEC SPA

SSSI; RSPB; CCT; Wildfowl Trust Reserve; National Wildfowl Refuge

An extensive area of washland habitat with large areas of unimproved grassland, and botanically rich dykes and rivers. Like the Nene Washes the area is used for the seasonal storage of flood-waters, and cattle-grazing in summer. Recent breeding success of ground-nesting species has been very poor owing to prolonged spring flooding. The reasons for the extensive late floods are uncertain, but increasing drainage and development upstream, automated sluices, and changing weather patterns are all thought to be contributory factors.

Important breeding area for *Anas strepera*, *A. crecca*, *A. acuta*, *A. querquedula* (4-7 pairs at RSPB Reserve in 1987), *A. clypeata*, and *Aythya fuligula*, as well as for waders, notably *Philomachus pugnax*, and *Limosa limosa*. Very important for wintering wildfowl with *Cygnus olor* (av. max. 562; max. 643), *C. columbianus* (av. max. 4458; max. 6164), *C. cygnus* (av. max. 310; max. 520), *Anas penelope* (av. max. 30,880; max. 42,175), *A. strepera* (av. max. 283; max. 356), *A. crecca* (av. max. 3099), *A. platyrhynchos* (av. max. 5547; max. 7815), *A. acuta* (av. max. 1160; max. 1803), and *A. clypeata* (av. max. 487; max. 685). The av. winter max. for wildfowl is 46,300.

164 The Wash; Lincolnshire, Norfolk (East Midlands, East Anglia)

52°47'-53°05'N, 00°00'-00°32'E 66,050 ha Ramsar Site; EEC SPA

SSSI; RSPB

A vast intertidal bay with extensive mudflats and sandbanks, saltmarshes, and sandy beaches. The land adjoining The Wash is used intensively for agriculture, with localised industrial and residential areas.

Breeding species include *Tadorna tadorna*, *Haematopus ostralegus*, *Charadrius hiaticula*, *Tringa totanus*, *Larus ridibundus*, *Sterna hirundo* (220 pairs), and *S. albifrons* (30 pairs). An extremely important area for passage and wintering wildfowl and waders with *Anser brachyrhynchus* (av. max. 6362; max. 9500), *Branta bernicla* (av. max. 19,465; max. 24,297), *Tadorna tadorna* (av. max. 19,111; max. 23,775), *A. acuta* (av. max. 2980; max. 4562), *Haematopus ostralegus* (av. max. 25,000; max. 29,159), *Charadrius hiaticula* (small numbers wintering; spring passage max. 1022), *Pluvialis squatarola* (av. max. 4191; max. 5512), *Calidris canutus* (av. max. 88,102; max. 117,886), *C. alba* (av. max. 469; max. 768), *C. alpina* (av. max. 34,525; max. 41,105), *Limosa lapponica* (av. max. 8593; max. 12,809), *Numenius arquata* (av. max. 3691; max. 5149), *Tringa totanus* (av. max. 3906; max. 5566), and *Arenaria interpres* (av. max. 970 winter/passage). The av. winter max. for wildfowl is 47,500 and for waders 152,884. Also very important for other wader species on passage e.g. *Tringa nebularia*.

165 North Norfolk Coast; Norfolk (East Anglia)

52°58'N, 00°37'-01°07'E 7701 ha Ramsar Site; EEC SPA; Biosphere Reserve

NNR; SSSI; AONB; RSPB; CCT; Heritage Coast

Includes Scolt Head, Holkham, Blakeney Point, and Cley – Salthouse Marshes. A complex of sand-dunes; shingle islands, spits, beaches, fresh- and saltwater lagoons, saltwater marshes, raised saltmarsh, and mudflats; also wet meadows, grassland, and arable land inland. Human activities includes agriculture, fishing, and tourism, and there are villages, towns, industry, and a harbour.

Breeding species include *Botaurus stellaris*, *Anas strepera*, *A. clypeata*, *Circus aeruginosus*, *Recurvirostra avosetta* (17 pairs at Titchwell RSPB Reserve in 1986; also breeds Cley – Salthouse), *Haematopus ostralegus*, *Charadrius hiaticula*, *Sterna sandvicensis* (4500 pairs), *S. hirundo* (1000 pairs), *S. albifrons* (400 pairs), and *Panurus biarmicus* (100 pairs). Important for passage waders, including *Recurvirostra avosetta*, *Calidris alba*, *Philomachus pugnax*, *Limosa limosa*, *Tringa erythropus*, *T. nebularia*, and *T. ochropus*. Large numbers of waterfowl occur in winter; wintering species include *Gavia stellata* (offshore), *Branta bernicla bernicla* (av. max. and max. for each area: Scolt Head 4350; 6000. Holkham 2957; 4250. Blakeney 3680; 5000), *Haematopus ostralegus* (av. max. 4367), *Calidris canutus* (av. max. 5430; max. 6121), and *Arenaria interpres* (av. max. 363). Other wintering species include *Circus cyaneus* and *Asio flammeus*.

166 Upper Thurne Broads and Marshes; Norfolk (East Anglia)

52°44'N, 01°35'E 1160 ha Ramsar Site; EEC SPA

SSSI; ESA; CCT; NT

A wetland complex with four large shallow lakes: Hickling Broad, Heigham Sound, Horsey Mere, and Martham Broad, surrounded by extensive areas of reedbeds, grazing marsh, and fen-meadow.

Breeding species include *Botaurus stellaris*, *Circus aeruginosus*, *Gallinago gallinago* (30 pairs), and *Tringa totanus* (25 pairs). Wintering waterfowl include *Cygnus columbianus* (170), *Cygnus cygnus* (55), *Anas strepera* (245), and *A. crecca* (1340). Also important in winter for *Circus cyaneus* (roosting) and *Falco columbarius*.

167 Ant Broads and Marshes; Norfolk (East Anglia)

52°43'N, 01°31'E 267 ha

SSSI; ESA

The area includes a variety of typical broadland fen habitats.

Breeding species include *Botaurus stellaris* (2 booming males), *Circus aeruginosus* (3 pairs).

168 Bure Broads and Marshes; Norfolk (East Anglia)

52°41'N, 01°28'E 412 ha Ramsar Site; EEC SPA

NNR; SSSI; ESA; CCT

The site comprises a large proportion of the fen and fen woodland in the Bure Valley.

The area supports a variety of breeding birds including *Circus aeruginosus*, *Sterna hirundo* (30-40 pairs), and an important U.K. population of *Cettia cetti*. In winter the site holds a good selection of wildfowl, up to 100 *Cygnus columbianus*, a roost of over 400 *Phalacrocorax carbo*, and a roost of *Circus cyaneus*.

169 Yare Broads and Marshes; Norfolk (East Anglia)

52°35'N, 01°27'E 736 ha (excluding Cantley Marshes)

SSSI; ESA; RSPB

An extensive area of unreclaimed fen, carr woodland, open water, and grazing marshes. Includes Surlingham and Rockland Broads, Strumpshaw Fen, and Cantley and Buckenham Marshes. Cantley Marshes are now more important than Buckenham for *Anser fabalis*, although the site is outside the SSSI and proposed SPA.

The only regular wintering site for *Anser fabalis* (av. max. 365; max. 420) in England. Also wintering *Anser albifrons* (max. 315 in 1988/89) and *Anas penelope* (av. max. 10,000).

170 Breckland Heaths; Norfolk, Suffolk (East Anglia)

52°28'N, 00°35'E 6600+ ha

NNR; SSSI; CCT

An imporant complex of grass, heather and lichen heath sites: Foxhole Heath, Weather and Horn Heaths, Stanford Training Area, Weeting Heath, Barnham Heath, Berners Heath, Cavenham/Icklingham Heaths, Deadman's Grave, Eriswell Low Warren, Lakenheath Warren, Little Heath (Barnham), Thetford Heaths, Wangford Warren and Carr.

Important for breeding *Burhinus oedicnemus* (*c.*80 pairs). Wintering species include *Circus cyaneus* and *Asio flammeus*.

171 Minsmere – Walberswick; Suffolk (East Anglia)

52°17'N, 01°38'E 1820 ha Ramsar Site; EEC SPA

NNR; SSSI; AONB; RSPB; NT; Heritage Coast

Two large marshes with *Phragmites* beds, fresh- and saltwater lagoons, beaches, sand-dunes, raised saltmarsh; with woodland, heath, grassland, and arable land. Includes the Blythe Estuary with extensive mudflats. An outstanding area for its diversity, with about 100 breeding species of birds.

Breeding species include *Botaurus stellaris* (5 pairs), *Anas strepera*, *A. crecca*, *A. clypeata*, *Circus aeruginosus* (5 pairs), *Recurvirostra avosetta* (65 pairs), *Tringa totanus*,

Sterna albifrons (20 pairs), and *Caprimulgus europaeus* (13 territorial males at RSPB Reserve; also breeds at Walberswick). Also important for wintering and passage waterfowl including *Cygnus columbianus* (Minsmere Levels: 150 in 1986/87), *Anser albifrons* (Minsmere Levels: max. 235), and *A. strepera* (av. max. 133). Other wintering species include *Circus cyaneus* (up to 15 roosting at RSPB Reserve in 1987).

172 Orfordness – Havergate; Suffolk (East Anglia)

52°04'N, 01°30'E 1600 ha EEC SPA (117 ha)

NNR; SSSI; AONB; RSPB; Heritage Coast

Estuary complex of the Rivers Alde, Butley, Ore, and Deben, and including a large island (Havergate) with saline lagoons. The area also includes shingle beaches, sand-dunes, mudflats, and saltmarshes.

Breeding species (figures refer to the RSPB Reserve in 1987) include *Recurvirostra avosetta* (94 pairs), *Sterna sandvicensis* (100 pairs), *S. hirundo*, and *S. paradisaea* (irregular). Also important for wintering/passage *Recurvirostra avosetta* (av. max. 334; max. 435).

173 Stour and Orwell Estuary; Suffolk, Essex (East Anglia, South East)

51°58'N, 01°15'E 3380 ha

SSSI; AONB; RSPB

Two estuaries with saltwater marshes and mudflats. Part of the Orwell is threatened by port expansion.

An important wintering area for wildfowl and waders including *Cygnus olor* (Stour: av. max. 253; max. 349), *Branta bernicla* (Stour: 2400 in 1986/87), *Tadorna tadorna* (Stour: av. max. 1887), *Charadrius hiaticula* (Orwell: av. max. 538; max. 782 / Stour: av. max. 312), *Pluvialis squatarola* (Stour: av. max. 1081; max. 1430), *C. alpina* (Stour: av. max. 16,171; max. 20,854), *Limosa limosa islandica* (Stour: av. max. 1104; max. 1660), *Tringa totanus* (Stour: av. max. 2058; max. 3221 / Orwell: av. max. 2158; max. 3105), and *Arenaria interpres* (Stour: av. max. 441; max. 483 / Orwell: av. max. 444; max. 675). The av. winter max. for waders on the Stour is 25,120 and for the Orwell 17,778.

174 Hamford Water; Essex (South East)

51°52'N, 01°14'E 2143 ha

NNR; SSSI

A large and complex estuarine basin with numerous tidal creeks, intertidal mud- and sandflats, extensive saltmarshes, islands, beaches, and marshy grassland.

Breeding species include *Sterna hirundo* and *S. albifrons*. *Tringa erythropus* and *T. nebularia* occur on passage, particularly in autumn. An important passage and wintering site for wildfowl and waders including *Branta bernicla* (av. max. 8300; max. 10,000), *Tadorna tadorna* (av. max. 2129; max. 3050), *Anas penelope* (av. max. 4877), *A. crecca* (av. max. 3428; max. 5700), *Pluvialis squatarola* (av. max. 852; max. 2282), *Calidris alba* (av. max. 197; max. 395), and *Limosa limosa islandica* (av. max. 671; max. 1477). The av. winter max. for wildfowl is 16,700 and for waders is 12,578.

175 Abberton Reservoir; Essex (South East)

51°49'N, 00°52'E 1228 ha Ramsar Site; EEC SPA

SSSI

Artificial reservoir with marshes, grassland, and arable land. Human activities include agriculture, fishing, and recreation including boating. Threats from increasing recreational disturbance, especially sailing.

Important for moulting and wintering waterfowl with *Podiceps cristatus* (av. max. 156; max. 229), *Cygnus olor* (av. max. 440; max. 547), *Anas penelope* (av. max. 12,510; max. 35,000), *A. strepera* (av. max. 303; max. 410), *A. clypeata* (av. max. 426; max. 612),

Aythya ferina (av. max. 2540; max. 3000 , moulting in autumn), *Bucephala clangula* (av. max. 508; max. 677), and *Fulica atra* (av. max. 9361; max. 10,055). The av. winter max. for wildfowl is 14,900.

176 Blackwater, Colne, and Dengie; Essex (South East)

51°44'N, 00°53'E 12,470 ha

NNR; SSSI

Dengie is a large and remote area of tidal mudflat and saltmarshes. Blackwater and Colne Estuaries.

Breeding species include *Larus ridibundus* (1020 pairs), *Sterna sandvicensis*, *S. hirundo*, *S. albifrons* (90 pairs), *Charadrius hiaticula* (30 pairs), and *Tringa totanus* (175 pairs). Important for wintering and passage waterfowl including *Branta bernicla* (Blackwater: av. max. 11,730; max. 13,410 / Colne: av. max. 4780; max. 7748), *Charadrius hiaticula* (Blackwater: av. max. 367; max. 717), *Pluvialis squatarola* (Blackwater: av. max. 1003; max. 1290 / Colne: max. 811 / Dengie: av. max. 950; max. 1700), *Calidris canutus* (Dengie: av. max. 5023; max. 10,280), *C. alba* (Colne: av. max. 184; max. 330), *C. alpina* (av. max. 15,581; max. 21,800), *Numenius arquata* (Blackwater: max. 2465), and *Arenaria interpres* (Colne: max. 530). The av. winter max. for wildfowl is 15,100 (Blackwater only) and for waders it is 22,067 (Blackwater), 13,504 (Colne), and 12,106 (Dengie).

177 River Crouch Marshes; Essex (South East)

51°39'N, 00°45'E 283 ha (Bridgemarsh Island SSSI only)

SSSI

Includes Bridgemarsh Island which is a large area of saltmarsh and intertidal mudflats in the River Crouch.

Wintering waterfowl include *Branta bernicla* (4900), *Anas penelope* (2120), *A. crecca* (1270), *Calidris alpina* (4340), and *Tringa totanus* (1250).

178 Foulness and Maplin Sands; Essex (South East)

51°34'N, 00°54'E 16,400 ha

SSSI

An estuarine area and island with saltwater marshes and mudflats.

Breeding species include *Sterna sandvicensis* (120 pairs), *S. hirundo* (270 pairs), and *S. albifrons* (70 pairs). Important for wintering *Branta bernicla* (av. max. 19,659; max. 23,810). Other wintering waterfowl include *Anas penelope*, *A. clypeata*, *Calidris alpina*, *Numenius arquata*, and *Tringa totanus*. The av. winter max. for wildfowl is 23,100.

179 Benfleet and Southend Marshes; Essex (South East)

51°32'N, 00°37'E 1580 ha

SSSI

An area of saltmarshes, mudflats, and dry grassland.

Wintering waterfowl and waders include *Branta bernicla* (5300), *Pluvialis squatarola* (800), *Calidris canutus* (5060), *C. alpina* (8400), and *Tringa totanus* (1060). Total waders (17,600).

180 Isles of Scilly Coastal Habitats; Cornwall (South West)

49°56'N, 06°17'W 320 ha

SSSI; AONB; Heritage Coast

Sections of coast in the Isles of Scilly with rocky shores, cliffs, sand and pebble beaches, sand-dunes, islets, lagoons, and mudflats. Human activities include fishing and recreation (boating).

Important for breeding seabirds with *Puffinus puffinus* (less than 300 pairs), *Hydrobates pelagicus* (1000+ pairs), *Phalacrocorax carbo* (510 pairs), *P. aristotelis* (1200 pairs), *Larus fuscus* (3800 pairs), *L. marinus* (990 pairs), *Sterna sandvicensis* (20 pairs), *S. dougallii* (6 pairs), *S. hirundo* (175 pairs), *Uria aalge* (110 pairs), *Alca torda* (180 pairs), and *Fratercula arctica* (90 pairs). Wintering waders include *Calidris alba* (330) and *Arenaria interpres* (940).

181 Tamar Complex; Devon, Cornwall (South West)

50°25'N, 04°12'W

SSSI

The estuaries of the Rivers Tamar, Tavy, and Lynher, with extensive areas of intertidal mudflats and saltmarsh. The most important areas are the Upper Tamar, Car Green area, and Weir Keys.

Important for wintering *Recurvirostra avosetta* (140-150 in recent years). Possibly also important for *Limosa limosa.*

182 Bodmin Moor; Cornwall (South West)

50°33'N, 04°33'W

AONB

An extensive area of moorland with deciduous and coniferous woodland.

Believed to be internationally important for wintering *Pluvialis apricaria.*

183 Exe Estuary; Devon (South West)

50°37'N, 03°25'W 2182 ha

SSSI

Estuary with saltwater marshes and mudflats. Includes the Exminster marshes, which are a botanically rich area of reclaimed land drained by dykes and ditches.

An important site for passage and wintering waterfowl with *Branta bernicla* (av. max. 2404; max. 2500), *Recurvirostra avosetta* (av. max. 120; max. 141), *Haematopus ostralegus* (av. max. 3004; max. 4478), *Charadrius hiaticula* (av. max. 601; max. 1037), and *Limosa limosa islandica* (av. max. 650; max. 800). The av. winter max. for waders is 13,090.

184 Taw and Torridge Estuary; Devon (South West)

51°05'N, 04°10'W 1000 ha

SSSI; AONB

Estuaries of two rivers with mudflats and saltmarsh.

Important for wildfowl and waders (high species diversity but relatively low numbers) with wintering *Branta bernicla hrota* (av. max. 45), *Anas penelope* (av. max. 2493; max. 6200), *Pluvialis apricaria* (av. max. 2921; max. 3350), *Charadrius hiaticula* (max. 400+), and *Vanellus vanellus* (av. max. 5632; max. 8930). Other wintering species include *Circus cyaneus*, *Falco columbarius*, and *F. peregrinus.*

185 Somerset Levels and Moors; Somerset (South West)

51°10'N, 02°50'W 7000+ ha

NNR; SSSI; ESA; RSPB; LNR

An area of low-lying agricultural land with waterlogged peat mires, raised bog, marsh and fen vegetation in periodically flooded wet meadows; also rivers and streams. Mostly grassland used for for hay, silage and cattle-grazing but with large areas intensively managed. Drainage has seriously damaged several parts of the site and lowered water-tables still pose threats to breeding wader habitat. Population of breeding waders has declined in recent years.

Breeding species include *Coturnix coturnix*, *Vanellus vanellus* (340 pairs), *Gallinago gallinago* (60 pairs), *Numenius arquata* (25 pairs), *Limosa limosa* (3 pairs), and *Tringa totanus* (40 pairs). Important for wintering wildfowl, especially *Cygnus columbianus* (1987 max. 144 at West Sedgemoor RSPB Reserve), *Anas penelope*, and *A. crecca*.

186 Chew Valley Lake; Avon (South West)

51°20'N, 02°37'W 565 ha EEC SPA

SSSI

A very large inland freshwater reservoir created by the flooding of a valley. There are several islands and embayments which support *Phragmites* beds, marshy ground, scrub, and woodland. The adjoining areas include arable land and localised settlements. The lake is used intensively for recreational purposes; notably water-sports.

Breeding species include *Tadorna tadorna*, *Anas strepera*, *Aythya ferina*, *A. fuligula*, and *Alcedo atthis*. Important for wintering and passage waterfowl with *Podiceps cristatus* (av. max. 482), *Ardea cinerea*, *Anas strepera* (av. max. 185), *A. crecca* (av. max. 1868), *A. clypeata* (av. max. 344), *Mergus merganser* (av. max. 75; max. 105), and *Oxyura jamaicensis* (av. max. 696; max. 1064).

187 Chesil Beach and The Fleet; Dorset (South West)

50°39'-50°35'N, 02°28'-02°37'W 763 ha Ramsar Site; EEC SPA

SSSI; AONB; Bird Sanctuary (Abbotsbury Swannery); Heritage Coast

Chesil Beach is a linear shingle storm beach some 28 km in length and from 150 m-200 m in width. The Fleet is a shallow (av. 1.5 m) lagoon on the landward side of Chesil Beach and is 13 km long and between 75 m-900 m in width. The character of the lagoon's water varies from saline to almost fresh. There are extensive submerged areas of *Zostera* and *Ruppia*. Potential problems in the area include eutrophication arising from fertiliser run-off, and the recent appearance of *Sargassum muticum*.

Breeding species include *Cygnus olor* (60+ pairs), *Charadrius hiaticula* (*c.*50 pairs), *Sterna hirundo* (*c.*50 pairs), and *S. albifrons* (max. 100 pairs). Wintering wildfowl include *Cygnus olor* (av. max. 751; max. 890), *Anas penelope* (av. max. 5430; max. 10,399), *Aythya ferina*, and *Mergus serrator* (av. max. 109; max. 185).

188 Poole Basin; Dorset (South West)

50°42'N, 02°00'W 7900 ha

NNR; SSSI; AONB; RSPB; Heritage Coast

An estuarine basin (Poole Harbour) with beaches, sand-dunes, islands, saltwater marshes, and extensive mudflats. Also surrounding and extensive valuable heathland (including Arne peninsula, and Povington, Grange, Stoborough, Creech, Hyde, Holton, Upton, Canford Heaths). Human activities include recreation (boating) and there is a harbour. Parts of the site are the subject of oil-exploration and extraction. The heaths are under severe pressure from housing, roads and industrial development; and are also suffering from disturbance and management neglect.

The heathland is an important breeding area for *Caprimulgus europaeus*, *Lullula arborea*, and *Sylvia undata*. Poole Harbour is important for wintering waterfowl, which include *Tadorna tadorna* (av. max. 2233; max. 3588) and *Limosa limosa islandica* (av. max. 648; max. 791). The av. winter max. for waders is 10,466.

189 Horton Common and Holt Heath; Dorset (South West)

50°51'N, 01°56'W 150 ha

SSSI

Two areas with dry and wet heathland, grassland, reed-swamp, coniferous and wet deciduous woodland. Formerly one of the most extensive unbroken tracts of heathland in

Dorset (supporting five per cent of the U.K.'s population of *Sylvia undata*), Horton Common was largely destroyed in 1981 by ploughing.

An important United Kingdom site for *Sylvia undata*. *Caprimulgus europaeus* also breeds.

190 Porton Down; Hampshire, Wiltshire (South East, South West)

01°40'W, 51°07'N 1250 ha

SSSI; AONB

An extensive area of chalk grassland with *Crataegus* and *Juniperus* scrub and several *Quercus-Fagus* woods.

Important for breeding *Falco subbuteo* and *Burhinus oedicnemus*.

191 Windsor Forest and Great Park; Berkshire, Surrey (South East)

51°24'N, 00°41'W

SSSI

Ancient forest with relicts of original primary forest. Contains ancient *Quercus* pollard, mixed woodland and open parkland. Also includes conifer woodland on heathland with valley bogs (Crowthorne Forest SSSI), and Virginia Water.

Important for woodland birds including *Aix galericulata*, *Falco subbuteo*, *Dendrocopos minor*, *Loxia curvirostra*, and *Coccothraustes coccothraustes*.

192 Avon Valley; Hampshire (South East)

50°48'N, 01°47'W

SSSI

A stretch of the Avon Valley with flood-meadows (many comparatively unimproved). Includes two stretches of the valley: Bickton - Blashford and Bisterne - Christchurch.

Breeding waders include *Gallinago gallinago* (15 pairs) and *Tringa totanus* (18 pairs). Wintering waterfowl include *Cygnus columbianus* (180) and *Anser albifrons* (190).

193 New Forest; Hampshire (South East)

50°52'N, 01°32'W 26,900 ha

SSSI

Forest and heath, marshes, and peatbogs. Human activities include forestry, stock-raising, recreation, and there is scattered human habitation.

Important for breeding *Pernis apivorus* and *Sylvia undata* (454 pairs in 1988).

194 West Solent Marshes and Southampton Water; Hampshire, Isle of Wight (South East)

50°47'N, 01°25'W 2250 ha

NNR; SSSI; AONB

Estuary with beaches, sand-dunes, mudflats, and raised saltmarsh. Includes Southampton Water, Needs Oar Point, Keyhaven, and Pennington Marshes.

Breeding species include *Larus ridibundus* (7250 pairs), *Sterna sandvicensis* (260 pairs), *S. hirundo* (400 pairs), and *S. albifrons* (75 pairs). In winter, waterfowl occurring include *Branta bernicla* (2100 in 1986/87), *Pluvialis squatarola* (Southampton Water: av. max. 485; max. 574), *Charadrius hiaticula* (Southampton Water: autumn passage av. max. 625), and *Limosa limosa islandica* (Southampton Water: av. max. 357; max. 515). The av. winter max. for waders at Southampton Water is 12,047.

195 Woolmer Forest; Hampshire (South East)

51°04'N, 00°05'W 300 ha

SSSI; AONB

Important areas of heathland (dry and humid heaths). Includes Woolmer Forest, Blackmoor, and Boxhead Commons.
Breeding species include *Caprimulgus europaeus*, *Lullula arborea*, and *Sylvia undata*.

196 Chichester and Langstone Harbours; Hampshire, West Sussex (South East)

50°47'-50°50'N, 00°49'-01°02'W 5749 ha Ramsar Site; EEC SPA

SSSI; AONB; LNR; RSPB; CCT

Two large estuaries with total shoreline of more than 60 km; with freshwater lagoons, saltmarshes, and mudflats. Human activities include fishing and recreation including boating. The area is frequently threatened by proposals for recreation, sailing and waterfront housing developments.
Breeding species include *Sterna albifrons*. Extremely important for non-breeding wildfowl and waders with *Branta bernicla* (Chichester: av. max. 10,603; max. 11,849/Langstone: av. max. 7825; max. 8646), *Tadorna tadorna* (C: av. max. 2856; max. 3772), *Charadrius hiaticula* (C: av. max. 458; max. 624/L: av. max. 449; max. 640; up to 1000 on passage), *Pluvialis squatarola* (C: av. max. 1822; max. 2647/L: av. max. 980; max. 1320), *Calidris alba* (C: av. max. 370; max. 600), *C. alpina* (C: av. max. 26,353; max. 30,084/L: av. max. 27,980; max. 30,250), *Limosa limosa islandica* (C: av. max. 672; max. 1360/L: av. max. 806; max. 1037), *Tringa totanus* (C: av. max. 2115; max. 2516), *T. erythropus* (passage), and *T. nebularia* (passage). The av. winter maxima for wildfowl are 15,900 (Chichester) and 11,200 (Langstone) and for waders 41,037 (Chichester) and 37,444 (Langstone).

197 Lee Valley; Greater London, Essex (South East)

51°38'N, 00°01'W 605 ha

SSSI

Two complexes of reservoirs, (Walthamstow and Chingford), with extensive areas of open, undisturbed water; and the Walthamstow Marshes.
Breeding species include *Ardea cinerea* (115 pairs), *Aythya ferina* (10 pairs), and *A. fuligula* (40 pairs). Wintering species include *Podiceps cristatus* (200), *Phalacrocorax carbo* (190), *Anas clypeata* (370), and *Aythya fuligula* (1730).

198 South-west London Reservoirs and Gravel Pits; Greater London, Berkshire (South East)

51°26'N, 00°30'W

part SSSI

Series of very large reservoirs (or complexes thereof): including Staines; King George VI; Wraysbury; Queen Mother; Queen Mary; Queen Elizabeth II; Walton; Hampton and Kempton; and Wraysbury Gravel Pits.
Nationally important for *Podiceps cristatus* (av. max. 333; Queen Mary), *Anas clypeata* (av. max. 403; Staines), *Aythya ferina* (av. max. 864; Staines), *A. fuligula* (av. max. 1216; Staines), and *Mergus merganser* (av. max. 91).

199 Chobham to Yateley Commons; Surrey, Hampshire, Berkshire (South East)

51°23'N, 00°36'W (Chobham); 51°19'N, 00°48'W (Yateley) 800+ ha

SSSI; LNR

Chobham and Yateley Commons are extensive, open tracts of heathland.
Breeding species include *Caprimulgus europaeus* (Chobham and Yateley Commons lie in one of the densest breeding areas in England for *Caprimulgus europaeus*). Also *Sylvia undata* and *Lullula arborea*.

200 Thursley, Hankley and Frensham Commons; Surrey (South East)

51°09'N, 00°45'W 1200 ha

NNR; SSSI

A lower greensand heath. Varied habitats range from dry to wet heath, bog (amongst the best in England), climax *Quercus* and coniferous woodland.

Breeding species include *Numenius arquata*, *Caprimulgus europaeus*, *Lullula arborea*, and *Sylvia undata*.

201 Amberley; West Sussex (South East)

50°55'N, 00°31'W 372 ha

SSSI; AONB; CCT

An extensive area of alluvial grazing marsh, crossed by numerous ditches and seasonally flooded by the River Arun, which forms the western border. A gravity drainage scheme initiated in the late 1970s has led to lower water levels and a general reduction in birds using the area, particularly breeding waders.

In times of winter flooding the area is important for wildfowl with *Cygnus columbianus* (100+), *Anas crecca* and *A. clypeata*.

202 Pagham Harbour; West Sussex (South East)

50°46'N, 00°46'W 616 ha Ramsar Site; EEC SPA

SSSI; LNR

An extensive area of saltmarsh and tidal mudflats, with adjoining shingle, open water, *Phragmites* swamp, and permanently wet grassland. There are also some small woodland areas dominated by *Quercus* and *Salix*.

Breeding species include *Ardea cinerea*, *Haematopus ostralegus*, *Tringa totanus* and *Sterna albifrons* (5 pairs). In winter the area is important for waterfowl with *Branta bernicla* (av. max. 3046; max. 4219), *Anas acuta* (av. max. 343), *Pluvialis squatarola* (av. max. 789), *Philomachus pugnax* (max. 302), *Limosa limosa islandica* (max. 617), and *Tringa totanus* (av. max. 2509; max. 2926). *Tringa erythropus* and *T. nebularia* occur on passage. The av. winter max. for waders (1976-86) was 24,620.

203 Pevensey Levels; East Sussex (South East)

50°50'N, 00°20'E 4112 ha

SSSI

An extensive area of flat, grazing meadows intersected by freshwater dykes.

Wintering waders include *Vanellus vanellus* (9400) and *Gallinago gallinago* (1050).

204 Dungeness to Pett Levels; Kent, East Sussex (South East)

50°51'N, 00°44'E – 51°02'N, 00°59'E 5880 ha

SSSI; LNR; RSPB

Includes the grazing marshes of Walland Marsh, and extensive tracts of shingle at Rye and Dungeness, which have areas of open water (gravel-pits) and scrub.

Important for breeding terns with *Sterna sandvicensis* (350 pairs), *S. hirundo* (350 pairs), and *S. albifrons*. Wintering waterfowl include *Cygnus columbianus* (140).

205 Stodmarsh; Kent (South East)

51°18'N, 01°12'E 604 ha

NNR; SSSI

A complex of open-water areas, extensive *Phragmites* beds, scrub and *Alnus* carr in the Stour Valley.

An important wintering site for *Circus cyaneus* (max. 20).

206 South Thames Marshes; Kent (South East)

51°28'N, 00°33'E 3600 ha

NNR; SSSI

Estuarine habitat with saltwater marshes, raised saltmarsh, mudflats, wet meadows. The site continues to be under pressure from general development in the area.

Wintering wildfowl and waders include *Anser albifrons* (av. max. 422; max. 730), *Haematopus ostralegus* (av. max. 12,260; max. 19,258), *Charadrius hiaticula* (av. max. 818; max. 955; autumn passage max. 1133), *Pluvialis squatarola* (av. max. 2752; max. 2998), *Calidris canutus* (av. max. 21,274; max. 29,098), *C. alpina* (av. max. 28,006; max. 34,987), *Limosa lapponica* (av. max. 6548; max. 16,217), *Numenius arquata* (av. max. 3361; max. 4864), *Tringa totanus* (av. max. 4281; max. 5105), *T. nebularia* (passage), and *Arenaria interpres* (av. max. 725; max. 888). The av. winter max. for waders is 82,882.

207 Medway Estuary and Marshes; Kent (South East)

51°24'N, 00°41'E 5633 ha

SSSI; RSPB

Extensive saltwater marshes, raised saltmarsh, mudflats, and wet meadows along the River Medway. Estuary still under many different types of threat; dredging disposal and dumping of power station flyash, through to marina and industrial development.

Very important for wintering wildfowl and waders (figures refer to scattered counts between 1976 and 1986) including *Podiceps cristatus* (260 in 1986/87), *Anser albifrons* (av. max. 333), *Branta bernicla* (av. max. 2187; max. 2888), *Tadorna tadorna* (av. max. 2814), *Anas penelope* (av. max. 3727), *A. acuta* (av. max. 463; max. 1000), *Charadrius hiaticula* (av. max. 1019; max. 1285), *Pluvialis squatarola* (av. max. 1229; max. 1813), *Calidris alpina* (av. max. 17,244; max. 22,049), *Tringa erythropus* (passage), *T. totanus* (av. max. 2509; max. 2926), and *T. nebularia* (passage). The av. winter max. for waders (1976-86) was 24,620.

208 The Swale and South Sheppey; Kent (South East)

51°21'N, 00°50'E 5835 ha Ramsar Site; EEC SPA

NNR; SSSI; LNR; RSPB; CCT

An estuarine area which includes the largest remaining fragments of freshwater grazing marshes in Kent. Other important habitats include mudflats, saltmarsh, and localised patches of shingle and sand beaches. The freshwater marshes are dissected by numerous dykes and fleets and are of major botanical interest. The area is likely to be affected by industrial pollution and excessive recreational disturbance.

Breeding species (at RSPB Reserve in 1987) include *Anas crecca*, *A. querquedula*, *A. clypeata* (40 pairs), *Aythya fuligula* (30 pairs), *Charadrius hiaticula* (30 pairs), *Vanellus vanellus* (220 pairs), *Tringa totanus* (200 pairs), *Larus ridibundus* (3500 pairs), *Sterna hirundo* (25 pairs), and *S. albifrons* (12 pairs). An important wintering site for wildfowl and waders including *Anser albifrons* (av. max. 1662; max. 2570), *Haematopus ostralegus* (av. max. 4558), *Pluvialis squatarola* (av. max. 1903), *Charadrius hiaticula* (max. 400+ on autumn passage), *Calidris alpina* (av. max. 14,907; max. 18,014), *Limosa limosa islandica* (av. max. 442; max. 773), *Numenius arquata* (av. max. 2188; max. 3119), *Tringa totanus* (av. max. 2375; max. 3730), and *Arenaria interpres* (av. max. 344; max. 448). *Tringa erythropus* occurs on passage. The av. winter max. for wildfowl is 19,100 and for waders 83,529.

209 Thanet Coast; Kent (South East)

51°16'N, 01°23'E 1648 ha (Sandwich Bay and Hacklinge Marsh SSSI only)

SSSI

The site includes the saltmarsh, mudflats, and sand-dune system of Sandwich Bay and Hacklinge Marshes.

Wintering waders include *Calidris alba* (710) and *Arenaria interpres* (780).

210 Dee Estuary; Clwyd, Cheshire, Merseyside (Wales, North West)

53°18'N, 03°10'W 13,055 ha Ramsar Site; EEC SPA

SSSI; LNR; RSPB

An estuarine site including extensive intertidal sandflats and mud, with large areas of saltmarshes (often dominated by *Spartina angelica* at the head of the estuary and along its eastern coast). The designated area includes the Hilbre Islands - three small low-lying sandstone islands lying about 2 km from the extreme north-west of the Wirral peninsula. The islands are cut off at high tide. Road proposals and marina-related dredging threaten the site.

Breeding species include *Vanellus vanellus*, *Tringa totanus* (45 pairs), and *Sterna hirundo*. A very important site for wildfowl and waders with *Tadorna tadorna* (av. max. 5798; max. 6130), *Anas crecca* (av. max. 3809; max. 5720), *A. acuta* (av. max. 7265; max. 11,265), *Haematopus ostralegus* (av. max. 30,078; max. 38,000), *Charadrius hiaticula* (av. max. 192; autumn passage max. 1260), *Pluvialis squatarola* (av. max. 1598; max. 2070), *Calidris canutus* (av. max. 20,593; max. 28,390), *C. alba* (av. max. 376; max. 435; spring passage max. 680; autumn passage max. 1180), *C. alpina* (av. max. 15,923; max. 21,950), *Limosa limosa islandica* (av. max. 672; max. 1285), *Numenius arquata* (av. max. 3183; max. 4680), *Tringa totanus* (av. max. 5040; max. 9220), and *Arenaria interpres* (max. 890; spring passage max. 949). The av. winter max. for wildfowl is 20,100 and for waders 83,529.

211 Berwyn; Clwyd, Powys, Gwynedd (Wales)

53°52'N, 03°25'W 21,510 ha

SSSI

A large area of upland (max. altitude 827 m) with extensive blanket mire.

Important for its breeding upland birds include *Circus cyaneus*, *Lagopus lagopus* (450 pairs), *Tetrao tetrix* (110 pairs), *Pluvialis apricaria* (25 pairs), *Asio flammeus* (5 pairs), and *Turdus torquatus* (25 pairs).

212 Traeth Lafan (Lavan Sands), Conway Bay; Gwynedd (Wales)

53°14'N, 04°04'W 2700 ha

SSSI; LNR

A large intertidal area with extensive sand- and mudflats. There are proposals for a road tunnel, which may result in the dumping of waste.

Wintering waders occurring include *Haematopus ostralegus* (5450), *Numenius arquata* (1500), and *Tringa totanus* (1180); with av. max. waders: 20,000.

213 Anglesey Islands and Cemlyn Bay; Gwynedd (Wales)

53°14'N, 04°32'W 75 ha

SSSI; AONB; RSPB; CCT

Small islands, and a tidal lagoon enclosed by a shingle bar, which is fringed by saltmarsh (Cemlyn Bay).

Important for breeding terns including *Sterna sandvicensis* (*c.*1000 pairs), *S. dougallii* (*c.*55 pairs), *S. hirundo* (180 pairs), and *S. paradisaea* (630 pairs).

214 Holy Island Coast; Gwynedd (Wales)

53°16'N, 04°37'W 400 ha

SSSI; AONB; Heritage Coast

Sections of rocky coast with cliffs.
Breeding species include *Uria aalge* (700 breeding birds), *Alca torda* (700 breeding birds), and *Fratercula arctica*.

215 Bardsey Island and Aberdaron Coast; Gwynedd (Wales)

52°47'N, 04°46'W 565 ha

SSSI; AONB; NT; Heritage Coast; Bardsey Island Trust

Sections of rocky coast with cliffs.
Breeding species include *Fulmarus glacialis*, *Puffinus puffinus* (4250 pairs), *Phalacrocorax carbo* (85 pairs), *P. aristotelis* (185 pairs), *Falco peregrinus*, *Haematopus ostralegus*, *Charadrius hiaticula*, *Larus fuscus* (225 pairs), *L. argentatus* (400 pairs), *Rissa tridactyla* (150 pairs), *Uria aalge* (315 breeding birds), *Alca torda* (350 breeding birds), *Fratercula arctica* (600 pairs), and *Pyrrhocorax pyrrhocorax*.

216 Cors Fochno and Dyfi; Dyfed, Gwynedd, Powys (Wales)

52°32'N, 04°01'W 2715 ha Ramsar Site; EEC SPA; Biosphere Reserve

NNR; SSSI; RSPB

The site comprises a large coastal estuary (Dyfi) with mudflats and saltmarsh, and one of the most extensive raised bogs in the United Kingdom (Cors Fochno).
Breeding species include *Tadorna tadorna*, *Mergus serrator*, and several species of wader, including *Actitis hypoleucos*. In winter the area is important for waterfowl, notably *Anser albifrons flavirostris* (95 in Mar. 1987) and *Anas penelope* (6900 in 1986/87). Other species wintering in small numbers include *Milvus milvus*, *Circus cyaneus*, *Falco columbarius*, *F. peregrinus*, a variety of waders, and *Asio flammeus*.

217 Elenydd – Mallaen; Powys (Wales)

52°16'N, 03°41'W 20,675 ha

SSSI

Moorland plateau covered by blanket bog and acid grasslands, separated by steep-sided valleys.
Important for breeding waders, which include *Pluvialis apricaria* (75 pairs), *Calidris alpina* (20 pairs), *Gallinago gallinago* (35 pairs), *Numenius arquata* (35 pairs), and *Actitis hypoleucos* (40 pairs). Other breeding species include *Lagopus lagopus* and *Turdus torquatus*.

218 Pembrokeshire Cliffs; Dyfed (Wales)

51°44'N, 05°15'W 1590 ha (excluding St David's Head)

SSSI; NP; Heritage Coast

Rocky coast, cliffs, and moorland. Includes Strumble Head, Stackpole Head, St David's Head, and Ramsey Island.
Important for *Falco peregrinus* and *Pyrrhocorax pyrrhocorax*. Other breeding species include *Fulmarus glacialis* (340 pairs), *Phalacrocorax aristotelis*, *Uria aalge* (6700 breeding birds), *Alca torda* (1700 breeding birds), and *Fratercula arctica*.

219 Skokholm and Skomer; Dyfed (Wales)

51°44'N, 05°17'W 420 ha EEC SPA

NNR; SSSI; LNR; Heritage Coast

Two islands surrounded by open sea, important for breeding seabirds.
Breeding species include *Fulmarus glacialis* (550 pairs), *Puffinus puffinus* (135,000 pairs), *Hydrobates pelagicus* (*c.*7000 pairs), *Phalacrocorax aristotelis*, *Larus fuscus* (16,700 pairs), *Uria aalge* (6400 breeding birds), *Alca torda* (4300 breeding birds), and

Fratercula arctica (19,600 breeding birds). *Asio flammeus* and *Pyrrhocorax pyrrhocorax* also breed.

220 Grassholm; Dyfed (Wales)

51°44'N, 05°29'W 9 ha EEC SPA

SSSI; RSPB

A rather low, small island with a large seabird colony.

Very important for breeding *Sula bassana* (28,600 pairs).

221 Carmarthen Bay; Dyfed (Wales)

51°43'N, 04°30'W 20,000 ha

SSSI

A large bay with sand beaches. Includes part of the Pembrey coast.

The area holds important moulting and wintering concentrations of *Melanitta nigra* (11,000+). Other wintering species include *Haematopus ostralegus* (max. 5191), *Calidris alba* (max. 165), and small numbers of *Tringa ochropus.*

222 Burry Inlet; West Glamorgan, Dyfed (Wales)

51°39'N, 04°10'W 5380 ha

SSSI; AONB; Heritage Coast

Estuary with dunes, saltwater marshes and mudflats. There are proposals for a barrage at the upstream boundary, and the construction of a road and car park.

Wintering wildfowl and waders include *Anas penelope* (av. max. 5351; max. 9200), *A. acuta* (av. max. 1885; max. 2535), *Haematopus ostralegus* (av. max. 17,327; max. 21,390), *Pluvialis squatarola* (av. max. 689; max. 925), *Calidris canutus* (av. max. 5288; max. 7100), *Numenius arquata* (autumn passage av. max. 2053), and *Tringa ochropus* (small numbers). The av. winter max. for wildfowl is 11,100 and for waders 36,415.

223 Swansea Bay – Blackpill; West Glamorgan (Wales)

51°36'N, 03°59'W 467 ha

SSSI

An area of intertidal mudflats.

Wintering waders include *Charadrius hiaticula* (240) and *Calidris alba* (390).

224 Severn Estuary; Gloucestershire, Avon, Somerset, South Glamorgan, Gwent (South West, Wales)

51°30'N, 02°52'W 35,000 ha Ramsar Site; EEC SPA

NNR; SSSI; Wildfowl Trust Reserve

The Estuary of the River Severn with mudflats, saltwater marshes, raised saltmarsh; also wet meadows, reclaimed grassland, and freshwater lakes (Slimbridge). Includes the Taff/Ely Estuary, Bridgwater Bay, and the islands of Flat Holm and Steep Holm. Human activities include cattle-grazing, fishing, and recreation. The ecological character of the area is likely to change completely if plans for a tidal barrage are implemented.

Breeding species include *Tadorna tadorna*, *Anas strepera*, *Vanellus vanellus*, and *Tringa totanus*. The islands of Flat Holm and Steep Holm have breeding *Phalacrocorax carbo*, *Larus argentatus*, *L. fuscus*, and *L. marinus*. The site is particularly important for wintering and passage waterfowl. Wintering waterfowl in the Upper Severn Estuary (New Grounds, Slimbridge) include *Cygnus columbianus* (av. max. 376; max. 475) and *Anser albifrons* (av. max. 3678; max. 4300). Passage and wintering waterfowl in the lower part of the Severn Estuary include *Charadrius hiaticula* (small numbers wintering; autumn passage max. 1471; spring passage max. 477), *Calidris alpina* (av. max. 45,788;

max. 56,830), *Numenius arquata* (av. max.* 2872; max.* 3416), and *Tringa totanus* (av. max.* 2104; max.* 2336). The av. winter max. for waders is 52,899.

The following sites in England, Scotland and Wales are not on the NCC list of sites qualifying for designation as Special Protection Areas and/or Ramsar Sites, but are believed to qualify for the reasons stated in the table following the introduction to this inventory.

225 Clett Stacks; Silwick, Shetland (Scotland)

60°09'N, 01°28'W 1.5 ha

Unprotected

Rocky coast, islets, and open sea.
A breeding site for *Phalacrocorax carbo carbo* (165 pairs).

226 Scapa Flow; Orkney (Scotland)
58°52'N, 03°02'W

Unprotected

Open sea bounded by archipelago islands.
Species occurring (some as winter visitors) include *Gavia immer* (200), *Podiceps auritus* (6), *Clangula hyemalis* (2400), *Somateria mollissima* (2000), *Phalacrocorax aristotelis* (4000), and *Cepphus grylle* (1000). (Information compiled in 1981)

227 Inchnadamph; Highland (Scotland)

58°08'N, 04°57'W 1300 ha

NNR

An area of limestone uplands with moorland and marshes supporting a high density of *Pluvialis apricaria* (4-10 pairs per 100 ha). (Information compiled in 1981)

228 Isay; Skye, Highland (Scotland)

57°32'N, 06°40'W

Unprotected
An island important for *Branta leucopsis* (245 in Mar. 1988).

229 North Sutor of Cromarty; Black Isle, Highland (Scotland)

57°41'N, 03°59'W

Unprotected

Rocky coast.
Supports breeding *Phalacrocorax carbo carbo* (203 pairs).

230 Black Isle sites; Highland (Scotland)

57°35'N, 04°20'W

Unprotected

Wet meadows, grassland, and arable land.
Due to the local agricultural practice of planting spring barley, and leaving the stubble from last year's crop over the winter, rich feeding areas for geese are available for *Anser anser* (Nov. av. 1000; max. 2560; information compiled in 1980). A change to planting winter cereals, already taking place in some areas, would significantly reduce the site's importance.

231 Monadhliath; Highland (Scotland)

57°09'N, 04°10'W 9700 ha

SSSI

A vast tableland covered largely with blanket mire, with tundra vegetation and snow-bed communities at high elevations.

An important breeding area for upland birds, including *Pluvialis apricaria* (1.5-4.0 pairs per 100 ha). (Information compiled in 1981)

232 Forfar, Rescobie, and Balgavies Lochs; Tayside (Scotland)

56°39'N, 02°47'W 212 ha

SSSI

Lakes, marshes and grassland, and arable land.

An important site for breeding and wintering waterfowl, particularly as a winter roost for geese, with *Anser brachyrhynchus* (Nov. av. 1800; max. 4800), *A. anser* (Nov. av. 530; max. 1800), and *Anas platyrhynchos* (250-500 in Jan.). (Information compiled in 1981)

233 Loch of Kinnordy; Tayside (Scotland)

56°41'N, 03°03'W 65 ha

RSPB

Lake with wet meadows and marshes.

An important roost for *Anser anser* (Nov. av. 2300; max. 5400). There is also a large breeding colony of *Larus ridibundus* (3000-5000 pairs). (Information compiled in 1981)

234 Loch Mahaick; Central (Scotland)

56°14'N, 04°06'W 95 ha

SSSI

A lake with marshes and moorland.

A roost site for *Anser brachyrhynchus* (Nov. av. 950; max. 2000). (Information compiled in 1980)

235 Haughs of Clyde; Carnwarth and Libberton, Strathclyde (Scotland)

55°41'N, 03°38'W

Unprotected

Grassland and wet meadows.

A site for *Anser brachyrhynchus* (Nov. av. 1525; max. 3000). (Information compiled in 1980)

236 Loch Lyoch and Cleuch Reservoirs; Strathclyde (Scotland)

55°36'N, 03°41'W 200 ha

Unprotected

Lakes and marshes.

A roosting site for *Anser brachyrhynchus* (Nov. av. 1100). (Information compiled in 1980)

237 Tetney Marshes; Lincolnshire (East Midlands)

53°31'N, 00°03'W 100 ha

RSPB

Saltwater marshes and beaches.

An important breeding colony of *Sterna albifrons* (90 pairs). *Charadrius hiaticula* also breeds.

238 Great and Little Orme; Gwynedd (Wales)

53°20'N, 03°47'W 25 ha

SSSI; Heritage Coast

Rocky coast, cliffs, and open sea. Human activities include recreation.

A breeding site for *Phalacrocorax carbo carbo* (198 pairs), *Rissa tridactyla* (2350 pairs), *Uria aalge* (2300 breeding birds), and *Alca torda* (230 breeding birds).

239 Puffin Island; Gwynedd (Wales)

53°20'N, 04°02'W 32 ha

SSSI; AONB

Island with rocky coast and beaches.

Breeding species include *Phalacrocorax carbo carbo* (370 pairs), *P. aristotelis* (120 pairs), *Rissa tridactyla* (310 pairs), *Uria aalge* (900 breeding birds), *Alca torda* (210 breeding birds), and *Fratercula arctica*; however, recently the island has become overrun by rats and its bird interest has drastically diminished.

240 St Margaret's Island; Dyfed (Wales)

51°39'N, 04°43'W 11 ha

SSSI; Heritage Coast

Island with rocky coast and cliffs, surrounded by open sea.

Breeding species include *Phalacrocorax carbo carbo* (238 pairs), *Larus marinus* (120 pairs), *L. argentatus* (500 pairs), *Rissa tridactyla* (260 pairs), *Uria aalge* (170 pairs), *Alca torda* (50 pairs), and *Phalacrocorax aristotelis* (18 pairs).

241 Kilpheder to Smerclate; Western Isles (Scotland)

57°09'N, 07°24'W 630 ha

Unprotected

Beaches, sand-dunes, grassland, and arable land.

Breeding species include *Anas crecca*, *A. clypeata*, *Aythya fuligula*, *Crex crex*, *Charadrius hiaticula*, and *Calidris alpina*. (Information compiled in 1984)

242 Slapton Ley; Devon (South West)

50°17'N, 03°39'W 266 ha

SSSI; AONB; LNR; Heritage Coast

Lagoon, beach, marshes, streams, grassland, arable land, and woodland.

Breeding species include *Alcedo atthis*. In winter, species occurring include *Gavia stellata*, *G. arctica*, *G. immer*, and *Asio flammeus*. Important for passage assemblages of passerines. (Information compiled in 1984)

243 Christchurch Harbour; Dorset (South West)

50°43'N, 01°45'W 260 ha

SSSI; LNR

Estuary with saltings, raised saltmarsh and mudflats; beaches, sand-dunes, heathland, and woodland.

Breeding species include *Tadorna tadorna* and *Charadrius hiaticula*. In winter, *Gavia stellata*, *G. arctica*, *Podiceps grisegena*, *P. auritus*, *P. nigricollis* occur, and *Falco columbarius*, *F. subbuteo*, and *F. peregrinus* appear on passage. Important for passage assemblages of passerines. (Information compiled in 1984)

244 Loch of Banks; Orkney (Scotland)

59°06'N, 03°16'W 90 ha

Unprotected

A partially drained loch with southern end drying out in summer. Good growth of marginal vegetation and an extensive *Phragmites* bed.

Breeding waterfowl include *Tadorna tadorna*, *Anas penelope*, *A. strepera*, *A. crecca*, *A. platyrhynchos*, *A. acuta* (5 per cent of U.K.'s breeding population), *A. clypeata*, and *Aythya fuligula*, with in addition, seven species of breeding waders. In autumn the area provides feeding for passage waders and wildfowl. In winter, the site supports a regular and important roost of *Circus cyaneus*.

245 Lough Foyle; Co. Londonderry (Northern Ireland)

55°05'-55°12'N, 07°00'-07°15'W 3000 ha

NNR; ASI; AONB; RSPB; mainly unprotected

Bay with saltwater marshes and coastal mudflats. There is disturbance from increased shooting and 130 ha are proposed to be used as a cross-border land-fill site by Londonderry and Co. Donegal Councils. Agricultural changes could threaten the foreshore in future.

Important for wildfowl (av. max. 24,100) and waders (four-yr. av. max. 17,500) in winter with *Cygnus columbianus* (av. max. 170; max. 293), *C. cygnus* (av. max. 1196; max. 2597), *Branta bernicla hrota* (max. 2500), *Anas penelope* (av. max. 21,000; max. 28,475), *Haematopus ostralegus* (max. 1900), *Pluvialis apricaria* (max. 720), *Vanellus vanellus* (max. 2500), *Limosa lapponica* (av. max. 3300), *Numenius arquata* (av. max. 3000), and *Tringa totanus* (max. 1050). (Figures refer to 1987)

246 Sheep Island; Co. Antrim (Northern Ireland)

55°13'N, 06°20'W 4 ha

NT

Island. A cull at a mainland fishery resulted in 90 birds being killed in 1987.

Supports one of the larger *Phalacrocorax carbo carbo* breeding colonies in the European Community (380 pairs).

247 Rathlin Island; Co. Antrim (Northern Ireland)

55°18'N, 06°12'W 1500 ha

NNR; AONB; RSPB

A large island with peatlands and unimproved grazing.

Supports important seabird populations (figures refer to 1985) with *Fulmarus glacialis* (1223 pairs), *Puffinus puffinus* (250-350 pairs), *Phalacrocorax aristotelis* (104 pairs), *Larus argentatus* (4037 pairs), *Rissa tridactyla* (6420 pairs), *Uria aalge* (39,840 birds), *Alca torda* (9071 birds), *Cepphus grylle* (46 pairs), and *Fratercula arctica* (2896 birds). *Falco peregrinus* (6 pairs) and *Pyrrhocorax pyrrhocorax* (5 pairs) also breed.

248 Larne Lough and Swan Island; Co. Antrim (Northern Ireland)

54°50'N, 05°45'W 1000 ha

RSPB; mainly unprotected

Sea lough with mudflats, mussel-beds, and a small area of saltings. Threatened by development plans, refuse tipping, and associated pollution. Swan Island is a tiny sand island.

Swan Island has an important tern colony with (figures refer to 1987) *Sterna sandvicensis* (74 pairs), *S. dougallii* (25 pairs), *S. hirundo* (159 pairs), and *S. paradisaea* (60 pairs). Wintering species at Larne Lough include *Branta bernicla hrota* (252-295 in the winters 1983/84-1985/86) and *Tringa nebularia* (20-30).

249 Belfast Lough; Co. Down and Co. Antrim (Northern Ireland)

54°40'N, 05°55'W 2000 ha

ASSI; largely unprotected.

A sea lough with a greatly reduced area of tidal mudflats following 150 years of land reclamation. The outer lough shores are mainly rocky with a few sandy bays. Four man-made lagoons in the Belfast Harbour Estate are the main wader roost. Problems include industrial and port development, domestic refuse disposal, hard-core tipping, pollution from a land-fill site, and motor cycling on the foreshore.

Wintering species (figures refer to 1987/88) include *Podiceps cristatus* (max. 703), *Haematopus ostralegus* (max. 10,543), *Tringa totanus* (max. 3037) and *Arenaria interpres* (max. 1183).

250 Outer Ards Peninsula; Co. Down (Northern Ireland)

54°28'N, 05°30'W 1300 ha

Unprotected

A flat (eastern-facing) shoreline of the Irish Sea with rocky outcrops interspersed with long sandy beaches. This site has only been surveyed in recent years.

Wintering waders include *Charadrius hiaticula* (max. 690), *Tringa totanus* (max. 730), and *Arenaria interpres* (max. 1950).

251 Killough Harbour, Coney Island Bay, and Strand Lough; Co. Down (Northern Ireland)

54°15'N, 05°38'W 150 ha

AONB

A small shallow freshwater lake draining into an expanse of mudflats and shingle banks. Threatened by marina proposals.

A site for passage *Branta bernicla hrota* (max. 400 in Mar.).

252 Strangford Lough and islands; Co. Down (Northern Ireland)

54°30'N, 05°38'W 13,700 ha

ASSI; ASI; AONB; Nature Reserves

A bay with saltwater marshes, coastal mudflats, and islands. Regularly subject to a variety of pressures which presently include fish-farming and an uncontrolled increase in recreation (boating, wildfowling, riding, and walkers with dogs).

A breeding site for *Phalacrocorax carbo* (124 pairs), *Sterna sandvicensis* (2127 pairs), *S. hirundo* (665+ pairs), and *S. paradisaea* (167 pairs). Large numbers of wildfowl (av. max. 22,300) and waders (av. max. 46,600) occur on passage and in the winter, with *Cygnus olor* (av. max. 326), *C. cygnus* (max. 230), *Branta bernicla hrota* (1986/87 max. 14,500), *Tadorna tadorna* (1300), *Anas penelope* (1800), *Bucephala clangula* (av. max. 400), *Mergus serrator* (av. max. 264), *Haematopus ostralegus* (max. 5000), *Pluvialis apricaria* (av. max. 7174), *Vanellus vanellus* (av. max. 10,400), *Calidris canutus* (av. max. 13,000), *C. alpina* (max. 5500), *Numenius arquata* (max. 1700), and *Tringa totanus* (max. 3700). (Figures refer to 1987 unless stated)

253 Dundrum Inner Bay; Co. Down (Northern Ireland)

54°15'N, 05°50'W 350 ha

AONB

A sandy bay with extensive mudflats, fed by four small rivers. Threats include recreational pressure, sewage pollution, refuse tipping, and commercial shellfish gathering.

Wintering species include *Branta bernicla hrota* (212-226 in the winters 1985/86 - 1987/88) and *Haematopus ostralegus* (max. 1960).

254 Carlingford Lough including Green Island; Co. Down (Northern Ireland)

54°04'N, 06°10'W 3800 ha

ASI; AONB; RSPB

A sea lough with the northern shore in Northern Ireland, which includes the most significant mudflats. Green Island is a small island, subject to chronic natural erosion and in danger of disappearing.

Green Island has an important tern colony with *Sterna sandvicensis* (286 pairs), *S. dougallii* (40 pairs), *S. hirundo* (458 pairs), and *S. paradisaea* (57 pairs). Wintering species include *Branta bernicla hrota* (365-407 in the winters 1984/85-1986/87).

255 Sandy Island including Gun's Island; Co. Down (Northern Ireland)

54°18'N, 05°34'W 35 ha

AONB

A low sandy island with sparse maritime vegetation. Linked by small causeway to Gun's Island which is well vegetated and grazed. Recreational pressure (especially day visitors) affects the area.

A breeding site for terns including *Sterna dougallii* (2 pairs), *S. hirundo* (20-25 pairs), and *S. paradisaea* (15 pairs).

256 Annaghroe, Blackwater River; Co. Armagh (Northern Ireland)

54°21'N, 06°52'W 50 ha

Unprotected

Grazed, periodically flooded, meadows along the River Blackwater. Threatened by drainage.

Wintering wildfowl include *Cygnus cygnus* (av. max. 50) and *Anser albifrons flavirostris* (Jan. av. 90).

257 Lough Neagh and Lough Beg; Co. Antrim, Londonderry, Tyrone, Armagh and Down (Northern Ireland)

54°30'-54°50'N, 06°15'-06°35'W 39,500 ha Ramsar Site; EEC SPA

NNR; ASSI; RSPB; two wildfowl refuges closed to hunting

Lakes with marshes and meadows. Human activities include fishing and hunting. Problems include shooting, disturbance, drainage, lignite mining, eutrophication, chemical pollution, gravel extraction, and recreation (water-sports).

Breeding species include *Podiceps cristatus* (750 pairs), *Tadorna tadorna*, *Anas crecca*, *A. clypeata*, *Aythya fuligula* (1000+ pairs), *Vanellus vanellus* (175 pairs), *Gallinago gallinago* (350 pairs), *Numenius arquata* (46 pairs), and *Tringa totanus* (215 pairs). On passage and in winter large numbers of waterfowl occur including *Podiceps cristatus* (max. 1100), *Cygnus olor* (max. 1069), *C. columbianus* (max. 338), *C. cygnus* (max. 1266), *Anas penelope* (2000-4000), *A. crecca* (max. 2290), *A. platyrhynchos* (max. 5282), *Aythya ferina* (max. 17,350), and *S. paradisaea* (57 pairs). Wintering species include *Branta bernicla hrota* (365-407 in the winters 1984/85-1986/87).

258 Lower Lough Erne; Co. Fermanagh (Northern Ireland)

54°28'N, 07°48'W 3300 ha

NNR; RSPB

Part of lough with highly indented shoreline, marshes, wet meadows, and islands. The main problem is eutrophication.

Breeding species include *Melanitta nigra* (10 pairs in 1987; a declining population), *Gallinago gallinago* (164+ pairs), *Numenius arquata* (74+ pairs), *Tringa totanus* (84 pairs), *Sterna sandvicensis* (78 pairs), and *S. hirundo* (5 pairs). Wintering waterfowl include irregular parties of *Cygnus cygnus* (*c.*100) and *Anser albifrons flavirostris* (less than 50).

259 Upper Lough Erne; Co. Fermanagh (Northern Ireland)

54°13'N, 07°29'W 11,300 ha

ASI; NNR; largely unprotected

Flooded drumlins in the course of River Erne, giving rise to a complex of islands, bays, and many lakes bordered by damp pastures. Problems include drainage, shooting disturbance, eutrophication, and recreation (with proposed marinas).

Very important for breeding ducks and waders including *Gallinago gallinago* (630+ pairs), *Numenius arquata* (173+ pairs), and *Tringa totanus* (146 pairs). Other breeding species include *Podiceps cristatus* (*c.*300 pairs), *Crex crex*, and *Sterna hirundo*. Wintering wildfowl include *Cygnus cygnus* (max. 876) and *Anser albifrons flavirostris* (less than 50).

260 Lower Lough McNean; Co. Fermanagh (Northern Ireland)

54°17'N, 07°50'W 500 ha

Unprotected

A freshwater lake with island. Problems include drainage, tourism with marina development.

Wintering wildfowl include *Anser albifrons flavirostris* (60) and *Cygnus cygnus*.

261 Pettigoe Plateau; Co. Fermanagh (Northern Ireland)

54°31'N, 07°58'W 2700 ha

Unprotected, partly protected in Irish Republic.

Blanket bog. Problems include afforestation, peat extraction, drainage, and agricultural improvement.

Breeding species include a few pairs of *Circus cyaneus* and *Pluvialis apricaria* (12 pairs). Wintering wildfowl include *Anser albifrons flavirostris* (less than 50).

MAIN REFERENCES

Osieck, E. R. and Mörzer Bruyns, M. F. (1981) Important bird areas in Europe. Unpublished report to the Commission of the European Communities.

CHANNEL ISLANDS

INTRODUCTION

General information

The Channel Islands are situated off the north-west coast of France some 80 miles from the English coast, and in places, less than 12 miles from the coast of Normandy. They consist of Jersey and Guernsey and the following dependencies of Guernsey: Alderney, Brechou, Great Sark, Little Sark, Herm, Jethou and Lihou. The Channel Islands cover a total area of 195 sq km and have a population of 126,000 (1977), the majority of which lives on the two largest islands, Jersey (11,630 ha) and Guernsey (6340 ha).

The islands are characterised by steep, rocky coastlines, alternating with sandy bays of varying sizes. Jersey, and Guernsey to a lesser extent, have wooded valleys. Marshy areas are scarce, having been reduced through drainage. Other semi-natural vegetation still present includes sand-dune communities, cliff-top heathlands and grasslands, with sand-dunes and coastal grasslands increasingly threatened by tourist developments. The greater part of the land is devoted to small-scale cultivation and stock-farming. Guernsey has an extensive glasshouse industry, producing tomatoes, sweet peppers, aubergines and other vegetables, and flowers. The Channel Islands, particularly Jersey and Guernsey, are popular tourist venues. The climate is mild with warm, prolonged summers.

Ornithological importance

The Channel Islands are important for their breeding seabirds, notably *Sula bassana* (4000 pairs). Other breeding seabirds include *Hydrobates pelagicus*, *Sterna hirundo* (70 pairs on Guernsey), *Alca torda*, and *Uria aalge*. *Sylvia undata* also breeds. In winter the coastal waters support small numbers (data for Guernsey only) of *Gavia arctica* (*c*.40), *G. immer* (*c*.40) and *Podiceps auritus* (c.20).

Conservation infrastructure and protected-area system

The Channel Islands are not part of the United Kingdom but are a direct dependency of the British Crown and have their own legislative systems (Guernsey and Jersey have their own legislative assemblies). The Channel Islands are not covered by the conservation legislation of the United Kingdom (Wildlife & Countryside Act etc.) but have their own bird protection legislation (1949 Protection of Wild Birds Ordinance [Guernsey], amended 1974; 1950 Protection of Wild Birds [Alderney] Ordinance; 1963 Protection of Birds [Jersey] Law, amended 1972).

International measures relevant to the conservation of sites

The Channel Islands are not part of the EEC (and are not, therefore, covered by the Wild Birds Directive). The Channel Islands are not covered by the Bonn Convention nor Bern Convention (although the U.K. Government is expecting to soon be able to ratify the Bern Convention on behalf of Jersey). Jersey is covered by the Ramsar Convention, but not Guernsey, and both are covered by the World Heritage Convention.

Overview of the inventory

Only one site is listed, that of Les Etacq and Ortac, which is important for its breeding colonies of *Sula bassana*. It is likely that other important bird areas exist in the Channel Islands which need to be identified and evaluated in a European context.

Acknowledgements

Data for the Channel Islands were provided by T. J. Bourgaize (La Société Guernesiaise). Information about the Channel Islands' relationship to the United Kingdom with regard to the above-mentioned intentional measures was provided by I. Muchmore (U.K. Government's Department of the Environment).

INVENTORY

No.	Site name	Criteria used to select site [see p.18] 0	1(i)	1(ii)	1(iii)	1(iv)	2	3	4
001	Les Etacq and Ortac, Alderney		*	*					

Comments on the inventory

1. The Channel Islands have been treated as a single 'region' when applying the site-selection criteria (category 3).

---

001 Les Etacq and Ortac, Alderney

49°45'N, 02°15'W

De facto bird sanctuary

Two rock stacks, off the coast of Alderney. Discarded nylon nets (used for nests) snare birds, particularly nestlings.

Two *Sula bassana* colonies (*c.*4000 pairs).

ISLE OF MAN

INTRODUCTION

General information

The Isle of Man covers an area of 572 sq km and is situated in the Irish Sea between England and Northern Ireland. The island consists of a main central mass of highland rising to a height of 621 m and separated by a central valley from the smaller range of the southern hills which reach 483 m and are adjacent to the west coast. A sound, 650 m wide, separates the south-western point of the main island from the Calf of Man, a hilly islet of 2.5 sq km rising to 128 m. Occupying the entire northern one sixth of the Isle of Man and a much smaller area in the south-east are flat lowlands.

For the most part, cultivated land ceases at about 200 m above sea-level. Mixed farming is practised, but since 1945 an increasing proportion of the land has been devoted to grass and hay at the expense of grain, potatoes and green crops. Cattle and to a lesser extent sheep have increased considerably. Non-grassland arable land (predominantly grain) accounts for 11 per cent of the island's area, hay and grassland 44 per cent and rough grazing 27 per cent. Woodland accounts for four per cent, mostly coniferous plantations which are occupying the moorland zone to an increasing extent. The hills are covered equally with grass heath and heathers. Often the transition zone with farmland is marked by extensive *Pteridium aquilinum* which occurs up to about 300 m.

Streams are fast flowing, often cutting through rocky gorges and forming waterfalls. In their lower reaches they usually pass through sheltered glens of mixed woodland. There are several artificial lakes ranging in size from one to 22 ha and scattered over the northern plain are numerous dubs which are either naturally occurring kettle holes or flooded marl or clay pits.

Marshland is represented by Ballaugh Curragh, Lough Cranstal, the Dog Mills Lough and the Lagagh in the north and by Greeba Curragh in the central valley. Although considerably reduced by drainage the Ballaugh Curragh still possesses quite extensive areas of bog and a few small pieces of open water; there is a dense growth of *Salix* sp. and *Betula* sp. is plentiful, while some areas are dominated by low shrubs such as *Salix repens* and *Myrica gale*.

The coast to the south of Ramsey and Peel consists mostly of slate cliffs interrupted by several large bays and a number of small shingle bordered coves. In the south there is a succession of low-lying promontories and bays. North Peel are cliffs of red sandstone, while within the two northern sheadings of Michael and Ayre the coast is composed of sandcliffs, shingle beaches and dunes.

Ornithological importance

In a European context, the Isle of Man is interesting for its breeding populations of four species: *Circus cyaneus* (6 pairs), *Falco peregrinus* (6-9 pairs), *Sterna albifrons* (57-60 pairs in 1985), and *Pyrrhocorax pyrrhocorax* (60 pairs). Other breeding species include *Phalacrocorax aristotelis* (600+ pairs), *Crex crex* (1-2 pairs), *Numenius arquata* (400 pairs), and *Asio flammeus* (2-5 pairs). The Calf of Man is of particular interest for passage migrants especially thrushes and warblers. Wintering species include *Gavia immer* (1-2), *Cygnus cygnus* (max. 15), *Circus cyaneus* (12), *Falco columbarius* (4), *F. peregrinus* (12), *Pluvialis apricaria* (3500), *Numenius arquata* (max. 6000), *Asio otus* (20-30), and *Pyrrhocorax pyrrhocorax* (160-185).

Conservation infrastructure and protected-area system

The Isle of Man is administered in accordance with its own laws, and is not bound by Acts of the United Kingdom unless specially mentioned in them. It is not, therefore, covered by the conservation legislation of the United Kingdom (Wildlife and Countryside Act etc.), and does not, for example, have a system equivalent to the SSSI/ASSI network in the U.K. Manx sites are unprotected with the exception of the Calf of Man and Langness peninsulas. The Calf has a resident warden from March to November and protection is of a very high order. Langness is a private bird sanctuary affording good protection from shooting but little else.

International measures relevant to the conservation of sites

The Isle of Man is not part of the EEC (and is therefore not covered by the Wild Birds Directive). The Isle of Man is not covered by the Ramsar Convention, Bonn Convention or Bern Convention, even though the United Kingdom is a party to these Conventions; it is, however, covered by the U.K. being a party to the World Heritage Convention.

Overview of the inventory

Three sites are included that cover a significant proportion of the island's breeding *Falco peregrinus*, *Sterna albifrons* (entire population) and *Pyrrhocorax pyrrhocorax*, as well as its breeding seabirds.

Apart from the three sites specifically described in the inventory the hills hold breeding *Circus cyaneus* (5+ pairs) and *Falco peregrinus* (2 pairs). Over 40 species have bred in the Ballaugh Curragh during the last decade and this site also holds one of the largest communal roosts of *Circus cyaneus* in the British Isles with counts of 23 (December 1986) and 19 (October 1987). J. P. Cullen prepared the introduction.

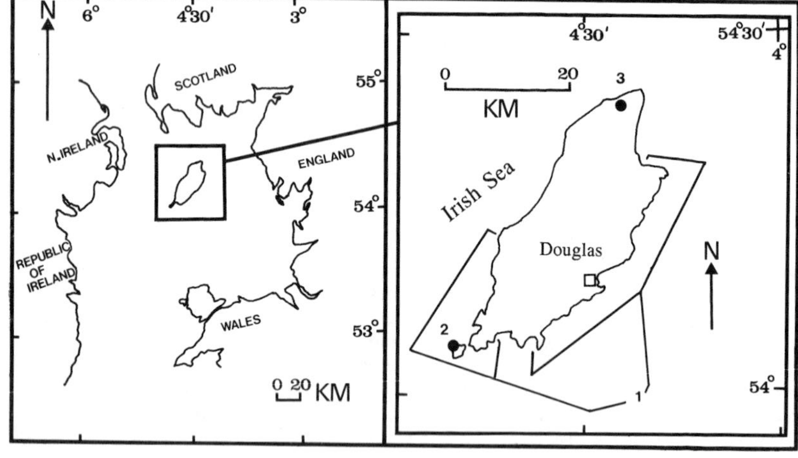

Figure 37: Map showing the location of the sites in the Isle of Man

Acknowledgements

Data-sheets for the following sites were compiled by J. P. Cullen, with the details of breeding seabird numbers provided by A. S. Moore and Calf of Man data provided by D. Walker. Information about the Isle of Man's relationship to the United Kingdom with regard to the above mentioned international measures was provided by I. Muchmore (U.K. Government's Department of the Environment). J. P. Cullen prepared the introduction.

INVENTORY

No.	Site name	Criteria used to select site [see p.18]							
		0	1(i)	1(ii)	1(iii)	1(iv)	2	3	4
001	Sea cliffs from Ramsey to Castletown and from Port St Mary to Peel							*	
002	Calf of Man							*	
003	The Ayres							*	

Comments on the inventory

1. The Isle of Man has been treated as a single 'region' when applying the site-selection criteria (category 3).

---

001 Sea cliffs from Ramsey to Castletown and from Port St Mary to Peel

54°20'N, 04°25'W-54°05'N, 04°40'W and 54°05'N, 04°45'W-54°12'N, 04°43'W

Partly Manx National Trust property

Slate cliffs. Important sections of coast (Maughold Head, Spanish Head and Eary Cushlin, between Bradda and Peel) are owned by the Manx National Trust. Nests of *Falco peregrinus* are robbed.

An important breeding area for *Falco peregrinus* (5+ pairs) and *Pyrrhocorax pyrrhocorax* (50+ pairs). Breeding seabirds include *Fulmarus glacialis* (1800 pairs), *Phalacrocorax carbo* (50 pairs), *P. aristotelis* (400 pairs), *Rissa tridactyla* (1100 pairs), *Uria aalge* (1500 pairs), *Alca torda* (300 pairs), *Cepphus grylle* (290 pairs), and *Fratercula arctica* (60 pairs). Wintering species include *Calidris maritima* (max. 120) and *Pyrrhocorax pyrrhocorax* (usually 25-40; max. 60).

002 Calf of Man

54°03'N, 04°50'E 246 ha

Manx National Trust property

An offshore island with rugged coast, steep slate cliffs, and grass- and bracken-covered slopes off the south-west tip of the Isle of Man. Mainly heather moorland with expanses of bracken and abandoned cultivation (farmed up until 1958). The land is grazed by feral sheep, and there is controlled burning of bracken and heather.

Breeding species include *Puffinus puffinus* (possibly 10-12 pairs), *Hydrobates pelagicus* (possibly max. 50 pairs), *Phalacrocorax aristotelis* (400 pairs), *Falco peregrinus* (1 pair), *Asio flammeus* (max. 3 pairs), *Uria aalge* (350 pairs), *Alca torda* (150 pairs), *Fratercula arctica* (40 pairs) and *Pyrrhocorax pyrrhocorax* (6 pairs, max. 10 pairs). An important site for migrants (there is a bird observatory managed by the Manx Museum and Manx National Trust) and large numbers of thrushes and warblers occur on spring and autumn passage.

003 The Ayres

54°25'N, 04°25'W 800 ha

Nature reserve (Manx Nature Conservation Trust reserve, Ballakesh Ayre: 16 ha); mainly unprotected

Coast and adjacent heath between the Lhen and Point of Ayre. Pebble beach with intertidal zone of sand, sand bar and coastal lagoon, sand dunes, bracken-covered fixed dunes and rough grass, sand and gravel pits, heath and gorse. There is sand and gravel extraction and recreational use (riding of motor bikes which is a nuisance at the site).

Breeding species include *Mergus serrator* (1 pair), *Charadrius hiaticula* (100 pairs), *Sterna hirundo* (max. 7 pairs), *S. paradisaea* (15-30 pairs), and *S. albifrons* (57-60 pairs in 1985). *S. dougallii* (1 pair) has bred. In addition, *Asio flammeus* (1-2) occurs in autumn and winter, and *Pluvialis apricaria* (300-1000) occurs in winter.

MAIN REFERENCES

Cullen, J. P. (1980) A review of the status of terns in the Isle of Man *Peregrine* 5(2): 68-73.

Cullen, J. P., and Jennings, P. P. (1986) *Birds of the Isle of Man*. Douglas.

Moore, A. S. (1987) The numbers and distribution of seabirds breeding on the Isle of Man during 1985-1986. *Peregrine* 6(2).

GIBRALTAR

INTRODUCTION

General information

The vegetation of the Rock of Gibraltar has been altered significantly since it was first settled by the Moors in 711 AD. The original native woodland probably consisted, judging from old references, of a combination of *Quercus ilex, Ceratonia siliqua* and *Olea europaea sylvestris*. This woodland was progressively removed so that the appearance of Gibraltar in the early twentieth century was that of a barren rock with very little vegetation. At that time, regeneration was held in check by goats but, following their removal, maquis became the dominant vegetation-type on Gibraltar and remains unique in the region. Over 600 species of flowering plants have been recorded and important fruit-bearing shrubs of the maquis include *Olea europaea, Pistacia lentiscus, Osyris quadripartita, Rhamnus alaternus* and *Asparagus albus*. There is no agriculture on Gibraltar and the maquis is only utilised for recreational and military purposes.

Ornithological importance

In a European context, Gibraltar is important as the continent's mainland stronghold of *Alectoris barbara*. The small breeding population of *Phalacrocorax aristotelis desmarestii* is the only known one on the Mediterranean Iberian mainland coastline. Huge numbers of raptors cross the Straits of Gibraltar in spring and autumn with varying numbers overflying the Rock (depending on the wind direction). The maquis is utilised by passerine migrants in spring, autumn and winter, and it is particularly favoured by warblers (especially *Sylvia* species).

It is the maquis (with natural or man-made clearings) and cliffs which are the most important bird habitats. Open vegetation (pseudosteppe and garigue), although limited in area, is essential for *Alectoris barbara*.

Conservation infrastructure and protected-area system

Gibraltar has its own legislative assembly, known as the Gibraltar House of Assembly. It is not therefore covered by the conservation legislation of the United Kingdom (Wildlife and Countryside Act).

The upper part of the Rock is managed with the interests of nature conservation in mind. It is protected from shooting and trapping and from building. Gibraltar does not have a network of protected areas. Certain species are protected, such as *Alectoris barbara*.

International measures relevant to the conservation of the sites

The United Kingdom is responsible for Gibraltar's external affairs. Gibraltar is, unlike the Isle of Man and the Channel Islands, covered by the EEC Wild Birds Directive. It is also covered by the U.K. being a party to the Ramsar Convention and World Heritage Convention, but not covered by the Bonn Convention and Bern Convention.

Overview of the inventory

The entire Rock is included as site 001. The most important bird localities within Gibraltar are the upper Rock which is covered by maquis and which is likely to become a nature reserve, Windmill Hill which is a military training ground with a large nucleus of *Alectoris barbara*, and the sea caves at Governor's Beach where *Phalacrocorax aristotelis* nest and large numbers of *Ptyonoprogne rupestris* roost in winter.

Acknowledgements

The following accounts were compiled by J. C. Finlayson. Information about Gibraltar's relationship to the United Kingdom with regard to the above-mentioned international measures was provided by I. Muchmore (U.K. Government's Department of the Environment). J. C. Finlayson prepared the introduction.

INVENTORY

No.	Site name	Criteria used to select site [see p.18]							
		0	1(i)	1(ii)	1(iii)	1(iv)	2	3	4
001	Rock of Gibraltar					*		*	
002	Strait of Gibraltar					*		*	

Comments on the inventory

1. Gibraltar has been treated as a single 'region' when applying the site-selection criteria (category 3).

---

001 Rock of Gibraltar

36°17'N, 05°21'W 600 ha

Protected (see comments above)
A British dependent territory at the southern tip of the Iberian peninsula. A rocky peninsula dominated by a dense cover of maquis and garigue with many important fruit-bearing shrubs which support large passerine populations on passage and during the winter.

Breeding species include *Phalacrocorax aristotelis desmarestii* (5 pairs), *Falco peregrinus* (4 pairs), *Alectoris barbara* (less than 50 pairs, with 21 pairs censused in 1980; the only mainland European breeding site), and a unique breeding population of *Sylvia atricapilla* (characterised by its dark appearance and short, rounded wings). An important bottleneck area used by large numbers of raptors as a crossing point to and from the African mainland. 250,000 raptors cross the Strait in a season and, of these, a varying proportion cross from the Rock depending on wind direction. The main species are *Pernis apivorus* (100,000), *Milvus migrans* (60,000), *Neophron percnopterus* (2000), *Circaetus gallicus* (5000), *Circus pygargus* (1500), and *Hieraaetus pennatus* (10,000). The Rock is also utilised by many trans-Saharan passerines and near-passerines as a stop-over site before crossing or having just crossed the Sahara Desert, and it is a major wintering site for *Hirundo rupestris* (over 3000 roosting in sea caves) and for large numbers of *Erithacus rubecula, Phoenicurus ochruros, Sylvia atricapilla,* and *Phylloscopus collybitus.*

002 Strait of Gibraltar

36°11'N,06°02'W – 35°47'N,05°56'W, 36°17'N,05°21'W – 35°53'N,05°19'W

Unprotected

Includes international waters and waters under the jurisdiction of the United Kingdom, Spain and Morocco. The Strait of Gibraltar is defined here as the sea area demarcated in the west by a straight line joining Cape Trafalgar on the European coast with Cape Spartel on the North African coast, and in the east by a straight line joining the Rock of Gibraltar on the European coast to Ceuta (enclave of Spain) on the North African coast. At its narrowest it is 15 km wide. The major threat is that of a major oil spillage since commercial shipping traffic is heavy.

This sea area is an important bottleneck for passage seabirds, in particular *Calonectris diomedea* (100,000), *Sula bassana* (7000), *Puffinus puffinus mauretanicus* (10,000), *Larus audouinii* (12,000), and *Fratercula arctica* (40,000). In addition, many other species use the Strait on passage between the Atlantic Ocean and the Mediterranean Sea and back. The Strait is also a wintering ground, in particular for *Sula bassana*, *Larus melanocephalus*, *Sterna sandvicensis*, and *Alca torda*.

MAIN REFERENCES

Bernis, F. (1980) *La migración de las aves en el estrecho de Gibraltar.* Volumen I: Aves planeadoras. Madrid-Universidad complutense.

Cortes, J. E., Finlayson, J. C., Garcia, E. F. J. and Mosquera, M. A. J. (1980) *The birds of Gibraltar.* Gibraltar Bookshop.

Elkins, N. and Etheridge, B. (1974) The Crag Martin in winter quarters at Gibraltar. *British Birds* 67: 376-389.

Finlayson, J. C. (1980) The recurrence in winter quarters at Gibraltar of some scrub passerines. *Ringing and Migration* 3: 32-34.

Finlayson, J. C. (1981) The morphology of Sardinian Warblers *Sylvia melanocephala* and Blackcaps *Sylvia atricapilla* resident on Gibraltar. *Bull. BOC.* 101(2): 299-304.

Finlayson, J. C. (1981) Seasonal distribution, weights and fat of passerine migrants at Gibraltar. *Ibis* 123: 88-95.

Finlayson, J. C., Garcia, E. F. J., Mosquera, M. A. J. and Bourne, W. R. P. (1976) Raptor migration across the Strait of Gibraltar. *British Birds* 69: 77-87.

Finlayson, J. C. and Cortes, J. E. (1984) The migration of Gannets *Sula bassana* past Gibraltar in spring. *Seabird* 7: 19-22.

Finlayson, J. C. and Cortes, J. E. (1987) The Birds of the Strait of Gibraltar – its waters and northern shore. *Alectoris* 6: 1-74.

Finlayson, J. C. in prep. The migration of the Audouin's Gull *Larus audouinii.*

Garcia, E. F. J. (1973) Seabird activity in the Strait of Gibraltar. *Seabird Report* 3: 30-36.

Linares, L. L. (1983) A checklist of the Gibraltar Flora. *Alectoris* 5: 24-39.

Pineau, J. and Giraud-Audine, M. (1979) *Les oiseaux de la péninsule tingitane.* Institut Scientifique-Rabat.

Telleria, J. L. (1981) *La migración de las aves en el estrecho de Gibraltar.* Volumen II: Aves no planeadoras. Madrid-Universidad Complutense.

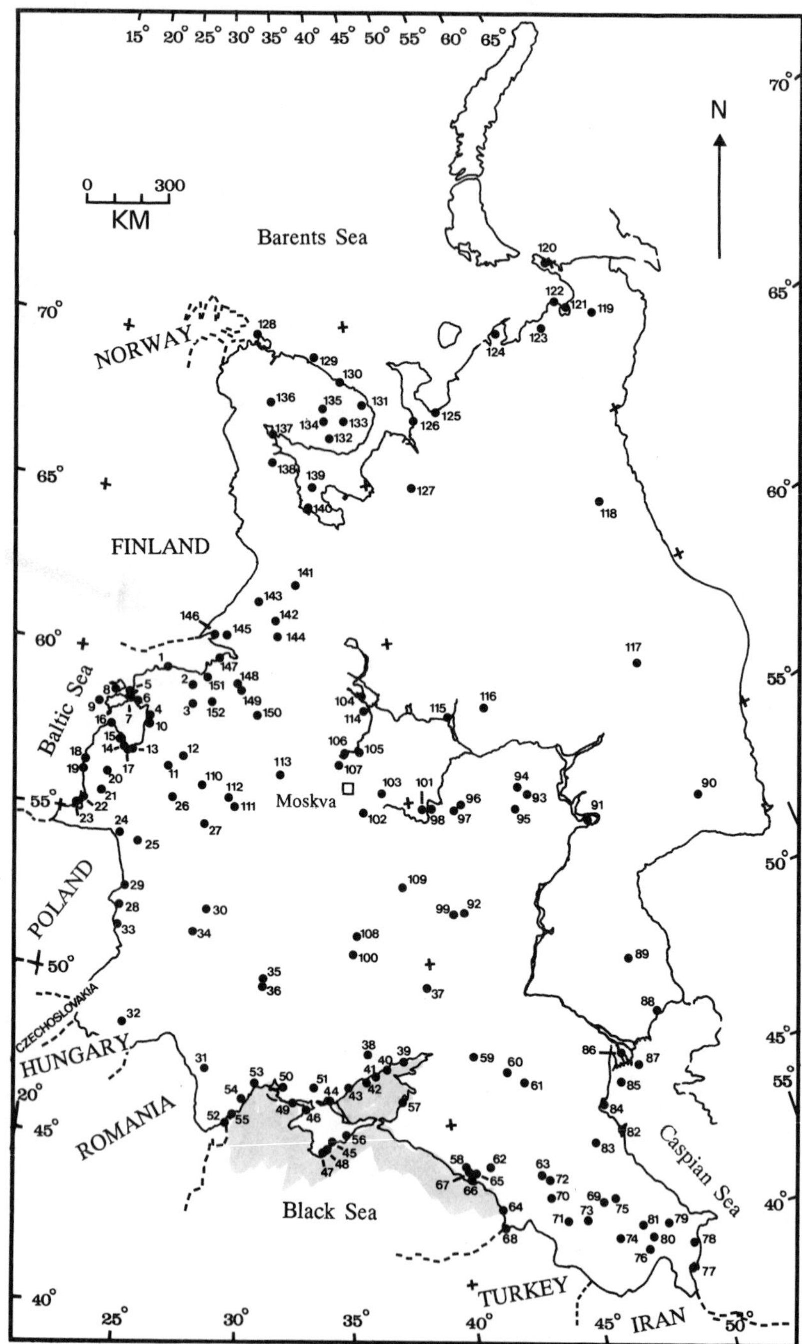

Figure 38: Map showing the location of the sites in the USSR

USSR

Caucasian Black Grouse *Tetrao mlokosiewiczi*

INTRODUCTION

General information

The Soviet Union is the largest country in the world, covering more than 22 million sq km and straddling approximate latitudes 35°20'N to 82°00'N, and approximate longitudes 19°50'E east to 169°00'W. This massive west-east extension, from the Baltic Sea to the Bering Strait exceeds 11,200 km and includes twelve time-zones. Not surprisingly, this vast territory contains an enormous diversity of natural, man-altered, and artificial environments, which provide habitats for an extraordinarily rich flora and fauna.

This account considers only that part of the Soviet Union which is included in Europe, i.e. the area from the country's western borders, east to the Ural Mountains and the western shores of the Caspian Sea. Although this is a relatively small section of the Soviet Union as a whole, the region is nevertheless the largest included in this volume. The following constituent units of the USSR are embraced by the area described: the Soviet Socialist Republics (SSRs) of Lithuania (Litva), Latvia (Latviya), Estonia (Estoniya), Belorussia (Belorussiya), Ukraine (Ukraina), Moldavia (Moldaviya), Georgia (Gruziya), Azerbaijan (Azerbaydzhan), Armenia (Armyanya), and part of Kazakhstan; together with (whole or part of) 45 of the Autonomous Soviet Socialist Republics (ASSRs) and Oblasts (regions) which make up the Russian Soviet Federal Socialist Republic (RSFSR).

The European section of the Soviet Union includes many of the country's larger centres of human population, (for example, Moskva, Leningrad, Kiyev, Kharkov, Odessa, Tbilisi, Baku, Kuybyshev, and Gorkiy) together with associated urban, industrial, and communication infrastructures. However, away from the areas around Moskva and the major Ukrainian cities, population densities are generally lower than those elsewhere in Europe. In particular, the inhospitable far-northern and mountain zones include vast tracts of sparsely populated land, with densities similar to those of northern Fennoscandia.

It is only possible, in the space available, to provide an extremely brief outline of the principal natural environments found in the European Soviet Union, using a highly simplified topographic and vegetational zonation.

There are two principal mountain ranges, the Urals (highest point *c.*2000 m; length *c.*2000 km) and the Caucasus (highest point *c.*5640 m; area *c.*440,000 sq km), together with a number of less significant upland areas, notably the Central Russian Uplands, part of the Carpathian range, and the mountains of the Crimean peninsula. The vast majority of the remaining territory lies between sea-level and 200 m above sea-level and contains numerous plains and complex river systems with associated lake networks. The principal rivers include the Dnepr, Don, Volga, Pechora, Severnaya Dvina, and Onega. Major sub-sea-level zones are restricted to the vicinity of the Caspian Sea.

It is possible to identify a number of simple vegetation zones, which largely reflect latitudinal climatic gradations. In the south-east, around the Caspian Sea, where the climate is markedly arid and continental, there are areas of desert and desert-steppe. With northward progress, the zones of steppe, broadleaved forest, mixed forest, boreal forest (taiga), and tundra are encountered. However, superimposed on this basic framework are the influences of topography, soil-type, geology, and human activities; thus, for example, in the Caucasus, altitude largely controls the climate to produce strong vertical zonation of vegetation.

Ornithological importance

The vastness of the European Soviet Union and the diversity of habitats which it embraces are reflected in the region's major importance for birds. No fewer than 18 globally threatened species (*Pelecanus crispus*, *Phalacrocorax pygmeus*, *Anser erythropus*, *Branta ruficollis*, *Marmaronetta angustirostris*, *Oxyura leucocephala*, *Milvus milvus*, *Haliaeetus albicilla*, *Aegypius monachus*, *Aquila heliaca*, *Falco naumanni*, *Crex crex*, *Otis tarda*, *Tetrax tetrax*, *Chettusia gregaria*, *Numenius tenuirostris* and *Acrocephalus paludicola*) have regular breeding, passage, or wintering populations, whilst one other, *Grus leucogeranus*, has been introduced as part of a long-term conservation programme.

Several species found in the Caucasus are endemic to the region or are part of a restricted, discrete population with a small and disjunct distribution. These species include *Tetrao mlokosiewiczi*, *Tetraogallus caucasicus*, *T. caspius*, *Prunella ocularis*, and *Sitta krueperi*.

The European Soviet Union (particularly the south-east of the region) also contains the western range-limits of a large number of species (some also breeding in eastern Turkey), including: *Anthropoides virgo*, *Charadrius leschenaultii*, *C. asiaticus*, *Larus ichthyaetus*, *Cuculus saturatus*, *Merops superciliosus*, *Melanocorypha leucoptera*, *M. yeltoniensis*, *Motacilla citreola*, *Hippolais caligata*, *H. languida*, *Sylvia mystacea*, *Phylloscopus nitidus*, *Parus cyanus*, and *Loxia leucoptera*. Whilst many of these species are very common in the central parts of their range, populations at the range-limits may be vulnerable and/or act as indicators of adverse ecological change.

Perhaps the Soviet Union's greatest importance for birds lies in the sheer extent of natural and semi-natural habitats. Thus hundreds of thousands of square kilometres of tundra or forest may support many millions of breeding birds, even if their actual density is rather low. Some examples of species which are present in internationally important populations are related below to habitat zones.

The Arctic Sea coast and islands are important for breeding *Fulmarus glacialis*, *Branta leucopsis*, *B. bernicla*, *Pagophila eburnea*, *Alle alle*, and *Uria lomvia*.

There are huge populations of breeding waterfowl in the tundra zones, including *Cygnus columbianus*, *Anser fabalis*, *A. albifrons*, *Anas* spp., *Aythya marila*, *Somateria spectabilis*, *Clangula hyemalis*, *Melanitta nigra*, *M. fusca*, and many species of

Charadriidae and Scolopacidae. Other species breeding in tundra areas include *Falco rusticolus*, *F. peregrinus*, and *Nyctea scandiaca*.

The taiga forests (or boreal zone) are characterised by low densities of animals. Typical breeding bird species, with very significant total populations, include *Bonasa bonasia*, *Tetrao tetrix*, *T. urogallus*, *Surnia ulula*, *Glaucidium passerinum*, *Strix uralensis*, *S. nebulosa*, *Aegolius funereus*, *Picoides tridactylus*, *Bombycilla garrulus*, *Tarsiger cyanurus*, *Turdus ruficollis*, *Phylloscopus trochiloides*, *P. inornatus*, *Perisoreus infaustus*, *Loxia leucoptera*, *L. pytyopsittacus*, and *Pinicola enucleator* (several of these species are on the western edge of their range in the European part of the USSR). The lakes and rivers of the boreal zone support important breeding populations of Anatidae (e.g. *Bucephala clangula*, *Mergus albellus*), *Circus* spp., Rallidae, Charadriidae, Scolopacidae, Laridae, and Sternidae, etc.

In addition to those species mentioned earlier, the Caucasus mountains hold very important breeding populations of raptors and a variety of passerines, including *Gypaetus barbatus*, *Neophron percnopterus*, *Gyps fulvus*, *Aegypius monachus*, *Oenanthe xanthoprymna*, *Irania gutturalis*, *Sitta tephronota*, *S. neumayer*, and *Emberiza buchanani*.

Typical breeding birds of the European USSR steppe include *Circus macrourus*, *Buteo rufinus*, *Aquila rapax nipalensis*, *A. heliaca*, *Falco naumanni*, *F. vespertinus*, *Coturnix coturnix*, *Anthropoides virgo*, *Tetrax tetrax*, *Otis tarda*, *Chettusia gregaria*, *Merops superciliosus*, *Melanocorypha calandra*, *M. leucoptera*, *M. yeltoniensis*, *Calandrella brachydactyla*, *C. rufescens*, and *Oenanthe isabellina*.

The major wetlands along the Caspian and Black Sea coasts support very important breeding populations of waterfowl with very large breeding colonies of Ardeidae, and Laridae including *Larus ichthyaetus*, *L. melanocephalus* (a majority of the world's population) and *L. genei*. Other breeding species include *Pelecanus crispus* and *Phalacrocorax pygmeus*. These wetlands also hold some of the largest concentrations of passage and wintering waterfowl in Europe.

Conservation infrastructure and protected-area system

All protected areas in the Soviet Union are owned, administered, and monitored by the state, but the large number of state organisations involved makes the system extremely complex. Details of the principal categories of protected area are given below. In addition to this aspect of its conservation programme, the Soviet Union has also introduced a series of legislative controls in attempts to regulate such matters as air pollution, water pollution, water conservation, tree-felling, soil erosion, hunting, fishing etc.

1. Zapovednik (State Reserve)

   This is the principal category of protected area in the Soviet Union. A Zapovednik is an area of land withdrawn from economic use for the study and preservation of fauna and flora. Literally meaning 'forbidden/restricted areas', Zapovedniks are closed to non-specialists, including tourists, except on organised visits. Each reserve is surrounded by an area of semi-protected land (or buffer-zone) where economic activity is allowed, providing that the reserve itself is unharmed. Zapovedniks are mostly administered by the Ministry of Agriculture, whilst final approval of reserve creation is given by the State Planning Committee for the Economy.

   The number of Zapovedniks is growing and this increase is projected to accelerate over the coming years, but this progress should be set against the past practice of abolishing Zapovedniks when economic exploitation of an area was seen as necessary. In some cases, Zapovedniks were de-designated, severely degraded by economic activity (e.g. open-cast mining) and then redesignated despite the destruction of their original ecological importance. In the early 1980s there were about 150 Zapovedniks in the Soviet Union (whole country) covering over 15 million ha.

2. Zakaznik (temporary reserve)

   These protected areas are normally set-up for a predetermined period of time, usually not exceeding ten years. Some Zakazniks are only protected for specified periods of the year (seasonal Zakazniks). Within a Zakaznik, all flora and fauna may be protected in order to allow, for example, the recovery of an area which had suffered some kind of environmental degradation. Zakazniks may also be established in order to protect a particular species or group of species. In such cases, economic activities, including hunting, may be allowed provided that the target species is unaffected. In 1980, there were over 1000 Zakazniks in the Soviet Union (whole country), covering some 25 million ha.

3. National Park
The first National Parks in the Soviet Union were established in the early 1970s in the Baltic SSRs of Estonia, Latvia, and Lithuania. More recently, parks have been set up elsewhere in the country. Most National Parks are centred on one or more Zapovedniks, where the standard Zapovednik regime applies. However, surrounding these core zones are large areas where limited economic activity, including tourism, is allowed.

4. National Hunting Reserve
There are seven areas of the Soviet Union designated as National Hunting Reserves. Hunting is theoretically limited to a level which will not deplete stocks. However, poaching appears to be a considerable problem.

5. Monument of Nature
This category of protected area refers to small zones around individual natural features of, for example, biological or geological importance. The total number of designated Monuments of Nature runs to several thousands.

International measures relevant to the conservation of sites

The Soviet Union is a contracting party to the Ramsar Convention. As of September 1988, seven Ramsar Sites (all included in the following inventory) had been designated, together with 11 Biosphere Reserves under UNESCO's Man and the Biosphere Programme (these figures refer only to the European part of the Soviet Union).

Overview of the inventory

One hundred and fifty-two important bird areas are included in the inventory. Of these, around two-thirds are principally wetlands, whilst the remainder are mostly steppe, forest, and mountain zones.

The geographical spread of the sites listed is sufficiently wide to ensure that representative examples of the major bird habitats found in the European part of the Soviet Union are included. Thus, amongst the 152 important bird areas are sites near the Polish border, in the southern Caucasus, in the foothills of the Urals, and on the islands of the Arctic Ocean. It is considered that the inventory satisfactorily reflects the aspects of ornithological importance discussed earlier in this introduction.

Many of the sites and regions listed are protected in some way. To a certain extent this reflects the main source document used to compile information on non-wetland sites (which covers Zapovedniks).

Many of the important wetlands in this inventory are unprotected or are seriously threatened (the latter applies to several of the country's Ramsar Sites). For example, the Volga Delta Ramsar Site is being affected by the large dams on the Volga and by agricultural reclamation, and the Kirov Bay Ramsar Site is being adversely affected by agricultural changes and irrigation schemes.

Acknowledgements

In the Soviet Union, the important bird areas project was coordinated by V. Zubakin (USSR Ornithological Society) with contributions and/or assistance provided by V. D. Ilyichev, O. Silajewa, N. N. Skokova, and V. G. Vinogradov. Data for Latvia were received from J. Vīksne and P. Blums.

Much of the material on which this inventory is based was translated by M. Turner, M. G. Wilson, and J. Dunning. Z. Karpowicz (World Conservation Monitoring Centre) provided advice in relation to administrative boundaries in the USSR and information on the country's protected areas. M. G. Wilson also made very useful comments on drafts of the inventory and was of considerable help with the standardisation of the site names.

INVENTORY

No.	Site name	Region	Criteria used to select site [see p.18] 0	1(i)	1(ii)	1(iii)	1(iv)	2	3	4
001	Laukasoo Marsh, Rakvere, and Harju	ES	*							
002	Muraka Marsh, Kokhtla-Järve	ES	*							
003	Mouth of the River Emajõgi, Tartu	ES	*							
004	Nigula Zapovednik, Pärnu	ES	*							
005	Matsalu Zaliv (Matsalu Bay)	ES			*	*		*	*	
006	Nätsi Marsh, Pärnu	ES	*							
007	Suurväin straits, Haapsalu and Kingissepp	ES				*				
008	Lake Käina, Hiiumaa	ES							*	
009	Vilsandi Archipelago, Kingissepp	ES	*							
010	Ollu and Kodu-Kapzemes Bogs	LA							*	
011	Teiču Bog, Jēkabpils and Madona	LA							*	
012	Gomelis Marsh	LA							*	
013	Lake Babite, Riga	LA	*							
014	Lake Kaņieris, Tukums	LA						*		
015	Lake Engure, Talsi and Tukums	LA				*		*	*	
016	Slitere State Reserve	LA					*	*	*	
017	Lielais Ķemeru Tīrelis Marsh, Jelgava, Riga, and Tukums	LA	*							
018	Lake Liepāja, Liepāja	LA	*							
019	Lake Pape and adjoining marshland, Liepāja	LA	*							
020	Kamanos Bog, Akmene	LV	*							
021	Lakes Biržulis and Styrvas, Telšiai	LV	*							
022	Nemunas Delta, Šilutė	LV				*		*	*	
023	Kuršių Bay (Litva),	RSFSR				*		*	*	
024	Lake Žuvintas and adjoining marshes, Alytus	LV	*							
025	Marshes on the River Čepkeliai, including the lower Merkys and Katra Reka Valley, Varėna	LV							*	
026	Lake Kretuonas, Švenčionys	LV						*	*	
027	Berezina	BA	*							
028	Telekhany, Ivatsevichi, and Lyakhovichi, Brest	BA						*		
029	Belovezhskaya pushcha, Brest, and Grodno	BA						*	*	
030	Pripyat; Zhitkovichi, Lelchitsy and Petrikov, Gomel	BA	*							
031	Kodry, Strasheny	MA						*		
032	Karpatski (Carpathians), Zakarpatskaya and Ivano-Frankovskaya Oblasts	UA	*							
033	Shatskiye Ozera (Lake Shatskiye), Volynskaya Oblast	UA				*			*	
034	Polesski, Zhitomir	UA	*							
035	Kanevskoye Vodokhranilishche (Kanev Reservoir), Kiyev	UA						*		
036	Kanev, Cherkassy	UA						*		
037	Lugansk, Voroshilovgrad Oblast	UA						*		
038	Ukrainian Steppe Reserve, Sumy, Donetsk, and Zaporozhe	UA							*	
039	Krivaya Kosa (Krivaya Peninsula), Novoazovsk Donetsk	UA			*	*		*	*	
040	Belosarayskaya Kosa (Belosarayskaya Peninsula), Volodarskoye, Donetsk	UA							*	

No.	Site name	Region	Criteria used to select site [see p.18]							
			0	1(i)	1(ii)	1(iii)	1(iv)	2	3	4
041	Berdyanskaya Kosa (Berdyansk Peninsula), Berdyansk, Zhdanov	UA	*							
042	Obitochnaya Kosa (Obitochnaya Peninsula), Primorskoye, Zhdanov	UA				*			*	
043	Molochny Liman, Melitopol	UA				*		*		
044	Sivash Zaliv, Azovskoye More (Sivash Bay, Sea of Azov)	UA		*	*	*		*	*	
045	Krymski (Crimean) Game Reserve, Krym	UA						*		
046	Karkinitski Zaliv, Chernoye More (Karkinitski Bay, Black Sea)	UA			*	*			*	
047	Yalta Mountain Forest, Bolshaya Yalta, Krym	UA	*							
048	Mys Martyan, Krym	UA							*	
049	Chumaki Ostrova, Dzarylgachski Zaliv (Chumaki Islands, Dzharylgach Bay), Skadovsk and Kalanchak, Kherson	UA				*		*		
050	Nizovya Dnepra (Lower Dnepr), Golaya Pristan, Kherson	UA				*				
051	Askania – Nova, Kherson	UA						*	*	
052	Dunay (Danube) and Yagorlytski and Tendrovski Zalivy (Yagorlytski and Tendra Bays)	UA		*	*	*		*	*	
052-1	Dunay (Danube)	UA								
052-2	Yagorlytski and Tendrovski Zalivy (Yagorlytski and Tendra Bays)	UA								
053	Tiligulski Liman (Tiligul Salt-lake), Berezanka and Kominternovskoye	UA				*			*	
054	Nizovya Dnestra (Lower Dnestr), Belgorod-Dnestrovski and Ovidiopol	UA				*				
055	Coastal lakes between the Rivers Dnestr and Dunay (Danube), Kiliya, Tatarbunary, and Belgorod-Dnestrovski	UA				*		*		
056	Karadag, Sudak, Krymskaya (Crimean) Oblast	UA						*		
057	Salt-lakes (Limany) in the Primorsko-Akhtarsk/Grivenskaya area (including Akhtarski Liman and Liman Sladki), Krasnoder Kray	RSFSR				*				
058	Kavkaz (Caucasus) Biosphere Reserve, Sochi, Krasnodar Kray	RSFSR						*	*	
059	Veselovskoye Vodokhranilishche (Veselovskoye Reservoir), Rostov Oblast	RSFSR				*		*		
060	Eastern Manych, Ozero (Lake) Manych-Gudilo, Kalmytskaya ASSR	RSFSR				*		*	*	
061	Burukshunskiye Limany (Burukshunskiye Salt-lakes), Kalmytskaya ASSR	RSFSR				*				
062	Teberda, Karachaevo, Cherkesskaya Oblast	RSFSR							*	
063	Kabardino-Balkarski, Sovetskoye and Chegem, Kabardino-Balkarskaya ASSR	RSFSR							*	
064	Nizovya Reki Rioni, Ozero Paliastomi (Lower Rioni, Lake Paliastomi)	GA	*							

No.	Site name	Region	Criteria used to select site [see p.18]							
			0	1(i)	1(ii)	1(iii)	1(iv)	2	3	4
065	Pskhuski, Abkhazskaya ASSR	GA							*	
066	Gumistin, Sukhumi, Abkhazskaya ASSR	GA							*	
067	Ritsa, Gudauta, Abkhazskaya ASSR	GA						*	*	
068	Kintrishi, Kobuleti, Adzharskaya ASSR	GA								*
069	Lagodekhi, Kvarelsk	GA							*	
070	Liakhvi, Tskhinvali, Yugo-Osetinskaya A. O. (South Osetin Autonomous Region)	GA							*	
071	Algeti, Tetri – Tskaro	GA	*							
072	Severo-Osetin (North Osetin), Severo-Osetinskaya ASSR	RSFSR							*	
073	Karayazi, Ikindzhi Shikhly	AN						*		
074	Geigelski, Kirovobad and Khanlar	AN						*		
075	Zakataly, Belokany, and Zakataly	AN						*	*	
076	Ozero Aggyol (Lake Akgyel)	AN				*		*	*	
077	Zaliv Kirova, Kaspiyskoye More (Kirov Bay, Caspian Sea)	AN				*		*	*	
078	Water bodies of the Shirvanskaya Steppe	AN				*		*	*	
079	Pirkuli, Shemakha	AN	*							
080	Shirvanski, Salyany	AN						*		
081	Turian-Chai, Evlakh, and Agdash	AN						*		
082	Agrakhanski Zaliv (Agrakhanski Bay), Dagestan ASSR	RSFSR				*			*	
083	Budary Ozera (Lakes, Budary) complex, Checheno-Ingushskaya ASSR	RSFSR	*							
084	Kizlyarski Zaliv (Kizlyar Bay), Dagestan ASSR	RSFSR				*				
085	Ostrova Chistaya Banka, Ivan-Karaul, Chapurenok, and Nordovyye, Kalmytskaya ASSR	RSFSR				*			*	
086	Volga Delta, Astrakhan Oblast	RSFSR				*		*	*	
087	Ostrov Morskoy Biryuchek (Biryuchek Island) and adjoining waters, Kalmytskaya ASSR	RSFSR				*				
088	Coastal shallows of north-eastern Kaspiyskoye More (Caspian Sea), Guryev	KN				*		*	*	
089	Kamysh-Samarskiye Ozera (Lakes Kamysh-Samarskiye), Uralskaya Oblast	KN	*							
090	Bashkir, Bashkir ASSR	RSFSR	*							
091	Zhigulevsk (I.I. Sprygin Zhiguli) Reserve, Kuybyshev Oblast	RSFSR	*							
092	Vicinity of Borisoglebovka, Saratov Oblast	RSFSR						*	*	
093	Flood-plain of the River Sura, Ulyanovsk Oblast	RSFSR				*				
094	Alatyr Dolina (River Alatyr Valley), Chuvash ASSR	RSFSR	*							
095	Sura Dolina (River Sura Valley), Mordovskaya ASSR	RSFSR	*							
096	Mordovian P.G. Smidovich Reserve, Temnikov, Mordovskaya ASSR	RSFSR						*		

No.	Site name	Region	Criteria used to select site [see p.18]							
			0	1(i)	1(ii)	1(iii)	1(iv)	2	3	4
097	Moksha Dolina (Moksha Valley), Mordovskaya ASSR and Ryazan Oblast	RSFSR	*							
098	Okskaya Dolina (Oka Valley), Ryazan Oblast	RSFSR				*				
099	Khoper, Voronezh Oblast	RSFSR						*		
100	Les Na Vorskle, Belgorod Oblast	RSFSR	*							
101	Oka, Ryazan Oblast	RSFSR						*		
102	Prioksko – Terrasny, Serpukhov, Moskovskaya Oblast	RSFSR	*							
103	Faustovo Flood-plains, Moskovskaya Oblast	RSFSR				*		*	*	
104	Volzhskoye Vodokhranilishche (Volga Reservoir), Uglich, Kalinin Oblast	RSFSR	*							
105	Dubna Marshes (Crane's Native Land), Moskovskaya Oblast	RSFSR				*			*	
106	Moskovskoye Morye, Konakovo, Kalinin Oblast	RSFSR	*							
107	Zavidovo reserve and scientific experimental station (including Diatlovo Ponds) Moskovskaya Oblast and Kalinin Oblast	RSFSR						*		
108	Prof. V.V. Alekhin Tsentralno-Chernozemny (Central Black Earth) Biosphere Reserve, Kursk and Belgorod Oblasts	RSFSR	*							
109	Galichya Gora, Lipetsk Oblast	RSFSR	*							
110	Osveyskoye Ozero (Lake Osveyskoye), Verkhnedvinsk, Belorussia Oblast	RSFSR						*		
111	Karachevskoye Boloto (Karachevskoye Marsh), Vitebsk and Gorodok	BA				*				
112	Obol (marsh), Polotsk and Shumilino	BA	*							
113	Tsentralno-Lesnoy (Central Forest) Reserve, Nelidovo, Kalinin Oblast	RSFSR	*							
114	Rybinskoye Vodokhranilishche (Rybinsk Reservoir), Kalinin, Vologda and Yaroslavl Oblasts	RSFSR				*		*		
115	Gorkovskoye Vodokhranilishche (Gorki Reservoir) and the Lower Unzha, Gorki, Ivanovo and Kostroma Oblasts	RSFSR	*							
116	Flood-plain of River Vetluga, Gorki and Kostroma Oblasts	RSFSR	*							
117	Votkinskoye Vodokhranilishche (Votkinskoye Reservoir), Perm Oblast	RSFSR	*							
118	Pechoro-Ilych, Troitsko-Pechorsk, Komi ASSR	RSFSR	*							
119	Vashutkiny, Padimeyskiye and Khargeyskiye Ozera (Lakes), Arkhangelsk Oblast	RSFSR				*				
120	Vaygach Ostrov (Vaygach Island), Arkhangelsk Oblast	RSFSR				*			*	

No.	Site name	Region	Criteria used to select site [see p.18]							
			0	1(i)	1(ii)	1(iii)	1(iv)	2	3	4
121	Khaypudyrskaya Guba (Khaypudyrskaya Bay), Arkhangelsk Oblast	RSFSR				*				
122	Varandeyskaya Lapta Kosa (Varandeyskaya Lapta Peninsula), Arkhangelsk Oblast	RSFSR				*				
123	River Chernaya, Bolshezemelskaya tundra, Arkhangelsk Oblast	RSFSR				*				
124	Russki Zavorot (Russki Zavorot Peninsula) Nenetski, Arkhangelsk Oblast	RSFSR				*			*	
125	Southern coast of Cheshskaya Guba (Bay), Nenetski, Arkhangelsk Oblast	RSFSR	*							
126	Kanin Poluostrov (Kanin Peninsula), Nenetski, Arkhangelsk Oblast	RSFSR				*				
127	Pinega, Arkhangelsk Oblast	RSFSR	*							
128	Ainovy Ostrova (Ainov Islands), Pechenga, Murmansk Oblast	RSFSR							*	
129	Sem Ostrovov (Seven Islands), Teriberka, Murmansk Oblast	RSFSR							*	
130	Coastal belt of eastern Murmansk, Lovozero, Murmansk Oblast	RSFSR				*				
131	Watershed of the Rivers Lumbovka and Ponoy Reka, Lovozero, Murmansk Oblast	RSFSR				*				
132	Watershed of the Rivers Strelna and Varzuga, Terski, Murmansk Oblast	RSFSR				*		*	*	
133	Middle reaches of the River Ponoy between the River Losinga and the Ponoy Zakaznik, Lovozero, Murmansk Oblast	RSFSR				*		*	*	
134	Chalmny-Varre, Lovozero, Murmansk Oblast	RSFSR				*		*	*	
135	Watershed of the Rivers Iokanga and Ponoy Reka, Lovozero, Murmansk Oblast	RSFSR	*							
136	Lapland, Monchegorsk, Murmansk Oblast	RSFSR						*		
137	Kandalakshskaya Guba (Kandalaksha Bay), Murmansk Oblast and Karelskaya ASSR	RSFSR				*		*		
138	Lakes of northern Karelia, Loukhi, and Kem, Karelskaya ASSR	RSFSR				*		*		
139	Solovetski Arkhipelag (Solovetski Archipelago), Onega, Arkhangelsk Oblast	RSFSR				*				
140	Onezhskaya Guba, Beloye More (Onega Bay, White Sea), Karelskaya ASSR	RSFSR				*		*	*	
141	Kivach, Kondopoga, Karelskaya ASSR	RSFSR	*							
142	Olonyets region, Karelskaya ASSR	RSFSR	*							
143	Kilpola Ostrov (Kilpola Island) and adjoining waters, Leningrad Oblast	RSFSR	*							
144	Svirskaya Guba (Svir Bay), Lodeynoye Pole, Leningrad Oblast	RSFSR				*		*		

No.	Site name	Region	Criteria used to select site [see p.18]							
			0	1(i)	1(ii)	1(iii)	1(iv)	2	3	4
145	Rakovyye Ozera (Rakovyye Lakes), Vsevolozhsk, Leningrad Oblast	RSFSR				*				
146	Vyborgski Zaliv (Vyborg Bay), Vyborg, Leningrad Oblast	RSFSR	*							
147	Koporski Zaliv (Koporski Bay), Kingisepp and Lomonosov, Leningrad Oblast	RSFSR	*							
148	Ozero Vyalye (Lake Vyalye) and adjoining marshes, Gatchina, Leningrad Oblast	RSFSR	*							
149	Sources of the River Oredezh, and Luga, Leningrad Oblast	RSFSR	*							
150	Ozero Ilmen (Lake Ilmen) and adjoining marshy plain, Novgorod Oblast	RSFSR				*				
151	Narvskoye Vodokhranilishche (Narva Reservoir), Kingisepp and Slantsy, Leningrad Oblast	RSFSR				*				
152	Chudsko-Pskovski Vodoyem (Lake Chudsko-Pskov) including the mouth of the River Velikaya, Pskov Oblast	RSFSR	*							

EA=Estoniya LA=Latviya LV=Litva
RSFSR=Russian Soviet Federal Socialist Republic BA=Belorussiya
MA=Moldaviya UA=Ukraina GA=Gruziya AN=Azerbaydzhan KN=Kazakhstan

Comments on the inventory

1. It has already been emphasised that the Soviet Union contains huge tracts of rather homogeneous habitats, where birds may be present in low densities but in highly significant overall numbers. There is the problem of defining an important bird area in, for example, the taiga. The conservation importance of the taiga as a whole cannot be in doubt, but in most circumstances to identify a small area or site of particular value is, at best, both difficult and inappropriate. Thus, the areas in tundra and forest zones which are detailed in this inventory should be seen more as representative examples than as part of a comprehensive list.

2. The vastness of the Soviet Union and difficulties of access to the more remote areas mean that many parts of the country are rather poorly known in ornithological terms by comparison with much of the rest of Europe. It is certain that some areas remain to be discovered which are of greater (or at least equivalent) importance for bird conservation when compared with some of the sites in this inventory.

3. Many of the site accounts have been compiled from published sources. The inventory therefore reflects the limited amount of translation work which could be undertaken with the available resources of time and money.

4. Proper names have, in general, been given as a transliteration of the name in the original language (e.g. Russian, Estonian, etc.) and are sometimes then followed by an English translation of the name in parentheses. Descriptive names are given in English. The site name is then followed either by the name of the Republic where it can be found or by the name of the Autonomous Soviet Socialist Republic/Oblast if the site is within the Russian Soviet Federal Socialist Republic (RSFSR); these are given in parentheses and are the 'regions' used when applying the site-selection criteria (categories 3 and 4).

5. The application of the criteria as depicted in the above table is very provisional. It was decided to include all the internationally and nationally important wetlands listed by Skokova and Vinogradov (1986) for the European part of the Soviet Union. Some of these sites are listed as not meeting the criteria (column 0), although it is felt that they would meet the criteria if further data were available. Furthermore, it was decided to include those nature reserves listed by Borodin and Syroechkovski (1983) if they supported species of interest in a European context. Again, it was difficult to apply the criteria to many of these sites (listed in column 0) because of insufficient data.
6. Some sites are listed as qualifying according to criteria category 1(iii), even though these criteria have been developed, for many of the species, without taking account of waterfowl populations in the USSR/Black Sea region. A greater understanding of waterfowl populations in the USSR is needed before numerical criteria can be developed which will cover the entire western Palearctic.
7. It is possible that there is some overlap of sites included in the inventory, e.g. in cases where a wetland site listed by Skokova and Vinogradov (1986) is part of or is included in a protected area listed by Borodin and Syroechkovski (1983).
8. No area (ha) is given for a small number of the sites because their boundaries have not been defined.

---

001 Laukasoo Marsh, Rakvere, and Harju (Estoniya)

59°40'N, 25°40'E 830 ha

Included in Lahemaa National Park

Marsh with a large number of small lakes, and *Pinus* plantations.
Breeding species include *Gavia arctica*, grebes, and ducks. A passage site for geese.

002 Muraka Marsh, Kokhtla-Järve (Estoniya)

59°05'N, 27°15'E 12,300 ha

Zapovednik

An extensive marsh with moraine ridges covered in woodland.
Breeding species include *Aquila chrysaetos*, *Pluvialis apricaria*, *Numenius phaeopus*, and *Tringa nebularia*.

003 Mouth of the River Emajõgi, Tartu (Estoniya)

58°30'N, 27°15'E 12,000 ha

Unprotected; proposed Ornithological Zakaznik

An extensive, low-lying marsh with lakes on the western shore of Lake Peipsi (Chudskoye Ozero).
An important site for passage swans, geese, ducks, and waders.

004 Nigula Zapovednik, Pärnu (Estoniya)

58°00'N, 24°45'E 2770 ha

Zapovednik surrounded by special protection zone (2100 ha)

Extensive marsh with marshy lakes and moraine ridges covered in woodland.
Breeding species include *Ciconia nigra*, *Aquila pomarina*, *Falco columbarius*, *Grus grus*, *Pluvialis apricaria*, *Tringa ochropus*, *T. glareola*, *Glaucidium passerinum*, *Strix uralensis*, *Dendrocopos leucotos*, *Picoides tridactylus* and *Lanius excubitor*.

005 Matsalu Zaliv (Matsalu Bay) (Estoniya)

58°40-58°54'N, 23°20-23°24'E 48,634 ha Ramsar Site

Matsalu Zapovednik (39,697 ha) in which economic activity and tourism are prohibited (5184 ha) and traditional forms of agriculture are maintained (34,513 ha); additional protected zone (8937 ha) in which hunting is prohibited and economic activities are managed.

A shallow, sea bay enclosed on the seaward side by an archipelago of large rocky islands, and the delta and flood-plain of the River Kasari. There are coastal islands, saltmarshes, extensive reedbeds (3000 ha), grazing pastures, and hay-meadows. The wetland is being adversely affected by: drainage which may damage the wet meadows of the River Kazari; pollution by the effluent from surrounding cattle-breeding farms; accelerating eutrophication, and sport-fishing from motor boats, although steps have been taken to resolve these problems. The site is important for international scientific research and has been the centre for bird ringing in Estonia.

Breeding species include *Botaurus stellaris* (common), *Anser anser* (300 pairs), *Branta leucopsis* (*c.*10 pairs), *Somateria mollissima* (1400 pairs), *Circus aeruginosus* (common), *Larus canus* (2000-2500 pairs), *Sterna caspia* (200 pairs, the only colony in the Soviet Baltic), *S. hirundo*, and *S. paradisaea*. Moulting birds include *Anser anser* (500-600) and *Aythya ferina* (9000). Extremely important during spring and autumn migration. In spring, birds occurring include *Cygnus cygnus* (5000-12,000, max. 40,000), *C. columbianus* (total numbers reaching 5000), *Anser fabalis* (several thousand), *A. albifrons* (2000-3000), *Branta leucopsis* (4000-12,000), more than 1 million diving ducks (predominantly *Melanitta nigra*, *Clangula hyemalis*, and sometimes *Mergus albellus*), *Grus grus* (several hundred), and *Philomachus pugnax* (several hundred thousand). In autumn, birds occurring include *Cygnus* spp. (max. 10,000), *Anser anser* (4000), *Branta leucopsis* (max. 1000), dabbling ducks (30,000-40,000), *Grus grus* (5000-6000, max. 11,000), and *Haliaeetus albicilla*.

006 Nätsi Marsh, Pärnu (Estoniya)

58°30'N, 24°00'E 9800 ha

Zakaznik

Marsh with small lakes and *Pinus* plantations in places.

Breeding species include *Podiceps auritus*, *Grus grus*, *Pluvialis apricaria*, and *Numenius phaeopus*.

007 Suurväin straits, Haapsalu and Kingissepp (Estoniya)

58°30'N, 23°30'E 7000 ha

Sea straits between Muhu Island and the mainland. There is a need to create a Zakaznik covering the period 1 July to 1 September.

Important for moulting *Anser anser* (max. 15,000) and diving ducks (10,000). Hundreds of thousands of waterfowl occur on passage.

008 Lake Käina, Hiiumaa (Estoniya)

58°45'N, 22°30'E 1280 ha

Ornithological Zakaznik

A shallow, overgrown relict lake which is quickly becoming eutrophic because of pollution.

Breeding species include *Cygnus olor* (60 pairs), *Anser anser* (60+ pairs), and *Recurvirostra avosetta* (60 pairs). Waterfowl occur on migration, including *Branta leucopsis*.

009 Vilsandi Archipelago, Kingissepp (Estoniya)

58°20'N, 21°30'E 10,700 ha

Zapovednik surrounded by special protection zone (5500 ha)

Small shingle islands (Vilsandi is the largest island: 890 ha) with granite boulders, surrounded by shallows, on the western edge of Saaremaa island. There is a need to enlarge the state reserve.

Breeding species include *Anser anser*, *Somateria mollissima* (4000 pairs; the most important site in the Baltic), and *Mergus* sp. Important for passage swans and geese (*Branta* spp.).

010 Ollu and Kodu-Kapzemes Bogs (Latviya)

57°58'N, 24°55'E 4300 ha

Zakaznik

The largest bogs in northern Latvia and hardly affected by human activities. Mainly open landscape with three lakes (162 ha, 90 ha, and 25 ha) and numerous smaller lakes and pools in the central part.

Breeding species include *Gavia arctica* (2 pairs), *Grus grus* (5+ pairs), *Aquila chrysaetos* (1 pair), *Pandion haliaetus* (1 pair), *Falco columbarius* (3+ pairs), *Pluvialis apricaria* (50+ pairs), *Numenius phaeopus* (25-30 pairs), *N. arquata* (30-40 pairs), *Tringa glareola* (30-50 pairs), and *T. totanus* (5-6 pairs). In the surrounding forests, *Strix uralensis* and *Picoides tridactylus* breed. An important resting site for migrants, especially *Anser* spp.

011 Teiču Bog, Jēkabpils and Madona (Latviya)

56°30'N, 26°00'E 18,968 ha

Ornithological Zakaznik

The largest raised bog in Latvia with numerous lakes and pools. One of the lakes (*c.*110 ha) is very shallow with rich vegetation. Human activities are limited.

Breeding species include *Gavia arctica* (2-5 pairs), *Tetrao tetrix* (*c.*300 males), *T. urogallus* (30-35 males), *Grus grus* (20-25 pairs), *Pluvialis apricaria* (25 pairs), *Limosa limosa* (*c.*10 pairs), *Numenius phaeopus* (10-15 pairs), *N. arquata* (20-25 pairs), *Tringa totanus* (*c.*5 pairs), *T. glareola* (45-50 pairs), four gull species (max. 700 pairs), and *Lanius excubitor* (3-4 pairs). An important resting site for migrants, especially for *Anser* spp. and *Grus grus*.

012 Gomelis Marsh (Latviya)

56°47'N, 26°59'E *c.*150 ha

Seasonal Zakaznik

Shallow overgrown marsh close to the north-eastern shore of Lubāna Ozero (Lake Lubāna) (separated by an artificial dam). No human disturbance during the breeding season.

Very important for breeding gulls and terns (supporting the largest breeding colonies of *Chlidonias* terns in Latvia), with *Larus minutus* (*c.*2000 pairs), *L. ridibundus* (*c.*500 pairs), *Chlidonias niger* (*c.*2000 pairs), and *C. leucopterus* (50-100 pairs). Other breeding species include *Botaurus stellaris* (1+ pair), about 50-100 pairs of ducks (*Anas platyrhynchos*, *Aythya ferina*, *A. fuligula*), and *Porzana parva*.

013 Lake Babite, Riga (Latviya)

57°00'N, 23°35'E 2655 ha

Ornithological Zakaznik: permanent (385 ha) and seasonal (2270 ha).

Eutrophic freshwater lake with partly artificial shoreline (and rich submerged vegetation) close to the southern shore of the Gulf of Riga (Rizhskiy Zaliv). Surrounded by farmland including wet meadows.

Breeding species include *Botaurus stellaris*, *Ixobrychus minutus*, *Cygnus olor* (80 pairs), *Aythya ferina* (200 pairs), *Larus ridibundus* (27,000 pairs), and *Fulica atra* (1000 pairs). An important site for passage swans, geese, and ducks.

014 Lake Kaņieris, Tukums (Latviya)

57°00'N, 23°30'E 1100 ha

Permanent Zakaznik (97 ha); Seasonal Zakaznik (759 ha)

A eutrophic, freshwater lake on the southern shore of the Gulf of Riga (Rizhskiy Zaliv) with several islands. The bottom of the lake is silty and covered with Characeae. Disturbance from commercial fishing is a negative factor.

Breeding species include *Ciconia nigra*, *Haliaeetus albicilla*, and *Grus grus*, as well as *Cygnus olor* (35 pairs), ducks (1500 pairs), *Fulica atra* (700 pairs), and gulls (4000 pairs).

015 Lake Engure, Talsi and Tukums (Latviya)

57°17'N, 23°07'E 3500 ha

Permanent Zakaznik (1080 ha); Seasonal Zakaznik (2186 ha).

Permanent freshwater lake, with seven islands, separated from the Gulf of Riga (Rizhskiy Zaliv) by a narrow strip of land (1.5–2.5 km) covered with woodland. About 30 per cent of the lake surface is covered by emergent vegetation, mainly *Phragmites*, *Typha*, and *Scirpus*. The bottom is silty and covered in Characeae. Sport fishing and hunting are allowed in part of the lake. There is a plan to reconstruct the lake for fishing, which, if realised, will destroy the waterfowl habitat.

One of the most important wetland breeding sites in the Baltic with *Podiceps cristatus* (500 pairs), *P. grisegena* (100-200 pairs), *P. auritus* (*c.*100 pairs), *Botaurus stellaris* (20-30 pairs), *Ixobrychus minutus* (5-10 pairs), *Ciconia nigra*, *C. ciconia*, *Anser anser* (5-10 pairs), *Aythya ferina* (1000-1300 pairs), *A. fuligula* (250-300 pairs), *Pernis apivorus*, *Haliaeetus albicilla* (1 pair), *Circus aeruginosus* (15-20 pairs), *Aquila pomarina*, *Falco columbarius*, *Bonasa bonasia* (*c.*30 pairs), *Tetrao tetrix* (*c.*15-20 'pairs'), *Grus grus* (*c.*5-8 pairs), *Porzana porzana* (40 pairs), *P. parva* (30 pairs), *Crex crex* (3-5 pairs), *Philomachus pugnax* (20-25 'pairs'), *Larus minutus* (255 pairs), *L. ridibundus* (34,400 pairs), *Sterna hirundo* (300-350 pairs), *Chlidonias niger* (70 pairs), *Bubo bubo* (max. 3 pairs), *Asio flammeus* (max. 3 pairs), *Aegolius funereus* (*c.*3 pairs), *Caprimulgus europaeus* (*c.*30 pairs), *Locustella luscinioides* (80-100 pairs), *Ficedula parva* (*c.*40 pairs), and *Lanius collurio* (*c.*80 pairs). Regularly supports 13,000 Anatidae and 12,000 *Fulica atra* in the post-breeding period.

016 Slitere State Reserve (Latviya)

57°42'N, 22°27'E 15,517 ha

Zapovednik

Situated at the northern end of the Kurzeme Peninsula; mainly woodland with farmland and bogs.

Breeding species include *Ciconia nigra* (2-3 pairs), *C. ciconia* (2-3 pairs), *Pernis apivorus* (10-13 pairs), *Circaetus gallicus* (1 pair), *Aquila clanga* (1-2 pairs), *A. chrysaetos* (1 pair), *Pandion haliaetus* (1-2 pairs), *Bonasa bonasia* (130-150 pairs), *Tetrao tetrix* (80-100 males), *T. urogallus* (30-40 males), *Grus grus* (4-7 pairs), *Crex crex* (6-10 pairs), *Pluvialis apricaria* (6-10 pairs), *Sterna hirundo* (3-5 pairs), *Bubo bubo* (1-2 pairs), *Aegolius funereus* (4-6 pairs), *Caprimulgus europaeus* (*c.*200-250, max. 300 pairs), *Dryocopus martius* (20-30 pairs), *Picoides tridactylus* (1-3 pairs), *Lullula arborea* (70-100 pairs), *Anthus campestris* (5-10 pairs), *Ficedula parva* (150-200 pairs), and *Lanius collurio* (30-40 pairs). The northern tip of the Reserve is a bottleneck site (Kolka Cape) where concentrations of over 12,000 raptors regularly pass during spring migration, with *Pernis apivorus* (*c.*500), *Haliaeetus albicilla* (5), *Accipiter nisus* (3500), *Buteo buteo* (8500), *Aquila chrysaetos* (10) and *Pandion haliaetus* (10). Also *c.*22,000 *Columba palumbus* and hundreds of thousands of passerines occur on passage.

017 Lielais Ķemeru Tīrelis Marsh, Jelgava, Riga, and Tukums (Latviya)

57°00'N, 23°34'E 6000 ha

Ornithological Zakaznik

Marsh with numerous lakes.

Breeding species include *Gavia arctica* and *Grus grus*, as well as dabbling ducks and waders. Also a passage site for geese and cranes.

018 Lake Liepāja, Liepāja (Latviya)

56°30'N, 21°00'E 3750 ha

Ornithological Zakaznik: permanent (394 ha) and seasonal (986 ha)

Eutrophic lake with extensive areas of submerged and emergent vegetation near the western coast of Latvia.

Breeding species include *Gavia arctica* and *Grus grus*, as well as Anatidae (500 pairs). Also a passage site for Anatidae.

019 Lake Pape and adjoining marshland, Liepāja (Latviya)

56°15'N, 21°00'E 2200 ha

Ornithological Zakaznik: permanent (1210 ha) and seasonal (995 ha)

Eutrophic freshwater lake with jagged shoreline and extensive beds of submerged and emergent vegetation, surrounded by marshes and forest.

Breeding species include *Aythya ferina* (500 pairs). A passage site for waterfowl.

020 Kamanos Bog, Akmene (Litva)

56°15'N, 22°30'E 5200 ha

Zapovednik (3660 ha)

Marsh with three small lakes.

A breeding site for *Ciconia nigra*, *C. ciconia*, *Bonasa bonasia*, *Tetrao tetrix*, *T. urogallus*, Rallidae, *Grus grus*, waders, and *Dryocopus martius*.

021 Lakes Biržulis and Styrvas, Telšiai (Litva)

55°40'N, 22°15'E 122 ha and 136 ha

Zakaznik (2500 ha) and proposed Zapovednik

Two small lakes with low-lying marshes.

Breeding birds include *Ciconia nigra*, *Grus grus*, waders and terns.

022 Nemunas Delta, Šilutė (Litva)

55°18'N, 21°15'E 14,100 ha

Botanical/Zoological Zakaznik

A delta complex. Extension of the polder system at the boundaries of the Zakaznik is adversely affecting the hydrological and hydrochemical regime.

Breeding species include *Botaurus stellaris* (20 pairs), *Ixobrychus minutus* (20 pairs), *Haliaeetus albicilla* (1 pair), *Porzana porzana* (10-20 pairs), *P. parva* (15 pairs), *Crex crex* (50-70 pairs), *Limosa limosa* (20 pairs), *Sterna hirundo* (250 pairs), *S. albifrons* (90 pairs), and *Chlidonias niger* (200 pairs). Passage waterfowl include *Podiceps cristatus* (1000), *Cygnus cygnus* (1000), *Anser fabalis* (5000), *Aythya fuligula* (20,000), *Bucephala clangula* (8000), and *Mergus merganser* (1000).

023 Kuršiu Bay, Nemunas (Litva), Zelenogradsk and Polessk, Kaliningrad (RSFSR)

55°15'N, 21°00'E 45,000 ha

Unprotected

Shallow, marine bay.

Breeding species include *Botaurus stellaris* (10 pairs), *Haliaeetus albicilla* (1 pair), *Circus aeruginosus* (10 pairs), *Tetrao tetrix* (50 'pairs'), *Porzana porzana* (100 pairs), *P. parva* (15 pairs), *Crex crex* (20-30 pairs), *Limosa limosa* (50 pairs), *Sterna hirundo* (30 pairs), and *Dryocopus martius* (15-20 pairs). Large concentrations of waterfowl occur on passage including *Podiceps cristatus* (5000), *Cygnus cygnus* (1500), *Anser fabalis* (10,000), *Aythya fuligula* (3000), *Bucephala clangula* (10,000), and *Mergus merganser* (2000, max. 5000).

024 Lake Žuvintas and adjoining marshes, Alytus (Litva)

54°20'N, 23°35'E 11,400 ha

Zapovednik (5424 ha)

An overgrown eutrophic lake surrounded by low-lying marshes. The breeding bird populations are declining because of eutrophication.

Breeding species include *Podiceps cristatus* (max. 170 pairs), *Ciconia nigra*, *Cygnus olor* (30-60 pairs), and *Grus grus*. A passage site for geese and ducks.

025 Marshes on the River Čepkeliai, including the lower Merkys and Katra Reka Valley, Varėna (Litva)

54°10'N, 24°45'E 14,800 ha

Zapovednik (8469 ha)

Extensive marshes with 22 small lakes and treeless dunes.

Important for breeding waders that are rare in the Baltic (*Pluvialis apricaria*, *Calidris alpina*, and *Numenius arquata*) and for *Grus grus* (10 pairs).

026 Lake Kretuonas, Švenčionys (Litva)

55°30'N, 26°20'E 829 ha (lake only)

Ornithological Zakaznik (2216 ha)

Eutrophic freshwater lake (with six islands, five covered in woodland) with *Scirpus* and *Phragmites* beds. The bottom is sandy, with Characeae. Surrounded by woodland, marshes, and wet meadows.

Breeding species include *Podiceps cristatus* (100 pairs), *Botaurus stellaris* (1-2 pairs), *Milvus migrans* (1 pair), *Circus aeruginosus* (2 pairs), *Tetrao tetrix* (2 'pairs'), *Crex crex* (3 pairs), *Philomachus pugnax* (16 pairs), *Gallinago media* (1 pair), *Limosa limosa* (3 pairs), *Sterna hirundo* (250 pairs), *S. albifrons* (2 pairs), *Chlidonias niger* (40 pairs), *Coracias garrulus* (2 pairs), and *Dryocopus martius* (2 pairs).

027 Berezina (Belorussiya)

*c.*54°50'N, 28°10'E 76,201 ha Biosphere Reserve

Zapovednik

An area of the Berezina lowlands, dissected by the Berezina river valley. Habitats include elevated glacial plains, river flood-plains, and peatlands, with undulating moraine hills. Woodland is mostly *Pinus*, *Betula*, and *Alnus*.

Two hundred species occur, including breeding *Ciconia nigra*, *C. ciconia*, *Anas crecca*, *A. querquedula*, *Bucephala clangula*, *Aquila pomarina*, *A. chrysaetos*, *Bonasa bonasia*, *Tetrao tetrix*, *T. urogallus*, *Grus grus*, and *Limosa limosa*. *Gavia arctica* and Anatidae occur on passage, whilst wintering species include *Bombycilla garrulus*, *Pinicola enucleator*, and *Plectrophenax nivalis*.

028 Telekhany, Ivatsevichi, and Lyakhovichi, Brest (Belorussiya)

52°15'N, 23°55'E 10,947 ha

Zapovednik

The reserve includes the Polesskaya marshy lowlands and the River Pripyat at the watershed of the Rivers Pripyat and Nemunas.

One hundred and ninety-four species occur, including *Podiceps cristatus*, *P. auritus*, *Anas crecca*, *A. querquedula*, *Aythya ferina*, *A. nyroca*, *Haliaeetus albicilla*, *Tetrao tetrix*, *T. urogallus*, *Sterna hirundo*, *Chlidonias niger*, and *Bubo bubo*.

029 Belovezhskaya pushcha, Brest, and Grodno (Belorussiya)

*c.*52°45'N, 24°05'E 87,577 ha

Zapovednik

A low-lying region (rising to 150-170 m) near the border with Poland. The area includes parts of the Rivers Narev, Narevka, and Lesna, two artificial ponds, meadows, and vast tracts of virgin forest. The avifauna is very rich, reflecting the diversity of habitats and the meeting of eastern and western faunal elements.

Species occurring include *Ciconia nigra*, *C. ciconia*, *Anas acuta*, *Pernis apivorus*, *Milvus migrans*, *M. milvus*, *Circus* spp. *Aquila pomarina*, *A. clanga*, *Hieraaetus pennatus*, *Falco peregrinus*, *Bonasa bonasia*, *Tetrao tetrix*, *T. urogallus*, *Philomachus pugnax*, *Gallinago gallinago*, *G. media*, *Strix uralensis*, *Dendrocopos leucotos*, and *Sylvia nisoria*.

030 Pripyat; Zhitkovichi, Lelchitsy and Petrikov, Gomel (Belorussiya)

*c.*52°10'N, 28°30'E 62,213 ha

Zapovednik

The northern part of the area includes marshy plains, and low narrow ridges alternating with flat lowlands. The southern part is characterised by irregularly distributed and variously shaped dunes. Other habitats include bogs, streams, lakes, three rivers (including the Pripyat), and *Pinus* woods.

Two hundred and fifty species occur (193 breeding), including *Ciconia nigra*, *C. ciconia*, *Milvus migrans*, *Tetrao urogallus*, and *Grus grus*.

031 Kodry, Strasheny (Moldaviya)

*c.*47°09'N, 28°39'E 5159 ha

Unprotected

Part of Kapriyanovsko-Lozovo forest in Central Kodry, north-west of Kishinev, with tracts of *Quercus*, *Fagus*, *Fraxinus*, *Tilia*, *Betula*, *Acer* etc.

Ninety-nine species occur, including *Aquila pomarina*, *A. clanga*, *A. heliaca*, *A. chrysaetos*, *Hieraaetus pennatus*, *Bubo bubo*, other Strigidae, and *Lullula arborea*.

032 Karpatski (Carpathians), Zakarpatskaya and Ivano-Frankovskaya Oblasts (Ukraina)

*c.*48°30'N, 24°30'E 18,544 ha

Zapovednik

The steep slopes of secondary uplands, including the highest point of the Soviet Carpathians. Subalpine and alpine vegetation belts are restricted to Chernogora.

One hundred and eighty species occur, including *Bonasa bonasia*, *Tetrao tetrix*, *T. urogallus*, *Strix uralensis*, and *Dendrocopos leucotos*.

033 Shatskiye Ozera (Lake Shatskiye), Volynskaya Oblast (Ukraina)

51°33'N, 23°50'E 5710 ha

Included in National Park (32,500 ha)

Overgrown freshwater lakes.

Breeding species include *Botaurus stellaris* (10-13 pairs), *Ciconia nigra* (3 pairs), *Circaetus gallicus* (1-3 pairs), *Porzana porzana* (*c.*10-15 pairs), *Limosa limosa* (60-70 pairs), *Bubo bubo* (2-3 pairs), *Caprimulgus europaeus* (40-50 pairs), *Dryocopus martius*

(5-6 pairs), *Lullula arborea* (10-15 pairs), and *Lanius collurio* (40-50 pairs). Waterfowl occurring on passage include *Anser fabalis* (2000-3000), *A. albifrons* (1000-2000), *A. anser* (800-1000), *Aythya ferina* (5000-10,000), *Fulica atra* (7000-12,000), and *Grus grus* (2000-3000). Large numbers of hirundines also roost on passage: *Hirundo rustica* (max. 50,000), *Delichon urbica* (5000-7000), and *Riparia riparia* (3000-4000).

034 Polesski, Zhitomir (Ukraina)

*c.*51°25'N, 27°55'E 20,104 ha

Zapovednik

An area of *Pinus* forest (73 per cent), bogs (21.5 per cent) and meadows (2 per cent) between the Rivers Ubort and Bolotnitsa.

Species occurring include *Ciconia nigra*, *Bonasa bonasia*, *Tetrao tetrix*, and *T. urogallus*.

035 Kanevskoye Vodokhranilishche (Kanev Reservoir), Kiyev (Ukraina)

50°00'N, 31°30'E *c.*200 ha

Unprotected

The western bank of the reservoir between Tripolye and Staiki, which remains unfrozen in winter.

One of the most important sites for wintering waterfowl in the Kiev region with *Anas platyrhynchos* (500-2000), *Bucephala clangula* (200-400), and *Mergus merganser* (400-600). *Haliaeetus albicilla* (max. 10) also winters.

036 Kanev, Cherkassy (Ukraina)

*c.*49°46'N, 31°28'E 1030 ha

Zapovednik

An area of *Quercus/Carpinus* forest to the west of the River Dnepr.

Two hundred and eighteen species (over 100 breed) occur, including *Botaurus stellaris*, *Ciconia nigra*, *C. ciconia*, *Haliaeetus albicilla*, *Circus aeruginosus*, *Aquila chrysaetos*, *Pandion haliaetus*, *Falco vespertinus*, and *Grus grus*.

037 Lugansk, Voroshilovgrad Oblast (Ukraina)

*c.*49°18'N, 39°52'E 1580 ha

Zapovednik

This reserve is divided into three nearby but independent sections: Streltsovskaya *Festuca/Stipa* steppe (494 ha); Stanichno-Lugansk riverine forest, and seven lakes (494 ha) in the valley of the River Severski Donets; and Provalskaya (stony) steppe (587.5 ha).

Species occurring include *Milvus migrans*, *Falco vespertinus*, *Grus grus*, *Asio flammeus*, and *Anthus campestris*. Also occasional *Tetrax tetrax* and *Otis tarda*.

038 Ukrainian Steppe Reserve, Sumy, Donetsk, and Zaporozhe (Ukraina)

*c.*47°30'N, 36°30'E 1634 ha

Zapovednik

Khomutovo steppe, 23 km north of the Sea of Azov (Azovskoye More); Kammenye mogili; Mikhaylovskaya tselina (virgin steppe).

Species occurring include *Botaurus stellaris*, *Ixobrychus minutus*, *Ardea purpurea*, *Milvus migrans*, *Falco vespertinus*, *Anthropoides virgo*, *Caprimulgus europaeus*, and *Melanocorypha calandra*.

039 Krivaya Kosa (Krivaya Peninsula), Novoazovsk Donetsk (Ukraina)

47°10'N, 38°10'E 154 ha

Zapovednik

Peninsula in the Sea of Azov (Azovskoye More). Heavy recreational pressure and the planned building of fish-ponds may substantially affect the site.

Breeding species include *Egretta alba* (max. 10 pairs), *Ardea purpurea* (max. 10 pairs), *Himantopus himantopus* (50-80 pairs; the largest colony in the Ukraine), *Recurvirostra avosetta* (30-120 pairs), *Glareola pratincola*, *G. nordmanni*, *Sterna sandvicensis* (70-1900 pairs), *S. hirundo* (1700-3000 pairs), and *S. albifrons* (500-1000 pairs). Passage species include *Ciconia nigra*, *Branta ruficollis*, *Haliaeetus albicilla*, *Aquila chrysaetos*, and *Pandion haliaeetus*.

040 Belosarayskaya Kosa (Belosarayskaya Peninsula), Volodarskoye, Donetsk (Ukraina)

47°00'N, 37°18'E 616 ha

Zapovednik

Peninsula in the Sea of Azov (Azovskoye More).

Breeding species include *Egretta alba* (8-20 pairs), *Recurvirostra avosetta* (12-35 pairs), *Sterna hirundo* (1600 pairs), and *S. albifrons* (500 pairs).

041 Berdyanskaya Kosa (Berdyansk Peninsula), Berdyansk, Zhdanov (Ukraina)

46°50'N, 36°45'E

Unprotected

Peninsula in the Sea of Azov (Azovskoye More) including the coastal shallows, low bare islands, and shores of Berdyansk Bay (Berdyanski Zaliv).

A breeding site for ducks, waders, gulls, terns, and passage and wintering waterfowl.

042 Obitochnaya Kosa (Obitochnaya Peninsula), Primorskoye, Zhdanov (Ukraina)

46°35'N, 36°20'E

Unprotected; proposed Zapovednik

Peninsula in the Sea of Azov (Azovskoye More) including the coastal shallows, low shores, and small islands of Obitochny Bay.

A site for *Egretta alba* (50 pairs), breeding ducks, waders, gulls, terns, and passage and wintering waterfowl.

043 Molochny Liman, Melitopol (Ukraina)

46°20'N, 35°20'E 22,450 ha

Zapovednik

A salt-lake (with fluctuating salinity) separated from the Sea of Azov (Azovskoye More) by a narrow spit, with extensive shallows and a group of islands. Irregular water supply via a canal leads to seasonal fluctuations in salinity (resulting in destruction of the water vegetation) and the upper part of the lake is greatly polluted with sewage from Melitopol.

A breeding site for grebes, waders, gulls, and terns. *Branta ruficollis* and *Numenius tenuirostris* occur on passage, as well as large numbers of commoner waterfowl (max. 30,000).

044 Sivash Zaliv, Azovskoye More (Sivash Bay, Sea of Azov) (Ukraina)

46°09-46°12'N, 34°21-34°50'E 45,700 ha Ramsar Site

Part of Azovskoye-Sivash Zapovednik Hunting Reserve (22,389 ha), althoug[illegible]
sites for birds remain unprotected, and some parts are not included in [illegible]

A shallow, saltwater bay with an indented shoreline, numerous spits and islands, largely isolated from the Sea of Azov by a low-lying spit (Arabatskaya Strelka). The water-level fluctuates according to the meteorological conditions (with strong winds exposing or inundating large areas) and the extent of evaporation in hot weather. A dam at Chongar Peninsula (Chongarski Poluostrov) also regulates the water allowed in from the Sea of Azov. The habitat is mainly saltmarshes, steppe and halophytic vegetation with extensive *Phragmites* beds. Agricultural development in the surrounding area, especially the creation of fish-ponds and rice-fields, has increased the area of freshwater. There is little economic exploitation except for industrial fishing and salt extraction in the eastern part, however excessive disturbance results from amateur fishing (up to 900-1200 boats per day) and recreation, and there is egg collecting. In addition, the ploughing of virgin steppe, and haymaking and sheep grazing on Kuyuk-Tuk Island (Kuyuk-Tuk Ostrov) are considered to be unfavourable factors.

Breeding birds include Ardeidae and Threskiornithidae (at least 10,000-11,000 pairs of *Nycticorax nycticorax*, *Ardeola ralloides*, *Egretta garzetta*, *E. alba*, *Ardea purpurea*, and *Plegadis falcinellus*), *Tadorna tadorna* (500 pairs), *Anthropoides virgo* (15-18 pairs on Kuyuk-Tuk and Churyuk islands, and additional pairs on the mainland), *Otis tarda* (2-3 'pairs'), *Recurvirostra avosetta* (700 pairs), *Larus ichthyaetus* (96-168 pairs), *L. melanocephalus* (1400-1650 pairs), *L. genei* (270-3915 pairs), *L. argentatus* (1600-2620 pairs), *Gelochelidon nilotica* (220-1060 pairs), *Sterna caspia* (56-159 pairs), *S. sandvicensis* (483-5463), *S. hirundo* (97-1030 pairs), and *S. albifrons* (70-900 pairs). There are additional colonies of *Larus melanocephalus*, *L. genei*, *Gelochelidon nilotica*, and *Sterna sandvicensis* with up to 20,000 pairs. In spring, up to 1000 *Otis tarda* occur on Kuyuk-Tuk. The bay serves as an important staging post for waterfowl, especially in spring, with up to 60,000-80,000 ducks (predominantly *Aythya fuligula*, *A. ferina*, *Tadorna tadorna* and *Anas platyrhynchos*) and *Fulica atra*, and hundreds of thousands of waders (predominantly *Philomachus pugnax*, *Calidris ferruginea*, *C. alpina*, and *Tringa totanus*), with the steppe parts of Churyuk and Kuyuk-Tuk islands used by *Charadrius morinellus*.

045 Krymski (Crimean) Game Reserve, Krym (Ukraina)

*c.*44°50'N, 34°30'E 42,957 ha

Zapovednik (14,998 ha)

The northern and southern slopes of the main Crimean range, including *Quercus-Pinus-Fagus* forest (27,957 ha), rivers (total area of open water approaches 10,000 ha), meadows (over 2400 ha), and a coastal zone including the Lebyazhi Islands (see site 046 below).

One hundred and eighty-five species occur (72 breeding), including *Gavia arctica*, *Egretta alba* (rare), *Ciconia nigra* (rare), *Aythya nyroca*, other Anatidae, *Haliaeetus albicilla*, *Neophron percnopterus*, *Gyps fulvus*, *Aegypius monachus*, *Circaetus gallicus*, and *Bubo bubo*.

046 Karkinitski Zaliv, Chernoye More (Karkinitski Bay, Black Sea) (Ukraina)

45°50'-45°46'N, 33°22-33°47'E 37,300 ha

Part of Crimean Zapovednik/Hunting Reserve; Karkinitski Zakaznik (27,646 ha); the sea [...]ound the islands is protected to a distance of 1 km offshore

[...]d of Karkinitski Bay with numerous spits, shallow bays, and salt lakes adjoining
[...]in steppe and agricultural land. There are some small, permanent islands
[...]a) which are either vegetationless or covered by *Phragmites* beds and
[...]he total area of the islands has been reduced by erosion. The
[...]bmerged vegetation, primarily Characeae and *Zostera*. The
[...]d rice-growing has resulted in the uncontrolled release of
[...]e productivity of the Characeae and *Zostera*. In
[...]f fish-eating birds, rice-growing, sheep-grazing,
[...]dversely affecting the wetland and its birds,
[...]emnant steppe. The site is regarded as

inadequately protected with no control on poaching. As a result of these problems many species are declining.

Breeding species include *Phalacrocorax carbo* (500-600 pairs), *Ardeola ralloides* (max. 200 pairs), *Egretta garzetta*, *E. alba*, *Ardea cinerea* (700-1500 pairs), *Plegadis falcinellus* (100-150 pairs), *Larus ichthyaetus* (120-130 pairs), *L. argentatus* (6800-10,000 pairs), *Gelochelidon nilotica* (800-900 pairs), *Sterna caspia* (100-300 pairs), and *S. hirundo* (200-300 pairs). Large numbers of *Cygnus olor* (4000-5000) moult. Anatidae occur during spring and autumn migration (max. 75,000), and several hundred thousand *Philomachus pugnax* occur. In winter more than 20,000 duck may be present.

047 Yalta Mountain Forest, Bolshaya Yalta, Krym (Ukraina)

*c.*44°30'N, 34°10'E 14,591 ha

Zapovednik

A band of forest (1–8 km wide), with stands of *Pinus*, *Quercus*, *Fagus*, and *Carpinus* on the southern slopes of the Crimea range.

Species occurring include *Gyps fulvus*.

048 Mys Martyan, Krym (Ukraina)

44°30'N, 34°09'E 240 ha

Zapovednik

An area of *Quercus* and *Juniperus* forest on the southern slopes of the Crimean Mountains, on the Black Sea coast.

One hundred and thirty-five species occur, including *Phalacrocorax aristotelis*.

049 Chumaki Ostrova, Dzarylgachski Zaliv (Chumaki Islands, Dzharylgach Bay), Skadovsk and Kalanchak, Kherson (Ukraina)

46°00'N, 32°55'E.

Unprotected

Small islands and coastal shallows in a bay of the Black Sea (Chernoye More). The islands are experiencing excessive recreational pressure and it is necessary to establish a seasonal Zakaznik.

Breeding birds include ducks (hundreds) and gulls (thousands). Hundreds of thousands of wildfowl occur during migration including *Branta ruficollis* (20,000).

050 Nizovya Dnepra (Lower Dnepr), Golaya Pristan, Kherson (Ukraina)

46°30'N, 32°20'E

Unprotected; proposed Zakaznik

Water channels, *Phragmites* beds, and marshy islands.

Breeding birds include grebes (hundreds) and Ciconiiformes (thousands). A passage site for *Anser anser* (thousands) and dabbling ducks (thousands).

051 Askania – Nova, Kherson (Ukraina)

*c.*46°27'N, 33°53'E 33,307 ha Biosphere Reserve

Zapovednik (only 1500 ha under total protection)

An area of arid (except for a few lakes) *Festuca-Stipa* steppe. The totally protected area has never been ploughed, whilst the remainder is used for grazing and haymaking.

Sixteen species breed in the virgin steppe area, including *Circus macrourus*, *Aquila rapax nipalensis*, *Anthropoides virgo*, *Tetrax tetrax*, *Otis tarda*, *Burhinus oedicnemus*, *Calandrella brachydactyla*, and *Anthus campestris*. The lakes and pond areas hold *c.*70 breeding species, including *Tadorna ferruginea*, *Circus macrourus*, and *Lanius minor*.

052 Dunay (Danube) and Yagorlytski and Tendrovski Zalivy (Yagorlytski and Tendra Bays) (Ukraina)

Information is provided for the following subsites:

052-1 Dunay (Danube) (Ukraina)

45°25'-45°30'N, 29°32'-29°40'E 14,851 ha

Part of Ramsar Site (with Yagorlyski and Tendrovski Zalivy)

Includes Dunay Zapovednik (14,851 ha)

The Soviet part of the Danube Delta with alluvial islands, numerous channels and a coastal zone (with shallow, open bays divided from the sea by low sand-spits or underwater bars). The islands are covered with dense *Phragmites* beds or with *Salix alba* woodland. At present there are no protected zones where human activities are completely prohibited, and the main problem is human disturbance since commercial fishing is permitted throughout the year and the best fishing areas are the same as the main breeding, feeding, and resting sites for birds.

Breeding species include *Nycticorax nycticorax* (350 pairs), *Ardeola ralloides* (50 pairs), *Egretta garzetta* (150 pairs), *E. alba* (40 pairs), *Ardea purpurea* (400 pairs), *Plegadis falcinellus* (100 pairs), *Platalea leucorodia* (60 pairs), *Recurvirostra avosetta* (100 pairs), *Sterna sandvicensis* (2000 pairs), *S. hirundo* (10,000-11,000 pairs), and *S. albifrons* (50 pairs). *Pelecanus onocrotalus* and *P. crispus* feed at the site, breeding in the Romanian part of the delta. Non-breeding *Philomachus pugnax* and *Limosa limosa* oversummer (6000 birds), and *Cygnus olor* (800) gathers to moult. A considerable variety of birds occurs on passage, the following being common: *Phalacrocorax pygmeus*, *Branta ruficollis*, and *Sterna caspia*. Up to 50,000 waterfowl occur in winter including *Cygnus cygnus* (max. 1000), *Anser albifrons* (10,000), and *A. anser* (3000).

052-2 Yagorlytski and Tendrovski Zalivy (Yagorlytski and Tendra Bays) (Ukraina)

46°07'-46°30'N, 31°49'-32°22'E 113,200 ha

Part of a Ramsar Site (with Dunay); Biosphere Reserve (87,348 ha)

Includes land areas of Chernomorski (Black Sea) Zapovednik and Yagorlytski/Tendrovski Zalivy islands Zapovednik (total area: 10,448 ha); Yagorlytski Zakaznik (30,300 ha)

Large sea bays (separated from the Black Sea by a narrow peninsula) with islands, adjoined by numerous small lakes and temporary waterbodies. Emergent vegetation is represented by beds of *Phragmites*, *Typha*, and *Scirpus*, with the bays surrounded by salt-meadow/steppe and forest-steppe. On the islands, halophytic vegetation is dominant. Since 1975, the hydrological balance has been upset (affecting the productivity of the ecosystem) by the release of fresh water from irrigation and rice-growing schemes, and saline water from a drainage system near Potiyevka. In addition, there is disturbance during the breeding season from commercial fishing.

Breeding species include *Podiceps grisegena*, *Botaurus stellaris* (common), *Ixobrychus minutus*, *Egretta alba* (common), *Somateria mollissima* (breeding since 1975, and of considerable biogeographical interest), *Mergus serrator* (800-900 pairs), *Recurvirostra avosetta* (400-700 pairs), *Glareola pratincola*, *G. nordmanni*, *Larus melanocephalus* (170,000-270,000 pairs on Orlov, Babin and Smaleny islands), *L. genei* (10,000-20,000 pairs), *Gelochelidon nilotica*, *Sterna caspia* (150 pairs), *S. sandvicensis* (max. 23,500 pairs), *S. hirundo* (3400-4900 pairs), and *S. albifrons*. About 500,000 birds of 45 species winter including *Cygnus olor* and *C. cygnus* (combined max. 23,000) and *Anas platyrhynchos* (250,000). *Branta ruficollis*, *Haliaeetus albicilla*, *Aquila heliaca*, *Tetrax tetrax*, *Otis tarda*, and *Numenius tenuirostris* also occur.

053 Tiligulski Liman (Tiligul Salt-lake), Berezanka and Kominternovskoye (Ukraina)

46°50'N, 31°00'E

Unprotected

Shallow salt-lake with *Phragmites* beds and sandy islands.
Breeding species include *Recurvirostra avosetta* (200 pairs). Up to 80,000 wintering waterfowl occur.

054 Nizovya Dnestra (Lower Dnestr), Belgorod-Dnestrovski and Ovidiopol (Ukraina)

46°15'N, 30°20'E

Unprotected; proposed Zapovednik

Salt-lakes and *Phragmites* beds.
Breeding birds include Phalacrocoracidae (220 pairs), Ciconiiformes (3500 pairs), *Cygnus olor* (170 pairs), *Anser anser* (1600 pairs), and ducks (max. 10,000 pairs).

055 Coastal lakes between the Rivers Dnestr and Dunay (Danube), Kiliya, Tatarbunary, and Belgorod-Dnestrovski (Ukraina)

45°40'N, 30°00'E 200,000 ha

Unprotected

Salt-lakes, canals, and reservoirs. It is necessary to determine the most important areas.
Breeding species include *Tadorna tadorna* (500 pairs). Very important for winter waterfowl (500,000), including swans (10,000). Other wintering species include *Haliaeetus albicilla* (50).

056 Karadag, Sudak, Krymskaya (Crimean) Oblast (Ukraina)

45°00'N, 35°15'E 1370 ha

Zapovednik

Includes 188 ha of forest, 300 ha of meadows, and 600 ha of adjacent sea.
One hundred and ten species occur, including *Pernis apivorus*, *Aquila heliaca*, *Falco cherrug*, *F. peregrinus*, and *Alectoris chukar*.

057 Salt-lakes (Limany) in the Primorsko-Akhtarsk/Grivenskaya area (including Akhtarski Liman and Liman Sladki) (Krasnoder Kray, RSFSR)

46°00'N, 38°00'E 118,340 ha

Partly a Zakaznik

Shallow salt-lakes connected by a dense network of channels alongside the Sea of Azov (Azovskoye More), with extensive beds of emergent and submerged vegetation. The development of irrigated agriculture is reducing the area of the wetland and the lakes are becoming shallower and more saline, whilst chemical run-off from farmland is causing eutrophication of the water bodies. If the degradation of the area is halted, it will be proposed for designation as a Ramsar Site.
A breeding site for pelicans, herons, and other waterfowl, with *Cygnus olor* (3200), *Anser anser* (5000), ducks (648,000), and *Fulica atra* (460,000) present after breeding. Important for moulting ducks (600,000-1,000,000) and wintering waterfowl (hundreds of thousands).

058 Kavkaz (Caucasus) Biosphere Reserve, Sochi (Krasnodar Kray, RSFSR)

*c.*43°40'N, 40°30'E 266,000 ha Biosphere Reserve

Zapovednik

The western part of the Main Caucasian Ridge and Peredovoy Ridge, with forested (162,319 ha) mountainous terrain including many glacier-fed rivers and streams. Also includes the south-east slope of Bolshoi Akhun Mountain.
One hundred and ninety-two species occur (132 breeding), including *Gypaetus barbatus*, *Gyps fulvus*, *Aegypius monachus*, *Aquila chrysaetos*, *Tetrao mlokosiewiczi*, and *Tetraogallus caucasicus*.

059 Veselovskoye Vodokhranilishche (Veselovskoye Reservoir) (Rostov Oblast, RSFSR)

47°00'N, 41°30'E 50,000 ha

Unprotected

A reservoir with extensive *Phragmites* beds.

Breeding species include *Anser anser* (7000-8000 birds after the breeding season), ducks (thousands), and *Fulica atra* (2500 pairs). Large numbers of geese (100,000) including *Branta ruficollis* (25,000) and ducks (150,000) occur on passage.

060 Eastern Manych, Ozero (Lake) Manych-Gudilo (Kalmytskaya ASSR, RSFSR)

46°15'N, 43°00'E 50,000 ha

Zakaznik

Lake with extensive shallows and *Phragmites* beds.

Important for breeding pelicans with *Pelecanus onocrotalus* (50 pairs; the only breeding site in the European part of the USSR except for the Danube Delta, where only a few pairs now breed), and *Pelecanus crispus* (200 pairs). Also breeding Ciconiiformes, Anatidae (hundreds of pairs), and Laridae. The site also supports large numbers of moulting *Cygnus olor* (500), *Tadorna tadorna* (22,000) and other ducks (20,000), and passage (autumn) *Anser albifrons* (45,000), *A. erythropus* (5000), and *Branta ruficollis* (25,000, with 1500 wintering if the weather is mild).

061 Burukshunskiye Limany (Burukshunskiye Salt-lakes) (Kalmytskaya ASSR, RSFSR)

45°55'N, 43°40'E 6000-8000 ha

Zakaznik (3500 ha)

A chain of saline, brackish, and freshwater water bodies with beds of *Phragmites* in the vicinity of Pravoyegorlyk Canal.

Supports large numbers of post-breeding waterfowl including Ciconiiformes (1200), ducks (70,000), waders (50,000), and *Fulica atra* (40,000). Up to 500,000 waterfowl occur on passage.

062 Teberda, Karachaevo (Cherkesskaya Oblast, RSFSR)

*c.*43°30'N, 41°35'E 90,300 ha

Zapovednik

The upper reaches of the Rivers Teberda, Arkhyz, and Zelenchuk on the north slopes of the Bolshoi Caucasus. Habitats include big glaciers, alpine meadows, and mountain forest.

One hundred and seventy species, including *Gypaetus barbatus, Aquila chrysaetos, Falco subbuteo, Tetrao mlokosiewiczi, Tetraogallus caucasicus, Alectoris chukar, Tichodroma muraria,* and *Carpodacus rubicilla.*

063 Kabardino-Balkarski, Sovetskoye and Chegem (Kabardino-Balkarskaya ASSR, RSFSR)

*c.*42°40'N, 43°40'E 74,081 ha

Zapovednik

The upper reaches of the Rivers Cherek Balkarski, Cherek Bizengiyski, and Chegem, with forests and meadows (mainly high mountain zones; several 5000 m peaks in the Bokovoy range) in a rugged landscape with deep ravines etc.

Breeding *Tetrao mlokosiewiczi, Tetraogallus* sp., and *Alectoris chukar.*

064 Nizovya Reki Rioni, Ozero Paliastomi (Lower Rioni, Lake Paliastomi) (Gruziya)

42°10'N, 41°40'E 500 ha

Zapovednik

Coastal marshes, channels, and lakes on the Black Sea (Chernoye More) coast.
A site for passage and wintering Ciconiiformes, ducks, and waders. There is also a bottleneck site for raptors in this region.

065 Pskhuski, Abkhazskaya ASSR (Gruziya)

*c.*43°25'N, 40°50'E 27,643 ha

Zapovednik

An area of forest (mostly broadleaved) with small tracts of meadows (208 ha) and open water (31 ha).
Species occurring include *Milvus migrans*, *Tetrao mlokosiewiczi*, and *Tetraogallus caucasicus*.

066 Gumistin, Sukhumi, Abkhazskaya ASSR (Gruziya)

*c.*43°20'N, 40°40'E 13,400 ha

Zapovednik
An area of the Bzybski range, between the Black Sea and the Caucasus, with forest (12,600 ha), meadows (80 ha), sands (7 ha), steep slopes, screes, cliffs, and open water. The principal tree species are *Fagus*, *Castanea*, *Carpinus*, *Quercus*, *Abies*, and *Rhododendron*.
Species occurring include *Tetrao mlokosiewiczi* and *Tetraogallus caucasicus*.

067 Ritsa, Gudauta, Abkhazskaya ASSR (Gruziya)

*c.*43°28'N, 40°34'E 16,289 ha

Zapovednik

An area of *Abies* forests surrounding Lake Ritsa on the southern spurs of the main Caucasus range. Forest covers 14,922 ha. There are also small areas of meadows, and deep river gorges.
Species occurring include *Gypaetus barbatus*, *Gyps fulvus*, *Aegypius monachus*, *Aquila chrysaetos*, *Tetrao mlokosiewiczi*, and *Tetraogallus caucasicus*.

068 Kintrishi, Kobuleti, Adzharskaya ASSR (Gruziya)

*c.*41°45'N, 41°50'E 7166 ha

Zapovednik

An area of the west and north-west slopes of the Meskhetsk range, with over 6500 ha of forest, subalpine lakes, and the gorge of the River Kintrishi.
Species include *Tetraogallus caucasicus*.

069 Lagodekhi, Kvarelsk (Gruziya)

*c.*41°27'N, 46°00'E 17,818 ha

Zapovednik

A belt of *Fagus*/*Quercus* forests, subalpine/alpine meadows, and lakes alongside the River Alazani on the spurs of the southern slope of the main Caucasus range. The relief is complex, with numerous gorges, and the river forms torrents and waterfalls.
One hundred and twenty species occur, including *Tetrao mlokosiewiczi* and *Tetraogallus* sp.

070 Liakhvi, Tskhinvali, Yugo-Osetinskaya A. O. (South Osetin Autonomous Region) (Gruziya)

*c.*42°15'N, 43°55'E 6804 ha

Zapovednik

An area on the southern slopes of the main Caucasus range, including the valley of the River Patara-Liakhvi. The relief is complex, with numerous gorges etc., and the principal habitat is forest (5283 ha).

Species occurring include *Tetrao mlokosiewiczi* and *Tetraogallus* sp.

071 Algeti, Tetri – Tskaro (Gruziya)

*c.*41°33'N, 44°30'E 6000 ha

Zapovednik

A gorge in the eastern part of the Trialeti range, with forest (5055 ha including stands of Eastern Spruce and Caucasian Fir, meadows (885 ha), and open water (25 ha).

Species occurring include *Sitta krueperi* and *Lanius minor*.

072 Severo-Osetin (North Osetin) (Severo-Osetinskaya ASSR, RSFSR)

*c.*42°50'N, 44°00'E 26,100 ha

Zapovednik

A mountainous area including forest, subalpine and alpine zones, glaciers, snow-fields, crags and screes on the northern slopes of the main ridge of the Caucasus range in the Ardon/Fiagdon (tributaries of the River Terek) basin.

One hundred and fifty-seven species occur, including *Gypaetus barbatus*, *Tetrao mlokosiewiczi*, *Tetraogallus* sp., and *Alectoris chukar*.

073 Karayazi, Ikindzhi Shikhly (Azerbaydzhan)

*c.*41°20'N, 45°10'E 4769 ha

Zapovednik

The reserve is bounded to the north by the Tbilisi-Baku railway, and to the south by the Kura waterway. Habitats include forest (*c.*30 per cent), pasture and arable land.

Species occurring include Ardeidae, *Ciconia nigra*, *Haliaeetus albicilla*, *Aquila heliaca*, and *A. chrysaetos*. *Coturnix coturnix* and *Gallinago gallinago* are numerous on passage.

074 Geigelski, Kirovobad and Khanlar (Azerbaydzhan)

*c.*40°34'N, 46°18'E 7131 ha

Zapovednik

An area of forest and meadows, with a few lakes, on the deeply incised slopes of Mount Kyapaz in the north-eastern Little Caucasus.

Thirty nine species occur, including *Gypaetus barbatus*, *Neophron percnopterus*, *Gyps fulvus*, *Aegypius monachus*, *Tetraogallus* sp., *Alectoris chukar*, and *Pyrrhocorax graculus*.

075 Zakataly, Belokany, and Zakataly (Azerbaydzhan)

*c.*41°39'N, 46°40'E 25,190 ha

Zapovednik

An area of the southern slope of the main Caucasian ridge. All the high-altitude vegetation zones are well defined, from broadleaved forest to alpine meadows. The relief is mountainous (630-3648 m) with deep chasms etc.

Eighty six species occur, including *Gypaetus barbatus*, *Gyps fulvus*, *Aegypius monachus*, *Hieraaetus pennatus*, *Tetrao mlokosiewiczi*, *Tetraogallus* sp., and *Bubo bubo*.

076 Ozero Aggyol (Lake Akgyel) (Azerbaydzhan)

40°05'N, 47°40'E 10,000 ha

Zapovednik (9100 ha)

Saline lake with *Phragmites*, *Typha*, and *Scirpus* beds. The wetland area has recently decreased in size, having previously increased from 4400 ha to 10,000 ha as a result of receiving water from irrigation systems.

Breeding species include *Anser anser*, *Tadorna ferruginea*, *T. tadorna*, *Marmaronetta angustirostris* (250 pairs; apparently now restricted as a breeding bird to this lake and a few others in Azerbaydzhan; probably the most important site in USSR), *Porphyrio porphyrio* (12,000 birds), and various Ciconiiformes. An important site for wintering waterfowl (100,000; formerly 300,000).

077 Zaliv Kirova, Kaspiyskoye More (Kirov Bay, Caspian Sea) (Azerbaydzhan)

38°53'-39°18'N, 48°40'-49°15'E 132,500 ha Ramsar Site

Kyzyl-Agach Bay Zapovednik (88,400 ha); Maly Kyzyl-Agach Bay Zakaznik (10,700 ha).

Kirov Bay, which includes Kyzyl-Agach Bay, an open bay connected to the Caspian, and Maly Kyzyl-Agach Bay, which is separated from the sea by an artificial dam and is greatly overgrown. Emergent vegetation includes beds of *Phragmites*, *Scirpus*, and *Juncus*. The submerged vegetation has changed since the 1960s with *Potamogeton* replacing *Zostera*.

Agricultural changes (from rice and grain to vegetable, grape, and cotton) have affected the availability of food for geese. In addition there is disturbance and poaching; while the removal of water for irrigation and the regulation of water (with, for example, releases of large quantities of fresh water into Kyzyl-Agach from the fish-ponds) have created unfavourable hydrological conditions with changes in the aquatic vegetation. As a result conditions are now less favourable for waterfowl (although there are plans to improve the freshwater wintering sites for dabbling duck, and fields have been sown with barley to attract the geese). For example, in the 1950s, the number of wintering duck and coot reached 10 million, but fell to 3 million in the 1960s, 1,500,000 by the end of the 1960s, and 200,000-400,000 at the beginning of the 1980s. The presence of fish-farms has adversely affected the surrounding steppe, which is now criss-crossed by channels, dams, and embankments and is gradually disappearing.

Breeding species include *Phalacrocorax pygmeus* (1400-2000 pairs), *Botaurus stellaris*, *Nycticorax nycticorax* (6000-7200 pairs), *Ardeola ralloides* (8000-9600 pairs), *Bubulcus ibis* (1400-4800 pairs), *Egretta garzetta* (3000-5000 pairs), *Ardea purpurea* (3000 pairs), *Plegadis falcinellus* (900-3000 pairs), *Phoenicopterus ruber* (170 pairs in 1982), and *Porphyrio porphyrio*. In favourable weather conditions, 170,000-500,000 diving ducks and 70,000-220,000 dabbling duck winter. Other wintering species include *Pelecanus onocrotalus*, *P. crispus*, *Phoenicopterus ruber* (1500-2000), *Cygnus olor* and *C. cygnus* (1500-5300 combined), *Anser erythropus* (11,000-25,000), *A. albifrons* and *A. anser* (8000-40,000 combined), *Branta ruficollis* (only 25-200; formerly 25,000), *Tadorna ferruginea* (common), *Tetrax tetrax* (30,000 in some years), and *Fulica atra* (50,000-400,000). *Grus leucogeranus* also occurs.

078 Water bodies of the Shirvanskaya Steppe (Azerbaydzhan)

39°30'N, 49°15'E 10,000 ha

Zakaznik and partly included in Shirvanski Zapovednik (4000 ha)

Large water bodies (holding water from irrigation systems) with rich aquatic vegetation.

Important for breeding *Porphyrio porphyrio* (4000 birds) and for passage and wintering waterfowl (100,000). Wintering species also include *Tetrax tetrax* and *Otis tarda*.

079 Pirkuli, Shemakha (Azerbaydzhan)

*c.*40°38'N, 48°37'E 1521 ha

Zapovednik

A reserve in three sections: the basin of the River Kyrkbulak (441 ha); Mount Pirkuli (529 ha); wooded spurs east of Chagan (551 ha). Habitats include open areas, ancient pasture, hay-meadows, cliffs, scree, open water, and *Carpinus* forest.

Species occurring include *Tetraogallus* sp. and *Alectoris chukar*.

080 Shirvanski, Salyany (Azerbaydzhan)

*c.*40°20'N, 47°50'E 17,745 ha

Zapovednik

The area includes a 4000 ha freshwater lake.

Important for wintering Anatidae, *Fulica atra*, *Tetrax tetrax*, and *Otis tarda*.

081 Turian-Chai, Evlakh, and Agdash (Azerbaydzhan)

*c.*40°38'N, 47°29'E 12,356 ha

Zapovednik

A reserve in the foothills of the Bolshoi Kavkaz (Great Caucasus), on the slopes of the Bozdag Ridge. The principal habitats are steppe and *Juniperus* forest.

One hundred and eight species occur (25 breeding; 16 wintering), including *Gyps fulvus*, *Aegypius monachus*, *Alectoris chukar* (population *c.*6000), and *Coracias garrulus*.

082 Agrakhanski Zaliv (Agrakhanski Bay) (Dagestan ASSR, RSFSR)

43°40'N, 47°30'E 15,000 ha

Unprotected

Shallow bay and coastal lakes. There is a plan to develop a health resort, and conservation measures, including the designation of a protected area, are needed.

The site holds breeding colonies of *Egretta garzetta*, *Ardea cinerea*, *A. purpurea*, and *Plegadis falcinellus* totalling 20,000 pairs. Important also for passage ducks (300,000).

083 Budary Ozera (Lakes Budary) complex (Checheno-Ingushskaya ASSR, RSFSR)

43°30'N, 46°05'E 1000 ha

Unprotected

Steppe lakes with *Phragmites* and *Typha* beds.

A site for breeding grebes and ducks, and passage and wintering grebes, herons, swans, and ducks.

084 Kizlyarski Zaliv (Kizlyar Bay) (Dagestan ASSR, RSFSR)

44°40'N, 47°00'E

Unprotected

Very shallow bay with a wide belt of *Phragmites*. There is a plan to develop a health resort, and conservation measures, including the designation of a protected area, are needed.

Important for passage waterfowl (hundreds of thousands) and wintering swans (max. 3000) and diving duck (max. 10,000).

085 Ostrova Chistaya Banka, Ivan-Karaul, Chapurenok, and Nordovyye, (Kalmytskaya ASSR, RSFSR)

45°10'N, 48°00'E.

Unprotected

Bare islands, and shallows, in the northern Caspian Sea (Kaspiyskoye More).

Important for breeding Laridae, including *Larus ichthyaetus* (8500 pairs) and passage (and wintering in favourable conditions) waterfowl (max. 750,000) including swans (max. 14,000).

086 Volga Delta (Astrakhan Oblast, RSFSR)

45°24'-46°24'N, 47°46'-49°20'E 652,500 ha

Ramsar Site; Biosphere Reserve (Astrakhan Zapovednik)

Astrakhan V.I. Lenin Zapovednik (62,500 ha); part of Northern Caspian Zapovednik; Hunting Reserves (100,000 ha); Zakazniks (70,500 ha)

A huge delta (with a seaward edge of more than 200 km and more than 800 channels) in the northern Caspian, with freshwater channels and lakes, extensive coastal shallows, alluvial islands and spits. There are extensive *Phragmites* beds (in places 10-15 km wide), wet meadows and *Salix alba* woodland (which is gradually drying out). The ecological balance of the delta is being affected by the large dams on the Volga (regulating the river flow and restricting the amount of silt deposited), and by agricultural reclamation (with an increase in rice-growing, melon cultivation and fish-farming), whilst there has also been an increase in the number of wildfowlers (about 200,000 waterfowl are killed every autumn).

Immense numbers of waterfowl breed, including *Podiceps grisegena* (common), *Phalacrocorax* spp. (8500-50,000 pairs), *Pelecanus crispus* (*c.*160 pairs), *Nycticorax nycticorax* (400-4200 pairs), *Ardeola ralloides* (200-4000 pairs), *Egretta garzetta* (200-3600 pairs), *E. alba* (200-4600 pairs), *Ardea cinerea* (500-3800 pairs), *A. purpurea* (*c.*2500 pairs), *Platalea leucorodia* (300-1200 pairs), *Plegadis falcinellus* (300-4500 pairs), *Cygnus olor* (2800-3000 pairs), *Anser anser* (10,000 pairs), *Aythya ferina* (8000 pairs), *Fulica atra* (150,000-180,000 pairs), and numerous *Chlidonias hybridus*, *C. niger*, and *C. leucopterus*. The original material (translated) for this site was ambiguous with regard to the status of breeding Ardeidae. The figures given may relate to individual birds rather than pairs, except for *Ardea purpurea* which is certainly given in pairs. The delta is used by large numbers of moulting ducks and geese (350,000-400,000), predominantly *Anser anser*, *Anas crecca*, *A. platyrhynchos*, *A. acuta*, and *A. querquedula*. The total number of Anatidae in spring and autumn reaches 5-7 million, and in relatively mild winters large numbers of waterfowl remain: in the 1974/75 winter, 314,700 birds occurred including 170,890 dabbling duck (mainly *Anas acuta*), 130,240 diving duck (mainly *Aythya fuligula*, *Mergus merganser*, and *M. albellus*), and in 1982/83 numbers reached 600,000.

087 Ostrov Morskoy Biryuchek (Biryuchek Island) and adjoining waters, (Kalmytskaya ASSR, RSFSR)

45°40'N, 49°00'E 35,000 ha

Zakaznik

Island in the Caspian Sea (Kaspiyskoye More) and adjoining waters.

Important in autumn for passage *Anser albifrons* (7000) and ducks (300,000).

088 Coastal shallows of north-eastern Kaspiyskoye More (Caspian Sea), Guryev (Kazakhstan)

46°20'-47°00'N, 49°15'-52°00'E 144,000 ha

Unprotected

Periodically flooded shores of the Caspian Sea between the Volga Delta and Ural Delta, with *Phragmites* borders and extensive open shallows with *Potamogeton* and *Chara* beds.

Autumn concentrations of waterfowl include *Pelecanus crispus* (500), *Phoenicopterus ruber* (40,000), *C. olor* (250,000) and duck (1,000,000).

089 Kamysh-Samarskiye Ozera (Lakes Kamysh-Samarskiye), Uralskaya Oblast (Kazakhstan)

48°57'N, 49°55'E

Unprotected

A system of overgrown lakes.
A site for breeding and passage waterfowl.

090 Bashkir (Bashkir ASSR, RSFSR)

*c.*52°50'N, 55°45'E 72,100 ha

Zapovednik

A reserve in the Southern Urals, divided into two sections. The first part includes *Pinus, Larix* and *Betula* forests in the mountain massif of South Kraka. The second area comprises forest-steppe in a bend of the River Belaya.

One hundred and fifty-five species occur, including breeding *Mergus merganser, Pernis apivorus* (rare), *Bonasa bonasia* (many), *Tetrao tetrix, T. urogallus* (many), *Grus grus* (rare), *Cuculus saturatus,* and *Picoides tridactylus* (rare).

091 Zhigulevsk (I.I. Sprygin Zhiguli) Reserve (Kuybyshev Oblast, RSFSR)

*c.*53°15'N, 49°30'E 19,400 ha

Zapovednik

A plateau adjacent to the River Volga. The area is heavily dissected by gorges and ravines, and includes forest-steppe with limestone cliffs and stands of *Quercus/Pinus*.

Species include *Bonasa bonasia, Tetrao tetrix, Merops apiaster*, and *Lullula arborea*.

092 Vicinity of Borisoglebovka (Saratov Oblast, RSFSR)

*c.*51°23'N, 42°02'E 30,500 ha

Unprotected; proposed Zapovednik

An area of agricultural land (cereals) which has replaced steppe.

An important site for breeding *Otis tarda* (up to 200). Other breeding species include *Aquila rapax nipalensis* (2 pairs) and *Anthropoides virgo* (5-6 pairs).

093 Flood-plain of the River Sura (Ulyanovsk Oblast, RSFSR)

54°30'N, 46°45'E 37,000 ha

Unprotected; Proposed Zakaznik

Flood-plain with numerous oxbow lakes.

A site for breeding *Ciconia nigra* and large numbers of waterfowl (170 birds/100 ha during the breeding season).

094 Alatyr Dolina (River Alatyr Valley) (Chuvash ASSR, RSFSR)

54°51'N, 46°15'E

Unprotected

River valley with water-meadows.
A site for breeding and passage geese and ducks.

095 Sura Dolina (River Sura Valley) (Mordovskaya ASSR, RSFSR)

54°12'N, 45°50'E

Unprotected

River valley with water-meadows.
A site for breeding and migrating ducks and geese.

096 Mordovian P.G. Smidovich Reserve, Temnikov (Mordovskaya ASSR, RSFSR)

*c.*54°40'N, 43°00'E 32,148 ha

Zapovednik

An area of *Pinus*/broadleaved forest, dissected by river plains and valleys, in the north of Mordovia near the border with Gorki Region.

One hundred and ninety-four species occur, including *Gavia arctica*, *Ciconia nigra*, *Cygnus cygnus*, *Pernis apivorus*, *Haliaeetus albicilla*, *Circaetus gallicus*, *Aquila heliaca*, *A. chrysaetos*, *Hieraaetus pennatus*, *Pandion haliaetus*, *Falco cherrug*, *F. peregrinus*, *Bonasa bonasia*, *Tetrao tetrix*, *T. urogallus*, *Coturnix coturnix*, *Grus grus*, *Gallinago media*, various Strigidae, seven species of Picidae, and *Pinicola enucleator*.

097 Moksha Dolina (Moksha Valley) (Mordovskaya ASSR and Ryazan Oblast, RSFSR)

54°32'N, 42°30'E

Unprotected

Moksha Valley with water-meadows, from Temnikov to the River Oka.

A site for breeding and migrating ducks and geese.

098 Okskaya Dolina (Oka Valley) (Ryazan Oblast, RSFSR)

54°43'N, 41°10'E

Partly included in the Oka State Zapovednik (22,900 ha)

The River Oka Valley from Ryazan to Pavlovo, comprising water-meadows and numerous oxbow lakes. This site overlaps with site 101.

The site holds large numbers of breeding ducks, and *Anser albifrons* (10,000-15,000 in spring) and ducks (tens of thousands) occur on passage.

099 Khoper (Voronezh Oblast, RSFSR)

*c.*51°20'N, 41°55'E 16,178 ha

Zapovednik

An area of the Khoper drainage basin, with channel-dissected plains rising to *c.*100 m above the river. The area includes over 400 lakes and other water-bodies (largest lake is 3.5 km in length), *Quercus*, *Alnus*, *Populus*, and *Pinus* forests, and meadows.

One hundred and eighty-four species occur, including *Podiceps nigricollis*, *Botaurus stellaris*, *Ixobrychus minutus*, *Ardea purpurea*, *Anas querquedula*, *Bucephala clangula*, *Pernis apivorus*, *Milvus migrans*, *Haliaeetus albicilla*, *Circaetus gallicus*, *Aquila pomarina*, *A. clanga*, *A. heliaca*, *Hieraaetus pennatus*, *Pandion haliaetus*, *Falco vespertinus*, *F. subbuteo*, *Coturnix coturnix*, *Porzana porzana*, *Grus grus*, waders, terns, *Merops apiaster*, *Coracias garrulus*, *Bubo bubo*, *Luscinia luscinia*, and *L. svecica*.

100 Les Na Vorskle (Belgorod Oblast, RSFSR)

*c.*50°40'N, 36°15'E 1038 ha

Zapovednik

Typical mid-Russian wooded steppe, with ancient *Quercus* predominant, adjacent to the River Vorskla in the Central Russian Uplands.

Seventy species occur, including *Milvus migrans*, *Falco subbuteo*, *F. cherrug*, and *Coracias garrulus*.

101 Oka (Ryazan Oblast, RSFSR)

*c.*54°45'N, 40°45'E 22,900 ha Included in a Biosphere Reserve (45,845 ha)

Zapovednik

The south-eastern part of the Meshchera lowlands. The River Pra (tributary of the Oka) forms the reserve's southern limit. Habitats include coniferous and deciduous forest (19,402 ha), bogs/marshes (2800 ha), and open-water areas (427 ha). The area is generally flat, with some low elevations in the north-west.

Two hundred and thirty species in total occur, 155 breed, including *Botaurus stellaris*, *Ixobrychus minutus*, *Ciconia nigra* (rare), *Milvus migrans*, *Haliaeetus albicilla*, *Pandion haliaetus*, *Bonasa bonasia*, *Tetrao tetrix*, *T. urogallus*, *Grus grus*, *Gallinago media*, *Xenus cinereus*, *Chlidonias* spp., *Bubo bubo*, *Glaucidium passerinum*, *Aegolius funereus*, *Coracias garrulus*, *Dryocopus martius*, and *Dendrocopos medius*. The reserve was chosen for the establishment of an artificial, but free-flying, breeding population of *Grus leucogeranus* as part of an international conservation programme. The first eggs (laid by captive-reared birds at the International Crane Foundation) were placed under *Grus grus* foster parents in 1985. Passage species include *Anas* spp., *Aquila chrysaetos*, *Falco cherrug*, and *F. peregrinus*. *Buteo lagopus* and *Nyctea scandiaca* occur in winter.

102 Prioksko – Terrasny, Serpukhov (Moskovskaya Oblast, RSFSR)

*c.*54°53'N, 37°25'E 4945 ha Biosphere Reserve

Zapovednik

An area of forest and steppe on the sandy terraces of the River Oka.

One hundred and thirty species occur (over 100 breed), including *Pernis apivorus*, *Circaetus gallicus*, *Pandion haliaetus*, *Bonasa bonasia*, *Bubo bubo*, *Caprimulgus europaeus*, and *Dryocopus martius*.

103 Faustovo Flood-plains (Moskovskaya Oblast, RSFSR)

55°19'N, 38°36'E *c.*9000 ha

Zapovednik (2120 ha)

Water-meadows, marshes, lakes and former beds of the Rivers Moskva and Nerskaya. Flooded or partly flooded in spring. The area is used for grazing, hay production, and hunting. Problems at the site include land-reclamation measures, ploughing of meadows, and early mowing. Proposed as a future Ramsar Site.

Breeding species include *Porzana porzana* (tens of pairs), *Crex crex* (tens of pairs), *Philomachus pugnax* (*c.*100 breeding females), *Gallinago media* (40-50 breeding females), *Limosa limosa* (100-200 pairs), *Tringa stagnatilis* (65-70 pairs), *Xenus cinereus* (10-15 pairs), *Sterna hirundo* (20-25 pairs), *Chlidonias niger* (20-45 pairs), and *C. leucopterus* (20-290 pairs). One of the most important sites for waterfowl in the Moscow region and in the central European USSR, with up to 20,000 waterfowl in spring, including *Anser fabalis* (250-300), *A. albifrons* (12,000-15,000), *Anas penelope* (2000-4500), *A. querquedula* (450-1200), *Pluvialis apricaria* (4000-5000), *Philomachus pugnax* (10,000+), and *Tringa glareola* (hundreds).

104 Volzhskoye Vodokhranilishche (Volga Reservoir), Uglich (Kalinin Oblast, RSFSR)

58°30'N, 38°00'E

Unprotected

Large reservoir.

Important for passage and breeding geese and ducks.

105 Dubna Marshes (Crane's Native Land) (Moskovskaya Oblast, RSFSR)

56°50'N, 37°30'E 14,540 ha

Crane's Native Land Zapovednik (11,000 ha) and Beaver Game Reserve (3540 ha)

The flood-plain of the River Dubna with *Sphagnum* bogs, boggy forest, black alder thickets, lakes and former riverbeds, and agricultural land.

Breeding species include *Aquila clanga* (2-3 pairs), *Falco columbarius* (1 pair), *Bonasa bonasia*, *Tetrao tetrix* (tens of 'pairs'), *T. urogallus*, *Grus grus* (*c.*20 pairs), *Limosa limosa* (25-30 pairs), *Numenius arquata* (40-50 pairs), and *Parus cyanus*. *Grus grus* (1700-2300) occurs before autumn migration (the largest concentration in central European USSR); also concentrations on spring migration of *Anser albifrons* (hundreds) and *A. fabalis* (hundreds).

106 Moskovskoye Morye, Konakovo (Kalinin Oblast, RSFSR)

56°50'N, 36°50'E 32,700 ha

Shoshinski Pool (6000 ha) is included in Zavidovski Scientific Research Zapovednik

A large reservoir with numerous islands and shallow pools.
A breeding area for ducks (4000 pairs) and passage site for geese and ducks.

107 Zavidovo reserve and scientific experimental station (including Diatlovo Ponds) Moskovskaya Oblast and Kalinin Oblast, RSFSR)

56°23'N, 36°06'E 125,442 ha

Zapovednik

Unprotected

An area of forest (79,604 ha), meadows (17,014 ha), and open water (1100 ha). A centre for the study of forest and meadow management, and game productivity.
Breeding species include *Podiceps auritus*, *Botaurus stellaris*, *Milvus migrans*, *Aquila clanga*, *Crex crex*, and *Chlidonias niger*. The most important area in the Moscow region for passage *Haliaeetus albicilla* during autumn migration. Also passage *Aquila clanga* and *Pandion haliaetus*.

108 Prof. V.V. Alekhin Tsentralno-Chernozemny (Central Black Earth) Bio sphere Reserve (Kursk and Belgorod Oblasts, RSFSR)

*c.*51°05'N, 36°30'E 4795 ha Biosphere Reserve

Zapovednik

An area of the Central Russian Uplands with wooded steppe. There are five sections: Streletski, Kazatski, Yamskoy, Barkalovka, and Bukreevy Barmy which occupy virgin herb steppes and *Quercus* stands.
One hundred and fifty species occur, including breeding *Milvus migrans*, *Falco vespertinus*, *Porzana porzana*, *Crex crex*, *Asio flammeus*, *Luscinia svecica*, and *Locustella fluviatilis*. *Buteo lagopus*, *Nyctea scandiaca*, *Eremophila alpestris*, *Calcarius lapponicus*, and *Plectrophenax nivalis* occur in winter or on passage.

109 Galichya Gora (Lipetsk Oblast, RSFSR)

*c.*52°35'N, 39°05'E 231 ha

Zapovednik

An area with forest-steppe (114 ha), meadows (110 ha), and open water (7 ha).
Forty-six species occur, including *Milvus migrans*, *Circus macrourus*, *Coturnix coturnix*, and *Caprimulgus europaeus*.

110 Osveyskoye Ozero (Lake Osveyskoye), Verkhnedvinsk (Belorussia Oblast, RSFSR)

56°00'N, 28°00'E 5600 ha

Hunting Zakaznik

Freshwater lake with extensive beds of emergent vegetation.
Breeding birds include grebes (3000-3500 pairs), *Haliaeetus albicilla*, and *Pandion haliaetus*. Swans, geese, and ducks (hundreds of thousands) occur on migration.

111 Karachevskoye Boloto (Karachevskoye Marsh), Vitebsk and Gorodok (Belorussiya)

55°18'N, 30°00'E 16,000-17,000 ha

Unprotected; proposed combined Zakaznik

Marshes with small lakes.
A site for breeding (5000 pairs) and moulting (*c.*10,000) ducks and passage geese and ducks (tens of thousands).

112 Obol (marsh), Polotsk and Shumilino (Belorussiya)

55°30'N, 29°37'E 76,000 ha

Hunting Zakaznik

Marshes with numerous small lakes and five large lakes. There are intensive land-improvement schemes in the surrounding area.
Breeding species include *Ciconia nigra*, *Aquila chrysaetos*, *Pandion haliaetus*, *Falco peregrinus*, and *Grus grus*.

113 Tsentralno-Lesnoy (Central Forest) Reserve, Nelidovo (Kalinin Oblast, RSFSR)

*c.*56°15'N, 32°35'E 21,348 ha Biosphere Reserve

Zapovednik

Mixed forest and numerous marshes on slightly undulating plains in the north-western part of Central Russian Uplands; the watershed of the Rivers Volga and Zapadnaya (western) Dvina.
One hundred and forty-one species occur, including *Pernis apivorus*, *Falco columbarius*, *F. vespertinus*, *Bonasa bonasia*, *Tetrao tetrix*, *T. urogallus*, *Grus grus* (breeds), *Bubo bubo*, *Nyctea scandiaca*, *Surnia ulula*, *Glaucidium passerinum*, *Aegolius funereus*, and *Cuculus saturatus* (has colonised from the east). Many waterfowl occur on passage.

114 Rybinskoye Vodokhranilishche (Rybinsk Reservoir) (Kalinin, Vologda and Yaroslavl Oblasts, RSFSR)

58°00'N, 38°00'E 455,000 ha

Partly included in Darwin Zapovednik (47,000 ha) and small Zakaznik (168 ha)

A reservoir with extensive shallows, pools, and islands.
Large numbers of ducks breed, and an important passage site for *Anser fabalis* and *A. albifrons* (10,000 combined), and *Grus grus* (2000+).

115 Gorkovskoye Vodokhranilishche (Gorki Reservoir) and the Lower Unzha (Gorki, Ivanovo and Kostroma Oblasts, RSFSR)

57°20'N, 43°05'E

Unprotected

Large reservoir.
Important for passage and breeding ducks.

116 Flood-plain of River Vetluga (Gorki and Kostroma Oblasts, RSFSR)

57°30'N, 45°10'E

Unprotected

Flood-plain of the River Vetluga from Sharya to Krasnyye Baki.
A breeding and passage site for geese and ducks.

117 Votkinskoye Vodokhranilishche (Votkinskoye Reservoir) (Perm Oblast, RSFSR)

57°20'N, 55°00'E

Zakaznik

Reservoir and flood-plain of the River Votka.
A site for breeding and passage geese and ducks.

118 Pechoro-Ilych, Troitsko-Pechorsk (Komi ASSR, RSFSR)

*c.*62°40'N, 56°10'E 721,322 ha Biosphere Reserve

Zapovednik

An extensive reserve in the upper reaches of the River Pechora, with *Pinus sibirica* taiga, stunted mountain forest, and north Ural tundra. The area is bounded by the Ural Mountains, and the Rivers Kozhim, Ilych, and Verkhnyaya Pechora.
Two hundred and four species occur, including breeding *Anser fabalis*, *Anas penelope*, *A. crecca*, *Bucephala clangula*, *Mergus merganser*, *Bonasa bonasia*, *Tetrao tetrix*, *T. urogallus*, *Lagopus lagopus*, *L. mutus*, *Coturnix coturnix*, and *Cuculus saturatus* (western limit of range).

119 Vashutkiny, Padimeyskiye and Khargeyskiye Ozera (Lakes) (Arkhangelsk Oblast, RSFSR)

68°00'N, 62°00'E 25,000 ha

Unprotected

Lake system in the Bolshezemelskaya tundra.
An important breeding and moulting area for *Anser fabalis* (50,000) and ducks (80,000-100,000).

120 Vaygach Ostrov (Vaygach Island) (Arkhangelsk Oblast, RSFSR)

70°00'N, 59°30'E 270,000 ha

Unprotected; proposed Zapovednik

Large tundra island between the Pechora and Kara Seas.
Important for breeding *Cygnus columbianus*, *Branta leucopsis,* and diving ducks. In autumn, large numbers of ducks (hundreds of thousands) occur.

121 Khaypudyrskaya Guba (Khaypudyrskaya Bay) (Arkhangelsk Oblast, RSFSR)

68°35'N, 59°45'E

Unprotected; proposed Zakaznik

A shallow bay in the Pechora Sea (Pechorskoye More) with wide, silty foreshore, surrounded by marshy tundra with lakes.
An area supporting large numbers of moulting diving duck (80,000), passage geese (including *Branta bernicla*), and diving duck (hundreds of thousands).

122 Varandeyskaya Lapta Kosa (Varandeyskaya Lapta Peninsula) (Arkhangelsk Oblast, RSFSR)

68°50'N, 59°00'E 350,000 ha

Low-lying peninsula with numerous lakes connected by channels with each other and to the Pechora Sea (Pechorskoye More). Proposed as a Ramsar Site.
One of the most important breeding sites in the northern European USSR for breeding swans, geese, and ducks, and moulting swans (2000), geese (30,000-40,000), and ducks (100,000).

123 River Chernaya, Bolshezemelskaya tundra (Arkhangelsk Oblast, RSFSR)

68°08'N, 57°00'E 200,000 ha

Unprotected

Low-lying marshy tundra with lakes.

Important for breeding and moulting swans (500), geese (20,000-30,000), and diving ducks (20,000).

124 Russki Zavorot (Russki Zavorot Peninsula) Nenetski (Arkhangelsk Oblast, RSFSR)

68°35'N, 53°00'E 50,000 ha

Unprotected

Extensive marine shallows, and low-lying tundra peninsula with numerous small lakes connected by channels with each other and to the Pechora Sea (Pechorskoye More). Proposed as a Ramsar Site.

The most important site in the northern European USSR for breeding (2000 pairs) and moulting (10,000) *Cygnus columbianus* and *C. cygnus*. Also important for breeding and moulting geese (100,000). Large numbers of Anatidae (tens of thousands) gather prior to autumn migration.

125 Southern coast of Cheshskaya Guba (Bay), Nenetski (Arkhangelsk Oblast, RSFSR)

66°50'N, 46°30'E

Unprotected

Low-lying coastal tundra in the vicinity of the Rivers Snopa, Oma, Vizhas and Perepusk.

Large numbers of geese and ducks occur on passage.

126 Kanin Poluostrov (Kanin Peninsula), Nenetski (Arkhangelsk Oblast, RSFSR)

66°40'N, 44°40'E 500,000 ha

Unprotected

Marshy, low-lying tundra with numerous rivers, lakes, and channels between the Rivers Yazhma and Nyes.

A breeding area for *Cygnus columbianus* and geese. Very large numbers of geese moult (50,000), and swans and geese (including *Branta leucopsis*) occur on passage.

127 Pinega (Arkhangelsk Oblast, RSFSR)

*c.*64°22'N, 43°10'E 41,244 ha

Zapovednik

An area adjoining the River Pinega, including a marshy plain, an elevated karst plateau, 83 lakes, and a *Larix russica* forest (200-300 years old).

Breeding species include *Bonasa bonasia*, *Tetrao urogallus*, *Dryocopus martius*, and *Picoides tridactylus*.

128 Ainovy Ostrova (Ainov Islands), Pechenga (Murmansk Oblast, RSFSR)

70°00'N, 32°00'E 260 ha

Included in Zapovednik

Two tundra islands in the Barents Sea (Barentsovo More).

Breeding species include *Somateria mollissima* (1500 pairs), *Melanitta fusca* (30-40 pairs), *Mergus serrator* (50-60 pairs), *Phalaropus lobatus* (tens of pairs), *Larus canus* (1000-2000 pairs), *L. argentatus* (15,000 pairs), *L. marinus* (5000-6000 pairs), *Sterna paradisaea* (100-1000 pairs), *Alca torda* (50-70 pairs), *Cepphus grylle* (100 pairs), and *Fratercula arctica* (12,000 pairs).

129 Sem Ostrovov (Seven Islands), Teriberka (Murmansk Oblast, RSFSR)

69°00'N, 37°00'E 1000 ha

Included in Zapovednik

An archipelago of tundra islands with cliffs in the Barents Sea (Barentsovo More).
Important for breeding auks (10,000-100,000 pairs) including *Uria aalge*, *U. lomvia*, and *Cepphus grylle*. Other breeding species include *Somateria mollissima* (3500 pairs), *Falco rusticolus* (1 pair), *Stercorarius longicaudus* (10-100 pairs), and *Sterna paradisaea* (1000-10,000 pairs).

130 Coastal belt of eastern Murmansk, Lovozero (Murmansk Oblast, RSFSR)

68°00'N, 39°00'E

Unprotected

Coastal shallows in the Barents Sea (Barentsovo More).
Breeding species include *Anser erythropus* (1 pair). Large numbers of *Somateria mollissima* and *S. spectabilis* winter (80,000-100,000).

131 Watershed of the Rivers Lumbovka and Ponoy Reka, Lovozero (Murmansk Oblast, RSFSR)

67°30'N, 40°30'E 260 ha

Unprotected

Marshy tundra with many lakes.
An important breeding and moulting site for *Anser fabalis* (15,000 birds) and many ducks.

132 Watershed of the Rivers Strelna and Varzuga, Terski (Murmansk Oblast, RSFSR)

66°30'N, 37°40'E 250,000 ha

Unprotected; Varzuga Zapovednik (107,000 ha) is planned

Extremely marshy northern taiga with a large number of lakes.
Breeding species include *Cygnus cygnus*, *Anser fabalis*, *Haliaeetus albicilla* (1 pair), and *Pandion haliaetus* (1 pair). *Cygnus cygnus* (max. 500) gathers prior to migration.

133 Middle reaches of the River Ponoy between the River Losinga and the Ponoy Zakaznik, Lovozero (Murmansk Oblast, RSFSR)

67°00'N, 39°00'E 60,000 ha

Zapovednik

Extremely marshy northern taiga with a large number of lakes and rivers.
Breeding species include *Cygnus cygnus*, *Anser fabalis*, *Haliaeetus albicilla*, *Pandion haliaetus*, and *Falco rusticolus*. *Cygnus cygnus* (max. 500) gathers prior to migration.

134 Chalmny-Varre, Lovozero (Murmansk Oblast, RSFSR)

67°00'N, 37°10'E 20,000 ha

Zapovednik

Lakes and marshes amongst forest and tundra in the watershed of the Rivers Ponoy and Varzuga.
Breeding raptors include *Haliaeetus albicilla*, *Pandion haliaetus*, and *Falco peregrinus*. Several thousand *Cygnus cygnus* breed and gather prior to migration.

135 Watershed of the Rivers Iokanga and Ponoy Reka, Lovozero (Murmansk Oblast, RSFSR)

67°30'N, 37°15'E 30,000 ha

Proposed Zapovednik

Marshy tundra with many lakes.

The most important breeding and moulting site for *Anser fabalis* in the Kola Peninsula. *Cygnus cygnus* also breeds.

136 Lapland, Monchegorsk (Murmansk Oblast, RSFSR)

*c.*67°55'N, 33°00'E 161,254 ha Included in a Biosphere Reserve (278,400 ha)

Zapovednik

An area of the Imandra Lake (Ozero Imandra) depression in the western part of the Kola Peninsula (Kolskiy Poluostrov), 120-160 km north of the Arctic Circle. Habitats include forest (53 per cent), montane tundra (28 per cent), Krummholz birch on slopes (7 per cent), marsh/bog (6 per cent), and lakes/rivers (biggest river is the Chuna; 5 per cent).

Breeding species include *Anas penelope*, *A. crecca*, *A. acuta*, *Melanitta nigra*, *Bucephala clangula*, *Mergus merganser*, *Haliaeetus albicilla*, *Pandion haliaetus*, *Bonasa bonasia*, *Tetrao tetrix*, *T. urogallus*, *Lagopus lagopus*, *L. mutus*, *Surnia ulula* (common), *Bubo bubo* (rare), *Dryocopus martius*, *Picoides tridactyla*, *Parus cinctus*, *Perisoreus infaustus*, and three *Loxia* species.

137 Kandalakshskaya Guba (Kandalaksha Bay) (Murmansk Oblast and Karelskaya ASSR, RSFSR)

66°45-67°08'N, 32°31-34°05'E 208,000 ha Ramsar Site

Kandalaksha Zapovednik (54,255 ha); Keretski Zakaznik (21,000 ha)

A large bay with rocky coastline and more than 860 islands of rock and alluvial sand. The islands range from rocky outcrops and low-lying treeless islets to large islands. On the large islands (Veliki, Ryazhkov, Oleni, Lodeiny, Vlasov) there are freshwater lakes and *Pinus* and *Picea* forests. The coastal belt of the islands and promontories comprises coastal meadows, grasslands, sedge-beds, and halophytic scrub with underwater beds of *Zostera*. The site does not include the waters adjacent to the town of Kandalaksha. All commercial activity and tourism are prohibited in the State Reserve with hunting prohibited in Keretski Combined Zakaznik. There is shipping throughout the year, and regulated fishing takes place. Disturbance results from the numerous small boats, and the main ecological problem is water pollutants (oil and products of its refining, industrial and domestic effluent, and phenols from submerged timber). There is also the planned commercial extraction of seaweed by underwater harvesting which will lead to severe ecological disturbance.

Breeding species include *Somateria mollissima* (*c.*9500 pairs), *Mergus serrator* (90-100 pairs), *Haliaeetus albicilla* (max. 12 pairs), *Pandion haliaetus*, *Haematopus ostralegus* (600-700 pairs), *Arenaria interpres* (250-300 pairs), *Phalaropus lobatus*, *Alca torda* (30+ pairs), and *Cepphus grylle* (350-500 pairs). About 25,000 duck moult in the bay, predominantly *Somateria mollissima* (10,000-12,000) and *Bucephala clangula* (max. 10,000). Waterfowl migration is not marked, although the southern edge of the wetland (Kem-luda) is a regular stop-over site for *Anser fabalis* and *Numenius phaeopus*.

138 Lakes of northern Karelia, Loukhi, and Kem (Karelskaya ASSR, RSFSR)

66°00'N, 33°00'E 1,000,000 ha

Hydrological Zakaznik Ozero Keret (Lake Keret); included in the plan for a North Karelian Zapovednik

Northern taiga with a large number of lakes and marshes. Lakes include Keret, Engozero, Nizhneye, Kumozero, and south-eastern part of Topozero. The boundaries of the most important wetlands need to be determined.

Breeding species include *Cygnus cygnus* (1000 pairs) and *Anser anser* (the most northerly breeding site). An important passage site for ducks.

139 Solovetski Arkhipelag (Solovetski Archipelago), Onega (Arkhangelsk Oblast, RSFSR)

65°15'N, 36°00'E 34,700 ha

Zapovednik

Marine shallows, extensive foreshore, beaches, and coastal meadows bordering the White Sea.

A site for *Somateria mollissima*: breeding (several hundred pairs) and moulting (2000 males). *Branta leucopsis*, *B. bernicla*, and diving ducks (tens of thousands) occur on passage.

140 Onezhskaya Guba, Beloye More (Onega Bay, White Sea) (Karelskaya ASSR, RSFSR)

64°30'N, 35°30'E

Includes Shuiostrov Zakaznik (10,000 ha)

Offshore islands and shallow sea (between the mouth of the River Kem and Myagostrov Island) with a wide foreshore and wet coastal meadows. Adversely affected by large--scale seaweed harvesting (especially by dredging), tourism and fast water transport. There is a need to restrict tourism during the breeding season. Recommended for designation as a Ramsar Site.

Breeding species include *Haliaeetus albicilla* and *Falco peregrinus*. Described as the most important site for waterfowl migration in northern European USSR, with hundreds of thousands occurring including *Cygnus* spp., *Branta leucopsis*, and *B. bernicla*. *Somateria mollissima* moults 5000-6000) and winters (20,000).

141 Kivach, Kondopoga (Karelskaya ASSR, RSFSR)

*c.*62°10'N, 34°15'E 10,460 ha

Zapovednik

The basin of the River Suna, which flows into the north-west of Lake Onega (Ozero Onezhskoye). The area includes forest (80+ per cent), open water (10 per cent), bogs (4 per cent), and meadows/clearings (3 per cent). The topography includes a variety of ridges, and lowlands with lakes.

One hundred and eighty-five species occur, including *Bucephala clangula*, *Mergus merganser*, *Bonasa bonasia*, *Tetrao urogallus*, *Crex crex*, *Strix uralensis*, *Caprimulgus europaeus*, *Picus canus*, *Dendrocopos leucotos*, and *Picoides tridactylus*.

142 Olonyets region (Karelskaya ASSR, RSFSR)

61°00'N, 32°45'E

Unprotected

Comprises the area around Olonyets including wet meadows and bays of Lake Ladoga.

Huge numbers of geese occur on autumn migration.

143 Kilpola Ostrov (Kilpola Island) and adjoining waters (Leningrad Oblast, RSFSR)

*c.*61°50'N 31°40'E 30,000 ha

Unprotected; proposed seasonal Zakaznik

Shallows with small islands in Lake Ladoga (Ladozhskoye Ozero), east of the Gulf of Finland.

An important area for diving duck during migration.

144 Svirskaya Guba (Svir Bay), Lodeynoye Pole (Leningrad Oblast, RSFSR)

60°35'N, 32°50'E 26,400 ha

Included in the Lower Svir Zapovednik (41,000 ha)

Bay of Lake Ladoga (Ladozhskoye Ozero) with shallow waters, *Phragmites* beds, sandy beaches and low-lying marshes upriver.

Breeding species include *Ciconia nigra*, *Haliaeetus albicilla*, *Pandion haliaetus*, and *Grus grus*. Huge numbers of waterfowl occur on passage (max. 500,000).

145 Rakovyye Ozera (Rakovyye Lakes), Vsevolozhsk (Leningrad Oblast, RSFSR)

60°40'N, 29°30'E 9500 ha

Zakaznik (5997 ha), and proposed Zapovednik

Freshwater lakes in the centre of the Karelian isthmus on a major migration flyway.

Breeding birds include *Grus grus* and waders. Large numbers of waterfowl occur on passage including *Cygnus cygnus* (hundreds), *Branta bernicla* (thousands), *B. leucopsis*, and ducks (tens of thousands).

146 Vyborgski Zaliv (Vyborg Bay), Vyborg (Leningrad Oblast, RSFSR)

60°35'N, 28°35'E 50,000 ha

Zakaznik

Shallow bay on the Baltic Sea with numerous small islands.

Concentrations of *Cygnus cygnus*, *C. columbianus*, *Branta bernicla*, and *Grus grus* occur on passage.

147 Koporski Zaliv (Koporski Bay), Kingisepp and Lomonosov (Leningrad Oblast, RSFSR)

59°55'N, 29°00'E 25,000 ha

Unprotected

Bay in the Gulf of Finland with sandy and rocky shores with *Phragmites* beds.

A passage site for swans and ducks.

148 Ozero Vyalye (Lake Vyalye) and adjoining marshes, Gatchina (Leningrad Oblast, RSFSR)

59°10'N, 30°10'E 20,000 ha

Zakaznik

Freshwater lake and low-lying marshes.

A breeding site for *Grus grus*. Large numbers of *Anser albifrons* occur on passage.

149 Sources of the River Oredezh, and Luga (Leningrad Oblast, RSFSR)

59°00'N, 30°25'E 34,400 ha

Unprotected; proposed Zakaznik

Marshes and mixed forest.

A site for breeding ducks, *Grus grus* and waders.

150 Ozero Ilmen (Lake Ilmen) and adjoining marshy plain (Novgorod Oblast, RSFSR)

58°10'N, 31°20'E 98,200 ha

Unprotected; proposed Zakaznik

Large lake, in places overgrown, surrounded by low-lying marshes and wet meadows. It is necessary to determine the most important areas.

A breeding site for *Anser anser* and ducks (tens of thousands).

151 Narvskoye Vodokhranilishche (Narva Reservoir), Kingisepp and Slantsy (Leningrad Oblast, RSFSR)

59°20'N, 28°15'E 20,000 ha

Unprotected

Reservoir with hydroelectric station.
An important breeding site for ducks (25,000 pairs).

152 Chudsko-Pskovski Vodoyem (Lake Chudsko-Pskov) including the mouth of the River Velikaya (Pskov Oblast, RSFSR)

58°30'N, 28°50'E 350,000 ha

Unprotected

Large lake and marshy plain with a river delta.
Large numbers of wildfowl breed, moult, and occur on passage.

MAIN REFERENCES

Borodin, A. M. and Syroechkovski, E. E. (eds.) (1983) *The nature reserves of the USSR* (Russian). 2nd revised and enlarged edition. Moscow: Lesnaya promysh lennost.

IUCN (1986) *Biosphere Reserves. Compilation 4.* Cambridge: IUCN Conservation Monitoring Centre.

Knystautas, A. (1987) *The natural history of the USSR.* London: Century Hutchinson.

Pryde, P. R. (1986) Strategies and problems of wildlife preservation in the USSR. *Biol. Cons.* 36: 351-374.

Skokova, N. N. and Vinogradov, V. G. (1986) *Waterfowl habitat conservation* (Russian). Moscow: Agropromizdat.

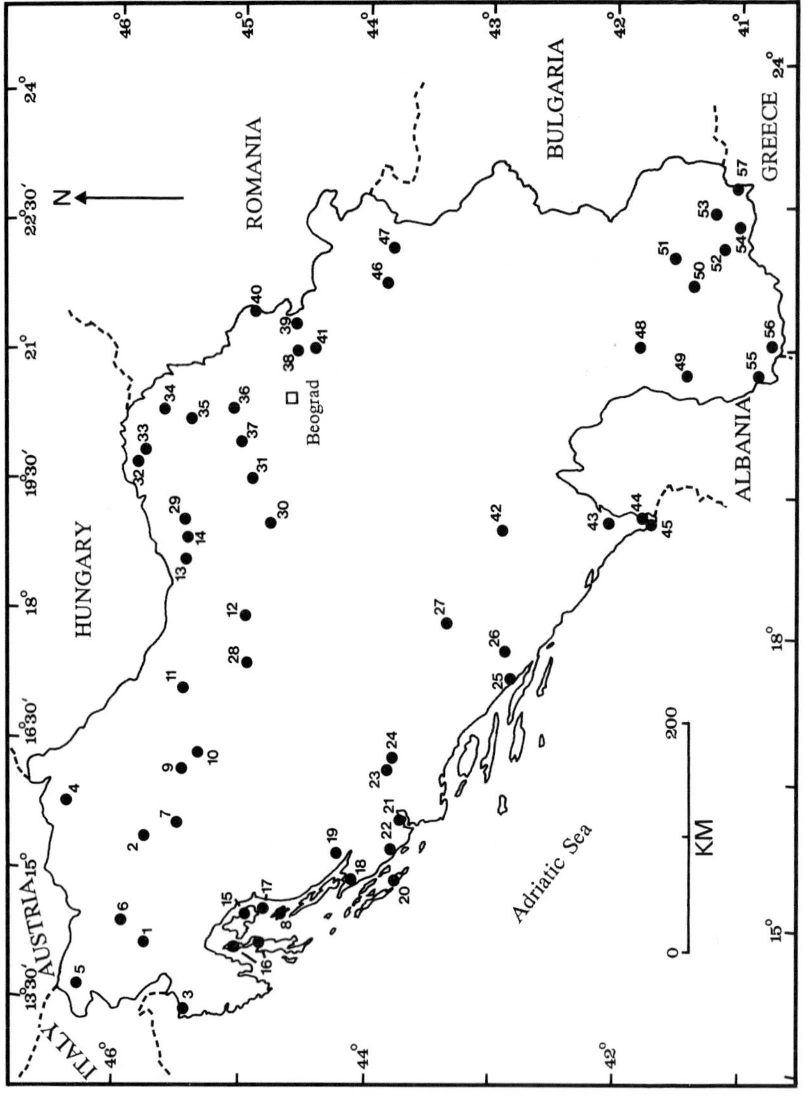

Figure 39: Map showing the location of the sites in Yugoslavia

YUGOSLAVIA

White-tailed Eagle *Haliaeetus albicilla*

INTRODUCTION

General information

Yugoslavia covers an area of 255,804 sq km and has a population estimated at 22.85 million (in 1983) (an average population density of 89 persons per sq km). Lowlands occupy 28 per cent of the country, principally the southern part of the Pannonian lowlands with the flood-plain of the Danube (Dunav) and Tisa, and the flood-plain of the Sava and Morava. The rest of the country is hilly to mountainous, with particularly high mountains in northern Slovenia (Julijske Alps), Montenegro, and Macedonia. The country has an extensive coastline bordering the Adriatic Sea (Dalmatian coast) with numerous rocky islands, the largest of which is Cres.

Agriculture is the most important industry in the country, and total agricultural land covers 142,000 sq km (56 per cent of total land area) of which 78,000 sq km are arable land, orchards and vineyards, and 64,000 sq km are meadows and pastures. There are five main agricultural regions: Adriatic coast, producing olives, citrus fruits, grapes, and vegetables; River Vardar valley, producing fruits, grapes, and vegetables; River Morava valley, producing fruits, wheat, maize, and cattle; highlands, producing barley, oats, potatoes, cattle, and sheep; and Vojvodina and Slovenia, producing wheat, maize, sunflowers, sugar-beet, cattle, and pigs.

Forests cover about 92,000 sq km or 36 per cent of the total land area. Along the Adriatic coast, there are Mediterranean mixed *Quercus* woods with other deciduous species including *Carpinus orientalis* and *Ostrya carpinifolia*. Man has had a major impact on the vegetation in this region, reducing the natural evergreen oak woodlands to maquis and garigue by grazing and the use of fire. Remnant mature stands are scattered (occurring, for example, at Dundo on the island of Rab). Woods of *Pinus halepensis* are common along the Adriatic coast, as are woods of *Pinus brutia* and *P. pinea*. Away from the Adriatic coast, coniferous woods are widespread and well developed on the lower and middle slopes of the higher mountains ranges; mainly woods of *Pinus nigra*.

In the continental parts, upland areas above the riverine lowlands are forested with *Fagus* and *Abies*, with *Picea* in subalpine areas. Over 54 per cent of Yugoslavia is suffering from overgrazing or other forms of timber destruction, resulting in serious erosion, particularly severe in the Morava and Vardar river basins.

The flood-plains of the main rivers (Sava, Drava, Dunav, Tisa, Morava) still support extensive riverine forests of *Salix* and *Populus*, which are perhaps the best-preserved riverine forests in central Europe. The lowlands also have forests of *Quercus robur* and *Q. pedunculiflora* (although large areas have been, and are still being, cleared for cultivation). The unimproved flood-meadows and the numerous, occasionally extensive, marshes, lakes, and fish-ponds associated with these rivers are also of great importance in a European context. The other main wetlands are the large karst lakes along the Dalmatian coast and on the border with Albania and Greece, which have extensive fringes of *Phragmites* and *Typha* in places.

Saltmarshes are scarce at the coast with small areas at the mouth of the Rivers Neretva and Bojana and on the islands of Rab and Pag. The Pannonian lowlands in Vojvodina are now mostly cultivated, but there are some relicts of steppe flora on saline soils and a number of salt-lakes.

Ornithological importance

The sea coasts of the Adriatic islands (e.g. Krk, Cres, Prvič, Rab, Pag) are important for breeding *Calonectris diomedea*, *Puffinus puffinus*, *Hydrobates pelagicus*, *Falco eleonorae*, and *F. peregrinus*, and as a wintering area for *Gavia stellata* and *G. arctica*.

Large parts of central and southern Yugoslavia are still remote and, unlike neighbouring Italy, Romania, and Bulgaria, still support viable populations of all four European vultures. The country's mountainous areas (e.g. Triglav, Durmitor, Dinara, Sar, Kozuf, Bosava) have breeding *Aquila chrysaetos*, *Hieraaetus pennatus*, *Bonasa bonasia*, *Lagopus mutus helveticus*, *Tetrao tetrix*, and *Alectoris graeca saxatilis*; whilst the lower hills have breeding *Circaetus gallicus*, *Aquila heliaca*, *Buteo rufinus*, *Falco biarmicus*, *Strix uralensis*, and *Bubo bubo*.

The lowlands of the north are particularly important in a European context. Yugoslavia has one of the largest populations of *Haliaeetus albicilla* (50+ pairs) in central Europe; the areas of lowland forest and flood-meadow also hold good populations of *Ciconia nigra*, *C. ciconia*, *Aquila pomarina*, *Falco cherrug*, and *Crex crex*. The lakes, marshes, and fish-ponds in the north are also of major importance for breeding Ardeidae, *Platalea leucorodia*, and *Aythya nyroca*, whilst Lake Skadar (Skadarsko Jezero) in the south is of international importance for *Pelecanus crispus* (15+ pairs) and *Phalacrocorax pygmeus*. Yugoslavia's wetlands are also important for passage and wintering birds; for example, very large numbers of *Platalea leucorodia* (in autumn), *Egretta alba* (in autumn and winter), and *Anser fabalis* (in autumn and winter) occur on passage at Kopacki rit, and the Dalmatian coast can be particularly important for a considerable variety of species when the weather is harsh in continental Europe.

Conservation infrastructure and protected-area system

Yugoslavia is a federal country with six republics: Serbia, Croatia, Slovenia, Bosnia and Herzegovina, Macedonia, and Montenegro, with Kosovo and Vojvodina as autonomous provinces within Serbia. Each republic and autonomous province has its own institute or office for nature conservation.

Because of this decentralised structure, the administration of protected areas across the country is extremely complex. Protected areas may be administered by experimental farms (under the Ministry of Agriculture) or by committees under the Ministry of Education or by one of the above-mentioned institutes for nature conservation.

Six main categories of protected areas are mentioned in this inventory: National Park, Regional Park, Nature Reserve, Ornithological Reserve, Zoological Reserve, and Special Reserve (two of these are defined below).

1. National Park (Nacionalni Park)
   These are extensive areas of exceptional natural beauty that are established to conserve nature in its totality (including flora, fauna, soil, water and air). Human activities are strictly controlled (no traffic, exploitation of natural resources, hunting, or fishing).
2. Regional Park (Regionalni Park)
   These are large areas of natural or man-created beauty that are established to regulate tourism and maintain the traditional cultural activities. Tourism and recreation are encouraged so long as they are not detrimental to the natural value and beauty of the area.

International measures relevant to the conservation of sites

Yugoslavia is a party to the Ramsar Convention, World Heritage Convention, and Barcelona Convention (and has ratified the Protocol concerning Mediterranean Specially Protected Areas). The country has designated two Ramsar Sites, four natural World Heritage Sites, two Biosphere Reserves, and ten Mediterranean Specially Protected Areas.

Overview of the inventory

The inventory includes 57 sites covering over 1 million ha of which six are in Slovenia, 19 are in Croatia, three are in Bosnia and Herzegovina, 13 are in Vojvodina, two are in Serbia (excluding Vojvodina), four are in Montenegro, nine are in Macedonia, and one is shared between Macedonia and Kosovo. Croatia and Vojvodina are believed to be well-covered by the inventory; the other republics and autonomous provinces are not so well covered, especially Serbia. A majority (32) of the sites are wetlands (coastal wetlands, lakes, freshwater marshes, wet meadows, riverine forests). The inventory includes a number of very important areas of flood-meadow and riverine forest along the Rivers Sava, Drava and Danube in Croatia and Vojvodina (e.g. 009, 010, 012, 013, 014, 028, 029, 030, 037, 039, 041); many of these sites are unprotected. Five sites are coastal islands (or sections of) with good populations of *Phalacrocorax aristotelis desmarestii* and *Gyps fulvus*, and 15 sites are upland or montane sites with valuable populations of birds of prey. Two sites stand out in a European context and are urgently in need of adequate protection measures. The first is Deliblatska pescara (038), an area of sandy-steppe with one of the most important populations of *Aquila heliaca* in Europe. The second is the alluvial wetlands of the River Sava (010; includes Lonjsko and Mokro Polje) with its sizeable populations of *Ciconia ciconia*, *Haliaeetus albicilla* and *Crex crex*.

Acknowledgements

This inventory was prepared from data-sheets compiled by many people. For Slovenia, data-sheets were compiled by B. Štumberger and J. Gregori; for Croatia by D. Antun, H. Ern, J. Fištrović, B. Gjetvaj, E. Kletečki, J. Mikuska, J. Mužinić, D. Radović, G. Robbrecht, M. Schneider, and G. Sušić; for Bosnia and Herzegovina by S. Albrecht and V. Brežančić; for Vojvodina by B. Garovnikov, I. Ham, J. Lakatoš, G. Nemeth, J. Purger, J. Rašajski, G. Robbrecht, and J. Soti; for Montenegro by I. Ham; for Serbia by B. Grubač; and for Macedonia, by B. Grubač and G. Robbrecht.

J. Gregori, J. Fištrovic, J. Mužinić, G. Sušić, B. Garovnikov, J. Soti, and B. Grubač helped with the coordination of the work in Yugoslavia or provided data on a large number of sites. J. Mužinić provided information which helped with the preparation of the introduction.

INVENTORY

No.	Site name	Region	Criteria used to select site [see p.18] 0	1(i)	1(ii)	1(iii)	1(iv)	2	3	4
001	Cerknisko jezero (Lake Cerknica)	SA						*	*	
002	Krakovski gozd (Krakovski Forest)	SA							*	
003	Sečoveljske soline (Sečovlje saltworks)	SA							*	
004	Severovzhodna Slovenija (North-east Slovenia)	SA							*	
004-1	Del Slovenskih Goric (part of Slovenske Gorice)	SA								
004-2	Reka Drava od Maribora do Zavrča (River Drava from Maribor to Zavrč)	SA								
004-3	Mura od Veržeja do Gibine (River Mura from Veržej to Gibina)	SA								
004-4	Črni log	SA								
005	Triglavski narodni park (Triglav National Park)	SA							*	
006	Ljubljansko barje (Ljubljana Moor)	SA						*	*	
007	Pokupsko Depression	CA				*		*	*	
007-1	Crna Mlaka	CA								
007-2	Draganići									
007-3	Pisarovina									
008	St Eufemia Bay, Rab	CA	*							
009	Turopolje	CA						*	*	
010	Poplavno podrucje rijeke Sava (Alluvial wetlands of the River Sava)	CA				*		*	*	
011	Ribnjaci Končanica (Končanica Fish-ponds)	CA				*		*	*	
012	Jelas polje (Jelas Field)	CA				*		*	*	
013	Dravske šume	CA						*	*	
014	Kopački rit	CA				*		*	*	
015	Ornitološki rezervat na Otoku Krku (Krk Ornithological Reserve)	CA							*	
016	Ornitološki rezervati na Otoku Cresu (Cres Ornithological Reserves)	CA							*	
017	Otok Prvič (Prvič Island)	CA							*	
018	Bokanjacko blato and Ninske solane (Nin saltpan)	CA	*							
019	Nacionalni park Paklenica (Paklenica National Park)	CA							*	
020	Nacionalni park Kornati (Kornati National Park)	CA							*	
021	Nacionalni park Krka (Krka National Park)	CA						*	*	
022	Vransko jezero (Lake Vrana)	CA							*	
023	Paško polje (Paško Field)	CA							*	
024	Dinara planina (Dinara Mountain)	CA							*	
025	Delta Neretve (Neretva Delta)	CA							*	
026	Hutovo blato	BA,HA						*	*	
027	Boračko jezero	BA,HA							*	
028	Bardača	BA,HA						*	*	
029	Gornje podunavlje or Monoštor	VA				*		*	*	
030	Bosutske šume (Bosutska Forest)	VA						*	*	
031	Fruška gora	VA						*	*	
032	Palič jezero (Lake Palič)	VA				*		*	*	
033	Ludaško jezero (Lake Ludaš)	VA				*			*	
034	Jazovo – Mokrin	VA				*		*	*	
035	Slano Kopovo or Šoškopo	VA				*		*	*	

No.	Site name	Region	Criteria used to select site [see p.18] 0	1(i)	1(ii)	1(iii)	1(iv)	2	3	4
036	Stari begej or complex of Carska bara	VA				*		*	*	
037	Koviljski rit	VA				*		*	*	
038	Deliblatska pescara	VA						*	*	
039	Donje podunavlje	VA				*		*	*	
040	Vršački breg	VA						*	*	
041	Obedska bara	VA				*		*	*	
042	Durmitor National Park	MO							*	
043	Skadarsko jezero (Lake Skadar)	MO				*		*	*	
044	Sasko jezero (Lake Sasko)	MO				*		*	*	
045	Ulcinjska solana (Ulcinj saltpans)	MO				*		*	*	
046	Resavska klisura i Beljanica (Resava Gorge and Beljanica Mountain)	SB							*	
047	Zlotska klisura (Zlot Gorge)	SB							*	
048	Šar planina [parts of] (Šara Mountains)	MA,KO							*	
049	Planina Korab i klisura Radike (Korab Mountain and Radika Gorge)	MA							*	
050	Klisura reke Babune i Topolke i Crn Kamen (Babuna Gorge, Topolka Gorge, and Black Rock)	MA						*	*	
051	Reka Bregalnica (River Bregalnica)	MA						*	*	
052	Klisura Crna reka (River Crna Gorge)	MA						*	*	
053	Demir kapija (Demir kapija Gorge)	MA						*	*	
054	Kožuf i Bošava Mountains (Kožuf Mountain and Bošava Region)	MA							*	
055	Ohridsko jezero (Lake Ohrid)	MA				*		*	*	
056	Prespansko jezero	MA				*		*	*	
057	Dojransko jezero	MA				*		*	*	

SA=Slovenia CA=Croatia BA=Bosnia HA=Herzegovina VA=Vojvodina MO=Montenegro SB=Serbia MA=Macedonia KO=Kosovo

Comments on the inventory

1. The site name is, in most cases, followed by an English translation of the site name in parentheses. This is then followed by the name of the republic or autonomous province where the site can be found. The republics/autonomous provinces are the 'regions' used when applying the site-selection criteria (category 3).
2. The figures for birds on passage for sites in Slovenia and Vojvodina are believed to be the total number occurring in a season (spring or autumn).
3. All of the sites are believed to meet the site-selection criteria except 008 and 018, which are included because of their importance for migratory birds.

---

001 Cerknisko jezero (Lake Cerknica) (Slovenia)

45°46'N, 14°24'E 3520 ha

Unprotected, but proposed for inclusion in Notranjska Regional Park

Eutrophic lake (dry in summer) with reedbeds, scrub, grazed fen, flood-meadows, and a small raised peatbog. Mainly agricultural land-use. There are plans to create a permanent reservoir; intensive agriculture and tourism are a problem at the site.

Breeding species include *Ixobrychus minutus* (2-5 pairs), *Crex crex* (5-10 pairs), *Numenius arquata* (2-5 pairs), *Alcedo atthis* (2-5 pairs), and *Saxicola rubetra* (20-50 pairs). *Ciconia ciconia* and *Falco peregrinus* formerly bred and *Tringa glareola* possibly breeds. A variety of waterbirds occur on passage with *Chlidonias niger* (50-200 in a season) and *C. leucopterus* (10-30 in a season) during spring passage.

002 Krakovski gozd (Krakovski Forest) (Slovenia)

45°54'N, 15°25'E 7000 ha

Nature Reserve (40 ha)

An area of primary *Quercus* forest and a remnant of the once vast Pannonian oak forest. The Nature Reserve is totally protected whereas the surrounding woodland is traditionally exploited. Drainage of the surrounding area may affect the site by lowering the water table.

Breeding species include (figures refer to the Nature Reserve only) *Ciconia nigra* (1 pair), *Dendrocopos medius* (10-20 pairs), *Ficedula albicollis* (50-100 pairs), and possibly *Dryocopus martius*.

003 Sečoveljske soline (Sečovlje saltworks) (Slovenia)

45°30'N, 13°39'E 850 ha

Unprotected, but proposed Nature Reserve

A partly abandoned area of saltpans with saltmarsh, reedbeds, and a small area of intertidal mudflats at the mouth of the River Dragonja. The western part of the saltworks is still used, whilst the future of the abandoned eastern part is undecided. There is indiscriminate hunting.

Breeding species include *Ixobrychus minutus* (2-5 pairs), *Sterna hirundo* (5-10 pairs), *S. albifrons* (2-5 pairs), *Alcedo atthis* (2-5 pairs), and *Anthus campestris* (2-5 pairs). *Botaurus stellaris* and *Acrocephalus melanopogon* possibly breed. *Philomachus pugnax* and *Tringa glareola* occur on migration.

004 Severovzhodna Slovenija (North-east Slovenia) (Slovenia)

46°27'N, 15°45'E 238,380 ha

Small areas are protected as Forest and Nature Reserves

An area to the north-east of the River Drava, with a variety of habitats including deciduous and coniferous forests, wet meadows, rivers, marshes, and ponds. Land-uses include agriculture, forestry, and intensive pisciculture. The intensification of agriculture, with drainage and the use of pesticides, threatens the remaining populations of *Ciconia ciconia* and *Coracias garrulus*.

An important area for breeding *Ciconia ciconia* (160 pairs); *Dendrocopos medius*, *Ficedula albicollis*, and *Lanius collurio* are numerous in the right habitat. *Crex crex* (now only single pairs) and *Coracias garrulus* (5-10 pairs; formerly hundreds) have declined dramatically.

Additional information is provided for the subsites 004-1 to 004-4.

004-1 Del Slovenskih Goric (part of Slovenske Gorice) (Slovenia)

46°35'N, 15°49'E 4200 ha

Partly protected as a Nature Reserve

A hilly region traversed by numerous streams and rivers (including the Globovnica and the Velka) with a great variety of habitats including rich riverine vegetation, wet meadows, dry hills, orchards, and vineyards. Land-uses include farming, fishing, and forestry. Agricultural intensification threatens the remaining *Coracias garrulus* population.

Breeding species include *Ciconia ciconia* (3 pairs), *Pernis apivorus* (1 pair), *Crex crex* (1 pair), *Coracias garrulus* (5 pairs; the last nesting site in Slovenia), *Picus canus* (5 pairs), *Acrocephalus arundinaceus* (8 pairs), *Ficedula albicollis* (5 pairs), *Lanius collurio* (35 pairs), and *L. minor* (3 pairs). A variety of herons and raptors occurs on passage.

004-2 Reka Drava od Maribora do Zavrča (River Drava from Maribor to Zavrč) (Slovenia)

46°33'N, 15°39'E – 46°23'N, 16°03'E 5800 ha

Partly protected (Šturmovec Regional Park: 350 ha and Zavrč Forest Reserve: 3 ha)

Meandering river with backwaters and large sandbanks, flanked by meadows, marshes, groves, and copses. Land-uses include agriculture, forestry, gravel extraction, hunting, fishing, and hydroelectric power generation. There is considerable pollution of the Drava and plans for the area include agricultural intensification, road building, the building of a chicken farm, and rubbish-dumps.

Breeding species include *Ixobrychus minutus* (5 pairs), *Ciconia ciconia* (5 pairs), *Pernis apivorus* (3 pairs), *Sterna hirundo* (70 pairs), *Alcedo atthis* (7 pairs), *Acrocephalus melanopogon* (4 pairs), and *Lanius collurio* (50 pairs). Passage species include *Ciconia ciconia* (20 during autumn), *Circus aeruginosus* (15 during spring), and *Pandion haliaetus* (8 during spring). Winter visitors include *Phalacrocorax pygmeus* (40), *Egretta alba* (15), *Anser fabalis* (1500), *A. anser* (200), *Anas crecca* (3000), *A. platyrhynchos* (13,000), *Bucephala clangula* (1000), *Haliaeetus albicilla* (1), and *Falco peregrinus* (2).

004-3 Mura od Veržeja do Gibine (River Mura from Veržej to Gibina) (Slovenia)

46°35'N,16°10'E – 46°31'N,16°16'E 3500 ha

Small areas are protected

Meandering river with large areas of *Salix/Populus* forest (in places mixed with *Quercus*), reedbeds, flood-meadows, and gravel-pits. Land-uses include forestry and there is intensive agriculture in the surrounding area. A possible threat is the building of a chain of hydroelectric plants, which would have a dramatic effect on the area.

Breeding species include *Alcedo atthis* (5-10 pairs), *Dendrocopos medius* (2-4 pairs per 100 ha), *Ficedula albicollis* (4-10 pairs per 100 ha), *Locustella fluviatilis* (10-20 pairs), *L. luscinioides* (5-10 pairs), and *Lanius collurio* (4-10 pairs per 100 ha). The area is important for feeding *Ciconia ciconia*.

004-4 Črni log (Slovenia)

46°36'N, 16°28'E 1200 ha

Unprotected

A large *Alnus* forest – the largest in central Europe – along the River Ledava. The forest is traditionally exploited. The creation of a reservoir nearby has caused a rise in the water-table, which may affect the area.

Breeding species include *Picus canus* (2-4 pairs per 100 ha), *Dendrocopos medius* (4-10 pairs per 100 ha), *Locustella fluviatilis* (4-10 pairs), and *Ficedula albicollis* (10-20 pairs per 100 ha).

005 Triglavski narodni park (Triglav National Park) (Slovenia)

46°21'N, 13°50'E 48,805 ha

National Park

A mountainous alpine area (up to 2860 m) with mixed and coniferous forests, heath, highland pasture, and rocky ground. Farming and forestry are practised in the border areas. The building of forest roads, hunting, and tourism are adversely affecting the area.

Breeding species include *Aquila chrysaetos* (3-5 pairs), *Lagopus mutus helveticus*, *Tetrao tetrix*, *Alectoris graeca saxatilis* (rare and has drastically declined), and *Picoides tridactylus*.

006 Ljubljansko barje (Ljubljana Moor) (Slovenia)

46°02'N, 14°26'E 14,560 ha

Unprotected

An area of flood-meadows, bisected by the Rivers Ljubljanica and Iscica, on the edge of Ljubljana, with remnant peatbogs, reedbeds, ponds, open grassland, and scrub. Agricultural land-use. Affected by early mowing and drainage, and there are plans to build roads and an airport.

Breeding species include *Ixobrychus minutus* (10-20 pairs), *Ciconia nigra* (1 pair), *Pernis apivorus* (2-5 pairs), *Crex crex* (20-30 pairs, but population considerably reduced), *Numenius arquata* (5-10 pairs), *Asio otus* (10-20 pairs), *Alcedo atthis* (5-10 pairs), *Saxicola rubetra* (50 pairs), *Acrocephalus arundinaceus* (10-20 pairs), *Sylvia nisoria* (5-10 pairs), *Lanius collurio* (40-50 pairs), and *L. minor* (2-5 pairs).

007 Pokupsko Depression (Croatia)

45°32'-45°42'N, 15°35'-15°50'E *c.*20,000 ha

Unprotected except for Crna Mlaka

A natural depression south of the Žumberak Mountains and extending towards the River Kupa. There are 11,500 ha of moist deciduous forests alternating with large tracts of semi-natural grassland, which are now either being reafforested or converted into maize fields. The area is crossed by numerous meandering streams, and there are four important commercial fish-ponds (Crna Mlaka, Draganići, Jastrebarsko, and Pisarovina) with more than 1400 ha of open water. There are many threats to the area: the main impact is from road building and canalisation of rivers and streams; other problems include modern methods of agriculture, forestry, and pisciculture, and there are projects to convert the southern part of the depression into a retention basin.

The area is important for breeding *Ciconia nigra*, *Haliaeetus albicilla*, and *Aquila pomarina*.

Further information is provided for the following subsites:

007-1 Crna Mlaka (Croatia)

45°37'N, 15°44'E 625 ha

Special Ornithological Reserve (fish-ponds)

Fish-ponds in the middle of the Pokupsko (Kupčina) Depression, surrounded by flooded woodland and meadows. Land-uses include pisciculture, with forestry in the surrounding area. Fish-eating birds pose a problem at the site and forestry could have a negative influence on the breeding success of *Haliaeetus albicilla*. This area is important for otters *Lutra lutra*.

Breeding species include *Botaurus stellaris*, *Ixobrychus minutus* (abundant), *Ciconia nigra* (2 pairs), *Aythya nyroca* (60-80 pairs), *Pernis apivorus* (1-2 pairs), *Milvus migrans* (1-2 pairs), *Haliaeetus albicilla* (1 pair), *Aquila pomarina* (1-2 pairs), *Crex crex*, and *Acrocephalus arundinaceus* (common). An important site during spring and autumn migration with (autumn figures unless stated) *Egretta alba* (max. 15; 5-10 in spring), *Platalea leucorodia* (max. 16), *Aythya nyroca* (3000-5000; one of the most important sites in Europe for this species), *Pandion haliaetus* (1-2), *Falco peregrinus* (1-2), and *Chlidonias niger* (max. 80). *Egretta alba* (5-8) and *Haliaeetus albicilla* (3-4) occur in winter.

007-2 Draganići

45°36'N, 15°38'E 363 ha

Unprotected

A complex of fish-ponds, one pond overgrown with rushes. There is a modern fish-breeding station connected to the ponds, and there is hunting by Italian visitors.

The bird fauna is similar to Crna Mlaka. Species recorded in October 1983 included *Egretta alba* (5) and *Aythya nyroca* (50).

007-3 Pisarovina

45°35'N, 15°50'E 355 ha

Unprotected

A complex of fish-ponds. There is considerable pressure from Italian hunters.

The bird fauna is similar to Crna Mlaka. Species recorded in October 1983 included *Phalacrocorax pygmeus* (3), *Egretta alba* (30), *Platalea leucorodia* (2), *Aythya nyroca* (*c.*200), and *Haliaeetus albicilla* (2).

008 St Eufemia Bay, Rab (Croatia)

44°45'N, 14°45'E 20 ha

Unprotected

A small tidal bay on the island of Rab with mudflats, and reedbeds at the northern end. Problems include human disturbance and hunting.

An important site for passage and wintering birds. Passage species include, or are thought to include, *Egretta garzetta*, *Plegadis falcinellus*, *Tringa glareola*, and *Chlidonias niger*.

009 Turopolje (Croatia)

45°40'N, 16°10'E – 45°30'N, 16°15'E 20,000 ha

Unprotected

Wet meadows between the Rivers Sava and Odra with *Quercus* woodland. Drainage and an airport for gliders are adversely affecting the site and it is a favoured location for a nuclear power-station.

Breeding species include *Ciconia nigra* (10+ pairs), *C. ciconia* (20 pairs), *Milvus migrans* (2-5 pairs), *Haliaeetus albicilla* (2-3 pairs), *Aquila pomarina* (2-3 pairs), and *Crex crex* (10+ pairs). *Saxicola rubetra*, *Acrocephalus arundinaceus*, *Ficedula albicollis*, and *Lanius collurio* are common.

010 Poplavno podrucje rijeke Sava (Alluvial wetlands of the River Sava) (Croatia)

45°30'N, 17°00'E 210,000 ha

Unprotected, except for three Bird Sanctuaries: Krapje Dol (25 ha), Vrazje Blato (77 ha) and Rakita (430 ha). Lonjsko and Mokro polje have been proposed as Nature Parks

The flood-plain of the Sava, Lonja, and Strug. A complex of alluvial forests of *Quercus* and *Populus* (mostly inundated annually), marshes, meadows, grazing land, fish-ponds, permanent water in depressions and oxbows, and rivers and streams without embankments. Lonjsko and Mokro polje are retention basins. Land-uses include forestry, grazing, and silage-making, and areas have been drained and are now cultivated (but have lost their ecological importance). There are large-scale plans for drainage and land reclamation outside Lonjsko and Mokro polje (to increase the area of cultivation) which will have a major impact, particularly on the population of *Ciconia ciconia*.

Breeding species include *Phalacrocorax carbo sinensis* (230 pairs), *Nycticorax nycticorax* (100-200 pairs), *Ardeola ralloides* (1 pair; formerly 20 pairs), *Egretta garzetta* (30-70 pairs), *Ardea purpurea* (10 pairs), *Ciconia nigra* (50-80 pairs), *C. ciconia* (570 pairs), *Platalea leucorodia* (150-170 pairs at Krapje Dol), *Pernis apivorus* (10+ pairs), *Milvus migrans* (10+ pairs), *Haliaeetus albicilla* (15 pairs), *Aquila pomarina* (25+ pairs), *Falco cherrug* (1 pair), *Porzana porzana* (10 pairs), *P. parva* (1 pair), *Crex crex* (120-150 pairs), and *Chlidonias hybridus* (150+ pairs). *Picus canus*, *Dendrocopos medius*, and *Ficedula albicollis* are common in the forest. Species occurring on passage include

Tringa glareola, *Philomachus pugnax*, *Chlidonias niger*, and *C. leucopterus*. *Haliaeetus albicilla* and *Egretta alba* occur in winter.

011 Ribnjaci Končanica (Končanica Fish-ponds) (Croatia)

45°37'-45°44'N, 17°02'-17°07'E 2100 ha

Unprotected

One of the oldest fisheries in Yugoslavia (with 24 fish-ponds), situated along the River Ilova, surrounded by meadows, marshes, and woodland (*Salix alba*, *Quercus robur*). *Phalacrocorax carbo* poses a problem at the fish-ponds.

Breeding species include *Phalacrocorax carbo sinensis* (157 pairs), *Botaurus stellaris* (1 pair), *Ixobrychus minutus* (7 pairs), *Ciconia nigra* (3 pairs), *C. ciconia* (28 pairs), *Aythya nyroca* (7 pairs), *Milvus migrans* (2 pairs), *Haliaeetus albicilla* (1 pair), *Circaetus gallicus* (1 pair), *Crex crex* (11 pairs), *Asio otus* (2 pairs), and *Alcedo atthis* (17 pairs). *Locustella luscinioides* and *Acrocephalus arundinaceus* are common. *Pandion haliaetus* occurs on passage and *Egretta alba* (21) in winter.

012 Jelas polje (Jelas Field) (Croatia)

45°09'N, 18°01'E 2300 ha

Unprotected

Situated in the central part of the Sava flood-plain, bordered to the west by the River Orljava and to the south by the River Sava. A large part of the area is agricultural land with two large blocks of alluvial forest of *Quercus*, *Fraxinus*, *Ulmus*, *Populus*, *Salix*, and *Alnus* (Migalovci lug and Msunjski lug: 2500 ha). There are fish-ponds of varying sizes (covering 2300 ha), large parts of which are covered in reeds, sedges, and floating waterplants. Also remnant alluvial *Quercus* forests. In spring and autumn the water-levels are lowered to catch fish, providing good feeding sites for migrant waterbirds. Frequent reconstruction of the embankments (to increase water depth) is detrimental to the marsh vegetation. An increasing *Phalacrocorax carbo* population is causing problems with the management, and the drainage of the alluvial wetlands in the surrounding area has had a negative impact on some species such as *Ciconia ciconia*. Shooting (during the shooting season) is intensive.

Breeding species include *Phalacrocorax carbo sinensis* (270 pairs), *Ixobrychus minutus* (120 pairs), *Nycticorax nycticorax* (170 pairs), *Ardeola ralloides* (80 pairs), *Egretta garzetta* (40 pairs), *Ciconia nigra*, *C. ciconia*, *Aythya nyroca* (120-160 pairs), *Haliaeetus albicilla* (in nearby forests), *Porzana porzana*, *P. pusilla*, *P. parva*, *Chlidonias niger* (10-20 pairs), and *Sterna hirundo* (70-120 pairs). Large numbers of herons, *Pandion haliaetus*, and possibly small numbers of *Numenius tenuirostris*, occur on passage, and *Egretta alba* (10-20) occurs in winter.

013 Dravske šume (Croatia)

45°35'-45°40'N, 18°10'-18°40'E 2500 ha

Unprotected

Deciduous forest of *Quercus* and *Populus* along the River Drava, west of Kopacki rit. Managed for forestry, and the main problem is disturbance of *Haliaeetus albicilla* nests by forestry activity. There is a plan to build a reservoir for a power-plant.

Breeding species include *Ciconia nigra*, *Haliaeetus albicilla* (5-6 pairs), *Falco cherrug*, *Picus canus*, *Dryocopus martius*, *Dendrocopos medius*, and *Ficedula albicollis*.

014 Kopački rit (Croatia)

45°32'-45°38'N, 18°44'-18°58'E 50,000 ha

Zoological Reserve (6234 ha) and Nature Park (10,766 ha)

The inundation area of the Rivers Danube (Dunav) and Drava, with extensive forests of *Salix*, *Populus*, and *Quercus*. In spring much of the Reserve is flooded; when drier, numerous channels, oxbows, and a lake (Kopački jezero) remain. There are extensive reedbeds and a large complex of fish-ponds (which is partly unprotected). Human activities include tourism, hunting, and pisciculture. The area is silting up, affected by eutrophication, and there is human disturbance from illegal fishing and frog-collecting activities. Fish predation by *Phalacrocorax carbo* and *Ardea cinerea* is a problem at the fish-ponds.

Outstandingly important for breeding herons with 545-1450 pairs in the period 1968-1985, including *Botaurus stellaris* (1-5 pairs), *Ixobrychus minutus* (100+ pairs), *Nycticorax nycticorax* (400 pairs), *Ardeola ralloides* (10-100 pairs; although there has possibly been a long-term decline with 190 pairs in 1970, but consistently low numbers since 1980), *Egretta garzetta* (30-200 pairs), *E. alba* (5-10 pairs), *Ardea cinerea* (200-400 pairs), and *A. purpurea* (10-200 pairs). Other breeding species include *Phalacrocorax carbo sinensis* (1200 pairs), *Ciconia nigra* (30 pairs), *C. ciconia* (20-50 pairs), *Anser anser* (20-40 pairs), *Aythya nyroca* (100-200 pairs), *Milvus migrans* (50 pairs), *Haliaeetus albicilla* (15-20 pairs; probably the most important locality in central Europe for this species), *Falco cherrug* (4-5 pairs), *Chlidonias hybridus* (100 pairs), and *C. niger* (50-100 pairs). Very important passage site for waterfowl including *Phalacrocorax pygmeus* (20), *Platalea leucorodia* (500-1000), *Grus grus* (50-500), and large numbers of waders, particularly *Philomachus pugnax*, *Limosa limosa*, *Tringa erythropus*, *T. nebularia*, and *T. glareola*. Large numbers of *Anser fabalis* (10,000-50,000) and *Anas platyrhynchos* (max. 50,000) occur in late autumn and winter (depending on conditions) and other wintering species include *Egretta alba* (max. 1000), *Haliaeetus albicilla*, *Aquila clanga* (2-5), and *Circus cyaneus* (20).

015 Ornitološki rezervat na Otoku Krku (Krk Ornithological Reserve) (Croatia)

45°02'N, 14°45'E 1000 ha

Ornithological Reserve

Canyons and high sea cliffs at the north-eastern side of the island of Krk. Tourism is a problem at the site.

Breeding species include *Phalacrocorax aristotelis desmarestii* (many), *Gyps fulvus* (10-15 pairs), *Circaetus gallicus* (1-3 pairs), *Falco peregrinus* (1-2 pairs), *Alectoris graeca* (many), *Burhinus oedicnemus*, and *Bubo bubo*. *Calonectris diomedea*, *Puffinus puffinus*, and *Hydrobates pelagicus* feed in the area, and many *Gavia stellata* and *G. arctica* occur in winter.

016 Ornitološki rezervati na Otoku Cresu (Cres Ornithological Reserves) (Croatia)

45°05'N, 14°22'E and 44°50'N, 14°27'E 900 ha and 550 ha

Ornithological Reserves

Forests of *Quercus ilex*, *Q. pubescens*, *Carpinus orientalis*, *Ostrya carpinifolia*, *Castanea sativa*, and *Juniperus* sp., and high sea cliffs. Tourism is a problem at the site.

Breeding species include *Phalacrocorax aristotelis desmarestii* (many), *Gyps fulvus* (2 colonies, 25 pairs), *Circaetus gallicus* (2-4 pairs), *Falco peregrinus* (1-2 pairs), and there are many pairs of *Caprimulgus europaeus*, *Calandrella brachydactyla*, *Anthus campestris*, and *Lanius collurio*. *Calonectris diomedea*, *Puffinus puffinus*, and *Hydrobates pelagicus* feed in the area, and many *Gavia stellata* and *G. arctica* occur in winter.

017 Otok Prvič (Prvič Island) (Croatia)

44°55'N, 14°48'E 7000 ha
Botanical and Zoological Reserve

The island of Prvič is situated south of the island of Krk. There are very high sea cliffs on the north-east and south-west sides. There is an upland plateau with stony grassland grazed by sheep, and garigue is the dominant vegetation. The island supports many endemic plants. Tourism is a problem at the site.

Breeding species include *Phalacrocorax aristotelis desmarestii* (many), *Gyps fulvus* (10-15 pairs), *Circaetus gallicus* (1-2 pairs), *Aquila chrysaetos* (1 pair), *Bubo bubo*, *Anthus campestris*, and possibly *Hieraaetus fasciatus* and *Falco peregrinus*. *Calonectris diomedea* and *Hydrobates pelagicus* feed in the area, and many *Gavia stellata* and *G. arctica* occur in winter.

018 Bokanjacko blato and Ninske solane (Nin saltpan) (Croatia)

44°15'N, 15°15'E 1000 ha

Unprotected, although Bokanjacko blato has been proposed for protection

Bokanjacko blato (blato = mud) is agricultural land with marshes, reedbeds, and ditches. Ninske solane is an area of saltpans with reedbeds and meadows. Hunting and agricultural intensification (use of pesticides) are a problem at the site.

Breeding species include *Coracias garrulus*, *Lanius collurio* (20 pairs), and *L. minor*. An important passage site, with *Circus cyaneus* (3-4), *C. pygargus* (3), *Falco columbarius* (2), *F. biarmicus* (2), and *Philomachus pugnax* (200) occurring in spring.

019 Nacionalni park Paklenica (Paklenica National Park) (Croatia)

44°20'N, 15°45'E 3617 ha Mediterranean Specially Protected Area

National Park

Two big river canyons with very high cliffs, with forests of *Fagus sylvatica*, *Pinus nigra*, *Quercus pubescens*, and *Carpinus orientalis*. Cliff-climbing throughout the year is a problem at the site (affecting the larger gorge - Velika Paklenica - which has meant that vultures no longer nest here).

Breeding species include *Neophron percnopterus* (1 pair), *Gyps fulvus* (*c.*20 pairs; see comment above), *Circaetus gallicus* (2 pairs), *Aquila chrysaetos* (1 pair), *Hieraaetus fasciatus* (possibly 1 pair), *Falco biarmicus* (possibly 1 pair), *F. peregrinus* (2 pairs), *Bonasa bonasia*, *Alectoris graeca*, *Bubo bubo*, and there are many pairs of *Lanius collurio*, *L. minor*, and *Emberiza hortulana*.

020 Nacionalni park Kornati (Kornati National Park) (Croatia)

43°45'N, 15°18'E 30,200 ha Mediterranean Specially Protected Area

National Park

An archipelago of several hundred islands (the outer islands with high cliffs) in the central part of the Adriatic Sea. All islands are without forests, but there are patches of *Quercus ilex*, *Olea europaea*, and *Juniperus* sp. Tourism is a problem at the site.

Breeding species include *Phalacrocorax aristotelis desmarestii* (many), *Circaetus gallicus* (max. 10 pairs), *Falco eleonorae* (max. 10 pairs), *F. peregrinus* (1-3 pairs), and *Sterna hirundo* (a few colonies), and there are many pairs of *Anthus campestris*, *Lanius collurio*, *L. minor*, and *Emberiza hortulana*. *Falco naumanni* and *F. biarmicus* possibly breed. *Calonectris diomedea*, *Puffinus puffinus*, *Hydrobates pelagicus*, and *Hieraaetus fasciatus* feed in the area, and many *Gavia stellata* and *G. arctica* occur in winter.

021 Nacionalni park Krka (Krka National Park) (Croatia)

43°48'N, 15°55'E 14,200 ha Mediterranean Specially Protected Area

National Park

Sea coast and river (River Krka), canyons, lakes, and forests of *Quercus pubescens* and *Q. ilex*, *Carpinus orientalis*, and *Ostrya carpinifolia*. Tourism is a problem at the site.

Breeding species include *Phalacrocorax aristotelis desmarestii*, *Botaurus stellaris* (1-2 pairs), *Ixobrychus minutus* (4-5 pairs), *Circaetus gallicus* (4-5 pairs), *Aquila chrysaetos* (possibly 1 pair), *Hieraaetus fasciatus* (possibly 1 pair), *Falco naumanni* (a few pairs), *F. biarmicus* (1-2 pairs), *F. peregrinus* (2-3 pairs), *Alectoris graeca* (a few pairs), *Bubo bubo* (1-3 pairs), *Calandrella brachydactyla* (20+ pairs), with many pairs of *Anthus campestris*, *Lanius collurio*, *L. minor*, and *Emberiza hortulana*. *Gyps fulvus* feeds in the Park. A variety of species occurs on passage including *Ardeola ralloides*, *Egretta alba*, *Circus aeruginosus* (many), *C. cyaneus*, *Pandion haliaetus*, and *Falco columbarius*, and many *Gavia arctica* occur in winter.

022 Vransko jezero (Lake Vrana) (Croatia)

43°51'-43°57'N, 15°31'-15°39'E 3000 ha

Partly protected by a small Ornithological Reserve (30 ha)

A Mediterranean lake (the largest natural lake in Croatia and connected by a canal with the sea), fringed with reeds, with agricultural land along the western shore. The lake is used for recreation (wind-surfing) and the surrounding area is used for fishing and agriculture. The development of agriculture and pisciculture, reed-cutting, hunting, and a tourist camp are problems at the site.

Important for breeding Ardeidae (colony protected by Ornithological Reserve) including *Ixobrychus minutus*, *Nycticorax nycticorax*, *Ardeola ralloides*, *Egretta garzetta*, and *Ardea purpurea*. Also breeding *Plegadis falcinellus*, *Crex crex* (possibly), and *Acrocephalus melanopogon*. *Anser albifrons*, *A. anser*, *Circus aeruginosus*, *C. cyaneus*, and *Falco peregrinus* occur in winter.

023 Paško polje (Paško Field) (Croatia)

43°55'N, 16°25'E 625 ha

Unprotected

Wet meadows (with many springs of cold water) at the head of the River Cetina. Agricultural use might pose a problem in the future.

Breeding species include *Circaetus gallicus* (1-2 pairs), *Tringa totanus* (30-50 pairs; the largest breeding population in Yugoslavia), *Caprimulgus europaeus* (many), *Lullula arborea* (many), *Anthus campestris* (many), *Acrocephalus arundinaceus*, *Ficedula parva*, *Lanius collurio* (many), *L. minor*, and *Emberiza hortulana*. *Aquila chrysaetos* and *Hieraaetus fasciatus* feed in the area, and passage species include *Ardeola ralloides*, *Ciconia nigra*, and *Tringa glareola*.

024 Dinara planina (Dinara Mountain) (Croatia)

43°53'-44°05'N, 16°25'-16°40'E 20,000 ha (central parts only)

Unprotected

High mountain meadows, cliffs and rocks, deciduous and coniferous woodland. Land-uses include sheep- and cattle-grazing.

Breeding species include *Circaetus gallicus* (approx. 5 pairs), *Aquila chrysaetos* (1-2 pairs), *Falco peregrinus* (2-3 pairs), *Bonasa bonasia*, *Tetrao urogallus*, *Bubo bubo*, *Caprimulgus europaeus*, *Anthus campestris*, and *Emberiza hortulana*. *Hieraaetus fasciatus* possibly breeds and *Gyps fulvus* feeds in the area.

025 Delta Neretve (Neretva Delta) (Croatia)

42°47'-43°07'N, 17°27'-17°40'E 11,500 ha Mediterranean Specially Protected Area

Partly protected by four Ornithological Reserves: Pod Gredon (650 ha), Prud (250 ha), Orepak (100 ha), and south-east delta (250 ha), and a protected landscape: Modro oko and lake (370 ha)

Although much changed and degraded by drainage and agricultural development, important marshes remain. A delta with coastal saltmarshes, saline lagoons, sandbanks, and wet meadows, contiguous with Hutovo blato in Bosnia and Herzegovina. Drainage, agricultural development, urbanisation, road building, and hunting are problems at the site.

Breeding species include *Ixobrychus minutus*, *Botaurus stellaris*, *Aythya nyroca*, *Alectoris graeca*, *Porzana pusilla*, *Acrocephalus arundinaceus*, and *Lanius minor*. A very important area during spring and autumn passage. During winter, the Delta is rich with species, and all five European grebes and almost all European species of ducks occur.

026 Hutovo blato (Bosnia and Herzegovina)

43°00'-43°05'N and 17°42'-17°50'E 6144 ha

Ornithological Reserve

Areas of open water with extensive stands of emergent vegetation (*Phragmites*, *Scirpus*), wet meadows, riverine and water-edge forests (*Salix*, *Populus*, *Alnus*), and degraded *Quercus* and *Carpinus* woodland on high ground. Human activities include fishing and hunting. Drainage, agricultural intensification, urbanisation, and tourism are problems at the site.

Breeding species include *Phalacrocorax carbo*, *P. pygmeus*, *Botaurus stellaris*, *Ardeola ralloides*, *Nycticorax nycticorax*, *Egretta garzetta*, *Ardea purpurea*, and *Aythya nyroca*.

027 Boračko jezero (Bosnia and Herzegovina)

43°34'N, 18°02'E

Lake with gravel edges and little or no vegetation, bordered by *Alnus* woodland, meadows, orchards, and surrounded by steep mountains covered in deciduous forest. The valley is used for farming and tourism.

Breeding species include *Strix uralensis*, *Dendrocopos medius*, and *D. leucotos*.

028 Bardača (Bosnia and Herzegovina)

45°07'N, 17°27'E 700 ha

Ornithological Reserve

Fish-ponds (with islands and reedbeds), marshes, grazing-meadows, and remnant alluvial forest along the River Sava. Drainage, hunting, and forestry are problems at the site.

Breeding species include *Ixobrychus minutus*, *Nycticorax nycticorax*, *Ardeola ralloides*, *Egretta garzetta*, *Ardea purpurea*, *Plegadis falcinellus*, *Platalea leucorodia*, *Aythya nyroca*, *Crex crex*, *Sterna hirundo* (30+ pairs), and *Chlidonias hybridus* (40+ pairs). *Ciconia ciconia* and *Haliaeetus albicilla* feed, and possibly breed, at the site. Also very important for passage migrants.

029 Gornje podunavlje or Monoštor (Vojvodina)

45°38'N, 18°58'E 1000 ha

Regional Park

Flooded area along the eastern bank of the Danube, adjacent to Kopacki rit, with extensive forests (*Quercus*, *Salix*, *Populus*), pools, marshes, rivers, and streams. Human activities include forestry, recreation, and hunting.

Breeding species include *Botaurus stellaris*, *Ixobrychus minutus* (100 pairs), *Nycticorax nycticorax* (300 pairs), *Ardeola ralloides* (10 pairs), *Egretta garzetta* (100 pairs), *E. alba* (10 pairs), *Ardea purpurea* (150+ pairs), *Ciconia nigra* (10 pairs), *C. ciconia* (40 pairs), *Haliaeetus albicilla* (4 pairs), *Circus aeruginosus* (10 pairs), *Falco cherrug* (3 pairs), *Porzana porzana*, *P. parva*, *P. pusilla*, *Crex crex*, *Dendrocopos medius* (common), *Acrocephalus arundinaceus*, *Ficedula albicollis*, *Lanius collurio* (very common), and *L. minor*. *Platalea leucorodia* (100) occurs on passage and *Circus cyaneus* (5) in winter.

030 Bosutske šume (Bosutska Forest) (Vojvodina)

45°00'N, 19°10'E
Unprotected

Riverine forest (predominately *Quercus robur*) along the River Sava close to Morovíč, with a complex of smaller rivers, pools, swamps, and marshes. Human activities include hunting, forestry, and fishing.

Breeding species include *Ciconia nigra* (5+ pairs), *Milvus migrans* (5+ pairs), *M. milvus* (possibly), *Circus aeruginosus*, *Haliaeetus albicilla* (3+ pairs), *Alcedo atthis*, *Coracias garrulus*, and *Dryocopus martius*, whilst *Dendrocopos medius* and *Lanius collurio* are common.

031 Fruška gora (Vojvodina)

45°05'N, 19°35'E 25,000 ha

National Park

Hilly area covered in deciduous woodland with clearings, surrounded by orchards, vineyards, and agricultural land. Land-uses include forestry, hunting, recreation (very popular because of its proximity to Novi Sad and Beograd), and agriculture. Problems at the site include intensive forestry, disturbance by recreational activities, and uncontrolled hunting.

Breeding species include *Ciconia nigra* (5 pairs), *C. ciconia* (10 pairs), *Pernis apivorus* (3+ pairs), *Aquila heliaca* (2-3 pairs), *Hieraaetus pennatus*, *Falco cherrug*, *Bubo bubo*, *Dendrocopos syriacus* (common), *D. medius* (very common), *Sylvia nisoria*, *Lanius collurio* (abundant), *L. minor*, and *Emberiza hortulana*. *Aquila pomarina* and *A. clanga* possibly breed.

032 Palič jezero (Lake Palič) (Vojvodina)

46°05'N, 19°45'E 80 ha

South-western part is protected (part of a Regional Park)

A man-made pool, highly eutrophic, with elongated and flat islets, aquatic vegetation, and small stands of *Populus* and *Salix*. Human activities include hunting. Problems include pollution, erosion of islets, and human disturbance.

Breeding species include *Ixobrychus minutus* (10+ pairs), *Nycticorax nycticorax* (100+ pairs), *Larus melanocephalus* (15+ pairs), *Sterna hirundo* (10+ pairs), and *Acrocephalus arundinaceus* (50 pairs). *Oxyura leucocephala* occurs in autumn and winter.

033 Ludaško jezero (Lake Ludaš) (Vojvodina)

46°05'N, 19°50'E 593 ha Ramsar Site

Included in a Regional Park

A shallow lake with extensive reedbeds and aquatic vegetation. Human activities include sport-fishing, hunting, reed-cutting, and recreation. Polluted by industrial and domestic effluent (from Subotica) which is passed through the lake; eutrophication, disturbance from fishing, recreation, and reed-cutting and -burning are also problems at the site.

Breeding species include *Podiceps nigricollis* (100+ pairs), *Botaurus stellaris*, *Ixobrychus minutus* (100+ pairs), *Ardeola ralloides*, *Ardea purpurea* (100-300 pairs), *Aythya nyroca* (50+ pairs), *Tringa totanus*, *Sterna hirundo* (less than 30 pairs), *Luscinia svecica*, *Locustella luscinioides* (50+ pairs), *Acrocephalus melanopogon*, *A. arundinaceus* (100+ pairs), and *Panurus biarmicus* (100+ pairs). *Oxyura leucocephala* and *Haliaeetus albicilla* no longer breed.

034 Jazovo – Mokrin (Vojvodina)

45°50'N, 20°15'E

Unprotected

Extensive pastures on alkaline soils (remnant steppe), large fish-pond (*c.*580 ha), cultivated areas, marshy depressions, small reedbeds, and *Salix*/*Populus* woodland along the River Zlatica. Human activities include sheep-grazing, agriculture, hunting, fishing, and reed-cutting. The main concern is that the pastures are protected from cultivation. Every year hunters take bustard eggs to hatch the young, but these die.

Breeding species include *Botaurus stellaris* (10+ pairs), *Ixobrychus minutus* (50+ pairs), *Ardea purpurea* (20+ pairs), *Ciconia ciconia* (20+ pairs), *Aythya nyroca* (10+ pairs),

Circus aeruginosus (5+ pairs), *Falco vespertinus*, *Otis tarda* (10+ pairs; the main site for this species in Yugoslavia), *Himantopus himantopus*, *Recurvirostra avosetta* (less than 10 pairs), *Limosa limosa* (5+ pairs), and probably *Asio flammeus*. *Anthus campestris*, *Lanius collurio*, and *L. minor* are common. Species on passage include *Nycticorax nycticorax* (100+), *Ardeola ralloides* (50+), *Ciconia ciconia* (300+), *Platalea leucorodia* (100+), *Grus grus* (300+), *Philomachus pugnax* (300+), and *Limosa limosa* (100+), and in winter *Egretta alba* and *Otis tarda* (20-30) are present and *Circus cyaneus* is common.

035 Slano Kopovo or Šoškopo (Vojvodina)

45°37'N, 20°13'E 600-700 ha

Unprotected, but protection proposed and hunting prohibited (March-October)

A saline lake with muddy shores, halophytic vegetation, and a narrow fringe of reeds, surrounded by pastures on alkaline soils and agriculture. The lake varies from 30-100 ha depending on the underground water-levels. Land-uses include livestock-grazing (sheep, cattle, pigs), agriculture, and hunting. Grazing animals, especially pigs, frequently destroy the nests of *Recurvirostra avosetta*.

Breeding species include *Botaurus stellaris* (1-2 pairs), *Ixobrychus minutus* (10+ pairs), *Nycticorax nycticorax* (30+ pairs; max. 150 pairs), *Ardea purpurea* (10+ pairs), *Ciconia ciconia* (45 pairs), *Circus aeruginosus* (2-3 pairs), *Porzana pusilla*, *Recurvirostra avosetta* (5-30 pairs), and *Luscinia svecica* (3-5 pairs). *Oxyura leucocephala* bred until the 1960s. Species recorded on passage include *Branta ruficollis*, *Aquila pomarina*, *A. heliaca*, *Grus grus* (250 in spring, 500 in autumn), *Recurvirostra avosetta* (300 in autumn), *Numenius tenuirostris* (occasionally small numbers in spring and autumn), *Sterna caspia*, and *Gelochelidon nilotica*. Species occurring in winter include *Anser erythropus*, *Circus cyaneus*, and *Asio flammeus*.

036 Stari begej or complex of Carska bara (Vojvodina)

45°16'N, 20°25'E 2000 ha

Regional Park (except Ečka fish-ponds) with a strict sanctuary (Carska bara: 300 ha)

A once-flooded area of the River Begej, with pools, marshes, fish-ponds, meadows, and *Salix* and *Populus* woodland. Includes Carska bara, Tiganjica, Perleska bara, and Ečka fish-ponds. Carska bara is a shallow, eutrophic lake surrounded by ancient *Salix*/*Populus* woodland. Land-uses include pisciculture, hunting, and reed-cutting. Carska bara is used for birdwatching, fishing, and recreation, and is affected by pollution, excessive disturbance from visitors, and inappropriate water management; there is excessive hunting and reed-cutting at the fish-ponds.

Breeding species include *Botaurus stellaris* (5+ pairs), *Ixobrychus minutus* (100+ pairs), *Nycticorax nycticorax* (100-1300 pairs), *Ardeola ralloides* (30-400 pairs), *Egretta garzetta* (50-200 pairs; max. 300 pairs), *Egretta alba*, *Ardea purpurea* (100+ pairs), *Ciconia nigra* (2 pairs), *C. ciconia* (70 pairs), *Aythya nyroca* (30+ pairs), *Haliaeetus albicilla* (1 pair), *Circus aeruginosus* (10+ pairs), *Falco cherrug* (1 pair), *Porzana porzana*, *P. pusilla*, *P. parva*, *Crex crex*, *Luscinia svecica* (10+ pairs), *Locustella luscinioides* (50+ pairs), and *Acrocephalus arundinaceus* (300+ pairs). Passage species include large numbers of herons, *Platalea leucorodia*, *Pandion haliaetus*, *Numenius tenuirostris* (autumn), *Sterna caspia*, and *Chlidonias leucopterus*. Winter visitors include *Anser erythropus*, *Haliaeetus albicilla*, and *Aquila clanga*.

037 Koviljski rit (Vojvodina)

45°12'N, 20°00'E 4000 ha

Unprotected except strictly Protected Nature Reserve (Kozjak: 150 ha); proposed Regional Park

Area flooded by the Danube in summer with pools, wet meadows, channels, islets, and extensive Salix/*Populus* woodland and plantations. Land-uses include forestry, recreation, commercial fishing, hunting, and seasonal pig-grazing. Current problems (outside the

Reserve) include replacement of natural woodland with plantations, planting of open areas, and uncontrolled hunting.

Breeding species include *Botaurus stellaris*, *Nycticorax nycticorax* (100-200 pairs), *Egretta garzetta* (100 pairs), *Ardea purpurea* (less than 10 pairs), *Ciconia nigra* (less than 3 pairs), *C. ciconia* (4 pairs), *Milvus migrans* (5 pairs), *Haliaeetus albicilla* (1-2 pairs), *Falco cherrug* (2 pairs), and *Porzana porzana*. *Ciconia nigra* (100 during autumn) and *Platalea leucorodia* (50 during autumn) occur on passage, and *Haliaeetus albicilla* occurs in winter.

038 Deliblatska pescara (Vojvodina)

44°49'N, 21°00'E 40,000 ha

Special Reserve (29,000 ha)

An elongated and elliptical tract of sand, spreading from the Danube north towards Vladimirovac; comprising grazing pasture, steppe, scrub, woodland, plantations, vineyards, and agricultural land. A large proportion of the area has been designated for afforestation and the area is used for grazing, bee-keeping, hunting, and recreation. Adversely affected by afforestation, transformation of pastures and steppe into agricultural land (affecting populations of *Citellus citellus* – the main prey of *Aquila heliaca* and *Falco cherrug*), and agricultural intensification.

Breeding species include *Haliaeetus albicilla* (1 pair), *Circaetus gallicus* (2 pairs), *Aquila pomarina* (1-2 pair), *A. heliaca* (6-7 pairs), *Falco cherrug* (6-9 pairs), *Crex crex* (20+ pairs), *Caprimulgus europaeus* (200+ pairs), *Picus canus* (50 pairs), *Lullula arborea* (500+ pairs), *Anthus campestris* (30+ pairs), *Saxicola rubetra* (200+ pairs), *Sylvia nisoria* (1000+ pairs), *Lanius collurio* (1000+ pairs), *L. minor* (10 pairs), and *Emberiza hortulana* (20-50 pairs). *Gyps fulvus* (2), *Haliaeetus albicilla* (2-4), and *Falco columbarius* (10) occur in winter.

039 Donje podunavlje (Vojvodina)

44°49'N, 21°17'E 1200-1300 ha

To be designated as a protected area

Flooded area, formed after the construction of a hydroelectric power-station on the Danube, with swampy meadows and *Salix/Populus* woodland.

Breeding species include *Phalacrocorax pygmeus* (150 pairs), *Ixobrychus minutus* (50 pairs), *Nycticorax nycticorax* (200 pairs), *Ardeola ralloides* (150 pairs), *Egretta garzetta* (250 pairs), *Ardea purpurea* (20 pairs), *Plegadis falcinellus* (5 pairs), *Aythya nyroca* (50 pairs), and *Crex crex* (10+ pairs). Species occurring on passage include *Egretta alba*, *Platalea leucorodia*, *Pandion haliaetus*, *Chlidonias hybridus*, and *C. niger*. Wintering species include *Phalacrocorax pygmeus* (100-500) and *Haliaeetus albicilla* (2-5).

040 Vršački breg (Vojvodina)

45°07'N, 21°25'E 4000 ha

Regional Park

Hilly area covered with deciduous forest, surrounded by extensive plains (including steppe habitat), agricultural land, and vineyards. Land-uses include forestry, hunting, and recreation.

Breeding species include *Ciconia ciconia* (6 pairs), *Milvus milvus* (1-2 pairs), *Aquila pomarina* (1-3 pairs), *A. heliaca* (1-2 pairs), *Accipiter brevipes* (2 pairs), *Crex crex* (25-40 pairs), *Dendrocopos medius* (common), *D. leucotos*, *Lanius collurio* (very common), *L. minor* (very common), and *Emberiza hortulana*.

041 Obedska bara (Vojvodina)

44°43'N, 20°01'E 17,000 ha Ramsar Site

Unprotected except strictly protected Nature Reserve (1400 ha)

Pools, marshes, wet meadows, and *Salix/Populus* and *Quercus* forests; large parts of which are regularly flooded by the River Sava. Obedska bara is a large oxbow lake. The regulation of the River Sava has affected fish stocks and therefore populations of fish-eating birds.

Breeding species include *Botaurus stellaris*, *Ixobrychus minutus*, *Nycticorax nycticorax* (300 pairs), *Ardeola ralloides* (30 pairs), *Egretta garzetta* (400 pairs), *Ciconia nigra* (8 pairs), *C. ciconia* (35 pairs), *Platalea leucorodia* (40 pairs), *Haliaeetus albicilla* (1 pair), *Aquila pomarina* (1 pair), *A. heliaca* (1 pair), *Porzana porzana*, *P. parva*, and *Dendrocopos medius*.

042 Durmitor National Park (Montenegro)

42°58'-43°17'N, 18°16'-19°27'E 33,000 ha World Heritage Site

National Park

A spectacular area with 15 mountain peaks over 2000 m, 16 glacial lakes, and a 60 km canyon which is more than 1000 m deep. Vegetation includes forests of *Quercus*, *Fagus*, *Pinus*, *Picea*, *Abies*, *Acer*, and *Juniperus*. The Park contains one of the last virgin *Pinus nigra* forests in Europe.

Species present include *Aquila chrysaetos*, *Tetrao tetrix*, *T. urogallus*, and *Alectoris graeca*. The avifauna is very diverse for southern Yugoslavia. *Ursus arctos* is also present.

043 Skadarsko jezero (Lake Skadar) (Montenegro)

42°15'N, 19°15'E 35,500 ha (21,655 ha in Yugoslavia)

National Park with hunting prohibited

A very large freshwater lake, about 20 km from the Adriatic coast, on the Albanian border. Rivers entering the lake from the north have created an extensive marshy delta with vast reedbeds and seasonally flooded land. There are important fisheries at the lake. Poaching is a problem, and there is increasing disturbance of the pelican colony by birdwatchers.

Breeding species include *Pelecanus crispus* (60 pairs in 1978 and 15+ pairs in 1986; the only breeding site in Yugoslavia), *Ixobrychus minutus* (many), *Ardeola ralloides* (many), *Ardea purpurea* (50 pairs), *A. cinerea* (120 pairs in 1978), and possibly *Plegadis falcinellus*. *Larus argentatus* (4 pairs in 1980) and *Chlidonias hybridus* (14 pairs in 1978) are recent breeders. The lake is perhaps the most important site in the world, after the Danube Delta, for *Phalacrocorax pygmeus* (believed to be *c.*2000 pairs; assumed to be breeding on the Albanian side of the lake and/or along the River Bojana; large numbers feeding on the Yugoslavian side, with 8000-10,000 in autumn concentrations). The numbers of wintering waterfowl are not well known and seem to vary considerably. Large numbers of *Tachybaptus ruficollis* (1000) and *Podiceps nigricollis* have been recorded, as well as internationally important populations of *Anser anser*, *Aythya ferina*, *A. nyroca*, and *A. fuligula*.

044 Sasko jezero (Lake Sasko) (Montenegro)

41°58'N, 19°22'E 350 ha

Unprotected

A small lake south of Skadarsko jezero and part of the River Bojana catchment. It is almost on the border with Albania, about 10 km inland from the Adriatic coast, and access is very difficult owing to intense border security.

Breeding species include *Egretta garzetta* (also nests along the River Bojana), *Nycticorax nycticorax* (20 pairs), *Platalea leucorodia* (*c.*25 pairs), *Plegadis falcinellus* (a few pairs; also nests along the River Bojana), and *Phalacrocorax pygmeus* (*c.*50 pairs; possibly max. 2000 pairs along the River Bojana).

045 Ulcinjska solana (Ulcinj saltpans) (Montenegro)

41°55'N, 19°18'E 1350 ha

Unprotected

An area of saltpans (with fresh water in winter and spring; saline in summer and autumn) largely without vegetation, bordered by agricultural land. Due to the salt-extraction plant, hunting and human disturbance are controlled, but the industry itself causes some disturbance.

Breeding species include *Tadorna tadorna* (1-2 pairs), *Himantopus himantopus* (45 pairs), *Glareola pratincola* (150 pairs), and *Sterna albifrons* (50 pairs). *Platalea leucorodia*, *Phalacrocorax pygmeus*, and large numbers of herons and waders occur on passage; the total number of geese, ducks, and swans in winter exceeds 10,000.

046 Resavska klisura i Beljanica (Resava Gorge and Beljanica Mountain) (Serbia)

44°10'N, 21°45'E 10,000-15,000 ha

Regional Park

A mountainous area, including the gorges of the Rivers Resava and Kločanica, with woodland (mainly *Fagus*) and grazing pasture. Land-uses include stock-raising and forestry. Illegal hunting, trapping and poisoning of wildlife, and forestry are problems in the area.

Breeding species include *Circaetus gallicus* (2-3 pairs), *Aquila pomarina* (1-2 pairs), *A. chrysaetos* (1-3 pairs), *Falco peregrinus* (2 pairs), *Bonasa bonasia*, *Bubo bubo* (3-4 pairs), *Strix uralensis* (possibly 1-2 pairs), *Caprimulgus europaeus*, *Alcedo atthis*, *Picus canus*, *Dryocopus martius*, and *Lanius collurio*.

047 Zlotska klisura (Zlot Gorge) (Serbia)

44°00'N, 22°00'E 2000-3000 ha

Unprotected, but a proposed Regional Park

Cliffs, rocky hills, woodland, and grazing pasture. There is a small amount of agriculture and cattle-grazing. Illegal shooting, hunting, and poisoning of wildlife are problems at the site.

Breeding species include *Pernis apivorus* (1 pair), *Aquila chrysaetos* (1 pair), *Falco peregrinus* (1 pair), *Bubo bubo* (1-2 pairs), *Caprimulgus europaeus*, *Alcedo atthis*, *Picus canus*, *Dryocopus martius*, *Dendrocopos medius*, *Ficedula albicollis*, and *Lanius collurio*. *Ciconia nigra* occurs on passage.

048 Šar planina [parts of] (Šara Mountains) (Macedonia, Kosovo)

42°00'N, 21°00'E 12,000 ha

Forest Hunting Reserve (Donja Lešnica) in Macedonia; Hunting Reserve in Kosovo; proposals to create a National Park in Macedonia

High mountainous region (includes the peaks of Titov Vrh, Popova Šapka, and Kobilica), with river gorges, cliffs and rocky hillsides, alpine pastures, and woodland (coniferous and deciduous). Land-uses include cattle-grazing and forestry. There is uncontrolled hunting in the Macedonian part, and forestry practices, road-building, and tourism (to be promoted) are adversely affecting the area.

Breeding species include *Pernis apivorus* (1-2 pairs), *Aquila chrysaetos* (3-4 pairs), *Falco peregrinus* (1 pair), *Bonasa bonasia*, *Alectoris graeca*, *Bubo bubo* (3-5 pairs), *Dryocopus martius*, *Saxicola rubetra*, *Lanius collurio*, and *Pyrrhocorax pyrrhocorax* (50-100 pairs), and possibly include *Tetrao urogallus*, *Strix uralensis*, *Aegolius funereus*, *Dendrocopos leucotos*, *Picoides tridactylus*, and *Pyrrhocorax graculus*. *Gypaetus barbatus*

(1) and *Gyps fulvus* (15-20) also occur. Mammals present include Brown Bear *Ursus arctos* and Lynx *Lynx lynx*.

049 Planina Korab i klisura Radike (Korab Mountain and Radika Gorge) (Macedonia)

41°45'N, 21°15'E 50,000-60,000 ha

Partly protected (Mavrovo National Park)

Cliffs, rocky gorges, mountains, woodland (deciduous and coniferous), and alpine pastures. Land-uses include cattle-grazing and forestry. Some illegal hunting and trapping of wildlife takes place.

Breeding species include *Gyps fulvus* (10 pairs), *Circaetus gallicus* (1 pair), *Aquila clanga/pomarina* (1 pair), *Aquila chrysaetos* (6-7 pairs), *Hieraaetus pennatus* (possibly 1-2 pairs), *Falco biarmicus* (1 pair), *F. peregrinus* (2-3 pairs), *Bonasa bonasia*, *Bubo bubo*, (*c.*10 pairs), *Caprimulgus europaeus*, *Alcedo atthis*, *Dryocopus martius*, and possibly *Dendrocopos leucotos*, *D. medius*, and *Picoides tridactylus*.

050 Klisura reke Babune i Topolke i Crn Kamen (Babuna Gorge, Topolka Gorge, and Black Rock) (Macedonia)

41°40'N, 21°45'E 2500-3000 ha

Unprotected, but proposed Ornithological Reserve

The gorges of the Rivers Topolka, Vardar and Babuna with cliffs, riverine vegetation, and scrub-covered hillsides. Land-uses include hunting and cattle-grazing. There is possibly illegal poisoning of wildlife and the eggs and young of birds of prey are regularly stolen by foreigners.

Breeding species include *Ciconia nigra* (1 pair), *Neophron percnopterus* (2-3 pairs), *Circaetus gallicus* (1 pair), *Buteo rufinus* (2 pairs), *Aquila heliaca* (possibly), *A. chrysaetos* (1 pair), *Falco naumanni* (a few pairs), *F. biarmicus* (1 pair), *F. peregrinus* (1 pair), *Alectoris graeca*, *Bubo bubo* (1-2 pairs), *Caprimulgus europaeus*, *Alcedo atthis*, and *Coracias garrulus*. *Gypaetus barbatus* and *Gyps fulvus* also occur.

051 Reka Bregalnica (River Bregalnica) (Macedonia)

41°45'N, 22°00'E 10,000 ha

Unprotected

River valley with damp woodland, steppe habitat, bare eroded land, bushes and trees. There is hunting, a small area of cultivation and cattle-grazing in winter. There is possibly illegal poisoning of wildlife.

Breeding species include *Milvus migrans* (1-2 pairs), *Neophron percnopterus* (2-3 pairs), *Circaetus gallicus* (1-2 pairs), *Circus pygargus*, *Aquila heliaca* (2-3 pairs), *A. chrysaetos* (1 pair), *Falco peregrinus* (1 pair), *Bubo bubo* (2-3 pairs), *Caprimulgus europaeus*, *Alcedo atthis*, and *Coracias garrulus*; *Buteo rufinus*, *Falco cherrug*, and *Tetrax tetrax* possibly breed. *Gyps fulvus* (18 birds) also occurs.

052 Klisura Crna reka (River Crna Gorge) (Macedonia)

41°20'N, 22°00'E 40,000 ha

Unprotected, although there is a small Hunting Reserve

Gorge of the River Crna, with cliffs, scrub and woodland (including *Fagus* and *Quercus*), bare and eroded land, an artificial lake without vegetation, and grazing pasture. Land-uses include hunting, fishing, and cattle-grazing. Problems at the site include illegal trapping and probably poisoning of wildlife, and house building.

Breeding species include *Ciconia nigra* (2-3 pairs), *Neophron percnopterus* (8-15 pairs), *Gyps fulvus* (9-12 pairs), *Circaetus gallicus* (6-7 pairs), *Buteo rufinus* (1 pair), *Aquila chrysaetos* (4-7 pairs), *Hieraaetus pennatus* (1 pair), *H. fasciatus* (1 pair), *Falco naumanni* (15-20 pairs), *F. biarmicus* (1-2 pairs), *F. peregrinus* (2-3 pairs), *Bonasa bonasia*,

Alectoris graeca, *Bubo bubo* (3-5 pairs), and *Coracias garrulus*. *Gypaetus barbatus* (1), *Aegypius monachus* (2), and *Aquila heliaca* (2-3) also occur.

053 Demir kapija (Demir kapija Gorge) (Macedonia)

41°20'N, 22°20'E 8000-9000 ha

Unprotected, but proposed Ornithological Reserve

Includes the Vardar Gorge, River Čelevečka and Krastavec Ridge, with cliffs and rocky hillsides, scrub, and woodland; there are also small areas of marsh, damp woodland, and some of steppe habitat in the Vardar Valley. Mainly inaccessible, but some of the area is used as agricultural land, while hunting and cattle-grazing take place. Hunting, theft of raptor eggs and young by foreigners, road and quarry building, and cutting of trees and bushes are problems at the site, and probably illegal poisoning and trapping of wildlife also occur.

Breeding species include *Ciconia nigra* (1-2 pairs), *Pernis apivorus* (1-2 pairs), *Milvus migrans* (2-3 pairs), *Neophron percnopterus* (3-4 pairs), *Gyps fulvus* (18 pairs), *Circaetus gallicus* (2 pairs), *Accipiter brevipes* (1 pair), *Buteo rufinus* (1 pair), *Aquila heliaca* (1-2 pairs), *A. chrysaetos* (2 pairs), *Hieraaetus pennatus* (1 pair), *Falco naumanni* (5-10 pairs), *F. biarmicus* (1-2 pairs), *F. peregrinus* (1 pair), *Alectoris graeca*, *Bubo bubo* (1-2 pairs), *Coracias garrulus* (3-4 pairs), and *Cercotrichas galactotes*. *Gypaetus barbatus*, *Aegypius monachus*, and *Falco cherrug* also occur.

054 Kožuf i Bošava Mountains (Kožuf Mountain and Bošava Region) (Macedonia)

41°10'N, 22°15'E 20,000 ha

Unprotected

A mountainous area with alpine pastures, cliffs, rocky hillsides, bare and eroded land, coniferous woodland (*Pinus nigra*, *P. sylvestris*, *Abies alba*), and *Fagus* woodland. Land-uses include forestry and cattle-grazing. Problems at the site include hunting, illegal trapping and poisoning, and forestry.

Breeding species include *Ciconia nigra* (2-3 pairs), *Pernis apivorus* (1-3 pairs), *Gypaetus barbatus* (1 pair), *Neophron percnopterus* (4 pairs), *Aquila pomarina* (1 pair), *A. chrysaetos* (3 pairs), *Hieraaetus fasciatus* (1 pair), *Falco peregrinus* (1 pair), *Bonasa bonasia*, *Alectoris graeca*, and *Bubo bubo* (3-5 pairs), and possibly *Aegolius funereus*, *Coracias garrulus*, *Dendrocopos leucotos*, and *Picoides tridactylus*. Small flocks of *Falco eleonorae* also occur during the summer.

055 Ohridsko jezero (Lake Ohrid) (Macedonia)

41°08'N, 20°45'E 4000 ha (including Albanian part) World Heritage Site

Ornithological Reserve

Large inland freshwater lake in a mountain basin, in south-western Yugoslavia.

No data available for breeding season. The International Waterfowl Census counts in winter 1987 and 1988 recorded (1988 data unless stated) *Tachybaptus ruficollis* (1090), *Podiceps nigricollis* (2635), *Phalacrocorax carbo sinensis* (70), *P. aristotelis* (10), *P. pygmeus* (600), *Cygnus olor* (100 in 1987), *Netta rufina* (1150; 1300 in 1987), *Aythya ferina* (7050), *A. fuligula* (2200), and *Fulica atra* (32,100).

056 Prespansko jezero (Macedonia)

40°50'N, 21°00'E 40,000 ha

Unprotected

Very large inland freshwater lake, surrounded by mountains and overlapping the borders with Albania and Greece, in the far south of Yugoslavia. Overlaps with site no. 032 Limni Megali Prespa in Greece, and site no. 003 in Albania.

No data available for breeding birds in the Yugoslavian sector. The International Waterfowl Census counts (in the Yugoslavian sector) in winters 1987 and 1988 recorded (1988 data unless stated) *Phalacrocorax carbo sinensis* (40), *P. pygmeus* (80), *Netta rufina* (80; 150 in 1987), *Aythya fuligula* (8000), and *Fulica atra* (5950). Additional reports of non-breeding birds include *Podiceps cristatus* (1300), *Phalacrocorax pygmeus* (200), *Pelecanus crispus* (58), *Anser anser* (200), and *Mergus merganser* (90).

057 Dojransko jezero (Macedonia)

41°12'N, 22°45'E *c.*4200 ha

Ornithological Reserve

Shallow eutrophic lake, with extensive reedbeds, in the far south of Yugoslavia, overlapping the border with Greece. There is an intensive traditional fishing industry.

Formerly important for breeding waterfowl including *Pelecanus onocrotalus*, *Egretta alba*, *Ardea purpurea*, *Cygnus olor*, and *Oxyura leucocephala*; however, no data on breeding species available for recent years. The International Waterfowl Census counts in winter 1987 and 1988 recorded (1988 data unless stated) *Gavia arctica* (10), *Podiceps nigricollis* (40), *Phalacrocorax carbo sinensis* (10), *P. pygmeus* (100), *Aythya ferina* (1150), and *Fulica atra* (6350).

APPENDIX 6 **English names of species mentioned in the text**

The scientific nomenclature follows Voous (1977, List of Recent Holarctic Bird Species) and the English names follow the British Birds list of birds of the Western Palearctic (1984), except where they differ from Collar and Stuart (1985) or Collar and Andrew (1988), in which case the nomenclature they have adopted has been used.

Accipiter brevipes	Levant Sparrowhawk
Accipiter gentilis	Goshawk
Accipiter nisus	Sparrowhawk
Acrocephalus agricola	Paddyfield Warbler
Acrocephalus arundinaceus	Great Reed Warbler
Acrocephalus melanopogon	Moustached Warbler
Acrocephalus paludicola	Aquatic Warbler
Acrocephalus palustris	Marsh Warbler
Acrocephalus schoenobaenus	Sedge Warbler
Acrocephalus scirpaceus	Reed Warbler
Actitis hypoleucos	Common Sandpiper
Aegithalos caudatus	Long-tailed Tit
Aegolius funereus	Tengmalm's Owl
Aegypius monachus	Black Vulture
Aix galericulata	Mandarin
Alauda arvensis	Skylark
Alca torda	Razorbill
Alcedo atthis	Kingfisher
Alectoris barbara	Barbary Partridge
Alectoris chukar	Chukar
Alectoris graeca	Rock Partridge
Alectoris rufa	Red-legged Partridge
Alle alle	Little Auk
Ammomanes deserti	Desert Lark
Ammoperdix griseogularis	See-see
Anas acuta	Pintail
Anas clypeata	Shoveler
Anas crecca	Teal
Anas penelope	Wigeon
Anas platyrhynchos	Mallard
Anas querquedula	Garganey
Anas strepera	Gadwall
Anser albifrons	White-fronted Goose
Anser anser	Greylag Goose
Anser brachyrhynchus	Pink-footed Goose
Anser caerulescens	Snow Goose
Anser erythropus	Lesser White-fronted Goose
Anser fabalis	Bean Goose
Anhinga melanogaster	Darter
Anthropoides virgo	Demoiselle Crane
Anthus berthelotii	Berthelot's Pipit
Anthus campestris	Tawny Pipit
Anthus cervinus	Red-throated Pipit
Anthus pratensis	Meadow Pipit
Anthus spinoletta	Rock Pipit
Anthus trivialis	Tree Pipit
Apus affinis	Little Swift
Apus caffer	White-rumped Swift
Apus unicolor	Plain Swift
Aquila adalberti	Spanish Imperial Eagle
Aquila chrysaetos	Golden Eagle
Aquila clanga	Spotted Eagle
Aquila heliaca	Imperial Eagle

continued

Appendix 6 (contd)

Aquila pomarina	Lesser Spotted Eagle
Aquila pomarina	Lesser Spotted Eagle
Aquila rapax	Steppe Eagle
Ardea cinerea	Grey Heron
Ardea purpurea	Purple Heron
Ardeola ralloides	Squacco Heron
Arenaria interpres	Turnstone
Asio flammeus	Short-eared Owl
Asio otus	Long-eared Owl
Aythya ferina	Pochard
Aythya fuligula	Tufted Duck
Aythya marila	Scaup
Aythya nyroca	Ferruginous Duck
Bombycilla garrulus	Waxwing
Bonasa bonasia	Hazel Grouse
Botaurus stellaris	Bittern
Branta bernicla	Brent Goose
Branta canadensis	Canada Goose
Branta leucopsis	Barnacle Goose
Branta ruficollis	Red-breasted Goose
Bubo bubo	Eagle Owl
Bubulcus ibis	Cattle Egret
Bucanetes githagineus	Trumpeter Finch
Bucephala clangula	Goldeneye
Bucephala islandica	Barrow's Goldeneye
Bulweria bulwerii	Bulwer's Petrel
Burhinus oedicnemus	Stone-curlew
Buteo buteo	Buzzard
Buteo rufinus	Long-legged Buzzard
Calcarius lapponicus	Lapland Bunting
Calandrella brachydactyla	Short-toed Lark
Calandrella rufescens	Lesser Short-toed Lark
Calidris alba	Sanderling
Calidris alpina	Dunlin
Calidris bairdii	Baird's Sandpiper
Calidris canutus	Knot
Calidris ferruginea	Curlew Sandpiper
Calidris maritima	Purple Sandpiper
Calidris minuta	Little Stint
Calidris temminckii	Temminck's Stint
Calonectris diomedea	Cory's Shearwater
Caprimulgus europaeus	Nightjar
Caprimulgus ruficollis	Red-necked Nightjar
Carduelis cannabina	Linnet
Carduelis carduelis	Goldfinch
Carduelis hornemanni	Arctic Redpoll
Carpodacus erythrinus	Scarlet Rosefinch
Carpodacus rubicilla	Great Rosefinch
Cepphus grylle	Black Guillemot
Cercotrichas galactotes	Rufous Bush Robin
Certhia brachydactyla	Short-toed Treecreeper
Certhia familiaris	Treecreeper
Ceryle rudis	Pied Kingfisher
Cettia cetti	Cetti's Warbler
Charadrius alexandrinus	Kentish Plover
Charadrius asiaticus	Caspian Plover
Charadrius dubius	Little Ringed Plover
Charadrius hiaticula	Ringed Plover
Charadrius leschenaultii	Greater Sand Plover
Charadrius morinellus	Dotterel
Chersophilus duponti	Dupont's Lark

continued

Appendix 6 (contd)

Chettusia leucura	White-tailed Plover
Chettusia gregaria	Sociable Plover
Chlamydotis undulata	Houbara Bustard
Chlidonias hybridus	Whiskered Tern
Chlidonias leucopterus	White-winged Black Tern
Chlidonias niger	Black Tern
Ciconia ciconia	White Stork
Ciconia nigra	Black Stork
Cinclus cinclus	Dipper
Circaetus gallicus	Short-toed Eagle
Circus aeruginosus	Marsh Harrier
Circus cyaneus	Hen Harrier
Circus macrourus	Pallid Harrier
Circus pygargus	Montagu's Harrier
Clamator glandarius	Great Spotted Cuckoo
Clangula hyemalis	Long-tailed Duck
Coccothraustes coccothraustes	Hawfinch
Columba bollii	Dark-tailed Laurel Pigeon
Columba junoniae	White-tailed Laurel Pigeon
Columba livia	Rock Dove
Columba palumbus	Woodpigeon
Columba trocaz	Madeira Laurel Pigeon
Coracias garrulus	Roller
Corvus corax	Raven
Corvus corone	Carrion Crow
Corvus frugilegus	Rook
Coturnix coturnix	Quail
Crex crex	Corncrake
Cuculus saturatus	Oriental Cuckoo
Cursorius cursor	Cream-coloured Courser
Cyanopica cyana	Azure-winged Magpie
Cygnus columbianus	Bewick's Swan
Cygnus cygnus	Whooper Swan
Cygnus olor	Mute Swan
Delichon urbica	House Martin
Dendrocopos leucotos	White-backed Woodpecker
Dendrocopos major	Great Spotted Woodpecker
Dendrocopos medius	Middle Spotted Woodpecker
Dendrocopos syriacus	Syrian Woodpecker
Dryocopus martius	Black Woodpecker
Egretta alba	Great White Egret
Egretta garzetta	Little Egret
Elanus caeruleus	Black-shouldered Kite
Emberiza aureola	Yellow-breasted Bunting
Emberiza buchanani	Grey-necked Bunting
Emberiza caesia	Cretzschmar's Bunting
Emberiza cineracea	Cinereous Bunting
Emberiza cirlus	Cirl Bunting
Emberiza hortulana	Ortolan Bunting
Eremophila alpestris balcanica	Shorelark
Erithacus rubecula	Robin
Falco biarmicus	Lanner
Falco cherrug	Saker
Falco columbarius	Merlin
Falco eleonorae	Eleonora's Falcon
Falco naumanni	Lesser Kestrel
Falco pelegrinoides	Barbary Falcon
Falco peregrinus	Peregrine
Falco rusticolus	Gyr Falcon
Falco subbuteo	Hobby
Falco tinnunculus	Kestrel

continued

Appendix 6 (contd)

Falco vespertinus	Red-footed Falcon
Ficedula albicollis	Collared Flycatcher
Ficedula hypoleuca	Pied Flycatcher
Ficedula parva	Red-breasted Flycatcher
Ficedula semitorquata	Semi-collared Flycatcher
Francolinus francolinus	Black Francolin
Fratercula arctica	Puffin
Fringilla coelebs	Chaffinch
Fringilla teydea	Blue Chaffinch
Fulica atra	Coot
Fulica cristata	Crested Coot
Fulmarus glacialis	Fulmar
Galerida theklae	Thekla Lark
Gallinago gallinago	Snipe
Gallinago media	Great Snipe
Gavia adamsii	White-billed Diver
Gavia arctica	Black-throated Diver
Gavia immer	Great Northern Diver
Gavia stellata	Red-throated Diver
Gelochelidon nilotica	Gull-billed Tern
Geronticus eremita	Northern Bald Ibis
Glareola nordmanni	Black-winged Pratincole
Glareola pratincola	Collared Pratincole
Glaucidium passerinum	Pygmy Owl
Grus grus	Crane
Grus leucogeranus	Siberian White Crane
Gypaetus barbatus	Lammergeier
Gyps fulvus	Griffon Vulture
Haematopus meadewaldoi	Canarian Black Oystercatcher
Haematopus ostralegus	Oystercatcher
Halcyon smyrnensis	White-breasted Kingfisher
Haliaeetus albicilla	White-tailed Eagle
Hieraaetus fasciatus	Bonelli's Eagle
Hieraaetus pennatus	Booted Eagle
Himantopus himantopus	Black-winged Stilt
Hippolais caligata	Booted Warbler
Hippolais icterina	Icterine Warbler
Hippolais languida	Upcher's Warbler
Hippolais olivetorum	Olive-tree Warbler
Hippolais pallida	Olivaceous Warbler
Hippolais polyglotta	Melodious Warbler
Hirundo rustica	Swallow
Histrionicus histrionicus	Harlequin Duck
Hoplopterus spinosus	Spur-winged Plover
Hydrobates pelagicus	Storm Petrel
Irania gutturalis	White-throated Robin
Ixobrychus minutus	Little Bittern
Lagopus mutus	Ptarmigan
Lanius collurio	Red-backed Shrike
Lanius excubitor	Great Grey Shrike
Lanius minor	Lesser Grey Shrike
Lanius nubicus	Masked Shrike
Lanius senator	Woodchat Shrike
Larus argentatus	Herring Gull
Larus audouinii	Audouin's Gull
Larus canus	Common Gull
Larus fuscus	Lesser Black-backed Gull
Larus genei	Slender-billed Gull
Larus glaucoides	Iceland Gull
Larus hyperboreus	Glaucous Gull
Larus ichthyaetus	Great Black-headed Gull

continued

Appendix 6 (contd)

Larus marinus	Great Black-backed Gull
Larus melanocephalus	Mediterranean Gull
Larus minutus	Little Gull
Larus ridibundus	Black-headed Gull
Larus sabini	Sabine's Gull
Limicola falcinellus	Broad-billed Sandpiper
Limosa lapponica	Bar-tailed Godwit
Limosa limosa	Black-tailed Godwit
Locustella fluviatilis	River Warbler
Locustella luscinioides	Savi's Warbler
Locustella naevia	Grasshopper Warbler
Loxia curvirostra	Crossbill
Loxia pytyopsittacus	Parrot Crossbill
Loxia scotica	Scottish Crossbill
Lullula arborea	Woodlark
Luscinia megarhynchos	Nightingale
Luscinia svecica	Bluethroat
Lymnocryptes minimus	Jack Snipe
Marmaronetta angustirostris	Marbled Duck
Melanitta fusca	Velvet Scotor
Melanitta nigra	Common Scotor
Melanocorypha bimaculata	Bimaculated Lark
Melanocorypha calandra	Calandra Lark
Melanocorypha leucoptera	White-winged Lark
Melanocorypha yeltoniensis	Black Lark
Mergus albellus	Smew
Mergus merganser	Goosander
Mergus serrator	Red-breasted Merganser
Merops apiaster	Bee-eater
Merops superciliosus	Blue-cheeked Bee-eater
Milvus migrans	Black Kite
Milvus milvus	Red Kite
Monticola saxatilis	Rock Thrush
Monticola solitarius	Blue Rock Thrush
Montifringilla nivalis	Snowfinch
Motacilla cinerea	Grey Wagtail
Motacilla citreola	Citrine Wagtail
Motacilla flava	Yellow Wagtail
Muscicapa striata	Spotted Flycatcher
Neophron percnopterus	Egyptian Vulture
Netta rufina	Red-crested Pochard
Numenius arquata	Curlew
Numenius phaeopus	Whimbrel
Numenius tenuirostris	Slender-billed Curlew
Nyctea scandiaca	Snowy Owl
Nycticorax nycticorax	Night Heron
Oceanodroma leucorhoa	Leach's Petrel
Oenanthe cypriaca	Cyprus Pied Wheatear
Oenanthe hispanica	Black-eared Wheatear
Oenanthe isabellina	Isabelline Wheatear
Oenanthe leucura	Black Wheatear
Oenanthe pleschanka	Pied Wheatear
Oenanthe xanthoprymna	Red-tailed Wheatear
Oriolus oriolus	Golden Oriole
Otis tarda	Great Bustard
Otus brucei	Striated Scops Owl
Oxyura jamaicensis	Ruddy Duck
Oxyura leucocephala	White-headed Duck
Pagophila eburnea	Ivory Gull
Pandion haliaetus	Osprey
Panurus biarmicus	Bearded Tit

continued

Appendix 6 (contd)

Parus ater	Coal Tit
Parus caeruleus	Blue Tit
Parus cinctus	Siberian Tit
Parus cyanus	Azure Tit
Parus lugubris	Sombre Tit
Parus palustris	Marsh Tit
Passer domesticus	House Sparrow
Passer hispaniolensis	Spanish Sparrow
Passer moabiticus	Dead Sea Sparrow
Pelagodroma marina	White-faced Petrel
Pelecanus crispus	Dalmatian Pelican
Pelecanus onocrotalus	White Pelican
Perdix perdix	Grey Partridge
Perisoreus infaustus	Siberian Jay
Pernis apivorus	Honey Buzzard
Petronia petronia	Rock Sparrow
Petronia xanthocollis	Yellow-throated Sparrow
Phalacrocorax aristotelis	Shag
Phalacrocorax carbo	Cormorant
Phalacrocorax pygmeus	Pygmy Cormorant
Phalaropus fulicarius	Grey Phalarope
Phalaropus lobatus	Red-necked Phalarope
Philomachus pugnax	Ruff
Phoenicopterus ruber	Greater Flamingo
Phoenicurus ochruros	Black Redstart
Phylloscopus collybita	Chiffchaff
Phylloscopus inornatus	Yellow-browed Warbler
Phylloscopus nitidus	Green Warbler
Phylloscopus sibilatrix	Wood Warbler
Phylloscopus sindianus	Mountain Chiffchaff
Phylloscopus trochiloides	Greenish Warbler
Phylloscopus trochilus	Willow Warbler
Picoides tridactylus	Three-toed Woodpecker
Picus canus	Grey-headed Woodpecker
Pinicola enucleator	Pine Grosbeak
Platalea leucorodia	Spoonbill
Plectrophenax nivalis	Snow Bunting
Plegadis falcinellus	Glossy Ibis
Pluvialis apricaria	Golden Plover
Pluvialis squatarola	Grey Plover
Podiceps auritus	Slavonian Grebe
Podiceps cristatus	Great Crested Grebe
Podiceps grisegena	Red-necked Grebe
Podiceps nigricollis	Black-necked Grebe
Polysticta stelleri	Steller's Eider
Porphyrio porphyrio	Purple Gallinule
Porzana parva	Little Crake
Porzana porzana	Spotted Crake
Porzana pusilla	Baillon's Crake
Prunella collaris	Alpine Accentor
Prunella ocularis	Radde's Accentor
Pterocles alchata	Pin-tailed Sandgrouse
Pterocles orientalis	Black-bellied Sandgrouse
Pterodroma feae	Gon-gon
Pterodroma madeira	Freira
Ptyonoprogne rupestris	Crag Martin
Puffinus assimilis	Little Shearwater
Puffinus puffinus	Manx Shearwater
Pyrrhocorax graculus	Alpine Chough
Pyrrhocorax pyrrhocorax	Chough
Pyrrhula pyrrhula	Bullfinch

continued

Appendix 6 (contd)

Rallus aquaticus	Water Rail
Recurvirostra avosetta	Avocet
Regulus ignicapillus	Firecrest
Regulus regulus	Goldcrest
Remiz pendulinus	Penduline Tit
Rhodopechys sanguinea	Crimson-winged Finch
Rhodospiza obsoleta	Desert Finch
Rhodostethia rosea	Ross's Gull
Riparia riparia	Sand Martin
Rissa tridactyla	Kittiwake
Saxicola dacotiae	Fuerteventura Stonechat
Saxicola rubetra	Whinchat
Saxicola torquata	Stonechat
Scolopax rusticola	Woodcock
Serinus canaria	Canary
Serinus citrinella	Citril Finch
Serinus pusillus	Red-fronted Serin
Sitta krueperi	Kruper's Nuthatch
Sitta neumayer	Rock Nuthatch
Sitta tephronota	Great Rock Nuthatch
Sitta whiteheadi	Corsican Nuthatch
Somateria mollissima	Eider
Somateria spectabilis	King Eider
Stercorarius longicaudus	Long-tailed Skua
Stercorarius parasiticus	Arctic Skua
Stercorarius skua	Great Skua
Sterna albifrons	Little Tern
Sterna caspia	Caspian Tern
Sterna dougallii	Roseate Tern
Sterna fuscata	Sooty Tern
Sterna hirundo	Common Tern
Sterna paradisaea	Arctic Tern
Sterna sandvicensis	Sandwich Tern
Streptopelia turtur	Turtle Dove
Strix nebulosa	Great Grey Owl
Strix uralensis	Ural Owl
Sturnus roseus	Rose-coloured Starling
Sturnus unicolor	Spotless Starling
Sula bassana	Gannet
Surnia ulula	Hawk Owl
Sylvia atricapilla	Blackcap
Sylvia borin	Garden Warbler
Sylvia cantillans	Subalpine Warbler
Sylvia conspicillata	Spectacled Warbler
Sylvia melanocephala	Sardinian Warbler
Sylvia melanothorax	Cyprus Warbler
Sylvia mystacea	Ménétries's Warbler
Sylvia nisoria	Barred Warbler
Sylvia rueppelli	Ruppell's Warbler
Sylvia sarda	Marmora's Warbler
Sylvia undata	Dartford Warbler
Tachybaptus ruficollis	Little Grebe
Tadorna ferruginea	Ruddy Shelduck
Tadorna tadorna	Shelduck
Tarsiger cyanurus	Red-flanked Bluetail
Tetrao mlokosiewiczi	Caucasian Black Grouse
Tetrao tetrix	Black Grouse
Tetrao urogallus	Capercaillie
Tetraogallus caspius	Caspian Snowcock
Tetraogallus caucasicus	Caucasian Snowcock
Tetrax tetrax	Little Bustard

continued

Appendix 6 (contd)

Tichodroma muraria	Wallcreeper
Tringa erythropus	Spotted Redshank
Tringa glareola	Wood Sandpiper
Tringa nebularia	Greenshank
Tringa ochropus	Green Sandpiper
Tringa stagnatilis	Marsh Sandpiper
Tringa totanus	Redshank
Troglodytes troglodytes	Wren
Turnix sylvatica	Andalusian Hemipode
Turdus merula	Blackbird
Turdus philomelos	Song Thrush
Turdus torquatus	Ring Ouzel
Tyto alba	Barn Owl
Uria aalge	Guillemot
Uria lomvia	Brunnich's Guillemot
Vanellus vanellus	Lapwing
Xenus cinereus	Terek Sandpiper

INTERNATIONAL COUNCIL FOR BIRD PRESERVATION

EUROPEAN CONTINENTAL SECTION

in collaboration with the

INTERNATIONAL WATERFOWL RESEARCH BUREAU

SITE DATA-SHEET

Please complete for each site as many sections as possible. Please return the site data-sheets to ICBP, 32 Cambridge Road, Girton, Cambridge CB3 0PJ, U.K.

---

1. Country:

2. Region:

---

3. Site name:

(if part of larger site complex please give this name also)

4. Approximate area of site: (hectares)

---

5. Geographical coordinates:

(if possible please indicate boundaries)

---

6. Map of site (photocopy or sketch map – please attach if more convenient):

---

7. International protection status (Ramsar Site, Biosphere Reserve, etc.):

8. National protection status and conservation measures taken or proposed:

9. Ownership/land tenure:

10. Description of site and main habitats:

11. Description of current land-use and management:

12. Current threats or problems at site:

(please indicate species especially affected and why)

13. Additional information and references:

14. Name and address of compiler:

15. Date:

16. Ornithological importance

For winter counts please state, if possible, whether it is an average, average maximum or maximum count and give the month(s) that these data refer to. For counts of birds on migration please state whether it is an average, average maximum or maximum count and specify if the count refers to the number per day or per season (spring or autumn). Counts of moulting birds or oversummering non-breeders should be entered in the 'migration' column, but please specify that this is what the figure refers to. If the number of birds has fluctuated greatly then a range can be given.

Red Data Book species:

Species	breeding	wintering	on migration (or moulting/ oversummering)

Species and subspecies which are threatened throughout all or a large part of their range in Europe:

Species	breeding	wintering	on migration (or moulting/ oversummering)

Other bird species (such as additional migratory species including waterfowl):

Species	breeding	wintering	on migration (or moulting/ oversummering)

THANK YOU FOR YOUR HELP

INTERNATIONAL WATERFOWL RESEARCH BUREAU — IWRB
BUREAU INTERNATIONAL DE RECHERCHES SUR LES OISEAUX D'EAU
INTERNATIONALES BÜRO FÜR WASSERVOGELFORSCHUNG
МЕЖДУНАРОДНОЕ БЮРО ПО ИЗУЧЕНИЮ ВОДОПЛАВАЮЩИХ ПТИЦ
BURO INTERNACIONAL PARA EL ESTUDIO DE AVES ACUATICAS

SLIMBRIDGE (Glos.) Tel: Cambridge, Glos. (045 389) 333 ext. 34
GL2 7BX
ENGLAND

WETLAND DATA SHEET
EUROPE 1987

1. Country: 2. Date: 3. Ref:

4. Name and address of compiler:

5. Name of wetland:

6. Geographical coordinates:

7. Location:

8. Area:

9. Altitude:

10. Biogeographical Province:

11. Wetland Type:

12. Description of site:

(a) water regime:

(b) water depth:

(c) salinity/acidity:

(d) fluctuations/permanence:

(e) tidal variations:

(f) climatic conditions:

13. Principal vegetation:
(a) aquatic vegetation:

(b) plant communities in adjacent areas:

14. Land tenure:
(a) of site:

(b) of surrounding areas:

---

15. Conservation measures taken:
(a) protected areas:

(b) other measures:

---

16. Conservation measures proposed:
(a) existing proposals:

(b) new proposals:

---

17. Current land use:
(a) at the wetland:

(b) in surrounding areas:

---

18. Possible changes in land use and proposed development projects:
(a) at the wetland:

(b) in the water catchment area:

---

19. Disturbances and threats:

20. Conservation values:

(a) economic and social values:

(b) wildlife:

- fish:

- waterfowl:

- other fauna:

(c) special floral values:

21. Research and facilities:

22. References:

23. Outline map of site:

24. Criteria for inclusion:

Please return completed data sheet to Stefan Brager, Project Coordinator, IWRB, Slimbridge, Gloucester GL2 7BX, England